D1312250

CLASSICAL AND MEDIEVAL LITERATURE CRITICISM

Guide to Gale Literary Criticism Series

For criticism on	Consult these Gale series
Authors now living or who died after December 31, 1999	*CONTEMPORARY LITERARY CRITICISM (CLC)*
Authors who died between 1900 and 1999	*TWENTIETH-CENTURY LITERARY CRITICISM (TCLC)*
Authors who died between 1800 and 1899	*NINETEENTH-CENTURY LITERATURE CRITICISM (NCLC)*
Authors who died between 1400 and 1799	*LITERATURE CRITICISM FROM 1400 TO 1800 (LC)* *SHAKESPEAREAN CRITICISM (SC)*
Authors who died before 1400	*CLASSICAL AND MEDIEVAL LITERATURE CRITICISM (CMLC)*
Authors of books for children and young adults	*CHILDREN'S LITERATURE REVIEW (CLR)*
Dramatists	*DRAMA CRITICISM (DC)*
Poets	*POETRY CRITICISM (PC)*
Short story writers	*SHORT STORY CRITICISM (SSC)*
Literary topics and movements	*HARLEM RENAISSANCE: A GALE CRITICAL COMPANION (HR)* *THE BEAT GENERATION: A GALE CRITICAL COMPANION (BG)* *FEMINISM IN LITERATURE: A GALE CRITICAL COMPANION (FL)* *GOTHIC LITERATURE: A GALE CRITICAL COMPANION (GL)*
Asian American writers of the last two hundred years	*ASIAN AMERICAN LITERATURE (AAL)*
Black writers of the past two hundred years	*BLACK LITERATURE CRITICISM (BLC-1)* *BLACK LITERATURE CRITICISM SUPPLEMENT (BLCS)* *BLACK LITERATURE CRITICISM: CLASSIC AND EMERGING AUTHORS SINCE 1950 (BLC-2)*
Hispanic writers of the late nineteenth and twentieth centuries	*HISPANIC LITERATURE CRITICISM (HLC)* *HISPANIC LITERATURE CRITICISM SUPPLEMENT (HLCS)*
Native North American writers and orators of the eighteenth, nineteenth, and twentieth centuries	*NATIVE NORTH AMERICAN LITERATURE (NNAL)*
Major authors from the Renaissance to the present	*WORLD LITERATURE CRITICISM, 1500 TO THE PRESENT (WLC)* *WORLD LITERATURE CRITICISM SUPPLEMENT (WLCS)*

ISSN 0896-0011

Volume 112

CLASSICAL AND MEDIEVAL LITERATURE CRITICISM

Criticism of the Works of World
Authors from Classical Antiquity through the
Fourteenth Century, from the First Appraisals
to Current Evaluations

Jelena Krstović
Project Editor

GALE
CENGAGE Learning

Detroit • New York • San Francisco • New Haven, Conn • Waterville, Maine • London

Comsewogue Public Library
170 Terryville Road
Port Jefferson Station, NY 11776

Classical and Medieval Literature Criticism, Vol. 112

Project Editor: Jelena O. Krstović

Editorial: Dana Ramel Barnes, Kathy D. Darrow, Kristen A. Dorsch, Jeffrey W. Hunter, Michelle Lee, Thomas J. Schoenberg, Lawrence J. Trudeau

Content Conversion: Katrina D. Coach, Gwen Tucker

Indexing Services: Zott Solutions, Inc

Rights and Acquisitions: Jacqueline Flowers, Margaret Chamberlain-Gaston, Jhanay Williams

Composition and Electronic Capture: Gary Leach

Manufacturing: Cynde Bishop

Associate Product Manager: Marc Cormier

© 2009 Gale, Cengage Learning

ALL RIGHTS RESERVED. No part of this work covered by the copyright herein may be reproduced, transmitted, stored, or used in any form or by any means graphic, electronic, or mechanical, including but not limited to photocopying, recording, scanning, digitizing, taping, Web distribution, information networks, or information storage and retrieval systems, except as permitted under Section 107 or 108 of the 1976 United States Copyright Act, without the prior written permission of the publisher.

This publication is a creative work fully protected by all applicable copyright laws, as well as by misappropriation, trade secret, unfair competition, and other applicable laws. The authors and editors of this work have added value to the underlying factual material herein through one or more of the following: unique and original selection, coordination, expression, arrangement, and classification of the information.

For product information and technology assistance, contact us at
Gale Customer Support, 1-800-877-4253.
For permission to use material from this text or product,
submit all requests online at **www.cengage.com/permissions.**
Further permissions questions can be emailed to
permissionrequest@cengage.com

While every effort has been made to ensure the reliability of the information presented in this publication, Gale, a part of Cengage Learning, does not guarantee the accuracy of the data contained herein. Gale accepts no payment for listing; and inclusion in the publication of any organization, agency, institution, publication, service, or individual does not imply endorsement of the editors or publisher. Errors brought to the attention of the publisher and verified to the satisfaction of the publisher will be corrected in future editions.

Gale
27500 Drake Rd.
Farmington Hills, MI, 48331-3535

LIBRARY OF CONGRESS CATALOG CARD NUMBER 88-641014

ISBN-13: 978-1-4144-3926-6
ISBN-10: 1-4144-3926-1

ISSN 0896-0011

Printed in the United States of America
1 2 3 4 5 6 7 13 12 11 10 09

Contents

Preface vii

Acknowledgments xi

Literary Criticism Series Advisory Board xiii

Preface

Since its inception in 1988, *Classical and Medieval Literature Criticism* (*CMLC*) has been a valuable resource for students and librarians seeking critical commentary on the works and authors of antiquity through the fourteenth century. The great poets, prose writers, dramatists, and philosophers of this period form the basis of most humanities curricula, so that virtually every student will encounter many of these works during the course of a high school and college education. Reviewers have found *CMLC* "useful" and "extremely convenient," noting that it "adds to our understanding of the rich legacy left by the ancient period and the Middle Ages," and praising its "general excellence in the presentation of an inherently interesting subject." No other single reference source has surveyed the critical reaction to classical and medieval literature as thoroughly as *CMLC*.

Scope of the Series

CMLC provides an introduction to classical and medieval authors, works, and topics that represent a variety of genres, time periods, and nationalities. By organizing and reprinting an enormous amount of critical commentary written on authors and works of this period in world history, *CMLC* helps students develop valuable insight into literary history, promotes a better understanding of the texts, and sparks ideas for papers and assignments.

Each entry in *CMLC* presents a comprehensive survey of an author's career, an individual work of literature, or a literary topic, and provides the user with a multiplicity of interpretations and assessments. Such variety allows students to pursue their own interests; furthermore, it fosters an awareness that literature is dynamic and responsive to many different opinions. Early commentary is offered to indicate initial responses, later selections document changes in literary reputations, and retrospective analyses provide the reader with modern views. The size of each author entry is a relative reflection of the scope of the criticism available in English.

An author or work may appear more than once in the series if they have been the subject of a substantial amount of criticism. Individual works or groups of works by an author may also be covered in separate entries. For example, Homer will be represented by three entries, one devoted to the *Iliad*, one to the *Odyssey*, and one to the Homeric Hymns.

CMLC continues the survey of criticism of world literature begun by Gale's *Contemporary Literary Criticism* (*CLC*), *Twentieth-Century Literary Criticism* (*TCLC*), *Nineteenth-Century Literature Criticism* (*NCLC*), *Literature Criticism from 1400 to 1800* (*LC*), and *Shakespearean Criticism* (*SC*).

Organization of the Book

A *CMLC* entry consists of the following elements:

- The **Author Heading** cites the name under which the author most commonly wrote, followed by birth and death dates. Also located here are any name variations under which an author wrote, including transliterated forms for authors whose native languages use nonroman alphabets. If the author wrote consistently under a pseudonym, the pseudonym will be listed in the author heading and the author's actual name given in parenthesis on the first line of the biographical and critical information. Uncertain birth or death dates are indicated by question marks. Single-work entries are preceded by a heading that consists of the most common form of the title in English translation (if applicable) and the author name (if applicable).

- The **Introduction** contains background information that introduces the reader to the author, work, or topic that is the subject of the entry.

- The list of **Principal Works** is ordered chronologically by date of first publication or composition and lists the most important works by an author. The genre and publication date of each work is given. In the case of foreign authors whose works have been translated into English, the Principal English Translations focuses primarily on twentieth-century translations, selecting those works most commonly considered the best by critics. For works originally written in Old or Middle English, the Principal English Editions section lists editions in modern English. Unless otherwise indicated, dramas are dated by first performance, not first publication. Lists of **Representative Works** by different authors appear with topic entries.

- Reprinted **Criticism** is arranged chronologically in each entry to provide a useful perspective on changes in critical evaluation over time. The critic's name and the date of composition or publication of the critical work are given at the beginning of each piece of criticism. Unsigned criticism is preceded by the title of the source in which it appeared. All titles by the author featured in the text are printed in boldface type. Footnotes are reprinted at the end of each essay or excerpt. In the case of excerpted criticism, only those footnotes that pertain to the excerpted texts are included. Criticism in topic entries is arranged chronologically under a variety of subheadings to facilitate the study of different aspects of the topic.

- A complete **Bibliographical Citation** of the original essay or book precedes each piece of criticism.

- Critical essays are prefaced by brief **Annotations** indicating the content of each piece.

- An annotated bibliography of **Further Reading** appears at the end of each entry and suggests resources for additional study. In some cases, significant essays for which the editors could not obtain reprint rights are included here. Boxed material following the further reading list provides references to other biographical and critical sources on the author in series published by Gale.

Cumulative Indexes

A **Cumulative Author Index** lists all of the authors that appear in a wide variety of reference sources published by the Gale, including *CMLC*. A complete list of these sources is found facing the first page of the Author Index. The index also includes birth and death dates and cross references between pseudonyms and actual names.

Beginning with the second volume, a **Cumulative Nationality Index** lists all authors and anonymous works featured in *CMLC* by nationality, followed by the number of the *CMLC* volume in which the entry appears.

Beginning with the tenth volume, a **Cumulative Topic Index** lists the literary themes and topics treated in the series as well as in *Nineteenth-Century Literature Criticism, Twentieth-Century Literary Criticism,* and the *Contemporary Literary Criticism* Yearbook, which was discontinued in 1998.

A **Cumulative Title Index** lists in alphabetical order all of the works discussed in the series. Each title listing includes the corresponding volume and page numbers where criticism may be located. Foreign-language titles that have been translated into English are followed by the titles of the translation—for example, *Slovo o polku Igorove (The Song of Igor's Campaign)*. Page numbers following these translated titles refer to all pages on which any form of the titles, either foreign-language or translated, appear. Titles of novels, dramas, nonfiction books, and poetry, short story, or essay collections are printed in italics, while individual poems, short stories, and essays are printed in roman type within quotation marks.

Citing *Classical and Medieval Literature Criticism*

When citing criticism reprinted in the Literary Criticism Series, students should provide complete bibliographic information so that the cited essay can be located in the original print or electronic source. Students who quote directly from reprinted criticism may use any accepted bibliographic format, such as University of Chicago Press style or Modern Language Association style.

The examples below follow recommendations for preparing a bibliography set forth in *The Chicago Manual of Style,* 15th ed. (Chicago: The University of Chicago Press, 2006); the first example pertains to material drawn from periodicals, the second to material reprinted from books:

Sealey, R. J. "The Tetralogies Ascribed to Antiphon." *Transactions of the American Philological Association* 114, (1984): 71-85. Reprinted in *Classical and Medieval Literature Criticism.* Vol. 55, edited by Jelena O. Krstović, 2-9. Detroit: Thomson Gale, 2003.

Bourne, Ella. "Classical Elements in *The Gesta Romanorum.*" In *Vassar Medieval Studies* edited by Christabel Forsyth Fiske, 345-76. New Haven: Yale University Press, 1923. Reprinted in *Classical and Medieval Literature Criticism.* Vol. 55, edited by Jelena O. Krstović, 81-92. Detroit: Thomson Gale, 2003.

The examples below follow recommendations for preparing a works cited list set forth in the *MLA Handbook for Writers of Research Papers,* 6th ed. (New York: The Modern Language Association of America, 2003); the first example pertains to material drawn from periodicals, the second to material reprinted from books:

Sealey, R. J. "The Tetralogies Ascribed to Antiphon." *Transactions of the American Philological Association* 114. (1984): 71-85. Reprinted in *Classical and Medieval Literature Criticism.* Ed. Jelena O. Krstović. Vol. 55. Detroit: Thomson Gale, 2003. 2-9.

Bourne, Ella. "Classical Elements in *The Gesta Romanorum.*" *Vassar Medieval Studies.* Ed. Christabel Forsyth Fiske. New Haven: Yale University Press, 1923. 345-76. Reprinted in *Classical and Medieval Literature Criticism.* Ed. Jelena O. Krstović. Vol. 55. Detroit: Thomson Gale, 2003. 81-92.

Suggestions are Welcome

Readers who wish to suggest new features, topics, or authors to appear in future volumes, or who have other suggestions or comments are cordially invited to call, write, or fax the Associate Product Manager:

Associate Product Manager, Literary Criticism Series

Gale

Cengage Learning

27500 Drake Road

Farmington Hills, MI 48331-3535

1-800-347-4253 (GALE)

Fax: 248-699-8054

Acknowledgments

The editors wish to thank the copyright holders of the criticism included in this volume and the permissions managers of many book and magazine publishing companies for assisting us in securing reproduction rights. We are also grateful to the staffs of the Detroit Public Library, the Library of Congress, the University of Detroit Mercy Library, Wayne State University Purdy/Kresge Library Complex, and the University of Michigan Libraries for making their resources available to us. Following is a list of the copyright holders who have granted us permission to reproduce material in this volume of *CMLC*. Every effort has been made to trace copyright, but if omissions have been made, please let us know.

COPYRIGHTED MATERIAL IN *CMLC*, VOLUME 112, WAS REPRODUCED FROM THE FOLLOWING PERIODICALS:

Archív Orientální, v. 53, 1985. Reproduced by permission.—*Bulletin of the School of Oriental and African Studies, University of London,* v. 56, 1993; v. 58, 1995. Copyright © 1993, 1995 School of Oriental and African Studies. Both reproduced by permission.—*Classical Quarterly,* v. 34, 1984 for "Ptolemy and His Rivals in His *History of Alexander*" by Joseph Roisman. Copyright © Cambridge University Press 1984. Reprinted with the permission of Cambridge University Press.—*Journal of Hellenic Studies,* v. 108, 1988. Reproduced by permission.—*Oral Tradition,* v. 11, October, 1996 for "Epos and National Identity: Transformations and Incarnations" by Lauri Harvilahti. Copyright © 1996 by Its author. Reproduced by permission of the author./ v. 16, October, 2001 for "History and the Tibetan Epic *Gesar*" by Li Lianrong. Copyright © 2001 by the author. Reproduced by permission of the author.—*Philologus,* v. 118, 1974 for "The Stoic View of the Career and Character of Alexander the Great," by J. Rufus Fears. Copyright © 1974 Akademie-Verlag, Berlin. Reproduced by permission of the author. (J. Rufus Fears is David Ross Boyd Professor of Classics and G. T. Libby Blankenship Chair at the University of Oklahoma.)—*Studies in English Literature, 1500-1900,* v. 11, winter, 1971. Copyright © 1971 by The Johns Hopkins University Press. Reproduced by permission.

COPYRIGHTED MATERIAL IN *CMLC*, VOLUME 112, WAS REPRODUCED FROM THE FOLLOWING BOOKS:

Akbari, Suzanne Conklin. From "Alexander in the Orient: Bodies and Boundaries in the *Roman de toute chevalerie*," in *Postcolonial Approaches to the European Middle Ages: Translating Cultures.* Edited by Ananya Jahanara Kabir and Deanne Williams. Cambridge University Press, 2005. Copyright © Cambridge University Press 2005. Reprinted with the permission of Cambridge University Press.—Atkinson, J. E. From *A Commentary on Q. Curtius Rufus' Historiae Alexandri Magni, Books 3 and 4.* J. C. Gieben, 1980. Copyright © 1980 by J. E. Atkinson. Reproduced by permission.—Bosworth, A. B. From *From Arrian to Alexander: Studies in Historical Interpretation.* Clarendon Press, 1988. Copyright © A. B. Bosworth, 1988. All rights reserved. Reproduced by permission of Oxford University Press.—Bosworth, Brian. From an introduction in *Alexander the Great in Fact and Fiction.* Edited by A. B. Bosworth and E. J. Baynham. Oxford University Press, 2000. Copyright © Oxford University Press 2000. All rights reserved. Reproduced by permission of Oxford University Press.—Bridges, Margaret. From "Empowering the Hero: Alexander as Author in the *Epistola Alexandri ad Aristotelem* and its Medieval English Versions," in *The Problematics of Power: Eastern and Western Representations of Alexander the Great.* Edited by M. Bridges and J. Ch. Bürgel. Peter Lang, 1996. Copyright © Peter Lang AG, Europaischer Verlag der Wissenschaften, Bern 1996. All rights reserved. Reproduced by permission.—Bunt, G. H. V. From "Alexander's Last Days in the Middle English *Kyng Alisaunder*," in *Alexander the Great in the Middle Ages: Ten Studies on the Last Days of Alexander in Literary and Historical Writing.* Edited by L. J. Engels, A. G. Jongkees, W. Noomen, and N. van der Wal. Alfa Nijmegen, 1978. Copyright © Alfa Nijmegen. Reproduced by permission of the author.—Bunt, Gerritt H. V. From *Alexander the Great in the Literature of Medieval Britain.* Egbert Forsten, 1994. Copyright © 1994 Egbert Forsten Groningen. All rights reserved. Reproduced by permission.—Cary, George. From "The Conception of Alexander in Moralists to the Fourteenth Century, with a Prospect of the Opinions of Later Writers," in *The Medieval Alexander.* Edited by D. J. A. Ross. Cambridge University Press, 1956. Reprinted with the permission of Cambridge University Press.—Chism, Christine. From "Too Close for Comfort: Dis-Orienting Chivalry in the *Wars of Alexander,*" in *Text and Territory: Geographical Imagination in the European Middle Ages.* Edited by Sylvia Tomasch and Sealy Gilles. University of Pennsylvania Press, 1998. Copyright © 1998 University of Pennsylvania Press. All rights reserved. Reprinted by permission of the University of Pennsylvania Press.—Cropp, Gylnnis M. From "Christine de Pizan and Alexander the Great," in

Christine de Pizan 2000: Studies on Christine de Pizan in Honour of Angus J. Kennedy. Edited by John Campbell and Nadia Margolis. Rodopi, 2000. Copyright © Editions Rodopi B.V, Amsterdam 2000. Reproduced by permission.—Dilke, O. A. W. From **The Battle of Pharsalia** *: A Verse Translation of Lucan, Book VII.* Leeds Philosophical and Literary Society, 1971. Copyright © Leeds Philosophical and Literary Society 1971. Reproduced by permission.—Dronke, Peter. From "Poetic Originality in the *Wars of Alexander,*" in **The Long Fifteenth Century: Essays for Douglas Gray.** Edited by Helen Cooper and Sally Mapstone. Clarendon Press, 1997. Copyright © The several contributors, 1997. All rights reserved. Reproduced by permission of Oxford University Press.—Graves, Robert. From **Lucan, Pharsalia** *: Dramatic Episodes of the Civil War.* Translated by Robert Graves. Penguin Books, 1957. Copyright 1957 by Robert Graves. Copyright renewed 1984 by Robert Graves. Reproduced by permission of Carcanet Press Ltd. and A.P. Watt Ltd on behalf of the Trustees of the Robert Graves Copyright Trust.—Hamilton, J. R. From **Plutarch, Alexander** *: A Commentary.* Clarendon Press, 1969. Copyright © Oxford University Press 1969. Reproduced by permission of Oxford University Press.—Hammond, N. G. L. From **Three Historians of Alexander the Great; The So-Called Vulgate Authors: Diodorus, Justin and Curtius.** Cambridge University Press, 1983. Copyright © Faculty of Classics, Cambridge University Press 1983. Reprinted with the permission of Cambridge University Press.—Hammond, N. G. L. From **Sources for Alexander the Great: An Analysis of Plutarch's** Life **and Arrian's** Anabasis Alexandrou. Cambridge University Press, 1993. Copyright © Cambridge University Press 1993. Reprinted with the permission of Cambridge University Press.—Heissig, Walther. From "From Verse Epic to Prosimetrum in Recent Mongolian Oral Literature," in **Prosimetrum: Crosscultural Perspectives on Narrative in Prose and Verse.** Edited by Joseph Harris and Karl Reichl. D. S. Brewer, 1997. Copyright © contributors, 1997. Reproduced by permission.—Joyce, Jane Wilson. From **Lucan: Pharsalia.** Cornell University Press, 1993. Copyright © 1993 by Cornell University. All rights reserved. Used by permission of the publisher, Cornell University Press.—Leigh, Matthew. From **Lucan: Spectacle and Engagement.** Clarendon Press, 1997. Copyright © Matthew Leigh, 1997. Reproduced by permission of Oxford University Press.—Maddox, Donald and Sturm-Maddox, Sara. From an introduction to Alexander the Great in the French Middle Ages in **The Medieval French Alexander.** Reprinted by permission from *The Medieval French Alexander* edited by Donald Maddox and Sara Sturm-Maddox, the State University of New York Press. Copyright © 2002 State University of New York. All rights reserved.—Pearson, Lionel. From **The Lost Histories of Alexander the Great.** American Philological Association/B. H. Blackwell, 1960. Reproduced by permission.—Ross, D. J. A. From **Alexander Historiatus: A Guide to Medieval Illustrated Alexander Literature.** Warburg Institute, 1963. Copyright © The Warburg Institute 1963. Reproduced by permission.—Widdows, P. F. From **Lucan's Civil War.** Translated by P. F. Widdows. Indiana University Press, 1988. Copyright © 1988 by Indiana University Press. All rights reserved. Reproduced by permission.

Gale Literature Product Advisory Board

The members of the Gale Literature Product Advisory Board—reference librarians from public and academic library systems—represent a cross-section of our customer base and offer a variety of informed perspectives on both the presentation and content of our literature products. Advisory board members assess and define such quality issues as the relevance, currency, and usefulness of the author coverage, critical content, and literary topics included in our series; evaluate the layout, presentation, and general quality of our printed volumes; provide feedback on the criteria used for selecting authors and topics covered in our series; provide suggestions for potential enhancements to our series; identify any gaps in our coverage of authors or literary topics, recommending authors or topics for inclusion; analyze the appropriateness of our content and presentation for various user audiences, such as high school students, undergraduates, graduate students, librarians, and educators; and offer feedback on any proposed changes/enhancements to our series. We wish to thank the following advisors for their advice throughout the year.

Barbara M. Bibel
Librarian
Oakland Public Library
Oakland, California

Dr. Toby Burrows
Principal Librarian
The Scholars' Centre
University of Western Australia Library
Nedlands, Western Australia

Celia C. Daniel
Associate Reference Librarian
Howard University Libraries
Washington, D.C.

David M. Durant
Reference Librarian
Joyner Library
East Carolina University
Greenville, North Carolina

Nancy T. Guidry
Librarian
Bakersfield Community College
Bakersfield, California

Heather Martin
Arts & Humanities Librarian
University of Alabama at Birmingham, Sterne Library
Birmingham, Alabama

Susan Mikula
Librarian
Indiana Free Library
Indiana, Pennsylvania

Thomas Nixon
Humanities Reference Librarian
University of North Carolina at Chapel Hill, Davis
  Library
Chapel Hill, North Carolina

Mark Schumacher
Jackson Library
University of North Carolina at Greensboro
Greensboro, North Carolina

Gwen Scott-Miller
Assistant Director
Sno-Isle Regional Library System
Marysville, Washington
Williamsburg, Virginia

Alexander the Great in Literature

The following entry presents critical discussion of classical and medieval literary works about Alexander the Great.

INTRODUCTION

Stories about the life of Alexander the Great were extremely popular in the centuries following his death, reaching the peak of their popularity during the Middle Ages. Collectively known as the Alexander romance, these tales and legends chronicle the exploits of Alexander of Macedon (356 B.C.-323 B.C.). Alexander ruled from 336 B.C. until his death, by which time he had conquered the majority of the known world. His life was the stuff of legend even in his own lifetime, and only grew more embellished in the telling and retelling. The Alexander romance is part history, part myth, and part literature, and has captivated readers for centuries in its many different variations and translations. Scholars are particularly interested in the sources and development of the Alexander romance, with its extraordinarily complex series of recensions and variations.

The romance begins with the story of Alexander's birth to Queen Olympias, the fourth wife of King Philip II of Macedon. The tale explains that the Egyptian Pharaoh Nectanebus, highly skilled in magic, posed as the god Ammon and seduced and impregnated Olympias, and thus was actually Alexander's father. According to legend, when Alexander was twelve, he accidentally killed Nectanebus by pushing him into a pit, unaware that this was his father. Another key story recounts Alexander's taming of a wild horse, also at the age of twelve. According to the story, Philip II is offered a magnificent, but untameable horse; when no one else is willing to break in the animal, Alexander announces that he will. Having watched the horse, Alexander knows that the animal is afraid of his own shadow. Therefore, the boy leads him toward the sun, calms him, and mounts him. Emotionally overpowered, Philip II tells Alexander that Macedon is too small a kingdom for him and that he should set his eye on a prize that is truly worthy of him. Alexander then names the horse he has tamed Bucephalus—according to the story, Bucephalus would remain Alexander's constant companion in battle until the animal died of wounds in 326 B.C. There are also many accounts of Alexander's battles; the key campaigns center on the defeat of Thebes, Athens, and Sparta, and the conquering of the lands of the Persian King Darius. Immediately before his death, Darius offers his daughter, Roxane, in marriage to Alexander, who accepts. Texts also describe Alexander's invasion of India and the marvels he encounters there; these descriptions are given in the body of a letter ostensibly written by him to his teacher, Aristotle. Numerous portents of Alexander's death are recounted, and his murder by poison concludes the tales.

The Greek historian Callisthenes accompanied Alexander on his expedition through Asia. His account, *Deeds of Alexander,* formed the basis of other histories of Alexander that followed, but is no longer extant. Lionel Pearson explains that the only connected narratives that survive were written hundreds of years after Callisthenes's death. An unknown Greek composed an Alexander romance sometime in about the second century B.C. The author was sometimes inaccurately called Callisthenes and his work served as the source for most of the stories that circulated in medieval times. Pseudo-Callisthenes, as he is now referred to, was largely responsible for emphasizing the legendary accounts of Alexander's life. The Alexander romance of Pseudo-Callisthenes was translated into Latin around the year 330 by Julius Valerius, under the title *Res Gestae Alexandri Macedonis.*

The more historically based versions of the Alexander story stem largely from the efforts of Quintus Curtius Rufus and his *Historiae Alexandri Magni* (c. 50). In late 12th century France, Curtius's work served as the basis for Gautier (or Walter) de Châtillon's *Alexandreis.* This Latin poem was enormously popular. It was Curtius's thesis that Alexander had been corrupted by success and although the Persians had been unable to defeat him militarily, they managed to corrupt him morally. The Roman historian Plutarch (c. 46-c. 120), author of the classic *Parallel Lives,* paired Alexander's story with the tale of Julius Caesar's life. J. M. Mossman writes that Plutarch introduced tragic patterning and imagery into the Alexander story. N. G. L. Hammond, in his analysis of Plutarch's work, notes that the author emphasized Alexander's natural endowments, both physical and mental. He also stresses that Plutarch was concerned about the gradual changes in Alexander's personality as he conquered land after land. Another Roman historian, Arrian (c. 86-after 146), composed the *Anabasis of Alexander.* Arrian excelled as a military historian and made use of sources now lost, including (the true) Callisthenes and Ptolemy. Ptolemy, one of Alexander's most important generals, wrote a biography of his leader, rich in battle descriptions; it is now chiefly known through the work of Arrian. Another important historical work on Alexander was from the early 5th century. It was composed by a Spanish priest, Paulus Orosius, as part of a multi-volume history of the world. His very negative evaluation of Alexander fills most of the third volume. Peter Dronke examines this version, describes its chief literary devices, and praises its style. Kratz (see Further Reading) additionally looks at three significant recensions of the work of Leo of Naples, as well the letter concerning India supposedly written by Alexander to Aristotle. Margaret Bridges argues that using the epistolary format was an inappropriate authorial decision. The *Roman d'Alexandre* is a product of 12th century France, written by Alexandre de Bernay, who broke free of the typical Alexander sources, instead using other poets' ideas, as well as his own imagination. De Bernay is critically acclaimed for greatly expanding the narrative of his subject's life, making it less episodic, and for his vivid characterization (albeit at the cost of historical accuracy) of Alexander. Another key Alexander work from the Middle Ages is the Spanish epic poem *Libro de Alexandre,* built upon Gautier de Châtillon's *Alexandreis.* G. H. V. Hunt studies *Kyng Alisaunder,* the earliest Alexander romance in English, dating from the 14th century. *The Wars of Alexander,* a fourteenth-century North West Midlands poem, was based on a variation from around 1200 of Leo's tenth-century translation. Christine Chism stresses that the vulnerabilities of Alexander that are revealed therein illustrate the conflicts of British chivalry. Chism explains that the Alexander story varied considerably based on who told it and for what purpose. The Alexander romance, nearly unrivaled in popularity in the Middle Ages, lost favor with the ushering in of the Renaissance.

REPRESENTATIVE WORKS

Anonymous
Alexander's Letter to Aristotle (translated by Lloyd Gunerson) (letter) 1980

Anonymous
Kyng Alisaunder (romance) 14th century

Anonymous
Libro de Alexandre (poem) c. 1178-1250

Arrian
The Campaigns of Alexander (translated by Aubrey de Selincourt) (prose) 1958

Alexandre de Bernay
Roman d'Alexandre (romance) 12th century

Callisthenes
Deeds of Alexander (biography) 330 B.C.

Gautier (Walter) de Châtillon
Alexandreis (poem) c. late 12th century

Dennis M. Kratz, trans.
The Romances of Alexander (romance) 1991

Paulus Orosius
Hostoriorum Adversum Paganos Libri VII [*The Seven Books of History against the Pagans*] (history) c. 4th-5th century

Plutarch
Greek Lives (translated by Robin Waterfield) (biography) 2008

B. P. Reardon, ed.
Collected Ancient Greek Romances (romance) 1989

Quintus Curtius Rufus
Historiae Alexandri Magni (history) c. 50

Julius Valerius
Res Gestae Alexandri Macedonis (history) 330

OVERVIEWS AND MAJOR WORKS

Jirí Bečka (essay date 1985)

SOURCE: Bečka, Jirí. "Alexander the Great in Persian-Tajik and Czech Literatures." *Archív Orientální* 53, no. 4 (1985): 314-38.

[*In the following essay, Bečka discusses how the theme of Alexander was used in Persian-Tajik and Czech literatures and assesses its impact on those cultures.*]

Among the themes of *belles-lettres,* a significant place has been occupied, for more than two millennia, by the depiction of the life and deeds of Alexander the Great, a controversial personality of ancient history. The campaigns of this warrior left a deep trace in the consciousness of mankind, which is palpable even after long centuries. Albert Pražák (1880-1956), an outstanding specialist in the *Czech Alexandreis,* wrote:

"There are times when everything on earth, in heaven and in mankind must seemingly rush down and collapse, so that it might be possible to continue to live. This is why, from time to time, there emerge, from the calm surface of nations, all-encompassing individuals who ambitiously shake borders as well as thrones, surging forth from their native countries like a huge flood, or even an all-threatening deluge, till its water, swelling high as if in order to create a new and different world, suddenly subsides, after their death, returning to its narrow bed. The march of these great and excessive individuals throughout the world, leaving behind streams of horror and blood, cannot be wiped from the face of the earth, and is taken up both by the historian and the poet, once with reverence, once with damnation, but always with a feeling of epoch-making greatness. The earth trembles continually remembering him and every new analogous shock recalls him to mankind, and even after centuries he suddenly shines above man like a bloody and indelible sign."[1]

Alexander the Great has been, for twenty-three centuries, a prototype of such an all-encompassing individual; to some extent he has remained so till today. Both in literature and historiography, his aggression connected West with East and East with West, putting an end to the old epoch and starting a new one.[2]

The present article has three purposes: to compare the utilization of the theme of Alexander in Persian-Tajik[3] and Czech literatures, to demonstrate the comparatively broad information on ancient Iran brought into Czech literature by novels on Alexander,[4] and to present a factual although partial picture of how deeply and largely this theme penetrated into Iranian and Czech culture. Czech and Slovak materials have been used in this study, as well, in order to show the contribution of Czechoslovak scholars and men of letters as well as the longstanding interest of readers in this particular field.

Alexander's great campaign affected the whole area of the Near and Middle East, above all ancient Iran up to its eastern satrapies in today's Afghanistan, as well as today's Soviet Central Asia and, for a short time only, but rather effectually, also North-western India.[5] After the death of Alexander, the events of the campaign were noted down both by its participants and by other authors; these records have not been preserved, but they became the basis of a book, rather a novel than a history, by an unknown Greek from Alexandria called Pseudokallisthenes, approximately in the second century B.C. His primary intention was to write an interesting and thrilling narrative. A Czechoslovak scholar[6] demonstrated in a convincing way the affinity of the book by Pseudokallisthenes with Xenofon's *Kyru paideia,* another work which offered further comprehensive information on ancient Iran to Czech readers, in a Czech translation dating from 1605.[7]

The deepest trace was left by Alexander in the consciousness of the peoples of the affected areas. Remarkable is the development of the opinion on this warrior in the area of Iran. No local historiography had existed in Iran and it was as late as in the sixth century A. D. that Khusrav I (531-579) ordered a history, entitled *Khvatāynāmak,* to be written. We may read therein about the destruction of the Achaemenid Empire "by the damned Alexander the Byzantine who ordered the sacred books to be burnt or made away with".[8] Zoroastrian religious literature, however, had condemned Alexander even earlier as a cruel usurper who had pillaged the Iranian Empire. In Arta Virāz nāmak we may read: ". . . then the cursed and mendacious Ahriman, in order to sow doubt about this creed, seduced that damned Alexander the Byzantine residing in Egypt, who came to the Iranian Empire with great cruelty and war and pillage, killed the ruler of Iran and destroyed and devastated the royal seat."[9]

Later Iranian historiography as well as general opinion were not able to face the idea that a foreign usurper might have been able to seize the empire. There arose a legend that Alexander was in fact the son of an Iranian king and a Macedonian princess. The Achaemenid ruler Darius II replaced the Egyptian pharaoh Nectanebus, from the novel by Pseudokallisthenes, and Alexander thus became the legitimate successor to the Iranian throne, as the elder brother of Darius III. The latter had no right to be made king and he was overthrown by his elder brother, justice being thus done to the divine laws and the legitimicy of the Iranian rulers. To some extent, this conception was justified by the fact that Alexander adopted Persian manners. And thus, in Firdausī's *Sāh-nāma,* the father of Alexander is Dārāb and his mother is a daughter of the Macedonian King Philip. She is sent back to her father by him because of her bad-smelling mouth. At that time, however, Dārāb did not know that she was pregnant. But according to a Zoroastrian rivayat (a reply of the Iranian magicians to the Indian Parsees), her father was not Dārāb but "an unclean spirit" who had had intercourse with Philip's daughter during her journey to Greece.[10]

A response to Alexander may be found also in two basic books of the Near East, the *Bible* and the *Koran.*[11] An Alexandrian cult arose also among the ruling families. The historian of the Mongol occupation of Central Asia, Muhammad Nasavī (died in 1249/50), relates, in his *Sīrat as-Sultān Jalāluddīn,* a ceremony at the court of Khvārazmšāh Alāuddīn Muhammad II (1200-1220), which was called "naubayi zulqarnayn" and which indicated the continuance of Alexander the Great's tradition by the ruler.[12] Another conqueror of Asia, Timur (1370-1405), bore, apart from other titles, also that of "Iskandar-ul-ahd," i.e. "Alexander of His Time."[13] In the *Sarafnāmayi šāhī* ('Abdullāhnāma) written by Ḥāfiẓi

Taniš to celebrate the Šaybānid ruler 'Abdullāh II (1583-1598), the Emir of Bukhara is declared to be a successor to Iskandar,[14] and the Turkish historian Sa'duddīn compares his ruler to Alexander, too:

> šād bā afsari muzaffar far
> dāvari 'ādili sikandar dar.[15]

A number of references to the great personality of Alexander, though an idolater; may be found also in a chronicle of the founder of the Afghan Empire, Aḥmadšāh.[16] The author of the chronicle 'Ubaydullāh-nāma, written in honour of 'Ubaydullāh the Aš-tarkhanide (1702-1711), mentions Alexander nine times, mostly by calling his ruler "Alexander of His Time."[17] In his *Tārīxi Mas'ūdī,* Bayhaqī considers the Greek Alexander and the Persian Ardašir to be the most excellent rulers.[18] The sojourn of Alexander in Sistan is described in the *Tārīxi Sīstān* dating from the end of the 13th century.[19] Marco Polo recalls Alexander six times in his travelogue of 1298; e.g., he states that there is a tradition among the inhabitants of the Tonokayn region[20] that a battle had taken place there between Darius and Alexander, and in the chapter on Balkh, he does not fail to mention that it was here that Alexander married the daughter of Darius.[21] A Czech traveller to Central Asia in 1913-1915 stated that Alexander was considered a saint by the inhabitants of Šahrisabz.[22] Many more testimonies of this kind could be mentioned.

There were few poets in Persian-Tajik literature as well as those connected with it who did not at some time refer to Alexander's personality. He was mentioned in the famous poem *Vīs va Rāmīn,* from the middle of the 11th century, by Faxruddīn Gurgānī,[23] and in the Divan of Abulḥasan Farruxī (died 1037) his name appears nine times in the ghazals ending in –r.[24] The *Musībat-nāma* by the poet Farīduddīn 'Attār (died 1220) describes Alexander's visit to the Land of Darkness.[25] Iskandar is often referred to by Šayx Muslihuddīn Sa'dī, in his *Gulistān* and *Bustān,* as well as by Hāfiz.[26] Stories and legends on Iskandar may be found in the mystic and literary treatises by Abubakr Vahīd Tartūsī (11th century),[27] in the *Kābūsnāma* by Kaykā'ūs from the same period,[28] and in Jāmī's *Bahāristān.*[29] In the *Badāyī' ul-vaqāyī'* by Zaynuddīn Vāṣifī (died between 1551 and 1566), thirteen references to Iskandar are to be found.[30] The Tajik folk-poetess Dilšod Barno (1800-1905/6) from Badakhšan wrote in a ghazal:

> Johonro asli odam bud doro,
> Nabud Iskandar, Dorobu Doro . . .[31]

Authors writing in the Pashto language also knew Alexander well, as is testified to by a ghazal by 'Īsā Āxundzāda and a legend in verse on the drowning of Alexander.[32]

In *The Arabian Nights,* there are many references to him as well as a whole narrative on the meeting of Iskandar Zulqarnayn with an ascetic king.[33] A fairy-tale on Iskandar, similar to that on King Lávra (in Greek, Midas), but with horns instead of long ears, may be found among the Uzbeks,[34] and his name appears also in Tajik proverbs.[35] The mountain lake Iskandarkul in today's Tajikistan is connected with a number of legends.[36] According to the testimony of the outstanding Tajik poet Mirsaid Miršakar born in Pamir, a tribe called Iskandarī was living there, being considered either descendants or soldiers of Alexander.[37] In a similar way, there arose a legend, or even a theory, that the whole ethnic group of today's Nuristanīs in Afghanistan were descendants of Alexander's Macedonians.[38] A significant place is also occupied by Iskandar in the culture of other Central Asian nations, such as the Kazakhs.[39]

Above all, however, Alexander the Great became the hero of novels, both in verse and prose, in dozens of languages all over the East and the West, with specialists mentioning eighty versions in twenty-four languages, from Great Britain to Malaya, Thailand and Ceylon.[40] Ye. E. Bertel's rightly stated that the novel on Alexander conquered a larger territory, in the 15th century, than the hero himself. The fact that this theme has not lost its vitality among the Eastern people till today is proved by the folk-narrator Mamad Yūsuf, aged ninety, who sang about the legendary royal hero Iskandar in the language of the Yazgulami, a Pamir ethnic group with about 2,000 members, till only recently.[41]

All of these works were no historiographic accounts of Alexander's life and campaigns, but a framework into which often stories of a fairy-tale character were inserted. All of these versions were based on the so-called Pseudokallisthenes's elaboration, which was itself a collection from that author's—as well as other people's—imagination. Many traits, however, reveal a common origin—e.g. the sending of symbolical gifts, the capture of the mother of Darius, his assassination by traitors, etc.

To the greatest extent, and probably with most success, the theme was taken over by Persian-Tajik poetry, also on the basis of Pseudokallisthenes, but with significant differences in the depiction of the parts concerning the territory of Iran itself. It is highly probable that the above-mentioned divergence in the conception of Alexander in relation to Iran was brought about by an unpreserved Pahlavi translation of the novel by Pseudokallisthenes, Alexander-Iskandar becoming a legitimate heir of the Achaemenes. Also based on this principle is the extensive description by the tenth-century Persian historian Abū Ja'far Tabarī, writing in Arabic,[42] as well as the respective part of Firdausī's epic *Šāhnāma* (Book of Kings). Iskandar is depicted therein as a righteous member of a local dynasty, but in some places, e.g. in the story of Ardašīr Bābakān (in Pādšāhīyi Aškāniyān), Firdausī returns to the older Pahlavi standpoint, depicting Alexander as an evil-doer.[43] Like other men of letters, Firdausī treated the theme very freely, expressing ideas in words other than the original ones, adding as well as leaving out much, inserting fabulous stories and making anachronisms.[44]

The spread of the theme in Persian-Tajik literature is testified to, for instance, by the fact that Abulḥasan Farruxī (died 1037/8), one of the best poets of the Ghazna period of Sultan Maḥmūd, even considered the subject to be antiquated and trite:

> fasāna gaštu kuhan šud hadīsi iskandar
> suxani nav ār ki navrā halāvatīst digar
> hadīsi kūhna sikandar kujā rassīdu čī kard
> zi bas šanīdan gardīda xalqrā bāvar.[45]

He was proved wrong, however, one hundred and fifty years later, by Ilyās b. Yūsuf Niẓāmī Ganjavī (died 1209), an Āzarbāyjān poet writing in Persian. Around the year 1200, he inserted into his *Xamsa*,[46] consisting of five epico-lyrical poems, also a depiction of Iskandar's adventures, which was rid of Pseudokallisthenes's schema to an even greater degree. According to the outstanding specialist in the poet's writings, Jan Rypka, Niẓāmī's two-part *Iskandarnāma* is a work attaining "such poetical and philosphical depths as are only granted to isolated geniuses in the literature of the world".[47] Influenced by Hammer-Purdstall, the Czech literary historian V. Nebeský said in the middle of the last century that in Iran "Alexander of Macedonia is not that Great one, but a Persian personality, so as to be liked by odalisques, nevertheless resulting in a pleasant and sweet fairy-tale full of blooms and gay play of wit, out of the fabulous contents of which the real action shows through here and there."[48] Niẓāmī's version was directly influenced by Firdausī's *Šāhnāma*, but Niẓāmī himself stated that he had used Jewish, Christian as well as Pahlavi books, leaving out no single source. He presents Alexander as a man of humble Byzantine origin and adds, in the concluding part of the *Iqbālnāma*, that he wishes to find shrewd and observant readers, thus indicting his intention to be different from Firdausī for whom Iskandar was a brave warrior and commander. Niẓāmī views him as a warrior at the beginning only, in the so-called *Šarafnāma* (Book of Honour), but in *Iqbālnāma* (The Book of Happiness) he is changed into a sage who has reached the peak of knowledge and, at last, the position of a prophet.[49]

> birūn z-ānki dād az jahānīyat
> payˉqambarī dāšt arzānīyat.[50]

A century after Niẓāmī, in India, the theme was taken up again by another outstanding poet writing in Persian, Amīr Xusrau Dihlavī, in his poem *Āyīnayi iskandarī.*

As far as its historical nucleus is concerned, however, the subject suffered a further loss and literally became but a framework for the expression of the poet's humanistic ideas:

> šaraf kardani mardum az mardumīst
> vagarna hama ādamī ādamīst,

or a direct appeal to the ruler:

> ba tanhā nabāšad kasī sarfarāz
> sar ān šud kī bāšad ra'yatnavāz.[51]

In an even stronger way, the philosophical element stands out in the depiction of Iskandar's adventures in *Xiradnāmayi Iskandarī* by 'Abdurrahmān Jāmī from Herat (1414-1492). In the introduction, Jāmī hints that he knows the two previous poems well, appreciating them highly;[52] nevertheless, he gives not only a quite different garb to his narrative, but also new content:

> Kunūn kardaam pušti himmat qavī
> Diham masnaviro libosi navī.
> Kuhan masnavihoi pironi kor
> Ki mondast az on raftagon yodgor,
> Agarči ravonbaxšu jonparvarast,
> Dar aš'ori nav lazzati digar ast![53]

Iskandar, the hero of the *Šāhnāma*, surviving in Niẓāmī though only in a faint way and fading away in Amīr Xusrau, has completely disappeared. The aim of Jāmī's poem is to express ideas of Islamic philosphy, even though mediated by such Greeks as Aristotle, Plato, Socrates and other sages. The wise emperor of China adds words of righteous validity to his presents:

> Čunon zī, ki gar bošadat šarq joy,
> Kunandat talabatti qarb az xudoy.
> Na z-on son ki dar Ray šavī joygir,
> Ba nafrinat az Rum xezad nafir.[54]

Like Niẓāmī, Jāmī brings Iskandar to the City of Pure Manners, a land of utopia.[55] New tones of humanistic ideology on a higher level resound from Jāmī's poem.[56] The ripeness of the poet's ideas is testified to by the circumstance that his Alexander always thinks before acting and is guided by the advice of older and experienced men. Jāmī's conviction is also expressed in the following verse:

> Sikandar ziyoni xudu sudi xalq
> Hame xost az bahri behbudi xalq.[57]

At the same time as Jāmī's version, the theme was elaborated by his contemporary and friend from Herat, 'Ališer Navoī, the founder of Uzbek literature. In his poem *Saddi iskandarī* (from around 1485), written in the Chaghatay (Old Uzbek) language, he presented the image of an ideal ruler; his book has clearly the character of a "mirror" (Fürstenspiegel), an instruction advising the ruler how to rule the country. This undoubtedly resulted from the high political offices held by the poet for a long time. Navoī gives here also a rare image of a brave and wise woman.[58]

There are a number of elaborations which are less known, such as a part of the *Rasūlnāma* by Badruddīn b. ʿAbdussalām al-Kašmīrī, who lived in Bukhara from 1553 on,[59] or the masnavī *Iskandarnāma*, a Ḥurūfī work by Fażlullāh of the 18th century preserved at the British Museum Library.[60] There are, however, also works entitled *Iskandarnāma,* which have nothing in common with Alexander the Great.[61] In Persian-Tajik literature, one may find many narratives connected with the personality and deeds of Alexander, such as *Ābi hayāt, Yaʿjūj va Maʿjūj,* and *Zindāni Iskandar,* or the alleged correspondence of Alexander with Aristotle, etc.

Attention should also be devoted to the prosaic *Iskandarnāma* of the 13th-14th centuries, edited by the Iranian scholar Īraj Afšār.[62] His edition is based on the only known manuscript from Saīd Nafīsī's library. This manuscript was probably based on an older text, as mentioned by the unknown author.[63] The origin of this version is unclear; according to the Tajik scholar Yusuf Salimov, it may have been the already mentioned Pahlavi text which was re-rendered, through the medium of Arabic, into Persian.[64] Alexander is presented here as a legitimate heir of the Iranian throne, an able commander, conqueror and righteous ruler. His true face is revealed, however, from time to time, when the plunder and cruelties perpetrated by Iskandar's army as well as by himself are described.[65] This version is characterized by an exceptionally large number of inserted tales taken over from other legends, among others also some from the *Šāhnāma,* such as the chapter on the meeting of Alexander with Siyāvuš. In it, Alexander reaches Oman, Yemen and even China, as well as fabulous and semi-fabulous countries such as the Land of Supernatural Beings.[66] Worth mentioning in this connection is the 13th-century novel, *Dārābnāma,* by Abū Tāhir Tarsūsī, containing a narrative on Buranduxt, a daughter of Darius III; after the death of her father she fought against Iskandar, but married him later on and accompanied him in his campaign to India.[67] This motif has remained alive till today, one of its elaborations being, for instance, a drama by the Afghan historian and writer Ahmad ʿAlī Kohzād written in 1946 or *Dreyema špa,* a short novel by another Afghan writer, Qulām Qaus Xaybarī.

With some delay, the short but eventful life of Alexander the Great aroused the interest of men of letters in mediaeval Europe, Alexander gradually becoming one of the most frequent subjects of literary creation. In Europe, too, one may trace a certain development of this particular theme. At first, Alexander was both condemned and extolled, gradually crystallizing into the prototype of an efficient soldier for the Christian creed. Novels emerged, both in prose and in verse, especially in Latin which was then dominating European culture, but soon also in various national languages.

The acceptance of the Alexander theme was undoubtedly connected with the interest in the East aroused by the Crusades. Verse novels were written in France and Germany in the 12th century; the theme spread to other nations which continued weaving the plot, with each person adding something of his own to the content. In a verse novel on Alexander, a special twelve-syllable line came into being in France, called the Alexandrine; later it found its way into other literatures. The Alexandrine also reached Czech poetry, where it was used especially by Karel Hynek Mácha (1810-1836), Otakar Březina (1868-1929) and Jaroslav Kvapil (1868-1950). In Europe, there was hardly any nation or country that was not affected by the Macedonian king, his life and deeds.

One of the oldest versions in a national language and the very first book of this kind in a Slavonic nation was the so-called *Czech Alexandreis.*[68] This poem was probably a contemporary of Amīr Xusrau's *Āyīnai iskandarī* of the end of the 13th century. It is likely to have spread to Moravia and Slovakia, too, as indicated by dialectical elements in the Esztergom fragment.[69] The Czech poem was based on the Latin text by Gualtherus de Castelione, an archbishop notary in Reims in the second half of the 12th century; naturally one cannot call it a translation, just as Nizāmī's *Iskandarnāma* and Goethe's Faust were not translations.

The Czech poem on Alexander occupies a significant place among verse novels written on this subject. It introduced heroic epics into Bohemia, while at the same time being one of the most important, most valuable and largest books of older Czech poetry. Finally, it represents the very best epic poem on a foreign theme in Old Czech literature in general.[70] At the time of the Czech enlightenment at the end of the 18th and beginning of the 19th century, the *Alexandreis* became a testimony to the antiquity of Czech culture and an object of scholarly research. The latter was participated in by contemporary Czech and Slovak scholars such as Josef Dobrovský,[71] Karel Jaromír Erben.[72] Pavel Josef Šafařík[73] as well as one of the most enlightened personalities in the field of the humanities of that time, František Palacký. The latter edited a fragment of the poem, which had been discovered in the Museum of České Budějovice shortly before.[74] The first comprehensive treatise on the Czech Alexandreis was written by Václav Nebeský in 1847.[75]

The author of the poem is not known and the epic has not been preserved in its full extent. Out of about 8,500 lines in the ten cantos of the original, only 4,050 lines have been found, not in a single manuscript but in eight fragments written by various scribes; among this number, 601 lines are identical. The number of fragments is a testimony to the popularity of the poem in the 14th and the beginning of the 15th century.

In the introductory part of his poem, the Old Czech author[76] refers to the wisest man of the world, the Biblical Salomon who, according to the poet, considered the most inscrutable phenomena of life to be the trace of a boat in water, a serpent among the rocks, an eagle in the clouds, and especially a young man brought up in riches. His task of writing about Alexander the Great was extremely difficult, he pointed out, but he was going to set about it, in spite of the foolishness, lack of understanding or envy of his critics. He would write the poem especially for those who wanted to know about the great Macedonian ruler and warrior. In this way, the Czech poet replaced the Latin introduction to the original with an independent one which at the same time was intended to defend himself against possible criticism. He then proceeded to depict the adventures of Alexander:

The Greek King, Philip, begot a son called Alexander, with Olympia. She, however, was abducted by Pausanias and Philip was killed. Alexander was brought up by his guardian, Aristotle. The country of Greece had been seized by Darius and after Alexander attained maturity, he decided to liberate his country from the hands of the usurper. Aristotle promised his protégé that he would be successful if he acted wisely. First of all, Alexander restored order in his own land, then he began a campaign against Iran. Darius put up a resistance, sending a letter to Alexander; he added as gifts a curb, so that Alexander might curb his rashness, a purse for his enrichment, and a ball to play with rather than wage a vain war against mighty Iran. However, Alexander explained the symbols in his own way: He would bind Darius with the curb, the purse implied his control over the enemy's wealth and the ball Alexander's rule over the world. When the fighting took place, Darius was defeated and fled. After the battle, his family was captured, but Alexander mercifully took it under his protection during the Greeks' plunder of the military camp.

Alexander then began to forget Aristotle's advice and, indulging in self-complacency, even declared himself a god. Darius collected a new army, but after the death of his wife he proposed peace to Alexander, offering him his daughter, the country being her dowry. Alexander answered that he would acquire power only through fighting. A new encounter took place, in which Darius was defeated and fled once again. During his flight, he was killed by the traitors Bessus and Nabarzanes, but he had left a message for Alexander saying that he should punish the assassins and that he hoped that Alexander would escape a simlar fate and live to conquer the whole world. Alexander fulfilled the bequest, avenging the death of Darius and continuing his campaign against the Indian King, Poros, finally making friends with him. He then cruised the seas, thinking which country to conquer next and longing to rule the world. He reached Babylon, where he drank a cup of poisoned wine during a feast. Before dying, he managed to address his soldiers and to appoint his successor. His death was a warning to all those who strive to conquer the world, but who are unable to control themselves.

It is apparent from the content of this book that, due to the common source, Pseudokallisthenes, the basic plot of the Czech Alexandreis is close to that of the Persian-Tajik poems, especially that part of Firdausī's *Šāhnāma* which deals with Alexander's adventures. In both cases, for instance, Aristotle is his tutor, who advises the young ruler not to care about lowly persons and not to accept unreliable men as advisers. After the death of Alexander's father, a war between the Greeks and the Iranians breaks out. In both the *Šāhnāma* and the *Czech Alexandreis,* the Macedonian commander takes Darius' family as prisoners after the battle, but behaves in a chivalrous way. As in the case of Nizāmī, in the Czech poem one of Darius' gifts—a large amount of seeds (a kind of poppy, in the Czech version)—is mentioned as a symbol of military superiority; Alexander lets the birds eat them to indicate that he shall easily defeat Darius' large army.[77] In both the poem by the Czech author and the one by Firdausī, Darius is killed by traitors, who are then punished by Alexander. In the Czech version, Darius bequeathes three wishes to Alexander, whereas in the *Šāhnāma,* Iskandar finds Darius still alive and hears his three pieces of advice, viz. to fear God, not to harm his family, and to marry his daughter, Raušanak. Darius' wealth is indicated in the Czech poem by a description of a showy procession with all its "Oriental" splendour, including a cart carrying fire— an object of pious devotion of the Zoroastrians, the golden emblems of an eagle, and a thousand men of the royal guard.[78]

The Czech poet extolled Alexander the warrior and conqueror, but in the third canto he devoted many a line to descriptions of merciless battles full of suffering and dying men, voiced his aversion to the Greeks' plunder of the conquered camp of the Persians and referred to the arduous work that was the lot of the peasants during the war. He often inserted gnomic remarks on the harmfulness and futility of chasing after property and power, as well as on chivalrous virtues, one's duty to defend the honour of one's native land, the ways of a righteous ruler and his relations to his subjects. Like the versions by the Persian-Tajik authors, the Czech Alexandreis was on a considerably higher moral level than the original version by Pseudokallisthenes.[79] Both Czech and foreign scholars agree that in more than one respect the Czech Alexandreis surpassed the other mediaeval writings of a similar character.[80]

In contradistinction to the novel by Pseudokallisthenes, which was written from a pro-Greek and anti-Iranian standpoint, one can see a shift towards neutrality in the Czech author. In his poem, the battles are not supposed to be encounters of the Hellenic spirit with the numerical superiority of "the barbarians";[81] here, one does not find Pseudokallisthenes' despect characterizing his utterances about Darius: "Like weak dogs bark aloud, in such a way Darius shows himself great in words when too weak for deeds."[82] The narrative of Pseudokallisthenes was also much drier, describing events in a rather abrupt way and not including various reflections of the type to be found in both the Persian-Tajik poems and the Old Czech verse novel.

In the *Czech Alexandreis,* Darius is presented as a mighty but peace-loving ruler, a man of honour and a worthy opponent of Alexander. For the Czech poet, Alexander was the ideal; the Persians were, in his view, pagans, with Alexander representing a defender of the Christian world, although this is not expressly stated anywhere. Nevertheless, the poet often presents Darius also as a model for Czech noblemen and the Czech ruler. The personality of that king is depicted, in the Czech poem, in a certain parallelism to Alexander, which is apparent also in its composition and some other elements of its form. At the same time, Darius is described as a living being with human problems, not unlike those which the contemporary man in Europe had to face. Darius wants to live in peace, but he considers a retreat from the battlefield to be inadmissible cowardice. The sympathy of the Czech poet, in this particular respect, is obvious form the following lines:

> Darius the king then stepped out
> And under a mountain
> Humbly addressed his army,
> And whoever was there, rich or poor,
> Hearing his humble speech
> Spoken to them very softly,
> Could not be endowed with a heart hard enough
> Not no feel sorry for him.
> He said: Listen, oh respectable men,
> Heirs of the glory of the best past!
> Let everyone of you,
> Remembering his nobility,
> Recall his ancestors
> And the family he has come from.[83]

The King Darius of the Czech poet is a patriot appealing to his people to recall the honour and bravery of their ancestors. He is prepared to give up his life rather than let his country's honour be tarnished:

> God himself knows best
> That neither I nor my people
> May fall into disgrace.
> However hard the death may be,
> I would rather suffer it
> Than become estranged from my people,
> Bring my country into disgrace
> And call forth evil words about my nation.[84]

The Czech poet was obviously addressing here his own ruler and the outstanding men of his country, urging them to become one with their people and to defend their homeland's independence.

Darius' end is described in more detail in the Czech version than in Firdausī's book.[85] Though having been warned against the conspiracy of the Greek Patron, Darius resigns himself to his fate, which is oppressing him ever more. Nevertheless he remains with his men, due to his honourable commitment to his country and his people whom he does not wish to abandon, although he is endangered from that side as well. Darius has a premonition about his last moments and, in his tent, he talks in an agitated monologue, settling accounts with his own life. He reflects on what has caused his woeful fate, the monologue being yet another broadly developed review of the ruler's duties:

> What is my fault, oh God?
> Or did I ever violate the law
> So that someone was deprived of legacy
> Against his rights and without fault?
> Did I ever reverse the judgment
> To deprive someone of his property?[86]

In another fragment, we meet badly wounded, dying Darius in a deserted dale. He has learnt to know the futility of the world and sends a message to Alexander, through a stray messenger, to beware of a similar fate.[87]

On Czech soil, in the milieu of the court of the last Premyslide, there also emerged a German Alexandreis, an apotheosis of King Přemysl Otakar II, written by Ulrich von Etzenbach.[88]

The *Czech Alexandreis* was frequently recite and copied throughout the 14th century. When the verse version, addressing especially the court and the country's leaders, ceased to be to the general liking, a new prosaic version reenlivened the theme still in the first half of the 14th century. This was a Czech translation of the Latin book, *Historia regis Macedoniae de preliis,* by the archpriest Leon, which is also one of the Latin elaborations of Pseudokallisthenes dating from about the year 900 A.D.[89]

The new novel contained many fabulous and fantastic elements and was void of any political topicality, the work being intended for entertainment rather than enlightenment.

In describing the events, considerable differences are to be seen here, compared to the poetic version. For instance, Alexander is said to be the son of Manon and Olympia and is conceived of rather as an adventurer. With his first letter to Alexander, Darius sends him a ball, a stick and a golden pot, which Alexander again explains in his own way. Darius, called *Darjáš,* King of Kings, derides Alexander for wanting to equal him, pointing out that "a dull ass and a mule cannot rise to the stars, having no wings".[90] We may find herein the story of Alexander secretly entering Darius' palace and participating in a feast. Darius is killed by two knights, Bisso and Onabrazantes. While dying, he is visited by Alexander, addresses him as "my son" and asks him to marry his daughter, Roxana. Alexander is deeply moved; he takes off his imperial cloak and invests the dying man with it. Alexander is then crowned King of Iran, to sit on the throne inherited from Cyrus. The splendour of the coronation hall is described in detail. Alexander orders the assassin of Darius to be executed, marries Roxana and sets out on his fantastic campaign toward the East. In the "Bragman" country King Dydimus writes to Alexander: "We do not rule over either people or animals . . . it is cruel to press into service man whom godly ways have made equally free as ourselves."[91] This book was printed in Plzeň (Pilsen), in 1513.[92]

Another prosaic version, based on various originals, was written by Matouš Philomates Walkenberger of Dačice.[93] He inserted in it a number of stories, as well as his own opinion concerning the contemporary court. The following foursome, he said, was most appreciated there: the liar, the fool, the adulator, and the drunkard.[94]

Before as well as after, the Czech intelligentsia was becoming acquainted with Alexander and his campaign against Iran and Central Asia, at higher schools directly from Latin or even Greek writings. Thus the glossed Latin poem by Gualtherus was used at mediaeval schools as a model of Latin versifying.[95] The textbook of rhetorics and poetics, *Laborintus,* written in the middle of the 13th century and well-known in our lands, extolled Gualtherus' *Alexandreis.*[96] Pupils learned about Alexander's campaigns also from *Historiarum Alexandri Magni Macedonis libri X,* by Quintus Curtius Rufus, based on an unpreserved book by Kleitarchos. The former contained fantastic tales as well as a lot of information on Iran. In general, Curtius praised Alexander but did not conceal his faults.[97] Another source of knowledge about Alexander in Iran was Justinus' (2nd century A.D.) Extract from the History of the Philippides, *Historiae Philippicae,* by Pompeius Trogus, dealing with the history of empires in the Near and Middle East.[98] In this connection, mention should be made of Aristotle's book De secretis seretorum, translated into Czech "from the Croatian language" by Bavor Jr. Ro-

dovský of Hustiřany;[99] his translation was preserved in a manuscript dated 1574 and it comprises advice to the ruler, with examples drawn from the life of Persian kings. In the 18th and 19th centuries, a source of information of this kind were the popular biographic works, Alexandros and Caesar, by Plutarchos;[100] also well-known was Arrian's book *Anabasis Alexandru*[101] containing thorough information on the Iranian campaign. Another popular book was that by Lukianos from Syria, written in Greek under the title Talks from the Other World; the parts translated in 1910 concern Alexander, too.[102]

Alexander's personality and deeds were also reflected in further Czech entertaining, didactic and scholarly literature, in the arts and in cultural activities in general. Mentions of Alexander as well as Cyrus may be found in the oldest extant chronicle written in verse in the Czech language, by Dalimil, at the beginning of the 14th century, and the Macedonian conqueror is mentioned also in the chronicles by Marignollia (died 1358), Neplach (died 1371) and Pulkava (died 1380), as well as in Klaret's dictionaries.[103] Many a reflection of the popular legends heaped around the personality of Alexander the Great may be found in the set of examples, Tales of the Romans *(Gesta Romanorum)*[104] from the second half of the 14th century, in which Alexander is presented as a sage, just as he is in the writings by Niẓāmī and his successors. As a wise man, he is depicted also in a considerable part of the manuscripts of *Životy starých mudrců* (Lives of Ancient Sages) by Walter Burleigh, written in the 14th-15th centuries. In all, 151 such Latin manuscripts have been found so far, of which 36 are preserved in Bohemia and one in Slovakia. Moreover, there are six Czech versions, a Czech translation having also been printed in 1516.[105] It is worth mentioning that "examples" of this kind were written also for the use of preachers, which were parables meant for a wide public. Alexander was recalled by the Masters of Prague University at the so-called *Bachelors' Determinations,*[106] and quite frequently by Jan Hus as well.[107] Alexander was well-known to the anonymous author of *Tkadleček,* an outstanding work of older Czech literature.[108] From various points of view, he was mentioned in poems written on the motif of "ubi sunt". A Disputation of the Soul and the Body, and in the poem Oh Deceitful Beauty of the World dating from 1719. His name may often be found in the writings and letters of Czech humanists of the 15th and 16th centuries, e.g. those of the scholar and writer Bohuslav Hasištejnský of Lobkovice (1460-1510).[109]

Alexander's campaigns were described in various books on the history of the world, e.g. among them the Czech translation of the well-known *Chronicle of the World* by the German mathematician, astrologer and physician Johann Karion, which appeared for the first time in

Litomyšl in 1541 and then in revised editions in Prague in 1581, 1584 and 1602.[110] A response to Alexander's campaign may be found in the Old Czech *Lucidarium*,[111] and he is mentioned several times in the then very popular *Kronika česká* (Czech Chronicle, 1541) by Václav Hájek of Libočany (died 1553), who was the first to publish, when describing the founding of a monastery for Slavonic liturgy in Prague in 1348, the so-called Record or *Manifesto of Alexander the Great to the Slavs,* allegedly written by Alexander in the twelfth year of his reign, i.e. in 324 B.C.[112] The British traveller Fynes Moryson found in the Church of Emaus in Prague, in 1592, an inscription containing this manifesto engraved on a monument.[113] Actually, the inscription probably originated during the Hussite Wars in Bohemia, when the very existence of the Czech nation was endangered with the impending threat of the fate of the Elbe Slavs. Its author might have been Vavřinec of Březová (1370-1437), an erudite Master of Prague University and the translator of Marco Polo's *Million*.[114] Ján Jesenský (Jessenius, 1566-1621), a scholar of Slovak origin who was executed for taking part in the struggle against the Hapsburg domination, compared, in 1611, Matthew II to Alexander the Great because of the former's resistance to Turkish expansion, and he said that Matthew had fulfilled what was asked of Cyrus by Xenofon. Also Jan Amos Komenský (Comenius, 1592-1670),[115] the greatest personality of older Czech literature, utilized literature concerning Alexander's life and deeds, selecting suitable examples to strengthen and corroborate his ideas and conclusions drawn in paedagogics. He presented Alexander, for instance, as a promoter of science and a friend of philosophy because of his relation to Aristotle, but later on he stressed rather his imperfect and bad personality characterized by an insatiable greediness. In his writing, *Truchlivý* (The Mournful) he takes an altogether negative view of Alexander, whom he describes as an enemy rejoicing at the destruction of all his opponents. Similarly in the *Labyrinth* Alexander is ranked among those who commit great wrongs to mankind.[116] The knowledge about Alexander was promoted also by one of the representatives of Czech humanistic literature, Mikuláš Konáč z Hodiškova (died about 1546), through his translation into Czech, in 1507, of a Pseudolukianian dialogue on the most famous warriors, Scipio, Alexander and Hannibal.[117]

The fine arts,[118] allegorical scenes, theatrical plays, as well as operas in Bohemia were also thematically inspired by Alexander's fate and the legends concerning him.[119]

Along with the spread of Czech and Slovak journalism at the beginning of the 19th century, popular as well as scholarly articles and shorter translations on the theme of Alexander started to appear.[120] Attention should be paid to a thorough paper by the classical philologist Vilém Gabler (1821-1897), responding to A. Lamartine's *Vie d'Alexandre le Grand* (Paris 1859). Gabler admired Alexander as little as Tamerlane; he considered him an arrogant conqueror and tried to correct certain assertions of Arrianos, Plutarchos and Curtius by analyzing all the reports and describing the cruelties perpetrated by Alexander in Iran as well as in other countries. He concluded his article with the following words: "If history is to be a teacher of life, it must renounce preaching vain glory of and unfounded legends about the so-called Great Kings."[121] A large number of special papers appeared also in reports of gymnasiums and other higher schools in the Czech lands.[122]

The theme of Alexander was also an inspiration to Czech poets and writers. The spiritual and moral superiority of a philosopher over a world ruler is shown in the comedy *V sudu Diogenově* (In Diogenes' Barel, 1883) by Jaroslav Vrchlický.[123] A satire entitled *Alexander Veliký* (Alexander the Great), written by Karel Čapek in the form of a letter sent from Iran by Alexander to Aristotle, was aimed at Hitler and his totalitarian rule.[124] Also Lom's radio play, *Alexander,* had the similarly humanistic purpose of defending human culture against the despotism of warriors. At the present time, a more detailed survey on a high level is presented by Vladislav Vavřínek in his book *Alexander Veliký* (Alexander the Great), in which samples of old literature concerning Alexander may also be found.[125] The suffering of Iran during Alexander's campaign is desribed in a novel by P. Bamm, the Slovak translation of which appeared under the title *Alexander Veľký alebo premena sveta* (Alexander the Great, or the Change of the World) in Bratislava in 1971.

Literature in the territory marked by Persian-Tajik culture was also strongly affected by the theme of Alexander. Just as in Europe and Bohemia, a number of large novels in verse,[126] as well as prosaic versions, appeared there, in all cases based on Pseudokallisthenes. The theme was dealt with by the best authors of lyrico-epical poems from the whole sphere of Persian-Tajik poetry and it was the Alexandreis which acquired an outstanding place in their writings. From more or less epic descriptions, though with fantastic elements, the best poems developed into writings imbued with highly humanistic ideas.

In comparison with Pseudokallisthenes and to some extent also with Gualtherus' book, the *Czech Alexandreis* in verse shows a shift towards didacticism and a higher moral level in expressing contemporary ideas, such as resistance against aggressive wars, sympathy with the lot of ordinary people, and patriotic emotions. The prosaic versions, however, both in our country and in the Iranian area, were meant rather for entertainment, depicting adventurous incidents or persons differing in social position and character and viewed from outside.

Alexander's personality and life story penetrated deep into the consciousness of both Persian-Tajik literature and that in our lands. Both here and there, there were few outstanding authors who did not utilize Alexander's deeds and personality in support of their own reflections. Alexander also permeated folk literature, however more in the East, where he has remained directly fixed in the memory of the people.

Niẓāmī often set his narrative in the milieu of Azerbaijan, Navoī's *Saddi Iskandarī* is a mine of information on the life and ideas of Central Asia in the 15th century, and Aḥmadī inserted incidents from the history of the Ottoman dynasty into his *Iskendernama,* which therefore may be considered the very first Ottoman chronicle that reflects, at the same time, the contemporary events in Tabriz.[127]

The Czech *Alexandreis* was a national adaptation of the theme of Alexander, which to a great extent was socially and personally connected with the Czech feudal milieu of the end of the 13th century.[128] In the mediaeval European surroundings, Alexander acquired, besides classical traits, many of the characteristics and embellishments of a Christian knight, but he was also tinted with a rich admixture of Eastern fabulous and supernatural elements. In the train of Alexander wandering through Iran and Central Asia, one may find courtiers having purely Czech names such as Radvan, Mladota or Radota; one may also find therein criticism of contemporary evils, such as bribes at the courts of justice. Allusions to the mutual relations between the Czechs and the Germans were easily inserted into the text, while describing the celebrations of the fall of Babylon—the Germans, who were only guests in Prague, would have preferred not to see a single Czech on a Prague bridge . . .[129] In the army of Alexander, one may meet princes, counts, dukes and knights[130] in the mediaeval sense. On the other hand, the Persians use tactics and weapons such as hammers, near to a Czech author, in their battles.[131] The *Czech Alexandreis* is an epic poem having a high style, depicting the ideal of the contemporary nobleman through the mediation of an ancient commander.[132]

Due to the novels on Alexander both in verse and in prose, some works of classical literature dealing with Alexander both in the original and in Czech translations, as well as writings on Alexander's campaign against Iran and Central Asia, the educated circles in our lands were able to read about the existence of ancient Iranian civilization and to come to know some of its products and the remote areas of Central Asia and

India.[133] Moreover, through the biblical references and preachings in which the so-called exempla played a role, this knowledge even spread among the broader strata of our country's inhabitants. Thus without the *Alexandreis,* our ancestors would have known practically nothing about Iran and Central Asia.[134]

Notes

1. From the introductory part of the excellent book, *Staročeská báseň o Alexandru Velikém* (An Old Czech Poem on Alexander the Great), Prague 1945, by the scholar Albert Pražák. Reviewed by J. Vilikovský, in: Naše věda 24, 1946, po. 235-237; J. Daňhelka, in: Věda a život 12, 1946, pp. 141-142; A. Škarka, in: Listy filologické 70, 1946, pp. 202-205; J. Viskovataja, in: Slavia (Praha) 18, 1947, pp. 496-503.

2. The author of the best ancient summary of Alexander's campaigns was probably Arrianos, in his *Anabasis Alexandru,* which was, however, apparently written from the Greek point of view. Alexander is considered to be the greatest Greek, whereas Darius is presented as a weak ruler unable to conduct war, but committing no wrongs in other respects. A Czech translation of this book is *Tažení Alexandra Velikého* (Campaigns of Alexander the Great), by A. Bělský (Prague 1972). A history of events in Iran, according to the most recent results of historiography, is contained in the book *Sláva a pád starého Íránu* (The Glory and Fall of Ancient Iran), by O. Klíma (Prague 1977, pp. 97-108). A thorough description may be found in the book *Aleksandr Makedonskij i Vostok,* by B. G. Gafurov and D. I. Cibukidis (Moscow 1980, 456 pp., with a detailed bibliography and indices). Alexander the Great even took credit for the progress of science. According to an old legend, the Egyptian god, Thoth (Greek, Hermes Trismegistos), had ordered the basic secret of alchemy to be engraved in an emerald tablet. This was hidden by Sarah, the wife of Abraham, in a cave near Hebron, where it was discovered by Alexander the Great.

3. The term Persian-Tajik culture and literature it meant to express the fact that today if forms a common cultural heritage of the Persians in Iran and the Tajiks in Tajikistan and Afghanistan. Iran, Iranian and similar terms cover not only today's Iran, but the whole Iranian area, including today's Afghanistan and the adjacent parts of Central Asia, which since remote times had been dominated by the Iranian culture.

4. Fragmentary pieces of information on Iran and its rulers were offered, since the 9th century, by the Old Slavonic and Latin Bible, since the 10th

century, by Czech translations of parts of the Bible, and since the 14th century, by its complete translation. The Czech *Bible* is also one of the Czech incunabules. In the Biblical Concordance by M. Bič and J. B. Souček (3 vols., Prague 1961-1967), words like Persian, Artaxerxes, Darius, Elam, Cyros, Median, etc. are quoted from more than a hundred places in the Bible.

5. Cf. Jawaharlal Nehru, *The Discovery of India*, Calcutta 1956, p. 101, etc. Concerning Alexander in India in relation to Czech culture, see also M. Krása, *Looking towards India*, Prague 1969, pp. 17-18 and 38. The fact that Alexander has remained in the memory of the Indians is testified to by the legend of Kautilya, who prevented Alexander the Great's invasion of India, in: *Příběhy bájné Indie* (Stories of Fabulous India), transl. by V. Miltner, Prague 1973, pp. 125-138. See also a whole chapter in the *History of the World* by al-Mas'ūdī, dating from the 10th century. In the book *Gold-fields and Gem-mines*, by Abu'l-Hasan 'Alī ibn al-Hussayn al-Mas'ūdī, the Czech translator J. Hrbek left out the chapter on India, as it does not contain historical facts (p. 215).

6. J. Ludvikovský, *Řecký román dobrodružný* (The Greek Adventure Novel), Prague 1925, pp. 125ff.

7. *Cyripaedia. Hodnověrná starožitná historie* (A Trustworthy Ancient History), transl. by Abraham of Gynterrode, Prague 1605. The book was published as well as translated several times, the last translation being Xenofon, *O Kýrově vychování* (On Cyrus' Education), by V. Bahník, Prague 1970.

8. O. Klíma, *Wie sah die persische Geschichtsschreibung in der vorislamischen Periode aus.* In: ArOr 36, 1968, pp. 213-232. *Dějepisectví v předislámské Persii* (Historiography in Pre-Islamic Persia), by the same author. In: Nový Orient 22, 1967, pp. 69-70. *Zarathuštra*, by the same author, Prague 1964, pp. 7, 126, 144.

9. O. Klíma, *Īrān*. In: *Prameny života. Obraz člověka a světa ve starých literaturách* (Sources of Life. Images of Man and the World in Ancient Literatures), Prague 1982, p. 147; on Alexander, see also pp. 150 and 154.

10. Ch. Bartholomae, *Mitteliranische Studie III (Die Erzeugung Alexander des Grossen in einer neuen Wendung).* In: Wiener Zeitschrift des Morgenlandes 27, 1913, pp. 23 ff.

11. The Bible presents Alexander the Great as an instrument of God's wrath against the Persians, especially in the apocryphal first book of the Maccabees (1, 1-10) and in Daniel's prophecy (2, 39;

7, 6; 8, 5-7; 11, 3ff). The 18th surah of the *Koran*, entitled The Cave, which is one of the most favoured ones in the Islamic world and is recited every Friday during the noon-prayer in all mosques, contains one of the episodes of the novel on Alexander, in lines 82-97. Cf. *Korán*, transl. by I. Hrbek, Prague 1972, pp. 278-279. The change of a warrior into a sage is reflected here. An explanation of the epithet "two-horned" his proposed by A. Salač in is article, *Alexander of Macedon and Al Iskandar Dhu-l-carnein.* In: Eunomia. Listy filologické IV, pars 2, Pragae 1960, pp. 41-43.

12. See V. M. Masson and V. A. Romodin, *Istoriya Afganistana*, Moscow 1964, Vol. 1, p. 277.

13. Muhammad 'Abdul Ghani, *A History of the Persian Language . . .* Allahabad 1929, pp. 12 and 38.

14. Xafiz-i Tanyš ibn Mir Muxammad Buxari, *Šarafnamayi šaxi*, Moscow 1983, T. 1 (another three volumes are to follow), edited by M. A. Salaxetdinov, fol. 4a (p. 34). Alexander is also mentioned in 51 other places here.

15. František Adam Kollár, a Slovak orientalist (1720-1783), in the text edition and Latin translation of Saad Ed-Dini *Annales Turcici Taschet-Tewarich . . . usque ad Muram I*, Viennae 1755, p. 46. Translation: Happy is he who has attained the honour of the crown / the righteous judge at Alexander's court.

16. *Tārīxi ahmadšāhī ta'līfi Mahmūd al-Husyanī al-munšī ibn Ibrāhīm al-Jāmī*, jildi 1, Muskū 1974, fol. 4a, 9b, 10a, 298b, 316b; jildi 2, 346a, 380b.

17. Mir Muxammed Amin-i Buxari, *Ubaydulla-name*, transl. by A. A. Semenov, Taškent 1957, p. 14 etc.

18. Abu-l-fazl Bayhakī, *Istoriya Mas'uda*. Translation from Persian; introduction, comments and appendices by A. K. Arends. 2nd Ed. Moscow 1969, p. 164.

19. *Ta'rixi Sistan* (Istoriya Sistana). Translated, commented upon and introduced by L. P. Smirnova, Moscow 1974, p. 55.

20. The towns of Tun and Kayn (i.e. Firdaus and Kayen) on the southern border of Khorasan. Actually, Darius was killed in a battle at Arbela (today's Erbil), far to the west of this place.

21. *Marka Pavlova z Benátek Milion* (The Million, by Marek Pavlov from Venezia). Edited by J. V. Prášek, Prague 1902, pp. 18, 30, etc. The book was translated into Czech in about 1400.

22. J. J. Malý, *Napříč říší tamerlánovou* (Across the Empire of Tamerlane), Prague 1939, p. 159.

23. Faxruddin Gurgani, *O lásce Vísy a Rámína* (On the Love of Vis and Ramin), transl. by V. Kubíčková, Prague 1979, p. 287.

24. *Dīvānī Hakīmi Farruxī*. Edited by Seyyed Abulqāsim, Tehrān 1320 h. q., p. 67. The ghazals are usually arranged according to the last letter of the rhyme. In the dīvān edited by Muḥ. Dabīri Siyāqī, Tehrān 1335, his name appears in 17 places.

25. Cf. J. A. Boyle, *Popular Literature and Folklore in 'Attār's Mathnawī*. In: Colloquio italo-iraniano sul poeta mistice Fariduddin 'Attār, Roma 1978, pp. 57-70.

26. In Czech translations, e.g., Sa'dī, *Růžová zahrada* (A Garden of Roses). Transl. by V. Kubíčková, Prague 1974, p. 28; *Z dívánu Háfize* (From the Divan of Hafiz). Transl. by J. Košut and J. Vrchlický, Prague 1881, pp. 9, 115, 116.

27. In more detail, see Ye. E. Bertel's, *Roman ob Aleksandre i yego glavyne versii na Vostoke*. In: Izbrannye trudy, Moscow 1965, pp. 306-314.

28. Kaykā'ūs, *Kniha rad* (Book of Advice). Transl. by J. Osvald, Prague 1977, pp. 45, 120, 129, 136 and 215.

29. Abdurrahmān Jāmī, *Jarní zahrada* (A Spring Garden). Transl. by J. Marek and K. Bednář, Prague 1957, pp. 21-23, 42 and 43.

30. *Badāyi' ul-vaqāyi'*. Ta 'līfi Zaynuddīn Vāsifī. Taṣḥīḥi Aleksandr Bodirūf (A. N. Boldyrev), Tāhrān 1349, 1350.

31. *Dilšodi Barno va merosi adabii ū*. Prepared by A. Muxtorov and Sulaymonqul Rojī, Dušanbe 1970, p. 53. Transl.: The Sustainer of mankind in the world is he who brings welfare / not Alexander, Darius or Dārāb. The Tajik texts are transcribed from the contemporary Tajik script.

32. V. J. Darmesteter, *Chants populaires des Afghans*, Paris 1888-1890, pp. 90, 94, 109-116.

33. *Kniha tisíci a jedné noci* (Arabian Nights), 8 volumes. Transl. by F. Tauer, Prague 1929, vol. 2, p. 10; Vol. 5, pp. 11-12, etc.

34. *Uzbekskie narodnye skazky*, Taškent 1955, pp. 179-181. This fairy-tale is included in a collection compiled by the ethnologist G. Jungbauer of České Budějovice, when he was a prisoner of war in Central Asia during the First World War: König Alexander mit dem Horn. In: *Märchen aus Turkestan und Tibet*, Jena 192, pp. 196-198. Detailed information on Alexander in folklore may be found in the book by E. A. Kostyuxin, *Aleksandr Makedonskiy v literaturnoy i fol'klornoy tradicii*, Moscow 1972.

35. Be pir narav dar amonī / harčand Iskandari zamonī. Transl.: Do not enter danger without an experienced man / even if you are the Alexander of your time. In: B. Tilavov, *Zarbulmasalhoi mašhur*, Dušanbe 1983, p. 27.

36. Cf. Yu. Ya'qubov, *Nomi aslii Kūli Iskandar čist?* In: Maorif va madaniyat, 1. 9. 1970, p. 4; Ozero tayn. In: Pamir 1983, No. 2, p. 70.

37. M. Miršakar, *Yodi yori mehrubon*. Dušanbe 1979, pp. 196-197. The author quotes a folk quatrain (ruboī), in which the name of the clan has been preserved:

Šoh Nosiri Xusravi šahi bandanovoz,
Iskandariyam, zi mulku duri Daroz.
Har on, ki ba dargahi tu oyad ba niyoz,
Navmed zi dargat tu kay gardad boz.

Translation: Oh King Nasir Khusrav, you merciful ruler, / I am from the clan of Iskandaris, from the distant land of Darvaz. / Whoever comes to your door with a request / he never goes back from your door without hope.

38. See, e.g., *Afghanistan*, ed. by Willy Kraus, Tübingen u. Basel 1972, p. 178; W. K. Fraser-Tytler, *Afghanistan*, London 1967, pp. 57 ff. This assumption is contradicted by the Afghan historian Ahmad'alī Kohzād, in his article *The Nuristanis are Aryans and not Greek Remnants*. In: Afghanistan (Kābul), 9, 1954, No. 2, pp. 36-40.

39. Cf. U. Kumisbaev, *Turmagambet Iztleuov i ego Rustem-Dastan*. Alma-Ata 1982, p. 44, etc.

40. In more detail, see A. Pražák, *Staročeská báseň o Alexandrovi Velikém*, Prague 1945, pp. 9-61; J. Cejpek, in: *History of Iranian Literature*, Dordrecht 1968, pp. 628-630. Contributions from Czechoslovakia on non-Iranian Eastern Alexandreis: Pavel Poucha, *Román o Alexandru Makedonském v mongolské literatuře* (A Novel on Alexander the Macedonian in Mongolian Literature). In: Zprávy Československé společnosti orientalistické 7, 1967, No. 2, pp. 22-27; E. Pantůčková, *Iskendername v tvorbě Ahmediho* (The Iskendername in Ahmedi's Writings). An unpublished Doctoral Thesis submitted to the Philosophical Faculty of Charles University in Prague, in 1967; Eva Pantůčková, *Zur Analyse eines der historischen Bestandteile von Ahmedis Iskendernāme*. In: ArOr [*Archiv Orientalni*] 41, 1973, pp. 28-41 (the manuscript of this writing by Ahmedi, dated 1486, is preserved at the University Library in Bratislava; see *Arabische, türkische und persische Handschriften der Universitätsbibliothek in Bratislava*. Bratislava 1961, No. 466/Tc 20); Karel Fischer, *Ohlas historické osobnosti Alexandra Ve-*

likého v židovské literatuře (A Response to the Historical Personality of Alexander the Great in Jewish Literature). A Doctoral Thesis submitted to the Philosophical Faculty of Charles University in Prague, in 1948/49 (No. 2434); B. Frank, *Zēnā Eskender, die äthiopische Alexander-Legende* (1941-2); Christian Greis; *Die äthiopische Schrift über Alexander* (1905-6). The two last mentioned monographs are unpublished Doctoral Theses submitted to the German University in Prague.

41. D. I. Edel'man, *Yazgulamskaya legenda ob Aleksandre.* In: Kratkie soobščeniya Instituta narodov Azii 67, 1963, p. 55.

42. The part concerning pre-Islamic Iran is probably based on an Arabic translation of the book *Xvatāynāmak.* Back in the 10th century, Abū' alī Muhammad Bal' amī translated this book, in a considerably shortened version, into Persian, under the title *Tarjumayi tārīxi Tabarī.* One of the manuscripts of it is preserved in the Manuscript Department of the State Library of the ČSR in Prague.

43. Kasī nīst zīn nāmdār anjuman / zi farzāne vo mardum rāyzan // ki našnīd k-Iskandar badgumān / če kard az furūmāyigī dar jahān // Translation: There is nobody in this esteemed gathering / consisting of sages and advisers of men / who has not heard about the evil deeds / perpetrated by vicious Alexander in the world. *Šāhnāmayi Firdausī.* Matni intiqādī,, jildi haftum, Muskū 1968, p. 130, 1.333. The *Šāhnāma* edited in Dushanbe quotes the following lines: Ki našnid, k-Iskandar andar jahon / čī kard az furūmoyagoni mehon, adding a note that the bayt is missing in one of the manuscripts used. Abulqosim Firdavsī, *Šohnoma,* jildi VII, Dushanbe 1966, p. 195, 1. 322. In her Candidate Thesis, *Istoki i evolyuciya obraza Iskandara v Šax-namexc"* Firdousi (The Sources and Development of Alexander's Image in Firdausi's Šāhnāma), Zulfiya Mullojonova presents the hypothesis that in the *Šāhnāma,* the whole part concerning Iskandar is a criticism of contemporary conditions or even a literary-political satire aimed at Maḥmūd of Ghazna (Self-report, Dushanbe 1985, p. 5).

44. E.g., a few centuries before Christ, he describes an oath with Christian attributes; see Šāhnāmayi Firdausī (Muskū 1968, jildi haftum, p. 59, bayt 959-961). According to Muhammad Ābādī Bāvīl, *Āyīnhā dar Šāhnāmayi Firdausī.* Tabrīz 1350, p. 44.

45. *Dīvāni Hakīmi Farruxī.* Edited by Seyyid Abulqāsim, Tehrān 1320 h. q. (lithographed), p. 67. Translation: The story of Alexander has been turned into a fairy-tale and become antiquated, / bringing new words of another new grace. / The people who listened to it frequently / have believed the old legend of Alexander, where he went and what he did. It is not without interest that Geoffrey Chaucer (1340-1404) wrote in his *Canterbury Tales:* The storie of Alexandre is so commune, / That every wight, that hath discretion / Hath heard somewhat or all of his fortune.

46. In Czechoslovak libraries, there are a few original manuscripts: The Library of the National Museum in Prague (Nostic), MSd2 from 831/1427-8; The State Library of the ČSR, from 1085/1674-5, No. 146 in the auxiliary list of the Manuscript Department; the Library of the Oriental Institute of the ČSAV in Prague, sign. R III 14, from about the 10th century H.

47. *History of Iranian Literature,* Dordrecht 1968, p. 212. A. Bausani, in the book *Storia della letteratura persiana,* by A. Pagliaro and A. Bausani, Milano 1960, p. 696, considers Niẓāmī to be the greatest Persian poet, and he devotes most space merely to his *Iskandarnāma.* In another paper, he draws attention to the remarkable position of the woman in this poem: "la figura di Širin idealizzata da Niẓāmī, sono espressioni piutosto rare non solo nella letteratura persiana ma forse in genere nella letteratura tradizionale." In: *Colloquio sul poeta persiano Nizami e la leggenda iranica di Alessandro Magno,* Roma 1977, pp. 172 ff.

48. W. Nebeský, *Alexandreis česká* (The Czech Alexandreis). In: Časopis českého museum 21, 1847, Vol. 2, p. 13.

49. Cf. Zabīhullāh Safā, *Tārīxi adabiyāt dar Īrān,* Tehrān 1336, p. 806, and the postscript by J. Rypka to the book, Iljás ben Júsuf Nizámí Gandžaví, *Chvály* (Praises), Prague 1953, pp. 169-170. F. Pfister, in his book, *Alexander der Grosse in den Offenbarungen der Griechen, Juden, Mohammedanern und Christen* (Berlin 1956), follows the way in which Alexander's personality gradually attained supernatural traits up to the point of deification in the literatures and traditions of various nations.

50. *Xamsayi Niẓāmī.* Ed. by Šayx Ḥasan, Tehrān 1316 h.q., p. 603. Translation: Besides entrusting you with world rule / he bestowed the dignity of a sage upon you. Some contemporary literary historians have adopted a contrary view. Thus H. Pažmān Baxtiyārī, in his edition of Niẓāmī's Xamsa, calls Alexander a bastard, and Zaynulābidīn Mu'taman, in *Tahavvuli ši'ri fārsī* (Tehrān 1339(1960), p. 156, wonders how Alexander could have been praised as a sage and a prophet in the

country which he had destroyed. See *Colloquio sul poeta persiano Nizāmī e la leggenda iranica di Alessandro Magno.* Roma 1977, p. 20.

51. According to E. E. Bertel's, *Navoi i Džami.* Moscow 1965, p. 341. Translation: It's for humaneness that people pay respect, / otherwise everyone would be a man. / Nobody can advance by himself, / he who is righteous becomes the head.

52. A. Sattorov, *Xiradnomai adibi xiradmand.* In: Maorif va madaniyat (Dushanbe), 17. 2. 1964, p. 4.

53. Abdurahmon ibni Ahmad Jomī, *Intixob az asarho,* Stalinobod 1956, p. 79. Transaltion: Now I have made a point / of giving new garb to my masnavī. / The old masnavīs by old masters / which have remained in memory after those who had passed away, / though vital and full of spirit, / there is other pleasure in my poems.

54. Abdurahmoni, Jomī, *Osori muntaxab,* Dushanbe 1964, Vo. 5, p. 301.

55. There is an old narrative by Yambul, from the 2nd century B.C., on a utopian island where people lead a carefree live, do not lack any material needs and live without wars and in friendship.

56. Cf. I. S. Braginskiy, *Klasika a současnost* (Classicism and Contemporaneity), transl. by J. Bečka. In: Společenské vědy v SSSR 1977, No. 2, pp. 179-185.

57. Abdurahmoni Jomī, *Osori,* etc., Vol. 5, p. 259.

58. Sadriddin Aynī, *Ališer Navoī.* In: Kulliyot, jildi 11, kitobi 1, Dushanbe 1963, p. 357. for more details on the poem, see also Ye. E. Bertel's, in his book *Roman ob Aleksandre,* Moscow 1948, pp. 123-186.

59. Cf. Č. A. Stori, *Persidskaya literatura,* Vol. II, Moscow 1972, pp. 1133 ff.

60. G. M. Meredith-Owens, *Handlist of Persian Manuscripts 1895-1966,* London 1968, p. 12.

61. E.g., in Taškent, a manuscript from the 17th century is preserved, which is a Persian translation of the Turkish *Tārīxi Qāzānī,* written for the Ashtarkhan Prince Iskandarsultān. See Č. A. Stori, op. cit., p. 780.

62. *Iskandarnāma.* Rivāyati fārsīyi Kalistenes durūqīn, pardāxti miyāni qarni 6-8 hijrī. Tehrān 1343 (1943) (1964), 35 + 800 pp.

63. Op.ócit., p. 497.

64. Yu. Salimov, *Nasri rivoyatii forsu tojik,* Dushanbe 1971, p. 49.

65. E.g.: Agar yak ta muyi bar sari padišah kaž gardad va-l-'iyazu billah xun duvist hazar mard dar in vilayat du jau nayarzad *(Iskandarnāma,* p. 66). In another place one may read a description of how Alexander, in anger, personally beheaded 130 foremen in Kashmir, who had refused him obedience (p. 49).

66. *Iskandarnāma,* pp. 354ff.

67. A part was edited and introduced by A. Devonaqulov, in Sadoi Šarq, 1969, No. 12, pp. 89-112. See also W. L. Hanaway, Jr., *Anahitā and Alexander.* In: Journal of the American Oriental Society 102.2 (1982), pp. 285-295.

68. It was probably called so by the author himself. The St. George fragment bears the inscription: Hic incipitur Boemicalis Alexander. There are the following editions: M. Hattala and A. Patera, *Zbytky rýmovaných Alexandreid* (Remnants of Alexandreises in Verse), Prague 1881. Rev. in: Obzor 3, 1880, pp. 334-335; F. Prusík, *Staročeské Alexandreidy rýmované* (Old Czech Alexandreises in Verse), Prague 1896; Reinhold Trautmann, *Die alttschechische Alexandreis mit Einleitung und Glossar,* Heidelberg 1916; V. Vážný, *Staročeská Alexandreida* (The Old Czech Alexandreis), Prague 1949. In the introduction to the last-mentioned edition, Albert Pražák says that during the Second World War, the Czech Alexandreis strengthened his belief that the enemy, who had rushed out of his country eastwards like an invincible devil, would sink down into the sands of the distant countries, just as Alexander did. The most complete edition, including also a fragment found in Esztergom in 1955, appeared under the title The Alexandreis (Prague 1963), prepared by V. Vážný and provided with an article by F. Svejkovský.

69. Cf. P. Király, *Ostřihomský zlomek staročeské Alexandreidy* (The Esztergom Fragment of the Old Czech Alexandreis). In: Studia slavica Academiae Scientiarum Hungaricae 2, 1956, pp. 158-184.

70. A. Pražák: "Among the world Alexandreises our poem is one of the most important and valuable relics, though preserved only in fragments." In his introduction to V. Vážný's edition (Prague 1949), pp. 13 ff. In *Dějiny české literatury* (A History of Czech Literature), Vol. I, Prague 1959, one may read: "The Alexandreis has a standing place in the development of Old Czech poetry." (p. 112) J. Hrabák mentions the admirable maturity of the Old Czech Alexandreis, stating that it has attained standing significance in Czech literature. In: *Studie ze starší české literatury* (Studies in Older Czech Literature), Prague 1962, p. 34. When enumerating the European versions; in the introduction to

his edition of *Iskandarnāma* (Tehrān 1343, i.e. 1964 A.D.), Īraj Afšār ranks the "tarjumayi bohemī" of the Pseudokallisthenes's recension in second place.

71. He wrote on the Czech Alexandreis in *Geschichte der böhmischen Sprache und Literatur,* Prague 1792, p. 148, often mentioning it in his correspondence with J. V. Zlobický and V. F. Durych, specialists in Slavonic studies (cf. *Korrespondence Jos. Dobrovského,* 3 Vols., Prague 1895-1908 - see Index).

72. Cf. A. Grund, *Karel Jaromír Erben,* Prague 1935. Erben's comments on the Alexandreis have retained their validity in the history of literature. It was he who drew attention to the affinity between the *Alexandreis* and *Dalimil's Chronicle* (p. 42).

73. P. J. Šafařík, *Klasobrání na poli staročeské literatury* (Gleaning in the Field of Old Czech Literature). In: Časopis českého Museum 21, 1847, pp. 303-310.

74. F. Palacký, *Zrada Bessova a Nabarzenova nad Dariem, králem perským* (The Treason of Bessus and Nabarzanes to Darius, the King of Persia). In: Časopis společnosti vlastenecké Museum v Čechách, 1828, vol. 3, pp. 84-96.

75. Wáclaw Nebeský, *Alexandreis česká* (The Czech Alexandreis). In: Časopis českého Museum 21, 1847, Vol. 2, pp. 1-24, 138-158. See also V.B. Nebeský, *O literatuře* (On Literature), Prague 1953, pp. 118-145 and 224. He mentions twelve Persian versions, considering Nizāmī's *Iskandarnāma* to be an excellent one.

76. Although only about two-fifths of the book have been preserved, it is possible to reconstruct the whole, in an approximate way, by comparing it with other European Alexandreises. Prokop Lang wrote a long treatise, *Co asi bylo obsahem ztracených částí Alexandreidy české?* (What May Have Formed the Contents of the Lost Parts of th Czech Alexandreis), in: Listy filologické a pedagogické 10, 1883, pp. 69-84, 275-301, 398-406. Lang even quotes passages in Gualter, which were probably left out of the Czech version.

77. The exchange of letters with symbolic gifts is dealt with by V. Janouch, *K pramenům a stylu Alexandreidy staročeské* (On the Sources and Style of the Old Czech Alexandreis), in: Věstník král. české spol. nauk. Třída pro filos., hist. a filologii 1943, No. III, pp. 1-25.

78. *Alexandreida.* Prague 1963, pp. 69-70, 1. 1220-1280.

79. *Op. cit.,* pp. 80-98, 1. 1536-1830 etc.

80. F. Šimek, *Zbásnil náš nejstarší cyklus legend i Alexandreidu jeden básník?* (Were Both our Oldest Cycle of Legends and the Alexandreis Written by the Same Poet?). In: Časopis Národního muzea. Oddělení věd společenských 125, 1956, p. 70.

81. Cf. J. Ludvíkovský, *Řecký román dobrodružný,* Prague 1925.

82. *Op. cit.,* p. 86.

83. *Alexandreida,* p. 72 (1. 1290 ff.).

84. *Op. cit.,* p. 129 (1. 127-134).

85. *Op. cit.,* p. 127 (1. 67 ff).

86. *Op. cit.,* p. 135 (1. 309 ff).

87. H. V. Tůma, in his article *O významu Alexandreidy české* (On the Importance of the Czech Alexandreis), attempted to analyze the characters of the Czech Alexandreis. In: Program vyššího gymnsia v Domažlicíca, Domažlice 1885, pp. 21 ff.

88. Cf. K. W. Titz, *Ulrich von Eschenbach und der Alexander boëmicalis,* Prague 1881; Václav Bok, *Germanistické poznámky k alexandrovské látce v jižních Čechách na počátku 14. století* (Germanistic Remarks on the Theme of Alexander in South Bohemia at the Beginning of the 14th Century). In: Listy filologické 107, 1984, pp. 90-100; V. Janouch, *O poměru Alexandreidy staročeské k Ulrichovi von Eschenbach* On the Relation of the Old Czech Alexandreis to Ulrich von Eschenbach). In: Věstník král. čes. spol. nauk. Tř. filosof., hist., filologická, 1950, Prague 1952, pp. 1-35. H. H. Bielfeldt, in *Die Quellen der alttschechischen Alexandreis* (Berlin 1951), attempts to prove the full dependence of the Czech Alexandreis on Ulrich's version at the same time showing that the poem by the Czech author is on a much higher artistic level than the contemporary German poem. Cf. J. Hrabák, *Nová práce o staročeské Alexandreidě* (A New Writing on the Old Czech Alexandreis). In: Česká literatura 1, 1953, pp. 37-45.

89. The Latin History has been preserved in nine manuscripts in Czechoslovak libraries. Its Czech version is known from six manuscripts from the 15th century. In more detail, see A. Vidmanová, *Latinská historie o Alexandru Velikém v našich rukopisech* (The Latin History of Alexander the Great in Our Manuscripts). In: Listy filologické 86, 1961, pp. 263-267. The less reliable Náchod Manuscript (District Museum, No. 284, from 1487) was edited by F. Prusík, *Kronika o Alexandru Velikém.* In: Krok 8-10, 1894-1896 (in 27 instalments). A sample containing chapters. 59-72,

on Darius' campaign against Alexander and the former's defeat, the imprisonment of his wife and mother, Darius' call for help to the Indian king, etc., was published in the *Výbor z literatury české* (An Anthology of Czech literature), edited by K. J. Erben, vol. 2, Prague 1868, pp. 530-543. See also Francis Peabody Magoun Jr. and S. Harrison Thomson, *Kronika o Alexandru velikém—A Czech Prose Translation of the Historia de preliis. Recension I 3*. In: Speculum 3, 1928, pp. 204-217. On the original from which the translation was made, see J. Ludvíkovský, *Řecký román dobrodružný,* Prague 1935, See also A. Vidmanová, *K tzv. německé interpreaci Alexandra Velikého v recenzi I 2 Historia de preliis* (The So-called German Interpretation of Alexander the Great in Recension I 2 of the Historia de preliis), in: Listy filologické 104, 1981, pp. 132-136.

90. *Kronika o Alexandru Velikém.* Ed. by F. Prusík. In: Krok 9, 1895, p. 46. New ideas were added by J. Kolár, *Román o Alexandru Velikém v souvislostech české středověké prózy* (The Novel on Alexander the Great in the Context of Czech Mediaeval Prose). In: Listy filologické 105, 1982, pp. 209-215. The author shows the apparent development undergone by the main character, as well as gradation as a significant element of the hero's development.

91. *Op. Cit.* 10, 1896, p. 3.

92. *Kronika o narození welikého Alle Macedonského a tudiješ o wssech skutzijech geho . . .* (A Chronicle of the Birth of the Great Alle of Macedonia as Well as All of his Deeds). W Plzni od Mikulasse Bakalarze . . . 1513 (paleotype).

93. *Hystorya o králi Alexandrowi Macedonském* (A History of King Alexander of Macedonia), Olomouc (about 1610). Dealt with in K. Sabina, *Dějiny literatury československé* (A History of Czechoslovak Literature), Prague 1866, pp. 911 ff. A new translation of the Latin original of the Historia de preliis, entitled *Život Alexandra Velikého* (The Life of Alexander the Great), pp. 237-311, appeared in the book *Láska a válka* (Love and War), Prague 1971. The reader may find therein also a survey of the genesis of the classical literary elaborations of Alexander's deeds and life, by B. Borecký (pp. 357-359).

94. In the quoted *Hystorya,* p. 69, Iran is dealt with e.g., in the following chapters: The battle of Alexander with King Darius's captains; The message of King Darius to Alexander on taxes and the reply (Alexander replied that he would send a hen laying golden eggs); The second message of Darius to Alexander (he sent him a Scythian curb, a purse with gold coins, a ball, a sack of poppy seeds and a birch rod); How Alexander behaved towards Darius' messengers; The reply of Alexander to the message of Darius (he sent the Persian king mustard and the following words: "I am that birch rod which has been sent against you by the God of heaven and earth"); The first battle of Alexander and Darius; How Darius submitted to Alexander sending him his delegates; Alexander's arrival at the portrait of Xerxes and what he said about him, etc.

95. *Dějiny literatury české I,* Prague 1959, p. 105. Gualtherus de Castelione is documented, in 1450, in the contemporary libraries of Bratislava, too. In the Middle Ages, Latin had a monopoly position in higher education, being therefore, the language used by the intelligentsia without any feeling of alienation. J. Hrabák, *Studie,* ed. cit., p. 104.

96. Lucet Alexander Lucani luce; meretur / laudes descriptus historicalis honor./. Cf. M. Šváb, *Některé vztahy naší Alexandreídy k soudobé latinské vzdělanosti v Čechách* (Some Links Between Our Alexandreis and the Contemporary Latin Education in Bohemia). In: Sborník pedagogické školy v Plzni. Jazyk a literatura 2, 1959, p. 75.

97. Parts were translated into Czech and edited in print by Abraham z Gynterrode, in 1605, as an appendix to his traslation of Xenofon's *Kyru paideia.* According to *Historie české literatury* (A History of Czech Literature), by J. Jungmann, 1st edition 1825 (2nd edition Prague 1849), p. 434. Curtius was translated into Czech by Cippelius in 1782, but the manuscript got lost. A complete Czech translation of all of the preserved eight books was edited in Prague by F. Š. Kott, *O činech Alexandra Velikého, krále macedonského* (On the Deeds of Alexander the Great, King of Macedonia), Praha 1899, 327 pp. Rev. by J. Kvíčala, in: České museum filologické 6, 1900, pp. 75-80. A small anthology for high schools appeared in Prague, in 1913, translated by A. K. Kvapil. On the Latin book, see R. Novák, *Poznamenání ke kritice Kurtia Rufa* (Remarks on the Criticism of Curtius Rufus), in: Listy filologické 12, 1885, pp. 385-387. On the presence of Curtius's book in the libraries of Czech scholars, see J. Hejnic and J. Šimáčková, *Ke knihovně Václava z Rovného* (On the Library of Václav z Rovného), in: Strahovská knihovna 3, 1968, p. 132.

98. A Czech translation in a separate book appeared as late as 1905: *M. Juniana Justina, Výbor z dějin filippských Pompeia Troga* (A Selection from the Philippide History by Pompeius Trogus), transl. by F. Š. Kott, Prague 1905, 338 pages. The book

contains a description of Alexander's campaign against Iran, in Books 1-12. Alexander's character is hinted at in the 12th Book: Before going off to the Persian war, he ordered all the relatives of his stepmother, who had been appointed as high dignitaries or made generals by Philippus, to be killed, not sparing even his own people . . . (p. 110).

99. See, e.g., Ant. Podlaha, *Soupis rukopisů knihovny metropolitní kapituly pražské* (A List of Manuscripts in the Metropolitan Capitular Library in Prague), Prague 1910 and 1922, No. 1625 from the beginning of the 15th century; A List of Manuscripts in the Mikulov Library, Brno 1954, p. 46 (1.25a-42b), from 1402. There is a testimony to the existence of the book Liber secretus secretorum Alexandri Magni, in Levoča in Slovakia, in 1450, etc. *Kiha Lidskeych Ctností a mnoheych naučžení* . . . (A Book of Human Virtues and Many Instructions). The State Library of the ČSR, Prague, sign. XVIII G 11. Bavor Rodovský translated The Life of Alexander the Great into Czech again, but his translation has not been preserved.

100. A Czech translation appeared as late as in 1933: *Alexandr a Caesar,* Prague 1933, 148 pages, transl. by F. Stiebitz.

101. Arrianos, *Tažení Alexandra Velikého* (The Campaign of Alexander the Great), transl. by J. Bělský, Prague 1972, 348 pp.

102. Lukianos, *Hovory záhrobní* (Talks from the Other World), transl. by F. Machala, Prague 1930. Luciani Samostatensis Dialogi selecti ad usum scholarum humaniorum Universitatis Pragensis appeared in Prague in 1770.

103. Bartoloměj z Chlumce (Claretus de Selentia): *Vokabulář gramatický, Bohemář, Glosář.* For more about him by V. Flajšhans, see *Klaret a jeho družina* (Klaret and his Followers), Prague 1928, p. 12, and A. Wesselski, *Klaret und sein Glossator. Böhmische Volks- und Märchmärlein in Mittelalter.* Brünn, Prag, Leipzig, Wien 1936.

104. There are more than a hundred manuscripts of the *Gesta Romanorum* on the territory of Czechoslovakia. The antiquity and number of Prague manuscripts point to Prague as the basis of the Middle-European version of the work. See A. Vidmanová, *Středolatinská beletrie a Čechy* (Middle Latin Bellest-lettres and Bohemia). In: Classica atque medievalia Jaroslav Ludvikovský octogenario oblata. Erno 1975, pp. 235-246; by the same author, *Staročeská Gesta Romanorum a jejich latinská předloha* (The Old Czech Gesta Romanorum and Their Latin Original). In: Listy filologické 95, 1972, pp. 65-92. The most recent edition, *Příběhy římské* (Roman Tales), Prague 1967, deals with Alexander on page 44, in addition to seven other mentions. See also J. J. Hanuš, in Krok 2, 1866, pp. 305-316 and 351-358, who mentions the fact that there are four tales on Alexander, the king and sage, in the *Gesta Romanorum.*

105. Cf. A. Vidmanová-Schmidtová, *Burleyovy Životy starých filosofů a jejich překlady* (Burleigh's Lives of Ancient Sages, and Their Translations), Prague 1962; F. Novotný, *Životy starých mudrců a jejich česká zpracování* (Lives of Ancient Sages and Their Czech Versions), in: Listy filologické 40, 1913, pp. 342-354 and 420-429; M. Okál, *Burleyove Životy filozofov v bratislavskom kodexe* (Burley's Lives of Philosophers in the Bratislava Codex, in: Listy filologické 104, 1981, pp. 222-232. See also J. Veitz, *Povaha povídek v Gesta Romanorum* (The Character of the Stories in the Gesta Romanorum), in: Listy filologické 37, 1910, p. 262. Many references to Alexander the Great may be found in K. Dvořák, *Soupis staročeských exempel* (A List of Old Czech Examples), Prague 1978. The role and usage of examples culminated here in the literature of the 14th century (p. 8).

106. See *Promoční promluvy mistrů artistické fakulty Mikuláše z Litomyšle a Jana z Mýta na universitě pražské z let 1386-1393* (Graduation Ceremony Addresses by Mikuláš z Litomyšle and Jan z Mýta, Masters of the Faculty of Arts of Prague University, in 1386-1393). Edited by B. Ryba, Prague 1948, p. 11.

107. He sometimes quotes Latin Gualter; see, e.g., *M. Jan Hus jako universitní rektor a profesor. Výbor z jeho projevů* (Master Jan Hus as University Chancellor and Professor. A Selection from His Addresses), compiled by E. Stein, Prague 1948, pp. 53-54, 64, 82-85; Magistr Ioannis Hus, *Quodlibet,* edited by B. Ryba, Prague 1948, pp. 40 and 180-181. In a sermon honouring the memory of the founder of the University, Charles IV, in 1409, John Hus devoted a large part of his sermon to the futility of glory and power, concluding it with Alexander's 28-line monologue. *Mistra Jana Husi Sebrané spisy* The Collected Writings of Master John Hus), edited and translated from Latin into Czech by M. Svoboda and V. Flajšhans, Vol. 1, Prague 1904, pp. 197-199.

108. See J. Gebauer, *Ludvík Tkadleček,* in: Listy filologické 2, 1875, p. 114; *Tkadleček. Hádka milence s Neštěstím* (A Lover's Quarrel with Misfortune), edited by Fr. Šimek, Prague 1974; *Tkadleček,* edited by V. Hanka, Prague 1824, I,

pp. 24, 30 and 42; II, pp. 11 and 119. Cf. also J. Vilikovský, *Písemnictví českého středověku* (Literature of the Czech Middle Ages), Prague 1948, pp. 221 and 230.

109. *Spisy Bohuslava Hasištejnského z Lobkovic* (The Writings of B. Hasištejnský of Lobkovice), edited by B. Ryba, Prague 1933, pp. 36, 38, 48, 50, 62 and 84. In his treatise on the administration of a state, he asks the ruler to be merciful towards his enemies, as Alexander was towards the defeated Darius and his family. Cf. also D. Martínková, *Nález spisu Bohuslava Hasištejnského z Lobkovic o správě státu* (The Finding of a Writing by B. Hasištejnský of Lobkovice on the Administration of a State), in: Zprávy jednoty klasických filologů 3, 1961, p. 125. Similarly in the correspondence of other humanists—see, e.g., *Dva listáře humanistické* (Two Humanistic Letters), edited by J. Truhlář, Prague 1897, pp. 25 and 53.

110. *Kronyka Swěta . . . o znamenitých wěcech . . . od Jana Karyona . . . od Burjana Sobka z Kornic přeložená . . . nyní znowu přehlédnuta od Danyele Adama z Weleslawína* (A Chronicle of the World . . . On Excellent Things . . . by Jan Karyon . . . Translated by Buryan Sobek of Kornice . . . Now Revised Again by Daniel Adam of Veleslavín), Prague 1541. On Alexander see pp. 125-134. etc.

111. *Staročeský lucidář.* Text rukopisu fürstenberského a prvotisku z r. 1498 (The Old Czech Lucidarium. The Text of the Fürstenberg Manuscript and the Incunabule dated 1498), edited by Č. Zíbrt, Prague 1903, p. 50, etc.

112. Hájek writes here: "The letter which had been given by Alexander, the King of Persia, to the same Slavs, his servants, long before the Advent of Jesus Christ to the world." Waclaw Hagek z Libočan, *Kronyka Cžeská,* p. 319.

113. According to J. Giesen and W. Pfeifer, *Der Bericht des Engländers Moryson über seine Reise durch Böhmen.* In: MVGDB 80, 1943, p. 47.

114. Cf. F. M. Bartoš, *Zápis Alexandra Velikého Slovanům a jeho původce* (The Record of Alexander the Great to the Slavs and Its Author). In: Časopis národního musea. Odd. duchovědné 115, 1946, pp. 45-49; also F. Pfister, *Das Privilegium Slavicum Alexanders des Grossen.* In: Zeitschrift für Slawistik 6, 1961, pp. 323-345. The record was thoroughly analyzed by O. Odložilík in his paper, *The Privilege of Alexander the Great for the Slavs.* In: Folia diplomatica, Universita J. E. Purkyně, Brno, 1, 1971, pp. 238-251.: "Bartoš' idea that Vavřinec of Březová compiled the privilege for

the Slavs is a brilliant conjecture, but only a conjecture," says Odložilík (p. 249).

115. In his Czech book *Didactica,* he referred to Alexander three times, as he did in his Latin dramas *Diogenes, Cynicus redevivus,* and *Abrahamus patriarcha,* where he mentions Alexander's battles in Iran. See *Dílo Jana Amose Komenského* (The Writings by Jan Amos Comenius), Vol. 11, Prague 1977, pp. 46, 82, 95, 531, etc. In his treatise, *Unum necessarium,* he refers to Alexander seven times.

116. Cf. M. Klučka, *Několik poznámek o pojetí Alexandra Velikého v díle pedagoga J. Komenského* (A Few Remarks on the Conception of Alexander the Great by the Pedagogue J. Comenius). In: Listy filologické 5 (80), 1957, pp. 90-97.

117. See *Antika v české literatuře* (Classical Antiquity in Czech Literature), Prague 1978, p. 243.

118. A rider with Alexander's banner may be seen in an illuminated manuscript dating from the beginning of the 15th century (see J. Krása, *Rukopisy Václava IV.,* Prague 1971, pp. 35 and 56). In the relief decoration of the Belvedere pavillion in Prague, Paolo della Stella presented a few scenes from Alexander's life, among them one of Alexander with Darius' wives. Charles IV decorated his coronation cross with a gem depicting Alexander's head, according to V. Vavřínek, *Alexander Veliký,* Prague 1967, p. 192.

119. In Czech collections of theatrical and musical works one may find a number of titles by Italian and other authors, dating from the 17th-19th centuries, e.g. G. A. Cicognini, *Le glorie e gli amori di Alessandre Magno e di Rossana* (Venezia 1661); *Alexandre le Grand,* 1789, 1791; *Alexander in India,* 1786 (see J. Šimáčková and E. Macháčková, *Teatralia zámecké knihovny v Českém Krumlové.* Knihovna Národního muzea 1976); *Alessandro nel India,* Prague 1734, 1750, 1760, 1764, 1769 (see P. Kneidl, *Libreta italské opery v Praze v 18. stol.* In: Strahovská knihovna 1, Prague 1966, pp. 126-163). The first opera by the Czech composer J. A. Koželuh was *Alessandro nell'India,* dated 1769. J. R. Racine's play, *Alexander in Indien,* Vienna 1760, was well-known here (see P. Kneidl, *Teatralia zámecké knihovny v Radeníně,* The Theatralia in the Library of Radonín Castle, Prague 1962). A play on Alexander was staged in Banská Štiavnica in 1755 (see J. Mišianik et col., *Dejiny staršej slovenskej literatury,* A History of Older Slovak Literature, Bratislava 1958, p. 240, etc.)

120. E.g., J. Z-r (J. Ziegler), *Rozmlauwanj mezi Diogenem a Alexandrem o marnosti slávy a pozemských statků* (The Dispute of Diogenes and Alex-

ander over the Futility of Glory and Worldly Estates). In: Český hlasatel 1806, pp. 106-109; *Alexander, Hannybal, Scypio*, by the same author. in: Český hlasatel 2, 1807, pp. 431-436; Ant. Marek, *Neohrožená mysl Alexandrových vojáků* (The Undaunted Spirit of Alexander's Soldiers), on the battles of Arimazes in Sogdiana. In: Čechoslav 2, 1821, pp. 231-232; F., *Krátká historka o Alexandrovi Makedonském* (A Short Story about Alexander of Macedonia). In: Čechoslav 5, 1824, p. 231; J. Hýbl, *Alexandr dobyvatel* (Alexander the Conqueror). In: Jindy a nyní 2, 1830, I, pp. 65-66; *Alexandr Macedonský*. In: Fejérpatakyho Slovenský pozorník 5, 1846, pp. 81-93; V. Gabler, *Smrt Alexandra Velikého* (The Death of Alexander the Great). In: Osvěta I, 1862/63, pp. 113-114; A. Velhartický's short story, *Požár Persepole* (The Burning of Persepolis). In: Topičův sborník 2, 1914-1915, pp. 358-362, etc.

121. Dr. Gabler, *Alexandr Veliký* (Alexander the Great). In: Památky archeologické 9. 1862, p. 225.

122. E.g., Jos. Jireček, *Ku kritickému rozboru Alexandreidy* (On a Critical Analysis of the Alexandreis). In: Krok 2, 1866, pp. 129-134; Jan Kořínek, *České Alexandreidy zlomek musejní*. Obsahuje části o Alexandrově tažení do Íránu, Dariově smrti, Rozmluvu Daria s Polystratem (A Museum Fragment of the Czech Alexandreis, Containing Parts on Alexander's Campaign against Iran, Darius' Death, and a Dialogue between Darius and Polystratos), Gymnasium Jindřichův Hradec 1870, pp. 3-18; P. Lang, *Jakou měrou držel se skladatel zbytku jindřichohradeckého latinské Alexandreidy Qualtera Castellionského* (To What Extent Did the Author of the Fragment from Jindřichův Hradec Adhere to Qualter Castillion's Alexandreis). Gymnasium Příbram 1881, pp. 3-30; H. V. Tůma. *O významu Alexandreidy české po stránce aestheticky-básnické* (On the Importance of the Czech Alexandreis from the Point of View of the Aesthetics of Poetry), *Exkurs metodický k Alexandreidě*. Gymnasium Domažlice, 1885, pp. 1-41; V. Hrnčíř, *Rukopis Kralovédvorský a Alexandreida česká* (The Manuscript of Dvůr Králové and The Czech Alexandreis). České Budějovice 1881, pp. 3-48; F. Ernst, *Der Untergang der Angehörigen Alexanders des Grossen*. Deutsche Realschule, Prag 1891, pp. 14-22, etc.

123. See also the poems by V. Zbraslavský, *Alexandr po boji* (Alexander after the Battle). In: Posel ze Sušice, 1889, No. 6, p. 51; V. Drbohlav, *Alexandr Veliký* (Alexander the Great). In: Anděl strážný 13, 1893/4, pp. 233-240, etc.

124. Lidové noviny 41, 1937, No. 220, pp. 1-2 (1. 5. 1937).

125. Prague 1967, 269 pp. Appended are translations of writings by the historians Arrian, Justinus, Curtius and Plutarchos; legends by the Jewish historiographer Josephus Flavius, by Lukianos, a sofist of Syrian origin, and by Valerius; extracts from the *Gesta Romanorum* and extracts from writings by clerical authors.

126. In the *Šāhnāma*, the description of Iskandar's adventures takes up about 2,400 couplets, Nižāmī's *Iskandarnāma* comprises around 10,500 couplets, and the *Xiradnāmayi Iskandarī* by Jāmī almost 15,000 couplets.

127. Cf. F. Taeschner, *Der Achidschuk von Tebriz und seine Erwähnung in Iskandarname des Aḥmedī*. In: Charisteria Orientalia (Miscellany edited, the 70th anniversary of Jan Rypka), Prague 1956, pp. 338-344.

128. Cf. M. Šváb, *Specifičnost české Alexandreidy ve vztahu ke Gualterovi* (The Peculiarity of the Czech Alexandreis in Its Relation to Gualtherus). An unpublished Doctoral Thesis submitted to the Philosophical Faculty of Brno University, in 1959.

129. *Alexandreida* . . . Praha 1963 p. 118 (1. 237-244).

130. Op. cit., p. 80 (l. 1547); p. 87 (l. 1786), etc.

131. Op. cit., p. 84 (l. 1677).

132. Jos. Hrabák, *Umělecké hodnoty našeho středověkého písemnictví* (The Artistic Value of Our Mediavel Literature). In: Studie ze starší české literatury (Studies in Older Czech Literature), Prague 1962, p. 120.

133. This is testified to also by the large number of manuscripts and old prints to be found in Czechoslovak historical libraries. They depict the life and adventures of Alexander the Great and contain Alexander's correspondence with Aristotle. There are many incunabules here, e.g. two prints of *Historia Alexandri Magni*, Argentinae 1489; three copies of Justinus, *Epitome in Trogi Pompeii Historiae*, Venetiis 1479; a number of writings printed in the 16th and 17th centuries, such as Curtius Rufus, *De rebus gestis*, Parisii 1508; the same book edited i Lugduni 1547; and other ones in Latin, Italian, German and French, in about eighty copies.

134. The author of the present article has written on this subject: *O Alexandru Makedonském v Íránu a v Čechách* (On Alexander of Macedonia in Iran and Bohemia). In: Nový Orient 26, 1971, pp. 218-220; *Aleksandr Makedonskiy v dariyskoy i češskoy literature*. In: Pamir (Dushanbe) 1973, No. 12, pp. 90-92.

Peter Dronke (essay date 1997)

SOURCE: Dronke, Peter. "Poetic Originality in *The Wars of Alexander.*" In *The Long Fifteenth Century: Essays for Douglas Gray*, edited by Helen Cooper and Sally Mapstone, pp. 123-39. Oxford: Clarendon Press, 1997.

[*In the following essay, Dronke describes the literary devices used in an English recension of Leo of Naples's* Alexander Romance.]

The title I have chosen may sound paradoxical. Can one really speak of the originality of a poetic text that is a translation—and for much of the time a close translation—of a Latin prose source? This Latin source, moreover—a variant, from around 1200, of the Alexander Romance that Leo of Naples had translated around 960[1]—is not one of the more compelling Alexander narratives that we possess: it is a compilation which is neither coherently shaped nor attractively written. How was it able to inspire sparkling, unpredictable writing in a vernacular poet-adapter some two centuries afterwards?[2]

The English poet had an innate gift for vivacious, humorous and pungent language. Yet it is not just a matter of his infusing the jejune diction of his source with new life. At many key moments we can see that it is more: the poet fires his source with a sense of imaginative purpose. He uses two opposing but complementary strategies. One is to make the remote, exotic world of Alexander more familiar, to reinterpret its features reassuringly in terms of realities known to his audience. The other is deliberately to heighten the unfamiliar, increasing its fascination. It is with this second aim in view that he repeatedly enriches the narrative of his source with passages of *ecphrasis* that have no counterpart there—descriptive excursions in which language and imagery, while always rigorously controlled, give the effect of going 'over the top'. The characteristic technique here is an accumulative one, that is ideally well matched to alliterative versification. The cumulations make the monstrosities and the marvels, the beauties and the cruelties, inexorably larger than life—as if the poet's subject-matter itself impelled him to pile word upon word, image upon image.

In some of the poetically densest passages, the devices of accentuating the familiar as well as the unfamiliar are used in combination. The poet wants to ensure the acculturation of his material, yet he is equally concerned to outdo and surpass the realms of experience that his audience know. I shall analyse two episodes in which this double strategy seems to me particularly remarkable, and, at the close, shall hazard a suggestion about the underlying imaginative intentions. But first I shall touch more briefly on a few examples of the one device and of the other.

There is nothing in the Latin prose which deliberately evokes the Christian world of the writer's time; the English poet, by contrast, uses anachronism with knowing delight. When near the opening King Nectanebus (Anectanabus in the English text) makes his escape from Egypt, he *clede him all as a clerke* (121) and takes with him *astralabus, quadrentis* (128-9) and the full working kit of a medieval astrologer. When he wins the favour of Queen Olympias in Macedon, she summons him as *hire awyn clerke* (398). The temple of Ammon becomes *a synagoge* (1182),[3] as does that of Apollo's oracle (2309), whose priestess, Zacora, is *a semely nonn* (2306). The god Dionysus becomes *Sire Denys, a duke* (3684)—perhaps with a touch of playful euhemerism: since the Latin source explains that he is also called Bacchus and Father Liber,[4] we may assume the poet knew who Dionysus was. On the other hand, when the Brahman Dindimus mocks Alexander's polytheism, the poet, who here had a faulty Latin text before him, failed to recognize Ceres, making her into *Serenon . . . sire of the wambe* (4639).[5] A moment later, however, comes another flicker of Christian wit, as Dindimus derides Alexander for sending a wild boar *to Mars in his mynstir* (4651). Among the various pagan *mynstirs* in the poem, there is one of surpassing beauty and splendour: the palace of the Sun (5025). The poet makes the vestments and couch of the solar priest inseparably exotic and Christian: where the source knows merely that they were made of gold,[6] in the poetry the hierophant has a blue mantle that

> Was browden all with brent gold full of bright aungels.
> The testre trased full of trones with trimballand wingis,
> The silloure full of seraphens and othire sere halows
>   . . .
>
> was brocaded with burnished gold full of bright Angels,
> the bedhead carved full of Thrones with trembling wings,
> the canopy full of Seraphim and diverse saintly beings
>   . . .
>
> (5040-2)[7]

The triple *full* and the *trimballand wingis* evoke no statuesque adornments but an image of consummate vital energy—as if the pseudo-Dionysian hierarchies were coming alive and thronging the pagan shrine.

Another device the poet uses to give a sense of familiarity lies in his manipulation of point of view. Occasionally, but tellingly, he writes as if he were himself one of Alexander's men. At the siege of Tyre, Alexander's siege-towers are *all oure werke without the wallis* (1546). Alexander is *oure emperoure* (3572), *oure conquirour* (4024). At the sight of the immensity of King Porus' army, 'our company from Macedonia' (*oure meneyhe out of Messedone*) were perturbed (3732).

Familiarity is likewise achieved at the close of several of the poem's 'fitts', where moments of solemnity or horror or splendour are left lightly suspended as the final verse is given its tag-ending. Thus when the treacherous murderers of King Darius make their escape:

> Than dryfes furthe tha domesmen[8] and halfe-dede him
>   levys,
> Famand out of fresch blod; and here a fitt endis.
>
> Then those justicers rush forth, leaving him half-dead,
> foaming out fresh blood—and here a section ends.
>
> (3330-1)

The Latin has neither the getaway nor the foaming blood: merely 'they left him in the palace half-alive' (*dimiserunt eum in palatio semivivum*).[9] The poet first heightens the brutal scene, then brings it down to earth, with a hint of irony, as he slips back into his role as entertainer.

His most elaborate use of the jongleur's persona (which naturally has no counterpart in the source) comes with the wedding-feast of Alexander and Darius' daughter, *Rosan the riche*. It is as if to set an *entr'acte* between what the poet sees as the two acts of his drama: Act I, which concludes Alexander's triumph over the Persians with his marriage, and Act II, which depicts the adventures that lead him through the perils of India to Babylon and (if the poem was ever completed) to his own death through treachery. Then the death at the hands of base courtiers, such as Darius suffered as the first act closed, would have been echoed in Alexander's murder, making the two acts symmetrical.

In the four verses that conclude Passus XIV and the eight that open XV (3592-603), the poet turns directly to the *lordis* of his audience. There is humorous self-deprecation—even if his matter *be . . . bot mene*, he'd like to *tary for a time and tempire my wittis* (are they his instrument, or perhaps his weapons?)[10]—conjoined with a memorable devotional formula: 'May he that mounted to the stars station us in heaven!' After the *entr'acte*, the poet appeals to the *lordis* anew, stressing his fidelity to his source (*followand the lettir*), and asking that in their prayers they call to mind him 'that made you this mirth' (3601-3). In the last resort, the narrative that follows—of the grim ordeals and monsters of India—is mirth, re-created for the delight of a world in which God's in his heaven.

My next instance of familiarizing takes us also to the complementary device of outdoing. The poet several times mitigates the more extreme surges of brutality that Alexander displays in his source. At an encampment deep in India, the king and his army encounter a wild man (*homo agrestis*),[11] huge and hairy as a pig, whose speech consists only of porcine squeals. When Alexander tells his men to capture him, 'he did not show fear or flee, but remained intrepid before them all'. Even though the uncouth figure poses no threat, Alexander decoys him by sending a naked girl to 'that animal'; she arouses him and he grabs at her; then, at Alexander's order, the girl is taken away and the man bound and burnt alive.

The English poet had little taste for such gratuitous cruelty and contempt for human life, so he introduces some telling changes of detail. He invents an exuberantly grotesque description, making the wild man sinister and authentically bestial:

> A burly best and a bigge was as a [berne] shapen;
> Umquile he groned as a galt with grysely latis
>
>   . . . . .
>
> And was as bristil[e] as a bare all the body ovire.
> Dom as a dore-nayle and defe was he bathe,
> With laith leggis and lange and twa laue eres.
> A hevy hede and a hoge as it a hors ware,
> And large was his odd lome the lenthe of a yerde.
>
> A burly beast and a big was shaped like a man;
> at times he groaned like a porker, with grisly cries
>
>   . . . . .
>
> and was as bristly as a boar all over his body.
> Dumb as a doornail and deaf was he too,
> with legs loathly and long and two low-hanging ears,
> a heavy head and a huge, as if it were a horse,
> and large was his outlandish tool, the length of a yard.
>
> (4869-77)

Even more, when he sees the lovely naked girl (*that hend*), his impulse is murderous, rather than naturally lustful: he 'hisses like an adder: he'd have strangled her straight, had stout men not been near' (4884-5). To this extent the poet has extenuated Alexander's behaviour: even in his callous command, he remains someone whom the audience could recognize as a 'prince' (4887) rather than a mindless butcher.

The portrait of the wild man is one of the many examples of vivid, exciting *ecphraseis*, with their cascades of alliterating words, that reveal the poet's individuality of vision as well as of language. They serve a number of poetic purposes. Thus, soon after the burning of the wild man, where the Latin text says, baldly, that 'a very great abundance of dragons, serpents and lions came upon the army, which afflicted them with very great distress',[12] the poet conveys the experience of that distress by keenly specific details, to show that these men—'our men', he says, involving his audience more grippingly—faced the utmost limits of physical trials and dangers. Moreover, he adds sound-effects that set the ordeals in an atmosphere of uproar and elemental disorder:

> Thare was hurling on highe, as it in hell ware,
> Quat of wrestling of wormes and wonding of knightis.
> As gotis out of guttars in golanand wedres,
> So voidis doun the vemon be vermyn[e]s schaftis.
> At othir time of oure tulkis was tangid to dede
> And slayn with tha serpents a sowme out of nounbre.
> So hard thai hampird oure heere and herid oure erles,
> Unneth it chansid thaim the cheke the cheffire to worthe.
> Quen he sckonfet and skerrid all tha skathill fendis,
> Then metis he doun of the mounte into a mirk vale,
> A dreghe dale and a depe, a dym and a thestir;
> Migh[t] thare na saule undire son see to anothire.

> There was havoc on high as if it were in hell,
> what with wrestling of serpents and wounding of knights.
> As streams out of channels in howling weathers,
> out pours the poison from vile creatures' jaws.
> At times some of our men were stung to death
> and slain by those serpents—a sum beyond number.
> So harshly they hampered our host and harried our earls,
> they had hardly the chance to prevail with their power.
> When the king trounced and terrified those dangerous fiends,
> he moves down from the mountain into a murky valley,
> a mighty deep dale, a dim and darkling one,
> no soul under the sun could there see another.

                                                    (4921-32)

With the last two lines cited the poet rejoins his Latin source. Yet its dry statement, 'they came into a valley so dark that one could scarcely see another',[13] is not enough for him: with hyperbolic fantasy he continues:

> They were enveloped in that land by so thick a cloud,
> they could feel it with their fists as flapping cobwebs.[14]

The most frequent and abundant *ecphraseis* that the poet adds to the Latin are battle-descriptions. These can evoke, for instance, the exhilaration of Alexander's first chance to prove himself in combat, in his encounter with *Sire Nicollas* (894), where the poet expands some four lines in his source to over forty, which begin (896 ff.):

> With that thai tuke up thaire trompes apon the twa sidis,
> Braidis banars abrade, buskis to mete,
> So knilid the clarons that all the cliffe rynges,
> The holtis and the haire [wode] and the hillis schenyn.
>
>   . . . . .
>
> Quat of stamping of stedis and stering of bernes,
> All dymed the dale and the dust ryses.
> With slik a bront and a brusche the bataill asembild,
> As the erth and all the el[e]mentis at anes had wrestild.

> With that they took up their trumpets upon the two sides,
> unfurl banners abroad, preparing to fight;
> so sounded the clarions that all the cliff rings,
> shattering the holts and hoar forests and hills.
>
>   . . . . .
>
> What with stamping of steeds and stirring of men,
> all the dale dimmed and the dust rises.
> With such racing and rushing the battle assembled
> as if earth and all elements had wrestled at once.

Here the interspersing of present-tense verbs in a narrative otherwise told in the past not only conveys the heightened vividness commonly associated with the historic present, but gives the very sense of a mêlée whose effects are still reverberating.

The descriptions can equally dwell on combat's harsher realities, as in one of the clashes of Greeks and Persians:

> Thare was stomling of stedis, stickinge of erles,
> Sharpe schudering of schote, schering of mailes,
> So stalworthly within a stond sterid thaim the Grekis,
> That of the barb[r]yne blod all the [bent] flowis.

> There was stumbling of steeds, stabbing of earls,
> sharp shuddering of shots,[15] cutting of coats of mail—
> so stalwartly soon did the Greeks show their mettle
> that with barbarian blood all the field flows.

                                                    (2748-51)

The graphic accumulations extend to a wide range of mood and tone. Where the Latin is perfunctory, the poet can choose to dwell on tender, as on savage, observation: for him the 'small and gentle bird'[16] that lays its egg in King Philip's lap

> thare hurkils and hydis as scho were hand-tame.
> Fast scho flekirs about his fete and fleytirs aboute,
> And thare it nestild in a noke, as it a nest were . . .

> crouches and hides there as if she were hand-tame,
> fast she flickers round his feet and flutters about,
> and there nestled in a nook as though it were a nest . . .

                                                    (504-6)

Or again, the poet can feast on the macabre, as in his verses about Bucephalus, in whose cage there lie not only 'hands of men and feet and other limbs dispersed',[17] as in the Latin, but

> Tharmes thrist owt, thee-banes and shuldres,
> Som hanchyd of the heved, som the handez etyn,
> Som thair riggez owt rytte, and som thair ribbez rent.

> intestines thrust out, thigh-bones and shoulders,
> some with the head gnawed off, some with the hands eaten,

some with their backs ripped out, and some with their
ribs rent.

(773-5)

With yet another spurt of invention, the poet can enrich
the insults aimed at Alexander's puny size with all the
verve of vernacular flytings and their pithy, often col-
loquial range of rudeness. Thus the Persians show
Darius Alexander's portrait:

Ane amlaghe, ane asalen, ane ape of all othire,
A wirling, a wayryngle, a wawil-eyid shrewe,
The cait[if]este creatour that cried was evire.

a nobody, a little ass, an ape beyond all others,
a dwarf, a butcher-bird, an odd-eyed shrew,[18]
the most contemptible creature ever created.

(1829-31)

Darius, in his letter of defiance, capitalizes on this:

And slike a dwinny[n]ge, a dwa[l]we, a dwerghe as
thiselfe,
A grub, a grege out of Gr[e]ce, ane erd-growyn so-
rowe . . .

such a wizened one, a weakling, a dwarf like yourself,
a grub, a gnat from Greece, an earth-grown disaster
. . .

(1876-7)

I should now like to try to adumbrate an imaginatively
more profound use of both familiarizing and outdoing
devices, in two episodes: Alexander's entry into Jerusalem, and his encounter with Candace.

In the poet's source,[19] both Alexander and the high
priest, Jaddus, have dreams that reveal their destiny. An
'angel of the Lord' appears to Jaddus, commanding him
to open the gates of Jerusalem and go without fear,
with all his people robed in white, to greet Alexander.
The King, instead of descending on the city as a
destroyer, sees Jaddus' mitre, with the tetragrammaton,
YHWH, inscribed in gold, and falls to the ground: he
adores the name of God, and venerates the priest who
bears it. Acclaimed by the Jews, he goes to sacrifice in
the Temple, and there Jaddus shows him that he is the
predestined victor over the Persians, he who had been
foretold in the Book of Daniel.

The English poet invests the key moments of this
episode with Christian associations: by his language
and imagery, I would suggest, he presents the city's
greeting of Alexander in a montage close to that of the
Palm Sunday liturgy. First he conveys a blithe tumult
and a sense of lavish welcome, Jerusalem and its high
priest striving to be worthy of the King who is about to
enter:

Than rynnes he furth in a rase, arais all the cite,
Braidis ovire with bawdkyns all the brade stretis,
With tars and with tafeta thare he trede sulde,
For the earth to slike ane emperoure ware ovire-feble.

Then runs he forth racing, arrays all the city,
braids over with baldachins all the broad streets,
with Tharsian silk and taffeta where he should tread,
for the earth for such an emperor would be over-poor.

(1636-9)

The verses cannot but recall the garments that the
populace in Jerusalem strewed upon Christ's route.

Jaddus is called *oure bischop* (1629),[20] and he is robed
in riotous episcopal splendour:

And sithen he castis on a cape of kastand hewes,
With riche r[y]b[an]s of gold railed bi the hemmes,
A vestoure to vise on of violet floures,
Wroght full of wodwose and othir wild bestes . . .

Then he casts on a cope of coruscating hues,
with rich ribbons of gold railed at the hems,
a vestment to view of violet flowers,
wrought full of woodsprites and other wild beasts
. . .

(1660-3)

His mitre was

Stight staffull of stanes that straght[en] out bemes,
As it ware shemerand shaftis of the shire son.

set surfeited with stones that sent out their beams
like shimmering shafts of the sheer sun.

(1666-7)

Where on Palm Sunday it is a liturgical procession of
boys that sings the hymn of acclaim, *Gloria, laus et
honor,* to the approaching Christ, here for Alexander

Thare passis the procession a piple beforne,
Of childire all in [c]halk-quyte, chosen out a hundreth,
With bellis and with baners and blasand torchis,
Instrumentis and ymagis within of the mynstire;
Sum with sensours and so, with silviryn cheynes,
Quareof the reke aromatike rase to the welken.

In front of the people passes the procession
of children all in chalk-white, a hundred chosen,
with bells and with banners and blazing torches,
instruments and images from within the minster,
some with censers and suchlike, with silver chains,
the spicy smoke of which rose to the skies.

(1684-9)

The poet expands the Latin acclamations of Alexander
by the citizens—

The wildire of all the werde and worthist on erthe!
. . . . .

The gretest and the gloriosest that ever god formed

. . .

the wielder of all the world and worthiest on earth!

. . . . .

the greatest and the gloriousest that ever God formed—

(1731-4)

the phrases coming close to the crowd's cries in Luke (19: 38): 'Blessed is the King who comes in the Lord's name: peace on earth and glory in heaven!' And in a sense Alexander entering Jerusalem *is* its saviour: he spares the city, even though previously the high priest, an ally of the Persians, had refused him tribute. But the paradox is that this sublime moment in Alexander's career, in which—for the medieval English poet, though not for his Latin source—Alexander becomes virtually *figura Christi,* comes about through his gesture of self-abnegation, prostrating himself in adoration of Yahweh. The poet makes the scene joyous and brilliantly co-loured in ways that leave the Latin text far behind; at the same time, all the details by which he outdoes his source become ways of giving the episode a new foundation, in the Christian *imaginaire.*

The Candace episode is very different in tone: with its tricking and countertricking, it comes close to fabliau. Alexander arrives at the Queen's palace pretending to be a Macedonian courtier, but she, who had secretly ordered a portrait of him in advance, unmasks him, leaving him defenceless. While the battle of wits between Candace and Alexander is depicted in all the principal western versions of the Greek Romance, it would seem to be the twelfth-century German poet Lamprecht (or his lost Provençal source, Alberic) who first gave the scene a sexual dimension. In Lamprecht's poem, Candace, having taken Alexander to her chamber, says:

> 'I know well who you are. No cunning that you have, bold hero, will help you now: you are in my power. What use to you is your might, or your victories over many lands? . . . Now a woman has vanquished you, without a fight . . . Don't be angry, noble hero, put on a manly disposition . . . I shan't give you away . . .'

> The lofty queen revealed her desire to me. Then in silence I made love with her. As I took her, she said I was her man; I was to leave off sulking, no evil would befall me.[21]

Whilst in every version Candace saves Alexander's life by keeping his identity secret, neither the English poet nor his Latin source tell that the pair become reconciled through lovemaking. Or rather, the English poet may imply it, though very discreetly, by way of another of his poetic feats in which, as in Alexander's entry into Jerusalem, the language of dazzling cumulations and that of familiar biblical echoes combine to create a surprising effect.

Both the Latin and the English tell that Candace's looks reminded Alexander of his mother, Olympias. Yet where the Latin has only the detached comment, 'the Queen was very beautiful',[22] the English poet launches into one of his most mettlesome evocations: he begins:

> Scho was so faire and so fresche, as faucon hire
>   semed,
> An elfe out of anothire erde or ellis an aungell.
> Hire palais was full precious, thof parades [it] ware
> . . .

> She was so fair and so fresh, like a falcon she seemed,
> An elf out of another earth, or else an angel.
> Her palace was all precious, as if it were paradise
> . . .

(5383-5)

This poet is fond of imagery of heaven and paradise, of which his Latin source knows nothing. For him, both the palace of Cyrus (3345) and the temple of the Sun (5032) are paradisal; Jerusalem, as Alexander is about to enter, *seems ane of the sevyn hevyns* (1651); in one of the loveliest lines in the whole poem, we learn that the Brahmans delight to walk in leaf-locked woods—

> Quen all is lokin ovire with levys, as it ware littill
>   heven.

(4512)

With Candace, the paradisal imagery colours the verse more and more. Of her summer hall: *Was nane so comly a close undire the cape of heven* (5392); it has precious stones *of paradise stremes* (5396); and at last, as Candace leads Alexander, all alone (5413), into her wondrous revolving chamber, comes a paradisal touch of a different kind from all the gold and gems that preceded: this *clochere*

> Was sammed all of sipris and seder tables.
> was assembled all of cypress and cedar tablets.

(5416)

Even the excellent recent editors did not recognize that with this verse the poet takes us into the Song of Songs:

> tigna domorum nostrarum *cedrina,*
> laquearia nostra *cypressina.* . .

(1: 16)

> si ostium est, conpingamus illud *tabulis cedrinis;*
> ego murus et ubera mea turris . . .

(8: 9-10)

> the beams of our dwelling are cedar,
> our panelling is cypress . . .

> If there is a door, let us adorn it with cedar tablets;
> I am the wall, and my breasts are the tower . . .

It seems to me likely that for at least some of the poet's audience the secret room *all of sipris and seder tables* must have evoked the bridal bower of the Canticle and its erotic associations. The poetic subtlety is that here the erotic moment is conjured up *before* Alexander is humiliatingly identified by the Queen. Unlike Lamprecht, the English poet does not, after Alexander is outwitted, go on to tell of sexual consummation. Instead, by his fleeting allusion to the unique *thalamus* of the Song of Songs, before the King's exposure, he has delicately enhanced his narrative with a hint of a more blissful love, that looks beyond the fabliau situation, while still not troubling the narrative flow. Candace's palace is indeed a paradise—though a precarious one. We now see why at the outset she was evoked as falcon, as angel, and as elf: she is as dangerous as a bird of prey, but she is also the angel who guards the hero's life and the elf who routs him with her lovingly malicious teasing: 'Why splutter so, Sir Conqueror, and make your soul so crabbish?' (5449).[23]

We have noted the cumulative language of outdoing alongside the familiarizing language that anchors Alexander's world in the medieval Christian one; we have seen some instances of how what is rich and strange in Alexander's world can, through poetic syncretism, assimilate Christ's entry into Jerusalem, or pseudo-Dionysian angels, or the inner chamber of the Song of Songs. It remains to ask, can we discern an imaginative principle underlying such combination? Is it simply a heady, virtuoso delight in the gamut of expressive possibilities in late medieval alliterative poetry, or is there a further poetic secret?

It seems to me that the twofold orientation in language and content which is one of the distinguishing features of *The Wars of Alexander* reflects and reinforces a twofold perception of Alexander himself, that we can document far more widely in medieval literature, and that I shall try to characterize briefly in more general terms.

The medieval Alexander was an *intrinsically* ambiguous figure—and it was precisely his ambiguity that made him seem so captivating. However diversely medieval writers and their audiences assessed Alexander, the stories about him catered to two contrary but complementary needs: they met the demands of wish-fulfilment and those of moral satisfaction. On the one hand, Alexander's career fulfilled a host of human longings. He seemed the nearest among men to have achieved unbounded existence: he broke every known confine of physical discovery, finding new realms of every kind and claiming them for himself—so many historical kingdoms, but also, in the legends, the heavens and the ocean's depths, and (almost) the earthly paradise. He is a visionary, driven within by a sense of destiny, a seemingly more than human force;[24] yet he is also a consummate trickster, often disguising himself as one of his own courtiers or messengers, even at the risk of his life.

He becomes a fabulous Oriental potentate, whose every caprice, for good or ill, magnificently generous or wantonly cruel, is instantly fulfilled; yet he is likewise (*avant la lettre*) a Faust, a restless conqueror of knowledge as well as power, who never asks the passing moment to linger, but is forever impelled, unquenchably and sublimely, towards a moment that appears more perfect still.

On the other hand, against the stories of the intoxicating fantasies and the aspirations realized, are set again and again the cautionary tales, the *exempla,* the reminders: he was small, often weak, often afraid, often flawed in character, at times even pusillanimous. And this account too is welcome, for it is reassuring. Alexander was not in essence different from ourselves. If the mythical projection had been purely that of a superman, it would carry little meaning for common humanity. So it was important to stress that the impaired, vulnerable condition which we experience was his as well as ours, that even a conqueror can be humbled, that even the mightiest of men can die young.

The Alexander of the great feats of outdoing is complemented by the Alexander of familiar human littleness. This complementarity is explored most profoundly near the close of the greatest of the medieval Alexander romances, Walter of Châtillon's *Alexandreis.*[25] Yet it is also, at least in some measure, manifest in a poetic presentation such as that of *The Wars of Alexander.* Here it is the language of outdoing and the language of familiarity, the flights of alliterative *ecphrasis* and the liturgical-biblical allusions, which, with notable aptness and power, suggest the ambivalence of this hero, who seems half to outstrip the poet's Christian cosmos and yet half to belong to it. It is especially in the 'ulterior motives' of the diction and the allusions that the originality of this poem lies.

Notes

1. *Die Historia de preliis Alexandri Magni: Rezension J³*, ed. K. Steffens (Meisenheim am Glan, 1975). This is cited below as *Historia,* followed by page and line references. On the relation of this version to the complex tradition of Leo of Naples' *Historia* and its revisions, see esp. D. J. A. Ross, *Alexander Historiatus,* Warburg Institute Surveys, 1 (London, 1963), 47-61.

2. On the basis of the carefully inconclusive observations of the editors, H. N. Duggan and T. Turville-Petre, *The Wars of Alexander,* EETS SS 10 (1989), pp. xlii-xliii, I assume for the poem a date of composition not too far from 1400. *MED,* when citing *The Wars,* gives the date of the Ashmole MS (*c.*1450), adding 'a. 1400?' in parenthesis. This would imply a date of composition around a

century after the ME metrical *Kyng Alisaunder* (ed. G. V. Smithers, EETS OS 227, 237 (1952, 1957)), and one or two generations after the other ME alliterative Alexander fragments (1340-70): *The Gestes,* and *Alexander and Dindimus* (ed. W. W. Skeat, EETS ES 1 (1867) and 31 (1878)). *The Wars* would also be approximately contemporary with the *Prose Life of Alexander* (ed. J. S. Westlake, EETS OS 143 (1913)), and slightly earlier than the Scottish *Buik of Alexander* of 1438 (ed. R. L. G. Ritchie, STS NS 12, 17, 21, 25 (1921-9)); it would precede by several decades Sir Gilbert Hay's *Buik of King Alexander the Conquerour* (ed. J. Cartwright, STS 4th ser. 16, 18 (1986-)). It should perhaps also be recalled that there are already OE versions of two Alexander texts: A. Orchard, *Pride and Prodigies* (Cambridge, 1995), has just given new editions with translation of the OE *Wonders of the East* and *Letter of Alexander to Aristotle.* Finally, Aristotle's letter to Alexander, the *Secretum Secretorum,* enjoyed a vast fortune in England in the later Middle Ages: M. Manzalaoui (EETS OS 276 (1977)) has edited nine English versions from MSS ranging from *c.*1400 to the early Tudor period. I was unable to see Gerrit H. V. Bunt's *Alexander the Great in the Literature of Medieval Britain,* Medievalia Groningana, 14 (Groningen, 1994), before the completion of this essay; Bunt includes only a brief, mainly genealogical discussion of *The Wars.*

3. The editors, in their note *ad loc.* (*Wars,* p. 205), claim that '*synagoge* should be translated as "pagan temple or shrine", without special reference to Judaism'; similarly *MED, s.v. sinagoge;* none the less, the specific poetic point here, I would suggest, is analogous to that of filling Alexander's world with minsters, clerks, nuns, and the rest: a *synagoge,* even if not quite a minster, is less unfamiliar than a fane.

4. *Historia,* 104. 25.

5. The editors (*Wars,* p. 275) valuably cite a Latin MS variant—*Cerenon deum dicitis esse ventris . . .*—not given in the apparatus of *Historia,* 140. 9-10, which accounts for the error.

6. *Historia,* 156. 9-10.

7. With comparative and non-specialist readers in mind, I have offered translations for the verse citations here and below. These also help to indicate succinctly my way of interpreting certain nuances and problematic expressions, which would otherwise require more detailed discussion.

8. On *domesmen* (literally 'judges'), see *Wars,* p. 220, *ad* 1937, where it translates Latin *nuncios;* thus the editors suggest that the word 'may merely emphasise their social importance'; by my rendering, 'justicers', I imply that the poet does have the more specific sense 'judges' in mind, but here informs it with savage irony.

9. *Historia,* 92. 3-4.

10. *MED, s.v. tempren* 9d, glosses this passage '? to sharpen (one's wits),? refresh'; the graphic quality of the poet's language, however, seems to me to admit the possibility of sense 7 ('to tune a musical instrument'), or 9a ('to work [metal . . .] to a proper degree of hardness and elasticity').

11. *Historia,* 148. 35-150. 14.

12. *Historia,* 150. 33-4: *venerunt super eos maxima copia draconum, serpentium et leonum qui angustia maxima afflixerunt eos.*

13. Ibid. 152. 1-2: *venerunt in vallem obscuram ita, ut vix unus alium conspicere posset.*

14. *Wars,* 4933-4:

    > Thai ware umbethourid in that thede with slike a thike cloude
    > That thai might fele it with thaire fiste as flabband webbis.

15. *Scharpe schudering of schote:* the editors (Glossary, pp. 367-8) render the words 'violent scattering of missiles'; *MED, s.v. shodering,* has '? movement;? crashing, clashing' for this passage. In the light of the previous phrase *stickinge of erles,* however, I incline to picture *schote*—in the collective sense of 'discharges, shots', *MED, s.v. shot,* 2 (a)—entering bodies with a quivering impact (the first sense of *shodering* in *MED* is 'a shaking, quivering').

16. *Historia,* 12. 22.

17. Ibid. 18. 15.

18. The editors (p. 371) gloss *shrewe* as 'wretch'; but in view of the three other animal terms of abuse in these verses (*asalen, ape,* and *wayryngle*), I suspect that the literal sense, 'shrew-mouse', may be in the poet's mind. On the other hand, *OED* has no example of this literal sense between 900 and 1538, and *MED, s.v. shreue,* gives figurative senses only.

19. *Historia,* 34. 7 ff.

20. In the Latin (34. 7 *et passim*), Iaddus is *pontifex Iudeorum.* The basis for this appellation may well lie in the Vulgate of St John's Gospel, where the high priest Caiaphas is several times called *pontifex* (John 11: 49 and 51; 18: 13). In her essay 'Alejandro en Jerusalén' (*Romance Philology,* 10

(1956-7), 185-96), María Rosa Lida de Malkiel pointed out that in various vernacular adaptations of the matter of Alexander Jaddus is designated bishop or even pope, and in particular in the thirteenth-century Spanish *Libro de Alexandre* there are a number of touches that show how 'the intention of making the source appear contemporary, without taking archaeological distance, gives the anachronisms their point' (p. 191 n. 7). Thus in the Spanish poem Jaddus puts on the vestment with which 'he said mass' (*la misa dizié*, 1137), and later not only a mitre but 'a dalmatic' (*una dalmática*, 1154). None the less, the Spanish poet does not invest the episode with any more pervasive *figura Christi* symbolism, nor does he have that element of 'taking sides' which the English poet once more indicates lightly by his expression '*oure* bischop'.

21. *Lamprechts Alexander,* ed. K. Kinzel (Halle am Saale, 1884), 6161 ff. (Strasbourg redaction).

22. *Historia,* 166. 10 (*Erat autem regina formosa nimis*—at *Wars,* p. 292 the editors cite the MS variant *pulchra, formosa plurimum et decora*).

23. 'Qui colkins thou, sire conquirour, and crabbis so thi saule?' *MED,* s.v. *colkenen,* relates this *hapax legomenon* to Danish *kulke* ('drink with a gurgling sound') and German dialectal *kolksen* ('burp'). The editors (*Wars,* p. 293) reject this on the ground that the Latin (*Historia,* 168. 13-14) has only '*Ut quid infra temet ipsum irasceris et turbaris?*' Thus they gloss *colkins* (p. 316) as 'become angry(?)'. But this is a dubious line of argument: examples of the poet's enlivening the language of his source are legion; in this verse alone, the sardonic addition of *sire conquirour,* and the rendering of *turbaris* by *crabbis so thi saule,* are sufficient indication that he was likely, too, to come up with something more piquant than 'Why do you become angry?'

24. The poet, translating Alexander's words to the Gymnosophists ('*Vellem siquidem in pace consistere, sed alius spiritus, qui sensui meo dominatur, me hoc facere non permittit*', *Historia,* 124. 11-12), endows them with a sombre, incantatory splendour (4193-4):

> 'My will ware to riste,
> Bot anothir gast and noght my gast thareof my gast lettis.'

25. I have tried to show this in some detail in a longer essay, the 'Introduzione' to the forthcoming anthology of texts with facing Italian translations, *Alessandro nel Medioevo* (Fondazione Valla, Mondadori, Milan).

Abbreviations

EETS: Early English Text Society

MED: *Middle English Dictionary,* ed. J. Kurath *et al.* (Ann Arbor, Mich., 1956-)

OED: *Oxford English Dictionary,* ed. J. A. H. Murray, H. Bradley, W. A. Craigie, and C. T. Onions (Oxford, 1933)

STS: Scottish Text Society

Christine Chism (essay date 1998)

SOURCE: Chism, Christine. "Too Close for Comfort: Dis-Orienting Chivalry in the *Wars of Alexander.*" In *Text and Territory: Geographical Imagination in the European Middle Ages,* edited by Sylvia Tomasch and Sealy Gilles, pp. 116-39. Philadelphia: University of Pennsylvania Press, 1998.

[*In the following essay, Chism contends that in the fourteenth-century North West Midlands poem* The Wars of Alexander, *Alexander begins to see certain correspondences between himself and his enemies as he faces a multiplicity of Eastern foes.*]

The *Wars of Alexander,* an alliterative North West Midlands poem, thought to date from the later fourteenth century, describes what is simultaneously a conqueror's dream and a xenophobe's nightmare.[1] While relating the exploits of Alexander the Great, a chivalric conqueror driven to separate himself from and place himself above all the kingdoms of the east, the poem incessantly embeds him in those worlds, disturbing his illusions of preeminence with the intimations of affinity. After describing its hero's Egyptian parentage and his effacement of this oriental origin, the poem is a mercilessly energetic description of his campaigns. Throughout the 5,800-line poem, Alexander drives onward, seeking new boundaries to obliterate, new kingdoms to encompass, in what becomes finally a need to escape the limits of history itself. As he ranges over the length and breadth of Asia, Alexander is impelled to transcend all chivalric expectations, to exceed every military precedent, and finally to set himself over every past, present, and future authority.

But Alexander is an iconoclast whose violence is painfully contained. As Alexander's campaigns incline farther and farther to the east, he is continually halted by the realization that his numerous adversaries know him, reflect back to him his own face, and adumbrate his own future. When this happens, he succumbs to an awful sympathy, arrested by the intensity of his emotions—a paralysis that ends only when he effaces the significance of the encounter and turns to meet the next enemy. His entire identity as a world conqueror and his chivalric enterprise are thus contingent upon his willful ignorance and rejection of his subversive resemblances to his enemies, of his oriental genealogy, and of his eventual fate—world conquest and sudden death.

Unlike the roughly contemporary alliterative poem the *Siege of Jerusalem,* where the struggle between West and East is driven primarily by religious, political, and economic imperatives, the conflicts of the *Wars of Alexander* are more pointedly generational—struggles that pit son against father, youth against maturity, inexperience and obscurity against historic fame, and finally chivalric iconoclasm against the delimiting structures of that iconoclasm's own origins and history. This generational conflict establishes indissoluble links between Alexander and his various adversaries—even as they succumb to him, they invoke his origin and mirror his future. In this way, the *Wars of Alexander* conflates genealogy and geography as contested territories, two linked fronts along which Alexander wages war, striving to efface the one and dominate the other. And while the poem shows his irresistible power to subdue the worlds of the east, it also insists on his complete temporal helplessness: his placement within a genealogy that links him to his enemies, his destined subjection to the same fate he imposes upon them.

Throughout the poem, then, Alexander is forced to face the idea that victory is not transcendence. He is repeatedly reminded of his own inscription within the processes of history and generation, and of his fundamental relationships to his oriental others. As the poem continues and Alexander runs the gamut of diverse adversaries from militant Persians, to ingenious Jews, to saintly Brahmans, to giant scorpions, his identity as a chivalric conqueror whose endeavor depends on singularity of will and solidarity of loyalty begins to break apart. His progress mobilizes an exploration of late medieval chivalric consciousness that is provocatively attentive both to its desire for labile, diversified, and polysemic others and to its need to ground its self-inventions upon their alienations.

The poem seems fascinated by moments in which the voices of Alexander's adversaries interrupt the strategic alienations that foreground his endeavor—moments in which his affiliations and likenesses to his enemies are revealed. Such moments are the militarily indomitable Alexander's only points of vulnerability, and the poem probes at them with sardonic persistence. In one confrontation of piercing clarity, as Alexander pauses on the banks of the impassable Ganges to question the Brahmans, the Indians convey to him their perception of his entire military enterprise: "It is ȝourselfe and noȝt ourself þat ai þe self hantis" (4794) [It is yourself and

not us that you are forever pursuing]. As Alexander confronts different adversaries, his military victories are often prologue to such stunning epistemological ambushes. The idea that Alexander is chasing his own carefully exoticized shadows animates the poem in a multitude of different ways, transforming Alexander's conflicts of identity into familial, political and ideological ones. Alexander is a patricide and his murder of his Egyptian prophet-father, Anectanabus, becomes the model and the drive for his subsequent conquest of his other oriental predecessors, the great rulers Darius of Persia and Porrus of India.

Alexander's dilemma reimagines the political and ideological conflicts of a whole late-fourteenth-early-fifteenth-century generation of British nobility, haunted by the specter of their military ineptitude during recent crusades—and ferociously refusing that knowledge. The sense of futility that plagues Alexander—the recurrent apprehension that he is shadow-boxing his own "fonned fantasies" (5639) through Asia—reflects and reconfigures the misgivings of a late-fourteenth-century audience increasingly aware of the necessary connections and complex debts between themselves and their numerous eastern adversaries.

It is striking that a British poet of this period should have been energized to translate and amplify a poem of such length into careful and at times delightfully ironic alliterative verse.[2] I will argue that Alexander is a uniquely situated figure for the gentry of the North West Midlands who were this poem's probable audience. Themselves identified with and eager to appropriate the historical and ideological appurtenances of the English nobility, they would have been drawn to Alexander as a chivalric model, one of the Nine Worthies about whom a rich legendary history had accumulated. Throughout the Middle Ages, Alexander's ongoing appeal is attested by the five-century history of the Alexander romances which form a continuing genre, analogous in breadth and richness to the other notable Matters of British chivalric legend, Arthur and Charlemagne.[3] In the course of the *Wars of Alexander,* Alexander himself emerges as the preeminent chivalric hero, in contrast to his Egyptian father Anectanabus, to Darius of Persia, and to all the multifarious eastern rulers and warlords whose defeats the poem will relate. Despite his eastern and magical origins, Alexander becomes the founder of a chivalric empire and a worthy predecessor to fourteenth-century nobility who wished to look further back than Arthur or even Rome for desirable chivalric forefathers.

In addition, Alexander, as a successful world conqueror, would have had a particular charm to a late fourteenth-century audience of gentry who had been gradually but forcibly taught the futility of ambitions to conquer, regain, or convert the immense diversity of non-Christian lands to the east. In subduing those rich and exotic civilizations, Alexander single-handedly performs what two hundred years of historical crusading and all the efforts of a supposedly righteous, God-inspired cause could not accomplish.

As a chivalric model, then, Alexander is alluring because he provides a positive image of chivalric imperial aggression repeatedly and irresistibly subduing the incredible might and cultural power of the empires of Persia, India, and the lands beyond. Yet as a Greek ruler (and in the late fourteenth century the Greeks themselves were given the ambiguous status of schismatics), he himself hovers on the tenuous border between what the fourteenth century defined as East and West. As this poem makes clear, if Alexander is situated as an identification for Western chivalry, he is also its other—a figure whose contradictions and perplexities mirror its own. Thus the poem's interrogation of Alexander's conquest enables a potential self-analysis and critique for a culture still desperately invested in oriental conquest but gradually forced to realize the futility of its dreams.

Alexander's very genealogical ambiguity would have posed interesting and fertile problems for the poem's audience. His Egyptian ancestry, polytheism, and the mounting scope of his ambitions make him a figure just as easily appropriable by eastern conquerors as western ones. To cite one contemporary and very influential example, Froissart's chronicle describes the defeat of the European army at Nicopolis in terms that attribute Alexandrian ambitions to the Ottoman leader Bayezid (Lamorabaquy) as he rejoices in the captured tents of the Christian leaders:

> Than Lamorabaquy . . . made as great myrthe as myght be, and sayd how he wolde shortely with great puyssaunce passe into the realme of Hungery, and conquere the countrey, and after other countreys upon the Crysten men, and to bringe them to his obeysaunce . . . he sayd he wolde reygne lyke Alysaunder of Masydone, who was twelve yere kynge of all the worlde, of whose lynage he sayde he was dyscended.

(237)

Bayezid's ambition gathers even more menacing overtones when Froissart attributes to him a desire to become the new Alexander and attain the "signory" over Christendom. He can claim Alexander as a literal ancestor and chivalric model as easily as the alliterative poets of England can make Alexander one of the Nine Worthies, an example of illustrious leadership for the west.

It is my contention that Alexander is so successful and fascinating a chivalric hero for the late-fourteenth-century poet precisely because he is self-perplexed:

traditionally, even his eyes were of different colors. He becomes a hybrid of eastern and western cultures who empowers himself as he attempts to obliterate his connections to his oriental origins, both ancestrally, by destroying his father and effacing his father's name, and politically, by trying to subdue to Greek rule all the kingdoms of the east. He represents western chivalry's admiration for and aversion to an oriental world it can never convert or conquer and from whose learning, science, and history Europeans had drawn a great part of their own.

ORIENTAL CONJUNCTIONS

In the *Wars of Alexander,* the ancient eastern cultures, including that of Macedon itself, are exoticized, becoming redolent not of particular differentiable geographical, ethnic, or social practices but rather simply of foreignness. Mary Campbell notes that in the literary traditions upon which the poet drew "'the East' is a concept separable from any particular geographic area. It is essentially Elsewhere" (*Witness,* 48). The *Wars of Alexander* joins other late-fourteenth-century alliterative poems such as the *Siege of Jerusalem* and the *Morte Arthure* when it retrenches the boundaries between east and west in a way that refuses knowledge of the exotic except as that which is to be conquered, reduced, and assimilated. Before Alexander's fierce, mismatched gaze Egyptians, Jews, Persians, Indians, and monsters blur together into a brilliant but hazy mass. He sees not a collection of individually distinctive (or obnoxious) religions and societies, but simply a series of enemies. They are conquered not for their usury, or their past crimes, or their adherence to false philosophies, but because their deaths will give power and definition to the emerging world order the poem is written to explore.

Alexander's obsession with the violently charged boundaries between his chivalric authority and the empires of the east places the poem within a complicated history of medieval boundary policing. During the twelfth and thirteenth centuries, most of the historical sources describing the relations of Christians and non-Christians work from a model of two irreducibly adversarial worlds, drawn into uneasy mutual orbit. Twelfth-century chronicles and memoirs from all sides of the conflicts positively bristle with horrified cultural incomprehension. Usamah Ibn-Muqidh, a Syrian scholar and warrior, recounts one incident:

> One day I entered this mosque, repeated the first formula, "Allah is great," and stood up in the act of praying, upon which one of the Franks rushed on me, got hold of me and turned my face eastward saying, "This is the way thou shouldst pray!" The Templars . . . came in to him and expelled him. They apologized to me, saying, "This is a stranger who has only recently arrived from the land of the Franks and he has never

seen anyone praying except eastward." . . . So I went out and have ever been surprised at the conduct of this devil of a man, at the change in the color of his face, his trembling and his sentiment at the sight of one praying towards the *qiblah.*"

(163-64)[4]

In Usamah's description, the violent exaggeration of the Frank's reaction forms a useful point of contrast to the diplomatic aplomb of the Templars. Throughout his memoirs, Usamah remains extremely wary of any European who has not been domesticated by at least some time in the Holy Land.

Where such accounts reinforce this aversion between east and west, the writings of many European church fathers and crusade-inspired clerics make it an ideological imperative. The twelfth-century abbot of Cluny, Peter the Venerable, was one of the first who fostered the model of east and west as two antagonistic worlds. Alarmed by the avidity with which well-to-do Christians all over Europe were embracing Islamic cultural products, philosophies, and rhetorical styles, he visited twelfth-century al-Andalus on a fact-finding mission to translate what he thought were the most crucial Islamic scriptures in order to reveal their erroneous deceptions and prevent bedazzled Christians from being seduced away from the glories of both their own tongues and their own faith. The works he translated as Islamic doctrine, however, included not only the Qur'an but four literary texts. Adapting his materials to a familiar medieval Christian schema, Peter offered his readers a vision of the Islamic heaven and hell. The results, as Maria Rosa Menocal understates it, were "a very imaginative vision of Islam" (42, 43). Peter's text represents the Islamic world as both threateningly foreign and degenerately enticing, a mixed message that persists in many subsequent representations, from such crusade chronicles as Odo of Deuil's to the *Wars of Alexander.*[5] This firm division of the world into east and west, then, was a very interested one, with advantages for those who deployed it. Even as it fostered persistent and often exploitable anxiety about the enemy without, it deemphasized the possibility of subversion from within. It posited essential differences between two monolithically defined cultures and faiths, differences that would, it was hoped, make cultural syncretism unthinkable. Throughout the period of greatest contact, this proposition was reassuring to conservative factions in Spain, southern France, and Italy, cultures that had been subject to thorough permeation by such threatening and enticing Arabic imports as the new Aristotelianism (Menocal, 27-70).

However, by the later fourteenth century, this conception of east and west as two worlds had undergone important challenges—challenges which the *Wars of Al-*

exander reflects. The first point of attack was the growing awareness of the sheer diversity and multiplicity of eastern lands. Different eastern cultures had been persistently orientalized for two centuries into sites for European projections; they served as literary landscapes for the fantasies of both chronicler and romance writer. European ignorance of the diversity and extent of its eastern neighbors was rapidly vanishing. There had been enough military trials of strength to prove that armed conquest or wholesale conversion was impossible. In addition, the countries of Europe had gradually realized how economically advantageous trade with eastern states could be, and had, in fact, come to rely heavily upon eastern luxuries, from spices to dyes to silks. As consciousness grew in Europe of the extent and richness of many eastern countries, and as merchant entrepreneurs sought ingress into an intricate and highly profitable system of trade that extended from Egypt and the Holy Land to China, there was a dizzying reversal in perspective. Perhaps Christian Europe and its desired crown, Jerusalem, rather than being the world's religious and cultural center and the heart of the *mappa mundi,* was to other navigators only a marginal silver on the northwest edge of a world system more enormous and multifarious than the Roman Empire at its most extensive.

R. W. Southern describes the traumatic effect of this slow realization upon twelfth- and thirteenth-century Europeans who still cherished the beguiling dream of converting to Christianity the world of Islam, assimilating its knowledge and wealth, and uniting the world under the banner of a newly invigorated Christian world system.

> There were ten, or possibly a hundred, unbelievers for every Christian. Nobody knew; and the estimate grew with each access of knowledge. One consequence of this was to make the Crusades seem either quite impossible, or in need of a drastic reassessment of its aims and methods.
>
> (*Western Views,* 43)

By the late fourteenth century, this need for reassessment was even more acute. In the first place, the loss of the last crusader stronghold at Acre to the Mamluks in 1291 had led to the cessation of the trade revenues that came from the control of the westernmost ports of Palestine. These trade revenues had helped finance and maintain the crusader kingdoms, which without them soon crumbled. With the kingdoms went the last real gains in a two-century bid to reestablish Christian European control of territory that was conceived both geographically and genealogically as the heart of the world and the cradle of Christianity.

In addition, Europeans could no longer easily participate in the elaborate system of trade and mercantile exchange, which had knit together countries from

England to China from the twelfth century to the mid-fourteenth century. France, Italy, Flanders, and England had become dependent upon the silks, spices, and artifacts that flowed along these routes. That these mercantile linkages were extensive and intimate is attested by the grisly evidence that if there had been such widespread and profitable traffic between the diverse countries, the bubonic plague certainly would not have spread from China to England with such devastating rapidity.[6]

By 1350, however, European countries had no direct access to either the northern or southern trade routes with the east and even their indirect access had become subject to strict and (they felt) humiliating regulation. The northern land routes over Asia had deteriorated with the fragmentation of the Mongol Empire (Abu-Lughod, 141). At the same time, the Mamluk sultanate in Egypt had consolidated its monopoly on the southern trade route through Egypt and the Red Sea. Venice successfully obtained a severely restricted access to trade through this route into the fifteenth century but only because it agreed to trade slaves to the Mamluks, slaves who were trained and employed to swell the ranks of the Mamluk military and thus strengthen them even further. The resentment caused by such mercantile regulation emerges very clearly in the accounts of the traders (European and otherwise) forced to undergo customs control at Alexandria.[7]

European responses to these altering circumstances bespoke both frustration and desperation. Possibilities of military conquest, always a favorite tactic, continued to entice despite repeated disasters. By the late fourteenth century, it had been over a century since a crusade had achieved notable success. The 1356 raid of Peter of Cyprus on Alexandria had won no permanent foothold and had led to no further campaigning. Yet the need for some response was felt to be acute, given the shifting power balances among Syria, Egypt, and Turkey. Most pressing to the English provincial gentry to whose interests the *Wars of Alexander* appeals was the newly emerging Ottoman Empire, whose armies in 1396 thoroughly trounced at Nicopolis an ill-judged crusade of knights from all over Europe, including sizable factions from the North-West Midlands reputedly led by the noblest families in England.[8]

However, alongside of this intensifying late-fourteenth-century defensiveness, there began to emerge for the first time in European and English writings an increasing sense of necessary connections between the countries of Europe and their easterly neighbors. The potential for connection had been there all along. Even geographically, it was difficult to maintain East-West distinctions in the face of many contested territories whose histories of occupation and repossession precluded clear categorization. For almost two centuries, Muslim-occupied Spain had formed the hybrid state of al-Andalus, a country where cultural interchange was so intense that for those two centuries it resisted geographical classification. Crusade narratives such as that of Odo of Deuil bespeak an intermittent but profound obsession not only with the Holy Land but also with the other "Eastern" center of Christianity, Byzantium, itself a challenge to clear lines of definition. In the second part of the fourteenth century, it seems to have become easier for European writers to acknowledge links to eastern cultures—not only geographically, but also in the most embattled territories of religion and theology.[9]

European and British writers and theologians began to propose relationships between Christianity and Islam that linked them by cause and effect, similarity, and fate. Southern discusses this convergence as a new development, discernible by 1350 and increasing into the fifteenth century (at the same time as the Ottoman conquests pressed Prussia and Hungary more and more closely).[10] At least one religious philosopher, the Benedictine monk Uthred of Boldon, who taught theology and promoted church reform at the University of Oxford in the mid-1360s, brought Christian, Jew, and Muslim together when he argued that salvation was offered to everyone, Christian, Jew, Saracen, or pagan, baptized or not, in a moment of intellectual illumination just before death. And Uthred was not the only writer to disregard two centuries of militant theological differentiation. In the fifteenth passus of the B-text of *Piers Plowman* (c. 1378), William Langland puts some startlingly even-handed sentiments into the toothless, tongueless mouth of Anima, a figure whose whole dialogue strives to transcend the confining and equally problematic Christian polemics that Will interrogates throughout the poem. The passus ends by affirming the essential unity of Christianity, Judaism, and Islam as monotheistic religions rooted in the first line of the Christian Credo:

> Ac pharisees and sarsens, scribes and Jewes
> Arn folk of oon feith—the fader God thei honouren.
> And sithen that the Sarsens and also the Jewes
> Konne the first clause of oure bileve, *Credo in Deum
>   patrem omnipotentem.*
>
> (15.603-6)

Here, the essential likeness of Judaism and Islam to Christianity is what enables their slow convergence. Building upon the monotheism they all hold alike, Anima imagines bringing them together to be as simple as conveying them "litlum and litlum" (608) through the Credo, just as one would teach it to a child. Anima's simplicity masks a surprising perception; merely by affirming the essential monotheism of Islam, Langland is going far beyond many of his contemporaries' more colorful representations of it as paganism or demonolatry.[11] Anima proposes a christianization that is not violent or adversarial, the education of a child rather than the conquest of an alien.

While Uthred and Langland envision possible intersections of Christianity and Islam as utopian and regenerative (giving the priority to Christianity, of course), three other fourteenth-century writers, John Mandeville, John Wycliffe, and Philippe de Mézières, deploy such resemblances to sharpen their calls for Christian reform. Langland himself, in tracing the origins of Islam to a Christian malcontent with corn in his ear (an astonishing view of Muhammad), makes the very existence of Islam a product of Christian chicanery—Christian corruption coming home to roost. Mandeville, Wycliffe, and Philippe castigate the divisions and problems of contemporary Christian Europe even more fiercely. In the work of all three writers, Islam reflects back to the works' Christian audiences their own negative images; Mandeville actually puts calls for Christian reform into the mouth of the sultan of Egypt. While each of these writers is heterodox and extraordinary in his thinking, it is significant that figures who move in such different social and political circles and write such different texts should construct and exploit similar connections between Christianity and Islam.[12]

Closest to the concerns of the *Alexander*-poet, Philippe de Mézières takes this same religious reflectivity a step further, using it as a call for crusade. After the defeat of the Christian armies at Nicopolis in 1396, Philip addressed a letter to King Philip of France, laying out the causes of the defeat—Christian division and decadence—and proposing reforms that would knit Christian knights into a militant order governed by the fourfold moral virtues of right rule (*règle*), discipline, obedience, and justice. Philippe in "L'épistre lamentable et consolatoire" places the same internal focus on the problems of Christianity as do Langland and Wycliffe and makes the same logical link between Christian reform and the dispelling of the Islamic threat. However, unlike his predecessors, Philippe's argument is driven by the need not only to mend Christian divisons but to avenge the defeat at Nicopolis and vindicate the honor of Christian Europe. He insists upon the intense shame of the 1396 defeat: "la grant vergoigne de la foy, la vergoigne de toy, de tous le roys crestiens et de la cretienté . . ." (458) [the great shame of the faith, your own shame, the shame of all Christian kings and of Christianity itself].[13]

This defeat is not just tactical. It strikes a mortal wound ("plaie") to the body of Christendom. This "plaie douloureuse" (458) can be cured, Philippe argues, by the nurturing of "une nouvelle génération de combattants qui possédera ces quatre vertus morales" (457) [A new

generation of fighters who possess the four moral virtues]. In Philippe's argument, the internal reformation of Christian knighthood into a newly regulated and energized military order automatically gives rise to a number of consummations devoutly to be wished: the defeat of the Turkish enemies of the faith, vengeance for their shaming victory, and the restoration of Christian sovereignty as the highest exemplars of chivalry, monarchy, and virtue. One of the reasons Philippe tried to negotiate peace between France and England in the 1390s was to help heal the internal divisions between Christian monarchs in preparation for a newly animated and successful crusade, which would reverse not only the recent defeat of the crusaders at Nicopolis, but the accumulated defeats on military, economic, and religious fronts of nearly a century.

In both the letter and his enormous work *Le Songe du vieil pelerin*, Philippe de Mézières characterizes his work as a voice crying in the wilderness, the voice of a solitary old pilgrim whose prophecies are the more crucial for being in the large part ignored. But similar crusading sentiments, although they failed to spark a royal crusade, were by no means alien or uncelebrated among the nobility and gentry of the English provinces, the probable audience of the *Wars of Alexander*, whose livelihoods were augmented not only by campaigns in France but increasingly, as the fourteenth century neared its end, by itinerant crusades in Prussia and Hungary, including the siege of Nicopolis.

In sum, by the late fourteenth century, the pressures and demands exerted by the various eastern dynasties and sultanates were multiple and ranged across a whole spectrum of European interests: political, social, economic, and religious. The *Wars of Alexander* reflects and explores this multiplicity. Even as it depicts a hero frantically trying to reduce endless empires to a single rule, the poem is captivated by the sheer diversity of Alexander's enemies, and it expands upon its source's descriptions of them with considerable inventiveness. Alexander's adversaries range from his secret Egyptian father, to the Jews in Jerusalem, to the great emperors Darius of Persia and Porrus of India, to the Brahmans of the Ganges, to the mysterious Master of the Temple of the Sun, and to the unnervingly self-possessed queen of Prasiaca, Candace, with whom he has a very close encounter indeed. As the poem continues and Alexander passes into unmappable eastern desolations, gruesome monsters erupt from the very earth to harry and decimate his forces. There is a clear sense that resistance to his encroachments is worked into the very soil of the landscape which yields monsters and portents with inexhaustible variety and fecundity. Such an overriding sense of eastern multiplicity—the east as a range of kingdoms, some very similar to Alexander's Macedon, others nightmarishly alien—subverts the cognitive division of the world into two halves, East and West.

At the same time, the poem problematizes the possibility of any singular conquest, because the conqueror himself is shown to be self-divided and fragmented, a hybrid creature whose identity ultimately rests on the constant erasure of his genealogical and situational affiliations to those he destroys. Even as the poem relentlessly depicts an empire in the process of foundation, it subverts the whole concept of a successful and lasting empire. It intimates an unnerving but irrefutable sense of the essential reflectivity of both East and West, their mutual dependence upon each other, their mutual generation of each other. In the end the poem points to one of the most insidious anxieties of a European sensibility anxious to reduce relations between itself and its eastern neighbors to the simple, unidirectional relation of conqueror and victim. It perhaps hints that their own foundational texts and tenets, their science and learning, their cultural genealogies have been obsessively translated, adapted and appropriated from cultures and countries now distanced as Eastern and other, from the Jews, from the Greeks, and from the Arabs. The poem insists on the essential relatedness of geographically opposed cultures and constructs that relatedness in a particularly threatening way—a relationship of blood in the senses of both violence and generation. It is Alexander's horrified recognition of his oriental progenitor that foregrounds, drives, and is ineffectually effaced by his subsequent military conquests.

BREAKING THE TERRESTRIAL MIRROR

The first part of the *Wars of Alexander* is occupied with the story of Anectanabus, the Egyptian king turned itinerant sorcerer, Alexander's secret, oriental, and untrustworthy father. Anectanabus's arcane knowledge obviates the web of chivalric solidarities between leader and follower that will make his son, Alexander, the greatest ruler of the world. King Anectanabus deserts his people when he learns by augury that they are about to be overrun by the Persians. He doffs the chivalric regalia of rulership and assumes the guise of a wandering astrologer—an unchancy magician who can vanish at will, transform himself into a dragon, deliver a baby, stage earthquakes and portents, and usurp the prerogatives not only of kings but of divinities, with perfect equanimity and impunity. By giving Alexander's father such socially disruptive energy, the poem constructs for its hero, Alexander, an oriental ancestry that is covert, lawless, volatile, and extremely unchivalric.

However, the poem complicates and obscures this ancestry when it details the trickery/divine intervention that brings about Alexander's birth. After fleeing Egypt,

Anectanabus seeks refuge at the court of Philip of Macedon. Immediately, he seduces Queen Olympados, by masquerading as the sun god Amon, and then convinces Philip that this is not just a visitation to be endured, a kind of divine *droit de seigneur,* but an actual honor. Anectanabus's stratagem meets with dazzling success, and Alexander is thus gifted with three fathers, one hidden, Anectanabus, and two publicly acknowledged, Philip of Macedon and Amon the sun god.

This overdetermined ancestry enables Alexander to recognize his two public fathers and displace the specter of Anectanabus. The two public (and false) fathers, Amon and Philip, render less problematic the complex of power and trickery that Anectanabus represents. Amon, the sun god of the Macedonians, provides a divinely purified non-Arabic source for Alexander's excessive energy, his military brilliance, and the supernatural invulnerability that guarantees his military successes. Philip of Macedon's chivalric finesse contrasts with Anectanabus's wanton disregard for the socially formative links of chivalric loyalty and service. Alexander internalizes the attributes of his two putative fathers as he is brought up in Philip's court, gaining an understanding of courtly virtue, both as a leader of knights and as a defender of noble women, so that several times he instructs Philip himself in loyalty to his queen. Even after he discovers his true father's identity, killing him in the process, Alexander declares his affiliation only to his two public fathers throughout the poem, virtually alternating them each time he announces his ancestry to some new soon-to-be-subject ruler. In other words (Alexander is nothing if not thorough), he follows his murder of Anectanabus's person with the obliteration of Anectanabus's name.

However, the poem's trajectory works insistently against Alexander's ancestral iconoclasm, translating, inverting, and bringing its objects back before Alexander's face each time he looks into a conquered enemy's eyes and sees an inscription of his own already determined destiny. This dialectic is set in motion in the actual scene of the patricide. Anectanabus takes Alexander up to a cliff above Philip's castle for some stargazing. He points out the fateful influences in the heaven that decree his own end at the hands of his son. Alexander, still ignorant of their relationship, is incensed at this resignation to fate and strikes Anectanabus on the back with such force that the astrologer "drives down to the depths of the dike bottom" (712). Anectanabus's astronomical (and hence Arab-originating) expertise is forcibly rejected, but it is clear that Alexander is not simply punishing fraudulence with death. He is also enacting an irrefutable proof that Anectanabus *is* fraudulent. Anectanabus must be killed by his own son; Alexander is not Anectanabus's son and Alexander has killed Anectanabus; therefore Anectanabus is a fraud.

Quod erat demonstrandum. His severity is a nicely reasoned and deliberately iconoclastic attempt to break the prophecy by anticipating it.

But Anectanabus, uncharacteristically, is not willing to vanish. Even as he succumbs to his fate, he chillingly demonstrates his preemptive power:

> Þan Anectanabus, as him aʒt wele; augirly granys.
> Dryues vp a dede voyce and dymly he spekis,
> "Wele was þis case to me knawen and kyd many wyn-
> tir
> Þat I suld dee slike a dethe be dome of my werdis.
> Sayd I þe noʒt so myselfe here before
> I suld be slayn of my son as now sothe worthis?"
> "What? and am I," quod Alexander, "ane of þi
> childer?"
> "ʒha, son! Als glad I my god, I gat þe myseluen"
>
> (717-24)

[Then Anectanabus, as it was necessary for him, groans greatly, drives up a dead voice and speaks darkly: "That my fate has doomed me to such a death is a thing I have known very well for many winters. Did I not say myself just now that I should be slain by my son as has now come truly to pass?" "What?" said Alexander, "and am I one of your children?" "Yes, son! As it please my god, I begot you myself."]

Here, Anectanabus becomes literally a voice from the grave animated only by words of his own deadly prophecy. And just as Alexander's blow was an attempt to enact a proof and destroy his father's authority, Anectanabus's revelation not only implicates Alexander in his death but finally and irresistibly reinstates Anectanabus's prophetic authority and, by extension, the validity of all the prophecies that will hound Alexander throughout the poem. The paradox of Alexander's position is underlined. By attempting to destroy Anectanabus's influence, Alexander has actually surrendered to it. His iconoclasm, however excessive and self-assured, is contained and rendered futile by his ignorance of his intimacy to that which he is destroying. The poet stresses the force of Alexander's horror by compressing it into direct dialogue. Alexander's aghast "What? Am I one of your children?" conveys the shock of the revelation and the way it reshapes his identity: from the son of a god and foster son of a king, to a king's bastard and parricide—a transformation that Anectanabus's vigorous "ʒha! son" drives home.

This scene of patricide determines the shape of Alexander's subsequent conquests. It provides a paradigm of conquest that stresses the fall from a height of a kingly forebear whom Alexander replaces and also outlines a pattern of reaction for Alexander—paralyzing tears and determined evasions. The poem's subsequent narrative reiterates this paradigm with obsessive variation. Alex-

ander will spend the rest of his career "driving into the deepest part of the dike bottom" all the tremendous oriental rulers and armies that oppose him. The poem, however, repeatedly underscores the tendency of such high/low binaries to invert themselves, given time. On numerous occasions, as the victorious Alexander stands over his fallen enemy, he receives the advice to regard the fall as the mirror of his own future and look to himself.

Darius of Persia's death is one of many that elaborates this somber injunction to self-examination:

> Þe same ensampill of myselfe [þou sees now betid].
> So gret I grew of my gods and gold in my cofirs,
> Þat kindly gods creatoure I kend noʒt myselfe,
> Bot for his feloʒe and his fere faithly me leued.
> Þus prosperite and pride so purely me blyndid,
> I couth noʒt se fra my sege to þe soil vndire;
> Þat at me failed þan to fynd fast at myn eʒen,
> Be þe myrrour no of meknes, I may a myle knawe
> . . .
> If all þe limpe as þe list, loke to þine ende,
> For die þe mose quen all is done, and ay þe day scor-
> tis.
>
> (3408-15, 3426-27)

[The same example of myself you can see happening now before you. I grew so mighty of my gods and had so much gold in my coffers, that I did not know myself for one of god's natural creatures, but rather believed myself firmly to be his equal and companion. Thus prosperity and pride blinded me so completely, I could not see from my throne to the soil underneath. I failed to discern what was clearly before my eyes and now through the mirror of submission I can see it from a mile away. When everything seems to be going as you wish, I warn you, look to your end. For you must die when all is done, and your day already shortens.]

This foreboding passage transforms the dialectic of high and low from a synchronic structure to a diachronic cycle, making the gulf between dominance and submission less a function of position than of time which inevitably passes. The "myrrour . . . of meknes" into which Darius now gazes also presses home the affinities between the two players. The temptation, as Darius argues, is to be blinded by the moment of victory, the throne from which the underlying earth is hidden, even as it waits to engulf one.

Here Darius connects himself to a powerful trope in late medieval writing: it surfaces in the *memento mori* effigies upon the tombs of medieval nobility and is, in fact, particularly linked to members of the nobility and gentry who would have the most temptation to let their exalted social position obscure the fact of their mortality. This is not to say that it necessarily works to undermine social rank as such; on the contrary, it is constantly incorporated into the paradigm of the noble life cycle as a necessary stage: the voice of age admonishing the eager and ambitious youth, and the mature and prosperous man. In the *Parliament of Three Ages,* another North Midlands alliterative poem of the late fourteenth century, we find a passage that echoes Darius. Here Age addresses Maturity and Youth:

> I sett ensample bi myselfe and sekis it no forthire . . .
> I was als euerrous in armes as ouþer of ȝoureseluen
> . . .
> And as myche wirschip I wane, iwis, as ȝe bothe . . .
> Bot elde vnderȝode me are I laste wist,
> And alle disfegurede my face and fadide my hewe
> . . .
> Make ȝoure mirrours bi me, men, bi ȝoure trouth
> This schadowe in my schewere schunte ȝe no while.
>
>   (269, 271, 276, 283-84, 290-91)

[Seek no further for an example (proof); I give you myself. I was as eager in arms as either of you, and won as much worship as both of you. . . . But age crept under me before I knew it, and disfigured my face. . . . Make your mirror by me, by your faith. Avoid no more this shadow [reflection] in my mirror.][14]

In this passage Age transforms himself, just as Darius does, into a mirror of the future of Youth, a dark reflection that should be faced straightly by those still "eager in arms." The *Parliament of Three Ages* insists upon the link between such spatial reflection and genealogy. The poem ends with Age declaring "I am thi sire and thou my sone, the sothe for to telle, / For Elde is sire of Midill Elde, and Midill Elde of ȝouthe" (646-47) [To tell the truth of it, I am your father and you are my son, for Age is father of Maturity, and Maturity of Youth].

The *Wars of Alexander* repeatedly traps its hero at this peculiar intersection. As Alexander subjugates all the rulers of the east, he repeats his initial parricide and expresses his need not just to avoid, but to deauthorize, break away from, and obliterate this "schadewe in [the] schewere" of his oriental enemies. And yet, with every king he drives down to the dust, the ground beneath his own throne becomes that much nearer. Genealogical conquests against his predecessors are reenacted as spatial and geographical ones, while genealogical affinities sharpen into actual reflections.

As Alexander presses ever further east, the text increasingly echoes with intimations of reverberation, reflection, projection, and equivalence between the conqueror and his enemies. Alexander encounters the Brahmans, who live a life without rank, culture, or luxury on the far side of the impassable Ganges. Alexander halts on the western bank and sends them letters asking to learn of their culture and society. They send him back a

description that links them with the primal innocence of the golden age but also aligns them with a fourteenth-century Christian reformatory perspective. They live like a literalization of Christ's sermon about the lilies of the field: no cultivation, no building, no rulers or servants, no greed, no disease, and no excess. They believe in a single god and regard life as a brief pilgrimage to be used and not enjoyed. Alexander replies with an aristocratic sneer, condemning them for both pride and foolishness: they are blasphemously and foolishly trying to imitate the gods.[15] Their answer to him throws his accusation back in his teeth:

> Þe same ensampill, as me semes, into ȝoureself touches.
> For so þe qwele of qwistounes ȝoure qualite encrees
> Þat noþir gesse ȝe gouernour no god bot ȝourselfe!
> Ȝe brixsill our benignite, our bonerte repreues,
> And beris apon vs blasfeme þat neuire bale thoȝt
>   . . . . .
> It is ȝourselfe and noȝt oureself þat ai þe self hantis.
>
>   (4786-94)

[The same proof, it seems to me, touches your own case, for as long as the wheel of fortune increases your quality, you believe in no governor or god but yourself. You upbraid our good will and reprove our gentleness, and attribute blasphemies to us who never intended evil. . . . It is yourself and not ourselves that you continually pursue!]

Until this episode, Alexander is able to evade the significance of such insights with relative impunity. Subsequent episodes, however, no longer simply foreshadow the futility of Alexander's conquest, they are actually deadly. Two hundred lines after the encounter with the Brahmans, Alexander and his armies are menaced in a narrow chasm by a basilisk that crouches on the brink and destroys vast companies simply by turning the glare of its eyes in their direction. Alexander climbs up to the beast and makes himself a shield as large as a barn door with a mirror on its outer surface: "Þe screwe in þe schewere his schadow behaldis, / And so þe slaȝtir of his siȝt into himselfe entris" (4981-82) [The wretch beholds his shadow in the mirror, and so the slaughter of his gaze enters into himself]. This lethal reflection is multivalent: the basilisk in its magical invulnerability and capacity to conquer lends itself to comparison with Alexander himself. Alexander's shield, which both hides himself and reflects his enemy, is a figure of his most crucial strategy, the willful nonrecognition upon which his conquest depends.

Alexander's closest encounter with a deadly reflection, however, marks his first direct venture into the realm of generation, genealogy, and by extension mortality. On his way back to Macedon, he pauses to subdue the nearby land of Prasiaca, called significantly by the poet

Preciosa, which is ruled by the conqueror-queen Candace. Yet as the two conquerors face each other, battle seems less on Alexander's mind than the queen herself and the queen's family. Disguising himself as one of his own knights, he rescues the queen's daughter-in-law from a neighboring king and visits Candace at her court to receive her thanks, knowing that her sons would kill him if they recognized him but believing himself unidentified. But unbeknownst to him, Candace knows him; she had sent a portrait-maker into Alexander's camp to secure his likeness and has judged him a highly desirable figure. On the second day of his clandestine visit, she takes him by the hand without explanation and leads him into a private chamber whose gilded walls "stremed as þe son" (5412) [shone like the sun]. Although they are quite secluded, she leads him further into a "clochere with a kay" (5415) [an enclosed place locked with a key] which is devised to whirl rapidly by the power of twenty tame elephants. Once they are within, the room begins to revolve, and, as Alexander is wondering at it, the queen calls him by his name, "Alexsandire." At this he starts and pales, but the queen only laughs, takes his hand, and leads him even further into a "preue parlour" (5430). And it is here in this triply enclosed sanctum that the by now sinister queen takes out his portrait, saying, "Se þiselfe a sampill þat I þe sothe neuyn" (5432) [See for yourself a proof that I name you truly]. Alexander is terrified. It is clear that by capturing his portrait and luring him from familiar ground into her own exotically revolving sphere, the queen has conquered him. She mocks him, not too gently:

> "Qui fadis so þi faire hew?" said the faire lady,
> "Þe werreour of all þe werd and wastour of Ynde,
> Þou þat has brettend on the bent þe barbrins fokke,
> Þe pepill out of Panty, þe Persens and þe Medis,
> Loo, now, þe here withouten hiȝt into my handis sesed,
> Bot in woman's ward for all þi wale dedis!"
>
> (5435-40)

["Why does your beautiful color fade?" asked the fair lady, "The warrior of all the world and the waster of India, you who have broken on the field all the barbarian folk, the people out of Parthia, the Persians and the Medes. Lo, now without warning you are taken into my hands, into the power of a mere woman for all your proud deeds."]

Alexander nearly explodes with rage, gnashing his teeth and shaking his head violently. When the queen teases him a little more, he declares:

> "I swete . . . þat I na swerd haue,
> For I na wapen haue, iwis my writh with to venge!"
> "Now, bald baratour on bent, if þou a brand hade,
> Quat prowis miȝt þi person apreue in þis stounde?"

> "For I vnwarly," quod þe [wee], "am to ȝoure will taken;
> I suld þe slaa þare þou sittis and þan myselfe eftir!"
>
> (5450-56)

["I sweat with rage that I have no sword, because I have no weapon to avenge my wrath." "Now, brave knight on the field! if you had a blade, what prowess would your person prove in this place?" "Because I unwarily," said the man, "am taken within your power, I should slay you where you sit, and then myself after!"]

The violence of Alexander's reaction is a terrified response to the intimate control Candace has established over him by isolating him and then showing him his own face. As a figure who throughout the poem destroys any external authority whatsoever, Alexander finds this subjection to a woman absolutely unbearable. The queen is able to allay his anger only by assuring him that she does not desire dominion. This promise enables a brief affair between them which the poem emphatically downplays—within one hundred lines Alexander is on the road again looking for new enemies.

This pivotal scene touches the heart of Alexander's "haunting": the tantalizing fear that drives him to pursue the shadow in the mirror which betokens his enemies, his origins, and his mortality. Simultaneously the greatest warrior in history and history's greatest dupe, in his attempts to evade such a fragmenting self-recognition he finally becomes as restless, rootless, unchivalric, and volatile as his own fiercely effaced father. The self-conflicts that have been driving him onward finally begin to tear him apart. The last eight hundred lines of the poem confront him with increasingly fantastic and nightmarish enemies, while his ambitions grow wilder and wilder. Much of the time he is battling terrifying lethal beasts: giant lions and scorpions, who pick away at his army, destroy his provisions, and reduce his followers by huge numbers. More and more he is hounded by a sense of inevitable attrition. His ferocious man-eating horse, Bucephalon, which has been with him since his boyhood, dies of a lingering disease. At the same time, he grows tired of transgressing earth's boundaries and frantically attempts to transcend the boundaries of the earth itself. He rigs a flying machine by harnessing four winged griffins to a chariot and extending a great hook baited with raw flesh over their heads. The narrator's disengagement from his hero's increasingly desperate fantasy surfaces clearly:

> Þare was a miȝti montayne at to þe mone semed,
> He gessis it gaynir to god þan to þe grounde vndire,
> And slike a fonned fantasy þan fell in his hert
> How þat he liftid miȝt be fra þe lawe vnto þe liȝt sternes.
>
> (5637-40)

[There was a mighty mountain that seemed as
tall as the moon. He believes it to be
nearer god than to the ground underneath, and
a certain foolish fantasy then grew in his
heart: how he might be lifted from the ground
up to the bright stars.]

Alexander's attempt to stellify himself is as unsuccessful as are his other forays at historic transcendence. The griffins rise up until "midilerth bot as mylnestane na mare to him semed, / and all the water of þe werd bot as a wrethen neddire" (5651-52) [The earth seemed no more than a millstone, and all the water of the world only a coiled serpent]—a vision as dismissive of the significance of his travails as Troilus' own. But the Christian God prevents Alexander from reaching his goal and, cursing like Lucifer, he falls to the earth, frustrated but unhurt—a *deus ex machina* interference that encapsulates Alexander's distance from his late medieval Christian audience. Undeterred, Alexander then attempts to plumb the depths of the seas.

In these reckless excursions, the poet plays on the latitude allowed by his hero's hybrid identity both to validate Alexander's chivalric leadership and to alienate reassuringly the more transgressive (and baroque) excesses of his ambition from his fourteenth-century audience. If one recalls the ambiguous ancestry and legacy that make Alexander a model and ancestor appropriable by both European and oriental conquerors, the poem's evident relish in Alexander's imminent demise is spiced with a kind of vengeful fantasy. Alexander's ambition driven to these extremes is ultimately blasphemous because, as the Brahmans point out, it finally refuses to acknowledge any authority but its own self-generated one.

However, Alexander's less celestial ambitions would probably have awakened a certain sympathy among the British crusaders at Nicopolis at the end of the fourteenth century, who regarded war as their livelihood, the Turks as their enemies, and the signory of the world as their God-given right. Like them, Alexander finally desires a life of war that is perpetual, profitable, and undeterred by any entrapping sense of debt, cultural affinity, or even knowledge of his adversaries. He wishes for an identity as self-sufficient, volatile, and perpetual as that of the fiery phoenix which he glimpses wistfully when he visits the Temple of the Sun just before he hears the dismal prophecy that he has just two more years to live.

If, as I argue, Alexander embodies the ideology of the fourteenth-century British chivalry, his hybrid genealogy and his impossible ambitions expose the conflicts within that increasingly defensive audience. Other North West Midlands alliterative works express a similar interest in the quandaries of their chivalric heroes: *Sir Gawain and the Green Knight* delights in pinching its hero between the twin imperatives of courtesy and loyalty; the alliterative *Morte Arthure* describes an Arthur whose blend of ardent chivalry and excessive ambition echoes Alexander's own. What sets the *Wars of Alexander* apart from these works is its more exclusive focus on the interpenetrations of eastern and western cultures. Despite the difficulties of the poem's dating, it is arguable that the poem responds to the late-fourteenth-century dilemmas of a British warrior-class whose livelihood depended on war, but which was threatened by the late century reverses and negotiations for peace in the Hundred Years' War with France. In the last decade of the century particularly, both Charles VI of France and Richard II of England sought to redirect the energies of veterans disaffected with the prospect of treaty by actively promoting crusades against the Ottoman Turks encroaching upon Prussia and Hungary. In fact, the gentry and itinerant soldiery of Cheshire and the North West Midlands—the region from which the *Wars of Alexander* is believed to originate—were so horrified by rumors of this peace that in 1393 they led an armed rebellion. No less a personage than John of Gaunt suppressed them and, significantly, enlisted the bulk of them into his army, first to quell his Gascon subjects, but then to accompany him on the crusade against Nicopolis.[16] The highest nobility of England advocated the crusade against the Turks as a pursuit eminently possible, chivalrously and religiously admirable, and politically canny—an escape valve for provincial warriors so dependent upon constant military exercise that they tended to armed rebellion when deprived of it. When the Christian armies were decimated at Nicopolis, their defeat thus put an end to a century of disastrous military reverses, economic dependence upon oriental luxury goods, and, most troublingly, internal dissensions within and between European and Christian countries. To such recent developments, the traditional world-bifurcating strategy of crusade had proven a wholly inadequate response.

In the *Wars of Alexander*, Alexander's dilemma is similarly irresolvable; the poem proposes no way for him to escape it, no sense in which he can acknowledge the deadly reflexivities between himself and his enemies and still remain the great world conqueror he is driven to be. In that, the history of the poem's two manuscripts have done Alexander a service: they are fragments whose end is missing and therefore provide no account of his death. It is useless to speculate whether the poem was deliberately left unfinished, or whether the ending has been simply lost. The poem does, however, gesture at closure before breaking off: it ends with the list of

Alexander's conquests that he inscribes upon the walls of his palace. Finally either the manuscript's history or the poem itself collaborates in the desires and aversions of its hero. The poem replaces Alexander's death with Alexander's monument, a gesture at immortality that even as it puts a final flourish to Alexander's conquests also redirects the reader's attention to his ambiguous and continuing legacy: a monument that is a wall—designed both to separate and commemorate—that refuses closure by echoing the interminable conquests of the poem itself. It is this ambivalent and reverberating legacy that ties the poem so closely to, the late medieval audience, the gentry of the North West Midlands. It is precisely because Alexander is in such an impossible, uncomfortable, and familiar position that his character so vividly encompasses the self-contradictions, anxieties, and fatal self-evasions of late fourteenth-century provincial chivalry.

Notes

1. The *Wars of Alexander* survives in two fragmentary manuscript copies, Ashmole 44 in a mid-fifteenth-century hand and Dublin MS 213 in a late-fifteenth-century hand. Like most of the late-fourteenth-century alliterative poems, the author is unknown, though the poem's most recent editors speculate on the grounds of an unusual number of shared phrases and some intriguing descriptive echoes that the author may have originated in the North West Midlands and have influenced or been influenced by the *Gawain*-poet. The poem's dating is extremely tenuous—suggestions have ranged from 1361 to just before 1450. My argument does not presuppose a particular date, but I treat the poem mainly as dating from the late fourteenth century or early fifteenth century. I focus upon the broader historical developments of the fourteenth century, because that seems to have been the period when alliterative poetry had its greatest English vogue, and when the other alliterative poems to which it is compared are generally believed to have been written. See Duggan and Turville-Petre (intro. ix-li), the edition from which all citations are taken; unless otherwise indicated, translations of this and other works are my own.

2. The poem's main source is the I³ version of the immensely popular late-twelfth-century *Historia de preliis Alexandri Magni,* of which forty-five manuscript copies survive. The *Wars* is a faithful translation, though the poet freely expands upon his source, introducing new episodes at several points, many of which are notable for their biting irony. The fact that it is a translation does not detract from its originality or from the significance attributable to the choice to translate it in the late

fourteenth century. See Duggan and Turville-Petre, intro. xiii-xvii.

3. Thrupp offers a possible reason for this continuing attraction during earlier periods: that early medieval Christians may have been growing tired of perpetually measuring their civilization and their achievements against the splendor of the lingering monuments of Rome. Instead they reached back to a hero who "outclassed any Roman hero" and whose exploits predate the Roman world (273).

4. For a description of Arabic attitudes to European incursions during the crusades, see Maalouf.

5. Odo of Deuil's narrative is particularly interesting in the way it works to associate the Greek Byzantine Christians with the Islamic Turks, as cultures "arrogant in wealth, treacherous in customs, corrupt in faith" [superba divitiis, moribus subdola, fide corrupta], who are nonetheless cultured, sophisticated, and above all, rich (86-87).

6. In fact, by far the greatest time lag between first documented cases occurs in the interval when the plague traveled from inland China (1320) to the Chinese port of Zaytun (1345). After that interval, it swiftly struck Caffa on the Black Sea in 1346, Cairo and Damascus in 1347, Italy, France, and Britain in 1348, Germany and Scandanavia in 1349, and Moscow in 1351. See Abu-Lughod, 172-73.

7. A complaint from a group of merchants forced to remain in Alexandria until their goods spoiled has been included in Lopez and Raymond, 335-36; see Abu-Lughod, 236-41, for a fuller account of the Alexandrian customs regulations.

8. Atiya, the historian who focuses upon this crusade most fully, emphasizes the role of the English knightly contingent in this venture (44-45).

9. Gibb outlines the ways these cultures might have spoken to each other even before the fourteenth century—their common respect for the heritage of the past, their need for continuity, and their balancing of faith and reason as ways to maintain it (160).

10. My argument here draws upon Southern's description of this convergence, augmenting the theologians he discusses with two other writers, William Langland and Philippe de Mézières. For Southern's discussion of fourteenth- and fifteenth-century developments, see *Western Views,* 67-107.

11. The civic cycle dramas of the late fourteenth and fifteenth centuries provide only one instance; in many Mahound is either an infernal demon or one of many deities.

12. Southern stresses the innovativeness of this reciprocity in Wycliffe's polemical writings (*Western Views,* 79-80).

13. Quoted from Thorlac Turville-Petre's edition; translations are mine throughout.

14. Quoted from Thorlac Turville-Petre's *Alliterative Poetry;* translations are my own.

15. I am not able here to explore how this exchange between Alexander and the Brahmans focuses fourteenth century ecclesiastical and seigneurial anxieties about the social effects of a literal *imitatio Christi,* but such concerns clearly animate the episode.

16. Palmer comments on their eventual fate: "Although John of Gaunt himself eventually withdrew from this venture, there is good reason to believe that most of his Cheshire troops marched towards the Balkans under the leadership of his illegitimate son John Beaufort, and fought and died on the banks of the Danube" (184-85). See his excellent discussion of the complex negotiations between the various Christian monarchs and the papacy which lead to the crusading fervor at the end of the century.

Bibliography

Abu-Lughod, Janet. *Before European Hegemony: The World System A.D. 1250-1350.* New York: Oxford University Press, 1989.

Atiya, Azia Suryal. *The Crusade of Nicopolis.* London: Methuen, 1934.

Gibb, Hamilton. "The Influence of Islamic Culture on Medieval Europe." In Thrupp, *Change.*

Lopez, Robert S., and Irving W. Raymond, eds. and trans. *Medieval Trade in the Mediterranean World.* New York: Norton, n.d.

Maalouf, Amin. *The Crusades through Arab Eyes.* New York: Schocken Books, 1985.

Odo of Deuil. *De profectione Ludovici VII in orientem.* Ed. and trans. Virginia Gingerick Berry. New York: Norton, 1948.

Palmer, J. J. N. *England, France and Christendom, 1377-99.* Chapel Hill: University of North Carolina Press, 1972.

Postan, M. M., E. E. Rich, and Edward Miller, eds. *Cambridge Economic History of Europe.* Cambridge: Cambridge University Press, 1963.

Southern, R. W. *Western Views of Islam in the Middle Ages.* 1962. Reprint, Cambridge, Mass.: Harvard University Press, 1980.

Thrupp, Sylvia L., ed. *Change in Medieval Society.* New York: Appleton-Century-Crofts, 1964.

Tibbetts, Gerald T. "Later Cartographic Developments." In Harley and Woodward, vol. 2, book 1, 137-55.

Wars of Alexander. Ed. Hoyt N. Duggan and Thorlac Turville-Petre. Oxford: Oxford University Press, 1989.

Brian Bosworth (essay date 2000)

SOURCE: Bosworth, Brian. Introduction to *Alexander the Great in Fact and Fiction,* edited by A. B. Bosworth and E. J. Baynham, pp. 1-22. Oxford: Oxford University Press, 2000.

[*In the following essay, Bosworth notes the dearth of contemporary sources for Alexander's actions and details some of the problems that scholars face with what sources are available.*]

The passionate popular interest in Alexander has never flagged. It may even be intensifying in this age of mass communication. Web sites proliferate on the Internet, where a plethora of aficionados advertise their fascination with the Macedonian conqueror. In the most powerful medium of all, television, there has been an enthusiastic response to Michael Wood's recent series with its striking visual images of the route of conquest, accompanied by a terse, energetic commentary on the more colourful episodes of the reign.[1] Translated into book form (Wood 1997) it has become a best-seller. Fact and fiction are here intertwined, and the result is a new Alexander Romance with all the fascination of the old. The object of the series is entertainment—in which it has succeeded admirably. It has also raised public interest in the charismatic figure of Alexander and challenged specialists to give new answers to old questions. That is the purpose of the present volume, to take new approaches, to analyse and explain some of the huge body of romance that has adhered to the historical Alexander and to address the perennial problems of kingship and imperialism. We cannot claim to be unveiling universal truth. Given the state of the evidence that is impossible. What is more feasible is to identify distortion and myth-making, to provide a general context of historical interpretation, and to clear the obstacles preventing a dispassionate and balanced assessment of the few questions which can be profitably discussed.

The besetting problem of Alexander scholarship is the dearth of contemporary sources. That has not changed in the last decades. There has been no influx of new documentary material like the marvellous bronze inscriptions from Spain which have so enriched our knowledge of early Imperial Rome.[2] The corpus of contemporary inscriptions has been increased by a handful of documents from Macedonia which raise interesting questions about Alexander's relations with his subjects in the distant homeland but leave us more perplexed than enlightened.[3] The same applies to the study of Alexander's prolific and enigmatic coinage. New issues have been discovered, predominantly in the great Babylon hoard; we now have more (and more revealing) examples of the Porus decadrachms and a whole series of tetradrachms with Indian themes.[4] However, the problems of dating and provenance remain as controversial and intractable as ever. There have been sensational archaeological discoveries, but again they are the subject of intense academic debate. More than twenty years after their discovery the contents of the Vergina Tombs are still incompletely documented, and there remains deep disagreement about their dating; the once conventional attribution of Tomb II to Philip II has come under increasing attack, and archaeological and historical arguments have combined in different patterns without any accepted dating peg emerging. That has been the stimulus for Olga Palagia's contribution[5] in which iconographic analysis is combined with historical interpretation to secure a late dating (after the eastern campaigns of Alexander) for the hunting fresco on Tomb II. Such progress is, however, rare. The gaps in our knowledge are usually too extensive for us to resolve the problems presented by the material evidence.

The history of the period remains based on literary evidence. Here too there is a lack of contemporary material which has not been rectified by papyrological discoveries. The one piece of evidence which has emerged (a fragmentary account of the Thracian campaign of 335 BC) is an enigma, elusive in genre and only explicable through extant literature.[6] It adds little or nothing in its own right. The basic evidence is what it always has been: derivative writings from the Roman period which draw upon the lost contemporary historians of Alexander. There is general agreement that this source material falls into two families. On the one hand we have the history of Arrian which is explicitly based on Ptolemy, Aristobulus, and (to a lesser degree) Nearchus, and on the other a tradition common to Diodorus, Curtius Rufus, and Justin, which is thought to derive from the popular Hellenistic writer, Cleitarchus of Alexandria. There is also the biography of Plutarch, which drew upon a mosaic of sources, and the voluminous geography of Strabo, which adapted significant passages of major historians, predominantly Onesicritus, Nearchus, and Aristobulus. This canonical list now has an extra member in Polybius, whose references to Alexander are analysed (amazingly for the first time) by Richard Billows, who argues that he drew upon Hieronymus and ultimately Demetrius of Phalerum.[7]

It is one thing to put a name upon a lost source, quite another to identify how that source was adapted in its extant context. Paradoxically one of our most powerful research tools, Jacoby's monumental collection of the fragments of the lost historians, is responsible for many misapprehensions. Direct quotations are identified by Sperrdruck, but the vast majority of 'fragments' are paraphrases by secondary writers, and we have no indication how faithfully they reproduce the content of the original or even how much of the context is attributable to the named author.[8] As a result there has been a strong tendency to take what Jacoby prints as the work of the cited author, not the actual writer. The extant intermediary tends to be forgotten, and it is assumed that the text of Arrian, say, is a reflecting mirror for Ptolemy. That tendency has now been obviated by studies dedicated to the literature that has survived. Detailed commentaries on Arrian and Curtius have shown how complex and sophisticated their composition was.[9]

Arrian, for instance, does not merely transpose material from his sources. He engages in an allusive dialogue with the great historical masters of the past: Herodotus, Thucydides, and Xenophon. There are subtle echoes of vocabulary; familiar themes from earlier periods are reworked in the context of Alexander's campaigns. There is also explicit literary rivalry. As a self-conscious stylist, by his own claim the equal of Alexander in the field of literature, he surpasses the writers of the past—in his own eyes at least. Consequently he subjects his source material to a counterpoint of allusive commentary. His description of the aftermath of Alexander's wounding at the Malli town is a good example. He drew on Nearchus for the vivid scene of the king's generals reproaching him for his excessive recklessness, but he dresses the scene in terminology that recalls Xenophon: Alexander's soldiers are made to represent their plight if their king died in language reminiscent of the Ten Thousand after the execution of their generals.[10] The implicit comment leads to an explicit statement of opinion by Arrian (6. 13. 4), that the criticism was justified: Alexander's thirst for glory drove him to embrace danger. That in turn looks forward to the complex passage at the beginning of book 7, in which Alexander's insatiate desire for glory is treated from several aspects. His ambition for further conquest is represented as inherently plausible, because of the underlying passion for glory; if there were no one else to surpass, he would compete with himself.[11]

The theme is then illustrated by three vignettes from different sources: the criticisms by the Indian gymnosophists, the meeting with Diogenes, and finally Megasthenes' account of Alexander's conversation with the Indian sage, Dandamis.[12] This last scene is also reported by Strabo, who gives essentially the same substance but places it in a different context, a formal contrast between Dandamis and his rival, Calanus.[13] The contrast is brought out by Arrian, but it is subordinate to the main theme, Alexander's failure to overcome his desire for fame. Dandamis' admonitions are an explicit commentary on the king's imperial ambitions, and form a bridge to the next episode in the history, the suicide of Calanus, who is portrayed as unconquerable (ἀνίκητον) in his resolution to die, as much so as Alexander in his determination to achieve world empire (Arr. 7. 3. 4). Here Arrian uses his sources with considerable sophistication. He does not misrepresent them, but he uses them discriminatingly to illustrate and underpin his view of Alexander. What is more, the material is not chosen with an eye solely for historical veracity. It is selected because it gives the most vivid illustration of his theme, and allows him to express his judgements both implicitly and explicitly. One cannot use his exposition as a primary source without taking account of his narrative perspective and indeed the tastes and expectations of his audience in the second century AD.

The same is true of the other extant writers. There is now a flourishing industry devoted to research on Plutarch, and the richness and diversity of his biographical method are widely recognized. The *Life of Alexander* has played an important role in that evaluation. It was the subject of one of the earliest and best modern commentaries (Hamilton 1969), and the programmatic utterance in its preface ('we are not writing histories but Lives') with its insistence on the value of the illustrative anecdote and apophthegm has been widely recognized as the key to the interpretation of the biographies.[14] Now there is less of a tendency to see a strict chronological sequence, more appreciation of the generic construction and the huge range of sources that Plutarch draws upon to illustrate Alexander's character. There is more to be done, of course. We still await a formal cross-comparison between the *Alexander* and its companion biography, the *Caesar,* to determine the degree of parallelism and the extent to which the interpretation of the one character has affected that of the other. However, there is probably more appreciation of the complexity of Plutarch than of any other source, and it is to be hoped that his rhetorical extravaganza in the first treatise, *On the Fortune or Virtue of Alexander,* will no longer be taken as the basic explanatory text for Alexander's treatment of his subject peoples.[15]

There are related problems in tackling the rest of the tradition. It is agreed (as, with rare exceptions, it has been for the last two centuries) that there is a common source which is drawn upon selectively by Diodorus, Curtius Rufus, Justin's epitome of Pompeius Trogus, and miscellaneous late sources, the most important of which is probably the so-called *Metz Epitome.*[16] This tradition, usually labelled the Alexander Vulgate, is

plausibly ascribed to Cleitarchus of Alexandria, writing towards the end of the fourth century BC.[17] Large segments can be identified, when we have parallel narratives in two or more extant accounts, but there remain intractable problems in assessing the degree to which the material is adapted and embellished. Diodorus has traditionally been treated as the most authentic conduit for the vulgate, since elsewhere he can be shown to have relied on a single source, sometimes over several books. But even he imposes his own style. Throughout his Universal History his vocabulary is uniform and recurrent; he has a preference for specific types of episode, which he describes in remarkably similar terms. Material from completely different sources is presented with the same terminology, and no distinctive stylistic fingerprints survive from the original works.[18] He is also capricious in his selection. Known fragments of Cleitarchus are often not included in his work, and that has encouraged speculation that Cleitarchus was at best one of several sources. But we do not know Diodorus' reasons for choosing his material. It should be remembered that he wrote at a politically volatile period, during the Triumvirate, and there were episodes which he would treat with caution. Cleitarchus mentioned that Alexander received a Roman embassy shortly before his death in 323,[19] but that incident was best omitted by Diodorus, who was writing in the Roman west at a time when the last of the Ptolemaic dynasty was threatening to hold sway in Rome itself (or so Octavian's propaganda asserted).[20] The omission cannot be shown to prove that Diodorus did not use Cleitarchus at this point of his narrative.

What matters is the material that Diodorus shares with Curtius and Justin. But here too there is a tendency to divide the tradition into what is favourable or unfavourable to Alexander; the campaign narrative can be precise, detailed, and informative or sensational and slapdash. This variation in narrative tone encourages the inference that there are two distinct sources at issue, a slovenly, romanticizing scandal-monger (Cleitarchus) and a much more scrupulous and impartial historian, who has been variously identified as Diyllus of Athens or Duris of Samos.[21] But most of these peculiarities can be explained by Diodorus' own style and practice. He tends to abbreviate drastically and capriciously, and he has a marked taste for the sensational. What is more, sober fact and sensationalism can coexist in the same work; the same Cleitarchus could write a vivid and compelling account of the siege of Tyre and an equally vivid description of the visit of Thalestris, the supposed Amazon queen. One could find an inexhaustible hoard of such anomalies in Herodotus or even Polybius. The record of 'great and marvellous deeds' (ἔργα μεγάλα τε καὶ θωμαστά) embraced the plausible and implausible alike.

The most enigmatic and frustrating of all the extant authors is Curtius Rufus, who has probably been more excoriated by modern scholars than any writer on Alexander.[22] His work is shockingly transmitted. The first two books are missing; there are numerous lengthy lacunae, and corruptions abound in the truncated corpus that remains. We lack any statement of the historian's aims and methods, and there are only two passages where sources are cited by name: Cleitarchus, Timagenes, and (perhaps indirectly) Ptolemy.[23] Since nothing outside Curtius is known of Timagenes' account of Alexander, this is not particularly helpful.[24] There is no way to isolate his contribution or even to determine whether Curtius used him at all outside the context of Ptolemy and the Malli town. It can be shown that Curtius' narrative follows sources identical or akin to those used by Ptolemy and Arrian, but it is well-nigh impossible to show how they have been adapted and transformed. It is agreed that he had a political agenda of his own, and interpreted the events of Alexander's reign, in particular the disturbances after his death, against the context of his own time under the Roman Empire. Unfortunately Curtius' own date is a notorious crux: practically every emperor from Augustus to Septimius Severus has been suggested at some time as the recipient of Curtius' eulogy in book 10 (some scholars have gone even later, suggesting Constantine or even Theodosius),[25] and it is difficult to give a precise political motivation if one cannot relate the text to any specific period. There is also Curtius' demonstrable penchant for rhetorical exaggeration, his punctuation of the narrative with rhetorical, moralizing comment, and his love of set speeches, long and short. What cannot be denied is that he has used every device at his disposal to make his narrative vivid and sensational. He also has recurrent themes which determine his choice and shaping of material. A recent study by Baynham has shed light on his treatment of prevailing motifs: the omnipresent influence of *fortuna*; kingship and its corollary, the autonomy of the individual in a despotism.[26] The overriding ideas explain the choice of material and much of the emphasis. That and the traditional historians' preoccupation with dramatic narrative account for many of the apparent anomalies of his account. In Baynham's view Curtius tailors the source material at his disposal to create a wider interpretative pattern, but does not fabricate pseudo-historical material. Others have been less charitable, and Curtius has been credited with deliberate invention to improve his story.[27] Much has still to be done in this area. One needs more of the sober, systematic comparison with Diodorus that Hamilton used in his discussion of the Indian narrative, to determine what Curtius may have added and why.[28] As it is, approaches to Curtius have varied sharply, and the variation is reflected in the differing treatment in several of the essays in this collection.

Other sources too have received rather more attention in recent scholarship. Justin's Epitome has been intensively studied, and it has been established that even Justin makes his own editorial contribution; he does not merely transcribe at random, but imposes his own vocabulary and perhaps at times his own ideas.[29] Consequently, his original, Pompeius Trogus, becomes even more elusive. What we have is a partial, distorted echo of his text, which makes it desperately difficult to establish the sources he used for his account of Alexander (other than the vulgate) and the contemporary pressures which might have determined his treatment of Alexander. Once we take into account the contribution of the intermediary, the problems of historical analysis become sharper and more complex. In the past the tendency was to isolate, or purport to isolate, the original authority for an assertion in the extant sources. One identified the authority, and judged the material on the basis of the authority's reputation—and the reputation was often based upon its attitude to Alexander, favourable or unfavourable. Arrian, based as he was on Ptolemy and Aristobulus, would automatically gain preference if he disagreed with other sources. But this principle ruled out much of the available source tradition. With some episodes, notably the arrest, trial, and execution of Philotas, there is a gross imbalance: Arrian's report (3. 26. 1-2), explicitly based on Ptolemy and Aristobulus, is perfunctory and unilluminating, little more than a dogmatic statement of Philotas' guilt. What he deals with in a dozen lines is the subject of a very extended narrative in Curtius which engrosses over twenty pages of Budé text.[30] It is a story of conspiracy and betrayal, replete with names and detail and housing a series of direct speeches which contain material otherwise unattested in the tradition of the reign.[31] This is an extreme case where one cannot simply accept the evidence of the 'good' sources, because it is practically non-existent, and, whatever one may think of individual details in Curtius, one can hardly reject the entire account as fiction.

The most suspect of sources may on occasion record unique and authentic data. One particularly intriguing detail comes from the so-called *Metz Epitome,* a late (tenth-century) manuscript, which preserves part of an epitome of a history of Alexander's reign. The style of the *Epitome* is late, best attributed to the fourth or early fifth century AD, but its unknown author was digesting a much earlier history which largely followed the vulgate tradition common to Diodorus, Curtius, and Justin.[32] On occasion it records details which are not attested elsewhere. For instance, it states that Alexander lost a son borne by Rhoxane while his river fleet was being built on the Hydaspes.[33] This is not attested elsewhere, but it is plausible enough. The incident is placed late in 326 BC, about eighteen months after the marriage, and it comes at a juncture where the rest of the source tradition is very thin. Alexander was stationary around the Hydaspes between September and November, but Arrian has no record of anything between Alexander's arrival at the Hydaspes and the departure of the fleet.[34] In contrast the Vulgate account, common to Curtius, Diodorus, and the *Epitome,* has a series of events; the arrival of reinforcements from the west, the building of the fleet (with rough agreement on numbers), and the reconciliation of the Indian kings, Porus and Taxiles.[35] The details are consistent, but not every episode is recorded in every source; Diodorus, for instance, has nothing about the reconciliation. Now, the *Metz Epitome* places the death of Alexander's son between the completion of the fleet and the reconciliation, and it seems that it was part of the so-called vulgate, an authentic detail passed over by Diodorus and Curtius. There is no obvious reason for the invention of a fictitious son of Alexander at this stage, and the death of a child in infancy or at birth may have seemed too unimportant to warrant notice in Curtius and Diodorus, in an age of high infant mortality.

Our most effective tool is critical cross-comparison. If we cannot accept or reject material on the basis of the reputation of its supposed source, we are faced with a much more complex exercise, examining the whole range of evidence in detail, assessing the extent of agreement, isolating the disagreements, and looking for explanations of the rejected variant traditions. Such explanations are rarely simple; we may be faced with deliberate distortion in the primary, contemporary tradition, misunderstanding by a secondary writer, adaptation and modification for purely literary purposes—or most often a combination. One of the most complex problems (and one which surfaces repeatedly in these essays)[36] is Alexander's burning of Persepolis. As is well known, there are two conflicting traditions, one regarding the conflagration as an act of policy, vengeance for the sack of Athens in 480,[37] and the other as a virtual accident, the culmination of a drinking party in which the Athenian courtesan Thais led the Macedonian revellers in an orgy of impromptu arson.[38] There are two main directions in which the argument can be directed. The first is to accept the role of Thais,[39] which is explicitly attributed to Cleitarchus, and can be interpreted as in part a tribute to Thais herself. She was one of the more powerful figures in the early Ptolemaic court; her children by Ptolemy were important pieces in the dynastic game by 308 BC.[40] She was present at the conflagration, and Cleitarchus could make her the chief agent, avenging the injuries of her city.[41] In that case the other tradition must be interpreted as apologetic. The wanton destruction was seen as an embarrassment,[42] and Ptolemy may not have welcomed Thais' association with it. Instead he (and Aristobulus) represented the destruction as a conscious plan, one which provoked dissent with Parmenio, who is shown presenting rational

arguments to counter the king's dogmatic insistence upon vengeance, an insistence which even Arrian (3. 18. 12) finds irrational. The second approach is to accept that Alexander did indeed destroy Persepolis out of policy, and that the exchange with Parmenio represents genuine disagreement on the Macedonian staff. In that case Cleitarchus' account of Thais' actions could be seen as a colourful fabrication.[43] Whichever line of argument one takes there are secondary arguments to be deployed. If the burning was policy, what was behind it? Was Alexander symbolizing the end of the Persian Empire or declaring to the world at large that vengeance was a serious issue, not to be compromised?[44] And why would Cleitarchus give Thais a role that she never played? On the other hand, if one accepts Cleitarchus' version, one has to explain why the burning was still an embarrassment some thirty years after the event, and why the fictitious debate between Alexander and Parmenion arose. The problem is the lack of a firm starting point, the difficulty of excluding anything as a priori impossible; could Cleitarchus, writing under Ptolemy, have given a totally false report about Thais, and could Ptolemy (if he is the source of Arrian) have retailed a debate which he and many others knew was unhistorical? One is faced with an intricate balance of probability, and not surprisingly judgements about what is possible and probable vary dramatically. There is no simple key to interpretation, and as a result there is no consensus. Indeed, given the state of the evidence, it is unlikely that a satisfactory resolution of the problem will ever be achieved.

There is another important point, often overlooked in traditional scholarship. Alexander's death does not form an absolute divide. His reign cannot be studied in isolation from what follows. That is clearly the case with the Lamian War, where the disturbances created by Alexander's decree restoring Greek exiles escalated at the news of his death and led to full-scale war within a matter of weeks. Similarly the tensions and rivalries generated by the court intrigues under Alexander erupted into open conflict, first during the turbulent political settlement at Babylon and then during the first civil war, when Perdiccas' extravagant dynastic ambitions drove Craterus and Antipater to war. One is constantly looking back to Alexander's reign to explain what happened after his death and conversely interpreting his reign by reference to later events. It is the main weakness of Helmut Berve's still indispensable prosopography that it closes with Alexander and has the briefest of references to events after his death, and the strength of Waldemar Heckel's study of Alexander's marshals (Heckel 1992) is that it pays particular attention to the period of transition, the years between 323 and 319, when the dynastic struggle was at its height. It can be argued that the enmities that determined the wars of the period also affected the historical tradition.

Service under Alexander was a potent element in dynastic propaganda. Alexander's generals had helped acquire world empire, and they considered themselves entitled to a share in it, the share commensurate with their achievements.[45] If we examine the historical record, it is not surprising that Ptolemy bulks so large; Cleitarchus, the source of the vulgate tradition, wrote under his regime, and Ptolemy himself was the main source of Arrian. It is not surprising that there is a constant stress on his exploits, a consistent insinuation that many of the great successes of the reign were directly due to his efforts.[46] On the other hand his enemies in the civil wars, notably Perdiccas, receive very grudging mention, and there are strong indications that some of the rare military setbacks of the reign were laid at his door.[47] Such animus is not easy to detect, and the evidence is far from uncontrovertible. However, it is a striking fact that the figures who are most prominent in the military narrative (apart from Ptolemy himself) are men who were dead within a few years of Alexander himself: Hephaestion, Craterus, and Leonnatus. Practically nothing is recorded of Ptolemy's contemporaries and rivals, Lysimachus and Seleucus,[48] despite the fact that one was a royal Bodyguard and the other a hypaspist commander, both holding positions which would keep them constantly in the front. This is deliberately selective treatment by a royal author who was not disposed to publicize the achievements of competing dynasts, even dynasts who were for many years his allies against Antigonus.

Ptolemy has deeply affected both the history and the historical tradition of the period. He was also, it seems, influential in devising the propaganda which evolved over the centuries into the Alexander Romance. The inspiration was the gossip and slander which circulated in the aftermath of Alexander's death. The prolonged fever which took him off after ten days was unsurprisingly attributed to poison administered by the family of Antipater, which was in deep disfavour during the last months of the reign, and the rumours were later exploited to discredit the regent and his sons. Olympias was to desecrate the grave of Iolaus, who had been Alexander's cupbearer and, as such, was the prime target of the calumny.[49] In the vulgate these stories are recounted with some reserve, as though Cleitarchus was unwilling to present them as fact but wished them to be known and to circulate.[50] The most elaborate treatment of the scandal is in the so-called *Liber de Morte,* an extensive account of Alexander's last days with a full reproduction of his purported testament.[51] This story ends all versions of the Alexander Romance, and despite the deeply corrupt textual transmission there is substantial agreement in detail.[52] Although our extant texts come from late antiquity, there is little doubt that the nucleus of what became the *Liber de Morte* originated close to Alexander's death. Some of the material recurs on Egyptian papyri of a relatively early date,[53] and the narrative contains traces of the propaganda war which followed Alexander's death. Unfortunately the details are controversial, and it has hitherto proved impossible to anchor the document in any one historical context. However Ptolemy appears in an extraordinarily favourable light, and the provisions of the testament can be shown to favour his interests and damage those of his dynastic enemies. Two of the contributions to this volume[54] examine the premiss that the propaganda that resulted in the *Liber de Morte* originated in Ptolemy's court around 309 BC, and that it was designed simultaneously to present him as the champion of the deceased Alexander and his family and to denigrate his enemies at that time, Antigonus and Cassander. Ptolemy, then, was circulating material which presented as fact what Cleitarchus had retailed as rumour—and which in his history (written in a different political context) he was to ignore or reject. For good and ill, in fact and fiction, our view of Alexander has been primarily determined by material emanating from him or his court.

The contributions to this volume represent almost all the approaches which have been described. They form a sequence, beginning with political analysis, progressing to the historical interpretation of iconography and literary propaganda, and ending with issues of historiography. Bosworth's essay on Alexander and Cortés sets the scene. It presents an interpretative model, arguing that the historical tradition of the conquest of Mexico in the early sixteenth century can shed light on the actions of Alexander in the far east (and vice versa), and also introduces some basic issues of imperial ideology—attitudes towards the subject peoples and justification of conquest. The dark side of monarchy is further explored in Badian's detailed examination of conspiracies at the Macedonian and Persian courts. The conflicting source material is analysed on the basis of cumulative probability, and a pattern gradually emerges: Alexander systematically exploited the tensions at his court, using conspiracies, both genuine and fictitious, to suppress opposition (in a manner only too reminiscent of the present century), while Darius was acutely conscious of the ever-present and real danger of conspiracy. He ultimately fell victim to a plot by his own nobles which he had virtually created by the very measures he had taken to prevent such intrigues (the noble hostages whom he had taken with him on campaign fell into Alexander's hands with disastrous consequences). Alexander, on the other hand, survived and prospered, the supreme political puppet master.

From political manœuvring we progress to ideology. Flower's contribution examines the political impact of panhellenism, the principle that Greek *poleis* should reconcile their differences and turn their united forces against Persia. A new examination of the evidence presents the case that panhellenism was a more potent ideal than has been recognized, and that it was far more than a pretext for war in the eyes of both Philip and Alexander. It was the ultimate justification for the burning of Persepolis, and, contrary to what is usually thought, it continued to be an element of policy throughout Alexander's reign, not incompatible with the promotion of selected Iranian nobles. Panhellenism and 'Verschmelzungspolitik'[55] could coexist, even in the political philosophy of Isocrates, and parallels could be drawn with the actions of Agesilaus earlier in the century. Fredricksmeyer by contrast provides us with a deep analysis of Alexander's concept of kingship. He attacks a firmly held view that Alexander assumed the Achaemenid monarchy and presented himself as Darius' successor. On the contrary, he aimed at something higher and more ecumenical, a kingdom of Asia which transcended the boundaries of the old Persian Empire. On this reading Alexander had evolved the concept as early as 332. He consistently promoted himself as King of all Asia, both replacing and superseding the Great King, and his destruction of Persepolis gave a clear signal that he considered the Persian Empire to be extinct.[56] Once again the orientalizing traits at Alexander's court can be reconciled with the larger picture. It was necessary that the Persians felt some affinity with the new regime, and so Alexander adopted dress and ceremonial which would appeal to them, but the orientalism stopped short of the full assumption of Persian court ceremonial. It was part of the larger picture, the absolute and unrestricted Kingship of Asia.

Palagia's contribution marks a transition from purely literary evidence to the interpretation of visual propaganda. She begins by arguing for the basic authenticity of Diodorus' description of Hephaestion's pyre, which she compares with the late fourth-century funerary pyre at Cypriot Salamis. The description of the animal hunt frieze in Diodorus becomes the starting point for an investigation of hunting scenes in early Hellenistic art. Such scenes are not attested in the western Greek world before Alexander, and it is argued that they were inspired by the epic hunts which Alexander staged in the Persian game reserves. That leads in turn to a reinterpretation of the famous fresco on the façade of Tomb II at Vergina. The hunting scene there portrayed belongs to an Asian context and dates to the reign of Alexander. From that perspective it is compatible with the solemn reburial which Cassander accorded Philip Arrhidaeus, Eurydice, and Cynnane in 316 BC, and can be interpreted as a joint commemoration of Arrhidaeus himself and the family of Cassander. The point of reference has been changed. The lion hunt theme establishes a date for the fresco no earlier than Alexander's eastern conquests, and once that is accepted, the supporting evidence that Tomb II post-dates Alexander becomes irresistible. Bosworth's chapter on the *Liber de Morte* adopts a similar method. Previous attempts to give a political context to the document (in 321 or 317 BC) had resulted in internal contradictions which could only be resolved on the assumption that it was heavily interpolated. However, these contradictions are largely resolved if we accept a precise dating to the year 309/8, when Ptolemy was paying court to Alexander's sister, Cleopatra, and championing the liberty of the Greeks against joint threats from Cassander and Antigonus. He is represented as the true heir of Alexander, the natural successor to the kingship after the murder of Alexander's son and the destined husband of Cleopatra. The propaganda can then be seen to promote Ptolemy's regal aspirations, which can be traced in literary and epigraphic evidence long before his formal assumption of the diadem. Baynham's chapter also addresses the *Liber de Morte,* and shows that the sensational portent with which it begins makes perfect political sense in the years after the death of Alexander IV but can be fitted to no other historical context. What is more, the portent fits nicely into the general tradition of the omens of Alexander's death and displays some knowledge of Babylonian mantic procedure. It comes in a literary context reminiscent of Xenophon's historical romance, the *Cyropaedia,* and the anonymous author can be seen to be working simultaneously in a literary and propagandist tradition, creating a novel with a strongly political purpose.

The remaining chapters tackle issues of source criticism. Carney deals with the complex relationship between fact and reported fact. She addresses two recurrent themes, the series of exchanges between Alexander and his senior general, Parmenio, and the three dramatic occasions when the king isolated himself from his troops. Here the analysis reaches contrasting conclusions, but in both cases there is an interplay between literature and life. The tradition of a hostile exchange between Alexander and Parmenio may have originated in the propagandist history of Callisthenes, who necessarily treated Parmenio as an opposition figure, but it has been elaborated by later writers who had their own propagandist objectives or were deliberately casting Parmenio in the Herodotean role of the warning adviser. The whole tradition is fundamentally warped and poisoned, and it is dangerous to accept any of the episodes as historical. On the other hand, the interplay between Alexander and his troops may have been affected by literary models: he, the new Achilles, was sulking in his tent, and his men reacted in a hysterical mode which recalls the figure of the excluded lover. Here the sources underscore the Homeric parallels, but the literary embellishment is justifiable; it enlarges on traits which were actually present. Alexander acted as Achilles, and the sources supply a counterpoint of allusion and rhetoric. In contrast, Billows focuses on a single historian, Polybius, whose references to Alexander have received very cursory attention in the past. However, his treatment of the king is interesting in that it is sober, free from apologia, recognizing atrocities like the sack of Thebes while keeping a generally favourable view of Alexander's generalship and character. The perspective is totally different from that of the extant Alexander sources, and several possible influences may be traced: the view of Alexander as the favourite of fortune may go back to Demetrius of Phalerum and his treatise *Peri Tyches,* and some of the historical detail could be ascribed to Hieronymus of Cardia, whose monumental history of the Successors repeatedly reached back into the reign of Alexander.

The final contribution by Atkinson takes the spotlight away from Alexander and concentrates upon the concerns of the primary historians. No writer can reconstruct the past without being influenced by his or her contemporary environment. That was clearly the case in antiquity. Atkinson shows how the interpretation of Alexander's reign was influenced by the wisdom of hindsight and the classical theory of the transmission of Empire, which began with Herodotus and was extended as each successive imperial power (Mede, Persian, Macedonian, and Roman) bit the dust. The interpretation can be in macrocosm, as with the sequence of empires, or in microcosm, when the actions of dominant contemporary individuals can be seen to be foreshadowed. In particular Curtius' description of the roles of Arrhidaeus and Perdiccas at Babylon is highly coloured by his experience of political intrigue and judicial murder in the early Empire. The past thereby becomes a vehicle for indirect and oblique comment upon the present. With that we come full circle. The history of Alexander remains anchored to the literary sources, and each student must establish his or her attitude to the extant tradition. The papers in this volume provide a rich variety of approaches and collectively, it is to be hoped, they make it more feasible to recapture something of that most elusive of figures, the historical Alexander.

Notes

I am grateful to Elizabeth Baynham, Michael Flower, and Olga Palagia for their advice and helpful criticism.

1. One may also mention Antony Spawforth's BBC production, 'Alexander the Great: the God-King' (1996), with its ironically sceptical treatment of the newest piece of Alexander fiction, the supposed tomb at Siwah.

2. In particular the *Lex Irnitana,* the *Tabula Siarensis,* and, above all, the great *Senatus Consultum* recording the condemnation of Cn. Piso. It has been observed by Miriam Griffin that 'The Spanish inscriptions on bronze are making a fair bid to

rival the Egyptian papyri in their contribution to our knowledge of the ancient world'.

3. The definitive edition with full bibliography is Hatzopoulos 1996: 25-8, no. 6; 84-5, no. 62. See also Hatzopoulos 1997; Errington 1998: 77-90.

4. See Price 1982; 1991. For recent summaries and bibliography see Lane Fox 1996 and Le Rider 1995-96: 856.

5. [Bosworth, Brian. *Alexander the Great in Fact and Fiction.* Oxford: Oxford University Press, 2000], Ch. 6.

6. Published by Clarysse and Schepens 1985. The text has been interpreted as part of a history or, less probably, a fragment of Strattis' commentary on the Royal *Ephemerides* (Hammond 1987; 1993: 201-2). I suspect that the work was a very detailed campaign history, which gave a full account of the movements of Alexander and his lieutenants, correlating the invasion of Triballian territory with simultaneous actions in Eordaea and Elimeia, in Macedonia proper. Unfortunately Arrian's account (1. 2. 1) is compressed to the last degree, and the papyrus is too defective to reconstruct any continuous narrative. All that remains is a tantalizing miscellany of familiar names without a meaningful historical context.

7. See [Bosworth, 2000], Ch. 10.

8. See the cautionary remarks of Brunt 1980 and Flower 1997: 4-9.

9. Bosworth 1980*a,* 1995 on Arrian; Atkinson 1980, 1994 on Curtius.

10. Arr. 6. 12. 1-3; Xen. *Anab.* 3. 1. 2-3; for detailed discussion see Bosworth 1996a, 54-6.

11. Arr. 7. 1. 4. The general sentiment was expressed by Aristobulus (Strabo 16. 1. 11 (741) = *FGrH* 139 F 56), and Arrian (7. 19. 6) duly records it as his own view (ὤς γέ μοι δοκεῖ). However, Arrian sharpens the comment, and expresses himself in Thucydidean style (Högemann 1985: 130); where Strabo merely states that Alexander 'desired to be lord of all things', Arrian has a more vivid turn of phrase: Alexander 'was for ever insatiate of conquest'. The phrase is probably a deliberate reminiscence of Herodotus' Cyrus, who was 'insatiable of blood' (Hdt. 1. 212. 2-4; cf. 1. 187. 5), and implicitly compares the two conquerors (note also the warning against insatiable exploitation of good fortune in Xen. *Cyrop.* 4. 1. 15). The terminology recurs in the final summation of Alexander, where Arrian insists that his hero was most continent with respect to bodily pleasures and when it came to the pleasures of the mind he

was completely insatiate—of fame alone (ἐπαίνου μόνου ἀπληστότατος). The lust for conquest was central in Arrian's picture of Alexander; it fascinated him, and despite himself a note of admiration underlies his moral censure.

12. Arr. 7. 1. 5-2. 1 (gymnosophists); 7. 2. 1 (Diogenes); 7. 2. 2-4 = *FGrH* 715 F 34b (Dandamis).

13. Strabo 15. 1. 68 (718) = *FGrH* 715 F 34a. On this episode see Bosworth 1998: 181-90.

14. Plut. *Alex.* 1. 1-2. On the comparable passage in the *Nicias* (1. 5) see Pelling 1992: 10-11, an essay in a collection which repeatedly invokes the opening of the *Alexander* (pp. 56, 109). On Plutarch's literary presentation of Alexander see Mossman 1988.

15. On this Badian 1958*a*: 433-40 remains primary. For the continuing influence of Plutarch's rhetoric see Bosworth 1996*a*: 2-5.

16. On the history of this discovery, perhaps the single most important contribution to the source criticism of Alexander's reign, see Bosworth 1976. There have been protests against the use of the label 'vulgate' (particularly Hammond 1983: 1-3; the term is defended by Bosworth 1988*b*: 8-9), but even the most confirmed critics of the terminology accept that there is a common tradition, used selectively and in different ways by a large proportion of our extant sources.

17. This seems now agreed: cf. Badian 1965; Schachermeyr 1970: 211-24; Hammond 1983: 84-5 Prandi 1996: 66-71.

18. See the detailed analysis in J. Hornblower 1981: 263-79. Perhaps the best example is his penchant for describing fighting in relays (ἐκ διαδοχῆς) in siege warfare throughout his history. It seems to have been his personal imposition upon his source material (cf. Sinclair 1966). On Diodorus' literary shaping of his sources see particularly Sacks 1994.

19. Pliny, *NH* 3. 57-8 = *FGrH* 137 F 31, on which see Bosworth 1988*a*: 85-91. The Romans are not named in the list of foreign embassies reported in Diod. 17. 113. 1-2 and Just 12. 13. 1 (the corresponding passage in Curtius is not extant).

20. So, memorably, Hor. *Od.* 1. 37. 5-8 (cf. Prop. 3. 11. 45-6; Ovid, *Met.* 15. 827-8). Cleopatra's favourite prayer was allegedly to dispense justice on the Capitol (Dio 50. 5. 4; cf. Florus 2. 21. 2). In those circumstances it would have been an effective gibe to point out that the Romans had in effect offered submission to Alexander. In the context of the Triumviral period the only options

were to rebut the tradition with indignation, as Livy was to rebut the insinuations that Rome would have been conquered by Alexander, or to pass over the detail silently; since Cleitarchus merely mentioned the Romans without elaborating on their presence, it was easy merely to omit the embarrassing detail.

21. See particularly Hammond 1983 (conclusions 160-5). This has the corollary that Diodorus and Curtius were using the same pair of sources, in which case one must assume that Cleitarchus and Diyllus were a canonical pair in the early Empire. Tarn 1948: ii. 116-22 had used similar arguments to reach the conclusion that Curtius drew directly upon Diodorus. In contrast Prandi, who believes that Diodorus supplemented Cleitarchus with Duris, takes it as axiomatic that Curtius cannot have used exactly the same pair of sources as Diodorus. She argues that Curtius did not use Duris, and consequently uses disagreements between Diodorus and Curtius as a tool to identify passages where Diodorus is supposedly dependent upon Duris (Prandi 1996: 125-6, 138-40).

22. On Curtius see now the detailed bibliographical survey by Atkinson (Atkinson 1998). See too his commentaries (Atkinson 1980, 1994), and in brief the useful Penguin translation by John Yardley and Waldemar Heckel (1984).

23. Curt. 9. 5. 21 = *FGrH* 137 F 24 (Cleitarchus) and 88 F 3 (Timagenes); Curt. 9. 8. 15 = *FGrH* 137 F 25. See Atkinson 1998: 3458-65 for traditional approaches to source identification.

24. On the general character of Timagenes' work see Yardley and Heckel 1997, 30-4 and the discussion in Atkinson's essay, Ch. 11 [Bosworth, 2000].

25. For summaries of the manifold suggestions see Atkinson 1980: 19-57; 1998: 3451-6; Baynham 1998*a* 201-19.

26. Baynham 1998*a*,

27. Some instances are given by Atkinson 1998: 3475; see also Baynham 1998*a*: 5-6.

28. Hamilton 1977: 129-35; cf. Bosworth 1988*a*: 9.

29. Yardley and Heckel 1997: 8-19, 333-43.

30. Curt. 6. 7. 1-11. 40. Other sources are less detailed, though in most cases more informative than Arrian (Oiod. 17. 79-80; Plut. *Alex.* 48. 1-49. 13; Justin 12. 5. 2-3 (garbled)).

31. In particular the detail that Philotas gave his sister in marriage to Attalus, Alexander's bitter enemy (Curt. 6. 9. 17). This is accepted in standard refer-

ence works (e.g. Berve 1926: ii. 94, 298; Heckel 1992, 23). On the political implications see Badian, Ch. 3 [Bosworth, 2000], p. 63, who rightly accepts the evidence of Curtius while conceding (n. 24) that the context is highly suspect. 'That the speeches at Philotas' trial are not authentic does not need to be argued.'

32. See particularly Baynham 1995, with references to earlier literature. The Teubner text, by P. H. Thomas, is unfortunately prone to adventurous emendation. A translation and commentary is being prepared by J. C. Yardley and E. J. Baynham.

33. *Metz Epit.* 70. The incident is usually ignored in histories of the reign, but it was picked up and accepted as fact by Berve 1926: ii. 347, no. 688.

34. Alexander arrives at the Hydaspes towards the end of the monsoon season, and can repair the rain-damaged buildings at Bucephala and Nicaea (Arr. 5. 29. 5); this was around the rising of Arcturus (Strabo 15. 1. 17 (691) = Aristobulus *FGrH* 139 F 35). Arrian then digresses to describe Alexander's earlier investigations on the course of the Indus, and then moves directly to the start of the Ocean voyage. Apart from the funeral of Coenus (6. 2. 1) there is no reference to any event by the Hydaspes.

35. Diod. 17. 95. 4-5; Curt. 9. 3. 21-2; *Metz Epit.* 70.

36. Flower, Ch. 4, pp. 113-15; Fredricksmeyer, Ch. 5, pp. 145-50; Carney, Ch. 9, p. 265.

37. Arr. 3. 18. 12; Strabo 15. 3. 6 (730).

38. Athen. 13. 576d = Cleitarchus, *FGrH* 137 F 11; Plut. *Alex.* 38; Diod. 17. 72; Curt. 5. 7. 2-11.

39. So, for instance, Schachermeyr 1973: 289-90, and most recently Bloedow 1995.

40. According to Athenaeus (13. 576e) she was actually married (ἐγαμήθη) to Ptolemy (Plut. *Alex.* 38. 2 describes her simply as his *hetaira*). At all events her children by Ptolemy were figures of distinction. A daughter, Eirene, was married to Eunostus, king of Cypriot Soli (Athen. 576e; cf. Seibert 1967: 77-8); one son, Leontiscus, ranked alongside Ptolemy's brother, Menelaus, among the Ptolemaic captives who fell into Demetrius' hands after the battle of Salamis (Justin 15. 2. 7), and the other, Lagus, won the chariot race at the Arcadian Lycaea while his father held court at Corinth in the summer of 308 (*SIG*³ 314, B V, lines 8-10).

41. So Plut. *Alex.* 38. 2-4; Diod. 17. 72. 2; Curt. 5. 7. 3.

42. As suggested by Curt. 5. 7. 10-11 (so Plut. *Alex.* 38. 8; see also Arr. 6. 30. 1).

43. So, for instance, Wilcken 1932: 145; Tarn 1948: ii. 48; Pearson 1960: 218-19; Hammond 1992: 363.

44. For the various suggestions see Bosworth 1980a: 331-2; Atkinson 1994: 120-4; Chapters 4 and 5 by Flower and Fredricksmeyer.

45. The classic instance is Seleucus' declaration to Antigonus that Babylonia was his by right in return for his services to the Macedonians during Alexander's lifetime (Diod. 19. 55. 4). Shortly before Antigonus had had problems removing Peithon from Media 'for it was no easy matter to arrest a man by force who had gained preferment while serving under Alexander' (Diod. 19. 46. 3). Cassander, who like Antigonus, played no role in the conquest of Asia, faced the same dilemma in removing Aristonous, 'seeing that he was respected because of the preferment he had received from Alexander' (Diod. 19. 51. 1). Both Peithon and Aristonous had been Bodyguards under Alexander, and it gave them dangerous prestige.

46. See the recent discussion in Bosworth 1996a: 41-53.

47. The fundamental discussion is Errington 1969; see also Bosworth 1976: 9-14. For more sceptical views see Roisman 1984; Hammond and Walbank 1988: 29, 61; Hammond 1993: 166-9.

48. Lysimachus is mentioned at the crossing of the Hydaspes and, shortly after, at the siege of Sangala (Arr. 5. 13. 1, 24. 5), while Seleucus only figures at the Hydaspes, where he is attested close to Alexander (Arr. 5. 13. 1, 4; 16. 3). I would not agree with a recent biographer 'that Lysimachus only reached military prominence in the latter years of the expedition' (Lund 1992: 5; so Heckel 1992: 274: 'Lysimachos attained his rank before Alexander's accession, his fame and power after, and as a result of, Alexander's death.')

49. Diod. 19. 11. 8; Plut. *Alex.* 77. 2. The orator Hypereides had earlier voted honours for him at Athens for his part in the alleged poisoning ([Plut.] *Vit. X Orat.* 849f).

50. Diod. 17. 118. 1 (φασὶ γάρ); Curt. 10. 10. 14 ('credidere plerique'); Justin 12. 13. 10-14. 8 has the same story, but he chooses to present it as fact, suppressed by the affected parties (so Curt. 10. 10. 18). Onesicritus had already written that Alexander died of poison, but he shrank from naming the conspirators (*Metz Epit.* 97 = *FGrH* 134 F 37).

51. The document was preserved on the same manuscript as the *Metz Epitome,* and standard editions run them together with sequential paragraphing.

However, there has never been any doubt that two separate and unrelated documents are at issue (cf. Merkelbach 1977: 122; Baynham 1995: 62-3).

52. The text is printed in composite form by Merkelbach 1977: 253-83, and the separate versions are presented sequentially in Heckel 1988: 96-107. Stoneman 1991: 148-55 supplies an English translation.

53. *P. Vindob.* 31954 (first cent. BC) contains the same material as *Metz Epit.* 116 (Merkelbach 1977: 151, 166; Baynham 1998*b*: 113-14).

54. Bosworth, Ch. 7, and Baynham, Ch. 8.

55. Meaning literally 'Policy of Fusion', a term invented to encapsulate Alexander's supposed plan of blending together Macedonians and Persians as a ruling elite (cf. Bosworth 1980*b*).

56. This reading, it should be emphasized, is not in formal contradiction with Flower. Both interpretations can be accepted, and it could be argued that the conflagration was simultaneously the triumph of panhellenism and the end of the Achaemenid monarchy.

Bibliography

Atkinson, J. E. (1980) *A Commentary on Q. Curtius Rufus' Historiae Alexandri Magni, Books 3 and 4.* Amsterdam

———. (1994) *A Commentary on Q. Curtius Rufus' Historiae Alexandri Magni, Books 5 to 7. 2.* Amsterdam

———. (1998) 'Q. Curtius Rufus' "Historiae Alexandri Magni"', *ANRW* [*Aufstieg ung Niedergang der Römischen Welt. Gesicte und Kultur Rms im Spiegel der neuren Forschung, ed. H. Temporini et al., Berlin 1972*] II, 34.4: 3447-83

Badian, E. (1958*a*) 'Alexander the Great and the Unity of Mankind', *Historia* 7: 425-44

———. (1965) 'The Date of Clitarchus', *PACA* [*Proceedings of the African Classical Association*] 8: 5-11

Baynham, E. J. (1995) 'An Introduction to the *Metz Epitome*: Its Traditions and Value', *Antichthon* 29: 60-77

———. (1998*a*) *Alexander the Great: The Unique History of Quintus Curtius.* Ann Arbor

———. (1998*b*) 'The Treatment of Olympias in the *Liber de Morte Alexandri Magni*—a Rhodian Retirement', in W. Will (ed.), *Alexander der Grosse: Eine Welteroberung und ihr Hintergrund.* Vorträge des Internationalen Bonner Alexanderkolloquiums, 19.-21. 12. 1996: Antiquitas, Reihe 1, Bd. 46. Bonn, 103-15

Berve, H. (1926) *Das Alexanderreich auf prosopographischer Grundlage.* 2 vols., Munich

Bloedow, E. F. (1995) 'That Great Puzzle in the History of Alexander: Back into "The Primal Pit of Historical Murk"', in Ch. Schubert and K. Brodersen (eds.), *Rom und der Griechische Osten.* Stuttgart, 23-41.

Bosworth, A. B. (1976) 'Arrian and the Alexander Vulgate', in *Alexandre le Grand: Image et Réalité.* Entretiens sur l'antiquité classique, 22. Geneva, 1-46

———. (1980*a*) *A Historical Commentary on Arrian's History of Alexander,* i. Oxford

———. (1988*a*) *From Arrian to Alexander.* Oxford

———. (1988*b*) *Conquest and Empire: The Reign of Alexander the Great.* Cambridge

———. (1995) *A Historical Commentary on Arrian's History of Alexander* ii. Oxford

———. (1996*a*) *Alexander and the East.* Oxford

———. (1998) 'Calanus and the Brahman Opposition', in W. Will (ed.), *Alexander der Grosse: Eine Welteroberung und ihr Hintergrund.* Vorträge des Internationalen Bonner Alexanderkolloquiums, 19.-21. 12. 1996: Antiquitas, Reihe 1, Bd. 46. Bonn, 173-203

Brunt, P. A. (1980) 'On Historical Fragments and Epitomes', *CQ* [*Classical Quarterly*] 30: 477-94

Carney, E. D. (1994) 'Olympias, Adea Eurydice, and the End of thhe Argead Dynasty', in I. Worthington (ed.), *Ventures into Greek History.* Oxford, 357-80.

Clarysse, W., and Schepens, G. (1985) 'A Ptolemaic Fragment of an Alexander History', *CE* [*Carmina Epigraphica*] 60: 30-47

Errington, R. M. (1998) 'Neue epigraphische Belege für Makedonien zur Zeit Alexanders des Großen', in W. Will (ed.), *Alexander der Grosse: Eine Welteroberung und ihr Hintergrund.* Vorträge des Internationalen Bonner Alexanderkolloquiums, 19.-21. 12. 1996: Antiquitas, Reihe 1, Bd. 46. Bonn, 77-90

Flower, M. A. (1997) Theopompus of Chios. History and Rhetoric in the Fourth Century B.C. Pb. edn. with postscript. Oxford

Hamilton, J. R. (1977) 'Cleitarchus and Diodorus 17', in K. Kinzl (ed.), *Greece and the Eastern Mediterranean in History and Prehistory.* Berlin. 126-46

Hammond, N. G. L. (1983) *Three Historians of Alexander the Great: The So-Called Vulgate Authors, Diodorus, Justin and Curtius.* Cambridge

———. (1987) 'Papyrus British Library 3085 verso', *GRBS* [*Greek, Roman, and Byzantine Studies*] 28: 331-47

———. (1992) 'The Archaeological and Literary Evidence for the Burning of the Persepolis Palace', *CQ* 42: 358-64

———. (1993) *Sources for Alexander the Great.* Cambridge

Hammond, N. G. L., and Walbank, F. W. (1988) *A History of Macedonia.* iii. Oxford

Hatzopoulos, M. B. (1996) *Macedonian Institutions under the Kings,* ii. *Epigraphic Appendix.* ΜΕΛΕΤΗΜΑΤΑ, 22. Athens

———. (1997) 'Alexandre en Perse: La Revanche et l'empire', *ZPE* [*Zeitschrift fuer Papyrologie und Epigraphik*] 116: 41-52

Heckel, W. (1988) *The Last Days and Testament of Alexander the Great.* Historia Einzelschr. 56. Stuttgart

———. (1992) *The Marshals of Alexander's Empire.* London

Högemann, P. (1985) *Alexander der Große und Arabien.* Zetemata, 82. Munich

Hornblower, J. (1981) *Hieronymus of Cardia.* Oxford

Lane Fox, R. (1996) 'Text and Image: Alexander the Great, Coins and Elephants', *BICS* [*Bulletin. Institute of Classical Studies*] 41: 87-108

Le Rider, G. (1995-96) 'Histoire économique et monétaire de l'Orient hellénistique', *Annuaire du Collège de France: Résumé des cours et travaux* 96: 829-60

Lund, H. S. (1992) *Lysimachus.* London

Merkelbach, R. (1977) *Die Quellen des griechischen Alexanderromans*[2]. Munich

Pearson, L. (1960) *The Lost Histories of Alexander the Great.* New York

Pelling, C. B. R. (1992) 'Plutarch and Thucydides', in P. A. Stadter (ed.), *Plutarch and the Historical Tradition,* London, 10-40

Prandi, L. (1996) *Fortuna e realtà dell'opera di Clitarchus.* Historia Einzelschriften, 104. Stuttgart

Price, M. J. (1982) 'The Porus' Coinage of Alexander the Great: A Symbol of Concord and Community', in S. Scheers (ed.), *Studia Paulo Naster Oblata,* i. *Numismatica Antiqua.* Leuven, 75-85

———. (1991) *The Coinage in the Name of Alexander the Great and Philip Arrhidaeus.* 2 vols. Zurich and London

Roisman, J. (1984) 'Ptolemy and his Rivals in his History of Alexander', *CQ* [*Classical Quarterly*] 34: 373-85

Sacks, K. S. (1994) 'Diodorus and his Sources: Conformity and Creativity', in S. Hornblower (ed.), *Greek Historiography,* Oxford, 213-32

Schachermeyr, F. (1970) *Alexander in Babylon und die Reichsordnung nach seinem Tode.* Sitzungsberichte der österreichischen Akademie der Wissenschaften, phil.-hist. Klasse, 268. 3. Vienna

———. (1973) *Alexander der Grosse: Das Problem seiner Persönlichkeit und seines Wirkens.* Sitzungsberichte der österreichischen Akademie der Wissenschaften, phil.-hist. Klasse, 285. Vienna

Seibert, J. (1967) *Historische Beiträge zu den dynastischen Verbindungen in hellenistischer Zeit.* Wiesbaden

Sinclair, R. K. (1966) 'Diodorus Siculus and Fighting in Relays', *CQ* 16: 249-55

Stoneman, R. (1991) *The Greek Alexander Romance.* Harmondsworth

Tarn, W. W. (1948), *Alexander the Great.* 2 vols. Cambridge

Wilcken, U. (1932) *Alexander the Great,* trans. G. C. Richards. London

Wood, M. (1997) *In the Footsteps of Alexander the Great: A Journey from Greece to Asia.* Berkeley.

Yardley, J. C. (1994) *Justin. Epitome of the Philippic History of Pompeius Trogus.* Atlanta

Yardley, J. C. and Heckel, W. (1997), *Justin: Epitome of the Philippic History of Pompeius Trogus, Books 11-12: Alexander the Great.* Oxford

Abbreviations

FGrH: F. Jacoby, *Die Fragmente der griechischen Historiker* (Berlin and Leidon, 1923-)

SIG[3]: *Sylloge inscriptionum graecarum,* ed. W. Dittenberger (3rd edn.: Leipzig, 1913-24)

Glynnis M. Cropp (essay date 2000)

SOURCE: Cropp, Glynnis M. "Christine de Pizan and Alexander the Great." In *Christine de Pizan 2000: Studies on Christine de Pizan in Honour of Angus J. Kennedy,* edited by John Campbell and Nadia Margolis, pp. 125-34. Amsterdam, The Netherlands: Rodopi, 2000.

[*In the following essay, Cropp discusses how Christine de Pizan incorporated Alexander material into her* Mutacion *to showcase the workings of Fortune.*]

During the centuries after Alexander the Great's death in 323 B.C., historical and biographical writing, notably of Arrian, Quintus Curtius Rufus and Plutarch, and the Greek prose romance of pseudo-Callisthenes, maintained the legend of his life, truth being augmented by fiction to create eventually the most complex and extensive of all the medieval European narrative traditions. In France the vernacular Alexander tradition dates from the early twelfth century, a fragment of 105 lines by Alberic de Pisançon, and culminates in that century with the verse *Roman d'Alexandre,* a vast compilation by Alexandre de Paris. French twelfth-century authors presented Alexander in a favourable light as a model king, despite his pagan origins. The Macedonian court resembles the Arthurian court of courtly romance, and historical events and fantastic happenings serve to display the chivalry of Alexander's knights.[1] Among other French versions of the thirteenth and fourteenth centuries is the work known as the *Prose Alexander,* a translation with interpolations of the *Historia de proeliis* (ca. 960), itself a Latin version of the pseudo-Callisthenes.[2] It is here that Christine de Pizan found her source material for the narrative section on Alexander in the *Mutacion.*[3]

In the romances, Alexander is not extensively described. He has an impeccable genealogy: descended from Andromache and Achilles on his mother's side, from Heracles on his father's side. He was a courtly prince and military leader admired for his courage, boldness, loyalty and magnanimity. By his generosity of gifts and money he cemented his relations with others. His dominant purpose was conquest and absorption of any opposition. A more nuanced viewpoint, perhaps closer to historical reality as far as historians can interpret it, is that he was an outstandingly successful young pagan king whose ambition was, with his army, to conquer the known world, who was motivated by earthly glory, and, some would add, corrupted by power. Alexander therefore very aptly illustrates the vanity of worldly success, and ranks below the Christian king and emperor, Charlemagne, the other preeminent paragon of chivalry and conquest in the fourteenth and fifteenth centuries.

Against this background, what image of Alexander the Great has Christine de Pizan presented in her writing? How consistent are her allusions?

In the late fourteenth and early fifteenth centuries Christine de Pizan was one of several French writers who expressed ideas on the education of princes and nobles, advocating understanding of philosophical, political, military and even scientific matters, as well as the development of moral virtue and chivalry. For these writers, Alexander provided an exemplary model of behaviour for leaders who must overcome the prevailing weakness of the monarchy and the contemporary strife among opposing factions and who were themselves subject to abrupt changes of material and personal fortune.

In seven of her long works, in one ballade (*Cent balades,* 92), and in the part of the *Mutacion* preceding the narrative passage which is the focus of this essay, all written between about 1400 and 1418,[4] Christine de Pizan referred to Alexander about fifty times, most frequently in a simple comparison, as an example of behaviour she advocated, or as the recipient of Aristotle's teaching which she in turn wanted to transmit. Several contexts recur, most frequently Alexander's connection with Aristotle, the tutor his father selected and who remained his mentor and authority on leadership. Christine referred also to Alexander as conqueror, to his magnanimity towards enemies he defeated, to his generosity, and to his combat skills and tactics. It is not surprising that in her later biography praising the virtues of Charles V, the *Fais et bonnes meurs,* she stressed Alexander's generosity,[5] and in her treatise on arms and chivalry (the *Fais d'armes,* known in Middle English as the *Book of Fayttes of Armes and Chivalrye*), his strategies in war and conquest.[6] In another didactic work concerned with princely ideals, the *Chemin de long estude,* she emphasised, through the example of Philip and Alexander, a father's responsibility for his son's education and a ruler's need of *sagesse,* "wisdom," as Aristotle had taught: ". . . qu'il affiert que le sage / Soit roy, et par tel avantage / Affiert que sage soit le roy."[7] In the *Epistre Othea* I, she very discreetly alluded to Alexander's paganism, in a moral gloss praising the wisdom of classical antiquity, listing him among the highest lords ever, "comme Dieux n'eust ancore ouverte la porte de sa misericorde" / "at the time when God had not yet opened the gate of mercy."[8]

The *Mutacion,* written in octosyllabic rhyming couplets, with a prose interlude, is a universal history comprising 23,636 lines. It has the form of allegory, includes autobiography, and in the latter part recounts the history of Troy, the lives of several famous Romans and "l'istoire d'Alixandre abrigee", 1186 lines in length, before brief mention is made of some contemporary people and events, all susceptible to Fortune's capricious power; Christine concludes by stating her preference for peace and solitude.

The Alexander narrative, in the form of a *vita,* follows chronological order and a campaign itinerary which is that of her primary source, the *Prose Alexander.* This itinerary diverges particularly in the early part from that established by modern historians. For example, after consulting Apollo, Alexander goes first to Italy where the Romans send him gifts in order to keep Rome untouched; he then conquers Africa (which is described in two lines), visits the temple of Amon before going to Egypt and founding the city of Alexandria, returning via Syria and Jerusalem to campaign against Darius of Persia. The historical Alexander, however, campaigned in the Balkans before landing in Asia, 334 B.C., descending into Syria, defeating Darius at the battle of Issus, 333 B.C., laying siege to Tyre and Gaza, then entering Egypt and founding Alexandria in 331 B.C. Apart from one or two changes to the order of events, Christine adhered to the itinerary of her source material, ahistorical though it seems to be.

It is noteworthy that in about 1400 Guillaume de Tignonville, friend of Christine de Pizan and of Eustache Deschamps and later provost of Paris, translated into French the *Liber Philosophorum Moralium Antiquorum* which also contains a narrative of Alexander's life, preceded by Aristotle's sayings to Alexander and followed by Alexander's sayings and anecdotes. This narrative is quite different, especially in its account of Alexander's end: he died of a bleeding nose,[9] whereas throughout the Middle Ages his death was usually attributed to poisoning.

Christine's narrative is divided into nine sections of unequal length, all introduced by a brief rubric. The first two sections describe early events from Alexander's birth to his departure from Jerusalem (ca. 350 lines), the third the campaign against Darius of Persia (ca. 300 lines); the fourth to seventh sections cover the expedition to India, ending with the two fantastic adventures of his flight in the air and his deep-sea diving (ca. 300 lines); the eighth is devoted to his coronation and death in Babylon (ca. 180 lines), and the final section to the ensuing discord and his mother's death (ca. 25 lines).

This essay will deal with five aspects of Christine's depiction of Alexander: his birth, his portraiture and appearance, his role as conqueror, his obsession with death and his dying, and the power of Fortune. Analysis of these aspects will show how Christine subtly adjusts her source material to make the life of a historical figure illustrate her portrayal of Fortune's mutability.

Christine de Pizan presents Alexander as "Filz de Phelippe, roy et sire de Macedoine" (22105-106), rejecting the common allegation that his father was Nectanebus, an astrologer and former king of Egypt: ". . . et, a voir dire, / Dyent aulcuns, par grant abus, / Qu'il fu filz de Nabtanabus" (22106-108). Then she relates an expurgated, abridged version of that story, emphasising Nectanebus' powers as astrologer and predictor of births. By his wiles he would have taken advantage of King Philip's absence to sleep with Queen Olimpias, deluding her to believe the god Amon had fathered her child. It is a long story in the *Historia de proeliis* and the *Prose Alexander,* and in the latter work attributed to the *Speculum historiale* of Vincent de Beauvais, who in fact mentioned this alternative explanation of Alexander's birth as found in vulgate histories, after affirming that Philip and Olimpias were Alexander's parents.[10] Similarly Christine de Pizan distanced herself from the

story by her final comment, contrasting what is said "en maint sermon" with the "droit voir" found "en toutes ses escriptures," and declaring Alexander to be Philip's son (22142-45). She has used the story effectively to express her respect for historical truth, and also to justify Alexander's visit to the temple of Amon on the island he conquered and named Sagittaire (22328-39). Medieval historians had continued to juxtapose the two accounts of Alexander's birth, although with growing scepticism about the Nectanebus story and Alexander's possible illegitimacy.[11]

Immediately after the account of his birth, Christine de Pizan describes Alexander who is, like a hero, "le preux et sage" (22149), with certain physical features: small stature, a strange face because one eye is lower than the other, a proud or fierce look, and a loud voice (22150-54).[12] To this description Christine added progressively other moral qualities: a heart more fierce than that of a lion (22216-17), his "bel lengage," or eloquence, his "bel accueil," "son sens et vallour" (22287-92). He is extraordinarily generous, and knowledgeable, which makes him recognised as a leader (22295-300). In her initial description she diverged from her source by omitting to say that one of his eyes was black and the other grey, that his teeth were sharp, and that both his hair and his countenance resembled those of a lion. The lion simile was originally used by the sculptor Lysippus to convey a fundamental trait of character, thus associating Alexander in particular with Achilles. Writing his life of Alexander in the second century A.D., Plutarch applied the simile to a physical characteristic: the tawny colour and style of Alexander's hair.[13] Christine de Pizán used it to refer to Alexander's moral virtue or courage: ". . . cuer avoit / Plus fier que lion . . ." (22216-17). It is possibly because the sculptor Lysippus portrayed him with his head slightly to one side that Alexander was subsequently thought to appear to have one shoulder higher than the other. But his most distinct and distinguishing feature was that he was short, by normal expectations of height, which Christine mentioned first: "Estoit de moult petit corsage" (22152). On three occasions others recognise this physical characteristic: Darius, king of the Persians, sees in a picture "sa petite forme," deems him ugly, and wonders that so many acknowledge him as their lord (22463-72); King Porus proposes single combat with Alexander, thinking to gain advantage from the latter's "petit corsage" (22843), and Queen Candace knows his stature from a portrait she commanded in secret of her artist (22920-28). Although his stature is distinctive, it is not a deficiency for one endowed with the *sens* and *savoir* Christine perceived in Alexander.

She introduces Alexander as the one who "Tout le monde conquist, par armes" (22096) and to whom Fortune was at first friend and then enemy. In addition,

Nectanebus had predicted before his birth that Alexander would conquer the world. He is thus destined to be a conqueror. His first feat recorded here is victory over one of his father's enemies, Nicholas, king of the Aridians, with whom he was meant to negotiate peace (22173-93). His behaviour in battle and humane treatment of the enemy had the effect in this instance and always of making people voluntarily surrender to his power, to which he responded with clemency and generosity. Christine repeats the phrase that he conquers as much "par amours" as by force and constraint (2233, 22312). With strategic planning, enormous energy, expenditure and speed, he assembled armies and moved long distances, with the goal ". . . pour conquerre / Entierement toute la terre" (22303-304).[14] Whereas the *Historia de proeliis* and the *Prose Alexander* mention liberation of towns and peoples under Persian rule as well as the lure of Persian gold and Darius's palace as motivation for the Persian campaign, Christine de Pizan made the extraordinary passion for conquest alone drive Alexander into battle. She gave less attention to combat than to Darius's fate and the peace settlements. Betrayed by his own soldiers, Darius is left as dead until Alexander finds him, tries to help him survive and restores his ruling power to him, but it is too late: Darius dies, and Alexander has him buried in noble style. Christine then sums up the stages of conquest: surrender of the country to Alexander, establishment of laws, gifts, restitution of property, "pour sa grandeur anoblir" and as evidence of his "liberalité . . . debonnaireté . . . signeurie si paisible . . . et si sensible" (22737-54). Christine has Alexander marry Darius's daughter, to the delight of the people whom he restrains from worshipping him, reminding them that it would be wrong to honour a living mortal in this way (22755-62). While the marriage accords with her source, Alexander's sensible attitude does not, for in both the *Historia* and the *Prose Alexander*, in this instance and elsewhere, Alexander is said to be worshipped as a god.[15] Description of the conquest of India and of victory over Porus is similar but more summary, with a swift narrative pace. Alexander overcomes with equal ease both the inhabitants and their rulers, and strange animals and other dangers. His arrival in Babylon is joyfully celebrated: "Conquis ot tout l'univers monde / Alixandre, en gloire joconde / Deust bien d'or en avant regner, / Si se veult faire couronner" (23073-76).

The story of a life leads inevitably to a death. Twice Alexander seeks predictions about his death, firstly at the temple of the god Sarapion in Egypt (22344-60), and secondly in India from the trees of the sun and moon (22959-90). On both occasions he learns he will drink poison and die. On the second occasion, he is also told an angry follower will administer the poison. In another episode, mid-way through the narrative, a traitor tried to have Alexander poisoned by one of his doctors

(22625-40). The supernatural and omens preyed on his mind, arousing suspicions about his death which were not unreasonable. Christine also had a fixation on poison, adding as a rare personal touch that the birds flocking around the new city of Alexandria carried poison, to Alexander's dismay (22359-72).

In line with the *Prose Alexander*, but not the *Historia*,[16] Christine situates Alexander's death immediately after his coronation in Babylon (23073-248). It is true that there were hosts of envoys and visitors at Alexander's court just before his death, when he was planning further expeditions and campaigns. In the tradition Christine de Pizan used, Alexander did not heed his mother's letter warning him against Antipater, his lieutenant and governor in Macedonia. As it comes about, Jobas, that is, Iolaus, one of Antipater's sons, taking offence at some slight, follows his father's earlier instructions and gives Alexander poison at the coronation feast, causing him sudden pain. Whereas in her Latin and French sources Alexander used a feather, *pennam* (Lat. accusative), "une penne," to try and induce vomiting, Christine de Pizan, probably misreading her source, has him ask for an apple, *une pomme*, as an antidote, but the traitor ensures the fruit also contains poison, so that the pain and burning sensation intensify (23183-92). Alexander contemplates suicide, but the queen, his comforter, diverts his thought from "tel orreur" (23198). He summons his lords, asks them to care for his mother and wife, makes gifts to them, including the traitor, and dies, leaving them to grieve. The account of Alexander's death is remarkable for its blend of narrative and direct speech, bringing out the drama and emotion of the event, in a style reminiscent of medieval romance.

Historians still disagree about the nature of Alexander's death, but the evidence remains too insubstantial for a definite verdict.[17] In the circumstances, rumours of foul play arose soon after Alexander's death, the inimity of Antipater and others being strong enough to suggest conspiracy.[18] In the troubled times in which Christine de Pizan lived and wrote, sudden death by assassination or poison was the end of many a famous person's life, for example, of a majority of the other noblemen and princes alluded to in the final part of the *Mutacion*.[19] It was then generally believed that Alexander had been poisoned.

What is the role of Fortune in Alexander's life? Christine de Pizan intervenes only occasionally to comment on Fortune's power. At the outset, Fortune is described as successively favourable and unfavourable: ". . . qui moult amie / Luy fu un temps, puis ennemye" (22097-98). Fortune's disposition to Alexander can therefore be expected to change. Until the end the goddess does not receive credit for Alexander's progressive rise to fame and power resulting from military success and moral virtues, but the brevity of his reign and his abrupt death are attributed to Fortune's wish that he fall from glory. As a prelude to the account of his death Christine intervenes as author, asking and answering questions, to forewarn the reader of the imminent change (23065-72). Three ominous comments follow, significantly placed before the reception of Olimpias's warning letter (23087-88), before the provocation of Jobas's anger (23147-50), and after Alexander's death: "Ainssy fina roy Alexandre, / Que Fortune fist si hault tendre / Que tout le monde avoit soubz soy, / Mais moult tost, si com apperçoy, / Le rüa jus, quant il luy plot, / Et tout despeça son complot" (23239-44). This is Fortune whom Christine has depicted elsewhere as "la royne de tout meseur," "descordable," "fausse," a cause of disaster, but whose influence is limited to this world.[20] For Christine there was a different movement or aspiration upwards towards virtue and knowledge within the realm of Christian spirituality. Accordingly she concluded the narrative with the following instruction to her reader: "Mire toy, mire en ceste istoire, / Vois se Fortune la perverse, / En peu d'eure, de moult hault verse!" (23274-76). Whereas Alexander's glory which was formed by the admiring gaze of his contemporaries on his achievements, proved transitory, Christine encourages her contemporaries to distrust worldly Fortune and look for more lasting inner rewards.[21] She herself believed in wisdom as a source of good judgement in the face of Fortune.

How does Christine de Pizan's view of Alexander compare with that of her contemporaries? Two writers from the same milieu, Eustache Deschamps and Philippe de Mézières, express respectively concordant and different viewpoints. In his poetry, Deschamps referred frequently to Alexander's reputation as conqueror of the world,[22] cited him among the Nine Worthies (1:86.3-5), and used his example to illustrate the themes of the vanity of worldly glory and the inevitability of death (3:183.11-13). Several times he mentioned that Alexander was fatally poisoned (3:282.1-3). In a ballade of advice to the young Charles VI, Deschamps cited Alexander's achievements to stir the king to defend his country and gain the following of his subjects, because "Le monde ainsi conquist jeune Alixandre" (2:22-23.9; CF. 3:161.36). Elsewhere, however, Deschamps attributed to Alexander's paganism he loss of his kingdom (8:162.1-10).

On the other hand, Philippe de Mézières offered a radical contrast with this overall approval and praise of Alexander. In *Le Songe du vieil pelerin* (1386-1389), a didactic work intended for the young king Charles VI, Philippe de Mézières strongly and frankly criticised Alexander: he was a bastard who mistreated Nectanebus, his reputed father;[23] he sought only vain glory, so that

God punished him by the manner of his death, which is not specified, and the short duration of his empire (2:25). In advice to her son (the young Charles VI), the allegorical Verite la royne (Queen Truth) enumerates Alexander's vices, for which his great courage and generosity do not compensate: firstly he conquered eastern kingdoms by force of vain glory and tyranny; secondly, he was extremely cruel, and thirdly he was addicted to sensual pleasure and lechery. She commends instead other models: Charlemagne, David, Joshua, Godfrey of Bouillon, Scipio Africanus (2:239-41).

Christine de Pizan followed selectively the *Prose Alexander* with little originality. As was her customary practice, she based her text more on the French than on the corresponding Latin source. The influence of Fortune is already integrated in the romance. I have highlighted five aspects: the paternity issue, Alexander's physical height and asymmetrical shape, his conquering, his death, and Fortune's power. Christine's individual viewpoint and feminine perceptions are hardly felt, although she gave due, but slight, place to Alexander's relation with his mother and to the queen's role as he is dying, and described his encounters with the queen of the Amazons and Queen Candace in India without embroidering the love element of the romances on to the second. There is no apparent discord between her allusions elsewhere to Alexander and the narrative, where in places she sacrificed coherence or explanation to the need for compression. She and Deschamps presented Alexander as an exemplary figure whose nobility, conquests and liberality made him a superior human being, though one not without flaws, and whose life offered valid lessons for contemporary princes and nobles at a time when France sought a strong leader to make peace with England and to resume crusades to the East. On the other hand, Philippe de Mézières condemned Alexander, and most vehemently through the voice of Verite la royne, for immorality, abuse of power and extravagance such as he observed at the French royal court. This expression of opposite views simply perpetuated the polarity of interpretation of Alexander the Great since his death.

For Christine de Pizan, Alexander was firmly in the grasp of Fortune, an unreliable and implacably hostile force against whose control even the greatest of achieves was powerless. It is Fortune which inevitably arrests conquest and puts an end to glorious supremacy. Unlike Chaucer at the end of *The Monk's Tale*,[24] Christine de Pizan did not grieve at Alexander's premature death. The fusion of history, allegory and fiction she found in the Alexander material enabled her to warn against the mutability of Fortune, a pagan goddess, and albeit tentatively, to point to an alternative in self-knowledge.

Notes

1. Gosman 1997, 28-33; Gaullier-Bougassas 1998, 20-22, 308-24, 524-27.

2. Hilka 1920/1974; Cary 1956, 46-48, 175-76; *Mutacion,* ed. Solente, 1: XCII-XCVII; Gosman 1997, 30-31.

3. *Mutacion,* ed. Solente, 4:29-68. Gaullier-Bougassas (29, n. 1) cites the *Mutacion* as one of two known 14-15th-century octosyllabic works to include a life of Alexander.

4. *Cent balades* 92, in *Œuvres Poétiques,* ed. Roy, 1: 92-93. See for example *Mutacion,* ed. Solente, passim ("Table des Noms Propres", 4: 105-6), plus indexes to editions of other works when available for references to Alexander.

5. *Fais et bonnes meurs,* ed. Solente, 1: 165.

6. *Fais d'armes,* ed. Byles, 35, 53, 56, 121-22.

7. *Chemin de long estude,* ed. Püschel, 219.5153-55.

8. *Epistre Othea,* ed. Parussa, 199; *Epistle of Othea,* ed. Bühler, 6.

9. Bühler 1941/1961, 152-225. See especially 206-9.

10. Hilka 1920, 19-30.

11. Cary 1956, 235-36.

12. Bosworth 1988, 19-21; Hammond 1997, 3-7.

13. Plutarch 1971, 12-13; Schwarzenberg 1976, 128-29, 248-53.

14. Darius of Persia intensified Alexander's hostility by scornfully sending him a soft ball and whip, 22477-500.

15. Hilka 1920, 138-39; also 172-73, 230-31.

16. Ibid., 246-60; *Mutacion,* ed. Solente, 1: XCV-XCVII.

17. Celebrations consisting of sacrifices followed by entertainment, feasting and carousing were Macedonian customs. It was claimed that on this occasion Alexander had drunk long into the night with harmful effects. Certain features, such as the sudden collapse and the violent spasm of pain as though caused by a sword, might be attributed to either alcohol or poison. On the other hand if, as a day-to-day account written soon after the death is said to have recorded it, Alexander gradually developed a fever and fell into a coma before death supervened, then he died of a natural illness, perhaps similar to that which had recently caused the death of his friend Hephaestion. New medical research has proposed typhoid, or possibly schistosomiasis, instead of malaria, as the probable disease. See Oldach 1998, 1763-69; Behrman 1998, 1248-49.

18. Bosworth 1988, 171-73; Hammond 1997, 196-98; Plutarch 1971, 77-79.

19. *Mutacion,* ed. Solente, 4: 68-78.23277-594; 86-95.

20. *Chemin de long estude,* ed. Püschel, 96.2204-22; Dulac 1998, 90.

21. Brucker 1998, 55.

22. Deschamps *Œuvres complètes,* 2: 117.11-12.

23. Philippe de Mézières 1969, 1: 167, 337, 617.

24. Chaucer 1987, 250.2663-70.

General Bibliography

Bosworth, A. B., and E. J. Baynham, editors. *Alexander the Great in Fact and Fiction.* Oxford: Oxford University Press, 2000.

Buhler, C. F. *The Epistle of Othea, Translated from the French Text of Christine de Pisan,* by Stephen Crope. EETS, 1970.

Byles, A. T. P., editor. *The Book of Fayttes of armes and of chyualrye, translated and printed by William Caxton from the French Original by Christine de Pisan.* London: H. Milford, 1932.

Cary, George. In *The Medieval Alexander,* edited by D. J. A. Ross. Cambridge: Cambridge University Press, 1956.

Gaullier-Bougassas, Catherine. "Jean Wauquelin et Vasque de Lucène: le 'roman familial' d'Alexandre et l'écriture de l'histoire au XVe siècle," in *Cahiers de Recherches médiévales (XIIIe-XVe siècle),* 5 (1998), 125-38.

Gosman, Martin. *La Légende d'Alexandre le Grand dans la littérature française du 12e siècle une réécriture permanente* (Faux titre 133, Amsterdam and Atlanta: Rodopi, 1997).

Hammond, N. G. L. *Three Historians of Alexander the Great; The So-Called Vulgate authors Diodorus, Justin, and Curtius.* Cambridge: Cambridge University Press, 1983.

Hilka, Alfons, editor. *Der altfranzösische Prosa-Alexanderroman nach der Berliner Bilderhandschrift nebst dem lateinischen Original der Historia de preliis (Rezension J²) herausgegeben von—.* Festschrift für Carl Appel zum 17. Mai 1917, Halle 1920.

Parussa, Gabriella, editor. *Christine de Pisan: Epistre Othea.* Librarie Droz, 2008.

Roy, Maurice, editor. *Oeuvres poétiques de Christine de Pisan.* Paris: Firmin Didot & cie., 1886-96.

Solente, Suzanne, editor. de Pisan, Christine. *Le livre de la mutacion de fortune.* Paris: A. & J. Picard, 1959.

————, editor. *Le livre des fais et bonnes meurs du sage roy Charles V, par Christine de Pisan.* Paris: H. Champion, 1936-.

ALEXANDER ACCORDING TO GREEK AND ROMAN HISTORIANS

Lionel Pearson (essay date 1960)

SOURCE: Pearson, Lionel. Introduction to *The Lost Histories of Alexander the Great,* pp. 1-21. Oxford: American Philological Association/B. H. Blackwell, 1960.

[*In the following essay, Pearson explores the nature and veracity of early written accounts of Alexander.*]

Plutarch begins his biography of Alexander by warning his readers that he will give them only a selection from the abundant material; and Arrian begins his *Anabasis of Alexander* by emphasizing how many authors have written about Alexander and how different one account is from another. This abundant material which they were able to consult is no longer available to us, and we possess no consecutive narrative of Alexander's expedition earlier than that of Diodorus, written in the age of Augustus. Our knowledge of Alexander, therefore, is largely based on so-called secondary sources, works written several centuries after his death—on the accounts in Plutarch and Arrian and in the seventeenth book of Diodorus; the Latin writers Quintus Curtius and Justin must be added, but the modern critic generally has less respect for these last two. It is true that we can learn much about the age of Alexander from other sources, epigraphic as well as literary; but we should have a very different impression of Alexander if these secondary authorities had selected their material differently.

Like most ancient writers they are not always explicit in acknowledging their obligations. Plutarch and Arrian, however, are more straightforward than the others in explaining their methods and their preferences. Plutarch, whose standards are really determined by his philosophic interests, admits that his selection of material may not please everyone:

> In this book, which will contain the lives of Alexander and Caesar, because of the mass of material available all I shall say by way of preface will be to ask my readers not to find fault if I fail to recount every incident or to report some famous incident in full, but prefer to tell most of the story in summary fashion. I am not writing histories, but lives, and it is not always in the most spectacular actions that virtue or vice is illustrated; on the contrary a brief act or word or even a jest is often more revealing of character than battles in which thousands fall or huge clashes between armies or sieges of cities. Just as painters seek the likenesses of their subjects in the face and in the appearance about their eyes, wherein character is revealed, paying little attention to the rest of their body, so I must be permitted to enter more deeply into the indications of inner personality (εἰς τὰ τῆς ψυχῆς σημεῖα μᾶλλον ἐνδύεσθαι) and by these means to delineate the life of each man, leaving the grandeurs and the struggles for others to describe.[1]

Thus Plutarch makes it quite clear what his principle of selection is to be: he is interested in significant incidents and in characterization, rather than in spectacular description. He does not take pains to show that he has been critical in his method of selection;[2] he does not, as a rule, say that he considers one author more trustworthy than another; but he clearly expects his readers to draw their own conclusions and is well aware that some of Alexander's achievements have been exaggerated; for example, he complains (*Alex.* 17) that the supposed miraculous passage along the coast of Pamphylia has been exploited by many historians for the sake of its dramatic effect.

Arrian, on the other hand, states quite clearly that he has relied almost entirely on two authors (*Anab.* 1 *proem.*):

> Everything concerning Alexander, son of Philip, which Ptolemy son of Lagus and Aristobulus son of Aristobulus have both described in the same way I have reproduced as being true in every respect; when they have not given the same account, I have chosen the version which seemed to me more worthy of belief and also more worthy of telling. Different writers have given different accounts of Alexander, and indeed there is no one about whom more writers have written or with greater disagreement among themselves; but to me Ptolemy and Aristobulus seemed more trustworthy for my story: Aristobulus, because he accompanied King Alexander on his expedition; Ptolemy, not only because he went on the expedition, but also because he was a king himself and it would have been more disgraceful for him to tell a lie than for another man; and both of them because they wrote after Alexander's death, when there was no compulsion or incentive to describe anything otherwise than as it happened. Other incidents recorded by other writers, because they seemed to me in themselves worthy of telling and not altogether unworthy of belief, I have reproduced as being merely "reported" about Alexander. Anyone who

wonders why, with all these writers available, I too have taken it into my head to write this account, let him suspend judgment until he has read everything that they wrote and then looked into this account of mine.

There is, therefore, no doubt about the principle which Arrian proposes to follow. His attitude is critical, up to a point; he wants to follow the most trustworthy sources and at the same time to include material which will add to the charm and interest of his story, though he will not be held responsible for its accuracy. It is a statement of principle which Herodotus might have written, though it would have irritated Thucydides, who took his critical responsibilities more seriously and knew that even eyewitnesses could disagree in accounts of what they had seen.[3] Moreover Aristobulus and Ptolemy were not the only writers who had been with Alexander's army and we may not share Arrian's respect for Ptolemy's honour as a king. But whether or not the reasons for his preference are good, he has stated it clearly and we must presume that he has described his procedure accurately.

Arrian does not often quote other authorities by name in the *Anabasis*; what he has learnt from Nearchus is mostly to be found in the *Indica*; when he mentions Callisthenes, Medeius, and Onesicritus, he is not concerned with their literary work but with their behaviour. Plutarch, by contrast, cites quite a number of writers, though he makes no critical remarks about them. Both Plutarch and Arrian, however, quote a long passage from the "Royal Diary" describing the last days of Alexander's life,[4] without making it clear where they have found it. Plutarch contrasts its sober account with the stories told by other writers, which "they thought it necessary to relate as a tragic final scene of a great drama;" and Arrian, after remarking that it did not conflict with the account of Ptolemy and Aristobulus, adds some less convincing details given by other writers "in order not to appear ignorant that these things are recorded."[5] Since Arrian makes no reference to the Diary in discussing the sources he used, modern critics have been ready to believe that he found the quotation in Ptolemy. My reasons for rejecting this view have been set forth elsewhere[6] and need not be repeated here. But the matter will need some further discussion in a later chapter when Ptolemy's work is under consideration.

Another source to which Plutarch sometimes refers as a final authority is the correspondence of Alexander himself, and here too the contrast is made between the king's straightforward account and the dramatic exaggerations of other writers.[7] There is mention of his correspondence with Olympias and Antipater and other persons in Macedonia; indeed Plutarch expresses surprise that he found time for so much personal correspondence with his friends "like the letters he wrote giving orders to search for the slave of Seleucus who had run away into Cilicia and commending Peucestas for catching Nicon, the slave of Craterus; and the letter to Megabyzus about the servant who had taken refuge in the temple, telling him to entice him out and seize him outside, if he can, but not to lay hands on him inside the temple."[8] Such intimate touches and evidence of kindliness towards his friends were naturally of great interest to Plutarch; but he never tells us where he found these letters or what reasons he had to believe they were genuine.

The official diary and some letters of Alexander himself (if these were genuine documents), and the accounts of Aristobulus and Ptolemy—if these texts were available to us now, we should certainly think ourselves lucky to have such good authorities. We might even think them comparable to our literary authorities for the age of Cicero or the Peloponnesian War. But if we try to compare the quantity and quality of the literature relating to Alexander which was available in Athens or Alexandria fifty years after his death with the literature relating to the Peloponnesian War that was available to Demosthenes or Aristotle, the difference is remarkable. Certainly, in 338 Thucydides and Xenophon did not stand alone as first-class historical authorities; there was, for example, Hellanicus' *Atthis* to be considered as well as the work of fourth-century writers like Androtion and Ephorus; and in addition to the extant plays of Aristophanes there was a large body of the Old Comedy capable of filling in details of Athenian political intrigue and gossip and illustrating changes in living conditions and shifts in public opinion. But despite the large quantity of Athenian literature produced in the first half of the fourth century—history, oratory, philosophy, drama, political pamphlets, and so on—Thucydides was never displaced from his position as the prime authority; his account was not subject to attack, its accuracy was not called into question. There were important supplements to it, of course, as is shown by Aristotle's account of the revolution of the Four Hundred, because any narrative of a complex political development must be selective, and selection and interpretation always vary with the interests and sympathies of each writer. But the problems which this period of history offers are mostly due to shortcomings or omissions on the part of writers, not to their dishonesty or their powers of invention.

Neither in the fourth century nor now has the student of the Peloponnesian War been embarrassed by a quantity of conflicting evidence; he has not been forced to spend much time in refuting fiction and legend; Thucydides had already taken care of that and he also generally let his readers know when he was offering a mere opinion; and his prejudices, when he indulged them, were not difficult to detect.[9] But the story of Alexander presented historians in the third century and later with a very different problem. Polybius, Strabo, Arrian, and Plutarch are all equally loud in their complaints.[10] Legends and lies about Alexander were given currency by authors who had actually seen him or accompanied his expedition; there had been no Thucydides to strangle such monsters at their birth, and if Ptolemy, in his later years, tried to clear them away and offer a sober narrative based on his own recollection, it was already too late.

Excuses for this violent outbreak of false and dishonest writing are not hard to find; there was to use Arrian's terms, both "compulsion" and "incentive" for writers to record things otherwise than as they actually happened. Flattery of Alexander, as later critics called it, the wish to write what would please the conqueror or further his political purposes, was hardly compatible with good history-writing.[11] Callisthenes, often called the official historian of the expedition, is blamed for initiating the fashion of flattering Alexander; and other writers followed his example.[12] Not that these writers tried to whitewash the king's personal character; Alexander's drinking habits were notorious; it was impossible to conceal the fact that he violated Greek custom by taking a second wife; the deaths of Cleitus and Parmenion were ugly stories which could not be explained away. No attempt, therefore, was made to present him as a model human being or the type of a just king; but he was portrayed as superhuman, above ordinary human standards of behaviour, and even immune to ordinary human temptations. Indeed, since Callisthenes was the first historian to make a god of him—before whom the sea made obeisance "nor failed to know its lord"[13]—, he has borne some of the blame for turning his head and corrupting his character.

Since Callisthenes was a relative and protégé of Aristotle and was supposed to be a philosopher, his guilt was held to be so much the greater. Onesicritus, equally severely castigated by later writers as a "flatterer," was also supposed to be a philosopher, a Cynic and a pupil of Diogenes, from whom, if he learnt nothing else, he should at least have learnt to speak the unadorned truth and abhor flattery. Strabo complains (2.1.9; 15.1.28) that he is a liar on the grand scale who told fantastic tales of India, of strange people, beasts, and natural wonders, which raised Alexander's journey into the realm of the miraculous and the mythical when he revisited places familiar from mythology and actually met the queen of the Amazons.

Onesicritus and others like him glorified Alexander by taking him into places where no ordinary human being could have been expected to go. This is an extension of the more obvious glorification which exaggerates the numbers and bravery of his enemies and the hardships of his journey over mountains and across deserts. And when it takes him to places where only gods like Dionysus and Heracles have been before him, it is linked up with his deification.[14]

Naturally individual writers were at liberty to choose their own particular methods of flattery. The king's personal prowess in battle was one obvious theme; a display of personal courage, however reprehensible in a modern general, was expected of great military leaders in his day;[15] flattery was all the easier when there was a nucleus of truth to begin with. He could be brought face to face with his personal opponent in battle, just as Achilles had fought with Hector; in that case his opponent must be made worthy of him, and Darius, despite his recognized incompetence and cowardice, must be brave and handsome. It is not difficult to see the opportunities of a writer with a sense of the dramatic and an understanding of the rhetorical tastes of his contemporaries and their appetite for the sensational. The soldier, the seaman, the administrative officer, the courtier, the philosopher, the politician—all had different opportunities and different experiences to draw upon when they told their stories. Not all of them would want to flatter Alexander, and we have some precious fragments of one hostile pamphlet intended to rouse Greek feeling against the king, written by a certain Ephippus from Olynthus.[16]

The character of Alexander did not remain static through the centuries, and as various conquerors challenged comparison with him his portrait was inevitably modified. Plutarch was bound to take notice of literary work written in Roman times and to be influenced by the attitudes of the philosophic and rhetorical schools. For Stoics and Peripatetics in particular Alexander became a useful figure for the illustration of moral lessons;[17] so also in schools of rhetoric, where pupils debated whether a man's success was due mainly to chance or personal merit, as well as more specific themes such as the chances of Alexander if he had attempted to conquer Italy. All this must be taken into account in any evaluation of Plutarch's biography or an investigation of his sources. Diodorus and Quintus Curtius were exposed to similar influences. The rhetorical interests of Quintus Curtius and his familiarity with Livy's work are obvious,[18] but we do not know enough about him personally to say whether he had any professional pretensions as a philosopher. Arrian, on the other hand, was a Stoic and a great admirer of Epictetus, and we naturally look for Stoic touches in his interpretation, particularly for traces of the Stoic ideal of kingship. He was also more keenly interested in military technicalities than any of the other writers; and where Plutarch compared Alexander with Julius Caesar, Arrian was likely to be thinking of Trajan.

Subsequent chapters in this book will be concerned with the peculiar characteristics of each of the earlier historians of Alexander, so far as it is possible to discover and illustrate them. Even without the evidence of the fragments[19] it should be clear from the very number of people who wrote about Alexander in the generation after his death that there were great differences between them. We certainly need not believe that all these writers were conscientious and wise historians, accurate observers of men and events, anxious to preserve the truth for posterity. More than twenty individual authors old enough to be called contemporaries of Alexander, who published works of one kind or another related to Alexander's expedition, are known by name, and there may be many more whose works have perished without leaving even this much trace. Never before in the Greek world did any subject draw so much attention from contemporary writers. The obvious attraction of the subject and its great political interest are not sufficient explanations for this sudden rich crop of so-called historians, especially when there is no startling renaissance in other branches of literature to keep it company; it is not as though independent literary work had been suppressed in Alexander's lifetime and we were witnessing a literary revival, as in the Roman world after the death of Domitian. While the story of Alexander offered a magnificent subject for treatment, it was also a subject towards which countless individuals had something to contribute, because the expedition had offered to Greeks a variety of experience and opportunity such as they had never known before. It is likely, then, that each individual wrote because he had had some unusual personal experiences, because he thought he had some special claim to a hearing or some special cause to plead, or even because some predecessor needed to be corrected. Even without the evidence of the fragments this would be a reasonable assumption; and it is borne out by the evidence.

The fragments and the conclusions to be drawn from them about individual writers and their works will be considered in the chapters which follow. Before individual differences between authors are considered, something may be said about characteristics and tendencies which they must have had in common. Naturally they shared a literary heritage which they could not discard, a common political tradition, a nucleus of scientific knowledge, a bare minimum (if nothing more) of philosophical interest. All were writing for a Greek public whose tastes and prejudices we must assume they understood. We can expect from them, as from any Greek with literary pretensions, a familiarity with the classic works of Greek literature; not only with the well-known masterpieces of epic, lyric, and drama and with Herodotus, Thucydides, and Xenophon, but also with some of the historians of the fourth century, with Ephorus and Theopompus if with no one else. Likewise,

in so far as they had philosophical, scientific, or rhetorical interests, we can expect some acquaintance with the dialogues of Plato, and with some of the works of Aristotle and even of Isocrates. But it will be best to take first the literary heritage that was bound to affect their choice of subject matter and their method of narrative—the inescapable influence of their reading of epic and history.

When they undertook to describe a great military expedition led by an extremely remarkable young man, their literary experience offered them two obvious parallels from earlier times: the ten-years' war to capture Troy as described in the Homeric poems, and the Persian expeditions against Greece as described by Herodotus. Agamemnon had led a panhellenic expedition to Asia, and Achilles had died young in a foreign land after winning great fame by his heroic deeds, which included a duel to the death with his great adversary, Hector. Herodotus had represented the Persian Wars as part of the eternal strife between East and West; the first oriental after the Trojan Wars to take the offensive against Greeks was Croesus, and then the part taken by Athens in the Ionian revolt gave Darius his excuse for revenge; the expedition which met with shipwreck on Mount Athos, the Marathon expedition, and the expedition of Xerxes were all attempts to take revenge, and they came near enough to success to justify retaliation on the part of the Greeks. Long before Alexander started out, the Greek world was educated to the idea that his task was to punish Persia for its arrogant aggression against Greece and its sacrilege in burning Greek temples. Isocrates had preached this kind of crusade, and indeed the only excuse for accepting Philip and then Alexander as *hegemon* of the League of Corinth was the projected war of revenge against Persia. Each individual historian of Alexander could choose his own way of writing; but whether he flattered or idealized, satirized or vilified, he could not avoid making some comparison of Alexander with Xerxes or Themistocles or Miltiades, with Achilles or Hector, possibly even with those earlier heroes who spread the seeds of Greek civilization, Heracles and Theseus, and Dionysus the god who travelled to India.

Herodotus had responded to the stimulus of Homer by borrowing some features of his epic style; by dramatizing conversations and conferences between Xerxes and his advisers; by bringing the gods and their wrath into his story, by showing Xerxes guilty of *hybris* that was bound to rouse divine anger, and letting a foreboding of disaster play its part. All this is well known and has been illustrated many a time in critical studies of Herodotus. Less familiar perhaps and less generally noticed by readers of Herodotus are the visits of Xerxes to places made famous by the *Iliad* and the *Odyssey*—to Troy, and to the land of the Cicones, the first place in

Europe where he halts (7.59), just as it is the first stopping place of Odysseus. Xerxes, unlike Alexander in our traditional version, does not travel with a copy of Homer under his pillow and is not indeed supposed to know much about Greek literature and tradition; but he does nevertheless, in the Herodotean account, make a special effort to visit certain places that are famous in Greek literature, like the vale of Tempe.[20]

A similar behaviour is attributed to Alexander by some of his historians, by Callisthenes in particular. It is likely enough that he did in fact visit Troy and did display a vivid curiosity in examining and identifying Homeric sites.[21] There are many occasions in the story of Alexander when it is hard to be sure just where history ends and romance begins. But there are enough fragments of Callisthenes to show that this point is passed in his account of Alexander's Homeric studies, because Alexander is made to behave as a descendant of Achilles and Priam ought to behave and, in contrast to Xerxes, as a conqueror should behave when visiting the scene of Homeric legend. The details of Callisthenes must await treatment in Chapter II,[22] but we must remember that he was a professional historian who had written a great deal before he joined Alexander's expedition, and who knew his Homer and his Herodotus perhaps better than any other historian of Alexander.

Some authors devised absurdly inappropriate imitations of heroic deeds. Quintus Curtius, after his description of the siege of Gaza, tells how Betis the brave commander of the city fell into Alexander's hands badly wounded, and Alexander, "though generally an admirer of courage in his enemies," treated him with horrible barbarity; "while he was still alive his ankles were pierced and leather thongs passed through them; he was tied to a chariot and dragged round the city, and the king bragged that in punishing an enemy he had imitated Achilles, from whom he traced his own lineage" (4.6.25-29). This story is not a late invention. It goes back at least as far as Hegesias of Magnesia, a third-century rhetorician whose account is quoted by Dionysius of Halicarnassus[23] as a horrible example of poor taste and bad writing. The only point of the story is that it shows Alexander imitating Achilles—imitating the evil in him as well as the good and actually outdoing him in cruelty, since Hector after all was dead before Achilles dragged him behind his chariot.

A similar instance of barbarity copied from a hero of legend is to be found in Plutarch, who makes Alexander kill Bessus in the manner that Theseus killed the robber Sinis, the *Pityocamptes*: "He bent two tall trees towards one another, fastened a portion of his body to each, then released them, so that each tree, as it swung back into place, took with it the part allotted to it."[24]

These two examples show the lengths to which some writers went in making Alexander follow the example of his heroic predecessors. On other occasions also Alexander is shown following heroic precedents which, if not directly discreditable, were never thought especially worthy of imitation. For example, Plutarch shows him "sulking in his tent" like Achilles, when his troops in India refuse to go any further.[25] It is likely enough that Alexander, with his tremendous enthusiasm for Homer, often thought of himself as re-enacting incidents from the *Iliad*; and his supposed descent from Achilles was no doubt frequently before his mind. He may be partly responsible himself for starting the fashion; with Callisthenes the constant reminiscence of Homer is no doubt intended to please him and flatter him; but in later authors, writing after his death, though ancient critics call it flattery, it would perhaps be more proper to call it romanticism.

Plutarch's narrative offers some reminiscences of Herodotus, and we find Alexander imitating the deeds of Persians as well as Greeks. Philip is supposed to have dreamt that he put a seal on his wife's womb before Alexander was born and that the image engraved on the seal was a lion (*Alex.* 2). To a Greek reader this should recall the dream of the mother of Pericles, as told by Herodotus (6.131)—that she gave birth to a lion. After the capture of Tyre Alexander is supposed to have sent home five hundred talents of incense and a hundred talents of myrrh to his teacher Leonidas, who had once rebuked him for being prodigal with incense when making sacrifice (*Alex.* 25); this recalls the lavish gesture of Datis when, after landing on Delos, he burnt three hundred talents of incense on an altar so as to impress the Delians (Hdt. 6.97.2). Demaratus of Corinth, the old and trusted friend who stood by him when he first sat on the Great King's throne (*Alex.* 37), inevitably recalls the Spartan Demaratus who gave such good advice to Xerxes. It is a little startling when Arrian compares the bridge over the Indus with the bridge of Xerxes over the Hellespont (*Anab.* 5.7.1), because Herodotus had represented Xerxes as defying the forces of nature; and the comparison, though strictly proper,[26] is hardly tactful in its implication that Alexander also may be calling down the nemesis of the gods. There were times when rhetoricians and rhetorical historians showed more learning than good taste in choosing historical parallels for Alexander's feats.

No ancient author reminds us that Alexander's sacrifice to Poseidon when crossing the Hellespont is a parallel to the sacrifice of Xerxes when crossing the bridge, but the details of both occasions are indeed similar; and we are bound to ask whether the resemblance is due to some historian or to a deliberate intention of Alexander to copy the act of Xerxes.[27] So also with Alexander's sacrifice to Athena of Ilium; the Spartan Mindarus had offered sacrifice to her, but so also (according to Herodotus) had Xerxes.[28]

If Alexander could be shown repeating exploits from mythology and history, he could also be made to repeat his own actions. Thus in Quintus Curtius we find him twice ignoring a wound he has received until he is overcome by the pain, and on a different occasion again in Arrian,[29] Quintus Curtius shows him refusing a precious draught of water in Sogdiana, though other authors reserved this incident for the Gedrosian desert;[30] and in Plutarch the magnificent funeral which the king arranges for Hephaestion has a counterpart in the funeral of Demaratus the Corinthian.[31]

Not all the historians of Alexander were professional writers, and only a few are actually known to have studied philosophy or to be trained in the technique of rhetoric. But special training or experience is not necessary to pick up some of the tricks of the literary trade, and a taste for mythological parallels and typical incidents could easily be learnt from fourth-century literature and the recognized older classics. A sure way to appeal to the imagination of Greek readers was to suggest parallels from mythology and early history, to describe the unusual incident of the present by comparing with it the familiar episode from the past; it was a favourite device of Pindar and of the dramatists in their choral odes. And since the story of Alexander was so particularly unusual and remarkable, the recourse to comparison with myth and legend was all the more difficult to resist.

Once the comparison with Achilles is accepted, it inevitably follows that Alexander's battles will include a *monomachia* and that his *aristeia* and his wounds will receive special prominence. Furthermore, as a traveller who penetrates beyond the limits of the known world, he must visit legendary sites and meet with creatures of legend and other fantastic wonders of nature; if he did not he would be a poor successor to the great travellers of legend, Heracles, Dionysus, Odysseus, and Jason; there are even some persons from historical times who cannot be despised as models, Herodotus, for example, and Xenophon, or even the less reputable Ctesias, no less than Xerxes and Cyrus the younger. Hence, like Herodotus, Alexander must be concerned with the sources of the Nile and the gold-digging ants of India.[32] Like Xenophon he will meet with strange and fierce tribesmen in the mountains. Like Ctesias and Herodotus he will learn of curious barbarian customs. His resemblance to Cyrus the younger and the great Persian kings is even less escapable; he marches up-country to challenge the ruling great king and then inherits from Darius the claim to be ruler of all Asia.

It is not denied that many of these parallels are just, and that Alexander was aware of them and in some degree actually influenced by them. But the historians are not content to record Alexander's actual actions or feelings. The story of the meeting with the queen of the Amazons provides a good example. It may well be that the Greek tradition of the Amazons originated with some actual historical tribe in Anatolia whose women were trained like warriors; and it is not beyond the bounds of possibility that some surviving offshoot of this tribe was encountered by Alexander's expedition at some point in its progress through Asia. This does not mean, however, that Alexander seriously pictured himself as re-enacting the exploits of Heracles against the Amazons or that the story told of his meeting with their queen bears even a remote resemblance to anything that really happened. This is an extreme case. But there are other occasions when we are uncertain whether the historians are trying to relate anything like the facts, as in the story of the Gordian knot or the account of the journey to the oasis of Siwa to consult the oracle of Ammon. At what point are we to say, "Here they cease to be conscientious and here they cease to believe what they are writing?" It is not always easy to answer these questions in dealing with Greek historians, not even with Herodotus whose text we possess complete.[33] Arrian declined to answer them, except in so far as Aristobulus and Ptolemy were concerned, and we cannot hope to answer very confidently on the evidence of mere fragments. The attempt must be made, however, but it will be limited to two aspects of the story: the geographical interpretation and the characterization of Alexander himself.

If Alexander was to be "lord of all Asia" it was to be expected that he should reach the furthest limits of the continent on his expedition; and if he was to be "conqueror of the world" he must reach the four corners of the *oikoumene*. In terms of fourth-century geography these four corners were represented by four peoples: to the northwest by the Celts, to the southwest by the Ethiopians, to the northeast by the Scythians, and to the southeast by the Indians. Ephorus had outlined the shape of the inhabited world by showing it framed on its four sides by these four peoples,[34] and it is noteworthy that the historians of Alexander made no effort to revolutionize geographical knowledge; their object, on the whole, was to make new discoveries harmonize with what was known and believed. For them, as convention dictated, the River Tanais (Don) divided Asia from Europe[35] just as surely as the Hellespont; these two water boundaries represent the northeast[36] and the northwest corners of Asia, and whoever controls the line connecting them controls the northern frontier of the continent. The eastern frontier can be defined only when the southeast corner is identified and this, as we shall see, is to be the Indus. The southwest corner was a debatable point, since one might treat Libya either as a third continent or as part of Asia (the older geographers counted only two continents, Europe and Asia, not three); but the combination of the Nile and the western desert made quite a good frontier, especially when it was discovered that the lower Indus, like the Nile, had a desert on its left flank.

Three corners of Asia, then, Alexander certainly reached—the Hellespont, the Nile, and the Indus. In the northwest he did even better, since he reached the northwestern corner of the entire civilized world when he made contact with the Celts on the Danube. Any claim that he controlled the western frontier of the Greek world (or the civilized world) is of course completely artificial; but he could formally claim to control the northern frontier of the Greek world—the Danube. So far as Asia was concerned, the only difficulty lay in the northeast, because Alexander never reached the River Don and could not therefore even formally claim to control the northern frontier of Asia. The only ruler who came near to controlling this line from the Hellespont to the Don was the great Mithridates of Pontus; and when Pompey conquered him Pompey's historians were ready to find in him a worthy successor of Alexander.[37]

Alexander's progress to the northeast came to a halt at the River Jaxartes (Syr Darya). But we find the view widely expressed among his historians that this river was in fact the Tanais (Don).[38] This identification was a brilliant solution of their difficulties as "flatterers" of Alexander. It justified his turning back at this point, because it represented this river (beyond which dwelt the Scythians) as the logical limit of conquest in this direction. Beyond this river, they could claim, was the mysterious northern Europe, land of Scythians and Celts, bounded by the Tanais, the Danube, and (if one chose to believe in it) the northern ocean.

The historians of Alexander were not geographers and it was not part of their task to explain how the Caspian Sea and the northern ocean fitted in with this scheme. Strabo, who believed the Caspian Sea was a gulf of the northern ocean, was bound to ridicule their scheme, because such a gulf of the ocean would make it impossible for their "Tanais" ever to reach the Palus Maeotis (Sea of Azov). One historian, Polycleitus, made an effort to include the Caspian in his geographical scheme by arguing that it was really a branch of the Palus Maeotis.[39] But generally, one suspects, the historians were prepared to leave the details of the solution to scientists.

Since Alexander turned back at the Riger Beas in India and gave up the idea of extending his dominion beyond the Punjab, the historians had to explain that the Indus, with its tributaries, offered just as satisfactory a boundary on the southeast as the Jaxartes on the northeast. There was some talk of identifying the Indus with the Nile and we are told that Alexander himself at one time shared this view[40] (whether he really thought so is another matter altogether); but when the expedition reached the mouth of the Indus, this theory had to be abandoned. If then the Indus could not be regarded as a boundary between Asia and Africa (like the Nile) or between Asia and Europe (like the Jaxartes), the alternative was to regard the land beyond the Indus as a new continent—a continent where it was too hot for anyone except specially adapted people to live, just as it was too cold beyond the Jaxartes. Thus both rivers could be regarded as boundaries of the habitable world.[41]

Once this attitude was adopted, it was no longer necessary to identify the Jaxartes with the Tanais, and some of the more cautious writers (like Aristobulus) evidently abandoned this identification;[42] there could be a No Man's Land, neither Asia nor Europe, between Jaxartes and Tanais just as well as between Indus and Nile; and it would not matter if some or most of the area was taken up by water, by the Arabian Sea in the south and the Caspian Sea (which might be a "gulf of the ocean") in the north.

It remained, however, to find some proof that the Indus was the boundary of the normally habitable world, that the country beyond was not a "white man's country." It was desirable that Alexander should reach the tropic of Cancer in India, and so we find Onesicritus asserting that he did so, while Nearchus claimed to have made observations on his voyages which proved not only that he had crossed the tropic but that he had actually crossed the equator.[43] Nearchus, as will appear later, had a model of his own, whose record as an explorer he wanted to equal—Scylax of Caryanda;[44] and his so-called "observations," like some of Alexander's feats, are to be explained in part by an ambition to be worthy of his predecessor. In fact, Alexander did not reach the tropic in India, and if a well had been dug on the banks of the Indus, like the famous well at Syene, in the hope of proving that the sun really was directly overhead at midday, the inconvenient truth would have been discovered. But the truth, though it may have been suspected, never finds expression in any historian of Alexander; and among all the lies of which later critics complain, this particular one is never denounced. What is more important, there is no sign of any historian rejecting the assumption which made these geographical opinions necessary.[45] It seems to have been axiomatic for all of them that Alexander conquered the whole of Asia and reached its northeastern corner as well as its southeastern limit. It makes little difference whether we regard this axiom as forced upon them by public opinion or gratefully accepted because it enhanced the story which they had to tell. Arrian confidently talks of writers after the death of Alexander as having no incentive to relate things otherwise than as they really happened.

He makes the mistake (pardonable perhaps in the Roman world)[46] of treating these historians as though they were politicians seeking advancement; their incentive was the hope of pleasing their readers by telling a good story; they could not do this if they whittled down Alexander's achievements, and so they accepted the conventional pattern of the story.

In interpreting the character of Alexander, however, they took greater liberty. Here it is a great mistake to think simply in terms of favourable or unfavourable characterization, as though all the historians were propagandists of one kind or another, determined to flatter Alexander or to vilify him.[47] Callisthenes, as his public relations officer, certainly had a special responsibility to glorify Alexander, and Ephippus set out to compose a hostile pamphlet, which may have been intended to rouse bitterness against Macedonia at the time of the Lamian War; such at least is a reasonable inference from his fragments, which show that he laid special emphasis on Alexander's extravagance and self-indulgence, his heavy drinking and his affectation of oriental magnificence.[48] Strictly speaking, however, even such behaviour on Alexander's part, objectionable though it might be to many persons, does not demand an unfavourable verdict on his character, if his portrait is conceived in heroic terms. Heracles was known to be a heavy drinker and Dionysus was notoriously effeminate; and just as we cannot call the *Frogs* of Aristophanes an attack on these gods, so we cannot agree that every writer who describes these weaknesses or eccentricities of Alexander is deliberately attacking him.

If we believe that many of the historians were aiming at a heroic scale of portraiture, we must not insist that they were also trying to be analytic biographers. And we have no right to conclude that any writer offered a sort of Euripidean portrait of the hero—least of all can we argue that Ptolemy gave such a portrait, when the fragments seem to show on the contrary that he avoided explanation and interpretation. There were some ugly incidents in Alexander's story, which were too well known to be suppressed but could not be explained as illustrations of Alexander's character without elaborate psychological complications: for example, the deaths of Cleitus and Parmenion. No one who was sufficiently interested to write a history of Alexander would have been content to agree that he was a bloodthirsty and treacherous tyrant. There were different opinions about the external details of these incidents; but the different versions do not imply different interpretations of Alexander's character; in all of them a large share of the blame rests with Alexander.[49] No matter how the story of Cleitus' death was told, it left the reader with the feeling that there was a strain of violence or even of savage cruelty in the king. But unless the evidence of the fragments is misleading, it was left to the reader to decide whether his wild outburst of rage was typical or exceptional behaviour.

Some writers, especially those who had known Alexander personally, were able to illustrate certain aspects of his personality. Nearchus showed his kindness and concern for his friends, Onesicritus his philosophical interests, Ptolemy his military genius. But who offered a reasoned comprehensive interpretation of his character? The fragments give no answer to this question. When Arrian tries to sum up Alexander's character at the end of his *Anabasis,* he falls back on the pattern which Xenophon had used in describing Cyrus;[50] he does not attempt to compare one source with another or one verdict with another, but simply offers his own opinions, clearly meaning us to believe that they are his own opinions, not borrowed from anyone else. Nor does he ever indicate that there was a conventional portrait of Alexander, against which he wishes to rebel. It cannot therefore be shown that there were axioms which early writers followed in characterizing Alexander, comparable to those which they followed in describing his deeds.

We may go further than this and ask whether it was likely that the first historians of Alexander would attempt a serious study of his character, in view of their apparent literary tastes and training and the prevalent conventions of their time. When they set out to write a historical work which revolved about a central dominant figure, there were two famous authors of the fourth century whose influence the historians of Alexander could not escape—Xenophon and Theopompus. Xenophon tried to offer a consistent and intelligible picture of Cyrus in his *Anabasis* and he gave admirable and striking character sketches of the Greek generals as well. Xenophon's work (whether the *Anabasis* or the *Cyropaedeia*) is known to have provided a model for Onesicritus,[51] who was a man with some philosophical training and interests. But the *Philippica* of Theopompus was more likely to appeal to writers of rhetorical taste and training. Theopompus was without question one of the leading literary figures in Greece when Alexander set out on his expedition. He was apparently a man who made enemies; there is the tale of his quarrel with Anaximenes; he was expelled from his native Chios, until restored by Alexander's order, and after Alexander's death was apparently unable to find a welcome in any country.[52] His generally rhetorical character, his violent manner of writing, his taste for abusive characterization, and his love of long digressions are well illustrated by the fragments and are too well known to need further discussion here. It is his treatment of Philip in the *Philippica* which concerns us. "Theopompus," says Polybius, "at the beginning of his history of Philip writes that he was driven to take up this work because Europe had never produced a man anything like Philip, the son of Amyntas; then on the top of this, not only in his preface but all through his narrative he shows Philip devoid of all restraints in his dealings with women (so much so that he might have ruined his entire family by his weakness for them and his promiscuous behaviour), completely unscrupulous and dishonest in his treatment of friends and allies, a man who cheated and enslaved numerous cities by underhand methods and violence, and a habitual toper of strong drink whom his friends frequently found drunk in broad daylight."[53]

There are plenty of quotations from the *Philippica* which show that Polybius is not overstating his case.[54] Polybius felt that this inconsistency in characterization was quite inexcusable, that it betrayed levity of mind and immaturity in an author if he was prepared to contradict himself so plainly that everyone could see he must be telling some deliberate lies (8.11[13].2). The criticism of Polybius is really a general criticism of the rhetorical style of history, of which Theopompus is the most famous exponent in the fourth century. This was a type of historical writing in which it was recognized that the author could tell lies for the sake of effect. Among the historians of Alexander Cleitarchus has a similar reputation,[55] and his familiarity with the work of Theopompus is plain to see. He found the story of Harpalus and Glycera ready made for him in Theopompus;[56] like Theopompus he found opportunities for historical digressions and novel treatment of incidents from earlier times; for example, he found the opportunity to bring in some account of Themistocles, in which he contradicted the established version of Thucydides. This was quite in the manner of Theopompus, who made a point of 'debunking' great men, representing Eubulus as dissolute and, stranger still, picturing Lysander as a man of great self-control and no vices.[57] A competent rhetorician was trained to speak on both sides of any question. When Callisthenes, after delivering an eloquent panegyric of the Macedonians before a court gathering, was invited to show his skill by delivering an indictment of them, he did so very willingly, never thinking apparently that the Macedonians present would take offence at such a *tour de force* (Plut. *Alex.* 53). So also Theopompus is recorded to have written both an encomium and a ψόγος of Alexander.[58]

If resourcefulness, rather than consistency in characterization, is the mark of a rhetorical historian, and if Theopompus set the example by abusing Philip and Alexander just as extravagantly as he praised them, it is indeed no wonder that the rhetorical historians of Alexander failed to satisfy Polybius, whose standards were generally quite like our own. But if ambitious writers like Callisthenes and Cleitarchus and professional rhetoricians like Anaximenes and Hegesias failed to paint a convincing portrait, what are we to expect of those writers who are not strictly professional literary men at all—of Ptolemy, the experienced military commander and administrator, of Nearchus the sea-captain, of Aristobulus the technical staff officer, and of Chares the official who arranged audiences at court?

We must in fact not expect from them any attempt at a general characterization of Alexander. There is no hint of it in their fragments; this must mean that, even if they offered full-scale portraits, their interpretations were not thought sufficiently interesting to be quoted by any later writer. They recorded their own adventures and what they observed themselves from their meetings with Alexander—their own impressions, which are indeed most valuable and interesting, but must not be mistaken for comprehensive judgments. It is likely, therefore, that different writers illustrated different sides of Alexander's personality; each writer had a different personal story to tell and it was his personal part in the expedition which gave him his excuse for writing. Just as their personal impressions might have been supplemented by a comprehensive study of his character, so their individual stories could be told in relation to the whole story of the expedition. But it does not follow that all of them took the opportunity of describing the expedition from beginning to end; Nearchus and Chares certainly did not, and Onesicritus perhaps did not pay much attention to the early stages.

Not all the works known to have been published within fifty years of Alexander's death can be dated with confidence. Ptolemy and Aristobulus did not publish their accounts until about 285 B.C., but it is certain that most of the personal stories had been in circulation for many years by that time; the work of Nearchus is generally dated about 310 or earlier, and Onesicritus evidently wrote before him. It has been widely believed that Cleitarchus wrote before the end of the century, but (as will be shown later) there are good reasons for supposing that he wrote after Aristobulus and Ptolemy, not before them. In any case it is most unlikely that he took part in the expedition, any more than Anaximenes did, since nothing is recorded of any part that either of them played. It follows, then, that except for the unfinished work of Callisthenes no comprehensive account of the expedition was written by an eye-witness who knew Alexander personally until Aristobulus and Ptolemy offered their versions, nearly forty years after his death. The fragments of earlier writers show that certain conventions about the story of the expedition had crystallized long before this time, despite numerous differences in detail and the refusal of some writers to accept some of the more fantastic incidents, like the meeting with the Amazon. But the interpretation of Alexander's character had not apparently kept pace with the concrete story of his adventures, and this is one of the reasons why it still remains a problem for the modern historian.

It is hardly profitable to carry this discussion any further without detailed critical examination of the fragments. But it seems worth while to ask at this stage why it was that Cleitarchus was so widely read and so popular in later times. His popularity must be admitted even by those who do not agree that he is the main source of Diodorus and Quintus Curtius. It is not sufficient explanation to say that the reading public in Hellenistic and Roman times delighted in rhetoric and bombast and often showed deplorable taste and very little discrimination. The writers who complain of the public's uncritical taste in this matter never suggest any better history of Alexander than that of Cleitarchus until Arrian introduces his readers to Ptolemy and Aristobulus, and tries to base his interpretation of Alexander on their sober factual accounts; but he makes it clear enough that these writers lacked the quality which the public admired in Cleitarchus—the ability to dramatize Alexander. It is likely that Theopompus was a more popular author than Thucydides in Hellenistic and Roman times; but he was not able to undermine the public's faith in the historical characters depicted by Thucydides; the Pericles, the Cleon, the Nicias of a later age are the men with whom we are familiar from the pages of Thucydides. Obviously Cleitarchus would not have succeeded so well if he had been preceded by some historian of real Thucydidean quality. But we can go further than that and explain his success by the failure of Alexander's contemporaries to offer a convincing interpretation of his character. Whether their failure was due entirely to their shortcomings as literary artists may perhaps be disputed by those who regard Alexander as a kind of superman, a "Titan" whom no contemporary could possibly inderstand. But whatever the reason for it, their failure goes far to explain why later ages were content with such a strange mixture of the heroic and the grotesque.

Notes

1. *Alex.* 1. For Plutarch's idea of biography see F. Leo, *Die griechisch-römische Biographie* (Leipzig 1901), esp. 146-49, 18-90.

2. It has been argued, therefore, that the selection was largely already made for him by some earlier writer. Cf. J. E. Powell, "The Sources of Plutarch's *Alexander,*" *JHS* 59 (1939) 229-40. This is not the proper place to discuss this view and it cannot be discussed at all until the attempt has been made to reconstruct the primary sources. But some compromise is possible between two extreme points of view; one need not believe that Plutarch knew the work of every author whose work he

quotes at first hand, but it is not necessary to believe that he took everything from an intermediary, and from one intermediary at that.

3. Cf. Hdt. 7.152.3; Thuc. 1.22.

4. Arr. *Anab.* 7.25.1—26.3; Plut. *Alex.* 76.

5. Arr. *Anab.* 7.27.1-3; Plut. *Alex.* 75.

6. "The Diary and the Letters of Alexander," *Historia* 3 (1955) 429-55.

7. *Alex.* 17; cf. *De Alex. fort.* 2.341c.

8. *Alex.* 42; cf. 39, 41.

9. Cf. L. Pearson, "Thucydides as Reporter and Critic," *TAPA* 78 (1947) 37-60.

10. E.g. Polyb. 12.12b; Strabo 11.7.4, 15.1.28, 17.1.43; Arr. *Anab.* 6.11.2-8; Plut. *Alex.* 75.

11. Greek writers were apparently not aware of the extent to which history was falsified in the Oriental empires in order to please or glorify a royal patron. The Greek tyrants seem not to have encouraged any such practice (though they naturally resented hostile criticism); and modern readers will not easily believe that Herodotus expected any concrete reward for "flattering" Athens or "favouring" the Alcmaeonidae, even if it is true that he received an enormous fee for a lecture in Athens.

12. See [Pearson, Lionel. *The Lost Histories of Alexander the Great.* Oxford: American Philological Association/B. H. Blackwell, 1960], Chap. II note 8.

13. See [Pearson, 1960], Chap. II 36-38.

14. Tarn wants to dismiss the work of Onesicritus as a "professed romance" (*Alex.* II 35); we must remember that romantic fiction in the fourth century, as in Xenophon's *Cyropaedeia,* sought to glorify its hero; fiction in later times about Alexander is less scrupulous (see [Pearson, 1960], Chaps. VIII and IX).

15. Tarn, *Alex.* I 125.

16. Chap. III section ii.

17. Cf. especially J. Stroux, "Die stoische Beurteilung Alexanders des Grossen," *Philologus* 88 (1933) 222-40.

18. Cf. e.g. R. B. Steele, "Quintus Curtius Rufus," *AJP* 36 (1915) 402-23.

19. By "fragments" whenever the term is used in this book are meant both *Fragmenta* (i.e. quotations) and *Testimonia* (i.e. criticism and remarks about a man or his work).

20. Hdt. 7.128. Legrand, note *ad loc.* (Budé ed.), thinks that the visit of Xerxes to Tempe was probably a military reconnaissance, not a mere pleasure excursion.

21. Cf. H. U. Instinsky, *Alexander der Grosse am Hellespont* (Godesberg 1949).

22. Especially pp. 41-45.

23. *De comp. verb.* 18. Cf. also Tarn, *Alex.* II Appendix 11.

24. Plut. *Alex.* 43. For Sinis see Apollodorus, *Bibl.* 3.16.2 and Frazer's note in the Loeb ed. (where this passage from Plutarch is not quoted).

25. *Alex.* 62. Cf. Arr. *Anab.* 7.16.8, where Alexander is represented as grieving for Hephaestion, as Achilles did for Patroclus (like Achilles, Arrian thinks, he would rather have died before his friend), and Q. Curt. 9.4.14: Cum amni bellum fuisse crederes.

26. Both kings are building bridges between continents, since India beyond the Indus was felt to be no longer Asia but another continent. See [Pearson, 1960], 15.

27. Cf. Arr. *Anab.* 1.11.6 with Hdt. 7.54. Instinsky (above, note 21) 46-53 thinks that Alexander did in fact imitate the sacrifice of Xerxes, and that this shows Alexander's knowledge of Herodotus.

28. Arr. *Anab.* 1.11.7; Plut. *Alex.* 15; Diod. 17.18.1; Xen. *Hell.* 1.1.4 (Mindarus); Hdt. 7.43.

29. Q. Curt. 4.6.17-20, 8.10.27-30; Arr. *Anab.* 6.10.2.

30. Q. Curt. 7.5.10-12; Arr. *Anab.* 6.26.1-3.

31. *Alex.* 56, 72. Cf. also the two Bacchanalian processions in Nysa and Carmania (Q. Curt. 8.10.15-18), and the incident of a man sitting on the king's throne on two separate occasions (Q. Curt. 8.4.15-17; Arr. *Anab.* 7.24.1-3).

32. It is Nearchus, a man of quite limited literary accomplishments, who reminds us of this. Cf. [Pearson, 1960], Chap. V 118-25.

33. Cf. L. Pearson, "Credulity and Scepticism in Herodotus," *TAPA* 72 (1941) 335-55.

34. Ephorus F.30 (*FGrHist* IIA, no. 70).

35. Cf. e.g. Strabo 11.7.4, and Jupiter's definition of Asia in Valerius Flaccus, *Argon.* 1.537-38:

> regio quae virginis aequor ad Helles
> et Tanain tenus immenso descendit ab Euro.

36. If the Don is to mark the NE edge of Asia, it must be imagined as rising in some mountain range that blocks further progress to the NE. The modern reader should remember that the ancient geographers regarded Europe (except the Mediterranean region) not as west of Asia but as north of it—and if on the NW, why not also on the NE?

37. Theophanes of Mytilene, Pompey's chief historian (see the fragments in *FGrHist* IIB, no. 188), was familiar with the work of Alexander's historians.

38. Strabo 11.7.4. The identification is still taken for granted in Plut. *De Alex. fort.* 2. 335E, 341C, which shows how firmly it must have been established as part of the pattern of panegyric.

39. Cf. [Pearson, 1960], Chap. III section iv, and my more detailed discussion in *CQ* n.s. 1 (1951) 80-84.

40. Nearchus F.20 = Strabo 15.1.25.

41. This view comes out most clearly in Onesicritus (see Chap. IV, [Pearson, 1960]).

42. See [Pearson, 1960], Chap. VI 163.

43. Onesicritus F.9 = Pliny, *N.H.* 2.183; Arr. *Ind.* 25.4-6.

44. See [Pearson, 1960], Chap. V 140-41.

45. Strabo of course rejected it without hesitation (11.7.4).

46. Cf. Tac. *Agr.* 1.

47. This is a serious weakness in the study of W. Hoffmann, *Das literarische Porträt Alex. des Grossen.*

48. Cf. [Pearson, 1960], Chap. III section iii.

49. Cf. [Pearson, 1960], Chap. VI 169-70.

50. Arr. *Anab.* 7.28-29; Xen. *Anab.* 1.9.

51. Cf. [Pearson, 1960], Chap. IV 87-92.

52. *FGrHist* IIB, no. 115, T.2, 10.

53. F.27 = Polyb. 8.9(11).1. For discussion of Theopompus see A. Momigliano, *RFIC* 59 (1931) 230-42, 335-53. Gilbert Murray's attempt to portray him as a Cynic historian is not very convincing (*Greek Studies* [Oxford 1946] 149-70).

54. E.g. F.81, 224 = Ath. 6.259F-260A, 4.166F-167C.

55. Cf. Cic. *Brut.* 42.

56. Cleitarchus F.30 = Ath. 13 586C-D.

57. Cleitarchus F.33 and 34; Theopompus F.100 and 20; and for his digressions in general see T.20, 30, 31.

58. T.8, F.255 = Suidas s.v. Ἔφορος; Theon, *Prog.* 2.

List of Abbreviations

AJP = *American Journal of Philology.*

CQ = *Classical Quarterly.*

FGrHist = *Die Fragmente der griechischen Historiker* (ed. Jacoby).

JHS = *Journal of Hellenic Studies.*

TAPA = *Transactions of the American Philological Association.*

J. R. Hamilton (essay date 1969)

SOURCE: Hamilton, J. R. Introduction to *Plutarch: Alexander—A Commentary*, pp. xiii-lxix. Oxford: Clarendon Press, 1969.

[*In the following essay, Hamilton examines two speeches that Plutarch wrote in the guise of Alexander—intended to persuade his audience that the latter was a "philosopher in action."*]

I. PLUTARCH OF CHAERONEIA[1]

LIFE[2]

Plutarch was born about 45[3] in the small town of Chaeroneia in western Boeotia, where Philip had defeated the Greek states in 338 B.C. (*Alex.* 9) and Sulla routed Mithridates' general, Archelaus, in 86 B.C. (*Sull.* 16 ff.). His family, evidently well-to-do,[4] had resided there for generations, and his great-grandfather, Nicarchus, could recall Antony's exactions during the campaign of Actium (*Ant.* 68. 7). His grandfather, Lamprias, a witty and cultured man, survived to appear as a lively conversationalist in the *Quaestiones convivales.*[5] Plutarch never mentions his mother,[6] but his father, probably called Autobulus,[7] figures in several of the dialogues,[8] and Plutarch recalls that when as a young man he had been prominent in an embassy to the Roman governor of Achaea his father gave him the sound advice not to seek to eclipse his fellow-ambassadors in his report to the Council (*Mor.* 816 d). Plutarch had at least two brothers, Timon,[9] to whose character he pays a warm tribute (487 d), and the more versatile Lamprias, whose interests embraced cooking, dancing, etymology, and philosophy, and who was priest at Lebadeia.[10] Plutarch's concern with ethical questions and his passion for study—reinforced by his later philosophical training—surely owed much to his family background.[11]

Plutarch married Timoxena, the daughter of a local magnate, Alexion (701 d), perhaps in the early seventies.[12] The marriage was evidently a happy one; the moving letter of consolation (608 b-612 b) which Plutarch addressed to her on the death of their daughter Timoxena reveals her as a devoted wife and mother and a good housewife. Of her intellectual qualities we know only that she wrote a short treatise on *Love of Orna-*

ment to a certain Aristylla (145 a). They had at least four children apart from Timoxena—Chaeron, who lived only a few years (609 d), Soclarus, who probably died in his teens,[13] and Autobulus and Plutarchus, who both reached manhood. Their interest in philosophy is shown (if it is not a dialogue convention) by their request to their father to explain Plato's teaching on the soul—the result is the *De animae procreatione in Timaeo* (1012 a-1030 c)—and by the prominence of Autobulus in the *Amatorius* (748 e-771 e).

At the age of about twenty Plutarch proceeded to Athens, famous as a 'university city'. There he presumably attended, like other well-to-do young men of his time, the classes of the famous sophists and philosophers, although of his teachers he mentions only the Egyptian philosopher, Ammonius.[14] Plutarch says nothing of his rhetorical studies and later expresses dislike of the excesses of rhetoric (below . . .), but he undoubtedly received a thorough training, and several of his early rhetorical treatises survive, including two dealing with the *Fortune of Alexander* (Section II, below). He declares his passion for mathematics (387 f), and his writings reveal some knowledge of physics, natural science, and medicine, but it was philosophy that particularly interested him.

In his early life Plutarch doubtless travelled widely, as did most young men of his class, to further his education. Later we know of visits to Tanagra (608 b), Helicon (749 b), Hyampolis in Phocis (660 d), Patrae (629 f), Aedepsus and Chalcis in Euboea (667 c, *Flam.* 16. 5), Eleusis (635 a), and Sparta (*Lyc.* 18. 2, *Ages.* 19. 10 f.). We may be sure that he made many visits to Athens, of which he became an honorary citizen and was enrolled in the tribe Leontis (628 a). He appears to have visited Asia (501 e) and certainly paid a visit early in life to Alexandria. More important were his journeys to Rome and Italy. Plutarch was probably in Rome in the late seventies (973 e ff.), and he was certainly there in the latter part of Domitian's reign (*Public.* 15. 3-6; cf. 522 d). He may, of course, have paid other visits to Rome, but the old view (not yet dead) that he spent some fifteen or twenty years there is certainly wrong; the fact that Plutarch never mastered the finer points of Latin, as he himself admits, tends to disprove it.[15] In Rome he made lasting friendships with many distinguished Romans,[16] notably L. Mestrius Florus, the friend of Vespasian (Suet. *Vesp.* 22) to whom Plutarch owed the Roman citizenship and whose *nomen* he adopted (*SIG* 829 a, Μεστρίου Πλουτάρχου; cf. 844 a), and Q. Sosius Senecio, the friend of Trajan and twice consul, to whom he dedicated the *Quaestiones convivales* and (probably) the *Parallel Lives.*[17]

However, a sense of duty, as he tells us (*Dem.* 2. 2), led Plutarch to spend most of his life in his native Chaeroneia, although so small a place could provide neither a good library nor the opportunity for an important political career. There Plutarch founded a school, in which members of his family and his many pupils and friends discussed a variety of philosophical, theological, and scientific problems. These discussions were set down by Plutarch, mainly after 96, in what are loosely but conveniently called his *Moralia* or *Moral Essays,* and during this period he also composed his *Parallel Lives.*[18] In spite of his substantial literary output Plutarch found time to take an active part in the religious and political life of the district.

Despite Plutarch's silence we may reasonably suppose, in view of his standing in the town and his interest in religious matters, that he held a priesthood at Chaeroneia.[19] Certainly he held one of the two life priesthoods of Apollo at Delphi,[20] where during the reigns of Trajan and Hadrian the oracle experienced a considerable revival of prosperity and many new buildings were erected (*RE* 4, 2579 f.). For this revival Plutarch was largely responsible; doubtless he used his influence with Sosius Senecio and other leading Romans to secure imperial favour.[21] At Chaeroneia Plutarch held the office of eponymous archon (642 f., 694 a), but he did not hesitate to perform the duties of a minor magistrate (811 b-c). As *epimeletes* of the Amphictyonic League he was responsible for setting up a statue to the emperor Hadrian in the early years of his reign (*SIG* 829 a), and if, as seems likely, Plutarch refers to himself at *Mor.* 785 c, he was a member of the Federal Council of Boeotia (Boeotarch), President of the Pythian Games (*agonothetes*), and enjoyed the privilege of a front seat at meetings of the Amphictyons (*proedria*).[22] There is no reason to question Suidas' statement that Trajan conferred on Plutarch the consular insignia, an honour sometimes granted to distinguished Greeks from the beginning of the second century A.D.,[23] but we need not believe him when he goes on to say that Trajan ordered that no magistrate in *Illyria* should act without Plutarch's approval.[24] Eusebius states, credibly enough, that Hadrian appointed Plutarch in his old age (in 119/20) ἐπιτροπεύειν Ἑλλάδος, by which he probably means that Plutarch became an imperial procurator (*epitropos*).[25]

The exact date of Plutarch's death is unknown, but there is good reason to suppose that he did not live much beyond 120. The omission of his name from Ps.-Lucian's *Macrobioi* suggests that he died before reaching the age of 80, and a piece of evidence, whose importance was first realized by Jones, is almost conclusive. He points out that it is virtually certain that it was as senior priest of Apollo that Plutarch dedicated the statue of Hadrian (*SIG* 829 a) and that when a similar statue was dedicated by the Amphictyons in 125 this was done not by Plutarch but by a certain T. Flavius Aristotimus (*SIG* 835 b). It follows that, unless the

Amphictyons had changed their practice in the interval, Plutarch had died and Aristotimus had become senior priest.

Plutarch was honoured, presumably after his death, by the citizens of Delphi and Chaeroneia, who set up a marble herm in accordance with a decree of the Amphictyons (*SIG* 843 a). His family continued to reside in Chaeroneia until at least the middle of the third century (*SIG* 845), and more than one of his descendants shared his interest in philosophy (*SIG* 844, 845).

THE POLITICAL AND CULTURAL BACKGROUND

The 'freedom' of the Greeks proclaimed by Nero at Corinth in November 67 was soon revoked by Vespasian.[26] Apart from this brief interlude (and the years 15-44 when it was under imperial jurisdiction) Greece had since 27 B.C. been a senatorial province governed by a proconsul of praetorian rank stationed at Corinth.

This fact dominated Plutarch's political outlook.[27] The Greek statesman, he writes, should always remember not only that he governs free men but also that he is a subject in a state ruled by Caesar's proconsul, whose power is supreme (813 d, 824 e). Plutarch's undoubted patriotism[28] did not blind him to the fact that the age of a free Greece had gone beyond recall; when he writes of the great figures of the past, of Pericles or Phocion or Demosthenes, he does not dream that the situation of the fifth and fourth centuries B.C. can be restored. Intelligent men, he holds, should admit the weakness of Greece,[29] they should make the best of it and live in peace and concord (825 a). Plutarch lists (824 c) the greatest benefits a city can enjoy: peace, freedom, good crops, a large population, and concord. Of these peace is assured by Roman rule,[30] the emperors have given the people as much liberty as is good for them, plenty and abundance of men must be prayed for: the major task facing a magistrate is the prevention of *stasis*. Indeed Plutarch lays great stress on the need to avoid a situation which will bring about Roman intervention. Magistrates who urge the people to emulate the warlike achievements of their ancestors harm their country and expose themselves to the danger of execution or exile; the glories of Marathon, Plataea, and the Eurymedon are topics best left to the sophists.[31] On the other hand he deprecates excessive dependence on the Romans; too often magistrates refer every decision, great or small, to the Roman authorities. What Greeks should aim at in his view is a proper balance between unbecoming subservience and dangerous independence.

The leading Romans, Plutarch maintains, were very eager to assist their friends in their political endeavours, and it was the duty of a patriotic Greek to co-operate with them; by this means the advancement of Greece could best be secured.[32] This advice clearly reflects Plutarch's own experience, and the results of such co-operation are evident in the revival of Delphi (above). Plutarch correctly assesses the Roman attitude. The emperors sought good government in the provinces—there was, after all, no profit in bad—but above all they sought stability. This they obtained not by military force, or even by the threat of military force (even the neighbouring province of Macedonia had no garrison), but by their support of the leading Greeks in the various cities. This patron-client relationship, of advantage to both sides, was no less vigorous under the Principate than it had been under the Republic,[33] and Roman intervention was seldom required except when the financial distress of the cities led to the sending of *correctores*.[34] In his *Praecepta* Plutarch defends the democratic ideal and clearly regards himself as living in a democracy; but it was a democracy, as he was well aware, very different from that of fifth-century Athens. The cities were ruled by the Councils, whose members were drawn from the small number of wealthy citizens, men like Plutarch himself.[35] Even if Plutarch does not exaggerate the importance of public opinion, as we may suspect, the assemblies evidently possessed little importance, and we hear little of them.

Despite his admiration for Roman society and his consciousness of Rome's achievements, Plutarch has no time for those Greeks who seek 'gainful commissions and the administration of provinces', i.e. for those who embark upon a career in the imperial civil service and turn their back on domestic affairs.[36] His outlook was national (or 'provincial') rather than imperial, and he felt that such men were lost to Greece. The local magistrate, in his view, had a real and important contribution to make to the life of Greece, to maintain the proper relation between the local administration and the central authority. The acceptance of an imperial procuratorship in his later years does not indicate a change of heart. An imperial request might be difficult to refuse, and in any case he was working in Greece; nor need his post have interfered to any great extent with his writing or with his civil and religious duties at Chaeroneia and Delphi. Plutarch's political outlook was clearsighted and realistic, even if it was perhaps easier for him than for some of his contemporaries to accept this rather restricted political horizon. He had no consuming political ambitions, and despite his conviction that a man ought to play his part in political life it is likely that he felt he could make a greater contribution to Greece as an educator.

Plutarch's 'school' at Chaeroneia was organized, predictably, on the pattern of the Academy, and instruction was given by means of formal lectures, dialogues, and symposia. A great variety of topics (ethical, political, scientific, theological, and psychological) was discussed, but the greatest importance was attached to ethics—for Plutarch, as for the majority of his contemporaries, the most essential part of philosophy.

Even Plutarch's admirers have seldom failed to remark that he was not an original thinker with original theories of his own to propound. Tucker[37] puts it thus: 'To his generation he served as a milch-cow of practical philosophy on the ethical side. He browsed on literature and thought, secreted the most valuable constituents, and yielded the cream to his readers or hearers.' He is representative of contemporary culture, not in advance of it, and as such his writings are valuable evidence for that culture. The extent of Plutarch's reading in philosophy, as in other subjects, is impressive. He was evidently familiar with the writings of many of the pre-Socratics,[38] and had a thorough knowledge of the teachings of the four major schools—the Academy, the Peripatetic, the Stoic, and the Epicurean. Although he did not adhere consistently to the tenets of any one school—like that other great humanist, Cicero, he was an eclectic and, like him, he often asserts the right of the philosopher to withhold assent—he probably thought of himself as a Platonist. Certainly for him the 'divine' Plato was the supreme philosopher (cf. 90 c, 700 b), and quotations from his works appear in most of Plutarch's writings, some 650 times in all.[39] Clearly the *Moralia* owe much to the dialogues of Plato, although Plutarch normally eschews the Socratic dialectic, and the use of myth is inspired by Plato. At the close of the *De sera numinis vindicta,* for example, the myth of Er is obviously his model. Nor did Plutarch neglect Plato's metaphysics, although it appears from the *De animae procreatione in Timaeo* that he did not always understand them. But it is no accident that the *Republic* and *Laws* are largely drawn upon; Plutarch was doubtless attracted by Plato's view that the philosopher should concern himself with the good of the state and its citizens. For he had no patience with philosophers who sought to live in an 'ivory tower', as his criticism of the Epicureans shows (below). On some questions Plutarch did not accept Plato's views. In the *Amatorius,* for instance, he refuses to concede that homosexual love is superior to that between man and woman,[40] while in the *De audiendis poetis* he adopts Aristotle's position that moral improvement should be sought through the charm of poetry in preference to Plato's prohibition of its teaching. But in most fundamental matters Plutarch sided with his master. He agreed with him that the gods were everlasting and the source of all good in the world, and he severely criticizes the Stoics for holding that only Zeus was immortal; they are 'more godless than the Epicureans',[41] who maintained that the gods did not concern themselves with the affairs of men. Even if, like Plato, he sometimes writes of 'God', he was a firm believer in the traditional Greek pantheon; nevertheless, while rejecting the wilder orgiastic cults, he tended to equate non-Greek deities with their Greek counterparts. Like all serious thinkers Plutarch was deeply concerned with the problem of evil which, in a world governed by beneficent gods, so often appeared to triumph. The solution he found in the old view that there existed *daimones,* beings intermediate between gods and men, who were responsible for the existence of evil in the world.[42] As a Platonist and an initiate into the mysteries of Dionysus, Plutarch naturally held fast to a belief in the immortality of the individual soul and rejected the views of the Stoics and the Epicureans that it perishes at death or soon after.

Indeed Plutarch often attacks Stoic teachings, although he scarcely less often accepts them. For example, myths which showed the gods behaving in a fashion opposed to traditional Greek morality he interpreted, like them, in an allegorical manner. To the Epicureans he is consistently hostile: indeed his attitude closely resembles Cicero's. Not only are their religious views attacked, but they come under fire for holding that virtue is not worth having if unaccompanied by pleasure. But perhaps their worst fault in Plutarch's eyes was that they advocated withdrawal from public life. The Epicureans, he complains,[43] have produced no one who has advanced human society; they fail to be of service to the state but enjoy the benefits in the cities. In the same way the early Stoics, especially Chrysippus, are found guilty of writing at length about political activity and then taking no part in politics. They have deserted their homeland to devote themselves to philosophy, and for all their talk they lead a life no better than that of the Epicureans.[44] For Plutarch the prime task of the philosopher was to lead himself, his pupils and friends, and those who after he became famous sought his aid, to *arete* and to the happiness which depends upon it. This *arete* manifested itself in right conduct, and man should not be concerned only with his own soul but should strive, as a duty, to benefit his fellow-citizens by engaging in political activity.

For readers of the *Parallel Lives* Plutarch's attitude to the passions is of particular importance.[45] These are not, as the Stoics maintained, to be eradicated; on the contrary, they are necessary, for without them reason would be condemned to inactivity like a steersman when the wind drops. Practical reason (*phronesis*) should regulate them so that a mean between excess and lack of passion is achieved. It is significant for Plutarch's portrait of Alexander that τὸ θυμοειδές (which is prominent in his character) is part of the irrational part of the soul and that anger, according to Plutarch, is the worst of passions. It destroys any society; it is not noble or manly, but attacks particularly the weak—women, the sick, and the elderly. To control anger is true bravery, and it is the function of philosophy to prepare the soul to meet storms of anger.

RHETORIC[46]

Since the fourth century B.C. philosophers and rhetoricians had been engaged in a constant struggle for supremacy, a struggle in which, surprising as it may seem to us, the rhetoricians had gained the upper hand. In Plutarch's day the practice of rhetoric offered to the ambitious young man the most rewarding career, and the most gifted pupils became sophists. Indeed, as Sandbach remarks,[47] 'something like a passion for eloquence seems to have possessed the Greek-speaking world'. This is he movement known as the Second Sophistic, represented for us mainly by Plutarch's contemporary Dion of Prusa (until his conversion to philosophy), and afterwards by Aristides and Lucian.

Although sophists might appear as advocates in the law-courts or act as counsellors in local politics the greatest fame and the greatest rewards were to be won by epideictic speeches. It was in these display-pieces that the sophist could best exhibit his powers of expression and his ability to improvise. This talent was the result of a long and arduous training, of which two aspects must be emphasized here in view of the theory that the majority of Plutarch's citations in the *Parallel Lives* are second-hand (see below . . .). The rhetorician was expected to read (and to continue reading) widely, if not deeply, particularly in the historians and orators. This reading provided him with a vast store of *exempla* with which to embellish his oratory. In particular, he had to know thoroughly the political history of Greece in the period from Solon to the death of Alexander.[48] To enable him to use these *exempla* when required the sophist had to have a prodigious memory, and to this end his memory was developed systematically. The student began by repeating a story dictated by his teacher and ended by offering proof or refutation of the facts of some assumed case (*controversiae*) or discussing the merits of some particular course of action (*suasoriae*).[49] In these exercises, since the student had to speak without notes, memory was of prime importance, and at all stages of his course he was obliged to practise constantly. Even when he was a famous sophist, Herodes Atticus declaimed daily. What results such training might produce may be seen in the remarks of the elder Seneca in the introduction to his *Controversiae* (1. 2): there he recalls that in his youth he could repeat 2,000 names, said once, in the same order, and could recite in reverse order over 200 verses spoken by his fellow-students. Indeed, the *Controversiae* were apparently written from memory.[50] There is no reason to suppose that Plutarch's memory was markedly inferior.

If in many respects Plutarch was representative of his age, this is not true of his attitude to rhetoric; for he came down strongly on the side of philosophy and several times (48 d, 80 a, 999 e-f) asserts the superiority of philosophic to sophistic education. It was not that he was hostile to artistic speech—in the *Praecepta* (801 e) he tells the young Menemachos that it is the duty of a statesman to make use of rhetoric[51]—but character (ἦθος), formed by philosophic training and expressed in words, is for him more important than rhetoric; it is the δημιουργὸς πείθους. Rhetoric, on the other hand, is its tool (ὄργανον), indispensable as a means to an end, but not to be pursued as an end in itself.[52] Many rhetoricians, however, appear to have concerned themselves little with the truth of what they said, but to have paid excessive attention to the way in which they said it. This applies both to their matter and their delivery. They quite intoxicated their hearers, modulating, smoothing, and intoning their voices (41 d), and Plutarch complains of their 'paltry thought, empty phrases, affected bearing', their 'elaborate and pretentious diction', their 'dainty, flowery words and theatrical matter' which is 'fodder for drones who play the sophist' (40 c-41 e). The word 'theatrical' recurs:[53] 'The speech of a statesman', he writes (802 e), 'should not be theatrical, as if he were making a harangue composed, like a garland, of curious and florid words, nor should it consist of over-subtle arguments and periods exactly framed by rule and compass.'[54] Here speaks the mature Plutarch, who has outgrown his early rhetorical training and has come to despise the rhetorical excesses which he himself once practised. 'Over-subtle arguments and periods exactly framed by rule and compass' might well describe his speeches *De Alexandri fortuna*.

11. THE SPEECHES *DE ALEXANDRI MAGNI FORTUNA AUT VIRTUTE*[55]

In default of a detailed commentary a brief summary of these two speeches may perhaps serve two purposes: to provide a example of first-century rhetoric, and to allow comparison of the achievement of Plutarch as a rhetorician and as a biographer.

DE ALEXANDRI FORTUNA *I*

(1) Plutarch announces that he is going to reply on behalf of Philosophy (or rather of Alexander) to Fortune, who has claimed Alexander as her work. In fact Alexander succeeded against great odds and at great cost with the support of the virtues of forethought, endurance, courage, and moderat on (*sophrosyne*). (2) Other kings (Darius, Sardanapalus, Ochus, Artaxerxes) owed their position to Fortune, but Alexander had to fight for his victories. His many wounds (ten instances given) show Fortune's malice. So far from favouring Alexander, she was actively hostile, especially at the Malli town where she shut him in with unknown barbarians and almost brought him to an ignoble end. (3) Even before the campaign began Alexander had to deal with troubles in Greece (Thebes, Athens), Macedonia (Amyntas, the sons of Aeropus), Illyria, and Scythia. His treasury was empty, he was in debt, and his forces were small (various estimates); nevertheless he formed the idea of ruling all men. (4) Despite his meagre (material) resources this was no rash or headstrong plan, for Philosophy had given him greater resources than any other king; indeed he owed more to Aristotle than to Philip. Because he wrote nothing and did not teach in the Academy or the Lyceum men reject the statement that his real equipment (*ephodion*) was Philosophy, although in deference to Homer they accept the view that the *Iliad* and the *Odyssey* were his *ephodion*. Yet other philosophers (Pythagoras, Socrates, Arcesilaus, Carneades) wrote nothing, although they were not busy, like Alexander, civilizing the barbarians, and still we account them eminent philosophers because of their utterances, their way of life, and their teachings. Judged by the same criteria Alexander too will be seen to be a philosopher.

[The remainder of the speech is devoted to proving the thesis that Alexander was not only *a* philosopher but *the greatest* of philosophers. His teachings are treated in chapters 5-9 (init.), his sayings in 9-10, and his deeds in 11-12.]

(5) Whereas the pupils of Socrates and Plato (Critias, Alcibiades, Cleitophon), who at least spoke Greek, rejected his teaching, Alexander taught the barbarians not to kill their fathers or marry their mothers, but to worship Greek gods, to bury their dead instead of eating them, and to read Greek literature. While Plato wrote a *Republic* (Πολιτεία) which no one used, Alexander founded more than seventy cities (πόλεις) and introduced Greek institutions. Few men read Plato's *Laws,* but countless men used (and still use) Alexander's laws. Since they enjoy the blessings of civilization, those whom Alexander conquered are more fortunate than those who escaped, and if philosophers pride themselves upon civilizing individuals Alexander should be considered the greatest of philosophers for civilizing whole peoples. (6) Zeno wrote a celebrated *Republic* advocating that all men should consider themselves citizens of a single commonwealth, but this was only a philosopher's dream; Alexander realized it. He rejected Aristotle's advice to act as a *leader* towards the Greeks and as a *master* towards the barbarians, and believing that he had a divine mission to control and reconcile all men, either by persuasion or by force, he 'mixed their lives and customs, their marriages and ways of life as in a "loving-cup"', and made the difference between Greeks and barbarians one of virtue and vice. (7) Demaratus of Corinth wept to think that past generations

of Greeks were deprived of the joy of seeing Alexander sitting on the throne of Darius. Yet this was due to Fortune; how much more desirable would it have been to see the marriages at Susa of Greeks and Macedonians to Persian women? This was the proper way to link Europe to Asia, not, as Xerxes did, to build a bridge of boats. (8) Alexander's adoption of a mixed Persian and Macedonian dress was designed to win over the conquered peoples and to create one united people. To have retained the Macedonian dress would have been silly and indeed childish, when he could by a slight change win their affection for Macedonian rule. He was no brigand who regarded Asia as mere booty, as Hannibal did Italy, and had he not died so soon all men would now look to a single law as to a common light. (9) The purpose of the expedition—to create concord, peace, unity among all men—shows Alexander a philosopher.

The characters of kings are revealed by their *sayings*. Those of Antigonus, Dionysius (the elder), and Sardanapalus reveal, respectively, injustice, impiety, and love of pleasure; those of Alexander, if one subtracts his diadem, his noble birth, and Ammon, might have been uttered by Socrates or Plato or Pythagoras. The inscriptions under his busts and statues and his reported remark, 'I am the son of Zeus', are poetic extravagance and flattery. His *genuine* utterances (Olympic Games, Philip's wound) reveal the mind of a philosopher rising above the weaknesses of the body. (10) Alexander's favourite Homeric line was 'A goodly king and a mighty warrior', which he took as a text for himself, and his rejection at Troy of the offer of Paris' lyre reveals his philosophic outlook. It is revealed also in his attitude to philosophers (Aristotle, Anaxarchus, Pyrrho, Xenocrates, Onesicritus) and in his remark, after meeting Diogenes at Corinth: 'If I were not Alexander, I would be Diogenes.' By this he did not mean 'If I were not king' or 'If I were not rich and an Argead' but 'If I were not carrying out my civilizing mission, I would be emulating the *frugalitas* of Diogenes'. Alexander too had to 'change the stamp of the common currency' and put the impress of a Greek *politeia* on barbarian material.

(11) Alexander's *actions* reveal not chance and warlike violence, but the bravery and justice, the moderation and gentleness of one acting with sober and wise reason. They confirm the Stoic *dictum* that in whatever the Wise Man does he acts with every virtue. Alexander exhibited valour with humanity gentleness with courage, generosity with economy, and so on and so on. . . . Consider his treatment of Porus, his marriage to Roxane, his treatment of the dead Darius, his trust in Hephaestion; if these actions do not reveal the philosopher, what actions do? (12) Contrast the actions of recognized philosophers. Socrates allowed Alcibiades to sleep with him, but Alexander furiously rebuked Philox-

enus for offering to send him a beautiful boy. We admire Xenocrates for refusing an offer of fifty talents from Alexander; should we not admire Alexander for offering them? Even under fire Alexander repeatedly remarked that he needed wealth to reward such men. This shows him a philosopher, for the judgements of ordinary men are confounded by imminent danger whereas philosophy renders those of philosophers strong against danger. . . . (here our manuscript of the speech breaks off).

De Alexandri fortuna 2

(1) Plutarch begins by saying that he omitted yesterday to mention the great number of artists who flourished during the reign of Alexander. This was due to the king, in whom they found a discriminating critic and patron and who, unlike other kings (Dionysius, Alexander of Pherae, Archelaus, Ateas the Scythian), encouraged them. (2) He concentrated on being a great warrior and honoured artists without envy. He refused to intervene in the contest between the tragedians Athenodorus and Thettalus (ch. 29), he rewarded the comic actor Lycon (ch. 29), and set up a statue to Aristonicus the harper, who fell in battle. In his reign lived Apelles the painter, whose 'bearer of the thunderbolt' was inimitable, and Lysippus the sculptor, who alone was allowed to sculpt Alexander since he alone preserved Alexander's character and *arete* (ch. 4). But Alexander refused the offer of Stasicrates to transform Mount Athos into a gigantic likeness of himself (ch. 72); the Caucasus, the Tanais, and the Caspian, he said, would be his memorials.

(3) Had this memorial been completed it would not have been due to Fortune any more than the works of Apelles and Lysippus; much less is a great man, indeed the greatest, the product of Fortune. To those who do not know how to use them the gifts of Fortune are a danger and a proof of their weakness; without *arete* everything else is useless, as we may see by comparing the lives of Semiramis and Sardanapalus. Fortune bestowed no greater gifts (arms, money, etc.) on Alexander than on other kings, but she could not make Arrhidaeus great, or Amasis, or Ochus, or Oarses, or Tigranes, or Nicomedes of Bithynia. (4) Fortune owes much to the rule of Alexander, since in him she was seen to be unconquered, noble, and so on. Leosthenes compared Alexander's army after his death to the Cyclops after his blinding, stretching out his hands uncertainly. We may perhaps better compare it, says Plutarch, to a dead body after the soul has departed; Perdiccas, Meleager, Seleucus, and Antigonus gave it a fitful existence, but it eventually decayed and put forth unworthy leaders like maggots. Alexander himself indicated as much when he reminded Hephaestion, quarrelling with Craterus, that he had no power without him

(ch. 47). Take away the *arete* of the conqueror, and he is utterly insignificant; as poor craftsmen, who put huge bases under small statues, emphasize their smallness, so Fortune, when she elevates a wretched creature, displays his instability. (5) Greatness consists in the *use,* not the possession, of good things. Even infants inherit kingdoms, as Charillus and Arrhidaeus (a virtual child), whom Meleager set on Alexander's throne although he was only a 'mute character'. Even a woman or child can give another wealth, power, etc. (as Bagoas gave Oarses and Darius the Persian throne), but to support and use great power requires *arete* and *nous.* Alexander, whom men accuse of drunkenness, was not intoxicated by power, as others were who could not bear even a little (Cleitus, Demetrius, Lysimachus, Clearchus the tyrant of Heracleia, Dionysius II, and Dionysius I). Some called themselves Euergetai, Kallinikoi, Soteres, Megaloi, in spite of their lusts, their dicing, and their constant feasting. (6) But Alexander breakfasted at dawn, sitting, and dined towards evening; he drank (only) when sacrificing to the gods and diced (only) with Medius when he had a fever. He married Roxane for love and Stateira for reasons of state. Towards Persian women he displayed great self-control ('he passed by those whom he saw more than those whom he did not'), and though in other matters most humane he treated beauty cavalierly. He would not hear a word about the great beauty of Darius' wife, and grieved so much at her death that his motives were misconstrued by Darius, who thought that Alexander's victory was due to Fortune (i.e. that he did not possess *arete*). When he learned the truth, he prayed that in the event of his defeat Alexander, and no one else, might sit upon the throne of Cyrus, i.e. he called the gods to witness that he adopted Alexander (ch. 30). (7) This is the way in which *arete* conquers. We may ascribe to Fortune Alexander's military successes, but moderation, self-control, superiority to pleasure and desire are not due to Fortune, and it was these that defeated Darius. In battle Tarrias, son of Deinomenes, Antigenes, and Philotas were invincible, but against pleasure, women, and money they were no better than slaves. Philotas boasted that Alexander owed everything to him, but although Alexander knew of this through Antigone he did not reveal his suspicions for seven years; yet men say he was a drunkard, had no self-control, and communicated everything to Hephaestion (as the episode of Olympias' letter is supposed to prove). (8) Even if Alexander became great through Fortune, he is greater because he used Fortune well. The more men praise his Fortune, the more they praise his *arete.*

But he did not gain the throne of Cyrus because of a horse's neigh, like Darius, nor because of the favour of a woman, like Xerxes. Fortune made others king, as she brought Aigon to the throne of Argos or Abdalonymus to that of Paphos, (9) but Alexander faced every danger and toil. He enjoyed *no* good Fortune either at the hands of man or Nature. Fortune should depart to Antiochus, son of Seleucus, or Artaxerxes or Ptolemy Philadelphos, who were proclaimed king when their fathers were alive. But Alexander was wounded from head to foot (eight instances). (10) Fortune did well to make Alexander great by exposing every part of his body to wounds! She did not save him from serious injury, as Athena did Menelaus. In fact, Alexander suffered more at the hand of Fortune than any other king. Yet despite her persistence she found Alexander, like Hercules, invincible. But for Alexander's great spirit, derived from his *arete,* he would have given up in the face of sieges, pursuits, countless revolts, and all the other difficulties. He would have tired of cutting off the hydra heads which grew again in fresh wars. (11) Fortune almost made men doubt that Alexander was the son of Ammon; for no son of a god, except Hercules, was called upon to perform such laborious tasks. But whereas one evil man imposed on Hercules the task of capturing lions to prevent him punishing Antaeus and putting an end to the murders of Busiris, *arete* imposed on Alexander the divine task of bringing all men under one rule, a desire which he had from childhood, as his questions to the Persian envoys showed (ch. 5). When Alexander was about to begin his expedition Fortune dragged him back by contriving wars with the Triballians and Illyrians, with Thebes and Athens, wars against fellow-Greeks that could bring him no glory. His financial resources were meagre, but he distributed his property and revenues to his Companions, of whom Perdiccas alone refused to accept them (ch. 15). (12) What hopes did Alexander take with him to Asia? Not an army and navy as large as Xerxes', but an army whose members vied with each other in *doxa* and *arete.* In himself he had great hopes; piety towards the gods, loyalty towards his friends, *frugalitas, continentia,* and so on. God formed Alexander's nature out of all the virtues—the spirit of Cyrus, the moderation of Agesilaus, the wisdom of Themistocles, etc., etc. He was more temperate than Agamemnon, more generous than Achilles, more pious than Diomedes, more missed by his relatives than Odysseus. (13) Solon, Miltiades, and Aristeides were great because of *arete,* not Fortune; yet if Alexander is compared to them he surpasses Solon's *seisachtheia* by paying his soldiers' debts, Pericles' use of tribute to adorn the Acropolis with temples by sending the wealth of the East to erect temples in Greece, and Brasidas' celebrated dash along the seashore to Methone by his leap into the Malli town, like Apollo landing on earth. Fortune's malice shut Alexander up in an insignificant village in which he could win no glory in death, as Pelopidas and Epaminondas did, and prevented his soldiers from entering. After Alexander was wounded, *arete* engendered in him courage, and in his companions strength and zeal. Limnaios, Ptolemy, and Leonnatus defended Alexander because of their love of Alexander's *arete*. A spectator would have said that it was a struggle between *arete* and Fortune. The speech ends with a description of Alexander's wound and a contrast between Alexander's courage and the despair of his followers.

Before examining the speeches we should perhaps ask whether in writing these speeches Plutarch was merely displaying his rhetorical talents or whether, as several distinguished scholars have held, he had in mind a more serious purpose.[56] Hirzel (*Der Dialog* 2. 78) and Tarn (*AJP* (1939) 56; *Alex.* 2. 296), impressed by the portrait of 'the philosopher in action' which Plutarch develops in the first speech, both consider that he was seeking to refute the charges made against Alexander's character by the philosophical schools (see below . . .). Hirzel thinks that Plutarch had in mind the Cynics and Stoics, while Tarn would add the Peripatetics.[57] Several considerations tell against this view. First, Alexander is contrasted favourably not only with philosophers of the Cynic, Stoic, and Peripatetic schools, but also with Plato and especially with Socrates (1. 4, 5, 9, 12); indeed, he is superior to *all* philosophers. The only philosophers, moreover, who are spoken of favourably are the Cynics Antisthenes and Crates (2. 3) and the Stoic Zeno (1. 6). It may be argued that to show Alexander as the supreme philosopher is one form of defence, but it should not be overlooked that 'the philosopher in action' occupies only a portion (although admittedly a major portion) of the first speech, while it is hardly mentioned in the second. Again when we bear in mind the full title of the speeches, *De A. M. fortuna aut virtute,* we can see that this portion is consistent with the main theme. Since the philosopher is the embodiment of virtue, the proof that Alexander was a philosopher constitutes proof of his *arete* and contributes to a solution of the *tyche-arete* problem. The attempt to prove Alexander a philosopher is not the chief aim of the speeches, but a means to an end. Nor are we compelled to believe that Plutarch is answering the criticisms of the philosophers; by his time these criticisms were commonplaces of the schools of rhetoric (see below . . .).

In the most recent substantial discussion of the speeches[58] Wardman has maintained that they are developed from two antitheses: *logos-ergon* and *tyche-arete*. The former theme is directed against earlier philosophical treatment of Alexander by the Stoics and Peripatetics, but is not apparently a serious defence of Alexander.[59] Plutarch's treatment of the second antithesis, Wardman suggests, is to be considered together with the *De Romanorum fortuna*. We can then see that 'Plutarch is viewing the whole of history as a trend towards world unity. Unity was accomplished by Rome, but—*this seems to be the implication* [my italics]—was

also the object of Greek history and Alexander's campaigns.' Plutarch's view, he argues, was that the Romans had succeeded because they possessed both Fortune and *arete*, while Alexander had the *arete* but lacked the Fortune necessary to succeed. This is to take Plutarch, particularly the young Plutarch, much too seriously as a political thinker and as a philosopher. His insistence in the *De Alexandri fortuna* on Fortune hampering Alexander[60] is adequately explained by rhetorical practice,[61] and the implication that Alexander's campaigns were a trend towards world unity is far from obvious. Moreover, the *De Romanorum fortuna* is unfinished (and perhaps in the process of revision), and if, as Wardman believes, the speech did not contain a portion in favour of *arete*, it must follow that Plutarch argued that Rome's success was due primarily to Fortune and that, just as in the first speech *De Alexandri fortuna,* Plutarch replies to a speech in favour of Fortune,[62] so in the *De Romanorum fortuna* his opponent argued in favour of *arete* and he put the case for Fortune.

A strong reason for considering these speeches rhetorical exercises is the perfection of Alexander. This is best explained not by the admiration of the youthful Plutarch[63] but by the maxim of the rhetorical schools that one should not rest content with refuting one's opponents, but should seek to prove the exact opposite. So there is no hint of criticism: Alexander is the embodiment of all the virtues. Moreover, a serious defence of Alexander would surely require that Plutarch should deal with such topics as the execution of Philotas, the murder of Cleitus, Callisthenes and the Pages' conspiracy, and *proskynesis*. Yet of these vital topics we hear not a whisper! Philotas is mentioned—but only to show that Alexander did not reveal his suspicions of him even to Hephaestion for seven years (!).

It seems most probable that the obvious view is the correct one, that the two speeches are 'epideictic display-pieces', devoid of any serious purpose.[64]

The wide reading expected of the rhetorician is evident not only from the many authors cited in the speeches but still more from the references to a large number of events in Greek and Persian (and even Roman) history. The orator was required to *display* his knowledge; hence the speeches contain many more incidents outside the reign of Alexander than does the *Life*. Many of these were no doubt commonplaces of the rhetorical schools, as e.g. the references to Xerxes (1. 7, 2. 12), but many must derive from Plutarch's recollection of his own reading; perhaps the references to Tigranes and Nicomedes come into this category. For a serious exercise the student must have been required to undertake a course of reading, amounting almost to research in our sense.

We can see to some extent how Plutarch has used his material to develop his thesis. Since Onesicritus (fr. 17) described Alexander as 'the philosopher in arms', the idea of him as 'the philosopher in action' may well be taken from him; perhaps also the statements that the *Iliad* was Alexander's *ephodion* and that he owed more to Aristotle than to Philip. At any rate both statements occur in chapter 8 of the *Life* in the same context. But the *development* of this conception of Alexander, the comparison with Pythagoras, Socrates, and other philosophers, and the somewhat forced parallelism between Plato's *Republic* and *Laws* and Alexander's city-foundations and his laws are best attributed to Plutarch himself. In his portrait of the 'cosmopolitan' Alexander (1. 6-9) Plutarch makes use of quite disparate pieces of information and combines them, not unskilfully, into a consistent whole. From Eratosthenes he derives Alexander's adoption of a mixed Persian-Macedonian dress and probably also the division between Greeks and barbarians according to virtue and vice. In both cases Plutarch has adapted his material. In the *Life,* which we may reasonably suppose represents his considered judgement on Alexander, Plutarch writes (ch. 45. 1) that either Alexander wished to win over the barbarians by adopting elements of native costume or else was seeking to promote the introduction of *proskynesis*; in the speech (1. 8) his adoption of this mixed dress is a measure to forward his universal commonwealth. Again, in the speech (1. 6) Alexander instructs all men to make the division between Greeks and barbarians a division between virtue and vice; yet we know from Strabo (1. 4. 9) that this was a remark made about him by Eratosthenes. Plutarch has quite simply attributed it to Alexander; for there is no reason to suppose that he ever uttered it or ever held the view expressed in it. At the beginning of ch. 9 Plutarch states that Alexander's goal *from the start of his expedition* was to create *in all men* ὁμόνοιαν καὶ εἰρήνην καὶ κοινωνίαν. Now in Arrian's description of the banquet at Opis (7. 11. 9) Alexander is said to have prayed for ὁμόνοιάν τε κα ὶ κοινωνίαν τῆς ἀρχῆς Μακεδόσι καὶ Πέρσαις. The similarity of expression suggests that Plutarch borrows, perhaps unconsciously, from Arrian's source.[65] In fact, Alexander's prayer, not uttered until 324, was limited to concord and partnership in rule between Macedonians and Persians (Iranians); it had nothing to do with a world commonwealth.[66] The splendid picture of the loving-cup (1. 6), too, may be a rhetorical device suggested to Plutarch by the banquet and his interpretation of it. The marriages at Susa, where ninety leading Macedonians married women of the Persian nobility, were part of Alexander's 'policy of fusion'.[67] Of this Plutarch was well aware; nevertheless this incident also is adapted to his thesis of 'Alexander the cosmopolitan'.

This adaptation of material by Plutarch can be illustrated by numerous less important examples. Alexander's remark after his meeting with Diogenes at Corinth, which in the *Life* (ch. 14) is used, reasonably enough, to show his reverence for philosophers, is developed in a quite ridiculous fashion into an expression of 'Alexander the civilizer' (1. 10). We can see, too, how Plutarch used this same remark in a different context in a completely different way. At *Mor.* 782 a-b (= *Ad principem ineruditum* 6) it is interpreted to mean that Alexander was vexed at his own position and power, because they were an obstacle to the virtue for which he could find no time. He envied the moral invincibility of Diogenes, although by the practice of philosophy he might have secured the moral character of a Diogenes while still retaining the position of an Alexander. A similarly strained interpretation is put on the incident in which Alexander questions the Persian ambassadors, which in the *Life* (ch. 5) illustrates his charm and seriousness of purpose. In the *Moralia* (2. 11) his questions show the desire he felt *from childhood* to create a universal commonwealth. His reply to those who urged him to compete in the Olympic Games (1. 9) is supposed to prove him a philosopher, while in the *Life* (ch. 4) it is properly used to show that he did not desire every kind of *doxa*. Finally his extended pursuit of the Scythians across the River Tanais while suffering from dysentery reveals in the *Life* (ch. 45) his indifference to hardship; in the *Moralia* (2. 9) it is one of many illustrations of the malice of Fortune.

These differences between the *Life* and the speeches, the list of which could be greatly extended, enable us to see the manner in which Plutarch, as a rhetorician, adapted and interpreted his material in the interests of his thesis. It follows that we cannot accept his *interpretation* of any event without confirmatory evidence, although we are justified in placing the *facts* in the speeches on the same level as those in the *Life*. We may, for example, place just as much (or as little) reliance on his statement that Alexander refused to compete at the Olympic Games as we do on Alexander's rejoinder to the wounded Philip (1. 9). We need not, and cannot, take these speeches seriously as representing Plutarch's view of Alexander. Indeed, it would need much faith to believe that at any period in his life Plutarch thought that Alexander was as perfect as he is portrayed. As Badian well remarks,[68] the difference between the speeches and the *Life* is not to be explained by Plutarch's additional reading or by his greater maturity, but by the difference between rhetoric and biography.

III. The *Parallel Lives*[69]

Although many of Plutarch's other biographies have perished,[70] the whole series of twenty-three pairs of *Parallel Lives* has survived with the exception of the (probable) first pair, Epaminondas and Scipio.[71] In this series Plutarch compares a distinguished Greek with his Roman counterpart, as he compares Alexander with Caesar.

CHOICE OF HEROES

This was based, as Erbse has convincingly demonstrated,[72] not only on the qualities which he considered the two men to share, although this was probably the decisive factor,[73] but also on the similarities in their careers; for, since Plutarch subscribed to the Peripatetic view of character as manifesting itself in action (see below . . .), their reactions to similar (or nearly similar) circumstances afforded an opportunity to compare their characters. Since Alexander and Caesar were the outstanding figures in the ancient world it might appear obvious (or indeed inevitable) that Plutarch would select them for comparison,[74] but it is evident that he discerned in them many common qualities. In particular, both appear greatly influenced by ambition and concerned with their reputation,[75] both are extremely generous (especially to their fellow-soldiers) and chivalrous towards their defeated enemies;[76] both display self-control;[77] finally, both later reveal certain tyrannical qualities.[78]

Each pair of *Lives* is normally followed by a summary comparison (*synkrisis*), which serves especially to set out the *differences* between the heroes, but in the case of the *Alexander-Caesar* this is absent.[79]

CHRONOLOGY OF THE LIVES

We do not know when Plutarch began writing the *Parallel Lives*, but Jones's suggestion[80] that 'Sosius' consulate in 99 furnished an occasion for Plutarch to dedicate the new undertaking to him' is attractive. Plutarch himself gives only one direct indication of the dates of composition: at *Sull.* 21. 8 he remarks that weapons were still being found in the marshes near Orchomenos 'almost 200 years' after Sulla's victory (in 86 B.C.). From this we should probably conclude only that the pair *Lysander-Sulla* was written within the decade 100-110. Recently, however, Jones has pointed out that those *Lives* in which Sosius Senecio is addressed (either directly or by the use of the second person pronoun) must precede his death, which occurred almost certainly before 116.[81]

From indications in the *Lives* we can reconstruct in outline their *relative* chronology. Plutarch's statements (*Dem.* 3. 1, *Per.* 2. 5, *Dion* 2. 7) enable us to place the pair *Demosthenes-Cicero* in the fifth position, the *Pericles-Fabius* in the tenth, and the *Dion-Brutus* in the twelfth. In many *Lives* (although not in the *Alexander*) there are references to other *Lives* as either completed

or, rarely, as in prospect. Unfortunately (on the assumption that the references are original) some of them contradict each other: in the *Caesar* (62. 8, 68. 7), for example, Plutarch indicates that the *Brutus* is complete, while in the *Brutus* (9. 9) he refers to the *Caesar* in similar terms.[82] Those scholars who investigated the problem in the nineteenth century[83] came to the conclusion that some of the references were not made by Plutarch but were marginal notes which had found their way into the text, and found a solution in the removal of the offending references.[84] In 1907, however, Mewaldt[85] put forward the hypothesis that the references were all genuine, that Plutarch worked on a number of *Lives* simultaneously and published them in groups, e.g. the *Theseus-Romulus, Lycurgus-Numa,* and *Themistocles-Camillus,* and as a second group the *Dion-Brutus, Aemilius-Timoleon,* and *Alexander-Caesar.* But in 1929 Stoltz, in an exhaustive study of the subject, rejected Mewaldt's solution and returned to the older view, deleting the references at *Dion* 58. 10, *Brutus* 9. 9, and *Camillus* 33. 10.[86] Stoltz found the method of working suggested by Mewaldt hard to credit, for while much of the material for the *Brutus* would be relevant to the *Caesar* and that of the *Dion* to some extent relevant to the *Timoleon,* the material for the *Aemilius* and the *Alexander* would have no relevance to any of the other *Lives* in the group. He further maintained that the pair *Theseus-Romulus* must be among the last of the *Lives,* whereas, in view of the references to the *Lysander* in the *Pericles* (22) and to the *Lycurgus* in the *Lysander* (17), the other pairs in this suggested group must precede the *Pericles-Fabius,* the tenth pair. Proof of the (late) position of the *Theseus-Romulus* he found in Plutarch's statement in the introduction to the *Theseus* (1. 2) that he is going to deal with the mythical period 'after passing through the periods accessible to probability in which history based on fact can find a footing'.[87] In Stoltz's view this must mean that Plutarch has dealt with all (or nearly all) the *Lives;* but surely Plutarch merely means that in the *Lycurgus-Numa* he has reached the limits of the historical period, without implying anything about the number of *Lives* already completed.[88] When Plutarch goes on to say (1. 4) that he thought he might reasonably go back to Romulus, being brought by his history so near to his time τὸν περὶ Λυκούργου τοῦ νομοθέτου καὶ Νομᾶ τοῦ βασιλέως λόγον ἐκδόντες, one would naturally conclude that the *Lycurgus-Numa* had already been published.[89] Mewaldt (572) and Flacelière (*REG* 61 (1948), 68 f.), however, hold that the two pairs were published simultaneously and that the preface to the *Theseus* is a preface to both pairs; they therefore translate ἐκδόντες as 'publishing'. But it is very doubtful whether the aorist participle can bear this meaning. Flacelière (loc. cit.) adduces a further argument. If the *Lycurgus-Numa* had already been published, he maintains, then Plutarch must have considered Lycurgus and Numa to be historical personages, for the *Lives* of Theseus and Romulus mark in this respect an innovation which is underlined in the preface; but this, he considers, is just what Plutarch did not do. As proof he points to his statements at the beginning of the *Lycurgus* and the *Numa,* that: 'It is impossible to affirm anything about Lycurgus which is not doubtful' and 'Opinions differ very greatly about the time when Numa lived.' A brief examination of the *Lives* in question will, in fact, prove exactly the opposite. In the *Theseus* Plutarch is clearly dealing with myth, not history;[90] in the *Lycurgus* and the *Numa,* on the other hand, he is dealing with history and the statements of historians. At *Lycurgus* 1. 1 he writes that 'Even the establishment of his laws and his constitution is variously reported *by historians*' and at 1. 7 'Although *history* is so disputed'.[91] So in the *Numa* the 'opinions which differ very greatly' are those of *historians.* It seems reasonable, then, to conclude that the *Theseus-Romulus* was written after the publication of the *Lycurgus-Numa.* If this is so, Mewaldt's thesis must be considered improbable.

Nevertheless whether we accept Stoltz's views or those of Mewaldt there is little doubt about the majority of the *Lives* which composed the first dozen pairs. There is general agreement that the missing pair, *Epaminondas-Scipio,* was composed first, and the fifth, tenth, and twelfth pairs are known (above, . . .). The *Cimon-Lucullus,* the *Lysander-Sulla,* and the *Pelopidas-Marcellus* must be included in the first ten pairs,[92] together with the *Lycurgus-Numa* and the *Themistocles-Camillus.*[93] Thus eight of the first ten pairs are settled. The two vacant places may be allotted to the *Sertorius-Eumenes* and the *Theseus-Romulus,* and either the *Solon-Publicola* or the *Philopoemen-Flamininus* may fill the eleventh position.[94]

If Mewaldt's theory is correct, the *Alexander-Caesar* and the *Aemilius-Timoleon* must have occupied the thirteenth and fourteenth (or fourteenth and thirteenth) positions immediately after the *Dion-Brutus,* and since Sosius Senecio is referred to in the *Aemilius* and the *Dion* we may date the *Alexander* (?some years) before 116.[95] If it is not correct, as seems probable, the position of the *Alexander-Caesar* within the series cannot be precisely determined; all that we can say *for certain* is that it was not later than the eighteenth pair. Nevertheless it would seem likely that it was published between 110 and 115.

PLUTARCH'S BIOGRAPHICAL AIMS AND METHODS

Plutarch is preoccupied with the *character* of his heroes. At the beginning of the *Timoleon* he tells us that he began writing at the request of others but continued for his own sake, 'the virtues of these great men serving me as a sort of looking-glass in which I may see how to adjust and adorn my own life'. His method, he says, is by the study of history and the familiarity acquired in writing to habituate his memory to receive and retain images of the best and worthiest characters. By turning his thoughts to view these noble examples he is enabled to free himself from any ignoble or vicious impressions.[96] Even bad examples may have their use. For Plutarch includes the *Lives* of Demetrius and Antonius not for variety or for the amusement of his readers, but because knowledge of the bad may encourage men to imitate the better lives (*Demetr.* 1).

The clearest statement of Plutarch's aims is contained in the first chapter of the *Alexander.* There he states plainly that he is not a historian, but a biographer; hence he will not attempt to include all the famous deeds of Alexander and Caesar.[97] It is the insignificant action, the casual remark or jest that affords the clearest insight into *character,* and so he will concentrate, as a painter does, on those features which reveal this. So, in the introduction to the *Nicias,* he disclaims any intention of rivalling Thucydides, as Timaeus had foolishly tried to do, and distinguishes between τὴν ἄχρηστον ἱστορίαν and τὴν πρὸς κατανόησιν ἤθους καὶ τρόπου (χρήσιμον ἱστορίαν). He means, of course, not that history is 'useless', but that certain facts which would be relevant to history do not concern him as a biographer.[98] Moreover, as Gomme observes,[99] Plutarch was not a biographer in the fullest sense, but an essayist; his *Parallel Lives* are moral essays—a complement to the *Moralia*—concerned with the hero's character, not with his place in history.

Plutarch repeatedly states his intention of illustrating the character ἦθος) of his subject through his actions (πράξεις), including in the case of an orator his speeches.[100] The terminology is Peripatetic.[101] The nature (φύσις) of a man is a basic and unchanging element in his character, which is not only revealed by his actions but is formed by habitual or repeated action and by his reactions to events. Education (παιδεία) and philosophy (λόγος), too, play an important part in the formation of character. For example, since the character of the elder Brutus was harsh by nature and was not 'softened' by philosophy he came to grief and killed his son; whereas the younger Brutus was a harmonious blend of action and reflection because of education and philosophy (*Brutus* 1. 2).[102] It is sometimes said that the development of character was unknown to ancient writers. This statement requires modification: a person's nature (φύσις) did not change, but character (ἦθος) might alter. So in ch. 52. 7 Plutarch writes that Anaxarchus made Alexander's character 'more conceited and lawless'.[103]

In general, in composing his biographies, Plutarch relates his hero's career from birth to death in chronological order. But he allows himself a good deal of scope, and the precise arrangement and the amount of space allotted to each topic depends on whether the hero is predominantly an orator, a politician, or a military man, and on the amount of material available to him.[104] The *Alexander* provides a good example of his practice. After the introductory chapter, Plutarch begins with a reference to Alexander's ancestry (brief presumably because it was well known), then mentions his parents' marriage, and deals at length (and rather sceptically) with the prophecies concerning the unborn Alexander. His birth is then dated, and various prophecies of his future greatness are mentioned (2-3). Next Plutarch treats of his physical appearance, his character as a boy and his early education (4-5). The breaking of Bucephalas is allotted a full chapter (6), and in chapter 7 Plutarch relates how Aristotle was summoned to educate the young Alexander, and deduces the content of his teaching from the letters. Alexander's education is treated in two parts principally because of the importance of Aristotle's influence; this is underlined by the digression on Alexander's interest in medicine, literature, and philosophy, which he owes to Aristotle. We then hear of Alexander's activities during Philip's reign, the domestic troubles caused by Philip's marriage to Cleopatra and Alexander's attempt to ally himself with the Carian dynast, Pixodarus, and finally of Philip's murder (9-10). The next four chapters (11-14) relate Alexander's campaigns in Illyria and Greece (with a digression on his treatment of Timocleia (12)), and his preparations for the Persian expedition. This begins with the crossing of the Hellespont (15), and henceforth Alexander's deeds are recounted in chronological order up to his death. The final chapter (77) discusses the story that he was poisoned and breaks off in the middle of an anecdote about his successor.

As is customary, the narrative is interrupted at various points by digressions, where a number of anecdotes are assembled out of chronological order to illuminate certain aspects of Alexander's character. Apart from those in chapters 8 and 12 (above), his treatment of the captive Persian women is followed by a discussion of his continence and subsequently of his self-control and habits (21. 5-23). Similarly the visit to Siwah is followed by a chapter (28) examining Alexander's attitude to his own divinity, and the burning of the palace at Persepolis occasions the longest digression (39-42. 4), illustrating the king's generosity and his loyalty to and care for his friends. Much briefer digressions occur at 45. 4-6, where Alexander's valour is demonstrated, and at 47. 5-12, where his measures to further his 'policy of fusion' are described. The German scholar Adolf Weizsäcker coined the terms 'Chronographisch' and 'Eidologisch' to describe the two elements in Plutarch's work.[105] These are useful to the historian who is attempting to date events, but the distinction is misleading to the extent that the illustration of character is not confined to the 'Eidology'. The narrative also is designed to bring out the character of the hero.

The portrait of Alexander is built up in several different ways, for Plutarch is too good an artist to rely on any single method. In view of his aims it is hardly surprising to find that the amount of space devoted to military operations, even in the case of so famous a leader as Alexander, is small. In the descriptions of the major battles interest is concentrated on the person of Alexander, and little effort is made to elucidate the topography or tactics involved. It is safe to say that we could not understand any of the battles from Plutarch's narrative. Although Gaugamela with its preliminaries occupies three chapters (31-3), the main stress is laid on Alexander's confidence before and during the battle, which Parmenio's request for aid serves to heighten. The actual fighting is disposed of in less than a chapter, in which the two kings are the protagonists. At Issus the battle itself is described in a single sentence (20. 8), which reveals how Alexander took advantage of Fortune's favour, and the actual fighting against Porus is allotted only two sentences (60. 10-11). The comparatively lengthy description of the operations at the Granicus (16. 1-14) is to be explained by the prominence of Alexander and his *aristeia* against Spithridates and Rhoesaces. The episode at the Malli town is fully treated, as we would expect, but the pursuit of Darius (42-3) serves merely to introduce Alexander's refusal of water, showing his ἐγκράτεια and μεγαλοψυχία, and the request of the dying Darius to Polystratus to reward Alexander for his ἐπιείκεια. The fierce and prolonged fighting in Bactria and Sogdiana is represented only by a series of episodes (45. 5-6; 58), showing the king's valour and daring and his φιλανθρωπία. The account of the siege of Tyre (24. 5-25. 3) well illustrates Plutarch's technique: we have a few words at the beginning and end about the military operations, but the bulk of the narrative is taken up with Alexander's dreams and the episodes involving Lysimachus and Aristander, which show the king's loyalty to his friends.

Apart from the major military operations Plutarch could hardly fail to include many well-known incidents such as the Gordian knot (18), the founding of Alexandria and the expedition to Siwah (26-7), and the visit of the Amazon queen (46). Nor could he avoid mentioning the 'conspiracies' of Philotas and the royal pages and the murder of Cleitus (49-55). Elsewhere he had more freedom of choice, and his *selection* of anecdotes, from which the narrative is built up, shows us how he intended to portray the character of Alexander. A number of themes, some dealt with more systematically in the digressions, recur. We see, for instance, his ἐγκράτεια and σωφροσύνη in his treatment of women,

Timocleia (12), and the Persian captives (21; 30), while the same qualities are attributed to him when he refuses the water in the desert (42. 7-10). His meetings with the Nysaean envoys (58. 7-9), Taxiles (59), and Porus (60. 14-15) all serve to bring out his generosity towards his enemies, both those who submitted and those defeated in battle. The expedition against the Arabs and his order to alter the calendar during the siege of Tyre (24-5) demonstrate his loyalty to his companions, while his trust in them is exemplified by the dramatic scene with his doctor, Philip (19). A less attractive side of Alexander's character appears in his superstitious belief in the series of omens in ch. 73 and his treatment of Cassander (74). The vast majority of anecdotes are relevant to Plutarch's main theme, the character of Alexander, but in a few cases, e.g. the purple of Hermione and the storing of Danube and Nile water in the Persian treasury (36. 2-4), information seems to be included simply because it interested Plutarch.

Although Plutarch generally allows his portrait of Alexander to emerge through his narrative of great events and the numerous anecdotes, he often comments in his own person on many of the most important aspects of his character, especially in the digressions to link or to introduce the anecdotes. In ch. 28, for example, Plutarch's remarks make it clear that in his view Alexander did not believe in his divinity but used other people's belief in it as a political device, and in ch. 23 he states his opinion that Alexander was not addicted to drink. Plutarch's technique can be seen most clearly in the 'great digression' (39-42. 4). He begins by stating that Alexander was extremely generous and that his generosity increased with his increasing means; this is shown by numerous examples. Plutarch goes on to illustrate the luxury of the king's followers (40), adding the comment that Alexander reproved them 'gently and philosophically'. He then relates that by exposing himself to danger Alexander tried to reform them, but that they were so devoted to luxury that they abused him (41). At first, Plutarch remarks, Alexander reacted 'gently', saying that to endure abuse when doing good was a king's duty, but finally (42. 4) became furious and was cruel and implacable, because he valued reputation (*doxa*) above life itself. Earlier (4. 8, 5. 5) the biographer has commented on and exemplified Alexander's love of reputation, although not from every kind of activity. Plutarch's own views are clearly expressed at 20. 7 and 26. 14, Alexander's superiority to Fortune and his invincibility due to his spirited nature (τὸ θυμοειδές), already deduced from his bodily heat (4. 7). Towards the end of Alexander's life Plutarch himself attests his suspicion and despondency (74. 1), and his addiction to superstition (75. 1-2). It is likely, too, that the alternative reasons given for Alexander's

generous treatment of Athens (13. 2), for his adoption of a mixed dress (45. 1), and for his slowness to take action against Philotas (49. 2) are Plutarch's own comment.

Finally Alexander's character is revealed directly by what he himself says and, less often, by what others say of him. His desire for the right kind of *doxa* is shown by his remarks that he would run at the Olympic Games if his opponents were all kings (4. 10), and that Philip would leave him nothing to accomplish (5. 4). His philosophic nature is illustrated by the famous remark 'If I were not Alexander, I would be Diogenes' (14. 5), and by his statement that he was indebted to Philip for life but to Aristotle for the good life (8. 4). His attitude to luxury is brought out by his comment on Darius' tent after Issus (20. 13), while his confidence is stressed by the celebrated reply to Parmenio, who advocated a night attack at Gaugamela, 'I do not steal victory' (31. 12), and perhaps also by his remark to him at 29. 8. His seriousness of character in childhood moves the Persian envoys to comment (5. 3), and his future greatness is foreshadowed when Philip says to him 'Macedonia is not large enough for you' (6. 8). The deserter Amyntas assures Darius that he need not worry about Alexander running away (20. 3); the eunuch tells Darius of Alexander's ἐγκράτεια καὶ μεγαλοψυχία (30. 11), and Darius' dying words emphasize his ἐπιείκεια (43. 4).

Plutarch's artistry consists largely in the way in which he skilfully employs these different methods of illustrating character in combination. Direct statement is confirmed by anecdote, and the major events are related in such a fashion that attention is concentrated on the person of Alexander and the biographer's conception of him gradually emerges through the narrative.

PLUTARCH'S HISTORICAL METHODS

In the *Moralia* and the *Lives* Plutarch cites no fewer than 150 historians (in the wider sense), including forty who wrote in Latin.[106] Despite this, or perhaps rather because of it, a highly sceptical view of the extent of Plutarch's historical reading prevailed for much of this century. For example, Busolt and Beloch in their standard histories held that Plutarch obtained most of his information at second hand.[107] The most obvious way of settling the question, the analysis of individual *Lives,* was by no means neglected but, unfortunately, produced widely differing and sometimes contradictory results.[108] In fact, it is rarely possible by source analysis to *prove* that one author has consulted another directly and not through an intermediary.[109]

Two doubts influenced those who favoured the theory that Plutarch used intermediate sources: first, how could he find time, while writing as much as he did, to read all the authors he cites, and secondly, if he could find time, was it conceivable that his library at Chaeroneia contained all these works, many of them far from common? The first difficulty has perhaps been exaggerated. Despite the claims of a busy public life the elder Pliny had written over 100 books before his death at the age of 55, an age when Plutarch had just begun to write his *Parallel Lives*.[110] The second difficulty, apparently more substantial when we consider the writer's isolation at Chaeroneia,[111] vanishes if we agree with Gomme[112] that Plutarch did not write surrounded by books, but relied to a great extent on his excellent memory and for the rest consulted his notes of books he had previously read. Gomme pointed, in particular, to Plutarch's wide reading[113] and to his statements that he had read various authors.[114]

What little we know of the methods of ancient writers supports Gomme's view. In a letter to Baebius Macer (*Ep.* 3. 5) the younger Pliny describes (§ 10) how his uncle worked: 'A book was read aloud while he made notes and extracts, as he did with every book he read.' It is not surprising to hear (§ 17) that his uncle left him '160 volumes of notes, written in a tiny hand on both sides of the page, so that these 160 volumes were equivalent to many more'.[115] Plutarch tells us (*Mor.* 457 d) that Minucius Fundanus made collections of material on various subjects, and we probably possess two such collections of his own in the *Regum et imperatorum apophthegmata* and the *Apophthegmata Laconica* (172 a-242 d).[116] We have no means of telling how detailed Plutarch's notes were, but we are probably safe to conclude that he relied mostly on his trained memory.[117] The assumption that he was writing from memory best explains the many errors of detail in the *Lives*. At *Them.* 12. 8, for example, Panaetius commands a trireme from *Tenedos,* while in Herodotus (8. 82), an author whom Plutarch had certainly read, he commands a *Tenian* trireme. In the same *Life* (15. 3) Lycomedes, an Athenian trierarch, is said to have made a dedication from the first Persian vessel captured at *Salamis*; yet from Herod. 8. 11 we know that he captured this vessel at *Artemisium.*[118]

Recent studies have confirmed that Plutarch worked in this way. In 1951 Theander examined his use of some sixteen Greek authors and proved beyond reasonable doubt that Plutarch had read these authors. He pointed out that Plutarch quotes *verbatim* and in particular criticizes authors or compares one with another in such a way that it is apparent that he had read them.[119] Several times, too, Plutarch indicates his use of an intermediate source, especially Hermippus, who is cited six times in this way.[120] This, Theander rightly claimed, must mean that he had read the more recent author. Unfortunately Theander's study, inevitably, does not embrace the many obscure writers cited by Plutarch. Argument in future is

likely to concern itself not with whether Plutarch habitually used *Mittelquellen*—this is settled[121]—but with what proportion of the authors cited he knew at first hand.

Ziegler, who had already rejected the idea that Plutarch always used second-hand material, attempted to draw up a table showing which authors Plutarch had certainly read, which he had probably read, and which he knew only through an intermediary.[122] Using as a criterion the number and spread of the citations, he concluded that rather more than half fell into the last category. But his criterion is evidently too simple, since it ignores the scope of an author's work, which Plutarch might have no occasion to consult except in one or two *Lives*;[123] moreover the results of the most recent investigation suggest that Ziegler was somewhat too cautious.

It has generally been thought (see Ziegler 859) that in the *Mulierum Virtutes* (242 e-63 c), twenty-seven little-known stories illustrating the heroic qualities of women, Plutarch and Polyaenus (who relates nineteen of them) used a common source, an existing anthology. Stadter, however, has proved that Polyaenus used Plutarch, who made his own selection, and has made it almost certain, by a detailed study of the individual stories, that Plutarch had read the writers he mentions.[124] Some of these are well known, but the majority are local historians. If Plutarch had read these, it is reasonable to conclude that he had also read at least the majority of the authors he cites elsewhere. This may be true even of much of the anecdotic material and the citations from the comic writers, which Büchner and Ziegler believe to be second-hand; but we must agree with Büchner that in many cases it is difficult or impossible to distinguish first-hand from second-hand material.[125]

Statements that 'no one took the duties of a historian more seriously than Plutarch' or that 'within their chronological limits the *Lives* provide a universal history of the Greco-Roman world' can excite only incredulity.[126] Plutarch himself does not claim so much (*Alex.* 1), and he made no attempt to provide the historical background to his heroes' actions or to explain the origins and long-term effects of their policies.[127] His reliance on memory is excessive, he is indifferent to detail, and, more important, he imposes his own interpretation of his hero's character on the narrative at the expense of the facts.[128] Nevertheless it would be wrong to conclude that Plutarch was credulous or even uncritical. Gomme[129] lists three main weaknesses: lack of insight into the political conditions of the classical age, indifference to chronology, and inability to value his authorities. About the first there can be no dispute. As for the second, it is disconcerting to find that Plutarch (*Sol.* 27) accepts the tradition that Solon met Croesus despite 'the so-called canons of chronology' because the meeting accords with his view of Solon's character.[130]

Yet he could use the archon lists to prove that Aristeides was archon in 489/8 B.C. (*Arist.* 5), and at *Them.* 2. 5 he refutes Stesimbrotus' statement that Themistocles was a pupil of Anaxagoras and Melissus by pointing out that Anaxagoras was a friend of Pericles, against whom Melissus commanded the Samian forces in 440/39.

About Gomme's third point I feel less sure. It may be true that Plutarch 'had no *scientific* appreciation of the difference between first-hand and second- or third-hand authorities', but it must be emphasized that he sought, where possible, to use contemporary or near-contemporary sources. It is significant that the *Themistocles* is based primarily on Herodotus and Thucydides, and that he followed Hieronymus of Cardia in the Hellenistic *Lives,* and Timaeus (? and Theopompus) in the *Timoleon.* So in the *Dion* (31. 2, 35. 6) the versions of Timonides and Philistus, who were contemporary with the events, are preferred to that of Timaeus.[131] Again, in the *Alexander* (see next section) his main authorities were men who had all (except Cleitarchus) accompanied Alexander. Note, too, his use of contemporary documents: in the *Solon* the poems of Solon, in the *Alexander* the king's letters (used in preference to other sources), and in the *Dion* the letters of Plato.[132] In the *Lives* of Cicero and Demosthenes he made considerable use of their speeches and in the *Demosthenes* of those of Aeschines as well.

Herodotus (7. 152) expressly states that he need not be thought to believe every statement he makes; Plutarch makes no such disclaimer, but we have no right to suppose that he would have vouched for the truth of every detail in the *Lives.* He often sets out variant views without comment,[133] as Herodotus had done, but frequently criticizes his authorities. His criticism is based to some extent on his knowledge of the character of their writings,[134] but he did not rely only on this knowledge. The dramatic descriptions of Alexander's passage along the Pamphylian coast (17. 6) and of his death (75. 5) are refuted in the one case by the evidence of the king's letter[135] and in the other by Aristobulus' statement.

Plutarch was well aware not only that the passage of time rendered the discovery of the truth difficult but also that contemporary historians might be swayed by hostility or by partiality (*Per.* 13. 16). At *Aratus* 38 he comments that Phylarchus' version would not be worthy of credit were it not supported by Polybius; for Phylarchus was an enthusiastic admirer of Cleomenes and constantly wrote like an advocate. Similarly he rejects (*Per.* 28. 3) Duris' allegations of Pericles' cruelty to the Samian captives, not only because Thucydides, Ephorus, and Aristotle say nothing of it, but also because it was likely that Duris would exaggerate the misfortunes of his fellow countrymen to blacken the Athenian character.[136] Plutarch makes much use of the *argumentum ex silentio*: at *Alc.* 32. 2, for example, he rejects Duris' version of Alcibiades' return to Athens in 408 because of the silence of Theopompus, Ephorus, and Xenophon;[137] typically, he adds the comment, based on his reading (? or misreading) of Alcibiades' character, that he would not have been likely to act in this way at this time.[138]

Perhaps the passage which best illustrates the merits and limitations of Plutarch's criticism is *Aristeides* 1. Demetrius of Phaleron had maintained that Aristeides was well-to-do: he had been chosen archon by lot, he had been ostracized, and he had set up a choregic monument. The last argument Plutarch counters by adducing the epigraphic evidence of Panaetius, which is conclusive; yet he does not regard this point as settled, and has indeed prefaced Panaetius' evidence with a quite inconclusive suggestion of his own. Against the other points made by Demetrius he shows that not all those ostracized were members of noble houses, and cites Idomeneus for the fact that Aristeides was *elected* archon. Plutarch's faults are clear: he does not appreciate the value of the epigraphic evidence, and he does not trouble to consult Aristotle's *Constitution of Athens,* which he had certainly read,[139] but relies on his recollection of a statement by Idomeneus, an author whom he criticizes elsewhere.[140] Yet he deserves credit for the clarity with which he sets out the arguments of Demetrius and Panaetius, and for his wide reading which provided this knowledge.

Plutarch's criticism contains much good sense, but it is easy to overvalue it; certainly it is too much to say, as Theander (78) does, that 'he became a historian almost against his will'. Nevertheless, Theander is right, particularly in view of the opinions sometimes expressed by his detractors, to emphasize Plutarch's curiosity about monuments (including portraits), topography, and ancient customs,[141] and his use of collections of documents.[142]

IV. The Sources of the *Alexander*

In the *Alexander,* apart from the letters written by or to Alexander which are mentioned over thirty times, Plutarch names no fewer than twenty-four authorities Of these he cites Aristobulus (15. 2; 16. 15; 18. 4; 21. 9; 46. 2; 75. 6), Chares (20. 9; 24. 14; 46. 2; 54. 4; 55. 9; 70. 2), and Onesicritus (8. 2; 15. 2; 46. 1; 60. 6; 61. 1; 65. 2) six times, Callisthenes (27. 4; 33. 1; 33. 10) three times, and Eratosthenes (3. 3; 31. 5), Duris (15. 2; 46. 2), and the Ephemerides or Royal Journal (23. 4; 76. 1) twice each. The following writers are mentioned once each:[143] Antigenes, Anticleides, Aristoxenus (4. 4), Cleitarchus, Dinon (36. 4), Hegesias (3. 6), Hecataeus of Eretria, Heracleides (26. 3), Hermippus (54. 1), Ister,

Philip of Chalcis, Philip of Theangela, Philon, Polycleitus, Ptolemy, Sotion (61. 3), and Theophrastus (4. 5).

Not all scholars believe that Plutarch had read all these authors. An extreme view is advanced by J. E. Powell (*JHS* 59 (1939), 229 ff.), who, observing certain similarities between his narrative and that of Arrian, concluded that both writers used a large variorum sourcebook and that Plutarch supplemented this from a collection of spurious letters.[144] Tarn (2. 306 ff.) made a brief but effective rejoinder to Powell; he pointed out *inter alia* that there are no precedents for the kind of volume envisaged by him, which would have to contain the whole of Ptolemy's history; and, we may add, a great deal besides. Recently Inge Rabe[145] has examined in detail the passages in Arrian and Plutarch on which Powell relies, and has demonstrated beyond question that in *no* case is the theory of a common source tenable.

The view advanced by Helene Homeyer,[146] that for the *Alexander* Plutarch used Eratosthenes and Duris, in whom the remaining authorities were already incorporated, needs more discussion. First, however, we should note Plutarch's statement in the introduction to the *Alexander,* that he does not propose to narrate *all* the famous exploits of Alexander and Caesar but to deal with only some of them, in summary fashion for the most part. This *ought* to mean, one would think, that he is selecting from a mass of material. Secondly, although Plutarch names twenty-four writers in the *Alexander,* this number is deceptive; for no fewer than seventeen are cited once only, ten of these at 46. 1-2 (the Amazon story).[147] This does not, of course, prove that Plutarch did not use these authors elsewhere, but in fact only Cleitarchus may have been used extensively (see below . . .). The other seven who are cited once[148] are referred to only for isolated incidents, and it is highly probable that all these references derive from Plutarch's own reading. Even Powell (p. 230) concedes that a few of them may be recollections from earlier reading; he instances Hegesias. This is certainly the case at 4. 4-5, where Plutarch combines Aristoxenus' statement that Alexander had a 'sweet smell' with Theophrastus' theory.[149]

Finally, if it can be shown that Plutarch consulted any of the major primary sources directly Miss Homeyer's theory collapses. For those who believe that he had before him a collection of Alexander's letters, and did not find them in his sources, Fränkel long ago established that Plutarch consulted Onesicritus directly. For he remarked (p. 135) that in the middle of the letter describing the battle at the Hydaspes (ch. 60) there occurs a quotation from Onesicritus. Obviously, if it is a genuine letter, Alexander cannot have included it, and it is surely inconceivable that a forger would have been so stupid as to insert it. Miss Homeyer, however, thinks that Plutarch found the extracts from the letters in his sources. Her position is not, I think, tenable. She remarks that they are cited 'nur oberflächlich', and it is self-evident that they are not quoted in full. But if they *were* contained in his sources, they must have been reported in full; for the manner in which Plutarch writes at 17. 8 strongly suggests that *he* is summarizing the letter, and conclusive proof is furnished at 46. 3, where he writes that Alexander seems to support those writers who say that the Amazon story is fiction. 'For', he continues, 'when writing in detail to Antipater, Alexander says that the Scythian offered him his daughter's hand, but makes no mention of the Amazon.' Evidently Plutarch had the whole letter before him, and it is very difficult to credit that Duris or Eratosthenes transcribed it (or any of the others) in full. The matter is settled, in my opinion, by Powell's observation (230 f.) that 'the quiet naïveté with which again and again he takes credit to himself for making use of the letters for the first time is the best proof that he used them directly'. Powell points out that the majority of the citations occur in the digressions on character, which must be Plutarch's own work.

There can be no doubt that the source of Plutarch's information in ch. 12 (the Timocleia episode) is Aristobulus, who is cited for the story at *Mor.* 1093 c.[150] A comparison with *Mor.* 259 d-260 d (= *Mul. Virt.* 24), where the incident is described in greater detail but with no significant difference, makes it evident that Plutarch is himself summarizing Aristobulus' version.[151] It is significant, as Rabe (pp. 130 f.) saw, that the episode is not even referred to by any other author.[152] Plutarch, therefore, was familiar with the works of Onesicritus and Aristobulus. That he had read Callisthenes and Chares cannot be demonstrated, but may reasonably be assumed.

Yet it is difficult to suppose that all the information contained in the *Alexander* was derived from these four authors, and it is likely that Plutarch used another source or sources. The most probable candidate is Cleitarchus; there are many incidents in the latter part of the *Life* where Plutarch's narrative is similar to that of the 'vulgate',[153] and in some of them at least Plutarch cannot be following Aristobulus (whose version, known from Arrian, was different), while it is unlikely that Chares and Onesicritus dealt with all the incidents. In particular, Plutarch gives Cleitarchus' version of the burning of Persepolis (ch. 38) and of the *komos* in Carmania (ch. 67), while at ch. 75. 5 he rejects his account of Alexander's death. It remains possible that Plutarch found this information in a later writer, perhaps Duris, as Miss Homeyer suggests, but while this possibility cannot be absolutely ruled out it seems to me much more probable that Plutarch consulted Cleitarchus directly.[154] It would be surprising, in view of his marked preference for primary sources (above . . .) and of the popularity of Cleitarchus in the late Republic and early Empire, if Plutarch had *not* read his book.

We cannot hope to assign every statement to its source,[155] but if we consider the character of the works of the contemporary sources and of Cleitarchus, as revealed by their extant fragments, some progress is possible.[156] We may reasonably suppose that where Alexander's divine sonship is mentioned or where he seeks to win over the Greeks (as at 34. 2) Callisthenes is his source; Onesicritus will have supplied information about Alexander's education and shown him as the 'philosopher in action', while Chares may be responsible for incidents concerning the court and Aristobulus for personal details. Plutarch's sources may also be surmised from the similarity of his narrative to that of the other extant sources. *Close* correspondence with Strabo may indicate that he is using Aristobulus or Onesicritus, and, in particular, resemblance to Arrian may show use of Aristobulus, and to the 'vulgate' use of Cleitarchus. Unfortunately this criterion is difficult to apply, especially in the first part of the *Life,* since all the historians drew on Callisthenes' account. Even after Callisthenes' history ceased the situation is complicated, as Cleitarchus used Onesicritus and Aristobulus used Cleitarchus.[157] Finally, in one or two instances Plutarch relates the same incidents in the *Moralia* and there names his source.

Using these criteria we may tentatively assign the following passages to their sources[158]—citations are marked with an asterisk:

Callisthenes: 17. 6; 26-7. 7*;[159] 30. 2-14 (cf. Arr. 4. 20. 1-3, Curt. 4. 10. 25-34); 31. 8-14; 32-3* (cited at 33. 1, 33. 10).[160]

Aristobulus: 4. 1 (cf. Arr. 1. 16. 4); 11 (for § 12 cf. Arr. 1. 9. 10); 12 (cited at *Mor.* 1093 c); 13. 1-2 (cf. *Dem.* 23. 3 ff.); 14. 8-9 (cf. Arr. 1. 11. 2); 15. 2*; 16* (cited at 16. 15; cf. Arr. 1. 16. 4, 7); 18. 2-4*; 20. 1-3 (cf. Arr. 2. 6. 3 ff., 2. 7. 1 ff.); 21. 9*; 23. 1 (cf. Arr. 7. 29. 4); 29. 7-9 (cf. Arr. 2. 25. 1-3); 31. 6-7 (cf. Arr. 6. 11. 4 ff.); 38. 8 (cf. Arr. 3. 18. 11); 42. 5 (cf. Arr. 3. 19. 5); 45. 5-6 (cf. Arr. 3. 30. 11, esp. the form Orexartes); 46. 2*; 57. 5-9 (cf. Arr. 4. 15. 7, Strabo 11. 518); 63. 2-14 (cf. *Mor.* 341 c, Arr. 6. 9. 1 ff.); 75. 6*.

Chares: 6 (cf. Gell. *NA* 5. 2); 20. 9*; 20. 13; 24. 10-14*; 46. 2*; 50-1 (cf. Berve 2. 207, n. 1); 54. 4-6*; 55. 1 ff.; 55. 9*; 70. 2*; 70. 3-6.

Onesicritus: 5. 7-8; 8. 2*; 15. 2*; 22. 7-10; 25. 6-8; 26. 1-2 (cf. 8. 2); 46. 1*; 59. 1-5 (cf. Strabo 15. 698); 60. 6*; 60. 12-16; 61. 1-2*; 62 (except §§ 4, 9); 65. 2*.

Cleitarchus: 37. 1-2 (cf. Curt. 5. 4. 10 ff., Diod. 68. 5); 38. 1-7 (cf. Curt. 5. 7. 2 ff., Diod 72); 39. 2. (cf. Curt. 4. 9. 24 ff.); 43. 3-4 (cf. Curt. 5. 13. 24, Justin 11. 15. 7 ff.); 46. 1*; 49 (cf. Curt. 6. 7. 1 ff., Diod. 79); 57. 1-2 (cf. Curt. 6. 6. 14 ff.); 66. 4-7; 67. 1-7 (cf. Curt. 9. 10. 24-8, Diod. 106. 1); 75. 3-5.

Theophrastus: 35. 15 (cf. *Mor.* 648 d).

Ctesias: 69. 1 (see n. ad loc.).

PLUTARCH'S MAIN SOURCES[161]

Callisthenes

(Jacoby no. 124. Robinson 45-77. Pearson 22-49. See also T. S. Brown, 'Callisthenes and Alexander', *AJP* 70 (1949), 225-48.)

Callisthenes accompanied Aristotle, his great-uncle, from Atarneus to Macedonia in 343/2, and must have known Alexander well, although he was too old to have been his fellow-pupil, as later tradition asserted (Berve 2. 191). He probably owed the invitation to join Alexander's staff (see 53. 1 n.) as much to his connection with Aristotle as to his reputation as a historian, although by 334 he had composed an encomium on Hermeias, a work on the Sacred War, and a ten-book *History of Greece* (387-357), and had co-operated with Aristotle in compiling a list of Pythian victors (see *GHI* 2. 187).

His task was evidently to produce for Greek consumption an account of Alexander's progress which would conciliate Greek public opinion, and it seems a necessary assumption that he sent his work back to Greece in instalments. He clearly understood what was required (*pace* Pearson 23), and wrote as Alexander wished him to write; the unfavourable portrait of Parmenio is his work (see 33. 10 n.). That his motives were 'patriotic' and that he hoped for a 'national regeneration' through Alexander, as Schachermeyr (127) maintains, cannot be proved or disproved. Later writers criticized him for his 'flattery' of Alexander, and his 'Exploits of Alexander' was to some extent at least a rhetorical encomium of the king. Of the dozen extant fragments the most important (14(*a*)) describes the visit to Siwah. From this we can see that Alexander was cast in *heroic* mould; the motive for the expedition was rivalry with his ancestors, Perseus and Heracles, and Alexander receives divine aid from two ravens. Even a rainstorm is the work of Zeus (see 27. 2 n.). Callisthenes was responsible for spreading the story that Alexander was the son of *Zeus* (cf. 33. 1, Alexander's prayer at Gaugamela)—which is not the same thing as making him a god (see esp. Badian, *Gnomon* 33 (1961), 661). The passage of Mount Climax (17. 8) is treated in similar fashion, and thunder at Sardes and Gordium is probably to be interpreted as an example of divine approval (see Pearson 36-8, 39). Callisthenes also dealt with Homeric sites in Asia Minor in order to emphasize Alexander's heroic ancestry, as Pearson (39-45) has well demonstrated. He was familiar with the terrain from his stay at Atarneus and was said to have collaborated in a recension of Homer (see 26. 2 n.). His account of the battle of Issus is severely, and in the main justly, criticized by Polybius (12. 17-22); his account of Gaugamela seems to have been no better, if we may judge by the versions of Plutarch (32-3) and Curtius—although they, admittedly, may be partly to blame.

Aristobulus

(Jacoby no. 139. Robinson 205-43. Pearson 150-87. See also G. Wirth, 'Anmerkungen zur Arrianbiographie', *Historia* 13 (1964), 213 ff.)

Aristobulus is called 'a man of Cassandreia', which means that he settled there after its foundation in 316, but he may have been a Phocian by birth (see Pearson, *AJP* 73 (1952), 71 ff.). He did not hold any military command, so far as is known, but was entrusted with various commissions, such as the restoration of Cyrus' tomb (69. 3), which suggest that he was an engineer or an architect.

Arrian selected him, together with Ptolemy, as the chief source for his *Anabasis* and evidently considered him a reliable authority, while Strabo used his book extensively in his account of India. Modern views of his abilities vary. The really important question (see Pearson 152 ff.) is whether he was a primary authority, writing before Ptolemy and Cleitarchus, or whether he drew on their works and was (in part) a secondary writer. The prevailing view, that Cleitarchus wrote towards the end of the fourth century, has been challenged by Tarn (2. 16 ff.) and, more effectively, by Pearson (226 ff.), who favour a date after 280, but it still appears to me to be more probable.[162] If this is so, Cleitarchus is clearly earlier than Aristobulus, who, it is agreed, wrote not earlier than 295 B.C.[163]

It seems certain on any view that Aristobulus did not indulge in rhetoric or exaggeration and did not aim at sensation. He is, for example, much more reticent than Onesicritus about the marvels of India, and did not relate the visit of the Amazon queen (46) or the *komos* in Carmania (67). He described accurately what he had seen, e.g. the tomb of Cyrus (see Pearson 180 f.) and the Gymnosophists at Taxila (fr. 41), and displayed 'a vivid interest in geography and natural history'. On the other hand, his portrait of Alexander appears to have been uniformly, and suspiciously, favourable.[164] He had little to say about the 'conspiracy' of Philotas (fr. 22),

while Cleitus deserved what he got (fr. 29) and the pages implicated Callisthenes (fr. 31). For all these events Plutarch preferred more detailed (and better) sources. But he no doubt welcomed Aristobulus' statement (surely false) that Alexander was not a heavy drinker (fr. 62; cf. fr. 59), and relates from Aristobulus the various anecdotes—Timocleia (ch. 12), Darius' women-folk after Issus and Barsine (ch. 21)—which show Alexander's self-control and generosity to captive women.

For major events, such as the expedition to Siwah and the battle of Gaugamela (and doubtless those of the Granicus and Issus as well) Plutarch preferred Callisthenes, although he was impressed enough to adopt Aristobulus' argument that the battle took place at Gaugamela and not at Arbela. In the events described in ch. 73 (Peithagoras and the man who sat on the king's throne) Plutarch rejected Aristobulus' version, perhaps because it did not square with his view that by this time Alexander had fallen victim to superstition. In fact, after Gaugamela there is little that can be positively attributed to Aristobulus, except Alexander's exploit at the Malli town (ch. 63).

Chares

(Jacoby no. 125. Robinson 77-86. Pearson 50-61.)

We know nothing of his life except that he was a native of Mytilene and was appointed Chamberlain (εἰσαγγελεύς), presumably in 330 after the death of Darius. His *Stories of Alexander* (so, rightly, Pearson 51), in at least ten books, was read by Aristobulus, Duris, and probably Cleitarchus (see *F.Gr. Hist.* 2D, 433). The majority of the nineteen fragments (all but two preserved by Plutarch and Athenaeus) are unimportant, and his only contribution to military history is the story that at Issus Darius was wounded by Alexander! Tarn (2. 70) concludes that 'one or two passages apart, like the *proskynesis* affair (which he presumably saw), the fragments only exhibit a trifler, immersed in court ceremonies and dinners, the minutiae of his office'. This is not unfair, and Schachermeyr (131) clearly goes too far in calling his book 'one of the three great works (the others are those of Ptolemy and Aristobulus) of the Alexander period'. Nevertheless, Chares is a valuable witness for events at court—the Susa weddings (fr. 4), the refusal of Callisthenes to drink unmixed wine (fr. 13), the *proskynesis* affair (ch. 54), and (almost certainly) the murder of Cleitus (ch. 50-1)—all the more valuable as Ptolemy (and Aristobulus) practised what Badian (*Gnomon* 33 (1961), 666) has aptly called 'a highly selective and purposeful reserve'. Chares seems to have been interested in description rather than character (Pearson 61), but if we may judge from his version of Callisthenes' death (55. 9), in which he seems to attempt to exculpate Alexander, his verdict on Alexander is unlikely to have been unfavourable.

Onesicritus

(Jacoby no. 134. Robinson 149-66. Pearson 83-111. See also T. S. Brown, *Onesicritus*.)

Onesicritus was a native of the town of Astypalaea on Cos; see the works cited in *Historia* 10 (1961), 457, n. 68. Otherwise we know only that he studied under Diogenes (65. 2) and that, as he became chief steersman of Alexander's fleet, he must have been an experienced sailor (see 66. 3 n.).

Whether he had a connection with Aegina is disputed. Suidas (s.v. Φίλισκος Αἰγινήτης) registers a Philiscus of Aegina who was one of Alexander's teachers, while Diogenes Laertius (6. 75-6) mentions 'a certain Onesicritus' of Aegina (Ὀνησίκριτόν τινα) who sent his son, Philiscus, to study under Diogenes and later joined him as a student. It has, therefore, been suggested that Suidas' Philiscus was the father of the historian and had the same name as his grandson. However, Strasburger (*RE* 18, 460 f.) and Jacoby (*F.Gr.Hist.* 2D, 469) reject the identification, since Onesicritus was too famous to be referred to as 'a certain O.', and, as he had two grown-up sons before he joined Alexander, he would have been too old to play the part he did in the expedition. Nevertheless, in view of the rarity of the name (see Strasburger *RE* 18, 461), it is tempting to conclude that Onesicritus was a relative of Alexander's teacher, since this would explain how he obtained his information about the young Alexander. That he possessed such information is a necessary deduction from the title of his book, which Diogenes Laertius (6. 84) gives as πῶς Ἀλέξανδρος ἤχθη and compares with the *Cyropaideia* of Xenophon.[165]

The comparison with the *Cyropaideia* is significant. Xenophon had depicted Cyrus as 'the shepherd of mankind', and in Onesicritus' book Alexander evidently appeared in Cynic fashion as 'the philosopher in arms', who had a mission to civilize the world; see Strabo 15. 1. 64 (= fr. 17 (a)). The idea is prominent in the first speech *De Alex. fort.* (see above . . .), but in the *Life*, although Alexander is devoted to philosophy and literature, it is largely absent. As a biographer Plutarch naturally was not interested in the strange customs and peculiarities of geography and natural history with which the extant fragments are mostly concerned, although it is probable that Onescritus was his source for much of chapters 59-62. There is no indication that Onesicritus was concerned with military matters or with political events. Presumably the charge of flattery which is levelled at him (see T. 7) means that he 'played down' the more unpleasant aspects of Alexander's character and his crimes, such as the murders of Cleitus and Parmenio.

Tarn (2. 35) justly describes his book as 'a professed romance' written by a professional seaman who made no claim to write history.[166] The evident attraction (and danger) of the work lay in the skilful blending of fact and fiction, as in the visit of the Amazon queen. Plutarch seems to have made little use of Onesicritus except in the early part of the *Life* (this can be demonstrated only for ch. 8 and ch. 15) and for India. For Onesicritus' influence on later writers see Strasburger, *RE* 18, 466 f.

CLEITARCHUS

(Jacoby no. 137. Robinson 171-83. Pearson 212-42. See also T. S. Brown, *Clitarchus, AJP* 71 (1950), 134-55.)

Nothing is known of his life except that he was the son of the historian Dinon and worked in Alexandria. He wrote apparently only a *History of Alexander* in at least twelve books, probably towards the end of the fourth century (on the date see above . . .). He was widely read in the late Republic and early Empire, but was adversely criticized both as a historian and a stylist (see Pearson 212 f.).

As Cleitarchus did not accompany Alexander's expedition he was dependent on earlier writers, Callisthenes (in the early part of his book), Onesicritus, Nearchus, and Polycleitus, and on oral information from the soldiers, mainly Greek, who had served with Alexander and Darius. The thirty-six extant fragments tell us little about his portrait of Alexander, and a much better idea can be gained from the seventeenth book of Diodorus.[167]

Hoffmann (26 ff.) and Jacoby (*RE* 11, 641) held that Cleitarchus wrote an unalloyed panegyric of Alexander, and it is undeniable that the prevailing tone of the work is favourable. In the first chapter of Diodorus (1. 3-4) Alexander is said to have surpassed the achievements of all kings from the beginning of time, and to have acquired a reputation rivalling that of the heroes and demi-gods of old. In fact, Alexander displays all the characteristics of a *hero*. He strives to rival Heracles (85. 2) and struggles with a river like Achilles (97. 3). His opponents are all brave, not only Darius (6. 1-2) and the Persians, but the Tyrians and Porus as well. Great stress is laid on his bravery (*passim*) and on his desire for glory (e.g. 42. 6, 78. 3, 85. 2, 93. 4). He decides (or intends to decide) by his own exertions the battles and sieges (examples in Tarn 2. 66, Hoffmann 27). Moreover, as Tarn (loc. cit.) has demonstrated, Alexander possesses also the stock virtues of a Hellenistic monarch, φιλανθρωπία, μεγαλοψυχία, and so on; see especially the treatment of the captive Persian women (37-8) and captured cities (22. 5, 24. 1).

Nevertheless, although Alexander was in the main portrayed favourably, Tarn has shown conclusively that he was at times depicted as cruel and possessed by anger.[168] In particular, Alexander frequently indulges in massacres (Tarn 2. 67), and cheats or resorts to trickery. But these examples do not prove that Cleitarchus was hostile to Alexander; they are rather to be seen as highly sensational stories, in some cases at least exaggerating what actually happened.[169] Similarly, when in ch. 77 Alexander adopts Persian customs, including a harem of 365 concubines (which may even be true—see Welles's note ad loc.), the tone is not hostile, since Diodorus remarks that Alexander used these customs sparingly to avoid offending the Macedonians. Nevertheless, Alexander's detractors might eagerly seize on this material and present it in a hostile way.

Cleitarchus does not appear to have influenced Plutarch's view of Alexander to any great extent. Plutarch adopts a number of picturesque anecdotes from his book, e.g. the Lycian guide (37. 1-2), Erigyius' single combat (39. 2), the *komoi* at Persepolis and in Carmania (38, 67), the death of Darius (43. 3), and the burning of the Macedonian baggage (57. 1-2). On the other hand, he rejects the view that Alexandria was founded *after* the visit to Siwah (26. 8), the Amazon story (46), and, more important, the 'cup of Heracles' (75. 5) and the poisoning of Alexander (77), while he does not mention Alexander's visit to the Persian captives (see 21. 2 n.). The most important borrowings are the story of the 'conspiracy' of Philotas (49), and the anecdotes in ch. 73 which show the king a prey to superstition. These may have determined, to some degree, Plutarch's view of Alexander's last months.

THE LETTERS OF ALEXANDER

In the course of the *Life* Plutarch refers to or quotes from more than thirty letters written by Alexander or his correspondents. It is clear from the manner in which some of them are introduced (see above . . .) that Plutarch found many of them in a collection.[170] Some, e.g. those contained in chapters 19, 29, and 34, he probably found in his historical source. All these letters he evidently believed to be genuine and used in preference to his other sources, as we can see most clearly in chapter 60.

The authenticity of these letters has often been disputed, especially by J. Kaerst (*Phil.* 51 (1892), 602 ff.) and Pearson (*Historia* 3 (1954/5), 444 ff.), and just as often asserted, notably by E. Pridik, *De Alex. epistularum commercio* (Berlin, 1893), and A. Zumetikos, *De Alex. Olympiadisque epist. fontibus et reliquiis* (Berlin, 1894). Both sides claimed too much. Kaerst and Pearson showed that for various reasons forgery was rife in the Hellenistic age, but they failed to prove their contention that all the letters in Plutarch were not genuine. Authentic letters certainly existed; see esp. Strabo 9. 2. 18, where the engineer Crates writes to Alexander about

the drainage operations at Lake Copais. Here forgery is surely out of the question.[171] On the other hand, Pridik and Zumetikos tended to assume that the letters were genuine because the information contained in them tallied with the evidence of Ptolemy and Aristobulus, without considering the possibility, acutely remarked by Pearson, that a forger might have used this evidence to provide verisimilitude.

The truth is that in the majority of cases no decision is possible. Many letters, e.g. those cited in chapters 39-42, cannot be tested by independent evidence and are referred to so briefly that nothing whatsoever can usefully be said about them. Others, such as those mentioned at 20. 9, 27. 8, 46. 3, 57. 8, and 71. 8, cannot be proved genuine, but there seems no obvious reason why they should not be. In the case of those in 17. 8, 47. 3, and 55. 7 it can at least be shown that many of the arguments directed against them are not valid. Finally those quoted at 28. 2 and 60. 1 ff. have strong claims to be considered genuine, and the authenticity of the letter to the generals (55. 6) can hardly be doubted.[172]

PHILOSOPHERS AND RHETORICIANS

As Plutarch was not only widely read in the historical literature on Alexander, but must also have been familiar with the views of Peripatetic and Stoic philosophers and of the rhetorical schools, these views may properly be included among his sources.

Theophrastus' judgement on Alexander was certainly unfavourable. In his *Callisthenes or about Grief* he described him (in Cicero's words) as a man 'summa potentia summaque fortuna sed ignarum quem ad modum rebus secundis uti conveniret',[173] and a later Peripatetic, Hieronymus of Rhodes, cites him for the statement that Alexander was semi-impotent.[174] Until recently it has been generally held that Theophrastus created a 'Peripatetic portrait' of Alexander as a man who was well educated by Aristotle but was corrupted by success and became a cruel tyrant.[175] This view has now been refuted by Badian (*CQ*, N.S. 8 (1958), 144 ff.), who shows the weakness of the evidence in its favour and points out that the title indicates that the work dealt only incidentally with Alexander, and by E. Mensching (*Historia* 12 (1963), 274 ff.), who shows that, of the Peripatetics contemporary with Alexander, Aristoxenus was favourable to him and that none, apart from Theophrastus, is known to have written unfavourably of him. Among the extant fragments of Peripatetic writers there are few references to Alexander,[176] and the members of the school evidently exhibited greater independence of judgement than did the Stoics.

The Stoics regarded Alexander as spoiled by τῦφος, by delusions of grandeur as we might say, and they blamed his teacher Leonidas for not knocking it out of him; see

J. Stroux, *Phil.* 88 (1933), 222 ff. This attitude is attested by Diogenes of Babylon in the first half of the second century B.C., but is doubtless older; it is repeated by Panaetius (ap. Cic. *Off.* 1. 26. 90), who compares Philip and Alexander and concludes that the father possessed *facilitas et humanitas* and was therefore *magnus,* whereas Alexander was often *tumidissimus.*[177]

By imperial times the criticisms of the philosophical and rhetorical schools are virtually indistinguishable.[178] They can be seen most clearly in Livy's well-known digression in Book 9 (ch. 17-19), in many passages of the younger Seneca, and in Lucan's attack on Alexander (10. 20 ff.). After depreciating Alexander's opponents and commenting on his drunken progress through India, Livy goes on (18. 1-5) to describe, in a manner reminiscent of Theophrastus, how he was corrupted by success, 'secundis rebus quarum nemo intolerantior fuit', and exhibited the characteristic features of τῦφος. He arrogantly adopted Persian dress, attempted to introduce *proskynesis,* murdered his friends 'inter vinum et epulas', and aspired to divinity. Finally Livy mentions his desire for drink, which increased daily, and his anger ('trux et perfervida ira'). In short, Livy asserts, his character virtually changed. Elsewhere he alludes to Alexander's unbroken *felicitas* (18. 8) and to his *temeritas* (18. 18).

Almost all these charges can be paralleled in Seneca's writings. Alexander is often described as 'vesanus adulescens',[179] and his *feritas,* particularly in connection with the murder of Cleitus, is a favourite topic.[180] Unlike the Stoic *sapiens,* Alexander failed to control his passions (*Ep.* 113. 29, where the deaths of Cleitus and Hephaestion are mentioned), his drunkenness leads to Cleitus' death and to his own (*Ep.* 83. 19, 23), and instead of *virtus* he enjoys *felix temeritas* (*Ben.* 1. 13. 3, 7. 3. 1; cf. Lucan 10 21). He has an inexhaustible desire for fame and possessions (*Ben.* 7. 2. 5 f.; *Q Nat.* 5. 18. 10), and is addicted to τῦφος (*Ben.* 5. 6. 1, 'homo super mensuram humanae superbiae *tumens*'; cf. 2. 16. 2, '*tumidissimum* animal').

v. The Character and Value of the *Alexander*

In the *Life* little emphasis is laid on Fortune, since it would be useless for illustrating character.[181] Fortune prevents serious consequences at Philip's wedding (9. 9) and luckily (κατὰ τύχην) Alexander lands on his feet when he jumps into the Malli town (63. 3), but although Fortune helps Alexander at Issus his generalship is the decisive factor in his victory (20. 7), while at 26. 14 Fortune yields to his assaults and at 58. 2 he strives to overcome Fortune by his daring. Plutarch's outlook is revealed most clearly at 17. 6, where he remarks sarcastically that many writers wrote bombasti-

cally that the sea retired before Alexander 'by some heaven-sent good fortune', and proceeds to refute them by citing a letter of Alexander.

In general the *Life* is apologetic in tone. Plutarch does not deny that Alexander spent a long time drinking after dinner, but he cites Aristobulus for the view that he did so only for the sake of conversation (23. 1, 6). Yet this is difficult to reconcile with his subsequent statement (23. 7) that the influence of drink made him unpleasant and boastful and ready to listen to flatterers, and is indeed incompatible with his own view (4. 7) that the king was ποτικός. He devotes a whole chapter (28) to the refutation of the Stoic charge that by believing that he was divine Alexander displayed τῦφος. It was only a political device, concludes Plutarch, for his own ends; Alexander himself was not deluded (οὐδὲν τετυφωμένος). Alexander's *temeritas* is defended: the risks he takes in battle are incurred to encourage his followers (40. 4). Nor is he sunk in luxury: his own habits are frugal (22. 7 ff., 23. 9) and he sets a limit to expenditure on banquets (23. 10). On the contrary, it is his friends who display extravagance (τρυφή), and it is the abuse which they heap on him when he attempts to remonstrate with them that makes him cruel (40-42. 4).

Plutarch, of course, had to tackle the question of Alexander's responsibility for the deaths of Philotas and Parmenio, Cleitus and Callisthenes. Here again he tends to be unduly charitable.[182] Before relating the story of Cleitus' murder (which was widely criticized as an example of unbridled passion; above . . .) Plutarch tries, not unreasonably, to mitigate Alexander's crime; it was not deliberate murder, but due to a mischance (δυστυχίᾳ τινι). In the case of Philotas the real culprits are his enemies, who seize the opportunity to convince the king that Philotas must be the instigator of the plot. So, after the fiasco of the *proskynesis* when Callisthenes has mortally offended the king, his enemies' accusations are believed (55. 3). Plutarch makes no explicit comment on the death of Parmenio, but his comments about Parmenio's services to Philip and Alexander and the deaths of his sons may imply reproach.

Indeed criticism is not absent from the *Life,* a fact which distinguishes it sharply from the speeches. Alexander is no paragon, but a real figure of flesh and blood (see Wardman, *CQ,* N.S. 5 (1955), 101). Alexander is twice described as 'cruel (fearsome) and implacable' (42. 4, 57. 3), and Callisthenes is said (54. 3) to have saved him from a great disgrace by refusing to perform *proskynesis.* Alexander's reaction to Hephaestion's death is stigmatized as 'utterly unreasonable' and his expedition against the Cossaeans is described as a consolation for his grief (72. 3-4), while he plans a monument for Hephaestion that is much stranger than Stasicrates' grandiose plans for Mount Athos (72. 8). His massacre of the Indian mercenaries is 'a kind of stain' on his otherwise unblemished record as a commander (59. 7).[183] Almost all Plutarch's criticisms occur in the last part of the _Life,_ for he recognized a deterioration in Alexander's character—see esp. 52. 7, where Anaxarchus is blamed—although, unlike Curtius (6. 2. 1 ff., 6. 6. 1 ff.), he does not date this precisely. But Alexander's action in delegating the decision about the fate of Thebes to those allies who were present is surely criticized by the use of the verb καλλωπισαμένου (11. 11). This suggests that Alexander sought to evade responsibility, and the criticism is perhaps due to Plutarch's sympathy for Thebes (Wardman, loc. cit.).

Again, when the army mutinies at the Hydaspes Alexander shuts himself up in his tent like Achilles through 'despondency and anger'. In fact, anger is the chief defect in Alexander's character. He is enraged with Philotas for failing to introduce Dimnus (49. 7), with Antigenes for his deceit (70. 4), and with Cassander for mocking a Persian performing _proskynesis_ (74. 3), while in the Cleitus affair anger is mentioned three times.[184] The reason for this is that, as Wardman (esp. 102 ff.) has shown, Plutarch sees Alexander as θυμοειδής;[185] this means (in Peripatetic terms) that he is both subject to fits of anger and endowed with 'spirit', which is responsible for his ambition. However, Wardman is mistaken in thinking that Plutarch regarded Alexander as 'the spirited man' (ὁ θυμοειδής), and attempted to explain his whole life in terms of this quality, as Peripatetic biographers such as Aristoxenus and Satyrus (see Dihle 70 f., 104 ff.) had attempted to generalize from a single quality. The Alexander of Plutarch is a many-sided character.

The value of Plutarch's biographies to the historian depends partly on the amount of other material available,[186] and the value of the _Alexander_ is enhanced by 'the regrettably inadequate documentation' of the expedition. All our extant sources are late, and only Justin is complete. Particularly unfortunate are the loss of the first two books of Curtius (as well as lacunae in the tenth book) and the great lacuna in Diodorus, which deprives us (as the Table of Contents shows) of his version of Cleitus' murder, the conspiracy of the pages, the arrest and death of Callisthenes, and Alexander's marriage to Roxane. In Arrian too there is a substantial lacuna in the last book.

Our first debt, then, is the preservation of material from primary sources. Much of the information is trivial, e.g. the fact that Alexander made the customary payment on entering Pasargadae (69. 1) or that he sent part of the spoils to Croton (34. 3). Other items are more important; we may mention the proclamation of Alexander as 'king of Asia' after Gaugamela, his letter to the Greeks (34. 1-2), and the length of his stay in Persepolis (37. 6). In particular Plutarch, most commendably, cites an extract from a letter of Alexander to the Athenians which runs counter to his thesis that Alexander did not believe in his divinity (28. 2). If this is genuine (see n. ad loc.), it throws much light on the state of the king's mind towards the end of his life, and supports the view that in 324 Alexander issued a 'request' to the Greek cities to worship him as a god.[187] Even if the statements of the writers cited by Plutarch are not true, they may enable us to see the tendencies of their work; to take one important example, the citations from Callisthenes in ch. 33 reveal his bias against Parmenio.

Much of what Plutarch tells us about Alexander's early life is to be found nowhere else, and its authenticity cannot be checked. There is, however, no reason to doubt that Olympias was a savage and passionate woman—her later career confirms this—or that she was a devotee of ecstatic rites. It would also be excessively sceptical not to believe that Alexander was devoted to Greek culture,[188] although his passion for philosophy may well be exaggerated. The ninth and tenth chapters are particularly valuable; but for Plutarch we should know little of Alexander's relations with Philip and the atmosphere in the royal palace. Alexander's reaction to his father's marriage, and the Pixodarus affair (for which Plutarch is our sole authority), throw much-needed light on the vital years 338-336.

It would be idle to complain that Plutarch tells us practically nothing of events in Greece during Alexander's expedition; the same criticism might legitimately be made of Arrian's book, a professed history, and the dominance of Alexander provides some excuse. But even as a biography of Alexander the _Life_ is inadequate. Little is said of his great military achievements (see above . . .), or of that hotly debated question, his future plans (see 68. 1 n.), while the wider aspects of his policies are ignored. We are told nothing of the administration of the Empire,[189] or of the significance of the Susa weddings. Plutarch is interested only in Alexander the man.

Plutarch's portrait of Alexander contains a good deal of truth. We need not hesitate to credit his generosity or his chivalry towards women: his treatment of Timocleia (12) and Darius' wife and mother (21) is surely historical. Nor should we question his care for his followers (41), even if Plutarch's instances may not all be genuine. The 'philosopher in arms' (see p. xxxi) has disappeared, which is all to the good; but we may suspect that Alexander was less of a philosopher than Plutarch in the _Life_ would have us believe (see esp. 27. 10 n.). Certainly the treatment of his enemies, for example Taxiles (59. 1-5) and Porus (60. 14-15), was largely motivated by policy. Plutarch appreciates that the adoption of a mixed dress (45) and the training of the 30,000 young Persians (47, 71), although not apparently the attempt to introduce *proskynesis* (54), are part of the 'policy of fusion'; he is aware too of the opposition that these measures aroused among the Macedonians, although he seems to think that this opposition was soon overcome because of respect for Alexander's *arete*. He does not deny the deterioration in Alexander's character (see p. lxiii), which certainly took place,[190] although his attempt to explain this in terms of Alexander's love for *doxa* (42. 4) is not convincing. Again, even if Plutarch is too ready to excuse Alexander (. . .), what he says about the part played by the 'flatterers' may not be altogether wide of the mark. That Alexander became increasingly addicted to superstition towards the end of his life may in general be true, although Plutarch's narrative is clearly influenced by his own attitude to superstition (see 75. 1 n.) and the picture is doubtless overdrawn. On the other hand Plutarch failed to understand the essentially 'heroic' character of Macedonian society and of Alexander himself. He did not realize just how savage and ruthless Alexander could be, if he felt his position was in any way threatened. This ruthlessness was in no way due to a deterioration in Alexander's character; at the very beginning of his reign he had removed all possible rivals.[191]

Plutarch makes his greatest contribution to our knowledge of Alexander in chapters 48-55. His accounts of Cleitus' murder and the *proskynesis* affair are accepted by almost all scholars, and we owe to him the vivid portraits of Philotas, Cleitus, and Callisthenes which help to fill in the background and bring them to life. We are enabled to see something of the conflicts in the entourage of Alexander, the jealousies between the philosophers and the *literati,* and between high-ranking Macedonians.[192] Plutarch, it is true, does not appear to have appreciated all the implications of the information he gives, but from this material a critical modern historian can create a truer portrait of Alexander.

VI. THE STYLE OF PLUTARCH[193]

Plutarch was largely unaffected by the prevailing Atticism.[194] This movement—an ostensible return to the style of the classical Attic writers—had arisen about the middle of the first century B.C. as a reaction against the bombast of the Asiatic orators. But the Atticists were more successful in imitating the vocabulary and syntax of the Attic writers than in recapturing their simplicity. More important, in their efforts to reproduce the classical Attic style they sought to cut out everything which had come into the literary language during Hellenistic times, and to confine themselves to authorized Attic material. While Plutarch, then, doubtless sympathized with their dislike of bombast,[195] he was not prepared to cut himself off from the living language. For him style

was less important than subject-matter.[196] Its function was to render the thought more vivid and persuasive; it must not obtrude or obstruct. Hence he did not join in their search for rare Attic words and expressions nor did he coin new words on anything like the same scale.[197] His vocabulary and syntax are basically those of the literary Koine, which itself contains a large Attic element. Particularly revealing is his use of the optative, which he employs roughly as often as Strabo and Philo but only about one-fifth as often as Plato.[198] His use of negatives also follows the practice of the Koine, μή being used not only in conditional clauses but in clauses expressing time, cause, or any attendant circumstance. Admittedly his vocabulary is much more extensive than that of other writers of the Koine and includes many common Attic words not used by them. Whether this is conscious archaizing or the result of his wide reading in Attic writers, especially Plato, is debatable.

The most striking feature of his style is the strict avoidance of hiatus, leading at times to an awkward distortion of the normal order of words.[199] Less obvious is his use of certain prose rhythms at the end of the sentence, particularly the double trochee, the cretic plus trochee, and the hypodochmius.[200]

Plutarch makes limited use of tropes. Chiasmus is seldom employed and in some cases, e.g. 31. 13, 45. 3, 51. 4, is perhaps due to the desire to avoid hiatus. Asyndeton, on the other hand, is relatively frequent at the beginning of the sentence, especially with ταῦτα. Asyndeton within the sentence is occasionally combined most effectively with repetition, as at 23. 2 οὐκ οἶνος ἐκεῖνον, οὐχ ὕπνος, οὐ παιδιά τις, οὐ γάμος, οὐ θέα . . . ἐπέσχε; cf. 67. 4. His similes are in general unremarkable,[201] as, for example, the comparison of the Tyrian Apollo to a deserter (24. 7) and Alexander after Cleitus' murder to a slave (52. 5). More effectively, the confused hubbub from the Persian camp before Gaugamela is likened to the sound of a vast ocean (31. 10), and the beautiful Persian women ignored by Alexander to lifeless statues (21. 11). The stage provides two similes: some writers described Alexander's death as 'the closing scene of a great drama' (75. 5), and the weak-minded Arrhidaeus is a mere 'mute character' (77. 7). Perhaps the most vivid is the comparison of the Macedonians after Issus to hunting-dogs on the scent of Persian wealth, which is enhanced by the use of the epic verb ἀνιχνεύειν (24. 3).[202] Metaphors are infrequent but effective, occurring at critical points in the narrative.[203] Philip's domestic troubles affect the kingdom (9. 5), and at his death (11. 2) he leaves a kingdom as disturbed as the sea (σάλος). The same sea metaphor describes the state of the Empire on Alexander's return from India (68. 3), and at Gaugamela the ebb and flow of the battle is likened to the surge of the sea and to the recurrence of an illness (32. 5).[204] Alexander allows himself to be 'ridden' by his flatterers (23. 7), and later opens his ears to Philotas' enemies (49. 10), a passage doubtless intended to recall 42. 2, where the king is said (literally) to have covered one of his ears when the prosecutor was speaking. Finally, the resentment of the discharged Macedonian veterans is cleverly evoked by their scornful reference to the young Persians as 'war-dancers' (71. 3).[205]

Plutarch has a remarkable power of visualizing a scene and a keen sense of dramatic effect. This is admirably illustrated by the scene between Alexander and his doctor Philip (which he himself describes as θαυμαστὴν καὶ θεατρικήν), where the effect is enhanced by the use of the tragic verb θεοκλυτεῖν, and by his account of the breaking of Bucephalas (ch. 6).[206] In the main Plutarch's narrative is simple and vivid, but the brevity which he praised in others escapes him. He is discursive by nature (some might say long-winded), and he has a habit of using two words where one would do; words of similar form are often chosen, e.g. 48. 1, φιλόδωρος δὲ καὶ φιλέταιρος, 72. 6, διατύπωσιν . . . διαμόρφωσιν. Stylistically the *Alexander* is not, I think, one of the best *Lives*; Plutarch deals with many episodes in summary fashion, as he promised in the introduction (1. 1), because of the mass of material. His expansive style requires space and is seen to greatest advantage in extended passages, as in his account of the murder of Cleitus.[207] His sentences sometimes extend to a considerable length and tend to straggle, but are seldom difficult to follow. A good example is 40. 1-2, a sentence of some fourteen lines; Plutarch begins with a temporal clause followed by four result clauses (the last with a dependent participle), then comes the main verb (qualified by two adverbs), a participle with dependent infinitive, and two causal clauses each followed by a noun clause (both with dependent participle), the second of which is subdivided by μέν . . . δέ. Despite the length and complexity of the sentence, the meaning is perfectly clear.[208]

Yet such sentences are the exception. In style, as in subject-matter, Plutarch sought variety,[209] for he was well aware of the dangers of being tedious. Indeed, we may apply to Plutarch himself his remark about Homer (*Mor.* 504 d): 'He continually avoids the tendency to surfeit which threatens talk of every kind, carrying his hearers from one story to another, and relieving their satiety by his constant freshness.'

Notes

1. *Note*: all dates in the Introduction are A.D. unless otherwise indicated. Figures in parentheses refer to sections of the *Moralia*.

2. Apart from brief notices in Suidas (s.v. Πλούταρχος Χαιρωνεύς) and Eusebius (*Chron. ab. Abr.* 2135 = 119/20 A.D., ed. Schoene 2. 164 ff.) and a few inscriptions (*SIG* 829 a, 843 a, b; cf. ibid. 844 b, 845), we are dependent on Plutarch's own writings.

3. Plutarch remarks that he was a young man (νέος) when Nero visited Greece in 67 (385 b, 391 e).

4. We may note that his father kept fine horses (641 f.)

5. 622 e, 669 c, 738 b.

6. Perhaps because she died young, as Ziegler 645 suggests.

7. See Ziegler 643.

8. 615 e, 641 f, 656 c, 657 e.

9. Ziegler (*Hermes* 82 (1954), 499-501) argues that Timon was a half-brother of Plutarch; his arguments are not accepted by B. Einarson, *CPhil.* 50 (1955), 253-5.

10. He is prominent in the *De defectu oraculorum,* the *Quaestiones convivales,* and the *De facie in orbe lunae*; refs. in Ziegler 645. The Lamprias attested as archon at Delphi is probably not Plutarch's brother; see G. Daux, *BCH* 73 (1949), 292.

11. As R. Flacelière, *Sagesse de Plutarque* (Paris, 1964) 4, has well remarked.

12. See Ziegler 648, C. P. Jones, *JRS* 56 (1966), 71.

13. The eldest child was dead when the *Consolatio* was written (609 d). If this was not Soclarus, who reached an age at which he could appreciate poetry (15 a), he must have been a sixth child. Flacelière (*REG* 63 (1950), 302) holds that Autobulus must have been the eldest son, since he bore his grandfather's name, and that the eldest child must have been a girl. But Plutarch's statement (608 c) that 'this daughter (i.e. Timoxena) was born after four sons, when you were longing to bear a daughter' strongly suggests that Timoxena was the *first* daughter.

14. Ammonius became an Athenian citizen and held the office of *strategos* at least three times. Refs. in Ziegler 651 ff. On Ammonius' career and family see C. P. Jones's important article in *Harv. Stud.* 71(1967), 205 ff.

15. *Dem.* 2. 2. For the old view see J. J. Hartman, *de Plutarcho* (Leiden, 1916), 662. Plutarch's difficulties with Latin, however, should not be exaggerated; some of his errors are no worse than Livy's mistranslations of Polybius. In particular, we should be chary of arguing from this admission that Plutarch read hardly any of the Latin authors he cites. The passage explicitly says that he *did*.

16. For a complete list of Plutarch's Roman friends see Ziegler 687 ff.

17. See Ziegler 688 f., who, however, wrongly assigns him a third consulship in 102.

18. On the chronology of Plutarch's writings see esp. Jones, *JRS* (1966) 61 ff.

19. The fact that the cults were of purely local significance may account for his silence (Ziegler 659).

20. *SIG* 829 a; cf. *Mor.* 792 f, where λειτουργοῦντα πολλὰς Πυθιάδας probably refers to his priestly office rather than to his position as *epimeletes*. J. Jannoray (*REA* 47 (1945), 257) dates the beginning of his office to between 85 and 90.

21. In the *De Pythiae oraculis* 29 (*Mor.* 409 c) Theon remarks φιλῶ δὲ τὸν καθηγεμόνα ταύτης τῆς πολιτείας γενόμενον ἡμῖν καὶ τὰ πλεῖστα τούτων ἐκφροντίζοντα καὶ παρασκευάζοντα. This is generally, and rightly, taken to refer to Plutarch; so (most recently) Jones, *JRS* (1966), 63 ff., who rejects Flacelière's view (*Rev. Phil.* 8 (1934), 56 ff. and subsequently) that Hadrian is referred to and that this passage supports a date after 125 for Plutarch's death.

22. Ziegler 660 agrees that Plutarch refers to himself in this passage, although at 657 he doubts whether Plutarch was Boeotarch.

23. See A. Stein, *Der römische Ritterstand* (München, 1927) 246 ff., 274 f. The honour did not confer membership of the senate.

24. Some scholars take Illyria to be a mere slip for Achaea, since until Diocletian the governor of Illyria had no jurisdiction over Achaea. Even so the statement is doubtful. We might, however, read 'Chaeroneia' for 'Illyria'. K. Latte (ap. Ziegler 658, n. 1) is sceptical of the whole matter, including the grant of consular insignia and Eusebius' statement (below).

25. So E. Groag, *Die römischen Reichsbeamten von Achaia* (1939) 145-7, and H. G. Pflaum, *Les Carrières procuratoriennes équestres* 3 (1961), 1071. Groag suggests that the work was done by Plutarch's staff or alternatively that the office was honorary.

26. Nero's speech: *SIG* 814; cf. *Flam.* 12, Suet. *Nero* 11. Freedom revoked: Suet. *Vesp.* 8. 4.

27. As expressed in his *An seni res publica gerenda sit?* (783 a-97 f) and, especially, his *Praecepta gerendae rei publicae* (798 a-825 f).

28. Nero bestowed freedom upon 'the best of peoples and the one most loved by the gods' (568 a).

29. At *Mor.* 414 a Plutarch writes that Greece can put only 3,000 hoplites into the field. It is impossible to believe that this represents all the men of military age, and J. A. O. Larsen, *An Economic Survey of Ancient Rome* 4 (1938), 481 f., suggests that Plutarch means those who had received training as ephebes. If so, there must have been a considerable decline in the number of the wealthy; but there still remained a small group with enough money to travel and to lead a life of leisure.

30. Magistrates no longer have the opportunity to wage wars, overthrow tyrants, or conclude military alliances (805 a).

31. See Lucian, *Master of Rhetoric,* ch. 18.

32. 776 a-779 c, 814 c-d.

33. See esp. G. W. Bowersock, *Augustus and the Greek World* (Oxford, 1965), ch. 1 and pp. 143 ff., and for the Republic E. Badian, *Foreign Clientelae* (Oxford, 1957).

34. On these officials see A. N. Sherwin-White, *The Letters of Pliny* (Oxford, 1966), on *Ep.* 8. 24. The earliest of them appears to have been Maximus in the first decade of the second century; see Pliny, ad loc.

35. See A. H. M. Jones, *The Greek City* (Oxford, 1940) 129 f., 170; T. Renoirte, *Les Conseils politiques de Plutarque* (Louvain, 1951).

36. 814 d. Although they were regularly employed among the Greek-speaking peoples; see Bowersock, op. cit. 147.

37. T. G. Tucker, *Selected Essays of Plutarch* (Oxford, 1913) 15.

38. See Ziegler 767 f., 919 f.

39. Details in Ziegler 749 ff.

40. For Plutarch's enlightened views on women see Stadter 5 ff.

41. *De comm. notit. adv. Stoicos* 32 = *Mor.* 1075 e.

42. On *daimones* see J. Oakesmith, *The Religion of Plutarch* (London, 1902), ch. 6-8, and esp. G. Soury, *La Démonologie de Plutarque* (Paris, 1942). On Plutarch's religious views in general see Nilsson 2. 402 ff. (with full bibliography).

43. *Adv. Coloten* 33 = *Mor.* 1126 e-f.

44. *De Stoicorum repugnantiis* 2 = *Mor.* 1033 c.

45. See especially the short treatises *De virtute morali* (440 c-452 d) and *De cohibenda ira* (452 d-464 d).

46. See especially Marrou 194 ff., 210; A. and M. Croiset, *Hist. de la litt. grecque,* 5. 556 ff.

47. *CAH* 11. 681.

48. In Philostratus' *Lives of the Sophists* there is no theme in Greek history later than 326 B.C.

49. For details see S. F. Bonner, *Roman Declamation* (Liverpool, 1949).

50. In the sixteenth and seventeenth centuries the Jesuits paid the greatest attention to the training of the memory. 'A top-notch pupil would volunteer to repeat a page of poetry after reading it only once; another would offer to repeat two pages' (Gilbert Highet, *The Art of Teaching* (London, 1951), 131).

51. Cf. *Mor.* 243 a, 743 d, 745 c.

52. *Mor.* 33 f; cf. *Per.* 8, *Fab.* 1, *Cat. Min.* 4.

53. In Plutarch, a term of censure; see the Commentary, n. to 75. 5.

54. See also his criticism of Isocrates at *Mor.* 350 d ff.

55. There is no external evidence for the date of these two speeches, but they are generally regarded, together with Plutarch's other rhetorical works, as among his *Jugendschriften*; cf. Schmid-Stählin, *Gesch. d. gr. Litt.* 2. 1. 486, 491; Ziegler 716 f. The effort of J. E. Powell, *JHS* 59 (1939), 235 f., to prove that they reveal knowledge of the *Life* is quite unsuccessful.

56. I merely mention the suggestions of Eicke (*Veterum philosophorum qualia fuerint de A. M. iudicia* (1909) 53 ff.) that in praising Alexander for his *continentia* Plutarch was dropping a hint to Trajan, who was supposed to be addicted to *amor,* and of Hirzel (*Der Dialog* (Leipzig, 1895) 2. 81) that by laying stress on deeds rather than words Plutarch was consoling Trajan for his defective education. They are 'too esoteric to be credible' (so Wardman, *CQ,* N.S. 5 (1955), 99, of Eicke's view), and in addition it is difficult to credit that these highly rhetorical speeches were written when Plutarch was over 50.

57. Tarn (*AJP* 60 (1939), 56, n. 86) doubts whether the speech is Plutarch's work. But there is no reason to doubt its authenticity, although Sandbach (*CQ* 33 (1939), 196, n. 3) may be right in thinking that it is an earlier work revised later.

58. A. E. Wardman, *CQ,* N.S. 5 (1955), 96-107.

59. At any rate Wardman (p. 99) claims that his explanation offers a middle way between Tarn's view and the view that Plutarch has no serious purpose.

60. The advantage claimed by Wardman for his view is that it helps to explain this.

61. Indeed it might well be argued that in the (lost) first speech Fortune has claimed Alexander as her handiwork and that in the second Philosophy counters by (*inter alia*) charging Fortune with actually obstructing him.

62. Wardman (100, n. 5) believes, against most scholars, that the opening words, οὗτος ὁ τῆς Τύχης λόγος, are simply 'a dramatic way of stating the view against which Plutarch is to argue'.

63. Tarn (*AJP* 60 (1939), 56) thinks that the first speech was written 'in a white heat of passion' to defend Alexander's reputation; so also 2. 296.

64. The phrase is Badian's (*Historia* 7 (1958), 436). This view is argued at length by Hoffmann 87-96.

65. That Ptolemy was Arrian's source is probable; see Tarn 2. 290 ff., Badian, op. cit. 429.

66. See esp. Badian, op. cit. 428 ff., 432 ff.

67. On this policy see esp. H. Berve, *Klio* 31 (1938), 135-68.

68. *Historia* 7 (1958), 437. Cf. T. S. Brown, *Historia* 16 (1967), 360.

69. On this section D. A. Russell, 'On Reading Plutarch's *Lives*', *Greece and Rome* 13 (1966), 139 ff., is valuable. See also his articles on the *Coriolanus* and the *Alcibiades* in *JRS* 53 (1963), 21 ff., and *Proc. Camb. Philol. Soc.,* N.S. 12 (1966), 37 ff.

70. For details of these, see Ziegler 895 ff. The extant *Lives* of Aratus, Artaxerxes, Galba, and Otho do not form part of the *Parallel Lives*.

71. Ziegler 895 f. considers that this was Scipio Africanus Maior. However K. Herbert, 'The Identity of Plutarch's lost *Scipio*', *AJP* 78 (1957), 83 ff., has argued persuasively in favour of Scipio Aemilianus.

72. In his important article, *Hermes* 84 (1956), 398-424, at p. 400.

73. Plutarch (*Sert.* 1. 3-10) is scornful of previous writers who compared men on the basis of mere coincidence in their careers, as e.g., the two Scipios were compared because the elder had defeated the Carthaginians and the younger had destroyed Carthage.

74. Velleius (2. 41. 1) had already compared them briefly. They are later compared at length by Appian (*BCiv.* 2. 149 ff.) and by Julian (*Conv.* 320 a-325 c). Nevertheless the comparison of Alexander with Scipio (the elder) was common

(Gellius, *NA* 7. 8); it had been made as early as the middle of the 2nd century by C. Acilius (Livy 35. 14. 7; cf. Plut. *Flam.* 21, Appian, *Syr.* 10, Lucian, *Ver. Hist.* 2. 9). Varro had compared him with Pompey (ap. Pliny, *HN* 7. 95), as had Pompey himself (cf. his *cognomen Magnus*) and his contemporaries; see Sallust, *Hist.* 3. 88.

75. *Alex.* 4. 8, 5. 5-6, 13. 4, 42. 4; *Caes.* 5. 8-9, 10. 9, 11. 3-6, 17. 1, 22. 6, 54. 4, 58. 4-5, 69. 1.

76. Generous: *Alex.* 39, 42. 5; *Caes.* 12. 4, 15. 4, 17. 1, 57. 8. Chivalrous: *Alex.* 21. 1-5, 43. 5-7, 59. 1-5, 60. 14-15; *Caes.* 15. 4, 18. 5, 34. 7-8, 48. 3-4, 54. 4.

77. *Alex.* 21-23; *Caes.* 17

78. *Alex.* 48-55; *Caes.* 4. 8, 57. 2-3, 60. 1 and 4, 61. 1.

79. For this view, which shows the limitations of Plutarch's scheme, see Erbse, *Hermes* 84 (1956), 406. He maintains that the *synkrisis* was an essential complement to the narrative of the two *Lives*; for a less favourable view of its importance see Ziegler 909 f. The *synkrisis* is absent also in the *Phocion-Cato Minor*, the *Pyrrhus-Marius*, and the *Themistocles-Camillus*, in Erbse's view because in the first instance the similarities and in the latter two the differences were too great. The more general view is that the *synkriseis* were written and are missing.

80. *JRS* 56 (1966), 70.

81. Jones, op. cit. 69 f. The *Lives* are *Dem.-Cic., Thes.-Rom., Dion-Brut., Aem.-Tim., Agis-Cleom.-Gracchi.*

82. Similarly while *Dion* 58 10 cites the *Timoleon, Timoleon* 13. 10 and 33. 4 cite the *Dion*, and while *Camillus* 33. 10 cites the *Romulus* and *Theseus* 1. 4 and *Romulus* 21. 1 cite the *Numa, Numa* 12. 13 cites the *Camillus.*

83. Details in Ziegler 899 ff.

84. The possibility that some of the references may have been added subsequently by Plutarch has been somewhat hastily rejected on the grounds that since the *Lives* were written in extreme old age (certainly not true of all) Plutarch would have had no time to make a *revision,* and that a revision would have eliminated the many inaccuracies and contradictions. But we need not envisage anything so elaborate as a second edition (see Ziegler 901), and this solution remains a real possibility.

85. J. Mewaldt, *Hermes* 42 (1907), 564-78. His solution is favoured by Stadter 32, n. 1 and by Flacelière (most recently in *Plutarque Vies I,* xxv-

xxvi). Jones adopts his scheme, but holds that the *Lycurgus-Numa* must have been published before the *Theseus-Romulus* (see below . . .).

86. C. Stoltz, *Zur relativen Chronologie der Parallelbiographien Plutarchs* (Lund, 1929). He is followed by Ziegler 901 ff., and (implicitly) by C. Theander, *Eranos* 56 (1958), 12-20.

87. τὸν ἐφικτὸν εἰκότι λόγῳ καὶ βάσιμον ἱστορίᾳ πραγμάτων ἐχομένη χρόνον διελθόντι. . . .

88. We should perhaps conclude that the *Lycurgus-Numa* immediately preceded the *Theseus-Romulus*; so Jones, *JRS* 56 (1966), 67, and W. Bühler, *Maia* 14 (1962), 281.

89. Especially as at *Romulus* 21. 1 Plutarch refers to the *Numa* as written (γέγραπται).

90. At 1. 5 he remarks 'Let us hope that *Fable* may, in what shall follow, so submit to the purifying process of *Reason* as to take on the appearance of *History*' (ὄψιν ἱστορίας). Cf. 2. 3—both Theseus and Romulus are said to have fallen foul of their fellow-citizens, 'if among the traditions that appear least fabulous there is any that helps to discover the truth'.

91. ἡ . . . πραγματεία διαφόρους ἔσχηκε ἱστορίας; cf. 1. 7, οὕτω πεπλανημένης τῆς ἱστορίας. . . .

92. The *Cimon* and the *Lysander* are referred to in the *Pericles* (9; 22), and the *Marcellus* in the *Fabius* (19; 22).

93. The *Lycurgus* is cited in the *Lysander* (17) and the *Camillus* in the *Numa* (9; 12).

94. See Jones's table, p. 68. Ziegler is in agreement except that (following Stoltz) he excludes the *Theseus-Romulus.*

95. For the relevance of the mention of Sosius Senecio see above . . . .

96. Moral good is a practical stimulus; it is no sooner seen than it inspires an impulse to practise (*Per.* 2. 4-5).

97. As he observes in the *Galba* (2. 3) it is the task of ἡ πραγματικὴ ἱστορία to provide a detailed record of events.

98. For the correct interpretation of this passage see Gomme 77, n. 2; Theander 32, n. 1, 49; Ziegler 910, n. 1, and for this sense of ἄχρηστος cf. *Dion* 21, *Tim.* 15. But Plutarch does not always exclude the stuff of history; at *Fab.* 16, for example, he includes a detailed description of Carthaginian tactics, which is quite irrelevant to Fabius'

character and which he attributes to those who wrote τὰς διεξοδικὰς ἱστορίας; cf. *Aem.* 8-9 (Antigonid history), *Cam.* 15-16 (Gauls).

99. pp. 54, 55.

100. See *Dem.* 11. 7 and the other passages cited by F. Leo, *Die griechisch-römische Biographie* (Leipzig, 1901) 184 ff.

101. See Leo 188 ff., and esp. Dihle 60 ff. Cf. Erbse, *Hermes* 84 (1956), 400, n. 1. This may be evidence for the prominent part played by the Peripatetics in biographical writing, but it does not mean that Plutarch used Peripatetic sources in the *Alexander.*

102. On the need for education and philosophy cf. *Tim.* 6; yet the Stoic philosophy might be dangerous to certain natures (*Cleom.* 2. 6). Compare also *Mar.* 2 and *Them.* 2. 7, where Themistocles is said often to have taken the worse course because he lacked λόγος καὶ παιδεία.

103. The clearest example of a change of character occurs in the *Demetrius*: see Dihle 76 ff., who has a good discussion of the difference between ancient and modern character-drawing. Note Plutarch's remarks at *Sert.* 10, esp. paras. 5 ff., a passage not discussed by Dihle. See also Russell, *Greece and Rome* 13 (1966), 144 ff., who notes (p. 147, n. 2) that Plutarch's terminology is not always consistent.

104. See the examples collected by Leo 184 f.

105. In his *Untersuchungen über Plutarchs biographische Technik* (Berlin, 1931). For his refinements on these basic terms and criticism of them see Ziegler 907 f.

106. Ziegler 911; for details of authors cited in the *Lives* see Index I to vol. 4. 2 of his Teubner edition (1939).

107. The most extreme view was advanced by Eduard Meyer in his *Forschungen zur alten Geschichte* (Halle, 1899); he asserted (2. 65, 67) that in his *Parallel Lives* Plutarch did not *use* (although he had *read*) even the 'classics' (Herodotus, Thucydides, Xenophon) at first hand, but depended on biographers such as Hermippus; even Hermippus, he claimed (2. 69), was known to Plutarch only through an intermediary. This view was demolished by Gomme (below, n. 112) and may be considered dead.

108. For work on the *Lives* between 1909 and 1934 see A. Hauser in Bursian's *Jahresbericht* 251 (1936), 35-86, and from 1934 to 1952 A. Garzetti, 'Plutarco e le sue "Vite Parallele"' in *RSI* 65 (1953), 76-104, esp. 79 ff.

109. See the forthright remarks of Fergus Millar, *A Study of Cassius Dio* (Oxford, 1964) viii.

110. For his career see A. N. Sherwin-White, *The Letters of Pliny* (Oxford, 1966), 219-21.

111. This should not be exaggerated; Athens was not too distant, and Plutarch doubtless made many visits. There must also have been a library at Delphi, and we should probably reckon on his receiving gifts of books from his many friends.

112. A. W. Gomme, *A Historical Commentary on Thucydides* 1 (Oxford, 1945), 54-84, a *locus classicus* on the subject; see esp. 54 ff., 78 ff. In 1865 H. Peter, *Die Quellen Plutarchs in den Biographien der Römer* (Halle), had taken a similar view; so, more recently, R. Zimmermann, *Rh. Mus.* 79 (1930), 55-64.

113. For the extent of his reading see esp. Ziegler 914-28, *Die Quellen der Bildung Plutarchs*, and W. C. Helmbold and E. N. O'Neill, *Plutarch's Quotations* (Philadelphia, 1959).

114. *Alex.* 4 (Aristoxenus); *Mor.* 422 e (Phanias); *Ages.* 19; *Mor.* 514 c (Ephorus); cf. *Mor.* 1093 c, from which it is clear that he had read Eudoxus, Aristotle, and Aristoxenus.

115. Even at dinner he took rapid notes (§ 11), and while being rubbed down, after bathing, he had a book read to him or dictated notes (§ 14).

    Cassius Dio also made notes for the whole of his Roman history before arranging his material and writing it up; see Millar, op. cit. 32.

116. On these see Ziegler 863-7, Gomme 78, n. 1. Ziegler considers that, since the corresponding portions of the *Lives* are more detailed, the former collection was not made by Plutarch; but I do not see why Plutarch may not have combined other material with it while at work on the *Lives*. Both collections were probably *based* on existing collections and published after Plutarch's death. At *Mor.* 464 f Plutarch refers to his note-books (ὑπομνήματα).

117. See above . . . , for the benefits of rhetorical training. Zimmermann, op. cit. 61 f., who refers to Seneca, thinks that Plutarch used *hardly any* notes. I find this difficult to believe.

118. There is no lack of examples. For those in the *Alexander* see the notes to 16. 15 and 67. 3, for those in the *Coriolanus* see D. A. Russell, *JRS* 53 (1963), 22.

119. Theander 42 ff. Quotations: Ephorus (*De Herod. mal.* 5), Charon of Lampsacus (ibid. 20, 24). Alexander's letters are quoted at *Alex.* 22. 5, cf. 47.

3, 60. 1. 11. Criticism: below . . . . Comparisons: Ephorus, Theopompus, Anaximenes (*Praecepta* 6); Ephorus, Timaeus, Philistus (*Dion* 36); Thucydides, Philistus, Timaeus (*Nic.* 1); Thucydides and Theopompus (*De Herod. mal.* 1).

See also E. Meinhardt, *Perikles bei Plutarch* (Frankfurt, 1957) 9-16, who adds the absence of any reference by Plutarch to a biographical source; which is not perhaps decisive. H. Erbse, *Hermes* 84 (1956), 420 ff., argues that Plutarch must have read widely in the available literature in order to discern the qualities in his heroes which enabled him to pair them satisfactorily.

120. Op. cit. 54 ff.

121. See the remarks of K. Büchner, *Gnomon* 32 (1960), 307. It is particularly encouraging that Flacelière adopts this point of view in his Budé edition of the *Lives*. However, M. Gelzer (*Gnomon* 36 (1964), 658 ff.) believes that the *Cicero* was based on an existing biography, while H. Homeyer (*Klio* 41 (1963), 145 ff.) still adheres to the theory of *Mittelquellen*; for her views on the *Alexander* see below . . . .

122. Rather *two* tables (912 f., 924 f.), for they do not coincide. e.g. Charon is doubtful 924 but second-hand 913, Phanias doubtful 925 but certain 912, Stesimbrotus certain 912 but doubtful 924.

123. e.g. Charon of Lampsacus, who wrote a *Persica* and a *Chronicle of Lampsacus*. He is, in fact, quoted in the *De Herod. mal.* 20, 24 (verbatim), in the *Mul. Virt.* 18, and at *Them.* 27.

124. Plutarch's statement that he is avoiding the best-known stories does not perhaps absolutely rule out the possibility that Plutarch is selecting from an anthology, but Stadter's points (pp. 126, 136), that 18 of the 27 stories are known only through Plutarch and that he had already used local historians to refute Herodotus in the *De Herod. mal.*, make his conclusion very probable.

125. Büchner loc. cit., Ziegler 914.

126. R. Hirzel, *Plutarch* (Leipzig, 1912) 48, 63. Theander (82), however, cites the former statement with approval.

127. Gomme 54 f. See, however, for exceptions n. 98 above.

128. The last point is admirably illustrated by Russell (*JRS* 53 (1963), 21 ff.) in his analysis of the *Coriolanus*.

129. p. 58.

130. At *Per.* 10 Plutarch rejects Idomeneus' statement that Pericles murdered Ephialtes because of envy and jealousy, since such an act is not consonant with his character. He adds, however, that Aristotle attributed the murder to Ephialtes' oligarchic enemies.

131. At *Cim.* 4 Plutarch expressly notes that Stesimbrotus was a contemporary of Cimon.

132. W. H. Porter, *Dion* (Dublin, 1952), rightly maintains that Plutarch consulted the Platonic epistles directly.

If Plutarch had not the critical equipment to determine the authenticity of these letters, we have not progressed much further.

133. See, e.g., *Alex.* 18. 3-4, 33. 10, 38. 8, 55. 9, 61. 1, 65. 2-4.

134. He distrusts the 'tragic' element in Duris (see esp. *Alc.* 32. 2 = fr. 70, *Eum.* 1 = fr. 53) and Phylarchus (esp. *Them.* 32. 4 = fr. 76); he is aware that Ctesias was inclined to the fabulous and the dramatic (*Artox.* 6. 9 = fr. 29), that Timaeus was justly nicknamed '*Epi*tin aeus' (esp. *Nic.* 1 = T. 18, *Dion* 36 = fr. 154), and that Theopompus dispensed blame more readily than praise (*Lys.* 30. 2 = fr. 333; cf. *Them.* 19. 1 = fr. 85, *Ages.* 33. 1 = fr. 323).

135. For the use of the letters in this way see also 20. 9, 27. 8, and 46. 5 (doubtfully).

136. Gomme (59) notes his failure to ask what value Duris had for fifth-century history; but may he not have assumed that Duris, as a Samian, had access to local information? Nor am I persuaded that Plutarch here thinks that the silence of Ephorus had the same value as that of Thucydides.

For Plutarch's appreciation of Ctesias' bias in favour of Clearchus and the Spartans see *Artox.* 13. 7 = fr. 23.

137. See also *Cic.* 49. 3 and *Phoc.* 4. 1-2, where he adds acutely that if Phocion had been of low birth he would not have attended the Academy or have indulged in aristocratic pursuits from his earliest years.

138. At *Dem.* 13. 1, 18. 3, and 21. 2 he quarrels with Theopompus' reading of Demosthenes' character.

139. See esp. Stadter 130 f.

140. *Arist.* 10. 7, *Phoc.* 4. 1, and esp. *Per.* 10. 7 (see p. xlvi, n. 7).

141. Theander 2-32 and *Eranos* 57 (1959), 99-131 (on his use of oral information). On portraits see the Commentary, n. to 4. 1.

142. Theander 78 ff. He points to the references to Craterus' collection of decrees at *Arist.* 10. 19. 26, *Cimon* 13, *Them.* 10, *Nic.* 12, *Dem.* 27; to the list

of Pythian victors and the *hypomnemata* of the Delphians at *Sol.* 11, and to the *anagraphai Laconicai* at *Ages.* 19.

143. Authors to whom no reference is given are all mentioned at 46. 1-2.

144. Powell was, essentially, reviving the theory of A. Schoene, to whom he refers at 238, n. 6; this had been refuted at length by Fränkel 30-92, and was firmly rejected by Schwartz (*RE* 2, 1238).

145. In her excellent doctoral dissertation, *Quellenkritische Untersuchungen zu Plutarchs Alexanderbiographie* (Hamburg, 1964), 42-125.

146. *Klio* 41 (1963), 145-57, esp. 154, n. 2. Schachermeyr 135 also considers that Plutarch used *Mittelquellen.*

147. For the view that some at least of these references may derive from a monograph on the subject, perhaps by Ister, see 46. 1 nn.

148. Aristoxenus, Dinon, Hegesias, Heracleides, Hermippus, Sotion, Theophrastus.

149. See n. ad loc. We may compare ch. 35. 10 ff., where Plutarch adduces two separate pieces of information in support of one view of the origin of naphtha. The whole of this passage is beyond question his own work.

150. Stadter (113, n. 291) rightly rejects attempts to connect the story with Cleitarchus because of its 'un-Aristobulian colouring'.

151. For full (and excellent) analyses see Stadter 112 ff., Rabe 126 ff.

152. Except Polyaenus (8. 40), whose version derives from Plutarch (above . . .).

153. Diodorus 17, Curtius, and Justin's *Epitome* of Trogus; see Tarn 2. 1.

154. We know little of Duris' account of Alexander's reign, but apart from the two citations (15. 2, 46. 2) there is nothing to suggest that Plutarch is using his history. Moreover, although he cites Duris 11 times in the *Lives,* he had a poor opinion of him; see esp. *Per.* 28, where he comments that his narrative was usually untruthful, and on *Alc.* 32 and *Eum.* 1 see [above] and n. 4.

155. See Tarn's remarks at 2. 296.

156. For a brief account of their writings see [below].

157. For this view of their relationship see [below].

158. A longer list will be found in Fränkel 327 f. I have omitted many of the instances he gives as the evidence seems insufficient for any decision.

In several instances (26. 2, 27. 8, 30. 14, 60. 12; cf. 31. 6, 61. 1, 77. 5) Plutarch evidently found substantially the same version in different authors and might have found it difficult to say whose version he finally presented; cf. Welles, *Diodorus,* vol. 8 (Loeb ed.), p. 10.

159. Callisthenes is cited at 27. 4, but much of these chapters is Plutarch's combination of various sources.

160. Although 32. 8-12 *may* derive from Chares.

161. The fragments are collected in F. Jacoby, *Die Fragmente der griechischen Historiker* 2B (Berlin, 1927) with a commentary in 2D; they are translated by C. A. Robinson Jr., *The History of Alexander the Great* 1 (Providence, 1953). The best commentary on these authors is L. Pearson, *The Lost Histories of Alexander the Great (Amer. Phil. Ass.* 1960); see Badian's important review in *Gnomon* 33 (1961), 660-7.

162. See my article in *Historic* 10 (1961), 448-59, and Rabe 8-40. Badian, *PACA* 8 (1965), 5 ff. argues against a late date for Cleitarchus but leaves the question of priority open. cf. D. Kienast, *Historia* 14 (1965), 185 (Cleitarchus writing before Megasthenes).

163. See, e.g., Tarn 2. 42, Pearson 152, Jacoby 509. Whether he wrote earlier than Ptolemy is disputed; Jacoby 499 and Strasburger 15 f. think it probable that he did not, but Tarn and Pearson hold the opposite view. Tarn considers that they wrote independently, but Pearson 172 argues that at Arr. 5. 14. 4 ff. Ptolemy is criticizing Aristobulus; this is very debatable, see *PACA* 4 (1961), 19, n. 24. In fact, there is no evidence for a late date for Ptolemy and he may have written much earlier; see Badian, *Gnomon* 665 f., and cf. Pearson's remarks (193).

164. For ancient views of him as a *kolax* see Jacoby T. 4-5.

165. Pearson's suggestion (87 ff.), that the title should be altered to πῶς ’Αλ. <ἀνήχθη and Παιδείαν Κύρου corrected to ’Ανάβασιν Κ., has been generally rejected. His alternative suggestion (89), that πῶς ’Α. ἤχθη may be the opening words of Onesicritus' book, has much to be said for it. For the date of the book see n. to 46. 4.

166. See also G. T. Griffith, *CR,* N.S. 1 (1951), 169 ff., reviewing Brown.

167. The close harmony at many points between Diodorus and Curtius makes it certain that they depend on a common source; see Schwartz's list in *RE* 4, 1873 f., which, however, requires to be

used with caution as by no means all his instances are valid. That this source was Cleitarchus is shown by the similarities between his fragments and Diodorus. Jacoby (*RE* 11, 631) and Pearson 217 believe that Diodorus used him directly, but Welles (Loeb ed., p. 10) and M. J. Fontana (*Kokalos* 1 (1955), 155 ff.) have given good reasons for thinking that Diodorus used an intermediary (their suggestions of Trogus and Duris are not convincing). Tarn's attempt to prove that Diodorus used a variety of sources, esp. Aristobulus and Cleitarchus and a 'Mercenaries' source', has been refuted by Strasburger, *Bibl. Or.* 9 (1952), 202 ff.; cf. Pearson 241, n. 123. Against a *written* 'Mercenaries' source' see Pearson 78 ff., P. A. Brunt, *CQ,* N.S. 12 (1962), 141 ff.

168. These two aspects are not irreconcilable, as Tarn held; they are the light and shade of the rhetorical Cleitarchan portrait and do not indicate two *sources.*

169. See Brown, *AJP,* 154 f.

170. Since seven letters are written to Antipater and one by him to Alexander, while those cited at 17. 8 and 60. 1 (which have no addressee) may have been written to him, it is possible that there was a separate collection of Antipater's letters. If it was published in the reign of Antigonus Gonatas, Antipater's grandson, the letters would not have been available to the first generation of Alexander-historians; see *PACA* 4 (1961), 11.

171. Private letters (e.g. to Olympias) must have been much more difficult to obtain, and the possibility of forgery in their case is higher.

172. For an examination of all the letters see *PACA* 4 (1961), 9-20.

173. *Tusc. Disp.* 3. 10. 21. Cf. *Ad Att.* 13. 28. 2-3, where Cicero writes that Aristotle's pupil, after he became king, became haughty, cruel, and uncontrolled (*immoderatus*).

174. Ap. Athenacum 435 a = fr. 38 (Wehrli); see Tarn 2. 320.

175. See Tarn 2. 100 f., who maintains (incredibly) that this portrait was first *written down* by Curtius.

176. See the Register to F. Wehrli, *Die Schule des Aristoteles* in Heft 10; one of these, Ariston of Ceos (fr. 13. IV). shows Alexander in a favourable light.

177. Adopting Stroux's convincing emendation (op. cit. 236 f.) of the MSS. *turpissimus. Tumor animi* = τῦφος; cf. Tarn 2. 123, n. 1.

178. See Hoffmann 53, n. 4, for the close parallels in the writings of the younger Seneca and the *Suasoriae* of his father.

179. *Ben.* 1. 13. 1, 2. 16. 1; *Ep.* 91. 17, 94. 62. Cf. Lucan 10. 20, 42-*vesanus rex.*

180. *Clem.* 1. 25. 1; *Ira* 3. 17. 1, 23. 1; *Ep.* 94. 62.

181. Perhaps also Plutarch implicitly answers the criticism that *continuous* good fortune spoilt Alexander.

182. This tendency is not confined to the *Alexander.* Cf. *Cim.* 2 (where the parallel with the portrait-painter recurs).

183. Tarn 2. 300 notes that Plutarch has already recorded without blinking Alexander's order to massacre the prisoners at Persepolis; it is, however, fair to say that immediately before this statement there is a lacuna in the text which may have contained some justification of Alexander's action.

184. 50. 2, ὀργήν; 51. 1, παροξυνθείς; 51. 10, εὐθὺς ἀφῆκεν ὁ θυμὸς αὐτόν; cf. 10. 6 and 16. 14.

185. The idea is evidently not Plutarch's own. In the *Moralia* (339 f) he relates how Alexander did not reveal his suspicions of Philotas for *seven* years— οὐκ ἐν οἴνῳ ποτε . . . ἐξέφηνεν ὁ μεθύων, οὐ δι' ὀργὴν ὁ θυμοειδής! Plutarch is clearly using the word ironically to refute someone, presumably a Stoic, who had said that Alexander *was* θυμοειδής.

186. The *Gracchi,* e.g., is of greater value to us than the *Cicero,* partly at least because for the Ciceronian period we have, relatively speaking, a mass of material while for the Gracchan period Plutarch's *Life* and Appian's *Civil War* are the only substantial literary sources.

187. Many scholars, however, do not believe this; see, e.g., J. P. V. D. Balsdon, *Historia* 1 (1950), 363 ff., E. Bickerman, *Athenaeum* 41 (1963), 70 ff. But, in favour, P. A. Brunt, *Greece and Rome* 12 (1965), 210 f.

188. See 4. 1, 11; 7-8; 11. 12; 26. 1; 29. 1-3.

189. On this see Badian, *Greece and Rome* 12 (1965), 166 ff.

190. Even Tarn 2. 97 admits this—'no one need deny that the Alexander of 324 was not the Alexander of 334'.

191. It is the appreciation of this fact that distinguishes the work of Badian (see esp. his articles in *TAPA* (1960) and *JHS* (1961)) and Schachermeyr (see Welles' review in *AJA* (1951), 433-6).

192. A subject on which Arrian's authorities were significantly reticent; cf. however Arr. 7. 13. 1, where (after a lacuna) the reconciliation between Hephaestion and Eumenes is mentioned.

193. See in general Ziegler 931 ff., and for the style of the *Marius* T. F. Carney, *JHS* 80 (1960), 24-31.

194. On Atticism see Marrou 200 f., and esp. A. Lesky, *A History of Greek Literature* (London, 1966), 829 ff. W. Schmid's four volumes, *Der Atticismus* (Stuttgart, 1896), are a mine of information on the usage of the Atticists; they also contain much useful material on Plutarch, esp. on his vocabulary.

195. For Plutarch's attitude see the Commentary at 3. 6, 17. 6.

196. See the revealing passage in his essay *On the Student At Lectures* (*Mor.* 42 d), where Plutarch criticizes those students who do not concern themselves with the subject-matter but demand a 'pure Attic style' from the lecturer.

197. For the coinages of the Atticists see Schmid 4. 685 ff. In the *Alexander* the following words *may* have been coined by Plutarch: φιλαναγνώστης (8. 2), ἰδιόστολος (34. 3), εὑροεῖν (53. 3). Moreover χαίτη (16. 7), ἀσύμβολος (26. 3), and πλαίσιον (67. 2) are not previously attested in the meanings used by Plutarch.

198. So Ziegler 932. A. Meillet, *Aperçu d'une histoire de la langue grecque*³ (Paris, 1930), 276, gives higher figures for Philo and Strabo.

199. For details of permitted hiatus see Ziegler 932 ff. A. J. Kronenberg, *Mnemos.* 5 (1937), 311, n. 2, adds that Plutarch allows hiatus after proper names and forms of θεός.

200. See Sandbach's table of frequencies in *CQ* 33 (1939), 197.

201. Some may derive from his sources: certainly the comparison of the shape of Alexandria to that of a *chlamys* (26. 8, where see n.), and probably Alexander compared to a lion sated with blood (13. 2).

202. Evidently Plutarch's own borrowing, as probably βρύχημα at 51. 10.

203. For the use of metaphor to indicate the unity of lengthy passages and for cross-reference see Carney, op. cit., 24 f.

204. σάλος is very frequently used by Plutarch with reference to political disturbance (see n. to 32. 5). For other medical metaphors see (e.g.) *Num.* 8. 2, *Cam.* 9. 3, *Caes.* 28. 6.

205. Other metaphors occur at 11. 11, 21. 10, 22. 9, 33. 8, 35. 8, 49. 9, 51. 2.

206. Cf. also ch. 12 (Timocleia); 16. 6-8 (battle of the Granicus); 9. 5 (Alexander's brawl with Philip); 67. 2-6 (*komos* in Carmania).

207. See also ch. 30. 2-13 (Darius and the eunuch), and esp. *Cam.* 10 (the schoolmaster of Falerii).

208. For similarly lengthy and involved sentences see *Caes.* 28. 2-4, 58. 4-7.

209. See D. A. Russell's perceptive remarks in *Proc. Camb. Philol. Soc.,* N.S. 12 (1966), 37 ff., esp. 47. Compare also Plutarch's habit of avoiding continuous exposition by digression in the philosophical works; see Sandbach, *CQ* 34 (1940), 21.

Abbreviations and Bibliography of Short Titles

Note: Books cited once are not included. References to articles are given in full in the Commentary.

AHR = *American Historical Review.*

AJA = *American Journal of Archaeology.*

AJP = *American Journal of Philology.*

Altheim = F. Altheim, *Weltgeschichte Asiens im griechischen Zeitalter.* 2 vols. Halle, 1947-8.

Ant. Class. = *Antiquité classique.*

BCH = *Bulletin de Correspondance hellénique.*

Bellinger = A. R. Bellinger, *Essays on the Coinage of Alexander the Great.* New York, 1963.

Beloch = K. J. Beloch, *Griechische Geschichte.* Ed. 2. 4 vols. Strassburg-Berlin and Leipzig, 1912-27.

Bengtson = H. Bengtson, *Griechische Geschichte von den Anfängen bis in die römische Kaiserzeit.* Ed. 2. München, 1960.

Berve = H. Berve, *Das Alexanderreich auf prosopographischer Grundlage.* 2 vols. München, 1926.

BIAO = *Bulletin de l'Institut français d'Archéologie orientale.*

Bibl. Or. = *Bibliotheca orientalis.*

BIE = *Bulletin de l'Institut d'Égypte.*

Brown = T. S. Brown, *Onesicritus, A Study in Hellenistic Historiography.* Berkeley-Los Angeles, 1949.

Burn = A. R. Burn, *Alexander the Great and the Hellenistic Empire.* London, 1947.

Bury = J. B. Bury, *A History of Greece.* Ed. 3. London, 1951.

CAF = T. Kock, *Comicorum Atticorum Fragmenta.* 1880-8.

CAH = *The Cambridge Ancient History.*

CHI = *The Cambridge History of India,* vol. 1.

CPhil. = *Classical Philology.*

CQ = Classical Quarterly.

CR = Classical Review.

Cumont = F. Cumont, *Les Religions orientales dans le paganisme romain.* Ed. 4. Brussels, 1929.

Denniston = J. D. Denniston, *The Greek Particles.* Ed. 2. Oxford, 1954.

Dihle = A. Dihle, *Studien zur griechischen Biographie.* Göttingen, 1956.

Droysen = J. G. Droysen, *Geschichte des Hellenismus.* Ed. 3. Basle, 1952.

Ehrenberg = V. Ehrenberg, *Alexander and the Greeks.* Oxford, 1938.

Etym. Magn. = Etymologicon Magnum, ed. T. Gaisford.

F. Gr. Hist. = F. Jacoby, *Die Fragmente der griechischen Historiker.* Berlin-Leiden, 1923-(in progress).

FHG = C. and Th. Müller, *Fragmenta historicorum graecorum.* 5 vols. Paris, 1841-70.

Fränkel = A. Fränkel, *Die Quellen der Alexanderhistoriker.* Breslau, 1883.

Fuller = J. F. C. Fuller, *The Generalship of Alexander the Great.* London, 1958.

Geog. Jour. = Geographical Journal.

GHI = M. N. Tod, *Greek Historical Inscriptions.* 2 vols. Oxford, 1946 (vol. 1, ed. 2), 1948 (vol. 2).

Glotz-Cohen = G. Glotz and R. Cohen, *Histoire grecque IV. i.* (in Glotz's *Histoire générale*). Ed. 2. Paris, 1945.

Gomme = A. W. Gomme, *A Historical Commentary on Thucydides* vol. 1. Oxford, 1945.

HA = C. A. Robinson Jnr., *The History of Alexander the Great* 1. Brown University Studies, no. 16. Providence, 1953.

Hammond = N. G. L. Hammond, A History of Greece to 322 B.C. Oxford, 1959.

Harv. Stud. = Harvard Studies in Classical Philology.

Harv. Theol. Rev. = Harvard Theological Review.

Head = B. V. Head, *Historia Numorum.* Ed. 2. Oxford, 1911.

Hoffmann = W. Hoffmann, *Das literarische Porträt Alexanders des Grossen im griechischen und römischen Altertum.* Diss. Leipzig, 1907.

IG^2 = *Inscriptiones graecae, editio minor.*

Jaeger = W. Jaeger, *Aristotle.* Ed. 2. Oxford, 1948.

Jax Festschrift = 'Natalicium Carolo Jax septuagenario a.d. VII kal. Dec. M.C.M.L.V. oblatum', Pars 1, *Innsbruck Beiträge zur Kulturgeschichte* 3 (1955).

JDAI = Jahrbuch des deutschen archäologischen Instituts.

JHS = Journal of Hellenic Studies.

JNES = Journal of Near Eastern Studies.

JOEAI = Jahreshefte des Österreichischen archäologischen Instituts.

JRS = Journal of Roman Studies.

Kaerst = J. Kaerst, *Geschichte des Hellenismus.* 2 vols. Leipzig, 1927 (vol. 1, ed. 3), 1926 (vol. 2, ed. 2).

Kornemann = E. Kornemann, *Die Alexandergeschichte des Königs Ptolemaios von Aegypten.* Berlin, 1935.

Kühner-Gerth = R. Kühner and B. Gerth, *Ausführliche Grammatik der griechischen Sprache.* Leverkusen, 1955. References are to the second part (Satzlehre) only.

LSJ = Liddell-Scott-Jones, *A Greek-English Lexicon.* Oxford, 1925-40.

Marrou = H. I. Marrou, *A History of Education in Antiquity* (tr. G. Lamb). London, 1956.

Marsden = E. W. Marsden, *The Campaign of Gaugamela.* Liverpool, 1964.

Mederer = E. Mederer, *Die Alexanderlegenden bei den ältesten Alexanderhistorikern.* Stuttgart, 1936.

Merkelbach = R. Merkelbach, *Die Quellen des griechischen Alexanderroman.* Zetemata 9. München, 1954.

Miscellanea Rostagni = Miscellanea di Studi Alessandrini in Memoria di Augusto Rostagni. Torino, 1963.

Mnemos. = Mnemosyne.

Nilsson = M. P. Nilsson, *Geschichte der griechischen Religion.* 2 vols. München, 1955 (vol. 1, ed. 2), 1950 (vol. 2).

Num. Chron. = Numismatic Chronicle.

OCD = The Oxford Classical Dictionary.

Olmstead = A. T. Olmstead, *A History of the Persian Empire.* Chicago, 1948.

PACA = Proceedings of the African Classical Associations.

Parke-Wormell = H. W. Parke and D. E. W. Wormell, *The Delphic Oracle.* Ed. 2. 2 vols. Oxford 1956.

Pearson, *LHA* = L. Pearson, *The Lost Histories of Alexander the Great.* New York, 1960.

Phil. = Philologus.

Pickard-Cambridge, *Dramatic Festivals* = Sir A. W. Pickard-Cambridge, *The Dramatic Festivals of Athens.* Oxford, 1953.

Pridik = E. Pridik, *De Alexandri epistularum commercio.* Diss. Berlin, 1893.

Proc. Am. Philos. Soc. = *Proceedings of the American Philosophical Society.*

Proc. Camb. Philol. Soc. = *Proceedings of the Cambridge Philological Society.*

Rabe = Inge Rabe, *Quellenkritische Untersuchungen zu Plutarchs Alexanderbiographie.* Diss. Hamburg, 1964.

Radet = G. Radet, *Alexandre le Grand.* Ed. 6. Paris, 1950.

RE = Paulys *Real-Encyclopädie der classischen Altertumswissenschaft.* Stuttgart, 1893-.

REA = Revue des études anciennes.

REG = Revue des études grecques.

Rev. Phil. = Revue de philologie, de littérature et d'histoire anciennes.

Rh. Mus. = Rheinisches Museum.

Robinson = C. A. Robinson Jnr., *Alexander the Great.* New York, 1947.

RSI = Rivista Storica Italiana.

SB Berlin = Sitzungsberichte der Preussischen Akademie der Wissenschaften, Phil.-hist. Klasse.

Schachermeyr = F. Schachermeyr, *Alexander der Grosse: Ingenium und Macht.* Graz-Wien, 1949.

Seltman = C. Seltman, *Greek Coins.* Ed. 2. London, 1955.

SIG = Sylloge inscriptionum graecarum, ed. W. Dittenberger. Ed. 3. 4 vols. Leipzig, 1915-24.

Smith *EHI* = V. A. Smith, The Early History of India from 600 B.C. to the Muhammadan Conquest. Ed. 3. Oxford, 1914.

Stadter = Philip A. Stadter, *Plutarch's Historical Methods.* Cambridge, Mass., 1965.

Strasburger = H. Strasburger, *Ptolemaios und Alexander.* Leipzig, 1934.

Stuart = D. R. Stuart, *Epochs of Greek and Roman Biography.* Berkeley, 1928.

Studies Ehrenberg = Ancient Society and Institutions, Studies presented to Victor Ehrenberg on his 75th birthday. Oxford, 1966.

Studies Robinson = Studies presented to D. M. Robinson, vol. 2. Washington University Studies, 1953.

TAPA = Transactions of the American Philological Association.

Tarn = Sir William Tarn, *Alexander the Great.* 2 vols. Cambridge, 1948.

Tarn, *Bactria* = Sir William Tarn, *The Greeks in Bactria and India.* Ed. 2. Cambridge, 1951.

TGF = A. Nauck, *Tragicorum Graecorum Fragmenta.* Ed. 2. 1889.

Theander = C. Theander, *Plutarch und die Geschichte.* Lund, 1951.

Thomson = J. O. Thomson, *History of Ancient Geography.* Cambridge, 1948.

Trans. Am. Philos. Soc. = Transactions of the American Philosophical Society.

UPZ = U. Wilcken, *Urkunden der Ptolemäerzeit,* 1-2. 2. Berlin, 1922-37.

Wilcken = U. Wilcken, *Alexander the Great* (tr. G. C. Richards). London, 1932.

Ziegler = K. Ziegler, *RE* 21 s.v. Plutarchos (2), cols. 636 ff. (1951). Previously published as *Plutarchos von Chaeroneia* (Stuttgart, 1949). The *RE* article contains a few revisions and additions.

Zumetikos = A. Zumetikos, *De Alexandri Olympiadisque epistularum fontibus et reliquiis.* Diss. Berlin, 1894.

J. R. Hamilton (essay date 1971)

SOURCE: Hamilton, J. R. Introduction to *Arrian:* The Campaigns of Alexander, translated by Aubrey de Sélincourt, pp. 13-40. London: Penguin Books, 1971.

[*In the following essay, Hamilton discusses some of Arrian's difficulties in writing* The Campaigns of Alexander *and offers a general critique of the work.*]

Arrian is remembered today only as the author of *The Campaigns of Alexander* and as the pupil of the philosopher Epictetus who preserved his master's teachings from oblivion. Yet he was a famous man in his own time. *The Campaigns of Alexander* was only one of a number of substantial historical works, while he held the chief magistracies at Rome and Athens and governed for a lengthy period an important frontier province of the Roman empire.

LIFE OF ARRIAN

Flavius Arrianus Xenophon, to give him his full name,[1] was a Greek, born at Nicomedia, the capital of the Roman province of Bithynia, probably a few years before A.D. 90.[2] His family was well-to-do, and Arrian himself tells us that he held the priesthood of Demeter and

Kore in the city. Like other wealthy Greeks, Arrian's father had received the Roman citizenship, evidently from one of the Flavian emperors, most probably Vespasian. Hence Arrian became at birth a Roman citizen with the prospect, if he wished it and possessed the requisite ability, of a career in the imperial service.

Arrian's boyhood and youth were spent in his native city, where he presumably received the customary upper-class Greek education in literature and rhetoric. Then, like many other young Greeks of similar social standing who planned a career in the imperial service, Arrian decided to complete his education by studying philosophy. He went about the year 108 to Nicopolis in Epirus, where the Stoic philosopher Epictetus had founded a school after the general expulsion of philosophers from Rome by Domitian in A.D. 92/3.[3] This remarkable man, a former slave, concerned himself mainly with ethics, and his teachings with their emphasis on the need for the individual to concern himself with his soul and their contempt for wealth and luxury had certain affinities with Christianity. Indeed, they have sometimes been thought, though wrongly, to have been influenced by the new religion. Like Socrates, Epictetus wrote nothing for publication, but fortunately he made such an impression on the young Arrian that he took down his master's words in shorthand and later published them in eight books of *Discourses*.[4] Four of these still survive to give us a vivid portrait of a striking personality. Also extant is the *Manual* or *Handbook* (*Encheiridion*) in which, for the benefit of the general public, Arrian combined the essentials of Epictetus' teaching. In the Middle Ages it enjoyed great popularity as a guide of monastic life. It is clearly from Epictetus that Arrian derived the high moral standards by which he judges Alexander. Epictetus, too, warmly commends repentance after wrongdoing, an attitude which finds an echo in Arrian's praise for Alexander's conduct after the murder of Cleitus. Since Epictetus drew on his experience of life in Rome under Domitian to illustrate his teachings, it is possible that Arrian's comments on 'the bane of monarchs', the courtier, have their origin in the same source.

Of Arrian's career in the imperial service until he reached the consulship in 129 or 130 we know only that he served on the Danube frontier and possibly in Gaul and Numidia. Arrian's career may have been forwarded by the phil-hellenism of Hadrian, the 'Greekling' as he was nicknamed, who succeeded Trajan as emperor in A.D. 117. But his appointment, in the year following his consulship, to the governorship of Cappadocia, it is safe to say, recognised his military and administrative abilities; for there is no evidence that Hadrian allowed sentiment to imperil the security of the empire. At this time the large and important frontier province of Cappadocia extended northwards to

the Black Sea and along its eastern coast from Trapezus as far as Dioscurias, and Arrian commanded two Roman legions and a large body of auxiliary troops, a rare, perhaps unexampled, command for a Greek at this period. It was an unsettled time 'produced by Trajan's momentary conquests beyond the Euphrates, and by Hadrian's prompt return to a defensive policy.'[5] In 134 the Alans from across the Caucasus threatened to invade Cappadocia and although they did not cross the frontier Arrian is recorded to have driven the invaders out of Armenia. The extant work of Arrian, *The Formation against the Alans,* describes the composition of his force, with its order of march and the tactics to be followed. Two other works dating from the period of his governorship are extant, the *Circumnavigation of the Black Sea* (*Periplus Ponti Euxini*) and a *Tactical Manual,* the latter dated precisely to 136/7 A.D. It is concerned only with cavalry tactics; for Arrian tells us he had already written a work on infantry tactics. The *Circumnavigation* is an account, based on the official report (in Latin) which he, as governor, submitted to the emperor, of a voyage from Trapezus to Dioscurias combined with two other passages to form an account of the whole Black Sea coast. This voyage took place at the beginning of his office—he mentions hearing of the death of king Cotys in 131/2 in the course of it—in order to inspect the defences of his area.

Arrian is attested as governor of Cappadocia in 137, but he retired or was recalled before the death of Hadrian in June 138. He seems not to have held any further office, for reasons we can only guess at, but to have taken up residence at Athens and to have devoted the remainder of his life to writing. He became an Athenian citizen and in 145/6 held the chief magistracy, the archonship. We last hear of him in 172/3 as a member of the Council, and in 180 the satirist Lucian refers to him in terms which reveal that he was already dead.

The writings of Arrian's Athenian period are numerous and varied. The order in which they were composed cannot be determined with certainty, but we may with confidence place early in his stay his biographies of Dion of Syracuse and Timoleon of Corinth, and possibly a life of Tilliborus, a notorious bandit who plagued Asia Minor. Of these no trace remains. In his writings he frequently refers in a spirit of rivalry to his namesake, the Athenian Xenophon, and a short work on hunting forms a supplement to the older writer's book on the same topic. By choosing the same title, *On the Chase* (*Cynegeticus*), Arrian stresses the connexion and challenges comparison. Indeed, he writes that he had from his youth onwards the same interests as the Athenian Xenophon—hunting, tactics, and philosophy. His major historical works came later. Apart from *The Campaigns of Alexander* (*Anabasis Alexandri*), whose title and division into seven books are clearly modelled on Xenophon's *Anabasis,* he wrote the still extant *Indica,* an account of the voyage of Alexander's fleet from India to the Persian Gulf (based on Nearchus' book) prefaced by a description of India and its people. Of his *Events after Alexander* in ten books we have virtually only the narrative of the first two years. The rest has perished—undoubtedly the greatest loss among the works of Arrian. We possess only fragments of his other works, a *Parthian History* dealing with Trajan's campaigns in seventeen books, and a *History of Bithynia* which traced the story of his native land from mythical times down to 74 B.C., when the last king, Nicomedes IV, bequeathed his kingdom to Rome.

THE CAMPAIGNS OF ALEXANDER

This book was intended to be Arrian's masterpiece, his lasting claim to fame. How important it was to him, his own words (I.12) make clear:

> I need not declare my name—though it is by no means unheard of in the world; I need not specify my country and family, or any official position I may have held. Rather let me say this: that this book is, and has been since my youth, more precious than country and kin and public advancement—indeed, for me it *is* these things.

He had, he felt, a splendid subject, and a splendid opportunity. No one had had more written about him than Alexander, yet no one, poet or prose-writer, had done him justice. The real Alexander was hidden behind a mass of contradictory statements, while the works of earlier writers contained downright error. They could not even get right the location of the decisive battle against Darius; they did not know which men had saved Alexander's life in India. Not to speak of Achilles' good fortune in having Homer relate his exploits, lesser men, such as the Sicilian tyrants, had fared better than Alexander. Arrian's book was intended to end this state of affairs. Such is the importance of Alexander that he will not hesitate to challenge the great historians of Greece.

For this task Arrian possessed substantial advantages. We cannot say with any certainty when he began his book, but a date before the middle of the second century would seem highly unlikely. Arrian, therefore, was probably in his sixties; he had read widely in the Alexander-literature and was thoroughly familiar with the classical historians, Herodotus, Thucydides, and Xenophon; he had written a considerable amount, although perhaps nothing as ambitious as this; he had at least some philosophical training and considerable military and administrative experience; finally, and not least important, he possessed, it is evident, a good deal of common sense.

But he faced formidable difficulties, difficulties he shared with the other extant writers on Alexander. Of

these the earliest is the Sicilian Greek Diodorus, who almost exactly three hundred years after Alexander's death, devoted the 17th Book of his *Universal History* to his reign. The Latin writer Quintus Curtius wrote his *History of Alexander* in the first century A.D., while early in the next century the Greek biographer Plutarch wrote a *Life of Alexander* which provides a useful supplement to Arrian. The *Philippic Histories* of the Romanised Gaul Pompeius Trogus, who wrote a little earlier than Diodorus, is extant only in the wretched summary of Justin (3rd cent. A.D.).[6] All these authors were faced with the problem of choosing from a multiplicity of conflicting sources. For Arrian does not exaggerate the mass of material that confronted the historian of Alexander. Much of this has perished almost without trace, but enough remains, in the shape of 'fragments' embedded in extant writers, to confirm his statement that many lies were told about Alexander and many contradictory versions of his actions existed.

Many of those who accompanied Alexander wrote of the expedition and its leader from their particular standpoint.[7] Callisthenes, Aristotle's nephew, acting as Alexander's 'press-agent' composed for Greek consumption—for Alexander's allies were by no means enthusiastic—an account of the expedition in which the king, who surely 'vetted' Callisthenes' narrative, bore a distinct resemblance to the 'heroes' of legend. This official version was necessarily broken off when its author was arrested, and later executed, on suspicion of treason. The last event certainly dealt with was the battle of Gaugamela. Chares, the royal chamberlain, wrote a book of anecdotes, valuable when he is dealing with events at court, otherwise useless, while Onesicritus, Alexander's chief pilot, who had been a pupil of Diogenes, created a dangerous blend of truth and falsehood with a Cynic flavour. For him Alexander was the 'philosopher in arms', a man with a mission. Nearchus, who commanded Alexander's fleet on its voyage from India to the Persian Gulf, followed with a more sober account, beginning, unfortunately, only with the start of his voyage. Lastly, to mention only the most important of the contemporary accounts, we have the histories of Ptolemy, who after Alexander's death became ruler and later king of Egypt, and of Aristobulus, apparently an engineer or architect. With these I shall deal later. But the history of Alexander which enjoyed the greatest popularity in succeeding centuries—Caelius, the friend of Cicero, read it—was written by a man who was not a member of the expedition, Cleitarchus, who wrote at Alexandria at the end of the fourth century, or perhaps even later. He portrayed Alexander as 'heroic', as Callisthenes had done, and (somewhat incongruously) as the possessor of the typical virtues of a Hellenistic king. But the main attraction of his book was almost certainly the vivid descriptions and the sensational incidents it contained—the Greek courtesan Thais leading Alexander, the worse for drink, in a Bacchic revel to set fire to the palace at Persepolis, Alexander's wholesale adoption of Persian luxury and practices, including a harem of 365 concubines, the week-long revel in Carmania, the poisoning of Alexander—to mention but a few.

All or much of this Arrian will have read. He will doubtless have been familiar, too, with the criticisms of the philosophical schools, particularly the Stoics, and the rhetoricians.[8] These found a congenial theme in Alexander's drunkenness, his conceit, his lack of self-control erupting into murderous violence, and his divine aspirations.

Faced with this mass of evidence Arrian decided, very sensibly, to use the histories of Ptolemy and Aristobulus as the basis of his narrative. Where their versions tallied, he tells us, he accepted their consensus as true. Where they differed, he sometimes gives both versions; more often, one suspects, he followed Ptolemy. Certainly for military matters Ptolemy is his principal source. His reasons for his choice, admittedly, do not inspire confidence. Since Alexander was dead when they wrote, neither, he claims, had anything to gain by not telling the truth, while it would be disgraceful for a king, as Ptolemy was when he wrote, to tell lies. It is not difficult to think of reasons why Aristobulus and, especially, Ptolemy might not care to tell the truth, at least the whole truth. But it would seem reasonable to suppose that Arrian had come to the conclusion, after long study of the available material, that these authors provided the most honest and most reliable accounts of Alexander. To supplement their works Arrian includes the 'stories' of other writers, such as Callisthenes and Chares, where these appeared 'worth relating and reasonably reliable'.

So far as we can judge, Arrian's choice of Ptolemy as his main source was fully justified, particularly as he concerned himself largely with military matters. For Ptolemy was an experienced soldier who had taken a part, although not at first a prominent one, in many of the operations he describes. His accounts of Alexander's major battles, as we see them through Arrian's eyes, are by no means free from problems, perhaps because of the difficulty a participant has in obtaining an overall view of the fighting. We should remember too that Ptolemy was not promoted to 'the Staff' until late in 330. The other military operations, particularly those in which Ptolemy took part, are reported with admirable clarity, although Ptolemy's tendency to exaggerate his personal contribution seems well established.[9] This is understandable, and unimportant. Less excusable is the apparently systematic denigration of Perdiccas, his bitter enemy in the struggle for power after Alexander's death.[10] The main fault of his book, it seems, lies elsewhere, in his reticence about some of the more

controversial, and perhaps discreditable, episodes in Alexander's career. Arrian does not cite him as a source for his narrative of the murder of Cleitus, although it is difficult to believe that Ptolemy did not mention the tragedy, while neither he nor Aristobulus is the basis of Arrian's account of Alexander's attempt to introduce the ceremony of prostration (proskynesis). It would seem that Ptolemy said no more than he had to about these incidents. The same is probably true of the 'plot' of Philotas and the conspiracy of the Pages, although he asserted the guilt of Philotas and Callisthenes.

Aristobulus' book provided a useful supplement to Ptolemy, since he was, it seems, more interested in geography and natural history. Most of the geographical and topographical detail in the Campaigns comes from Aristobulus and it was he who described Alexander's measures to improve the canal system of Babylonia and the navigation of the River Tigris. Aristobulus was ordered by the king to restore the tomb of Cyrus near Pasargadae which had been plundered by robbers, and it is to him that we are indebted for the description of the tomb before and after it was robbed, a description that modern archaeology has confirmed. It is probable that the vivid narrative of the march through the Gedrosian desert with its valuable botanical observations comes from the same source. It is Aristobulus too who related the exploration of the coasts of Arabia and the plans which Alexander had made for its conquest. One of Alexander's motives for the expedition, Aristobulus tells us—we learn this from Strabo, for Arrian does not mention the name of his source—was the expectation that the Arabians would recognize him as a god.

But it is on the personal side that Aristobulus' account is open to question. Whereas Ptolemy had been content to pass over the less pleasant aspects of Alexander's character, Aristobulus' book seems to have had a distinctly 'apologetic' character which earned him in antiquity the soubriquet of 'flatterer' (kolax). He justifiably stressed the generosity of the king towards the captured Persian royal family, and put forward the tenable view that Cleitus asked for trouble, but although he asserted the guilt of Philotas and Callisthenes he was apparently as reticent as Ptolemy about the reasons for his judgement. Then his statement that the king was not a heavy drinker, but remained long at banquets only for the sake of the conversation, must provoke a smile. The murder of Cleitus alone disproves it. In fact, it represents an excessive reaction from the quite indefensible view that Alexander was habitually drunk. Many writers depicted the king towards the end of his life as a prey to superstitious fear. According to them Alexander, on the advice of his seers, put to death the sailor who had worn the royal diadem and the man who had sat upon the royal throne. Aristobulus, however, stated that the sailor was merely flogged and then let go and that the second man was tortured to reveal his motive, implying, it would seem, that he suffered nothing worse. But, as the man was a scapegoat, this seems doubtful. On the other hand, Aristobulus relates that he learned from the seer Peithagoras himself that Alexander had treated him with great favour because he had told the king the truth, namely that his sacrifices had disclosed impending disaster for him.

Arrian brought to his task patience, common sense, and a shrewd knowledge of human affairs, as well as considerable military and administrative experience. In military matters his adherence to Ptolemy produced good results. Here he followed a first-rate source well up in the inner circle of the Macedonians, whom he seems almost always to have understood. We might be tempted to depreciate Arrian by saying that he did little more than summarize Ptolemy's narrative. To do so would be unfair. We have only to compare his account of Issus or of Gaugamela with that of Quintus Curtius, who certainly had access to Ptolemy's book at first or second hand, to see his achievement. This is not to say that his account of military operations is everywhere satisfactory or that he tells us all we would like to know about the Macedonian army. We do not know, for example, what the soldiers in the various units were paid, and, more important, we hear almost nothing of the logistics of the army. Again, at Gaugamela Arrian fails to explain how a messenger from Parmenio could reach Alexander after he had begun the pursuit of Darius. Only occasionally does he appear to misunderstand Ptolemy, for it is unlikely that the Macedonian supposed that Alexander, after crossing the Hydaspes, rode ahead with his cavalry in the expectation that he could defeat Porus' entire army with it alone. On the other hand he offers sensible criticism of Aristobulus' statement that Porus' son was sent with only 60 chariots to oppose Alexander's crossing of the R. Hydaspes, and rightly commends Alexander for refusing to risk attacking the Persians by night at Gaugamela, as Parmenio advised. Moreover, Arrian nearly always uses technical terms correctly, an immense help to the student of military history, and takes care to name the commanders of the various units. His use of *taxis* ('unit') as a utility word and of 'Companions' (*Hetairoi*) to refer either to the Companion cavalry or to Alexander's 'Peers' does give rise to difficulties, but for this Arrian can hardly be held responsible. The same painstaking attention to detail is evident in administrative matters. Appointments of governors are duly mentioned, and throughout his book Arrian is careful to give the father's name in the case of Macedonians, e.g. Ptolemy son of Lagus, and in the case of Greeks their city of origin. One can imagine the confusion that would have resulted had he not done so, in view of the shortage of Macedonian proper names and the resultant abundance of Ptolemys and Philips.

We must regret, however, that Arrian has interpreted his subject in a somewhat narrow fashion, perhaps because his model, Xenophon, had concentrated on *his* expedition. Unlike Polybius, he does not discuss *why* Alexander invaded Asia—he might, however, have said that this was a matter for the historian of Philip and that Alexander never thought of not continuing an operation already begun—nor does he mention previous operations in Asia or the existence of a Macedonian force in Asia in 334. His account of the events of 336, which determined Alexander's relations with the Greek states, formally at least, are dealt with so summarily as to be barely intelligible. Consequently the reader, I suspect, is in the dark when, without having heard of the League of Corinth, he is told of 'the resolutions of the Greeks'. In fact, Alexander's relations with the Greek states and events in Greece during the expedition are almost entirely neglected. This is to some extent understandable and justifiable, although Persian hopes of transferring the war to Greece in 333 are not fully intelligible without the background of Greek discontent. Indeed, Arrian's preoccupation with Alexander leads him to treat this important, though admittedly abortive, episode in the war very sketchily. Again, the reader must be curious, one would think, to learn what happened to King Agis of Sparta who vanishes from the pages of Arrian after receiving 30 talents and 10 ships from the Persians, even if we regard the Spartan revolt in 331, as Alexander is said to have regarded it, as 'an affair of mice'.

Arrian clearly made no attempt to give a comprehensive account of the war, or of its antecedents. We hear only incidentally of the troubles in the Persian empire that preceded Darius' accession in 336, and every reader must have asked himself the question: 'Why did the Persians allow Alexander's forces to cross into Asia unopposed?' Even after the start of the expedition we hear what the Persians have been planning and doing only when they come into contact with Alexander. It is only on the eve of Issus in November 333 that we are told of Darius' plans in the preceding months. Arrian deliberately chose to disregard the Persian background, as Professor Brunt has proved.[11] He was not ignorant of Persian matters; but his method 'was to follow the movements and describe the activities of Alexander himself'.

Arrian's portrait of Alexander is in general more open to criticism than his narrative of military operations, partly through his reliance on Ptolemy and Aristobulus. Yet Arrian's portrait is more than the sum of his sources; for he possesses a distinct personality of his own which we can detect most clearly in his attitude to religion and morals. Many of the characteristics of his Alexander are undeniably true. We can see clearly the qualities which enabled Alexander to maintain for so many years his hold upon his men, the dashing leadership which was expected of a general in his day—although Arrian does not conceal the fact that his officers thought that the king sometimes went too far in hazarding his life—the confidence (seldom disappointed) of success, with which he inspired his troops, and his care for their welfare. We remember how after the victory at the Granicus Alexander 'showed much concern about the wounded, visiting each, examining their wounds, asking how they were received, and encouraging each to relate, and even boast of, his exploits'. We recall his determination and persistence in many sieges, notably in the face of the desperate resistance by the Tyrians for seven long months, and his courage in adversity, exemplified by his 'noblest deed', the refusal to drink the helmetful of water, too little for his troops to share, in the burning heat of the Gedrosian desert—a proof, as Arrian remarks, of his endurance and his generalship. Arrian, too, rightly praises his generous treatment of the defeated Indian rajah Porus—although this was not altogether disinterested—and his compassion for the captured Persian royal family. There are many instances of Alexander's affection for his friends, particularly his *alter ego* Hephaestion, and his trust in them is portrayed in the celebrated scene with his doctor Philip, while Arrian warmly commends his repentance after his murder of Cleitus.

It is when Arrian's imagination is kindled by incidents such as these that he raises the pitch of his narrative and achieves eloquence. For the most part he is content to let the story speak for itself. Certainly he deliberately avoided sensationalism and he explicitly denied the truth of such favourite stories as the visit of the Amazon queen or the week-long revel through Carmania. Perhaps no passage better illustrates Arrian's admiration for his hero and the heightened tone of his narrative than that in which he describes the king's return to his army after his recovery from the wound which so nearly caused his death. I quote the end of the passage:

> Near his tent he dismounted, and the men saw him walk; they crowded round him, touching his hands, his knees, his clothing; some, content with a sight of him standing near, turned away with a blessing on their lips. Wreaths were flung upon him and such flowers as were then in bloom.

But Arrian's evident admiration for Alexander and his achievements did not prevent him from criticizing his hero where he failed to reach the high standard which, as a Stoic, Arrian felt a king ought to attain. In particular, Alexander is censured several times for his excessive ambition. Arrian does not know, and commendably will not speculate about, Alexander's future plans, but he is convinced that he would never have rested content with his conquests. The Indian wise men are expressly commended for their view that 'each man

possesses just so much of the earth as he stands on', and Alexander, despite his applause of this sentiment, is said to have acted always in a way completely opposed to it. It is clear that for Arrian Alexander's conquests are merely an expression of Alexander's insatiable appetite for fame. There is some truth in this, but it is not the whole story. It is, however, entirely to Arrian's credit that he wholeheartedly condemns Alexander's letter to Cleomenes, the governor of Egypt (7.23.6-7), in which the king offers to pardon him for his past misdeeds and to give him a free hand in the future if he erects temples in Egypt for the dead Hephaestion. The historian's understanding and humanity is apparent in his attitude to the murderer of Cleitus. Alexander's act excites in him pity for the man who has given way to two grave vices, passion and drunkenness. The king has failed to achieve that self-mastery which, as Arrian has remarked a little earlier, is necessary before one can be happy. A similar sentiment occurs in the speech of Coenus at the River Hyphasis when he says to Alexander 'when things go well with us, the spirit of self-restraint is a noble thing'—surely Arrian's own view, whether or not it was shared by Coenus.

The main weaknesses in Arrian's portrait of Alexander seem to me two-fold—a tendency, which he derives from his sources, to gloss over the less attractive side of the king's character, and a failure to appreciate Alexander's intentions, especially with regard to the Persians.

The first of these is apparent before the expedition gets under way. The slaughter of the Thebans, perhaps rightly, and the destruction of the city and the enslavement of the survivors is blamed on the Greek allies of Alexander. Nothing is said of his responsibility for permitting them, as in fact he did, to pass this sentence. Yet even Plutarch, whom no one could accuse of hostility to Alexander, implicitly holds him responsible; as he saw, Alexander's intention was to terrify the other Greek states into submission. At the battle of the Granicus Arrian relates without comment the massacre of the Greek mercenaries, nearly 18,000 according to his own account; he does not remark on the cruelty or the inadvisability of the massacre. In the same way at Massaga in India the massacre of 7,000 Indians passes without comment. Nor should we guess from Arrian that some writers had doubts about the involvement of Philotas in a plot against the king. He is content to accept Ptolemy's statement, although the 'manifest proofs' of his guilt adduced by him do not amount to much. Again, the burning of the palace at Persepolis is very briefly referred to with no mention of the alternative tradition that it was set on fire during a drunken revel. On the other hand, Arrian gives a much more balanced account of the murder of Cleitus than Aristobulus seems to have done, and he is obviously reluctant to accept the statements of Ptolemy and Aristobulus that Callisthenes was involved in the conspiracy of the Pages.

What the modern reader misses in Arrian's book is an appreciation of the larger issues. Alexander emerges as a great leader, a great conqueror possessed of boundless ambition, a man who reached the height of human prosperity and who, if he committed great crimes, had the magnanimity to repent of them. Certainly the conquest of the Persian Empire was his most lasting achievement, but what we want to know is whether he was more than the supreme conqueror. What plans did he have for his empire? What part did he intend the conquered peoples to play in it? Amid a great deal that is obscure about Alexander, one thing is certain, that he was very much in earnest about what modern writers have called his 'policy of fusion'. The clearest expression of this policy is his prayer at Opis—a prayer that Arrian records without comment—that Macedonians and Persians might live in harmony and jointly rule the empire. This was a revolutionary idea, not shared by his Macedonians, nor, we can be sure, by many Greeks either. For the most distinguished of Alexander's many teachers, the eminent philosopher Aristotle, who inspired him with a love of Greek literature and particularly of Homer, is said by Plutarch to have written to Alexander advising the young king to behave towards the Greeks as a leader but towards the 'barbarians' as a master. This contemptuous attitude towards 'barbarians' was no doubt widespread. But Alexander, who may have felt doubts about it even before the expedition—Artabazus and other leading Persians lived as exiles at Philip's court when Alexander was a boy—soon came to reject it. After Gaugamela we find him appointing Persians as governors, certainly not through a lack of suitable Macedonians.

Arrian clearly shared Aristotle's prejudice against 'barbarians' and had no conception of Alexander's vision of a partnership between the two peoples. In the characterisation of Alexander at the end of his book he sees Alexander's adoption of Persian dress and his introduction of Persian troops into the Macedonian army as a mere 'device', designed to render him less alien to his Persian subjects. Indeed, Arrian has earlier (4.7) condemned his adoption of oriental dress as a 'barbaric' act not so different from his 'barbaric' punishment of the pretender Bessus. Both acts, in Arrian's view, indicate a deterioration of Alexander's character. Even in the case of Bessus Arrian does not see that the punishment was a Persian punishment inflicted on him by Alexander in his position as 'Great King'. Elsewhere, he refers to Alexander 'going some way towards "barbarian" extravagance', and his comment on the king's marriage to Roxane, the Bactrian princess, is illuminating. 'I approve', he writes, 'rather than blame'. This 'policy of fusion' with the adoption of Persian

dress and Persian court ceremonial was bitterly resented by the Macedonians, as Arrian is well aware. Drink led Cleitus to give utterance to grievances which were deeply felt and widely shared, while the extent of the Pages' conspiracy leads one to think that their motives were not so much personal as political. Yet Arrian does not ask himself whether Alexander would have persisted in a policy so universally detested if it were nothing more than a 'device' to win Persian favour.

Plutarch, perhaps exaggerating, puts the number of cities founded by Alexander at seventy. In his *Campaigns* Arrian mentions fewer than a dozen foundations; not a cause for complaint, for he was not compiling a catalogue. But we are not told what Alexander's motives were, military or economic or, as some scholars believe, part of his mission to spread Greek culture throughout Asia. It is from the *Indica* that we learn that cities were established among the conquered Cossaeans to encourage them to forsake their nomadic habits and become a settled people.

Alexander took his religious duties very seriously indeed, as the account of his last days makes plain. Arrian frequently records that the king offered sacrifice or made drink-offerings, and the prophecies made by his seers, notably Aristander, are faithfully reported. Only once, before the siege of Tyre, is he provoked to sarcasm; 'The plain fact', he writes, 'is that anyone could see that the siege of Tyre would be a great undertaking'. But Arrian's hostile or sceptical attitude to the ruler cult of his day—an attitude he shares with Plutarch and the historian Appian—prevents him from doing justice to Alexander's divine aspirations. That Alexander believed himself to be the son of Ammon-Zeus, as his ancestor Hercules was son of Zeus, is very probable, although admittedly not susceptible of proof. Arrian will have none of this. Alexander set out for Siwah 'hoping to learn about himself more accurately, or at least *to say that he had so learnt*'. For him Alexander's claim was merely another 'device', to impress his subjects. He displays the same sceptical attitude towards Alexander's divinity. In 324 the Greek states, probably in response to a 'request' from the king himself, sent *theoroi* (envoys sent on sacred missions) to crown him with a golden crown at Babylon. That the envoys were *theoroi* admits of no doubt; the fact that they themselves wore crowns proves it. If Arrian writes that 'they came as *theoroi* forsooth', using a Greek particle implying disbelief or sarcasm, he is suggesting that Alexander, as a mortal, could never be a god. Gods were immortal, men were not, and 'after all', as Arrian drily comments, 'Alexander's death was near'.

Arrian set out to produce the best and most reliable account of Alexander's expedition, avoiding the exaggerations of his predecessors and correcting their errors.

That he succeeded few will dispute. The histories of Diodorus and Curtius and, particularly, the biography of Plutarch throw light (and sometimes darkness) on the character of Alexander and occasionally even on his military exploits, but Arrian's book is the basis of our knowledge. It impresses one as the work of an honest man who has made a serious and painstaking attempt to discover the truth about Alexander—a task perhaps impossible by his time—and who has judged with humanity the weaknesses of a man exposed to the temptations of those who exercise supreme power. We need not deny the limitations of the work, but it is proper to remember that Alexander's idea of an empire in whose rule conquering Macedonians and conquered Persians were to share perished with him. To spare the conquered was one thing, to associate them with one in government was another, an idea that was not to reach fulfilment until long after Alexander's death.

ALEXANDER'S ARMY[12]

In the spring of 334 Alexander set out from Macedonia, leaving Antipater with 12,000 infantry and 1,500 cavalry to defend the homeland and to keep watch on the Greek states. The size of the army with which he crossed the Hellespont has been variously reported, totals ranging from 30,000 to 43,000 for infantry and 4,000 to 5,500 for cavalry. But the detailed figures given by Diodorus (17.17), 32,000 infantry and 5,100 cavalry, agree essentially with the totals in Arrian (Ptolemy), and may be taken as substantially correct. The size and composition of the force holding the bridgehead at Abydos—there surely must have been some troops there in 334—is not known, but the likelihood is that it was small and consisted mainly of mercenary infantry.

The backbone of the infantry was the Macedonian heavy infantry, the 'Foot Companions', organized on a territorial basis in six battalions (*taxeis*) of about 1,500 men each. In place of the nine-foot spear carried by the Greek hoplite, the Macedonian infantryman was armed with a pike or *sarissa* about 13 or 14 feet long, which required both hands to wield it. The light circular shield was slung on the left shoulder, and was smaller than that carried by the Greek hoplite which demanded the use of the left arm. Both Greek and Macedonian infantry wore greaves and a helmet, but it is possible that the Macedonians did not wear a breastplate.[13] The *phalanx* (a convenient term for the sum total of the Macedonian heavy infantry), like all the Macedonian troops, had been brought by Philip to a remarkable standard of training and discipline. Unlike the phalanx which the Romans encountered over a century later, Alexander's phalanx was capable of rapid movement and was highly manoeuvrable, as one can see from a reading of the first half-dozen chapters of Arrian's book.

In battle the right flank of the phalanx was guarded by the *Hypaspists* or 'Guards'. These were an élite corps, consisting of a Royal battalion (*agema*) and two other battalions, each of approximately 1,000 men. Alexander used them frequently on rapid marches and other mobile operations, often in conjunction with cavalry and light-armed troops. This suggests, although it does not prove, that they were more lightly armed than the heavy infantry; but if they were less heavily armed, we do not know where the difference lay.

The member states of the Corinthian League contributed 7,000 heavy infantry, while 5,000 Greeks served as mercenaries. The remainder of Alexander's infantry consisted of 7,000 Thracian and Illyrian light troops armed with javelins and two bodies of archers from Crete and Macedonia respectively. The outstanding unit among the light troops was the Agrianians, 1,000 strong, who have been well compared in their relation to Macedon and in their quality to the Gurkhas of the Indian army. Alone of the allies they served throughout the campaign and Arrian mentions them almost fifty times. With the archers and the Guards they took part in all the reconnaisances and skirmishes as well as fighting superbly in the set pieces.

Pride of place among the cavalry was held by the Macedonian 'Royal Companions', originally 1,800 troopers divided into 8 squadrons or *Ilai,* all under the command of Parmenio's son, Philotas. Among them the Royal Squadron, consisting of perhaps 300 men, was Alexander's own bodyguard, which spearheaded the devastating cavalry charge in the major battles. Their position was on the immediate right of the Guards, who had the task of maintaining contact between the Companions and the phalanx. The counterpart of the Companions on the left of the phalanx was the Thessalian cavalry, also 1,800 strong at the start of the expedition. Under the general command of Parmenio, they had the difficult task at Issus and Gaugamela of holding much superior forces of Persian cavalry while Alexander delivered the decisive blow on the right. The Greek allies furnished 600 horsemen, and the remaining 900 were made up of Thracians, Paeonians, and 'Scouts' (*Prodromoi*) who were also called 'Lancers' (*Sarissophoroi*) since they were armed with the *sarissa,* presumably shorter than those carried by the infantry which required the use of both hands. Whether these light cavalry were Macedonians or Thracians is not clear; certainly they were distinct from 'the Thracians'. Finally, although Diodorus does not mention mercenary cavalry in his list of forces, Alexander may have had some from the beginning. By Gaugamela at least he had perhaps 1,000 of these.[14]

Despite the need for garrisons in Asia Minor and Egypt, Alexander's army at Gaugamela numbered 40,000 infantry and 7,000 cavalry. The only substantial reinforcements of Macedonian and allied troops recorded by Arrian reached Gordium early in 333, and there is no good reason to suppose that Alexander received any worthwhile number of Macedonians or allies apart from these before Gaugamela. For Quintus Curtius, who after 331 records the arrival of many reinforcements not mentioned by Arrian, mentions reinforcements only of mercenaries in this period. Indeed, it is clear that the increase in the number of Alexander's troops was due principally to the recruitment of mercenaries from Greece and to the enlistment of mercenaries who had fought for Persia. Alexander had begun by treating the latter as traitors, but finding that this merely encouraged desperate resistance decided within a few months to change this unsuccessful policy. Many of the garrisons doubtless consisted in large part of mercenaries.

Soon after Gaugamela Alexander received strong reinforcements of Macedonian troops, no fewer than 6,000 infantry and 500 cavalry. This enabled him to create a seventh battalion of infantry, which was certainly operating early in 330.[15] The other battalions must have remained over strength for some time. This is the last draft of Macedonians he is known to have received until he returned to the west after his Indian campaign, and there is no compelling reason to think that he received any others. In 330 the allied troops from the Greek states and from Thessaly were discharged at Ecbatana. Many, we are told, chose to re-enlist as mercenaries. Increasing use was made of Greek mercenaries, and the garrisons of the many cities founded by Alexander in the eastern satrapies consisted of them together with the native inhabitants and some unfit Macedonians. Presumably few of the 10,000 infantry and 3,500 cavalry left behind to protect Bactria in 327 were Macedonians.

After Gaugamela the pattern of warfare changed. In Bactria and Sogdiana Alexander found himself faced with a national resistance which, under the leadership of Bessus and then of Spitamenes, wisely avoided major conflicts and concentrated on widespread guerrilla activity. It was probably to cope with this altered mode of fighting that in 329 Alexander made an important change in the organization of his Companion cavalry. We no longer hear of eight *squadrons* (*Ilai*), but of (at least) eight *regiments* (*Hipparchiai*), each consisting of two, or perhaps more, squadrons. Some of these squadrons, it seems likely, now included or consisted of the excellent Persian cavalry.[16] Certainly Alexander made use of Persian cavalry outside the Companions. As early as 330 we hear of a unit of Persian mounted javelin-men (3.24), and at the battle of the River Hydaspes in 326 he had in his army a body of Daae,

mounted archers, as well as horsemen from Bactria, Sogdiana, Scythia, Arachotia, and the Parapamisus, or Hindu Kush, region.

At Massaga in India Alexander is said to have attempted to enlist Indian mercenaries in his army, but when they attempted to desert to have massacred them. No further recruitment of Indian mercenaries is recorded, and the only Indian troops that we hear of in his army are those provided by the rajahs Taxiles and Porus and the city of Nysa, some 11,000 in all. However, if Nearchus is correct in saying (*Indica* 19.5) that at the start of the voyage down the River Hydaspes Alexander had 120,000 fighting men with him (a figure given by Curtius (8.5.4) for the army at the start of the Indian campaign and by Plutarch (Alexander 66.4) for the (Infantry) force with which Alexander left India), Alexander must have had a great many Indian troops in his army. But their presence was only temporary, since there is no indication that any Indians returned to the west with him.

Among the grievances of the Macedonians in 324 Arrian (7.6.4) mentions the (recent) creation of a fifth cavalry regiment consisting, if we accept Professor Badian's emendation of Arrian's text,[17] almost entirely of Iranians. This means that the division of the Companion cavalry into eight regiments had been abandoned and that for a brief period after the return from India there were only four. It is sometimes said that the change reflects the losses sustained in the march through the Gedrosian desert. This need not be the case. Hephaestion's command is described (7.14.10) as a 'Chiliarchy', a group of 1,000 men, and, although it is true that he was 'Chiliarch' or 'Vizier', it is not self-evident that the preservation of his *name* required that his unit be called 'the chiliarchy of Hephaestion' rather than 'the regiment of Hephaestion'. It is probable, it seems to me, that the new regiments were (nominally) 1,000 strong. If this is so, the change will have been a change in organization, a consolidation of the cavalry into fewer and stronger units.

In 324 the 30,000 young Persians (the 'Successors'), who had been undergoing training in Macedonian fashion for the last three years, joined Alexander at Susa. Later in the same year, after the mutiny at Opis, Alexander sent home those Macedonians who were unfit or past the age for service, about 10,000 infantry and perhaps 1,500 cavalry, probably the bulk of his Macedonian forces. In 323 strong reinforcements reached Babylon. Philoxenus brought an army from Caria and Menander one from Lycia, while Menidas came with the cavalry under his command. It is likely that, as Brunt suggests,[18] these were fresh drafts from Macedon to replace the veterans now on their way home; Alexander had not drawn on the manpower of the homeland since 331 and it is not likely that he wished the Macedonian element in his army to be reduced to negligible proportions. In addition, Peucestas brought 20,000 Persian archers and slingers, as well as a considerable force of Cossaean and Tapurian troops, presumably infantry. Alexander now carried out his last reform. The Persians were integrated into Macedonian units in such a way that each platoon consisted of 4 Macedonian NCOs and 12 Persians, each armed in their national fashion.

For the future, then, or at least for the immediate future, the army in Asia was to consist predominantly of Iranian troops. The only indication of the size of the Macedonian component is given in a speech in Quintus Curtius purporting to have been delivered by Alexander but certainly the historian's own composition. There (10.2.8) the king mentions an army of 13,000 infantry and 2,000 cavalry, surely all Macedonians, excluding the garrisons already in being.

Notes

1. Philip A. Stadter (*Greek, Roman and Byzantine Studies* 8, 1967, 155ff) has shown that Xenophon was not merely a nickname, but part of the historian's name.

2. Arrian was suffect consul in 129 or 130 A.D., and in his day it was usual for a man to hold the consulship at about the age of 42; see *JRS* 55 (1965), p. 142 n. 30.

3. We do not know why Arrian chose to study under Epictetus rather than, as we should have expected, at Athens. In an important article on Arrian's governorship in the *English Historical Review* 1896 (reprinted in his *Essays,* ed. F. Haverfield, Oxford, 1906), Professor H. F. Pelham has suggested that Arrian was probably influenced by the traditions of his mother's family, the 'gens' Arria, famous in the history of Roman Stoicism. He conjectures that the *cognomen* Arrianus indicates the family of the historian's mother, as *cognomina* often did in the first and second centuries A.D.

4. In a letter to a Lucius Gellius Arrian gives his reasons for publishing them. We now know that this Gellius was an eminent citizen of Corinth, L. Gellius Menander, who with his son, L. Gellius Iustus, set up an inscription in honour of Arrian at Corinth; see G. W. Bowersock in *Greek, Roman and Byzantine Studies* 8 (1967), 279-80.

5. The quotation is taken from page 218 of Pelham's article mentioned in n. 3.

6. Diodorus' 17th Book is translated (with useful notes) by C. Bradford Welles in the Loeb Classical Library, Curtius by J. C. Rolfe in the same series, and Justin (with Cornelius Nepos and Eutropius) in Bohn's Library. Plutarch's *Alexander* has been frequently translated (usually with a number of other Lives), most recently by Ian Scott-Kilvert in *The Age of Alexander* (Penguin Books).

7. These authors are the subject of detailed study by Lionel Pearson, *The Lost Histories of Alexander the Great* (New York, 1960).

8. On these see my *Plutarch* Alexander: *A Commentary* (Oxford, 1969), lx-lxii.

9. See the convincing analysis by C. B. Welles, 'The reliability of Ptolemy as an historian', in *Miscellanea . . . A. Rostagni* (Turin 1963) 101ff. Curtius, who had the advantage of reading Ptolemy's book, presumably refers to this aspect of Ptolemy's writing when he describes him (9.5.21) as a man 'who was certainly not inclined to depreciate his own glory'.

10. R. M. Errington, 'Bias in Ptolemy's History of Alexander', in *CQ* 1969, 233ff., gives several instances of misrepresentation by Ptolemy. He considers that Aristonous was deprived of the credit for helping to save Alexander's life, but he contests the usual view that Antigonus' hard-fought victories over the survivors of Issus were ignored by Ptolemy, because of his rivalry with Antigonus in the years following 314.

11. See his 'Persian Accounts of Alexander's Campaigns' in *CQ* 1962, 141ff. The quotation which follows is taken from p. 141.

12. For details of Alexander's troops see especially Major-General J. F. C. Fuller, *The Generalship of Alexander the Great* (London, 1958); E. W. Marsden, *The Campaign of Gaugamela* (Liverpool, 1964), Appendices I and II; A. R. Burn, 'The Generalship of Alexander', in *Greece and Rome* 1965, 140-54.

13. See G. T. Griffith, *Proceedings of the Cambridge Philological Association,* 4 (1956/7), pp. 3ff.

14. P. A. Brunt, 'Alexander's Macedonian Cavalry', in *JHS* 83 (1963), 27-46 discusses the many problems concerning Alexander's cavalry.

15. As R. D. Milns has demonstrated in *Greek, Roman and Byzantine Studies* 7 (1966), 159-166.

16. On the Hipparchies see Appendix A.

17. E. Badian in *JHS* 85 (1965), 161.

18. *JHS* 83 (1963), 39.

Abbreviations

AJP: *American Journal of Philology.*

CQ: *Classical Quarterly.*

Ehrenberg Studies: Ancient Society and Institutions. Studies presented to Victor Ehrenberg, edited by E. Badian (Oxford, 1966).

Fuller: Major-General J. F. C. Fuller, *The Generalship of Alexander the Great* (London, 1958).

JHS: Journal of Hellenic Studies.

Tarn, *Alexander*: Sir William Tarn, *Alexander the Great,* 2 Vols. (Cambridge, 1948).

Tod: M. N. Tod, *A Selection of Greek Historical Inscriptions,* vol. 2 (Oxford, 1948).

Wilcken, *Alexander*: Ulrich Wilcken, *Alexander the Great,* translated by G. C. Richards (London, 1932); reprinted with an introduction to Alexander studies, notes, and a bibliography by Eugene N. Borza (New York, 1967).

J. Rufus Fears (essay date 1974)

SOURCE: Fears, J. Rufus. "The Stoic View of the Career and Character of Alexander the Great." *Philologus* 118, no. 1 (1974): 113-30.

[*In the following essay, Fears rejects the claim that Middle Stoic writers were hostile to Alexander.(J. Rufus Fears is David Ross Boyd Professor of Classics and G. T. and Libby Blankenship Chair at the University of Oklahoma.)*]

The study of the sources for Alexander's career has long been dominated by the view that two of the Greek philosophical schools, the Peripatetics and the Stoics, were hostile to the memory of Alexander. Accordingly many of the unfavorable elements in the tradition could be traced to the intentional blackening of Alexander's memory by Stoic and Peripatetic writers of the Hellenistic period:

> Portraits favorable to Alexander were anything but common. Literature, generally speaking, was in Greek hands, not Macedonian; and Greece, with exception of one or two bodies of men who produced no literature, . . . was hostile, often bitterly hostile, to Alexander . . . Of the great schools of philosophy and learning who guided thought, two, the Stoics and Peripatetics, were bitterly hostile to him from start to finish, and that coloured the whole of the literature of Alexandria, which grew out of Peripateticism, just as the Stoics were responsible for the blind hatred of Alexander so vehemently expressed by eclectic Stoics of the early Empire, like Lucan and Seneca . . . To the Stoics, he was bad from the start; his *paidagogos* Leonidas ought to have knocked the *typhos* out of him and did not . . . The Peripatetic portrait has long been known: Aristotle turned out a perfectly good pupil, but he was ruined by his own fortune[1].

In 1958 Badian examined the elaborate picture of a Peripatetic portrait of Alexander and conclusively exploded it as a myth of modern scholarship, based on the flimsiest of evidence[2]. However, Alexandrian source criticism, as well as studies of the memory of Alexander in later Greek and Roman tradition, continues to accept the arguments of Stroux and Tarn and to assume that the hostile portrait of Alexander found in such Roman Stoics as Lucan and Seneca can be traced directly to the school teachings of the Middle Stoa[3]. According to this view, Quintilian, Clement of Alexandria, and Cicero preserve the unfavorable judgement passed upon Alexander by Diogenes of Babylon and Panaetius.

> *Siquidem Leonides Alexandri paedagogus, ut a Babylonio Diogene traditur, quibusdam eum vitiis imbuit, quae robustum quoque et iam maximum regem ab illa institutione puerili sunt persecuta[4].*

> . . . Λεωνίδης δέ οὐ περιεῖλεν τὸν τῦφον τοῦ Μακεδόνος . . .[5]

> *Philippum quidem, Macedonum regem, rebus gestis et gloria superatum a filio, facilitate et humanitate video superiorem fuisse; itaque alter semper magnus, alter saepe tumidissimus* [Stroux's emendation for *turpissimus* found in all the manuscripts][6].

Following Stroux, Quintilian offers a summary, while Clement gives the specific reason, Alexander's *typhos,* for Diogenes' disapproval. Reading *tumidissimus* in the passage from Cicero, Stroux argues that both Diogenes and Panaetius, the alleged source of Cicero's comment, judged Alexander guilty of *typhos,* a cardinal sin in Stoic ethics[7]. Seneca's savage indictment of Alexander *tumidissimum animal,* developed directly from this Middle Stoic tradition[8].

Unfortunately, upon careful examination these passages in Quintilian, Clement, and Cicero do not prove that the Middle Stoa was hostile to the memory of Alexander. Diogenes' reproaches are directed against the tutor Leonides, not against his pupil Alexander. Leonides typifies the bad *paedagogus,* who attempts to hide his own lack of education by tyrannizing his students:

> *Nihil est peius iis, qui paulum aliquid ultra primas litteras progressi falsam sibi scientiae persuasionem induerunt. Nam et cedere praecipiendi partibus indignantur et velut iure quodam potestatis, quo fere hoc hominum genus intumescit, imperiosi atque interim saevientes stultitiam suam perdocent. Nec minus error eorum nocet moribus[9].*

Drawing upon Quintilian, Jerome even more clearly makes Leonides responsible for Alexander's faults:

> *Graeca narrat historia Alexandrum potentissimum regem orbisque domitorem et in moribus et in incessu Leonidis paedagogi sui non potuisse carere vitiis, qui-*

bus parvulus adhuc fuerat infectus. Proclivis est enim malorum aemulatio et, quorum virtutem adsequi nequeas, cito imitere vitia[10].

The important point in both Quintilian and Jerome is that the best possible teacher must be chosen, for even the greatest of kings could never rid himself of faults inculcated through imitation of a bad teacher. These passages then in no way support the contention that for the Stoics "Alexander was bad from the start". For Diogenes, Alexander's faults were not basic to his nature but were rather learned from a bad teacher. Reprobation of particular faults in the tutor does not imply a general judgment on the pupil; and furthermore, such an inference drawn from a single philosopher is certainly not evidence for the judgment of an entire school.

Clement, like Quintilian and Jerome, emphasizes the faults of teacher, not pupil. His mention of Leonides is part of a list of bad teachers of famous men: Phoenix, Adrastus, Leonides, Nausithoon, Zopyrus, Sicinnus, and the Persian royal pedagogues. All either failed to rid their pupils of vices or were themselves sinful. Again the emphasis is on finding the correct teacher, in this case God himself.

Pointing out the influence of Middle Stoic psychology and ethics on the theoretical and practical-ethical sections of the *Paedagogus*, Stroux suggests that Clement used Diogenes of Babylon in this passage. Both Clement and Quintilian, he argues, drew upon an originally Stoic concept which proved the worth of a good choice for a teacher by the example of bad teachers who had planted enduring vices in the pupil[11]. However, pace Stroux, the charge Clement makes against Leonides differs fundamentally from that of Diogenes quoted in Quintilian. Leonides did not plant vices into Alexander. Instead he failed to wash away Alexander's pre-existing sin of pride. It is difficult then to see how Clement can be said to be using Diogenes here; and in fact it is far from certain that this passage is drawn from any Stoic source. Stoicism, like Platonism, did exercise a notable influence on Clement in the *Paedagogus* and in his other works[12]. However, there is nothing specifically Stoic in this passage. The other unfortunate pupils, mentioned along with Alexander, do not seem to have been standard Stoic exempla Achilles, the son of Croesus, Philip, Alcibiades, and the children of Themistocles[13]. More importantly, a passage in Dio Chrysostom's second oration on kingship, an exposition of Stoic doctrines of kingship, compares favorably the education of Achilles by Phoenix and that of Alexander by Aristotle[14]. Moreover, Stroux and those who follow him contradict themselves in claiming that both this passage (sc. Clement Paed. 1. 7. 55) and that in Cicero's de Officiis represent the same strain in Stoic thought. In Cicero, Philip is *semper magnus* and far superior to this son in *facilitas* and *humanitas*[15]. In Clement, Philip is placed alongside his son, differentiated only by his vice, drink instead of pride. Finally it should be pointed out that the disparagement of *typhos* was not uniquely Stoic. Cynics and Plato, as well as Zeno, were connected with the condemnation of this vice[16]. Furthermore, apart from philosophical discussion, it seems to have been a commonplace maxim among military writers that the great commander must avoid the fault of *typhos*[17].

Clearly then we must look elsewhere, for Clement's comment on Alexander's arrogance cannot be attributed to a Stoic source. A rhetorical handbook is the most obvious source for Clement's list of bad pedagogues. It is also possible that Clement drew up the list from his own wide reading. Clement's writings are filled with an extremely large number of citations from classical writers[18]. A considerable controversy has centered on the extent to which these numerous classical references reflect the use of literary anthologies by Clement, whom Eusebius, Jerome, Cyril of Alexandria, Socrates, Anastasius of Sinai, and Photius praised for his knowledge of the Classics[19]. For our present purpose it is immaterial whether Clement had read these authors in their entirety. It is enough that his wide-ranging citations from Herodotus, Plato, Homer, and Plutarch show that he was familiar with large sections of their works. With the exception of Nausithoon, mentioned nowhere else, the material in the passage under discussion comes from popular authors, frequently cited by Clement throughout his works.

> It is generally agreed that Clement knew Homer and Plato, including Alcibiades I, at first hand. Iliad 9. 449-54 is the obvious source for Phoenix gynaikomanes, while Alcibiades I, 121-2, provides the necessary material for Clement's description of Zopyrus and the Persian pedagogues[20]. Clement's references to Adrastus and to Sicinnus derive from Herodotus, frequently cited by Clement, who had clearly read at first hand Herodotus' account of Croesus[21]. Leonides, the tutor of Alexander, is known from Plutarch's biography[22]. There are at least twenty-three references to Plutarch's parallel lives in Clement; and it seems very likely that he at least knew the Life of Alexander at first hand, for he repeats verbatim Plutarch's account of Alexander's questioning of the gymnosophists[23]. It is true that Plutarch accords Leonides a favorable mention. However, the same biography provides examples of Alexander's proverbial pride, and Clement himself could have made the connection between the tutor and the king's arrogance[24].

Whatever the source of Clement's list of bad pedagogues, the important point is that, in view of the uncertainties which have been raised, this passage in Clement cannot be used as evidence for general Stoic condemnation of Alexander.

Clement's view of Alexander cannot then be traced to a Stoic source, but the question remains whether, as

Stroux assumes Panaetius' opinion of Alexander is reflected in Cicero's derogatory portrait of the young Macedonian in de Officiis 1. 90[25]. Panaetius is indeed Cicero's major source for the entire de Officiis[26]. However, as Cicero explicitly states, he is not translating Stoic treatises verbatim but adapting them and presenting evidence from a number of sources[27]. Thus unlike Panaetius, Cicero begins with a definition of duty, and at points throughout he departs from Panaetius' model[28]. If the passage under discussion is examined in context it becomes clear that Cicero's remarks on Alexander represent his personal opinion and not that of Panaetius. The statement on Alexander occurs as part of Cicero's treatment of *fortitudo*. This entire section (1. 18. 61-1. 26. 92) is extremely eclectic, filled with examples drawn from Plato and from Cicero's own political experiences. The specific context of the Alexander passage is that of a discussion on the necessity of abstaining from pride in times of good fortune:

> *Atque etiam in rebus prosperis et ad voluntatem nostram fluentibus superbiam magnopere, fastidium arrogantiamque fugiamus. Nam ut adversas res, sic secundas inmoderate ferre levitatis est praeclaraque est aequabilitas in omni vita et idem semper vultus eademque frons, ut de Socrate idemque de C. Laelio accepimus. Philippum quidem Macedonum regem rebus gestis et gloria superatum a filio, facilitate et humanitate video superiorem fuisse. Itaque alter semper magnus, alter saepe turpissimus, ut recte praecipere videantur, qui monent, ut, quanto superiores simus, tanto nos geramus summissius. Panaetius quidem Africanum auditorem et familiarem suum solitum ait dicere, 'ut equos propter crebras contentiones proeliorum ferocitate exultantes domitoribus tradere soleant, ut is facilioribus possint uti, sic homines secundis rebus ecfrenatos sibique praefidentes tamquam in gyrum rationis et doctrinae duci oportere, ut perspicerent rerum humanarum imbellicitatem varietatemque fortunae'*[29].

Cicero explicitly introduces his unfavorable comparison of Alexander as a personal observation. Immediately after his remarks on Alexander, Cicero, to confirm his point that the higher we rise, the more humbly we should act, explicitly cites Panaetius for a simile used by Africanus[30]. If Panaetius held the same damning view of Alexander, the most famous of Greek kings, why does Cicero not use him for this opinion, instead of mentioning him quite specifically only in connection with the story of Africanus? Thus JUNGBLUT, in his detailed examination of the sources of the de Officiis quite rightly follows Cicero's own clear indication (*video*) and sees the observations on Alexander as the personal view of Cicero, without any reference to Panaetius. In the same way Cicero's reference to Philip and Alexander is not attributed to Panaetius by either modern edition of the fragments of Panaetius, FOWLER or VAN STRAATEN[31].

Discarding then the view that in this passage Cicero reproduces Stoic tradition on Alexander, we must also reject STROUX's emendation *tumidissimus* for *turpissimus* in the key description of Alexander, an emendation which has been accepted in all subsequent treatments of the Stoic view of Alexander. *Turpissimus* is found in all the manuscripts. Palaeographically *tumidissimus* is possible but certainly not compelling. The only arguments which Stroux advances for rejecting the unanimous manuscript tradition is clearly circular: (a) *tumidissimus* should be read because Cicero is here giving the Stoic view of Alexander, whom the Stoic Seneca called *tumidissimum animal*; (b) we know that Cicero is here giving the Stoic view of Alexander because he uses the Stoic catchword *tumidissimus*. Pace Stroux, *turpissimus* is the correct reading; and editors of the de Officiis since STROUX have rightly rejected his emendation[32].

Cicero's description of Alexander in de Officiis 1. 90 is his own private opinion and tells us nothing about the view of Panaetius or any other Stoic writer. However, in the same work, Cicero himself provides evidence that Panaetius, *gravissimus stoicorum*[33], held a favorable opinion of Alexander:

> *Quis est enim, cui non perspicua sint illa, quae pluribus verbis a Panaetio commemorantur, neminem neque ducem bello nec principem domi magnas res et salutares sine hominum studiis gerere potuisse? Commemoratur ab eo Themistocles, Pericles, Cyrus, Agesilaus, Alexander, quos negat sine adiumentis hominum tantas res efficere potuisse. Utitur in re non dubia testibus non necessariis*[34].

The exalted company in which Panaetius placed Alexander in this passage suggests that this judgement of the Macedonian differed greatly from the expressed by Cicero. Xenophon portrayed Cyrus and Agesilaus as prototypes of the good kings and models after whom the just statesman should fashion himself[35]. Panaetius' pupil Africanus constantly kept Xenophon at his side[36]. For Stoics, at least from the Middle Stoa onward, Cyrus was the model of the just monarch[37]. The inclusion of Alexander in a list along with Cyrus and Agesilaus suggests then that Panaetius viewed the Macedonian king and his career with favor.

Although we have no firm evidence which permits us to reject Cicero's clear indication that Polybius and Panaetius often discussed political matters with Africanus[38], nonetheless the extent of Polybius' indebtedness to the younger philosopher is a moot point[39]. As in the case of Polybius' description of the Roman constitution, we cannot be certain that Panaetius' conception of Alexander influenced Polybius. However, it is noteworthy that both Polybius and Panaetius refer to Alexander is the same context of the great general's need for great lieutenants. In refutation of Theopompus' scandalous charges against Philip and his companions, Polybius argues that much of the credit for the success of Alexander and his father was due to their companions, magnanimous men, truly royal in their self-restraint. Nonetheless, Polybius continues, a large portion of the glory for such great achievements belongs to Alexander, who, although so young, was the leader of the entire undertaking[40]. Here, as elsewhere, Polybius praises Alexander for his virtues, including magnanimity and piety[41].

Regardless of the question of Panaetius' influence on Polybius, there is no evidence to support the view that Cicero's explicit disapproval of Alexander is derived from the teachings of Panaetius. The low opinion of Alexander expressed in the de Officiis is paralleled by Cicero's remarks written in a letter of the same period:

> Quid? Tu non vides ipsum illum Aristoteli discipulum summo ingenio, summa modestia, posteaquam rex appellatus sit, superbum, crudelem, immoderatum fuisse?[42]

Since Stroux, it has been commonly accepted that this gives the Peripatetic view of Alexander even as that in the de Officiis gives the Stoic portrait[43]. Nothing in this passage labels it as Peripatetic; and in point of fact both passages reflect the contemporary Roman political scene, not Greek philosophical traditions. As Badian has pointed out, *rex* is the key word in the "Peripatetic" passage[44]. The reference is clearly to Caesar's pretensions. Cicero makes this evident by the parallelism of his very next sentence:

> Quid? Tu hunc de pompa Quirini contubernalem his nostris moderatis epistulis laetaturum putas?

The major part of the letter is concerned with the question of what Cicero should write to Caesar. He contrasts his fate with the good fortune of those who were able to write letters of advice to Alexander. However, even the best of young men was corrupted by the title of king. In both passages Cicero's hatred is not for the historical Alexander but for the symbolic figure, the prototype of those who would destroy the Republic, of Pompey and now of Caesar[45]. The disparaging comment on Caesar as the tentmate of Quirinus struck directly at Caesar's association with Alexander, for the statue of Caesar placed in the temple of Quirinus bore the identical inscription as that of Alexander in Athens: *Deo Invicto*[46]. That Caesar was the reason for Cicero's dislike of Alexander is further made clear by the dates of his remarks. References to Alexander in Cicero's earlier works are either neutral or favorable. The hateful remarks occur in works written under the *regnum Caesaris*: de Divinatione, de Officiis, and Tusculanae disputationes[47].

This linkage of Caesar and Alexander and the direction of vituperative remarks against both jointly, found in Cicero, also appears in Lucan and Seneca. Caesar's visit to the tomb of Alexander serves as the point of departure for Lucan's invective against Alexander, in which each point echoe`s earlier remarks on Caesar[48]. Like Caesar later, ambition led him to soak the earth in blood so that liberty might be extinguished and that the world could be under the rule of one man[49]. Like Caesar, Alexander was a thunderbolt and a star:

> . . . fulmenque quod omnis percuteret pariter populos et sidus iniquum gentibus[50].

In one of his most savage attacks on Alexander, Seneca explicitly links him with Pompey and Caesar. All these were impelled by unlimited ambition to wage constant war and to seek ever greater power. All three exemplify those who, lacking self-restraint and virtue pursue the false path of self-aggrandizement[51].

> Isti cum omnia concuterent, cuncutiebantur . . . qua plerisque nocuerunt, ipsi quoque sentiunt[52].

For both Lucan and Seneca, the truly great man is, of course, Cato, who said no to both Pompey and Caesar and stood for liberty when all others were rushing into servitude[53]. He is developed into the Stoic counterpart to Alexander, bravely and wisely enduring desert marches and thirst, drinking only after all his troops have quenched their first[54]. As Marti, Brisset, and Levi have shown, for Lucan and Seneca, Alexander was not a historical personage. He was instead the symbol of Caesarism, of that unrestrained *ambitio* which led to the destruction of the Republic by Pompey and Caesar, who sought to have themselves compared with the Macedonian[55].

We find also in Marcus Aurelius this same tendency to consider Alexander, Pompey, and Caesar jointly as prototypes of the prideful ruler. From Severus, Marcus learned to know Thrasea, Helvidius, Cato, and Brutus and to accept a concept of monarchy which is based on equality for all and freedom of speech and which values the liberty of its subjects above all else[56]. Like Seneca, Marcus castigates Alexander for his pompous pride; and he links Alexander with Pompey and Caesar as antitheses to Diogenes, Heraclitus, and Socrates. The latter saw the true nature of things, while the former were enslaved to wordly cares[57].

This vilification of Alexander by such Roman writers as Seneca, Lucan, and Marcus Aurelius contrasts strongly with the opinion of such Greek Stoics of the imperial period as Arrian and Dio Chrysostom. For Arrian, the pupil of Epictetus and the transmitter of the Discourses and the Manual, Alexander was far more than the great general and conqueror. Handsome, courageous, pious, temperate, honorable in his relations with other men, and generous with others but frugal with himself, Alexander was truly a man like unto no other mortal. Certain acts of his must indeed be criticized, but these can be explained and excused as the result of youth, unbroken good fortune, and the harmful advice of courtiers. Moreover, alone of all kings of past times, Alexander's nobleness of character led him to admit and to be repentant for the errors which he had committed[58].

Arrian's enthusiasm for Alexander has been a source of embarrassment to those who would make Alexander the prototype of the tyrant in Greek Stoic tradition. Arrian's undisguised admiration has been explained as the victory of truth over philosophical convictions[59]. Without disparaging Arrian's love of truth, the weakness of such an explanation is obvious. It is difficult to understand how such a conscientious Stoic would have admired and apologized so enthusiastically for Alexander if indeed Stoic teaching were traditionally hostile to the memory of the Macedonian king.

Although a more eclectic Stoic than Arrian, Dio Chrysostom, in his second oration on kingship further supports the view that the Middle and Later Greek Stoa could view Alexander and his career with favor[60]. The oration takes the form of a dramatic dialogue between father and son, in which Alexander expounds the main tenents of the Stoic doctrine of the good monarch. At the conclusion, Philip exclaims that he has rightly esteemed so highly Aristotle, who has instructed his son so well in the acts of good government and kingship[61]. Again if Stoics traditionally portrayed Alexander as evil from the start and the model of the tyrant, it would have been absurd for Dio, without explanation, to make him a preceptor of Stoic teachings on good government. Moreover, we know that Dio wrote a work in eight books on the virtues of Alexander[62].

Clearly then there existed no single, uniform Stoic view of Alexander, and we must look for an explanation of why Seneca, Lucan, and Marcus Aurelius portrayed Alexander in such a very different light than did Panaetius, Arrian, and Dio Chrysostom. The emperor Marcus' references to Thrasea, Helvidius, Cato, and Brutus, together with the almost mythological Cato of Lucan and Seneca and the fact that they and Marcus all link Caesar and Alexander as exempla of the prideful tyrant; may provide the clue. Thrasea, consul in 56 A.D. along with Seneca, and author of a laudatory life of Cato, was forced to commit suicide under Nero[63]. Lucan wrote of the constant struggle between Caesarism and *libertas*[64]; and according to Tacitus, *libertas* as a political catchword played an important part in Capito's verbal attack which led to Thrasea's death:

> *Ut quondam C. Caesarem inquit [Capito Cossutianus], et M. Catonem, ita nunc te, Nero, et Thraseam avida discordiarum civitas loquitur. . . . Aut transeamus ad*

illa instituta, si potiora sunt, aut nova cupientibus auferatur dux et auctor. . . . Ut imperium evertant, libertatem praeferunt: si perverterint, libertatem ipsam adgredientur[65].

In his martyr's death, Thrasea was joined by his son-in-law Helvidius Priscus the elder, executed under Domitian[66]. By their deaths, Thrasea and Helvidius joined Cato as exempla of the just man who died for *libertas*. Under Domitian panegyrics by Arulenus Rusticus on Thrasea and by Herennius Senecio on Priscus Helvidius were made capital crimes and the works of Helvidius and Thrasea celebrating *libertas senatus*, were publicly burned[67]. Their opposition to tyranny even enabled admirers to join them with Brutus and Cassius in banquet toasts:

> *Quale coronati Thrasea Helvidiusque bibebant Brutorum et Cassi natalibus. . . .*[68]

The careers of Thrasea and Helvidius belong of course to the so-called senatorial opposition to the principate, so brilliantly described by Boissier, MacMullen, and others[69]. For many of these upper-class Roman critics *libertas* served as a battle cry and Cato the younger as a hero[70]. Reconciled to the necessity of a *princeps* and even seeing positive benefits in monarchy, their opposition was often not diverted against the principate itself but against tyranny, which used its absolute power not to benefit its subjects but to destroy all personal freedom and security[71]. Literature was an outlet for their criticism and for sharers of a common cultural and social outlook, mythology and history provided an effective and often safer vehicle than direct polemic. To the initiate a declamation on the tyranny of Agamemnon or Atreus spoke volumes on the horrors of the regimes of Tiberius and Gaius[72]. However, even allegory could be dangerous. Thus Helvidius Priscus the younger wrote a farce about Paris and Oenone, which was interpreted as a joke on Domitian's divorce and which cost him his life[73]. Under Tiberius a poet was executed for writing a tragedy portraying Agamemnon as a tyrant[74], while Cremutius Cordus met death for praising Brutus and calling Cassius *ultimus Romanorum*[75].

In treating this literature of opposition, one must avoid the danger of presenting a single stereotyped image of the nature of this Roman upper-class criticism of the principate. In particular Seneca is by no means consistent in his attitude towards the principate and *libertas*. In the de Beneficiis Seneca writes of monarchy: *optimus civitatis status sub rege iusto [est]*[76]. In the same work, he implies that *libertas* and monarchy cannot be reconciled[77]; and yet in the de Clementia he writes that under Nero *laetissima forma reipublicae ad summam libertatem nihil deest nisi pereundi licentia*[78]. Lucan presents fewer problems, but superficially at least, it is difficult to reconcile his panegyric to Nero[79] with his dominant theme of the extinction of *libertas* by the tyranny of Caesar[80] and his reflection:

> *Sic et Thessalicae post te pars maxima pugnae*
> *Non iam Pompei nomen populare per orbem*
> *Nec studium belli, sed par quod semper habemus,*
> *Libertas et Caesar erit . . .*[81]

Leaving aside the question of their overall relationship to the "senatorial opposition to the principate", it is obvious that the personal careers of Seneca and Lucan under Nero will have affected their view of the principate. Lucan's eulogy of Nero may have been written while he was still close to Nero[82]. His invective against Alexander comes in Book X, clearly written after his break with Nero; and it may be read as a thinly veiled attack on Nero, who sought to establish a guard regiment called the Phalanx of Alexander and whose Eastern policy invited comparison with the Macedonian. While Alexander met unlimited success in the East, Nero's reign saw the capitulation of a Roman force at Rhandeia. Nero himself did not take the field against the Parthians. Instead he left it to his general Corbulo to restore Rome's fortunes in the East. The sham of Nero's *imitatio Alexandri*[83] is perhaps implied by Lucan's rebuke:

> *Sed cecidit* [Alexander] *Babylone sua Parthoque ver-*
> *endus.*
> *Pro pudor! Eoi propius timuere sarisas*
> *Quam nunc pila timent populi. Licet usque sub Arcton*
> *Regnemus Zephyrique domos terrasque premamus*
> *Flagrantis post terga Noti, cedemus in ortus*
> *Arsacidum domino. Non felix Parthia Crassis*
> *Exiguae secura fuit provincia Pellae*[84].

Seneca's opinion of Nero may not have been without its effects on his image of Alexander. Savage indictments of the Macedonian are to be found in the de Beneficiis, which Seneca possibly finished after his retirement[85], and in Epistle 94, clearly written after his secessus[86]. Yet also in the de Clementia, composed in the halcyon days of Nero's reign, Seneca vilifies Alexander and his cruelty: *iste animus ferox, insatiabile gentium malum*[87]. In the de Clementia, Seneca's discussion of Alexander's cruelty is part of his general distinction between the tyrant and the king:

> *"Quid ergo? Non reges quoque occidere solent?" Sed*
> *quotiens id fieri publica utilitas persuadet; tyrannis*
> *saevitia cordi est*[88]

Here, as elsewhere in Seneca, Alexander serves merely as an exemplum of the tyrant.

Taylor, Pfligersdorffer, Schönberger, MacMullen, and others have shown that in picturing Cato as a paragon of virtue and Caesar as an exemplum of tyranny, Seneca and Lucan reflect the legends of Cato and Caesar shaped by the rhetoric and popular philosophy of those "new nobles who had acquired public office through the policy of Caesar and his successors . . . [and] who looked back to the 'Age of Cato' when Roman magistrates . . . had had prestige and power; and [who] honored Cato because he had ended his life rather than see such prestige and power die"[89]. Since Lucan and Seneca portray Alexander as the very antithesis of Cato and since they link him with Caesar as exempla of the prideful tyrant, it seems likely that their image of Alexander was a product of these same intellectual and political currents. By closely associating himself with Alexander, Caesar ensured the Macedonian's status as the prototype of the tyrant and provided critics with a convenient means of attack. It is not coincidental that, after Augustus, Gaius and Nero, monsters par excellence in the senatorial tradition, are the only two Julio-Claudian emperors said to have associated themselves with Alexander[90]. A declamation on the tyranny and pride of Alexander was a less direct and hopefully safer means of criticizing a tyrannical emperor.

In short, the Alexander of Lucan, Seneca, and Marcus Aurelius is not derived from the philosophical teachings of the Middle Stoa. It is Roman, and it is perhaps best seen as part of that well-known development which transformed Caesar and Cato from historical figures into stock characters in a Roman allegory. At times, the image of Cato could be invoked without any political overtones, as a stereotype of virtue facing insurmountable odds[91]; and in the de Clementia, this Roman image of Alexander simply provided Seneca with a convenient exemplum of the evil tyrant, just as the Roman image of Cato provided a prototype of the virtuous man. Elsewhere in Seneca, especially in Epistle 94, and in Lucan, there is probable justification for seeing a criticism of Nero in their vilification of Alexander.

Apart from the difficult question of the position of Seneca and Lucan in later Stoic thought[92], we should not overemphasize the importance of philosophy in shaping this portrait of Alexander. For many writers on Alexander, philosophy was far less influential than the training of the rhetorical schools[93]. Lucian and Plutarch are cases in point[94]. Seneca implies that his description of the death of Cato parallels that of the rhetorical schools[95]. Like the death of Cato, the career of Alexander offered numerous topics for sharpening the young rhetorician's skills. The elder Seneca preserved two Suasoriae dealing with Alexander, Deliberat Alexander Magnus an Babylona intret and another with the conjectural title Deliberat Alexander an Oceanum naviget. It is important to note that, like Seneca the younger, he castigated Alexander for his arrogance: *facile Alexandrum ex iis esse quos superbissimos et supra mortalis animi modum inflatos accepimus*[96]. The influence of rhetorical loci on tyranny is clear in Lucan's portrait of Alexander. Livy's rather deprecatory comparison of Alexander with great generals of Rome's part has also been seen as a product of Livy's rhetoric school days[97]. According to Livy, Alexander was no greater than a number of Roman generals with whom he would have had to do battle had he invaded Italy: M. Valerius Corvus, C. Marcius Rutulus et al. Alexander's equals in military science, these noble Romans further lacked those fatal flaws which marred his character, so transformed after the victory over Dareus.

> *Referre in tanto rege piget superbam mutationem vestis et desideratas humi iacentium adulationes, etiam victis Macedonibus graves, nedum victoribus et foeda supplicia et inter vinum et epulas caedes amicorum et vanitatem ementiendae stirpis. Quid si vini amor in dies fieret acrior? Quid si trux ac praefervida ira? Nec quicquam dubium inter scriptores refero . . .*

This passage represents what was a considerable quantity of literature, much of it set rhetorical pieces, comparing Alexander with Roman heros and debating whether Alexander could have conquered the Romans. Greeks took part as actively as Romans, some championing the cause of Alexander who had reduced to a quiet province Parthia, pround conqueror of Crassus and Antony[98]. Livy refers to *levissimi ex Graecis* who claimed that the Romans could not have withstood even the name Alexander, much less have defeated him in battle[99]. Whatever influence Stoic philosophical tenets exerted on Livy, there is nothing specifically Stoic in his description of Alexander[100]. He makes no mention of any philosophical school in the Alexander passage; and his vague reference *scriptores* parallels the fact that each of the faults which he attributes to Alexander was a well-known element in the so-called Vulgate tradition. Livy's patriotic conclusion of the same passage, *Mille acies graviores quam Macedonum atque Alexandri avertit avertetque, modo sit perpetuus huius qua vivimus pacis amor et civilis cura concordiae*[101], suggests that for Livy national pride and the desire to idealize the heroes of Rome's past, rather than any philosophical consideration, shaped his description of Alexander. By self-assertion Tacitus was committed to no philosophical position[102]; and yet he too castigated the well-known faults of Alexander and chose to compare the Macedonian unfavorably with his hero Germanicus, who, excelling Alexander in clemency, in self-restraint, and in all other virtues, was kindly towards friends and moderate in his pleasures[103]. In a speech which Polybius credits to Lykiskos the Acarnanian, Alexander emerges as a Greek national hero[104]; and as the passage in Livy implies, for many rhetorical writers national pride may have been more important than philosophical considerations in shaping their image of Alexander.

Nonetheless Alexander and his career served as a philosophical exemplum and the schools no doubt exerted an influence on both rhetorical and strictly historical treatments of Alexander. However, it cannot be assumed that each school presented a single uniform judgment on Alexander. Cynics clearly had varying views of Alexander[105]. Onesicritus, the pupil of Diogenes, gave an extremely flattering portrait of Alexander as a philosopher in arms[106]. Another, almost certainly Cynic tradition, contrasted Alexander with such truly wise men as Diogenes and the Gymnosophists[107]. Alexander is here represented as blinded by worldly ambition, but nonetheless as one who respects the wisdom and the freedom of philosophers and is eager to learn from them[108]. In the same way, as we have seen, individual Stoics had differing opinions of Alexander. Moreover, it should be emphasized that we can speak with certainty only of the Middle and Late Stoa. There is no firm evidence for the image of Alexander held by any member of the Old Stoa, but his career may have been viewed with mixed feelings. Eratosthenes, who was certainly under Stoic influence, praised Alexander in the highest terms[109]. On the other hand, according to Plutarch, Chrysippus gave Idanthyrsus the Scythian and Leucon of Pontus as examples of monarchs with whom the wise man should associate[110]. A much more famous example was at hand, if Chrysippus were indeed favorably impressed with Alexander and his career. In the future then, studies in the sources for Alexander's career as well as treatments of his memory in Antiquity should discard once and for all the theory of uniformly hostile Stoic, Peripatetic, and Cynic portraits of Alexander.

Notes

This article was written with the aid of grants from the Penrose Fund of the American Philosophical Society and from Indiana University. I should like to thank Professor G. Downey for reading and commenting upon it. Abbreviations are those found in *L'Année philologique.*

1. W. W. Tarn, *Alexander the Great* (Cambridge 1950) II 69 with n. 1.

2. E. Badian, *CQ* 52, 1958, 144-7. See also E. Mensching, *Historia* 12, 1963, 274-82.

3. The most detailed exposition of the theory of the uniformly hostile Stoic attitude towards Alexander is found in the extremely valuable study of J. Stroux, *Philologus* 88, 1933, 222-40. Earlier the same view was advanced by E. Schwartz, *RE* [*Real Encyclopedie*] IV 1890; W. Hoffmann, *Das literarische Porträt Alexanders des Großen im griechischen und römischen Altertum* (Leipzig 1907) 14-8; and L. Eicke, *Veterum philosophorum qualia fuerint de Alexandro Magno iudicia* (Rostock 1909) 12. Stroux's arguments are ac-

cepted by, e.g., Tarn (above n. 1) II 69, and *AJPh* 60, 1939, 54-6; A. Heuss, Antike und Abendland 4, 1954, 74; E. Sanford, *HSPh* 48, 1937, 86 n. 2; P. Treves, *Il mito di Alessandro e la Roma d'Augusto* (Milan-Naples 1953) 18-9, 32, n. 14; R. Hoïstad, *Cynic King and Cynic* (Uppsala 1948) 210-2; A. Gitti, *Alessandro Magno all'oasi di Si-wah* (1951) 134; L. Pearson, *The Lost Histories of Alexander the Great,* American Philological Association Philological Monographs 20, 1960; M. Morford, *The Poet Lucan* (New York 1967) 16; H. Bengston, *Griechische Geschichte*² (Munich 1960) 319; J. Hamilton, *Plutarch Alexander: A Commentary* (Oxford 1969) lxi-xii. Protests against this view were raised by F. Weber, *Alexander der Große im Urteil der Griechen und Römer* (Diss. Giessen 1909) 44; and M. Fisch, AJPh [*American Journal of Philology*] 58, 1937, 50-1. However, their arguments are dismissed by Stroux 234; Tarn *AJPh* 60, 1939, 55 n. 77; and Hoïstad 24 n. 6, and have received no acceptance.

4. Quint. *Inst.* 1. 1. 9 = Diogenes frg. 51, von Arnim SVF III p. 220.

5. Clem. *Al. Paed.* 1. 7. 55.

6. Cic. *Off.* 1. 26. 90.

7. Stroux (above n. 3) 236-40. The emendation *tumidissimus,* accepted by writers on the Stoic view of Alexander the Great, must be rejected. Below . . . . Diogenes Laertius 7. 22 = Zeno frg. 317, von Arnim SVF I p. 69, preserves Zeno's view that especially in the young nothing was so unseemly as *typhos.*

8. Sen. *Ben.* 2. 16. 2.

9. Quint. *Inst.* 1. 1. 8. For a Stoic source for this entire section, see J. Cousin, *Études sur Quintilien* (Paris 1936, rptd. Amsterdam 1967) I 16-8. More recently, see F. Grypdonck, *AC* 35, 1966, 487-05.

10. Jerome *Ep.* 107. 4. 7. For Jerome and Quintilian see F. H. Colson ed., *Liber I Institutionis Oratoriae* (Cambridge 1924) xliv-v. Cf. the remark of Hincmar of Rheims drawn from *Jerome: Leoniden citatis moribus et incomposito incensu notabilem quae puer quasi lac adulterinum surgens ab eo sumpsit.*

11. Stroux (above n. 3) 226-7.

12. For Stoic influence on Clement see esp. M. Pohlenz, *Die Stoa* (Göttingen 1964) 414-24; M. Spanneut, *Le stoïcisme des pères de l'Eglise de Clément de Rome à Clément d'Alexandrie* (Paris 1957); J. R. Donahue, *Traditio* 19, 1963, 438-47. For Platonic influence R. Casey, *HThR* [*Harvard Theological Review*] 18, 1925, 39-101, is still important. More recently, A. Mehat, *Étude sur les Stromates de Clément d'Alexandrie* (Paris 1966) 346-94; and H. Steneker, *Peithous demiourgia: observations sur la fonction du style dans le Protreptique de Clément d'Alexandrie* (Nijmegen 1967) 85-90.

13. Alcibiades was a favorite rhetorical antithesis to the good king Cyrus. See Dio *Chrysostom Or.* 21. 11; 25. 4. See further Hoïstad (above n. 3) 73-94.

14. Dio *Chrysostom Or.* 2. 15. For the Stoic character of this oration, see below n. 37.

15. Cicero *Off.* 1. 26. 90.

16. Diogenes *Laertius* 6. 26.

17. Polyb. 3. 81. 9; Onosander 42. 24.

18. For Clement's citation of classical writers see the indices in volume IV. 30-59, of O. Stählin's edition of Clement in: *Die griechischen christlichen Schriftsteller d. ersten drei Jahrhunderte, xxxix.* W. Krause, *Die Stellung d. frühchristlichen Autoren zur heidnischen Literatur* (Vienna 1958) argues that, against an average of 14.9% among other early Christian writers, 26% of Clement's citations come from pagan authors.

19. For Clement's erudition, see Jerome de Vir. ill. 38; Socrates H. E. 2. 35; Anastasius Sinaita Hom. in Psal. 6 (Migne LXXXIX 1105); Photius Bibl. Cod. 109; Eusebius H. E. 6. 13; Cyrill Alex. Contra Julianum X p. 342 ed. Aubertus (Migne LXXVI 1028). An excellent recent study of the question of the sources of Clement's classical quotations, direct or through anthologies, is provided by Steneker (above n. 12) 77-93. Recent scholarship has rightly rejected the extreme view that Clement's knowledge of classical writers came only through anthologies, found in J. Gabrielssohn, *Über die Quellen des Clemens Alexandrinus* (Uppsala-Leipzig 1906-9). However, for the view that Clement's knowledge of Pindar and Menander was entirely derived from anthologies, see R. Grant, *CPh* 60, 1965, 157-63; I. Opelt, *Byzantinische Forschungen* II, 1967, 284-98.

20. It is generally agreed that Homer and Plato were read at first hand by Clement. See P. Gussen, *Het leven in Alexandrie volgens de cultuurhistorische gegevens in de Paedagogus* (Boek II en III) *van Clemens Alexandrinus* (Diss. Leiden 1955) 28-36, 47-53, with the earlier literature, of which F. Clark, *TAPhA* [*Transactions of the American Philological Association*] 33, 1902 xii-xx is still extremely valuable. See also H.-I. Marrou, ed. and trans. *Clement d'Alexandrie, Le Pédagogue* I (Paris 1960) 73; Steneker (above n. 12) 79-81, 85-7.

21. Herod. 1. 34-5 (Adrastus); 8. 15 (Sicinnus). Clement also reproduces elements from Herodotus' account of Croesus at Protrepticus 3. 43 and Strom. 3. 3. 16. In all, Clement refers to Herodotus forty times. See Stählin (above n. 18) 40. Zopyrus and Sicinnus are also mentioned in Plutarch Alcib. 1; Lyc. 16; Themist. 12.

22. Plut. Alex. 5.

23. Cf. Plut. Alex. 64 and Clem. Alex. Strom. 6. 4. 38. In general for the very difficult question of Clement's use of Plutarch, see K. Hubert, *Hermes* 73, 1938, 321-5; and Gussen (above n. 20) 56-61.

24. For Alexander's pride, see esp. Plut. Alex. 52. Alexander's pride and love of glory were, of course, proverbial. See, e.g., Arrian 4. 9. 1; Livy 9. 18; Dio Chrysostom 4. 6, Sen. Suas. 1. 5.

25. The view of Eicke (above n. 3) 12, that Cicero's judgment of Alexander reflects the views of Panaetius is re-iterated by Stroux (above n. 3) and Hoïstad (above n. 3) 211.

26. Cic. Att. 11. 16. 4; Off. 2. 17. 60, 3. 2. 7. H. Jungblut, *Die Arbeitsweise Ciceros im ersten Buch über die Pflichten* (Frankfurt a. M. 1907); *Cicero und Panaetius im zweiten Buch über die Pflichten* (Frankfurt a. M. 1910) is a detailed attempt to separate the Ciceronian in the de Officiis. For Cicero and Panaetius, see most recently, F. Steinmetz, *Die Freundschaftslehre des Panaitios nach einer Analyse von Cicero's Laelius de Amicitia* (Wiesbaden 1967).

27. Cic. Off. 1. 2. 6.

28. Ibid., 1. 2. 7. Cf. e.g. 1. 43. 152, 2. 24. 86, 3. 2. 7-8.

29. Cic. Off. 1. 26. 90.

30. M. van Straaten, ed., *Panaetii Rhodii Fragmenta*[3] (Leiden 1962) frg. 12.

31. Rightly, Cicero's reference to Philip and Alexander is not attributed to Panaetius by either modern editor of the fragments, H. N. Fowler (Bonn 1885) or van Straaten. So too Jungblut (above n. 26) 56-7.

32. See e.g. C. Atzert (Leipzig 1963): and M. Testard (Paris 1965). In view of the Caesarean association in this passage, it is interesting to note that in a letter of March 17, 49 B.C., Cicero describes the unnamed agent of Caesar as *turpissimus*. Att. 9. 9. 3.

33. Cic. Off. 2. 14. 51.

34. Cic. Off. 2. 5. 16.

35. See most recently F. Dvornik, *Early Christian and Byzantine Political Philosophy: Origins and Background* (Washington 1966) I 187-91.

36. Cic. ad Q. 1. 1. 8; Tusc. disp. 2. 26-62.

37. Stoic idealization of Cyrus is treated in detail in my forthcoming article in *American Journal of Philology,* "Cyrus as a Stoic Exemplum of the Just Monarch". In general, see, e.g. Dio Chrysostom Or. 2. 77, where Cyrus is portrayed as the bearer of Stoic royal virtues and is listed with other Stoic exempla of good kings (cf. Plut. de Stoic repug. 20. 3-7 p. 1043 D). For more on the Stoic character of Dio de Regno II, see Hoïstad (above n. 3) 89. For Stoic political philosophy in Dio, V. Valdenberg, "Philosophia politicheskaja Diona Chrysostoma", *Izvestija Akademii Nauk SSR*, Otdelenie Hum. Ser. 6, 20 (1926) 943-74; 1281-1302; 1523-54 (abridged French version *REG* 40, 1927, 142-62). More recently, Dvornik (above n. 35) II 533-42.

38. Cic. de Rep. 1. 21.

39. For Panaetius and Polybius, see Pohlenz (above n. 12) I 193; M. Schäfer, *Gymnasium* 62, 1955, 334-5; F. W. Walbank, *A Historical Commentary on Polybius* (Oxford 1957) I 6; K. Ziegler, *RE* XLII 1470-2.

40. Polyb. 8. 12.

41. Ibid., 5. 10.

42. Att. 13. 28. 3 (May 26, 45 B.C.).

43. Stroux (above n. 3) 234.

44. Badian (above n. 2) 155.

45. For the identification of Pompey and Caesar with Alexander, see the very full collection of material in D. Michel, *Alexander als Vorbild für Pompeius, Caesar und Marcus Antonius,* Collection Latomus 94, 1967, 35-107.

46. For the statue of Alexander the Invincible God at Athens, see Hypereides Or. I col. 32: [στῆσαι εἰκόνα Ἀλεξάνδρον βασιλέως τοῦ Ἀνικήτου θεοῦ]

For Aniketos as the title of Alexander, widespread in the first century B.C., see F. Pfister, *Historia* 13, 1964, 37-47. For the statue of Caesar, Cassius Dio 43. 45. 3; Cic. Att. 12. 45. 3; 13. 28. 3. In general, see the excellent remarks of S. Weinstock, *Divus Iulius* (Oxford 1971) 186-8.

47. Cicero's view of Alexander before Caesar: de Or. 3.35. 141; Rep. 3. 9. 15; Arch. 10. 24; Att. 5. 20. 3. After Caesar, in additior to the citations in the text, Div. 1. 23. 47; Off. 2. 15. 53; Tuse, disp. 5. 32. 91. See also Weber above n. 3) 44.

48. Luc. 10. 14-53.

49. Ibid., 10. 21-43 (Alexander); 1. 143-57; 7. 233-41, 7. 385-6 (Caesar).

50. Luc. 10. 34-6; 1. 143-57. For the portrait of Caesar in Lucan, see esp. E. Griset, *RSC* 3, 1955, 56-61; G. Peligersdorffer, Hermes 87, 1959, 344-77; J. Brisset, *Les idées politiques de Lucain* (Paris 1964) 85-107; A. Lintott, *CQ [Classical Quarterly]* 65, 1971, 498-504.

51. Sen. Ep. 94. 62-6.

52. Sen. Ep. 94. 67. For the portrait of Caesar in Seneca, see esp. W. Alexander, *Transactions of the Royal Society of Canada [TRSC]* 35, 1941, Sec. II 15-28.

53. Sen. Ep. 14. 12-3; 95. 69-73; 104. 29-33; de Constantia sapientis 1. 2-2. 3. The idealization of Cato by Lucan is well known. See esp. W. Alexander, *TRSC* 40 (1946) Sec. II 59-74; L. Pavan, AIV 110 (1954-5) 209-22; Brisset (above n. 50) 148-57; Pfligersdorffer (above n. 50) 346-55; J. Souhain, *Pallas* 14, 1967, 59-68; P. Pecchiura, *La figura di Catone Uticense nella letteratura latina* (Turin 1965) 52-71; M. Griffin, *CQ* 62, 1968, 373-5.

54. Sen. Ep. 104. 33; Luc. 9. 445-619.

55. For Alexander as the prototype of the tyrant Caesar in Seneca and Lucan, see esp. B. Marti, *AJPh* 66, 1945, 362-3; M. A. Levi, *Nerone e i suoi tempi* (Milan 1949) 63-5; J. Brisset (above n. 50); Morford (above n. 3) 19.

56. M. Ant. 1. 18.

57. Ibid., 9. 29, 8. 3.

58. Arrian 7. 28-30.

59. Tarn (above n. 1) II 69.

60. For the Stoic character of de Regno II, see above n. 35.

61. Dio Chrysostom Or. 2. 79. Dio may have known the letters of Aristotle to Alexander on kingship and governing cities. On this see now Bielawski and M. Plezia, *Lettre d'Aristotle à Alexandre sur la politique envers les cités* (Warsaw 1970).

62. Suda s. v. Δίων. In his voluminous writings Dio by no means presents a consistent portrait of Alexander. The good king Alexander of the Stoic de Regno II is to be contrasted with the Alexander of the cynic de Regno IV. See in general Hoïstad (above n. 3) 202-20, who overemphasizes the unfavorable elements in Dio's portrait of Alexander in de Regno IV. Diogenes sees Alexander as good and kingly by nature but at present without

reason, because he lacks proper instruction (37-38, 56). Hoffmann (above n. 3) 74-80, argues that Dio's relations with Trajan were responsible for his increasingly favorable portrait of Alexander.

63. For Thrasea, *Tac. Ann.* 13. 49, 14. 48-9, 15. 20-3, 16. 19-27; Dio Cassius 62. 20. For the biography of Cato, Plut. Cato Min. 37. For the general importance of Thrasea, see A. Sizoo, *REL* 4, 1926, 229-37, 5 1927, 41-52; C. Saumagne, *REL* 33, 1955, 241-57; R. Syme, *Gymnasium* 69, 1962, 246; R. MacMullen, *Enemies of the Roman Order* (Cambridge, Mass. 1966) 21-3; T. Adam, *Clementia Principis* (Stuttgart 1970) 63-72.

64. Luc. 7. 695-6.

65. Tac. *Ann.* 16. 21-2.

66. For Helvidius Priscus the elder see Tac. *Ann.* 16. 27. Hist. 4. 5-6, Agr. 2; Pliny *Ep.* 1. 19. 5; Dio Cassius 66. 12, 67. 13. 2; Suet. Vesp. 15. In general see J. Toynbee, *Greece and Rome* 13, 1944, 52; R. Rogers, *CPh [Classical Philology]* 55, 1960, 19-23. An imaginary dispute between Helvidius and Vespasian is given by Epictetus Diss. 1. 2. 19-22.

67. Tac. Agr. 2.

68. Juv. 5. 36-7.

69. G. Boissier's excellent *L'Opposition sous les Césars*[5] (Paris 1905) has been followed by a large literature dealing with various aspects of opposition. See among more recent studies, Toynbee (above n. 66) 43-58; Ch. Wirszubski, *Libertas as a Political Idea at Rome During the Late Republic and Early Principate* (Cambridge 1950) 124-71; MacMullen (above n. 63) 1-94; Adam (above n. 63) 56-82; and the extremely valuable studies of K. Becker, *Studien zur Opposition gegen den römischen Principat* (Diss. Tübingen 1950) and A. Bergener, *Die führende Senatorenschicht im frühen Principat* (Diss. Bonn 1965).

70. For a detailed discussion of the figure of Cato in this literature of opposition, see Pecchiura, (above n. 53) 52-71. More recently, see the penetrating remarks of Adam (above n. 63) 67-71.

71. For the distinction between monarchy and tyranny as one of deeds rather than name see esp. Sen. de Clem. 1. 12. For *libertas et principatus* in opposition thought, see Wirszubski (above n. 69) 123-71.

72. MacMullen (above n. 63) 32-45.

73. Suet. Domit. 10. 3.

74. Suet. Tib. 61. 3. Cf. Dio Cassius 58. 24. 3-4.

75. Tac. Ann. 4. 34. Cf. Dio Cassius 57. 24. 2-3; Suet. Tib. 61. 3; Calig. 16. 1; Sen ad Marc. 1. 2. 4; Quint. 10. 1. 104. See also F. Klingner, *MH [Mediavelia et Humanistica]* 15, 1958, 197.

76. 2. 20. 2.

77. Ibid.; cf. *Ep.* 14. 13.

78. 1. 1. 8.

79. 1. 33-66.

80. Contrast Lucan's attitude towards the ruler cult expressed at 1. 45-6 with that at 7. 457. For the panegyric to Nero, see e.g., P. Grimal, *REL* 38, 1960, 296-305; Brisset (above n. 50) 178-85, with the earlier literature. Pfligersdorffer (above n. 50) 344-77 is an important treatment of Lucan's position as poet of the "opposition". See also P. McCloskey and E. Phinney, *Hermes* 96, 1968, 80-7; and Morford (above n. 3) 15. There is no need to discuss here the complex questions of the meaning of the eulogy to Nero and of the unity of the Pharsalia. For this latter see, among recent studies, B. Marti, *Entretiens sur l'antiquité classique* 15, 1968 (Geneva 1970) 3-38.

81. Luc. 7. 693. 6.

82. For Lucan's break with Nero, see G. de Plinval, *Latomus* 15, 1956, 513-20; G. Gresseth, *CPh* 52, 1957, 24-7; and Brisset (above n. 50) 12.

83. Schönberger, Hermes 86, 1958, 233; E. Sanford, in: *Classical and Medieval Studies in Honor of E. K. Rand* (New York 1938) 255-64.

84. 10. 46-52.

85. Ben. 1. 13. 1; 2. 16. 1; 5. 6. 1; 7. 2. 5. The best introduction to the problem of dating the de Beneficiis is still M. Schanz—C. Hosius, *Gesch. d. röm. Lit.*[4] (Munich 1935) II 697-8, with the earlier literature.

86. Ep. 94. 13. For the generally accepted view that the Epistles were compared after Seneca's retirement, see Schanz-Hosius, II 704.

87. 1. 25. For the date of the de Clementia, see W. Richter, *RhM* 108, 1965, 146-70.

88. 1. 12.

89. L. Taylor, *Party Politics in the Age of Caesar* (Berkeley—Los Angeles 1949) 180-2 from which the quotation in the text is taken; Pfligersdorffer (above n. 50) 344-77; Schönberger (above n. 83) 233; Rutz (above n. 50) 236-51; MacMullen (above n. 69) 18-21, 23-7. See too Alexander (above n. 53) 63; Adam (above n. 69) 67-71; Pecchiura (above n. 53) 50; Sizoo (above n. 63) 233; Wirszubski (above n. 69) 126; and McCloskey and Phinney (above n. 79) 80-7.

90. It is too often assumed that it was common for emperors to associate themselves with Alexander. Augustus did so (Suet. Aug. 18. 50, 94. 7; Cassius Dio 51. 16. 5; Pliny N.H. 34. 3. 8, 34. 18. 8, 35. 36. 93). For the later Julio-Claudians, there is little evidence. Gaius is said to have worn the breastplate of Alexander (Suet. Gaius 51); and Nero sought to establish a guard regiment called the Phalanx of Alexander (Suet. Nero 19). The next literary evidence is for Trajan. Cassius Dio 68. 29-30. However, hitherto neglected numismatic material gives additional evidence for the cult of Alexander under Domitian, Trajan, and Hadrian. See my forthcoming article. "Numismatic Notes on the Role of Alexander in the Imperial Propaganda of Domitian and Trajan" in: *The American Numismatic Society Museum Notes. For the memory of Alexander at Rome* see A. Bruhl, *Mélanges d'Archéologie et d'Histoire de l'École Française de Rome* 47, 1930, 202-21; Treves (above n. 3) 2-129; Heuss (above n. 3) 80-105; L. Cerfaux and J. Tondriau, *Le culte des souverains dans la civilisation gréco-romaine* (Tournai, Belg. 1957) 397. For the influence of Alexander on Augustan portraiture, H. P. L'Orange, *Apotheosis in Ancient Portraiture* (Oslo 1947) 57-63; and O. Brendel, *Ikonographie des Kaisers Augustus* (Nürnberg 1931) 61.

91. Thus Vergil, hardly inimical to the Augustan principate, celebrates Cato as lawgiver of the good in the underworld. Aen. 8. 670. Horace C. 1. 12. 35-6, 3. 3. 1-8; Livy frg. 45 (ed. Weissenborn); Pliny Ep. 4. 27; Pers. Sat. 3. 49. Further R. Syme, *Tacitus* (Oxford 1958) II 527.

92. For Stoicism in the Pharsalia, see, among recent studies H. Schotes, *Stoische Physik, Psychologie u. Theologie bei Lucan* (Bonn 1969); and O. Due, *Entretiens sur l'antiquité classique* 15, 1968 (Geneva 1970) 204-24. An interesting criticism of the general tendency to consider Seneca as a typical and convinced Stoic is given by Adam (above n. 63) 63-8.

93. On the influence of the rhetorical schools on the memory of Alexander, see most recently Pearson (above n. 3) 6-7, 243-50.

94. Lucian's portrait of Alexander is generally favorable. Contrast Alex. 1; V.H. 2. 9; Cal. 17-21, with D. Mort. 12-4. For the rhetorical nature of Plutarch's de Alexandri Fortuna, see esp. E. Badian, *Historia* 7, 1958, 432-40. Mention might also be made of the almost consistently anti-Alexander anecdotes throughout Aelian Variae Historiae: 1. 25, 2. 3, 2. 19, 3. 23, 3. 32, 4. 29, 7. 7, 9. 4, 9. 37-8, 10. 4, 12. 7, 12. 16, 12. 37, 12. 54, 12. 57, 12. 64, 13. 7.

95. Sen. Ep. 24. 6.

96. For Alexander's arrogance, Sen. Suas. 1. 5. For the influence of rhetoric on the Alexander of Lucan, Morford (above n. 3) 13-9.

97. Livy 9. 17-19. The best discussion of this passage is Treves (above n. 3) 2-38, with the earlier literature. Treves 15, 27 argues against the view that the excursus is merely a rhetorical piece composed during Livy's student days, first suggested by W. Anderson, *TAPhA* 34, 1908, 94-9. Most recently, see H. Breitenbach, *MH* 26, 1969, 146-57. Whenever it was composed, the rhetorical nature of the passage is beyond question. See P. Walsh, Livy (Cambridge 1970) 40.

98. For this Greco-Roman literary match on the merits of Alexander, see Schwartz (above n. 3) 1881; Hoffmann (above n. 3) 37-43; Weber (above n. 3); Tarn (above n. 1) II 396-7; Treves (above n. 3) esp. 13-9, 99-114.

99. Livy 9. 18. 6. G. Schwab, *De Livio et Timagene historiarum scriptoribus aemulis* (Stuttgart 1834) originally suggested that Timagenes is to be understood under Livy's reference to *levissimi ex Graecis,* and Jacoby, *FGrHist* [*Die Fragmen le der grechischen Historiker*] 88 T. 9, lists this passage among the testimonia for Timagenes. Weber (above n. 3) 42, protested against this view, and Tarn (above n. 1) II 396, rightly rejects it. *Dictitare solent* cannot refer to a single writer. Livy here refers to a "circle of ideas spread over a certain period of time, not a single utterance".

In Alexander's complete success over the Persians, Greek champions of Alexander, writing after Carrhae, had a sharp barb which has left its traces in Lucan's wistful comment at 10. 50-3.

100. A convenient, recent discussion of Stoic views in Livy, is Walsh (above n. 97) 49-64.

101. Livy 9. 19. 17.

102. Tac. 6. 22. Good general discussions of Tacitus' attitude towards philosophy are B. Walker, *The Annals of Tacitus*[2] (Manchester 1960) 250-1; R. Syme (above n. 91) II 525-6; R. Scott, *Religion and Philosophy in the Histories of Tacitus* (American Academy in Rome 1968).

103. Tac. Ann. 2. 73. For Germanicus' imitatio Alexandri, see G. Aalders, *Historia* 10, 1961, 382-4. For Tacitus and Stoic historiography, O. Murry, *Historia* 14, 1965, 58-9.

104. Polybius 9. 34. 1.

105. Hoffmann (above n. 3) 7-14, and Hoïstad (above n. 3) 202-20, argue that the Cynics uniformly portrayed Alexander as a savage tyrant. This view requires the dismissal of Onesicritus, the only clearly named Cynic who presents an opinion on Alexander, as well as the misrepresentation of the evidence of Megasthenes and the Berlin Papyrus.

106. Onesicritus Jacoby, *FGr Hist* frg. 17 = Strabo 15. 1. 63-5. Onesicritus as the pupil of Diogenes, Diogenes Laertius 6. 75-6; Plutarch de Alex. fort. 1. 10. p. 331 E.

107. For a Cynic source for the antitheses Alexander—Diogenes and Alexander—Gymnosophists, see Hoïstad (above n. 3) 202-20; and U. Wilcken, *Sitzungsberichte Preuß.* Akademie d. Wiss. Berlin (1923) 177.

108. Dio's Cynic portrait above n. 62. Megasthenes (= Strabo 15. 1. 68; Arrian 7. 2) gives one account of Alexander's confrontation with the Gymnosophists. Neither here nor in Berlin Papyrus P. 12044 is Alexander represented as a savage tyrant.

109. Eratosthenes Jacoby, *FGrHist* 241 T. 10—Strabo 2. 2. E. Zeller, *Die Philosophie der Griechen* III i[3] 43, 298-9, classifies him as Stoic. Pohlenz (above n. 12) I 136, sees him as strongly influenced by Stoicism. For Eratosthenes' view of Alexander, see Strabo 1. 4. 9; Plut. de Alex. fort. 1. 6.

110. Chrysippus frg. 691, von Arnim SVF III p. 173 = Plut. de Stoic. repug. 20. 3 p. 1043 D.

J. E. Atkinson (essay date 1980)

SOURCE: Atkinson, J. E. "Curtius's Sources and the Composition of the Histories." In *A Commentary on Q. Curtius Rufus's* Historiae Alexandri Magni, *Books 3 and 4,* pp. 58-73. Amsterdam, The Netherlands: J. C. Gieben, 1980.

[*In the following excerpt, Atkinson examines Curtius's sources and influences for his* Historiae Alexandri Magni.]

This survey of the source problems is necessarily brief, and on many points depends on argument in the Commentary. It is further assumed that the reader has access to Pearson's *The lost Histories of Alexander* together with Badian's review of it, and Hamilton's *Plutarch "Alexander"* (I regret that I have not yet been able to consult R. Egge's *Untersuchungen zur Primärtradition bei Q. Curtius Rufus*).

In the Commentary Curtius' sources and style are considered together, for it is necessary to determine Curtius' own contribution to the development of the myth, when one considers points of divergence between

Curtius and the other sources (Rabe's careful analysis of the sources illustrates the danger of treating the secondary sources as structures built from units from earlier writers, as though Curtius and the other secondary sources were no more than simple copyists).

Whilst many inconsistencies can be regarded as the product of Curtius' concern about the composition (cf. on iii, 2.9, 7.1 and 8-10), there are still many cases where contradictions cannot be so explained and they indicate the *contaminatio* of differing traditions (vide on iii, 7.5; 9.12; 11.13; 12.13, iv, 1.15, 2-4 with Rutz; 6.18 and 21; 12.2; contrast vii, 10.10 with vii, 5.43, Schwartz [*RE* [*Real Encyclopaedie*] IV, 1879] cited as examples of Curtius' failure to harmonize conflicting traditions the difference in bias between the tale of the trial of Amyntas and his brothers and the story of the fall of Philotas' family, and the difference in the judgement on Alexander's superstition between vii, 7.8 and 10.4: but *contaminatio* is difficult to establish where the inconsistency is in interpretation rather than facts).

Curtius says little in the extant books of the *Historiae* about his approach to historiography. He professed concern, as did Herodotus, to preserve and pass on traditions which were no less real for being dubious evidence (ix, 1.34). He would not censor what might seem uncouth to his readers' minds (vii, 8.11), but left out what he considered irrelevant (viii, 9.37). Where appropriate he presented his material thematically and not synchronistically (v, 1.1). We shall return to consider his thematic treatment, but here the important point is that Curtius tells us that he worked from diverse and sometimes conflicting traditions (ix, 5.21, viii, 5.8, 6.24-25; x, 10.5; iv, 16.9 etc.). Curtius refers to only three earlier prose writers: Cleitarchus, Timagenes and Ptolemy, and of these Timagenes is least known to us as a writer on Alexander's campaigns, for Curtius' reference (ix, 5.21 = Jacoby *FGH* [*Fragmente der griechiskhen Historiker*] 88, F.3) is the only one we have, though Livy records that Timagenes thought the Romans incapable of standing up to the brilliance of an Alexander (Livy ix, 18.6. Detail in C.R. iii, 1.22 and 6.1 and iv, 8.9 may possibly derive from Timagenes). He was brought to Rome in 55 B.C. and taught rhetoric there but although he was accepted into Antony's circle of friends and managed to switch sides when Octavian emerged as the new power, he advertised his contempt for Rome and was outspoken enough to anger Augustus. Banished from the Princeps' court he destroyed his manuscript of his history of Augustus' career. He apparently wrote as a separate work a general history, which was available to Strabo after the latter's return to Rome in 29 B.C. (the evidence on Timagenes is collected in Jacoby *FGH* no. 88; I have here summarised points made by G. W. Bowersock 108 sq. and 123 sq.).

It has at various times been suggested that Timagenes was the source for Trogus' *Philippica*, a work which Curtius certainly read, as we shall see (the arguments for Trogus' use of Timagenes are rehearsed by Jacoby *FGH* IIC 220 sq.; limited use of Timagenes on the Parthians is argued by Th. Liebmann-Frankfort *Latomus* xxviii, 1969, 894 sq.). The fragments of Timagenes, however, are insufficient to establish whether Trogus used him on the history of Alexander, and whether Curtius used him directly or through perhaps Trogus (cf. Schwartz *RE* IV, esp. 1887 sq., Edson 200-1, Levi, esp. 164 sq., sees Timagenes as explaining much in Curtius that could not be attributed to Cleitarchus).

13. Curtius' Use of Trogus

Trogus' *Philippica* was a product of the Augustan age, completed after 20 B.C., to which date he carried his history of Parthia. The *Philippica* is known to us through the *Epitome* of Justin, who completed his work by A.D. 321 (Edson 203) or perhaps before A.D. 226 (Steele [4]).

Tarn (ii, 124 and 79) found no evidence to prove use of Trogus by Curtius or use of Curtius by Trogus, and other scholars have generally supposed that similarities between Curtius' account and Justin's arose from Curtius' and Trogus' use of the same or related sources (Schwartz *RE* IV, esp. 1883 sq., Bardon [3] esp. 123 sq., Jacoby *RE* XI, 631 argues that Curtius and Trogus both took Cleitarchus through an intermediary source. Von Gutschmid argued the case for rejecting Peterdorff's theory [in *Eine neue Hauptquelle des Curtius Rufus* 1884, known to me indirectly] that Curtius picked up Cleitarchus' account via Trogus and Gutschmid's refutation was accepted by Schwartz [*RE* IV, 1884]). The view that Curtius used Trogus' source directly is attractive (but not justified thereby) in that the study of the sources on Alexander has tended to proliferate hypothetical intermediary sources. Then too the valid point has been made that Curtius could hardly have derived sufficient material for his ten books from the two books of Trogus' *Philippica* which related to Alexander; and Steele (1) 417-420 emphasizes the differences between Curtius and Justin.

However there are significant links and coincidences of phraseology (Dosson 146-7 and references below). Clearly Curtius was familiar with a Latin history of Alexander whose phraseology coincided with Trogus' in many instances; in the absence of other candidates the natural conclusion is that the source was Trogus himself. What must now be recognised is that Curtius often adopted the language of Trogus' narrative and used Trogus' phrases, whilst taking the historical material from other sources. Thus in the tale of Alexander's sickness at Tarsus Curtius adopts Trogus' expressions though he used some other source for the historical detail (see on iii, 5 and 6). Then Curtius attributes to Alexander as part of his address to his troops before the battle of Issus ideas which occur in Justin's version of Alexander's speech before Gaugamela (C.R. iii, 10.9 with J. xi, 13.11: *hortatur spernant illam aciem auro et argento fulgentem, in qua plus praedae quam periculi sit.* Trogus may have been influenced here by Livy, whose work he knew [J. xxxviii, 3.11] but this same book of Justin at least provides a guarantee that Justin was concerned to preserve something of the rhetoric of Trogus' speeches [Seel *Trogus* F.152]: thus it is unlikely that Justin departed from Trogus' text to incorporate passages from Curtius). Curtius' account of Alexander's dealings with the Persian royal captives after Issus is closer to Justin's account in phraseology than in detail (see iii, 12.8, 11 and 19). Similarly C.R. iv, 14.20 echoes J. xvii, 2.3, from a different context.

Edson picked out Curtius' account of the battle of Megalopolis to point to Curtius' dependence on Trogus, for this passage is almost identical with Justin's sketch of the battle of Sellasia (C.R. vi, 1.7-8 with J. xxviii, 4.2; C. Edson 199: unfortunately he gives an incorrect reference to Justin and confuses the battle of Mantinea with that of Megalopolis). Edson went on to suggest that whilst Curtius made direct use of Trogus, he did not manage, or trouble to harmonize the hostility of Trogus' presentation of Alexander with the more favourable picture which he found elsewhere: "This accounts for many of the unfavourable and derogatory features of the view of Alexander given by Curtius, a hasty and irresponsible rhetorician who could not or would not coordinate the information derived from his various sources into a coherent picture of the king" (Edson 200). It is too readily assumed that Curtius and Trogus were incapable of using a source without adopting its peculiar bias: thus Trogus' use of Timagenes is generally rejected because Timagenes' admiration for Alexander and contempt for Rome are allegedly not mirrored in Justin's epitome (Trogus' consistency is indeed somewhat illusory: the story of Gaugamela, for instance, is favourable to Alexander, though the tragedy of Darius' fall is an important motif [J. xi, 13-14] and J. Therasse (1) 560 sq. points out that Justin's account of Alexander's adoption of oriental practices is not hostile to Alexander nor moralist in tone). In the case of the story of Alexander's illness at Tarsus Curtius borrowed from Trogus' account without, however, picking up the bias in Trogus' version, which was clearly to highlight Parmenion's integrity and efficiency (see on iii, 5-6). The tradition favourable to Parmenion was presumably cynical about his opponents, and this may explain Curtius' unfavourable treatment of Menidas (iv, 12.4, 15.12) and Craterus (vi, 8.1 sq.). The tradition favourable to Parmenion was not Callisthenes' work, and Ptolemy and Aristobulus were unsympathetic (A. iii, 26.1 sq.);

Duris was favourable to Craterus (Nepos *Eum.* 3, 3). We cannot tell if it was Trogus who recast the Tarsus story, but Curtius apparently read it but did not give the story the same angle. The explanation may be that Trogus set out to counter Timagenes' presentation of Alexander and recast many episodes by giving Parmenion a more positive rôle; Curtius then read both Timagenes—as he said he did—and Pompeius Trogus, whose work he used without giving it free advertisement. Thus Curtius' version of the Tarsus story was influenced by these rival accounts.

14. CURTIUS AND ARRIAN'S SOURCES, ARISTOBULUS AND PTOLEMY

In many cases Curtius' phraseology matches fairly closely Arrian's, and as Curtius wrote earlier than did Arrian the similarities may have arisen from Curtius' use of sources later employed by Arrian (similarities are noted for instance at iii, 8.20; 9.2; 11.3; iv, 1.14; 5.13-22; 10.8-14; some other parallels in phraseology and detail are indexed by Dosson 141-3). It was not Arrian who copied Curtius for in many cases it can be demonstrated that Curtius mistranslated a Greek source or mutilated the sense by abbreviation whilst Arrian copied the same source accurately (contrast C.R. vi, 4.23 with A. iii, 23.6, for example; other references in Section 8 above; Steele (3) 50 sq., following a point made by Dosson 187 sq.).

Steele properly noted that Curtius is closer to Arrian than is immediately apparent as a divergence from Arrian may often be owing to Curtius' inclusion of an idea picked up from Livy (Steele (3) 41 sq.). Thus the difference between C.R. ix, 1.8 and A. v, 20.6 may be accounted for as Curtius' knowledge of Livy xxi, 24.4, and Curtius' development of the story of the mutilation of the prisoners-of-war taken at Issus shows the influence of Livy (A. ii, 7.1, Livy xxx, 29.2, cf. commentary on iii, 8.15); similarly Livian influence drew Curtius away from the source he shared with Arrian on the death of Spitamenes (C.R. viii, 3; A. iv, 17.7; Livy xxxviii, 24; Steele [1] 407). Steele went on to argue that Curtius read Arrian's *Anabasis* (Steele [3] 153 sq.), but the evidence on Curtius' dates shows this is to be a false conclusion.

The evidence is there that Curtius used a source later employed by Arrian. Curtius himself refers to Ptolemy (ix, 5.21) and his use of Ptolemy is elsewhere discernible, as we shall see, but it is less easy to determine whether Curtius knew Arrian's other main source, Aristobulus: a link with Aristobulus is suggested below at iii, 9.2 (cf. A. iii, 11.7) and at iv, 2.7-9. Tarn (ii, 107) stated that Curtius' account of the capture of Bessus (vii, 5.19 sq.) is "Aristobulus' account written up", for Aristobulus recorded that Bessus' officers handed him over to Alexander, whereas Ptolemy wrote that he took Bessus after a forced march against the camp of Spitamenes and Dataphernes (A. iii, 30.5 and 29.6 sq.). Tarn suggested that more might be from Aristobulus. Since Tarn's case ultimately rests on his view of the story of Bessus, it must be noted that Welles has challenged the view that Aristobulus' version was unique, whilst Ptolemy's was the correct and generally believed version (Welles [2] 109 sq., A. iii, 29.7 sq., C.R. vii, 5.19 sq., and D.S. 83.8). If Aristobulus altered the record one might have expected him to excise reference to the barbaric punishment of Bessus which Alexander permitted, for he was generally concerned to counter elements in the history of Alexander which detracted from his glory (Bessus' punishment: C.R. vii, 5.40, D.S. 83.9, cf. A. iv, 7.3. On the readiness of Aristobulus to defend Alexander: Jacoby *FGH* Frags. 7, 8, 33, 55, 58, 59, 62; Pearson (1) 156 sq., and Badian (1) 255-6; incidentally none of these fragments is matched by Curtius); conversely Ptolemy had something to gain from changing the record to set the capture of Bessus to his own credit. Furthermore in the case where Curtius contradicts Ptolemy he cites against him Cleitarchus and Timagenes (ix, 5.21), not Aristobulus.

Dosson saw a fragment of Aristobulus in Curtius' account of Alexander's wound received in the assault on the city of the Malli, for ix, 5.9 matches the quotation from Ptolemy at A. vi, 10.1 save that Curtius gives the length of the arrow as does Aristobulus (Plut. *Mor.* 341c; Dosson 144). This argument is unsatisfactory for it presupposes that Arrian was incapable of shortening quotations, whereas we shall note that he did drop out details (vide on iii, 7.3 and 8). Curtius might have taken all the information here from Ptolemy: collateral use of Aristobulus is not established.

In Bk. 3 Curtius did not employ Aristobulus on the way in which Alexander broke the Gordian knot nor on the background to Alexander's collapse at Tarsus (1.18 and 5.2); it is further argued below that Curtius did not make use of Aristobulus' catalogue of Persian units at Gaugamela, and most likely did not use Aristobulus for his description of the Persian army assembled in 333 (see on 2.9 and p. 106 sq. infra), and that Aristobulus was not Curtius' source on the tale of Darius' dream (cf. notes on iii, 3.2-7). Then Curtius did not include the story of the Sardanapalus monument at Anchialus, though Aristobulus gave it (Jacoby *FGH* F.9, though Cleitarchus admittedly gave it too and his work was apparently known to Curtius). Aristobulus was probably not Curtius' source on the administration of Egypt (iv, 8.4-5), pace Fränkel.

By contrast there is a direct reference to Ptolemy at ix, 5.9, and several passages suggest a link with Ptolemy's work: compare C.R. iii, 8.20 with A. iii, 11.2; C.R. iv, 1.10-14 with A. ii, 14.4-9 and Hamilton (1) 77; C.R. vii, 10.10 with A. iv, 7.3 (Hamilton (1) p. 115); C.R. x, 2.24 with A. vii, 9.6 (Hamilton (1) 36-7 and Tarn ii, 296); C.R. viii, 13-14 with A. v, 8 sq. (Pearson (1) 198 sq. On the problems of identifying fragments of Ptolemy see too Strasburger (1) and (4)). It is tempting to attribute to Ptolemy data which Curtius and Arrian give in common on the battles and on military and civil administration.

However, in many cases detail given by Curtius does not tally with that given by Arrian (cf. Strasburger (1) 6-7). Further it is rather disturbing to find that Curtius preserves details about Ptolemy's later opponents which do not appear in Arrian's account. Thus Curtius preserves information missing in Arrian, on Perdiccas (notably C.R. ix, 1.19), Antinous, and Eumenes (Schachermeyr (2) 104), who clashed with Ptolemy after Alexander's death, and comparison of Curtius and Arrian shows too that Ptolemy suppressed information on Leonnatus, Polyperchon and Antigonus (the evidence is discussed by Tarn ii, 110, Welles (2) esp. 107-8, Errington (1) and Bosworth (7); see on iv, 1.35, 3.1, 13.7 and 28). It emerges too that Ptolemy's work belongs to his early years in Egypt, when he had greatest cause to enhance his own reputation at the expense of others (Errington (1) esp. 241; Badian in Fondation Hardt *Entretiens* 22, pp. 35-6, commenting on Bosworth [7]).

The sobering conclusion must be that Curtius had access to a source which was on many points more detailed and reliable than Ptolemy. That source was not Callisthenes, for much of the relevant detail relates to the period after his death, and there are contradictions between Curtius and Callisthenes on other points (see on iii, 1.24), nor was it Chares who was certainly not followed by Curtius for example at iii, 11.10 nor on Philotas' fall (cf. Badian (1) 253). It may have been Onesicritus, but it seems at least that he was not a source for Bk. 3 (see on iii, 6.1) and elsewhere detail given by Curtius disagrees with Onesicritus' information (contrast C.R. vi, 4.22 and D.S. 75.6, with Onesicritus, Jacoby *FGH* no. 134, F.3; the divergence is discussed by T. S. Brown (1) 91 sq.). In other cases they are closer: compare C.R. ix, 1.9-10 with Onesicritus F.22; C.R. x, 1.10 mentions Onesicritus on a mission which Nearchus reported without mentioning Onesicritus by name (A. viii, 34.6): this might suggest that Curtius' information derived from Onesicritus. There are however divergences from Onesicritus shared by Diodorus and Curtius which suggest that Onesicritus' work was known to these two writers indirectly, perhaps via Cleitarchus (so Hamilton [2] 457-8, Jacoby *RE* XI, 652-3). A corollary of the argument concerning Curtius' inclusion of Onesicritus' name where Nearchus omitted it, is that Nearchus was not one of Curtius' sources. The fragments of Nearchus' work do not provide a *prima facie* case for considering him further. It is possible that the missing link is Medeius, who served with Nearchus under Antigonus (D.S. xix, 69): he had less cause to omit Onesicritus than did Nearchus, and he presumably covered Antigonus' campaigns in Asia Minor, which Ptolemy apparently left out. But the central point is that Curtius used a source that was often close to what Arrian preserves, and, if Aristobulus was not much used by Curtius, we must conclude that Curtius read Ptolemy, as he appears to claim, or a source that drew heavily on Ptolemy, or both Ptolemy and a related source. This brings us to a consideration of Cleitarchus.

15. CURTIUS, DIODORUS SICULUS AND CLEITARCHUS

The parallels between Curtius and Diodorus are numerous and striking; indices may be found in Schwartz's article on Curtius (*RE* IV, 1873-5, cf. *RE* V, 682-4), in Fränkel's *Quellen* (esp. 395 sq., and 407 sq., where differences are listed) and in Dosson 138-140. Book 3 of Curtius' *Histories* has numerous links with Diodorus' account, especially on the battle of Issus (see for example on 2.10-19, 3.9, 7.7, 8.24, 11.4 and 20-26, and 12.17); the same can be seen in Bk. 4, for instance in 2.1-21, 3.20-26, 4.1-5 and so on.

Tarn (ii, 116 sq.) attempted to show that Curtius read and used Diodorus, but his argument was rejected by Strasburger (3). Tarn's argument concerning Curtius' mention of "argyraspids" (iv, 13.27) involved the assumption that Curtius had not read Hieronymus, who certainly used the term, and whose work was known to Diodorus; however Errington (2) argues that Curtius' Book 10 was based on Hieronymus. Comparison with the Hieronymus based accounts of 323 makes it more likely that Curtius used Cleitarchus (Schachermeyr (2) 92-104, and Bosworth (4) 63, n. 6), but whether he used Hieronymus or Cleitarchus for Bk. 10, there is no need to assume that he picked up the anachronistic reference to "argyraspids" from Diodorus.

As Curtius' account of Alexander's campaigns could not have been derived from Diodorus' meagre and patchy history of the period, one assumes that Curtius had access to one or more of Diodorus' sources, or, perhaps one should say, to Diodorus' source for Book 17 (we may leave open the question whether either author only knew the common source indirectly). The common source was Cleitarchus, in the opinion of most scholars.

Cleitarchus was apparently not with Alexander in 334, but may have joined the army at some point before Alexander's death, and "his active lifetime might possibly span the year 300 B.C." (Badian [10], the quotation is

from p. 10. Further on Cleitarchus' dates see Rabe, pp. 8-36, who rejects Schnabel's case for dating Cleitarchus' work later than 260 B.C. Tarn's bid to date Cleitarchus later than Ptolemy, who was, in Tarn's view, later than Aristobulus, was soundly countered by Strasburger [3]). Schachermeyr (Fondation Hardt *Entretiens* 22, p. 34) explains why Cleitarchus can be presumed to have written before 310. Ptolemy's insistence that he was not present at the action in Mallian territory when Alexander was wounded (C.R. ix, 5.21) is generally taken to show that Ptolemy wrote later than Cleitarchus.

Cleitarchus was a popular author; as critics saw him, a rhetorician rather than a scholar. Curtius cites him twice (ix, 5.21 and 8.15) and Curtius and Diodorus might reasonably be expected to have read Cleitarchus (on his popularity see refs. in Jacoby *FGH* no. 137). Pearson (1) c. 8 analyses the fragments of his work and shows where Curtius and Diodorus appear to have used him.

There has, however, been a tendency to attribute too much to Cleitarchus without any justification (cf. the comments of Welles (1) 7 sq.) and it is salutary to record how few are the links between the fragments of Cleitarchus and Curtius. Fragment 9 in Jacoby's collection concerns the Carthaginian practice of immolating children as a thank-offering to "Cronus", and this rite is mentioned by Curtius (iv, 3.23; noted as a quotation from Cleitarchus by Dosson 135 and Edson 199-200), but many differences between Curtius and Cleitarchus will be noted in this passage. On the number of prostitutes attached to the Persian court Curties tallies with Cleitarchus, but only if Curtius' text is emended (C.R. vi, 6.8; Cleitarchus F.10, vide notes on iii, 3.10 and 24). Cleitarchus, Frag. 11, described Thais as inspiring the arson of Persepolis, and Curtius and Diodorus agree (C.R. v, 7.3 sq., D.S. 72), and again on the visit of the Amazon queen to Alexander the three writers give basically the same story (Cleitarchus, Frag. 15; C.R. vi, 5.24 sq. and D.S. 77.2-3; cf. Pearson (1) 220-1). On the geography of Hyrcania Curtius and Diodorus both tell of trees, similar to oaks, which drip with honey (C.R. vi, 4.22 and D.S. 75.6); Diodorus goes on to deal with a bee-like insect called the "anthredon", and his description is similar to Cleitarchus' (Frag. 14): perhaps Curtius and Diodorus used Cleitarchus on the flora and fauna of Hyrcania, but the item on the honey-dripping trees goes back to Onesicritus (ap. Pliny *n.h.* xii, 34; Pearson (1) 93 and 220) and Cleitarchus actually called the insect the "tenthredon", not "anthredon" (cf. Fontana (1) 177). Aphorisms in a speech of Scythians are similar to *sententiae* attributed to Cleitarchus (compare C.R. vii, 8.12 and 15 with Cleitarchus Frags. 40, 43 and 48; Pearson (1) 222, n. 42). From ix, 1.1-13 and again from 24 Curtius' account runs parallel to Diodorus 89.4 sq., and there are significant links between D.S. 90.1-3 and 90.5-6 and Cleitarchus Frags. 18 and 19. Nearchus and Onesicritus both covered the same area and the differences between ix, 1 and D.S. 89.4 sq. might be attributed to Curtius' and Diodorus' not following the same source; but as they proceed often with the same sequence of detail it is more likely that they were using the same source, and Cleitarchus F.18 makes him the probable source. Then on the number of Sambus' subjects killed by Alexander Curtius cites Cleitarchus and with a slight emendation it tallies with that given by D.S. (C.R. ix, 8.15, D.S. 102.6). Incidentally Curtius and Diodorus proceed to describe the attack on the city of Harmata or Harmatelia and they agree on many points of detail: the position of the city in the kingdom, the number of light-armed troops sent against them by Alexander, the number of Indians who were enticed out of the city, the Indians' unsportsmanlike act of smearing poison on their weapons, the wounding of Ptolemy and Alexander's concern for him, and Alexander's dream of a snake offering a remedy for Ptolemy's wound (C.R. ix, 8.17 sq., D.S. 103.1 sq.). The two accounts are so close in detail and formulation that, if Cleitarchus was in fact Curtius' source for ix, 8.15, he would seem to be the common source for the capture of Harmata too. Finally, Curtius cites Cleitarchus on the story of Ptolemy's actions at the city of the Malli, and shows by reference to Ptolemy's own work that Cleitarchus was inaccurate (ix, 5.21; it is unlikely that Curtius intended his comment as a sarcastic dig at Ptolemy, cf. Pearson (1) 207, n. 83).

Thus very little can be firmly attributed to Cleitarchus (see esp. Borza [3]), and I have noted in the Commentary instances where we can say with varying degrees of certainty that Cleitarchus was not Curtius' source (vide on iii, 3.19 and 24;4.1 and 3, and the discussion on the sources of iii, 13).

Fontana (1) esp. 171 sq. went so far as to argue that the differences between Diodorus and the fragments of Cleitarchus are so great that Cleitarchus can be excluded as Diodorus' main source, and he posited that Duris was his source. But items once attributed to Duris in Curtius' third book cannot be shown to derive from him (vide on 3.11 and 11.4; at vi, 5.24 sq. Curtius gives the story of the Amazons' visit which Duris rejected as a fiction [ap. Plut. *Alex.* 46, 2]. Diodorus gives the same story [77], without noting that it was unhistorical. A certain contradiction appears between Diodorus xvi, 34.5 and Duris, Frag. 36).

Despite the frailty of the evidence to identify Cleitarchus as the source shared by Diodorus and Curtius, there is no stronger candidate, and as Cleitarchus was from Alexandria and apparently loyal to Ptolemy he may have provided Curtius with details that Ptolemy, perhaps writing later, chose to leave out.

Thus far we conclude that Curtius used several sources. He borrowed ideas and phraseology from Trogus, and knew, if not directly, Timagenes' work. He knew Ptolemy's work, perhaps directly, and at the same time had access to a source which gave detail that Ptolemy suppressed. This latter source was apparently not Aristobulus, but could have been Onesicritus. Curtius also made extensive use of a source which formed the basis for Diodorus' Book 17, and this source may have been Cleitarchus.

16. The "Peripatetic Tradition" and the Mercenaries' Source

Two sources which Tarn considered basic to Curtius' work have not survived subsequent rigorous examination: the Peripatetic tradition, as Tarn described it, does not emerge from the evidence (Badian (7), E. Mensching *Hist.* xii, 1963, 274 sq., Atkinson (1) 134 sq. and Fears (4); see too on iv, 14.18), and the "mercenaries' source" appears curiously ill-informed about what the mercenaries did and less informative about the Persian army than authors who relied presumably on what was divulged by prisoners-of-war (Brunt (2)). Wolf's thesis that Cleitarchus incorporated mercenaries' tales in his history breaks down on many points (for example see on iii, 8.15; 11.11 and iv, 1.27-40; 12.4).

17. Elements of Curtius' Style

Each book of Curtius' *Histories* is centred on a few episodes, but whilst the narrative is episodic, Curtius carefully interrelates the parts for example by programmatic notes and references back (for example iii, 3.28, 6.3, 12.18 and 13.17; iv, 7.32, v, 1.1-2, vi, 2.4, viii, 10.18; and for references back, iii, 7.7, iv, 9.9 and v, 9.1 [perhaps a reference to something in the missing books, but Artabazus' connection with Philip is mentioned in detail at vi, 5.2]). Indeed Curtius is superior to Arrian in his ability to construct a cohesive work (cf. Strasburger (5) 459).

Book 3 illustrates Curtius skill at structuring his material. The major episodes concern the Gordian knot, the assembly of the Persian army, Alexander's collapse in Tarsus, the battle of Issus and the subsequent capture of Damascus. Then there is a series of minor episodes, including Darius' exchange with Charidemus, the cowardice of the governor of Cilicia, the murder of Sisines, the council-of-war in Issus and so on. These narrative units are linked together by two major motifs running through the book: first the contrast between the luxury, extravagance and savagery of the orientals and the rugged simple culture of the men who fought with Alexander; secondly the relationship between a king and his subjects, be they his nationals, or collaborators or prisoners. The cultural contrast explains in part what the war is about and why Alexander could defeat the Persians at Issus; the book finishes by showing that after Issus Alexander was strong enough to resist the temptations of wealth, but anticipates the irony of his eventual submission to the forces of corruption in the empire he conquered. A subsidiary motif is the importance of the Greek mercenaries to Darius and Alexander's need of Greek aid (see on 1.1 and 19 sq., 2.10 sq., 3.1 etc.). The second motif provides a series of sketches of political situations where Curtius looks at the problems of leadership, explains Alexander's qualities, and illustrates his own ideas on the integrity and independence of thought which an officer or aristocrat should protect. Darius' exchanges with Charidemus, the mercenaries and his courtiers, Alexander's dealings with Parmenion, the doctor, Philip, Sisines and Sisygambis, and Parmenion's approach to Darius' governor in Damascus all concern problems of leadership, and in particular the nicety of the balance which has to be preserved between state security or self-preservation and the dignity that goes with trust. On the other side of government Curtius illustrates the ideal of "libertas" for example in the antithesis between the value of Charidemus' honest advice to Darius and the inane loyalty and orthodoxy of the Persian nobles. The development of this theme surely belongs to Curtius himself, writing with the experience of times when it was easy for senators to capitulate before the spectre of "maiestas" trials. When Caligula died no doubt many senators had cause for soul-searching. These motifs are further analysed in the Commentary (see on iii, 2.10 sq., 6.1 sq., 7.11 sq., 8.1-11, 12.7 sq., and chapter 13. An echo of the terror of Tiberius' rule from Capri is perhaps found in Curtius' frequent reference to secret correspondence: for example iii, 6.4 sq., 7.12, and 13.2 sq. [the last two cases are not mentioned by the other sources] and iv, 10.16). A subsidiary motif here is the condemnation of cowardice and treachery: Darius' officers in Cilicia and Damascus are criticised for capitulating without a fight.

In the development of these motifs consistency of characterisation is sometimes set aside in favour of a neat antithesis. Thus, for example, whilst a central theme of Book 3 is the simplicity of the Graeco-Macedonian culture as opposed to the luxury of the Persian culture and this is repeated in the tale of Gaugamela (for example iv, 14.16), yet Curtius presents a picture of Alexander's troops after the battle of Issus, looting and raping without restraint (11.20 sq.). The inconsistency here is perhaps the byproduct of the antithesis Curtius wished to establish between the material greed of his troops and Alexander's concern to hunt down Darius (12.1).

The episodic units can serve not only to build up the central motifs, but also to control the pace of the story: thus the story of Sisines' murder (iii, 7.11 sq.) holds up the beginning of the battle; similarly Curtius holds up the battle narrative after mentioning the exchange of war-cries, by inserting at that point a lengthy account of Alexander's address to his troops (iii, 10.3 sq.).

The influence of Roman rhetoric on the construction of the speeches is obvious (Helmreich's *Reden* is of value on this topic: for the general influence of rhetoric on Curtius see Dosson 217 sq.). The influence of rhetoric shows itself in places where Curtius appears uncertain about the motivation or explanation of some action. This was a rhetorical device, found for example in Lucan and in Seneca's work, where alternative theories are advanced without indication of Seneca's own view even where one of the theories represents a Stoic doctrine or his own belief (Marti *AJP* lxvi, 1945, esp. 357 and n. 20, where she quotes for example Seneca *ad Polyb.* 9, 3 and 5, 1, *Ep.* 16, 5; examples in Curtius occur at iii, 1.18, iv, 13.3, v, 1.9, vi, 7.35, vii, 2.34, viii, 6.20 and 12.3); Tacitus used the device to suggest what the evidence did not. Another feature of Curtius' work that shows the influence of rhetoric is surely the psychological observations expressed as neat *sententiae*; and rhetoricians were interested in the description of the emotions and the manifestations of these emotions (see infra on iii, 3.2, 6.5 and 11.12), but this is not to say that comments on psychology and emotions only came into the story with Roman writers (see on iii, 6.10 and 8.20).

Curtius was certainly competent at dramatising his material; dramatic irony is an important element, often suggested by antithetical scenes (witness the contrasting pictures of the two armies in iii, 2 and 3, and the series of scenes describing Darius' and Alexander's relationship with various advisers: iii, 2.10 sq., 6.4 sq., and 7.8 sq. and 8.2 sq., iv, 1.15-26, 10.16-17, 11.10-15, 13.1-10); the pace of the story is well controlled with climaxes carefully built up and factual matter used to brake the narrative or to heighten the suspense (the story of Alexander's sickness at Tarsus illustrates these points, cf. pp. 163-4. Similarly Curtius' organisation of his material in the story of the preliminaries to the battle of Issus shows dramatic skill and shows that Curtius was ready to sacrifice plausibility to dramatic effect: see on iii, 9.12 and 10.1-3); *peripeteia* is another element of his dramatic style (for example iii, 8.16 and 24, 12.6 sq. and 13.4 sq.). Dramatic pathos is also created by the use of real or invented geographical detail and time references (for this type of geographical description, known as *Topothesie,* see on iii, 8.18 and Servius on V. *Aen.* i, 159 and Ziegler *RE* 2.R. VI 1722-3; time references: see on iii, 5.10. On these and other features of Curtius' dramatic skill see Rutz 370 sq., with reference to the story of the siege of Tyre).

18. CHARACTERISATION

Much has been written about inconsistencies in characterisation in the *Histories*. The general picture of Alexander is an heroic figure who was corrupted by success after the final defeat of Darius, and then could no longer control his arrogance and anger (this picture is epitomised by Curtius at iii, 12.18 sq.). Yet Curtius notes points of weakness before Alexander's degradation began, and in his final summary of Alexander's merits and weaknesses, Curtius plays down the elements of Alexander's corruption which are highlighted in the main narrative (x, 5.26 sq.). Tarn expounded the theory that the inconsistency arose from Curtius' inability to harmonize two contrasting traditions: one the Peripatetic tradition, which presented Alexander as the victim of success, a man who started well but was corrupted by fortune and became a dissolute, vicious tyrant; and the other a tradition similar to the Stoic view, which saw in Alexander from the start the viciousness and arrogance that later characterised his megalomanic rule (Tarn ii, 96 sq., cf. McQueen 33 sq., Schwartz *RE* IV, 1880 sq.; on the Stoic picture of Alexander, J. Stroux, Die stoische Beurteilung Alexanders *Philologus* lxxxviii, 1933, 222 sq.). However the evidence does not confirm the existence of a Peripatetic tradition, such as Tarn described (cf. Badian (7) and section 16 supra), and the idea of fortune corrupting a man was a commonplace which Curtius could have picked up anywhere (see on iii, 2.18 and 12.18 sq.); furthermore Curtius was quite capable of forming his own moral judgements and of writing them into his story: Therasse (1) and (2).

McQueen, like Tarn, has identified strands favourable and unfavourable to Alexander in Curtius' portrayal of Alexander, and he reduces the charge of inconsistency by arguing that Alexander was indeed a complex character, inconsistent in his behaviour, and Curtius appreciated this and attempted to delineate the various facets of his character (Curtius Rufus, esp. 37-38; cf. Bardon (3) 134 sq.: Curtius was concerned to produce a coherent and consistent portrait of Alexander. One might compare Tacitus' picture of Germanicus, on which see Timpe *Der Triumph des Germanicus* 1968, with K. Wellesley's comments in *JRS* lix, 1969, 278).

Neither approach is adequate since the end-product of character portrayal can hardly be discussed meaningfully until the technique of characterisation has been analysed. This is not the place for a thorough study of techniques of character portrayal, and it may suffice to identify some of the elements of characterisation in Curtius' work. First we must note again the psychological observations couched in neat *sententiae,* and the use of the formula "sive . . . sive" to suggest alternative motives behind an action. These are elements of rhetorical style rather than of scientific analysis. Thus, for

example, one can hardly argue (as Tarn does, ii, 100) that Curtius was using different sources when he described Alexander as "interritus ad omnia" at iv, 10.4, and when he commented on Alexander's anxiety before the battle of Issus: ut solet fieri, cum ultimi discriminis tempus adventat, in sollicitudinem versa fiducia est (iii, 8.20). The latter is a rhetorical commonplace that suits the drama of the preparations for battle, thus it is misleading to say or imply that Curtius used a source which presented Alexander as fearful or anxiety prone (pace McQueen 37 and 42, n. 61).

Secondly we must recognise that Curtius was influenced by the exercises of rhetoricians and philosophers who used historical *exempla* to describe moral qualities (the prose encomium was similarly constructed: "The facts of character and career were utilized to exemplify and to demonstrate . . . presupposed qualities" [D. Stuart *Epochs of Greek and Roman Biography* Berkeley, 1928, 64]). The connection between history and this type of moralizing is shown by the fact that Trogus' account of Alexander's cure by Philip at Tarsus was read both by Curtius and by Valerius Maximus, who recorded the tale under the heading *de constantia*. Curtius writes such an essay in iii, 12, on the theme *continentia,* where he deals with Alexander's treatment of the women captured at Issus. The story was a commonplace and its inclusion in the *Histories* tells us nothing about Curtius' source, nor does it indicate *per se* that Curtius saw *continentia* as one of Alexander's qualities. As will be seen in the *Commentary* it is the modifications in the story which tell us something about Curtius' style of characterisation.

Another feature of Curtius' style of character portrayal is the situational presentation, as opposed to general psychological description (compare A. Dihle's comment: Die Antike und vor allem die Römer haben Charakterbilder stets besser mit Situationsschilderungen als durch reine psychologische Deskription entworfen [*RE* 2.R. VIII A. 1 (1955) s.v. Velleius Paterculus, 652]). Thus, for example, a relatively dull passage, like the opening chapter of Bk. 3, says a great deal about Alexander: the episodes covered show Alexander acting resolutely to achieve his main objective, patiently clearing the ground and making careful preparations for action, and self-confident. Then in the story of the capture of Damascus in iii, 13 Curtius reveals through the narrative various facets of Parmenion's character: sound judgement, loyalty, his concern to act decisively and his tendency to overreact in an apparently dangerous situation.

Because the narrative is basically episodic it can happen that the individual story generates its own picture of the characters involved and inconsistencies may then occur between different episodes. Thus, for example,

Alexander's readiness to quit when things went wrong during the siege of Tyre, contrasts with his determination to face Darius in 333, or again with his self-confidence in a difficult situation in the land of the Sudracae (Tyre: iv, 3.11 and 4.1-2: Curtius did not invent the detail for compare D.S. 42.6 and 45.7, but he restructured the tale to use Alexander's supposed hesitancy for greater dramatic effect [cf. Rutz 377 and 380]; Sudracae: ix, 4.25). One must therefore consider the dramatic structure of each episode as a factor that may upset consistency of characterisation (see below on iii, 8.1-11). Curtius' fondness for antithesis might too lead him into inconsistency (see iii, 6.5).

It is possible too for characterisation to be sacrificed to rhetoric. Thus, for example, Curtius' version of the clash between Alexander and Parmenion, over Darius' final offer before Gaugamela of a negotiated settlement, almost excludes Parmenion. His famous line is recast, and the term "pecunia" inappropriately employed: "et ego pecuniam quam gloriam mallem, si Parmenio essem" (iv, 11.14; contrast D.S. 54.4-5, A. ii, 25.2 and Plut. *Alex.* 29, 8). This passage is worked out like a rhetorical exercise: Darius' envoy argues that Alexander should halt his advance if he is to retain his "moderatio" and "continentia": "difficile est enim continere, quod capere non possis" (iv, 11.7, 2 and 8); Parmenion's advice serves as a bridge passage: the quantification of "continentia" allows Alexander to make the transition from "pecunia" to "gloria", and in the following reply to Darius Alexander refers to his own "clementia" and "liberalitas", virtues akin to "moderatio", and argues that Darius is not a "iustus hostis"—reason enough for Alexander to claim the "gloria" of a military victory (iv, 11.16 sq.).

Finally there are elements in Curtius' characterisation of Alexander and other figures in the story which are reflections of his own society rather than part of the historical tradition. It was as difficult for a Roman historian as it is for a modern writer to avoid interpreting history in terms of his own society: the famous passage in x, 9 shows the immediacy of Alexander's story to Curtius' own experience (other references to Curtius' own day are found at iv, 4.21; v, 7.9; 8.1; vi, 6.11; vii, 5.42; 10.16; viii, 6.6 and 10.12; cf. Lana *RFIC* 1949, 60 sq. and his observation in *Velleio Patercolo* 1952, 189-190). A writer who had seen "imitatio Alexandri" projected as part of the emperor's image could hardly fail to point the similarities or contrasts between Alexander and his emulator. Thus, the reference to Alexander's respect for his sisters would seem to be a reference to Caligula's relationship with his sisters (iii, 6.15). This item adds to the characterisation of Alexander, but, as is argued in the commentary, Curtius did not find it in his source, and one need not worry about whether the item is favourable or unfavourable to Alexander,

nor whether it is consistent with other facets of Alexander's character in Curtius' picture. Similarly the anachronistic reference in speeches delivered before the battle of Issus to plans for the capture of Bactria and India (iii, 10.5) seems to be Curtius' own invention; it has a bearing on the characterisation of Alexander for it suggests that he had from the start extraordinarily wide aims. This may be unhistorical and Curtius was perhaps writing with Caligula in mind, who had romantic ideas of imperialism that were never brought to fruition. Curtius himself judged that consolidation was more prudent than further conquest: at least his comment on Alexander's plan to advance beyond the Hyphasis was "vicit cupido rationem" (ix, 2.12 and 2.9 sq. and 3.7 sq.; on the implications of Rome's policy of consolidation under Tiberius see G. Alföldy *Latomus* xxiv, 1965, 824 sq.: it was not motivated by liberal sentiments).

Curtius, writing under Claudius—the brother of Germanicus no less than the successor to Caligula—could only conclude that Alexander was a great man. Whatever he said in the individual episodes about Alexander, the only prudent conclusion at the end of his work was that Alexander's merits outweighed his weaknesses.

Abbreviations and Bibliography

ANCIENT SOURCES

C. R. = Curtius Rufus. The *lemmata* are taken from Bardon's text with a few minor alterations.

A. = Arrian *Anabasis*.

Dio Cassius: references are to U. P. Boissevain's edition, 5 vols. Berlin, 1895 sq.

D. S. = Diodorus Siculus. Unless otherwise stated all references are to Bk. 17.

Epitomal/Liber de morte/Testamentum Alexandri: references are to the edition *Incerti auctoris epitoma rerum gestarum Alexandri Magni . . .* ed. P. H. Thomas Leipzig, Teubner, 1960. The *Epitoma* is also known as the Metz epitome.

Itin(erarium Alexandri): references are to C. W. L. Müller's edition in *Arriani Anabasis et Indica . . . reliqua Arriani . . . Pseudo-Callisthenis historiam . . .* ed. Fr. Dübner and C. Müller. Paris, 1877.

J. = Justin.

Panegyricus: references are to the edition, *XII Panegyrici Latini*; ed. Mynors. Oxford, 1964.

Plut. = Plutarch: references to his life of Alexander are based on the edition by C. Lindskog and K. Ziegler, *Plutarchi, Vitae Parallelae* Vol. ii. Fasc. 2^2 Leipzig. Teubner, 1968.

Ps.Call. = Pseudo-Callisthenes: references are to Kroll's edition, *Historia Alexandri Magni (Pseudo-Callisthenes)* 2nd ed. Berlin, 1958.

Tacitus: references are to the Teubner texts.

Atkinson, J. E. (1) = Primary sources and the Alexanderreich, *A Class* vi, 1963, 125-137.

(2) = The Curtii Rufi again, *A Class* xvi, 1973, 129-133.

(3) = Curtius Rufus' *Historiae Alexandri* and the Principate, in *Actes de la XIIe Conférence Internationale d'Études Classiques 'Eirene'* . . . *1972.* Bucharest/Amsterdam, 1975, 363-7.

Badian, E. (1) = *Studies in Greek and Roman history,* Oxford, 1964.

(7) = The eunuch Bagoas, *CQ [Classical Quarterly]* viii, 1958, 144-157.

(10) = The date of Cleitarchus, *PACA [Proceedings of the African Classical Association]* viii, 1965, 5-11.

KEY TO THE BIBLIOGRAPHICAL REFERENCES

Bardon, H. (3) = Quinte Curce historien, *LEC [Les Etudes Classiques]* xv, 1947, 120-137.

Borza, E. N. (1) = Alexander and the return from Siwah, *Hist. [Historia]* xvi, 1967, 369.

(3) = Cleitarchus and Diodorus' account of Alexander, *PACA* xi, 1968, 25-45.

Bosworth, A. B. (4) = The government of Syria under Alexander, *CQ* xxiv, 1974, 46-64.

(7) = Arrian and the Alexander vulgate, in Fondation Hardt *Entretiens XXII.* Geneva, 1976, 1-33.

Bowersock, G. W. = *Augustus and the Greek world,* Oxford, 1965.

Brown, T. S. (1) = *Onesicritus: a study in hellenistic historiography,* Berkeley, Univ. of California Press, 1949.

(2) = Clitarchus, *AJP [American Journal of Philosophy],* lxxi, 1950, 134-155.

Brunt, P. A. (2) = Persian accounts of Alexander's campaigns, *CQ* xii, 1962, 141-155.

Dosson, S. = *Étude sur Quinte-Curce, sa vie et son oeuvre,* Paris, 1886.

Edson, C. = review of O. Seel *Trogus,* in *CP [Classical Philology]* lvi, 1961, 198-203.

Errington, R. M. (1) = Bias in Ptolemy's history of Alexander, *CQ* xix, 1969, 233-242.

(2) = From Babylon to Triparadeisos 323-320 B.C. *JHS [Journal of Hellenic Studies]* xc, 1970, 49-77.

Fears, J. R. (4) = The Stoic view of the career and character of Alexander the Great, *Philologus* cxviii, 1974, 113-130.

Fontana, M. J. (1) = Il problema delle fonti per il xvii libro di Diodoro Siculo, *Kokalos* i, 1955, 155 sq.

(2) = Sulla cronologia del xvii libro di Diodoro, *Kokalos* ii, 1956, 37 sq.

Gutschmid, A. von = *Kleine Schriften,* Vol. 3. Leipzig, 1892.

Hamilton, J. R. (1) = *Plutarch 'Alexander': a commentary,* Oxford, 1969.

(2) = *Alexander the Great,* London, 1973.

(3) = Three passages in Arrian, *CQ* xlix, 1955, 217-221.

Lana, I. = Dell' epoca in cui visse Quinto Curzio Rufo, *RFC [Revista de Filologia Classica]* xxvii, 1949, 48-70.

Livy. References are made to the following commentaries:

Ogilvie, R. M., *Livy Books 1-5,* Oxford, 1965.

Briscoe, J., *Livy Books 31-33,* Oxford, 1973.

I have made good use of D. W. Packard's *Concordance to Livy,* 4 vols. Cambridge (Mass.), 1968.

McQueen, E. I. = Quintus Curtius Rufus, in *Latin Biography*; ed. T. A. Dorey. London, 1967, 17-43.

Pearson, L. (1) = *The lost histories of Alexander the Great,* New York, 1960.

Rabe, I. = *Quellenkritische Untersuchungen zu Plutarchs Alexanderbiographie,* Diss., Hamburg, 1964.

RE = Pauly-Wissowa, *Real-Encyclopädie der classischen Altertumswissenschaft.*

Rutz, W. = Zur Erzählungskunst des Q. Curtius Rufus: die Belagerung von Tyrus, *Hermes* xciii, 1965, 370sq.

Schachermeyr, F. (2) = *Alexander in Babylon und die Reichsordnung nach seinem Tode,* Vienna, 1970.

Seel, O., *Trogus* = *Pompei Trogi Fragmenta,* Leipzig, 1956. (vide C. Edson)

Steele, R. B. (1) = Quintus Curtius Rufus, *AJP* xxxvi, 1915, 402-423.

(3) = Curtius and Arrian, *AJP* xl, 1919, 37-63 and 153-174.

(4) = Pompeius Trogus and Justinus, *AJP* xxxviii, 1917, 19-41.

Strasburger, H. (1) = *Ptolemaios und Alexander,* Leipzig, 1934.

(3) = review of Tarn's *Alexander,* in *Bibliotheca Orientalis* ix, 1952, 202-211.

(5) = Alexanders Zug durch die Gedrosische Wüste, *Hermes* lxxx, 1952, 456-493.

Stroux, J. = Die Zeit des Curtius, *Philologus* lxxxiv, 1928/29, 233-251.

Therasse, J. (1) = Le moralisme de Justin (Trogue-Pompée) contre Alexandre . . . , AC [*Antiquite Classique*] xxxvii, 1968, 551-588.

(2) = Le jugement de Quinte-Curce sur Alexandre: un appréciation morale indépendante, *LEC* xli, 1973, 23-45.

Welles, C. B. (1) = *Diodorus of Sicily,* Vol. 8. Cambridge (Mass.), 1963 (Loeb series).

(2) = The reliability of Ptolemy as an historian, in *Miscellanea di studi Alessandrini in memoria di Rostagni,* Torino, 1963, 101-116.

Wolf, R. = *Die Soldatenerzählungen des Kleitarch bei Quintus Curtius Rufus,* Diss., Wien, 1964.

N. G. L. Hammond (essay date 1983)

SOURCE: Hammond, N. G. L. Introduction to *Three Historians of Alexander the Great; The So-Called Vulgate authors Diodorus, Justin, and Curtius,* pp. 1-11. Cambridge: Cambridge University Press, 1983.

[*In the following essay, Hammond attempts to ascertain the sources for Diodorus's, Justin's, and Curtius's accounts of Alexander.*]

THE NEED FOR SOURCE ANALYSIS

The basic task for the historian of Alexander (henceforth A) is to assess the value of each of the five main accounts which have survived. It is rendered formidable not only by the length and the complexity but also by the unevenness of Arrian, *Alexandri Anabasis* (henceforth Arrian), Diodorus (henceforth D.), Justin (henceforth J.), Curtius (henceforth C.) and Plutarch, *Life of Alexander* (henceforth P*A*). There is only one way to discharge this task fully, and that is to analyse each individual account and determine, as far as it is possible,[1] which earlier source it was using at any given point. In this book I attempt to do so only for D., J. and C.

The reason for selecting these three is that they have often been grouped together as 'The Vulgate', and have been set apart from the other two. In itself such a grouping is innocuous; and its own inner rationale is that at some points D., J. and C. do have some features in common. But what has been damaging to the evaluation of each has been the exploitation of this grouping.

Thus they have been given the label 'The Vulgate Tradition'. The implication that a single tradition is conveyed in these three works is fallacious; for they differ frequently one from the other, and often in major matters. Worse still is the label attached by E. Schwartz and F. Jacoby, 'The Cleitarchan Vulgate'; for this indicates not only that all three derive from one source but also that that one source was Cleitarchus.[2]

The first attempt to break the spell of 'The Vulgate' was made by W. W. Tarn. Although many of his arguments were unconvincing, he seemed to me to demonstrate that 'The Vulgate Tradition' and 'The Cleitarchan Vulgate' are both myths of a simplistic kind. Two of his conclusions may be quoted. 'How two such totally different historians as D. and C., with such different points of view and such different main portraits of A, ever got bracketed together is very hard to understand.' 'There never was any such thing as an Alexander-vulgate or Cleitarchan vulgate, exhibited by D., C. and J.'[3] But it then became incumbent on Tarn to provide his own analysis and identify the sources of each work. Here he failed lamentably. His analysis was too superficial (he analysed only one chapter of D.), and the sources he identified included two—'The Mercenaries Source' and 'The Peripatetic Tradition'—which were not mentioned in ancient literature and have not been accepted in modern literature either.[4]

A younger generation of writers, reacting against the work of Tarn, have thrown out the good with the bad. What is worse, they have not only resumed 'The Vulgate Tradition' but have also introduced 'The Vulgate Sources', by which is meant not, as one would expect, 'the sources of the vulgate tradition' but the 'vulgate' accounts themselves. And worst of all, some writers have lost the origin of the term 'vulgate', and they have included among 'the vulgate sources' P*A*, the *Metz Epitome* and almost anything which is not Arrian.[5] The final step is to match the entire array against Arrian and see how he stands up to the assault, if at all. And as the name of Cleitarchus still clings to 'The Vulgate Tradition', Cleitarchus gets the benefit of the good things which do occur in D., C., J., P*A* and the minor works concerning A. He becomes quite a gifted writer! Recently advances have been made in the studies of two of our authors. In the Budé edition of D. 17 P. Goukowsky has summarised views which he had already published in specialist articles. In particular he refuted the idea that D. excerpted throughout from Cleitarchus. 'Ainsi,' he wrote, 'de nombreux détails inconnus des autres historiens de la "Vulgate" (ou même d'Arrien) peuvent être le fruit des lectures personnelles de Diodore et provenir soit des sources historiques utilisées dans d'autres sections de la Bibliothèque soit de traités techniques.' In his Commentary on C. 3-4 J. E. Atkinson has concluded from his study of these two books (out of nominally ten but really eight) that 'Curtius used several sources' and that one of these sources 'may have been Cleitarchus'. If either one or both of them are right, as I believe they are, then the concept of 'The Vulgate' as enunciated by Schwartz and Jacoby is mistaken—and even more so the later elaborations of it. In consequence, the term 'vulgate' is not used in this book. What I attempt is an analysis of the sources of each writer separately—D., J. and C.

The need for a detailed analysis of these three Alexander-accounts has been stated often in recent years. For instance, E. N. Borza writing of Cleitarchus and Diodorus 17 remarked that 'more is needed of the order of Hammond's study of the sixteenth book [of Diodorus]', and P. Goukowsky in considering the same topic asked for 'une analyse détaillée du livre 17'.[6] And E. Badian in *Entretiens Hardt* 22 (1975) 301 noted that C. and D. were still practically untreated, and that comments on them tended to be either limited or arbitrary; and he expressed the need for a thorough investigation of each. That is, *inter alia*, the purpose of this book.

D., J. and C. are inevitably contrasted with Arrian, from whom they differ radically. 'The generally high quality of Arrian's history', wrote P. A. Stadter in his admirable study, 'is due in no small degree to a discriminating use of sources.'[7] What is more, Arrian alone of Alexander-historians stated who his sources were and why he had chosen them: namely Ptolemy and Aristobulus, because they had campaigned with A and were the most trustworthy of all the authors whose works he read. For these reasons, as well as for its 'generally high quality', Arrian's work has generally been regarded as far superior in the main to the works of the other writers on A. Indeed it has often been used as a touchstone for testing the quality individually of D., J. and C. However, the trend of recent scholarship, especially in the writings of E. Badian and A. B. Bosworth, has been to try to reverse this verdict in regard to many issues, such as A's complicity in the murder of Philip, the course of the battle of the Granicus river, the cause of the fire at Persepolis and the cause of A's death. The weakness of this trend is that its advocates have not tackled the problem of identifying the sources used by D., J. and C. Until they have done so and have shown that those sources are more trustworthy than the known sources of Arrian, there is a danger that their judgements are unduly subjective.

ALEXANDER'S LAST DAYS AS AN EXAMPLE

It will be illuminating for the reader to take now as an example the accounts of Arrian on the one hand and of D., J. and C. on the other hand which were concerned with the last days of A. For the reader will see at the outset that the differences are sharp not only between the ancient authors but also between modern scholars.

When Arrian's narrative approached the illness of A, he abbreviated and paraphrased a passage in the *King's Journal*, which he called simply αἱ βασίλειοι ἐφημερίδες (7.25.1-26.3). Plutarch had already done likewise in writing his *Life of Alexander* (76-77.1).[8] The similarity of the paraphrases confirms what we have no reason to doubt, that each was telling the truth and each was drawing independently on the same passage in the same *King's Journal*. At the end of his paraphrase Arrian commented as follows. 'The accounts of Ptolemy and Aristobulus', i.e. in their own works which Arrian preferred to those of other writers, 'were not far from this [account];[9] but others recorded remarks by A in conversation with his Companions', i.e. about the succession; and yet others attributed A's death not to a natural illness but to poisoning at the instigation of Antipater.

At the end of his paraphrase Plutarch discussed the allegation of poisoning, which most writers, he said, regarded as a fabrication. Plutarch helped to confirm Arrian's point about Aristobulus' account being 'not far from' that in the *King's Journal*; for at 75.6 he cited Aristobulus as saying that having a raging fever and an excessive thirst A drank wine, 'after which he became delirious and died on the thirtieth day of the month Daesius'. It was this excessive fever and delirium which prevented him from being able to speak. However, D., J. and C. all provided remarks allegedly uttered by A in conversation with his Companions (D. 17.117.3-4; J. 12.15; C. 10.5.1-6), and in particular his dying words (D. 17.117.4; C. 10.5.6 'suprema haec vox fuit regis, et paulo post exstinguitur'). J. and C. present the story of the poisoning as a matter of general belief or as a fact (J. 12.14; C. 10.10.14-17), while D. is more cautious (17.117.5 - 118.2).

Thus the accounts of the *King's Journal*, Aristobulus, Ptolemy, Plutarch and Arrian are totally incompatible with those of D., J. and C. In the former group Alexander was represented as speaking only of military and naval affairs and then being speechless for four days before he died; and he neither said nor did anything about the succession. The symptom too of a continuous high fever is incompatible with death by poisoning. According to the latter group Alexander retained his power of speech till the last and made astute remarks about the succession, and in particular he gave his signet-ring to Perdiccas; and the tradition that A was poisoned is treated as being worthy of serious consideration.

Which group is to be regarded as correct? Pearson, Samuel, Hamilton, Bosworth, Brunt and Lane Fox favour the latter group. They all maintain that the *King's Journal* was a forgery made in antiquity.[10] In addition, Badian and Bosworth, for instance, accept the statements of this group that A did give his royal signet-ring to Perdiccas, and Badian thinks that Perdiccas retained it until his own death. Bosworth accepts the poisoning as historical.[11] I am perhaps alone in regarding the first group as superior and in judging the *King's Journal* to be genuine. Let us look at the arguments. And let us bear in mind that until Pearson wrote his article in 1954 'it has been almost universally held that Arrian derived his version from Ptolemy, who had access to the original Diary [*King's Journal*]'.[12] It seems to me that Pearson's case for denying the genuineness of the *Journal* has been uncritically accepted by subsequent writers.

THE KING'S JOURNAL

That a *King's Journal* was kept for Philip and then for A, and that *Alexander's Journal* did record the last words and the last days of A is beyond question.[13] It was from the latter that Plutarch and Arrian believed themselves to be making their paraphrases. The fact that they had *Alexander's Journal* in front of them and were practised in assessing the genuineness or otherwise of such documents might be enough in itself to convince us that they were right.[14] Then we have the further fact that the accounts given by Aristobulus and Ptolemy (though lost to us) were judged by Arrian to be 'not far from' the account in *Alexander's Journal*. Could these two men, being contemporaries of A and close to him, have been taken in by a forgery which misrepresented the last words and the last days of A? That is to me inconceivable. On the other hand, if Aristobulus wrote from memory and if Ptolemy either used the genuine *Journal* or wrote from memory only, is it possible that the memory of each was faulty precisely in those reports which coincided by chance with the misrepresentations of the forged *Alexander's Journal* from which Plutarch and Arrian made their paraphrases? That too is really beyond belief.

It is, of course, an exciting idea that a modern scholar, operating only with paraphrased fragments, may be able to prove an ancient work to have been a forgery so ingeniously constructed that it deceived four ancient scholars (Plutarch, Arrian, Aelian, *VH* 3.23 and Athenaeus 10.434b, cited together in *FGrH* 117). But excitement is not enough; we need very strong arguments to support the idea. Hamilton listed those of Pearson's arguments which he found 'decisive', and it will be enough in this context to consider them. The first argument arises from the *Journal*'s mention of a shrine of Sarapis, the Egyptian god of healing, whom some Companions of A consulted during the night before A died. Pearson argued that the presence of such a shrine in Babylon was an anachronism, and that in consequence the *Journal* was composed only when such a shrine existed—*c.* 280 in his belief—and so was a forgery. But we have to remember that Egyptians, like Jews, may have visited and resided in Babylon in the Persian period; that A was deeply impressed by the Egyptian priests of Zeus Ammon, practised Egyptian forms of worship in Egypt, and had Egyptian seers in his entourage from 331 onwards (C. 4.10.4); and that he intended his body to be embalmed by Egyptian priests when he lay dying at Babylon. Thus it is probable rather than improbable that a shrine of Sarapis should have existed in Babylon in 323.[15] On the other hand, if a shrine of Sarapis was such a glaring anachronism as Pearson and others have supposed, would a forger have made the stupid error of introducing it into his account? Would not Peithon, Attalus, Demophon, Peucestas, Cleomenes, Menidas and/or Seleucus[16] have protested that there was no such deity in Babylon and they never went near such a shrine?

The second 'decisive' argument cited by Hamilton is that Arrian seems to mention the *King's Journal* as 'a familiar literary work'. Arrian passes no such comment. It is a matter of modern taste whether one considers such sentences as 'next day he bathed again, sacrificed the appointed sacrifices and after sacrificing continued in constant fever' to be the mark of a literary work rather than a factual diary of events and sayings.[17] Rareness of citation from it is another point; but this applies equally to a genuine *Journal* and to a forged *Journal* supposed to be genuine. We have to remember the difference between the research scholar and the ancient writer. The latter did not go back in the primary material, if he could avoid it by using a literary account, and particularly so in the case of a *Journal* which covered in diary form the thirteen years of A's exceedingly active reign and was packed with original documents. Next, it is argued that 'the other references to the *Journal* do not suggest an official document'. Here again we must keep a historical perspective. Modern scholars may not be interested in A's hunting, sleeping, drinking, illness and health, but there is no doubt that in the fourth century B.C. the royal hunts were of the greatest importance (cf. the fresco at Vergina and C. 8.1.14-16), that the royal banqueting and the heavy drinking at banquets with the consequent daytime sleeping were normal at court (cf. the palace of Vergina[18] and the affair of Cleitus), and that the last days of such a king were important to his followers. Lastly, 'it is surprising, if Ptolemy used the *Journal*, that he failed to mention his use of so reliable a source'. This too applies to a forged *Journal* as much as to a genuine one; and again it rests on the tacit assumption that an ancient writer behaved like a modern writer who is continually citing and evaluating his sources. In any case we possess very little indeed of Ptolemy's own writings.

More general aspects of such a forgery may be considered. It had to be very different from the real *King's Journal* in order to make the undertaking worthwhile; and the undertaking was enormous, to construct bogus diaries for thirteen years of intense and documented activities—a work perhaps twice the length of Winston Churchill's *Second World War.* To fake spurious but plausible reports, letters, orders and documents was by itself a daunting task. Bosworth tried to evade this difficulty by postulating a truncated Diary, a mere fragment covering 'the last few months'. But this only creates difficulty. 'What is this fragment?' people would say when it was published, 'Where is the rest of the *Journal* if this fragment is from it?'[19]

When was the fake *Journal* produced? Pearson opted for *c.* 280 when men's memories might have become dim. But who was interested then? Surely the real *King's Journal* was already known and even written about by 280? Bosworth went to the other extreme. He had the forger write and publish between June 323 and winter 322-321. As this early date was incompatible with Pearson's chief argument, namely that the worship of Sarapis did not arise at Babylon until much later, Bosworth argued—as Bickerman had already done and I have done here—that such a worship was practised at the time of A's death in Babylon. Forger though he was, Bosworth's faker got that right. But could a forger have imposed his version on the minds of the Macedonians in the very year after A's death? Hundreds of leading Macedonians knew the true facts, their memories were green and they would surely have rejected a false version. At that time the corpse of A and his possessions were still in Babylon, and the real *Journal* was there. It could have been used at once to expose the forgery.[20]

Who was the forger? Bosworth proposed Eumenes. Now Eumenes and his team of secretaries had already composed the entire *Journal* since A's accession. Did Eumenes in the twelvemonth after A's death sit down and compose a false version of A's last few months? Any secretary or anyone having access to the *Journal* could have exposed him at once as a falsifier. Pearson was more subtle. He made use of a little-known writer called Strattis of Olynthus (*FGrH* [*Die Fragmente der griechischen Historiker*] 118), who wrote three works according to the Suda. One of these works, as cited by Pearson, was 'five books about *The Journal of Alexander*', περὶ τῶν Ἀλεξάνδρου ἐφημερίδων βιβλία πέντε.[21] This title is found also in Athenaeus 10.434b, where we are told that Eumenes of Cardia and Diodotus of Erythrae wrote up *The Journal of Alexander,* ἐν ταῖς ἐφημερίσιν αὐτοῦ (i.e. Alexander). At first sight one would make two deductions: that *The Journal of Alexander* was very lengthy and that Strattis being an Olynthian wrote his commentary before *c.* 300, since he took his citizenship as an adult from a city which Philip had destroyed in 348. Not so Pearson. He supposes that the forger used 'a faked author's name for a fictitious diary' which he was publishing *c.* 280; so he chose to call himself 'Strattis of Olynthus'. This

double supposition is a strain on anyone's belief. Further, why did the forger choose to call himself an Olynthian? Would not people have wondered at the time: 'Who is this Strattis, no youngster but a man of 86+, as he became a citizen at Olynthus?' It is more in accordance with the dictates of reason to believe that there was a real Strattis and that he did write five books of commentaries on the real *Journal of Alexander,* than to suppose with Pearson that an unknown man wrote five books about a (?his own) faked *Journal of Alexander* and assumed a faked name and an unlikely citizenship *c.* 280.[22]

Let us limit ourselves to a real *Journal of Alexander.* The corpse and the possessions of the deceased king were to be taken to Aegeae, but they were intercepted and removed by Ptolemy to Memphis and then to Alexandria (Paus. 1.6.3). Among them surely was the *Journal.* Ptolemy himself used it in writing his history and he may have given favoured persons access to it; perhaps Strattis of Olynthus was one. The original or a copy of it went, one imagines, into the Library of Alexandria; and copies were available later for Plutarch, Arrian, Aelian and Athenaeus to consult. On the other hand, early writers such as Cleitarchus did not have access to the *Journal.*

If the conclusion is correct that what Arrian and Plutarch were paraphrasing was a passage in a genuine *King's Journal,* then the reader will see that Arrian and Plutarch in this instance are to be regarded as dependable and D., J. and C. as not. For the source of Arrian and Plutarch was a factual record of the day-by-day happenings in which the King was involved, made at the time and not intended for publication. He will see also that, since Ptolemy's account and Aristobulus' account were 'not far from' the version of the *King's Journal,* Ptolemy and Aristobulus were dependable authors in this instance, and that Arrian's choice of them as participants at the time and as trustworthy writers was justified. On the other hand, D., J. and C. provided items of fiction; not because they invented the items, but because they obtained them from one or more sources who were writing fiction or propaganda. The points which D., J. and C. have in common evidently came from a common source of this kind, one who wrote probably before the detailed accounts of Aristobulus and Ptolemy were published and so had a free field for invention. This source must have been a writer who was popular in the time of D., J. and C. As we shall see later, he was probably Cleitarchus, who was regarded by ancient authors as having a lively style but little or no regard for the truth. Thus the reader will have no hesitation in discarding as unhistorical the giving of the signet-ring to Perdiccas, the sayings of A about the succession and the alleged poisoning of A; and in rejecting the views of Badian and Bosworth, for instance, which were based on their belief that D., J. and C. were in this instance more dependable than Arrian.

This example provides an introduction to the methods which any historian of Alexander should employ. Whenever differences occur between the five main accounts, the historian has to consider which version has the best claim to be accepted as historical. Some writers have made their own arbitrary choice; and they have then written a life of A which is built around their own concept of what A was like and what in their opinion he would have done. But if one is concerned first to ascertain what A did and what in some cases he wrote or said, then one has to analyse the sources of the various accounts and determine as far as possible which accounts are dependable and which are not at each stage. Then it is the results of the analysis and the determination which lead to an understanding of A's actions and from them to some concept of his personality. The chapters which follow are, it is hoped, a contribution to that understanding.

Notes

1. As Tarn 4 remarked, 'it is impossible to suppose that a source can be found for everything given by our extant writers'.

2. Epigrammatically expressed by Jacoby in *RE* [*Real-Encyclopädie*] 11.630 and repeated in *FGrH* [*Die Fragmente der grieschischen Historiker*]: 'die vulgata die im wesentlichen ein immer wieder bearbeiteten Kleitarchos ist'.

3. 132.

4. Most recently Atkinson 67, referring to earlier work especially of Brunt and Badian.

5. As two examples of many I mention Brunt and Bosworth. 'It is conventional to refer to the accounts of Alexander which do not depend on Ptolemy, Aristobulus and Nearchus as "the vulgate"' (Brunt xxxii). Bosworth *C* 28f. began by defining 'the so-called vulgate tradition, the tradition common to Diodorus 17, Curtius Rufus and Justin', but he then went on to include under this heading P*A* at 159, 271 (with *Frag. Sabb.*), 329, 331 and 345 (but not consistently since at 263 he set P*A* apart from 'the vulgate sources'). His views on the vulgate were further developed in *EH* [*Ecclesiastical Hierarchy*] 22 (1975).

6. Borza 44f. and Goukowsky in *REA* [*Revue des études anciennes*] 71 (1969) 337.

7. *Arrian of Nicomedia* (Chapel Hill, 1980) 148.

8. The abbreviations are obvious, since the sacrifices and the orders would have been described in the original, and since the talk with Nearchus con-

tained A listening to Nearchus (in P*A*) as well as A giving detailed instructions to the naval officers (Arr. 7.25.4). For Plutarch and Arrian were interested not in those matters but in what Plutarch called succinctly τὰ περὶ τὴν νόσον.

9. Having given his paraphrase of the primary narrative, Arrian went on to note how the secondary accounts were related to this narrative: those of Ptolemy and Aristobulus were close to it, and others were different from it. Thus the meaning of οὐ πόρρω δὲ τούτων in this context is clearly 'not far from it', as at Arr. 5.20.9 οὐ πόρρω τοῦ ἀληθοῦς is 'not far from the truth'. Robson's translation in the Loeb edition 'beyond this neither Ptolemaeus nor Aristobulus have recorded' is incorrect; for the length of their work is irrelevant. See L. Pearson, 'The diary and the letters of Alexander the Great', *Historia* 3 (1954-55) 437f.; one of his translations, 'no detail in addition to these', will not do, because τούτων simply resumes the preceding account. Bosworth *C* 23f. and n. 29 supports Robson.

10. Pearson 194f.; A. E. Samuel, 'Alexander's royal journals', *Historia* 14 (1965) 1ff.; Hamilton 210; Bosworth, 'The death of Alexander', *CQ* [*Classical Quarterly*] n.s. 21 (1971) 117-123; Brunt xxvi-xxviii; R. Lane Fox, *Alexander the Great* (London, 1973) 464ff.

11. E. Badian in *Gnomon* 34 (1962) 381 ff.; Bosworth in *CQ* n.s. 21 (1971) 128 and 136; for the ring see also *EH* 138.

12. Hamilton 210.

13. So Pearson in *Historia* 3 (1954-55) 434 'there is certainly no reason to doubt that some kind of diary was kept, recording the events of each day, the king's conferences, the orders he issued, the reports he received, and so on'. It seems that Eumenes was trained first under Philip and then became chief secretary for the *Journal*. When papers were burnt, A had 'his satraps and generals everywhere send copies' for Eumenes to use, no doubt for the *Alexander-Journal* (Plut. *Eum.* 1-2). For A's orders see the remarks in Hammond, *Alex.* 48 and 57. Only events involving the king were recorded—not such things as the ultimate fate of Callisthenes A. E. Samuel, 'Alexander's royal journals', *Historia* 14 (1965) 1ff. has shown a possible source in the East from which Philip may have adopted the practice of keeping an official journal; but it may equally well have been a Macedonian invention.

14. Plutarch and Arrian use the normal phrases for direct citation; so do Aelian and Athenaeus. There

are no grounds for supposing that each of them is misleading us and really found a passage in an intermediary source.

15. Bosworth in *CQ* n.s. 21 (1971) 119f. is also critical of Pearson's argument. One should note that in the story about a man sitting on A's throne at Babylon the god in the background was Sarapis (P*A* 73.9), foreshadowing his later advice to let A die.

16. As named by Arr. 7.26.2; they are those with Python (an error for Peithon) and Seleucus in P*A* 76.9. The latter lived until 280.

17. That this was a typical sort of extract is clear from the citation by Aelian, *VH* 3.23.

18. For the banquet-rooms see R. A. Tomlinson, 'Ancient Macedonian symposia', *Ancient Macedonia* I (Thessaloniki, 1970) 308ff.

19. Bosworth is able to represent the citations and references to the *Journal* as restricted to the last few months only if two emendations are made to the text; see Hammond, *Alex.* 298 with n. 131.

20. As Pearson remarked in *Historia* 3 (1954-55) 347, 'at such an early date a forgery would readily have been detected'.

21. *FGrH* no. 118, with variant readings. Pearson in *Historia* 3 (1954-55) 437 proposed an alternative translation: 'Five books of diaries about the exploits of Alexander'. But this is a very unlikely usage, because the normal term is 'the diary of A', meaning about A, and not 'the diary about the things of A'.

22. Though in a make-believe world I suppose anything may be possible.

Bibliography

Atkinson, J. E. *A Commentary on Q. Curtius Rufus' Historiae Alexandri Magni Books 3 and 4* (Amsterdam, 1980).

Badian, E. 'The eunuch Bagoas', *CQ* n.s. 8 (1958) 144.

'The death of Parmenio', *TAPA* [*Transactions of the American Philological Association*] 91 (1960) 324.

'The death of Philip II', *Phoenix* 17 (1963) 244.

'The date of Clitarchus', *PACA* [*Proceedings of the African Classical Association*] 8 (1965) 5.

'Agis III', *Hermes* 95 (1967) 170.

Borza, E. N. 'Cleitarchus and Diodorus' account of Alexander', *PACA* 11 (1968) 25.

Bosworth, A. B. 'The death of Alexander the Great', *CQ* n.s. 21 (1971) 112.

'Arrian and the Alexander Vulgate', *Fondation Hardt Entretiens* 22: *Alexandre le Grand, image et realité* (Geneva, 1975).

'Alexander and Ammon', *Festschrift F. Schachermeyr* (Berlin, 1977) 51.

A Historical Commentary of Arrian's History of Alexander I, on Books I-III (Oxford, 1980).

Brunt, P. A. 'Persian accounts of Alexander's campaigns', *CQ* n.s. 12 (1962) 141.

'Alexander, Barsine and Heracles', *RFIC* 103 (1975) 22.

Arrian I in the Loeb ed. (London, 1976).

Goukowsky, P. 'Clitarque seul? Remarques sur les sources du livre xvii de Diodore de Sicile', *REA* 71 (1969) 320.

Hamilton, J. R. 'Cleitarchus and Aristobulus', *Historia* 10 (1961) 448. *Plutarch, Alexander: a Commentary* (Oxford, 1969).

Hamilton, J. R. 'Cleitarchus and Diodorus 17', *Festschrift F. Schachermeyr* (Berlin, 1977) 126.

Hammond, N. G. L. *Alexander the Great: King, Commander and Statesman* (New Jersey, 1980; London, 1981).

Jacoby, F. *Die Fragmente der griechischen Historiker* II (Berlin, 1929).

Pearson, L. 'The diary and letters of Alexander the Great', *Historia* 3 (1954/5) 249.

Samuel, A. E. 'Alexander's Royal Journals', *Historia* 14 (1965) 1.

Tarn, W. W. *Alexander the Great,* I and II (Cambridge, 1948).

Joseph Roisman (essay date 1984)

SOURCE: Roisman, Joseph. "Ptolemy and His Rivals in His History of Alexander." *Classical Quarterly* 34, no. 2 (1984): 373-85.

[*In the following essay, Roisman defends Ptolemy's history of Alexander against charges that it is politically biased for the ancient author's benefit.*]

Scholarly opinion about Ptolemy Soter's history of Alexander has been far from unanimous. Not long ago Ptolemy was held to stand in the first rank of ancient historians. His history was described as brilliant, rational, straightforward, and exhaustive, while he himself was proclaimed a 'second Thucydides'.[1] In recent years, however, Ptolemy's reputation has seriously declined. His shortcomings, acknowledged also by his admirers, have been stressed and extensively analysed. Fritz Schachermeyr clearly reflected current opinion when he equated a 'version from the *Hauptquartier*'s circles' with a lie, a fraud, and an intentional omission.[2] The purpose of this paper is to examine the recent reassessment of the nature and the aims of Ptolemy's work.

The date and the aim of Ptolemy's history are interrelated in modern research. The assumption is that if we knew when the work was written we should be able to appreciate its purpose. Not too long ago it was largely believed that Ptolemy must have written the history towards the end of his reign, when, presumably, he had time at his disposal. In those years, it was reasoned, there was no political urgency or gain in composing a work on Alexander. The main purpose of Ptolemy's history was to refute or correct certain widely accepted and romantic accounts about Alexander.[3]

What seems to vitiate this interpretation is its basic premiss: the purpose of the work is deduced from its alleged date and vice versa. From the assumption that Ptolemy wrote the history late in life it is deduced that he had nothing to gain thereby. Hence, it follows that he must have wanted to set the record straight as regards the late king. Similarly, if he planned to criticize other traditions, what better time for doing so than the peaceful period towards the end of his reign? But the thesis is flawed, and not only because of its circular nature. Active politicians did not necessarily write histories and memoirs at the end of their careers; they often produced them early on, fully aware of their political value. Moreover, the story of Alexander did not cease to be of political relevance after 323. It has been shown that friendship with, and service under, the Macedonian king carried weight long after Alexander's death.[4]

Thus an alternative theory was put forward, namely, that Ptolemy wrote his history at the height of the war of the diadochs. Such a context throws light on his seemingly biased treatment of persons who became his rivals after the death of Alexander.[5] Yet it seems that this interpretation suffers from flaws similar to those of its counterpart. Once again the date of the work is inferred from its apparent character, which is explained, in turn, by the work's time of publication. Still, focusing the attention on what is called 'the bias of Ptolemy' is fairly new and deserves investigation. Hence it may be worth examining once more if, or to what extent, Ptolemy distorted facts to promote his political interests.

E. Badian called to notice the 'mixture of *suppressio veri* and *suggestio falsi* . . . in his [i.e. Ptolemy's] treatment of character and politics'.[6] His observation was elaborated in an influential and much quoted study by R. M. Errington which aimed at demonstrating Ptolemy's biased writing through his treatment of his chief rivals in the wars of the successors.[7] The most serious distortions are said to involve the person of Perdiccas.

When Arrian deals with Alexander's siege of Thebes he stresses the wish of the king for reconciliation as opposed to the unwise stubbornness of the Thebans (*Anabasis* 1. 7). Then, we are informed, Perdiccas attacked the enemy on his own initiative and drew Alexander into battle, which ended catastrophically for the Thebans (*Anab.* 1. 8. 1-2).

Arrian may have shown caution in his description of the events. In his narrative Perdiccas' assault is prefaced by the remark: 'But Ptolemy son of Lagus says . . .' (1. 8. 1). Diodorus Siculus, on the other hand, suggests that Perdiccas, rather than initiating the hostilities with the Thebans, joined the battle in its midst, and did so under a direct order of the king (17. 12. 3). It was concluded, then, that Ptolemy deliberately changed the course of the battle so that Perdiccas would be made responsible for Thebes' destruction, which shocked the Greek world.[8]

This is the sole instance where Ptolemy is charged with actually lying to his readers concerning Perdiccas' career. Other distortions were traced in Ptolemy's practice of omitting facts which could have enhanced the reputation of Perdiccas. Thus Perdiccas' name was not found in the list of casualties of the battle of Gaugamela. Ptolemy did not mention that Perdiccas was already a *somatophylax* in 330, nor that he was in charge of the siege of a Sogdianian city. He ignored Perdiccas' and his own roles in the notorious Cleitus affair, and he said nothing of Perdiccas' promotion to Hephaestion's high position in 324 or his receiving the royal signet ring from the dying Alexander.[9] The reason for the above distortions and omissions is not hard to guess. Not long after Alexander's death Perdiccas waged a war against Ptolemy, the satrap of Egypt, and invaded his country. As it happened, Perdiccas was murdered by his officers and Ptolemy's rule was saved. But Perdiccas' invasion exacerbated certain problems which faced Ptolemy in Egypt. The satrap sought recognition as the legitimate lord of the land, that is, as a true successor to Alexander. He also needed Macedonians and Greeks to serve in his army and to populate Alexandria. This provided the background for Ptolemy's biased history of Alexander. It was a work which glorified and flattered Alexander and his army, exaggerated Ptolemy's contribution to the campaign, and spoke ill of, or minimized, the achievements of the opponents of Ptolemy. Ptolemy, in sum, wrote a history of Alexander to be used in the diadochs' war of propaganda.[10]

However, a thorough examination of Ptolemy's 'biased account' seems to suggest that the author must have been a master of subtle propaganda, of a propaganda indeed so subtle that its usefulness may be doubted. The account of the siege of Thebes is a case in point. Arrian's narrative leaves no room for doubt. Responsibility for the disaster in Thebes lay with the Thebans themselves, or more specifically, the Theban exiles who returned to the city and their supporters (*Anab.* 1. 7. 1, 11). The massacre of the Theban population was mainly the doing of Alexander's Boeotian allies, who are also made responsible for the decision to destroy the city and to enslave its inhabitants (1. 8. 8; 9. 9-10). Perdiccas' blame, therefore, for the tragic fate of the city was practically negligible.

Moreover, a close examination of the course of the battle in Arrian's narrative shows that Alexander sent in his main force under circumstances which were only indirectly associated with Perdiccas' attack. Perdiccas did, in fact, commence fighting with the assistance of Amyntas, son of Andromenes (1. 8. 1 ff.). To prevent their being cut off Alexander sent in the archers and the Agrianians but still did not involve the *agema* and the *hypaspistai*. Meanwhile, however, Perdiccas was wounded and carried off the field; his role in the affair was over. The rescue-force pursued the Thebans, but only after it was pushed back and the Thebans threatened to destroy it did Alexander involve his main army, which defeated the enemy.[11] Thus a close examination of the course of the battle considerably reduces Perdiccas' responsibility for its consequences. But it is unlikely that many readers of Ptolemy's history would have paid close attention to such minute details, or concluded from the description of the battle, or the whole work, that Thebes' destruction originated in Perdiccas' charge.

Whatever the date of Ptolemy's history was, not many of Perdiccas' soldiers would have forsaken him or his memory because of his (supposed?) initiative in Thebes. In fact the Macedonians felt no remorse for the fate of the city, while the Greeks held no one but Alexander responsible for its destruction.[12] If Ptolemy lied about Perdiccas' role in the attack (and did not record the battle as he remembered it), he did so primarily to exculpate Alexander from the charge of initiating the battle rather than to damage the reputation of his rival. The bias, if any, was pro-Alexander, not anti-Perdiccas.

The rest of the so-called Ptolemaic distortions consist of omission of information that could have contributed to Perdiccas' fame. It has been maintained reasonably that it is impossible to deduce bias from omission when the work is not extant in its entirety.[13] Alternatively, the omissions can be blamed on Arrian's careless use of the history of Ptolemy, or possibly on his citing a faulty

copy of the work. Yet such suggestions seem to offer too easy a solution. It is necessary to discuss in detail whether, in fact, Ptolemy concealed information about Perdiccas' career, and if so, to what end.

Ptolemy is said to have cheated Perdiccas out of glory by omitting his name from the list of officers wounded during the battle of Gaugamela. But the fact is that it is impossible to determine what source Arrian was using in the *Anabasis* 3. 15. 2 where the casualties are mentioned. H. Strasburger suggested the intervention of Arrian or of a source of inferior standing in this passage.[14] Diodorus (17. 61. 3), who mentioned Perdiccas, also remarked that there were other wounded commanders. He did not name them and it is not likely that either he or his source omitted them deliberately. The omission of Perdiccas' name, then, could have been due either to literary considerations, or to a slip of memory, or to the fact that Arrian was using an alternative source.[15]

Ptolemy is also blamed for not reporting that Perdiccas had been one of Alexander's *somatophylakes* since at least 330. Yet Arrian, and probably his sources, did not bother to record the occasions for the bestowal of this honorific title, save for two exceptions: the case of Ptolemy himself, who might be expected to report such a fact significant to his career, and of Peucestas, who received the title in remarkable and famous circumstances.[16]

Curtius Rufus (7. 6. 19-23) tells of a town of the Memaceni in Sogdiana that refused to surrender to Alexander. The king sent Perdiccas and Meleager to besiege it, went to Cyropolis to complete its capture, rejoined his generals and destroyed the city. Curtius is the only source to record the mission of Perdiccas, and the failure to refer to it in Arrian was attributed to a deliberate omission on the part of Ptolemy.[17]

However, a comparison between the versions of Arrian and Curtius suggests that the latter's account (or his source) is not free from flaws. The following is a summary of the parallel passages in both sources:

Arrian

4. 2. 2: Alexander sent Craterus to Cyropolis

4. 2. 3-4: the king captured Gaza

4. 2. 4: Alexander took two more cities

4. 2. 5-6: Alexander dispatched cavalry, which surprised fugitives from two other cities

4. 3. 1-4: the king captured Cyropolis after penetrating its walls through a dry riverbed; was struck with a stone

4. 3. 5: Alexander captured a seventh city

4. 3. 6: war with the locals had resumed

Curtius

7. 6. 16: Alexander sent Craterus to Cryopolis ibid.: the king took another city

7. 6. 17-18: the Memaceni revolted and killed Alexander's fifty horse embassy

7. 6. 19: Alexander ordered Perdiccas and Meleager to besiege the Memaceni while he joined Craterus

7. 6. 20-2: the king destroyed Cyropolis and returned to the Memaceni, where he fought hard and was struck with a stone

7. 6. 23: the walls were undermined and the city was taken

7. 6. 24: war with the locals had resumed

Since Curtius and Arrian are our only sources for the events, it is difficult to decide whose account is more accurate. A compromise between the versions may be attained if the Memaceni are identified with one of the two cities which according to Arrian (4. 2. 4) were captured after the fall of Gaza.[18] But few details of Curtius' account of the siege of the Memaceni make it likely that the author is dealing with what Arrian records as the battle of Cyropolis. Thus the Memaceni lost their city after 'cuniculo . . . suffossa moenia' (7. 6. 23), while in Arrian's narrative Cyropolis was captured after its penetration by way of a dry riverbed. Moreover, it was during the siege of Memaceni (Curtius) or Cyropolis (Arrian) that Alexander was hit by a stone. Now both historians agree that Cyropolis was besieged by Craterus and not by Perdiccas and Meleager. The conclusion must be either that Curtius confused the siege of Cyropolis with that of another city which is otherwise unknown, or that Arrian/Ptolemy not only ignored Perdiccas' mission in Sogdiana but also confused the battle of Cyropolis with another operation. I suggest that the first alternative is the more likely. There is even an indirect proof of Arrian's general credibility in describing the events under discussion. The town of Gaza, which is mentioned in his report alone, has been identified with a locality named *Ghazaq* in the vicinity of *Kurkath*-Cyropolis.[19]

It is hard to know how Curtius obtained the story of the siege of the Memaceni by Perdiccas and Meleager. It could be that their mission involved the submission of one of the seven Sogdianian cities which Arrian chose to allude to only generally in 4. 2. 3-4. 3. 5. If so, the omission of their names indicates not malice but literary considerations. For even if we accept Curtius' version as authentic,[20] it is evident that he did not regard the incident as significant, and hence its omission would not have been likely to damage Perdiccas' reputation.

Ptolemy, allegedly, also used the so-called Cleitus affair for the denigration of Perdiccas. Curtius (8. 1. 45-6) says that Ptolemy, Perdiccas, Lysimachus and Leonnatus tried to restrain the raging king before he killed Cleitus. Arrian's account of the affair is full of *legomena,* so that it is difficult to determine the identity of his source. But he gives two, slightly different, versions of the last phases of the quarrel. One has Alexander checked by his companions (4. 8. 8). The other, based on Aristobulus, maintains that Ptolemy took the drunken Cleitus out of the royal tent (4. 8. 9). If the first version is Ptolemy's—and this cannot really be proven—, then Ptolemy omitted not only Perdiccas' name but also his own. It was suggested that Ptolemy was not proud of his part in the affair and preferred to omit his own name and also play down the role of others.[21] But why would Ptolemy conceal his part in the incident? In both Arrian's and Curtius' accounts he plays a positive, restraining role in his attempt to prevent the coming catastrophe. Conversely, if Perdiccas' participation in the banquet could have damaged his reputation, why was he not mentioned among those present? It seems that the problem lies not with Perdiccas' real or imaginary role in the affair but with the extant evidence for the episode. Ptolemy's version is lost and it is impossible to determine what it included or lacked. If Ptolemy dealt with the story, it is reasonable to assume that he emphasized the provocative behaviour of Cleitus which led to his doom. That, probably, was the essence of his report and not the absence of Perdiccas' name from his narrative.

The most significant omission concerning Perdiccas' career is said to be found in Arrian's statement (*Anab.* 7. 14. 10) that Alexander did not appoint a new chiliarch of the *hetairoi* cavalry after the death of Hephaestion, so that his friend's name might not be taken from his unit. Diodorus (18. 3. 4) and Plutarch (*Eumenes* 1), among others, state expressly that Perdiccas inherited the office of Hephaestion. Since the incumbent of the office was second in command to the king, it was maintained that Ptolemy concealed the information to undermine Perdiccas' later claim of supremacy. To this may be added the fact that the story of Alexander handing Perdiccas his signet ring on his death-bed is told by, e.g., Diodorus (17. 117. 3), Curtius (10. 5. 4), and Justin (12. 15. 2), but not by Arrian.[22]

Not everyone accepted the above reports as authentic. It was argued that Perdiccas was the commander of the cavalry *de facto* but not in name, and the story of the ring has been labelled unhistorical.[23] But the main reason given for the rejection of these traditions was the fact that Arrian does not cite them—a not particularly convincing argument. Arrian's silence is undeniable, and should be accounted for. It was suggested, then, that the blame lay with Ptolemy, who was both Arrian's source and an enemy of the chiliarch.[24] Such an assumption, however, calls for at least two additional inferences: (*a*) that Arrian zealously reproduced the statements and the silences of his main sources; (*b*) that he ignored other traditions concerning Perdiccas either because of the silence of his sources, or because he was slack in collecting additional information. By themselves, these are not unlikely conjectures. When he chose to, Arrian doubted information about Alexander since it was not written down by his main sources, and his over-reliance on Ptolemy and Aristobulus led him to some errors of judgement.[25] But perhaps the omission of Perdiccas' ascent to power in 324/3 should not be attributed to Arrian's usual handling of his sources. Perdiccas became pre-eminent towards the end of Alexander's reign. This period in Alexander's life is recorded in the seventh book of the *Anabasis,* which is somewhat different from the rest of the work.

It seems that Arrian intended Book Seven of the *Anabasis* to be a proper conclusion to the story of Alexander, interwoven with his own reflections on the hero. The narrative, which records just one campaign (7. 15. 1-3), leads the reader to Alexander's unavoidable death, with particular emphasis on Alexander's behaviour and character. Accordingly, the philosophical features of the *Anabasis* are salient and Arrian's intervention in the course of the narrative is highly visible.[26] Such an approach called for a change in the use of the sources. Book Seven includes an unusual number of *legomena,* while Ptolemy and Aristobulus are cited only selectively.[27] Thus Ptolemy is mentioned three times only in Book Seven as an authority, twice for the purpose of refuting traditions which were not recorded in his work, and a third time to mark a point in his narrative.[28] This is, I believe, a valuable indication of how little the book relies on him. Aristobulus, on the other hand, is mentioned sixteen times and is Arrian's authority, *inter alia,* for Alexander's meeting with the Chaldeans, his preparations for the Arabian campaign, the sailing on the Euphrates, the story of the man who sat on Alexander's throne, and many more details.[29] Arrian, then, must have relied only sparingly on Ptolemy in Book Seven. The bulk of the narrative appears to come from Aristobulus and the subsidiary sources.

If the analysis of his sources in Book Seven is correct so far, Arrian's silence concerning Perdiccas' prominence should not necessarily be attributed to the vindictiveness of Ptolemy. It is equally possible that Arrian used other sources, such as Aristobulus, who seemed to have no known reason to damage Perdiccas' reputation, but who, nevertheless, did not mention the stories of Perdiccas' inheritance of Hephaestion's chiliarchy or Alexander's ring.[30] Arrian's silence, therefore, is a poor indication of any bias on the part of Ptolemy. As far as Perdiccas' ascent is concerned, it may very

well reflect Arrian's literary preferences rather than his source's ill will.[31]

So far the present investigation has tried to call into question instances where Ptolemy was said to treat Perdiccas unfairly. But the issue of Ptolemy's anti-Perdiccan bias must be examined from yet another perspective, namely, its purpose and/or its influence on Ptolemy's readers. For Ptolemy's anti-Perdiccan campaign would have been most effective and necessary when his reign was exposed to a danger from that direction. It is important, then, to discuss briefly the nature of their relationship after the death of Alexander the Great.

Our sources indicate clear signs of dissension between Ptolemy and Perdiccas only in 321, when Antipater and Craterus wished to ally themselves with Ptolemy against Perdiccas, who seemed to have wanted Macedon to himself.[32] Earlier, in Babylon, Ptolemy and Perdiccas may have disputed on the way to rule Alexander's empire.[33] But this rift between them, possibly the first—if rift it was—was soon healed, as proved by Ptolemy's support of the regent Perdiccas against the challenges of Meleager (Curtius 10. 7. 16). Pausanias charges Ptolemy with eliminating Cleomenes, the former ruler of Egypt, because of his ties with Perdiccas (1. 6. 3). But since Pausanias' account is not free from errors or difficulties of interpretation, it is uncertain whether Cleomenes was murdered for his contacts with Perdiccas or for his hold on the treasury and other sources of local power.[34] There is also no assurance that Ptolemy's subsequent annexation of Cyrene was done against Perdiccas' express wishes.[35] Arrian (*Succ.* 16-19) and Diodorus (18. 19-21), who deal extensively with the conquest of Cyrene, say nothing of Perdiccas' resistance to Ptolemy's policy. The first overt breach in their relationship followed the 'snatching' of the body of Alexander, which took place at the beginning of 321.[36] Ptolemy's growing power and independence, the bitter fighting in Asia Minor, and the conflict with Antipater, directed Perdiccas' steps toward Egypt. At the beginning of 320 Perdiccas invaded the country and met his death near Memphis by the hands of his lieutenants. No source reports that the soldiers of Perdiccas lamented his loss. In fact Ptolemy had no difficulty in persuading them to change their allegiance from the late general to Pithon, who conspired against him.[37]

Perdiccas' disappearance from the political scene seems to have made but scant impression on the Greeks and the Macedonians. Till 320 he was a prime mover in the region. His death left his brother, Alcestas, his brother-in-law, Attalus, and his friend, Eumenes, who fought for themselves and not for his memory. Indeed, when unrest is reported among Perdiccas' former soldiers, it was due to their demand for *chremata* and not to their loyalty to the memory of their former master.[38] For unlike Alexander, or even Ptolemy, Perdiccas had no *Nachleben*. The reputation he left of having been a hard and violent man evoked no sentiments of political value.[39] Indeed, after his brother's defeat Alcestas was deserted by his Macedonians and had to rely on the loyalty of the Pisidians for his survival.[40]

Thus the period of open conflict between Ptolemy and Perdiccas, during which it would have been most profitable to slander Perdiccas, lasted two years at the most. Was Ptolemy's history written between 321 and 320? These dates seem to be rejected even by scholars who ascribe contemporary political bias to his work.[41] What was the purpose of such history? Were the Macedonians, or the Greeks of Alexandria, so agitated by Ptolemy's treatment of Perdiccas that they consequently stood by Ptolemy or moved over to his side? It is not likely that many soldiers took their arms and deserted to Ptolemy's camp if they could not find mention in his book of Perdiccas' succeeding Hephaestion or receiving Alexander's ring. The distortions associated with Ptolemy's work were likely to influence only a small number of people who were anxious to damage Perdiccas' cause by fair means or foul. It is doubtful that the prospective audience of Ptolemy fitted such a category. It is also worth remembering that Arrian, largely relying on Ptolemy, is the only source to record Perdiccas' participation in the battles of Alexander north of Macedonia, in Granicus, in Halicarnassus, and at the Persian Gates. Arrian is also the only authority to report Perdiccas' command over one-fifth of Alexander's army in Sogdiana and half of the charging force in the attack on the city of the Malli.[42] Why Ptolemy chose to record these facts and to conceal others is unclear. His bias must have been highly selective or erratic.

Another contemporary figure who is said to suffer from Ptolemy's history is Aristonous.[43] His name is not mentioned among the combatants who saved Alexander from the Malli, and the fact that he was triarch on the Indus and a *somatophylax* was recorded by Nearchus and Aristobulus but not by Ptolemy. Again the omission is explained by political motives. Aristonous' speech quashed Ptolemy's proposal of forming a group of marshals to succeed Alexander, and he also fought for Perdiccas against the kings of Cyprus, who were the allies of Ptolemy.[44]

The omissions, however, can be interpreted differently. Curtius (9. 5. 15) names Alexander's saviours in the Mallian town as Peucestas, Leonnatus, and Aristonous. All were wounded, he says, except for Timaeus, who lost his life. Arrian names the defenders of the king as Peucestas and Leonnatus, and Abreas, who died in the battle (6. 10. 1). Later he adds that historians agree about Peucestas' participation but not on that of Leon-

natus or Abreas (6. 11. 7). His evaluation of the sources' handling of the episode is still valid. Of the participants in the battle, Diodorus (17. 99. 4) mentions only Peucestas, while Plutarch adds Lymnaeus, who fell in battle (v. *Alex.* 63. 7-8), Leonnatus, and Ptolemy (*Moral.* 327b; 344d). Thus, except for Peucestas, there is no agreement over who saved Alexander. Ptolemy indeed is Arrian's source for the episode. But no ulterior motive can explain why he omitted Timaeus' name, which is mentioned only by Curtius, or Lymnaeus' name, which is mentioned only by Plutarch. The variants in the sources stemmed either from the primary sources, who gave different accounts of the affair, or from the secondary sources' treatment of these accounts. Ptolemy, then, may have given an accurate account of the episode rather than concealed Aristonous' heroism.[45]

Ptolemy cannot be held responsible for depriving Aristonous of the title *somatophylax*. Arrian's source for this detail was indeed Aristobulus (6. 28. 4), but only because the latter made a list of Alexander's bodyguards which Arrian gratefully copied. It should be noted that Aristobulus (ibid.), and not Ptolemy, was also Arrian's source for Pithon's title of bodyguard, that Pithon who was Ptolemy's chief ally in Perdiccas' camp.[46]

Nor should excessive significance be attributed to the omission of Aristonous' triarchy on the Indus. Arrian left the detailed description of that enterprise to the *Indica*. Hence no triarch is mentioned in his account of the voyage, not even Ptolemy, who according to Curtius' testimony 'scilicet gloriae suae non refragatus' (9. 5. 2; Arr. *Ind.* 18. 5).

The extensive discussion of the treatment of Perdiccas and Aristonous by Ptolemy was aimed at examining whether his work was substantially influenced by the history of his wars during the post-Alexander era.[47] I think that Ptolemy's 'distortions' do not justify such characterization. If Ptolemy's chief aims were to increase his following, to lure supporters away from his opponents, or to justify his hold over Egypt by virtue of his past services to Alexander, it is hard to see how he would have achieved these ends by recording detailed descriptions of battles and journeys (which he probably did), in which neither he nor his later rivals and friends seemed to have played a truly significant role. It may be argued that a direct approach or blatant propaganda would have exposed the historian's hidden intentions. But it is unclear why Ptolemy should wish to be discreet. For who was his audience? Surely not soldiers looking for ideals or people who needed only gentle persuasion to move to his side.[48]

If Ptolemy had other aims than writing history *qua* history, they should be sought in what his work contained rather than in what it supposedly lacked. Ptolemy's entire history is not extant, but the surviving fragments are characterized by their emphasis on military affairs and warfare, a tendency to glorify Alexander and/or justify his actions (especially the questionable ones), and by an element of autopsy which depicts the author as a successful and loyal general.[49] These general traits of the fragments were taken to reflect the original purpose of the work. The stress on the military, Arrian's matter-of-fact style, which was held to reflect that of his source, and especially his use of Ptolemy's statements and silences to refute what he called 'popular versions', created the impression that Ptolemy aimed at improving upon previous and inaccurate accounts of the exploits of Alexander.[50] But the only direct proof of Ptolemy's attempt to correct the so-called vulgate version concerned his participation in Alexander's battle with the Malli. Both Arrian (6. 11. 8) and Curtius (9. 5. 2) reject the tradition that Ptolemy saved Alexander on the basis of Ptolemy's statement that he was not with Alexander at that time. However, there is no assurance that Ptolemy denied the story of his presence in the battle *suis verbis*. Arrian and Curtius could have used his statement about his absence from the fighting to disprove the versions that claimed otherwise. But even if Ptolemy wished to deny his participation in the battle, a single example of dissent on his part is hardly an indication of the nature of the entire work.[51]

Ptolemy's inclination to idealize Alexander and absolve him from wrongdoing, while accentuating his own role in the campaign, was also interpreted as an attempt by the satrap to base the legitimacy of his rule on his relationship with Alexander. After all, Alexander was both Egypt's conqueror and Alexandria's founder, and his cult and tomb were closely associated with the cult and the state symbols of the Ptolemies.[52] It was claimed, then, that by making all marshals equal in the eyes of the king while emphasizing his own close friendship with Alexander, Ptolemy rendered his reign in Egypt legitimate.[53]

But if Ptolemy's aim was to impress his readers with proofs of his *arete* as well as his intimate relationship with Alexander, he must have disguised his purpose quite skilfully. For it is noteworthy that two episodes which could have contributed most significantly to Ptolemy's image as Alexander's close friend were absent from his work: one had Ptolemy saving Alexander from the Malli and the other had Alexander miraculously curing Ptolemy from a poisoned weapon.[54] Furthermore, as far as can be judged from Arrian's *Anabasis* or Ptolemy's fragments, the theme of Ptolemy's personal contribution to Alexander's campaign hardly dominated his work. Indeed scholars seem to exaggerate the importance of the element of autopsy in Ptolemy's history. In the *Anabasis* the tales of Ptolemy's own *erga* are hardly numerous or of pivotal

significance to the narrative. Arrian was not very likely to have omitted autobiographical portions of Ptolemy's work as immaterial to the history of Alexander. The personal accounts of Ptolemy which he had left in the *Anabasis* are of modest or little consequence to its central theme.[55] What distinguished Ptolemy's own stories from the rest of his fragments, besides their concentration on Ptolemy's exploits, was their use of minute details, some of them remarkable, others not very significant, which created an especially vivid picture of the actions of Ptolemy and Alexander. Conversely, what the autobiographical tales and the rest of Ptolemy's fragments had in common was the dominant position that they allotted to Alexander within the narrative.[56] I believe that the lively description, Ptolemy's own participation in the events (which lent them authenticity), and the strongly felt presence of Alexander encouraged rather than discouraged Arrian to incorporate Ptolemy's private stories within the *Anabasis*. The small number and the uniqueness of Ptolemy's pieces of autopsy, as well as his apparent avoidance of reporting personal stories of clear propaganda value, should caution against designating his work as an autobiography or memoir aimed at sustaining his position at home or abroad.[57]

Neither does the fact that Ptolemy depicted Alexander in most favourable terms make his history a contemporary political pamphlet. Other contemporary authors such as Chares, Onesicritus, Nearchus, Aristobulus, and probably Cleitarchus, shared his attitude toward the king. Yet their approbation of the king was not considered a propaganda ploy. Their bias, including Ptolemy's, could have stemmed from personal sentiments and the fact that they made their reputation by serving Alexander.[58] Ptolemy owed his prominence and ultimately his rule to Alexander. He could not (and certainly did not intend to) slander Alexander, minimize his achievements, or depict him as a tyrant, unless he wished to face disturbing questions concerning his own role and standing during the campaign. Hence he glossed over Alexander's faults, ironed out his failures, and often seemed to write as the spokesman of Alexander.[59] But such attributes, as well as his detailed, non-epic account of Alexander's combats and actions, could only complement rather than form the basis of Alexander's heroic stature as the last Pharaoh of Egypt and the *ktistes* of Alexandria.

What was, then, the nature of Ptolemy's history? It is my opinion that it was not the purpose of the work to strengthen Ptolemy's position in Egypt or to weaken that of his rivals. To be sure, Ptolemy could scarcely have escaped all contemporary influence. He certainly welcomed any political advantage that could be gained from the work, especially when it enhanced his reputation or interests. But to judge from his fragments and the *Anabasis* of Arrian, Ptolemy's composition was not the tool of propaganda in the sense hitherto alleged. Perhaps it would be better to leave the riddle of Ptolemy's aims unsolved as long as his work exists in its present fragmentary form. For all we know, Ptolemy could have written his history simply for the sake of writing history. If so, the time of its composition was of little political relevance.[60]

Notes

1. Restrictions of space preclude listing all of Ptolemy's 'admirers'. The best known are E. Schwartz, 'Arrianos', *RE* [*Real-Encyclopädie*] 2 (1895), 1238; F. Jacoby, *F. Gr. Hist.* II B, esp. pp. 498-500; E. Kornemann, *Die Alexandergeschichte des Konigs Ptolemaios I von Ägypten* (Leipzig, 1935), pp. 170, 208 ff., 260; W. W. Tarn, *Alexander the Great* 2 (Cambridge, 1950), pp. 1-2, 268, 443. For further readings see J. Seibert, *Alexander der Grosse* (Darmstadt, 1972), pp. 19-21. All dates in this paper are B.C.

2. *Alexander in Babylon und die Reichsordnung nach seinem Tode* (Wien, 1970), pp. 89 ff.; cf. E. Badian, 'Agis III', *Hermes* 95 (1967), 86.

3. Compare F. Jacoby, *F. Gr. Hist.* [*Die Fragmente der griechischen Historiker*] II B, pp. 499-500; H. Strasburger, *Ptolemaios und Alexander* (Leipzig, 1934), pp. 15-16; Tarn, 2. pp. 19, 43; L. Pearson, *The Lost Histories of Alexander the Great* (N.Y., 1960), pp. 152, 193, and the bibliography cited in P. Goukowsky, *Essai sur les origines du mythe d'Alexandre (336-270 av. J.-C.). I: Les origines politiques* (Nancy, 1978) (hereafter cited as Goukowsky), p. 338 n. 345.

4. H. Montgomery, *Gedanke und Tat* (Lund, 1965), p. 224; J. Seibert, *Untersuchungen zur Geschichte Ptolemaios' I* (München, 1969), pp. 152-6; esp. R. M. Errington, 'Alexander in the Hellenistic World', in *Alexandre le Grand. Image et réalité* (Fondation Hardt no. 22, Genève, 1976), pp. 137 ff. Cf. Goukowsky, pp. 75 ff.; K. Rosen, 'Politische Ziele in der frühen hellenistischen Geschichtsschreibung', *Hermes* 107 (1979), 462 ff.

5. Pearson (note 3 above), pp. 192-3, was hesitant concerning the traditional dating of Ptolemy's history. E. Badian's review of his book, *Gnomon* 36 (1962), 666, tied in the work with Ptolemy's war with Perdiccas and his taking possession of Alexander's body. In 'Alexander the Great', *CW* [*Classical World*] 65 (1971), 40, Badian dates the history at the time between the 'snatching' of the body and 308, in the context of Ptolemy's presumable ambition to become Alexander's successor.

(See, however, his remarks in ibid. p. 38 and in *Alexandre le Grand* [note 4 above], p. 36.) R. M. Errington, 'Bias in Ptolemy's History', *CQ* [*Classical Quarterly*] n.s. 19 (1969), 241, clearly related the work to the war with Perdiccas and dates it to *post* 320.

6. *Gnomon,* 36 (1962), 666.

7. 'Bias in Ptolemy's History', *CQ* n.s. 19 (1969) (hereafter cited as Errington), 232-42.

8. Errington, 237. Cf. Jacoby, *F. Gr. Hist.* II B, p. 501; H. Berve, *Das Alexanderreich auf prosopographischer Grundlage* 2 (München, 1926), p. 313; Goukowsky, p. 238 n. 344. Strasburger, *Ptolemaios und Alexander,* p. 22 sees here a typical Ptolemaic description based on 'psychological alternatives' which stresses Perdiccas' impetuousness as against Alexander's hesitation. But Alexander hesitated not at all.

9. For all these, with references, see Errington, pp. 236-8 and below. Errington notes another Ptolemaic omission: Perdiccas' command over the siege of Tyre in Alexander's absence (Curtius Rufus 4. 3. 1). The omission, if by Ptolemy, need not be attributed to ill will. Alexander's campaign in Lebanon lasted just ten days, and Arrian 2. 20. 4-5 also omits the name of Craterus, who shared command with Perdiccas. There is no known Ptolemaic bias against Craterus.

10. See Errington, pp. 241 ff.; E. Badian, *CW* 65 (1971), 38, 40; A. B. Bosworth, 'Arrian and the Alexander Vulgate', in *Alexandre le Grand* (note 4 above), pp. 15-16, 27, 29, 32; idem, *A Historical Commentary on Arrian's History of Alexander* 1 (Oxford, 1981, hereafter cited as Bosworth, *Commentary*), pp. 23, 25 ff. Compare also M. A. Levi, *Introduzione ad Alessandro Magno* (Milano, 1977), pp. 44, 52, 56-8, 81-2. Errington in *Alexandre le Grand,* p. 45 seems to retract slightly his earlier position when he states that Ptolemy's work was not a flagrant political pamphlet. He still implies, however, that it was used for propaganda.

11. Arrian 1. 8. 5. The present analysis aims, not at reconstructing the course of the battle (for which see, for example, Bosworth, *Commentary,* pp. 80 ff.), but at dealing with its presentation in Arrian.

12. See Antigonus' remarks concerning the rebuilding of the city by Cassander: Diod. Sic. 19. 61. 1-3. For the Greeks' reaction see, for example, Ephippus, *F. Gr. Hist.* no. 123, F3, P1b. 37. 2. 13; Pausanias 9. 7. 2.

13. N. G. L. Hammond, *Alexander the Great, King, Commander and Statesman* (London, 1981), p. 4. Cf. more generally P. A. Brunt, 'On historical frag-

ments and epitomes', *CQ* n.s. 30 (1980), 476-94. Levi (note 10 above), p. 45 and Goukowsky, p. 141, point to the difficulties of appreciating the nature of Ptolemy's work but go on to analyse its characteristics. The latter scholar argues reasonably against dating Ptolemy's work by its presumed bias (p. 142). Nevertheless, he dates it to the period after Ipsus because of Ptolemy's alleged failure to mention Antigonus' and Lysimachus' achievements under Alexander (p. 143).

14. Strasburger, *Ptolemaios und Alexander,* p. 35.

15. Bosworth, *Commentary,* p. 311, suggests that Arrian's source (and perhaps it was Arrian himself?) digressed in 3. 15. 2 to the general list of casualties. If the list was originally located (*apud Callisthenem*?) at the conclusion of the battle description, as it is now placed in Diod. 17. 61. 3 and Curt. 4. 16. 32, Perdiccas' name could have been missed in the process of copying.

16. Ptolemy as a bodyguard: Arr. 3. 27. 5; Peucestas: Arr. 6. 28. 3-4.

17. Errington, p. 237.

18. Gaza is presumably the unnamed city in Curt. 7. 6. 16.

19. E. Benveniste, 'La ville de Cyreschata', *Journal Asiatique* 234 (1943-5), 165 f.; cf. J. R. Hamilton, *Plutarch, Alexander. A Commentary* (Oxford, 1969), p. 122. Plut. *Moral.* 341b is of no help here.

20. Cf. Berve (note 8 above), p. 34; but see Hamilton, op. cit.

21. Errington, pp. 238-9.

22. Berve, p. 316; Strasburger, *Ptolemaios und Alexander,* p. 47; Kornemann (note 1 above), p. 247; Pearson (note 3 above), p. 193; Errington, p. 240; Bosworth, 'The death of Alexander the Great; rumours and propaganda', *CQ* n.s. 21 (1971), 128 n. 7, 132, 134.

23. W. W. Tarn, 'Alexander's *Hypomnemata* and the World Kingdom', *JHS* [*Journal of Hellenic Studies*] 41 (1921), 4 ff.; cf. M. J. Fontana, *La lotta per la successione di Alessandro Magno* (Palermo, 1960), pp. 117, 252 ff. Goukowsky, esp. pp. 117-18, cf. 31-4 accepts Arr. 7. 4. 10 as authentic but on the basis of a questionable distinction between the chiliarch's duties.

24. See note 22 above.

25. See *Anab.* 6. 28. 2; 7. 13. 3; 7. 15. 6 and Bosworth, *Commentary,* p. 30. Compare Bosworth, ibid. pp. 33 f. on Arrian's biased attitude towards Alexander, which was adopted from his sources.

26. For example, 7. 1-3, 12. 5, 13. 4, 27-30. For the characteristics of Book Seven compare Badian, 'A King's notebooks', *HSCP* [*Harvard Studies in Classical Philology*] 72 (1968), 192-4, and especially P. A. Stadter, *Arrian of Nicomedia* (University of North Carolina Press, 1981), pp. 86-8.

27. I have counted forty-six cases of Arrian using words and expressions which imply that he was following a source other than Ptolemy and Aristobulus: 7. 1. 2, 1. 3, 1. 5, 2. 1, 2. 3, 2. 4, 3. 2, 12. 5, 13. 1, 13. 2, 13. 6, 14. 1, 14. 2, 14. 3, 14. 4, 14. 5, 14. 6, 14. 7, 14. 8, 15. 4, 15. 5, 17. 2, 18. 6, 20. 1, 20. 2, 20. 4, 20. 5, 24. 4, 25. 1, 26. 1, 26. 3, 27. 1, 27. 2, 27. 3. Not every occurrence of *oratio obliqua* means a subsidiary source; cf. the famous example of Arr. 7. 20. 1 and Strabo 16. 1. 11 (p. 741), both using Aristobulus. Still, the burden of proof rests upon whoever wishes to show the derivation of the majority of the *legomena* in Book Seven from Arrian's main source.

28. *Anab.* 7. 13. 3, 15. 6, 26. 3. The favourable reference to Ptolemy in 7. 15. 3 implies that he was Arrian's source for the campaign against the Uxii (7. 15. 1-3).

29. *Anab.* 7. 13. 3; *F. Gr. Hist.* no. 139, frs. 52-5, 60-1. By way of comparison Book Six of the *Anabasis* includes Ptolemy's fragments nos. 24, 25, 10, 26a, 27 (*F. Gr. Hist.* 138) and Aristobulus' fragments nos. 16, 49a; 50, 51a (*F. Gr. Hist.* 139). The narrative mentions Nearchus five times (6. 2. 3, 13. 4, 13. 5, 24. 2, 24. 3), Onesicritus once (2. 3), and includes expressions which convey the use of subsidiary sources in 6. 11. 1, 11. 3-4, 7-8 (all in the context of Arrian's demonstration of his historiographical pretensions), 22. 8, 26. 1, 28. 1. The contrast with the use of the sources in Book Seven is striking.

30. Levi's attempt (note 10 above), pp. 81-3, to trace Seleucid propaganda in Aristobulus' history lacks sufficient evidence.

31. Arrian's silence might even be anchored in historical grounds. Badian, though uncommitted, raised doubts concerning the story of the ring: *HSCP* 72 (1968), 185, 204.

32. Diod. 18. 25. 4. Diod. 18. 14. 1-2 is confused chronologically. Ptolemy's hostility towards Perdiccas is deduced from later events, and the negotiations with Antipater are antedated to the period preceding the Cyrenian campaign: J. Seibert, *Historische Beiträge zu den dynastischen Verbindungen in hellenistischer Zeit* (Historia Suppl. 10, Wiesbaden, 1967), p. 17; P. Briant, *An-*

tigone le Borgne (Paris, 1973), p. 183, n. 2. I follow here the chronology of E. Manni, 'Tre note di cronologia ellenistica', *RAL* ser. 8, 4 (1949), 53 ff. in spite of Briant's objections to his reconstruction (pp. 218 ff.).

33. The main source for the deliberations in Babylon is Curtius 10. 6 ff. They were recently analysed by F. Schachermeyr (note 2 above), esp. pp. 134 ff.; R. M. Errington, 'From Babylon to Triparadeisos', *JHS* 90 (1970), 46-56; Bosworth, *CQ* n.s. 21 (1971), 112 f.; Briant, esp. pp. 235 ff.; Goukowsky, pp. 75-84, 193-4.

34. Pausanias (1. 6. 2) makes Ptolemy responsible for the division of the empire at Arrhidaeus' expense. Yet he neglects to mention that the Macedonians, who were persuaded by Ptolemy to hand over Alexander's body to him (ibid. 3), were led by Arrhidaeus, who should have known better. Pausanias' narrative also conveys the distinct, but misleading, impression that Perdiccas had been first pushed back from Egypt and then murdered: 'Ἐξωσθεὶς δὲ Αἰγύπτου . . . ἀπέθανεν ὑπὸ τῶν σωματοφυλάκων' (1. 6. 3). The Egyptian treasury: Diod. 18. 14. 1, and see Seibert (note 4 above), pp. 77, 97-100.

35. Thus Errington, *JHS* 90 (1970), 65. *Pace* Seibert, pp. 109-10, the Heidelberg epitome (*F. Gr. Hist.* no. 155) and Justin 13. 6. 20 do not make the conquest of Cyrene a cause for the war between Ptolemy and Perdiccas. It is perhaps significant that in a Perdiccan propaganda pamphlet (*Iulii Valerii Alexandri Polemi* [ed. B. Küler], p. 166, for which see R. Merkelbach, *Die Quellen des griechischen Alexanderromans* [München, 1954], pp. 125 ff., 145), Alexander's testament deprives Ptolemy of Egypt but gives him Libya.

36. Diod. 18. 29. 1, Arr. *F. Gr. Hist.* no. 156, F10. 1. On the affair see Badian, *HSCP* 72 (1968), 186-7; Seibert, pp. 66-7, 97 ff.; Errington, *JHS* 90 (1970), 64-5; O. Müller, *Antigonos Monophthalmos und 'das Jahr der Könige'* (Bonn, 1973), pp. 59-61. On Alexander's tomb and its significance see P. M. Fraser, *Ptolemaic Alexandria* 1 (Oxford, 1972), esp. pp. 15-17, 225-6; Errington in *Alexandre le Grand*, pp. 141-5; Goukowsky, pp. 91 ff.

37. Diod. 18. 36. 6-7. For Goukowsky, p. 89 see Diod. ibid. and Errington, *JHS* 90 (1970), 65-6.

38. Arr. *Succ.* 32-3; Diod. 18. 39. 2-3; cf. Polyaen, 4. 6. 6.

39. Perdiccas' reputation: Diod. 18. 33. 3; Arr. *Succ.* 28; Justin 13. 8. 1; Suda *s.v.* 'Perdiccas'. Cf. F. Geyer, 'Perdiccas', *RE* 19 (1937), 613-14. Perdiccas' memory could have been cherished by some,

hardly significant, communities in Cocle-Syria: Goukowsky, p. 302 n. 39.

40. Diod. 18. 46. 1. On possible friction between Alcestas and Perdiccas before the Egyptian campaign: Briant, pp. 196 ff. (see, however, Diod. 18. 37. 2). It is worth noting that all our information concerning the pre-323 career of Alcestas, who surely had no love for Ptolemy, comes from Arrian (Ptolemy?). In fact Curtius (8. 11. 1) grants Polyperchon a victory over Ora (Hora) which Arrian (*Anab.* 5. 27. 5-6) attributes to Alcestas. For more references see Berve (note 8 above), pp. 22-3. Attalus managed to gather soldiers after Perdiccas' death, but that only by virtue of his control over the treasury: Diod. 18. 37. 4; Arr. *Succ.* 39.

41. Errington and Bosworth, note 10 above.

42. *Anab.* 1. 6. 9, 14. 2, 20. 5; 3. 18. 5; 4. 16. 2; 6. 9. 1 (cf. 5. 22. 6). If Curtius' 'Sambagrai' (9. 8. 4-7) and Diodorus' 'Sambastai' (17. 102. 1-4) are Arrian's 'Abastanes' (6. 15. 1), then, according to Arrian's version, they were vanquished by Perdiccas, while the other two sources have them surrender to Alexander. Moreover, if Ptolemy is the source of Arrian 4. 16. 2, then the reporting of Perdiccas' command over one-fifth of the army is much more significant than the omission of his title of a bodyguard in that context (Errington, p. 238).

43. Errington, pp. 235-6; cf. Tarn (note 1 above), 2 pp. 109-10, but also Goukowsky, p. 302 n. 37.

44. See Curtius 10. 6. 10; Arr. *F. Gr. Hist.* 156 F 10. 6 and the previous note.

45. Berve (note 8 above), p. 69, assumes that Aristonous' participation in the battle was deduced from his title of bodyguard.

46. Seibert (note 4 above), pp. 122 ff.; Errington, *JHS* 90 (1970), 65-6. The fact that Pithon became Antigonus' ally c. 317 would hardly make this year a *terminus post quem* for Ptolemy's history.

47. Tarn, 2 p. 110, blames Ptolemy for omitting Antigonus' achievements; but see Errington, p. 234 and compare Briant, p. 99. There is little doubt that Ptolemy had ample reason to dislike Perdiccas and that the two waged a war of propaganda: Merkelbach (note 36 above); Bosworth, *CQ* n.s. 21 (1971), 112 ff.; Goukowsky, pp. 88 ff., 305 n. 61, 336 n. 302. But neither Ptolemy's work nor probably the *ephemerides* were used as weapons in that war.

48. For Ptolemy's *autopsia* see below. K. Rosen, *Hermes* 107 (1979), 463-5, maintains that Ptolemy stressed the military achievements of Alexander in the service of the *Alexanderideologie*, which was

used to retain the loyalty of the soldiers and to make his rule legitimate. Judging from the extant sources, few histories of Alexander could avoid bringing the military into the foreground. Similarly, Bosworth's attempts to show a Ptolemaic bias against the sons of Andromenes (in *Alexandre le Grand,* pp. 13-14) call for much co-operation on the part of his audience in order for the bias to be effective.

49. Ptolemy's military fragments are: *F. Gr. Hist.* 138, nos. 1, 3, 4, 6, 10, 15, 18, 20, 21, 24-6, 34-5. Alexander is especially idealized and justified in frs. 1, 3, 13, 16, 23. Ptolemy's autopsy: frs. 14, 18, 35; Arr. 4. 29. 1-6. For the following compare Levi (note 10 above), pp. 43 ff.; Bosworth, *Commentary,* pp. 22 ff.

50. Ptolemy frs. 20, 27, 28 b, 29; and esp. 26a. On Ptolemy's dissatisfaction with the vulgate see, e.g., Schwartz, *RE* 2 (1895), 1237-8; Jacoby, *F. Gr. Hist.* II B, pp. 500-2; Strasburger, *Ptolemaios und Alexander,* pp. 14 f., 27; Pearson (note 3 above), pp. 180, 205-6. Cf. R. D. Milns and F. Schachermeyr in *Alexandre le Grand,* pp. 42-3.

51. The conclusion holds true even if Ptolemy argued with Aristobulus on the details of Alexander's battle with the son of Porus: *Anab.* 5. 14. 3 ff.

52. See Errington, Bosworth, and Levi, note 10 above; Goukowsky, pp. 91 ff., 143.

53. See the above note and Levi, pp. 51-2; Goukowsky, pp. 134, 141.

54. See Arr. 6. 11. 8 and Curt. 9. 5. 2 above, and Diod, 17. 103. 6-8; Curt. 9. 8. 20-8 for Ptolemy's recovery. For other sources and an explanation for the absence of the last episode in Arrian see Goukowsky, 'Clitarque seul? Remarques sur les sources du livre XVII de Diodore de Sicile', *RÉA* [*Revue des études ancienes*] 71 (1969), esp. p. 320.

55. This is especially true for F 35, which seems to stand out from Arrian's narrative in a splendid descriptive isolation. For Ptolemy's autopsy see note 49 above and C. B. Welles, 'The reliability of Ptolemy as an historian', in *Miscellanea di studi alessandrini in memoria di Augusto Rostagni* (Torino, 1963), pp. 101-16, whose analysis is disputed by Seibert (note 4 above), pp. 4 ff.

56. Compare Strasburger, *Ptolemaios und Alexander,* pp. 38-9, 42.

57. See also Jacoby, *F. Gr. Hist.* II B, p. 499; Strasburger, pp. 53-4; Pearson (note 3 above), pp. 200-2.

58. Cleitarchus, however, may not have taken part in the campaign. For his date see, for example, Scha-

chermeyr (note 2 above), pp. 211 ff.; Levi (note 10 above), pp. 84 ff.

59. See, e.g., Ptolemy frs. 1 (with Strasburger, *Ptolemaios und Alexander,* p. 21), 13, 16-17. Compare Bosworth in *Alexandre le Grand,* pp. 9 ff.

60. I wish to thank the editors of *Classical Quarterly* for their most helpful remarks. No one but the author is guilty of the opinions expressed here.

J. M. Mossman (essay date 1988)

SOURCE: Mossman, J. M. "Tragedy and Epic in Plutarch's Alexander." *Journal of Hellenic Studies* 108 (1988): 83-93.

[*In the following essay, Mossman examines Plutarch's* Life *of Alexander, noting that the historian uses epic coloring to describe Alexander's great deeds and tragic coloring to describe his darker side.*]

Achilles is the poetic paradigm of a hero, Alexander his real-life counterpart as well as his descendant. This idea is a commonplace of all our sources for Alexander's life. There are numerous examples of it: Diodorus says at xvii 1.4:

> ἐν ἔτεσι γὰρ δώδεκα καταστρεψάμενος τῆς μὲν Εὐρώπης οὐκ ὀλίγα, τὴν δὲ Ἀσίαν σχεδὸν ἄπασαν εἰκότως περιβόητον ἔσχε τὴν δόξαν καὶ τοῖς παλαιοῖς ἥρωσι καὶ ἡμιθέοις ἰσά . . . ουσαν . . . Ἀλέξανδρος οὖν γεγονὼς κατὰ πατέρα μὲν ἀφ' Ἡρακλέους, κατὰ δὲ μητέρα τῶν Αἰακιδῶν οἰκείαν ἔσχε τὴν φύσιν καὶ τὴν ἀρετὴν τῆς τῶν προγόνων εὐδοξίας.[1]

Diodorus xvii 97.3 extends the parallelism to a specific incident: Achilles' fight with Scamander, Alexander's lucky escape from drowning.[2] Arrian's account of Alexander's landing at Sigeum (i 11-12) strongly suggests that Alexander himself encouraged the parallel:

> θῦσαι δὲ αὐτὸν καὶ Πριάμωι ἐπὶ τοῦ βωμοῦ τοῦ Διὸς τοῦ Ἑρκείου λόγος κατέχει, μῆνιν Πριάμου παραιτούμενον τῶι Νεοπτολέμου γένει, ὃ δὴ ἐς αὐτὸν καθῆκεν . . . οἱ δέ, ὅτι καὶ τὸν Ἀχιλλέως ἄρα τάφον ἐστεφάνωσεν· Ἡφαιστίωνα δὲ λέγουσιν ὅτι τοῦ Πατρόκλου τὸν τάφον ἐστεφάνωσε· καὶ εὐδαιμόνισεν ἄρα, ὡς λόγος, Ἀλέξανδρος Ἀχιλλέα ὅτι Ὁμήρου κήρυκος ἐς τὴν ἔπειτα μνήμην ἔτυχε.

Compare also Diodorus xvii 17.3. The sacrifice is a public act affirming his lineage.

Plutarch in the *de Alexandri Magni fortuna aut virtute* (*Mor.* 327f-328a) makes it clear that Alexander's love of Homer was well-known (though for the purposes of his argument he subordinates Homer to philosophy here):

ἀλλὰ τοῖς μὲν γράφουσιν, ὡς Ἀλέξανδρος ἔφη
ποτὲ τὴν Ἰλιάδα καὶ τὴν Ὀδύσσειαν ἀκολυθεῖν
αὑτῶι τῆς στρατείας ἐφόδιον, πιστεύομεν, Ὅμηρον
σεμνύνοντες· ἂν δέ τις φῆι Ἰλιάδα καὶ τὴν
Ὀδύσσειαν παραμύθια πόνου καὶ διατριβὴν
ἕπεσθαι σχολῆς γλυκείας, ἐφόδιον δ'
ἀληθῶς γεγονέναι τὸν ἐκ φιλοσοφίας
λόγον . . . , καταφρονοῦμεν;

Compare also the *Life,* 8.2 and 26.2.

Elsewhere in the treatise there are comparisons of some
length between Alexander and a number of Homeric
heroes: for example 331cd, which also stresses Alexander's knowledge of Homer and his espousal of Homeric ideals:

Καὶ μὴν εἴ ποτε γένοιτο τῶν Ὁμήρου σύγκρισις
ἐπῶν ἐν ταῖς διατριβαῖς ἢ παρὰ τὰ συμπόσια,
ἄλλον ἄλλου στίχον προκρίνοντος, αὐτὸς ὡς
διαφέροντα πάντων ἐνέκρινε τοῦτον,

ἀμφότερον βασιλεύς τ' ἀγαθὸς κρατερός τ'
αἰχμητής

(*Il.* iii 179; *cf.* Xen. *Mem.* iii 2.2)

ὃν ἄλλος ἔπαινον τῶι χρόνωι προέλαβε, τοῦτον
αὑτῶι νόμον κεῖσθαι λογι . . . όμενος, ὥστ' εἰπεῖν
"Ὅμηρον ὅτι τῶι αὐτῶι μέτρωι τὴν μὲν
Ἀγαμέμνονος ἀνδραγαθίαν κεκόσμηκε, τὴν δ'
Ἀλεξάνδρου μεμάντευται.

The description is indeed of Agamemnon—Helen says
it in the Teichoskopia. Later in the section we find
another Achilles comparison.

καί τινος αὑτῶι τῶν ἐγχωρίων ὑποσχομένου τὴν
Πάριδος λύραν εἰ βούλοιτο δώσειν 'οὐδέν' ἔφη 'τῆς
ἐκείνου δέομαι· τὴν γὰρ Ἀχιλλέως κέκτημαι, πρὸς
ἣν ἐκεῖνος ἀνεπαύετο

ἄειδε δ' ἄρα κλέα ἀνδρῶν

(*Il.* ix 189)·

ἡ δὲ Πάριδος πάντως μαλακήν τινα καὶ θήλειαν
ἁρμονίαν ἐρωτικοῖς ἔψαλλε μέλεσι.'

At 343ab we find a more elaborate system of comparisons: Alexander is more self-restrained in dealing with
his female captives than Agamemnon, more magnanimous to Darius than Achilles was to Hector, more generous than Achilles because he enriched even his enemies,
whereas Achilles accepted gifts from his friends in
compensation after his anger had passed, more reverent
than Diomedes and more deeply mourned by his relatives than Odysseus, for Odysseus' mother died of grief,
but the mother of Alexander's greatest enemy loved
him so much that she chose to share his death.

We should notice two points here: firstly, that there are
two points of comparison with Achilles, one with each
of the other heroes; secondly, that although this type of

comparison is a commonplace of encomium, particularly
when the subject of the encomium claims to be related
to a hero like Achilles or to a god,[3] at 343ab the scale
of the passage and the detailed references to the poems
perhaps suggest a more conscious identification with
the heroes as they appear in the Homeric epics.

Plutarch's source for Alexander's love of Homer is
presumably Onesicritus. It is interesting that, although
most Onesicritus material is treated more lightly in the
Life than in the *de Alexandri Magni,* notably Onesicritus' picture of Alexander as the philosopher man of action, the material on Alexander's love of Homer and
literature generally is given just as much weight.[4]

Since Alexander's association with Homer was well-
known, and since he does seem to have encouraged
such Iliadic parallelism,[5] and since a certain encomiastic
strain inherent in epic poetry encouraged such comparisons to become well-rooted in the later encomiastic
tradition, it comes as no surprise to find Plutarch
developing and exploring the epic dimension of Alexander in the *Life.* It is considerably more unexpected to
find him introducing *tragic* atmosphere as a counterbal-
ance to the epic view, as I would argue he does. This
may seem surprising because, as Phillip de Lacy has
pointed out ('Biography and tragedy in Plutarch', *AJP*
[*American Journal of Philology*] lxxiii [1952] 159 ff.),
although tragedy obviously has an important place in
Plutarch's literary background, allusions to it usually
imply an adverse moral judgement and in literary
contexts it is used as a term of censure in his writings.[6]
This view is associated with Plutarch's Platonism, as de
Lacy has shown.[7]

A distinction needs to be made, however, as we shall
see, between the sensationalism of so-called 'tragic
history' which Plutarch dislikes so much and the
sustained tragic patterning and imagery which is a
perfectly respectable feature of both biography and history. Plutarch himself not infrequently chooses to characterise some of the subjects of the *Lives* and their actions by using such tragic imagery: Dionysius, Pompey,
Lysander, Antony, and Demetrius are examples.[8] Some
of these we will discuss more fully below. De Lacy
comments: 'Plutarch's tragic figures are not his great
heroes, such as Alexander and Epaminondas; they are
his villains: the elder Dionysius, Antony, and Nero.' As
I hope will become clear, this is an inadequate description of the way in which Plutarch uses tragedy. Central
to the *Alexander* is the tension, first made explicit as
early as 4.5-8 (an important passage), between Alexander's hot temper and his self-control;[9] his θυμός is
the source of great achievements, but also of disaster,
when, combined with heavy drinking, it breaks down
his σωφροσύνη. Plutarch often chooses to illustrate
this tension by interweaving and contrasting epic and

tragic elements throughout the *Life*.[10] In short, I would argue that in the *Alexander* Plutarch is interested not only in what Alexander does, but in what he does to himself, and that just as he may use epic colouring to chronicle Alexander's great deeds, so he also uses tragic colouring to delineate the darker side of Alexander's character.

In putting forward this argument we shall encounter one fundamental methodological problem: identifying and distinguishing 'epic' and 'tragic' tone. Since antiquity the intimate nature of the connection between tragedy and epic has been recognised.[11] Aristotle in the *Poetics* lays great stress on it: cf. 1448b34-1449a1, 1449b9-20, 1456a10-19, 1459b-1460a5, 1461b26 ff. However, Aristotle also makes it clear that there is a difference between the two: this is perhaps most clearly formulated at 1449b16-20:

μέρη δ' ἐστὶ τὰ μὲν ταυτά, τὰ δὲ ἴδια τῆς τραγωιδίας· διόπερ ὅστις περὶ τραγωιδίας οἶδε σπουδαίας καὶ φαύλης, οἶδε καὶ περὶ ἐπῶν· ἃ μὲν γὰρ ἐποποιία ἔχει, ὑπάρχει τῆι τραγωιδίαι, ἃ δὲ αὐτῆι, οὐ πάντα ἐν τῆι ἐποποιίαι.

The remarks of Stephen Halliwell (*The Poetics of Aristotle, translation and commentary* [London 1987] 81) are helpful and perceptive; 'Epic poetry . . . developed from the original impulse to portray and celebrate the actions of outstanding or noble men; but the essence of tragedy, *both in its Homeric* (my italics) and in its later Attic form, involves such characters in great changes of fortune, or transformations, which arouse pity or fear in those who contemplate them.' Halliwell is right to remind us that tragic feeling lies at the very heart of the *Iliad*: it is not by any means the exclusive preserve of Attic drama, but can be traced in Herodotus and, as Macleod pointed out ('Thucydides and Tragedy', *Collected Papers* [Oxford 1983] 140), in Thucydides: '. . . his theme, like the tragedians', is suffering on the grand scale, and . . . like them, he is not afraid to represent it as the utmost of human experience'. Nonetheless, in the *Alexander*, theatrical imagery or a tragic quotation or an obvious reminiscence or quotation from Homer will usually be sufficient to pin down a passage firmly as 'epic' or 'tragic'.

In the chapters following 4.5-8 the epic tone prevails: for example we are told that Lysimachus called himself Phoenix, Alexander Achilles, and Philip Peleus, and the taming of Bucephalas is narrated. Horse-taming is a very Iliadic activity: heroes are given the epithet ἱπποδάμος, 'tamer of horses'. Achilles of course has divine horses, so it is appropriate that there should be something distinguished about Alexander's. In ch. 8 we hear more of Alexander's love of Homer: (8.2)

καὶ τὴν μὲν Ἰλιάδα τῆς πολεμικῆς ἀρετῆς ἐφόδιον καὶ νομί . . . ων καὶ ὀνομά . . . ων, ἔλαβε μὲν

Ἀριστοτέλους διορθώσαντος ἦν ἐκ τοῦ νάρθηκος καλοῦσιν, εἶχε δ' ἀεὶ μετὰ τοῦ ἐγχειριδίου κειμένην ὑπὸ τὸ προσκεφάλαιον, ὡς Ὀνησίκριτος ἱστόρηκε

(FGrH 134 F 38)

In the chapters describing the end of Philip's life the tragic tone is uppermost: in contrast to the campaigns at the start of ch. 9 we hear of αἱ δὲ περὶ τὴν οἰκίαν ταραχαί, the stuff of tragedy, Olympias' βαρυθυμία and Philip's drunkenness sketching the origins of, and foreshadowing, Alexander's own proclivities in these directions. Philip's drunken attempt to attack Alexander is a doublet of the death of Cleitus: here Philip stumbles, and the incident comes to nothing εὐτυχίαι δὲ ἑκατέρου—Cleitus dies δυστυχίαι τινι . . . τοῦ βασιλέως. Philip's troubles arise διὰ τοὺς γάμους καὶ τοὺς ἔρωτας. The quotation from the *Medea* (288)

τὸν δόντα καὶ γήμαντα καὶ γαμουμένην

attributed to Alexander is thus an apposite one to complete the mood: cf. also eg. *Med.* 626 ff.[12]

The destruction of Thebes is a display of θυμός (tempered by the story of Timocleia, which prefigures Alexander's chivalry to Darius' household): Plutarch suggests that Alexander forgave Athens μεστὸς ὢν ἤδη τὸν θυμόν, ὥσπερ οἱ λέοντες (cf. *Demosthenes* 23.5). The simile must look back to the portent of Alexander's birth at 2.4 and is important for what follows, for lions are very much associated with Alexander as Dionysus.[13] It is immediately followed by 13.4:

ὅλως δὲ καὶ τὸ περὶ Κλεῖτον ἔργον ἐν οἴνωι γενόμενον, καὶ τὴν πρὸς Ἰνδοὺς τῶν Μακεδόνων ἀποδειλίασιν, ὥσπερ ἀτελῆ τὴν στρατείαν καὶ τὴν δόξαν αὐτοῦ προεμένων, εἰς μῆνιν ἀνῆγε Διονύσου καὶ νέμεσιν.

This is the first of several connections between Alexander and Dionysus, always (with the single exception of 17.9, crowning Theodectas' statue in his cups) with sinister force. In the *Life* Dionysus comes to represent the traits in Alexander which lead him to take his most disastrous actions: his drinking and his temper.[14] Olympias is also particularly associated with Dionysus: cf. 2.9,

ἡ δ' Ὀλυμπιὰς μᾶλλον ἑτέρων . . . ηλώσασα τὰς κατοχάς, καὶ τοὺς ἐνθουσιασμοὺς (i.e. the Orphic rites and the orgies of Dionysus) ἐξάγουσα βαρβαρικώτερον, ὄφεις μεγάλους χειροήθεις ἐφείλκετο τοῖς θιάσοις . . .

This special link with Dionysus constitutes a bold reinterpretation of the relationship between Alexander and the god: the Diadochi usually made the connection a complimentary one to Alexander and hence to his current royal successor: Dionysus is seen as the world-conqueror, the bringer of joy, rather than as the Dionysus of the *Bacchae* of Euripides.[15] Plutarch also makes a similar link between Dionysus and Antony in the *Antony,* with the same sort of effect. To those familiar with the Alexandrian identification, this view of Dionysus as a malevolent force in Alexander's make-up would have been very striking.

The epic tone, as one would expect, is reintroduced with the beginning of the expedition and Alexander's arrival at Troy. The parallelism with Achilles is very strong here, with Alexander's reverence for Achilles' tomb and the anecdote about the lyres (15.8-9), for which compare *Mor.* 331d above. Coming at the very beginning of the expedition, this acts as a declaration of Alexander's heroic intentions: the pun on his name and Paris' helps to drive home the point. This Alexander will be as completely different from the mythological one as Achilles was: his preoccupations will be with glory and conquest; he will shun the pleasures of the palace and the bedroom with which Paris is particularly associated in Homer. The heroics in the battle of the Granicus should be read in this context (there is a similar arrangement in Arrian). 16.7 is significant: Alexander has wonderful armour like Achilles:

ἦν δὲ τῆι πέλτηι καὶ τοῦ κράνους τῆι χαίτηι
διαπρεπής, ἧς ἑκατέρωθεν εἰστήκει πτερὸν
λευκότητι καὶ μεγέθει θαυμαστόν.

In the incident of Philip the Acarnanian and the cup of medicine (ch. 19) we find the exception to the usual use of tragic imagery in the *Life*: for, as Plutarch depicts θαυμαστὴν καὶ θεατρικὴν τὴν ὄψιν of Philip reading the letter accusing him of trying to posion Alexander and Alexander simultaneously drinking the cup which may be poisoned, we find tragic imagery used to illustrate Alexander's best qualities, with admirable economy, in one action: Alexander's trust in his friends, his fondness for the grand gesture and his physical courage are all brought out. The scene is at once a fine exercise in the sort of character drawing described in 1.2-3 and simply a tremendous stage-picture. Its economy and ἐναργεία, realised particularly by the skilful narration in 19.4, fully justify the epithet θεατρικήν.[16]

As Alexander's successes mount up, we find more Homeric reminders—Lysimachus as Phoenix once again at 24.10, and the placing of the *Iliad* in the precious coffer of Darius at 26.2 leading into the dream of Homer telling Alexander to found Alexandria in the proper site at 26.4-5. The 'arming scene' at 32.8-11 before Gaugamela certainly owes something to those in the *Iliad,* with its careful descriptions of the appearance of the armour and weapons, who made them and who gave them to the wearer: we may compare for example *Il.* xi 16 ff.

The burning of Persepolis (ch. 38), however, continues the theme of dubious deeds committed by Alexander while drunk. Dionysus is very much in our minds here: the palace is burned by a band of revellers κώμωι καὶ βοῆι, with Alexander in a garland (38.5-6). The remark at 23.1 ἦν δὲ καὶ πρὸς οἶνον ἧττον ἢ ἐδόκει καταφερής, despite Plutarch's careful discussion and rejection of the extremity of the prevailing view in chapter 23, is not really borne out by his narrative. Once again, as after Thebes, repentance speedily follows: *cf.* 38.8.

Alexander's relationship with his friends is carefully dwelt on throughout the *Life* (right from 5.4), and their difficulty in adapting to foreign ways forms a major theme. The transplanting of Greek plants by Harpalus at 35.15, with limited success (ivy will not grow in the πυρώδης Babylonian soil), is a metaphor for this. Chs. 47 and following skilfully sketch deteriorating relationships with what may conveniently be thought of as a series of scenes. They contrast with 40-42—Alexander's amazement at his friends extravagance—where one is only just aware of trouble on the horizon and the present is all sweetness and light.

The affair of Philotas and Parmenio leads into the more traumatic episode of Cleitus, who, we remember, saved Alexander's life at the Granicus. Plutarch's introduction is extremely interesting: at first sight the affair is ἀγριώτερα, he says, but if we consider τὴν αἰτίαν καὶ τὸν καιρόν, we see that it happened οὐκ ἀπὸ γνώμης, ἀλλὰ δυστυχίαι τινι . . . τοῦ βασιλέως, ὀργὴν καὶ μέθην πρόφασιν τῶι Κλείτωι δαίμονι παρασχόντος (50.2). In other words both men suffered from forces beyond their control. One is reminded of Alexander's conviction that this incident was part of Dionysus' revenge for the burning of Thebes. This and the evil omen, the sacrifices ordered by Alexander (in vain) for the safety of Cleitus, and the sinister dream linking Cleitus and Philotas, and the fact that Cleitus goes to his final feast straight from his unfinished sacrifice all reinforce the impression that both men are caught in some inexorable divine plan, a favorite theme of tragedy, exemplified by the *Oedipus Tyrannus.* Of course it is not a theme confined to tragedy: historians may make use of such story-patterns too: *cf.* e.g. Hdt. i 35 ff., the story of Adrastus; but it is one particularly characteristic of it. The quarrel is reported with a high proportion of direct speech, which adds vividness. The climax comes when Alexander loses control: οὐκέτι φέρων τὴν ὀργήν. Despite the precautions taken by Aristophanes, the pleadings of his friends and the reluctance of the trumpeter, and despite Cleitus' removal, the killing still occurs: the emphasis on the precautions taken intensifies the idea of inevitability: it happened despite everything that mortal man could do. Cleitus' re-entry and continued defiance, marked by the tragic quotation, seem to be so irrational as to be the work of his *daimon*. The terrible remorse which instantly follows the deed emphasises his horror and how alien it is to Alexander's true intentions and feelings: his attempt at self-destruction, his extreme grief, and the seer's reminder of τήν τε ὄψιν ἣν εἶδε περὶ τοῦ Κλείτου, καὶ τὸ σημεῖον, ὡς δὴ πάλαι καθειμαρμένων τούτων (52.2), all reinforce the initial impression that here we are in the world of tragedy, with inexorable divine forces working on the characters of men to produce disaster which brings bitter regret. As in a number of tragedies, the gods work through the men themselves and their characteristics: in Alexanders case through his propensity for drink and his θυμός. In tragedy Dionysus works on Pentheus' prurience, and Hera, Iris, and Lyssa on Heracles' great strength and force in the *Heracles Mainomenos*. It may well be no accident that the Cleitus episode, with its pattern of madness/murder—remorse—consolation is highly reminiscent of the *Heracles*: Heracles is of course Alexander's other ancestor and is closely associated with him.[17]

A comparison between Plutarch's account of this incident and Arrian's is instructive: Arrian has no evil omens, no dream: Cleitus makes no unfinished sacrifice, though Alexander fails to sacrifice to Dionysus as is usual on that day. Arrian interrupts Cleitus' tirade with his own criticisms of Cleitus, and has almost none of Plutarch's elaborate precautions: Alexander's friends merely try to hold him back and fail. Cleitus' voluntary return is mentioned as an alternative version of Aristobulus, who, however, left the drinking bout without a context, according to Arrian. Cleitus does not use a tragic quotation. It seems very likely from this that Plutarch has carefully constructed his version from various sources to produce the maximum tragic effect.

The consolations of the philosophers Callisthenes and Anaxarchus bring no real relief: for the narrative continues with the destruction of Callisthenes and the Pages' conspiracy which are brought about by too great reliance on the doctrines of Anaxarchus: his words at 52.6-7 are specifically said to have a bad effect on Alexander: τὸ δὲ ἦθος εἰς πολλὰ χαυνότερον καὶ παρανομώτερον ἐποίησεν . . . καὶ τοῦ Καλλισθένους τὴν ὁμιλίαν . . . προσδιέβαλε.

As to Anaxarchus' actual words (also in Arrian), Dike is the πάρεδρος of Zeus as early as Pindar (*Ol.* viii 21 ff.) and Sophocles (*OC* 1381 ff.). But for the idea that the king can do no wrong we must turn to Hdt. iii 31 (of Persia) and to Creon in the *Antigone*: (666-7)

ἀλλ' ὃν πόλις στήσειε, τοῦδε χρὴ κλύειν
καὶ σμικρὰ καὶ δίκαια καὶ τἀναντία.[18]

Plutarch transplants in time the downfall of Callisthenes and the Pages' conspiracy to act as an illustration of the deterioration in Alexander's morals (*cf.* 56.1)—they really belong to the spring of 327. On the present arrangement the episodes grow organically one out of the other (Arrian too saw the benefits of this plan and also adopted it, apologising for the change at iv 14): Callisthenes is first played off against Anaxarchus in the aftermath of the death of Cleitus: his character is then developed. He is represented as an honest, upright and independent, if rather irritating, character. Plutarch's portrait of him is far more favourable than Arrian's, who calls him ὑπαγροικότερον and refers to his ὕβρις καὶ σκαιότης and his ἄκαιρος παρρησία καὶ ὑπέρογκος ἀβελτερία (iv 10.1, 12.6-7). The episode of the speeches (ch. 53) does not show Alexander in a good light, for it is by his request that Callisthenes speaks against the Macedonians and alienates both them and Alexander himself. The quotation from the *Bacchae* which Alexander applies to Callisthenes is by no means really complimentary: it is from Teiresias' speech to Pentheus (and thus indicates an interesting role-reversal when it is put into Alexander's mouth in this context) and continues: (278)

σὺ δ' εὔτροχον μὲν γλῶσσαν ὡς φρονῶν ἔχεις
ἐν τοῖς λόγοισι δ' οὐκ ἔνεισί σοι φρένες.

The story of the kiss (ch. 54) confirms Callisthenes as the proud philosopher, Alexander as the demanding monarch. The treatment of the Pages' conspiracy, far less detailed than Arrian's account, keeps Callisthenes rather than Hermoläus and the boys in the forefront of our minds, and it is his fate that is dwelt on rather than theirs. His miserable end is immediately contrasted with that of Demaratus and his magnificent funeral: we are reminded that Alexander can be loyal and generous to his friends.

The expedition into India moves into the epic sphere again after these dark interludes: Alexander's courage is to the fore, contrasted with the cowardice of Sisimithres in 58. His generous behaviour to Taxiles and Porus recalls his earlier munificence: the death of Bucephalas and the dog Peritas remind us of his gentleness. Then there is his Achillean withdrawal into his tent in protest at his soldiers' reluctance to advance and his relenting to their pleas. The climax of this epic phase of the narrative is of course the battle in the Malli township, where he leapt from the wall into the mêlée: τιναξαμένου δὲ τοῖς ὅπλοις, ἔδοξαν οἱ βάρβαροι σέλας τι καὶ φάσμα πρὸ τοῦ σώματος φέρεσθαι (63.4). (*Cf.* also *Mor.* 343e.)

This is surely to be compared with Achilles' appearance in the closing books of the *Iliad*, shining in his divine armour: cf. *Il.* xix 375 ff.:[19] note the repeated use of σέλας (375, 379) and that the flashing light comes from the movement of the armour. Alexander is never more like Achilles than this, in his magnificent courage: it is a fine touch to mark the resemblance with so plain a reference to his Iliadic model. Arrian, too, makes such a reference, though, as one would expect, in less romantic fashion:

δῆλος μὲν ἦν Ἀλέξανδρος ὢν τῶν τε ὅπλων τῆι λαμπρότητι καὶ τῶι ἀτόπωι τῆς τόλμης . . .

he says at vi 9.5.

The hardships of campaign and exploration are contrasted with the unlikely Bacchanalian revel in Carmania in ch. 67. We are not here concerned with its historical credentials: its function in the scheme of Plutarch's narrative is, I think, to introduce a darker phase of the *Life*. Dionysus, as we have seen, is scarcely a propitious deity for Alexander in Plutarch's account: it is ominous, therefore, to hear at 67.6:

τῶι δὲ ἀτάκτωι καὶ πεπλανημένωι τῆς πορείας παρείπετο καὶ παιδιὰ βακχικῆς ὕβρεως, ὡς τοῦ θεοῦ παρόντος αὐτοῦ καὶ συμπαραπέμποντος τὸν κῶμον.

Note ἀτάκτωι and πεπλανημένωι pointing the contrast between this and the usual military discipline and swiftness with which Alexander moves.

Further, his public display of affection towards Bagoas, which we must be meant to contrast unfavourably with his earlier σωφροσύνη and his outrage in ch. 22 when Philoxenus and Hagnon offer him boys, occurs when he is drunk: 67.8 λέγεται δὲ μεθύοντα αὐτὸν θεωρεῖν ἀγῶνας χορῶν . . .

Alexander's difficulties multiply in the next chapter: he has ignored the advice of the Gymnosophist Calanus in 65[20] and spread his realm too far, and rebellion is rife (68.2-3). Troubles at Macedon, Oxyartes' death by Alexander's own hand, Abuletes' punishment (all in ch. 68) are succeeded by the episode of Cyrus' tomb, whose inscription ἐμπαθῆ σφόδρα τὸν Ἀλέξανδρον ἐποίησεν, ἐν νῶι λαβόντα τὴν ἀδηλότητα καὶ μεταβολήν: a distinctively tragic theme. Calanus' death and funeral, with its disastrous aftermath, follow: his prophecy that he would soon see the king at Babylon and the deaths from drinking at the funeral continue the feeling of impending doom. Even Alexander's marriage to Stateira scarcely lightens the tone; and the misunderstanding with the Macedonian veterans at 71.1 ff., though it is resolved, is an unhappy incident. Arrian, we should note, gives the Macedonians less reason to complain by omitting the thirty thousand boys who in Plutarch are the cause of the trouble: vii 8-11.

The death of Hephaestion (ch. 72) after eating casseroled fowl and drinking ψυκτῆρα μέγαν οἴνου while his physician was at the theatre and Alexander's mourn-

ing for him follow. Here we are irresistibly reminded of Achilles mourning for Patroclus: the destruction of the Cossaeans is an ἐναγισμός for Hephaestion's shade (72.4), recalling Achilles' human sacrifice in *Il.* xxiii 175-7. Here, it might be said, we have an example of an epic reminiscence being used to develop the darker side of Alexander's character. This is an exception, however, which proves a rule: Achilles in his mourning for Patroclus is very much a forerunner of the great tragic heroes, as Rutherford (*art. cit.* [n. 11] 145-6) has pointed out: we have a reference here to the most tragic part of epic. At the same time it is appropriate that here the ethos is not purely tragic: for Alexander's mourning for Hephaestion is not part of the self-destructive side of his nature in the same way that the murder of Cleitus is.

The portents of Alexander's own death follow immediately on from this (contrasting bitterly with Stasicrates' elaborate plans for Mount Athos). The effect of the portents on Alexander is traumatic: 74.1 αὐτὸς δὲ ἠθύμει καὶ δύσελπις ἦν πρὸς τὸ θεῖον ἤδη καὶ πρὸς τοὺς φίλους ὕποπτος. This was the man who drank Philip of Acarnania's medicine προθύμως καὶ ἀνυπόπτως! Suspicion, fear and excessive belief in prodigies possess him: 75.1-2. The trusting man is paranoid, the brave man a prey to fear, the man who created his own portents (24.6-7) sees omens in the tiniest occurrence. The calamities of tragedy sometimes bring about similar collapses: Creon the 'hard man' crumbles quickly into submission in the *Antigone*; the strong man Heracles must be led away like a child, as he once led his own children, by Theseus; under the influence of the god Pentheus' puritanism gives way to the streak of prurience which was always in him.

And it is Dionysus, once again, who dominates Alexander's death. 75.5, where Plutarch rejects some of the more romantic versions of Alexander's end (notably that found in Diodorus) is interesting (and very typical of the style of his criticism of tragic history elsewhere: *cf.* note 6): he says: ταῦτά τινες ὤιοντο δεῖν γράφειν ὥσπερ δράματος μεγάλου τραγικὸν ἐξόδιον καὶ περιπαθὲς πλάσαντες. We shall have reason to mention the 'tragic historians' involved in a moment. The point of Plutarch's criticism of his sources here is not, I think, that they saw Alexander's life as a δρᾶμα λέγα and he did not: Plutarch himself, as I have tried to show, thought it appropriate to illustrate Alexander's life by means of sustained dramatic patterning, as well as seeing matter for straightforward dramatic spectacle in it, for example in the Philip of Acarnania scene. The emphasis, I think, must be on πλάσαντες: there was no need to fabricate a pathetic end to Alexander's life, says Plutarch: and he substitutes for the absurdities of the 'tragic' historians an account which far exceeds theirs in pathos and which has the additional merit of being true—or at least culled from the royal journals. The unforgettable picture of the soldiers filing past Alexander's couch far surpasses the fictions of the sources Plutarch has rejected.

One should not pass from the description of Alexander's death without mentioning a very striking parallel from the end of the *Demetrius,* a life whose whole structure, as de Lacy notes, seems to be conceived in terms of a tragedy: at Demetrius' death we are told that the Macedonian δρᾶμα is at an end. The more oblique link between Alexander and δρᾶμα reflects the less schematised, more complex play which Plutarch makes with tragedy in this *Life.*

For one cannot say simply that tragic colouring means automatically that Plutarch is 'attacking' Alexander. It very often means that Alexander's darker side is to the fore, but the theatrical imagery in the episode of Philip of Acarnania is used to pack some of Alexander's best qualities into one memorable scene. I use the word 'scene' advisedly, for as I hope has become clear, there are scenes in the *Alexander*: great set-pieces told with tremendous ἐναργεία which more than anything else constitute the ingredients of the εἰδοποιία described in chapter 1.

We must now consider tragic history, and whether we should be surprised to find Plutarch, its arch-enemy, apparently succumbing to its charms. The answer to this question, it seems to me, is that put forward by Walbank in his articles on the origins of tragic history:[21] 'tragic' history constitutes no more than a souping-up of the facts for a cheap thrill; although it sometimes made use of theatrical imagery, it has nothing to do with sustained tragic patterning in the sense in which it may be observed in the *Alexander,* the *Demetrius,* or the *Antony,* where it is also extremely important. There is no inconsistency in Plutarch's despising this debased genre and adopting the techniques we have observed perfectly deliberately in his own work for a serious artistic purpose. It is also possible that Plutarch considered that biography, with its greater concentration on individuals, was a more suitable *genre* in which to set up such patterning than history; hence his remarks at 1.2-3.

Plutarch is sparing in this use of such tragic frameworks, however: he does not, for example, use it in the *Caesar,*[22] which seems surprising: the tragic colouring in the *Demetrius* continues into the *Antony.* It seems clear that something about Alexander's career suggested that it would be a fruitful approach to take, and that Caesar's did not: Alexander was a patron of the arts and a lover of literature (4.6) and Caesar was not: and Alexander saw himself in epic terms and Caesar did not (the nearest he comes is *Caesar* 11.2). But perhaps the most decisive reason was that tragic patterning could not fit in to Plutarch's conception of Caesar's downfall: for Plutarch, external factors destroyed Caesar, whereas internal forces worked on Alexander, as they did on Demetrius and Antony; Plutarch evidently felt it more appropriate to explain Caesar's end in terms of historical causation and politics, and Alexander's vicissitudes in terms of tragedy, epic, and divine wrath. Onesicritus gave Plutarch the epic strand and the general literary ethos of Alexander's life; the interweaving and balancing of epic and tragic is Plutarch's own original contribution to the tradition: individual versions of incidents are combined, where they exist, to produce the desired result: the elements may spring from others but the product is Plutarch's own.

Possibly, too, Plutarch was inclined towards working with these tragic overtones by Herodotus' account of the Persian Wars, in which there are many tragic elements. The works cover some of the same geographical area, and in many ways Alexander's conquest of Persia is seen as a reversal of, and a reply to, the Persian attempts on Greece: hence Demaratus the Corinthian's remarks at 37.7. There are a number of Herodotean elements in the *Life*: the relationship of Amyntas and Darius recalls a number of wise but disregarded Greek councillors in Herodotus, for instance, and both works show careful Oriental colouring when dealing with Persian affairs. Above all, there is the episode with the statue of Xerxes at 37.5, where Alexander, seeing a fallen statue of Xerxes, deposed by looting soldiers, debates whether to set it up again:

'πότερόν σε' εἶπε 'διὰ τὴν ἐπὶ τοὺς "Ελληνας
στρατείαν κείμενον παρέλθωμεν, ἢ διὰ τὴν ἄλλην
μεγαλοφροσύνην καὶ ἀρετὴν ἐγείρωμεν;' τέλος δὲ
πολὺν χρόνον πρὸς ἑαυτῶι γενόμενος καὶ
σιωπήσας, παρῆλθε.

Xerxes, the tragic king who wept at the ephemeral nature of his great army in Herodotus (vii 46), is presented in an encounter with Alexander, who, just as he later empathises with Cyrus (ch. 69), silently ponders the fate of Xerxes. The episodes both form part of the large theme of the contact and conflict between Greek and Persian which Plutarch, like Herodotus before him, found fascinating. I do not find the idea that Plutarch had Herodotus in mind and wanted to elaborate and expand the intimations of tragedy in that author incongruous; as Russell has pointed out (*op. cit.* [n. 21] 60 ff.), Plutarch's indignation against Herodotus in the *de malignitate Herodoti* is distinctly artificial, and surely assumed for rhetorical purposes.[23]

In no other prose author,[24] though, are the poetic genres, tragedy and epic, used in so sophisticated and refined a way to illuminate the tensions within a character. This illustrates not only the different preoccupations of history and biography (Plutarch is concerned with Alexander's internal development more than with his external career, as he makes clear from the beginning) but also just how good Plutarch is at what he does: using the genres in this way Plutarch can produce an account of Alexander, that most complex of characters, which is one of the most memorable he ever wrote, rich in ambiguity, contradiction and irony and thus magnificently real.

Notes

1. *Cf.* Plut. *Alex.* 2.1. An earlier draft of this paper was delivered at the conference of the International Plutarch Society held at the Canadian and American Schools of Classical Studies at Athens, 26th-28th June 1987. I am most grateful to the Society and to the organisers of the conference. I owe a special debt to Dr C. B. R. Pelling and Mr E. L. Bowie, whose perceptive criticisms were invaluable, to the very useful remarks of an unnamed referee, and to Mark Edwards for his generous interest and stimulating conversation.

2. D.S. xvii 97.3:

   σωθεὶς δὲ παραδόξως τοῖς θεοῖς ἔθυσεν ὡς μεγίστους ἐκπεφευγὼς κινδύνους καὶ πρὸς ποταμὸν ὁμοίως Ἀχιλλεῖ διαγωνισάμενος.

3. Compare for example Theocritus xvii 53 ff.:

   Ἀργεία κυάνοφρυ, σὺ λαοφόνον Διομήδεα μισγομένα Τυδῆι τέκες, Καλυδώνιον ἄνδρα, ἀλλὰ Θέτις βαθύκολπος ἀκοντιστὰν Ἀχιλῆα Αἰακίδαι Πηλῆι· σὲ δ' αἰχμητὰ Πτολεμαῖε αἰχμητᾶι Πτολεμαίωι ἀρί . . . ηλος Βερενίκα.

4. A. Momigliano, *The development of Greek biography, Four Lectures* (Harvard 1971) 82-3 shows the importance of accounts of education to Greek biography, and this may explain Plutarch's selection of material. But in that case it is perhaps surprising that he did not make more use of Onesicritus in the early part of the *Life:* cf. J. R. Hamilton, *Plutarch, Alexander: a commentary* (Oxford 1969) lvii.

   Onesicritus' ὡς Ἀλέξανδρος ἤχθη is paralleled by the Ἀλεξάνδρου ἀγωγή of Marsyas of Pella, another companion of Alexander.

5. This cannot of course be deduced simply from the *de Alexandri Magni* but the conjunction of Diodorus and Arrian is convincing.

6. Plutarch and tragedy: the material is false: *de Aud. Poet.* 16a-17e passim; tragedy contrasted with historical truth: *Theseus* 1.3-4, 2.3, 15.2, 16.3-4 (cf. Plato, *Minos* 318de, 320e-321b); cf. *Romulus*

8.9. Theopompus condemned as 'tragic' for giving a false account: *Demosthenes* 21.2; Phylarchus ditto, cf. *Themistocles* 32.4; Herodotus, cf. *de Mal. Herod.* 870c; Ctesias, *Artaxerxes* 6.9; others, cf. *Alexander* 75.5. Also of philosophical arguments: *de Pyth. Or.* 399e-400c; *Adv. Col.* 1119c, 1123b.

The audience is deceived: *de Aud. Poet.* 15cd, 16a-17c, esp. 17c. So are the poets: 17d. Tragedy = pretence: in philosophy *Mor.* 528bc (*de genio Socratis*), 724d (*Quaestiones Conviviales*); in wild stories *Mor.* 926c (*de facie in Orbe lunae*) cf. *Lucullus* 11.2; putting extra tragoedia in oracles cf. *de Pyth. Or.* 407b.

The actor pretends: *Mor.* 50e (*Quomodo Adulator ab Amico Internoscatur*): cf. Ps.-Plut. *de Liberis Educandis* 13b; *Non posse suaviter vivi* 1102b.

Against actors: cf. *Sulla* 2.3-4, 36.1; *Galba* 16.3; *Apophthegmata Laconica* 212f (cf. *Agesilaos* 21.8); *Solon* 29.7; *Demosthenes* 28.3-29.7; *An Seni Resp.* 785a.

Tragedy = madness and anger: *de Cohib. Ira* 462b

Tragedy vs. philosophy *Mor.* 545f; = naughty stories *de Aud. Poet.* 27f.

Cf. also A. E. Wardman, *Plutarch's Lives* (London 1974) 168-79.

7. *Art. cit.* 167-8. For Plutarch's Platonism in general cf. eg. R. M. Jones, *The Platonism of Plutarch* (Diss. Menasha, Wisconsin 1916).

8. Deception = 'constructing a tragic machine', cf. *Them.* 10.1; *Lysander* 25.2, 26.6; Numa's meetings with the Muses etc. a 'drama': *Numa* 8.10; cf. Marius and the Syrian prophetess: *Marius* 17.5.

Pomp and circumstance to deceive the eye: *Aratus* 15.3 'tragedy and scene-painting'; *Pompey* 31.10; *Nicias* 21.1; *Lucullus* 21.6; *de Cupid. Div.* 527ef, 528b.

Tyrants and tragedy: *Demosthenes* 22.5 (*cf. de Alex. Mag.* 337d); *Lucullus* 21.3; *Poplicola* 10.3; *Antony* 54.5 (cf. *de Alex. Mag.* 329f: Persian dress 'tragic'). Nero: *Quomodo Adul.* 56e: cf. also *Galba* 14.2-3; *Quaest. Conviv.* 717c; *Pelopidas* 34.1; *Quomodo Adul.* 63a; *Praecepta Rei p. Gerendae* 823e.

Opposition of tragic to military: *Eumenes* 2.2; *Otho* 5.8.

Tragic calamities: *QC* 714e; *Galba* 1.7-8, 12.5; *Crassus* 33 passim, esp. 33.7; *Marius* 27.2; *Pompey* 9.3-4.

9. 4.5-8 (Plutarch is speculating as to the cause of Alexander's pleasant body-odour: he concludes that the κρᾶσις of Alexander's body was respon-

sible, πολύθερμος οὖσα καὶ πυρώδης, and continues by saying): Ἀλέξανδρον δ' ἡ θερμότης τοῦ σώματος ὡς ἔοικε καὶ ποτικὸν καὶ θυμοειδῆ παρεῖχεν.

Ἔτι δ' ὄντος αὐτοῦ παιδὸς ἥ τε σωφροσύνη διεφαίνετο . . .

This passage is heavily influenced by philosophy: it refers to Theophrastus' *de Odoribus* and is akin to such works as the *Airs, Waters, Places,* and . . . is a Platonic word: cf. *Rep.* 375c, 411c, 456a. As Wardman has pointed out (A. E. Wardman, 'Plutarch and Alexander', *CQ* [*Classical Quarterly*] n.s. v [1955] 96-107), θυμός and *ira* are frequently cited in Hellenistic philosophy (for example by Plutarch himself in the *de Cohibenda Ira, Mor.* 458b) as denoting bad qualities, which Alexander is used to exemplify; though in the *Life*, as in epic and often in tragedy, θυμός is more ambiguous.

10. The alternation of motifs is a favorite technique of Plutarch's: one may compare the early chapters of the *Antony,* where Antony's military virtues are dwelt on alternately with his submissiveness first to Fulvia, then to Cleopatra. On this *cf.* the forthcoming commentary by C. B. R. Pelling.

11. For recent, perceptive accounts of this relationship *cf.* R. B. Rutherford, 'Tragic Form and Feeling in the *Iliad*', *JHS* cii (1982) 145-60, and J. Gould, 'Homeric Epic and the Tragic Moment', in T. Winnifrith *et al.* (edd.) *Aspects of the Epic* (London 1983).

12. Eur. *Med.* 626 ff.:

ἔρωτες ὑπὲρ μὲν ἄγαν
ἐλθόντες οὐκ εὐδοξίαν
οὐδ' ἀρετὰν παρέδωκαν
ἀνδράσιν.

13. *Cf.* E. E. Rice, *The Grand Procession of Ptolemy Philadelphus* (Oxford 1983) 112-3: Athenaeus 201f: there were twenty-four extremely large lions in the procession with statues of Alexander and Ptolemy. For lions' role in Dionysiac cult *cf.* the lion in the Hellenistic Dionysiac procession in the dromos of the Memphian Serapeum and the frieze of the Great Altar of Pergamum. Lions are frequent on later sarcophagi depicting Dionysus' Indian Campaign, either as part of his triumph or drawing the god's chariot.

Lions and Alexander: *cf.* Curt. Ruf. v 1.21 (A. fights a lion in Bactria) and viii 1.14 (he is given presents of lions by the Babylonians). Lions are royal animals in the east. A. hunts lions on the Alexander sarcophagus; a Delphian statue of Cra-

terus records that C. saved A.'s life on a lion-hunt (*FD* 111 [4] 137). A. wore the lion-skin as Heracles: Ath. 537f.

14. The two are closely associated by Plutarch, as we have seen, at 4.7-8: they are seen as springing from the same natural cause.

15. Clearly in the *Bacchae* both elements are present; but the terrifying aspect is uppermost in the end.

For Alexander as Dionysus in Alexandria *cf.* Rice, 43, 48 (Dionysus' Indian triumph in the light of Alexander's successes in the east), 67 (Alexander as new Dionysus following in the god's footsteps, identifying landmarks associated with the god. *Cf.* Arrian v 1.1 ff., vi 28.1 ff., vii 20.1 ff., *Ind.* i 1 ff., v 8 ff.). The key text is Athenaeus 200d-201c, the procession of Dionysus (*cf.* Rice *passim,* esp. 83-6 and P. M. Fraser, *Ptolemaic Alexandria* [Oxford 1972] 202-6, 211): Alexander is more the hero of the procession than Dionysus. Dionysus in military contexts: *cf.* Eur. *Cyc.* 5 ff., *Ba.* 13-20.

The Ptolemies connect themselves with A. through Dionysus: *cf.* the genealogy in Satyrus. The procession is 'the indirect celebration of A. through the glorification of D.' (Rice).

Rice sums up: (191-2) 'The importance of the emphatic presentation of Alexander as the Neos Dionysos who followed in the footsteps of the god and succeeded as an equal conqueror in the east can hardly be over-estimated. These scenes from the Dionysiac procession give support to the claims that this picture of Alexander had an Alexandrian origin . . . the Ptolemaic kings adopted and publicised this view of Alexander, and shared in the glory of this vision themselves through their claim to a blood-relationship with both A. and D. This in turn enhanced their position as the legitimate heirs of Alexander in Egypt and endowed them with a convenient legitimisation of the divine status of their dynasty.'

Cf. also P. Goukowsky, *Essai sur les origines du mythe d'Alexandre* (Nancy 1978-81) vol. II *passim,* esp. 79 ff.

For the similar link in the *Antony, cf.* esp. *Ant.* 24.

16. It is perhaps possible that the use of θεατρικὴν here rather than τραγικὴν is significant, either because Plutarch is thinking of another genre, mime, for instance, or because he does not want to label the episode directly as tragic, as, after all, it does turn out happily; if either of these possibilities is correct, then this is an exception which proves a rule.

17. Most frequently in art, for example on his coins, and on the Alexander sarcophagus.

Shakespeare (*Henry V* IV vii) makes Fluellen compare Henry's rejection of Falstaff with the death of Cleitus:

Alexander—God knows, and you know—in his rages, and his furies, and his wraths, and his cholers, and his moods, and his displeasures, and his indignations, and also being a little intoxicates in his prains, did, in his ales and his angers, look you, kill his best friend, Cleitus. . . . I speak but in the figures and comparisons of it; as Alexander kill'd his friend Cleitus, being in his ales and his cups, so also Harry Monmouth, being in his right wits and his good judgments, turn'd away the fat knight with the great belly doublet; . . .

18. For discussion on Plutarch's views on ruler-cult *cf.* K. Scott, 'Plutarch and the Ruler Cult', *TAPA* lx (1929) 117-35; G. W. Bowersock, 'Greek Intellectuals and the Imperial Cult in the Second Century AD', *Entr. Hardt.* xix (1972), esp. 187-90; S. R. F. Price, *Rituals and Power* (Cambridge 1984) 116-7.

19. Homer, *Il.* xix 375 ff.:

ὡς δ' ὅτ' ἄν ἐκ πόντοιο <u>σέλας</u> ναύτηισι φανήηι καιομένοιο πυρός, τό τε καίεται ὑψόθ' ὄρεσφι σταθμῶι ἐν οἰοπόλωι· τοὺς δ' οὐκ ἐθέλοντας ἄελλαι

πόντον ἐπ' ἰχθυόεντα φίλων ἀπάνευθε φέρουσιν· ὡς ἀπ' Ἀχιλλῆος σάκεος <u>σέλας</u> αἰθέρ' ἵκανε καλοῦ δαιδαλέου· περὶ δὲ τρυφάλειαν ἀείρας κρατὶ θέτο βριαρὴν· ἡ δ' ἀστὴρ ὡς ἀπέλαμπεν ἵππουρις τρυφάλεια, περισσείοντο δ ἔθειραι χρύσεαι, ἃς Ἥφαιστος ἵει λόφον ἀμφὶ θαμείας.

20. The Calanus-incident, and Alexander subsequently ignoring his advice, is typical of a *topos* which goes back to Herodotus and (for example) Croesus' encounter with Solon (Hdt. i 29-32); on the other hand, despite Alexander's heedlessness of Calanus' counsel, Plutarch obviously does wish to portray him as being well-disposed towards philosophers, as we see from 7-8, 14 and 64. There are certainly traces of Onesicritus in 64-5: Alexander *philosophus* is being hinted at here, and it is Onesicritus who visits the sophists in 65.

21. *Cf.* F. Walbank, 'Tragic history: a reconsideration', *BICS [Bulletin of the International Classical Society]* ii (1955), 4-14; 'Tragedy and History', *Historia* ix (1960) 216-34, repr. *Selected Papers* ch. 15, 224-41; C. B. R. Pelling, 'Plutarch's Adaptation of his Source-Material', *JHS [Journal of Hellenic Studies]* c (1980) 127-40, esp. 132 n. 26; and D. A. Russell, *Plutarch* (London 1972) 123.

22. For Caesar destroyed by external factors, *cf.* Pelling, *art. cit.* 136-7. He also notes how material

on Caesar's personal (especially sexual) habits, extensively used elsewhere, is largely suppressed in the *Life.*

There is a strong atmosphere of divine threat in the last chapters of the *Caesar* (the many omens, the accounts of how Caesar is *nearly* warned more than once of the conspiracy, culminating in Pompey's statue as it were presiding over his death), which could be seen as comparable to the handling of the Cleitus incident in the *Alexander,* but this is never pinned down as tragic in the same manner: an important difference, I think.

23. The handling of the material in the *Themistocles* perhaps supports this.

24. With the possible exception of Heliodorus, whose use of stage-terms is extensive and complex. On this *cf.* J. W. H. Walden, 'Stage-terms in Heliodorus' *Aethiopica*' HSCP [*Harvard Studies in Classical Philology*] v (1894) 1-43.

A. B. Bosworth (essay date 1988)

SOURCE: Bosworth, A. B. "The Peroration: Arrian's View of Alexander." In *From Arrian to Alexander: Studies in Historical Interpretation,* pp. 135-56. Oxford: Clarendon Press, 1988.

[*In the following excerpt, Bosworth notes inconsistencies in Arrian's portrayal of Alexander and contends that the historian was conflicted in his dual role as a panegyrist and a moral critic.*]

Arrian's work ends in a carefully contrived panegyric, extended and fulsome (vii. 28. 1-30. 3). In the ninth century AD Photius noted dryly that the author praises his hero for virtually every known virtue,[1] and the modern reader will concur heartily. After recording Alexander's death and the length of his reign Arrian embarks on a catalogue of the king's excellences, phrased consistently in the superlative. Qualities of mind balance bodily virtues (28. 1). In rapid succession Alexander is characterized as a brilliant, almost prophetic, strategist, an inspiring and successful commander, a ruler dependable in his compacts but perceptive of falsehood, who combined personal frugality with generosity to others (28. 2-3). From encomium Arrian proceeds to apology (29. 1-4), discounting various moral objections to the king's behaviour on a number of grounds, some of them highly sophistical. He ends with an almost impassioned demand that Alexander's actions be viewed in their totality, their greatness contrasted with the insignificance of the critic. His overwhelming achievement sets him apart from the rest of humanity,[2] proving that there was divine agency at work in his birth. There may be flaws in the diamond, but its size and brilliance are matchless, its value unimpaired.

This encomium has many peculiarities. It is extremely fulsome but at the same time strangely defensive. The chapter of apology is far longer and far more elaborate than the initial panegyric, and it is conceived in a strongly polemical vein, designed to counter criticisms of Alexander that were entrenched in popular thought and literature. Some of the same flavour can be traced in Curtius Rufus (x. 5. 26-36), who also gives a summary of Alexander's virtues as a commentary on the refusal of the queen mother, Sisygambis, to survive the death of her conqueror. There is a similar contrast of virtues and vices, but the apology is more conventional: the virtues come from Alexander's nature, the vices from his fortune and youth. The virtues of nature do bear a close relation to those in Arrian: *vis animi*, physical stamina, liberality, fearlessness, piety, sexual temperance. Similarly the faults of fortune are much the same as those discounted by Arrian: the encroachment on the divine, excessive irascibility, orientalizing in dress and policy (33). At first sight one is tempted to posit a common source, but there are too many divergences for that hypothesis to be sustained. Curtius' catalogue is a list of moral virtues: there is no appreciation of Alexander's qualities as a general, except for a perfunctory passing reference to his *consilium* and *sollertia* (x. 5. 31). Arrian's encomium is slanted towards the practical virtues which were responsible for his accomplishments. The moral virtues are less prominent. Some, in particular *clementia,* are notable for their absence. On the other hand Curtius is prepared to accept the vices for what they are and admits the degenerative role of fortune. He goes so far as to suggest that Alexander's irascibility and appetite for wine might have been mitigated by the advancing years (34), but that is the limit of it. There is none of Arrian's committed and sophistical apology, which comes close to claiming the vices as virtues and falling under his own censure.[3] The two passages are clearly independent elaborations of a common theme, and both authors draw upon a stock of approved virtues and criticisms which has little or nothing to do with the historical material they record.[4]

Arrian's catalogue of virtues stands in isolation. There is no attempt to connect it with the campaign narrative, and it is hard to see how it could be connected. Some motifs may admittedly be foreshadowed in the fuller narrative. The praise of Alexander's talents of anticipation recalls episodes like the march on Thebes, the advance into Uxian territory or the stratagem used at Massaga,[5] while the description of his creative generalship (vii. 28. 2) probably owes something to Ptolemy's penchant for explaining Alexander's calculations in advance and underlining how they were vindicated.[6] The commendation of the king's temperate attitude to sensual gratification also echoes the earlier encomiastic treatment of his behaviour towards the royal captives (iv. 19. 6). There Arrian praises Alexander's temperance in the face of all the enticements of youth and good fortune and attributes it to a desire for good repute. Two themes are linked together and are recapitulated in the final encomium, rhetorically juxtaposed.[7] But other themes have no obvious counterparts. Arrian's narrative certainly does not highlight Alexander's reliability in keeping promises, and, as has been noted, the survivors of Massaga, on Arrian's own account, had justifiable complaints against his good faith.[8] Nor is Alexander's immunity from deception a feature of the regular narrative.[9] Most striking of all is the paradoxical claim that Alexander was sparing in the use of money for his pleasures. This is at total variance with the record of banqueting during the last years, which Arrian himself documents. I suspect that he has been influenced by his own (and others') rhetoric. At Opis he had made Alexander disclaim any wealth of his own and portray himself as the servant and benefactor of his subjects.[10] In general the qualities adduced by Arrian are imperfectly attested in his narrative. The inspiration for the encomium should be looked for outside his range of specifically historical material.

Some literary models spring immediately to mind. As most commentators note, the description of Alexander's skill in foretelling the outcome of present actions is irresistibly reminiscent of Thucydides' famous characterization of Themistocles.[11] That passage, like so much of Thucydides, was deeply ingrained upon Arrian. He was to use it in a similar context in the *History of the Successors*[12] where he praises Demosthenes and fuses its terminology with echoes of another Thucydidean character-sketch, that of Antiphon.[13] But, important as Thucydides undoubtedly was, Xenophon was the greater inspiration. One of the most impressive passages of the *Anabasis* is the sustained eulogy of Cyrus the Younger, which Xenophon places immediately after his report of that prince's death.[14] This begins like Arrian's encomium with a string of superlatives (βασιλικώτατός τε καὶ ἄρχειν ἀξιώτατος κτλ.) and proceeds with a catalogue of boyhood and adult virtues, consistently framed in the superlative. Many qualities stressed by Arrian reappear here: intrepidity, reliability in keeping promises, unsurpassed magnanimity to friends.[15] In fact Cyrus' behaviour in giving and receiving presents, as described by Xenophon,[16] could serve as a commentary on Arrian's final antithesis (at vii. 28. 3). But the praise of Cyrus is a simple catalogue of virtues exemplified in action without the forced rhetorical antithesis of Arrian.

A closer parallel is furnished by Xenophon's most extended encomium, his essay on the Spartan king Agesilaus. There Xenophon presents Agesilaus as a canon of moral virtue.[17] He expounds his hero's excellences in deliberate précis, to assist his readers' memory (11. 1), and he uses antithesis constantly, building up a climactic deluge of superlatives.[18] The similarities with Arrian both in form and in content are undeniable. In the body of the text there are successive eulogies of Agesilaus' restraint towards money and generosity to his friends (4. 1-6), his total temperance with regard to food, drink, and sex (5) and his inspirational leadership in battle (6. 4-8). All these elements have their brief counterpart in Arrian's characterization of Alexander. His catalogue of virtues amounts to a fusion of Thucydides' Themistocles with Xenophon's Agesilaus; the strategic foresight of the one is wedded to the moral excellence of the other. The form too was dictated by Xenophon. Arrian has refined the style, with more balanced antithesis and borrowings from Thucydides, but his immediate model is evident. One immediately recalls the famous passage of Book i where Arrian complains that, thanks to the genius of Xenophon, the achievements of Cyrus and the Ten Thousand are more celebrated than those of Alexander and explicitly sets up his own work in competition.[19] His Alexander could not be second to Xenophon's Cyrus or Clearchus, and his final encomium needed to surpass that of Xenophon. Surpass it it did, but only by superimposing moral virtues which had little support in the actions of Alexander that Arrian recorded.

The form of the encomium, based on antithesis and phrased in superlatives, is, as we have seen, borrowed from Xenophon. Other passages similar in style and sentiment but shorter in scope occur elsewhere in the Alexander history and were perhaps a feature of Arrian's mature historical writing.[20] If the relevant entries in the 'Suda' are correctly ascribed to him (and linguistically and stylistically they are difficult to fault), he gave shorter but comparable appreciations of Demosthenes and Craterus in the *History of the Successors* and of one of the early Arsacid monarchs in the *Parthica*.[21] The latter passage is very strikingly similar, echoing the vocabulary of vii. 28. 1-2 and stressing similar virtues with similar (occasionally identical) superlatives.[22] But there is something very different in the appreciation of Alexander, and that is the defence or mitigation of his vices. All the other examples in Arrian or, for that matter, in Xenophon are undiluted encomia. There is no hint of anything which required apology. In the case of Alexander the praise is emphatic in the extreme but it is outweighed by the defence.

Is Arrian here borrowing from one of his sources, taking over a brief already prepared? At first sight one might think so.[23] The chapter ends with a famous citation of Aristobulus, in which that author maintained that Alexander drank little wine but sat up late out of

courtesy to his friends.[24] Some of the material which precedes it may also come from Aristobulus, notably the observations on Alexander's motives for drafting Persian troops into Macedonian units.[25] That passage takes up two episodes recounted somewhat earlier: the admission of selected nobles into the cavalry *agema* (vii. 6. 4-5) and the drafting of native levies from Persis into the phalanx (vii. 23. 3-4). The reference here is not simple recapitulation but reflects a substantial shift of emphasis.[26] The Persian troops incorporated in the phalanx are the crack guards, the *melophoroi*, whereas in the earlier narrative it is implied that the new levies from Persis were simple tribesmen. More significantly Arrian terms the Persian nobles ὁμότιμοι, a designation which recurs only once in his work, in the context of the Persian ladies captured at Issus.[27] The word is obviously taken from one of his sources, and it was not the source for vii. 6. 4. There the Persian nobles were admitted into the cavalry *agema* alone: here both the cavalry and infantry *corps d'élite* (τοῖς ἀγήμασι[28]) are at issue. There the admission of the nobles was one of a number of Macedonian grievances; here it is interpreted as a conscious device to conciliate the barbarians and create a defence against the arrogance of the Macedonians. The latter motif occurred in the vulgate tradition[29] and may well have occurred in Aristobulus also. If that is so, Arrian used at least some material from his second source which he passed over in the earlier narrative, reserving it for his defence of Alexander.

Other themes in the chapter might also be attributed to Aristobulus, the defence on the score of youth and fortune or even (at a pinch) the crass mitigation of the murder of Cleitus. What seems to me impossible for Aristobulus is the blatantly cynical interpretation of Alexander's claims to divine sonship (vii. 29. 3). No contemporary of Alexander could view the great king's relation with Ammon as a mere *sophisma*; and there were obvious dangers in such an attitude while contemporary monarchs were making similar pretensions— Demetrius as son of Poseidon and Seleucus as son of Apollo.[30] On the other hand in Arrian's day the claim to be son of a deity was a historical curiosity, unrelated to the contemporary ruler-cult. He could discuss. Alexander as son of Zeus/Ammon in an entirely neutral way, placing any interpretation he liked upon the relationship, whereas the worship of the living Alexander was a far more perilous theme.[31] Criticism of the deification of the king came close to criticism of the living emperor. While such criticism might be embodied in a speech by the historical Callisthenes, to be implicitly disavowed,[32] it could hardly be voiced by Arrian in his own person.

Indeed Alexander's pretensions to divinity are rarely the subject of discussion during the early Empire. Seneca, the most persistent critic, never refers to them but selects other traits for denunciation.[33] On a less exalted level Lucian satirizes Alexander in his *Dialogues of the Dead* and contrasts the fact of his mortality with his claims to divinity. But those claims are based solely on his presumed relations with Ammon; it is not suggested that he demanded worship in his own right. And Lucian, like Arrian, is cynical about his motivation: 'I accepted the oracle for my own purposes . . . the barbarians thought they were fighting against a god, so I conquered them the more easily.'[34] That was neutral ground. Like the imposition of *proskynesis* the claim to divine sonship was remote from contemporary practice and could serve as a moral *exemplum*. That is how Arrian approaches the subject. He accepts that it was a defect in his hero to have referred his birth to the divine. He concedes the possibility that it was a trick to impose upon his subjects (which made it justifiable) and adds that Alexander had as much reason for his belief as had the heroes of antiquity. Once again Arrian seems keen to steer his argument away from deification proper. The examples that he chooses are not the familiar examples from Alexander's lifetime, Heracles, Dionysus, and the Dioscuri,[35] all of whom were in some sense deities. Instead he parades the two founding fathers of Athens and Ionia (Theseus and Ion), implicitly contrasting Alexander, the paradigm of the city founder. Somewhat more surprising is the selection of the three judges of the underworld, Minos, Aeacus, and Rhadamanthys. Arrian may be implicitly recalling his eulogy of Alexander's critical acumen and perception of deceit, suggesting that his hero is at least the equal of the infallible and incorruptible judges of the dead.[36] His preliminary researches for the *Bithyniaka* may have enlarged his acquaintance with the relevant myths. At least he was to write in detail about the family of Europe, claiming (somewhat eccentrically) that Aeacus and Minos were brothers,[37] and he may already have been predisposed to think of the underworld triad as a set of full brothers, sons of Zeus and Europe. At all events the selection of parallels must be Arrian's own, his aim to show Alexander as the equal and more than the equal of the most distinguished mythological heroes but not encroaching upon the territory of the gods.

The defence of Alexander is not plagiarism. It may, as we have seen, include material from Aristobulus, deliberately held in reserve for the peroration, but the disposition is original. The problem remains as to why Arrian is so strongly on the defensive and why he spoils the effect of the catalogue of virtues by appending an exculpation of avowed misdeeds. In this he is not unique. There is, for instance, a similar passage in Aelius Aristeides' *Panathenaic Oration,* where the speaker defends Athens against conventional criticisms of her destruction of Melos and Scione.[38] To some extent he follows traditional lines, almost echoing Isocrates in his insistence that the Athenians ruled more moderately

than could have been expected of them, so that their aberrations—against men who were recognized enemies—were particularly noticeable.[39] But the main line of defence recalls Arrian's challenge to the critics of Alexander. The city should not be reproached for one or two faults but the totality of her actions must be examined. If one or two are alone reprehensible, it is an implicit encomium of the rest.[40] Aristeides ends the passage with an analogy that Arrian himself might have envied. Like the sun and moon Athens must be judged by the sum total of her actions, which eclipses the very few deeds of harm.[41] That could hardly be closer to Arrian's position in his final chapter. There is also a common stress on the virtue of remorse, Aristeides praising Athens for her annulment of the verdict of Mytilene (310). The coincidences strongly suggest a common stock of rhetorical *topoi* which both authors deployed to combat automatic objections to their laudation. No encomiast of fifth-century Athens could avoid confronting the atrocities of Melos and Scione, and no encomiast of Alexander could evade equally standard criticisms.

Now the conventional criticisms of Alexander view him as a classic instance of the corruption of power.[42] Whether his arrogance or immoderation was inbred or the effect of unbroken and good fortune,[43] it was manifested in a series of arbitrary and tyrannical acts. The best catalogue is probably given by Livy, in his indignant contrast of Roman virtue with the degeneracy of the Macedonian king. If he had crossed into Italy at the end of his reign, he would have been more like Darius than the original Alexander, now that he had been submerged in the flood of fortune: *referre in tanto rege piget superbam mutationem vestis et desideratas humi iacentium adulationes . . . et foeda supplicia et inter vinum et epulas caedes amicorum et vanitatem ementiendae stirpis* (ix. 18. 4). Livy proceeds to stigmatize his addiction to wine and his increasingly intractable anger. These are precisely the allegation Arrian tries to defend: the crimes of irascibility, the claim to divine sonship, the assumption of Persian dress, and the propensity to heavy drinking. There was evidently a standard list of *exempla* which would be adduced to enlarge upon the theme of Alexander the immoderate despot. That comes out clearly in the work of Dio of Prusa. In that author's attractive second discourse on kingship (a dialogue between Philip and Alexander) the young prince appears as a high-minded and virtuous enthusiast of Homer. However, in the first discourse, Alexander is briefly brought on scene as the traditional bundle of vices: he would punish with exceptional severity, rage at his friends and comrades, and disdain his mortal and real parents.[44] Once it fitted his rhetorical purposes, Dio would regurgitate the stock description; and the choice of *exampla* was clearly determined by the subject-matter of the discussion.

Rhetorical convention provided Arrian with a standard list of vices, and his defence is deeply coloured by rhetorical practice. The acts of anger and despotism are admitted but discounted on three grounds. All had been foreshadowed in the body of his narrative. As we have seen, the defence on the grounds of youth and good fortune was anticipated in the encomium of Alexander's sexual restraint and it was obviously a standard theme, echoed by Curtius.[45] The argument is strengthened by an observation on the ill effects of flattery. Once again the theme recurs in the narrative. Darius' fatal error at Issus is attributed to the malign effects of flattery, that inevitable evil of sovereignty, and, more significantly, the origins of the Cleitus tragedy are traced to unprincipled flattery by Alexander's courtiers.[46] The sentiments and wording are echoed in Arrian's defence and they must have been commonly used in contemporary rhetoric. Plutarch also ascribes the ruin of Callisthenes, Parmenion, and Philotas to the insidious actions of flatterers, the gangrenes and cancers of the court.[47] But Plutarch's picture is highly unflattering to Alexander, who is said to have been 'worshipped, dressed up, and moulded like a barbarian idol'; and Arrian himself must have been embarrassed by the argument, which implied that his hero had a penchant for self-deception. If he were a prey to flattery, it was perverse to claim simultaneously that he was invulnerable to deception.

Not surprisingly, Arrian moves to a stronger debating-point, Alexander's capacity for remorse. Once more this recalls his earlier narrative, where he reprehends Alexander's loss of control and his inebriation but praises his immediate admission of fault after Cleitus' death.[48] The theme is now developed as the basis of the defence. Remorse does not excuse the error but it makes it more tolerable.[49] Here Arrian is at his most rhetorical, far removed from the ethical teaching of Epictetus, which might be thought to have underpinned his appreciation of Alexander.[50] The Stoa had traditionally regarded repentance as a characteristic of the base individual (φαῦλος), a typical manifestation of his emotional instability which was the polar opposite of the unchanging virtuous disposition of the sage.[51] Admittedly from the time of Aristotle and Epicurus there had been some concession that the consciousness of error was the beginning of virtue: *initium est salutis notitia peccati.*[52] But this was a long way from the acceptance of remorse as a moral virtue. It was a *sine qua non* of moral improvement, and, according to Seneca and Plutarch, one of the primary functions of philosophy was to inculcate a consciousness of error and desire for moral improvement. But remorse was not a virtue in itself; good cannot be generated from ill, any more than a fig-tree from an olive.[53] At best Alexander's remorse at Cleitus' death might be seen as a sign that he was not beyond redemption but had the capacity for improvement.[54] For Arrian, however, the capacity for remorse is

an actual virtue, and he does not seriously expect improvement. There would have been more rash acts had Alexander lived and they would have been mitigated by more repentance. As far as I can see, Arrian had no precedent for this view. He contributed a new theme to literature. Julian later elaborated it, making his Alexander apologize for his harsher acts on the ground that they were followed by remorse, 'that altogether temperate spirit which is the saviour of wrongdoing'.[55] 'It is, however, a highly sophisticated argument, which only the converted could entertain. Cleitus and the other victims of Alexander gained no consolation from his regrets.

Arrian's defence, despite its recapitulation of earlier themes, sits very uneasily with what went before. Most of his material was tackled in the great excursus in Book iv (7. 4-14. 4), and Arrian's moral attitudes are significantly different in that context. In the peroration he accepts Aristobulus' view that Alexander did not drink heavily, whereas in the prelude to Cleitus' death he emphasizes that his drinking was becoming more barbaric (iv. 8. 2). The two statements are irreconcilable. More interesting is Arrian's attitude to the assumption of Persian court dress. This is an episode which is not mentioned at its correct chronological place in 330. Instead Arrian uses it as a moral *exemplum,* to be reprobated or explained away. In the peroration it is a political device to conciliate the barbarians and neutralize the Macedonians, and Arrian goes some way towards Plutarch's interpretation of court dress as a symbol of political fusion.[56] In the earlier passage (iv. 7. 4) it is simply the standard illustration of degeneration into autocracy.

Arrian's attitude is interesting at a more general level. His condemnation of court dress comes in the wider context of condemnation of barbarian excess, seen at its worst in the mutilation of Bessus. Arrian was clearly shocked by what he read. One of his most appealing features is revulsion against cruelty. Though a passionate huntsman, he was distressed by the death of his quarry, and he takes Xenophon to task for his exultation in the kill.[57] The mutilation of Bessus revolted him and he reacted strongly, condemning it as an act of oriental extravagance. He appends another example of the same trait (Persian dress) and concludes with a quasi-philosophical homily: Alexander's entire career is an object-lesson that the greatest good fortune is no guarantee of happiness (εὐδαιμονία) unless its recipient is also endowed with moderation (iv. 7. 5-6). That comes close to the moral position taken by Epictetus, who stated forthrightly that happiness was to be found in none of the externals, not in wealth, in office, or in kingship.[58] The poverty of a Diogenes is infinitely preferable in terms of happiness to the pomp of the Great King. For Arrian also, when he comments on

Bessus' punishment, Alexander is the antithesis of the sage, the type of barbarian arrogance, and his assumption of Persian court dress is one of the most notable symptoms of immoderation.

The same moral stance is evident when Arrian focuses upon Alexander's lust for conquest. He was insatiable and, if there were no other rival, he would have competed with himself (vii. 1. 4). This note of reluctant admiration is then stifled by an approving reference (ἐπὶ τῷδε ἐπαινῶ) to the virtuous admonition of the Indian gymnosophists who reminded Alexander of his mortality and stressed the futility of conquest as an end in itself. Arrian then remarks that the king praised the sentiments but ignored the advice, just as he had ignored the virtuous example of Diogenes.[59] Once more the passage reflects Epictetan scorn for externals. The attitude of the gymnosophists is the attitude of the sage typified by Diogenes, who treats as slaves the powerful and feared of this world—'who on seeing me does not imagine that he sees his king and master'.[60] Arrian's conclusion is conventional. The episode proves that Alexander was to some degree capable of seeing the better but was marred by his desire for glory. His appetite for fame becomes a besetting vice, marring his acquisition of true virtue. Once again there is a contradiction of the rhetoric of the peroration,[61] where Alexander is approvingly dubbed φιλοτιμότατος and his unshakeable desire for praise is singled out as laudable (vii. 28. 2). The canons of the rhetorical encomium were substantially different from those of popular moral philosophy.

This oscillation of values can be seen in the various works of the emperor Julian, more than two centuries later. When the context is an overt panegyric of Macedon, Alexander is the paradigm of virtue, excelling in generalship as in everything else, and his military achievement is the crown of his success.[62] Elsewhere, when the aim is to praise the virtues of philosophy, the emphasis changes and the conquests are discounted: 'Who has ever found salvation through Alexander's victories? What city was ever more wisely governed because of them? What individual improved? Many indeed you might find whom those conquests enriched, but not one whom they made wiser or more temperate.'[63] The king's lust for fame also leads to perplexity. According to one's intentions, whether praise or blame, it could be interpreted as innate greatness of virtue or excess leading to empty vainglory.[64] By this time the rhetoric is predetermined. The centuries of literary, rhetorical, and philosophical debate have produced admitted clichés, and the conventional picture of Alexander is divorced from the detailed record of his reign. This type of rhetorical moralizing is a minor but significant element in Arrian's writing. Its direction is determined by the immediate context. In particular,

when he criticizes Alexander's desire for fame, his language inevitably echoes the platitudes of Stoic and Cynic moral philosophy.

A philosophical basis to Arrian's moral criticisms is less evident elsewhere, but it does leave its traces, notably in the excursus in Book iv, where the more extravagant features of the tradition are treated together. The picture of the king is at its most adverse: the indictment for barbarian arrogance is repeated, the malign influence of the flatterers underscored.[65] There is no denying the fact that he acted repeatedly out of *hybris*, and Arrian regards his subjection to wine and intoxication as pitiable (iv. 9. 1). That is not far from Epictetus' observations on tyranny: it is not the victim of despotic violence who is harmed; rather it is the person who inflicts the violence who is in the most pitiable state.[66] Arrian does praise Alexander for his repentance after Cleitus' murder, but he does not (as in the peroration) claim the capacity for remorse as a moral virtue. It is rather a sign of his capacity for improvement, in the same category as his appreciation of the gymnosophists. Arrian, at least in this restricted context, was not inconsistent with the old Stoic view that the *need* for repentance is an evil, the characteristic of an unhappy and unstable *psyche*. Alexander's disposition may have been reprehensible but it contained the ingredients for improvement.

On the other hand Arrian is severely critical of other actors in the drama. Anaxarchus was a moral disaster, urging that justice was a totally relative concept, the whim of the ruler.[67] Cleitus was to blame for his insulting remarks (iv. 8. 5, 9. 1), as, most emphatically, was Callisthenes. Now at first sight this censure of free criticism seems a total contradiction of Epictetus' practice of *parrhesia*, which Arrian himself praises in his prefatory *Letter to Gellius*,[68] and the virtuous behaviour of men like Helvidius Priscus and Paconius Agrippinus, who would not compromise their ideals of the duties of their station by complying with tyranny.[69] But the moral situation is not altogether clear-cut. Arrian has nothing against plain speaking in itself. The edifying reproofs of the gymnosophists are retailed very favourably, and the frankness of Coenus at the Hyphasis, though displeasing to Alexander (v. 28. 1), is documented without adverse comment, indeed with implicit approval. What was wrong with Callisthenes' criticism was that it was misplaced (ἄκαιρος), an act of gratuitous stupidity.[70] It is clear that Arrian regarded Callisthenes' behaviour as blatant self-advertisement. He exalted himself at the king's expense and had no concern for the moral improvement of his royal master. Arrian had recorded Epictetus' recommendation that a man should not assume a *persona* beyond his powers,[71] and no doubt felt that Callisthenes was monstrously ill equipped to take on the role of a sage at court. His motives were not virtue but self-gratification, rather like Epictetus' convert to Cynicism who considered the career of the sage a licence for promiscuous abuse.[72] Cleitus' actions were worse, *hybris* and drunken *hybris* at that (iv. 8. 7), incompatible with any concept of the duty of a subject. The correct action was to preserve one's own dignity and attempt quietly to promote the king's fortunes (iv. 12. 6). There is a flavour of Epictetan thought here. If one has assumed the role of courtier, one must play that role, not shaming oneself by flattery but without undermining the regime by ostentatious public opposition. Silence may often be the best policy (iv. 8. 5). Now, even in his most critical moments, Arrian never thought of Alexander as depraved or lacking virtue and, on his interpretation, the most punctilious Stoic would not wash his hands of him. The general attitude is reminiscent of Thrasea Paetus in the early years of Nero's reign: *silentio vel brevi adsensu priores adulationes transmittere solitus.*[73] Thrasea only publicized his objections after the crowning enormity of the murder of Agrippina, Previously he was prepared to compromise with the regime, not stooping to flattery but offering no overt opposition. That was close to the ideal praised by Arrian.

Elsewhere the moral comment has no philosophical content. The criticism of the burning of Persepolis is based on common sense, as is the shocked reaction to the letter to Cleomenes (vii. 23. 8): any man in his right senses would think the same. Similarly he endorses the general censure of Alexander's recklessness at the Malli town (vi. 13. 4), commenting that he could see the merits of prudence but was carried away by the excitement of battle and desire for glory.[74] Once again the obsessive search for fame is represented as Alexander's besetting sin, a positively harmful characteristic, and Epictetus with his repeated insistence that glory is external and desire for it futile could only have agreed.[75] But there is no strong or consistent philosophical underpinning. When Arrian is moved to criticism, he assumes modes of thought that find parallels in Epictetus. The bulk of his narrative is devoid of moral judgements for good or ill. The tone of the peroration, however, is remarkable for its total absence of Stoic thought and almost revels in Alexander's devoted pursuit of glory. It reflects the values of the rhetorical schools, and the contradictions, as we have seen, are many and blatant.

The inconsistency of judgement betrays a certain inconsistency of purpose. In Arrian's work panegyric and moral criticism blend together in an uneasy union. Other writers insisted on a distinction of genres. Polybius, for instance, distinguishes his early encomiastic biography of Philopoemen from a history proper. The former, being panegyrical, demanded a brief report, designed to enhance the actions, whereas history, which

contains praise and blame alike, requires a true statement, clearly put, with the considerations that accompanied each action.[76] The contrast is highly pertinent to Arrian. At one level his work is avowed panegyric. He claims to give an account of Alexander's achievements which will do them credit and is explicit that his work is a literary tribute. On the other hand there were facets of his sources' picture which he could not accept, and it was his duty as a conscientious historian to single them out for criticism. That was a commonplace of historical thinking, whether voiced by a professed Stoic such as Poseidonius or an eclectic like Tacitus;[77] and it is hardly surprising that Arrian felt it incumbent upon him to reprove some of Alexander's actions in the interests of truth and utility (vii. 30. 3). But the greater aim was the encomium of Alexander, and the peroration marks its climax. The string of excellences eclipses the virtues of a Cyrus or an Agesilaus, and the conventional criticisms are placed in perspective, flaws but not detracting from the total picture. In the last analysis Alexander's greatness depends on his conquests, for it was as a conqueror that his name had penetrated to every race and city of mankind (vii. 30. 2). Viewed in that light his desire for fame and the military qualities that achieved his fame are elevated into primary virtues Yet earlier, when the focus of discussion was different, those ambitions could be stigmatized as supererogatory and inimical to true happiness. The emphasis and indeed the whole hierarchy of values changes with the context of discussion.

Arrian was not, of course, alone in his dilemma. Curtius Rufus' inconsistencies are no less blatant and far more numerous,[78] given his greater penchant for interlarding his narrative with moral comment. But any historian who had historical favourites and a modicum of honesty was forced into inconsistency. A particularly good example is provided by Tacitus, whose comparison between Germanicus and Alexander could almost serve as a commentary upon these final chapters of Arrian. Tacitus' portrait of Germanicus, like Arrian's of Alexander, was in general highly favourable, although there is an occasional hint of criticism.[79] Germanicus' death is the occasion for a brilliant eulogy, characteristically phrased in *oratio obliqua,* in the guise of remarks by bystanders at the funeral (*Ann.* ii. 73. 1-3). The deceased prince is compared with Alexander on the superficial basis of age and fashion of death: both were physically handsome, of distinguished lineage, and died in their early thirties. But Tacitus then embarks on a *deterior comparatio,*[80] using all the standard criticisms of Alexander's immoderation and treating him solely as a foil to Germanicus. Unlike Alexander, the type of irascibility, Germanicus was mild with his friends; and he was the paradigm of moral virtue, moderate in his pleasures, content with a single marriage and with children of determinate parentage.[81] Next the historian has to face the inevitable criticism. How could Germanicus, whose military achievements were insignificant, be compared favourably with Alexander? The answer is that he had been prevented from following up his victories and reducing Germany to servitude. If, like Alexander, he had been a free agent and had enjoyed regal power, he would easily have overhauled his military glory, just as he eclipsed him in moral virtue, notably temperance and clemency.

Tacitus sustains the comparison by concentrating on his hero's undoubted uprightness. The defects of strategy are forgotten. The record in Germany was one of victory, and the only reason why no permanent conquests accrued was the malicious obstructiveness of Tiberius.[82] What emerges is a caricature of the earlier narrative,[83] an implicit denial of military error or military reverses, and Germanicus is seen resplendent as a potential world conqueror frustrated by the political limitations of his command. Tacitus of course avoids direct responsibility for the comparison, which is placed in the mouths of unnamed commentators, and it is quite possible that his sources reported comparisons with Alexander, whom Germanicus did apparently emulate.[84] But the reported comment is entirely favourable. There is no attempt to balance it with saner criticism (as was done so effectively in the report of Augustus' funeral).[85] There can be no doubt that Tacitus was favourably disposed to the views he reports, but he was sensitive enough to state them indirectly. There is no such artifice in Arrian. He operates openly, focusing upon Alexander's undoubted military achievements and his universal reputation. The moral strictures were then neutralized by a sophistical two-pronged approach. Arrian denies the validity of the individual criticisms when viewed against the totality of Alexander's achievement and he actually claims some of the purported vices as virtues. The effect and the intention is not historical appreciation, but rhetorical encomium.

Arrian saw himself in two lights, as panegyrist for Alexander and as moral critic, serving both the posthumous reputation of the king and the edification of his readers. In his earlier monographs on Dion and Timoleon there was probably no conflict, for both men were generally acknowledged as standard types of virtue and no apology would have been needed.[86] In Alexander's case there was a whole literature of invective and, while it was possible for him to discount the criticism in the rhetorical passion of the peroration, Arrian was honest enough to reflect the common sentiment in his historical exposition. In the finale, however, he speaks as enthusiast and apologist, and the Alexander he creates is as fictitious as the philosopher in action of Plutarch's first treatise *On the Fortune of Alexander*. As rhetoric it is impressive. It would not have appealed to Epictetus, in whose eyes all epideictic rhetoric was futile. Nobody

listening to such performances, he claimed, is troubled about his moral welfare or moved to self-examination. Even if the speaker is at the height of his reputation, the comments go no deeper than 'a pretty talk, that one about Xerxes',[87] Intellectually the record of Alexander's campaigns was trivial, the classic example of the glorification of externals, and a committed disciple of Epictetus should have scorned the theme.[88] But Arrian had a thoroughly conventional view of the desirability and glory of conquest. It was better if accomplished with the Stoic qualities of moderation and temperance but it was still an eminently worthy end in itself. In that respect Alexander was the great exemplar, the standing challenge to all future empire-builders, and his achievement deserved to be commemorated in literature with the appropriate meed of praise. Moral criticism was not out of place but subordinated to the greater end of encomium. Inconsistency was the inevitable result. Each passage when viewed in isolation may appear logical and effective, but the total work is a farrago of conflicting commonplaces.

Notes

1. Phot. *Bibl.* cod. 91: ἐπαινεῖ δὲ αὐτὸν ἐπὶ πάσαις σχεδόν τι ταῖς ἀρεταῖς ἐς τὰ μάλιστα ὁ συγγραφεύς.

2. vii. 30. 2 (ἀνὴρ οὐδενὶ ἄλλῳ ἀνθρώπων ἐοικώς); cf. i. 12. 4. The sentiment echoes (perhaps consciously) Theopompus' celebrated verdict on Philip II (Polyb. viii. 9. 1; 11. 1 = *FGrH* 115 F 27).

3. Cf. vii. 29. 2 (οἱ δὲ τῷ προηγορεῖν αὐτοῦ . . . ἐπικρύψειν οἴονται τὴν ἁμαρτίαν); so, even more rhetorically, iv. 9. 6.

4. On Curtius see S. Dosson, *Étude critique sur Quinte-Curce* (Paris, 1887) 203-6, reviewing other passages where Curtius gives positive or negative appreciations of Alexander's character. He admits that the final composite picture is more flattering and less complete than the earlier *aperçus*. Tarn, *Alexander* ii. 100, claimed that this final encomium 'stultifies nearly everything Curtius has said about Alexander'.

5. i. 7. 5-6; iii. 17. 4-5; iv. 26. 2-4; cf. vii. 28. 3 (προλαβεῖν δεινότατος).

6. i. 1. 9 (καὶ οὕτω ξυνέβη ὅπως παρῄνεσέ τε Ἀλέξανδρος καὶ εἴκασεν); cf. ii. 10. 3-4; iii. 18. 9; v. 23. 7-24. 2 (= *FGrH* 138 F 35). Compare vii. 28. 2 (τὸ εἰκὸς ξυμβαλεῖν ἐπιτυχέστατος).

7. σωφροσύνῃ τε πολλῇ χρώμενος καὶ δόξης ἅμα ἀγαθῆς οὐκ ἀτόπῳ ἐφέσει (iv. 19. 6); ἡδονῶν . . . ἐγκρατέστατος . . . ἐπαίνου μόνου ἀπληστότατος (vii. 28. 2). For the latter theme see further vii. 2. 2 (above p. 73).

8. Cf. iv. 27. 3-4. Brunt's exclamation mark (*Arrian* ii. 298) is well placed.

9. On Arrian's own account he was taken by surprise when the Sogdian revolt broke out, instigated by the very men he had pardoned (iv. 1. 5), and also when the Persian army cut across his rear at Issus (ii. 7. 1-2).

10. See Particularly vii. 9. 9 ([Bosworth, A. B. *From Arian to Alexander*. Oxford: Clarendon Press, 1988], p. 104). The rhetorical contrast between personal frugality and liberality to others also occurs in Plutarch, *de Al. f.* ii. 4 (337ᴮ). As we shall see, it was a common *topos*.

11. Thuc, i. 138. 3: τῶν μελλόντων ἐπὶ πλεῖστον τοῦ γενησομένου ἄριστος εἰκαστής . . . ἐν τῷ ἀφανεῖ ἔτι προεώρα μάλιστα.

12. 'Suda' s.v. Δημοσθένης = Arr. *Succ.* F 23 (Roos)—the fragment is not explicitly attributed to Arrian but it is stylistically impeccable (see, however, Stadter 236 n. 58).

13. εἰπεῖν ὅσα ἐνθυμυθείη δυνατώτατος . . . ἱκανώτατος τὸ ἀφανὲς εἰκάσαι καὶ τὸ γνωσθὲν ἐξηγήσασθαι. Cf. Thuc. viii. 68. 1, 4.

14. Xen. *Anab.* i. 9. 1 ff. On the use of the encomium by Xenophon see G. Fraustadt, *Encomiorum in litteris graecis usque ad Romanam aetatem historia* (diss. Leipzig, 1909) 56-7, 67-70; A. Dihle, *Studien zur griechischen Biographie*[2] (Abh. der Ak. der Wiss. in Göttingen, 3. Folge, Nr. 39: 1970) 24-9. Dihle's conclusion ('Das Leben der dargestellten Personen . . . interessiert die Autoren viel weniger als der Tugendenkanon einer Idealgestalt', 28) applies as well to Arrian's encomium as it does to Xenophon and Isocrates.

15. Cf. *Anab.* i. 9. 6, 9. 7.

16. *Anab.* i. 9. 22-7.

17. Xen. *Ages.* 10. 2: παράδειγμα . . . τοῖς ἀνδραγαθίαν ἀσκεῖν βουλομένοις.

18. e.g. *Ages.* 11. 12: βαρύτατος μὲν ἀνταγωνιστὴς ἦν, κουφότατος δὲ κρατήσας. ἐχθροῖς μὲν δυσεξαπάτητος, φίλοις δὲ εὐπαραπειστότατος.

19. i. 12. 3-4. See [Bosworth, 1988], ch. 2.

20. Cf. vii. 22. 5 (on Seleucus).

21. Arr. *Succ.* F 23 (Demosthenes), 19 (Craterus); *Parth.* F 19 (Arsaces).

22. The similarity was noted by A. von Gutschmid, *Philologus* 8 (1853) 439 (= *Kl. Schr.* iii. 130) and endorsed by Roos. Note the repetition of τὸ σῶμα

κάλλιστος at the beginning of the character-sketch and the highly poetical δαημονέστατος, borrowed from Xenophon (*Cyrop.* i. 2. 12) and used by Arrian in the most diverse contexts (*Ind.* 24. 5; *Tact.* 12. 1, 35. 6).

23. Kornemann 33-6 claimed that the last chapters were practically all derived from Ptolemy. This 'surprising result', which he alleged was the most important of his investigation, has been unsurprisingly ignored.

24. vii. 29. 4 = *FGrH* 139 F 62. The same tradition appears in Plut. *Al.* 23. 1, 6 (see further, ch. 7 below).

25. ἐφ' ὅτῳ (sc. to counter the insubordination of the Macedonians) δὴ καὶ ἐγκαταμῖξαί μοι δοκεῖ ταῖς τάξεσιν αὐτῶν τοὺς Πέρσας τοὺσ μηλοφόρους καὶ τοῖς ἀγήμασι τοὺς ὁμοτίμους.

26. Unlike vii. 8. 2, which plainly recapitulates vii. 6. 4-5 and deliberately echoes the earlier terminology.

27. ii. 11. 9; cf. *HCArr.* i. 218.

28. This is the only occasion in Arrian that the plural is used (the manuscript reading at i. 8. 3 is clearly false: see *HCArr.* i. 81-2).

29. Diod. xvii. 108. 3, on which see P. Briant, *Rois, Tributs et Paysans* (Paris, 1982) 30-9; Bosworth, *JHS* [*Journal of Hellenic Studies*] 100 (1980) 17-18.

30. For the Seleucid evidence (particularly *OGIS* 227 = Welles *RC* 22) see W. Günther, *Das Orakel von Didynia in hellenistischer Zeit* (Ist. Mitt. Beih. 4; Tübingen, 1971) 66 ff. On Demetrius see Athen. vi. 253ᴇ (Duris, *FGrH* 76 F 13). The coinage, which prominently features Poseidon, is particularly important. One series depicts Demetrius with the bull's horn of Poseidon exactly as contemporary Alexander heads display the ram's horn of Ammon. Cf. E. T. Newell, *The Coinages of Demetrius Poliorcetes* (London, 1927), esp. 65-73 (nos. 53-8).

31. There are curious parallels in modern scholarship. Greek attitudes to Macedon in the fourth century are an uncontroversial subject—until one impinges on the question of the Hellenism (or otherwise) of the Macedonians. Then the debate acquires contemporary relevance and an element of hysteria obtrudes.

32. See [Bosworth, 1988], ch. 5.

33. Cf. A. Heuss, *Antike und Abendland* 4 (1954) 88-9. Livy similarly avoids the subject of deification, castigating only the fraudulent arrogation of

divine birth (ix. 18. 4). Valerius Maximus (ix. 5. *ext.* 1) talks vaguely about claims to divinity other than those as son of Ammon. His language, however, is opaque (*spreto mortali habitu divinum aemulatus est*) and need not be a criticism of cult honours *per se.*

34. Luc. *Dial. Mort.* 12. 1, cf. 25. 2. The remarks on the 'deification' of Hephaestion (*de calum.* 17-18) are based on some intemediate source.

35. Cf. iv. 8. 3, 10. 6-7 with my remarks (pp. 114 ff., [Bosworth, 1988]).

36. Isocrates (12. 205) suggests that the trio were a proverbial paradigm of virtue.

37. *Bithyn.* F 29 (Roos); cf. Serv. *ad Aen.* vi. 566 (*Rhadamanthus Minos Aeacus filii Iovis et Europae fuerunt*). Aeacus was traditionally son of Zeus and Aegina.

38. Aristid. 1. 302-12.

39. Aristid. 1. 308-9; cf. Isocr. 4. 100-6; 12. 62-6.

40. Aristid. 1. 304; cf. Arr. vii. 30. 1-2.

41. Aristid. 1. 311.

42. The evidence is fully compiled, if somewhat schematically arranged, in two German dissertations: W. Hoffmann, *Der literarische Porträt Alexanders des Grossen im griechischen und römischen Altertum* (diss. Leipzig, 1907) and F. Weber, *Alexander der Grosse im Urteil der Griechen und Römer bis in die konstantinische Zeit* (diss. Giessen, 1909). A brief but somewhat deeper survey is provided by A. Heuss, 'Alexander der Grosse und die politische Ideologie des Altertums', *Antike und Abendland* 4 (1954) 65-104.

43. These views, often inaccurately labelled Stoic and Peripatetic, are multiply attested. See the critical essays of E. Badian, *CQ [Classical Quarterly]* 8 (1958) 144-7, E. Mensching, *Historia* 12 (1963) 274-82, and J. R. Fears, *Philologus* 118 (1974) 113-30 (with the comments of Brunt, *Athenaeum* 55 [1977] 39-44).

44. Dio Chrys. 1. 6-7. See also the pseudo-Dionic oration *On Fortune*, 64. 19-22.

45. iv. 19. 6 (quoted above, n. 7); cf. Curt. x. 5. 29 (*ut iuveni et in tantis . . . rebus*).

46. ii. 6. 4 (τῶν καθ᾽ἡδονὴν ξυνόντων τε καὶ ξυνεσομένων ἐπὶ κακῷ τοῖς ἀεὶ βασιλεύουσιν); iv. 8. 3; cf. vii. 29. 1.

47. Plut. *quom. adul. ab amico intern.* 24 (Mor. 65D); cf. *Al.* 23. 7. As Brunt notes, there is a similar indictment of flattery in Seneca (*de Ben.* vi. 30.

4-31. 12), where Xerxes serves as the example of the despot brought to ruin (vi. 31. 1-10 strongly recalls Arr. ii. 6. 4-6). See Plut. 18 (60B-C) for another instance of flattery at Alexander's court.

48. iv. 9. 2, 5-6.

49. vii. 29. 2: μόνη γὰρ ἔμοιγε δοκεῖ ἴασις ἁμαρτίας ὁμολογεῖν τε ἁμαρτάνοντα . . .

50. See, particularly, P. A. Brunt, 'From Epictetus to Arrian', *Athenaeum* 55 (1977) 19-48, esp. 38.

51. Cf. Chrysippus, *SVF* iii. 548 (οὐδὲ μετανοεῖν δ᾽ὑπολαμβάνουσι τὸν νοῦν ἔχοντα), 563 (so 414). See also Sen. *Ep.* 90. 34.

52. Sen. *Ep.* 28. 3 = Epicurus F 522 (Usener). Cf. Arist. *NE* vii. 1150^a 21-2 (negatively phrased: without repentance one is irredeemable), with iii. 1110^b 18 ff. See also Diog. Laert. v. 66 = Lycon F 23 (Wehrli).

53. Sen. *Ep.* 87. 25. See further, P. Grimal, *Sénèque ou la conscience de l'Empire* (Paris, 1978) 193 ff.

54. Plut. *quom. quis suos in virtute sentiat profectus* 11 (*Mor.* 82A-C): τὸ δ᾽ ἑαυτὸν ἁμαρτάνοντα παρέχειν τοῖς ἐλέγχουσι . . . οὐ φαῦλον εἴη προκοπῆς σημεῖον. See further, W. Schmidt, *Rh. M.* [*Rhenische Museum*] 100 (1957) 301-27, esp. 309 ff.

55. Julian *Caes.* 325A-C.

56. Arr. vii. 29. 4; cf. Plut. *de Al. f.* i. 8 (*Mor.* 330A) = *FGrH* 241 F30. For the development of the *topos* see *JHS* 100 (1980) 3-6. For the historical dating (autumn 330) see Plut. *Al.* 45. 1; Diod. xvii. 74. 4; Curt. vi. 6. 1; Justin xii. 3. 8.

57. Arr. *Cyneget.* 16. 5-8; cf. Xen. *Cyneget.* 5. 33.

58. See particularly Epict. *Diss.* iii. 22. 26-30, 60-1 (this is explicit Cynic doctrine).

59. vii. 1. 5-2. 2. On this passage and its Cynic inspiration see above, pp. 72 ff.

60. Epict. *Diss.* iii. 22. 45-9.

61. Cf. Brunt (above, n. 50) 44: 'In these passages . . . he did embrace the Stoic view, but only to forget it when he came to the final appreciation of his hero'.

62. Julian *Pan. ad Eusebiam* 106D-107C.

63. Julian, *Ep. ad Themistium* 264D. In a different context compare *Pan. ad Constantium* 45D-46A, where Alexander's arrogance and pretensions to divine sonship are contrasted with the mildness and filial piety of Constantius. For Alexander in the familiar role of the slave of fortune see 257A-B.

64. Julian, *ad Sallustium* 251B-C.

65. iv. 8. 3-4, 9. 9.

66. *Epict. Diss.* iv. 1. 127: ἐκεῖνος δὲ (sc. the tyrant) ὁ βλαπτόμενός ἐστιν ὁ τὰ οἰκτρότατα πάσχων καὶ αἴσχιστα. So Chrysippus, *SVF* iii. 289. It was common Stoic doctrine.

67. iv. 9. 7-8; cf. Plut. *Al.* 52. 3-7, *ad princ. inerudit.* 4 (781A-B).

68. *Ep. ad Gell* 2. A good example of this trait in action is the dialogue with the *corrector* Maximus (*Diss.* iii. 7; cf. Millar, *JRS* [*Journal of Roman Studies*] 55 [1965] 145; Stadter 25-6).

69. Cf. Epict. *Diss.* i. 1. 26-32, 2. 12-24.

70. iv. 12. 7: ἐπὶ τῇ ἀκαίρῳ τε παρρησίᾳ καὶ ὑπερόγκῳ ἀβελτερίᾳ. For a highly unpleasant picture of Callisthenes self-advertisement see iv. 10. 1-2.

71. Epict. *Ench.* 37; cf. Panaetius, *SVF* i. 111-14 (quoted by Brunt, *PBSR* 30 [1975] 14).

72. Epict. *Diss.* iii. 22. 9-12.

73. Tac. *Ann.* xiv. 12. 1. For Thrasea's role in the first years of the reign see Brunt, *PBSR* 30 (1975) 26; M. Griffin, *Seneca: a Philosopher in Politics* (Oxford, 1976) 100-3.

74. This comment is foreshadowed in the narrative of the siege, where Alexander's yearning for fame, even posthumous fame, is adduced as a motive (vi. 9. 5—the sentiment is often ascribed to Ptolemy, who certainly provided the details of the account).

75. Cf. *Diss.* ii. 9. 15, 19. 32, iii. 22. 29.

76. Polyb. x. 21. 8. The thought is echoed (and trivialized) by Lucian *hist. conscr.* 7. On these passages see Avenarius 13-16, 157-62. On Polybius' biography see R. M. Errington, *Philopoemen* (Oxford, 1969) 232 ff.

77. Poseidonius, *FGrH* 87 F 108u and w; Tac. *Ann.* iv. 33. 2 (cf. iii. 65. 1). Other passages are adduced by Avenarius 158-9. On Poseidonius see Brunt (above, n. 50) 35 f.; Strasburger, *JRS* 55 (1965) 47.

78. This was strongly emphasized by Tarn, *Alexander* ii. 96-100, who thought that Curtius used two separate and inconsistent portraits of the king. Contrast the reasoned discussion of Atkinson (above, ch. 1, n. 2) 70-3, esp. 72: 'the individual story generates its own picture of the characters involved and inconsistencies may then occur between different episodes'.

79. See particularly *Ann.* i. 78. 2; ii. 8. 2 with the commentary of Goodyear (below, n. 81).

80. The technique was not Tacitus' invention. Note Velleius' short comparison of Caesar and Alexander, *magno illi Alexandro (sed sobrio neque iracundo) simillimus* (Vell. ii. 41. 1) and (at a much later date) Julian's extended panegyric of Constantius (45D-46C).

81. 73. 2: *sed hunc mitem erga amicos, modicum voluptatum, uno matrimonio, certis liberis egisse.* The reference to children is problematic. It may be a hit at the illegitimacy of Heracles, son of Barsine or even an insinuation against the virtue of Rhoxane (cf. Goodyear, *The Annals of Tacitus* ii. 419). Perhaps Tacitus is focusing on the notorious marital chastity of Germanicus and Agrippina, leaving his readers to entertain what conclusions they wished about Alexander.

82. 73. 3: *praepeditusque sit perculsas tot victoriis Germanias servitio premere.*

83. Syme, *Tacitus* 492: 'The artifice is patent, the laudation gross in disproportion—and the historian evades responsibility.'

84. The question posed by Syme, *Tacitus* 771; cf. Goodyear (above, n. 81) ii. 417. The recent essay by M. L. Paladini, in *Alessandro Magno tra storia e mito* (ed. M. Sordi; Milan, 1984) 179-93, is not particularly helpful. For Germanicus' emulation of Alexander see *POxy.* 2435r. 20-1 (*EJ*[3] 379), with G. J. D. Aalders, *Historia* 10 (1961) 382-4; Weippert (ch. 4, n. 96) 257-8.

85. Tac. *Ann.* i. 9. 1-10. 7

86. Timoleon, however, suffers when Plutarch compares him adversely with Aemilius Paulus (*Comp. Tim. Aem.* 2).

87. Epict. *Diss.* iii. 23. 33-8.

88. So Brunt (above, n. 50) 37-9, 47-8. Stadter 110-14 is more indulgent ('Arrian, always a philosopher . . .').

Bibliography

What follows is a compromise. The footnotes give full coverage of the literature. I have extracted what seem to me the most significant contributions, arranged according to the interests of potential readers. Standard works of reference are excluded, as is specialist literature of peripheral importance.

I have used throughout the text established by A. G. Roos: (i) *Alexandri Anabasis*; (ii) *Scripta Minora et Fragmenta* (Teubner; 1967, 1968: second editions, revised by G. Wirth). This is a fundamental re-evaluation of the manuscript tradition, accepted as the basis of recent editions and translations:

BRUNT, P. A. *Arrian*: History of Alexander *and* Indica i-ii (Loeb Classical Library; Cambridge, Mass., 1976-83).

ARRIEN, *Histoire d'Alexandre,* trans. P. Savinel; postlude by P. Vidal-Naquet (Paris, 1984).

ARRIAN, *Der Alexanderzug: Indische Geschichte* (Greek and German), trans. and ed. G. Wirth, O. von Hinüber (Munich/Zürich, 1985).

(I) BOOKS AND ARTICLES RELEVANT TO ARRIAN AND HIS HISTORIOGRAPHICAL MILIEU

BRUNT, P. A., 'Stoicism and the Principate', *PBSR* 30 (1975) 7-35.

————, 'From Epictetus to Arrian', *Athenaeum* 55 (1977) 19-48.

————, 'On historical Fragments and Epitomes', *CQ* 30 (1980) 477-94.

DOSSON, S., *Étude critique sur Quinte-Curce* (Paris, 1887).

GUTSCHMID, A. VON, 'Zu den Fragmenten aus Arrians parthischer Geschichte', *Philologus* 8 (1853) 435-9 (= *Kleine Schriften* iii. 125-30).

STADTER, P. A., 'Flavius Arrianus: the new Xenophon', *GRBS* [*Greek, Roman, and Byzantine Studies*] 8 (1967) 155-61.

————, 'Xenophon in Arrian's *Cynegeticus*', *GRBS* 17 (1976) 157-67.

————, 'The *Ars Tactica* of Arrian: Tradition and Originality', *CP* [*Classical Philology*] 73 (1978) 117-28.

————, *Arrian of Nicomedia* (Chapel Hill, 1980).

————, 'Arrian's Extended Preface', *Illinois Classical Studies* 6 (1981) 157-71.

SYME, R., *Tacitus* (Oxford, 1958).

(II) BOOKS AND ARTICLES RELEVANT TO ALEXANDER AND THE HISTORIOGRAPHY OF HIS REIGN.

BADIAN, E., 'The Eunuch Bagoas: A Study in Method', *CQ* 8 (1958) 144-57.

BOSWORTH, A. B., 'Alexander and the Iranians', *JHS* 100 (1980) 1-21.

BRIANT, P., *Rois, Tributs et Poysons* (Centre de Recherches d'Histoire Ancienne 43: Paris, 1982).

DIHLE, A., *Studien zur griechischen Biographie* (Abh. der Ak. der Wissenschaften in Göttingen Phil.-Hist, Kl., Dritte Folge, nr. 37; Göttingen 1970).

FEARS, J. R., 'The Stoic View of the Career and Character of Alexander the Great', *Philologus* 118 (1974) 113-30.

FRAUSTADT, G., *Encomiorum in litteris Graecis usque ad Romanam aetatem historia* (diss., Leipzig, 1909).

HEUSS, A., 'Alexander der Grosse und die politische Ideologie des Altertums', *Antike und Abendland* 4 (1954) 65-104.

KORNEMANN, E., *Die Alexandergeschichte des Königs Ptolemaios I von Aegypten* (Leipzig, 1934).

MENSCHING, E., 'Peripatetiker über Alexander', *Historia* 12 (1963) 274-82.

TARN, W. W., 'Alexander's Hypomnemata and the World Kingdom', *JHS* 41 (1921) 3-17.

————, *Alexander the Great* i-ii (Cambridge, 1948).

WEBER, F., *Alexander der Grosse im Urteil der Griechen und Römer bis in die konstantinische Zeit* (diss. Giessen, 1909).

Abbreviations

References to ancient sources and modern literature follow standard conventions. In each chapter the footnotes are interrelated to provide direction to full bibliographical information. The following list has two functions: it gives special abbreviations of works frequently used and also explains abbreviations which might be considered abstruse.

Brunt, *Arrian*: P. A. Brunt, *Arrian* i-ii (Loeb Classical Library; Cambridge, Mass., 1976-83)

FGrH: F. Jacoby, *Die Fragmente der griechischen Historiker* (Berlin/Leiden 1923-, rev. edn. 1957). (References to the text are given by the number of the author in the collection [e.g. 'Duris, *FGrH* 76 F 1'], references to the commentary by the volume number [e.g. '*FGrH* ii.D 563'].)

HCArr.: A. B. Bosworth, *A Historical Commentary on Arrian's History of Alexander* (Oxford, 1980-)

Kornemann: E. Kornemann, *Die Alexandergeschichte des Königs Ptolemaios I. von Aegypten* (Leipzig, 1935)

Stadter: P. A. Stadter, *Arrian of Nicomedia* (Chapel Hill, 1980)

SVF: *Stoicorum veterum fragmenta* i-iv, ed. H. von Arnim (Leipzig, 1903-24)

Tarn, *Alexander*: W. W. Tarn, *Alexander the Great* i-ii (Cambridge, 1948)

N. G. L. Hammond (essay date 1993)

SOURCE: Hammond, N. G. L. "Plutarch's Reflective Passages and Alexander's Personality." In *Sources for Alexander the Great: An Analysis of Plutarch's* Life *and Arrian's* Anabasis Alexandrou, pp. 163-87. Cambridge: Cambridge University Press, 1993.

[*In the following excerpt, Hammond notes that Plutarch recognized personality changes in Alexander, most notably his gradual loss of moderation and self-mastery.*]

1. Natural Endowment and Formative Factors until the Accession of Alexander

In his Introduction Plutarch maintained that the personality of such a man as Alexander or Caesar may be revealed by 'a small incident, a saying or a joke' rather than by a great battle-narrative (1.2). Plutarch should therefore be allowed to 'enter into the indicators of a man's soul (εἰς τὰ τῆς ψυχῆς σημεῖα) and thereby to characterise his life'. Where he was acting on this principle in this *Life,* I have called the passages 'the reflective passages' in contrast to 'the narrative passages'.

The key to Plutarch's characterisation of Alexander's life is provided in chapter 4.1-7. He assumed, as Pindar and many Greek writers had done, that a man's natural endowment (φυά or φύσις), both physical and mental,[1] was the basis of his development. He therefore began his study of A by commenting on A's physique. He took as his sources the statues of Lysippus, the paintings of Apelles and the *Memoirs* of Aristoxenus,[2] which he read directly (ἀνέγνωμεν). This Aristoxenus was ten years or so older than A, joined the school of Aristotle and wrote 'Lives' of some philosophers; and his idea of the body being 'tuned' by the soul may have influenced Plutarch in his approach to A.

According to Plutarch A was remarkable for the poise of his neck, the liquidity of his eyes, the fairness of his skin, the ruddiness of his face and particularly of his chest, and the very pleasant aroma of his body (εὐωδία), which imbued his clothing. Plutarch attributed these characteristics 'perhaps' to A's bodily heat; for 'the temperament of his body was hot-blooded and fiery' (πυρώδης). It was this heat which generated the pleasant aroma, 'as Theophrastus supposes'.[3] It was probably from Theophrastus that Plutarch derived his analogy that the hot sun, acting on moist decaying matter, produced the finest perfumes (i.e. in Arabia). 'The bodily heat, so it seems (ὡς ἔοικε), made A both fond of drink and passionate' (4.7 ποτικὸν καὶ θυμοειδῆ). Here we see one aspect of the interaction between body and soul (the latter including one's mind), which underlay Plutarch's theory of personality.

The other aspect of the interaction was illustrated by a description of A as a boy (4.8-11). He had in his mentality a sense of restraint (σωφροσύνη) which enabled him to resist the pull 'of bodily pleasures', despite the fact that he was otherwise 'violent and exceedingly impetuous' (ῥαγδαῖον . . . καὶ φερόμενον σφοδρῶς). And he also had a 'desire for honour' (φιλοτιμία) beyond his years, and this desire made him serious in mind and 'magnanimous in spirit' (μεγαλόψυχον). (These were among the mental qualities which were to be seen 'tuning' such bodily urges as his sexual desires at 21.10f. and 22.6.)[4]

Plutarch then turned to anecdotes which illustrated A's physical and mental qualities. His love of honour for himself was not unbridled, like that of Philip, but selective, so that, when being swift of foot he was urged by other boys to compete at the Olympic Games, he replied 'Yes, if I am to have kings as competitors.' Plutarch did not enlarge here on this cryptic reply; but in *Moralia* 179d it was Philip who urged A to compete and received that answer, and in *Moralia* 331b A showed his bent for philosophy by saying that defeat in an open competition would be defeat of a king by commoners. Thus Plutarch used the same anecdote here to illustrate a different point. And he went on to mention A's aversion to the rougher form of athletics, such as boxing and the pancration. and his delight in competitions of drama, music, recitation, hunting and duelling with sticks. In 5.1-3 Plutarch illustrated A's serious-mindedness and desire to do great things (μεγαλοπραγμοσύνην) by the story of the Persian envoys being questioned by the boy A (above, p. 20), and by A's fears that Philip's triumphs would leave no opening for A to show his excellence and win glory. He would rather inherit a kingdom which offered not wealth, luxury and enjoyment but struggles, wars and ambitious prospects (5.6). That wish was fulfilled at A's accession when the kingdom was the centre of discontents, enmities and dangers (11.1).

Education was another factor in developing one's natural endowment into an adult personality. Plutarch therefore commented on the qualities of two among many teachers[5] of A—Leonidas and Lysimachus (both were to appear later in the *Life*). Then the story of Bucephalus illustrated A's passionate nature (6.3 περιπαθοῦντος) and his courage at a young age (above, pp. 21f.). The secondary education of A, in whom Philip saw 'a nature (φύσιν) resistant to any form of compulsion (δυσκίνητον) but capable of being led by reason to appropriate action', was entrusted to Aristotle (in 342 B.C. when A became fourteen). The subjects of instruction were a matter of Plutarch's own speculation (ἔοικε) and of inference from a letter of A to Aristotle, quoted from 'a copy' (ἀντίγραφον), and Aristotle's summarised reply—both now regarded as not authentic.[6] Plutarch also thought (δοκεῖ μοι) that

A's love of medical theory and of actual healing was due mainly to Aristotle, and he looked forward to the concern which A was to show for the illness of his friends in his letters (as in 41.7). A's love of literary scholarship and of reading was illustrated by the *Iliad* of the Casket (defined in 26.1f.), the text of which had been revised by Aristotle, and by a list of the books, mainly of poetry, which were sent by Harpalus to A in Asia. Although A's affection for Aristotle declined later, his zest for philosophy, innate by nature (ἐμπεφυκώς) and cultivated from the outset, continued unabated, as was seen from his dealings with Anaxarchus, Xenocrates, Dandamis and Calanus.

The discharge of the duties laid upon him as regent at the age of sixteen and at the Battle of Chaeronea[7] at the age of eighteen won for him the exceeding love of his father (9.4). However, quarrels ensued between them. Plutarch drew upon the unsatisfactory work of Satyrus for highly-coloured examples of these quarrels in 9.5-14 and in 10.1-5 (see [Hammond, N. G. L. *Sources for Alexander the Great.* Cambridge: Cambridge University Press, 1993], pp. 7-13). He was not prepared to give his own approval to the report that A had connived in the planned assassination of Philip (10.6-8).[8]

Thus, although Plutarch had formed a general opinion of A's personality in his earlier writings in *Moralia* and in his preliminary reading, he took great trouble at the start of the *Life* to define the natural endowment of A in body and mind. He relied mainly on his own theories of physiognomy and especially on A's bodily heat as one of the controlling humours. He drew on his own observation, the *Memoirs* of Aristoxenus and the ideas of Theophrastus. He chose anecdotes and incidents which supported his own preconceptions, and he no doubt shaped the narrative to produce the desired effects. His source for A's boyhood was, we have argued, Marsyas Macedon, an exact contemporary of A and later a capable commander—a good choice; and he referred to Onesicritus for a point about the keeping of the *Iliad* in a casket under A's pillow. Then Plutarch seems to have relied on his own reading and knowledge of philosophy to estimate the influence of Aristotle on A. He may well have been shown the Nymphaeum at Mieza[9] and he mentioned 'A's oak' by his home-town Chaeronea. The stories which he took from Satyrus illustrated A's hot blood, passionate nature and fondness of drink, and in the Pixodarus affair A's φιλοτιμία, which demanded that he should have first place after his father. Whatever Plutarch thought of Olympias, he hesitated to think A capable of conniving in parricide.

2. VICTORIES OF 335-333 AND ALEXANDER'S SELF-MASTERY (11-23)

Plutarch wrote narrative passages not for their own sake but as illustrations of A's personality in action. He drew therefore on the accounts which seemed best to fit the parameters of A's personality as he had described it in 1-10, but he modified them in his own version for his own purpose. Thus in 11-13 he drew on Cleitarchus for A's impetuosity and speed, his 'most savage and most dismal act' (13.2, the sack of Thebes), the passionate anger which he sated as lions do, and his policy of *Schrecklichkeit* in Greece. Because Cleitarchus was used also by Diodorus (17.8.2-14.4) and Justin (11.3f.),[10] we can see that Plutarch reduced the emphasis on anger and introduced into his version A's 'daring and greatness of mind' (11.4 τολμη καὶ μεγαλοφροσύνη), gratifying of his allies (11.11), remorse and clemency. Even so, Plutarch wanted to show A in a less terrifying light; so he drew on Aristobulus for the story of Timoclea and A's humane treatment of her and her children.

Plutarch packed a variety of episodes and anecdotes into 14-15. He adopted Onesicritus' account of A's visit to Diogenes and the saying of A 'Indeed, were I not Alexander, I would be Diogenes', in order to illustrate A's love of philosophy. He took from Cleitarchus the stories of A's impetuous violence at Delphi (βία . . . τῆς σπουδῆς) and his excessive gratifying of his friends. Plutarch saw the latter as a further example of A's 'impetuosity and mental preparedness' (ὁρμη καὶ παρασκευη διανοίας).[11] He obtained from Aristobulus two anecdotes which illustrated A's desire for glory (14.9 and 15.9).

For the Battle of the River Granicus Plutarch drew on Aristobulus, probably because Aristobulus provided two sayings of A and concentrated more on A's actions in the battle than Ptolemy did. A showed here above all his 'mental preparedness' in acting at once and in contradiction to his advisers (as he had done at 11.3f.), his daring impetuosity (16.3 ἐμβάλλει . . . ἔδοξε μανικῶς καὶ πρὸς ἀπόνοιαν μᾶλλον ἢ γνώμη στρατηγεῖν) and his acting in passion rather than in calculation when he was the first to charge at the Greek mercenaries (16.14 θυμῷ μᾶλλον ἢ λογισμῷ). After the victory A's desire for honour prompted the wording of the inscription on the spoils (16.17 φιλοτιμοτάτην ἐπιγραφήν). Plutarch drew on Aristobulus for the description of the Battle of Issus (20.1-9), because Aristobulus had the anecdote of Amyntas, 'familiar with A's nature', declaring 'Alexander will march against you, indeed is almost already on the march' and represented A as eager to engage (σπεύδων ἀπαντῆσαι). It seems likely that Plutarch himself introduced the figure of Fortune favouring A (20.5 τη συντυχία; 20.7 ἡ τύχη πάρεσχεν), because he had written on the Fortune of A in *Moralia*.

The intervening narrative, 17-19, is far from consecutive. A managed to restrain his impetuosity (17.3) and was encouraged by a prophetic tablet to follow the slower course of conquering the coastal area first. As he passed along the Pamphylian coast Plutarch mentioned the statements of many historians that the sea gave way before him, and he then cited a letter of A which made no such marvel of it (17.8).[12] Plutarch preferred to write of a drunken after-dinner spree by A, in which A put garlands on the statue of a distinguished local philosopher;[13] for this illustrated Plutarch's regard for a piece of fun (παιδιά χις) as an indication of personality (1.2), and A's regard for philosophy and Aristotle. The treatment of A by Philip the doctor was described in such a way as to stress A's goodwill towards and trust in the doctor (19.7).

At 20.12f. Plutarch told the story of A bathing in Darius' gold-fitted bathroom and saying in jest to his Companions: 'This is what it was to be king, it seems.'[14] Thus A mocked Darius' priorities and showed his own disregard for luxury. A's courtesy to the royal ladies is praiseworthy but puzzling because the wife of Darius, 'it is said', was the most beautiful of all royal women and her daughters were equally lovely. Yet A kept his hands off them. Plutarch advanced his own explanation: A, as it seems, reckoned it more kingly to be master of himself than to be master of the women (21.7). Nor was A lacking in the sexual urge; for he said in jest that Persian women were torments to the eyes and yet he passed them by, parading by contrast his own self-mastery and restraint (ἀντεπιδεικνύμενος . . . ἐγκρατείας καὶ σωφροσύνης).

A's resistance to luxury in the bathroom and the charms of the captive ladies prompted Plutarch to write a reflective passage, 22-3. He began with letters by and to A which were in his judgement genuine. The first exchange showed a Macedonian officer forwarding an offer of two pretty boys for sale, and A reprimanding the officer and ordering him to get rid of the procurer. The second exchange was on the same subject and had the same result. Then A wrote to Parmenio with an order to execute, if they were found guilty, two Macedonian soldiers who were reported to have raped the women of two mercenary soldiers. This was a matter of military discipline. But in his letter to Parmenio A wrote this phrase (κατὰ λέξιν): 'So far from having seen Darius' wife or desired to see her, it will be found that I have not allowed anyone to speak of her beauty.'[15] Indeed A used to say that sleep and sex made him conscious of his being a mortal (22.6).

Having demonstrated A's restraint in sexual matters, both heterosexual and homosexual, Plutarch went on to other forms of self-mastery. In conversation with the Carian Queen, Ada, A rejected her offer of lavish titbits and quoted his tutor's precepts: the best preparation for breakfast was a night-march, and for dinner a light breakfast. And he went on to say that this tutor, Le-

onidas, used to check in his wardrobe that there was nothing luxurious or special which had been sent by his mother. Next, 'he was less given to wine than he was thought to be' because of the long time he spent over each glass, in conversation when he had leisure; for nothing distracted him when he had a job in hand. Plutarch then gave a specimen leisure-day: sacrifice to the gods on rising, breakfast sitting, daylight hours spent in hunting, judging, arranging a matter of war, or reading. If he was on a leisurely march, he would practise archery[16] or mounting and dismounting from a chariot in motion. Often for sport he used to hunt foxes and birds, 'as can be gathered from the *Ephemerides*'. Dinner at nightfall was well served and well provided, and he prolonged the drinking for conversation, 'as has been said' (23.6). After the drinking he bathed and slept, sometimes until midday, sometimes until the evening (23.8). In 23.7 there was a digression about A, when he was drinking, becoming over-boastful and letting himself be 'ridden' by his flatterers, which annoyed the better guests.

Plutarch then went back to the subject of titbits, only to say that A gave them all away to his Companions and kept none for himself. But his dinners were magnificent. The cost rose with his military successes to 10,000 drachmae both for a dinner he provided and for a dinner to which he was invited.

What were the sources of this reflective passage? In 22-23.2 Plutarch seems to be drawing on letters and incidents which he had already mentioned in the *Moralia*. Thus the offer of the pretty boys and the reprimand occurred in *Mor.* 333a (but only one boy) and 1099d. The saying on sleep and sex being signs of A's mortality was explained in *Mor.* 65f and 717f.[17] The conversation with Queen Ada was mentioned thrice but without the appendage of Leonidas at *Mor.* 127b, 180a and 1099c. Then the moderate use of wine was part of a discussion at *Mor.* 337f and 623e One may conclude that Plutarch was writing here either from his own memory or after consultation of the *Moralia*. The only letter in chapter 22 which did not figure in the *Moralia* was that to Parmenio. As there are other instances of execution for breaches of discipline in A's army,[18] there is no reason to regard this letter as unhistorical.

Chapter 23.3-6 and 8 is not an echo of the *Moralia*, nor of any writing by anyone else. Plutarch must have turned to a different source. At 23.4 he named his source as the *Ephemerides*. Commentators seem to have thought that Plutarch obtained from the *Ephemerides* only the hunting of foxes and birds;[19] but it is much more likely that Plutarch went to that source in constructing this typical leisure-day. I suggest, then, that 23.3-6 and 23.8 all came from the *Ephemerides*. This suggestion is much strengthened by the fact that

Philinus was cited by Plutarch in *Mor.* 623f as having obtained from the *Ephemerides* the information that after drinking A slept all day and sometimes the next day as well. There is no doubt that Plutarch and his contemporary Philinus had access to a copy of Alexander's *Ephemerides*.[20]

In 23.7 the comment on A's boastfulness and the influence of the flatterers may have resulted from Plutarch's reading of some account of the conversation between A and Cleitus;[21] but boastfulness and flatterers were not reported in his own account in 50-1. The flatterers were named as active only after the killing of Cleitus, at 53.1. In 23.10 the limit on expenditure for a dinner makes no sense unless one knows how many guests were to be entertained. That information was supplied by Ephippus (*FGrH* 126) F 2, namely 60 or 70 guests. It is probable that Plutarch had read Ephippus but did not trouble to mention the matter of guests.

3. Divine Birth (28) and Excessive Generosity to Friends (39-42)

In chapters 24-7 Plutarch had less to add in illustration of A's personality. He chose Chares' story of A risking his own life to save that of his ageing tutor, Lysimachus; stressed the trust and the affection A had for his favourite diviner, Aristander (25.2); and told the anecdote of A's generosity to his teacher, Leonidas.[22] A's love of poetry and learning appeared in his placing of the *Iliad* as the most precious of all his possessions in the Casket (26.1f.). A's faith in omens and dreams as indications of the gods' wishes and purposes is never questioned throughout the *Life,* and in these chapters it is conspicuous in the preliminaries to the siege of Tyre, on the day of its fall, during the siege of Gaza, before and during the founding of Alexandria, and especially during the journey to Siwa. Indeed Plutarch was as confident as A himself was that 'the aids which coincided with his difficulties came from the god' (i.e. from Ammon), and that the responses of the oracle were inspired by Ammon. What those responses were was another matter. Plutarch gave first the report of 'most writers' about A's questions and the answers of Ammon's priest. But honesty led him to mention the Letter to Olympias in which 'A himself says that the prophecies that had been made were not to be divulged; but on his return he would tell them to her alone' (27.8). Plutarch reported also the saying of 'some' that a silly slip in pronunciation by the priest led to the story that A was addressed as 'the son of Zeus by the god' (i.e. by Ammon).[23] These varied versions naturally raised the question whether A was born of man or god, the question which he was to tackle in the reflective passage (28).

Before he did so, Plutarch introduced a *legomenon*:

A is said to have listened to Psammon in Egypt, the philosopher, and to have accepted this particularly of his utterances, that all men are subject to the kingship of god, since the ruling and controlling force in each [man] is of god (θεῖον). But A himself is said to hold and express a more philosophical belief on this matter, that while the god is the common father of all men he adopts as his own the best men.

Since Psammon is so named as a spokesman of Ammon, 'the god' to whom Psammon referred was Ammon, a deity very familiar as 'Zeus Ammon' to the Greeks and especially to the Macedonians, who worshipped him at the oracular shrine of Aphytis in Chalcidice.[24] The idea of 'Zeus the King' ruling over the world was nothing new; indeed A had chosen to portray on his coins Zeus the King in such a way as to suggest that he was the same as the Belus (Ba'al) of the Asians.[25] That the ruling force in each of us is some form of spirit or soul, and that this is the divine element in each of us was a widespread idea from the time of Pythagoras in the Greek world and a fundamental idea in Egypt. While A accepted this belief, he is said to have improved on it by making the best of men particularly the children of the god—not in terms of physical paternity but metaphorically.[26] To see 'excellence' (ἀρετή) in men without distinction of race was certainly characteristic of A. The source of this *legomenon* is unknown.

As compared with the teaching of Psammon, Plutarch's reflections in chapter 28 are disappointing. 'A dealt haughtily with the barbarians and behaved like someone fully persuaded of his origin and begetting from god'; and it was in this connection that he represented A as using the belief in his divinity (τη δόξη τῆς θειότητος) as a means of 'enslaving the others' (i.e. the barbarians).[27] 'With the Greeks he made a god of himself with moderation and rather sparingly.' Plutarch gave examples which did indeed show A treating the idea lightly and humorously. The sources of two of them are known. When wounded by an arrow and in great pain, A quoted a line of the *Iliad* about ichor flowing in the veins of gods and remarked that in his own case it was blood, not ichor. Athenaeus gave the earlier part of the story as coming from Aristobulus (251a).[28] The other concerned a clap of thunder and A being asked by Anaxarchus whether, as the son of Zeus, he could do likewise. To that question A replied with a laugh that he had no wish so to frighten his friends. And A then referred to an earlier remark of Anaxarchus about A supplying at dinner a dish of fish and not a dish of satraps' heads, the implication being that there was no point in making the effort of conquest if one then ate a humble dish of fish. This second example was given also by Athenaeus (250f), citing Satyrus as his source.[29]

It is evident that Plutarch obtained these passages from his reading of Aristobulus and Satyrus. After recounting these two examples Plutarch concluded that 'in view of what has been said A did not suffer in any way nor was he in a deluded state' (28.6 τετυφωμένος).

There was, however, one exception to this light treatment of the idea of being a god, which Plutarch cited: 'except that in writing to Athenians about Samos he says: "I would not have given you a free and famous city: you hold it after receiving it from him who was then in control and is being called my father"—meaning Philip' (28.2). This letter has been a subject of much controversy.[30] Plutarch did not provide a historical context. It seems that Athenians had written to A, saying that he had granted them Samos, i.e. had confirmed their possession of it, and that A replied that Philip made the grant, i.e. in the settlement after the Battle of Chaeronea, and that he himself would not have done so. The only attested period of such negotiations was in 324-323 B.C. Yet Plutarch's next sentence began 'But later A was wounded by an arrow', such a wound being attested at Massage in 327. The natural conclusion is that the negotiations occurred in 334-332, when A had dealings with the islands off the coast of Asia.

Did Plutarch misunderstand the letter? The Athenians would probably have said 'Philip your father made the grant', implying that the son would not undo his father's grant; and it would then be reasonable for A to reply that 'The man you call my father may have done so but I would not have.' What Plutarch apparently read into the phrase is 'Philip is being called my father but is not so, since Ammon is my father.' Such an inference is far from justified. My view is with those who regard the letter as not genuine, or who think that, if genuine, it was misinterpreted by Plutarch. Finally it is odd that, if A did parade a divine origin for himself to the Greeks, this letter is the best—apparently the only—evidence that Plutarch could produce.

In the narrative passages which follow Plutarch illustrated A's devotion to an actor friend, Thessalus, and his generosity in paying a fine which Athens had laid on the winning actor—a generosity far exceeded when A gave ten talents to an actor who inserted a request for that amount into a comedy (29.4-6). Here Plutarch repeated what he had mentioned in *Moralia* 334e. Next, the death of Darius' wife led to Darius' praise for A's self-mastery, restraint and great-mindedness (30.10f. σωφροσύνη, ἐγκράτεια, μεγαλοψυχία). For the Battle of Gaugamela Plutarch chose to follow the colourful account by Cleitarchus, in which A refused to steal victory by night despite the recommendation of Parmenio (31.12), whether he acted in youthful bravado or far-sighted policy. There was praise for A's greatness in his calm calculation and confidence in the planning (32.4),

for the terror he inspired in action (33.6), and for his forbearance with the inefficient Parmenio (33.11). After the battle he sought honour for himself (φιλοτιμούμενος)[31] in paying tributes to some of the Greeks who had fought against Persia in 480-479; 'so much was A respectful of all excellence (ἅπασαν ἀρετήν), and so much a guardian and a kinsman of noble deeds'.

There is nothing indicative of A's personality until his arrival in Persepolis, where a mob of people had pushed their way into the palace and overturned the statue of Xerxes. A addressed the statue. 'Are we to pass on as you lie there because of the expedit on against the Greeks, or are we to raise you up because of your other high-mindedness and excellence?' (37.5 μεγαλοφροσύνην καὶ ἀρετήν). After a long time in silence, communing with himself, he finally passed on. The point of the story is that A attached more importance to Xerxes' crimes against Greece than to all his merits in Asia. It was perhaps told originally in order to explain A's action in burning the palace of Xerxes ἀπὸ γνώμης 'deliberately, as others say' (28.8). But Plutarch preferred to follow Cleitarchus in attributing the burning of the palace to an Athenian prostitute and to A leading a band of revellers behind her.

In a long reflective passage, 39-42.4, Plutarch began by enlarging on the munificence of A, on which he had already touched (15.3-6, 23.9f. and 29.5f.). The first two anecdotes (39.2f.) are not told elsewhere. Next Plutarch alludes to a letter, in which A told Phocion that he would not be treated as a friend if he rejected A's favours.[32] For this the full story was given by Plutarch in the *Life of Phocion* (18.1-4), and mention of it occurred in *Mor.* 188c. Two anecdotes follow. One names a young ball-player as Serapion; the story is too trivial probably to have been invented, and we know from 73.7 and Athen. 19a that A did play ball with a team of young men. The other names Proteas. He was mentioned by Athenaeus 129a as a son of Lanice, A's nurse, and as a boon-companion of A in drinking. Both anecdotes may be true. Plutarch then cites a letter of Olympias in which she chides A for so enriching others and depriving himself. She wrote often to this effect, said Plutarch; but as he adds that A kept her letters secret (ἀπόρρητα) it is not clear how such letters survived for Plutarch to see and read. He reinforced his statement about their secrecy by saying that A put his ring on Hephaestion's lips, when Hephaestion happened to be reading with A one of her letters (39.8)—an incident previously mentioned in *Mor.* 180d, 332f and 340a. He was generous in sending presents to Olympias, and he was gentle but firm with her meddling in his practical affairs. When Antipater wrote a long letter criticising her, A commented: 'Antipater does not realise that one of my mother's tears wipes out ten thousand letters'

(39.13). To leading men he was particularly generous, as Plutarch showed by supplying anecdotes concerning a son of Mazaeus and the gift of a mansion to Parmenio, and by mentioning a letter in which he ordered Antipater to have bodyguards. No doubt A was exceedingly generous to those he trusted.

In 40 A is represented as chiding gently but logically those of his Companions who indulged themselves in vulgar extravagance—Hagnon, Leonnatus and Philotas being named as such. On the other hand, A engaged even more energetically in military and hunting expeditions and risked his life, for instance, in despatching a great lion (with his spear). Plutarch provided an anecdote about that event, and noted that Craterus dedicated at Delphi a group of bronzes which showed the lion, the dogs, the king engaging the lion, and himself coming to help.[33] The artists were Lysippus and Leochares. In 41 the practice of A in courting danger and in urging the others to do likewise led them to become intolerant of him and even to speak ill of him. At first (ἐν ἀρχῇ) he bore this mildly, and he showed to them the marks of great goodwill and respect. Plutarch then gave a number of examples. These were drawn from letters to Peucestas, Hephaestion and doctors who treated Peucestas and Craterus, and from a dream which led A to sacrifice and to urge Craterus (who was sick) to sacrifice for recovery. When his boyhood friend Harpalus absconded with treasure in 333,[34] A distrusted those who informed him and put them in chains. Plutarch completed his list with a story which he had narrated twice in *Mor.* 180f and 339c. Then he had named A's friend as Antigenes of Pellene, but here he called him Eurylochus of Aegae. However, the name of the prostitute with whom the friend was in love was the same in all versions, Telesippa. Perhaps Plutarch took trouble to check on the man's name for the *Life.*

In 42 Plutarch expressed surprise that A found time to write so many letters to the Friends. He cited three such letters, which were concerned with the slaves owned by Seleucus, Craterus and Megabyzus. As a judge, 'he is said' to have kept one ear free for the defendant's case 'at first' (ἐν ἀρχῇ). But later he was made harsh by the numerous prosecutions, since the many that were true led him towards accepting those that were false. In particular, when he was maligned, he abandoned reason and was harsh and inexorable, because indeed he loved his own glory above life and kingship. Here we have a pointer towards the later deterioration of A.

4. Gradual Changes in Personality

In the second part of the *Life* Plutarch let the narrative take control and he made reflective comments *en passant.* Although the *leitmotif* was a change in A for the worse in some respects, he was anxious to give a proper place to A's continuing fine qualities. He illustrated A's self-mastery and great-mindedness (42.10 ἐγκράτειαν καὶ μεγαλοψυχίαν) in giving back the water which was offered to him when all were overcome with thirst. The story was told of several places.[35] Plutarch chose to include it in the pursuit of Darius. It was followed by the picture of Darius on the verge of death praying that the gods would reward A for his decency towards the royal family (43.4 ἐπιεικείας). The theft of Bucephalus, reported here rather than earlier, showed A at his most merciful; for he not only pardoned but even rewarded the thieves[36] when they returned the horse unharmed (44.5 φιλανθρώπως). The change to which Plutarch attached great importance was the adoption by A of Asian dress and the wish of A to receive obeisance (προσκύνησις). When this change began, Plutarch offered two explanations (45.1-3):

> Either A wished to associate himself with the local customs because common custom and common race are a great step towards the civilising of mankind. Or this was a furtive attempt to introduce obeisance for the Macedonians, as they were gradually accustoming themselves to put up with his changing mode of life.

These were not presented as exclusive alternatives. Plutarch implemented both explanations as his narrative proceeded.

The first explanation was developed when Plutarch came to report the training of 30,000 Asian boys (in 330) and the marriage with Roxane (in 327).

> In his mode of life A was making himself still more like the local peoples, and he was bringing them (reading ἐκείνους) closer to Macedonian customs, thinking that he would stabilise the situation rather by goodwill than by force through an intermingling and partnership with them, at a time when he was about to march far away.

(47.5)

Here Plutarch was repeating in more measured terms the praise he had expressed in *Moralia* 329f-330e for A 'the philosopher' envisaging 'for all men concord and peace and partnership'.[37] The barbarians saw A's marriage with Roxane as an example of such partnership (τῇ κοινωνίᾳ), loved A exceedingly and respected him for his restraint (47.8 σωφρονέστατος), in that, passionately in love though he was, he waited to marry Roxane legally. His power of conciliation was shown too in his dealings with Hephaestion and Craterus, although Hephaestion sympathised with the change in A's mode of life and Craterus clung to old Macedonian ways.

Plutarch came next to the affairs of Philotas, Cleitus, the Pages and Callisthenes. He was no doubt familiar with the many varying accounts, and it seems that he composed his own versions therefrom, except that he adopted Aristobulus' descriptions of the early suspicion of Philotas and of the Cleitus affair. He never mentioned the Assembly of Macedonians, except in a letter of A to Antipater, and he attributed all decisions to A alone. A appeared in a favourable light at first; for he disbelieved the accusations which were made against Philotas in Egypt, and he gave important commands to Philotas and Parmenio. But in 330 A is represented as opening his ears to the arguments of Philotas' enemies, receiving '10,000 false accusations' (μυρίας διαβολάς), and taunting Philotas for uttering cries under torture. The killing of Parmenio followed. These aspects 'made A an object of fear to many of the Friends' (49.14).[38]

The rift between A and the older Friends was made manifest in the account of the Cleitus affair, and it was widened when the younger Friends sided with A and insulted Cleitus. A had lost that power of reconciling the old and the young which he had shown in dealing with Craterus and Hephaestion. The grounds of the rift were represented by Plutarch as in part charges of cowardice and mainly the policy of A in promoting Persians and in adopting Persian ways himself (51.2 and 5). The disaster was predestined, given the wilfulness of Cleitus (50.9 and 51.5). There was hearty drinking (50.8 πότου νεανικοῦ) and both men were flushed with liquor, but these were attendant circumstances, not the cause. Plutarch thus exonerated A from any charge of murder but not from adopting a policy which split the Friends.

The remorse of A was alleviated by Aristander, who said the fate of Cleitus was predestined,[39] and by Anaxarchus, who suggested that the king, like Zeus, was above the law, thus rendering A's character 'in many ways more conceited and more lawless' (52.7 χαυνότερον καὶ παρανομώτερον). The rift with the Friends was seen again in the matter of obeisance. A's attempt to introduce it was frustrated by Callisthenes, who thus 'saved the Greeks from a great disgrace and A from a greater disgrace' (54.3).[40] But Callisthenes 'destroyed himself' thereby. For the flatterers of A made accusations, and when the Pages' Conspiracy was discovered the false charges gained verisimilitude.[41] Here Plutarch was less interested in Callisthenes' innocence or guilt than in the deterioration of A under the influence of the flatterers. 'He was now regarded with fear and he was inexorable in punishing those who offended him' (57.3).

As a military commander A was still his old self. 'In his ambition to overcome fortune by daring and force by valour (ἀρετη) he thought that nothing was insuperable for the confident and nothing was secure for those who lacked daring' (58.2). He grieved for the loss of a young man killed in action and for the deaths of Bu-

cephalus and a dog he had trained. He showed gentleness and courtesy to Acouphis (πραότητα καὶ φιλανθρωπίαν),[42] outdid Taxiles in generosity, and gave gifts in the end to the Indian philosophers. When he had to turn back at the river Hyphasis, he was overcome with despondency and anger (62.5 δυσθυμίας καὶ ὀργῆς), but he showed all his courage at the city of the Malli. The only 'stain' on his military record was the killing of the Indian mercenaries, after he had granted them a truce (59.7).

During the return from India A and his Companions engaged in drunken revels day and night, and once when A was drunk he kissed his beloved Bagoas passionately in public (67.8). Plutarch concerned himself more with A's drunkenness than with pederasty, which his source, Dicaearchus, had made into the moral of the story (Athen. 603a-b φιλόπαις . . . ἐκμανῶς).[43] Then Plutarch told a story about Antigenes, which he had told of Tarrias in _Moralia_ 339b-c—presumably now correcting himself: the story showed A being lenient to a very brave man for a peccadillo (70.6). The mutiny at Opis was attributed to the Macedonians' fear that A was paying more attention to his 30,000 Asian boys than to themselves. A was angry and abusive to the Macedonians, and he persisted in promoting the Persians, until the Macedonians were humbled and he wept with them over a reconciliation (71.8).

Qualities which A had once had and now lacked were moderation and self-mastery. The change was clear in Plutarch's account of his mourning for Hephaestion. He showed a complete 'lack of reason' (72.3 οὐδενὶ λογισμῷ). He demanded the clipping of the manes and tails of all horses and mules and the dismantling of all battlements, crucified 'the wretched doctor', massacred the young Cossaeans, and intended to spend a colossal sum on a grandiose funerary monument. He became suspicious of his Friends. He who had been a cause of terror to them, was now afraid of them, particularly of Antipater. He lost his temper with Cassander and treated him with brutality. His faith in the favour of the gods who had carried him from triumph to triumph weakened, as the diviners interpreted omen after omen as presaging disaster for him personally. He became 'downhearted and as regards the gods despondent' (74.1 ἠθύμει καὶ δύσελπις ην πρὸς τὸ θεῖον). Finally, giving in to the signs of the gods, he became so bewildered and terrified in mind, that he interpreted anything unusual or out-of-the-way as a portentous sign. Priests sacrificing, purifying and prophesying filled the palace. Pious though he was, Plutarch saw that A was the victim of nonsensical superstition and panic fears (75.2).[44]

Relief came only with the announcement from Ammon's oracle, that Hephaestion should be honoured as a hero (72.3 and 75.3). He engaged again in sacrifices and drinking parties. Cleitarchus, whom Plutarch had been following as his main source, went on to complete the religious and moral disintegration of A by having him cap a night and day of continual drinking with 'a bowl of Heracles', whereupon he suffered a seizure and later died. Plutarch, however, preferred the view of Aristobulus, that the fever was not due to excessive drinking, and the day-by-day account of the illness in the *Ephemerides*.[45]

5. ATTRIBUTIONS AND DEDUCTIONS ABOUT ALEXANDER'S PERSONALITY

In the reflective passages Plutarch relied a good deal on his own memory of what he had written in *Moralia* and in other chapters of the *Life*. However, he drew also on particular sources as follows:

(1) 4.1-8	A's endowment	Statues, paintings, Aristoxenus, Theophrastus
(2) 21.5-23.10	self-mastery	Aristobulus (21.9), Letters, *Ephemerides* (23.3-6 and 8)
(3) 28	divine birth	Aristobulus (28.3), Letter, Satyrus (28.4f.)
(4) 39-42.4	generosity	Letters

In (1) Plutarch put before the reader the main features of A's personality as Plutarch saw them. He did this at the outset, and not, as in a modern biography, at the end. The main features may be described as a passionate nature, a fondness for drink, a tendency to violence, an excessive impetuosity, a serious, indeed philosophical mind, a sense of restraint, a desire to do great things, and a desire to be honoured, while he was high-principled ($\mu\epsilon\gamma\alpha\lambda\acute{o}\psi\upsilon\chi o\varsigma$) and difficult to deflect ($\delta\upsilon\sigma\kappa\acute{\iota}\nu\eta\tau o\varsigma$). The first four of these features were basic in that they stemmed from an innate 'high bodily heat'—what we might describe literally, as well as metaphorically, as 'an unusually hot blood' and 'an unusually hot temper'. In (2) Plutarch showed that A's sense of restraint was in control of his sexual urges, his appetite for food and drink, and any desire to be inactive; this sense of restraint led here to self-mastery. In (3) Plutarch considered how far A's mind was affected by the report that he was of divine birth. The conclusion was that A was not affected at all in his relations with Greeks and Macedonians, and that he used such a belief as a means of subjecting the barbarians. In (4) A's consideration for and generosity to others were carried almost to excess, and as a judge he made a point of reserving one ear to listen to the defendant stating his case.

Why did Plutarch place these reflective passages where he did in the narrative? Any answer must be tentative. In my opinion he wrote (1) as the backcloth to the boy-

hood and young manhood of A, so that the reader could see the interplay of the elements of A's personality in these formative years: the serious mind questioning the Persian envoys, the longing for fame when overshadowed by his father, the impetuous daring with Bucephalus, the philosophical mind developed by Aristotle and others, the drunken quarrel with Attalus and Philip, the hurt pride in the Pixodarus affair, the lion-like rage at Thebes, the mercy for Timoclea, the violence at Delphi, the impetuosity at the River Granicus, the passionate attack on the Greek mercenaries, the drunken revel at Phaselis, and the trust in his doctor at Tarsus. Up to this point we are seeing the elements in A's personality pulling in different directions.

In (2) the high principles of A and especially his self-mastery are displayed, and in the ensuing narrative they continue to be dominant. During this period of well-balanced maturity A was the happy recipient of dreams and omens, sent from the gods, which foreshadowed success after success, and in the journey to Siwa he received help from the gods which matched each difficulty (27.1). Perhaps A was thereby justified in his belief that 'the god' adopted as his own the best among men. Plutarch interrupted his narrative with (3) in which he showed that the balance of A's mind was not affected at all by a belief in a divine origin. The period of well-balanced maturity continued until the end of the Greek part of the campaign, the capture of Persepolis. Plutarch represented the burning of Xerxes' palace there as the act of the Greek girl, Thaïs, in which the Companions urged A to take part and which delighted the Macedonians. They were all of one mind then.

In (4) Plutarch wrote of the generosity and the consideration which A showed to common soldiers as well as to the Companions. The examples extended over the career of A in Asia. They showed A as the successful and unselfish leader of men. But in the latter part of (4) Plutarch struck a new note. 'In the beginning', i.e. up to the burning of Xerxes' palace, A heard a man's defence when he was accused. 'Later' he believed false accusations and became harsh. 'At first' he took it mildly if anyone spoke ill of him; but later, if this happened, he went out of his mind and became cruel and inexorable (41.2 and 42.4). Plutarch was looking forward—and directing us to look forward—to A's treatment of Philotas and Cleitus, and then to his hatred of Callisthenes. Thus at the end of (4) Plutarch marked a great divide.

In the ensuing narrative, although Plutarch praised A's ideas about relations with the barbarians, he drew attention to the cracks in A's personality which were revealed in his treatment of the Companions and the Macedonians. His attempt to introduce obeisance by the Companions was utterly disgraceful (54.3) and alienated the older and the better Companions. He became an object of fear to his associates and to the whole army (57.3), for he was inexorable. Passionate anger was mastering his judgement. He was more conceited and lawless, he lost his sense of proportion in his mourning for Hephaestion, and he suspected his Companions of disloyalty. As his hot blood took control of his personality, he engaged more in drinking-bouts. But the most sinister development was A's fear of adverse omens and portents, his yielding to superstition, and his panic fear and bewilderment.

To the modern historian there is a great deal that is unsatisfactory in Plutarch's analysis and protrayal of A's personality. We do not regard an infant's natural endowment, such as unusually hot blood, as a powerful element in the development of the adult personality. Plutarch chose to keep in separate compartments A's treatment of his Greek and Macedonian associates and troops on the one hand, and his policy towards the barbarians on the other hand; but A's determination to found and govern a kingdom of Asia meant that he had to co-ordinate his policies and his attitudes towards both groups of peoples. Plutarch was unduly influenced by the contemporary view that monarchical power corrupts the monarch and converts even a generous personality into a conceited, lawless and inexorable tyrant. His picture of a deteriorating A was certainly overdrawn. But Plutarch had access to more information than we do. He had more understanding of the religious beliefs of the time. And he was honest in believing what he wrote. Inevitably the worth of much of the *Life* depends on the value of his various sources. . . .

Notes

1. Pindar, *O*. 2.86 σοφὸς ὁ πολλὰ εἰδὼς φυᾷ coupled poetic inspiration and physical prowess as due to natural endowment. See C. Gill, 'The question of character-development: Plutarch and Tacitus', *CQ* [*Classical Quarterly*] 33 (1983) 473ff. for Plutarch's views on φύσις.

2. See Wardman 102 and Hamilton *C* 11.

3. Theophrastus wrote a treatise *De Odoribus*; see Wardman 102 and Hamilton *C* 12 for possible passages in Theophrastus' works. Plutarch made the same points about A in *Mor*. 623e.

4. These two qualities σωφροσύνη and μεγαλοψυχία were associated with self-control, ἐγκράτεια, in the reported speech of the eunuch to Darius at 30.10.

5. See Berve 14 for the names of others.

6. See Hamilton *C* 19, giving references.

7. Plutarch was probably relying on his memory; and he expressed his hesitation about A being the first

to charge the Theban Sacred Band (λέγεται πρῶτος ἐνσεῖσαι).

8. See [Hammond, 1993], pp. 8-11.

9. Rediscovered in this century and shown to members of the First Symposium on Ancient Macedonia in 1968.

10. *THA* 13-16 and 26; 95.

11. Perrin omitted διανοίας altogether. 'Mental preparedness' was one reason for it being difficult to deflect A from his purpose.

12. See [Hammond, 1993], p. 46.

13. See Hamilton *C* 45 for this philosopher, Theodectes.

14. See [Hammond, 1993], p. 51.

15. Because Plutarch accepted this letter as genuine, he had not included a visit by A and Hephaestion to the royal ladies (see [Hammond, 1993], p. 52).

16. Probably for use in hunting birds and deer, since A did not carry a bow in battle.

17. At *Mor*. 65f 'A said that he did not believe those who proclaimed him to be a god in the matter of sleep especially and sexual intercourse.'

18. Even a Page was executed by Philip II for disobeying an order to stay under arms (Aelian, *V.H.* 14.48), and a Companion disobeying orders was killed by Alexander (*PA* 57.3).

19. It would certainly be odd if this was all that Plutarch found in the *Ephemerides* which he considered worthy of mention about A's daily round.

20. So too later writers such as Athenaeus, who confirmed at 434b that such bouts of sleep were shown in the *Ephemerides,* and Aelian, *V.H.* 3.23, who claimed to report A's drinking and sleeping from the *Ephemerides.*

21. Such is the account which was transmitted by Curt. 8.1.22-5 (boasting) and Arr. 4.8.3 (flatterers).

22. This anecdote was mentioned earlier by Pliny, *N.H.* 12.62; it figures also in *Mor*. 179e-f.

23. The story offsets the statement of A to his mother that there were prophecies (μαντεῖαι). The moral of the story is that it was due to a mistake that A was supposed to be a son of Zeus. For a different view see Hamilton *C* 73.

24. See *HM* II 180 and 192.

25. *AG*² 158f.

26. In *Mor*. 180d 'Zeus is the father of all by nature (φύσει) and makes the best his own.'

27. At 28.6 τοὺς ἄλλους picks up the distinction made at the start of the chapter. Perrin mistranslates as 'o hers', and Hamilton *C* 75 does not bring out the point.

28. Plutarch gave the same account in *Mor.* 180e and 341b, but in the latter passage with the addition that A was speaking to his flatterers (πρὸς τοὺς κόλακας εἶπεν). Athenaeus told the anecdote to illustrate the behaviour of flatterers, Dioxippus citing this line of Homer to A. These are evidently two parts of the same anecdote, in which Dioxippus cited the line in flattery and A responded with the line in mockery. This was suggested by Tarn 358 n. 5. The story was told differently as a criticism of A by Callisthenes (Seneca, *Suas.* 1.5) and by Anaxarchus (D. L. 9.60). See Hamilton *C* 74, who remarked that 'Tarn is doubtless right.' Brunt in *CQ* 24 (1974) 68, who did not mention the views of Tarn and Hamilton, supposed that Athenaeus had erred in naming as his source 'Aristobulus'; but Brunt did not say what name would have been more to his liking.

29. Athenaeus cites 'Satyrus in the *Lives*', of which one was evidently that of Alexander.

30. The text is as follows. ἐγὼ μὲν οὐκ ἄν, φησίν, ὑμῖν ἐλευθέραν πόλιν ἔδωκα καὶ ἔνδοξον ἔχετε δὲ αὐτὴν λαβόντες παρὰ τοῦ τότε κυρίου καὶ πατρὸς ἐμοῦ προσαγορευομένου. Perrin translated thus: 'I cannot have given you that free and illustrious city; for ye received it from him who was then your master and was called my father, meaning Philip.' 'Cannot' is clearly wrong, and to say to Athenians 'Philip was your master' was untrue and would have been most undiplomatic. Hamilton in *CQ* 3 (1953) 151 n. 2 translated as follows. 'I would not have given you that free and illustrious city but you have it as a gift from its former master, my "so-called" father, meaning Philip.' This translation assumes that Philip had become 'master of Samos' before the settlement; but Philip did not go anywhere near that island in the years before the battle of Chaeronea.

The diction of A's letter to Athenians has to be studied in relation to other Macedonian documents of the period. In A's letter ἔδωκα is used exactly as in two inscriptions of 335-334 B.C. within Macedonia (see my article in *CQ* 38 (1988) 384f.) and in an edict of 319 B.C. by Philip III Arrhidaeus in Diod. 18.56.7 σάμον δὲ δίδομεν 'Αθηναίοις, ἐπειδὴ καὶ Φίλιππος ἔδωκεν ὁ πατήρ. The use of κύριος in A's letter is paralleled by A's words in his letter to Darius ἐμοῦ τῆς 'Ασίας ἀπάσης κυρίου ὄντος (Arr. 2.14.8; cf. 2.14.9 κυρίῳ ὄντι) and in his dedication of spoils at Lindus after the battle of Gaugamela (*FGrH* 532 F 1.38 κύριος γενόμενος τᾶς 'Ασίας). In A's letter I take it that τότε goes only with κυρίου, and the meaning is that Philip was then in control of Greek affairs. To refer to Philip as 'my father' is not surprising; for A did so in his letter to Darius (Arr. 2.14.5 τὸν ἐμὸν πατέρα), and Philip III did the same in 319 B.C. (Φίλιππος ἔδωκεν ὁ πατήρ; cf. Diod. 18.56.2 Φίλιππος ὁ ἡμέτερος πατήρ). I see no point in Philip being called A's father (πατρὸς ἐμοῦ προσαγορευομένου) in 338 B.C., when A was relatively unimportant. He was evidently being called so in the negotiations of 334-332 B.C. by Athenians, who hoped A would be reluctant to change his father's decision about Samos.

These analogies show either that the letter is genuine and is to be explained in terms of Macedonian terminology, as I have suggested, or that it was forged by someone conversant with Macedonian terminology of that time. Earlier literature on the subject is well summarised by Hamilton in *CQ* 3 (1953) 151-7. He himself concluded that the letter was genuine, but in my opinion he misunderstood the meaning of the letter.

31. I take it that the participle here is absolute (the meaning being comparable to that at 16.17 fin. above) and πρὸς τοὺς ''Ελληνας goes with ἔγραψε (as at 29.9 πρὸς τὸν Δαρεῖον ἔγραψεν), the Greeks here being contrasted with the Plataeans in particular. Perrin and Hamilton *C* 91 took πρὸς τοὺς ''Ελληνας with φιλοτιμούμενος (Perrin translating 'being desirous of honour among the Greeks').

32. Hamilton *L* 14 reached no decision about the authority of this and the other two letters in chapters 39, 41 and 42.

33. The actual dedication was made by Craterus' son after his father's death; see Hamilton *C* 107.

34. If this had been the second time Harpalus absconded, A would hardly have arrested the informers; see Hamilton *C* 109.

35. Curt. 7.5.10-12 in Sogdiana; Arrian 6.26.1-3 in Gedrosia; Polyaenus without a location; and Frontinus, *Strat.* 1.7.7 on the way to Siwa. The accounts vary also in detail.

36. A feature not in the versions of Curt. 6.5.20, Diod. 17.76.8 and Arr. 5.19.6.

37. Although Plutarch wrote in the *Moralia* of the Alexander-cities and of the spread of Greek education into remote parts of Asia, he was content in the *Life* to leave the matter at the philosophical level.

38. Plutarch did not discuss the question whether Philotas was guilty of treason or innocent; he simply said that the reason for Philotas not informing A was 'unclear' (49.5 ἄδηλον). Plutarch's concern was with A's personality and its effect on others. He blamed the flatterers in *Mor.* 65d.

39. This was the view of Aristobulus, which Plutarch was following in 50.1-7; see [Hammond, 1993], p. 93.

40. Although Plutarch had praised A's Asian policy in the *Moralia,* he regarded obeisance as shameful for any Greek even to contemplate.

41. Perrin translated διαβάλλω and its derivatives as 'accuse' at 49.10 and 55.3, but the word has the connotation of accusing falsely.

42. Following Hamilton *C* 161.

43. Plutarch had already mentioned A's disgust at being asked to obtain pretty boys for his sexual pleasure at 22.1-3. If we discount the difference in the moral they drew, the versions of Plutarch and Athenaeus are so close that a common source is to be presumed, namely Dicaearchus, a pupil of Aristotle. See Hamilton *C* 180 and for a different view E. Badian in *CQ* 8 (1958) 156.

44. Plutarch condemned superstition roundly in his essay *De Superstitione.*

45. Rather different views of Plutarch's portrayal of A are to be found in Hamilton *C* lxii-lxvi, e.g. 'in general the Life is apologetic in tone', and in Tarn 296-309, e.g. 'Plutarch being quite inconsistent'.

Abbreviations and Select Bibliography

A: Alexander the Great

AG[2]: N. G. L. Hammond, *Alexander the Great: King, Commander and Statesman* (2nd edn, Bristol Classical Press, 1989)

Arr.: Arrian, *Anabasis Alexandrou*

Berve: H. Berve, *Das Alexanderreich auf prosopographischer Grundlage,* 2 vols. (Munich, 1926)

FGrH: F. Jacoby, *Die Fragmente der griechischen Historiker* (Berlin, 1923-30; Leiden, 1940-58)

Hamilton *C*: J. R. Hamilton, *Plutarch, Alexander: a Commentary* (Oxford, 1969)

Hamilton *L*: J. R. Hamilton, 'The letters in Plutarch's *Alexander*', *PACA* [*Proceedings of the African Classical Association*] 4 (1961) 9-20

HM: *A History of Macedonia* I by N. G. L. Hammond (Oxford, 1972); II by N. G. L. Hammond and G. T. Griffith (1979); III by N. G. L. Hammond and F. W. Walbank (1988)

P A: Plutarch, *Life of Alexander,* in the Loeb edition (1971)

Perrin: B. Perrin, *Plutarch's Lives* VII (1971), Loeb edition

Tarn: W. W. Tarn, *Alexander the Great* II (Cambridge, 1948 and 1979)

THA: N. G. L. Hammond, *Three Historians of Alexander the Great: the so-called Vulgate authors, Diodorus, Justin and Curtius* (Cambridge, 1983)

Wardman: A. E. Wardman, 'Plutarch and Alexander', *CQ* 5 (1955) 96-107

THE MEDIEVAL ALEXANDER

George Cary (essay date 1956)

SOURCE: Cary, George. "The Conception of Alexander in Moralists to the Fourteenth Century, with a Prospect of the Opinions of Later Writers." In *The Medieval Alexander,* edited by D. J. A. Ross, pp. 80-117. Cambridge: Cambridge University Press, 1956.

[*In the following excerpt, Cary surveys the opinions of fourteenth-century moralists on Alexander.*]

1. INTRODUCTION

The historical accounts of Alexander presented medieval Europe with established philosophic judgements of his character which preserved, though they were confused in the derivative histories of Curtius, Justin and Orosius, the characteristics of the Peripatetic and Stoic attacks upon him. Alexander was either fundamentally weak or fundamentally bad, and his continued prosperity, ascribed not to his own ability but to Fortune, encouraged his inherent weakness to yield to vicious influences, or his inherent wickedness to worsen as his power increased.

Ethical teaching is more stable and constant than metaphysical speculation. Based upon an abstract idea of good, and not necessarily dependent on the postulation of a God, ethical norms transcend the civilization that gives them birth, and survive the decay of those religious or philosophic ideals upon which they were originally established. Though the coming of Christianity, and the transformation of pagan morality into a rule of Christian conduct through which a man might attain to heaven, affected the orientation of speculative and didactic morality, it did not deprive medieval moralists of sympathy, often of complete agreement, with principles first laid down by pagan writers. They substituted Christian motives and the workings of God for philosophic motives and the working of Fortune, of Natura, or other impersonal forces; but the basic teaching of morality remained much the same.

And Christian morality was especially in sympathy with those philosophers who were most intimately connected with Alexander in the minds of Christian readers. Aristotle, 'maestro di color che sanno', and Seneca, 'maximus ille paupertatis et continentiae sector, et summus inter uniuersos philosophos morum aedificator', were the most venerated of pagan philosophers; while of those with whom Alexander came into recorded personal contact, Diogenes and the Brahmans were considered admirable examples for the Christian ascetic, and Callisthenes was honoured as the pupil of Aristotle. The philosophers with whom the name of Alexander was connected, in a fashion normally unfavourable to his reputation, were readily understood and appreciated. Thus it was in the denunciations of Alexander by Diogenes, Dindimus and Dionides, supported by Seneca's Stoic attacks, by the summary judgements of the accessible historians, and by the comments of the Fathers of the Church upon the antique material that they transmitted, that medieval moralists found it easiest to establish a judgement upon Alexander; since these were men they could understand, and who presented a judgement of Alexander which, even if it was confused upon particular issues, was at least decisive in condemnation, and ready-made to an exemplar end.

It is, therefore, from the broken survivals of antique tradition that the conception of Alexander in the writings of medieval moralists is principally derived. We shall discuss the perseverance of this tradition in judgements both upon the whole career of Alexander, and upon particular aspects of his character, and show the effect of the impact of other traditions upon this philosophic material, which is merely the continuance of a Greek tradition transmitted through Rome to Christendom. First, however, it is necessary to note the chief problem which faced Christian moralists; a problem for which no solution was ever put forward and which is inherent in every serious medieval judgement of Alexander. The substitution of Christian for pagan ideas necessarily involved the replacement of Fortune, that controlling force in the development of Alexander's character, by Divine Providence. But in the parallel Jewish tradition, in the testimony of the Bible and of Josephus, Alexander is God's instrument of wrath against the Persians and his career is watched over by God. In Josephus Alexander is, in addition, conscious of the power of God, who accomplishes miracles on his behalf. The same idea is echoed in the Oriental Alexander tradition, and thence in the *Historia de Preliis*;

but it is difficult to reconcile with the idolatrous, vicious Alexander of classical tradition, whose vices are ascribed in great part to that very influence of Fortune, and therefore, in the Christian tradition, of God. The questions raised by the conflict between these two traditions will be discussed fully in the second section in dealing with the theological approach to Alexander.

The anecdotal information about Alexander from which almost all knowledge of him in the moralists of this period was derived was supplied principally by Seneca, Valerius Maximus, and Cicero. Of these authors, Seneca naturally reflects the Stoic opinion of Alexander in his anecdotes, Cicero the Peripatetic approach, while Valerius Maximus, as an anthologist like many of the medieval writers themselves, is subject to both philosophic currents. Thus, although there are a certain number of anecdotes which have no connexion with any particular view of Alexander current in antiquity, most of the material known to medieval moralists was derived either from Stoic or Peripatetic sources; and, as we have seen, these anecdotes were necessarily those best adapted for moral use, and of the greatest influence upon medieval opinion of Alexander.

As a very general rule the following principles of anecdotal transmission may be noticed: that the anecdotes derived primarily from Seneca and from Cicero, and retransmitted by the Fathers of the Church, were those best known in the Middle Ages; while those told by Valerius Maximus were widely used only by John of Salisbury among moralists, and passed through his or other intermediacy into the books of *exempla*.

Upon these premises I have adopted the following arrangement in considering the conception of Alexander in the earlier medieval moralists. I have first discussed the history of the anecdotes most popular in the Middle Ages, and the significance of the morals attached to them; I have then dealt with the scattered anecdotal material that appears in the moralists; and finally, I discuss certain special issues and individual judgements. This arrangement has been made necessary by the entire dependence of this class of writers upon scattered references, which makes the assessment of the picture of Alexander presented in any one moralist so fragmentary, so contradictory and so elusive as not to deserve consideration; whereas the discussion of the history of each anecdote shows how its moral became changed, the effect of its popularity upon the general opinion of Alexander, and the fate of individual points of ancient propaganda; so that these parallel vertical traditions, each possessing its particular interest, will by their combination show the trend of the conception of Alexander among medieval moralists down to the fourteenth century, and look forward to the deeper influence of morality upon poetry in the later Middle Ages.

2. The Most Popular Moral Anecdotes of Alexander, and Their Medieval History and Usage

In this section the following anecdotes and anecdotal groups have been placed: Alexander's interview with Diogenes; the group of anecdotes in Cicero and Seneca that concern his liberality; his interview with Dindimus; and his encounter with Dionides the Pirate. The reasons for the popularity of these philosophical interviews in the Middle Ages have already been discussed; and it remains now to show how medieval moralists reacted to this material, and how deeply it affected their consideration of Alexander.

(A) Alexander and Diogenes

Ancient philosophers worked upon the reputation of the Cynic Diogenes until they had made him the hero of many legendary episodes;[1] and the legend was caught up and enlarged by medieval writers. The fact that Diogenes did not regard his asceticism as a means to a Christian end was not appreciated by medieval observers, who accepted the Senecan and patristic portrait of Diogenes, and were accustomed to see in all asceticism something of Christian saintliness. For it was the ascetic side of him that they took for their example and admiration; the old man sitting in meditation upon a philosophy presumed to be as Christian in its intimations of immortality as it was in its denial of human comfort.

The story of Diogenes in his tub and Alexander interfering with his sun is too well known to need retelling here. Its popularity in learned medieval circles was assured by its appearance in authors well established in medieval favour: Cicero, and Valerius Maximus.[2] Valerius Maximus added a proverbial comment: 'Alexander Diogenem gradu suo diuitiis pellere temptat, celerius Darium armis.'[3] And Seneca, in reference to the story, which he does not repeat, also made use of epigrammatic abuse of Alexander: 'multo potentior, multo locupletior fuit [Diogenes] omnia tunc possidente Alexandro: plus enim erat, quod hic nollet accipere quam quod ille posset dare.'[4] And in another place: 'Alexander Macedonum rex gloriari solebat a nullo se beneficiis uictum.'[5]

These comments were often reproduced in the Middle Ages, sometimes with the anecdote and sometimes independently. They point to a moral best expressed by Seneca, and typical of the Stoic treatment of Alexander's character. The world-conqueror, accustomed to boast that nobody could surpass him in liberality, was surpassed by Diogenes, who, by his refusal to accept anything from him except what he could not give, proved himself richer in true riches, and a better man. The emphasis is therefore upon Alexander's making

liberality a part of vanity, and on the rebuff that he receives from Diogenes, who asks him to give him back what he cannot give—the sunshine. There is a close parallel in the story of the Gymnosophists later to be discussed, who ask Alexander to give them immortality;[6] and a similar implication—all good gifts come from God.

This moral conclusion was fully maintained where the story was used by learned medieval writers who do no more than repeat the story and the original comments; but it was lost when the story was applied to the purposes of the books of *exempla*. There it took on a wider moral as eminently suited to an edifying purpose as Seneca's judgement was to moral disquisition. This new interpretation was reached by the addition to the anecdote of new material from an Oriental source, which completely changed its character by altering the focus, placing the incident of the sun in the background, and making the episode a lecture on incontinence of a general and conventional type. In this version, which reached Europe through the *Disciplina Clericalis*, the main part of the narrative is occupied by Diogenes' explanation of his statement that Alexander is 'the servant of his servant'. He explains that his own will is subject to his reason, while Alexander's reason is subject to his will, and therefore Alexander is 'the servant of his servant'. This remark, expounded at considerable length, is preceded by the story of Diogenes' sunshine. This, however, is here not even told of Diogenes and Alexander, but of Diogenes and the servants of Alexander who find him seated in his tub, and to whom he first delivers himself of his epigram on their master. This exemplar anecdote will be examined later; for the moment it is sufficient to note how the incident of the sunshine here became a brief, insignificant, and scarcely noticed introduction to the real theme of the story—Alexander's inability to subject his will to reason.

In its simple form, however, as a comment upon false liberality, and with the comments of Seneca and Valerius Maximus either attached or understood, the application of this story was consistently learned rather than popular, as will be seen from the examples given of its use; it was only when it became attached to the wide moral of the Oriental material that it became known outside learned literature. This restricted application must be considered in conjunction with other Stoic and Peripatetic material relating to Alexander's liberality that was known in medieval times; since, as we shall see, the question of Alexander's liberality was one of great importance in the medieval period, and frequently discussed.

(B) ALEXANDER'S LIBERALITY IN THE MORALISTS

The moral of the Diogenes story is closely connected with that of other Senecan passages; it is also to be related to an anecdote derived from Cicero, and to episodes in the historians known to the Middle Ages. All this material, by its medieval use, illustrates the view of Alexander's liberality held by moralists of this period; and it is of especial importance to establish the evolution of their attitude, because the secular reputation of Alexander for liberality was so pronounced and so remarkable as to suggest some traditional evidence in support of its proverbial fame.[7]

We will first discuss the texts relating to Alexander's liberality best known to medieval writers, and then proceed, from a philosophic definition of liberality, to examine the medieval treatment of these texts, and to consider how far Alexander's liberality was thought true liberality, and how far the effect of mistaken policy or of arrogant vanity.

That this last is the view of Seneca, who represents the Stoic attitude towards Alexander, may be seen not only from his comment upon the Diogenes story, but from two anecdotes which he tells of Alexander's liberality. The first concerns the envoys of an Asiatic city, who advance to offer half their city to the invading Alexander. Alexander replies: 'It is no question of your giving me your city, but of your keeping what I choose to give you back'.[8] The second is the story of the poor veteran who comes to Alexander to beg his release from the army, since he has served his time;[9] he asks for a small gift. Alexander is in the humour to give the man a city. The veteran exclaims in astonishment: 'I am not worthy of so great a gift.' Alexander replies: 'The question is not what it is fitting for you to receive, but what it is fitting that I should give.' This story is compared with that of Antigonus and the Cynic who asks for an obol; when Antigonus suggests that this is no fit gift for a king to give, the Cynic asks for a talent, whereupon Antigonus avoids giving him anything by saying that a talent is no fit gift for a Cynic to receive. Seneca attacks both impartially; Antigonus for his higgling, evasive parsimony, and Alexander for his refusal to consider the feelings of other people, his making liberality a part of vanity, and thence his neglect of all those precepts which should govern the act of giving, the consideration not only of what may reasonably or fittingly be given, but of the ultimate benefit of the recipient: 'Tumidissimum animal! si illum accipere hoc non decet, nec te dare: habetur personarum ac dignitatum portio et, cum sit ubique uirtutis modus, aeque peccat quod excedit quam quod deficit.'[10] The history of this second anecdote, which was widely known in the Middle Ages, belongs not only to the moral, but also to the exemplar and secular attitudes to this question; and there will therefore be frequent reference to it.[11]

An echo of this Stoic approach to Alexander is the passage in Justin where he tells how Alexander gave a kingdom to a peasant, that the gift might be seen to be wholly dependent upon the king's liberality, and not in part upon the rank or true worth of the recipient; while in his preface Justin contrasts the extravagance of Alexander with the parsimony of Philip: 'Frugalitati pater, luxuriae filius magis deditus erat.'

Seneca therefore represents Alexander's liberality as the direct effect of his ὕβρις; and the vigour with which he attacks Alexander for his supposed virtue, and concentrates most of his references to Alexander upon that attack,[12] shows that Alexander had already by this time an established reputation for liberality. And, apart from those references to it which are here unimportant because of their independence of medieval tradition, this reputation is indicated in a passage of Cicero, where he quotes, in a discussion of the true nature of liberality, a famous letter of Philip to the young Alexander.[13] Philip reproaches him for his prodigality, aimed at the acquisition of faithful followers, and points out that he is succeeding only in corrupting the recipients of his prodigality and in diminishing the royal dignity: 'Praeclare in epistula quadam Alexandrum filium Philippus accusat, quod largitione beneuolentiam Macedonum consectetur: "Quae te, malum!" inquit "ratio in istam spem induxit, ut eos tibi fideles putares fore, quos pecunia corrupisses? An tu id agis, ut Macedones non te regem suum, sed ministrum et praebitorem sperent fore?"'

This letter therefore attacks Alexander's liberality on different grounds; it is not derived from vanity, but from mistaken political motives—it is the indiscretion of youth, not the innate conceit of a man. There may be compared with this the correspondence between Zeuxis, Philip, Alexander, and Aristotle in Pseudo-Callisthenes . . . and Julius Valerius, where the two former reproach the young Alexander for his prodigality; and Alexander and Aristotle reply that it is no prodigality, no careless extravagance of youth, but a careful policy of judicious liberality based on the teaching of Aristotle. It is thus evident that opinion was as divided upon Alexander's liberality in the sources immediately available to the writers of the Middle Ages as in those writers themselves.

The moral of the Ciceronian anecdote, that mistaken liberality does not make friends but prepares enemies, is echoed in Curtius; although in his concluding summary Curtius praises Alexander's liberality wholeheartedly and without reserve.

It was these passages from Cicero and Seneca, transmitted in part through Valerius Maximus and the Fathers of the Church, that provided learned medieval writers with the most accessible material for forming a judgement upon Alexander's liberality. The references to his liberality in legendary texts were unknown or unnoticed by serious writers; the references in the historians, though they have been here adduced as supporting evidence for the principal trends of ancient opinion, similarly went unnoticed outside their contexts, because they are comments on incidents, and were not cast into that anecdotal form so necessary for the wide dissemination of textual material in the Middle Ages.

Before considering the use made of these anecdotes by learned medieval writers it is essential that the fundamental beliefs which determined the medieval attitude to liberality should be examined. William of Conches defined liberality, following Cicero, as: '. . . uirtus animi beneficiorum erogatrix, quam eandem pro affectu benignitatem, pro effectu beneficentiam appellamus. Haec uirtus tota in distribuendo consistit.'[14] This definition, and especially this division of liberality into two necessary parts, *affectus,* the natural benevolence of the giver, and *effectus,* the objective act of giving, must be taken as the starting-point for any consideration of the medieval attitude to Alexander's liberality; since opinion upon it was to be divided as to the relative importance to be accorded to *affectus* and to *effectus.*

To a philosopher, the emphasis must naturally be upon the *affectus,* the state of mind in the giver; if this is corrupt in any way, if it is not true benignity, but a desire for self-glorification, the groping towards a political end, or careless pleasure in giving, then the *effectus* must lose the name of true liberality. And this *effectus,* be it noticed, comprises in its original definition all the beneficent results of benevolence; not only material benefits, gifts of money or rank or possessions, but any act of kindness. It includes all those things that benefit the recipient.

To Seneca this definition of liberality was further conditioned by the considerations which attend the act of giving; benevolence does not suffice to make liberality, if the benevolence results in a liberality foolish either because the recipient does not deserve it or because the donor cannot afford it. For Seneca liberality is a careful, philosophic process; and his condemnation of Alexander is especially bitter because he breaks all the rules—his giving does not spring from true benevolence; it considers neither the good of the recipient, nor how much the donor can afford or ought to give.

In contrast to this, Cicero's story of Philip's letter to Alexander is a political comment upon the mistaken use of prodigality for political advantage. The act of liberality is hardly here considered at all; the motives upon which it is based, though they are not benignant, would be excusable as politically expedient. But a measure of political expedience has to be judged by its results, and

in this case the results are prophesied to be fatal. This is the view neither of the philosopher, observing the state of mind of the giver, nor of the preacher or the secular writer, who is especially concerned with the amount of the gift; it is that of the counsellor, who examines the action not so much in connexion with liberality as with its expediency as a political act. The medieval use of the story is therefore restricted, and we find it where we should expect to find it—in the *Policraticus*[15] of John of Salisbury, and in encyclopaedists like Vincent de Beauvais and Brunetto Latini.[16] In these citations the original moral is naturally retained.

We return, therefore, to the anecdotes of Diogenes and of the man to whom Alexander gave a city (the anecdote of the Asiatic city appears only in *exempla*[17]), both of which were adorned with savage Senecan comments. The history of the Diogenes anecdote and its attendant comments has already been traced, and it has been seen how the emphasis was laid not only upon the character of Alexander, but as much, or more, upon that of Diogenes. It was not the act of giving, but the act of refusing, which was the more significant. This point is well illustrated by the fact that the anecdote is hardly ever introduced into a discussion of the character of Alexander, but often forms part of a panegyric on Diogenes.

The history of the other anecdote is very different, and if we may say that the moral of the Diogenes anecdote is maintained at the same philosophic level, that of the second anecdote declines; it becomes altered for exemplar and secular uses, and ends by bearing a moral the opposite of that intended by Seneca. Seneca's bitter comment upon Alexander's so-called liberality is reproduced, so far as I am aware, only in Petrus Cantor, where the story is still joined to that of Antigonus.[18] The stories are similarly connected, in William of Conches, Giraldus Cambrensis, and others; but the edge has been taken off the anecdote by the omission of Seneca's comment, and the use of a simple transitional phrase, 'melius Alexander', inserted between the story of Antigonus and that of Alexander. This is the intermediate stage in the gradual transformation of the moral attached to the anecdote, which finally emerged, separated now from the Antigonus anecdote, in exemplar and secular writers in a form directly favourable to Alexander.

In its passing through learned into unlearned literature the point of this anecdote was lost; while the moral of the anecdotes of Diogenes was maintained at two different levels, one for learned, and the other for exemplar transmission and interpretation, the anecdote of the man to whom Alexander gave a city was altered for exemplar uses and given an interpretation in keeping with the needs of the parish priest seeking alms for his poor, or the dependent begging money from his patron—transformed into an example of that unphilosophic liberality that we shall later consider more fully. So sharp and subtle a criticism as Seneca's was not to be maintained for long by even the most earnest of medieval moralists, who would consider the Christian uses of extravagance; and to the general observer, Alexander would always seem more pardonable than Antigonus, whatever Seneca might have to say upon the question.

Thus Alexander's prodigality was partly admitted; but a more charitable view was taken of it than would be expected from a survey of the surviving material. For medieval views upon prodigality, conditioned by the needs of Christian society, were more fluid and less strict than those of the authors from whom this material was derived; and even the most learned of moralists had, from the ancient viewpoint, a relatively unphilosophic approach to liberality.

(C) ALEXANDER AND DINDIMUS

That the attack of the Brahman Dindimus on Alexander should have so much in common with Greek philosophic attacks on him should cause no surprise; for it was the pleasure of timid and ingenious philosophers among the Cynics to put their abuse of Alexander in the mouth of one of those whom Alexander met in his wanderings, and especially the Brahmans. In their rejection of intellectual life, and their attempt to divest the person of all personal attributes, the Brahmans had certain affinities with the Cynics, and offered an admirable mouthpiece because they were a nation of philosophers.

Dindimus' attack is more valuable than the anecdotal material which we have discussed, for it presents an analysis of the whole character of Alexander, instead of isolated aspects of that character—and the fact that it also contains an account of the ideal ascetic life, with its strange similarity to that preached by Christianity, makes it the more effective as propaganda, in that it demonstrates not only the wickedness of Alexander's life, but also the goodness of the life that should be led.

The *Collatio,* the most influential of the Brahman tracts, also differs from the anecdotes in its literary form, as a comparison between the lives of two men; while in the anecdotes the condemnation of Alexander had been summary and unanswered, the correspondence with Dindimus takes rather the form of a trial in which both sides are heard. If, as we may well believe not only from the tone of the narrative itself, but from the textual researches of M. Liénard, the original author of the *Collatio* aimed at discrediting Alexander's pagan or Christian accusers, personified in Dindimus, his subtle intention was lost to Christian readers, who might well not sympathize with Alexander's vivacious retorts, and who were soon not permitted the opportunity of disap-

proving, because, in abridged or anecdotal usage, either Alexander's contemptuous remarks upon Dindimus and ascetics in general were suppressed, or Dindimus was allowed to have the last word.

The *Collatio,* like the other Brahman pamphlets which are Cynic accusation in earnest, belongs to the philosophic tradition represented by all the anecdotes in this section; but it was most closely related textually to the legendary tradition, into which it was incorporated in the interpolated *Historia de Preliis.* It enjoyed, however, an independent circulation both before and after that incorporation, and though it is usually linked in the manuscripts to one or other of the main legendary texts, its separate popularity is early shown by the fact that Alcuin sent a copy of the correspondence to Charlemagne.

Before the material which afforded a direct comparison between the Brahmans and Alexander was widely known, the Brahmans had been often proposed by Christian writers as a fit subject for admiration. Tertullian refers to them, St Jerome praises them for their ascetic virtues, while Origen had known of the encounter between Alexander and Dindimus;[19] and in the *De moribus Bragmanorum,* ascribed popularly to St Ambrose,[20] one of the lesser Brahman tractates was connected with one of the greatest of the Fathers.

Thus, when the correspondence between Dindimus and Alexander first began to be known, Christians naturally interpreted it, not as the author had intended, but from the Brahman (or Cynic) point of view. The subtle mockery was lost to that edified mind which saw in the *Collatio* another proof of the admirable asceticism of the Brahmans. From the standpoint of this established reputation, and with a sympathetic prejudice in favour of the ascetic Brahman philosophy, Christian moralists looked upon Alexander's controversy with Dindimus as yet another text that demonstrated the wickedness of Alexander when compared with the Brahmans.

The influence of the correspondence upon the secular conception of Alexander will be separately considered. Its appearance in those moralists who are our immediate study is infrequent, not for any reason inherent in the character of the text, which was suitable for moral purposes, but because it was neither cast, nor capable of being cast, into a short anecdotal form, and also because it did not follow the usual route of transmission through a well-known classical or patristic writer.

In the twelfth century Dindimus was highly regarded. Abaelard makes his admiration clear; in a discussion of prophecies of the Messiah, he brings forward four pre-Christian kings who foresaw Christ's coming. Two of these are Jewish, two Gentile; David and Solomon,

Nebuchadnezzar and Dindimus: 'Iuuat autem et Didimi regis Bragmanorum inferre testimonium, ut in quatuor regum auctoritate nostrae assertio fidei praemineat. Duorum quidem Iudaeorum, et duorum gentilium, David scilicet et Salomonis, Nabuchodonosor et Didimi. . . . Ait itaque Didimus in prima ad Alexandrum epistola . . .', and he gives Dindimus' declaration of the god that he worships, saying in conclusion: 'Quibus quidem epistolis, si fides exhibenda sit, nulla hominum uita quantumcumque religiosorum innocentiae atque abstinentiae Brachmanorum aequiparanda uidetur.'[21] And he then quotes St Jerome's praise of the Brahmans. Abaelard's deep respect for the nation of ascetics is shown not only by the repetition of this passage in another place, but by a reference to '. . . illud Brachmanorum sacrificium, hoc est orationes et lacrymae . . .'.[22]

John of Salisbury, discussing the necessity of justice in a king, cites the correspondence, and says that Alexander left the Brahmans in peace—'. . . nullam ratus uictoriam, si eorum pacem perpetuam turbaret . . .'.

Christian admiration for Dindimus showed itself not only by the usual suppression of Alexander's forceful conclusion of the correspondence, but also by such alterations in the text as made Dindimus and his Brahmans into true Christian philosophers. The most interesting of such remanipulations is in the *Pantheon* of Godfrey of Viterbo, who has completely changed the character of the *Collatio*;[23] not only is Dindimus made the mouthpiece of Christian thought, but Alexander's answers are altered into the arrogant trumpet-blasts of the man who calls himself the son of Jupiter, and Dindimus is allowed the last word by increasing the number of letters to six. A similar Christian treatment appears notably in Jacques de Vitry, Martinus Polonus (von Troppau), and the *Contrefait de Renart*. In these authors varying proportions are given to the several letters of the *Collatio*, but Dindimus is always made singularly Christian, and Alexander is always deprived of his effective retort.

This suppression of Alexander's answers shows the adaptation of a rhetorical controversy to a moral use; the answers of Alexander are too disturbing, too convincing, and too pagan to be allowed a place. The *Collatio* left its impression upon late medieval didactic writers but it did not pass into exemplar literature.

The slight independent popularity of the treatise *De moribus Bragmanorum* is shown by its use in the *Eulogium Historiarum*,[24] a universal chronicle written by a monk of Malmesbury, and in the *Speculum morale*;[25] but the *Collatio* was by far the most influential of the tractates, and the only one whose effect upon the medieval conception of Alexander merits consideration.

The subtlety of Dindimus in the *Collatio* was accepted by Christian moralists; they cut the element of controversy out of the episode, and brought him forward as the conventional ascetic. Alexander appears as the man who received his reproofs; he is reduced almost to the unimportance of the lay-figure that he becomes when this material is re-used in books of *exempla*. Dindimus' reputation was independent of any special connexion with Alexander, but was largely supported by the *Collatio*. Thus the story of Alexander and Dindimus is not so forceful nor therefore so important, even if we neglect the rarity of its appearance in the works of the moralists, as the anecdotal material borrowed from classical and patristic sources, which is closely and personally connected with the character of Alexander. It falls into the category of material of edifying type, the string of moral precepts and pronouncements directed at Alexander, but intending no especial or individual dispraise of him, that we shall meet so often in exemplar literature. The character of the piece caused it to be referred to in works of didactic or encyclopaedic intention, while its lack of true anecdotal quality, as well as its textual history, deprived it of lasting popularity among moralists.

(D) ALEXANDER AND DIONIDES THE PIRATE

St Augustine, in the *De Ciuitate Dei*, speaks of the necessity of just government to the establishment of a true kingdom. In illustration he tells a story from the *De Republica* of Cicero, about Alexander and a certain pirate:

Quam similia sunt latrociniis regna absque iustitia

Remota itaque iustitia, quid sunt regna, nisi magna latrocinia? Manus et ipsa hominum est, imperio principis regitur, pacto societatis astringitur, placiti lege praeda diuicitur. Hoc malum si in tantum perditorum hominum accessibus crescit, ut et loca teneat, sedes constituat, ciuitates occupet, populos subiuget, euidentius regni nomen adsumit, quod ei iam in manifesto confert non adempta cupiditas, sed addita impunitas. Eleganter enim et ueraciter Alexandro illi Magno quidam comprehensus pirata respondit. Nam cum idem rex hominem interrogasset, quid ei uideretur, ut mare haberet infestum: ille ibera contumacia, Quod tibi, inquit, ut orbem terrarum: sed quia id ego exiguo nauigio facio, latro uocor, quia tu magna classe, imperator.

St Augustine accepts the validity of the pirate's argument; dominion without justice does not make a kingdom, but a *latrocinium*, a robber-kingdom. But a personal application of this moral to Alexander was not easily to be established in the Middle Ages, nor was the question of Alexander's injustice, and of the legitimacy of his empire, to be decided upon the evidence of this anecdote alone, but upon such variable evidence, and with such a variety of resultant opinion, that the discussion of it must be reserved; and comment will here be restricted to the history of the anecdote itself, and to showing that the attached moral, like those of the Senecan anecdotes, veered away from an interpretation unfavourable to Alexander.

St Augustine borrowed the anecdote from Cicero, where it occurs in one of the lost sections of the *De Republica*.[26] But it seems possible that the citation of the anecdote in John of Salisbury, its next use and one which had far-reaching effect, is from the text of Cicero; since the wording differs so substantially from that of St Augustine as to preclude any possibility that John borrowed the anecdote from the *De Ciuitate Dei*.

In the *Policraticus* the speech of the pirate, who is here called Dionides while St Augustine had not named him, is given in more detail.[27] He develops the argument against Alexander at greater length, and inveighs against his ambition and pride: 'Me fortunae iniquitas et rei familiaris angustia, te fastus intolerabilis et inexplebilis auaritia furem facit . . . tu quo fortunatior, nequior eris.' On hearing the man's arguments, Alexander pardons him, and gives him a place among his own men. This is significant; but even more significant is the position of the anecdote in the *Policraticus*. For it comes after the story of Antigonus, Alexander's tutor, reproving him for playing a lyre:[28] 'Quod et ille (Alexander) patientissime tulit, licet plerumque impatientissimus fuerit, et patrem sicut uirtute ita uitiis superaret.' And the two anecdotes are grouped together under the heading of *patientia*; so that the moral in John's mind becomes evident. He is not here occupied with the question of justice in a king (he shows elsewhere that he thought Alexander unjust[29]), but with the question of self-control; and the two anecdotes are intended to show that Alexander was capable of great self-restraint. The pirate's remarks are not the less true—he speaks 'eleganter et uere', in John as in St Augustine—but their importance here is that they offer, as Antigonus' reproof offered, such an affront to the king as would not have been pardoned by a man less controlled than Alexander. It was a new emphasis; and with this citation of the story in the *Policraticus* the history of the anecdote divides into two streams. In the first tradition the emphasis is, as in St Augustine, upon the pirate's epigram, not necessarily treated as an individual attack upon Alexander, or leading to the conclusion reached by St Augustine upon the illegality of Alexander's empire. In the second the emphasis is concentrated upon the forbearance and kindness shown by Alexander in offering to change the man's fortune for him, and enrolling him among his own men—this when he has been subjected to an eloquent attack. The second tradition, since it is almost confined to exemplar and secular writers, is of less immediate importance to us.

In the first tradition, Tolomeo da Lucca, Vincent de Beauvais, and Guibert de Tournai reproduce the text of the story given by St Augustine; the first adds the comment that it was for this reason that God transferred world empire from the Greeks to the Romans, and thus he attaches to the story the individual application to Alexander given it by St Augustine. All other citations, however, derive from John of Salisbury. Though this almost universal dependence upon the *Policraticus* version was common to both traditions, and necessary to the second, the pirate's speech, as it is given by John, is most stressed in the first tradition, while in the second it is the conclusion of the *Policraticus* narrative, the mercy shown by Alexander to Dionides, which receives the most attention.

Within the first tradition we may also place the insertion of the anecdote, in its *Policraticus* form, in various Alexander-books, where it is accepted merely as an unstressed passage of narrative; and it was used, with emphasis upon St Augustine's moral, by Chaucer and Gower. In Gower, as would be expected, the didactic element in the story is expanded into a lengthy passage; but in Chaucer it has lost all force of personal criticism, and is a witty remark made to Alexander without any personal application to him being intended:[30]

> To Alisaundre told was this sentence;
> That, for the tyrant is of gretter might, . . .
> Lo! therfor is he cleped a capitain;
> And, for the outlawe hath but smal meynee, . . .
> Men clepen him an outlawe or a theef.

The second form of the anecdote had its origins in the innovations of the *Policraticus* version, and seems to have had an especial vogue in Italy, where it occurred most frequently. I have included under this second tradition all those uses of the anecdote where there is a manifest emphasis upon the forbearance shown by Alexander. Two such uses of the anecdote are of especial interest: that by Boccaccio, cited in the notes, and that by François Villon in his *Testament*. The story is here told at length:[31]

> L'empereur si l'araisonna:
> 'Pour quoy es tu larron de mer?'
> L'autre responce luy donna:
> 'Pour quoy larron me faiz nommer?
> Pour ce qu'on me voit escumer
> En une petiote fuste?
> Se comme toy me peusse armer,
> Comme toi empereur je fusse.

But Fortune is against him; so Alexander, when he has heard the story, changes the pirate's fortune for him. And Villon comments:

> Se Dieu m'eust donné rencontrer
> Ung autre piteux Alixandre. . . .

There can be no more striking example of the way in which the morals of the Alexander anecdotes were constantly being altered during the medieval period, generally, except in Germany, in a manner favourable to Alexander, than in the story of Alexander and the pirate: which in contrast to its first use by St Augustine to condemn the injustice and thence the illegality of Alexander's empire, became a signal instance of his mercy shown in his treatment of a malefactor.

3. MISCELLANEOUS REFERENCES TO ALEXANDER IN MORALISTS TO THE FOURTEENTH CENTURY

Most of the material here gathered together is unimportant in its effect upon the medieval moral conception of Alexander, which was, in fact, established by the anecdotes which we have discussed. But it is necessary at least to note the existence of references to other material, both favourable and unfavourable to Alexander, in the works of the earlier moralists.

(A) MISCELLANEOUS MATERIAL UNFAVOURABLE TO ALEXANDER

(i) 'Victor uictus', a Rhetorical Accusation

'The conqueror of all the world was conquered.' Comments based upon this simple rhetorical pattern were eagerly manufactured by every scribbler who aspired to taste; they were made by the turn of a word or two to apply to whatever vice the writer had especially in mind, or to incidents in Alexander's life—the trickery of Candace, or the poison that killed him. A similar turn of phrase—'he pressed upon the earth with his armies, now he is pressed upon by the earth'—was introduced into Europe in the scene of the philosophers gathered about Alexander's tomb; and was taken up by the author of the school-epigram found among the I[3] interpolations of the *Historia de Preliis*. These epigrams, dependent upon the simplest possible verbal play, will be seen from the references given to touch on many aspects of Alexander's life, character and death. How far they reflect the real opinion of their writers, and how far they show merely the desire to make a rhetorical play on words, is not clear.

(ii) Alexander, Women, and Wine

As Dr Tarn has pointed out,[32] one of the most unfair attacks upon Alexander in ancient historians was that upon his chastity; every sort of lie was invented to prove his lecherous incontinence, and these lies appear at their worst in the historical writers accessible to the Middle Ages, but they received no acknowledgement in the anecdotal tradition. The chroniclers of the Middle Ages naturally maintained the libels of Curtius, Justin and Orosius, but without comment; nor did their accounts of Alexander's amorous adventures come to be related outside their historical context. Thus it was that

there was no deliberate medieval moral attack upon this aspect of Alexander's reputation before the time of Petrarch;[33] on the other hand, there was in John of Salisbury an overt recognition of Alexander's continence and political wisdom in sending back, untouched, a captive virgin betrothed to a barbarian prince.[34]

As has been seen, there are some rhetorical references to women's conquest of Alexander; but on the whole his reputation did not suffer until the attack of Petrarch, and until the courtly embroideries of the love passage between Alexander and Candace fell into the hands of moral poets.[35] In the late medieval period the anecdote of Campaspe who rode on Aristotle's back, blamed both Alexander and Aristotle impartially for their weakness in dealing with women; while the story of the poison-girl sent to Alexander showed him, if capable of lust, also capable of restraint, and added nothing decisive to the issue.

There were two especial instances of Alexander's addiction to wine which received attention from medieval moralists. The first was the fact that his love of wine was indirectly responsible for his murder, since the poison was introduced into his cup during a drunken orgy; this received due attention from rhetoricians and writers of epitaphs.[36] More important was the anecdote telling how Alexander sentenced a man one night in a drunken rage, and, when the man appealed next morning 'from Alexander drunk to Alexander sober', pardoned him. This incident was used by Giraldus Cambrensis[37] to show how Alexander was at bottom a just man, but was ruined by his vices, and thus to illustrate the Peripatetic viewpoint that is clearly to be perceived in the medieval picture of Alexander's attitude to women and to wine. There is something of pity in such comments, pity for the weak man who gave way to the strongest of all temptations. Wine and women were easily to be pardoned in the Middle Ages; only Petrarch could have no sympathy, and, in his abuse of Alexander for the burning of Persepolis, remarked that it was unpardonable '. . . tanta de re, Baccho et meretriculae paruisse'.[38]

But the earlier medieval moralists were content with but slight dispraise in their introduction of such rhetorical condemnations of Alexander.

(iii) Miscellaneous Unfavourable Evidence

In addition to those anecdotes already discussed, and those general topics treated below, there are various individual criticisms of Alexander, based upon rare anecdotes or upon the rarer expression of personal opinion, that need, in the interests of completeness, to be here catalogued. They refer to the characteristic vices of which Alexander was accused; his pride, ambition, envy and injustice.

The *Policraticus* of John of Salisbury well illustrates the point made at the beginning of this section, that it is impossible accurately to define the attitude of any given medieval moralist to Alexander before the time of Petrarch; we can only observe their importance as transmitters of material, and detect certain tendencies in the medieval interpretation of classical anecdotes. The *Policraticus* contained both favourable and unfavourable comment upon Alexander; but whereas the favourable material is scattered throughout the book, John's unfavourable criticism is almost wholly concentrated in one passage, where, after quoting stories illustrative of the sense of justice in Alexander and Pythagoras, and deciding in favour of the latter as the greater man: 'michi quidem semper (ut tamen pace eorum loquar, qui temeritatem uirtuti praeferunt) ditissimo Alexandro pauper Pitagoras maior erit', he goes on to quote the well-known comparison made by Justin between Alexander and Philip, to which he subjoins a comment apparently his own:[39] the comment begins at 'Ast in uno . . .

> Quibus artibus orbis imperii fundamenta pater iecit, operis tanti gloriam filius consummauit. Ast in uno non modo patris sed omnium ingenuorum transcendit uitia, quod incontinentissimae fuit inuidiae, adeo ut etiam paterni triumphi ei lacrimas extorquerent ac si ei uirtus paterna omnium gerendorum praeriperet gloriam. Eos etiam aut propriis manibus interficiebat aut rapi praec piebat ad penam, qui paternae uirtutis praeconia praedicabant.

John quotes elsewhere the well-known story (not so well known in the Middle Ages) of Alexander and Anaxarchus, and his bitter disappointment in learning that there were so many worlds to conquer, when he had not yet conquered one.

The same accusation of ambitious envy was taken up by Alexander Neckham, who showed, however, his profound admiration for Alexander in most respects, and considered it his only great vice. He said that Death took Alexander to show men that he was not a God,[40] a reference not to the Ammon episode, but to Alexander's superhuman endeavours.

A reproof supposed to have been administered to the boasting Alexander is cited by Giraldus Cambrensis:[41]

> 'Quid fui, quid sum, quid ero?' 'Vile sperma, uas stercorum, esca uermium.' Dicitur enim Alexandro Macedoni, gradatim ad dignitates ascendenti et inde iactanti ac glorianti, a Dionysio philosopho sic responsum fuisse.

The emphasis in this anecdote upon Alexander's decline into vice is but rarely paralleled in the early Middle Ages. We have shown that the individual characteristics of the Peripatetic portrait of Alexander were well known; but the Peripatetic account of his vicious

deterioration after the conquest of Persia was not normally quoted except in texts immediately derived from Curtius. The reason for this, as has been previously stated, is the preference for a fixed anecdote, with an individual moral application, to an unanecdotal historical evolution, of interest only to the student of the development of personality. Although the group of 'uictor uictus' phrases contain the kernel of the Peripatetic attack, they are judgements upon the final effects of Alexander's decline, and not upon the history of it. The few places outside historical contexts where there is reference to this decline before the late Middle Ages are cited in the notes.

A few further unfavourable comments may be added to this list, but no detailed unfavourable criticism of Alexander appeared before the late Middle Ages; and from the scarcity and individual nature of these comments it is apparent that early unfavourable criticism was principally founded upon those popular anecdotes and anecdotal groups which have already been discussed, and which, by their greater weight and dissemination, are of far greater importance than the isolated condemnations here collected.

(B) MISCELLANEOUS MATERIAL FAVOURABLE TO ALEXANDER

The material under this head is so sparse and individual, that it cannot be arranged in any satisfactory grouping, nor can it be regarded as evidence of any weight in assessing the moral attitude to Alexander. It is almost entirely confined to the small group of humanistic writers represented by John of Salisbury and Giraldus Cambrensis; and is derived principally from Valerius Maximus, whose anecdotes are generally favourable to Alexander.

These anecdotes illustrate various aspects of Alexander's continence: his feeling for justice, his chastity, his humility, his trust in his friends, and other amiable qualities. But such material was directly contradicted, and easily overborne in popularity, by the material derived from sources antagonistic to Alexander which we have discussed, and which could be used to point a series of completely contrasting conclusions about Alexander's character. Outside the authors mentioned the influence of this favourable material was negligible, and hardly extended beyond the *Dialogus Creaturarum* which borrowed much of its material from the *Policraticus*. In the later Middle Ages, when the anecdotes derived from Cicero, Seneca and Oriental sources were widely known, this material remained unextracted from the *Policraticus,* and though we may see no deliberate intention in this neglect of evidence favourable to Alexander, it is obvious that the anecdotes of Valerius Maximus were not so popular as those derived from other sources, since their only easy transmission to unlearned medieval authors lay through the *Policraticus,* whereas the anecdotes of Cicero and Seneca, and other unfavourable material, were made known not only through the popularity of the classical authors in which they appear, but also through their quotation in the works of the Fathers, their rapid circulation through books of *exempla,* and their incorporation into legendary texts.

The list of all instances found in which this favourable material is used before the fourteenth century shows clearly that such use is restricted to a few anthologists.

4. ALEXANDER'S PREMATURE DEATH, AND THE QUESTION OF MONARCHY AND EMPIRE

Alexander's early death, at a time when it seemed that nothing could stop him achieving his heart's desire, has always been a subject for earnest reflexion, coloured for Christian moralists by the consideration of its cause and its effect, for writers of *exempla* by a musing upon the futility of all human effort in the face of death, and for the secular writer by regret at the death of so noble a warrior.[42]

Certainly so premature and unforeseen a death argued, to medieval moralists, some direct intervention of God, an intervention that was easily enough explained by Alexander's intolerable vices. But there was a reason more urgent because it was dogmatic to assume such intervention. This was the coincidence in time of the foundation of the Empire by Augustus and of the Church by Jesus, which established the opinion that God ordained it should be so. It followed that, before the Roman Empire, there could have been no Empire and no true Monarchy, a belief which necessarily involved the depreciation of Alexander's achievements.

To medieval thinkers, therefore, beyond the personal moral causes of Alexander's premature death to be found in his evident imperfections, there was frequently a clear connexion of that death with the wide doctrinal reason, that God prevented him from achieving world empire because the time was not yet come. Four causes were directly adduced by medieval moralists for Alexander's death, and in certain cases some comment is added upon God's purpose in depriving him of Empire in favour of the Romans. The four reasons given were:

(i) His injustice, as it was illustrated by the story of the Pirate,[43] to which Tolomeo da Lucca added the comment: 'Ista ergo ratione Romanis a Deo collatum fuit dominium.'[44] This view was also in the mind of John of Salisbury, when he wrote that God deprived an unjust king of heirs to his dominion, and cited the example of Alexander.[45]

(ii) His ambition and his consequent envy of others was suggested by Alexander Neckham as the reason for his death;[46] death took him to show the world that he was not immortal, nor a God. This may be compared with the view that his fate was due to his presumptuous arrogance in allowing himself to be worshipped as the son of Ammon; a view which was especially prevalent in the later Middle Ages.[47]

(iii) The rational reason of treachery assisted by drunkenness was generally brought forward by writers upon kingship, concerned with the threat of treachery, the need for continence in all things, and the troubles that surround a king.[48]

(iv) Dante, satisfied with the glorious fact of the simultaneous establishment of Church and Empire by God's forethought, does not linger over any explanation of why God deprived Alexander of monarchy; he merely accepts the happy truth as evidence of God's intention to make perfect the coincidence of the spiritual and the temporal monarchy.

The nature of these explanations of Alexander's untimely end is important if they are contrasted with the secular theories upon the subject. It will be seen that moralists, seeking a reason for God's intervention, found it in Alexander's faults, while secular writers were to find a cause for his death in the variability of Fortune, in God's determination to remove Alexander to a greater glory, or in the conspiracy of traitors against him.

But in spite of the reasons given for the cutting-off of Alexander before he had achieved monarchy, he was occasionally described as a monarch in medieval writers; and considering the size of his empire, and the supposed weakness of those peoples who remained unconquered, it is not surprising that many should have chosen to think of him as a monarch even if he did not achieve the solitary dominion of the Romans.

5. ALEXANDER AND ARISTOTLE

The writing of philosophic treatises upon government for the benefit of contemporary rulers, the secluded dictation of cloistered monks to their royal patrons upon the administration of affairs, was a popular occupation in the Middle Ages, and sometimes not unconnected with the prospect of consequent advancement; so that there may be contained among the moral precepts a judicious portion of flattery, aimed at the exaltation of the writer by the exaltation of his patron.

It is with the view of Alexander expressed in works of this type that we are now concerned. The *Secret of Secrets* is evidently the most important document that might have influenced this conception, since it is itself a work supposedly written by the greatest of philosophers for the greatest of princes, and since for Aristotelian writers it became the model of works upon government. And the attitude towards Alexander which we are here to consider is that which is reflected in the circumstances under which the *Secret of Secrets* was supposed to have been composed; it is the attitude of the philosopher, or the learned writer anxious to achieve recognition, towards a king who listened to the counsels of the greatest philosopher so willingly that he ordered all his dominions by the advice of Aristotle, and asked the latter to write him a book on true government. It is Alexander's reverence for letters and for learning that is most considered in these authors, who hope to impress their patron by their own words of wisdom, or to receive some tangible reward for their celebration of his greatness.

There are here three motifs which, while they are founded on such immediate considerations, belong to every writer who considers his dignity as a writer, and every philosopher who wishes to advise a king. The first is the importance of a tutor to a king as demonstrated by the example of Alexander and Aristotle; the second is the necessity, if a prince is to preserve his fame, that he shall surround himself with a circle of learned writers; and the third is the praise of Alexander as a learned prince, and one who encouraged learning in other men.

The first of these points is not only evident in the *Secret of Secrets* (and explicitly in the episodes there recorded of the treatment of conquered Persia,[49] and the girl sent to Alexander by the Queen of the North[50]), but also in other legendary material; the story of the basilisk,[51] and the interpretation of the Wonderstone,[52] besides numerous inverted adjurations and counsels of Aristotle that are scattered throughout the various Alexander-books. Yet most of this material is Oriental in ultimate origin, and it is noticeable that it is in the antique and the Oriental traditions that the importance of Aristotle's tutorship is most stressed. He is revered in the Western legends, but he is son ething of a philosophic figurehead, without real effect upon the career of Alexander; and in the *Lai d'Aristote* he becomes a burlesque figurehead.[53] The separation of learned from secular tradition upon this point has been well demonstrated by Hertz's researches into the number of tutors who are supposed to have supervised Alexander's education.[54] Among the Alexander-books it is only in the *Alexandreis* and similar works drawing on older or on moral tradition that Aristotle becomes the only, or even the chief, tutor. In the works of writers upon government, however, as would be expected, Aristotle stands as the philosopher who controlled Alexander's destinies and the relationship between the king and the philosopher is frequently referred to in learned admonition, more frequently as the Middle Ages became more familiar with the *Secret of Secrets*.

Beside the emphasis upon the importance of having a tutor, we may place the use of the story of the murder of Callisthenes which takes on in works of this type the moral that one should not murder tutors. The emphasis in the Callisthenes episode is here individual and professional. Not here, as in Petrarch and his followers, popular moralists with a foot in the pulpit, is it the aim to demonstrate Alexander's horrible folly the excess of vanity that led him to so great a crime, but rather to show that sudden anger, and especially anger against a tutor, is undesirable; and that outspokenness in tutors may also be undesired. The Oriental tradition of Aristotle, the tutor whom Alexander obeyed and who always counselled Alexander, and the Peripatetic tradition of Callisthenes, the philosopher sent by Aristotle to teach Alexander and murdered because his counsel was unwelcome, are scarcely compatible, but neither tradition was challenged.

Nor should a prince only have a philosopher to advise and educate him; he should also have philosophical writers of history to commemorate him. The prologue to the *Policraticus* of John of Salisbury:[55] 'Quis enim Alexandros sciret aut Caesares, quis Stoicos aut Peripateticos miraretur, nisi eos insignirent monimenta scriptorum?' is typical of an attitude which was especially illustrated by Alexander's famous remarks at the tomb of Achilles, his envy of Achilles that he found so great a poet to celebrate his deeds. The most famous medieval echo of this is in a sonnet of Petrarch's to Laura:

> Giunto Alessandro alla famosa tomba
> Del fero Achille, sospirando disse:
> O fortunato, che sì chiara tromba
> Trovasti, e chi di te sì alto scrisse.[56]

Generally such a statement or such an anecdote appears as an apology for the efforts of the writer, who commends himself by saying that he is conferring literary immortality upon his patron. A pleasing contrast to this self-satisfied attitude is provided by the author of a life of St Martin: 'Postremo Alexandrum, Xersen, Augustum asseclasque eorum comparatione sui (S. Martinus) facit inglorios, dum illi a solis scholasticis recitantur, nec tamen laudantur, istius uero uirtutes ab uniuersa ecclesia memorantur, benedicuntur, et praedicantur.'[57]

But it is best of all that a king, besides surrounding himself with learned men, listening to their counsels and assuring himself of immortality in their panegyrics and histories, should himself be learned; and on this count also mention is made of Alexander, as an example of a learned prince. Giraldus Cambrensis, in his treatise *De Principis Instructione,* uses him as an example of a literary prince, and shows how learning profits a ruler;[58] Alexander Neckham admires his diligence in examining natural phenomena;[59] and many other instances may be cited. The theme appears also in vernacular romance; in every medieval period Alexander's education was represented as including all those subjects which the imagination of the writer considered essential to the perfect prince; and in every case he learnt them well.

These, therefore, are certain additional elements which colour the conception of Alexander in writers upon government and in other humanistic writers. Like the troubadours, they hope for, if they are not dependent on, the liberality of princes, and therefore seek to impress upon them the value of learning, and the importance of its encouragement. But it would be vulgar and untrue to ascribe their attitude merely to ulterior motives—they are really interested in the importance of the message that they have to give to rulers, and uplifted by the thought that their writings may confer immortality.

Apart from this emphasis upon Alexander's relationship with learned men, and his attitude to learning, is it possible to reach any general conclusion upon the conception of Alexander formed by writers on kingship? For as they are in some sort specialists upon kings, their judgement might reasonably be expected to be at once more elaborate and more just than that of other classes of writers.

It is unfortunate that many of the works written upon kingship in the Middle Ages are as far removed from contact with the actual problems of government as possible, and are composed of quotations from the works of the Fathers and the Scriptures, dreamy theorizing on the ideal state, and platitudinous praise of Christian virtue. In the more considered and more worthy treatises the *Secret of Secrets,* and the definition of an ideal prince contained in it, had a great and lasting influence which began to be felt in the middle of the thirteenth century. But this work had more influence upon general moral judgements than upon any especial consideration of Alexander, who occupies almost as negligible a position in it as the prince to whom any medieval treatise on government was dedicated; and thus these writers' conception of Alexander was inevitably derived—apart from the separate issue of Alexander's regard for learning—from the usual learned sources. And even in that separate issue the *Secret of Secrets* supplied only the fact and the supposed reason for Aristotle's instruction; the tradition of Alexander's interest in learning was chiefly derived from Pliny the Elder, and from the legendary text of Alexander's *Letter to Aristotle,* which gave evidence of such interest in natural history.

These were men of the same learning and the same approach to moral questions as those we have already discussed; it is only that here we are concerned with questions affecting Alexander not as a man, but as a king; and the authors' object is the determination of the nature of true kingship. Where such writers have indulged in usual moral consideration of Alexander they conform to the general tone of learned opinion. They are independent only in so far as they have access to the *Secret of Secrets,* and its portrait of Alexander listening to Aristotle, the perfect relationship of the king and his tutor.

6. ALEXANDER, THE ORACLE OF AMMON, AND CALLISTHENES

We have now to consider the attitude of medieval writers to those incidents on which Stoics and Peripatetics alike based their hatred of Alexander: the interview with the oracle of Ammon, the murder of Cleitus, and the murder of Callisthenes for resisting Alexander's wish to be treated as a god.

This is not an anecdote, but a passage in the life of Alexander; and thus it is impossible to attack the question of its transmission according to previous methods, and to trace its reception as we may trace the moral accorded to a single anecdote. In the form in which it reached the Middle Ages, this train of incidents was linked together in the following order: Alexander goes to the oracle of Ammon, and hears the priest (Justin: after having bribed the oracle) permit his companions (Justin: order his companions) to worship him as a god, the son of Ammon. This deification accentuates Alexander's arrogance; and from it there results indirectly the murder of Cleitus, for comparing Alexander disparagingly with Philip, and the murder of Callisthenes, for advising Alexander against exacting the worship accorded to an Oriental monarch; a murder which is made worse by the fact that Callisthenes had prevented Alexander from committing suicide over the death of Cleitus. He is subjected to lingering tortures, from which he is finally delivered by Lysimachus who gives him the means of committing suicide.

The visit to the oracle of Ammon was to ancient philosophers a turning-point in Alexander's career, an episode of far greater importance than those isolated anecdotal interviews that were quoted by medieval moralists. But before the fourteenth and fifteenth centuries, the story of Alexander's visit to the oracle, the prologue to the story of Cleitus and Callisthenes, was not quoted outside its historical context in the chronicles. The reasons for this silence of the learned are to be found in the nature of the material, and are twofold.

First, why should the story of the visit to the oracle have been cited? Its importance in the deterioration of Alexander's character and its place as the ultimate cause of the murder of Callisthenes are an insufficient answer to the question. We have seen how rarely material from the historians themselves was excerpted for medieval use; anecdotal material was taken, not from the accessible narratives, but from previous excerpts, from Seneca and Cicero through the medium of patristic writers, and from Valerius Maximus. Both these authors and medieval writers chose their anecdotes upon a reasonable principle, that they should bear a general application, and that they should have some sort of intrinsic interest. This episode has, considered by itself, neither of these qualities. What does it say? that Alexander bribed the priests of Ammon to salute him as a god. What does that imply? that Alexander bribed the priests of Ammon to recognize him as a god. What is its moral? that one should not bribe priests to recognize one as a god—this is the only direct moral. This *reductio ad absurdum* shows that the episode is properly only an incident in an historical progression as Lessing says of the Laocoön, it is the turningpoint that teaches us nothing. The indirect consequence, Alexander's punishment for setting himself up as a god, has a moral, and is remembered; but the mere fact of the recognition of his divinity has only the individual and momentary application that is of no service to the moralist. It was therefore rejected by Cicero, Seneca (who ought to have relished it), and Valerius Maximus, and after them by the medieval moralists.

Secondly the preachers, the compilers of books of *exempla,* and such lesser thinkers were further discouraged from reproducing the passage by the stories known to them which represented Alexander as refusing divine honours. One such anecdote, quoted by Seneca from Quintus Curtius, in which Alexander, when he has been wounded, says that the pain of his wound proves him to be no god, was known to the writers of *exempla*.[60] Another is his well-known reply to the Persians who offered him divine honours, which would be known to any reader of the legend;[61] a third is his reply to the Gymnosophists;[62] and a fourth is the reverent attitude of Alexander to God in Josephus,[63] and to a different God in the *Dicts and Sayings.*

These two reasons together account for the uselessness of the Ammon episode as a moral or exemplar anecdote. But there were more possibilities in the murder of Callisthenes, which did, in fact, have a limited independent existence as an anecdote. And this is as easily explained for the merely textual reason that Valerius Maximus used it, and John of Salisbury borrowed it,[64] and for the subjective reason that it shows the contrast between the philosopher and the tyrant—and the philosopher happened to be a protégé of Aristotle, and after his death of the Peripatetic propagandists.

The fullest account of the murder of Callisthenes available to the Middle Ages was in Quintus Curtius.[65] As the incident stands in Justin, we are merely told that Callisthenes was put to death with certain Macedonian nobles for refusing to adore Alexander as a god,[66] although, at a later stage of his narrative, when no longer dealing with the life of Alexander, Justin returned to the death of Callisthenes and described the gruesome tortures to which he was subjected.[67] In Orosius the episode appeared as in the first account of Justin.[68]

This episode, circulated by Peripatetic pamphleteers, did Alexander more harm than any other. From his own time it alienated from him the sympathy of philosophers who felt that a philosophical preceptor, if anyone, should be free from the anger of a tyrant. While no one could rebuke Alexander for his treatment of Diogenes, Dindimus or Dionides, here was a glaring example of his blind vanity, of his refusal to listen to reason and of his cruelty.

The early medieval chronicles, all founded upon Justin and Orosius, reproduce the narrative in which the murder of Callisthenes is dismissed in a sentence. Thus Ekkehart of Aura wrote, following Orosius, but omitting the reason given by Orosius for Callisthenes' murder:

> Alexander . . . sanguinem siciens. Unde non solum de extraneis, sed de suis quoque multos occidit, inter quos Amintam consobrinum, Clytum quoque annis grauem et amicicia sibi coniunctum, Callistenen etiam phylosophum sibique apud Aristotilem condiscipulum, cum plurimis regni principibus.

Here the murder of Callisthenes is made to appear, without any reason given, as an example of Alexander's bloodthirsty cruelty. It will be noticed that the name of Cleitus is already closely connected with that of Callisthenes; later this connexion is insisted upon, the events are brought into sequence, and the Cleitus episode made to blacken still further Alexander's murder of Callisthenes.

The story of Callisthenes did not follow the commonest anecdotal route because it appeared only in Valerius Maximus, among classical moralists and anthologists known to medieval writers. It appears in the Middle Ages as an anecdote for the first time in the *Policraticus,* and in an interesting context. The episode does not illustrate vanity or cruelty, but the 'praeceps nobilitas' and 'concitatum ingenium' of noble youths, which should be kept in check by a tactful tutor. John says of Callisthenes that he was sent to Alexander by Aristotle with instructions that he should be cautious and discreet with Alexander: 'At ille, dum Alexandrum Persica salutatione exultantem obiurgat et mores eius studet componere, uita priuatus est.'[69]

This is therefore a moral of quite a different type; it demonstrates the care that tutors should take in their dealings with kings. John of Salisbury introduces the anecdote as a piece of political advice; and from him its history in political writings may be traced through Guibert de Tournai,[70] who used it in the same way in his book on the education of princes, to Aeneas Syluius, who used it as a warning to learned men to keep away from courts, where there are always such lurking dangers.

So far the Ammon episode has not been brought in, nor is the murder of Callisthenes seen in relation to Alexander's visit to the oracle. In the Orosian tradition the episode is an example of Alexander's vanity and cruelty; in the anecdotal field it appears as a warning to tutors not to try their kings too high. The question of προσκύνησις is given as the immediate reason for the murder of Callisthenes, but it is not linked to the story of the oracle of Ammon, nor is the emphasis upon Alexander's vanity in wishing to be so worshipped, but upon the folly of Callisthenes in being so indiscreet.

Gautier de Châtillon, true to his admiration for Alexander, keeps very quiet about the episode, dismisses it in a few lines, and adds to it a moral similar to that in Aeneas Syluius—the favour of princes does not last. The first movement towards a stronger condemnation of Alexander for the murder of Callisthenes was in Vincent de Beauvais.[71] The reason given is Alexander's demand 'non salutari, sed adorari', and Vincent, with a good knowledge of Justin, mentions the tortures of Callisthenes for the first time in the Middle Ages, adds the story of Lysimachus thrown to the lions for his part in easing Callisthenes' torment, and connects with the murder of Callisthenes the previous murder of Cleitus, when Callisthenes had dissuaded Alexander from committing suicide in his subsequent gloomy repentance.

The change of phrase from 'Persica salutatio' to 'non salutari, sed adorari' is significant; προσκύνησις is beginning to be understood, not as an act of extreme obeisance to a monarch with divine honours, but as an act of worship to a man who wishes to be worshipped as a god, and specifically (though unhistorically) as the son of Ammon. In the long historical narrative of Vincent de Beauvais some chain of supposed historical causation naturally appeared; and the episodes of Ammon, Cleitus, and Lysimachus were combined to place the murder of Callisthenes in a fictitious historical setting, as an act of extreme cruelty inspired by an insane vanity caused by Alexander's visit to the oracle of Ammon. It was the gradual evolution of the murder of Callisthenes from an isolated anecdote of special application to a link in an historical chain that blackened the case against Alexander by revealing, more clearly than appeared in such authors as John of Salisbury and Guibert de Tournai, the misunderstood circumstances of that murder. Vincent de Beauvais heralded a period in which the Ammon incident first began to be known outside

historical texts, and in which the character of Alexander was to suffer from the use of historical narrative in unhistorical writers. The age of anecdote had made way for the age of lengthy historical digression.

Petrarch is the first who, as an ardent follower of the Peripatetic portrait of Alexander, told the Callisthenes story in its full horror.[72] Alexander bribed the priests of Ammon in his insane pride; in the same wild fancy to be thought a god he condemned Callisthenes to a death delayed by lingering tortures—a sentence which was the more revolting and cruel because Callisthenes was his benefactor, not as his tutor alone but as the man who had dissuaded him from committing suicide after he had murdered Cleitus. This incident is cunningly brought in as an obituary comment upon Callisthenes, so that it may linger in the mind of the reader.

The historical scheme has now been accepted. Alexander's murder of Callisthenes is inspired by his mad vanity, which has made him desire to be worshipped as a god. The full lie now became widely known, and was told in detail by Walter Burley[73] and by Boccaccio,[74] from whom it passed through Laurent de Premierfait to Lydgate's *Fall of Princes*.[75] In Petrarch and in Lydgate we have a summary of the feelings aroused in the writer by this supposed truth, this combination of the Stoic accusation of arrogance consequent upon the visit to the oracle with the Peripatetic concentration upon the fate of Callisthenes: Alexander was a prey to all desires, and the worst of those desires was to be thought, or at least to be treated as if he were thought, a god. The policy in arrogating to oneself divine honours could never have been understood by men who regarded kingship as temporal and a king as a deputy holding the reins under God. And if political reasons were set aside, the vain blasphemy and the added horror of the martyroom of so philosophic a tutor, were clear enough and damning enough.

Thus the combination of the various historical sources, and their introduction into unhistorical literature realized in the fourteenth and fifteenth centuries, caused the Stoic view to triumph over the original Jewish view of Alexander's relationship with God. Alexander was no longer quoted as an example of the reverence in which all, even pagan, kings approached the Jewish God, but as an example of a hideous blasphemer who wished himself to be worshipped as a god. Alexander's blasphemous pride was consequently argued by late medieval moralists as the cause of his death, and in the later editions of the French translation of the *Dicts and Sayings*, we find a contemporary tag attached to that portrait of a reverent and venerable Alexander: 'Plusieurs bons enseignemens et doctrines donna Alexandre, mais enfin il fut deceu par haine et mondaine gloire, car il se souffri adorer comme Dieu et filz de Jupiter

Hammon.' The focus had changed; it was no longer the drunkenness, or the injustice, of Alexander that brought him to his death, but his shocking blasphemy—a Stoic accusation become Christian.

Thus the Callisthenes episode comes gradually to be attached to its supposed historical concatenation, to the bribing of the priests of Ammon, the murder of Cleitus, and the savage punishment of Lysimachus, and evolves from an unconnected act of cruelty into the climax of a cruel blasphemy. In the second, minor chain of development it becomes an admonitory anecdote in the hands of writers upon government, 'Keep out of the hands of princes', or (to the princes), 'Don't torture tutors.' Finally it becomes a piece of advice to men aspiring to become courtiers—like Mr Punch's advice to those about to marry—Don't!

7. Summary

In this section it has been seen how the material upon which the ancient moral attack on Alexander was based survived into the medieval period not so much in historical narrative excerpts as in the anecdotes borrowed from Seneca, Valerius Maximus and others. But this persistence of the fundamental material was not, at least before the fourteenth century, paralleled by a similar persistence in the morals attached. The Callisthenes episode was lightly treated, the criticism of Seneca lost all its force, and while the morals of the Diogenes and Dindimus episodes were textually retained, it is evident that the ancient philosophic attack on Alexander lost much of its fervour in the twelfth and thirteenth centuries.

But it must be remembered that the writers concerned formed only a very limited section of medieval society, and that the men most likely to use anecdotal material on a large scale in this period (and especially that material which did not reach them through the intermediacy of the Fathers of the Church, but was borrowed direct from classical authors) were precisely those who could be expected to take a moderately enlightened view of Alexander: the humanistic writers of the twelfth and thirteenth centuries who took some interest in personality, John of Salisbury, Giraldus Cambrensis, and others to whom the study of pagan antiquity made the same appeal. In this small literary group the morals attached to the anecdotes of Alexander were somewhat discounted, but they made this material known to other writers of a less humanistic approach, and their role, considered against the whole medieval background, was that of transmitting most of the material upon which the unfavourable late medieval view of Alexander was founded.

Considered from the standpoint of its regional distribution, use of this moral anecdotal material during the twelfth and thirteenth centuries was almost confined to England and France. The earliest Italian moralist to use it was Brunetto Latini, and when the anecdotes reached Germany in the later Middle Ages, they reached it not through the direct intermediacy of moralists, but through those books of *exempla* and vernacular story-books which had received, adapted and retransmitted that material.

Notes

1. For the ancient legends of Diogenes, see K. von Fritz, *Quellenuntersuchungen zu Leben und Philosophie des Diogenes von Sinope* (*Philol., Suppl.-Band* XXVIII), 1926.

2. Cicero, *Tusc. Disp.* V, 32; Valerius Maximus, IV, iii, ext. 4.

3. Valerius Maximus, loc. cit.

4. Seneca, *De Ben.* V, iv, 4.

5. Seneca, *De Ben.* V, vi, 1.

6. See [Cary, George. *The Medieval Alexander.* Cambridge: Cambridge University Press, 1956] p. 148.

7. This question is fully discussed in Appendix II [Cary, 1956], pp. 358-68.

8. *Ep. ad Luc.* LIII, 10.

9. *De Ben.* II, xvi; the Antigonus story is in *De Ben.* II, xvii.

10. *De Ben.* II, xvi, 2.

11. See [Cary, 1956], pp. 146-8, 348, 351, 361-2.

12. Namely *De Ben.* II, xvi; V, iv, 4; V, vi, 1; *Ep. ad Luc.* LIII, 10.

13. Cicero, *De Off.* II, xv, 53 ff.; the letter is also given in Val. Max. VII, ii, ext. 10. Compare the letter of Olympias in Plutarch, *Vita Alex.* XXXIX, 5.

14. William of Conches, *Liber Moralium Dogmatis Philosophorum* (under the name of Hildebert of Lavardin) in Migne, *P.L.* [*Patrologia Latina*] CLXXI, col. 1015. For Cicero's definition of liberality, . . . *De Officiis* I, xiv, 42 ff.

15. John of Salisbury, *Policraticus* VIII, ii (ed. Webb, II, p. 235): 'Valerius Maximus, sed et Cicero. . . .'

16. Vincent de Beauvais, *Speculum Historiale* IV, 19 (ed. Douai, 1624, p. 123).

Brunetto Latini, *Li Livres dou Tresor* II, ii, 80 (ed. Chabaille, p. 418).

Higden, *Polychronicon* III, . . . (ed. Lumby, vol. III, p. 406).

Upon the possible connex on of a passage in Philippe de Novare with this letter, see Meyer, *A. le G.* II, pp. 361-3 and below, p. 362.

17. See p. 155.

18. Petrus Cantor, *Verbum Abbreviatum* XLVII; 'contra eos qui dant non indigentibus', in Migne, *P.L.* vol. CCV, col. 150.

19. Tertullian, *Apologeticus* XLII, i (Migne, *P.L.* vol. I, cols. 490-1).

    St Jerome, *Contra Iouinianum* II (Migne, *P.L.* vol. XXIII, col. 304).

    Origen, *Contra Haereses* I, xliv-xlvii (Migne, *P.G.* vol. XVI, part 3, cols. 3051-2).

20. On the *De moribus Bragmanorum* ascribed to St Ambrose, see above, p. 12. The text is in Migne, *P.L.* vol. XVII, cols. 1131-46.

21. Abaelard, *Introductio ad Taeologiam* I, xxii-xxiii (Migne, *P.L.* vol. CLXXVIII, cols. 1032-3).

22. Abaelard, *Theologia Christiana* III (Migne, *P.L.* vol. CLXXVIII, col. 1225).

23. See L. Meyet, *Les Légendes des Matières de Rome, de France, et de Bretagne dans le 'Panthéon' de Godefroi de Viterbe* (Paris, 1933), pp. 82-97, where this original version of the *Collatio* is discussed in full.

24. *Eulogium Historiarum*, cap. CXXVI (ed. Haydon, vol. I, pp. 432-4).

25. See [Cary, 1956], pp. 297-8.

26. The context in the *De Republica* suggests that Cicero used the story much as St Augustine used it; and that in spite of its favourable ending in his version, he did not give it the moral suggested in the *Policraticus*.

27. John of Salisbury, *Policraticus* III, xiv (ed. Webb, vol. I, p. 225).

28. *Policraticus* III, xiv (ed. Webb, vol. I, pp. 224-5).

29. See [Cary, 1956], p. 104.

30. Chaucer, *The Manciple's Tale*, ll. 226-34 (ed. W. W. Skeat, *Works*, vol. IV, p. 562).

    Gower, *Confessio Amantis* III, ll. 2363 ff. (*English Works*, ed. Macaulay, vol. I, pp. 290ff.).

31. François Villon, *Le Testament* (*Œuvres*, ed. L. Thuasne (Paris, 1923), vol. I, pp. 181-2).

32. See W. W. Tarn, *Alexander the Great*, II (Cambridge, 1948), App. 18, pp. 319-26.

33. On Petrarch's attack see G. Cary, 'Petrarch and Alexander the Great', *Italian Studies*, V (1950), pp. 43-55.

34. John of Salisbury, *Policraticus* V, vii (ed. Webb, I, pp. 309-10); the anecdote also occurs in the *Dialogus Creaturarum*, dial. 121: 'De homine et muliere' (ed. Grässe, *B.L.V.* vol. CXLVIII, p. 277).

35. For the courtly and late medieval treatment of this question, see [Cary, 1956] pp. 218-20, 231-3.

36. See [Cary, 1956], pp. 282-4, n. 19.

37. Giraldus Cambrensis, *De Principis Instructione* I, xvii (*Opera*, vol. VIII, ed. Warner, pp. 58-9). Cf. Ranulph Higden, *Polychronicon* III, xxviii (ed. Lumby, vol. III, pp. 440-2). The story was of course originally told of Alexander's father Philip (see Valerius Maximus, VI, 2, ext. 1).

38. Petrarch, *De Viris Illustribus*, ed. Razzolini, *Collezzione di Opere Inedite o Rare*, vol. I (Bologna, 1874), p. 122.

39. *Policraticus* V, xii (ed. Webb, vol. I, p. 336). Further on Justin's comparison between Philip and Alexander, see [Cary, 1956], p. 87.

40. Alexander Neckham, *De Naturis Rerum*, ed. by Thomas Wright (Rolls Series, 1863), p. 338.

41. Giraldus Cambrensis, *De Principis Instructione*, praefatio prima (*Opera*, vol. VIII, ed. Warner, p. 5).

42. For reflexions upon Alexander's death in exemplar and secular writers, see [Cary, 1956] pp. 151-2, 189-95.

43. For St Augustine's use of this anecdote, see [Cary, 1956] pp. 95-6.

44. Thomas Aquinas (Ptolemaeus Lucensis), *De Regimine Principum* III, v (ed. Mathis, p. 48).

45. John of Salisbury, *Policraticus* IV, xii (ed. Webb, vol. 1, p. 276): 'Quis Alexandro maior in Grecia? Et tamen non suus legitur successisse sed filius saltatricis.'

46. Alexander Neckham, *De Naturis Rerum* (ed. Wright, p. 338).

47. See [Cary, 1956], pp. 115-16.

48. Medieval comments upon the treachery that brought Alexander to his death are grouped [Cary, 1956], pp. 315-17. For comments upon his drunkenness, and the part it played in bringing him to his death, see [Cary, 1956] pp. 282-3.

49. This incident was used by Guibert de Tournai, *Eruditio regum et principum* (ed. A. de Poorter (*Les Philosophes Belges*, IX, Louvain, 1914)), p. 68; further references to separate articles of advice given by Aristotle to Alexander in the *Secret of Secrets* occur in the *Disciplina Clericalis* (ed. A.

Hilka and W. Soederhjelm (*Sammlung mittellat. Texte,* 1, Heidelberg, 1911), pp. 10, 37), in the *Gesta Romanorum* (see p. 302).

50. On the history of the story of the poison-girl see W. Hertz, 'Die Sage vom Giftmädchen', *Gesammelte Abhandlungen* (Stuttgart and Berlin, 1905), pp. 156-277. See also [Cary, 1956], p. 231.

51. For the basilisk episode, which was used in the I³ *Historia de Preliis* and in the *Gesta Romanorum,* see W. Hertz, loc. cit. pp. 192 ff., and F. Pfister, in *Münchener Museum,* 1 (1912), p. 265.

52. The best survey of the history of the Wonderstone story is by Hertz, *Ges. Abh.,* pp. 73-130. See also [Cary, 1956], pp. 149-51, 347.

53. For the well-known story of Alexander, Aristotle, and Campaspe or Phyllis, see [Cary, 1956] pp. 231-2.

54. See W. Hertz, *Ges. Abh.,* pp. 1-33.

55. John of Salisbury, *Policraticus,* Prologue (ed. Webb, I, p. 12, l. 17).

56. Petrarch, *Sonetti in vita di Laura* CXXXV, vv. 1-4.

57. Radbodus, *Libellus de miraculo S. Martini,* in *M.G.H. Scriptt.* XV, ii (1888), p. 1242, ll. 3-4.

58. Giraldus Cambrensis, *De Principis Instructione* I (*Opera,* vol. VIII, ed. Warner, 1891, p. 7).

59. Alexander Neckham, *De Naturis Rerum* (ed. Thomas Wright, pp. 141-2; cf. p. 403).

60. See [Cary, 1956], pp. 152-3.

61. J. Valerius II, 39 (ed. Kuebler, p. 110).

   Historia de Preliis II, 22 (ed. Pfister, *Alexanderroman,* p. 100, ll. 23-5): 'Nolo, ut exhibeatis mihi honorem sicut diis, quia corruptibilis et mortalis ego sum. Dubito enim sociare me diis.'

62. See [Cary, 1956], p. 148.

63. See [Cary, 1956], pp. 125-30.

64. John of Salisbury, *Policraticus* VIII, 14 (ed. Webb, vol. II, p. 333).

65. The story of the alleged conspiracy, and the subsequent death of Callisthenes, is in Quintus Curtius VIII, v, 5-viii, 23.

66. Justin XII, vii, 2.

67. Justin XV, iii, 3-6.

68. Orosius III, xviii, 11.

69. John of Salisbury, loc. cit.

70. Guibert de Tournai, *Eruditio Regum et Principum* (ed. de Poorter, p. 22).

71. Vincent de Beauvais, *Speculum Historiale* IV, 33 (Ammon), 45 (Clitus), 46 (Callisthenes) (ed. Douai, 1624, pp. 126 and 129). Cf. Higden, *Polychronicon* III, 27, 28 (ed. Lumby, vol. III, pp. 420 and 446-8).

72. Petrarch, *De Viris Illustribus,* de Alexandro Macedone (ed. G. Razzolini, *Collezione di Opere Inedite o Rare* Bologna, 1874), I, pp. 126ff.). Cf. G. Cary, 'Petrarch and Alexander the Great', *Italian Studies,* V (1950), pp. 43 ff.

73. W. Burley, *De Vita ac Moribus Philosophorum* LXVI (ed. H. Knust, *B.L.V.* vol. CLXXVII (Tübingen, 1886), pp. 278-80).

74. G. Boccaccio, *De Casibus Virorum Illustrium* IV (Paris, Jean Gourmont and Jean Petit, n.d.), f. xxxviiᵛ to f. xxxviiiᵛ.

75. John Lydgate, *Fall of Princes* IV, vv. 1109-1421. See on this passage [Cary, 1956], p. 257.

Bibliography

ABAELARD. *Introductio ad Theologiam,* Migne, *P.L.* CLXXVIII. *Theologia Christiana,* ibid.

AQUINAS, THOMAS. *Opera Omnia* (Parma, 1852-71).

BOCCACCIO, G. *De Casibus Virorum Illustrium,* ed. J. Gourmont and J. Petit (Paris, s.d.).

BRUNETTO LATINI. *Li Livres dou Tresor,* ed. P. Chabaille (Paris, 1863).

BURLEY, WALTER. *De uita ac moribus philosophorum,* ed. H. Knust, *B.L.V.* CLXXVII (Stuttgart, 1886).

CARY, G. 'Petrarch and Alexander the Great', in *Italian Studies,* V (1950), pp. 43-55.

CHAUCER, GEOFFREY. *Works,* ed. W. W. Skeat (Oxford, 1900).

Dialogus Creaturarum, ed. J. G. T. Grässe, *B.L.V.* CXLVIII (Tübingen, 1880).

FRITZ, K. VON. *Quellenuntersuchungen zu Leben und Philosophie des Diogenes von Sinope, Philol., Supplement-Band* XXVIII (1926).

Gesta Romanorum. Ed. W. Dick, *Die Gesta Romanorum nach der Innsbrucker Handschrift vom Jahre 1342 und vier Münchener Handschriften herausgegeben. Erlanger Beiträge zur englischen Philologie,* VII (Erlangen, 1890).

[*Gesta Romanorum*] Ed. H. Oesterly (Berlin, 1872).

English version, ed. S. H. J. Herrtage, E.E.T.S. [Early English Text Society], E.S. XXXIII (1879).

GIRALDUS CAMBRENSIS. *Opera,* ed. Brewer, Dimock and Warner, Rolls Series, 7 vols.

GOWER, JOHN. *English Works,* ed. G. C. Macaulay, E.E.T.S., E.S. LXXXI-LXXXII (1901).

GUIBERT DE TOURNAI. *Eruditio regum et principum,* ed. A. de Poorter, *Les philosophes belges,* IX (Louvain, 1914).

HERTZ, W. 'Aristoteles in den Alexanderdichtungen des Mittelalters', in *Abhandlungen der königlichen bayerischen Akademie der Wissenschaften,* I Cl., XIX. Bd., I Abt. (Munich, 1890).

JEROME, ST. *Contra Iouinianum,* Migne, *P.L.* XXIII.

JOHN OF SALISBURY. *Policraticus,* ed. C. C. J. Webb (Oxford, 1909).

LYDGATE, JOHN. *Fall of Princes,* ed. H. Bergen (Washington, Carnegie Institute, 1923).

MEYER, L. *Les Légendes des Matières de Rome, de France, et de Bretagne dans le 'Panthéon' de Godefroi de Viterbe* (Paris, 1933).

MEYER, P. *Alexandre le Grand dans la littérature française du moyen âge,* 2 vols (Paris, 1886).

Migne, J.-P. *Patrologia Latina.*

NECKHAM, ALEXANDER. *De Naturis Rerum,* ed. T. Wright, Rolls Series (1863). *De Vita Monachorum,* ibid.

ORIGEN. *Contra Haereses,* Migne, *Patrologia Graeca,* XVI.

PETRARCH. *De uiris illustribus,* ed. G. Razzolini, *Collezione di opere inedite o rare,* I (Bologna, 1874).

PETRUS CANTOR. *Verbum Abbreviatum,* in Migne, *P.L.* CCV.

RADBODUS. *Libellus de miraculo S. Martini,* in *M.G.H. Scriptt.* XV, ii (1888).

RANULF HIGDEN. *Polychronicon,* ed. J. R. Lumby, Rolls Series (1871).

TARN, W. W. *Alexander the Great* (Cambridge University Press, 1948).

TERTULLIAN. *Apologeticus,* in Migne, *P.L.* I.

VILLON, FRANÇOIS. *Œuvres de François Villon,* ed. L. Thuasne (Paris, 1923).

VINCENT DE BEAUVAIS. *Speculum Historiale* (ed. Douai, 1624).

———. *Speculum Morale* (ed. Douai, 1624).

WILLIAM OF CONCHES. *Liber Moralium Dogmatis Philosophorum,* in Migne *P.L.* CLXXI.

D. J. A. Ross (essay date 1963)

SOURCE: Ross, D. J. A. "Historical Accounts of Alexander." In *Alexander Historiatus: A Guide to Medieval Illustrated Alexander Literature,* pp. 67-83. London: Warburg Institute, 1963.

[*In the following excerpt, Ross presents capsule descriptions of medieval and Renaissance historical accounts of Alexander.*]

HISTORICAL ACCOUNTS OF ALEXANDER

The historical accounts of Alexander's career fall into two groups. Those in the first group were available throughout the Middle Ages and were often used by the writers of vernacular Alexander-books, either as principal sources or to supplement legendary accounts based on some version of Pseudo-Callisthenes. To this first group belong Quintus Curtius, Justin's *Epitome* of the *Historiae Philippicae* of Trogus Pompeius and Orosius, *Historiarum adversum paganos libri septem,* Book III.

In the second group are placed those Greek historical writers whose works only became available in Western Europe at the Renaissance. These include Arrian's Ἀνάβασις Ἀλεξάνδρου, the most reliable source we possess for the historical figure of Alexander, Plutarch's *Life of Alexander* and Books XVI and XVII of the *Bibliotheca Historica* of Diodorus Siculus.

As a general rule the historical Alexander texts are rarely illustrated in their original Latin or Greek form, but vernacular translations and adaptations of them are not uncommonly illustrated more or less generously. This is in accordance with the general tendency whereby books intended for wealthy patrons speaking only the vernacular are alone likely to be provided with the expensive luxury of a cycle of illustrations, while those meant to be within the reach of the scholar's purse are destitute of such costly adjuncts.

GROUP I: HISTORICAL ALEXANDER-TEXTS OF THE MIDDLE AGES

1. QUINTUS CURTIUS RUFUS, RES GESTAE ALEXANDRI MAGNI

The highly-coloured and somewhat romanticized biography of Alexander by Quintus Curtius Rufus,[1] who was probably a contemporary of the emperor Claudius,[2] has reached us in a defective form. Of its ten books the first two, together with some shorter passages in other parts of the work, were already lost in the archetype of all the surviving manuscripts.

Curtius' work was well known in the Middle Ages and had a wide influence on the writers of Alexander-books, chiefly through the version in hexameter verse of Gautier de Châtillon.[3]

No tradition of Quintus Curtius illustration appears to have descended from antiquity. One manuscript of the twelfth century, destroyed in the Strasbourg library fire of 1870, is described in old catalogues as 'cum figuris'[4] but nothing is recorded concerning it, and it is not even clear if the 'figurae' were illustrations or merely illuminated decorations. Apart from this no illustrated manuscript of Quintus Curtius has come to light, although a few of the very numerous Italian humanist copies of the fifteenth century have some sort of illustration, usually a fancy portrait of Alexander in pseudo-antique costume, incorporated in the decoration of the title-page.[5]

2. THE EXPANDED AND INTERPOLATED QUINTUS CURTIUS

Five manuscripts of Quintus Curtius[6] contain supplementary matter extracted from Justin's *Epitome* of the *Historiae Philippicae* of Pompeius Trogus, Julius Valerius, Solinus, other parts of Quintus Curtius himself and elsewhere which is intended to replace the lost Books I and II and fill the lacunae elsewhere in the text. This expanded text was apparently used by Alberic for his account of the battle of the Granicus[7] and was translated into French by Vasque de Lucène for Charles the Bold of Burgundy.[8] The Latin manuscripts are unillustrated.

DIRECT TRANSLATIONS OF QUINTUS CURTIUS

3. THE ITALIAN VERSION OF PIER CANDIDO DECEMBRIO

The first vernacular translation of Quintus Curtius was the Italian version made in 1438 by the humanist and scholar Pier Candido Decembrio for Filippo Maria Visconti, Duke of Milan.[9] Most of the known manuscripts of this work are typical humanist ones with decoration confined to an elaborate title-border and illustration to, at most, a fancy portrait of Alexander in a medallion or historiated capital.[10]

One manuscript in the Biblioteca Comunale in Siena, I.VII.23, has, however, a charming and detailed miniature at the beginning of each book. Decembrio filled the lacunae in Book X from Plutarch's *Life of Alexander* and also composed a 'Comparison of Alexander and Julius Caesar' in the Plutarchan manner, which he appended to his translation. The artist follows the text closely, in each case illustrating a major episode in the book to which the picture belongs. There is no attempt at classicizing the style of the pictures. Costumes and settings are typical of fifteenth-century Italy. Even the double portrait of Alexander and Caesar preceding the 'Comparatione' shows them as medieval knights in full plate armour.[11]

4. SPANISH VERSIONS OF PIER CANDIDO DECEMBRIO'S ITALIAN TRANSLATION OF QUINTUS CURTIUS

Pier Candido Decembrio's Italian translation of Quintus Curtius appears in several forms in Spain. Three are in Castilian. One is attributed to Alfonso de Liñan in

manuscript 7565 of the Biblioteca Nacionál in Madrid. A fragment of a second version by Martin de Avila is found in manuscript 11265 of the same library and a third Castilian version of Tomás de Lira Aleman is in manuscript 8549. An edition of 1481 in Valencian dialect is attributed to Luis de Fenollet.[12] One more anonymous version in Castilian was published in Seville by Meinhard Ungut and Stanislaus Polonus on 16 May 1496.[13] With the exception of the last which has one woodcut, none of these Spanish versions appears to exist in an illustrated form.

5. LES FAITZ D'ALEXANDRE. FRENCH VERSION OF QUINTUS CURTIUS BY VASQUE DE LUCÈNE

Vasco Fernandez, Count of Lucena, a Portuguese gentleman attached to the Burgundian court in the household of Isabella of Portugal, wife of Philip the Good, is responsible for a translation of the expanded Quintus Curtius into French prose, which he dedicated to Charles the Bold in 1468.[14] Although written in the heavy, verbose and turgid style usually employed in literature intended for the Burgundian court in the fifteenth century, the book, appearing at a moment when the New Learning and the spirit of the Renaissance were beginning to turn men's minds against the medieval wonder-book conception of Alexander, achieved great success by its deliberate rejection of the fictions of the romance in favour of the text of a respectable ancient historian. At least twenty-seven manuscripts of it survive; the majority of them costly productions expensively illustrated for members of royal and noble houses, and it was printed seven times between 1500 and 1555.

The numerous illustrated manuscripts show picture-cycles of three types. The first has normally ten large miniatures, a presentation miniature of Vasque de Lucène offering his book to Charles the Bold and a miniature at the beginning of each of the nine books depicting an event at the beginning of that book. Manuscripts of this type are:

1. Chantilly, Musée Condé, MS. 755 (467). Vellum. 12 + 256 fols. Large presentation miniature and 9 others.[15] Second half C15.

2. Copenhagen, Royal Library, Thott 540. Vellum. 253 fols. 9 miniatures.[16] Second half C15.

3. London, B.M., Royal 20 C III. Vellum. 257 fols. Presentation and 9 other miniatures.[17] Late C15.

4. Paris, Arsenal, MS. 3687. Paper. 162 fols. Presentation and 9 other miniatures. Second half C15.

5. Paris, B.Nat.Fr. 258. Paper. 283 fols. One damaged miniature of nine or ten survives.[18] Late C15.

6. Vatican, Regin.lat. 736. Vellum. 259 fols. Presentation miniature and 2 others, and one lost.[19] Late C15.

One manuscript has only a presentation miniature:

7 Bern, Stadtbibliothek, MS. A.25. Paper. 210 fols. One miniature, fol. 9.[20] Dated 1459.

The majority of the manuscripts have usually a presentation miniature, a large miniature at the beginning of each book, and a varying number of, usually, small column-wide miniatures illustrating events of importance within the book. Such manuscripts have usually from about fifteen to about eighty miniatures. They include the following:

8. Florence, Biblioteca Laurenziana, Medic.Palat.155. Vellum. 261 fols. 23 miniatures.[21] Second half C15.

9. Geneva, Bibl. Publique et Universitaire, Fr. 76. Vellum. 279 fols. 10 large and 30 small miniatures.[22] Late C15.

10. Gotha, Landesbibliothek, MS.I.116. Vellum. 37 miniatures. Late C15.

11. London, B.M., Royal 15 D IV. 219 fols. 49 miniatures.[23] Circa 1480.

12. 17 F I. 238 fols. 9 large and 11 small miniatures.[24] Late C15.

13. Burney 169. Vellum. 204 fols. 52 miniatures. Circa 1470-5 (Bought 1475).

14. New York, H. P. Kraus, Catalogue No. 95 (1961).[25] MS. No. 21. Vellum. 225 fols. 11 large and 3 small miniatures. Circa 1470.

15. Oxford, Bodleian, Laud.Misc. 751. Vellum. 245 fols. + 4 fly-leaves. 19 miniatures. Circa 1470.

16. Paris, Bibl.Nat.Fr. 47, 48, 49. Vellum. 59 + 89 + 100 = 248 fols. 53 miniatures.[26] Second half C15.

17. 257. Vellum. 222 fols. 45 miniatures.[27] Circa 1475-80.

18. 708, 709, 710, 711. Vellum. 159 fols. 83 miniatures. Circa 1500.

19. 6440. Vellum. 256 fols. 18 miniatures. Late C15.

20. 20311. Vellum. 304 fols. (+ 29 lost). 57 surviving miniatures. Second half C15.

21. 22547. Vellum. 270 fols. 85 miniatures.[28] Supposed to be copy presented to Charles the Bold in 1470.

Thirdly, there are three manuscripts with provision for a very extensive picture-cycle indeed, almost one small picture to every chapter, besides the usual large presentation frontispiece and large miniature at the beginning of each book. Only one manuscript has this programme fully carried out. These manuscripts are:

22. Oxford, Bodleian, Douce 318. Vellum. 246 fols. Spaces for 196 miniatures, none carried out. Second half C15.

23. Paris, Bibl.Nat.Fr. 9738. Vellum. 221 fols. 57 clumsy miniatures and spaces for a further 205; 262 in all. Nine folios with frontispieces of the nine books are lost. Second half C15.

24. Vienna, Nationalbibliothek, MS. 2566. Vellum. 166 fols. 291 miniatures of fine quality by three hands.[29] Before 1481.

Finally, there are two unillustrated manuscripts:

25. Chantilly, Musée Condé, MS. 756 (507). Paper. 223 fols. Late C15.

26. Leningrad, State Public Library, F.p.IV.45. Paper. 269 fols. Late C15.

One more manuscript is illustrated but I have no information about it:

27. Jena, Universitätsbibliothek, MS. N.B.91. Vellum.

The iconographic study of this vast mass of illustrative material is excessively difficult and might not prove very rewarding. In no case does there appear to be any sign of the use of any previously existing cycle of Alexander pictures, and, apart from the three main groups outlined above, the manuscripts do not appear to fall into any very clearly defined groups so far as the iconography of their pictures is concerned. The picture-spaces left by the scribes appear in most cases to have been filled by the painters without recourse to any model, and only rarely do two manuscripts appear to be closely related iconographically.[30]

The French Quintus Curtius retained its popularity until the middle of the sixteenth century and was printed seven times between about 1500[31] and 1555. Only three of these editions have, so far as I can discover, any illustrations. They are:

1. Paris, Vérard, circa 1500. 252 fols. Two of Vérard's stock cuts and one repeat.[32]

2. Paris, Michel Le Noir, 1503, 200 fols. One of Le Noir's stock cuts on title-page.[33]

3. Paris, Jacques le Messier, 1534, 116 fols. Title-border on fol. a[i] and one cut from Vérard's *Josephus* on fol. a[vi] verso.[34]

None of these woodcuts have any real connection with the text or any interest for the study of Alexander iconography.

6. RUDOLF VON EMS, ALEXANDER

The *Alexander* in Middle High German verse of Rudolf von Ems or von Montfort was completed shortly after 1250. Quintus Curtius is the principal source of the poem but Rudolf has used several supplementary sources to complete Curtius' defective text and to include all the additional information about Alexander that he could find. The most important of these supplementary sources is *Historia de Preliis* I[2] and Rudolf also used Pseudo-Methodius *Revelationes,* for Gog and Magog, and Petrus Comestor's *Historia Scolastica.*[35]

Two illustrated manuscripts of the poem exist, both made on paper about 1430 in the workshop of Diebolt Lauber of Hagenau in Alsace.[36] One, Munich, Cgm. 203, has only a fancy author-portrait and a frontispiece depicting an unidentified siege, perhaps that of Tyre. The other, Brussels, Royal Library 18232,[37] has forty-six water-colour pictures. The majority of them, those which illustrate passages of which the source is Quintus Curtius, Pseudo-Methodius or Petrus Comestor are based directly on the German text without a visual model. The few whose subject derives from *Historia de Preliis* I[2] on the other hand show some iconographic connection with the late antique cycle which was presumably available to the illustrator in the form of an illustrated *Historia de Preliis* manuscript.

7. The Alexandreis of Gautier de Chatillon

It was left to the Middle Ages to repair the neglect of Antiquity and treat the life of Alexander as subject of an heroic epic in hexameters in Virgilian style.

Gautier de Châtillon, or de Lille, wrote his poem between 1178 and 1182. It is a typical product of the twelfth-century Renaissance of classical literary studies and is dedicated to William, Archbishop of Rheims. The principal source used is Quintus Curtius[38] but Justin, Josephus and Julius Valerius also contribute to this fine epic whose popularity and success were fully deserved. The *Alexandreid* became a standard school text on a par with the *Aeneid* and a very copious marginal and interlinear gloss and commentary for school use is found in a large number of the surviving manuscripts.[39] Its popularity waned with the Middle Ages. Humanist preoccupation with original sources, and with Antiquity to the exclusion of the 'Gothic barbarism' of the previous age killed it, although it was still printed four times in the sixteenth century and once in the seventeenth.[40]

The character of the one hundred and thirty-five manuscripts that I have traced is that of the severest austerity school-text. Nothing in the nature of real illustration ever occurs in them, although, like schoolbooks of later ages, these manuscripts sometimes bear in margin or on fly-leaf the amateur illustrative efforts of their owners.[41]

Vernacular Derivatives of the *Alexandreis* of Gautier de Châtillon

Gautier's poem was not only important in itself; it was also the source of five vernacular Alexander-books of considerable significance.

8. El Libro de Alexandre

The authorship of the mid-thirteenth-century Spanish Alexander poem *El libro de Alexandre*[42] is uncertain though it may be the work of Gonzalo de Berceo.[43] It is a fine poem based mainly on the *Alexandreis* of Gautier de Châtillon[44] supplemented with material from *Historia de Preliis* and the French *Roman d' Alexandre.*[45] Two manuscripts and a fragment exist, of which one, the Osuna manuscript, Madrid, Biblioteca Nacionál Vª.5.10 has two pen-drawings representing Alexander telling the story of the siege of Troy over Achilles' tomb, and Alexander's nearly fatal bathe in the river Cydnus. They are the work of the scribe who wrote the manuscript and are based directly on the text, no model being used.[46]

9. Jakob Van Maerlant, Alexanders Geesten

The *Alexanders Geesten* of Jakob van Maerlant, the best known of Middle-Dutch writers, is a close translation of the *Alexandreis* into rhyming couplets which was made between 1256 and 1260. Other sources used by Maerlant to supplement the *Alexandreis* include the *Iter ad Paradisum* and one of the French Vengeance sequels. No illustrations occur in the surviving manuscripts and fragments.[47]

10. Ulrich Von Eschenbach, Alexander

The *Alexander,* an excessively long and diffuse poem in Middle High German by Ulrich von Eschenbach, was completed in its original form between 1270 and 1287. A lengthy epilogue was added later. The principal source of this work is the *Alexandreis* of Gautier de Châtillon but *Historia de Preliis* I[2], the *Iter ad Paradisum* and a variety of other sources are also drawn on. The manuscripts are all unillustrated.[48]

11. Brandr Jónsson, Alexanderssaga

A version of the *Alexandreis* of Gautier de Châtillon was made about 1260 in Icelandic prose by Brandr Jónsson, bishop of Holar.[49] One of the manuscripts has an initial D historiated with a picture of an enthroned monarch, probably intended for Alexander.[50] The others are unillustrated.

12. The Czech Alexandreis

The last of the vernacular derivatives of the *Alexandreis* of Gautier de Châtillon was made in Czech verse probably about 1265. No illustrated manuscripts of it appear to exist.[51]

ITALIAN ALEXANDER-POEMS OF THE
RENAISSANCE BASED ON QUINTUS CURTIUS

13. DOMENICO FALUGIO, TRIONFO MAGNO

This poem, in twenty-seven cantos in *ottava rima,* was
published in 1521. Its principal source is Quintus Curtius, whose account of Alexander has been treated here
in the spirit of the burlesque epic of the Renaissance.[52]
The title-page of the only edition has a woodcut showing Alexander in a triumphal car drawn by elephants.[53]

*14. THE ROME ALEXANDER ROMANCE ROME, BIBLIOTECA
VITTORIO EMANUELE, MS. 1751 (MO.M.10)*

A romantic poem on Alexander in *ottava rima* survives
incomplete in manuscript 1751 of the Biblioteca Vittorio Emanuele in Rome. It is a poem with the love
interest well developed and draws on Curtius only for
the barest framework on which to hang its romantic
fantasies. Originally each of its six cantos was preceded
in the manuscript by a pen-drawing illustrating an
episode in the canto. Those before cantos I and II are
lost and the remainder are love scenes except the last,
fol. 107, which shows a combat between two warriors
in antique armour.[54]

*15. OROSIUS, HISTORIARUM ADVERSUM PAGANOS LIBRI SEP-
TEM, BOOK III*

In the early fifth century Paulus Orosius, a Spanish
priest, wrote, at the request of his friend St. Augustine,
a brief universal history entitled *Seven books of histories
directed against the Pagans.* His object was the same as
Augustine's in writing the *City of God;* to defend
Christianity against the current pagan complaint that the
disasters which had overtaken Roman civilization were
the outcome of the anger of the old gods at the apostasy
of their worshippers to Christianity. His method was
simply to retell the history of the ancient world, laying
particular stress on the horrors and disasters of that history, and so to show that things had been no better
under the old dispensation, and that current misfortunes
were to be attributed rather to the anger of the Christian
God at man's perennial folly and wickedness.[55]

Despite its ephemeral polemic purpose Orosius' book
achieved great and lasting success. Probably because it
contained all the essential facts of history in a brief and
readable form, no less than on account of its acceptable
Christian philosophy of history, the *History against the
Pagans* became the standard universal history textbook
of the Middle Ages, and no school, university or
monastic library could afford to be without a copy. Two
hundred and forty-five complete and fragmentary
manuscripts of it survived down to 1939[56] and it was
printed twenty-five times before the publication of the
critical edition of Sigebert Havercamp at Leyden in
1737, which was for long the best available text.

The history of Macedon, of Philip II, Alexander and his
successors is told in Book III, chapters 12 to 20 and 23.
It is an important source, frequently used in the Middle
Ages to supplement the legendary accounts of Alexander, although it appears only rarely as principal
source.

No definite tradition of Orosius illustration existed in
the Middle Ages. A very few manuscripts were illustrated in their margins by their owners but the different sets of pictures devised by them have no connection
with one another, no relationship with any pre-existing
cycle of Alexander illustrations, and no influence on the
illustrations of any other Alexander-book.

Only one of these manuscripts is really interesting. It is
in the Vatican, Vat.lat.3340, a manuscript of the early
eleventh century in a Beneventan hand. It was, about
1050, illustrated with very small and delicate pen-
drawings in the lower and outer margins. The loss of
three quires at the beginning and other losses has left
only twenty-eight folios with illustrations. The history
of Macedon begins on fol. 16v and ends incomplete on
fol. 23v, after the battle of Alexander and Porus, Book
III, cap. 19, § 3. The other illustrated Orosius manuscripts, Florence, Biblioteca Laurenziana, Plut. LXV.37;
London, B.M., Burney 216; and Stuttgart, Württemb.
Landesbibliothek, Cod.hist.fol.410 have no more than
small marginal sketches or visual marginalia.[57]

*16. VERNACULAR TRANSLATIONS OF OROSIUS INTO OLD ENGLISH,
FRENCH, SPANISH AND ITALIAN*

The most famous vernacular version of Orosius is that
made by King Alfred in Old English prose in the late
ninth century as part of his educational programme for
the English.[58] Both the surviving manuscripts are unillustrated.

The French version, *Les Empereors de Rome,* was made
by a certain Calendre in Lorraine between 1213 and
1220. Very surprisingly this poem is based not, as one
would expect, on the original Latin text of Orosius but,
directly or indirectly, on King Alfred's Old English version.[59] It is confined to Roman history and omits that of
Macedon. The only manuscript, Paris, B.Nat.Fr. 794, is
unillustrated. Orosius is also a major source of the *Histoire Ancienne jusqu'à César* and its derivatives.[60]

A Spanish version was made by Pero Diáz de la Torre
of Aragon for Fernan Alvarez de Toledo, Count of Alva
in 1442.[61]

An Italian translation was made by Bono Giamboni for
Lamberto degl'Abati in the fourteenth century.[62] I have
found no illustrated manuscripts of either the Spanish
or the Italian version.

17. Orosius as Principal Source: The Latin Alexander Compilations

Orosius is rarely used as a main source and only in works of relatively little interest. His book supplies the chief element in a Latin biography of Alexander compiled, with the supplementary use of various other sources, about 1150, possibly by Radulfus Abbot of St. Albans, and known as the *St. Albans Compilation.* It survives in two unillustrated manuscripts in Cambridge.[63]

The *St. Albans Compilation* was translated into Anglo-Norman French before the end of the thirteenth century. This version exists in one unillustrated manuscript,[64] and was drawn on for the prologue added to the *Old French Prose Alexander* in its second redaction.[65]

Two similar Latin compilations exist; one in Oxford, Bodleian, Douce 299, in which the *St. Albans Compilation* is supplemented from the *Epitome* of Julius Valerius, and the second in the British Museum, MS. Sloane 289. Neither of these manuscripts is illustrated.[66]

18. The Middle-Irish Prose Alexander

An Irish prose life of Alexander, based principally on Orosius with supplementary use of Josephus, the *Epistola ad Aristotelem* and the *Collatio cum Dindimo* is found in two slightly differing versions in the *Book of Ballymote* and the *Leabhar Breac* where it is unillustrated.[67]

19. Parva Recapitulatio

A brief Latin prose text called *Parva recapitulatio de eodem Alexandro et de suis* is found in five English manuscripts, each containing much the same series of Alexander texts, as a supplement to the *Epitome* of Julius Valerius. It contains three episodes, a special variant of the Nectanebus story from an unknown source, Alexander's visit to Jerusalem adapted from Josephus, and a brief account of the struggles of the Diadochi taken textually unaltered from Orosius. The manuscripts are all unillustrated.[68]

20. Justinus, Epitoma Historiarum Philippicarum Pompeii Trogi

Pompeius Trogus or Trogus Pompeius was probably a contemporary of Augustus but not much is known about him. He wrote a world history giving special attention to the conquests and empire of Alexander, the history of Macedon generally and that of the Alexandrian succession states of the Diadochi, and which he called *Historiae Philippicae.* It is in forty-four books and survives in two forms. The first consists of the summary prologues to the books composed by Pompeius Trogus himself. The second is an epitome of the work as a whole which is attributed to a certain Justinus, of whom nothing is known. It was made some time before the early fifth century A.D., when it was used as a source by Orosius.[69]

The loss of the complete text of Pompeius Trogus is most regrettable, not so much for his account of Alexander himself, which is based mainly on the bad, so-called Cleitarchus tradition, as for that of Alexander's successors, for whose reigns and doings the very inadequate text of Justin is often our sole source of knowledge. Justin was quite well known in the Middle Ages but, as a respectable classical historian, became really popular only with the Renaissance. Three-quarters of the manuscripts, of which I have traced over two hundred and thirty, are Italian humanist codices of the fifteenth century.

The vast majority of these manuscripts are of the usual humanist type with no more illustration than, at most, a fancy author-portrait incorporated in the decoration of the title-page. There exist, however, three manuscripts with a certain amount of real illustration.[70]

The first is a twelfth-century manuscript from the Abbey of St. Vincent, No. 400 in the Bibliothèque Publique of Laon. Each book has at the beginning a pen-drawn historiated capital. Several of them show a king or prince enthroned who is prominent in the book in question.[71]

A mid-fifteenth-century Italian humanist manuscript in the Vatican, Ottob.lat.1529, has an elaborate title-page with six medallions showing scenes from the first few chapters of Book I and, at the beginning of each book, a small panel with a capital and a picture, usually a fancy bust-portrait of a monarch or other prominent person mentioned near the beginning of the book in question. Philip II of Macedon appears in Books VIII, IX and XI; in the last case his head is thrown back and his eyes are closed, a convention adopted by the illustrator to show that he is dead in Book XI. Similarly, Alexander is shown as a young man with a lion's head helmet alive in Book XII and dead in Book XIII.[72] There is no connection between the iconography of this manuscript and that of the manuscript in Laon.

The last illustrated Justin manuscript is also in the Ottoboni collection in the Vatican, lat. 1417. It is a paper manuscript dated 1461 and has a number of pictures in water-colour, under the strong stylistic influence of the *Legend of the Cross* by Piero della Francesca in Arezzo, which illustrate the text in a contemporary Italian non-classicizing style.[73] These miniatures are the work of a very able amateur, Giovanni dei Castaldi da Fano, who was also the scribe of the manuscript.[74] The relevant subjects illustrated are: the siege of Larissa by Philip II; the assassination of Philip by Pausanias; Parmenio's letter accusing Philip the physician of conspiring to poison Alexander and the duel on horseback of Alexander and Porus. Unfilled spaces were probably intended to illustrate the death of Darius; Alexander's foolhardy leap into the city of the Mardians and Alexander's death. This manuscript has no iconographic connection with the other two and none of the illustrated Justin manuscripts appear to draw on any previously existing iconographic source.

21. JUSTIN AS A SOURCE IN VERNACULAR ALEXANDER-BOOKS AND VERNACULAR VERSIONS OF HIS BOOK

Justin's epitome of Pompeius Trogus is much less frequently used as a source in medieval Alexander-books than is Orosius. The most important example of such use is the *Trésor des Histoires* made for Baudouin d'Avesnes, where Justin supplements the account of Alexander taken from the *Histoire ancienne jusqu'à César.*[75]

A humanist Italian version of Justin is found in three unillustrated manuscripts of the fifteenth century, Paris, B.Nat.Ital.1486; Siena, Biblioteca Comunale, MS. I.VII.1; and Valencia, Biblioteca Universitaria, MS. 1241. Other manuscripts of it may well exist.

Claude de Seyssel made a version in French in the early sixteenth century which is preserved in one unillustrated manuscript, Paris, B.Nat.Fr. 715, *L'Ystoire de Justin.*

22. SOLINUS, COLLECTANEA RERUM MEMORABILIUM

Caius Julius Solinus wrote a geographical description of the world, probably early in the third century A.D. This work, variously entitled *Collectanea rerum memorabilium, Polyhistor* or *De mirabilibus mundi,* is taken almost entirely, without acknowledgement, from the *Historia Naturalis* of the elder Pliny and from Pomponius Mela, *De situ orbis.*[76] Solinus' work was extremely popular in the Middle Ages and manuscripts are numerous of every century from the ninth to the fifteenth. At least one hundred and sixty-six manuscripts exist, of which Mommsen lists one hundred and fifty-three in his edition.[77]

Solinus has many references to Alexander in his descriptions of the various countries through which the conqueror passed, and the very numerous outlandish peoples and monstrous races which he describes were drawn on to supply additional marvels in medieval Alexander-books. Thomas of Kent makes a particularly extensive use of Solinus for this purpose in his *Roman de Toute Chevalerie* in the second half of the twelfth century.[78]

There appears to have been a cycle of illustrations for Solinus dating back to late antiquity. One early fourteenth-century Italian manuscript, Milan, Biblioteca Ambrosiana, lat.C 246 inf.[79] preserves this cycle in a medievalized form apparently complete. Miniatures occur on 68 out of 128 pages and the total number of subjects depicted is about 260, including maps. Wittkower has pointed out its resemblance, allowing for stylistic medievalization, to the ninth-century Cosmas Indicopleustes manuscript in the Vatican which is regarded as copied from a sixth-century model. The Ambrosiana Solinus has the same spaceless character with figures placed on the bare page unframed and barely related to one another. Another indication of early date is the omission of Paris in the map of Gaul on fol. 30, and the borrowing of a picture from the late antique cycle of Alexander pictures to illustrate Macedonia on fol. 18v. This picture, which represents Bucephalas presented to Philip and occurs also in the Venice Pseudo-Oppian codex of the early eleventh century,[80] has been mis-interpreted by the illustrator as representing Alexander himself. As the late antique Alexander picture-cycle cannot be later than the fourth century[81] and may even be earlier, Solinus too may have been illustrated from within a century or so of the appearance of the work.

There are some traces of this picture-cycle in two other Solinus manuscripts. MS. Egerton 818 in the British Museum, formerly in the possession of Coluccio Salutati,[82] is an Italian manuscript of about 1100. It has on fol. 2 a miniature showing Solinus on the left seated on a throne and holding a book in his left hand and a pen in his right. Facing him and standing on the right is Adventus, to whom Solinus presents his work in a dedicatory letter. Both wear long robes of antique type. Adventus is bare-headed, Solinus has a pointed cap resembling a tiara. The picture is curiously like the standard presentation-picture formula, with the author in the place usually occupied by the recipient and vice versa. This picture appears indeed to be altered, under the influence of that formula, from an author portrait of Solinus which occurs at the beginning of the Ambrosiana manuscript (fol. IV). In this Solinus is dressed almost exactly as in the Egerton manuscript but holds an OT map like an orb instead of the pen in his right hand, and the open book in his left is inscribed with the beginning of the dedication to Adventus. This picture is clearly adapted from the standard 'enthroned monarch' formula, and the Egerton picture is evidently adapted from it. Apart from this Egerton 818 has a few capitals historiated with busts of kings and some marginal drawings (a griffin, a lion and Bucephalas) by a later hand, none of which is connected with any picture in the Ambrosiana manuscript. A tenth-century manuscript in the

Vatican, Vat.lat.3342, has in its margins a few maps of islands which may derive from the picture-cycle in the Ambrosiana manuscript.

Solinus was first printed in Rome by J. Schurener de Bopardia, probably before 1473, if Mommsen is right in regarding this undated edition as the earliest.[83] It was printed over thirty times in the fifteenth and sixteenth centuries. Two editions may have some connection with the Solinus picture-cycle. The first, Basel, M. Isengrinius and H. Petrus, 1538, has on p. 6 a plan of Rome bearing some resemblance to that on fol. 3v in the Ambrosian codex; apart from that there are a number of maps of no interest. The other, also published by H. Petrus in Basel, in 1541, has eleven maps of small islands which appear to have some connection with similar maps in the Ambrosiana manuscript and in Vat-.lat.3342.[84]

There is no evidence that this very interesting and early picture-cycle had any direct influence on the illustrators of Alexander-books of the Middle Ages. The illustrator of Thomas of Kent's *Roman de Toute Chevalerie* evidently was not familiar with it, as the numerous pictures in the manuscripts illustrating passages deriving from Solinus bear no resemblance to the illustrations of those passages in the Ambrosiana manuscript. Certain common representations of well-known monstrous peoples, the one-eyed Arimaspians or the 'men whose heads Do grow beneath their shoulders', for example, do certainly occur among the Solinus illustrations and also in illustrated Alexander-books, but these were well-known iconographic types and no direct connection with the Solinus pictures need exist.[85]

23. THE COSMOGRAPHIA *ATTRIBUTED TO 'AETHICUS ISTER'*

The curious geographical description of the world, supposed to have been written by a certain 'Aethicus or Ethicus the Istrian' in Greek, and translated into Latin by a 'Hieronymus Presoyter' who was intended to be taken for the maker of the Vulgate, was believed by its editor, H. Wuttke, to be a product of the decline of the empire, made in about the fourth century A.D.[86]

It is in reality a bogus travel-book, a Mandeville of the Dark Ages, and its probable author was the Irish monk, Virgil, bishop of Salzburg, in the second half of the eighth century.[87] It is a strange work and contains much that would be of considerable interest could one only disentangle fact from fiction. Several Alexander traditions are reported in it; in particular, Alexander's contacts with the mysterious Meopari with their submarine pirate vessels, who help him to enclose Gog and Magog, and an interesting variant version of the Gog and Magog legend itself.[88]

Manuscripts are quite numerous from the eighth century to the fifteenth, when its presence with the *Notitia Dig-*

nitatum in the lost Codex Spirensis ensured its being reproduced in the numerous fifteenth-century humanist copies of that fascinating book. Neither there nor anywhere else is there any evidence that it was ever illustrated.

Aethicus was used extensively by Thomas of Kent in the *Roman de Toute Chevalerie* for the Meopari, whose submarines replace the traditional glass diving-bell in Alexander's submarine exploration, for the enclosing of Gog and Magog and for some other adventures. All this material is illustrated in the Paris and Cambridge manuscripts following directly the French text.[89]

GROUP II: HISTORICAL WORKS ON ALEXANDER FIRST KNOWN IN WESTERN EUROPE AT THE RENAISSANCE

24. ARRIAN, ᾽ΑΝΑΒΑΣΙΣ ᾽ΑΛΕΞΑΝΔΡΟΥ

The most important historical account of Alexander's career which became known in Latin Europe only at the Renaissance is the ᾽Ανάβασις ᾽Αλεξάνδρου of Arrian, a contemporary and trusted servant of the Emperor Hadrian in the first half of the second century A.D.[90]

Arrian was a fine scholar with the good historian's critical eye for reliable authorities, and he alone has preserved for us the 'good' tradition of the history of Alexander going back to unbiased contemporary sources, principally the account of Alexander's lieutenant Ptolemy I Soter of Egypt and to a much lesser extent to Aristobulus.

Most of the thirty or so Greek manuscripts of Arrian are late in date and unillustrated. One only, Vienna, Nationalbibliothek, Hist.Gr.4, is of the late twelfth or early thirteenth century and has an equestrian portrait of Alexander as frontispiece.[91] This picture was added on a paper leaf to the vellum manuscript in the fifteenth century but there is some reason to think that it may replace and derive from a much earlier frontispiece of late antique origin. In its existing form it is a curious mixture of late medieval with ancient elements. It shows Alexander as a knight in full plate armour of the late medieval period mounted on Bucephalas with hawk on wrist and preceded by a greyhound who is coursing two hares, a purely medieval conception of him. On the other hand above his head a winged victory (now mutilated) is shown about to crown him with a laurel wreath, a conception which is purely antique and would be unthinkable to a medieval illustrator. Another ancient element is the ox-head brand on the horse's flank. Such a brand is undoubtedly the true explanation of the name of Alexander's favourite charger,[92] and appeared also in the late antique Pseudo-Callisthenes picture-cycle where we find it in the Venice Pseudo-Oppian codex of the early eleventh century,[93] in the *Armenian Alexander* in Venice, San Lazzaro 424[94] and in a seventeenth-century Russian manuscript of the *Serbian Alexander*.[95] Taken together the evidence seems to point to the existence in late antiquity of a frontispiece for Arrian showing Alexander mounted on Bucephalas and crowned by Victory.

25. LATIN VERSIONS OF ARRIAN

The humanists recognized the importance of Arrian at an early date and his book was translated into Latin, first by Pier Paolo Vergerio for the Emperor Sigismund, probably in the 1430's. Vergerio deliberately used a simple and medieval Latin style to suit the low cultural standard of his patron. In 1450 Aeneas Sylvius Piccolomini (Pius II) found the text of Vergerius' version somewhere in Austria and sent it to Alfonso I of Naples who commissioned his historiographer Bartolomeo Facio to revise the translation and improve its Latinity. Facio died in 1457 with only a third of the task completed and the revision was finished by Giacomo Curlo after the death of Alfonso himself.[96]

Manuscripts of both versions exist with humanist decoration and fancy portraits of Alexander but the text is never regularly illustrated.[97]

26. DIODORUS SICULUS, ΒΙΒΛΙΟΘΗΚΗ, BOOKS XVI AND XVII

The world history written between about 60 and 30 B.C. by Diodorus Siculus is only partially preserved. Books XVI and XVII contain an account of Alexander's career based mainly on the 'bad' or so-called Cleitarchus tradition. Books XVII-XX deal with the Diadochi. These five books are preserved in full. Diodorus, like Arrian, began to be current in Western Europe at the Renaissance. I have not traced any manuscripts with illustrations.[98]

Claude de Seysel, the French translator of Justin,[99] also produced, in the early sixteenth century, a French version of Books XVIII-XX of Diodorus, entitled *L'Istoire des successeurs d'Alexandre*. The manuscript, Paris, B.Nat.Fr.712, is unillustrated.

27. PLUTARCH, LIFE OF ALEXANDER

Plutarch's *Parallel Lives* of eminent Greeks and Romans were written in the early second century A.D. The *Vitae Parallelae* were unknown in Western Europe in the Middle Ages but leaped into immediate popularity in the Renaissance.

The *Life of Alexander* parallels that of Julius Caesar and is one of the longest of the series. It was valued by humanist historians for its contribution to knowledge of Alexander's life and character and was translated into Latin, Spanish (Aragonese dialect) and German. It was

not much used as a source except in a curious little French tract called *Les Trois Grands*. There appears to be no evidence that the *Lives* were illustrated in any Greek manuscript.[100]

TRANSLATIONS OF PLUTARCH'S LIFE OF ALEXANDER

28. THE ARAGONESE VERSION OF PLUTARCH'S LIVES MADE FOR JUAN FERNANDEZ DE HEREDIA

Rather surprisingly the first Western European version of the *Lives* of Plutarch was made by a Dominican bishop of Tudernopoli for the Aragonese Grand-Master of Rhodes Juan Fernandez de Heredia in the third quarter of the fourteenth century, before 1377. No doubt de Heredia's connection with Rhodes accounts for this early interest in a Greek historical text. The manuscript, Paris, B.Nat. Espagnol 70-72 has lost the first of its four volumes which may have contained the life of Alexander. It is unillustrated.[101]

29. LATIN VERSIONS OF PLUTARCH'S LIVES: GUARINO DA VERONA, PIER CANDIDO DECEMBRIO AND DARIO TIBERTI

Humanist interest in Plutarch was shown at an early date. Coluccio Salutati had a copy of the Aragonese version sent to Florence in 1395. In 1397 Chrysoloras arrived in Florence to teach Greek and is said to have translated some of the *Lives* while living with Palla Strozzi.

The versions of the *Lives* which finally became current as the standard humanist Latin translations were mostly the work of Guarino da Verona, who was responsible for the *Life of Alexander*, and of some of his pupils.[102]

An abbreviated Latin version of some of the *Lives* was made in the 1450's by Pier Candido Decembrio. The surviving manuscripts, two of which have capitals historiated with fancy portraits of the heroes, omit the life of Alexander. One of them, however, Vatican, Barb-.lat.112, refers at the end to a now lost fourth book which may have contained it.

A second epitome of the *Lives* was made in 1492 by Dario Tiberti of Cesena. It survives in an unillustrated edition printed in Ferrara in 1501 by Laurentius de Valentia.[103]

Neither Guarino's version nor the epitomes exist, so far as I can discover, in a regular illustrated form, although Guarino's occurs in several manuscripts with a capital historiated with a fancy portrait of Alexander in the usual style of humanist book-decoration.[104]

30. ANONYMOUS GERMAN VERSION OF PLUTARCH'S LIVES

A German version of Plutarch's *Lives* was made in the late fifteenth or early sixteenth century. The Vienna manuscript[105] has full-page standing portraits of the heroes. That of Alexander, in contemporary dress of about 1500, occurs on fol. 9.

31. Les Trois Grands

In France the influence of Plutarch was surprisingly small until the late Renaissance period, when Jacques Amyot translated the *Lives* (published 1559) and the *Moralia* or Philosophical Essays (published 1572).

A few of the lives, not including that of Alexander, were translated into French from the humanist Latin versions by Symon Bourgouyn for Louis XII about 1500 but they appear to have had little influence.[106]

One late medieval example of Plutarch's influence that I have discovered is in a brief anonymous tract called *Les Trois Grands.* This is apparently imitated from Lucian's first *Dialogue of the Dead,* the contest for preeminence between Alexander, Hannibal and Scipio Africanus before Minos. In *Les Trois Grands* each of the three personages who have been surnamed 'the Great', Alexander, Pompey and Charlemagne, sets out his claim to that title and to precedence over the other two in a prosy rhetorical speech. Alexander's harangue is based almost entirely on Plutarch with no trace at all of the romance.[107] The whole is probably a Paris university production, as a large part of Charlemagne's discourse is devoted to the glories of that seat of learning and his own special merit as its reputed founder.

The oldest manuscript is interpolated into a text of *L'Histoire des Neuf Preux et des Neuf Preues* of Sebastien Mamerot. This is in Vienna, Nationalbibliothek, MS. 2577 and is dated 1472, fols. 195-199v. It has a space for a large miniature before each of the three speeches. Two other manuscripts, Paris, Arsenal, MS. 5025, fols. 24-36 and Paris, Ste. Geneviève, MS. 3005, fols. 19v-24v, have a standing portrait of each 'Grand' in ate fifteenth-century dress. An early sixteenth-century undated edition, Chantilly, Musée Condé, No. 1905, shows them in woodcuts as enthroned monarchs.[108]

Notes

1. On Curtius see S. Dosson, *Etude sur Quinte Curce, sa vie et son oeuvre,* Paris 1887. Dosson's book, written three-quarters of a century ago, remains the best and fullest study of Curtius and his work. His list of manuscripts on pp. 315-56 is invaluable. On the value of Curtius for the history of Alexander see Tarn, II, pp. 91-122. Edition: J. C. Rolfe, *Loeb Classical Library,* 1946.

2. Dosson (pp. 18-45) dates him after the death of Tiberius and between 37 and 65 A.D., probably before 42 A.D. Tarn, pp. 111-16, places him in the principate of Augustus.

3. On the medieval influence of Curtius in general see Dosson, *op. cit.,* Appendix II, pp. 357-380. This is not wholly reliable on medieval popular works.

4. Dosson, *ibid.,* p. 325. The catalogues are: G. Haenel, *Catalogus librorum manuscriptorum,* Leipzig 1830, col. 472 (Q. Curtius: de rebus gestis Alexandri Magni script. per dom. Vitum, iussu And. Math. Aquaeviti Ruis de Aragonia c. fig. membr. fol.) and J. Rathgeber, *Die handschriftlichen Schätze der früheren Strassburger Stadtbibliothek,* Gütersloh 1876, p. 34: 'Wahrscheinlich aus dem Ende des 12. Jahrhunderts war cas Manuscript . . .' etc. (as in Haenel).

5. It would be useless waste of space to attempt to list all such humanist manuscripts of Curtius. A few examples of such fancy Alexander portraits are: Florence, Laurenziana, Plut. LXIV. 28, fol. 1; Plut. LXIV. 32, fol. 1; London, B.M., Harley 2727, fol. 1; Additional 9950, fol. 1; Paris, B.Nat.Lat. 9677, fol. 1; Vatican, Vat. lat. 1867, fol. 1; Ottob. lat. 1678, fol. 1; Urbin. lat. 427, fol. 1. Chigi lat. H. VII 228, vellum, C15, humanist, with arms of Cardinal Francesco Gonzaga, has on fol. 2 an elaborate title-border with a capital I historiated with a fancy portrait of Alexander as Hercules. There are also three medallions in the border with scenes not easily identifiable. Similar borders with medallions, some containing possible portraits of Alexander and others with symbols and *imprese* occur on fols. 19, 50v, 91v, 115, 132 and 139v.

6. The manuscripts are Oxford, Corpus Christi College 82; Paris, B.Nat.Lat. 14629; Vatican, Vat. lat. 1869, Regin. lat. 728 and Ottob. lat. 2053. On these see Dosson, *op. cit.,* pp. 322-24 and 344. Also Cary, p. 62 and P. Meyer, *Alexandre le Grand* II, Paris 1886, p. 21, n. 2 and pp. 381-86.

7. A. Foulet, 'La bataille du Granique chez Albéric', *Romania* LX, 1935, pp. 237-41.

8. Below . . . .

9. See Dosson, *op. cit.,* p. 375 and, for list of manuscripts, V. Zaccaria, 'Sulle opere di Pier Candido Decembri' *Rinascimento* VII, 1956, p. 16, n. 1.

10. An example of a manuscript of this type with a fancy portrait of Alexander is Florence, Nazionale, Magliabecchi XXIII. 45, fol. 1.

11. On this manuscript see P. Toesca, *La pittura e la miniatura in Lombardia,* Milan 1912, p. 534, figs. 436-37; and C. Mitchell, *A fifteenth century Italian Plutarch,* London 1961, pp. 15-16 and n. 34. On the non-classicizing style of humanist illustration, Mitchell, *ibid.,* pp. 5-7. The manuscript in the Biblioteca Ventimiliana in Catania (G. Mazzatinti, *Inventari dei Manoscritti delle biblioteche d'Italia,* XX, Florence, 1913, p. 159, No. 84) is described as 'con belle miniature' in the catalogue.

I have not seen it. It is wrongly listed by Bossuat (below, n. 14) as a manuscript of the French version of Vasque de Lucène.

12. Printed in Barcelona by Pere Posa Prevere and Pere Bru Sauoyench, 16 July 1480. Dosson, *op. cit.,* pp. 377-78.

13. *GKW* VII, Leipzig 1938, No. 7879, cols. 224-25.

14. The only detailed study of Vasque de Lucène and his translation of Quintus Curtius is R. Bossuat, 'Vasque de Lucène, traducteur de Quinte Curce', *Bibliothèque d'Humanisme et Renaissance* VIII, 1946, pp. 197-245. He lists twenty-four manuscripts (pp. 204-9) and all the editions (pp. 209-10). He omits manuscripts 14, 15, 22 and 26 in my list. Others probably exist in private libraries. On the translator see also C. Samaran, *Vasco de Lucena à la cour de Bourgogne (Documents inédits),* Lisbon 1938. Also Cary. pp. 63, 229 and 238-39. Bossuat's manuscript 13 (Catania) is of the Italian version of Pier Candido Decembrio. Above, n. 346.

15. See H. d'Orléans, *Chantilly. Musée Condé. Le cabinet des livres. Manuscrits,* III, pp. 47-48.

16. Abrahams, *Description des manuscrits français du moyen âge de la bibliothèque de Copenhague,* Copenhagen 1844, p. 65.

17. G. F. Warner and J. P. Gilson, *Catalogue of the Western Manuscripts in the Old Royal and King's Collections,* London 1921, II, p. 371.

18. Paulin Paris, *Manuscrits français de la Bibliothèque du Roi,* Paris 1836-48, II, p. 293.

19. A. Thomas in *Romania,* XIX, 1890, pp. 601-2.

20. H. Hagen, *Catalogus Codicum Bernensium,* Bern 1875, p. 19. The date 1459 is wrong. Probably it is an error for 1469.

21. A. M. Bandini, *Bibliotheca Leopoldina Laurentiana,* Florence, 1793, III, col. 389-91.

22. H. Aubert in *Bulletin de la Société Française de reproductions de manuscrits à peintures,* II, Paris, 1912, pp. 97-101 and pl. XLV. Also L. M. J. Delaissé, *La miniature Flamande: Le mécénat de Philippe le Bon,* Brussels 1959, p. 188, No. 261.

23. Warner and Gilson, *op. cit.* above, n. 17, p. 173.

24. *Ibid.,* p. 261.

25. H. P. Kraus, *Twenty-five Manuscripts,* Vaduz (1961), No. 21, pp. 72-76, with reproductions of fols. 2v and 109.

26. P. Paris, *op. cit.* above, n. 18, I, pp. 49-51.

27. *Ibid.,* II, pp. 280-84. Delaissé, *op. cit.* above, n. 22, pp. 186-87, No. 258.

28. L. Delisle, *Le cabinet des manuscrits de la Bibliothèque Nationale,* 1868-81, III, p. 341. P. Durrieu, *La miniature flamande au temps de la cour de Bourgogne,* Paris and Brussels 1927, pp. 48-49 and pls. XXV and XXVI.

29. F. Unterkircher, *Inventar der illuminierten Handschriften der oesterreichischen Nationalbibliothek in Wien,* Vienna, 1957, Part I, p. 75. Delaissé, *op. cit.* above, n. 22, pp. 160-61, No. 204.

30. The aesthetic interest of some of these manuscripts is very great as they are in many cases the work of some of the most eminent miniaturists of the Burgundian court in the second half of the fifteenth century. I do not list all the studies devoted to this aspect of these manuscripts.

31. This is assuming that the supposed Vérard edition of circa 1490 (Hain 5887, Copinger II, 1859) is fictitious.

32. J. Macfarlane, *Antoine Vérard (Bibliographical Society Monographs* VII), London 1900, p. 122, No. 278; Brunet, *Manuel du Libraire* II, col. 451; *GKW* VII, Leipzig 1938, col. 225, No. 7880. Copy Paris, B.Nat.Réserve J.85. For brief description of the editions see Bossuat, *op. cit.* above, no. 14, pp. 209-10.

33. Copy: Paris, B.Nat.Réserve J.1730.

34. Copy: Paris, B.Nat.Réserve J.814.

35. Edition: V. Junk, *Rudolfs von Ems Alexander (Bibliothek d. Lit. Vereins zu Stuttgart,* CCLXXII and CCLXXIV), Leipzig 1928-29. See also O. Zingerle, *Die Quellen zum Alexander des Rudolf von Ems (Germanistische Abhandlungen* IV), Breslau 1885 and A. Ausfeld, 'Ueber die Quellen zu Rudolf von Ems Alexander', Programm Donaueschingen 1883. Cary, *passim,* especially pp. 66-67, 186-187 and 205-7.

36. R. Kautsch, 'Diebolt Lauber und seine Werkstatt in Hagenau', *Centralblatt für Bibliothekswesen* XII, 1895, pp. 1-32 and 57-113. On the Rudolf von Ems manuscripts see pp. 69 and 77-79.

37. Described in detail by G. Gaspar and F. Lyna, *Les principaux manuscrits à peintures de la Bibliothèque Royale de Belgique (Société Française de reproduction de manuscrits à peintures),* Part 2, Paris 1947, pp. 85-89. See also V. Junk, 'Die Ueberlieferung von Rudolf von Ems Alexander', *Beiträge zur Geschichte der deutschen Sprache und Literatur* XXIX, Halle 1904, pp. 374-81.

38. Edition: F. A. W. Müldener, Leipzig 1863 and A. Gugger in Migne, *PL* CCIX, 1855, cols. 459-574. See also H. Christensen, *Das Alexanderlied Walth-*

ers von *Châtillon,* Halle 1905 and C. Giordano, *Alexandreis, poema di Gautier da Châtillon,* Naples 1917; Cary, *passim,* especially pp. 63-66, 173-74, 191-95 and 321-22.

39. On the gloss see R. de Cesare, *Glosse latine ed antico-francesi all'Alexandreis di Gautier de Châtillon,* Milan 1951.

40. Editions: Strasbourg 1513; Ingolstadt 1541; Lyon 1557 and 1558; St. Gall 1659.

41. One very common illustration occurs in the gloss. It is an OT map of the world accompanying the brief geographical description of Asia beginning: 'Tertia pars orbis, cuius ditione teneri . . .' Book I, l. 406. Ed. Migne, col. 472.

42. Edition: R. S. Willis, *El libro de Alexandre (Elliott Monographs* 32), Princeton 1934. Prints both the Paris and the Madrid manuscripts in parallel. For bibliography, Cary, pp. 64-65; also pp. 179-80, 187-88 and *passim.*

43. The authorship question is discussed in B. Dutton, 'The profession of Gonzalo de Berceo and the Paris manuscript of the *Libro de Alexandre', Bulletin of Hispanic Studies* XXXVII, 1960, pp. 137-45.

44. See R. S. Willis, *The Relationship of the Spanish 'Libro de Alexandre' to the 'Alexandreis' of Gautier de Châtillon (Elliott Monographs* 31), Princeton 1934; A. Morel-Fatio 'Recherches sur le texte et les sources du *Libro de Alexandre', Romania* IV, 1875, pp. 7-90.

45. R. S. Willis, *The debt of the Spanish 'Libro de Alexandre' to the French 'Roman d'Alexandre' (Elliott Monographs* 33) Princeton 1935.

46. Reproduced in edition of R. S. Willis (above n. 377) pls. I and IV; discussed *ibid.* pp. xiv-xx. Also M. Schiff, *La Bibliothèque du Marquis de Santillana (Bibl. de l'Ecole des Hautes Etudes,* CLIII), Paris 1905, pp. 386-87.

47. Edition: J. Franck, *Alexanders Geesten (Bibliothek van Middelnederlandsche Letterkunde),* Groningen 1882.

48. Edition: W. Toischer, *'Alexander' von Ulrich von Eschenbach (Bibl. Lit. Vereins Stuttgart,* CLXXXIII), Tübingen 1888. See also W. Toischer, 'Ueber die *Alexandreis* Ulrichs von Eschenbach', *Sitzungsberichte der kaiserlichen Akademie der Wissenschaften in Wien, Phil.-Hist. Klasse* XCVII, 1881, pp. 311-408. Cary, pp. 65-66 and *passim.*

49. Edition: Finnur Jónsson, *Alexanders Saga. Islandsk Oversaettelse ved Brandr Jónsson. Biskop til Holar* 1263-64, Copenhagen 1925. Description of manuscripts pp. III ff.

50. The manuscript is No. AM 226 fol. of the Arnamagnus collection in Copenhagen, fol. 129. Reproduced in H. Hermansson, *Icelandic Illuminated Manuscripts of the Middle Ages,* Copenhagen 1935, p. 30 and pl. 29b. Hermansson interprets the picture as Darius, since the capital D at the beginning of the text is the initial of his name, but it seems more likely that the hero of the story would be depicted in preference to his opponent.

51. Edition: R. Trautmann, *Die alttschechische Alexandreis,* Heidelberg 1916. On the sources see H. H. Bieleveldt, *Die Quellen der alttschechischen Alexandreis (Deutsche Akademie der Wissenschaften. Veröffentlichungen des Forschungsinstituts für Slawistik,* I), Berlin 1951.

52. On this poem see J. Storost, *Studien zur Alexandersage in der älteren italienischen Literatur (Romanistische Arbeiten* XXIII), Halle 1935, pp. 231-82. Cary, pp. 67 and 272.

53. Edition: Rome, printed by 'Marcellus Silber dictus Franck', 1521.

54. Storost, *ibid.,* pp. 283-304 for analysis and extracts from the poem, which is unpublished. Cary, pp. 67 and 272.

55. The best edition is that of C. Zangemeister, Leipzig, Teubner 1889. A generally satisfactory English translation is that of I. W. Raymond, *Seven Books of History against the Pagans,* New York 1936.

56. The manuscripts are listed in J. M. Bately and D. J. A. Ross, 'A check-list of manuscripts of Orosius, *Historiarum adversum paganos libri septem', Scriptorium* XV, 1961, pp. 329-34.

57. For detailed study of the illustrated manuscripts see D. J. A. Ross, 'Illustrated manuscripts of Orosius', *Scriptorium* IX, 1955, pp. 35-56 and pls. 11-15.

58. H. Sweet, *King Alfred's Orosius,* Part I, E.E.T.S., O.S. 79, 1883. See also: J. M. Bately, 'King Alfred and the Latin MSS. of Orosius' History', *Classica et Mediaevalia* XXII, 1961, pp. 69-105.

59. Edition: G. Millard, *Les Empereors de Rome par Calendre,* Ann Arbor 1957. On the relation to Alfred's Orosius, *ibid.,* pp. 6-18, and J. M. Bately, 'Alfred's *Orosius* and *Les Empereors de Rome', Studies in Philology* LVII, 1960, pp. 567-86.

60. [Ross, D. J. A. *Alexander Historiatus.* London: Warburg Institute, 1963], pp. 18-20.

61. See M. R. James, *Fitzwilliam Museum, Maclean Bequest, Catalogue of the Manuscripts,* Cambridge 1912, pp. 346-47, No. 180. Another manuscript is

in Madrid, Biblioteca Nacionál 10200 (Osuna Collection). The Cambridge manuscript has a few capitals historiated with busts but no real illustrations.

62. Manuscripts: Florence, Nazionale, Magliabecchi II.I.109, Paper, C14; Magliabecchi II.IV.68, Paper, C15; Rome, Biblioteca Corsini, MS. 43.C.9, Paper, C15.

63. P. Meyer, *Alexandre le Grand* II, Paris 1886, pp. 52-63. Cary, p. 68. The manuscripts are Corpus Christi College 219 and Gonville and Caius College 154.

64. D. J. A. Ross in *French Studies* VI, 1952, p. 353. MS. Fitzwilliam Mus. CFM. 20.

65. *Ibid.* Also F. P. Magoun in *Speculum* I, 1927, pp. 225-32.

66. P. Meyer, *op. cit.*, pp. 63-68. Cary, p. 69. Dr. F. Arnold informs me (letter 4 March 1963) that the Sloane compilation is in fact an extract from the *Polychronicon* of Ranulf Higden; Book III, caps. xxvi-xxx. (Ed. Rolls Series Vol. III, p. 382-Vol. IV, p. 16.)

67. Edition: K. Meyer in W. Stokes and E. Windisch, *Irische Texte,* 2. Serie, H. II, Leipzig 1887. Also R. T. Meyer, 'The sources of the Middle Irish Alexander', *Modern Philology* XLVII, 1949, pp. 1-7.

68. See Cary, p. 70.

69. Edition: F. Ruehl, Leipzig 1886. Also F. Ruehl, *Die Verbreitung des Justinus im Mittelalter,* Leipzig, 1871.

70. See D. J. A. Ross, 'An illustrated humanist manuscript of Justin's *Epitome* of the *Historiae Philippicae* of Trogus Pompeius', *Scriptorium* X, 1956, pp. 261-62.

71. *Catalogue des manuscrits de la bibliothèque de Laon,* in *Catalogue général des manuscrits des bibliothèques publiques des départements,* I, Paris 1849, p. 206.

72. Described in detail in D. J. A. Ross, *op. cit.* above n. 405, pp. 262-67 and pl. 32.

73. The date of this manuscript helps to date Piero's masterpiece, which must have been nearing completion when the manuscript was made.

74. For full description see D. J. A. Ross, 'An unrecorded follower of Piero della Francesca', *Journal of the Warburg and Courtauld Institutes* XVII, 1954, pp. 174-81 and pls. 21-24.

75. [Ross, 1963], pp. 20-21.

76. The best edition is T. Mommsen, *C. Iulii Solini Collectanea Rerum Memorabilium,* 2nd edition, Berlin 1895.

77. *ibid.,* pp. xxv-lii. He lists a further twenty-five manuscripts containing excerpts and epitomes, *ibid.,* pp. liii-lv.

78. On Thomas' use of Solinus see J. Weynand, *Der Roman de toute chevalerie des Thomas von Kent,* Diss. Bonn 1911, pp. 50-62.

79. In the manuscript Solinus extends from fol. 1 to fol. 64. It has not been much studied. See, however, P. Rivelli, *I codici ambrosiani di contenuto geografico,* Milan 1929, pp. 36-38; and P. Rivelli, 'Figurazioni cartografiche dell'età imperiale in un codice ambrosiano di Solino del primo trecento', *Raccolta di scritti in onore di Felice Ramorino,* Milan 1927, pp. 615-26. Also R. Wittkower, 'Marvels of the East', *Journal of the Warburg and Courtauld Institutes* V, 1942, pp. 171-72 and pl. 42a (reproducing fol. 57).

80. References [Cary, 1956], p. 6 and n. 20.

81. [Cary, 1956], p. 6.

82. Described and discussed by H. Idris Bell, 'A Solinus manuscript from the library of Coluccio Salutati', *Speculum* IV, 1929, pp. 451-61.

83. Mommsen, *op. cit.,* p. lvi. Mommsen lists a few of the most important editions on pp. lvi-lviii.

84. I have a study of the illustrations of Solinus nearing completion.

85. On the whole pictorial tradition of the monstrous races in ancient and medieval art see R. Wittkower, 'Marvels of the East', pp. 159-97. Also R. Wittkower, 'Marco Polo and the pictorial tradition of the Marvels of the East', *Oriente Poliano,* Rome 1957, pp. 155-72.

86. The only edition is still the unsatisfactory one of H. Wuttke, *Die Kosmographie des Istriers Aithikos,* Leipzig 1853. On Wuttke's dating see Introduction, pp. lxxxix-xciv. A new edition is needed.

87. On date and authorship see H. Loewe, *Ein literarischer Widersacher des Bonifatius. Virgil von Salzburg und die Kosmographie des Aethicus Ister (Akad. d. Wissensch. u. d. Lit., Geistes- und Sozialwissenschaftliche Kl. H. 11),* Mainz 1951, pp. 903-88. F. Pfister, 'Studien zur Sagengeographie', *Symbolae Osloenses* XXXV, 1959, pp. 9-10, n. 5 suggests a possible connection with the tradition of the 'Scythian' philosopher-traveller Anacharsis. On the sources of the *Cosmographia* see K. Hillkowitz, *Zur Kosmographie des Aethicus,* Diss. Bonn 1934.

88. See, especially, ed. Wuttke, chapters 33-41, pp. 19-29.

89. [Cary, 1956], pp. 25-27. On Thomas of Kent's use of Aethicus see J. Weynand, *op. cit.* above n. 78, pp. 62-67.

90. Edition: E. Iliff Robson, *Loeb Classical Library,* 1929-33.

91. On this picture see P. Buber and H. Gerstinger, *Beschreibendes Verzeichnis der illuminierten Handschriften in Oesterreich,* Neue Folge, IV. 2, Leipzig 1938, pp. 138-39, No. 102.

92. On the name Bucephalas and its meaning see A. R. Anderson, 'Bucephalas and his legend', *American Journal of Philology* LI, 1930, pp. 1-21. For texts see also L. Sternbach in *Wiener Studien* XVI, 1894, pp. 8-37.

93. K. Weitzmann, *Illustrations in Roll and Codex,* Princeton 1947, figs. 133 and 134.

94. F. Macler, *L'Enluminure arménienne profane,* Paris 1928, pls. V, fig. 27, VI, fig. 32 and *passim.*

95. *Aleksandria.* Obshchestvo liubitelei drevnei pisy-mennosti. St. Petersburg (Leningrad) No. 66, 1880 and No. 87, 1887, *passim.* First manuscript.

96. For the history of these Latin versions see D. J. A. Ross, 'A Corvinus manuscript recovered', *Scriptorium* XI, 1957, pp. 104-6.

97. Vergerio's version occurs in Paris, B.Nat.nouv.a-c.lat.1302, made for Pope Nicolas V. Facio's is found in the Vatican, Urbin.lat. 415; Naples, Nazionale V.G.1 and in Vat.lat. 5268. The last is an important manuscript made for Matthias Corvinus king of Hungary, with a portrait of Corvinus as Alexander on the title-page. Ross, *ibid.,* pp. 106-8 and pls. 28 and 29.

98. Edition: F. Vogel, Leipzig 1888-1906. The *Loeb Classical Library* edition of C. H. Oldfather and others is incomplete. Books XVI and XVII have now appeared.

99. [Cary, 1956], p. 77.

100. Edition: B. Perrin, *Loeb Classical Library,* 1914-26. The life of Alexander is in Vol. VII, 1919.

101. See A. Luttrell, 'Greek histories translated and composed for Juan Fernandez de Heredia, Master of Rhodes, 1377-1396', *Speculum* XXXV, 1960, pp. 401-7.

102. On the Latin versions of Plutarch's *Lives* see C. Mitchell, *A fifteenth century Italian Plutarch,* London 1961, pp. 7-8. See also V. R. Giustiniani, 'Sulle traduzioni latine delle "Vite" di Plutarco nel

Quattrocento', *Rinascimento* Serie 2, Vol. I, pp. 3-62; especially, for Alexander, pp. 34-35. This contains a valuable check-list of manuscripts and editions with a full bibliography.

103. See V. Zaccaria, 'Sulle opere di Pier Candido Decembrio', *Rinascimento* VII, 1956, pp. 32-38. On both epitomes see G. Resta, *Le Epitomi di Plutarco nel Quattrocento,* Padua 1962. This contains full descriptions of manuscripts and editions with reproductions of historiated capitals from the two illustrated manuscripts of Decembrio's version: Vatican, Barb.lat.112 and Verona, Biblioteca Capitolare CCXXXIX (200).

104. C. Mitchell, *op. cit.,* discusses humanist manuscripts of Plutarch and their decoration, but the manuscript, London, B.M. Additional 22318, with which he is concerned, has no life of Alexander. Fancy portraits of Alexander are found, for example, in B. M. Harley 3485, fol. 367; Vatican, Vat. lat. 1880, fol. 1, and Ottob. lat. 2025, fol. 1; Cesena, Malatestiana, Plut. XV, cod. 1, fol. 1; Florence, Laurenziana, Plut. LXV. 27, fol. 192; Vatican, Urbin. lat. 448, fol. 2. Bologna, Bibl. Universitaria 2220 has, on fol. 1, a fine miniature showing Alexander in a group with the heroes of other lives in the volume, which is reproduced by M. Salmi, *Italian Miniatures,* London 1957, p. 61 and pl. LVI.

105. Vienna, Nationalbibliothek 2856*, dated 1502.

106. A manuscript in Leningrad, State Public Library F.v.IV, 4, is described by A. de Laborde in *Les principaux manuscrits à peintures conservés dans l'ancienne Bibliothèque Impériale de Saint-Petersbourg (Soc. Française de reproduction de manuscrits à peintures,* Vol. II), Paris 1936, pp. 138-39.

107. Another example of the influence of Plutarch in France in the fifteenth century is the biography of Alexander in *Le Triomphe des Neuf Preux.* Below, Appendix I, pp. 109-10.

108. I hope to publish this text shortly.

G. H. V. Bunt (lecture date 1977)

SOURCE: Bunt, G. H. V. "Alexander's Last Days in the Middle English *Kyng Alisaunder.*" In *Alexander the Great in the Middle Ages: Ten Studies on the Last Days of Alexander in Literary and Historical Writing,* edited by L. J. Engels, A. G. Jongkees, W. Noomen, and N. van der Wal, pp. 202-29. Nijmegen, The Netherlands: Alfa Nijmegen, 1978.

[*In the following essay, originally presented as a lecture in 1977, Bunt focuses on the final episodes of* Kyng Alisaunder, *the earliest Alexander romance in English.*]

I Introduction

Despite the ample attention that Alexander's career received from medieval English poets and prose-writers[1], treatments of his last days are relatively scarce. Chaucer, Gower, and Lydgate, who all devote a smaller or larger number of lines to Alexander, do not undertake a full biography; the 15th-century translations of Guillaume de Tignonville's *Dits Moraulx,* of which that by Anthony Woodville, Earl Rivers, is the most famous[2], include a life of Alexander and a collection of his wise sayings, but are brief on his last days. Of the Alexander romances[3] that have come down to us, *Alisaunder,* or *Alexander A,* is merely a fragment which deals only with its hero's youth, while both manuscripts of the 15th-century *Wars of Alexander* have lost their final leaves. *Alexander and Dindimus,* or *Alexander B,* restricts itself to Alexander's debate with the Brahmin king and a few adjacent episodes. The voluminous *Buik of King Alexander* by the 15th-century Scottish poet Sir Gilbert Hay is still unedited, and has been little studied; the Scottish *Buik of Alexander,* which according to its epilogue was composed in 1438, is a lengthy translation of two episodes of the Alexander story in which the king himself plays only a minor part, the French *Fuerre de Gadres* and *Les Voeux du Paon.* The *Prose Life of Alexander* does contain a full account, derived from the *Historia de Preliis I*[3], of Alexander's last days and of his death, but this text has lost a considerable number of leaves containing earlier parts of the narrative. The only complete treatment of Alexander's career in medieval English of which a good modern edition is available, is *Kyng Alisaunder.* From a literary point of view, too, *Kyng Alisaunder* is the most interesting and most successful account of Alexander's career in medieval English. It is on the final episodes of this poem, the earliest Alexander romance in English, that the following study is based.

The Text of Kyng Alisaunder

Kyng Alisaunder (henceforth to be referred to as KA) is an anonymous work, which has reached us in complete form in one manuscript, Laud Misc. 622 in the Bodleian Library, Oxford (B). This manuscript, of the later 14th century, is almost entirely written in a single hand, which is identical with that in two other manuscripts[4]. Ms. B contains mainly pieces of a religious and didactic character[5], and MEHL 1967, 189 may well be right in suggesting that KA was included here because of its instructive value[6]. KA is given here in a reasonably good text. According to SAMUELS 1963, 87, B and its two sister manuscripts, together with a number of other manuscripts, among which two hands of the Auchinleck Manuscript (for which see below), are written in a kind of London English which he terms 'Type II'.

Another, much inferior, text of KA is included in Lincoln's Inn Ms. 150 (L). Here a long stretch of text corresponding to B 4763-5979 has been omitted, no doubt, as MEHL 1967, 190 points out, as the result of a deliberate editorial decision; there is no noticeable break in the text, and the prologue to the second part of the story, after the final defeat and the murder of Darius, is immediately followed by the narrative of the events leading up to Alexander's expedition against Gog and Magog, an episode so well-known that our supposed L redactor must have felt his Alexander poem would be incomplete without it. The sections which L omits are the list of authorities for the *mirabilia,* the episodes dealing with Alexander's experiences in India, his first encounter with Porus, and the description of India and its marvels. MEHL supposes that the omission was made as a concession to a public which prized entertainment more than learned information about exotic lands and peoples; but it remains strange to see a redactor reject precisely those elements of the Alexander material which many other readers counted among its chief attractions. The contents of L, in contrast to B, are of a predominantly secular character, although it also includes an A-text of *Piers Plowman.* Ms. L can be dated c. 1400, and was probably written in the West of England.

Fragments of KA, including the episodes dealing with Alexander's last days, are also found in what remains of the famous Auchinleck Manuscript, officially Ms. Advocates 19.2.1 of the National Library of Scotland (A). This manuscript has suffered a great deal in the course of time; many leaves, including most of KA, are lost, and most of its illustrations have been cut out. A few of the lost leaves have in recent times been rediscovered[7]. The Auchinleck Ms. contains a large number of texts, among which many romances, and was probably written in a London bookshop c. 1340[8]. This date also furnishes a *terminus ante quem* for the composition of KA. KA is written in what BLISS 1951 has analysed as hand 1, which, like B, employs Type II London English.

Two fragments of a printed edition of c. 1525, which include an interpolated adaptation of the *Epistola Alexandri ad Aristotelem,* are preserved in the *Bagford Ballads* in the British Library. They do not contain any material relating to Alexander's last days.

For the story of Alexander's last days as recounted in KA we therefore have the testimony of three manuscripts, B, L, and A. All three manuscripts and the early printed text are reproduced in the excellent edition of KA by G. V. SMITHERS for the Early English Text Society (SMITHERS 1952, 1957, EETS OS 227, 237).

There is not sufficient evidence for a precise date of the composition of KA. Since it is in the Auchinleck Ms., it must be earlier than c. 1340. The usual date given in the handbooks, late 13th century or early 14th, seems reasonable. The poem was probably composed in London or its immediate neighbourhood.

II The Author

The author of KA cannot be identified. On the grounds of stylistic and linguistic similarities he is often supposed to be also the author of the romances *Arthour and Merlin* and *Richard Coeur de Lion,* both of which also deal with great royal heroes, and of the collection of tales *The Seven Sages of Rome*[9]. All these texts are found in the Auchinleck Ms., and they all seem to have been composed in London round the year 1300, and to appeal to the same kind of audience. Within this group KA is easily the most successful.

For information about the author of KA we must depend on internal evidence, a notoriously slippery source of information on medieval writers. What we can gather from KA is that its author must have been well read in Latin and French literature, and that he was familiar with the stylistic traditions of Latin and Old French epic. He must have had some training in rhetoric, and is acquainted with some of its terminology. He may also have had some knowledge of Middle Dutch, and his vocabulary contains an interesting group of Middle Dutch loanwords as well as an unusually large number of French adoptions. As SMITHERS 1957, 56 puts it, 'KA contains a rich and variegated store of rare, unusual, problematic, or otherwise notable words'. He must have been well educated, and shows himself to be at home in many branches of medieval learning, although his learning has its inevitable limits, and naturally much, but by no means all of it, is directly derived from the poem's Anglo-Norman source.

The Historical Background

KA contains only few allusions to contemporary events or circumstances. In the episodes dealing with Alexander's last days, however, two details occur which are reminiscent of political issues of the early fourteenth century.

The first of these is the *tallage* (7803) which Alexander levies on all classes of society to finance his intended campaign in Africa. In its strictest sense a *tallage* is a tax that a king could levy on his demesne boroughs and manors at his will (KEEN 1973, 9 and OED s.v. *tallage*). King Edward I (1272-1307) made frequent use of this and other royal prerogatives to finance his numerous wars while avoiding the drawbacks of assented taxa-

tion. However, this exploitation of the king's rights was widely resented and called forth much protest, and this method of taxation came to be associated with the abuse of royal power. Edward III (1327-1377) finally relinquished the right of *tallage* in 1340. The term could, however, also be used in a looser sense of almost any tax, and it would be unwise to conclude too much from its use in KA.

In ll. 7810-7818 Alexander, on receiving complaints from the inhabitants of his homeland about their justice Antipater, at their request has him deposed immediately. This recalls the debate that was carried on during the reigns of Edward I (1272-1307) and Edward II (1307-1327) on what means of redress there were for the subject against oppressive acts of the king and his officials (KEEN 1973, 82 ff. and TANNER *et al.* 1932, 678). KA appears to represent Alexander as a good ruler who provides immediate redress against the malpractices of one of his high servants, and recognises the right of his subjects to petition against acts of injustice by corrupt judicial and administrative officials.

The Audience

The prologue to KA offers a few general indications as to what kind of audience the author of KA envisaged for his poem. Taking the general argument of the prologue, that listening to a good story is a noble diversion amidst the troubles and uncertainties of life, from his Anglo-Norman source, the *Roman de toute chevalerie* by Thomas of Kent[10], he adds, among other things, that he wishes to exclude those from the company of listeners

> *þat hadden leuer a ribaudye*
> *þan here of God oiþer Seint Marie,*
> *Oiþer to drynk a copful ale*
> *þan to heren any gode tale*
>
> (21-24)

'. . . who would rather have a ribald story than hear of God or Saint Mary, or drink a cupful of ale rather than hear a good tale'

and stresses, without, however, returning to the point later in the poem, that Alexander acted *by his maistres techyng* 'according to his master's instruction' (32). As Cato says, he points out, *opere mannes lijf is oure shewer* 'another man's life is our teacher' (18). Elsewhere he assures his hearers and readers that

> *þis is nouȝth romaunce of skof,*
> *Ac storye made of maistres wyse*
>
> (668-669)

'This is not an idle tale, but a history composed by wise masters'.

The poem, he announces at the end of the prologue, will deal with Alexander's victories and with the *wondres of worme and beest* 'the wonders of serpent and beast' (37).

The author, therefore, seems to have appealed to an audience who expected not only exciting adventure, but who could also be assumed to be interested in the learned information and the moral uplift that he had to offer.

What social classes did the intended audience of KA belong to? DIEKSTRA, in PAYEN and DIEKSTRA 1975, 102-103, expresses the generally held opinion that most English romances were intended for an audience which ranged from the lower nobility to the prosperous urban bourgeoisie; and in her famous article on the Auchinleck Ms., Laura Hibbard LOOMIS 1942 argues that the manuscript, which contains a text of KA, was compiled for a reading public consisting mainly of well-to-do London guildsmen. It is among the newly prosperous upper middle class in the towns, and among the landed gentry and lower nobility in the country, then, that KA will have found most of its readers. MEHL 1967, 190 has found in KA indications that this audience was accustomed to lighter fare, and he surmises that the remarkable combination of didacticism and a light popular tone that we find in KA was designed to win them over to this more serious and more demanding type of literary entertainment.

III THE GENRE

KA is usually classed among the romances[11]. The medieval English romance is notoriously difficult to define as a genre; it overlaps variously with the epic, the chronicle, the saint's life, the exemplum, the ballad, and even the fabliau. DIEKSTRA lists as characteristics of the romance mode 'the concentration on the adventures of single knights or ladies in distress, the theme of love and the inspiration of women, the code of the gentleman with its core of "gentilesse" and works of mercy, the idealisation of heroic behaviour, and the concomitant black and white characterisation. The characters engage in their adventures from motives of self-realisation, and they fight for love, religion, friendship, and often for what seems to be sheer thirst for adventure' (PAYEN and DIEKSTRA 1975, 77-78). Some of these characteristics are clearly present in KA; but, like many other texts which are generally agreed to be romances, it answers only partly to DIEKSTRA's description. Perhaps the vaguer definition of D. PEARSALL 1977, 113, who describes romances simply as 'secular narratives, with a hero, designed for entertainment', is preferable.

English romances are usually later in date than their French counterparts. They are often derivatives of French originals, and they tend to be rather shorter than their sources and to concentrate on action and incident at the expense of descriptive and reflective matter. They are often less aristocratic and courtly in appeal and atmosphere, and many of them have a strongly moral tone.

A CHARACTERISATION OF KA

As was said above, KA evidently does not exhibit all of the romance characteristics indicated by DIEKSTRA. Indeed, in many respects the poem is more like an epic, or even a historical work, than like a romance of the usual type. It certainly shows more affinity with the type of historical narrative in which the rise and fall of Fortune's wheel occupies a prominent place, and which PICKERING 1967 associates with the name of Boethius. Many features that are characteristic of the romance genre are absent or nearly so in KA. The theme of love, for instance, plays only a subordinate role; the only women who figure at all prominently in the story are Alexander's mother Olympias, whose affair with Neptanabus is certainly not idealised, and queen Candace, who is able to trap the hero into a brief liaison. As a hero, Alexander is *sui generis,* and the only romance hero he could be compared to is the Arthur of the alliterative *Morte Arthure* (cf. MATTHEWS 1960). A closer analysis of the treatment of Alexander and of the story of his last days will be attempted below, and we shall not anticipate it here, but restrict ourselves to outlining a few striking peculiarities of KA.

What strikes us at once is the usually large place that KA, following RTC, gives to the marvellous. The story opens with Alexander's begetting by the magicianking Neptanabus, and in its second part much space is given to an elaborate treatment of the *mirabilia* of India, Ethiopia, and Egypt. In the prologue to what he calls *þe opere gest* 'the second romance'[12] (4762), the author carefully lists his authorities (although in fact he takes over the list from RTC) for the *mirabilia,* lest his audience should think that he has invented them. It is clear that he regards these *mirabilia* not primarily as marvels which might appeal to a taste for the sensational (they seem not to have appealed to the L redactor, who omitted a large part of them), but, as MEHL 1967 has pointed out, as serious geographical information about the distant countries that his hero traversed.

The author is anxious to hold the attention of his audience, and carefully punctuates his narrative with the famous 'head-pieces', with brief moral comments on the story, with short prayers and blessings, with announcements of what exciting events are now about to be recounted, and with exhortations to his audience to listen attentively.

The 'head-pieces', lyrical and/or sententious insets, often monorhymed, which frequently introduce a new section of the narrative[13], constitute an all but unique feature of the style of KA. An important function of the head-pieces seems to be to articulate the narrative and to introduce a new episode; but they also build up a kind of moral frame of reference which guides the audience in their interpretation of the story. Their subjects are diverse; some present little vignettes of courtly life, or occasionally of the life of a merchant, sometimes with an ironic undertone; some give an evocation of the spring season; many are mainly a string of aphorisms, a frequent theme being that of mutability and transience. This is also the theme of the only head-piece in the section of KA that deals with Alexander's last days. The L redactor, who omits a long stretch of text after the second prologue, shows that he understands the structural function of the head-pieces; when he resumes the story, he begins again with the head-piece which introduces the narrative of the events leading up to Alexander's expedition against Gog and Magog.

KA is one of the most successful among the Middle English romances. It may have its obvious weaknesses; too often its metre and rhyme depend on feeble tags, and the structure of the poem is not perfect. Yet KA is an attractive poem through its lively and varied style, its combination of a light popular tone and didactic seriousness, its rapid mode of narration which ensures a vivacious, fast-moving story, and above all through its head-pieces with their lyricism and with the ironical view of life that meets us in some of them.

THE SOURCES

The chief source of KA is the Anglo-Norman *Roman de toute chevalerie* by Thomas of Kent[14], a poem of the last quarter of the 12th century in alexandrines in rhymed *laisses*. The author of KA refers to this source as *þe gest* or *þe Freinsshe*. In addition to this he has drawn on Walter of Châtillon's *Alexandreis*[15], which is referred to as *þe Latyn*. In ll. 3506-3516 he compares the versions of *þe gest* and *þe Latyn* of an incident involving the doctor Philippoun and the baron Permenyoun, and decides the Latin is to be preferred; and in l. 2195 ff. he tells us that he has used the Latin for rhetorical ornament and for the names and deeds of the knights who fought in the first great battle against Darius.

SMITHERS 1957, 16 f. has pointed out a number of details not in RTC or in the *Alexandreis* which may be reminiscences of Julius Valerius' *Res Gestae Alexandri Magni*[16], of the *Epitome* of that work[17], and of the *Fuerre de Gadres*[18]. In the story of Alexander's last days he has discovered a detail which to him implies contact with the *Historia de Preliis* I[2] or I[3][19]. It has not been noticed up to now that a reference to the legend of the foundation of Alexandria in l. 7998 may go back to HdP I[2] or to Petrus Comestor's *Historia Scholastica*[20].

THE RECEPTION OF KA

We have proof of the existence of three manuscripts of KA, and of one early print. Three of these texts probably come from London, where KA was composed; L appears to be of Western provenance. Since many medieval English literary works are preserved in only one manuscript, the existence, however fragmentary, of three manuscript versions indicates that KA enjoyed a certain measure of success; and the existence of the printed fragment suggests that c. 1525 KA was still considered worth printing. Apart from the three mss. and the printed text, nothing is known of any later redactions.

We have already . . . seen that the nature of the manuscript collections in which KA is included offers contradictory evidence as to the qualities which attracted the compilers of the collections; whereas B contains mainly religious and didactic pieces, the contents of L, which omits much of the learned information contained in the *mirabilia* sections, are largely secular in character, and A contains a wide variety of texts. It remains to be added that the L scribe was so much impressed by the figure of Alexander that after he had completed his copy of the poem he gave expression to his regret that he should have died a pagan:

> *Alisaunder, me reowiþ þyn endyng,*
> *þat þou nadest dyȝed in cristenyng!*
>
> (L 6745-6746)

'Alexander, I am sorry for your ending, that you did not die a Christian!'

IV ALEXANDER'S LAST DAYS: A SUMMARY OF THE STORY

The story of Alexander's last days as studied in this collection of essays begins at his arrival in Babylon. In KA this episode follows immediately after the Candace episode: Alexander returns to India, joins his army, and leaves for Babylon the next day. There is, however, no break in the narrative here; no authorial comment, no head-piece, not even a large initial, creates a pause in the recital of events. The head-piece which introduces the account of Alexander's death does not appear until after Antipater's motives for plotting the king's death have been related.

We shall now summarise the narrative of Alexander's last days as KA gives it. For ease of reference the summary is divided into numbered episodes.

1. Alexander marches to Babylon, with Antiochus commanding the vanguard and Tholomeus the rear; he passes through Persia and Assyria. In Babylon he expects to find Darius' treasure.

Babylon and Babel (i.e., the tower) were first 'made' by the giant Nimrod[21], who was prevented by the intervention of God from completing it, 62 languages resulting from his *outrage*. A lady, Amiramys, then humbled Nimrod and won the city and its dependencies with 15 surrounding kingdoms. There is a brief description of Babylon. Alexander intends to make it his capital (7778-7801).

2. Alexander sends messengers to levy a tax (a *tallage*) and raise a large army for a campaign in Africa the next summer (7802-7809).

3. Alexander receives complaints about a justice in his homeland, Antipater. The inhabitants request his removal. Alexander deposes him and summons him to court. The narrator invites his listeners to hear the king's *encoumbrement* 'misfortune' (7810-7819).

4. A head-piece on the transitoriness of earthly prosperity and human glory, with a string of brief *exempla*. *Aventure* (probably Fortune, but here masculine), has turned his steps and raised his mace against the king (7820-7832, with 7833 fourteen lines on one rhyme).

5. Olympias warns Alexander against Antipater (7833-7837).

6. Antipater, realising that the king is *fel and cruel* 'harsh and cruel', decides to forestall him. He mixes poison with a precious wine, named *Eleboryne,* and sends it to the king (7838-7848).

7. At his bidding, Alexander is given a drink of the wine in a gold cup. He drinks *er þan he sholde* 'before he ought to'. He throws the cup from him, realising that he must die. No drink, he says, can ever cause so much harm. He expresses his concern for his mother, his sister, and above all for his barons, who will now be lordless. Let no one drink of it! (7849-7867)

8. Alexander swoons. His barons take him in their arms and bewail his fate. Rich and poor weep bitterly; the clamour can be heard two miles round (7868-7887).

9. The king comes to and comforts his entourage. He wants to be brought to his bed, where he will declare his last will. The barons stand round the bed (7888-7895).

10. Alexander's testament occurs in KA in a unique form for which no parallels have been found elsewhere. The dying Alexander names only nine heirs, one of whom, Sampson of Ennise, is here mentioned for the first time. Space forbids a full discussion of all the problems that the testament offers, and we must restrict

ourselves to a brief summary and to a few points which bear on the structure of the poem and on the author's characterisation of Alexander.

The dying king begins his testament by restoring to the local lords and those *of Tire, of Mede, of Sydoneye* who had served him in his wars their lands and revenues, plus a thousand pounds each by way of compensation for their hardships. Appreciation of faithful service amidst hardship is also shown in Alexander's words to several individual heirs.

The division of lands is as follows:

Perdicas: Greece, Corinth, Macedoyne, Cartage, Tebes. Perdicas is also to look after his king's mother and to avenge indignities offered to him.

Tholomeu (Ptolemaeus): Portyngale and Egypt to the river Jordan.

Antioche: Rome, Romeyn (Romagna), Lumbardye. Antioche is termed *ostage by dome* 'hostage by judicial award'; this may be an echo of I Maccabees 1, 10, where it is said of Antiochus Epiphanes, son of King Antiochus, that he had been a hostage in Rome before he succeeded to the throne. The phrase *by dome* is puzzling, but it may just be a mere tag, put in to supply a rhyme for *Rome*.

Aymes of Archade (the Emenidus de Archadia of the Latin text of the *Fuerre de Gadres*[22]): Calabre, Poyle (Apulia), the land of Labur (the Terra di Lavoro near Naples).

Thiberie: Sullye (Syria), Acres (Acre), Japhes (Jaffa), Jerusalem, Nazareth, Bedlem (Bethlehem) and Galilee.

Mark of Rome: Esclavoyne (Slavonia), Constantyn-noble, Lymochyus and Gryfaine. Gryfaine is named earlier (6270) as the land of one of the 22 nations enclosed with Gog and Magog. Lymochyus remains unidentified; for a suggestion see SMITHERS' note to l. 7933 (1957, 157 f.). Mark of Rome is the leader of the contingent of knights that Alexander received from Rome (1483).

Philoth (Philotas): Caucasus, all the land to Malleus (according to KA 4894-4906 an extremely high mountain in India), all the land from Caspias to Baudas (a city in Porus' kingdom, not, as is usually the case, Baghdad), and the isles of Taproban (Ceylon).

Sampson of Ennise (= Emesa in Syria??): Albyenne (Albania on the Caspian Sea), Armenia *in to þe fenne* 'as far as the marsh, i.e. the Sea of Azov', Occanie (not certainly identified; see SMITHERS' note to l. 7946, 1957, 158), and Newe Alisaunder.

Salome (a kinsman of Darius, who has served Alexander after the Persian king's death) receives his heritage, Perce, Mede, and Babiloyne.

The testament as we have it in KA makes reasonable sense from a geographical point of view, even if we cannot localise Lymochyus, Gryfaine and Occanie. The author apparently had no very clear idea of the situation of Portugal and Carthage. But generally, the territories assigned to the nine heirs are continuous stretches of land. The author's geographical knowledge, we may conclude, was considerable, if not impeccable.

Not only does Alexander's testament in KA name several heirs who are unknown in other versions of the testament, the assignment of the territories also departs from the usual traditions. Perdicas and Tholomeu alone receive those lands which are generally theirs in the Alexander traditions. The others are either not mentioned at all in medieval versions of the testament (Thiberie, Mark of Rome, Sampson of Ennise, Salome) or receive other territories (Antioche, Aymes of Archade, Philoth). It is curious that Antioche, whose name through the Book of Maccabees is so firmly associated with the history of Syria and the Holy Land, should here be given lands in Italy. Perhaps the statement in Maccabees that we cited on p. 212 is responsible for this association with Italy. However that may be, the author of KA clearly departs from the historical or pseudo-historical information about the division of Alexander's dominions that could have been available to him.

We have seen that Sampson, one of the heirs, is here mentioned for the first time. Among the territories divided here, too, there are several whose conquest is not related earlier in KA, such as Portyngale and the unlocalised Lymochyus and Occanie; while Libya and Sicily, which are conquered earlier in the story, are not included in the testament. It seems, therefore, that the testament is only imperfectly integrated into the poem (7896-7959).

11. Having declared his last will, Alexander distributes his entire treasure among his retinue, *kniȝth, sweyn, and knaue.* Immediately after this, *þe lijf he lete of body goo* 'he let life go from the body', and is lamented profusely (7960-7971).

12. The heirs argue about the place where Alexander's body is to be buried. Salome, Sampsoun, Philoth, Perdicas, Aymes and Antioche each claim the body for their own territory. A bird[23] that sits above them tells the barons to abandon their strife; God's will must be done, and Alexander is to be buried in Alexandria in Egypt, the city that he built in the desert, *þoo he destroyed þe vermyne* 'when he destroyed the vermin'[24] (7972-8000).

13. The barons bring the body to Egypt, lay it in fine gold, and bury it in a temple of Apolyne. Tholomeu has the possession of it (8001-8009).

14. After the king's burial each duke goes to his own lands. They fight among themselves for the king's inheritance. That is the way of the world: when the head is fallen, all the limbs are in distress (8010-8021).

V ALEXANDER'S LAST DAYS: THE AUTHOR'S TREATMENT OF ALEXANDER

The aim of this paper is to discover what view of Alexander is conveyed to us in the narrative of his last days in KA. Having presented some essential information about the work under discussion and a summary of the account that it gives of Alexander's last days, we now turn to a more detailed investigation of what the author of KA tells us about his hero; we shall examine how he refers to him, what character traits he attributes to him implicitly or explicitly, what views of Alexander are expressed by the narrator himself or by his characters, what attitudes other characters take up towards Alexander, and what actions, speeches, thoughts and intentions of Alexander are reported.

REFERENCES TO ALEXANDER

The references to Alexander in the final sections of KA do not contain anything very remarkable. KA usually refers to him as *þe kyng* (genitive *þe kynges*) (13 instances) or *Alisaunder/Alisaundre* (3 instances). Twice he is *Alisaunder þe kyng,* and once *Alisaunder þe riche sire* 'the mighty, or magnificent, lord'[25]. Once he is referred to as a *heþen kyng* 'pagan king', but the phrase is used in a general sense: never was a pagan king known to have such a rich burial. After his death, we also find such colourless phrases as *his body* (7977), *þe bodyes* (genitive) (7974), *þat body* (8002), *þe corps* (7995). Extended appositive phrases (other than those quoted above) or relative clauses qualifying Alexander are notably absent in the 244 lines under discussion; only the L scribe states at the end of the poem,

> *þus eyndiþ kyng Alisaunder,*
> *Of whom was so muche sclaunder*
>
> (L 6738-6739)

'Thus ends king Alexander, about whom there was so much rumour'.

ALEXANDER'S ACTIONS, SPEECHES, THOUGHTS, AND INTENTIONS

It is related several times that Alexander does things without delay; after leaving Candace, he loses no time in setting out for Babylon; he promptly deposes Antipater after receiving complaints about him; he immediately asks for a drink of Antipater's wine, and the unsuspecting promptness with which he drinks of it earns him the narrator's sole critical remark (7851). All this leads to the conclusion that Alexander is represented as a man of action with a propensity for rashness. This impression is strengthened by the remarkably active phrase in which his dying is described (episode 11).

We are also told of his eagerness for further conquests (episode 2), and of the measures that he plans to give his dominions an administrative centre and to confirm his kingship by appropriating Darius' treasure (episode 1). He is anxious to suppress injustice, and responds immediately to the complaints of his subjects about Antipater (episode 3).

Throughout the sequence of events from the moment when he drinks the poison to his death, Alexander remains in control of the situation. It is he who directs all events; he immediately realises that he must die, and does not hesitate to make the necessary arrangements for the disposal of his lands and treasures. His composure in the face of death is no doubt meant to indicate true greatness of mind.

Far from being 'absolutely involved with himself', as RICHMOND 1975, 42 suggests, he exhibits a proper concern for his relatives and his barons, and comforts them in their grief; and in his testament he shows his gratitude to his followers for their faithful and devoted service. His last act, the dispersal of his treasure among his retinue, is an instance of the liberality for which Alexander was famous throughout the Middle Ages.

ALEXANDER'S REFERENCES TO OTHER CHARACTERS

Alexander appropriately refers to his murderer as *a traitour fals and qued* 'a wicked and treacherous traitor' (7863); but the narrator does not make it clear whether Alexander knows that Antipater is his murderer.

His references to his followers are affectionate or appreciative; his concern is for his barons *þat Ich miȝth in herte loue* 'whom I might sincerely love' (7861), because they will now be lordless. In the testament, Perdicas and Mark of Rome are *bele amy* 'good friend', and Thiberie is said to be *wiþ flessh hardye* 'of great physical courage'. The lords of Babylon and adjacent regions and Perdicas, Sampson and Salome are also praised for their devoted service. More neutral are the epithets applied to Tholomeu, *my maresshale* 'my marshal', to Antioche, *ostage by dome* (see above . . .), and to his vanquished enemy Porus, *þe kyng*.

Olympias is simply *my moder* or *my moder Olympias*, but a certain wistful affection is apparent in the phrase applied to his sister, *þat so fair was*.

THE ATTITUDES OF OTHER PERSONAGES TOWARDS ALEXANDER

The wicked justice Antipater, when deposed and summoned to court, is mortally afraid. He knows that the king is *fel and cruel* 'harsh and cruel' (7839). It is fear and the desire to forestall the king's measures against him that leads him to plan his murder.

Olympias alone understands that Aventure no longer favours Alexander; she is moved by her love for her son to write to him *as to her owen swete derlyng* (7835) to warn him against Antipater.

The barons and other followers are chiefly reduced to bewailing Alexander's imminent end. The barons weep for

> *his prowesse,*
> *His ȝingþe, and his hardynesse,*
> *His gentrise, and his curteisie*
>
> (7878-7880)

'. . . his prowess, his youth and his valour, his nobility and his courtesy'

emphasising his military and courtly qualities. They are joined by *riche and pouer, lesse and more* 'rich and poor, high and low' (7884). There are further laments after Alexander's death, and all his followers are stricken with grief at the death of their beloved king. After his death, his heirs, for reasons which the narrator does not explain, are keen to bury him each in their own territory.

NARRATORIAL COMMENT

The narrator only infrequently comments on the story in such a way as to guide his audience in their interpretation of it. The most important narratorial intervention is in the head-piece, which reminds us of the transitoriness of joy and prosperity in this world, and states that Aventure has turned against the king. Alexander's end is thus placed in a context of the mutability of all earthly things.

We have already noted that the only point at which the narrator criticises Alexander is when he drinks of the poisoned cup *er þan he sholde* 'before he ought to'. He also briefly comments on the wars between his successors with a generalising remark to the effect that such chaos all too often follows upon the death of a great leader (see above . . .).

The narrator's final remark at the end of KA is a simple *þus ended Alisaunder þe kyng* (8020), which L varies adding a reference to his fame; and the last line contains a blessing. The L scribe adds his regret that Alexander did not die a Christian.

VI ALEXANDER'S LAST DAYS: A COMPARISON WITH THE CHIEF SOURCE

The chief source for KA is the Anglo-Norman *Roman de toute chevalerie* by one Thomas of Kent, of whom nothing is known except his name. Even about his name there was some confusion, until WEYNAND 1911 finally established it as Thomas and not Eustache. Its editor, the late Dr Brian FOSTER, dates it in the last quarter of the twelfth century (1977, 73-76)[26]. FOSTER's edition, which was announced by ROSS 1963, 89, has now appeared (FOSTER 1976-1977), but the second volume, containing Introduction, Notes and Glossary, became available too late for me to make full use of it. Before the publication of FOSTER's edition, the only parts of RTC that were available in print were those in MEYER 1886, who gives the list of rubrics from Ms. D, as well as extracts from Ms. P with variants from Ms. C in an appendix[27]. These extracts include those *laisses* in RTC which correspond to the story of Alexander's last days in KA.

The three manuscripts which preserve RTC in more or less complete form (although C has lost more than half of its leaves) all contain interpolations which are not represented in KA. The relationships between the three manuscripts and the supposed original state of RTC are discussed by SCHNEEGANS 1906, who gives separate treatment to the complex situation in the final section of RTC. The extant mss. of RTC contain two endings; in C the 'second' ending, which is derived from the *Roman d'Alexandre*, Branch IV, follows the 'first', which corresponds to the ending of KA, whereas in D and P the second ending is embedded within the first[28]. D and P lack two *laisses* which C preserves, and which probably furnished the material for KA 7852-7867 and 7961-7967 (episodes 7 and 11).

The most important divergence in KA from the first ending of RTC as contained in C is its inclusion of the Testament in a form unparalleled in other versions of the story. SMITHERS 1957, 18 concludes that either the author of KA inserted a form of the testament on his own initiative, or he may have found one of this type in the early, uninterpolated form of RTC that he must have used as his source; in that case the extant mss. of RTC must have replaced it by the more orthodox form in which the *Roman d'Alexandre* gives it. Since the Julius Valerius *Epitome,* which WEYNAND 1911 has identified as the chief source of RTC, does not contain a testament of Alexander either, the first alternative has much to commend it. In our study of the relation of KA to RTC we shall assume that the author of KA based his account of Alexander's last days on the 'first ending' of RTC as we have it in Ms. C (in FOSTER's edition, *laisse* 528, ll. 7828-7831, and *laisses* 529-536, 539-543, 545-546).

While conforming to the main outlines of the story as he found it in RTC, the author of KA treats the material with considerable freedom. Like many English adapters of French source material, he reduces the descriptive element, and he presents a lively, fast-moving narrative

punctuated by the head-piece and the brief narratorial comments. The reduction of the descriptive element is perhaps most striking in KA's handling of episode 7, where Alexander drinks the poison; RTC carefully sets the scene, but KA restricts the narrative to bare essentials, so that the action comes to take place in what is virtually a spatial void.

We have already indicated that the head-piece, and the reference to the role of Aventure that it contains, as well as the testament, are independent of RTC. The same is true of nearly all the narratorial comment; only the final *laisse* of RTC, which bewails the inconstancy of mankind and the miseries inflicted upon the poor by the wars among Alexander's heirs, finds a faint echo in the generalising comment in KA on the chaos which results from the death of a great leader (episode 14).

A notable omission in KA is the scene in RTC where messengers from all over the world come to Babylon to placate Alexander with submission and tribute, lest he should do them *damage.*

Many episodes are treated in KA in a manner which differs markedly from that in RTC. Thus the description and history of Babylon, which in RTC follows the outlines provided by Orosius, is transformed into an unorthodox account in which Nimrod[29] is prevented by God from completing the tower, and is later humbled by a lady Amiramys[30], who

> *Aleide his boost and al his prys,*
> *And wan þe cite wiþ al þe honoure,*
> *And fiftene kyng-riches, tut entoure*
>
> (7793-7795)

'. . . humbled his pride and all his renown, and won the city with all its seignories, and 15 kingdoms all round'[31].

Semiramis, on whom see Irene SAMUEL 1944, is usually the wife of Ninus, the grandson of Nimrod, who succeeded her husband, continued his policy of conquest, and completed the building of Babylon. Here she seems to conquer the city from Nimrod.

KA also introduces Antipater into the story differently from RTC. In RTC Olympias' warning induces Alexander to depose him and summon him to court, whereas in KA it is the complaints of the *londe-folk* 'inhabitants' that lead to Antipater's removal. This is only one of those cases where Alexander as KA draws him appears to take an interest in wider sections of the population than the narrow aristocratic circle to which his contacts are all but confined in RTC. Thus all present, of whatever rank, join the barons in a lament which is new to KA (episode 8); and when Alexander distributes his treasures (episode 11), the beneficiaries are *kniȝth, sweyn and knaue*; the terms *sweyn* and *knaue* do not seem to have a very precise meaning, but they certainly denote men of low rank. In RTC Alexander here shares out his lands and treasures among his *bons compagnons* and *chers amis,* which phrases probably refer to his inner circle of noble associates. But in KA the *tallage* that in episode 2 Alexander orders for his African campaign is also levied on all classes of society; RTC uses a similar formula for the summoning of the army, mentioning a variety of nobiliary ranks, to which mss. C and P add *les bons soudeers* 'the good soldiers, or mercenaries'.

Alexander's speech in episode 7, when he realises that he has been poisoned, also shows notable differences beside a similarity in general outline. In RTC he says that all who love him may now be sad, above all his mother and other relatives; there will be great sorrow and a strong revenge. In KA he expresses his concern for his mother, his sister, and his now lordless barons; no drink will ever cause so much harm. Alexander here manifests his love and concern for his dependents, whereas in RTC he anticipates their concern and grief for him.

Another scene which shows marked differences of treatment is that where Alexander is brought to his bed (episodes 8 and 9). In RTC the king, having drunk the poison, leaves the palace and with great difficulty reaches his bed, where he summons his relatives, friends and nobles and makes his *devis*. In KA he swoons; his barons take him into their arms and lament his fate, in which they are joined by all others present; Alexander comes to, comforts his retinue, and asks to be brought to his bed, where he will declare his last will. KA's version is more dramatic, and gives more prominence to the affection of the barons for their dying king.

The quarrel about Alexander's burial place (episode 12) is again handled differently in the two poems. In RTC it is peoples who each claim the body for their own territory, but finally decide to draw lots in order to learn the will of the gods, and unite in prayer. A voice then tells them not to quarrel, and to bury the body in the city that Alexander built in Egypt. In KA it is not peoples but six of the individual beneficiaries of the testament that engage in the dispute over the body. They do not resolve the quarrel of their own accord: a bird sits above them and tells them to abandon their strife. It is God's will (in RTC, in the text it is also the will of God, but the rubric which heads this *laisse* tells us that the—pagan—gods ordained the burial of Alexander[32]) that the body be brought to Egypt. Two other unambiguous references to the pagan gods in RTC are omitted in KA. On the other hand, KA adds that Alexander's burial took place in a temple of *Apolyne*. The allusion to the legend of the foundation of Alexandria is also new (see above . . . , and note 24).

VII ALEXANDER'S LAST DAYS: MEDIEVALISMS

We have already emphasised that KA's account of Alexander's last days is told briefly and rapidly, with only a minimum of description. Apart from verse-form and style, the story, as distinct from digressions and narratorial interventions, can hardly be said to be given a strongly medieval flavour. The distinctively medieval element is limited to the use of a number of words which describe medieval social and political realities, to the attribution to Alexander of courtly virtues, and to a thin layer of Christian colouring.

MEDIEVAL SOCIAL AND POLITICAL STRUCTURES

As in RTC, Alexander's generals are usually referred to as *baroun(s),* or sometimes as *duk(es).* In the testament, which is new to KA, Tholomeu is addressed as Alexander's *maresshale* 'marshal, a high court official or military commander'. The term *honoure* 'honour, seignory', used in the Babylon digression for that city's dependencies, and the *rentes* 'revenues' and *londes* 'lands' that are restored to the lords of Babylon and adjacent regions in the testament, seem to reflect a feudal, or post-feudal, structure of society.

Other terms for social classes are found in formulas, as when Alexander levies his tax

> *On kynges, dukes, princes and erles,*
> *On barouns, kniʒttes, sweynes and cherles*
>
> (7804-7805)

when he distributes his treasures among *kniʒth, sweyn and knaue* (7962), or when the narrator remarks that it happens everywhere, *amonge þe lew[ed] and þe lerde* 'among laity and clergy' (8017) that when the head is fallen all the limbs are in distress.

We have already commented (above . . .) on KA's use of the term *tallage* for the tax that Alexander levies for his intended African campaign. RTC uses the same term at this point. This is an additional reason for interpreting the use of this term cautiously. I suspect that we should be reading too much into KA's use of the term here if we assumed that the author or his audience thought of Alexander as a medieval king abusing his prerogative rights. Such a view of Alexander would also be inconsistent with what is implied in the story of his prompt deposition of Antipater at the request of his subjects, the parallels of which with early fourteenth-century history we also noted above . . . . RTC gives a different reason for the deposition of Antipater.

Among the virtues of the dying Alexander that are bewailed by his barons are, besides his military qualities, his *gentrise* 'nobility' and his *curteisie* 'courtesy', words which reflect the courtly ideals of a medieval aristocratic culture.

CHRISTIAN ELEMENTS

Unlike RTC, KA refers to Alexander as a *heþen kyng* 'pagan king' (8006), but nevertheless has him use the name of God in an asseverative formula *so God me assoile* 'so may God absolve me' (7920). More significantly, the bird who tells the quarrelling heirs of Alexander to abandon their strife says that it is God's will that Alexander should be buried in Egypt. God is thus made to show an active interest in Alexander's burial-place, which suggests that somehow the author of KA regarded him as a servant of God; but it must be added that such an idea is alluded to nowhere else in the story of Alexander's last days.

The name of God is also used twice in narratorial blessing formulas, and in the Babylon digression God is said to prevent Nimrod from completing the Tower of Babel. None of these instances corresponds to anything in RTC, which has only one, not unproblematic, mention of God (see above . . . and note 32), and two, or if we include the rubric to *laisse* 542, three, references to the pagan gods, none of which we find in KA. On the other hand, KA adds that the burial took place in a pagan temple; but burial in a place of worship is again, it seems, a medievalism.

There are in our story of Alexander's last days several allusions to the Bible or to legends which embroider biblical stories, such as the references to Nimrod and the Tower of Babel (episode 1) and Absalon (the head-piece). The legend of the foundation of Alexandria, which is alluded to in 1. 7998, is of Christian origin (PFISTER 1914 and 1976). We also recall that in the testament the lines about Antioche may contain an echo of I Maccabees 1, 10, and that Thiberie is given a number of places in the Holy Land. Among the places and countries mentioned elsewhere in the testament, Esclavoyne (Slavonia) was well-known as a country to be traversed on the way to the Holy Land[33]; and several other toponyms, e.g. Constantynnoble, indicate medieval rather than ancient geographical units.

VIII ALEXANDER'S LAST DAYS: CONCLUSIONS

What, then, is the view of Alexander that confronts us in KA's account of his last days? Let us briefly sum up what our analysis of the story and the comparison with its chief source has taught us. Meanwhile, we should bear in mind that the author of KA tells us very little directly of his view of Alexander, so that we shall perforce have to rely to a large extent on what is implied in his treatment of his material.

ALEXANDER'S CHARACTER

Alexander is represented as young and eager for action, and impetuous to the point of rashness, his only quality to receive critical comment from the narrator. He is devoted to his mother, and she to him. He shows true greatness of spirit in the face of imminent death. KA tells us nothing of his appearance.

ALEXANDER AS KING

The only epithet that is applied to Alexander more than once is *kyng*. As king, Alexander shows himself to be eager for further conquest, and he takes the necessary measures for his prospective African campaign, and for the stabilisation of his territory by the choice of a capital and the appropriation of Darius' treasure.

He is keen to suppress injustice, and he responds to the complaints of his subjects by removing Antipater from his position. It is this sense of justice and this responsiveness to the request of the people of his homeland that leads ultimately to his death, not, as in RTC, his readiness to heed the warning of his mother.

Alexander is feared by Antipater, who knows that he is cruel and harsh, but his relations with his barons are affectionate, and they weep for him profusely. All this appears to be as it should be: a king should love his loyal subjects, and they him, but evildoers should be filled with fear. This picture of ideal kingship appears in numerous medieval English romances, and, indeed, in medieval literature generally.

Before he dies, Alexander duly takes care to make proper arrangements for the disposal of his possessions, restoring some of his followers to their former inheritance, and rewarding others with lands and treasure. This again agrees with what good kings do shortly before they die in many other romances, and it also highlights that most famous quality of Alexander, his liberality.

The ephemeral nature of his empire becomes evident when, immediately after his death, his barons fall to quarrelling. It is he who held the empire together, and now that he is dead, all his achievement comes to nothing.

KA contains no instruction for rulers, nothing that resembles a 'mirror for princes'. This should not surprise us, since the poem was not addressed to a royal or noble audience; and, indeed, no English king appears to have taken an active interest in literature in English before Richard II (1377-1399), whose reign stands at the end of the century at the beginning of which KA was composed.

Velma Bourgeois RICHMOND, in her *The Popularity of Middle English Romance*, argues, a little one-sidedly, that the medieval English romances owed their success with their middle-class audience largely to their moral and edifying character; she finds that KA also has a primarily moral purpose, and suggests that the author leads his audience to a moral condemnation of Alexander[34]. Not entirely without justice, she describes him as 'relentless in his obsession with worldly glory'; but she also charges him with an 'absolute involvement with himself', on which we commented above, on p. 215, and she appears to misunderstand KA more seriously when she says that it 'concludes with an expansive lamentation for himself that emphasizes the distribution of his kingdom and wealth among those who survive' (RICHMOND 1975, 35-42)[35]. On the contrary, what fills Alexander with concern is the lot of his relatives and his barons, not his own approaching death. Had the author of KA wished to represent Alexander as a proud, self-centred despot, he would have found ample opportunity to do so; he need only have elaborated the scene in RTC where messengers and envoys from all over the world come to Babylon to offer Alexander submission and tribute; but instead he chose to omit this scene altogether.

ALEXANDER AS KNIGHT

Alexander's military and courtly qualities are bewailed in the first lament of his barons, but, unlike his generosity, they are not shown in action.

ALEXANDER AND NIMROD

Nimrod is said to have begun the building of Babylon and Babel, but to have been unable to complete the work through the intervention of God, 62 languages originating from his *outrage* 'excess, lack of moderation, presumption'; later he was brought low by a lady. Did the author of KA intend us to remember, we wonder, that Genesis 10, 8 describes Nimrod as 'a mighty one on the earth', and did he mean us to see a parallel between Nimrod and Alexander, another mighty one whose megalomaniac efforts were frustrated in Babylon? Is Alexander's career also characterised as *outrage*? Or does Alexander resemble Nimrod in wickedness? The poem gives no answer to these questions; but Alexander certainly is not represented as brought low by a lady as Nimrod was, and Nimrod and Alexander may have no more in common than a brief period of power and a rapid fall.

Similar questions might be asked, with even more reason, apropos of the three men who are named in the head-piece as examples of the transitoriness of earthly glory, Ypomodon, Pallidamas, and Absolon. But we are told nothing at all about them; and while the biblical Absolon might be considered guilty of *outrage,* it is his beauty which is singled out for mention.

ALEXANDER AND AVENTURE

In the head-piece Aventure is said to have turned his steps and raised his mace against the king. It is curious to find Aventure, who is probably to be identified with Fortune as she was conceived since Boethius, treated here as a masculine agent. RTC does not mention Aventure at this point. The reference to Aventure is reminiscent of Jacob van Maerlant's *Alexanders Geesten*[36], where Aventure favours Alexander throughout his career, but finally withdraws her protection. In KA Aventure does not play such an important part; he is mentioned twice before the last head-piece by adversaries of Alexander who attribute his superior strength to Aventure's help (3918, 4505). Olympias is reported to understand that Aventure has turned against her son (7833), but no such insight is attributed to Alexander.

THE AUTHOR'S VIEW OF ALEXANDER

It seems evident that the author's view of Alexander, as it appears to us in his account of the king's last days, is what CARY 1956 describes as the secular conception of Alexander. However, none of the 'subjective judgements upon the forces that brought Alexander to his death' that CARY distinguishes seem to fit KA's account. Neither his vices or the direct intervention of God, nor a conspiracy of Nature and Leviathan, nor Fortune (or Aventure) and her wheel, nor simply Antipater with his poison are made responsible for his end[37]. Aventure is, indeed, referred to as being now the king's enemy, but there is no suggestion that he prompts Antipater to his treasonable act. It is Antipater's poison which causes the king's death. But Antipater is driven to his deed by fear of punishment for his malpractices, and it is Alexander's justice which, by responding to the complaints of his subjects and deposing Antipater, sets the train of events in motion that ultimately leads to his death. It is, therefore, not his vices, but a virtue, that is, at least in part, responsible for his death.

Alexander's ambitions are brought to nothing by his untimely end; and the author's comments in the head-piece are the familiar ones of the limitations of fame and the transitoriness of human achievement. The figures of Nimrod and Absolon add a faint and doubtful suggestion that Alexander overreached himself; but our dominant impression is that of a great conqueror and a good, if pagan, ruler, who, however, proved to be subject to the same inexorable laws of mutability and transience as all other mortals.

POSTSCRIPT (DECEMBER 2008)

This article was originally published in 1978. I feel that its overall argument and its conclusions can still largely stand, but that some of its details need updating.

Sir Gilbert Hay's *Buik of King Alexander the Conqueror* is now available in an edition by John Cartwright for the Scottish Text Society. It contains an elaborate account of Alexander's last days, very different, because it is based on different sources, from that in *Kyng Alisounder.* Lincoln's Inn MS 150, which also contains a text of *Kyng Alisounder,* has recently been the subject of an article by Simon Horobin and Alison Wiggins. They argue that the texts in this manuscript have been consciously revised to enhance their impact to a listening audience. The vocabulary of *Kyng Alisounder* is rich in unusual and often problematic words, for which the scribe tended to substitute more ordinary ones, with the result that compared to the Laud and Auchinleck MSS, the language of the Lincoln's Inn MS often strikes us as flat and commonplace. There are also places where the Lincoln's Inn scribe must have been completely at a loss and reserved to guesswork. On the Auchinleck MS see now chapter 4 in Thorlac Turville-Petre's *England the Nation* and www.nls.uk/auchinleck. This splendid website also contains transcriptions of all the texts of the MS together with the fragments of the Auchinleck text of *Kyng Alisounder* which have been preserved elsewhere, and a facsimile. Recent scholarship tends to emphasize that the MS must have been a costly one, and that only the wealthiest could have afforded such a sumptuous book. A predominantly middle-class audience therefore seems less likely, although the richest merchants do fall within the class of possible owners. Loomis' bookshop theory is no longer generally accepted. For an overview of medieval literature of Alexander the Great written in Britain, see my *Alexander the Great in the Literature of Medieval Britain.* In this book I argue that Cary's quest for "the medieval conception of Alexander", which also informs some of my conclusions in the present paper, was, at least in part, misguided.

REFERENCES:

Bunt, Gerrit H. V. *Alexander the Great in the Literature of Medieval Britain*, Groningen: Egbert Forsten, 1994 (Mediaevalia Groningana, XIV).

Cary, George. *The Medieval Alexander.* Edited by D. J. A. Ross. Cambridge: CUP, 1956, reprinted 1967.

Hay, Sir Gilbert, *The Buik of King Alexander the Conqueror.* Ed. John Cartwright. 2 vols. Edinburgh: 1986-90 (Scottish Text Society, 4th Series, 16, 18).

Horobin, Simon and Alison Wiggins. "Reconsidering Lincoln's Inn MS 150". *Medium Aevum* LXXVII (2008), 30-53.

Turville-Petre, Thorlac. *England the Nation. Language, Literature and National Identity, 1290-1340.* Oxford: Clarendon Press, 1996.

Notes

1. A useful survey of Alexander references in Middle English literature is given by MATTHEWS 1960, esp. pp. 68-80 and 200-201. CARY 1956 and ROSS 1963, with its supplement ROSS 1967, are indispensable guides to medieval Alexander literature generally, and for this purpose supersede MAGOUN 1929. The brief survey in HAMILTON 1927 is not always reliable. Bibliographical references, with short summaries of the story and surveys of the scholarship, are given in the *Manual of the Writings in Middle English,* vol. I (ed. J. B. SEVERS 1967). The *New Cambridge Bibliography* (ed. G. WATSON 1974) also covers the pieces in Old English.

2. The translation by Earl Rivers was printed by Caxton in 1477, one of the first books to be printed in English. A reprint appeared in 1877. For other translations see BÜHLER 1941 and BATESON 1899.

3. Editions: *Alexander A,* ed. W. W. SKEAT 1867; *Alexander and Dindimus,* ed. W. W. SKEAT 1878; both fragments were re-edited by MAGOUN 1929. *The Wars of Alexander,* ed. W. W. SKEAT 1888. Extracts from Sir Gilbert Hay's poem were published by A. HERRMANN 1900; I have not seen this book. The *Buik of Alexander* was edited, together with its French sources, by R. L. G. RITCHIE 1921-1929. *The Prose Life of Alexander,* ed. J. WESTLAKE 1913.

    A fragmentary Middle English version of *Les Voeux du Paon* survives in the *Cassamus-fragment,* ed. K. ROSSKOPF 1911. There is also a short passage on Alexander as one of the Nine Worthies in *The Parliament of the Three Ages,* ed. M. Y. OFFORD 1959.

4. See SMITHERS 1957, 2, SAMUELS 1963, 87. *Kyng Alisaunder* was edited by G. V. SMITHERS 1952-1957.

5. For a full description of the mss., see SMITHERS 1957, 1-8.

6. Velma Bourgeois RICHMOND 1975, 35-42 argues for a primarily moral purpose of the author. See the discussion [above].

7. For a description see SMITHERS 1949, SMITHERS 1957, 4-6, 13, and SMITHERS 1969.

8. A full description of the Auchinleck Ms. and of its contents is given by KÖLBING 1884 and BLISS 1951. The London bookshop theory was evolved by LOOMIS 1942; for further literature see SEVERS 1967, 262 ff.

9. Editions: *Of Arthour and of Merlin,* ed. O. MACRAE-GIBSON 1973; *Richard Coeur de Lion,* ed. K. BRUNNER 1913; *The Seven Sages of Rome* (Southern Version), ed. K. BRUNNER 1933.

10. Henceforth to be referred to as RTC. Ed. FOSTER 1976-1977 (see note 14).

11. A list of publications on the English romances is given in PAYEN and DIEKSTRA 1975, 71-72. For a survey of attempts to define the genre see MEHL 1967 and 1968. Bibliographies are given in the *Manual* (SEVERS 1967) and the *New Cambridge Bibliography* (WATSON 1974). A motif index for the Middle English metrical romances is provided by G. BORDMAN 1963.

12. The term *gest,* which is used more often in KA for the poem itself and for its source, has so vague and general applications that it is of no use as a guide to the author's intentions.

13. A useful discussion of the head-pieces and their functions in KA is given in KITCHEL 1973, 66-80.

14. RTC has reached us in three manuscripts: Paris, Bibliothèque Nationale, Ms. fr. 24364 (P), Durham Cathedral C IV 27 B (D), and Trinity College Cambridge 0.9.4 (C); there are two brief fragments, the Robartes fragment in the Bodleian Library, Oxford, and the recently discovered leaf in Additional Ms. 46701 of the British Library. RTC has been edited by Brian FOSTER 1976-1977 under the title *The Anglo-Norman* Alexander (Le Roman de Toute Chevalerie) *by Thomas of Kent,* in two volumes (I, Text and Variants, 1976; II, Introduction, Notes and Glossary, 1977). I have been able to make full use only of vol. I. For the text I have also used the extracts in MEYER 1886. SCHNEEGANS 1906 deals with the manuscript tradition of RTC, WEYNAND 1911 treats its sources, and HILDENBRAND 1911 discusses its relation to KA. FOSTER 1955 deals with problems of date and authorship; see also the comments by LEGGE 1955 and ROSS 1955[2], and FOSTER's later view in the second volume of his edition, 1977, 73-76.

15. Ed. F. A. W. MÜLDENER 1863. A translation and commentary are given in JOLLY 1968.

16. Ed. KÜBLER 1888

17. Ed. ZACHER 1867

18. Ed. ARMSTRONG and FOULET 1942

19. The *Historia de Preliis I*[2], ed. A. HILKA 1920, and HILKA and BERGMEISTER 1976-1977. *HdP I*[3], ed. K. STEFFENS 1975. A synoptic edition, based on earlier work, of the first half of Leo's translation and the interpolated versions I[1], I[2], and I[3], is given by H.-J. BERGMEISTER 1975.

20. Ed. MIGNE, P.L. 198

21. The name of Nimrod, which is given as *Nebrot* in 1. 5954 (B only), here takes the peculiar, but not unparallelled, forms *Menbrok* (L) and *Membrot* (A); B has the corrupt *Men brou3th,* which SMITHERS emends to *Menbrot.*

22. For this identification, see ROSS 1959. I am grateful to Professor ROSS for drawing my attention to this article, and for saving me from a few errors. Professor ROSS explains the form *Aymes* as due to a development *Emenidus Emelidus Aymes li dus li dus Aymes* &c.

23. RICHMOND 1975, 41 misinterprets *a gentyl bryd* as 'a gentle human being'; the phrase means 'a noble bird'.

24. This is an allusion to the legend of the foundation of Alexandria, as told in an interpolation in Pseudo-Epiphanius' Life of Jeremiah in his *Vitae Prophetarum.* From this source it was taken over by Petrus Comestor in his *Historia Scholastica* (Liber Tobiae III) and in *HdP I*[2] (24, 15-16). Alexander introduced from Argos in the Peloponnesus good snakes to fight the poisonous snakes and crocodiles which infested the site of Alexandria, but these were unable to eradicate them. Then he buried the bones of Jeremiah at various points round the city, thus banishing the evil creatures. For a discussion see PFISTER 1914, reprinted in revised form in PFISTER 1976. This collection also includes the relevant extract from the Greek Pseudo-Epiphanius. KA never refers to this legend elsewhere.

25. *þe kyng* 7814, 7816, 7832, 7839, 7843, 7848, 7849, 7851, 7888, 7972, 8010; *þe kynges* (gen.) 7819, 8014. *Alisaundre* 7800, *Alisaunder* 7834, (gen.) 7882. *Alisaunder þe kyng* 7971, 8020. *Alisaunder þe riche sire* 7782.

26. Earlier writers date RTC variously between the mid-twelfth century and the early thirteenth. FOULET 1969 proposes a date between 1175 and 1185.

27. MEYER (1886 II, 278-280) also prints the Robartes fragment, which contains nothing relevant to our subject.

28. SMITHERS' statement that in P the first ending follows the second is erroneous (SMITHERS 1957, 17).

29. See SMITHERS' note to ll. 7786-7791 (1957, 155), and BARNOUW 1955. BORST 1957-1963 gives a full discussion of the legends connected with the Tower of Babel.

30. I have been unable to find parallels for this form of the name Semiramis. The nearest is Orosius' *Sameramis.* Professor ROSS suggests that an initial capital *S* may have dropped out somewhere in the transmission (personal communication).

31. Irene SAMUEL 1944 takes this to mean that Semiramis outdid Nimrod's work. But KA's statement may also mean that she took Babylon from Nimrod by conquest.

32. RTC 7976 has *le voloir a Dieu* (according to FOSTER 1976, who uses D as his basis, and records no other variants here); MEYER 1886, printing from the often corrupt P, has *le voleir as deus*. The rubric in D (originally a picture caption; see ROSS 1955) reads *Coment les dieux ordinerent la sepulture Alisandre*; the other mss. do not differ materially.

33. Another place that pilgrims to the Holy Land must have been aware of is Sampson's home town of *Ennise,* if, indeed, my tentative identification with Emesa is correct. It is also interesting to note that in Ms. B KA is followed by a short, and, as far as I know, still unedited, text entitled *þese arn þe pylgrimages of þe holy lond.* Elsewhere in this volume, E. R. SMITS mentions several mss. of *HdP I²* which also contain pieces relating to the Holy Land or itineraries for pilgrims (p. 102).

34. A somewhat similar view of KA is expressed in BUCK 1972. My reading of the final sections of the poem agrees to a large extent with that in KITCHEL 1973.

35. See also note 23, which suggests a misunderstanding of a more elementary character.

36. Ed. J. FRANCK 1882. See the contribution by K. R. DE GRAAF in this volume, and VERMEEREN 1972

37. Cf. CARY 1956, 191

Works Cited

ARMSTRONG-FOULET 1942: Armstrong, E.C.&A. Foulet, *The Medieval French Roman d'Alexandre, Volume IV/V: le Roman du Fuerre de Gadres d'Eustache,* =Elliot Monographs, 39= Princeton 1942

BARNOUW 1955: Barnouw, A. J., "*Unorthodox Genesis Stories,*" in: *The Germanic Review* 30 (1955), 14-26

BATESON 1899: Bateson, Mary (ed.), *George Ashby's Poems,* = Early English Text Society, Extra Series, 76 = London 1899

BERGMEISTER 1975: Bergmeister, Hermann-Josef (ed.), *Die Historia de preliis Alexandri Magni (Der lateinische Alexanderroman des Mittelalters) Synoptische Edition der Rezensionen des Leo Archipresbyter und der interpolierten Fassungen J1, J2, J3 (Buch I und II),* = Beiträge zur klassischen Philologie, 65 = Meisenheim am Glan 1975

BLISS 1951: Bliss, A.J., *Notes on the Auchinleck Manuscript,* in: *Speculum* 26 (1951), 652-658

BORDMAN 1963: Bordman, Gerald, *Motif-Index of the English Metrical Romances,* = FF Comunications, 190 = Helsinki: Suomelainen Tiedeakatemia 1963

BORST 1957-1963: Borst, Arno, *Der Turmbau von Babel. Geschichte der Meinungen über Ursprung und Vielfalt der Sprachen und Völker,* Stuttgart 1957-1963

BRUNNER 1913: Brunner, Karl (ed.), *Richard Coeur de Lion,* = Wiener Beiträge zur englischen Philologie, 42 =, Wien 1913

BRUNNER 1933: Brunner, Karl (ed.), *The Seven Sages of Rome (Southern Version),* = Early English Text Society, Original Series, 191 =, London 1913

BUCK 1972: Buck, David Earle, *Studies in Middle English Alexander Literature* (unpublished doctoral dissertation, University of Missouri-Columbia; abstract in *Dissertation Abstracts* (34) 1233 A) (1972)

BÜHLER 1941: Bühler, Curt F. (ed.), *The Dicts and Sayings of the Philosophers. The translations made by Stephen Scrope, William Worcester, and an anonymous translator,* = Early English Text Society, Original Series, 211 =, London 1941

CARY 1956; 1967²: Cary, George, *The Medieval Alexander* edited by D. J. A. Ross, Cambridge 1956; 1967²

FOSTER 1955: Foster, Brian, "*The 'Roman de toute chevalerie': its date and author,*" in: *French Studies* IX (1955), 154-158

FOSTER 1976; 1977: Foster, Brian (ed.), *The Anglo-Norman Alexander (Le Roman de Toute Chevalerie) by Thomas of Kent* with the assistance of Ian Short. I: Texts and Variants, = Anglo-Norman Texts, 29-31 =; II: Introduction, notes and glossary, = Anglo-Norman Texts, 32-33 =, London, Anglo-Norman Text Society, 1976; 1977

FOULET 1969: Foulet, Alfred, La date du *Roman de toute chevalerie,* in: *Mélanges offerts à Rita Lejeune,* 2 vols., Gembloux 1969, 1205-1210

FRANCK 1882: *Alexanders geesten van Jacob van Maerlant.* Opnieuw uitgegeven door J. Franck, Leiden 1882

HAMILTON 1927: Hamilton, George L., *Quelques notes sur l' histoire de la légende d'Alexandre le Grand en Angleterre au moyen âge,* in: Mélanges de philologie et d'histoire offerts à M. Antoine Thomas, Paris 1927, 195-202

HERRMANN 1900: Herrmann, A. (ed.), *The Forraye of Gadderis, The Vowis, Extracts from Sir Gilbert Hay's Buik of King Alexander the Conqueror,* in: Wissenschaftliche Beilage zum Jahresbericht der II. Städtischen Realschule zu Berlin, Berlin 1900

HILDENBRAND 1911: Hildenbrand, T., *Die altfranzö-sische Alexanderdichtung 'Le roman de toute chevalerie' des Thomas von Kent und die mittelenglische Romanze 'Kyng Alisaunder' in ihrem Verhältnis zu einander,* Bonn 1911

HILKA 1920: Hilka, Alfons (ed.), *Der altfranzösische Prosa-Alexanderroman nach der Berliner Bilderhand-schrift nebst dem lateinischen Original der Historia de preliis (Rezension J²) herausgegeben von—.* Festschrift für Carl Appel zum 17. Mai 1917, Halle 1920

HILKA-BERGMEISTER 1976: *Historia Alexandri Magni (Historia de Preliis) Rezension J² (Orosius-Rezension). Herausgegeben von Alfons Hilka. Erster Teil. Zum Druck besorgt durch Hermann-Josef Berg-meister,* = Beiträge zur klassischen Philologie, 79 =, Meisenheim am Glan 1976

KEEN 1973: Keen, M. H., *England in the Later Middle Ages. A Political History,* London 1973

KITCHEL 1973: Kitchel, Luann Marie, *A Critical Study of the Middle English Alexander Romances* (unpublished doctoral dissertation, Michigan State University; abstract in Dissertation Abstracts (34) 3347 A) (1973)

KÖLBING 1884: Kölbing, E., *Vier Romanzen-Handschriften,* Englische Studien VII (1884), 177-201

KÜBLER 1888: Kübler, B. (ed.), *Iuli Valerii Alexandri Polemii Res gestae Alexandri Macedonis,* Leipzig 1888

LEGGE 1955: Legge, M. Dominica, *"Discussions: Thomas of Kent, I,"* French Studies IX (1955), 348-349

LOOMIS 1942: Loomis, Laura Hibbard, *The Auchin-leck Manuscript and a Possible London Bookshop of 1330-1340,* in: Publications of the Modern Language Association of America LVII (1942), 595-627

MACRAE-GIBSON 1973: Macrae-Gibson, O. D. (ed.), *Of Arthour and of Merlin, vol. I: Text,* = Early English Text Society, Original Series, 268 =, London 1973

MAGOUN 1929: Magoun, Francis Peabody, *The Gests of King Alexander of Macedon,* Cambridge Mass., 1929

MATTHEWS 1960: Matthews, William, *The Tragedy of Arthur. A Study of the Alliterative 'Morte Arthure',* Berkeley-Los Angeles 1960

MEHL 1967: Mehl, Dieter, *Die mittelenglischen Ro-manzen des 13. und 14. Jahrhunderts,* = Anglistische Forschungen, 93 =, Heidelberg 1967

MEHL 1968: Mehl, Dieter, *The Middle English Ro-mances of the Thirteenth and Fourteenth Centuries,* London 1968

MEYER 1886; 1970 Meyer, Paul, *Alexandre le Grand dans la littérature française du moyen âge, 2 tomes,* Paris 1886 (repr. 1970)

MIGNE P. L. 198, PETRUS COMESTOR: *Historia Scolastica Petri Manducatoris,* ed. J. P. Migne, = Patro-logiae Cursus Completus; Series Latina, 198 =, Paris 1864

MÜLDENER 1863: Müldener, F. A. W. (ed.), *Gualteri ab Insulis Alexandreis,* Leipzig 1863

OFFORD 1959: Offord, M.Y. (ed.), *The Parlement of the Thre Ages,* = Early English Text Society, Original Series, 246 =, London 1959

PAYEN-DIEKSTRA 1975: Payen, J. Ch. & F. N. M. Diekstra et collaborateurs, *Le Roman,* = Typologie des sources du moyen âge occidental, 12 =, Turnhout 1975

PFISTER 1914: Pfister, Friedrich, *Eine jüdische Gründ-ungsgeschichte Alexandrias, mit einem Anhang, über Alexanders Besuch in Jerusalem,* in: Sitzungsberichte der Heidelberger Akademie der Wissenschaften, Phil.-Hist. Klasse V (1914), 20-22; reprinted in revised form: *Eine Gründungsgeschichte Alexandrias und Alexanders Besuch in Jerusalem,* in: PFISTER 1976

PFISTER 1976: Pfister, Friedrich, *Kleine Schriften zum Alexanderroman,* = Beiträge zur klassischen Philologie, 61 =, Meisenheim am Glan 1976

RICHMOND 1975: Richmond, Velma Bourgeois, *The Popularity of Middle English Romance,* Bowling Green, Ohio 1975

RITCHIE 1921-1929: Ritchie, R. L. G. (ed.), *The Buik of Alexander,* = Scottish Text Society, new series, 12, 17, 21, 25 =, Edinburgh 1921-1929

ROSS 1955[1]: Ross, David J. A., *Some Unrecorded Mss. of the Historia de preliis,* in: Scriptorium 9 (1955), 149-150

ROSS 1955[2]: Ross, David J. A., *Discussions: Thomas of Kent, II,* in: French Studies IX (1955), 349-351

ROSS 1959: Ross, David J. A., *A New Manuscript of the Latin Fuerre de Gadres and the Text of Roman d'Alexandre, Branch II,* in: Journal of the Warburg and Courtauld Institutes XXII (1959), 211-253

ROSS 1963: Ross, David J. A., *Alexander Historiatus. A Guide to Medieval Illustrated Alexander Literature,* = Warburg Institute Surveys, 1 = London 1963

ROSS 1967: Ross, David J. A., *"Alexander Historiatus. A Supplement,"* in: Journal of the Warburg and Cour-tauld Institutes XXX (1967), 383-388

ROSSKOPF 1911: Rosskopf, K. (ed.), *Editio Princeps des mittelenglischen Cassamus (Alexanders-Fragmentes),* München 1911

SAMUEL 1944: Samuel, Irene, *"Semiramis in the Middle Ages: The History of a Legend,"* in: Mediaeva-lia et Humanistica II (1944), 32-44

SAMUELS 1963: Samuels, M. L., "*Some Applications of Middle English Dialectology,*" in: *English Studies* XLIV (1963), 81-94, reprinted in: Lass, Roger (ed.), *Approaches to English Historical Linguistics. An Anthology,* New York 1969

SCHNEEGANS 1906: Schneegans, Heinrich, "*Die handschriftliche Gestaltung des Alexander-Romans von Eustache von Kent,*" in: *Zeitschrift für französische Sparache und Literatur* XXX (1906), 240-263

SEVERS 1967: Severs, J. Burke (ed.), *A Manual of the Writings in Middle English, 1050-1500, I, Romances,* New Haven, Conn., 1967

SKEAT 1867: Skeat, Walter (ed.), *The Romance of William of Palerne . . . to which is added a fragment of the alliterative romance of Alisaunder,* = Early English Text Society, Extra Series, 1 =, London 1867

SKEAT 1878: Skeat, Walter (ed.), *Alexander and Dindimus,* = Early English Text Society, Extra Series, 31 =, London 1878

SMITHERS 1949: Smithers, G. V., "*Two Newly Discovered Fragments from the Auchinleck Ms.,*" in: *Medium Aevum* 18 (1949), 1-11

SMITHERS 1952-1957: Smithers, G. V. (ed.), *Kyng Alisaunder,* = Early English Text Society, Original Series, 227 and 237 =, London 1952-1957

SMITHERS 1969: Smithers, G. V., *Another Fragment of the Auchinleck Ms.,* in: Pearsall, D. A. and R. A. Waldron (edd.), *Medieval Literature and Civilization: Studies in Memory of G. N. Garmonsway,* London 1969

STEFFENS 1975: Steffens, Karl (ed.), *Die Historia de preliis Alexandri Magni Rezension J³,* = Beiträge zur klassischen Philologie, 73 =, Meisenheim am Glan 1975

TANNER-PREVITÉ-ORTON BROOKE 1932: Tanner, J. R., C. W. Previté-Orton & Z. N. Brooke, *Cambridge Medieval History, VII,* Cambridge 1932

VERMEEREN 1972-1973: Vermeeren, P. J. H., "*Jacob van Maerlants Alexanders Geesten. Overpeinzingen van een lezer,*" in: *Spiegel der Letteren* 14 (1972-1973), 273-297

WATSON 1974: Watson, George (ed.), *The New Cambridge Bibliography of English Literature,* I: 600-1600, Cambridge 1974

WESTLAKE 1913: Westlake, J. S. (ed.), *The Prose Life of Alexander from the Thornton Ms.,* = Early English Text Society, Original Series, 143 =, London 1913

WEYNAND 1911: Weynand, Johanna, *Der Roman de toute chevalerie des Thomas von Kent in seinem Verhältnis zu seinen Quellen,* Bonn 1911

ZACHER 1867: Zacher, J. (ed.), *Iulii Valerii Epitome,* Halle 1867

Gerritt H. V. Bunt (essay date 1994)

SOURCE: Bunt, Gerritt H. V. "*Le roman de toute chevalerie* and *Kyng Alisaunder.*" In *Alexander the Great in the Literature of Medieval Britain,* pp. 19-26. Groningen, The Netherlands: Egbert Forsten, 1994.

[*In the following essay, Bunt presents overviews of* Le roman de toute chevalerie *and* Kyng Alisaunder.]

After the Norman Conquest, a demand for literature pertaining to Alexander continued to exist in the British Isles. HAMILTON 1927b refers to a number of manuscripts of English origin containing Alexander material in Latin which date from the eleventh to the fifteenth centuries. No Alexander texts in English, however, have come down to us from the centuries between the Conquest and approximately the year 1300. During this period French was the dominant literary language in England, and English texts are relatively few in number.

It should, therefore, cause us no surprise to find that the earliest surviving treatment of the life of Alexander which was written in England after the Conquest is in that insular variety of French which is usually known as Anglo-Norman. *Le roman de toute chevalerie,* as the poem is entitled in the colophons at the end of the text in two of its manuscripts, was written between 1170 and 1200 by a certain Thomas of Kent, who cannot be further identified. There is some confusion in the manuscripts and in the scholarly literature between this Thomas and an equally shadowy Eustache; the Eustache the manuscripts mention is most probably the author of the original *Fuerre de Gadres,* which was interpolated, in the form in which it was also incorporated into the *Roman d'Alexandre,* into Thomas' text. Like the continental *Roman d'Alexandre* as it was revised by Alexandre de Paris, *Le roman de toute chevalerie* is composed in rhymed *laisses* of varying length, consisting of twelve-syllable lines which took their name of alexandrines from their use in the *Roman d'Alexandre.*

The textual tradition of Thomas of Kent's poem is complex. It has come down to us in three manuscripts, in all of which it stands alone. Two of the manuscripts, Durham Cathedral MS C.IV.27B and Trinity College Cambridge MS O.9.34, are clearly Anglo-Norman, while the third, Paris, Bibliothèque Nationale f.fr. 24364, appears to be an adaptation for a continental readership. In addition, there are two brief fragments of one leaf only. All manuscripts contain later interpolations from the *Roman d'Alexandre* and from other sources, which are not represented in the poem's Middle English derivative, *Kyng Alisaunder.*

The edition of the *Roman de toute chevalerie* by Foster is based upon the Durham manuscript, but omits the interpolations from the *Roman d'Alexandre,* while retaining some passages which are peculiar to the Durham manuscript and are not paralleled in *Kyng Alisaunder*. Foster identifies the poem's main sources as the Julius Valerius *Epitome* together with the *Epistola*. Thomas has, however, expanded the treatment of the wonders of the Orient that he found in these sources by drawing on such accounts as Solinus' *Collectanea rerum memorabilium* (collection of marvellous things; otherwise known as *Polyhistor* or *De mirabilibus mundi* (on the marvels of the world), and largely derived from Pliny's *Naturalis Historia*) and the *Cosmographia* of a certain Aethicus Ister, translated from Greek into Latin by a 'Hieronymus Presbyter'. Thomas names these and other sources in a passage introducing the marvels of the East in which he is at pains to show that his account is based upon authoritative sources and is not a mere figment of his imagination (ll. 6641-66). Fantastic though it may seem to twentieth-century readers, to medieval writers the geographical and natural-historical lore that they found in such sources as Pliny, Solinus and Aethicus Ister was serious information that they saw no reason to view with scepticism. The *mirabilia* of the East form an important ingredient in many texts, for instance *Mandeville's Travels*—which also alludes to Alexander's campaigns (see [Bunt, Gerritt H. *Alexander the Great in the Literature of Medieval Britain.* Groningen, The Netherlands: Egbert Forsten, 1994] Chapter 10)—, and they were used by Shakespeare's Othello to impress Desdemona and her father (*Othello,* I.iii.140 ff.). Among the other sources that Thomas names are Orosius and 'Trege' (Pompeius Trogus, no doubt as epitomised by Justin). A full study of Thomas' sources is given by WEYNAND 1911.

The Middle English *Kyng Alisaunder*, in rhymed octosyllabic couplets, was probably composed in the early 14th century. It is preserved in three manuscripts; the earliest is the famous Auchinleck Manuscript (Edinburgh, National Library of Scotland, MS Advocates 19.2.1) of c. 1340. This large collection, which mainly consists of romances and religious pieces must have been compiled in London, and it has been argued (LOOMIS 1942) that it is the result of the collaboration of a number of professional scribes in a commercial bookshop. Unfortunately, it has lost a large number of its leaves and even whole quires, and most of the small miniatures with which it was illuminated have been cut out. This circumstance has led to the loss of most of the Auchinleck text of *Kyng Alisaunder*, although parts of it have been rediscovered on leaves which had been used in the bindings of later books. A complete text is given in the later MS Laud Misc. 622 in the Bodleian Library at Oxford, which can be dated to the late 14th century; it was probably also written in London. The contents of MS Laud Misc. 622 are predominantly religious in character, and, as MEHL 1968, 189 suggests, *Kyng Alisaunder* may have been included here because of its instructive value. A very corrupt text is included in MS Lincoln's Inn 150 (c. 1400), which can be localised in Clun in SW Shropshire; unlike the Bodley MS, its contents are chiefly secular, although it also includes an A-text of *Piers Plowman*. The Lincoln's Inn MS omits a large part of the *mirabilia* corresponding to ll. 4763-5979, no doubt as a result of a deliberate editorial decision. There is no noticeable break in the text; the prologue to the second part of the story, after the final defeat of Darius and his death, is immediately followed by the narrative of Alexander's expedition against God and Magog. MEHL 1968 supposes that the omission was made by way of concession to a public which was more interested in vigorous action than in learned information about exotic lands and nations. It remains strange, however, to see a medieval redactor reject precisely those elements of the Alexander story which to others constituted one of its main attractions. On the other hand, we have noted, in the French *Fuerre de Gadres* and *Les Voeux du Paon,* a strand in the medieval Alexander traditions of Western Europe which appears to avoid stories of the marvellous; and although the text of *Kyng Alisaunder* in the Lincoln's Inn MS preserves a considerable miraculous element, the excision of so many *mirabilia* may perhaps be seen as an instance of this tendency. Two printed fragments of *Kyng Alisaunder* are preserved in the so-called *Bagford Ballads* in the British Library (STC 321). Contrary to what we noted in the Lincoln's Inn MS, here the narrative of the marvels of India is expanded by the interpolation of a version of the *Epistola Alexandri ad Aristotelem*; the *Epistola* had already been drawn upon in Thomas of Kent's Anglo-Norman poem which was the main source of *Kyng Alisaunder,* and in this late adaptation of the romance it is thus used twice over. The texts of all three manuscripts and the printed fragments are given in the edition by G. V. Smithers for the Early English Text Society.

Kyng Alisaunder is the earliest surviving Alexander romance in English, and the only one of which we possess a complete text. It is also easily the most attractive full-length treatment of Alexander's career in Middle English. As we noted above, its main source is Thomas of Kent's *Roman de toute chevalerie,* which the anonymous author of *Kyng Alisaunder* refers to as 'þe gest' or 'þe freynsshe'. The interpolations from the *Roman d'Alexandre* and other sources which are found in the extant manuscripts of the Anglo-Norman poem are, however, not represented in *Kyng Alisaunder,* which must therefore go back to an earlier version into which these interpolations had not yet been inserted. Its author appears to have used his source critically, and he must have compared the story as it is told there with that in Walter of Châtillon's *Alexandreis.* In ll. 3506 ff. he discusses the divergent accounts in 'þe gest' and 'þe latyn' of an incident involving the physician Philippoun and the baron Permenyoun. As SMITHERS, in vol. ii of his edition (p. 26), points out, the author must have been worried by the discrepancy of the baron's death in the *Roman* and his later reappearance in the *Alexandreis*. In ll. 2195 ff. he tells us that he has drawn on 'Latyn' for details of the names of knights and their deeds on the battlefield:

> Þis bataile distincted is
> Jn þe Freinsshe, wel jwys.
> Þerefore [J] habbe [hit] to coloure
> Borowed of Latyn a nature,
> Hou hiȝtten þe gentyl kniȝttes,
> Hou hij contened hem in fiȝttes,
> On Alisaunders half and Darries also.
>
> [2195-2200]

(This battle is set apart (?) in the French, quite certainly. Therefore I have, to embellish it, borrowed a way of recounting it (?) from the Latin, what the noble knights were called, how they acquitted themselves in battles, on Alexander's side as well as on Darius's.)

Smithers has also identified details in the poem that may imply that the poet knew a variety of other sources, such as Julius Valerius, both the full text and the *Epitome,* the *Fuerre de Gadres* and the *Historia de Preliis* I² or I³. As we noted in Chapter 1, an allusion at the end of the poem (ll. 7996-7998) to the legend of the foundation of Alexandria in Egypt and the bones of Jeremiah may go back to the I² version of the *Historia de Preliis* or to Peter Comestor's *Historia Scholastica.* For the origins of this legend, see PFISTER 1976, 80-103 (especially 93-95); an extract from the Greek Pseudo-Epiphanius on the life of Jeremiah is printed in PFISTER 1976, 351-352.

On one occasion we may suspect the author of *Kyng Alisaunder* of having misunderstood his source. Thomas of Kent tells us that Nectanebus succeeded in having peace until the time of Philip (63), but is then attacked by thirty kings. In *Kyng Alisaunder,* l. 95, Philip is made the leader of the thirty kings who march against Neptanabus (this is the form of the name that *Kyng Alisaunder,* in common with a number of other sources, uses), whose later seduction of Olympias is partly motivated by a desire to 'ȝelde his iniquite' (132; repay his iniquity), since Philip has destroyed his country (130). On the other hand, *Kyng Alisaunder* presents exceptional versions of several well-known episodes, and here, too, the author's departure from his source may have been inspired by a wish to give a stronger motivation to Neptanabus' actions.

The romance opens with a prologue of forty lines, which is only partly based on the *Roman.* Cato—that is to say, the collection of wise sayings known as *Disticha Catonis*—is quoted to the effect that 'oþere mannes lijf is oure shewer' (l. 18; other men's life is our preceptor). The poet wishes to exclude from his audience those:

> Þat hadden leuer a ribaudye
> Þan here of God oiþer Seint Marie,
> Oiþer to drynk a copful ale
> Þan to heren any gode tale.
>
> (21-24)

(. . . who would rather have a ribald story than hear of God or Saint Mary, or drink a cupful of ale rather than hear a good tale.)

and he invites us to

> heren noble geste
> Of Alisaundre, þe rich[e k]yng,
> þat dude by his mais[t]res teching.
>
> (30-32)

(. . . hear a noble story of Alexander, the powerful king, who acted according to his master's teaching.)

We are also promised 'þe wondres of worme and beest' (37; the marvels of serpent and beast). After Alexander has finally conquered Persia and has been accepted as king, the poet pauses to introduce 'þe oþere partye / Of Alisaunders dedes hardye' (4747-4748; the second part of Alexander's valiant deeds) with a brief summary of what is to follow and the list of sources that he has taken over from his Anglo-Norman source.

The poem thus falls into two main parts. Shorter divisions are equally well marked by the so-called headpieces. These are insets of a lyrical and/or sententious character which punctuate the narrative and usually introduce a new episode. Some evoke the spring season, others present little vignettes of life at court, or occasionally of the life of a merchant, sometimes with an ironic undertone; many are essentially a string of aphorisms, a frequent theme being that of the surprises of life, of transience and mutability. Most of the headpieces occur in the first half of the poem; in the second half, which is largely devoted to the *mirabilia,* they are found at longer intervals. But here, too, they introduce important episodes such as the enclosing of Gog and Magog, the final battle against king Porus of India and the poisoning of Alexander by a trusted servant. Their length varies from two to eleven lines; the last, which stands at the head of the story of Alexander's death, is also the longest. Some head-pieces are monorhymed, with the single rhyme continuing into the resumption of the narrative, so that the head-piece is firmly anchored to the story. This is also the case in the last head-piece, in which the theme of mutability is elaborated. Two obscure Greek heroes and the biblical Absalom are recalled to exemplify the shortness of life and the vulnerability of human existence, although the statement that all three were soon forgotten (7825) is belied by the poem itself. 'Aventure' is said to have suddenly turned against Alexander.

The head-pieces are all but unique to *Kyng Alisaunder*; only in the Arthurian romance *Of Arthour and of Merlin,* which is often believed to be by the same author, do we find anything comparable in Middle English. Smithers (vol. ii, 35 ff.) finds their origins in Old French and Classical Latin epic. There is a useful discussion of the head-pieces in L. M. Kitchel's unfortunately unpublished doctoral dissertation (KITCHEL 1973, 66-80).

Some episodes which occupy an important position in other versions of the Alexander story are absent in *Kyng Alisaunder* and in its Anglo-Norman source. We hear nothing of Alexander's visit to Jerusalem, and the account of his contact with the Brahmans is restricted to a brief passage (5904-5927); there is no exchange of letters and no debate between Alexander and the Brahman king, which have no place in the *Epitome-Epistola* tradition to which *Kyng Alisaunder* belongs.

More space is given to Alexander's inclusion of Gog and Magog and the events which led up to this famous exploit. Immediately after conquering the land of the Brahmans (in most other accounts he leaves them in peace), Alexander receives a 'man ferlich' (5938; an extraordinary man), black as pitch, whose head 'was in his body yshote' (5943; was thrust into his body). This remarkable visitor, no doubt a member of that nation, 'whose heads', as Othello told Desdemona's father, 'do grow beneath their shoulders' (I,iii,141-142), warns the king that unless he subdues the wicked nations in the country of Taracun in the north, between Gog and Magog, his fame will be of no value. After consulting his dukes, barons and knights, Alexander decides to march against them. He assembles a large army, which includes the queen of Sichis with ten thousand maidens who had never been overcome but by Alexander himself (6036-6039) and two Amazon queens with twenty thousand maidens who were 'wiȝth in bataile, / And comelich in bed, saunz faile' (6044-6045; valiant in battle and pleasing in bed, without fail), and sails northwards. However, his campaign has little success and many of his men are eaten by their cannibalistic enemies, whose evil habits receive full emphasis. Then the Meopante, who possess contraptions rather like submarines, provide him with a bitumen with the aid of which he succeeds in blocking the sole passage to the country of the wicked peoples. They will be confined there until Doomsday, when Antichrist will overthrow Alexander's wall and the wicked nations will break out of their confinement and cause much bloodshed. It will be seen that this account differs on a number of points from the Gog and Magog episode in other Alexander stories. For instance, Alexander is able to block the passage to the country of Gog and Magog without the help of God. The nations that he encloses include the Getas, the Turks, dwarves, and a nation of men who are wolves from the navel upwards; all in all, twenty-two nations (the usual number) of people of evil habits and horrible appearance.

Another well-known episode which in some form or other is present in most Alexander romances is that of the hero's involvement with queen Candace. We are told that she and Alexander are secretly in love, although they had never met. For security reasons, however, Alexander avoids her country. She then sends messengers to him declaring her love and offering rich gifts, in response to which Alexander sends her a metal image of himself; in most other versions of the episode, Candace secretly has a portrait of Alexander made by an artist. After he has defeated and killed king Porus, Alexander helps Candace's son Candulek to recover his wife, who had been kidnapped by a hostile king. Masquerading as his general Antygon, Alexander then visits Candace. His favourite trick of disguising himself, which had worked well with Darius and Porus, fails to deceive Candace, who now has him in her power and compels him to become her lover. To the outside world Alexander's pretence of being Antygon is maintained, until another son of Candace's, who is married to a daughter of Porus, discovers Alexander's true identity and insists on avenging his father-in-law's death. Alexander is obliged to leave the queen's court and returns to his army. There is a slight courtly element in the story, but the emphasis is on Alexander falling a victim to a woman's wiles. Candace even recites a conventional catalogue of men who were similarly entrapped by women, thus introducing an antifeminist touch; yet she is by no means bent on his destruction, and actively helps him to escape her son's revenge.

As is to be expected in a romance in the *Epitome* tradition, Alexander's death by poison is recounted quite briefly. After he has drunk from the fatal cup, he realises immediately that he has been poisoned; he is brought to his bed and makes his testament. A testament of Alexander, in which he divides his lands among his followers, is present in many versions of the story, but not in *Le roman de toute chevalerie* as the author of *Kyng Alisaunder* is likely to have known it. The Durham MS of the *Roman* has interpolated Alexander's division of his empire among his twelve peers from the *Roman d'Alexander*; but the testament that we find in *Kyng Alisaunder* is very different in content. Alexander names only nine heirs, some of whom are unknown in other versions of the testament. Most of these heirs receive different territories from those assigned to them in other sources. One heir, Sampson of Ennise, here makes his first appearance in the poem, and among the lands divided here there are several whose conquest is not related earlier in *Kyng Alisaunder*. We must conclude that the testament is not too well integrated into the story.

Kyng Alisaunder is thus not without structural infelicities. We may also consider our poet's account of how Candace came by her portrait of Alexander less satisfactory than the usual version of this scene, which gives a better motivation for Alexander's disguise. We have seen that its author may on occasion have misunderstood his source. Its rhyme and metre, too, show imperfections, frequently depending as they do on feeble tags; yet the poem easily holds the reader's attention through its lively and varied style and its combination of a light tone and didactic seriousness. The manuscript context in which it has come down to us also seems to highlight these two aspects of its treatment of the Alexander legend. The narrative moves rapidly and is attractively punctuated by the head-pieces, which in a general way comment upon the story and emphasise its themes and structure. Alexander emerges as a great hero, immoderate and rash at times, and not impervious to the wiles of women, but a generous and magnanimous leader and ruler. However, he is far from superhuman, but subject to the same inexorable laws of transience and mutability as other mortals; his untimely death brings his ambitions to nothing, and his empire disintegrates as soon as he is dead.

Margaret Bridges (essay date 1996)

SOURCE: Bridges, Margaret. "Empowering the Hero: Alexander as Author in the *Epistola Alexandri ad Aristotelem* and its Medieval English Versions." In *The Problematics of Power: Eastern and Western Representations of Alexander the Great,* edited by M. Bridges and J. Ch. Bürgel, pp. 45-59. Bern, Switzerland: Peter Lang, 1996.

[*In the following essay, Bridges analyzes the* Epistola Alexandri ad Aristotelem *and argues that authorial power is inadequately articulated in it.*]

In medieval England, Alexander's worthiness to function as a romance hero—surely not the least sense in which we are to think of him as one of the nine worthies—is established relatively late.[1] Less empowering forms of literary representation do, however, occur in earlier English writings: I am thinking of the Anglo-Latin, Old English and early Middle English histories, encyclopedic compendiums and cosmographic writings which constitute an early medieval "discourse of the real." One of these works associating the extension of our knowledge of reality with the figure of Alexander is a first-person travel narrative relating the Macedonian's journey through India, that realm on the far eastern periphery of the known world: the Latin *Epistola Alexandri ad Aristotelem* (henceforth *Epistola*), circulating independently of, or appended to, the Epitome of Julius

Valerius's *Res gestae Alexandri Macedonis,* has come down to us in medieval vernacular versions from Ireland, Iceland, Italy, France and England. The two extant English versions belong to two distinct phases of medieval English culture, the Anglo-Saxon version in British Museum Cotton Vitellius A xv being at least four and a half centuries older than the late Middle English version in Worcester Cathedral Library MS. F.172 (fifteenth century).[2] There is evidence that the *Epistola* was known to Anglo-Saxon *literati* at an early date already, together with the Alexander and Dindimus *Collatio* (associated with Alcuin c. 800) and romance material incorporated in the Old English Orosius (c. 900).

Like the career of the historical Alexander, the story of his literary representation in medieval England is marked by a struggle for legitimation that moves from originary uncertainty and doubt to imperialistic self-assertion and bombast. While the Middle English *Letter of Alexander to Aristotle* (henceforth ME *Letter*) appears at a time when the heroic status of Alexander is well established in literary and iconographic representations, and when Latin syntax and vocabulary are providing writers with the structures and resonance which their so-called "aureate diction" seeks to approximate, representations of Alexander in the Anglo-Saxon period get off to an inauspicious start. The Old English version (henceforth OE *Letter*) predates the first explicit formulation (by Leo of Naples) of the principle that Alexander has exemplary value as an "excellent heathen (. . .) who lived before the birth of Christ" and whose conduct is worthy of imitation and emulation.[3] When underscoring the imitation principle, medieval authors tone down the good pagan's "otherness" in favour of his "sameness." Alexander's struggle for literary respectability is, therefore, related to the author's willingness to represent him as a projection of the self—a willingness which is problematical in the texts I shall be discussing.

It would, however, be naive to reduce the rationale for the translation into medieval English of the *Epistola* to the exemplary status of the protagonist and the prestige of the medium involved, for although Kenneth Sisam (84) has attributed to the older of the two works similar "pretensions to high style," Alexander is indubitably a lacklustre figure in Anglo-Saxon England. He is outshone by the Brahman Dindimus, that remote other epitomizing all the strivings of the Christian self, and he is subsumed under that vainglorious rout against whom Orosius directed God's authoritative narrative of history (*adversus paganos*).

In spite of these difficulties, several models of protagonistic power have been associated with the hero of the *Epistola* in attempts to provide the work's translation appeal with a heroic rationale. In this paper I propose to show how inadequately these models account for the articulation of the narrative around the potentially empowering figure of the hero as author. If that potential (for authorial power) is not fully realized in the case of the epistolary Alexander, as I shall be arguing, it may have something to do with the epistolary mode itself, and with the distinctive role of the marvellous in this mode. For the *Epistola* and its vernacular translations belong not to heroic tradition, but to a vast body of eccentric, medieval ethnographic writings that, like all works of imaginative geography and history, dramatize "the distance and difference between what is close to [the author] and what is far away" (Said 55), the self and the other, the familiar and the strange. Their ideological biases, unlike those of the centripetal sermons and universal histories of the period, tend towards the periphery, the knowledge of which is no longer mediated through *auctoritas,* but is represented as being the object of experience, achieved through desire and fear, and always, like the *aporia,* resisting appropriation.

Three different models of protagonistic power have been proposed for the early English epistolary Alexander: the Alfredian hero (modelled on King Alfred of Wessex), the Beowulfian hero (modelled on the titular hero of the Old English poem *Beowulf*) and the virtuous pagan. Sisam advocated the first of these models when he pointed out features unique to the Old English version which he attributed to the translator's overriding interest in the martial aspects of Alexander's Indian career. When water fails in the desert, the ideal leader of the Greeks and Romans thinks first of his army, but the Anglo-Saxon redactor, remarks Sisam, feels "that the general should come first" (86). The episode in which Alexander visits Porus's camp in disguise in order to spy out the enemy's position (a motive not found elsewhere) is not only felt to be confirmation of the translator's military bias, but underscores Sisam's hypothesis that the historical referent and the empowering model for this particular representation of Alexander may well have been the late ninth-century Wessex King during his Viking campaigns; a similar story of King Alfred visiting the Danish camp in disguise with the intention of spying was reported by William of Malmesbury in his *Gesta Regum Anglorum.* Finally, Sisam argues that the truncated ending of the OE *Letter,* which omits several *mirabilia,* and the lack of what he calls "moralizing," are further evidence that Alexander's successful military campaign provides the rationale for this particular translation. This identification of Alexander with Alfred, which was formulated in the interests of philological concern for such issues as date and place of composition, will not, in my opinion, sustain critical enquiry. Although Alexander's territorial conquest of India cannot be accomplished without confronting and

despoiling the Indian king, one might venture beyond the observation that "military prowess plays a relatively minor role in the epistolary narrative" (Kratz xxxi) and pause to reflect on one striking feature of the Indian king that has not yet received critical attention and that problematizes the notion that Alexander derives his protagonistic power from his assimilation to a national leader capable of resisting foreign invasion. I am thinking of the fact that Porus, the monarch of an exotic "other" world, is paradoxically represented as Alexander's double, or other self.

Not only do the *Epistola* and its vernacular translations reduce the preliminary epistolary exchange of abuse between the adversaries in battle (an exchange that figures prominently in the Alexander romances) to a single letter, from Porus to Alexander, but that letter's contents, which provoke laughter and a passing derogatory comment, are not even reported; they are, however, by virtue of the role he assumes in the disguise scene, practically dictated by Alexander himself. The *Epistola* therefore attributes to him the role of "author" and of transmitter of this letter within a letter, whereas the romances, in epic mode, represent the Macedonian general as the mere recipient of the Indian king's insults.[4] Instead of responding to the letter with outrage, the epistolary Alexander can laugh *before* having read it:

> When he pressed me more strongly about his affairs, I told him that I did not know much about Alexander's affairs and seldom saw him, for I was only the cowherd of one of his retainers. When he heard this, he gave me a letter that he had written and asked me to give it to King Alexander, promising me a reward if I gave it to him. I promised to do as he bade me. I left there and returned to my camp, and both before I read the letter and afterwards I was overcome by laughter.

> (Davidson and Campbell 12)

In spite of Alexander's subsequent reference to Porus as a "barbarian king," his role-playing in this episode largely contributes to the fusion of the protagonist and antagonist, author and audience. Moreover, actual combat between Porus and Alexander is evoked at the outset of the OE Letter in one brief phrase ("with remarkable speed we overcame and conquered King Porus," *we þa mid wunderlicre hreðnisse porum þone cyning ofercwomon and oferswyðdon*) relating adversatively to "the things that are worth your remembering" (*ac ic wolde þæt þu þa þing algeate þa ðe weorðe sindon in gemyndum to habbanne*: Rypins 5). More worthy of representation are Porus's army and palace (a simulacrum of Darius's palace in Pseudo-Callisthenes), whose abundance is admired and appropriated in more senses than one. For throughout the rest of the narrative the royal city Fasiacen functions as a place of refuge, a "home" to both Porus and Alexander: movement during the Indian campaign takes one of two forms, either *away* from Fasiacen, towards the remote and ultimately circumambient—as at the outset of the *Epistola*—or *towards* Fasiacen, which implicitly figures the familiar, as when Alexander is enjoined to return there towards the end of the *Epistola*.[5] The Macedonian and the Indian, contrasted in the romance tradition as small and tall, modest and bragging, exemplary and reprehensible, merge into a single subject in the *Epistola,* where nearly all the subsequent adventures are undertaken jointly by both Macedonian and Indian.[6] The latter's alliance with the former is signalled in Old English not only by contrastive collocation of the near-homophones *feond* and *freond* ("fiend" and "friend"), but also by use of the first-person plural pronoun:

> After all the hostility that was between us, it turned out that he became my friend and ally and a friend to all the Greek army.
>
> (Davidson and Campbell 12)

> of þæm feondscipe þe us ær betweonum wæs þær he seoðþan wæs me freond ond eallum greca herige ond min gefera ond gefylcea.
>
> (Rypins 29)

This gratuitous (the Anglo-Saxon writer calls it "unexpected," *unwened*) conversion of their hostility to friendship, uniting the two men in a single consciousness and making Porus's dwelling place into the displaced centre of the narrative, suggests that Porus represents the self, rather than the other, and makes nonsense of the hypothesis that an English King defending his land against an invading adversary might be the empowering model for the epistolary hero Alexander. It is with the Indian King as it is with all representations of the remote in this work: what begins as desire to extend our knowledge of the other ends up by demonstrating the inability of the other to be anything but a variant or extension of the self.

If King Porus in the *Epistola* is less of an other than he is in the romances, it is perhaps also because he partakes of the ambiguity of the good Indian. As Thomas Hahn has shown, the good Indian was a variant of the figure of the virtuous pagan, which enjoyed wide currency in post-Carolingian Europe. Imagining the heathen as virtuous to the point of redeemability amounted to recognizing their natural grasp of familiar Christian truths while acknowledging their remoteness in time (as the *simplices,* living before Christ) or in place (as barbaric peoples, beyond the confines of the civilizing Word). But the otherness and sameness which coexist in the idea of the virtuous Indians whose "exoticism is closely bound up with their virtue and their hope for salvation" (Hahn 233) are, in the epistolary Porus, not so much a function of virtue and hope for salvation—

neither of which is much in evidence—as they are a function of his ability to duplicate features associated with Alexander. The real question therefore must be to what extent this text subsumes Alexander under the figure of the excellent pagan, as do other medieval English authors, like Caxton in his preface to Malory's *Morte Darthur.*

What standards of virtue does the pseudonymous speaker himself invoke that might inform his concept of the virtuous pagan? As a specimen of medieval ethnographical writing, the *Epistola* evokes a number of remote tribes, one of which is explicitly presented as a *gens iustissima omnium gentium.* The virtues of this last tribe encountered by Alexander before his return "home," the Seres (identified in one group of manuscripts as the Chinese),[7] are defined *ex negativo* as abstention from *manslawghter, advowtry* (adultery), *periury* and *gloteny,* and positively as vegetarianism and helpfulness in guiding the visitors back to Porus:

> ffrom thens bi many perels we cam to Ceres, where most Rightwis folke of al maner of people is to be witnessed, wher nother manslawghter, nor advowtry, nor periury, nor gloteny is commytted nor done, as it is saide with brede, water, and herbis only thei bien fed. Whiche vs token with the best felawshippes and with right Iorneys bi the yaatis of Caspie vnto ffasiacen, to the Kyng Porrus ledden.
>
> (143-145)

The negative definition serves both to remind us that behind every evocation of the good pagan lies an implicit contrast with its opposite, the deficient Christian back home, as well as of the fact that cartographically remote tribes often partake of a self-authenticating game of civilizational identification through the definition of themselves as what they are *not*.[8] In the same passage, the positive evocation of the Seres' eating habits and their helpfulness may moreover be said to serve the purpose of alleviating authorial anxiety about the remote creature as "wild man." Psychoanalysis and ethnography concur in attributing fear of cannibalism and of exile (or "severance from home") to the developing individual subject and emergent societies respectively: this dual fear is alleviated in the passage in question by confinement of the Seres' diet to vegetarian food as well as by the amiable conduct which consists in leading Alexander and his army back "home." From this evocation of the idealized Seres alone, it is apparent that Alexander cannot be subsumed under the category of virtuous pagan, by definition an *object* of ethnography, inasmuch as his authorial status forces him to assume the persona of the ethnographic observer, or *subject,* with all its attendant fantasies.

Not just ethnography, but theology also complicates the identification of the epistolary Alexander with the good pagan. Devout monotheism is an essential feature of the western image of the good pagan, but there is hardly a passage in the *Epistola* that represents Alexander as monotheist. On the contrary, several episodes evidence the epistolary author's polytheistic superstition, as when he feels the need to placate with sacrificial offerings Hercules and Liber (the author of the ME *Letter* appears not to have recognized the Roman deity of that name, which he renders as "[free] son") after perforating their effigies to test whether they are of solid gold. Or as when Alexander's curiosity is confirmed with regard to Liber's retributive power to kill those who fail to perform the proper sacrifices before entering the cave consecrated to him. Alexander's repeated impulse to sacrifice, which is checked by the wise Indian priest in the grove of the prophetic trees, is only once replaced by behaviour which is not "monotheistic," although it does show the Macedonian ruler in a more secularized light than he is wont to appear in the *Epistola*. I am thinking of the episode in which Alexander rejects his men's superstitious interpretation of the freakish weather as a manifestation of the anger of the gods, by countering it with superior knowhow: he recommends torn clothes as a protection from fire-spitting clouds. (The fact that a large number of men actually die from exposure to the elements leaves the question of his wisdom wide open.) The author of the ME *Letter* actually has Alexander ordering his men to kindle sacrificial fires with their clothes in a kind of metonymous gesture of propitiation which, together with their prayers, succeeds in appeasing the gods:

> We shamed to say that the wrath of þe goddis vs overpressed, that I a man and hercules wer knowen to passe the steppis. Also I bad the knyghtis to cut their clothis and cast hem in the fuyre. Than a cliere nyght anon contynuauly was graunted to oure praiers.
>
> (135)

Only once does one of the English versions of the *Epistola* allow us to think of Alexander as sensitive to the grand design of a single cosmic intelligence, responsible for the *liber mundi*. This occurs in a passage which elsewhere unequivocally attributes foresight and intelligence to Alexander himself as author:

> On þæm ærrum gewritum þe ic þe sende ic þe cyþde ond getacnode be þære asprungnisse sunnan ond monan and be tungla rynum ond gesetenissum ond be lyfte tacnungum, *þa ðing eall* ne magon elcor beon buton micelre gemynde swa geendebyrded ond forestihtod
>
> (Rypins 4. My emphasis.)

> In the earlier letter which I sent to you, I disclosed to you the eclipse of the sun and moon, and the paths of the stars and their positions and the signs in the heavens. All these things cannot be otherwise than they have been arranged and foreordained by some great intelligence.
>
> (Davidson and Campbell 7)

The attribution of the activities of ordering (*geendebyrdian*) and foreordaining (*forestihtian*) to a divine intelligence, rather than to an authorial one, depends on whether all "these things" refer to the astronomic realities or to their narrative representation. The difference in this respect between the Middle English (closely following the Latin) and Old English versions is striking. This single great intelligence evoked at the outset of the ME *Letter* is that of Alexander himself, who as author of an earlier *Epistola* and of the present one selects his material and arranges it into a narrative sequence:

> The former and first lettris I signified and marked to the of the Sonne and Moone and of þe Eclips (. . .) the whiche nat withoute grete charge and cure ordeigned to the I have sent. And thiese newe histories, now inplied and folden, al the deedis and wrytinges I shall commende.
>
> (117)

With the possible exception of this one equivocal passage in the OE *Letter*, there is no attempt to assign monotheistic beliefs to the epistolary Alexander. In this, the English redactors of the *Epistola* are quite unlike the *Beowulf* poet, who carefully emphasizes the consonance between his Germanic hero's pre-Christian beliefs and behaviour, and the tenets of his own faith. All in all, for reasons that are largely related to Alexander's status as epistolary author, it is more difficult to argue for the good pagan as an empowering model for protagonistic representation in the case of the worthy Macedonian than it would be to argue a similar case for the Geat Beowulf.

The idea that the epistolary Alexander is a Beowulfian hero enjoys wide currency. It is premised on the observation that Alexander, like Beowulf, was "confronted with more than the usual tests of the courage of a man because his fierce conflicts involved not only men but monsters (. . .) who were as deadly as they were unreal. [The OE *Letter*] resembles *Beowulf* because it involves a hero, his travels and his amazing encounters" (Davidson and Campbell 3-4). Moreover, the marvellous—considered to be a distinctive feature of the *Epistola*—has often been singled out as the common denominator of all the works anthologized around 1000 AD by the compiler of MS Cotton Vitellius A xv, which includes *Beowulf*. Although several problems attend the Germanic notion that a folk-hero triumphing over the monstrous or marvellous informs the epistolary Alexander, I shall here limit myself to questions relating to the form and function of the marvellous. I shall moreover have to forgo discussion of other forms assumed by the marvellous in the *Epistola*, such as gold, which is so important in the heroic economy of *Beowulf*, and which would provide interesting material for a comparative study. Like the fabulous creatures of India, gold in the *Epistola* appears in response to protagonistic curiosity about the world, and, like those creatures, gold resists appropriation, even in the legitimate form of spoils. As the object of this study, however, marvellous gold has to give way to the marvellous creatures, since it is they who are most often invoked to confer heroic status on Alexander.

It is customary to think of the role of the marvellous as dependent on generic considerations. Testing of the hero through the marvellous is generally associated with romance or the folktale.[9] Throughout much of the *Epistola* Alexander, through heroic ruse and strength, *sapientia et fortitudo,* defeats strange creatures whose wildness (figuring society's negative definition of itself) poses a considerable threat to the Macedonians, who stand for "civilization." Equally often, however, it is not heroic behaviour which triumphs over the threat to civilization. For every episode in which heroic norms of strength and ruse get the better of the beast (as when storming elephants are dispersed through the grunting of swine and the sound of the trumpet or when a *dentityrannus* of the strength of three hundred Macedonians is killed for a loss of only fifty-two Macedonians) there is one in which Alexander can provide no explanation for his survival, as when the beasts leave of their own volition (when "countless thousands of elephants (. . .) for some reason did not try to harm [the Macedonians]. Otherwise [they] would have been viciously trampled": Kratz 123-124).

In the Anglo-Saxon epic, the poet has emplotted the hero's struggle with monsters in such a way as to suggest that they make Beowulf's fame and fortune. The epistolary Alexander's fame is, however, strangely independent of victory over, or defeat by, the marvellous monsters of India, which are frequently mere objects of *curiositas,* conjured up by the desire to see, know and possess. When that desire is experienced as transgressive, the object is figured as aggressive, and the marvellous creatures attack. Most of Alexander's battles are represented as the consequence of both his desire to pursue an object that resists perception and appropriation and the feeling that that pursuit is fraught with danger, against which he is, of course, fully armed. New departures are frequently rationalized by no more than Alexander's desire to see what lies beyond his view, and are initiated by collocations of verbs of volition (OE *wilnian/willan*; ME *coveit/will*) with verbs of seeing (OE *seon/sceawian*; ME *behold/see*), which also have cognitive status.

If we turn now to the implicit and explicit claims marking the works' attitude towards the marvellous, then we must acknowledge an essential difference between those writings which, like the vast majority of Hellenistic and medieval Alexander narratives, claim to be imaginative literature, and those, like the *Epistola,* which claim to constitute a different kind of discourse, a discourse of the real rather than of the marvellous. The reality claim, which could be inferred from the letter's addressee alone, is made most emphatically in the epistolary preface, in the lines which immediately precede Alexander's narration of his adventures proper. These lines contain a disclaimer with regard to the pseudonymous author's intentions in reporting his mindstretching adventures on the periphery of geographical knowledge: these are not reported for the sake of heroic magnification but in the interests of furthering Aristotle's already considerable knowledge. Through the philosopher's doctrine (*ratio doctrinae*) and prudence (*prudentia*), this will in turn be transmitted to the world at large. All the episodes dramatizing the acquisition of knowledge are presented in the epistolary preface as credible and memorable because personally experienced and because related with regard for veracity:

> aliquid per novarum rerum cognitionem studio et ingenio possit accedere. Quamquam in te consummata prudentia nullumque adiutorium expostulet ratio doctrinae quae a te et tuo saeculo ac futuris temporibus conveniat, tamen, ut mea gesta cognosceres quae diligis en ne quid inusitatum haberes (. . . .) non crediderim cuiquam esse tot prodigia, nisi subiecta meis oculis ipse prius cuncta ponderavissem (. . . .) Sed ego de his quae primum cognovi eloquar daturus operam, ne aut fabulae aut turpi mendacio dignus efficiar.
>
> (Boer 1-2)

> By making you aware of new things perhaps I can add something to your intellect and scholarship. You possess perfect wisdom and have devised a system of science, suitable for your own time and future eras, that needs no help. I want you to understand those accomplishments of mine that you value and not regard them as anything extraordinary (. . . .) I would not have believed anyone that so many monsters existed on earth had I not examined them all first as they lay before my very eyes (. . . .) I will speak about the first things I learned to make sure that I do not seem the sort of man who tells fantastic tales or shameful lies.
>
> (Kratz 107)

Although commentators have been sensitive to this veracity claim, few have taken the cue from recent critical developments and noted its ability to function as a so-called device of "self authentication," a concept referring the process by which all discourse constitutes its own object, becoming, in other words, a metadiscourse.[10] Using more traditional critical concepts, Gunderson does, however, arrive at a similar distinction between the *Epistola* and the Alexander romance, on the grounds of the latter's "implicit claim to be imaginative literature and its propensity for adapting to its narrative the devices and even the plots used in writing tragedy" (25). Subordination of all the characters to Al-

exander and the foregrounding of "the sensational possibilities of the story" are considered further generic
traits. By contrast, the *Epistola* proper, which Gunderson assimilates to a generic category he calls "teratological," is said to make no effort at characterization
through speech during its report of "as many remarkable experiences as possible" (26).

In summary, teratological literature is marked by an approach to the marvellous which does not subordinate its
occurrence to the protagonist's heroic career. Like other
objects of *curiositas,* the marvellous emerges as an
object worthy of knowledge in its own right. In the
form of the strange and wild creatures granted a place
on the borders of the *mappa mundi,* the marvellous is
moreover part of the process of civilizational identification which I have already had occasion to refer to: the
concept of wildness, or barbarism, or monstrosity is appealed to by a civilization that is uncertain as to the
precise quality of its sensed humanity, in order to
designate an area of subhumanity characterized by
everything civilized men hope they are not. This is as
true for the monsters of *Beowulf* as it is true for the
oriental creatures of the *Epistola.* What distinguishes
the two works is not the epistemological status of the
marvellous as object of self-knowledge and self-
definition. It is rather the way in which the central
authoritative consciousness, which somehow represents
the civilization that produces the text (the self),
organizes its relationship to the marvellous, the remote,
the other. In the *Epistola* that central consciousness is a
function of the pseudonymous author of the travelogue,
or first-person narrative of things seen and experienced
on the confines of the known world. As Hayden White
has shown, borrowing linguistic concepts from Benveniste and Genette, no matter how fictitious the signa-
tory of a pseudonymous letter may be, he constitutes
the (first) person who maintains the discourse; so the
Epistola, like any other narrative organized from the
retrospective view of its speaker, presents itself as a
metacode arising between an experience of the world
and the efforts to describe that experience in language.

The epistolary narrative of territorial conquest is, of
course, but one of many forms that a travel story can
take, but all travel narratives necessarily involve sapiential polarization of an outsider, deficient in local
knowledge, and of knowledgeable native guides and
informants who are instrumental in the transference and
transformation of knowledge. This traditional distribution of sapiential roles comes into conflict, however,
with the epistolary organization of the narrative around
the central authoritative consciousness of Alexander.
The *Epistola* is thus fundamentally ambiguous with
regard to the problematics of authorial power, and the
limits of the knowable (signalled by the liminal nature
of the places visited, which are all either peripheries or

periphery symbols) are simultaneously those of the ef-
fable. As a document transmitting and extending
knowledge of the world, this centrifugal narrative uses
Alexander as little more than a formal principle of
organization, linking the objects of observation in
sequential episodes that mimic the *ordo naturalis* of
experience for want of any other, culture-specific
authoritative stance that would govern the literary
representation of events. Morally neutral, and of equivocal cultural allegiance, the figure of Alexander barely
holds together a narrative whose several episodes, like
so many arbitrarily listed *mirabilia,* are susceptible of
being rearranged, added to, or omitted altogether. (Small
wonder that the history of the *Epistola*'s transmission is
marked by so many permutations and combinations of
episodes, as was pointed out by Gunderson.)" Yet the
pseudonymous author has provided his text with the
linguistic markers of a narrative whose sequence is
determined by the retrospective view of the speaker,
recollecting past experience. The articulation of his
discourse is not marked by the kind of discontinuity
that we find in the ethnographic discourse of the *liber
monstrorum* or the *Wonders of the East,* which have
many episodes in common with the *Epistola.* Were we
to compare some of these episodes in detail, we would
see that the principal differences lie in the way the
authors emplot their objects of observation, which are
either presented as having been observed or as simply
observable, in a narrativized spatio-temporal context or
in an arbitrary, interchangeable sequence. These formal
differences in narrative organization reflect varying
degrees of authorial allegiance to the social system,
which, as the metahistorian White has shown (1981
passim), alone provides the diacritical markers for rank-
ing the importance of events, transforming a world of
qualities (where things just "are") into one of agents; a
world in which things just happen to people into one in
which people *do* things. The *Epistola* and its vernacular
versions neither constitute an authoritative discourse of
the real, like the "universal" history, which ranks events
hierarchically from within a perspective that is culture-
specific (and not universal at all), nor does it wholly
belong to that earlier discursive order, of the annal or
chronicle, which is marked by the absence of an
authoritative stance from which the significance of
events and things could be gauged. Rather, the *Epistola*
belongs to one of those alternative discursive forms in
which the organization of the narrative around a culture-
specific authority is problematized. Alexander may be
an author in this work, but he is one whose authority is
undermined by the peculiar discursive nature of his
own text.

Notes

1. *Kyng Alisaunder* (c. 1300), the alliterative *Alexander and Dindimus* (or *Alexander B*) and *Alex-*

ander A (both late fourteenth century), the *Wars of Alexander* and *The Prose Life of Alexander* (both fifteenth century) are the principal English Alexander romances.

2. The only two modern editions of the Middle English *Letter from Alexander to Aristotle,* by Thomas Hahn (1979) and by Vincent di Marco and Leslie Perelman (1978), appeared virtually simultaneously and with no apparent knowledge of one another. Unless otherwise stated, references are to the former edition.

3. Leo's introductory comments on the didactic value of relating "what beneficent works pagans have undertaken out of love for the world from the beginning until the birth of Christ" do not constitute unmitigated praise of the good heathen, inasmuch as these are evoked as creature worshippers who, like the devil, fail to serve the Creator (Kratz 136).

4. Only one group of manuscripts reports the contents of Porus's letter, granting Alexander leave to withdraw rather than face inevitable defeat in view of his "advanced" age; the contrast with Alexander's real age, well below that associated with his office, is attributed by Gunderson to the rhetorical nature of this particular letter, considered to be "a corrupt insertion" (55).

The function fulfilled by these letters is consonant with the epic convention of flyting before combat, even if critics are correct in assuming that the "source" from which most of the letters in the romance are derived is an "epistolary romance" (see Gunderson 28-33).

5. By omitting the adventures Alexander undertook without Porus, after the prophecy of the trees of the sun and moon, the OE *Letter* has underscored Fasiacen's ability to function as home.

6. The two men explore distant regions together until the episode of the prophetic trees, which will individualize Alexander's destiny: preparing to travel to the sacred grove with a reduced escort, Alexander "sent the troops with a few prefects, the entire army, the elephants, King Porus and all the baggage back to the Fasian region" (Kratz 119). The oracle concludes by ordering Alexander to return to the Fasis and to Porus, whose name coincidentally resembles the Greek word for "passage," "access to an other and possibility of return" (see the remarkable chapter on *poros* and *aporia* in the writings of Herodotus, by Hartog 34-60).

7. See Gunderson 74.

8. See White (1972), 5.

9. Beowulf's status as a romance or folktale hero depends largely on the role assigned to the monstrous or marvellous. For a recent survey of criticism on the subject see Niles (3-30), who believes that Beowulf's own marvellous nature undermines his exemplary heroic function.

10. This concept is central to the new historicist Greenblatt in his 1991 study of travel literature in *Marvellous Possessions,* as well as to Hayden White's metahistorical studies of the Wild Man (1972) and of the medieval annals and chronicles (1981).

11. Gunderson 29 *et passim.*

Works Cited

Boer, W. Walther, ed. *Epistola Alexandri ad Aristotelem ad codicum fidem edita et commentario critico instructa.* The Hague, 1953.

Davidson, Donald, and A. P. Campbell. "The Letter of Alexander the Great to Aristotle." *The Humanities Association Bulletin* 23/3 (1972). 3-16.

Di Marco, Vincent, and Leslie Perelman. *The Middle English Letter of Alexander to Aristotle.* Amsterdam, 1978.

Greenblatt, Stephen. *Marvelous Possessions: The Wonder of the New World.* Oxford, 1991.

Gunderson, Lloyd L. *Alexander's Letter to Aristotle about India.* Beiträge zur klassischen Philologie 110. Meisenheim am Glan, 1980.

Hahn, Thomas. "The Indian Tradition in Western Medieval Intellectual History." *Viator* 9 (1978). 213-234.

———. "The Middle English Letter of Alexander to Aristotle: Introduction, Text, Sources, and Commentary." *Medieval Studies* 41 (1979). 106-160.

Hartog, François. *The Mirror of Herodotus: The Representation of The Other in the Writing of History.* Trans. Janet Lloyd. Berkeley, 1988.

Kratz, Dennis M., trans. *The Romances of Alexander.* New York, 1991.

Niles, John D. *Beowulf: The Poem and Its Tradition.* Cambridge, Mass., 1983.

Rypins, Stanley, ed. *Three Old English Prose Texts in MS Cotton Vitellius A xv.* Early English Text Society os. 161. London, 1924.

Said, Edward. *Orientalism.* London, 1978.

Sisam, Kenneth. *Studies in the History of Old English Literature.* Oxford, 1953.

White, Hayden. "Forms of Wildness: The Archeology of an Idea." In E. Dudley and M. Novak, eds. *The Wild Man Within: An Image in Western Thought from the Renaissance to Romanticism.* Pittsburgh, PA, 1972. 3-38.

————. "The Value of Narrativity in the Representation of Reality." In W. J. T. Mitchell, ed. *On Narrative.* Chicago, 1981. 1-23.

Donald Maddox and Sara Sturm-Maddox (essay date 2002)

SOURCE: Maddox, Donald, and Sara Sturm-Maddox. "Introduction: Alexander the Great in the French Middle Ages." In *The Medieval French Alexander,* edited by Donald Maddox and Sara Sturm-Maddox, pp. 1-16. Albany: State University of New York Press, 2002.

[*In the following essay, Maddox and Sturm-Maddox examine how Aristotle is treated in French Alexandrian romances and comment on the Alexander-Aristotle relationship.*]

The figure of Alexander "the Great" is extraordinary on any terms. The global dimensions of that "greatness" are aptly summed up by Laurence Harf-Lancner, a contributor to this volume:

> On June 13 in the year 323 B.C., Alexander died in Babylon at the age of thirty-three. He had conquered a great part of the known world and had, by advancing through India as far as the Ganges basin, pushed back the eastern limits of the universe. His accomplishments were also to give rise to a myth about his own person that after his death would proliferate and endure to our own time.[1]

The awesome magnitude of Alexander the Great thus obtains in two spheres that are in most contexts inextricably interrelated: in ancient history, but also in the expansive mythic strands that proliferate outward from the historical record. The powerful legendary matrix resulting from this blend of history and myth is by no means an ideological monolith, however, for over the *longue durée* it retains a remarkable elasticity, capable of accommodating an astonishing variety of contrastive, and sometimes contradictory, worldviews. As David Williams has observed, Alexander is the only hero whose appeal seems truly multicultural and transhistorical.[2] Indeed, across a vast expanse of space and time, throughout Europe and the Near East and from Alexander's own century through the Middle Ages and beyond, his adventures continued to yield rich veins that generations of writers exploited in a strikingly diverse array of literary and didactic texts. For a schematic overview of the medieval French Alexander texts and their principal antecedents, see the Chronology at the end of this introduction.

Throughout the Middle Ages, Alexander's adventures found prominence in a wide variety of historical and literary settings. The medieval European tradition originates in the third century A.D. with a Greek romance known as the "Pseudo-Callisthenes," which brought together history and legend in a combination that was to have enormous influence. Translated into Latin in the fourth century and abridged in the ninth,[3] it affords the essential elements of the vernacular image of Alexander that emerges shortly after 1100 and thereafter looms large in both Latin and vernacular texts. In influential works like the Latin *Alexandreis* of Gautier de Châtillon (ca. 1170, extant in some 200 manuscripts), depictions of Alexander helped to shape medieval attitudes toward history. He figures among the legendary Nine Worthies in the late medieval canon of heroes—a theme of long duration that was itself introduced in an Alexander romance;[4] Chaucer's Monk proclaims that "The storie of Alisaundre is so commune / That every wight that hath discrecioun / Hath herd somewhat or al of his fortune."[5] By the end of the Middle Ages his importance had by no means diminished; of particular interest in this regard is the popularity of Alexander texts in fifteenth-century Burgundy, where he "plays a key role in the rich political reflections of the theoreticians of power" connected with Philippe le Bon and Charles le Téméraire.[6]

Already in the mid-tenth century, the legend of Alexander was recognized by clerical authors as an apt vehicle for addressing a wide range of contemporary concerns. A telling example of this is examined in this volume by Michel Zink, who explores the ways in which the author of the Prologue to the Latin translation of the Pseudo-Callisthenes sets forth the combats and victories of the great pagan heroes as models for emulation by Christians, but models nonetheless to be transcended through the exercise of Christian virtues.[7] Here a figurative implementation of the legend of Alexander transforms chivalric combat into spiritual *agon,* casting clerics as "officers" and the lay public as "simple soldiers" in a striking metaphor whose repercussions will be evident in numerous texts, including Saint Bernard's *Praise of the New Militia.* The potential of the Macedonian's heroic legend for development in positive or negative didactic commentary was to have a long posterity in secular texts as well, and Zink discusses one early vernacular example of its prominent reappearance, in the prologue to the late-twelfth-century *Conte du Graal* of Chrétien de Troyes in which the poet's patron, Philip of Flanders, is favorably compared to Alexander in terms of the practice of largesse.

Almost half a century ago, the substantial corpus of medieval texts devoted to Alexander was surveyed by George Cary; in 1963, D. J. A. Ross assessed the illustrated Alexander manuscripts.[8] Subsequently, a few sporadic contributions addressed specific features of the legend in medieval contexts.[9] In recent years, a quickening of scholarly interest has produced much new work on the figure of Alexander as represented both in the ancient world and thereafter.[10] The present volume partakes of this renewal. As the first systematic collective study of the medieval French Alexander tradition and its background, it provides an essential complement to comparative study of the larger textual archive in the comprehensive medieval Alexandrian tradition that includes, for example, the Castilian adaptations of the legend[11] and its avatars in medieval Britain, Persia, and elsewhere.[12] And a substantial inquiry devoted exclusively to the medieval French corpus of works dealing with Alexander the Great is fully justified: within the richly variegated plurality of Latin and vernacular texts that comprise the Alexandrian tradition from late antiquity through the later Middle Ages, the corpus of French texts that engage the Macedonian's legend is unique in terms of both its amplitude and its diachronic scope. It involves a substantial number of works that together span nearly the entire period of medieval French literary production, from the early-twelfth century through the late fifteenth—hence a thread whose multiple strands are intricately woven into the fabric of medieval literary history.

This volume is the product of an international initiative, and its contributors include many of the major participants in the recent renewal of scholarly attention to the medieval Alexander. Most of the essays are revised contributions to an international colloquium held at the University of Massachusetts, Amherst. That gathering provided a provocative forum for collaborative rethinking of how the classical legacy was repeatedly renewed and transformed in a corpus of narratives spanning four centuries. The contributions subject the various types of medieval writing exemplified, in this substantial and important group of works, to sensitive textual analyses informed by a variety of methodological perspectives: anthropology, art history, codicology, the history of mentalities, postcolonial theory, and sociology are among the disciplines represented. The topics addressed include the generic interplay between romance and epic conventions; the ideological implications of successive rewritings of ancient history; the composition of a "mirror for the prince" in the accounts of the hero's education and accomplishments; the thirteenth-century *mise en prose* of the heroic story; the fourteenth-century cyclification of the legend's components; the use of a legendary hero as warrant for the historicity of a character in later Arthurian romance, notably the monumental *Roman de Perceforest*; and medieval

beliefs and phantasms concerning the fabulous and exotic Orient. We also see how legend was tendentiously recast in particular episodes, such as Alexander's visit to Jerusalem and his battles against Persians assimilated to Saracens, so as to appropriate the classical hero's engagements as a prefigurat on of the conflicts of the Crusade era.

Within the full context of the medieval French Alexander, the twelfth century stands out as the powerfully formative period. From the beginning to the end of the century, a number of texts in verse develop the basic elements of the legend and add new ones. The earliest of these, dating from near the beginning of the century, is a Franco-Provençal work by Albéric de Pisançon of which only the opening survives, a fragment of 105 octosyllables in fifteen monorhymed *laisses* depicting the hero's *enfances*.[13] Albéric's poem was subsequently adapted in a decasyllabic Poitevin *Roman d'Alexandre,* also portraying only the *enfances* (ca. 1160),[14] followed, during the 1170s, by three dodecasyllabic works unknown in their original states: *Le Roman du Fuerre de Gadres,* an account, attributed to Eustache, of a raid on Gaza (*MFRA IV* and *MFRA V*); an *Alixandre en Orient* by Lambert le Tort of Châteaudun; and an anonymous *Mort Alixandre*. The Poitevin *enfances* and the latter two works were amalgamated into a composite *Roman d'Alixandre*.[15] Late in the century, Alexandre de Paris drew substantially upon these earlier works in order to elaborate a massive dodecasyllabic poem of some 16,000 verses in monorhymed laisses treating the comprehensive biography of the hero in four "branches."[16] The enormous success of this so-called "Vulgate" version is evident in the number of interpolations and continuations by poets, moralists and historians that appear throughout the Middle Ages. It is reflected too in the designation of the French twelve-syllable verse in which it is cast as "alexandrine"—a designation dating from the fifteenth century.[17]

This twelfth-century corpus as synthesized in the monumental achievement of Alexandre de Paris comprises the dense and intricate "core" that has received the lion's share of the textual scholarship devoted to the medieval French Alexander during the twentieth century. Much of this emerged from a single project with multiple editors, *MFRA I-VII* published in the Elliott Monograph Series between 1927 and 1976, an achievement that provides an invaluable frame of reference for study of the entire tradition.[18] Despite the seminal vitality of that editorial project, however, scholarship on the French Alexander material during the twentieth century is relatively modest compared to that devoted to other areas of medieval French narrative.

Why, in view of the impressive size of the medieval French Alexander corpus, did it not command considerably more attention until near the end of the century? One reason may be that the twelfth-century *Alexandre* is a *roman* that embodies many formal and thematic features of Old French epic, such as monorhyming *laisses* and lengthy segments devoted to collective combat.[19] The coexistence of epic and romance elements throughout the poem precludes any uncomplicated identification with a single genre.[20] In recent decades, an intensified scholarly interest in questions relating to medieval genres has disclosed the myriad ways in which the fluidity of *matières* in medieval vernacular writing persistently defies modern textbook notions of generic purity, prompting a new interest in Alexander de Paris's composite poem.

Mindful of this generic lability, Emmanuèle Baumgartner turns her attention to the vast epic canvas of the Gadres episode, which Alexandre de Paris extensively reworks into the second branch of his narrative. Her interest is kindled precisely by the fact that, even though this lengthy episode redolent of Old French epic enjoyed considerable popularity in the Middle Ages, it has generally been overshadowed by modern readings centered on the poem's affinities with romance. Baumgartner shows that, while in terms of its generic properties the episode in many ways compares favorably with the *chansons de geste,* it conveys a didactic and ideological perspective that is fundamentally at odds with an epic worldview. Here we discover many subtle, though powerful, intimations of a cautionary perspective on the unbridled fervor of conquest for its own sake. According to Alexander's rewriting, the exercise of individual and collective prowess to win personal glory and to benefit from the conquerer's legendary largesse ultimately proves vain in the absence of transcendental ideals. To provide an effective vehicle for this lesson, in Baumgartner's view, the extensive recourse to the technical and thematic elements of epic would most likely have maximized the appeal of this episode to a chivalric public.

Thus we see that the values represented by this colossal—and in some respects monstrous—story from the ancient world were to find an accommodation through medieval epic discourse that was procrustean at best. This generic incommensurability partakes of a larger tendency apparent in the medieval reception of the Alexandrian legend, whose inherent ambiguities were sometimes met with ambivalence on the part of medieval authors.[21] At first glance, Alexander's most fundamental traits would seem to be relatively stable, whether he be considered an "epic" or a "romance" hero: a largesse deemed exemplary in texts ranging from epic and troubadour lyric to romance;[22] an indomitable drive to conquer; and an equally insatiable desire for knowledge. From the earliest accounts of his life and adventures, however, the story of this "greatest

of rulers" is rich in ambiguities, some of them profoundly disquieting. First there is the question of his birth: was Alexander the son of the mighty conqueror Philip of Macedonia, and thus his legitimate heir, or was he the son of the Egyptian Pharaoh and magician-astrologer Nectanabus, who seduced Alexander's mother in the guise of Ammon—a divinity with whom Alexander himself often proclaimed his filiation?[23] Or again, were his temperament and his inclinations shaped by that eminent philosopher Aristotle, who served as his tutor and later as his advisor, or were they formed by Nectanabus's pretensions to all-embracing knowledge? Was his largesse a primordial trait of his character, as Aristotle affirms—"Largesse estoit ta mere et tu ieres ses fis: / En doner iert ta gloire, ta joie et tes delis" (br. IV, 51, 1032-33: Largesse was your mother, and you were her son. In giving was your glory, joy, and delight)—or was it the calculated gesture later held up as an example for the Prince by a cynical Machiavelli?[24]

It is of course true that we also find ambiguities in some representations of the two other rulers, Charlemagne and Arthur, whose legends were tributary to major medieval French narrative traditions. In some poems Charles is the object of mild humor, or subject to lapses of temper or judgment, or even, according to one legendary current, guilty of incest; Arthur's fortunes in the hands of medieval authors are also variable, and include moments of weakness, lethargy, and, again, the shadow of incest. But these ambiguities are far less culturally remote than those of a colossal hero who could be portrayed, on the one hand, as representative of the best of the pagan past and a *figura Christi,*[25] and on the other, as at the hands of a twelfth-century clerical writer expanding upon Old Testament implications, as a figure of the Antichrist.[26] Unlike the more "exotic" Macedonian, Charlemagne and Arthur were both readily perceived in proximity to medieval religious and social institutions: in terms of values, Charlemagne is most often depicted as the Christian Emperor who through both piety and conquest represents God and France; Arthur is characteristically portrayed as a monarch whose *regnum,* however problematic politically and socially, was impelled by, and in many ways exemplified, ideals of chivalry, courtliness and social order. Thus the fact that twentieth-century scholarship devoted to medieval French narrative traditions accorded considerably more attention to the Carolingian and Arthurian material than to the Alexandrian legacy may to some degree be attributable to the latter's greater originary remoteness from medieval institutions and values, rendering its reception more difficult to apprehend and interpret.[27] It is worthy of note that that remoteness would finally be mitigated, in the fourteenth-century *Roman de Perceforest,* by making Alexander Arthur's ancestor, a development that Michelle Szkilnik explores in this volume.

Branch III of the Vulgate *Alexandre* offers a particularly interesting example of the difficulties involved in interpreting medieval perceptions of Alexander's story. In an extensive rewriting of the *Alixandre en Orient* of Lambert le Tort, Alexandre de Paris variously illustrates the question of Alexander's relentless curiosity about the universe in terms of his oriental adventures. Here, descriptions of the farthest known reaches of civilization are, as Emmanuèle Baumgartner points out, "designed to awaken, as well as to satisfy, the medieval public's curiosity and in this regard are among the very first instances of literary exoticism in the vernacular."[28] The conqueror and his forces encounter widespread evidence of supernatural influences. Among them are three fountains: one that restores youth, one that revives the dead, and one that confers immortality. This romance, which in the expansive adaptation from Lambert le Tort introduces the theme of the "Fountain of Youth" into vernacular literature, makes of this triad of fountains a special case, a triple adventure considerably amplified with regard to earlier versions, to become "the very symbol of Alexander's quest, and of that obsession with transcending the human condition the Greeks called *hybris* and the French of the twelfth century *outrage*, hence a symbol of Alexander's excess."[29] Or we may consider the introduction, in his Eastward itinerary, of the "bornes Artu" which he has sought to reach, a name suggestively introducing the prestige of Arthur while evoking the pillars of Hercules set in place by that hero to mark the limits beyond which man should not pass.[30] Dante was to render memorably in the *Commedia* the fateful consequences of willfully passing that limit.[31] His Ulysses, whose affinities with Alexander have been observed,[32] embodies that type of hunger for knowledge—that "turpis curiositas"—condemned by Saint Bernard as "the first degree of pride."[33]

Yet despite the Macedonian's ironclad will, the marvelous Orient refuses to yield, and finally closes back upon its own enigmas; soon thereafter, Alexander will learn of his impending death from another marvel, the Trees of the Sun and the Moon.[34] If Chaucer's Monk finds Alexander's insatiable ambition a sign of his greatness, demanding "Who shal me yeven teeris to compleyne / The death of gentillesse and of franchise, / That all the world weelded in his demeyne, / And yet hym thoughte it myghte nat suffise?" (1663-66), two Latin Alexander texts draw different conclusions. The twelfth-century *Iter Alexandri ad Paradisum*, which will appear with some variation in two Old French versions, is a prime example.[35] Reaching a reputed Paradise of Delights at the source of the Ganges, Alexander learns from an aged Jew that his boundless ambition can never be satisfied, whereupon he renounces all forms of greed and ambition.[36] We find a more somber moment in the Latin *Alexandreis* of Gautier de Châtillon, which otherwise

tends to exalt the Macedonian hero: after a triumphant Alexander at last declares himself eager to conquer other worlds, since all the earth is subject to his power, Nature herself conspires with Leviathan to exact vengeance.[37]

It is hardly surprising, then, that even Alexander's splendid education, which had already earned special praise from the earliest of the French authors, Albéric de Pisançon, frequently comes under unfavorable scrutiny. As might be expected, the reservations have less to do with its substance than with the values reflected in its applications by Alexander. Douglas Kelly examines this question in the Vulgate *Alexandre* and the *Roman de Toute Chevalerie*, specifically in terms of the interplay of ideals of *chevalerie* and *clergie* as they inform the motivation and implementation of the Macedonian's conquests. He begins with a lesser-known romance also attributed to Alexandre de Paris, *Athis et Prophilias*, in which the "humanistic" view of *clergie* proves less than ideal for the formation of the knight or nobleman. In both the Vulgate *Alexandre* and Thomas's *Roman*, although *clergie* is indeed vital to the hero's brilliant education as well as to his active life, the intellectual component ultimately facilitates and glorifies the vast agenda of militant conquest. In terms of what motivates Alexander and what he accomplishes, Kelly concludes that in these two late-twelfth-century work; it is *chevalerie*, not *clergie*, that prevails as an ideal.

Catherine Gaullier-Bougassas also considers the question of Alexander's education, with emphasis on the role of Aristotle, in a selection of texts from the twelfth to the fifteenth century.[38] Whereas in numerous didactic texts the complementarity of monarch and philosopher is more consistently praised, these literary works show a greater diversity of attitudes and tend to take more nuanced—and often far less optimistic—positions. At times, Aristotle does serve to project a favorable view of the influence of clerics on rulers, as is initially the case in the Vulgate *Alexandre* in which his functions as Alexander's tutor, and later as his advisor, are crucial. Yet in due course he acquires dubious associations with the magician Nectanabus, while in the final branch his image undergoes "symbolic destruction" when his idolatrous panegyric of the late ruler reveals how extensively his wisdom has been corrupted by the latter's excesses. An ambivalent image of the philosopher also features in the later *Voyage d'Alexandre au Paradis terrestre*, while in the *Lai d'Aristote* Henri d'Andeli subjects him to pitiless ridicule.

In general, then, valorizations of the conqueror's education range between two extremes, the one demonstrating how it enhances the learned king's profile and furthers his achievements, the other condemning his rampant ambition and lack of restraint. Here again, we see the persistence of ambiguity and ambivalence in these medieval literary reconfigurations of ancient traditions. Despite the continued emphasis in French texts on Alexander's acquired learning, these texts also accord considerable attention to his innate gifts—to his *nature* as well as to his *noreture*—as manifested in the inexhaustible curiosity that motivates his explorations but also in the cleverness he displays in his dealings with others. François Suard focuses on this aspect of his character. We see how Alexandre de Paris individualizes and nuances the traditional image of the omnipotent conqueror in his adaptation of two scenes, inspired by classical sources, in which the hero presents himself to an adversary in disguise. The medieval author's rewriting of each of these otherwise quite different scenes introduces the humorous vein of the *gab* found in the early epico-romanesque tradition. His aim in depicting the disguised Alexander as both learned and clever, associating his mastery of ruse and of language with his mastery of prowess, is, Suard suggests, not only literary but didactic, and deliberately enigmatic, so as to heighten the exemplary nature of the scenes by suggesting them to the reader as instructive.

In the social and political spheres too, the portrait is ambiguous. Is Alexander the embodiment of prideful ambition and an agent of destruction, as the Old Testament depicts him[39]—a role that seems to find an echo in Gautier de Châtillon's designation as "that bloody sword of the Fates"?[40] Or is he a civilizing hero whose extraordinary military and intellectual accomplishments are due to Providence? For Dante, his was the closest approximation before the Roman Empire to a universal monarchy (*De Monarchia* II, 8. 8). But was he conquering hero, or conquering oppressor?[41] Fashioned by the courtly French tradition as the embodiment of *courtoisie* and held up by some authors as a model for princes because of his celebrated largesse and learning, Alexander was identified by others as a cautionary figure because of his insatiable hunger for both knowledge and power.

Medieval implementations of his legend also transformed it into a powerful medium for direct expression or symbolic representation of contemporary social and political aspirations and—more commonly—anxieties. Alexandre de Paris, in his prologue, presents Alexander—his "riche estoire"—to those who would "prendre bon essample" with regard not only to prowess but to what to love and to hate, and how to keep one's friends and do harm to one's enemies (br. I, vv. 1-8). In the twelfth-century vernacular romances, subtle semantic changes detectable within a modest, though culturally charged, lexicon inherited from early epic discourse provide valuable indices of social change, as Rupert T. Pickens demonstrates in his examination of how terms relating to *vasselage* and *cortoisie* are variably semanti-

cized as we move from the decasyllabic texts to the Vulgate *Alexandre*. His inquiry discloses a major transition from the epic celebration, typical of the early *chansons de geste,* of *vasselage*—a feudal value centered in male strength and loyalty to the overlord—to a more "courtly" concept in which *vasselage* is subsumed into elegant speech and refined manners, in a form of *courtoisie* strongly identified with women. On the ideological plane, Pickens proposes, we may also discern an attempt to revitalize a conservative ethos.

Evidence of such a tendency is also apparent in William W. Kibler's study of the Vulgate *Alexandre,* which was the first to introduce the legend to the economically volatile Paris region. In Alexandre's poem Kibler identifies striking reflections of the profound institutional changes taking place on the French political horizon. While the text can be categorized as one of the many "mirrors for the prince" written during the medieval period, it also reflects the anxieties of the French aristocracy, which in the latter decades of the twelfth century was progressively being displaced by a rising monied class elevated by the Capetian monarchy to the status of administrators and advisors. In response to this major economic shift, the romance tenders a conservative ideal of kingship valorizing traditional forms of largesse while also repeatedly emphasizing the perils of reliance on low-born men rather than on the higher aristocracy.

Institutionalized largesse is addressed by Stephen D. White, who considers the *Roman d'Alexandre* in the light of current theoretical discussions of models for the study of feudal society. He examines in particular the lengthy deathbed scene in Branch IV of the Vulgate, where Alexander makes generous gifts of land, as promised, to each of his twelve peers. White suggests ways in which, by holding up Alexander's fief-giving as an example of largesse and contrasting it with the bribe-like gifts of avaricious lords, Alexandre de Paris draws on a long-standing and complex feudal discourse. In this text the Eastern potentates encountered by Alexander are generally framed not only as his opposites but as counterexamples to his own exemplary conduct.[42] White shows how the Vulgate *Alexandre,* by radically dichotomizing Alexander's expansive largesse and Darius's avaricious use of bribes to procure selfish ends, oversimplifies and moralizes real political experience. He concludes that the romance reproduces and mystifies, but fails to resolve, a fundamental underlying ambiguity between honorable fief-giving and bribery camouflaged as largesse.

Together, then, the late-twelfth-century corpus reflects acutely felt tensions engaengendered by accelerated social change, as these found expression within a conceptual sphere encompassing such basic yet mutable notions as *clergie, chevalerie, vasselage, courtoisie,* and *largesse.* And while the early Alexander texts afford considerable insight into the definition of an ethos, the texts that derive from that fertile legacy and focus on this same gigantic figure during the three enusing centuries offer equally suggestive views of its metamorphosis over time.

We begin to note new attitudes toward the Alexandrian legend early in the next century. According to Michelle R. Warren, the political preoccupations apparent in the twelfth-century verse romance shift in the thirteenth-century prose version, adaptively translated from the tenth-century Latin prose *Historia de Preliis.* In essence, Warren suggests, the prose *Alexandre* moves significantly away from courtly concerns toward embodiment of a more resolutely expansionist ideology. Her essay on relations of unequal power and the coercive dynamics that sustain them is usefully informed by contemporary postcolonial studies. She argues, moreover, that prose is particularly well suited to the kind of totalizing effects cultivated in this thirteenth-century text's representation of imperial desire and colonial ambition.

Much recent scholarship has disclosed that the emergence of French prose around the turn of the thirteenth century owes a great deal to increasing concern with the writing of history in the vernacular. Catherine Croizy-Naquet shows how the figure of Alexander comes into prominence in this regard, as Roman history enters upon the French historiographic horizon with the *Faits des Romains* at the beginning of the thirteenth century. The compiler of this text attaches the Roman material to elements of ancient story that were already well-known, notably the legend of Troy and the great deeds of Alexander. Although Alexander's presence in the text is limited, evocations of his heroic career in the account of the life of Caesar enable the compiler to redefine the contours of both exemplary figures. This essay demonstrates that the thirteenth-century reconfiguration of Alexander also played an important role in the development of medieval historiography.

The late medieval "epigones," works that derive from the earlier French tradition while also modifying it in multiple ways, comprise an important subset of texts which Martin Gosman addresses.[43] While retaining the basic legendary *fabula,* these epigonic writers, who for the most part nourish an optimistic view of the tradition's political implications, variously reinvest it with illustrations of social order founded on the principle of *utilitas regis.* Hence a corpus of late-medieval narratives that resonate profoundly with a period in which monarchy definitively transforms itself from a weak feudal institution into a highly theorized sociopolitical machine. In literary and pseudohistorio-graphical texts from across this period, Gosman discloses the conservative as well as the innovative functions of works that produce idealized images of monarchy, operative within a courtly framework emphasizing political cohesiveness sustained by protocol, ritual, and pageant. These works are thus indicative of how major political transformations in late-medieval France were conspicuously valorized in its cultural productions.

Among these epigones, three of the works in Gosman's corpus, composed in the fourteenth century, form an ensemble inserted into Branch II of the *Roman d'Alexandre* and generally referred to as the "Cycle du Paon." While in general they are marked by a "spirit of idyllic courtesy which pervades the knightly atmosphere," as John L. Grigsby observed,[44] the last of the three, Jean de la Mote's *Parfait du Paon* (1340), reintroduces elements that underline the ambiguous traits of the hero.[45] Here Renate Blumenfeld-Kosinski looks closely at the nature of the poetic project involved in the *Parfait,* which in its network of references to earlier Alexander texts in many ways represents the endpoint of the tradition. In the episode of the *chambre amoureuse,* she suggests, the description of the elaborate murals provides through *ekphrasis*—word painting—a reading of both the Alexander and the related *Paon* cycles, while also configuring a legendary memory inviting readers to reflect on the tradition in new ways. Though they are part of only one interlude in a larger canvas of bloodshed and destruction, these highly allusive figural reminiscences also allow the temporary emergence of a different figure of Alexander: now himself engaged in poetic creation, he is dramatically transformed into a dynamic artificer commemorating, and consecrating, the sort of culture represented in the chamber itself, thus investing a role that in turn generates new texts.

Two other contributions focus on one monumental fourteenth-century text, the *Roman de Perceforest,* which is progressively becoming available in modern editions. Michelle Szkilnik considers how in the *Perceforest* Alexander is at last integrated into the Arthurian tradition: here he becomes not only Arthur's ancestor, but the founder of the rites of Arthurian society. Not only does he institute an illustrious lineage and establish a brilliant civilization; he initiates the recording of events that constitute the very material of romance. It is in this linkage and through its demonstration of Alexander's adoption of Arthurian values, Szkilnik argues, that the Macedonian hero's name and enterprise are saved for the Western legacy.

Implementing inethodologies of sociology and feminist theory, Jane H. M. Taylor examines an episode in the *Perceforest* that is new in the tradition and represents

Alexander as lover: the account of his clandestine, idyllic love affair in England with Sibille. In earlier Alexander texts, Taylor points out, women were perceived either as marginal or as dangerous distractions to male autonomy in an ideal social order based on masculine chivalric identity. The *Perceforest* makes the tensions between public and private spheres, between eros and empire-building, even more explicit. It also brings more fully into prominence a dichotomous universe, one in which the bond of "brotherliness" is ultimately incompatible with erotic love. Yet here again the male, homosocial ethos prevails, with the systematic exclusion of the lady from the public arena. Taylor situates this eventuality within the context of a much larger assortment of medieval French narratives that show similar tendencies.

The *Perceforest* is one example of how, during the later Middle Ages, the Alexandrian material continued to offer writers, as it had to Lambert le Tort, Alexandre de Paris, and the anonymous architect of the prose *Alexandre,* a powerful vehicle for depicting engagements with geographical and cultural alterities. "Alterity," writes Corrado Bologna, "is the measure of Alexander. Bent upon knowing and on conquering, on taking the measure of reality, Alexander is one of the most extraordinary mediators of alterity for the ancient and medieval West" (*Alessandro,* p. 167). Eventually, the legend's luxuriant "exotic" landscape began to intersect, often contrastively, with later medieval eyewitness descriptions of travel to remote lands. Developing a comparative perspective on one of the most important of these accounts, the *Devisement du monde* of Marco Polo, Laurence Harf-Lancner discovers two quite distinct approaches to the marvels of the Orient and to that which is, more generally, "other." The Alexander romances magnify the emblematic, often exemplary or cautionary figure of the discoverer avid for knowledge, who enters marvelous worlds that ultimately escape his capacity to master them fully. In contrast, the originality of the *Devisement* lies in its tendency to classify, and thus to demystify, the Oriental *merveilleux,* though without in any way diminishing the sense of wonder and awesome strangeness that prevails throughout. The intricate and arresting manuscript illustrations of the two works also show contrasts. While Marco Polo's text tends to reduce the marvelous to the exotic—the never-before-seen, the unheard-of—his imagers, recurring to earlier practices reflected in many *Alexandre* manuscripts, sometimes contradict his text so as to remain faithful to the traditional iconography of *mirabilia,* marvelous objects and events. Hence, in this essay, we find many detailed examples of the frequently subtle interplay between texts and their manuscript illuminations.

Like Harf-Lancner, Keith Busby is attentive to the evidence afforded by manuscripts, and in addressing the complex textual history of the *Roman d'Alexandre* he makes the codex containing each known version of a work the central object of study. The threads of his wide-ranging inquiry converge in a typology of the French *Alexandre* manuscripts, and he offers many suggestive comments on codicological features that might cast light on the reception of the legend within the historical context that produced a given manuscript. For manuscripts in which the *Roman d'Alexandre* figures among other works, Busby argues that close scrutiny of the manuscript's material properties and the way it contextualizes a given work may be required in order to apprehend the latter's intrinsic significance and larger implications.

In sum, these essays invite us to rethink medieval literary history and the norms of medieval culture from the multiple vantage points offered by the medieval French Alexander. As an ensemble, these works enable us to revisit, by working through one of its richest veins, the entire opening period of French literary history, from its inception near the beginning of the twelfth century to its glorious late-medieval expansion and diversification and its anticipation of early modern syntheses and transformations. The medieval French engagement with the legend of Alexander the Great, as it moves us in successive phases across the medieval centuries, emerges as a barometer of social and political change; as a measure of the complex coherence of mentalities and even a few pockets of local knowledge; and, on occasion, as a skeleton key for gaining access to contradictions within the social formation. The object of both adulation and censure even in his own time, Alexander emerges from these depictions as a figure about whom crystallize configurations, variously valorized, of an ideal whose ramifications are both political and personal. For it is Alexander—more than Charlemagne, more than Arthur, despite the celebrity of both of these rulers—who serves as a mirror, or perhaps better, as a prism, in which both the ancient world and the medieval are refracted in multiple and monumental ways.

Notes

1. *RA,* p. 5; translation by the editors.

2. David Williams, "Alexandre le Grand dans la littérature anglaise médiévale. De l'ambivalence à la polyvalence," in *Alexandre,* p. 356.

3. Pseudo-Callisthenes, *The Romance of Alexander the Great,* trans. A. M. Wolohojian (New York: Columbia University Press, 1969); *Julii Valerii Epitomè,* ed. J. Zacher (Halle, 1867).

4. See Laurence Harf-Lancner on Jacques de Longuyon's *Voeux du paon* (1312) in "Alexandre et l'Occident médiéval," in *Alexandre,* p. 19. The

Nine Worthies are Hector, Alexander, and Caesar; Joshua, David, and Judas Maccabeus; Arthur, Charlemagne, and Godefroy de Bouillon.

5. Geoffrey Chaucer, "The Monk's Tale" (vv. 743-45), *The Canterbury Tales,* in *The Riverside Chaucer,* ed. Larry D. Benson (Boston: Houghton-Mifflin, 1987).

6. Christine Raynaud, "Alexandre dans les bibliothèques bourguignonnes," in *Alexandre,* p. 187.

7. On the prologue see also A. Frugoni, "La biblioteca di Giovanni III duca di Napoli (Dal *Prologus* dell arciprete Leone al *Romanzo di Alessandro*)," in C. Settis Frugoni, *La fortuna di Alessandro Magno dall'antichità al Medioevo* (Firenze: La Nuova Italia, 1978), pp. 133-41.

8. Cary, *The Medieval Alexander,* Ross, *Alexander Historiatus.* See also idem., "Alexander historiatus: A Supplement," *Journal of the Warburg and Courtauld Institutes* 30 (1967), 383-88.

9. These concern specific matters such as his extraterrestrial voyages; the eulogies spoken in his memory; his horse Bucephalus; or his tent. On the latter, see Aimé Petit, "Le pavillon d'Alexandre dans le *Roman d'Alexandre* (ms. B. Venise, Museo Civico VI, 665)," *Bien dire et bien aprandre* 6 (1988), 77-96.

10. The scope of this tradition is illustrated in *Alexandre;* see the introductory essays by Claire Kappler and Laurence Harf-Lancner.

11. See Christine Abril, "Les Enfances d'Alexandre: Essai de comparaison entre le *Roman d'Alexandre* et le *Libro de Alexandre,*" *PRIS-MA* 13 (1997), 1-12; Amaia Arizaleta, "La figure d'Alexandre comme modèle d'écriture dans la littérature médiévale castillane," in *Alexandre,* pp. 173-86, and her *La Translation d'Alexandre. Recherches sur la genèse et signification du "Libro de Alexandre"* (Paris: Klincksieck, 1999).

12. For recent syntheses on the comprehensive Alexandrian tradition, with special emphases on the medieval heritage, see *Alessandro; Alexandre;* and the article "Alessandro Magno" in *Miti e personaggi del Medioevo: Dizionario di storia, letteratura, arte, musica,* ed. Willem P. Gerritsen and Anthony G. van Melle; Italian ed. Gabriella Agrati and Maria Letizia Magini (Milan: Mondadori, 1999), pp. 4-16. On the British Alexander, see Gerrit H. V. Bunt, *Alexander the Great in the Literature of Medieval Britain* (Groningen: Egbert Forsten, 1994).

13. See *MFRA III,* pp. 37-60, for the text, along with a French translation of Lamprecht's Middle High German adaptation, the *Alexanderlied* (ca. 1155).

14. Only the beginning of this poem survives, in two manuscripts: Arsenal 3472 and Venice, Museo Civico, VI, 665. For a reconstruction of the decasyllabic archetype see *MFRA III,* pp. 61-100. In ms. BNF fr. 789, components of the decasyllabic poem and Alexandre de Paris's Branch I are combined with new material. See *MFRA III,* pp. 101-54, and *RA,* pp. 20-21.

15. Evidence of this "archetype" is found in three manuscripts. See *MFRA I* for the texts of mss. Arsenal 3472 and Venice, Museo Civico, VI, 665 (which also recounts the "Fuerre de Gadres" episode). For the first 72 laisses of ms. BN fr. 789, see *MFRA III,* pp. 101-54. For a fac-simile of the Venice ms.: *Le Roman d'Alexandre: Riproduzione del ms. Venezia Biblioteca Museo Correr 1493,* ed. Roberto Benedetti (Udine: Roberto Vattori, 1998), with an introduction by Emmanuèle Baumgartner.

16. The four components of Alexandre de Paris's poem were identified as "branches" by Paul Meyer, "Etude sur les manuscrits du *Roman d'Alexandre,*" *Romania* 11 (1882), 213-332. Each branch is clearly representative of antecedent works: Br. I, the *enfances,* reflects the decasyllabic *Alexandre;* Br. II draws on the "Fuerre de Gadres" episode by Eustache; Br. III, on the expedition to the Orient, extensively reworks Lambert le Tort; and Br. IV, on the death of Alexander, is a rewriting of the anonymous *Mort Alixandre. MFRA II* gives the text of BN fr. 24365 for Branch I, and of BN fr. 25517 for Branches II-IV. *RA* follows the text of BN fr. 25517 exclusively, giving substantial excerpts from branches I, II, and III and all of Branch IV. See *RA,* pp. 59-61.

17. See Catherine Gaullier-Bougassas, "Jean Wauquelin et Vasque de Lucène: le 'roman familial' d'Alexandre et l'écriture de l'histoire au XVe siècle," in *Cahiers de Recherches médiévales (XIIIe-XVe siècle),* 5 (1998), 125-38.

18. In addition to *MFRA I-VII,* other works in the French Alexander tradition appear in the Elliott Monograph Series (Princeton: Princeton University Press): Gui de Cambrai, *Le Vengement Alixandre,* ed. Bateman Edwards (23, 1928); Jean le Nevelon, *Venjance Alexandre,* ed. Edward Billings Ham (37, 1931); *La Prise de Defur* and *Le Voyage d'Alexandre au Paradis Terrestre,* ed. Lawton P. G. Peckham and Milan S. La Du (35, 1935). All except *MFRA VI* (1976) were subsequently reprinted (New York: Kraus Reprints, 1965).

19. See Harf-Lancner's discussion of "Chanson de geste ou roman?" in *RA,* pp. 27-43.

20. For a sensitive discussion of the question of genre, see François Suard, "Alexandre est-il un personnage de roman?" *Bien dire et bien aprandre,* 7 (1989), 77-87, esp. p. 79.

21. On the legend's ambiguities see also, in *Alessandro,* Peter Dronke's "Introduzione" (pp. xv-lxxv).

22. See Corrado Bologna, "La generosità cavalleresca di Alessandro Magno," *L'Immagine riflessa* 12 (1989), 367-404.

23. See Catherine Gaullier-Bougassas, "Nectanabus et la singularité d'Alexandre dans les *Romans d'Alexandre* français," in *Alexandre,* pp. 303-19.

24. "And to that prince who marches with his troops, who lives by plundering, sacking and ransom, who controls what belongs to others, such generosity is essential; otherwise, his soldiers would not follow him. And with that which does not belong to you or to your subjects you can be a more liberal giver as was Cyrus, Caesar or Alexander, because spending what belongs to others does not detract from your reputation, rather it enhances it; only spending your own is what will hurt you." Niccolò Machiavelli, *The Prince,* ed. and trans. Mark Musa (New York: St Martin's Press, 1964), pp. 133-35.

25. See Piero Boitani, "L'aura e le ombre di Alessandro" in *Alessandro,* pp. 441-43.

26. Hugh (or Richard?) of Saint Victor, *Allegoriae in Vetus Testamentum* (*PL* [*Patrologia Latina*] CLXXV). See Dronke, *Alessandro,* p. li, and for other examples see Cary, pp. 118-42.

27. For the Vulgate *Alexandre*'s contrast to the texts with which it is frequently associated in literary history, the so-called *romans antiques* of *Thèbes, Enéas,* and *Troie,* see Aimé Petit, "Les romans antiques et Alexandre," in *Alexandre,* pp. 289-302.

28. See Emmanuè e Baumgartner, "L'Orient d'Alexandre," *Bien dire et bien aprandre* 6 (1988), p. 9, our translation.

29. Laurence Harf-Lancner, "La quête de l'immortalité: les fontaines merveilleuses du *Roman d'Alexandre* d'Alexandre de Paris," in *Sources et fontaines du Moyen Age à l'Age baroque* (Paris: Champion, 1998), p. 39, our translation.

30. For discussion of the name see Shigemi Sasaki, "'E si veira les bones, (. . .) / Que artus aveit faites en Orïent fichier'," in *Studi di storia della civiltà letteraria francese: Mélanges offerts à Lionello Sozzi* (Paris: Champion, 1996), pp. 1-20.

31. *Inferno* XXVI, in Dante Alighieri, *The Divine Comedy,* trans. Charles S. Singleton (Princeton: Princeton University Press, 1970): "dov' Ercule

segnò li suoi riguardi / acciò che l'uom più oltre non si metta" (108-109) [where Hercules set out his marks, that no man should venture beyond them]; our translation.

32. For the parallels between Dante's Ulysses and Alexander, see D'Arco Silvio Avalle, *Modelli semiologici nella Commedia di Dante* (Milan: Bompiani, 1975), pp. 33-63.

33. Saint Bernard, "De Gradius humilitatis et superbiae," in Etienne Gilson, *La Théologie mystique de Saint Bernard* (Paris: J. Vrin, 1969), pp. 181-82, 85. See Sasaki, "'E si veira les bones . . .'," pp. 18-19.

34. See Baumgartner, "L'Orient d'Alexandre": "A la différence peut-être de l'autre monde celte, l'Orient d'Alexandre ne paraît ainsi prodiguer ses merveilles que pour mieux en montrer le caractère déceptif. Il ne s'offre que pour mieux se reprendre," (p. 13).

35. For the texts see *Prise,* pp. xlii-xlviii, xlix-lii, and 73-90.

36. For the relation of this text to the "horizontal" conception of a dialectic between this world and the Christian Otherworld, see Maria Luisa Meneghetti, "Cieli e terre nei secoli XI-XII: Orizzonti, percezioni, rapporti," in *Miscellanea del Centro di studi medioevali* (Milan: Università Cattolica del Sacro Cuore, 1998), pp. 184-85.

37. See Marylène Perez, "Alexandre le Grand dans l'Alexandréide," *Bien dire et bien aprandre* 6 (1988), pp. 73-76. Jean-Yves Tilliette argues that the hero of the Latin poem is essentially ambiguous and discloses the limitations of the character made popular by the *Roman d'Alexandre;* see "L'*Alexandréide* de Gautier de Châtillon: Enéide médiévale ou 'Virgile travesti'?" in *Alexandre,* pp. 275-86 (here p. 286).

38. Her vernacular corpus includes *MFRA II; RTC; Prosa;* Rutebeuf, *Dit d'Aristote;* Henri d'Andeli, *Lai d'Aristote;* and *Prise.*

39. See the *Book of Daniel* VIII, 5-8 and 11; the *Book of Maccabees* I, 1, 3-5.

40. VIII, 492-94: "ille cruentus / Fatorum gladius, terrarum publica pestis."

41. See Pierre Briant, "Alexandre à Babylone: images grecques, images babyloniennes," in *Alexandre,* pp. 23-32.

42. See Catherine Croizy-Naquet, "Darius ou l'image du potentat perse dans le *Roman d'Alexandre,*" in *Alexandre,* pp. 161-72 (here p. 164).

43. Gosman's corpus includes: *Prise,* from the second half of the thirteenth century; the three works—*Voeux* (1313-14), *Restor* (before 1338), and *Parfait* (before 1348)—comprising the so-called Paon Cycle; and two fifteenth-century prose compilations, the *Historia du bon roy Alixandre* by Jean Wauquelin (ca. 1448), and the anonymous *Fais et Concquestes du Noble roy Alexandre* (1450-70).

44. John L. Grigsby, "Courtesy in the *Voeux du Paon,*" *Neuphilologische Mitteilungen* 86 (1985), p. 568.

45. See also Michelle Szkilnik, "Courtoisie et violence: Alexandre dans le *Cycle du Paon,*" in *Alexandre,* pp. 321-39.

Abbreviations

MFRA I: The Medieval French "Roman d'Alexandre," vol. I: *Text of the Arsenal and Venice Versions,* ed. Milan S. La Du [Elliott Monographs 36] (Princeton: Princeton University Press, 1937; New York: Kraus Reprints, 1965).

MFRA II: The Medieval French "Roman d'Alexandre," vol. II: *Version of Alexandre de Paris,* ed. Edward C. Armstrong, Douglas L. Buffum, Bateman Edwards, L. F. H. Lowe [Elliott Monographs 37] (Princeton: Princeton University Press, 1938; New York: Kraus Reprints, 1965).

MFRA III: The Medieval French "Roman d'Alexandre," vol. III: *Version of Alexandre de Paris: Variants and Notes to Branch I,* ed. Alfred Foulet [Elliott Monographs 38] (Princeton: Princeton University Press, 1949; New York: Kraus Reprints, 1965).

MFRA IV: The Medieval French "Roman d'Alexandre," vol. IV: *"Le Roman du Fuerre de Gadres" d'Eustache,* ed. Edward C. Armstrong and Alfred Foulet [Elliott Monographs 39] (Princeton: Princeton University Press, 1942; New York: Kraus Reprints, 1965).

MFRA V: The Medieval French "Roman d'Alexandre," vol. V: *Version of Alexandre de Paris. Variants and Notes to Branch II, with an Introduction,* ed. Frederick B. Agard [Elliott Monographs 40] (Princeton: Princeton University Press, 1942; New York: Kraus Reprints, 1965).

MFRA VI: The Medieval French "Roman d'Alexandre," vol. VI: *Version of Alexandre de Paris: Variants and Notes to Branch III,* ed. Alfred Foulet [Elliott Monographs 42] (Princeton: Princeton University Press, 1976).

MFRA VII: The Medieval French "Roman d'Alexandre," vol. VII: *Version of Alexandre de Paris: Variants and Notes to Branch IV,* ed. Bateman Edwards and Alfred Foulet [Elliott Monographs 41] (Princeton: Princeton University Press, 1955; New York: Kraus Reprints, 1965).

Prise: La Prise de Defur and Le Voyage d'Alexandre au Paradis terrestre, ed. Lawton P. G. Peckham and Milan S. La Du [Elliott Monographs 35] (Princeton: Princeton University Press, 1935; New York: Kraus Reprints, 1965).

RA: Le Roman d'Alexandre, ed. (from the text of *MFRA II*) and trans. Laurence Harf-Lancner [Livre de Poche, "Lettres Gothiques" 4542] (Paris: Librairie Générale Française, 1994).

Alessandro: Alessandro nel Medioevo Occidentale, ed. Mariantonia Liborio, Piero Boitari, Corrado Bologna, and Adele Cipolla; intro. Peter Dronke (Verona: Mondadori, 1997).

Alexandre: Alexandre le Grand dans les litteratures Occidentales et Proche-Orientales: Actes du Colloque de Paris, 27-29 novembre 1997, ed. Laurence Harf-Lancner, Claire Kappler, and François Suard [Litterales Hors Serie—1999] (Paris: Centre des Sciences de la Litterature, Universite de Paris X, Nanterre, 1999).

Suzanne Conklin Akbari (essay date 2005)

SOURCE: Akbari, Suzanne Conklin. "Alexander in the Orient: Bodies and Boundaries in the *Roman de toute chevalerie.*" In *Postcolonial Approaches to the European Middle Ages: Translating Cultures,* edited by Ananya Jahanara Kabir and Deanne Williams, pp. 105-26. Cambridge: Cambridge University Press, 2005.

[*In the following essay, Akbari explains how geography—particularly in terms of the West versus the East—informs the* Roman de toute chevalerie.]

One of the great criticisms leveled against Edward Said's groundbreaking study, *Orientalism,* was that it posed one monolithic entity, "the West," against another, variously identified as "the Orient," "the East," or "Islam." This formulation was seen as both homogenizing the "Oriental" subject, and conflating a broad spectrum of Western views, ranging from antiquity to the late twentieth century, into a single discourse, Orientalism.[1] Ironically, the most influential postcolonialist interventions made during the 1980s, including Bhabha's theory of colonial mimicry and the notion of subalternity as formulated by Spivak, were founded on Said's strategically reductive presentation of the "Oriental" subject.[2] For those studying premodern cultures, however, the more pressing concern has been Said's conflation of Western views. As I have argued elsewhere, the binary opposition of East and West, fundamental to Said's theory, cannot be projected back onto a Middle Ages which seldom conceived the world as bipartite. Medieval maps and encyclopedias almost invariably present a tripartite world, divided between the three known continents: Asia, Europe, and Africa. The opposition of a coldly rational Occident and an overheated, passionate Orient has its origins not in classical antiquity but in fourteenth-century reconceptualizations of north-western Europe and its relationship to the surrounding world.[3]

Admittedly, neither the binary opposition of East and West, nor the discourse of Orientalism, is completely absent from medieval texts. Several historical chronicles discuss the transmission of imperial might through the westward movement of *translatio imperii*; in addition, a wide range of texts, including the Alexander romances, the Prester John Letters, and travel narratives such as the *Milione* of Marco Polo and *The Book of John Mandeville,* present an Orient replete with luxurious goods, wealth, and wonders. There are, however, significant differences between modern and premodern manifestations of both the East-West opposition and its attendant Orientalism. This chapter probes these differences by focusing on Thomas of Kent's *Roman de toute chevalerie.* This late twelfth-century Anglo-Norman poem depicts a world in the process of being conquered by Alexander the Great, who places ceremonial markers defining the boundaries of his empire at "treis fins del mond" (line 5945) (three ends of the earth): the extreme East, North, and South.[4] The fourth cardinal direction is absent: Alexander does not bother to venture to the West, where dwell the Irish, Spanish, and British. Despite this curious absence, the romance takes what I term a "westward turn" in its closing sections, which describe Alexander's mortal remains being returned from the East, Babylon, to the central regions of his empire. The narrative's own genealogy, from the putative Greek original of Alexander's letter to his tutor, Aristotle, to the letter's Latin translation, to the Anglo-Norman poem, traverses a similar path, moving from remote regions to the familiar space of the vernacular. This multiple westward turn in the *Roman*—geographical, corporeal, and linguistic—lays the foundation for the establishment of imperial might in a long-forgotten corner of Europe, and for the emergence of a new construction of Western identity.

LOCATING THE WEST

Thomas of Kent's account of Alexander's conquests draws heavily on a template of universal history and geography and a binary opposition of East and West furnished by a particular group of medieval texts: twelfth-century histories consciously patterned after Paulus Orosius' *Seven Books of History against the Pagans,* a historiographic counterpart to Augustine's *City of God.*[5] Orosius uses the dichotomy of East and West in order to structure his narrative in terms of *translatio imperii,* the gradual movement of imperial domina-

tion from the kingdom of Babylon to the rule of the Caesars in Rome. Orosius begins with a tripartite division of the world into Asia, Africa, and Europe.[6] However, his presentation of the chronological succession of empires soon reveals a westward movement based upon the poles of the ancient city of Babylon and the modern city of Rome: "siquidem sub una eademque conuenientia temporum illa cecedit, ista surrexit . . . tunc Orientis occidit et ortum est Occidentis imperium" [thus, at the exact same moment, the one fell and the other arose . . . thus the empire of the East fell and that of the West was born] (I:87-8; II.2.10). However, closer examination reveals this opposition of East and West is rooted in a four-part historical sequence, itself ordered about the four cardinal points of the earth.

Between the might of eastern Babylon and western Rome, Orosius declares, came the short-lived empires of Macedonia in the North and Carthage in the South:

> Inter Babylonam regnum quod ab oriente fuerat, et Romanum quod ab occidente consurgens hereditati orientis enutriebatur, Macedonicum Africanumque regnum, hoc est quasi a meridie ac septentrione breuibus uicibus partes tutoris curatorisque tenuisse. Orientis et occidentis regnum Babylonium et Romanum iure uocitari, neminem umquam dubitasse scio; Macedonicum regnum sub septentrione cum ipsa caeli plaga tum Alexandri Magni arae positae usque ad nunc sub Riphaeis montibus docent; Carthaginem uero universae praecelluisse Africae et non solum in Siciliam Sardiniam ceterasque adiacentes insulas sed etiam in Hispaniam regni terminos tetendisse, historiarum simul monumenta urbiumque declarant.
>
> (III:17-18; VII.2.4-6)

[During the time between the Babylonian Empire that existed in the East and the Roman Empire which, raising itself up in the West, was nourished by the heritage of the East, there intervened the Macedonian and African Empires . . . in the North and the South they held, for a brief time, the roles of guardian and protector. I know that no one has ever doubted that the Babylonian and Roman Empires are rightly called that of the East and that of the West. We are taught that the Macedonian Empire was in the North not only by its very geographical location (lit. "celestial zone"), but also by the altars placed by Alexander the Great at the foot of the Riphaean mountains, which still remain to this day. The testimony of books of history as well as city monuments attest that Carthage had preeminence over all of Africa, and had extended the boundaries of its rule not only as far as Sicily, Sardinia, and the other nearby islands, but even as far as Spain.]

Here, the ostensibly simple movement from Babylon to Rome, following the natural path of the sun, proves to be more complex. Although Macedonia and Carthage are not true heirs to the Babylonian empire, they hold its authority in custody until the true heir, Rome, reaches maturity. The opposition of North and South, Macedonia and Carthage, counterbalances that of East, Babylon, and West, Rome, adumbrating a pattern in world history that makes visible the hidden truth of Christian history. As Fabrizio Fabbrini argues, this pattern follows the perfect geometrical design of a cross, rendering visible a deeper Christian *telos* invested in "a fifth Empire, qualitatively different from the others."[7] This city is not ruled by an earthly emperor, but by Christ. In this evocation of the Christian empire of the spirit, it is possible to see the conformity of Orosius' view of history to that of his mentor, Augustine.

Orosius undeniably describes both time and space as quadripartite, with the four cardinal points corresponding to the four empires. While, in its broadest terms, *translatio imperii* moves from East to West, its actual trajectory moves from East, to North, to South, to West—from Babylon, to Macedonia, to Carthage, to Rome. Speaking as a Roman, however, Orosius mentions only three of the four regions in describing his place in the world: "latitudo orientis, septentrionis copiositas, meridiana diffusio . . . sedes mei iuris et nominis sunt quia ad Christianos et Romanos Romanus et Christianus accedo" [The breadth of the East, the vastness of the North, the extensiveness of the South . . . are of my law and name because I approach Christians and Romans as a Roman and a Christian] (II:86; v.2.3). For Orosius, the West is, as it were, a personal center. Although it is not the center of the world, it is the place from which he encounters the world as a Roman citizen.

The *Roman de toute chevalerie* also describes the far reaches of the earth using only three of the four cardinal directions, omitting the West. Alexander is said to have conquered "tuit le mond" [all the world] (line 5943), having placed his standard at each of the "treis fins del mond" [three ends of the world] (line 5945), that is, at the extreme East, North, and South. The only region left unexplored and unconquered is the West, simply because (as Thomas says) there is nothing there worth conquering:

Ore n'i ad [a] dire si sul occident non
Ou meinent ly Yreis, Espaniol e Breton,
Qe la terre habitable ne seit alé environ.

(lines 5948-51)

[Now there is nothing at all to be said about the West, where the Irish, Spanish and British live, for the habitable land does not extend around there.]

This omission is made even more striking by the detailed accounts of Alexander's placement of commemorative markers or "mercs" at the other extreme edges of the known world. He ventures into the East as far as the "mercs" of Hercules, and exceeding even the latter's reach, places his own "temples" and "auters" (line 5947) at the "fin d'orient" and constructs "col-

umpnes de metal" (line 6546) at the far reaches of the North to enclose the unclean tribes of Gog and Magog. Finally, having surrounded the East and the North, he turns southward to the kingdom of Ethiopia (line 6639). In each of these locations, Alexander makes ritual sacrifices and receives divine messages that prophesy his inevitable downfall. In the East, he encounters the oracular trees of the sun and moon; in the North, on Mount "Chelion," he hears the voice of God; and in the South, Alexander sacrifices on the "ardant mont" [burning mountain] (lines 6883-93) where a disembodied voice tells him that he will never see his home again. Alexander's encounters with these liminal points, located at the extreme margins of the known world, are significant in two respects. For humanity as a whole, they represent man's greatest and most extreme accomplishments. For the individual, however, they represent danger and inevitable destruction. In these places at the "fin del mond," the divine is audible and one's own end is in sight.

There is a deeper significance to be found in this patterning of world geography in the *Roman de toute chevalerie* after the Orosian scheme. Thomas of Kent's description of Alexander's sequence of conquests follows the same sequence reported in Orosius' quadripartite account of *translatio imperii* from East, North and South, and finally to Rome in the West. Alexander's path of conquest follows a similar trajectory—up to a point. Following his encounter with Darius and the conquest of Babylon, Alexander ventures into the furthest East, going beyond the varied lands of India to the shores of the eastern Ocean. He then heads North to subdue the unnatural races of Gog and Magog, and then to the South to survey the heterogeneous nations of Ethiopia. Alexander, however, never ventures into the West: a disjunction between the *Roman de toute chevalerie* and Orosius' chronicle that repays closer scrutiny. On a superficial level, Alexander never ventures into the West because, as Thomas states, the West houses only the straggling populations of Ireland, Britain, and Spain. On a deeper level, however, the absent voyage into the West signals Alexander's role as a harbinger of imperial conquests to follow: the conquest of the known world by Rome, the great city of the West, and the subsequent rise of European might in the far western regions.

This point is supported by Alexander's special place in medieval historiography, as evidenced by the detailed comparisons of Alexander and Augustus Caesar found in Orosius' *Seven Books against the Pagans*. As a proud man and relentless conqueror who ultimately falls prey to the excesses of the flesh, Alexander is no hero to the devout Christian: Orosius accordingly emphasizes both his appeal and his limitations. Alexander's undeniable might, however, makes him a fitting counterpart to the

Roman emperor who achieved universal peace and concord, preparing the way for the establishment of Christianity on the foundations of the Empire. Once again, Orosius makes the comparison through symbolic geography. Representatives from all over the world assembled in homage to Alexander after his eastward return to Babylon (I:172; III.20.3). Correspondingly, Augustus Caesar receives homage from the far corners of the world not in his imperial seat at Rome, but in the distant lands of the West:

Caesarem apud Tarraconem citerioris Hispaniae urbem legati Indorum et Scytharum, toto Orbe transmisso, tandem ibi inuenerunt, ultra quod iam quaerere non possent, refuderuntque in Caesarem Alexandri Magni gloriam: quem sicut Hispanorum Gallorumque legatio in medio Oriente apud Babylonam contemplatione pacis adiit, ita hunc apud Hispaniam in Occidentis ultimo supplex cum gentilicio munere eous Indus et Scytha boreus orauit.

(II:233; VI.21.19-20)

[After having crossed the whole world, the ambassadors of the Indians and Scythians finally found Caesar in Tarraco, a city of furthest Spain, beyond which they could not have continued to seek him, and they transferred to Caesar the glory of Alexander the Great. In the same way that a legation of Spaniards and Gauls intending to make peace came to him (i.e., Alexander) in Babylon, in the middle of the East, just so the Indian of the Eastern Ocean and the Scythian of the Boreal River beseeched him (Caesar) on their knees in Spain, at the extremity of the West, offering tribute from their peoples.]

Alexander appears here as both counterpart and harbinger of Augustus. Just as Rome is said to be the heir to Babylonian might, as *translatio imperii* moves from East to West, so all the lands of the East come to the furthest point West to pay tribute to Augustus Caesar, just as long ago all the lands of the West came to "the middle of the East" to pay tribute to Alexander. Augustus thus perfects, not simply repeats, Alexander's triumphs. As Orosius puts it, in spite of all his great achievements, "Alexandro uero apud Babylonam . . . interiit" [Alexander died in Babylon] (I:172; III.20.4); by contrast, Augustus exercised imperial power so complete that "ab oriente in occidentem, a septentrione in meridiem ac per totum Oceani circulum cunctis gentibus una pace conpositis" [from the East to the West, from the North to the South, and over the entire circuit of the Ocean, all nations were arranged in a single peace] (II:234; VI.22.1). At that moment, the world is prepared for the crucial moment in salvation history: that is, the Incarnation.

By the twelfth century, the negative view of Alexander as tyrannical conqueror, possessed by pride and destroyed by lust, had begun to give way to a more positive image that emphasized his daring, bravery, and might.[8] Simultaneously, the symbolic geography of Orosius, in which imperial power moved from the East to the North, South, and then West, was fundamentally altered. Where Orosius had stated that the mantle of empire was handed from Babylon to Macedonia, to Carthage, to Rome, twelfth-century chroniclers such as Otto of Freising replaced these nations with Babylon, Persia, Greece, and Rome.[9] As a result, the notion of *translatio imperii* was made more emphatically and more simply a movement from East to West, with Greece as a new middle ground, belonging fully neither to the East nor to the West. This change erases the imperial history of Carthage, deleting Africa from the sequence of imperial power in European historiography.[10]

It was in this context that the *Roman de toute chevalerie* was composed. The story of Alexander reemerges as both cautionary and inspirational, with Alexander exemplifying the qualities not just of the ideal conqueror, but of the ideal knight. His "chevalerie" (that is, his possession of the qualities appropriate to a knight) is exercised both on the battlefield and in the bedroom, as he rallies his troops in wartime and gives pleasure to his lady in time of peace. In addition, for the medieval reader of the romance, Alexander is a mediator between the familiar space of home and the exotic terrain abroad, as the reader sees the curiosities of the world—from the monstrous races of Ethiopia to the marvelous luxuries of India—through his eyes.

FROM THE TOMB OF DARIUS TO THE CHAMBER OF CANDACE

The *Roman de toute chevalerie* is both a heroic portrait of one man—Alexander—and a history of the rise and fall of the Macedonian Empire. It also has an encyclopedic character, including several long accounts of the monstrous races and natural marvels to be found at the extreme limits of the *ecumene*, drawn from a version of the legend of Alexander composed in the fourth century by Julius Valerius, the marvels of the East described in the *Letter of Alexander to Aristotle,* and a variety of works of natural philosophy, including Pliny's *Historia naturalia,* Solinus' *Collectanea rerum memorabilium,* and Aethicus Ister's *Cosmographia.*[11] This idiosyncratic compilation has been attributed to a now-lost Old French original, hypothetically titled *Alexandre en Orient,* which provided a common source of parallel passages in the two main Alexander romances of the twelfth century, the *Roman d'Alexandre* and the *Roman de toute chevalerie.*[12] However, while the author of the *Roman d'Alexandre* refers to a vernacular ("romans") antecedent, Thomas of Kent refers to a Latin source: "d'un bon livre en latin fist cest translatement" [I made this translation from a good book in Latin (line P 21)].[13]

More significant than the (probably insoluble) question of whether the *Alexandre en Orient* really existed is the fact that Thomas self-consciously presents his *Roman de toute chevalerie* as a work of translation ("cest translatement"). The fictitious assertion of a Latin source appears to be an effort to claim greater authority for Thomas's narrative, giving the vernacular romance a stabilizing foundation in an ancient text.

Latinity, in the Middle Ages, does not necessarily connote Rome. Nonetheless, the absent West in Thomas's adaptation of Orosius' symbolic geography is still evident on a linguistic level, in the Latin language—the language of the Roman Empire—that, Thomas asserts, lies behind the *Roman de toute chevalerie*. The claim of a Latin original thus does more than simply ground the poem's authority on a firmer basis: it embeds Alexander's story in Latin prose as well as in Roman history. This move is central to Thomas's effort to domesticate the unpredictable and dangerous peripheries of the globe by connecting them to the stable center of imperial Rome. The monstrous races of Ethiopia, the marvelous diversity of India, and the hideous uncleanness of the races of Gog and Magog are reined in by the discipline of Alexander's military conquest, and by the order imposed by the poet's metrical line.

Thomas's comment on his sources immediately follows his account of the death and interment of the Persian king Darius. This moment is significant both on the level of *translatio imperii* and on the level of the individual, for it marks not only the transfer of imperial power (in Orosius' terms) from the East to the North, but also the transformation of Alexander into an Oriental king. Other narratives of Alexander similarly signal the interment of Darius as a crucial moment. In Walter of Châtillon's *Alexandreis,* for example, the monumental tomb of the Persian king, topped with a crystalline globe and inscribed with an elaborately rubricated map of the earth, both memorializes Darius and pays tribute to Alexander's new status as king of all the Orient, and ruler of the world.[14] Alexander's intention is to be not simply Darius' conqueror but his heir: an almost filial piety motivates not only the construction of this magnificent memorial, but also his first act following the tomb's erection, as Alexander sets out to find and punish Darius' killer. In the *Roman de toute chevalerie,* too, the tomb of Darius demarcates a turning point in the narrative. Unlike Orosius' presentation of him as a northern king ruling over rapidly expanding eastern territories, Alexander becomes, after the death of Darius, part of the Orient he now rules.

This transformation, however, seems far off during the initial stages of the conflict between Alexander and Darius, where Darius is depicted as a Saracen king, patterned after the depictions of Saracens found in the *chansons de geste* and romances. Like those "pagans," Darius is early on said to be "orgoillus" (proud, line 27); he rules over a vast and heterogeneous army of "cent mil Sarazin" [a hundred thousand Saracens] (lines 1604-8) that, in every respect, is identical to the Saracens of the *chansons de geste,* even down to their worship of "Apolin" and "Tervagant" (lines 1605, 1391-2, 2270).[15] These associations project Alexander, Darius' opponent, forward in time as a crusader king, identifiable with the contemporaneous European Christian effort to take the Holy Land.[16] And yet Alexander is also heir to Darius and his dominion, becoming the ruler over his heterogeneous group of subjects, and king not only of the whole Orient, but of the whole world: "tuit le mond est Alisandre a bandon, / De touz roys terriens ad il subjecion" [all the world has surrendered to Alexander; he has subjected all earthly kings] (lines 5943-4).

The fate of Darius, then, becomes an uncanny harbinger of Alexander's own fate. The process of Darius' interment—the ritual preparation of the body, the exacting design and construction of a fitting monument—anticipates the final disposition of Alexander himself.

> A deus ciriziens fet Alisandre overir le corps,
> Mult bien le fet laver dedenz e dehors;
> Font arder la boele qe ne la mangent pors.
> E cusent le en un paille e enbalment le cors,
> E puis [l]'envolupe[nt] en quir de deus tors,
> En bere le metent entre deus chevals sors.

(lines 3710-15)

[Alexander had the body opened by two surgeons, and had it very well washed, both inside and outside. He had the guts burned, so that pigs would not eat them. And they placed the body on a silken cloth and embalmed it, and then wrapped it in the hide of two bulls and placed it on a bier drawn by two sorrel horses.]

The ritual preparation of Darius' body—interred "en guise de Persien" (line 3722) [in the Persian manner], his body placed "en sarcu de fin or" (line 3725) [in a sarcophagus of pure gold]—anticipates that of Alexander's body after his death by treachery, embalmed in a "sarcu de fin or" (line 7982). Being king of the Orient, Alexander is naturally buried as an Oriental king, with one crucial difference: location. While Darius' tomb is a fixed mausoleum, a monument to the fallen glory of Persia, Alexander's golden sarcophagus is mobile. Carried by his men back westward, it lies in Alexandria, one of the twelve cities founded by the conqueror and named after him. This bodily translation emblematizes the *translatio imperii* narrated in the *Roman de toute chevalerie*—both the transmission of imperial power from Persia to Macedonia explicitly recounted, and its transmission further west, to Europe, which is implicit in the depiction of Alexander as a model of "toute chevalerie."

Between the golden sarcophagus of Darius and the golden sarcophagus of Alexander lies a sprawling account of the marvels of the world, as Alexander ventures into the furthest regions of the East, North, and South in his passionate endeavor to explore everywhere and conquer everything. The magnificent *mappa mundi* which adorns Darius' tomb in the *Alexandreis* comes alive, as it were, in the *Roman de toute chevalerie*'s account of the abundant luxuries found in the "fin d'Orient," the hideous tribes of Gog and Magog found in the northern wastes, and the monstrous races populating the torrid regions of the South. Significantly, the trajectory of Alexander's route of exploration and conquest—East, North, and South—follows that found in Orosius' universal chronicle, as the Persian Empire gives way to Macedonia, to Carthage, and finally to Rome. Alexander thus embodies the spirit of conquest, summing up the path of *translatio imperii* in the life of a single man. The westward track of *translatio imperii*, however, in which imperial power devolves upon Rome, is mirrored not in Alexander's acts, but in the fate of his dead body.

Alexander's voyage into the East is characterized in terms of doubleness. The land itself is double, for India is divided into two parts: "En la fin d'orient, de Inde i ad deus paire, / Inde superior e Inde la maire" [In the furthest East, there are two Indias, Upper India and Greater India] (lines 4601-2).[17] This doubling has a temporal dimension as well, for there are two summers, and two harvests (lines 4619-20). The resulting plenty extends not just to the abundant crops but also to the numerous cities and great number of "diverses genz" [diverse peoples] (line 4623). The East is filled with "merveiles" (line 4626), as Thomas illustrates in his long catalogues of the various peoples and wondrous animals to be found in India. When Alexander encounters the Indian king Porus, he has only one demand: he asks Porus to take him to the "fin d'orient" (line 5359), as far as the "mercs" left by Hercules long ago (line 5377). There, an aged native comes up to Alexander to tell him about the further marvels to be found further east, beyond the pillars of Hercules, in the land of Taprobane.[18] Predictably, Alexander insists on going "ou Hercules n'osa" [where Hercules did not dare] (line 5484). In Taprobane, the doubleness of the East is reinforced, with two summers, two harvests, and, furthermore, two winters. In this easternmost region, Alexander encounters further marvels, exploring until there is no more to be found: "Par tote [Ynde] est alez cerchant la region" [He went throughout all India, exploring the region] (line 5938).

Alexander's exploration of the Orient is interrupted when a messenger comes down from the North, begging the conqueror to come back with him to deal with the hideous tribes of Gog and Magog, who live "vers aquilon" [in the place of the north wind]. This horrible "nacion" is "vers humeine nature" [against human nature]: their favorite food is "char d'ome" [human flesh] but they also eat dogs instead of venison, serpents, toads, frogs, and slugs (lines 5961-70). The uncleanness of these tribes is manifested not just in their cannibalism (and in eating man's best friend), but also in their consumption of foods that are unclean because they fall outside normal categories, such as frogs and toads.[19] The tribes of Gog and Magog are, in some ways, homogeneous: Thomas describes them as a single "nacion" (line 5961), united in their unclean behaviors and in their common descent from Nimrod, "Nembroth le traitur" (line 5980).[20] Despite this apparent homogeneity, however, the northerners demonstrate a range of diversity similar to that encountered earlier during Alexander's travels throughout the East. One group lives on the sea and eats human flesh; another eats mice; still another is made up of metalworkers, and so on. Among this diverse lot, Thomas gives special emphasis to the Turks, who eat both humans and dogs, "char vive" [living flesh] and "ordure" [filth] (line 6021). They are "cruel e dure" [cruel and hard], given to "lecherie e chescune luxure" [lechery and every wanton behavior] (lines 6019-20). Thomas goes beyond his source, the *Cosmographia* of Aethicus Ister, in his emphasis on the Turks and in his description of the climatic qualities associated with the northern region they inhabit. In this chilly, arid land, "Il n'i put nul blé crestre, ne nul fruit n['i] m[e]ure; / En esté, en yver ont toz jors la froidure" [no wheat can grow there, nor any fruit or berry; in summer and in winter, they have constant cold] (lines 6048-9).[21]

The catalogue of the tribes of Gog and Magog goes on to include those who swim in the sea, those who build "estranges nefs" [strange boats] (line 6057) that travel underwater, unnamed dwarves, and "Rifaires" who constantly fight "vers autres Sarazins" [against other Saracens] (line 6090).[22] Alexander's role as conqueror demands his cleansing the world of the tribes of Gog and Magog: "De cest[e] ordure est trestuit le mond soillez" [the entire world is made dirty by this filth] (line 6338). Having established the borders of the known world through conquest, Alexander also must bear the burden of maintaining the order of his territory within. Accordingly, he withdraws to Mount Chelion to make sacrifices, where the voice of God instructs him on how to enclose Gog and Magog. Forging columns of metal, reinforced with bitumen, Alexander seals up the unclean tribes in an enclosure from which they will emerge only in the time of Antichrist (lines 6574-8).[23] It is this accomplishment, for Thomas, that makes Alexander "the Great," himself as marvelous as the marvels he discovers.

Having swept through the regions of the East and North, Alexander turns his glance southward:

> Les deus parties del mond ad pres environé . . .
> Al regné de Ethiopie ad il ost mené,
> E veu tel[es] choses qe point nen ay conté
>
> (lines 6637-40)

[He surrounded two parts of the world . . . and turned his host toward the kingdom of Ethiopia, and saw such things as I have not yet begun to tell.]

Ethiopia—used here, as usual in twelfth-century maps and geographies, to represent the southernmost habitable region—is replete with marvels, and marvelous diversity. Its many kingdoms are filled with

> Gent de meintes maneres e de diverse colur:
> Aquanz i sunt noir, autres blanc cum flur,
> Aquanz sunt coloré, aquant ont palur.
>
> (lines 6681-4)

[People of many different characters and of different colors: some there are black, others white as a flower; some are ruddy, others pale.][24]

Unlike medieval encyclopedists, who attribute the racial diversity of the southern regions to the effects of climate, Thomas describes it as the consequence of their unusual behavior:

> En Ethiope ad gent de diverse nature,
> De diverse lignee, de diverse parleure,
> Car trestoz en sunt de diverse engendrure.
>
> (lines 6702-4)

[In Ethiopia are people of diverse natures, of diverse lineages, of diverse languages, because everyone there is diversely engendered.]

Thomas explains that Ethiopians' great diversity is due to their sexual promiscuity, such that no man knows his father, nor any father his sons: "Tuit sunt commun entr'els cum bestes en pasture" [All is common among them, like beasts in the field] (line 6708). As in the regions of the East and North, the southern expanse contains a numerous, heterogeneous collection of peoples: some who have a dog for their king, others who have four eyes and worship Mercury; those who eat lions and have one eye, those who bark like dogs, those who ride elephants, those who have no mouths and communicate by sign language, and so on.

As Alexander moves through Ethiopia, its resemblance to the Indian regions where he began becomes more evident. The marvelous races, the wondrous animals, and even the land itself recall the India he left behind, for there are said to be two Ethiopias (line 6776) just as there were two Indias (line 4601). In a reenactment of his behavior in the northern wastes, Alexander with-

draws to a mountain to make a sacrifice. A voice speaks to him once again, but this time it tells him that he will never return, that his insatiable thirst to see the world will end not in the safe haven of home, but abroad. At last, Alexander has received tribute from every nation, and seen everything there is to see: "Ne remeint a veer nule merveille seue, / De mostre ne d'engin ne de beste mue" [No more marvels remained to be seen, neither monsters nor quaint inventions nor crouching beasts] (lines 6923-4). Therefore, Alexander returns; but he returns not back to Macedonia, but back to "Inde major" (line 6929). In a curious sense, the Orient has itself become home to this king of the Orient. Accordingly, the following episodes are focused on Alexander's identity and his ultimate fate, as he encounters the oracular trees at the very farthest limits of the East, and is entertained by the Oriental queen Candace in her private chamber. Both the grounds surrounding the trees and the chamber of Candace are said to be enclosures; these enclosures, however, represent not the secure, domestic spaces of home but instead unsettling locations where identity is revealed to be contingent, and danger is close at hand.

Initially, Alexander's encounter with Candace seems as though it could have taken place in the courts of France or England. This Oriental queen is "bele e blanche" (line 6943; cf. line 7751), fair-skinned and blonde as any European. As Alexander approaches the queen's palace, disguised as a messenger called Antigone, she listens to her minstrels play "un nouvel son / Coment danz Eneas ama dame Didon" [a new song of how Lord Aeneas loved Lady Dido] (lines 7650-51).[25] Perhaps remembering the fate of Dido, "Pensive en est Candace del torn de l[a] chançon" [Candace is made thoughtful by the turn of the song] (line 7655). She approaches Alexander first, sending messengers bearing luxurious gifts ranging from camels loaded with baskets of emeralds to a thousand armed Ethiopians (lines 6971). Candace's purpose here is not merely to propitiate Alexander: she also sends an artist along with her delegation, commissioned to make a portrait of the Macedonian. On his return, the portrait is used as a model for the construction of a life-size statue that will greet the conqueror during his encounter with Candace, which immediately follows his visit to the oracular trees of the sun and moon.[26]

After displaying all her rich treasures, Candace confronts Alexander with the truth of his identity: "Vous estes Alisandre; le non por quei changez?" [You are Alexander; why have you changed your name?] (line 7685). Alexander insists that he really is just "Antigone," the king's messenger, whereupon Candace takes Alexander off to a "privé manage" or private room (line 7698): "Alisandre," says Candace, "veez cy vostre ymage" [Alexander, see here your image] (line 7699).

By not only tricking Alexander, but actually trapping him alone in her private room, deep within the palace walls, Candace gains ascendancy over Alexander. Generously, however, Candace tells him not to be ashamed, because "tuit temps est usage / Qe femme deceit homme" [it always happens that woman deceives man] (lines 7710-11). Now that you're under my "discipline," says Candace, "Aloms ore juer suz cele cortine" [Let's go play now behind those bed-curtains] (lines 7748-49). They go "desur le lit parler d'amur fine; / Recordent la lesçon qu'afiert a tel doctrine" [onto the bed to speak of "fine amour," to rehearse the lesson that goes along with that doctrine] (lines 7755-6). Alexander has entered a kind of carnal paradise, where the deceptive nature of woman renders man powerless, and where no secrets can be held back.

Several scenes of enclosure punctuate Alexander's journeys throughout the world, ranging from the walling up of the tribes of Gog and Magog in the North, to the oracular cave in the deepest South, to the grove containing the trees of the sun and moon in the land furthest East, which is said to be "enclos . . . tot entur" [entirely enclosed] (line 7134). Like the grove of trees, where "flairent . . . les espices cum ceo fust Paradis" [the spices smelled as fragrant as if it were Paradise] (line 7101), Candace's bedchamber is a location which is at once paradise-like and threatening, offering both sensuous pleasure and imminent danger. The series of enclosures near the end of the narrative, including the grove of trees and the bedchamber of Candace, will end with a final enclosure: the "sarcu de fin or" (line 7982) which encloses Alexander's dead body, like the one in which he enclosed the body of his predecessor, Darius. The private room in which Alexander and Candace meet is a place at once strange and familiar: strange, because it is located in an eastern locale, decorated with curious and rare treasures, but familiar because it is a place where the knight Alexander can play at "fine amour" with a lady who is both "beautiful and white." The distant center of oriental luxury proves to epitomize the courtly ideal found (for the European reader) at home. In spite of its reassuring familiarity, this locale proves to be dangerous, for here Alexander's own identity becomes peculiarly fluid. In Candace's realm, he is known as Antigone, the messenger of Alexander, in order to protect himself from enemies in this alien land. Only in the queen's bedroom is he known by his right name, for she alone knows his true identity. He wavers between being Antigone and Alexander, messenger and king, depending upon his location.

THE TRANSLATION OF ALEXANDER

The destabilization of identity experienced by Alexander in the distant Orient signals the incipient end of the narrative. Having reached the "treis fins del mond"

[three ends of the earth] (line 5945) and placed monumental markers at the extreme East, North, and South, the great conqueror's own end is in sight. His dead body, lavishly anointed with oriental unguents and spices, is returned to Egyptian Alexandria, a formerly foreign land recently absorbed into the Macedonian Empire, and soon to become a province of greater Rome. Exploration to the very periphery of the world is necessarily followed by a return to the central regions of the realm. However, that exploration included only three of the four cardinal directions: Thomas declares that Alexander does not journey to the West, where the Irish, Spanish, and British are found, because of the lack of habitable territory there. How, then, to understand the significance of the westward turn which concludes the *Roman de toute chevalerie,* in the form of Alexander's bodily translation to Alexandria and the text's literal translation from Greek to Latin, from Latin to Anglo-Norman? The movement westward represents domestication and stabilization, an assimilation through translation of the dangerous Orient—at the price, however, of the traveler's own identity.

Translation, in the *Roman de toute chevalerie,* is a process carried out both in the macrocosm and in the microcosm, in the passage of empires and in the passage of the single man. Alexander's bodily translation proceeds from Babylon to Alexandria, as his golden sarcophagus makes its way westward. This movement is reflected in the *Roman de toute chevalerie's* account of its own textual transmission: Thomas declares that he translated his text from a "good book in Latin" (that is, the *Letter from Alexander to Aristotle*), which itself was thought to be a Latin translation of a Greek original. In it, Alexander tells of the great marvels of the East, none of them more amazing than the oracular trees of the sun and moon located at the very tip of the Orient. Those trees speak not only Greek but "indiene parole" (line 7178), words translated from the Indian language into Greek, into Latin, into Anglo-Norman. Thomas himself reflects on the nature of such translation in the passage where he names himself and describes the genesis of his book:

> E tut içoe ai dist, quei i fu et coment.
> La verité ai estrait, si l'estorie [ne] ment.
> N'ai sez faiz acreu, çoe vus di verreiement,
> Mes beles paroles i ai mis nequedent.
> N'ai acreu l'estoire ne jo n'i ost nient;
> Pur plaisir as oianz un atiffement;
> Home ne deit lange translater autrement;
> Qui d[ir]eit mot por mot, trop irreit leidement.

(lines P 10-17)

[I have told all of it, what happened there and how.
I have extracted the truth, if the story doesn't lie.
I have not exaggerated his deeds, that I tell you truly,
although I did add some pretty words here and there,
   nevertheless.

I have not embellished the story, nor have I omitted
  anything.
For the pleasure of the hearers there is some decora-
  tion;
One may not translate any other way;
He who does it word for word does very badly.]

Translation necessarily entails transformation; not
alteration of the substance of the story, the "verité," but
the incorporation of new words that both convey truth
and give pleasure. The beauty of the language, like the
beauty of Alexander's golden sarcophagus, lies in the
act of movement, in the translation across tongues, and
across cultures.

The Alexander romances, and the *Roman de toute chevalerie* in particular, offer crucial insights into the
dynamism of medieval conceptualizations of the shape
of the world. The modern dichotomy of East and West
can be fitted to medieval texts only awkwardly, owing
to the much more common conceptualization of a
tripartite world, made up of the known continents of
Asia, Europe, and Africa. Even Orosius' chronicle,
which posits a movement of empires from the East into
the West, begins with the tripartite division of the world,
a formula repeated in the opening of the *Roman de
toute chevalerie*:

> En trois la departirent . . .
> L'une est Aufrike, Asye est la seconde,
> Europe est la tierce.

(lines 34-6)

[They divide (the world) in three . . . One is Africa,
Asia is the second, Europe is the third.]

The opposition of East and West in the work of Orosius
is strikingly different from the modern dichotomy in
that the westward flow of imperial might is interrupted
by what Orosius calls the "guardianship" of the northern
kingdom of Macedonia and the southern empire of
Carthage. This quadripartite structure, as Fabbrini
argues, is intended to represent the cross, a symbol of
how Christian history is embedded within the development of the secular world. The opposition of East and
West in the later medieval chroniclers who base their
work on Orosius, such as Otto of Freising and Orderi-
cus Vitalis, differs even more greatly, for these chroniclers had to adapt their symbolic geography to accom-
modate the special role of Jerusalem in the context of
the crusades. In the *Roman de toute chevalerie,* the
quadripartite structure of the world found in the Orosian account is even more elaborately developed, as the
variable effects of climate are illustrated in the course
of Alexander's voyages to the ends of the earth.

He travels, however, into only "treis fins del mond":
conspicuously, Alexander does not venture into the
West. For Orosius, the West is Rome, the fourth and

greatest of the world empires that paves the way for the
advent of the spiritual empire of Jesus Christ. In the
history of Alexander, however, the West represents the
future, both the proximate future of Alexander's body,
translated westward in its golden sarcophagus, and the
more distant future of the European nations to come.
Alexander's world, in the *Roman de toute chevalerie,* is
the prehistory of the European nations; accordingly, its
symbolic geography anticipates the fulfillment of imperial ambitions in the West, as the uninhabitable
wasteland of the "Irish, Spanish, and British" gives rise
to the modern nations familiar to the twelfth-century
reader. The richly elaborated vision of the Orient found
in texts like this Anglo-Norman poem made it possible
to conceive of an idea of the West that was founded
upon humble origins, but imbued with the infinite
potential for growth and expansion.

Notes

1. Assessments of Said's binary opposition of East
   and West are many: see especially Robert Young,
   *Colonial Desire: Hybridity in Theory, Culture,
   and Race* (London and New York: Routledge,
   1995) and Aijaz Ahmed, *In Theory: Classes, Nations, Literature* (New York: Verso, 1992).

2. See the cogent assessment of the relationship of
   Bhabha's work, especially *The Location of Culture,* to Said's *Orientalism,* in Ato Quayson, *Post-
   colonialism: Theory, Practice or Process?*
   (Cambridge: Polity, 2000), 39-47. Spivak has
   mediated the European and North American reception of the work of the Subaltern Studies collective by translating its radical historiography into
   poststructuralist terms; see Gayatri Chakravorty
   Spivak, "Subaltern Studies: Deconstructing
   Historiography," *Subaltern Studies* 4 (1985): 330-
   63, and "Can the Subaltern Speak?" in *Marxism
   and the Interpretation of Culture,* ed. Cary Nelson
   and Lawrence Grossberg (Urbana: University of
   Illinois Press, 1988), 271-313. For the interrela-
   tion of Spivak and Said's work, see *Selected
   Subaltern Studies,* ed. Ranajit Guha and Gayatri
   Chakravorty Spivak, Foreword by Edward W. Said
   (Oxford and New York: Oxford University Press,
   1988), v-x, and Spivak, *A Critique of Postcolonial
   Reason: Toward a History of the Vanishing Present*
   (Cambridge, MA: Harvard University Press,
   1999), 264-72 and *Death of a Discipline* (New
   York: Columbia University Press, 2003), 105 n6.
   Thanks to Ritu Birla for help with these refer-
   ences.

3. Suzanne Conklin Akbari, "From Due East to True
   North: Orientalism and Orientation," in *The Postcolonial Middle Ages,* ed. Cohen, 19-34.

4. *The Anglo-Norman Alexander (Le Roman de toute
   chevalerie) by Thomas of Kent,* ed. Brian Foster

and Ian Short, 2 vols. (Anglo-Norman Text Society 29-33, London: Anglo-Norman Text Society, 1976-77). References to the *Roman de toute chevalerie* are cited in the body of the text by line number; translations are my own.

5. One of the most famous examples is Fulcher of Chartres, where the historian reflects on the paradoxically backward flow of *translatio imperii* to be found in the European-ruled Holy Land: "Consider, I pray, and reflect how in our time God has transferred the West into the East. For we who were Occidentals now have been made Orientals." See *Historia Hierosolymitana, (1095-1127),* ed. Heinrich Hagenmeyer (Heidelberg: Carl Winter, 1913), 748 (III.27.2-3); translated in *The First Crusade: The Chronicle of Fulcher of Chartres and Other Source Materials,* ed. Edward Peters, trans. A. C. Krey, second edn (Philadelphia: University of Pennsylvania Press, 1998), 281.

6. Paulus Orosius, *Historiarum adversum paganos libri vii,* in *Orose: Histoires (Contre les Païens),* ed. and trans. Marie-Pierre Arnaud-Linder, 3 vols. (Paris: Les Belles Lettres, 1990), 1:15-16; 1.2.1-12. Citations refer to the volume and page number of the edition, followed by book and chapter numbers. Translations are adapted from Arnaud-Lindet's very literal modern French translation; a more idiomatic English translation can be found in *The Seven Books of History Against the Pagans,* trans. Deferrari.

7. Fabrizio Fabbrini, *Paulo Orosio: uno storico* (Rome: Edizioni di Storia e Letteratura, 1979), 364-5; translation mine.

8. On views of Alexander in the twelfth century, see George Cary and D. J. A. Ross, *The Medieval Alexander* (Cambridge: Cambridge University Press, 1956), 208-9 and *passim*; Martin Gosman, *La Légende d'Alexandre le Grand dans la littérature française du 12e siècle une réécriture permanente* (Faux titre 133, Amsterdam and Atlanta: Rodopi, 1997), 143-67.

9. On the significance of this change, see Fabbrini, *Paulo Orosio,* 14 n57.

10. Compare the often minimalist depiction of Africa on medieval world maps described in Scott D. Westrem, "Africa Unbounded on an Unstudied European *Mappamundi* (ca. 1450) and in Related Cartography," in *Making Contact: Maps, Identity, and Travel,* ed. Glenn Burger, Lesley B. Cormack, and Natalia Pylypiuk (Edmonton: University of Alberta Press, 2003), 3-21, esp. 4 and 12-14.

11. A full study of the sources of the *Roman de toute chevalerie* can be found in Johanna Weynand, *Der Roman de toute chevalerie des Thomas von Kent in seinem Verhältnis zu seinen Quellen* (Bonn: Carl Georgi, 1911).

12. On the conjectural *Alexandre en Orient,* see Armstrong's comments in *The Medieval French Roman d'Alexandre,* vol. VI: *The Version of Alexandre de Paris,* ed. Edward C. Armstrong (Princeton: Princeton University Press, 1976), vii and 22ff.

13. *Roman d'Alexandre,* ed. Armstrong, 88-9 (line 15 in the version of Alexandre de Paris). Note that Foster and Short's edition of the *Roman de toute chevalerie* numbers the lines of the poem according to manuscript D; where D lacks an episode, they restart the numbering, adding the letter of the supplementary manuscript. Hence lines P1-178 follow line 3921 in D. On the limitations of Foster and Short's edition, see Gosman, 290-2.

14. Walter of Châtillon, *Alexandreis* VII.42-77, ed. Marvin Colker, *Galteri de castellione Alexandreis* (Padua: Antenore, 1978); *The Alexandreis of Walter of Châtillon: A Twelfth-Century Epic,* trans. David Townsend (Philadelphia: University of Pennsylvania Press, 1996), 126-7. On this passage, see Christine Ratkowitsch, *Descriptio picturae: Die literarische Funktion der Beschreibung von Kunstwerken in der lateinischen Grossdichtung des 12. Jahrhunderts* (Vienna: Verlag des Österreichischen Academie der Wissenschaften, 1991), 167-8, and Maura K. Lafferty, "Mapping Human Limitations: The Tomb Ecphrases in Walter of Châtillon's *Alexandreis,*" *Journal of Medieval Latin* 4 (1994): 64-81.

15. On the pagan "anti-Trinity" of Apolin, Mahum, and Tervagant in the *chansons de geste,* see Suzanne Conklin Akbari, "Imagining Islam: The Role of Images in Medieval Depictions of Muslims," *Scripta Mediterranea* 19-20 (1998-99): 9-27; on the names of the gods, see C. and Y. Pellat, "L'idée de Dieu chez les Sarrasins des chansons de geste," *Studia Islamica* 22 (1965): 5-42.

16. Noting a similar case of the interchangeability of ancient heroes with contemporary knights, Christine Chism argues that the figure of Alexander in the Middle English *Wars of Alexander* served as a vehicle for the concerns and the "ideology of the fourteenth-century British chivalry" (136) in "Too Close for Comfort: Dis-Orienting Chivalry in the *Wars of Alexander,*" in *Text and Territory,* ed. Tomasch and Gilles, 116-39.

17. On maps and in prose geographies, India is divided into two, three, or even more parts. See von den Brincken, *Fines Terrae,* 162.

18. In connection with the figure of the local informant, a native who offers direction and informa-

tion in an unfamiliar territory, compare Ora Limor's description of the "knowing Jew" in "Christian Sacred Space and the Jew," in *From Witness to Witchcraft: Jews and Judaism in Medieval Christian Thought,* ed. Jeremy Cohen (Wolfenbütteler Mittelalter-Studien II, Wiesbaden: Harrassowitz, 1996), 55-77.

19. See Mary Douglas, "The Forbidden Animals in Leviticus," *Journal for the Study of the Old Testament* 59 (1993): 3-23.

20. This unusual detail comes not from the *Cosmographia* of Aethicus Ister, the source for much of Thomas's account of Gog and Magog, but from the *Apocalypse* of pseudo-Methodius; noted in Smithers' edition of *Kyng Alisaunder* 2: 135-36 (note to line 5954).

21. Compare the source passage in the *Cosmographia* of Aethicus Ister, where the chill of the northern climate is not emphasized, and the natives even celebrate a late-summer religious festival: *Die Kosmographie des Aethicus,* ed. Otto Prinz (MGH, Quellen zur Geistesgeschichte des Mittelalters 14, Munich: Monumenta Germaniae Historica, 1993), 120-1, cap. 4.

22. Thomas of Kent uses the term "Sarazin" to refer to pagans in general, not just those found in the Orient, and also applies it to the pre-Christian period. Diane Speed suggests that such generic usage of the term was standard in twelfth- and thirteenth-century England; see "The Saracens of *King Horn,*" *Speculum* 65 (1990): 564-95, esp. 566-7.

23. The standard source on the tradition of the encounter of Alexander with the tribes of God and Magog is Andrew Runni Anderson, *Alexander's Gate, Gog and Magog and the Inclosed Nations* (Cambridge, MA: Medieval Academy of America, 1932). See also Andrew Gow, *The Red Jews: Antisemitism in an Apocalyptic Age, 1200-1600* (Leiden: E. J. Brill, 1995) and "Gog and Magog on *Mappaemundi* and Early Printed World Maps: Orientalizing Ethnography in the Apocalyptic Tradition," *Journal of Early Modern History* 2 (1998): 61-88; Scott D. Westrem, "Against Gog and Magog," in *Text and Territory,* ed. Tomasch and Gilles, 54-75.

24. Compare the climatic maps which illustrate Isidore, *Etymologiae* XIII.6, in which the northern habitable extreme is labeled with the Riphaean Mountains and the southern extreme with Ethiopia; examples in von den Brincken, *Fines Terrae,* plates 13-15.

25. This may refer to the twelfth-century romance of *Eneas*; see *The Anglo-Norman Alexander,* ed. Foster and Short, vol. II, 73.

26. On the oracular trees in the *Liber floridus, Roman de toute chevalerie,* and *Kyng Alisaundre,* see my *Idols in the East,* chapter 2 ("From Jerusalem to India") (forthcoming, University of Pennsylvania Press).

FURTHER READING

Criticism

Bosworth, A. B. "The Death of Alexander the Great: Rumour and Propaganda." *Classical Quarterly* n.s. 21, no. 1 (May 1971): 112-36.
    Concentrates on the death of Alexander—particularly the contemporaneous rumors that he was poisoned—and assesses the trustworthiness of the Royal Ephemerides.

Kratz, Dennis M. Introduction to *The Romances of Alexander,* translated by Dennis M. Kratz, pp. ix-xxxvii. New York: Garland Publishing, 1991.
    Presents an overview of several works featuring Alexander, noting two divergent views of him in medieval times, and gauging the merit and influence of the romances.

Michael, Ian. Introduction to *The Treatment of Classical Material* in the *Libro de Alexandre,* pp. 1-11. Manchester, United Kingdom: Manchester University Press, 1970.
    Discusses the *Libro de Alexandre,* one of the works that popularized Alexander's life in medieval Spain and France, exploring how best to approach it critically.

Wolohojian, Albert Mugrdich. Introduction to *The Romance of Alexander the Great by Pseudo-Callisthenes,* pp. 1-21. New York: Columbia University Press, 1969.
    Discusses the manuscript tradition of Pseudo-Callisthenes's romance, the source for most of the Alexandrian episodes of the Middle Ages.

Gesar

Tibetan epic, c. tenth century. Original language title is *Gling rje Gesar rgyal povi mam tar.*

INTRODUCTION

The *Gesar* epic is the lengthiest oral narrative in the world. No definitive, complete, scholarly edition has been published to date, but a planned version is expected to span over forty volumes, consisting of eight hundred thousand lines of poetry, containing sixteen million words. With other variants included, this edition is estimated to reach twenty million words. *Gesar* has no single author but is the collective product of the Tibetan folk culture, with its oral roots dating as far back as the fifth century; portions of it were first committed to paper in about the tenth century. *Gesar* has evolved and developed over the centuries, and it continues to change even to the present day, with a large number of variant renditions from area to area. Tibetan bards still recite the verses and have continued to be the major means of transmission of the epic. Well over a hundred individuals are engaged in the practice currently; many of them have an almost unfathomable ability to recite hundreds of thousands of lines from memory. The work's hero is King Gesar of Ling, the ultimate Buddhist warrior, who wages war against the evil forces of the four directions. Scholars focus on the epic's origins and development, while historians examine what it reveals about the Tibetan culture of the past, including the spread of Buddhism. As an entertaining work of literature and a seminal part of the Tibetan cultural heritage, the *Gesar* epic is beloved by millions, most especially the Chinese.

TEXTUAL HISTORY

In recent decades many Tibetologists and other scholars have attempted to ascertain the origin of the *Gesar* epic. There are numerous theories, but the dominant one was advanced by Chinese scholar Jiangbian Jiacuo (see Further Reading), who led the movement away from finding a single ur-text, instead characterizing the work as a "running river," developing and evolving over the centuries through oral presentation. Jiacuo identifies three previous schools of thought regarding its creation: 1) the *Gesar* epic comes from the later period of the Tubo Regime in Tibet, sometime in the eighth or ninth century; 2) it comes from the time of the Song and Yuan dynasties in the eleventh century; 3) it comes from the Ming and Qing dynasties, after the fifteenth century, with the entire creative process extending through the start of the twentieth. Jiacuo believes that the *Gesar* epic existed in embryonic form in about the fifth or sixth century and began taking a more definite shape in the seventh century. No single, all-encompassing text of the epic has ever been printed. Beginning with the founding of the People's Republic of China, however, the Chinese have extended great effort in documenting the work, with dozens of volumes systematically planned, arranged, and published as part of a national plan. Numerous audio recordings have also been made of portions of the work. The *Gesar* epic is renowned as a living epic, continuing to undergo modifications with each new telling.

PLOT AND MAJOR CHARACTERS

The *Gesar* epic begins with an account of the creation of the world, followed by a history of Tibet and the ascendancy of Buddhism from chaos. Evil spirits eventually dominate again, however, and demonic kingdoms cover the land. Gesar, who is sometimes referred to as Joru before becoming King, is sent from heaven by the gods to eventually wage war against the evil forces of earth. As a youth he causes mischief but it is already clear that he commands extraordinary magical powers. He has two uncles, sPyi dPon rong tsha and Khro thung. The former nurtures him, while the latter serves as a comic foil. As a result of his wild behavior, the boy and his mother are exiled from the kingdom of Ling. Despite his difficult circumstances, Gesar continues to develop his skills, strength, and willpower. He becomes the ruler of Ling at age twelve by winning a horse race with his magical horse, Kyang Go Karkar. King Gesar at once begins to conquer adjacent kingdoms. Many battles are waged against his bitterest opponent, the King of Hor; in one of them Gesar's halfbrother, rGya tsha, dies. Later the Hor King captures Gesar's Queen, Qomo. Gesar makes him pay for the affront with his life, and rescues his wife. Much later, in his eighties, after saving and bringing peace to the suffering people of Tibet, Gesar returns to heaven.

MAJOR THEMES

The primary themes explored throughout the *Gesar* epic involve the contest of good versus evil, the vanquishing of evil spirits through heroism and magic, and the promotion of truth and justice for the common people. In addition to its moral lessons, *Gesar* has also served as a repository of information about social and historical changes, class relationships, and the culture and customs of Tibet.

CRITICAL RECEPTION

Analyzing the basic structure of the *Gesar* epic, Samten G. Karmay notes problems in the chronological order of some of the events. He argues that the chronology issue and certain geographical confusion betray the fact that some of the episodes were inserted at a later date. In another essay, Karmay discusses how the meaning of the kinship concept *phu-nu* changes during the course of the epic. Walter Heissig examines the Mongolian *Gesar* epic's relation to the Tibetan versions and explores the introduction of prose portions into otherwise versified content. Critics have also written about *Gesar* in relation to other ancient epics and the oral tradition, and have debated the merits of traditional epic singers (who aim to perfectly reproduce a text) versus performers (who improvise, allowing themselves considerable artistic liberty in their presentation). Other critics have focused on how traditional epic singers commit such huge portions of the epic to memory, explaining how fixed formulas and mental composure play an important part in the performance. In an examination of new trends in *Gesar* research, Li Lianrong writes that scholars "need to shift [their] methodology away from treating the epic as a history whose content may be used to determine its time of origin." Lianrong further offers that, "when history enters the domain of traditional art, it does not submit to documentation; historical figures in an epic no longer belong to history, but to art and culture."

PRINCIPAL WORKS

Principal English Translations

The Superhuman Life of Gesar of Ling (translated by Alexandra David-Neel) 1934

The Warrior Song of King Gesar (translated by Douglas J. Penick) 1996

The Tibetan Epic of Gesar of Ling (translated by Robin Kornman) 2009

CRITICISM

Samten G. Karmay (essay date 1993)

SOURCE: Karmay, Samten G. "The Theoretical Basis of the Tibetan Epic, with Reference to a 'Chronological Order' of the Various Episodes in the *Gesar Epic*." *Bulletin of the School of Oriental and African Studies, University of London* 56, no. 2 (1993): 234-46.

[*In the following essay, Karmay discusses the difficulties in correctly ascertaining the chronological order of certain sections of the* Gesar *epic.*]

In the 1950s when Professor Stein was engaged in his research on the *Gesar* epic,[1] he wrote: 'If there ever existed a complete recension of all Chapters, they remain unknown to us. Neither written texts nor oral versions contain the totality of the epic story. And the ones that we know of at present, present themselves in the form of a literature that is still alive and mobile.'[2]

Since then, the situation has totally changed with the publication of many previously unknown chapters, not only those that have come down to us from the past but also the new products of a literature that is still expanding, as Professor Stein so accurately observed. What I am concerned with here, however, is the theoretical basis which underlies the ordering of the episodes relating to the hero and his life, and the notion of a correct 'chronological order' which the tradition presents, however fictitious the events may be. It is the materials which existed before our time which are most pertinent here and which permit us to identify the theoretical basis of which I speak. That basis provides a perspective on the question as a whole, and a guide through the tangled structure of the Tibetan epic. We are now, as I said, in a better position than in the 1950s to make an assessment of the whole body of Tibetan epic literature. We may not know the exact number of chapters and still less their correct 'order', though in Tibet the bards themselves do talk about the order and the number of chapters, as we shall see. Moreover, when they tell their own stories these are related to one or other major episodes and it would be incorrect to say that the bard invents a story which has no connexion with any of the episodes involving Gesar or his people. But this is not the place to enter on the 'circular argument' as to whether the written or the oral tradition came first.[3]

This epic literature has a beginning, namely, the chapter *lHa-gling,* and proceeds through various episodes in a 'chronological order' following the activities of the hero during his lifetime. It also has an end, since at a certain age Gesar no longer leads any expeditions. This does not mean that the bards or those who read the epic always do so in the correct order, or transmit it orally in a 'chronological order'. On the contrary, one episode will be more popular than another in a given locality and the bards choose which episodes to tell according to the circumstances.

There is, nevertheless, a correct sequence for the episodes, especially the great ones which are regarded as major campaigns and the purpose of Gesar's central mission on earth, prophetically foretold by the hero's divine aunt (Ma ne-ne rgyal-mo).

The Tibetan scholar gCod-pa Don-'grub recently met a number of bards living in different parts of Tibet and collected a great deal of research material on **Gesar.** He has given special attention to the question of the 'chronological order' of the various episodes and recently published a most interesting article on the subject in a collection of his other writings, all of which deal with what Professor Stein calls 'the traces of Gesar' found in Amdo.[4] This particular article gives the following 'chronological order' for the episodes relating to the life of Gesar.

When Gesar is in heaven he is called Thos-pa-dga'. He comes down to earth and is born to Seng-blon and 'Gog-za in order to bring happiness to the world.[5]

When Gesar is three years old, he subdues the demon child lCags-kyi lto-ldir.

At the age of one, he shoots and kills the three black birds sent by sGom-pa ra-tsa by means of magic with the help of Ma-bzhi Khro-thung, in order to undermine the life of Gesar. He subdues sGom-pa ra-tsa, who is himself a magician.

At the age of two, A-bra Srin-po mgo-dgu causes various misfortunes to the people of Gling [hereafter: Ling]. Gesar, in accordance with a prophecy received from Gong-ma rgyal-mo, subdues the animal with the help of his walking stick, called lCang-dkar, on the west bank of the river 'Bri-chu.[6]

At the age of three, he captures the fort Tsha-ba mda'-rdzong in Tsha-ba and makes its king Mig-brgya btsan-po a vassal. In this place he finds three special bamboo arrows. One of these he offers to the gods, another to the gNyan and the third is kept for men.[7]

At the age of seven, he captures the Fort of Goats, Kha-ser ra-yi ra-rdzong and its king, Kha-ser rgyal-po. He then drives back to Ling thousands of goats amongst

which there are white ones with conch horns and black ones with *garuḍa* horns. He distributes the animals equally among the people of Ling.[8]

At the age of eight, his paternal uncle Khro-thung fears that he may lose his political influence among the Ling people to his nephew. He accordingly banishes Gesar, together with his mother, to rMa-smad g.yu-lung sum-mdo and so causes them to live like yaks.[9]

At the age of nine, obeying the order given by sPyi-dpon Khra-rgan, Gesar, with the help of his uncle Khro-thung, sets out on a campaign against the king of 'Dan-ma. From the region of 'Dan-ma he brings barley grains back to Ling.[10]

At the age of ten, a great snowfall occurs in Ling country, such as had never been seen before and men and their herds are unable to move about. On the other hand, in rMa-smad where Gesar and his mother live there is sunshine, showers of flowers as well as rainbows and blossoming fruit trees. sPyi-dpon, the doyen of the Ling people, despatches rGya-tsha zhal-dkar, Gesar's elder half brother, and Tsha-spyang 'Dan-ma, a hero from the 'Dan country, to rMa-smad in order to rent the grassland in rMa-smad for the Ling people. Gesar gives them the use of the grassland.[11]

At the age of 12,[12] a great horse race is organized by the three principal clans of Ling. The stake is the throne of Ling and the hand of 'Brug-mo, famed for her beauty among not only the Ling but also the Hor people, the deadly enemies of the Ling. Gesar wins the race and picks up the first scarf (*ka-btags*) from the ground at the gallop. He therefore marries 'Brug-mo and is enthroned as King of Ling with the name of Seng-chen Nor-bu dGra-'dul.[13]

At the age of 13, the time comes to open the treasury of rMa Shel-brag. There Gesar finds various armaments: a coat of mail made of gold, silver and conch-shell; a helmet made of coral, a noose with a ring at its end, a hook, a sword, a garment made of broacade and a belt.[14]

At the age of 14, Gesar gathers together all the heroes of Ling in order to perform the ceremony of purification and the *bsang* offering to all the gods in heaven, the mountain spirits on earth, and those of the underworld. This ceremony is called *'Dzam-gling spyi-bsang,* the 'universal ceremony of purification for the world'. On this occasion, he shoots and kills a huge wild yak (*'brong*), because this beast is the 'residence' of the soul of the great demon, Klu-btsan who lives in the North and is the target of Gesar's next campaign.[15]

EPISODE I

At the age of 15, Gesar embarks on an expedition in order to subdue the most dreaded old demon called

Klu-btsan who lives in the North of Ling. After making friends with A-stag lha-mo, the demon's sister, he eventually kills the demon.[16]

EPISODE II

At the age of 24, while Gesar is still engaged on his campaign against the demon Klu-btsan the king of Hor, Gur-dkar-rgyal-po, makes an incursion into Ling and plunders it. He takes away Gesar's wife, 'Brug-mo, by force together with many children of the Ling people. Gesar is informed of the events in Ling when he has already spent nine years in the country of the demon. Leading an army consisting mainly of the subjects of the demon, he goes on a campaign against the Hor. The king of Hor surrenders. After appointing Shan-pa, a great general of the Hor army, as governor of Hor he returns with 'Brug-mo. This campaign takes nine years.[17]

EPISODE III

At the age of 33, following the prophetic instructions of sMan A-ne rgyal-mo, Gesar sets out on an expedition to 'Jang in the East, one of the four enemies of the four cardinal points. The king of 'Jang, gives himself up after a fight. This expedition takes three years.[18]

EPISODE IV

At the age of 36, heeding the prophetic instructions given by the White Brahman, he leads an army consisting of soldiers from 'Jang and Hor to Mon in the South. The king of Mon, Shing-khri, finally submits. Gesar invites a lama of Mon named Nor-bu to Ling.[19]

At the age of 39, following divine prophetic instructions, Gesar goes into retreat for a year on Mount Potala, paradise of Avalokiteśvara. (Note: in certain versions of the story, it is said that Gesar went into retreat because otherwise he would not be able to lead the soul of the king of sTag-gzig to heaven, this country being the objective of his next campaign.)

1. At the age of 40, he campaigns against sTag-gzig. Its king surrenders together with his fort, Nor-rdzong. Gesar brings back to Ling a great quantity of precious objects which he distributes among his people. This campaign lasts one year.[20]

2. At the age of 42, he campaigns against Kha-che. Its king, Khri-btsan, surrenders with his fort, gYu-rdzong, which is rich in turquoise. Gesar brings back to Ling a great quantity of turquoise which he distributes to his subjects. This campaign takes one year.[21]

3. At the age of 43, when many people from Ling carrying much gold leave for Lhasa in order to make offerings of gold to the 'face' of the three holy images in

Lhasa, they are robbed and many are killed in ambush by the people of Mi-nub rma-bya. Gesar, hearing of these events, leads a campaign against the latter. The king of Mi-nub surrenders together with his fort, Dar-rdzong, which is famed for its wealth of silk. Gesar obtains a large amount of silk in compensation.[22]

4. At the age of 44, the time has come for him to capture the fort Mu-tig-rdzong in Zhang-zhung which possesses a lot of pearls. Its king, lHun-grub grags-pa, gives himself up and Gesar obtains a great many pearls for distribution among his people in Ling.[23]

5. At the age of 46, Gesar's paternal uncle, Khro-thung, takes the daughter of the king of A-grags, Nyi-ma rgyal-mtshan, by force and the Ling people clash with those of A-grags. This gives Gesar an excuse to lead his army to attack the A-grags people. The fort gZi-rdzong, envied for its quantity of the precious stone *gzi,* is taken. He carries away the precious stones for distribution among his people.[24]

6. At the age of 47, he campaigns against Gru-gu. Its king Thog-rgod surrenders together with his fort, Go-rdzong, which contains an armoury. Gesar takes away much of the armour for his people.[25]

7. At the age of 49, he campaigns against Me-gling. Its king is defeated and after capturing gSer-rdzong, a fort famous for its gold, Gesar carries away much of the gold for the Ling people.[26]

8. At the age of 51, he campaigns against sMyug-gu. After the capture of the fort Drel-rdzong, the king Nyi-ma rgyal-mtshan surrenders with his mules. Gesar introduces different breeds of mules into Ling, as well as inviting back the daughter of the king, lHa-lcam Me-tog.[27]

9. At the age of 52, he campaigns against Sog-po. The king of Sog-po, Nyi-ma lhun-grub, gives himself up after fighting and offers Me-ri thog-rdzong, a fort known for its wealth of weapons. Gesar takes away a great number of catapults and 400 guns.[28]

10. At the age of 53, he campaigns against mNga'-ris, Brag-gi rgyal-po, the king of mNga'-ris, surrenders and the fort of gSer-rdzong, which contains a statue of the buddha made of gold, is taken.[29]

11. At the age of 55, he campaigns against Gangs-ri. Its king, Gangsdkar, is defeated and Shel-rdzong, the fort, is captured. Gesar finds there a coat of mail and a helmet made all of crystal.[30]

12. At the age of 56, he campaigns against Tsa-ri. Its king, dBang-chen stobs-grags, surrenders together with his fort, sMan-rdzong, famous for its wealth of medicines. Gesar introduces various medicines into Ling.[31]

13. At the age of 58, he campaigns against Bye-ri sTag-rtse. The king of Bye-ri surrenders together with his fort, Byur-rdzong. The fort houses statues of Amitāyus and Hayagrīva, both made of coral, which Gesar takes to Ling with other different types of coral.[32]

14. At the age of 61, he campaigns against China. Its king sTag-bdud surrenders and the fort Ja-rdzong is taken. Various kinds of tea are introduced into Ling.[33]

At the age of 63, Gesar goes into retreat in order to undertake acts of expiation because he has harmed so many living beings whilst on campaign.

15. At the age of 64, he campaigns against Dung-dkar. Its king, sTag-thub, surrenders and his fort sTag-rdzong is taken. Gesar takes from the fort 168 coats of mail, 9,800 arrows, a statue of Tārā and a noose, all made of conch-shell.[34]

16. At the age of 67, he campaigns against India. The king Chos-lung is defeated and his fort Chos-rdzong is taken. It contains thousands of volumes of *Prajñā-pāramitā* texts, written in gold, silver and turquoise.[35]

17. At the age of 68, he campaigns against Nepal. Its king, Bal-ri, surrenders together with his fort 'Bras-rdzong. From there Gesar introduces rice into Ling.[36]

18. At the age of 69, he campaigns against Bhara. Its king, Khyung-khri, is defeated and his fort Lug-rdzong is taken. From there Gesar introduces three breeds of sheep into Ling.[37]

Between the age of 69-80, Gesar is supposed to have continued taking small forts, listed below, but in fact many of the titles in this list are episodes connected with the cavalries (*dpa'-thul*) rather than the hero himself.

1. *Thog-gling g.yul-'gyed*

2. *Sog pyi-gling gser-rdzong*

3. *Po-ri gzi-rdzong*

4. *Phyi-gling khrab-rdzong*

5. *sMar-kham byu-ru-rdzong*

6. *sDe-dge chos-rdzong*

7. *Khyung-chen sgro-rdzong*

8. *sPyi-dpon shel-rdzong*

9. *sGa-sde khro-rdzong*

10. *rGya-tsha'i dngul-chu khro-rdzong*

11. *Go-gu khyi-rdzong*

12. *A-stag sha-rdzong*

13. *Li-khri rta-rdzong*[38]

14. *Srin-mo ra-rdzong*

15. *Bal-po lug-rdzong*[39]

16. *A-bse 'bri-rdzong*

17. *Zhang-zhung sman-rdzong*[40]

18. *rGya-tsha'i gri-rdzong*

19. *'Dan-ma'i mda'-rdzong*

20. *Khro-thung lcags-rdzong*[41]

At the age of 87 Gesar returns to heaven after having appointed his nephew dGra-lha rtse-rgyal king of Ling.[42]

Here ends gCod-pa Don-grub's discussion concerning the activities of the hero and his cavalries. It is perhaps here that I should mention some of the works on the epic that do not deal with a particular episode but present themselves as an account of the hero's life as a whole. Among these is one edited by Tashi Tsering, which has a very interesting introduction.[43]

THE FOUR ADVERSARIES

The 'chronological order' according to which the successive campaigns are presented shows that the Gesar epic is not recounted as a story consisting of random episodes. The narrative sequence of the epic is primarily related to the four major episodes, known as the 'four adversaries of the four quarters' (*phyogs-bzhi dgra-bzhi*).[44] These four then lead on to the military expeditions against the 18 countries or tribes (*rdzong-chen bco-brgyad*),[45] i.e. those occurring between the age of 40 and 69. These are considered minor actions by comparison with the four major episodes. The majority of the 18 tribes are situated in Tibet whereas the four major campaigns are against what are treated as foreign countries.

In the classical theory of the 'Four Sons of Heaven', Gesar is usually presented as the king of Phrom in the north.[46] This theory is further related to the four foreign kingdoms lying beyond the borders of Tibet, the most feared adversaries of the early Tibetan kings. In this framework, the Tibetan kingdom is conceived of as being at the centre and opposed to China in the east, India in the south, the Iranian world in the west and Turkestan in the north. These are known as the 'Four kingdoms of the borderlands' (*mtha'-bzhi rgyal-khab*)[47] and the early Tibetan kings were thought to be predestined to counter the challenge that these kingdoms might present. Historically, of course, Tibet had relations of various kinds with these countries, but the idealized world view reflected in the beliefs of the ancient Tibetans seem to me to have survived, at least in popular literature such as the epic under discussion.

A different classification of the 'four kingdoms of the borderlands', however, occurs in a manuscript from Tun-huang, where it is enmeshed in a cosmographic description of the four great rivers whose sources are situated in the regions of Mount Tise (Kailas).[48] This ninth-century document is the earliest source mentioning Phrom Gesar in the framework of the 'Four Sons of Heaven'. Interestingly, Phrom Gesar is here thought to be in the west rather than the north: i.e. (1) China in the east; (2) India in the south; (3) Phrom Gesar in the west; (4) Ta-zig and Tru(Dru)-gu in the north.

In another fairly ancient historical work, the *lDe'u chos-'byung* (written in 1261), Gesar is situated in the north, but no mention is made of Phrom. At any rate, the way in which the four kingdoms are presented is particularly worthy of consideration. According to the work in question, 'when Tibet did not have a king, it was governed by the twelve principalities who, however, were unable to oppose the enemies in the four directions (*phyogs-bzhi'i dgra*). India coiled round Tibet, like a snake; China slunk around Tibet, like a wolf lying in wait for sheep; Tazig (Iran) ranged over Tibet, like a hawk over a flock of birds; Gesar (of Phrom) attacked Tibet, like an axe swinging to cut down a tree'.[49] It is not my intention here to take up the arguments concerning whether Ling Gesar has any connexion with Phrom Gesar that have occupied scholars in recent times, although there is little doubt that the name Gesar is borrowed from Phrom Gesar.[50] The main concern of this [essay] is the basic structure of the Tibetan epic edifice.

Gesar is born with the mission of subduing his four adversaries of the four quarters. These are, according to the *lHa-gling*, (1) the demon in the east, China; (2) the demon in the south, 'Jang; (3) the demon in the west, Yar-khams byang-ma; (4) the demon in the north, Hor.[51]

The same classification is found in the *bDud-'dul*.[52] Here, too, China is included as the adversary in the east. However, the presentation of Klu-btsan as the demon of the west, but residing in what seems to be the north, Yar-khams byang-ma ri-brgyad, has been the source of considerable confusion as we shall see. The demons of the four quarters are further described as belonging to four categories of spirits: (1) the king of Hor, demon of the gods (*lha-bdud*); (2) the king of 'Jang, demon of the *btsan* (*btsan-bdud*); (3) the king of China, demon of the *dmu* (*dmu-bdud*); (4) the king of Yar-khams, demon of the *klu* (*klu-bdud*).[53]

But there is a change in this traditional presentation of the four adversaries in the episode of the horse race. China is replaced by Mon and the latter is put in the west and Hor in the east: (1) Yar-khams in the north; (2) Hor in the east; (3) 'Jang in the south; (4) Mon in the west.[54]

The term Hor is known to refer to a country inherited by Mongols or a people of Turco-Mongol origin, but within Tibet certain regions are also known by this name, and they are situated to the north-east in relation to Ling. It is also in this context, that is in relation to Ling, that Mon is thought to be situated in the west.

These four kingdoms or countries are conceived of as being in opposition to Ling, the 'Central continent,' like Tibet and its neighbours in ancient times. However, there has been some uncertainty surrounding one of the four adversaries. As we have seen, in the *lHa-gling* it is China, but in other texts China is replaced by Mon. Although the *Ma-yig*,[55] a prophecy which to my mind could represent the original written version of the *Gesar* epic if such ever existed, is said to have indicated the four great adversaries and the 18 small principalities that Gesar is destined to capture, there exists yet another tradition according to which the hero at first had three adversaries: (1) the first adversary (*dgra-mgo*), Klu-btsan in the north; (2) the second adversary (*dgra-sked*), Hor-ser in the east; (3) the last adversary (*dgra-mtha'*), 'Jang, in the south.[56]

In another version still, the last adversary is China and we find a very long text devoted to the episode in which Gesar's military adventure in China is recounted,[57] but this episode seems to have been ignored by those researching the *Gesar* epic in Tibet and China, perhaps for political reasons.

In this scheme, it is clear that only the first three of the four adversaries are involved, suggesting that the next major episode, contained in texts such as the *Mon-gling*, did not yet exist, but that as the epic continued to develop it acquired many more episodes and the adversary, Mon, then seems to have been added to make up the four. But in the process some confusion has resulted. This is evident in the way in which the author of the article which was commented on above, wavers even between the directions in which Yarkhams, Hor and 'Jang should be located. He places them as follows: the country of the demon in the west; Hor in the east; 'Jang in the north; Mon in the south (p. 9). This is quite simply impossible, though we have to allow that there is a certain amount of illogicality in the presentation of sources such as the *lHa-gling* concerning Klu-btsan, demon of the west but who lives in the north. 'Jang, on the other hand, simply cannot be in the north, or anywhere but in the south. It is strange that the author of the article should have run into this geographical confusion. He clearly follows the version of the four which contains both 'Jang and Mon and so is obliged to put 'Jang in the north which in turn makes him locate the country of the demon in the west. There may have been an element of political expediency in leaving out China as an enemy of Ling and accepting Mon instead, but the resulting arrangement is obviously unsatisfactory.

In conclusion, there is definitely a correct sequence of episodes in the **Gesar** epic even though, in oral tradition, a bard may tell any part of the story in any order he wishes, and a reader of the epic texts may choose to read whichever part he pleases first. The sources show, too, that there has existed more or less a set of the epic story as a whole, consisting of the *lHa-gling, 'Khrungs-skor, rTa-rgyug,* the four major episodes and the 18 minor ones. The list of these last differs from one version to another, but they are essentially the same.

The writers of the **Gesar** epic have chosen and can still choose an individual theme from any of the episodes centring upon the exploits of one or two characters in the epic, and so we find many different short chapters, such as the 20 titles listed earlier in this paper, which are not connected with the main corpus, but are concerned with adventures for the most part undertaken by various cavalries.

The three chapters in the Alexandre David-Neel collection in the Musée Guimet on which our team of scholars has been working in Paris for the last few years belongs to a similar category,[58] but the protagonist in these chapters is the hero himself. The author of these chapters has chosen the themes he wished to elaborate on in his own way, often in a condensed form, but always within the context of the epic itself. This brings us back to Professor Stein's observation that the Tibetan epic literature is still expanding. We may therefore conclude that there will never be an end to its elaboration so long as there is Tibetan culture. A good example of this is the chapter *'Jar-gling g.yul-'gyed,* an episode of **Gesar** set in Phyi-gling 'Jar, probably Hitler's Germany,[59] and the voluminous *Ti-dkar,* which is concerned with the hero's exploits in a country called Ti-dkar whose king is a *mu-stegs-pa (tīrthika).*[60]

A living epic tradition is indeed a remarkable phenomenon, and provides scholars with an engrossing object of research. But the result is that an already tangled web of material is constantly growing in complexity. The basic structure outlined above shows that this tangle at least has its origins in a systematic principle.

Notes

1. This article was presented as a paper at the second International Symposium of the Epic of King Gesar, organized by the Tibetan Academy of Social Sciences and held in Lhasa, 7-13 August 1991.

All the Tibetan texts on the Gesar Epic referred to in this article have been published. Those published by Bod-ljongs mi-mang dpe-skrun-khang, I have simply indicated as Lhasa, mTsho-sngon mi-rigs dpe-skrun-khang as Xining, Kans'u mi-rigs dpe-skrun-khang as Lanzhou, Si-khron mi-rigs dpe-skrun-khang as Chengdu, and Mi-rigs dpe-skrun-khang as Peking.

The Bhutanese edition (*The Epic of Gesar,* vols. 1-30, Thimphu, 1979-81) has not been used here because of the unreliability of the way in which it is edited and the confusion in its arrangements of the texts. Volumes 27, 28 and 30 are simply reproductions of recent Tibetan and Chinese editions without any indication of the references given in the originals.

I have not attempted to mention all the manuscripts containing different episodes and existing in various libraries or in private collections, nor do I assume the published texts mentioned in this paper are exhaustive. If a text is indicated here, it came to my notice before October 1991.

2. *Recherches sur l'épopée et le barde au Tibet* [hereafter *Recherches*] (Paris, 1959), 4. (The English translation is mine.)

3. Cf. Silke Hermann, 'Possibilities for a new perspective in epic research on the Tibetan Gesar', in H. Uebach and J. Panglung (ed.) *Tibetan studies* (Studia Tibetica, Bd. II), Munich, 1988, 197-201.

4. 'Gling ge sar rgyal po 'i skyes rabs lo rgyus rags tsam brjod pa' (*Gling ge sar rgyal po 'i shul rten gyi ngag rgyun ngo mtshar me tog phreng mdzes,* Xining 1989), 1-17.

5. R. A. Stein provides an edition of the *lHa-gling* and a summarised translation (*L'épopée tibétaine de Gesar dans sa version lamaïque de Ling* [hereafter *Version lamaïque*], (Paris, 1956), 19-39; 169-215. For recent publications of the same text, see *lHa-gling gab-tse dgu-skor* (Chengdu, 1980, 152 pp.); (Lanzhou, 1982, 155 pp.). Another version of the same episode told by the bard Grags-pa has also been published (Peking, 1984), 84 pp.

6. These last three episodes are concerned with the *'Khrungs-gling.* R. A. Stein has edited this text and made a summarised translation (*Version lamaïque,* 40-86; 216-74). For a recent publication of the same work, see *'Khrungs-skor* (Lanzhou, 1981, 171 pp.). For another, slightly different version of the same text, see *'Khrungs-gling me-tog ra-ba* (Chengdu, 1980, 186 pp.).

7. *Tsha-ba mda'-rdzong* (Lhasa, 1982, 213 pp.).

8. There does not seem to be any text concerned with this episode.

9. The text on this period of Gesar's banishment is probably contained in the Bacot manuscript in Paris, but this still awaits study.

10. *'Dan-ma'i nas-rdzong* (Xining, 1989, 116 pp.).

11. No text has so far been seen on this theme.

12. The connexion of the horse-race episode with the age of 12 by this author is a mistake. When Gesar is 12, the concern is with finding him a horse for the race, but the race itself is postponed until the following year, and therefore takes place when he is 13, see *rTa-rgyug* (Lanzhou, 1981), 12-14.

13. The text containing this episode is entitled *rTa-rgyug nor-bu-cha-bdun*. R. A. Stein has edited it and provided a translation/summary (*Version lamaïque*, 87-140, 275-355). The same text has also recently been published in other editions: *sTa-rgyug nor-bu cha-bdun* (Chengdu, 1981, 258 pp.), *rTa-rgyug* (Dharamsala, 1983, 185 pp.), *rTa-rgyug nor-bu cha-bdun* (Lhasa, 1981, 173 pp.) and *rTa-rgyug dpyid-kyi nyi-ma* (Xining, 1981, 276 pp.). The songs in the episode of the horse race in the text published by Stein have been translated into French; see M. Helffer, *Les chants dans l'épopée tibétaine de Gesar d'après le livre de la course de cheval* (Genève-Paris, 1977.)

14. *rMa shel-brag* (Xining, 1982, 202 pp.). The attribution of this event to the age of 13 is uncertain. The text mentioned gives the age as eight (p. 2) and uses the name Jo-ru as if the event were taking place prior to the race.

15. *'Dzam-gling spyi-bsang* (Lanzhou, 1980, 196 pp.).

16. bDud-'dul (Lanzhou, 1981, 201 pp.).

17. *Hor-gling g.yul-'gyed* (Xining, 1980, vol. I, 562 pp., vol. II, 668 pp.). The same version of events appears in vol. I of the edition published in Lhasa (1980, 441 pp.; I have not seen vol. II). Another, much shorter version is *Hor-'dul-gyi rtogs-pa brjod-pa g.yul-rgyal lha'i ruga-sgra* (Chengdu, n.d., 251 pp.).

18. *'Jang-gling g.yul skor* (Delhi, 1965, 382 pp.): *Gesar 'Jang-gling sgrung.* by Ngag-dbang bsam-gtan phun-tshogs (Gangtok, 1977, vol. I, 596 pp., vol. II, 607 pp.).

19. Four long texts which are for the most part identical and have the same title, *Mon-gling g.yul-'gyed* (Lhasa, 1980, 470 pp.; Chengdu, 1982, 519 pp.; Xining, 1982, 353 pp.; Lanzhou, 1983, 419 pp.).

20. *sTag-gzig nor-rdzong* (Lanzhou, 1979, 443 pp.). Another, slightly different version of the same work is published under the title *sTag-gling g.yul-'gyed* (Lhasa, 1979, 385 pp.).

21. *Kha-che g.yu-rdzong* (Lhasa, 1979, 236 pp.).

22. ? *Mi-nub rma-bya* (I have not seen this text).

23. *Zhang-gling g.yul-'gyed* (Lhasa, 1982, 143 pp.); *Zhang-zhung mu-tig-rdzong* (Lanzhou, 1984, 328 pp.).

24. *A-grags gzi-rdzong* (Xining, 1985, 662 pp.).

25. *Gru-gu go-rdzong* (Lhasa, 1988-89, vol. I, 883 pp., vol. II, 246 pp.). The same work was published in Dharamsala (1982-83) in three volumes.

26. *Me-gling gser-rdzong* (Xining, 1983, 223 pp.); *Me-gling g.yul-'khrugs* (Lhasa, 1982, 328 pp.).

27. *sMyug-gu drel-rdzong* (Lhasa, 1982, 662 pp.).

28. *Me-ri thog-rdzong* (I have not seen this text).

29. *mNga'-ris gser-rdzong* (Chengdu, 1981, 233 pp.).

30. *Gangs-ri shel-rdzong* (Chengdu, 1982, 377 pp.).

31. *Tsa-ri sman-rdzong,* written by dBang-chen stobs-rgyal of mGo-log and completed in 1987 (Xining, 1990, 408 pp.).

32. *Bye-ri byur-rdzong* (Xining, 1983, 518 pp.). Another text related to this episode is *Ge-sar sgang-gling sgrung* (Gangtok, 1977, 675 pp.).

33. ? *rGya-nag ja-rdzong* (I have not seen this text).

34. ? *Dung-dkar stag-rdzong* (I have not seen this text).

35. ? *rGya-gar chos-rdzong* (I have not seen this text).

36. ? *Bal-ri 'bras-rdzong* (I have not seen this text).

37. ? *Bhara lug-rdzong*. At the second International Symposium of the Gesar Epic, held in Lhasa in August 1991, the bard bSam-grub recited an episode of the epic which he called *Bal-ra lug-rdzong*. Cf. no. 15 in the list of minor texts.

38. *Sog li-khri rta-rdzong,* by sGrung-gter Nyi-ma rang-shar in mDo-smad (Amdo), (Chengdu, 1990, 254 pp.). Similar but much longer texts include *Sog-stod rta-rdzong* (Dharamsala, 1982, 585 pp.); *Sog-smad khrab-rdzong,* by Don-rgyud nyi-ma, the eighth Khams-sprul (b. 1931), (Dharamsala, 1985, 823 pp.). For his other works on Gesar, see below.

39. Cf. n. 37.

40. It is not Zhang-zhung, but Shang-shang and is probably identical to the text entitled *Shang-shang sman-rdzong* written by Grub-rigs khyu-mchog

(Lanzhou, 1984, part 1, 1-395, part 2, 396-638). Another text related to this episode is *mThing-gling g.yul-'gyed* (Lhasa 1985, 241 pp.).

41. To this list can be added several more texts that have appeared recently: *Sum-gling g.yul-'gyed* or *Sum-pa mdzo-rdzong* (Lhasa, 1981, 135 pp.); another version of the same episode and the same title (Chengdu, 1982, 204 pp.); *Shan-'dan stag-seng kha-sprod* (Chengdu, 1982, 244 pp.); *Ri-nub (a-dkar rdo-rdzong)* (Xining, 1985, 176 pp.); *By-ang sgo-ra rgyal-po'i tshva-g.yang*, by lHa-dge bDud-mdul rnam-rgyal (Dharamsala, 1985, vol. I, 683 pp., vol. II, 284 pp.); *Ja-rong 'bru-rdzong*, by Nang-so Blo-bstan (Lhasa, 1987, 522 pp.); *rMi-li gser-rdzong*, by 'Brong-stod lHa-dge (Dharamsala, 1985, vol. I, 513 pp., vol. II, 808 pp.); *Glang-ru* (Xining, 1985, 132 pp.).

42. The bards (*sgrung-mkhan*) do not talk about Ge-sar's death because he 'never dies'. However, the *dMyal-gling* episode is about his 'departure from the earth', see *dMyal-gling rdzogs-pa chen-po* 'rediscovered' by Rig-'dzin drag-rtsal rdo-rje in mGo-log (*The Epic of Gesar*, Thimphu, 1977, vol. 31, 357 pp.). There are other texts which have similar titles but contain different minor episodes: *dMyal-ba'i le'u* or *dMyal-gling*, by 'Dan Chos-kyi dbang-phyug (Tibetan Bonpo Monastic Centre, 1973, 526 pp.). This is concerned with Gesar's rescue of some of his cavalry who fall into hell after their deaths. A similar text is *dMyal-gling mun-pa rang-gsal* (Xining, 1983 109 pp.), which deals with Gesar's rescue of A-stag lha-mo, demon Klu-btsan's sister, from hell, and Gesar's complic-ity. The *dmyal-gling* or *dmyal-le* types of text are therefore not always connected with his own departure for heaven, but with his actions spread over other periods of his life.

43. *rTsa-ba'i rnam-thar*, 1-44 (*Gling-rje ge-sar-gyi rtsa-ba'i mdzad-pa mdor-bdus*, Burmiok Athing Collection Series, vol. III, Dharamsala, 1981). Other texts of the same type are: *Gling ge-sar rgyal-po'i rnam-thar* (Lhasa, 1989, 117 pp.); *'Dzam-gling skyes-bu'i chos-sgrung sil-ma las gser-chos 'og-min bgrod-pa'i them-skas gsang-ba'i rgya-can* (*Chos-sgrung dang bshad-pa rnam-bdun*. Chengdu, 1990, 1-87); *Srid-pa Chags-lugs* (Xining, 1987, 332 pp.) This last work deals with the hero's life only up to the horse race (*rTa-rgyug*).

44. *lHa-gling* (Lanzhou, 1982), 42; *bDud-'dul* (Lanzhou, 1980), 15ff.

45. R. A. Stein's translation of the line *mtha'-bzhi rgyal-khag bco-brgyad* as 'Les ennemis humains venus des dix-huit royaumes des quatre confins' is incorrect (*Version lamaïque. lHa-gling*. 195); *bDud-'dul* (Lanzhou, 1980), 12.

46. *Recherches*, 254-61; Ariane Macdonald, 'Note sur le diffusion de la "théorie des Quatre Fils du Ciel" au Tibet', *Journal Asiatique*. CCL, 1962, 531-48.

47. The bilingual inscription of the Sino-Tibetan peace treaty (H. Richardson, *The corpus of early Tibetan inscriptions*, London, Royal Asiatic Society, 112, l. 37; 108, ll. 13-14); *lHa-gling* (Lanzhou, 1982), 79, 84, 87, 104.

48. Pelliot tibétain 958, fol. 1a-1b, A. Macdonald and Y. Imaeda, *Choix de documents tibétains con-servés à la Bibliothèque Nationale*, tome 1 (Paris, 1979), pl. 241-2: cf. also Ariane Macdonald, 'Note sur la diffusion . . .', 532-5.

49. *mKhas-pa lde'us mdzad-pa'i rgya-bod-kyi chos-'byung rgyas-pa* (*Gangs-can rig-mdzod*, 3, Lhasa, 1987), 220-26.

50. R. A. Stein, *Recherches*, 252-3 and 'Une source ancienne pour l'histoire de l'épopée tibétaine: Le Rlangs Po-ti bse-ru', *Journal Asiatique*, CCL, 1962, 85.

51. *lHa-gling* (Lanzhou, 1982), 15.

52. Lanzhou, 1980, 12, 83, 98, 108, 116, 119.

53. Ibid., 108.

54. *rTa-rgyug* (Lanzhou, 1981), 2, 238-9.

55. Ibid., 239.

56. See *Mon-gling g.yul-'gyed* (Lhasa, 1980), 1-2.

57. *Gesar rgya-gling sgrung* or *Nag-po rgya-gling* (Gangtok, 1977, 527 pp.). (*da dgra-mtha' nag-po rgya-la gtad / rgya-nag khrims-sgo phye-ran thal*, 21).

58. They are *sMan-lis*, *Tshe-lis* and *Hor-lis* and belong to a large work of many more chapters, but the three named are the only ones to have reached Paris. The author of these chapters is dBang-chen Nyi-ma, a Bonpo layman and chief of the dMar-ru region in Khams who lived around the beginning of this century. The French translation of these chapters is now complete and it is hoped that it will be published in the near future.

59. Written by Byang-chub sems-dpa' chos-kyi blo-gros, alias Don-rgyud nyi-ma, the eighth Khams-sprul (Lhasa, 1983, 448 pp.). His other works on Gesar are: *U yan-gling* (Palampur, H. P., 1974, vol. I, 659 pp., vol. II, 512 pp.). For other similar recent works, see also Karma rang-byung phrin-las (Kalu Rinpoche), *dBus 'chi-bdag cham-la phab-pa* (Bir, 1975, vol. I, 870 pp., vol. II to appear).

60. Written by Kha-tsha pra-pa Ngag-dbang blo-bzang from Ri-bo-che in Amdo (Lhasa, 1986-89, vol. I, 411 pp., vol. II, 761 pp., vol. III, 533 pp.; *Bhe-gling g.yul-'gyed,* another recent work, is by sNam-snang rdo-rje (Xining, 1989, 386 pp.).

Samten G. Karmay (lecture date 1993)

SOURCE: Karmay, Samten G. "The Social Organization of Ling and the Term *Phu-Nu* in the *Gesar Epic.*" *Bulletin of the School of Oriental and African Studies, University of London* 58, no. 2 (1995): 303-13.

[*In the following excerpt, originally delivered as a lecture in 1993, Karmay examines the social and political structure of Ling society and the change in the meaning of* phu-nu *(a kinship concept) in the course of the* Gesar *epic.*]

In recent studies of the Tibetan epic, much effort has been spent on analysing the origins and types of material that make up the epic literature, but no study presents an overall view of Ling (Gling) society.[1] In the paper I gave at the second Symposium on the *Epic of King Gesar* at Lhasa in 1991, I therefore discussed the theoretical basis upon which the whole of Tibetan epic literature is built. I demonstrated that the Tibetan epic reveals a basic principle as well as a 'chronological order' in its development. Without this theoretical basis, Tibetan epic literature appears as a tangled web of material which is moreover still growing in complexity.[2]

In the present [essay], I shall deal with another aspect of this epic literature: the social organization of the society as expressed through the concept of *phu-nu.* In order to understand the significance of the whole body of material, we must know what kind of society is being represented in it, on what basis that society is organized and to what extent Tibetan traditional society is reflected in the epic. Is this society clanic (*rus*) or tribal (*tsho*), or both? Is it merely a static society with a unique hero? The epic undoubtedly reflects Tibetan society and its social organization at a given period, but at what level of development, clanic, ethnic or national, can we take Tibetan epic literature as a basis of identity?

In the epic, King Gesar, the hero, has celestial parents in heaven as well as others in the subterranean world, but he is born as a man into a terrestrial family. It is this family which plays a major role in the social and political life of the society in Ling over which he rules. The hero is, of course, often idealized as an edifying Buddhist figure. This presentation of him is more noticeable in some episodes than in others, especially when the author of the episode is explicitly a Buddhist, but this does not prevent the epic from making him an ideal Tibetan layman who upholds the honour of his ancestral lineage and observes other social norms in matters such as patriotism, bravery, fame, shame, treachery, treason, and above all leadership in the society. It is for this reason that the Tibetan Buddhist clergy in general have often disapproved of the epic and reserved no place for its literature within their own communities, monastic or otherwise.

Ling society is made up of various tribes (*tsho-ba*). How these tribes collaborate with each other, in alliances or by marriages with their tribal chiefs as distinct from their king, Gesar, will also be discussed, as will their place in the social hierarchy and their political status.

1. THE CELESTIAL FAMILY

Like the first Tibetan king, gNya'-khri btsan-po, Gesar also descends from heaven to earth, but the parallelism in the two myths is not complete: gNya'-khri btsan-po reigns as a descendant from heaven,[3] whereas Gesar is born as a man. In heaven, Gesar's father is Tshangs-pa dkar-po and his mother, 'Bum-skyong. There are other members of the family, including an aunt called Ma Ne-ne. The father is identified with Brahma; the aunt is known by different names and has various functions as a goddess in both the Bonpo and Buddhist legends. These two—the father and the aunt—play a very important role in Gesar's life on earth. The father often appears in Gesar's visions and gives him advice, while the aunt's intervention in his life is literally incessant: she constantly appears in his visions and dreams, telling him what he must and must not do. Tshangs-pa and Ma ne-ne are presumably brother and sister (she is not the sister of 'Bum-skyong), but this is never made explicit. Other members of the celestial family do not have specific functions apart from being evoked occasionally by name at the beginning of particular songs.

2. THE TERRESTRIAL FAMILY

Seng-blon has three sons, Gesar being the second, by three wives. He has no daughters. Gesar has another father on earth, a *gnyan*, i.e. a mountain spirit named Ger-mdzo. One of the early Yar-lung kings also had as father a *gnyan*. It is very common among the population in Amdo that when a man becomes politically powerful and prestigious, he is regarded as the son of the local mountain divinity and there is a special term for this: *gnyan-bu* 'the son of a *gnyan*'.[4]

3. THE SUBTERRANEAN FAMILY

'Gog-bza, Gesar's mother is regarded as a daughter of Klu gTsug-na, an aquatic divinity in the subterranean world.

THE SOCIAL ORGANIZATION OF LING

Tibetan society has often been stigmatized for its practice of polyandry, especially by foreign travellers. It is true that polyandry was once quite common, but it was by no means the only prevailing custom.[5] In the epic literature, on the contrary, the kinship system is based entirely on polygyny and quite often also on monogamy, as we shall see shortly. No instance of polyandry has so far been found in the epic which might suggest that in that context, it is not considered an ideal basis for the human family unit.

Gesar's earliest named ancestor, Ra-khra, has three sons, all by the same mother.[6] She is his only wife, but his father, Seng-blon has three women: Gesar is born to the second, a woman from the 'Gog clan (*rus*), who is hence called 'Gog-bza'. The first woman bears a son to Seng-blon called rGya-tsha Zhal-lu. The third woman, a woman from the Rong clan, bears a son called Rong-tsha sKar-rgyan. Gesar himself has only one wife, but has a number of women friends described as 'cooks' (*ja-ma*).[7] His elder half-brother has three wives.

From the story of the conflict between 'Gog and Ling, we know that 'Gog was invaded by Ling[8] and that 'Gog-bza', Gesar's mother, was taken by force, thus reflecting the custom of marriage by capture still practised in Amdo until very recent times. She then became a *ja-ma* in the family of 'Bum-pa. sKya-lo, the tribe from which Gesar's wife, 'Brug-mo, comes is regarded as not being in Ling. In Ling society the most important clan is the gDong, the clan which has precedence over every other clan and social unit in all social and political matters. It is into this clan that Gesar is born and in his time it is represented by three brothers, each with his own family.

sPyi-dpon Khra-rgan, the elder brother: he is depicted as the wisest man of Ling, he who knows the entire genealogical history of the clan. He has three sons by one woman. All three sons serve as knights (*dpa'-thul*) of Gesar's. The third is killed in the campaign against the Hor.

Khro-thung, the second brother: he is the father of nine sons by five different women, one of whom is from the 'Dan tribe. His nine sons serve as knights of Ling. Khro-thung is the adversary of his cousin, Gesar. He is depicted as a cunning rogue and poltroon. Nevertheless, he is an important character in the epic and figures in various legends. When he was a baby, his mother was unable to give him enough milk herself, so he was nourished at the breasts of a female yak, a she-goat, and a bitch, hence his epithet of Ma-bzhi (Four Mothers).[9] He is depicted as a great talker, but nobody believes what he says. He was in the past an important leader of Ling, but was ousted and continues to dream

of being the king of Ling. He plots to undermine his younger brothr, Seng-blon, the true ruler. By various signs he prophesizes that Gesar will be born to Seng-blon and that he will never have a chance to become king. Later he secretly covets 'Brug-mo, his cousin's future wife. When Ling is in conflict with one of its enemies, he is often suspected of treason.

Seng-blon, the third brother: he is the reigning king of Ling whom Gesar succeeds. He is depicted as a person of mild character and Khro-thung exploits his weakness. However, Seng-blon is the father of three sons by different women. In Tibetan society, the second brother, more than the other brothers, often tends to assume responsibility for the family. So in the epic both Khro-thung, the uncle, and Gesar, the cousin, are depicted as the second of three brothers, a kinship feature more emphasized to date in the epic literature of other societies; for instance, in the epic of Buryatia.[10]

The gDong clan in the Tibetan epic therefore exemplifies the basic kinship system around which the social and political organization of Ling society revolves. It is founded on patrilineal descent through the transmission of the bone substance of the father, as in all populations of Tibetan culture. Great stress is often laid on the *prima* of the kin (*pha-khu, pha-tshan, sras-dbon*), rather than on affines (*ma-zhang, ma-tshan, lcam-sras*), but the affines are regarded as no less important, from the standpoint of the socio-cultural context, as we shall see.

The Ling people therefore identify themselves through the intermediary of an origin myth of the gDong clan:

Ra-khra rgan-po has three grandsons. Each one is married to one of the three daughters of the mountain divinity rMa-chen sPom-ra.[11] One day, Ra-khra tells his grand-daughters-in-law to go to rMa and bring back whatever each one finds. The elder goes to the highlands in rMa and finds a golden yoke, a span in length; the second goes to the middle lands and finds a handful of tamarisk bush; and the third goes to the lowlands and finds the tail of a wolf. So the descendants of these women are called respectively gSer-ba (the Gold), 'Om-bu (the Tamarisk) and Mu-spyang (the Wolf). The descendants of the first couple occupy the highlands of Ling, those of the second the middle lands and those of the third the lowlands.[12]

The myth also relates that the grandfather of the three brothers is killed by wolves and the corpse is buried on Mount A-myes rMa-chen. That is why, it explains, the land of Ling is so prosperous and full of brave men. I am unable to interpret the significance of this part of the myth's content: Gesar does, of course, discover a great armoury on the mountain along with other things, but this brings one no closer to understanding the connexion between the corpse, the armoury, and Ling's prosperity.

On the other hand, the myth not only provides an explanation for the matrimonial alliance between Ling and rMa in the epic but also throws light on the socio-cultural context in which women play a significant part. In the myth, it is the women who provide the names for their offspring, but the offspring nevertheless remain within the gDong clan: that is, they identify themselves by patrilineal descent. The lineage of the three brothers constitutes the basis of the primitive clan structure of Ling from which branches all other clan groups in Ling descend. The three also represent the senior, middle and junior patrilineal lines of descent respectively (*che-rgyud, 'bring-rgyud, chung-rgyud*).

In real geographical terms, the land of Ling (Gling-yul) is situated in Khams, to the west of the river rDza-chu (Mekong), whereas the land of rMa (rMa-yul) is in Amdo, to the north-east of the river. The centre of rMa (rMa-sked), which is generally known as 'Go-log, is dominated by the snow mountain A-myes rMa-chen. The distance between Ling and rMa is therefore considerable, but this has not prevented the myth from envisaging an association of the two regions in the epic. The divinity of A-myes rMa-chen is the protective deity of the gDong clan as well as their wife-giver. In my view 'Gog-bza', Gesar's mother, comes from there, as do the other women in the myth. The clan name 'Gog is probably connected with the toponymy of 'Go-log. The land of rMa is also where Gesar and his mother are banished. In many episodes, Ling and rMa are represented as if they were one and the same place.[13]

As was said above, in the terrestial world, Gesar has a *gnyan* as father, that is, a mountain spirit represented by Mount Ger-mdzo which, being on the father's side, is situated in the Shar-zla region of Ling and not in rMa; and his human mother is regarded as an embodiment of a water spirit of the lakes. In accounts of the genealogy of the hero, this concept is often expressed in the following manner: 'the lineage of the father is from a mountain and that of the mother from a lake.'[14] This notion of the mountain as male and the lake as female is further expressed in popular rituals particularly in Amdo where it is only men who propitiate the mountain spirits up in the mountains and only women who propitiate water spirits down in the valleys.[15] The mountain spirits are often regarded as male and the *klu* as female in the local beliefs. (When the word *klu* is used to translate the Sanskrit term *nāga* in the Indian Buddhist texts, we find not only the Indian-based notion of male *klu* but of a caste-system of the *klu* as well.)

The epic envisages Ling society in its early stage as composed of six tribes (*gling tsho-drug*). They are linked together by the concept of *phu-nu* to which we shall return below. As for the identification of the six, to my knowledge, it is never very clearly stated precisely which tribes are meant. Like the number three, the number six enjoys great popularity in the epic. There are invariably only three brothers in the epic's pedigrees. Tibet's primitive clans are also six in number. In reality, the tribes that are enumerated as under the domination of Ling are always many more than six: the numbers of these tribes, as well as their names, vary in different episodes. In one episode, the six tribes are given as follows: (1) 'Bum-pa; (2) 'Dan-ma; (3) sTag-rong; (4) rGya; (5) sKya-lo; (6) 'Bri ('Gru).[16]

These six tribes constitute the core of Ling social organization. 'Bum-pa is the name of the family into which Gesar is born and whose clan is gDong. The lineages of this clan, which are represented by the three brothers mentioned above, constitute the upper social stratum of Ling society; but not all the three brothers use the name 'Bum-pa.

'Dan-ma is the name of a region in Khams and in the epic it is made subject to Ling after a conflict between them; a series of ministers of the ruling house of Ling is provided through a marriage alliance and, in Gesar's time, a knight of the same name—'Dan-ma—becomes one of his ministers. His name is therefore often preceded by the word *tsha-zhang*, 'nephew and maternal uncle'.[17]

sTag-rong, too, is the name of a region which becomes attached to Ling after a conflict between the two.[18] Khro-thung is then appointed governor of this region, hence sTag-rong Khro-thung.

The rGya tribe, however, is not known at all. There does not seem to be anything about it in the epic which gives only the name of a person of this tribe. Certainly rGya as a tribal name occurs only in this episode and in this list.

sKya-lo is a tribe whose location, as in the case of sTag-rong, is distinct from that of Ling. In certain episodes sKya-lo seem to be situated in rMa.[19] Gesar's wife comes from one of the families of this tribe called sGa, hence sGa-bza' 'Brug-mo.

The connexion of the tribe 'Bru ('Gru) with Ling is not explicit, but it is represented by a tantric magician who is one of the 30 knights.

This rough sketch gives some idea of how the epic represents Ling social and political structure. It is clear from this list that only the 'Bum-pa are members of the Ling élite class. Ling itself is divided into three regions. Each region has its subdivisions, but in theory all the social strata of Ling belong to the same clan, gDong, as is envisaged in the myth discussed above.

Under Ling rule, there are therefore five tribes, two of which are presented as having been annexed after a war and these 'non-Ling' tribes are not only vassals, but form marriage alliances with Ling. The three women of the origin myth come from rMa, and Gesar's mother also comes from another land. The myth depicts a Ling society as practising exogamy. However, when the six tribes are listed, a number of the clan names indicate that endogamy is prevalent: for instance, the sKya-lo, one of the six tribes, provided Gesar's wife.

In the epic, the mode of livelihood in Ling is presented as that of an agro-nomadic society as is in fact the case today for many of the people in Khams and Amdo. The epic boasts of the people of Ling keeping herds up in the mountains and houses, castles and farmlands down in the valleys, but the predominant aspect of Ling society is nevertheless nomadic pastoralism. References to numerous tent-dwellings and changing camps recur constantly.

Gesar, the king of Ling, is served by 30 knights who are mostly from Ling itself, but some are chiefs of the five tribes. Some of these, 'Dan-ma, for example, are ministers, while others are military chiefs leading the army of their own tribe under the overall command of Gesar. In the course of Ling's expansion, the epic recounts the growth of an empire and military conflicts become a recurring theme. Many of the 30 knights die heroic deaths in action and are replaced by men from the newly conquered people to maintain the earlier chain of command.[20]

All this social and political movement in Ling is organized, determined and regulated through the concept of *phu-nu*. This concept is therefore the basis of development in the beginning, at the tribal stage, but it inevitably becomes difficult to maintain as Ling gradually becomes an empire and extends its territorial possessions in different parts of Asia.

THE CONCEPT OF *PHU-NU*

To belong to the *phu-nu* is an indication of a certain social status: and those who belong to it have the right to ranks and other social claims. A man from each of the six tribes is sent to invite back the young Joru (Gesar's childhood name) to Ling from the land of rMa to which he has been banished. These six men are described as being the six *phu-nu*.[21] Therefore the expression *phu-nu* is applied not only to the members of Ling society itself who are all members of the same clan, gDong, but also to the people of the annexed tribes who belong to clans other than those of Ling. These are connected with Ling only through their marriage alliances.

Phu-nu is the term by which the social organization is determined and by which its coherence is expressed.

Phu-nu means literally 'the elder and younger brothers', but in the kinship terminology employed in the epic it is applied to a very wide circle of relatives. At an early stage, *phu-nu* membership is confined only to members of certain lineage groups. Whatever the reasons or motivations for this, solidarity within the *phu-nu* is depicted as absolute. It is only members of the *phu-nu* who can attend certain meetings and take part in particular rites. This *phu-nu* organization is marked by three paradigms: solidarity, commensality and equality in status. These are expressed in four lines of a poetic oration delivered by sPyi-dpon, the doyen of Ling society, on the occasion of the birth of his cousin and Gesar's half brother, rGya-tsha:

> 'From the time of Chos-'phan- nag-po,
> If an enemy appears we hold spears together,
> We eat food together from the same plate,
> We sit together on the same seat.'[22]

This solidarity among members of the same clan is enhanced by the concept of their belonging to the 'same bone of the father', this being emphatically stressed in the same speech:

> 'In Ling there are three lineages, the great, the medium
>   and the small,
> They are not distinguished by high or low ranks . . . ,
> Because they all have the same bone of the father'[23]

This fraternal bond is regulated through two social imperatives, moral and jural: before Joru becomes king, the power to rule over the kingdom is loosely shared by the three brothers who are Gesar's father, the designated king, and his two paternal uncles (*pha-khu, pha-tshan,*). Khro-thung, one of the paternal uncles, knows by instinct that Gesar, his obstreperous cousin, is a potential threat to his own secret ambition. He contrives two ways of getting rid of his cousin. He questions the legitimacy of Joru's belonging to the *phu-nu* because Joru's mother 'Gog-bza' is a servant and not a lawful wife of Seng-blon. Khro-thung then accuses the young Joru of the theft of a calf, a foal and a lamp from his people. Joru is also accused of murdering three hunters from the same group. He is therefore banished according to the law of Ling, together with his mother, to the Land of rMa, because he has violated the law between *phu-nu,* an unpardonable action, and his mother is not a lawful wife.[24] From this conflict between the paternal uncle and the cousin (*khu-tsha, khu-tshan*)—a common theme in Tibetan stories (one thinks of Milarepa and his uncle)—it is clear that Khro-thung endeavours to exclude Joru from the *phu-nu,* first by questioning the legitimacy of his birth and then accusing him of theft and murder. Both such actions would have the effect of disqualifying him from membership of the *phu-nu*. In the conflict, uncle and cousin come close to murdering each other, but both know that such an act, which is termed 'pollution from within' or 'fratricide' (*nang-dme*), would cause the disintegration of the *phu-nu*. The notion of 'pollution from within', which occurs only when a murder has taken place within the *phu-nu,* is an important jural factor in maintaining the solidarity of the *phu-nu.*[25] This idea is further illustrated by the great feud between 'Dan-ma and Shan-pa. The latter is a military commander of the Hor who is taken prisoner after the conquest of Hor. In a dreadful fight with spears Shan-pa manages to kill rGya-tsha. However, Gesar intends to admit him into the *phu-nu* in spite of the killing of his half-brother and appoint him as a minister of Ling. In the eyes of 'Dan-ma Gesar is confused concerning the distinction between those who are outside the *phu-nu* and those who are within it. He rebels against Gesar and declares: 'I am going to sever the *phu-nu* connexion between us.'[26] From this context, we understand that not only are blood relatives members of the *phu-nu* but also those who are connected with Ling through marriage. In fact, all the 30 knights of Ling are considered as being *phu-nu.*[27]

Another element which characterizes the *phu-nu* is the importance of *snying-nye,* lit. 'close to heart', meaning loyalty towards one another. However, the most important factor which binds the members of the *phu-nu* together in the face of external aggression is the idea of *mgo-'phang,* 'the height at which the head is held', meaning honour. It is this last which is shamed most when 'Brug-mo, Gesar's wife, is taken by force by the Hor, and when Me-bza', Gesar's other favourite, is abducted by Klu-btsan, the Demon of the North. The recapture of the two women restores the honour of Ling and ultimately leads also to the conquest of the two enemies.

Let us now examine more closely the meaning of the term *phu-nu.* As we have seen, at an early stage in the epic, *phu-nu* designates a restricted group of people within Ling, bound together by the fact that they are of 'the same bone of the father'. In other words, consanguinity is emphasized. However, the term gradually comes to be applied to those who are linked not only by patrilineal descent but also by affinity. The use of this term therefore goes through different stages in the epic.

The term is translated in various ways in Western works on Tibet. In the *'Khrungs-gling,* R. A. Stein invariably translates it as 'frères' ('brothers'), but he also states that it in fact refers to a class of young people and he emphasizes that it is not about blood relationship.[28] However, in the epic the term is applied not only to the young but also to the older generation, as we know from the fact that all the 30 knights are regarded as *phu-nu,* including sPyi-dpon, the elderly doyen of Ling society. *Phu-nu* is, of course, a contraction of *phu-bo*

and *nu-bo,* 'elder' and 'younger brother', but it does not have the same connotation in every context in which it occurs. For example, Stein translates the line: *phu-nu nang-dme yong-dogs* as 'Ainsi il y aura souillure d'homicide entre frères cadets et aînés,'[29] but in this context, it is not a question of problems between brothers but between uncle and cousin. Again, he translates the line: *phu-nu nang-dme mi-gtong-ba'i nges-pa mi-'dug* as 'Il n'est pas certain que tu ne sèmeras pas la souillure interne (la guerre civile) entre les "frères".'[30] Here, too, the text is concerned with the conflict between Khro-thung and Gesar: they are not brothers, and in the epic Khro-thung is an old man. In this last context Stein uses 'frères' in a figurative sense.

In a slightly different form the term occurs in early Tibetan texts from Dunhuang: *Pu-ma-nu* which J. Bacot translates as 'enfants'. This seems to be the only place where this variant of the term occurs. It certainly does not mean 'children'; in my opinion, it simply means 'relatives'. In the same passage of the document the form *pu-nu* also occurs, but this is not translated by Bacot. The passage in question is concerned with some *phu-nu* who are being disloyal (*pu-nu snying rings-pa*).[31]

However, the earliest dated source for the term is the inscription of Zhol rDo-ring erected *c.* A.D. 764 at Lhasa. In this inscription the term *pu-nu-po,* and not just *phu-nu,* occurs twice in contexts where the concern is the nearest kin to whom the property of a family is to be given should the line of descendants of that family become extinct. In these two passages, H. Richardson translates the term as 'kin' and 'kinsmen'.[32] This is certainly correct: as pointed out above, the term in early times had this connotation of 'kinsman'.

The form of *pu-nu-po* is corroborated by its occurrence with the gender change, *phu-nu-mo.* It is entered in the ninth-century Sanskrit-Tibetan dictionary, *Mahāvyutpatti,* with the form of *phu-nu-mo'i sru,* to translate the Sanskrit term *bhaginī,* 'sister', 'maternal aunt'.[33]

CONCLUSION

As stated above, in the epic the term *phu-nu* occurs frequently in the episode of *'Khrungs-gling*—when giving accounts of the society—with the meaning of 'kinsman' but, as Ling expands, different tribes appear and become an integrated part of Ling society. The term *phu-nu* then covers the new members of the alliance. It brings together both sides: filiation and alliance. The term has therefore the meaning of a very wide circle of relatives covering not only male and female members of a clan but affines as well.

After the conquest of Yarkham and the land of Hor, a new development begins and introduces a change in the social structure of Ling society. A-stag Lha-mo, a sister of the great Demon of the North, is appointed governor of Yarkham. In the hierarchy, she is raised to knightly rank with ministerial status, and is the only woman among the 30 knights. In the same way, two chiefs of the Hor, Thang-rtse and Shan-pa, are also given knightly status, although Shan-pa, as we have seen, is the killer of rGya-tsha, the half brother of Gesar. Still others among the 30 knights, who are killed, are also replaced by various 'non-Ling people'. From this point on the *phu-nu* organization of the tribal stage in the epic breaks down and the epic is now concerned with the supra-clanic organization and the word *phu-nu* is less often used, but great concern is shown for the patrilineal descent of the 'Bum-pa family and for the throne of Ling. Yul-lha of 'Jang, another important character, who joins Ling society after the conquest of 'Jang, participates in the campaign against the Mon, as do A-stag, Thang-rtse and Shan-pa. Through the admission of these 'non-Ling people' to the circle of knights in the service of the king, the epic is no longer portraying a clan or tribal society at its local level but a kingdom with many vassals and with a chief now styled as a universal monarch. The idea of *phu-nu* organization, however, lingers on, but in a different form. When the Ling people reject the proposal to appoint Shan-pa as a minister, Gesar indicates that although Shan-pa does not belong to the *phu-nu* of Ling he was related to Gesar in heaven in a previous age and that is why he refuses the request and forbids others to kill him, for that would amount to committing 'pollution from within' (*nang-dme*).[34]

It should be clear from what I have said that no consideration of the **Gesar** material can dispense with an awareness of *phu-nu* and the subtle, elusive, but deep-rooted and influential principles which determined its use.

Notes

1. This article was presented as a paper at the third International Symposium on the Epic of King Gesar, organized by the Chinese Academy of Sciences and the Gesar Institute of Inner Mongolia and held in Xilinhot, Inner Mongolia, 22-26 July 1993.

   I am very grateful to Professor A. W. Macdonald who kindly read the manuscript of the article and made invaluable suggestions.

2. 'The theoretical basis of the Tibetan epic, with reference to a "chronological order" of the various episodes in the Gesar epic', *BSOAS*, [*Bulletin of the School of Oriental and African Studies*] LVI, 2, 1993, 234-46.

3. S. G. Karmay, 'The origin myths of the first king of Tibet as revealed in the *Can-lnga*', in P. Kvaerne (ed.), *Tibetan studies*, vol. 1, *Proceedings*

of the sixth seminar of the International Association for Tibetan Studies in Fagernes (Norway), 21-28 August 1992 (Oslo, 1994), 410-11.

4. cf. Shar-rdza bKra-shis rgyal-mtshan (1859-1935), *Legs-bshad-madzod* (S. G. Karmay, *The treasury of good sayings: a Tibetan history of Bon*, London Oriental Series, vol. 26, London: Oxford University Press, 1972, 69-70).

5. On this theme, see N. E. Levine, *The dynamics of polyandry* (Chicago: University of Chicago Press, 1988).

6. cf. *lHa-gling gab-tse dgu-skor*, Kan-su'u mi-rigs dpe-skrun-khang, 1982, 94 (R. A. Stein, *L'épopée tibétaine de Gesar dans la version lamaïque* [hereafter *Version lamaïque*], Paris: Presses universitaires de France, 1956, 197).

7. *rTa-rgyugs dpyid-kyi nyi-ma* (hereafter *dPyia-nyi*), mTsho-sngon mi-rigs dpe-skrun-khang, 1981, 10.

8. *Gling ge-sar rgyal-po'i sgrung 'khrungs-skor* (hereafter *'Khrungs-skor*), Kansu'u mi-rigs dpe-skrun-khang, 1981, 17. This text, under the title of *'Khrungs-gling*, is studied by R. A. Stein, *Version lamaïque*, 221; *dPyid-nyi*, 10, 46.

9. cf. *Shan-'dan stag-seng kha-sprod* (hereafter *Shan-'dan*), Si-khron mi-rigs dpe-skrun-khang, 1982, 15; *Bod-rgya shan-sbyar-gyi ge-sar tshig-mdzod* (hereafter *Bod-rgya*), Si-khron mi-rigs dpe-skrun-khang, 1989, 41.

10. cf. R. Hamayon, 'The one in the middle: unwelcome third as a brother, irreplaceable mediator as a son', in W. Heissig (ed.), *Fragen der mongolischen Heldendichtung*, III (Wiesbaden: Harrassowitz, 1985), 373-409.

11. In *'Khrungs-skor* (p. 5), these three women, however, appear as wives of one man . . . .

12. *dPyid-nyi*, 6-7.

13. e.g. *Shan-'dan*, 5-7, 10, 157, 161-2, 166-7.

14. *yab-rgyud-ni ri-nas chad-pa, yum-rgyid mtsho-nas chad-pa* (*dPyid-nyi*, 4).

15. cf. S. Karmay, Ph. Sagant, 'La place du rang dans la maison sharwa', in D. Blamont, G. Toffin, (ed.), *Architecture, milieu et société en Himalaya: Etudes himalayennes* (Paris: Editions du CNRS, 1987), 247-50.

16. *'Khrungs-skor*, 1981, 143-44 (*Version lamaïque*, 265).

17. *Shan-'dan*, 144, 149; *Bod-rgya*, 223-4.

18. cf. *Bod-rgya*, 41.

19. *dPyid-nyi,* 9-10.

20. *Hor-lis,* f. 214, manuscript in the David-Neel Collection, Musée Guimet, Paris. The translation into French of this episode with two others is in the process of publication.

21. *phu-nu mi-drug* (*'Khrungs-skor,* 144; *Version lamaïque,* 265).

22. *gling chos-'phan nag-po tshun-chad nas / dgra byung-na mdung-mo mnyam-'dzin yin / zas sder-nang gcig-tu mnyam-za yin / skyid gdan-thog gcig-tu mnyam-'dug yin /* (*'Khrungs-skor,* 7; *Version lamaïque,* 218).

23. *thob go-sa'i che-chung ma-yin-te / . . . de-phyin pha-rus gcig-pa yin /* (*'Khrungs-skor,* 9; *Version lamaïque,* 219).

24. *'Khrungs-skor,* 104-5 (*Version lamaïque,* 250-55).

25. In this context the following terms are often used: *khu-tshan nang-'gal,* 'conflict between uncle and cousin'; *phu-nu nang-dme,* 'murder with kinsmen'. Cf. *Shan-'dan,* 141.

26. *phu-nu 'brel-thag bcad-le yin /* (*Shan-'dan,* 137); *Hor-lis,* f. 5a.

27. *phu-nu sum-cu* (*'Khrungs-skor,* 155; *Version lamaïque,* 81).

28. '. . . il ne s'agit pas de liens de parenté par le sang.' (*Version lamaïque,* 40, n. 2).

29. *'Khrungs-skor,* 93; *Version lamaïque,* 246.

30. *'Khrungs-skor,* 98; *Version lamaïque,* 64, 248.

31. J. Bacot, F. W. Thomas, Ch. Toussaint, *Documents de Touen-houang relatifs à l'histoire du Tibet* (Paris, 1940, 110, 146). This same document also attests the existence of the term *phu-ma-nu* which J. Bacot translates as 'garçons ou filles'. In my view it simply means 'kinsman'.

32. H. E. Richardson, *A corpus of Early Tibetan inscriptions* (London: Royal Asiatic Society, 1985), 20, 24.

33. Sakaki, *Mahāvyutpatti* (Kyoto, 1916-26).

34. *sMan-lis,* manuscript in the David-Neel Collection, Musée Guimet, f. 164, 169, 174, 181 (see n. 20); *Shan-'dan,* 180-81.

Lauri Harvilahti (essay date October 1996)

SOURCE: Harvilahti, Lauri. "Epos and National Identity: Transformations and Incarnations." *Oral Tradition* 11, no. 1 (October 1996): 37-49.

[In the following essay, Harvilahti discusses how the folklore process informs the life-cycle of the Gesar *epic.]*

MYTH, HISTORY, AND NATIONALISM

In his 1990 book E. J. Hobsbawm outlines the history of nationalism. He begins with the French Revolution, proceeds through stages like "proto-nationalism," "transformation" (1870-1918), and the "apogee" of nationalism (1918-50) to the late twentieth century, and finally ends up with a prophecy according to which (in light of the progress in the study and analysis of nations) nationalism is past its peak: "The owl of Minerva which brings wisdom, said Hegel, flies out at dusk. It is a good sign that it is now circling round nations and nationalism" (182-83).

Obviously something unexpected happened to Minerva's owl. The book was published in 1990, and as we now know, Hobsbawm's vision did not come true. One of the reasons might be that in his book the word *myth* appears only in the subheading—not anywhere else. It is perhaps to history that we have to return in order to discover the roots of our ideas and ideologies, triumphs and tragedies—but the problem is that national history is a myth suppressing and surpassing time rather than a true history.[1]

For an epic scholar the mythic patterns of history are well known: heroic ancestors and their monstrous antagonists, golden ages of cultural prosperity and the darker ages, migration and settlement stories, defeats and victories (cf. Smith 1984:292-93). There is no single, specific heroic or mythic age, but a constant interplay between myth and reality, past and present—no history, but "a perpetually re-created song of truth" (Zumthor 1990:84). We may take as an example the South Slavic epic poetry that experienced a dynamic, productive period continuing well into the twentieth century (e.g., Lord 1960:14-17). The chief reason for this phenomenon was that there were clear points of comparison and analogy between the contents of the old poems about earlier history and what was occurring in more recent history: the uprisings of 1804-6 and 1815-16, the constant resistance to Turkish rule (in which some of the singers likewise took part, sometimes actively, sometimes watching from the sidelines). Continuous warfare with occupying forces, conflict between different sectors of the population, social, cultural, and economic heterogeneity—all helped to strengthen the vitality of improvisatory poetry (among Christian as well as Moslem singers). This situation also inspired a large number of new epic songs. Narrative poetry did not find itself in a state of stagnation; it was in use as a productive pattern adapting to new situations.[2] From that point of view the meaning of, for example, the Battle of Kosovo (1389) for the Christian Serbs is more myth than history—a myth of defeat.

TRANSFORMATIONS OF EPIC MODELS

As is well known, German romanticism took Homer as a paragon or pattern for the epos in the eighteenth century and, as Lauri Honko has stated (1992:2), the birth of an epic signaled the emergence of literature, but also the emergence of nation. This paragon was not a blueprint, but a flexible tool in the hands of educated, nationalistic authors.

In the second half of the nineteenth century the German politician, poet, and wandering bard Wilhelm Jordan (1819-1904) created the epos *Die Nibelunge* consisting of two parts: *Die Sigfridsage* (1868) and *Hildebrands Heimkehr* (1874). In his *Epische Briefe* Jordan declared that he was in fact "The German Homer," a kind of embodiment or incarnation of an epic poet, matured at the correct stage of development of the people, in a fateful hour occurring only once in a thousand years. According to his epic vision, the German people were on the way toward becoming the leading world power and supreme religion. The task of the national bard was to disclose the "ripened fruit" that was the work of the people (*Volksarbeit*) over those thousand years (1876:27-37, 56; cf. Martini 1974:387-88). Jordan traveled from town to town throughout half of Europe performing his own epics and also made a tour to America in 1871. His works remained relatively unimportant in the history of world literature, but they form an interesting example of using (or adapting) some of the poetic devices of epic folk poetry, plot structures, tropes, images, and allusions in a new sociohistorical context.

It is worth noticing that this model of creating an epos, based on romantic-heroic historicism and nationalism and eulogizing the politics of Bismarckian Germany, was the one championed by Andrejs Pumpurs, the author of the Latvian national epos *Lāčplēsis* (*Bear Slayer*). In the preface to his work Pumpurs stated that he wanted to prove that the Baltic peoples also belonged to the Aryan epic peoples of Europe—and not only the Greeks and the Germans, as Jordan insisted (Pumpurs 1988:141; Rudzītis 1988:17-18). He went on with creating his epic on the basis of Latvian etiological tales, folktales, local legends, wedding songs, and other items excerpted from folklore. The origin of the main plot is to be found in folktales describing a powerful, supernatural hero, brought up by a she-bear. In folktales this hero fights against various monsters, while in *Lāčplēsis* he strives not only against mythic but also against human enemies, the German Knights of the Sword. Even with its abundant folklore motifs his epic is—because of its passages of national romantic proclamation and artistic metrical devices—very far from a folklore-based work, resembling in this sense the works of Wilhelm Jordan. Pumpurs' natural, mythical philosophy is,

however, significantly removed from the militant, expansionist overtones of the German nationalist.

The epos of Andrejs Pumpurs did not fall into oblivion. At the end of the nineteenth century the *Bear Slayer* had the same kind of significance as the *Kalevala* for the Finns or the *Kalevipoeg* for the Estonians. Despite its romantic-nationalistic groundwork the epos continued to be published even during the Soviet period. One reason for this phenomenon was probably that the antagonists in Pumpurs' tale are the knights of the sword and feudal rulers. Recently, in the years of struggle for independence, the *Bear Slayer* acquired new political connotations. During the celebrations of the centennial of the epos (1988), the periodical *Avots* (*Fountain*) published a libretto of a rock opera based on the poem. Taking place at the same time was the premiere of the dramatization of Pumpurs' work, and the Latvian writers' union organized an international seminar dedicated to the *Bear Slayer*.

Once again the old paragon has been adapted according to the changing political and sociohistorical contexts. Models of textualization appear to be productive when their conventions, basic contents, and networks of interpretation are related to the dynamic (or emerging) trends of thought or dominant ideological concepts (cf. Bauman and Briggs 1990:75-78). The process of using these models is very often stimulated by a general idealistic current represented by a nucleus group of cultural activists or by an organization, although the national-political stimulus may come from the power machinery of society.

THE *EPIC OF GESER*

The term *epos* has normally been used of literary epics created by known or unknown authors, in some cases even of oral-derived epic collations or conglomerates. In fact, the borders between these categories are flexible. Sometimes the term has been used to refer to a cycle of epic poems (for example, incorporated around one main hero) belonging to some particular nation or ethnic group; this takes place when the poems have an epic-like significance for the community in contact with them. Such significance can reach from mythic and cosmogonic meanings to the contemporary use of folk epics, for instance to propagate national identity and integrity.

The epic of *Geser* is among the best known and most widespread epic traditions in the world. The influence of Tibetan civilization can be seen in most of the oral and literary versions of this epic. It is known in Tibet, Mongolia, Inner Mongolia (in China), Buryatia (in Russia), and Ladakh (India). There are also versions in Sikkim, Bhutan, Nepal, and among various Tibeto-

Burmese, Turkish, and Tunghus tribes (Herrmann 1990:485; Nekljudov 1984:145; Stein 1959:59-60). In many cases the translation of the hero to some particular tradition has been so natural that scholars formerly disputing matters like "original form," "initial stage," or "origin," or trying to locate the "original manuscript" or searching for the idealistic "poeta anonymus" (see Herrmann 1990:496-501), have been able to produce evidence in order to explain the epic of *Geser* as a national treasury of this or that nation.

On the basis of new (oral as well as literary) collections and materials, it is possible to create a more complete and complex picture of this epic. At present there is enough evidence to state that *Geser* is best preserved in Tibet and its adjacent areas in oral and in literary form. Formerly, unfamiliarity with the Tibetan literary monuments and the scarcity of collected oral versions led to various speculative fallacies created at the writing table by European scholars (Herrmann 1990:500-1). The western concept of epos modeled on Homer was misleading, and research was conducted without sufficient knowledge of cultural history, religion, educational conditions, oral tradition, and so forth. During the past few decades, research based on new materials and methods has been able to override these earlier concepts,[3] sometimes even in cases in which the prior results seemed to be on solid ground. In addition to the research on the epic of *Geser,* we find parallel examples on Central Asian epic.[4] In the following I intend to examine a few examples of *Geser* epic as a manifestation of cultural identity, but dozens of other cases may be found as well.

In outline the Tibetan version (from Amdo) could be summarized in the following way (see Nekljudov 1984:169-80):

> In the kingdom of gLing there was no king and chaos prevailed. One of the sons of the Heavenly God was sent down to the earth. He was reborn into a noble family (or as a son of a mountain spirit). As a baby he was slobbering and deformed, and was given the name Džoru. Even as a child he began to destroy demons and various monsters. As an adolescent he came to the throne and earned the beautiful Brugmo as consort. He also obtained his magic horse, heroic shape, and proper name. The first heroic deed was annihilation of the demon of the North. The demon's wife Meza Bumskiid helped him to accomplish this task, but after the victory she gave Geser the herb of forgetfulness and so he stayed in the North. At home Geser's uncle Khrotung tried to seduce Brugmo—without any success. Khrotung betrayed his land and led the Hories to gLing. The Hories carried off Brugmo. Geser was finally able to break the spell with the help of heavenly forces and hurried to the camp of the enemies disguised as a scabby boy. By means of magic and supernatural power he destroyed the king of the Hories, subdued his kingdom and returned to gLing.

Most of the main elements of the above-mentioned summary (its "plot-structure" or "macrostructure" or "chain of macropropositions" or "mental text") are also found in the Ladakh and Mongolian versions. There are, however, huge differences in different regions that I have not mentioned. The variation is abundant, especially on the level of surface structure, and not only in the oral versions but also in the literary texts.[5] As a result we get a multi-dimensional network of possible actualizations of this epic.

According to the materials now available, there are in Tibet dozens of volumes, more than one million verses in different "versions" of the epic. The collection of the *Geser* epic started during a critical stage: the work that had begun in the 1950s was totally interrupted during the cultural revolution and continued only after 1978. By 1986 Tibetan scholars had already recorded 29 chapters (as they say) of the oral forms of this epic, a total of 985 sound cassettes (see Tunzhu 1988:154; 'Jam-dpal rgyal-mtsho 1990:472). It is clear that research conducted on the basis of these collections will give unprecedented results.

THE TIBETAN ORAL EPOS

As to their artistic skill, the Tibetan performers can be divided into several classes—from respectable and skillful masters to untalented and poor ones. The performances formerly had a ritual character: when the singers started to sing, an incense table was set up with a big portrait of Geser, his thirty heroes and concubines on either side. Different paraphernalia (bows, arrows, swords believed to have been used by the hero) were brought, butter lamps were lit, and bowls with alcohol were served for the Gods. By reading the Buddhist scriptures, with eyes closed, legs crossed, beads in hands, the singer got into a trance and during the possession Geser or some other hero entered his body. Once the sacred spirit had entered him, the performer started to sing. Usually the mode of performance was flexible and varied. The singers could perform on various occasions and for different audiences, who were able to choose the chapter to be performed according to the situation.[6] Such a description of "the epos in the making" clearly shows how important it is to modify our Western literary-based concept of the epos (cf. Honko 1992).

GESER AS A BUDDHIST EPOS OF THE MONGOLS

In the *Nomči qatunu Geser,* one of the Mongolian literary versions, there is an appendix, a sort of religious legend or sutra, called "Scripture of the meeting of the Dalai Lama and Geser Khan." In this chapter Lama Erdeni (Dalai Lama) is meditating when he suddenly hears a booming sound from heaven: Geser Khan appears to him in the night sky and gives strict rules and instructions concerning ritual behavior and sacraments. Then he disappears back into the night with his magic horse at a fantastic speed. According to this holy scripture, Geser Khan is in fact the reincarnation of Avalokitešvara. Those who believe in these words will find the way to salvation, but Geser Khan's spirit will bring the unbeliever misfortune.[7]

This sutra added to the heroic epic of *Geser* aimed at the creation of a lamaistic religious epic text. Bayartu (1989:232-33) and Halén (1990:159-63) have even found a historical basis for this sutra. In 1578 the dGelugs-pa leader bSod-nams rgya-mtsho (later the third Dalai Lama) and the leader of the Tümet Mongols, Altan Khan, met each other near Köke-nuur. The Altan Khan became a Buddhist, and the yellow sect and Geser spread over the Mongolian world. According to Halén (160-61), Geser Khan might have been identified with Altan Khan through folk etymology, based on the identical meaning of Mongolian *altan* "gold" and Tibetan *gser* "gold." The joining together of Geser and the Dalai Lama may have been conscious lamaistic propaganda, as Bayartu indicates, or an unambitious expression of piety and cultural identity: Geser was as an object of worship equal to the Supreme Divinities. Later Geser was also identified with the war god Guan Yu, and in consequence the warlord Baron Roman Ungern von Sternberg was also considered to be an incarnation of Geser.[8]

THE BEIJING XYLOGRAPH EDITION OF GESER

The epos was printed in Beijing as a block-printing edition in old Mongolian script in 1716. This edition does not contain any information about the compilers.[9] The reasons were political: the publishers had good reason to be cautious with the censorship of the Qing dynasty (see Bayartu 1989:2, 197, 249). On each page of this edition is, in Chinese characters, the title *Sān gúo zhì*, "The Chronicle of Three Kingdoms," a title that referred not to the epic of *Geser* but to a chronicle published under the first Qing emperor. According to Bayartu, this was a trick invented in order to mislead the censors: the chronicle was in fact translated into Mongolian (*yurban ulus-un bičig*), but remained unpublished. Under this disguise the epic of *Geser* was published in Mongolian, although the work clearly propagated the heroic ideals of the Mongols and maintained the national spirit, longing for restoration of the Mongolian Yuan dynasty (see Bayartu 1989:246-47, 249-50).

THE BURYAT EPIC OF GESER IN THE ORAL AND LITERARY TRADITION

In Buryat oral epic tradition the versions produced may range from more than ten thousand lines among one group of the northern Buryats (Ehirit-Bulagats) to less than a thousand among the Hori Buryats. Ehirit-Bulagat epic poetry also contains more archaic, mythical features than that of the other groups. In some of the oral versions this epic has clearly maintained the macrostructure of a literary version (for example, the Beijing xylograph), but the stylistic figures and the poetic devices are used in accordance with the Buryat oral epic tradition alongside elements attributable to the singer's personal style (see Lörincz 1975:64-65, Nekljudov 1984:208, 211). Many of the Buryat versions represent the structures and contents of the local tradition and are relatively independent of the literary sources. The Ehirit-Bulagat version is especially interesting with its abundant shamanistic features (Nekljudov 1984:206-7).

On the basis of versions collected among the Buryats, a compilation bearing the title "The Heroic Epos of the Buryats" was published in Russian in 1973. A Russian poet named Semën Lipkin has declared himself to be the translator. The text of this version of *Geser* is based on Namdžil Baldano's collation in the Buryat language (24,000 verses), and is founded (as stated in the book) "almost entirely" on original versions. Four chapters (the first, second, sixth, and ninth) have actually been translated into Russian by the folklorist Aleksei Ulanov in a word-for-word prose format, and five are included only as summaries. In his preface Ulanov states that in the translation process "the content, style and poetic devices have been observed" and that "only side-episodes hampering the integrity of the plot have been removed." Finally, Lipkin has contrived a poetic translation using regular rhyme and other poetic features unknown not only in Buryat but also in Russian epic poetry. Baldano thus played the role of the Elias Lönnrot of the Buryats, Ulanov translated his text into Russian prose, and Lipkin versified the result called "*Geser*: The Heroic Epos of the Buryats." The title page does, however, announce "Translation from the Buryat language by Semën Lipkin."

The different forms of the *Geser* epic I have mentioned give a glimpse of the different dimensions of the concept of "epos": 1) oral, living epic poetry, 2) literary epos containing elements of sacral text, 3) literary epos serving the purpose of ethnic or national integrity, and 4) collation (in a language other than the original) created in accordance with the ideological program of a multinational state.

In the life-cycle of the *Geser* epic, the situation is right now rather interesting. The ritual forms of performance and genuine oral traditions are on the decline, although there still are productive singers in Tibet. During the 1980s the singers won social appreciation as members of the Political Consultation Committee and the Tibet Society for Folk Literature and Art. Through modern editions, radio and television programs, orchestral arrangements, and conferences the epic of *Geser* reappears in new forms and in new incarnations. As for the Mongols, Geser and Chenggis Khan are the main national heroes. In the folk tradition there is also a belief that, according to a decree given by Buddha and Hormusta, the Heavenly God, Geser will reappear as an incarnation of Chenggis Khan in order to rule over the world (Bayartu 1989:243-44). The present-day revitalization of the worship of Chenggis Khan, the new editions of the *Geser* epic, festivals, concerts, and so forth are indications of the new life of the heroic culture. These new avatars of the old epic heroes will certainly imply new meanings and consequences.

Conclusion

It is possible to identify a whole network of epic genres serving the purpose of epos: oral and literary creations, short epic poems, and long conglomerates. The works also vary in genre: sacral texts and secular forms, poetic forms but also prose-texts and mixed forms in which verse and prose alternate. In addition to these, as a rule, excerpts from different genres play an important role (chapters in verse hagiography or panegyric, fragments of lyric elegy or laments, for example). In oral epos narrated, recited, and sung modes are possible—with or without the accompaniment of an instrument. There are evidently folklore-based written versions, but also abundant examples of literary creations in which the poet has used only a limited number of the basic elements of folk poetry. Whatever the case, the desire to reinforce the people's self-esteem and to arouse respect for their own heritage and culture is among the main tasks of an epos (even within an oral epic poetry culture): the hero is unconquered, invincible, since he is ours—and even if he was once defeated, he will be back one day, as a liberator of his people, driven by revenge. When events warrant—in times of political awakening, conflicting ideological interests, or even a state of war—an epos may be employed as a kind of myth-like weapon for ideological purposes, but that is only one of the manifestations of the use of epics in the folklore process (cf. Honko 1991:32-33, 44). The political role of the epics in strengthening cultural and national identity varies over a large spectrum according to the prevailing sociocultural situation. The use of epics in cultural life involves many positive values but also elements demanding careful deliberation. But we may well ask who will conduct the deliberations, since we are dealing with a phenomenon capable of surviving historical periods, empires, and ideologies.

Notes

1. On returning to history, see Hutchinson 1992:103; on national history as myth, Herzfeld 1987:82.

2. Koljević (1980:215-321) gives a comprehensive account of the context of Christian Serbian epics.

3. See, e.g., Bayartu 1989; Halén 1990; Heissig 1980, 1983, 1987; Nekljudov 1984.

4. For example, the Oirat/Kalmyk epic Džangar or the oral epic poetry of the Turkic peoples—see, e.g., Bitkeev 1992:6-14; Džamtso 1988:139-48; Harvilahti 1993; Reichl 1992.

5. See Nekljudov 1984:146; Herrmann 1990:486-87, 490-96; 'Jam-dpal rgyal-mtsho 1990:478.

6. 'Jam-dpal rgyal-mtsho 1990:474-78; see Stein 1959:7-9 and Nekljudov 1984: 150.

7. See in detail, e.g., Bayartu 1989:228-30 and Halén 1990:159-61.

8. See in detail Bayartu 1989:234, 244; Halén 1990:163; Riftin 1991:163-64.

9. According to Heissig (1983:513, 1987:1156), this edition is most probably based on a West Mongolian Oirat oral version; see also Damdinsüren 1957:56. Halén (1990:163) states additionally that the language of the Beijing version differs from the classical written Mongolian and is close to the spoken vernacular of the Köke-nuur Öölöts.

References

Basham 1989: A. L. Basham. *The Wonder That Was India*. Calcutta: Rupa.

Bayartu 1989: T. Bayartu. *Mongγol-un angγan-u siditü roman. Begečing-ber-un "Geser-un" sudulul*. Köke-hota.

Bauman and Briggs 1990: Richard Bauman and Charles Briggs. "Poetics and Performance as Critical Perspectives on Language and Social Life." *Annual Revue of Anthropology,* 19:59-88.

Bitkeev 1992: N. C. Bitkeev. "Epičeskie tradicii mongol'skih narodov (na materiale èposa 'Džangar')." In *VI Meždunarodnyj kongress mongolovedov. Ulan-Bator, avgust 1992 g. Doklady rossijskoj delegacii,* vol. 2. Moscow.

Damdinsüren 1957: C. Damdinsüren. *Istoričeskie korni Geseriady*. Moscow.

Džamtso 1988: T. Džamtso. "Mengguzu yingxiong shishi 'Jianggeer' ziliao souji baoguan he chuban." In *Zhong fen minjian wenxue souji baoguan xueshu yantao hui wenji*. Beijing.

Halén 1990: Harry Halén. "Altan Khan and the Mongolian Geser Khan Epic." In *Altaica Osloensia: Proceedings from the 32nd Meeting of the Permanent International Altaistic Conference*. Oslo.

Harvilahti 1993: Lauri Harvilahti. "Džangar-epiikka ja kansallinen identiteetti. Kansanperinteen keruu- ja tutkimusmatka Luoteis-Kiinaan." In *Katse Kaukoitään. Suomalaista Itä-Aasian tutkimusta*. Ed. by Lauri Harvilahti and Jouko Seppänen. Helsinki.

Heissig 1980: Walther Heissig. *Geser Rëdzia-wu. Dominik Schröders nachgelassene Monguor (Tujen) Version des Geser-Epos aus Amdo. In Facsimilia und mit der Einleitung herausgegeben von W. Heissig*. Asiatische Forschungen, Band 70. Wiesbaden: Harrassowitz.

Heissig 1983: ———. *Geser-Studien*. Abhandlungen der Rheinisch-Westfälischen Akademie der Wissenschaften, Band 69. Opladen: Westdeutscher Verlag.

Heissig 1987: ———. "Geser Khan." *Enzyklopädie des Märchens*, 5. Berlin and New York: de Gruyter.

Herrmann 1990: Silke Herrmann. "The Life and History of the Epic King Gesar in Ladakh." In *Religion, Myth, and Folklore in the World's Epics: The Kalevala and its Predecessors*. Ed. by Lauri Honko. Berlin: Mouton. pp. 485-502.

Herzfeld 1987: Michael Herzfeld. *Anthropology through the Looking-glass: Critical Ethnography in the Margins of Europe*. Cambridge: Cambridge University Press.

Hobsbawm 1990: E. J. Hobsbawm. *Nations and Nationalism since 1780: Programme, Myth, Reality*. Cambridge: Cambridge University Press.

Honko 1980: Lauri Honko. "Upptäckten av folkdiktning och nationell identitet i Finland." *Tradisjon*, 10.

Honko 1991: ———. "The Folklore Process." Unpublished paper, Folklore Fellows' Summer School, July 28-August 18. Turku.

Honko 1992: ———. "The Making of Oral Epics." Unpublished paper, Rome, Villa Lante, March 4.

Hutchinson 1992: John Hutchinson. "Moral Innovators and the Politics of Regeneration: The Distinctive Role of Cultural Nationalists in Nation-Building." In *Ethnicity and Nationalism*. Ed. by Anthony Smith. Leiden: E. J. Brill.

'Jam-dpal rgyal-mtsho 1990: 'Jam-dpal rgyal-mtsho. "The Singers of the King Gesar Epic." In *Religion, Myth, and Folklore in the World's Epics: The Kalevala and its Predecessors*. Ed. by Lauri Honko. Berlin: Mouton. pp. 471-84.

Jordan 1876: Wilhelm Jordan. *Epische Briefe*. Frankfurt am Main.

Koljević 1980: Svetozar Koljević. *The Epic in the Making*. Oxford: Clarendon Press.

Lipkin 1973: Semën Lipkin. *Geser, burjackij geroičeskij èpos*. Moscow.

Lord 1960: A. B. Lord. *The Singer of Tales*. Cambridge, MA: Harvard University Press. Rpt. 1968 et seq. New York: Atheneum.

Lörincz 1975: L. Lörincz. "Die burjatischen Geser-Varianten." In *Acta Orientalia Academiae Scientiarum Hungariae*, vol. 29, fasc. 1. Budapest: Akadémiai Kiadó.

Martini 1974: Fritz Martini. *Deutsche Literatur in bürgerlichen Realismus 1848-1898*. Stuttgart: J. B. Metzler.

Nekljudov 1984: S. J. Nekljudov. *Geroičeskij èpos mongol'skih narodov*. Moscow: Nauka.

Pumpurs 1988: Andrejs Pumpurs. *Lāčplēsis: Latvju tautas varonis. Tautas eposs*. Ar Jāzepa Rudzīša ievadapcerējumu un komentāriem. Rīga: Zinātne.

Reichl 1992: Karl Reichl. *Turkic Oral Epic Poetry: Traditions, Forms, Poetic Structure*. New York and London: Garland.

Riftin 1991: B. L. Riftin. "Guan Di." In *Mifologičeskij slovar'*. Ed. by E. M. Meletinskij. Moscow: Sovetskaja Ènciklopedija.

Rudzītis 1988: Jāzeps Rudzītis. "A. Pumpura eposs Lāčplēsis." In Pumpurs 1988.

Smith 1984: Anthony D. Smith. "Ethnic Myths and Ethnic Revivals." *European Journal of Sociology*, 25.

Stein 1959: R. A. Stein. *Recherches sur l'épopée et le barde au Tibet*. Paris: Presses Universitaires de France.

Tunzhu 1988: Tunzhu (Dun Zhu). "Zangzu yingxiong shishi 'Gesaer wang zhuan' ziliao de baoguan." In *Zhong fen minjian wenxue souji baoguan xueshu yantao hui wenji*. Beijing.

Zumthor 1990: Paul Zumthor. *Oral Poetry: An Introduction*. Minneapolis: University of Minnesota Press.

Walther Heissig (essay date 1997)

SOURCE: Heissig, Walther. "From Verse Epic to Prosimetrum in Recent Mongolian Oral Literature." In *Prosimetrum: Crosscultural Perspectives on Narrative in Prose and Verse*, edited by Joseph Harris and Karl Reichl, pp. 349-64. Cambridge: D. S. Brewer, 1997.

[*In the following essay, Heissig examines the Mongolian* Gesar *epic's relation to the Tibetan versions.*]

INTRODUCTION

Orally transmitted Mongolian epic poetry, the cultural heritage of a past society, has been fairly well documented and studied, at least by comparison to other heroic poetry from Asia.[1] A great number of epics has been collected; in the Mongolian Academy of Science in Ulanbator alone, 273 epics are preserved.[2] Many versions have been published by scholars, both in Mongolia and in the districts of China with a Mongolian population. In Europe, over eighty Mongolian epics have been translated.[3] Mongolian epics are in verse; when they are performed they are generally sung to the accompaniment of a bowed or plucked instrument. According to their subject matter, we can distinguish three types of epics: suitor-epics; epics on the recovery of a family which has been abducted or led into captivity, or of herds, land and property which have been robbed; and epics which combine features of the first and second type with the theme of the killing of a many-headed, man-eating monster (*mangɣus*). Two cycles of epics enjoy the greatest popularity, a cycle on the West Mongolian hero Jangɣar[4] and one on Geser Khan. The latter treats, in many versions and variants, of the adventures of heaven-sent Geser, a demiurgic figure who fights against evil, impersonated in the many-headed *mangɣus*.[5] The Mongolian *Geser* epic must be seen in relationship to the Tibetan versions of the Geser legend, to which it shows clear affiliations.[6]

Although, as we have seen, the Mongolian oral epic is traditionally in verse, there is some indication of the spread of prosimetrum. In the course of the officially sponsored recording campaign of all *Geser* epics still extant, which has been carried out in the Mongolian-speaking provinces of China since 1981, oral variants of the *Geser* epic have come to light which have so far been unknown to scholars. Among these are six episodes ('chapters'), sung by the blind rhapsode Süke from the Kukunoor area,[7] which show some affinities with Tibetan versions of the *Geser* epic.[8] The greater part of these recordings, however, come from Inner Mongolia: Šulfungɣa, an elderly Bagharin-born Mongol, remembered two *Geser* songs which he had learned in his youth from Perlei, a singer well known in this area.[9] Two more chapters have been preserved by Bökečilaɣu, another Mongol of Bagharin origin, who had heard them from Čimedsürüng, a Lamaist monk, long since dead.[10] Five chapters of a cycle of *Geser* stories, called *Qor Geser*,[11] have been recorded from Lubsang (born in 1943), who had learned them starting at the age of five from an old monk named Lubsangdorji during Lubsang's noviciate, 1948-1958. Lubsang has in the meantime enlarged the number of his *Geser* chapters to twenty-one (running to about fifty tapes),[12] which have not yet been published. These new chapters show signs of cyclisation: Geser has a son who begins to take part in his father's adventures. There is no space here to discuss the contents of these new chapters and their value for the tradition of the *Geser* epic. But I would like to emphasize the fact that the oral transmission of the new chapters of the version of the epic sung by Lubsang can certainly be traced to two Lamaist

monks and that the transmission itself can be dated to the late 1930s and 1940s. As to their form, all these *Geser* chapters are in alliterated verse only; there is no addition of prose.

That the *Geser* epic, apart from the written versions, had been given individually different poetical forms, in particular by East Mongolian minstrels, has already been shown convincingly by S. Ju. Nekljudov, Ž. Tömörceren and B. Riftin. Between 1974 and 1976, these scholars recorded five short *Geser* epics in verse from two East Mongolian singers living in the Republic of Mongolia. The five short epics they took down and published in an exemplary edition[13] confirm the existence of new oral *Geser* epics in the eastern parts of Inner Mongolia. The origin of all the singers mentioned above points to the Bagharin district on the fringes of the East Mongolian territory as one of the centres of this new development, and as a matter of fact this area abounds in legends and placenames connected with Geser Khan.[14] The still existing close affiliation with the mythic figure of Geser is illustrated by the recent rebuilding, in 1993, of the Geser Khan temple, which was ruined during the Cultural Revolution.[15]

In addition to the singers of the *Geser* epic (*geserči*) mentioned above, there is another Bagharin rhapsode, named Sampilnorbu (1925-1993), whose work is totally devoted to stories and legends about Geser. Sampilnorbu lived in the vicinity of the famous White Pagoda (*čaɣan suburɣa*) in the West-Bagharin district. He was the son of a herdsman. During the Cultural Revolution he was declared an 'anti-ideological singer' (*terselegüü quɣurči*) and had to undergo a number of privations. In 1955, he became the pupil of the well-known rhapsode Toɣtaqu,[16] who was at that time already a very old man. Rumour has it that he was born before the end of the nineteenth century. Sampilnorbu remained until 1960 the pupil of this old singer, learning only *Geser* stories (*Geser-ün tuɣuji*), apart from the 'romance' *Šang ma juwan*.[17] The Mongolian term for 'romance' is *bensen üliger* 'book-based story'; it denotes a narrative which re-tells the contents of a Chinese chivalric novel and embellishes this re-telling with poems. Later Sampilnorbu became renowned for the repeated performance of the didactic poem *The Teachings of Geser,* a poem also known under the name of *Dendüb-yin silüg* (The poem of Dendüb) among the Bagharin. Sampilnorbu has left (in manuscript) his own version of the *Geser* epic in 110 chapters, of which chapters 34 to 41 agree in content with the oral version discussed here.

In September 1988 I was able to record one of his *Geser* stories at the Inner Mongolian Academy of Social Sciences in Kökehota, where Sampilnorbu was staying at that time. After the customary 'Opening song'[18]—which begins with the words 'I play my long-necked fiddle, I shall make it sound . . .' and offers a welcome to the listeners present—Sampilnorbu recited his epic, accompanying himself on the four-stringed violin (*quɣur*; Chinese *šangse*) which is used for the reciting of the *bensen üliger*, as opposed to the two-stringed horse-head fiddle (*morin toluɣaitu quɣur*) which is reserved for the performance of the 'great epic' on semireligious occasions.[19] In keeping with this non-epic use of instruments Sampilnorbu performed the **Geser** epic not entirely in verse, but in the manner of a *bensen üliger* in twenty-two sections of prose and verse.

The general tendency of Sampilnorbu's *Geser-ün tuɣuči* is to repeat the old teaching of filial piety, which had reached the Mongols in the form of a bilingual Mongolian-Chinese edition of the Chinese classical book of filial piety (1307), one of the earliest xylographs (or wood-block prints) of the Yüan-reign.[20] Sampilnorbu appears strongly influenced by the didactical *Teachings of Geser*, which he had learned from his teacher Toɣtoqu. In this poem the importance of parents as the origin of one's own existence, the necessity of showing love and gratitude to one's father and mother and the condemnation of all violations of the rules of filial piety are emphasized. In it attention is also drawn to the teachings of one's parents and forefathers, and the audience is warned of the evil effects of an abuse of drinking, a subject treated quite often in Mongolian didactical literature.[21]

THE PROSIMETRIC *BIRTH OF GESER*: CONTENTS AND STRUCTURE

Sampilnorbu's *Birth of Geser* can be divided into an introductory poem and sixteen sections, each consisting of a prose and a verse passage. In the following I will give an analysis of the structure and contents of the prosimetric epic, with some comments on parallels to other works and a short discussion of the most significant motifs of the singer's version of *Geser-ün tuɣuči*.

Sampilnorbu opens his narration with a poem of 89 lines, in which the sufferings of the primeval world under the rule of blood-drinking *mangɣus* monsters are described, as well as Geser's descent from heaven and his re-incarnation on earth to fight these evils. The motif of the rebirth of a supernatural power for this purpose is common to all Mongolian and Tibetan versions of the **Geser** epic. Some lines of Sampilnorbu's initial poem parallel the phraseology of the *Teachings of Geser*,[22] a fact which confirms the view that singers use the traditional expressions which they learned from their teachers.

I (Prose) Having been successful in fighting the evil *mangɣus*, Geser decides to get married and celebrate his wedding feast together with his parents, friends and the people. This is a structural motif (No. 13.3), with which the Mongolian heroic epic of the courting type usually ends.[23]—(Verse) The splendour of the banquet, the merriment during the feast and the richness of the meal are described in a lengthy poem (60 lines). But when in the course of the wedding celebration we witness drunkenness (No. 4.22-1) and sleep through intoxication (No. 4.17), we are reminded of the condemnation of the evils of strong drink in the *Teachings of Geser*.

II (Prose) Upon joy and merriment follow sadness and distress. During the night Geser's father and mother together with five members of their household disappear.—(Verse) The next morning, everybody is questioned (No. 4.12-5), but nobody has seen the missing party leave (No. 4.12-7) (19 lines).

III (Prose) Geser has his horse saddled, takes his arms and rides out in search of his missing parents.—(Verse) But wherever he asks for his parents and the members of their household, nobody has seen the seven missing persons (63 lines).—(Prose) The search continues.

IV (Verse) Geser returns distressed, imagining that his parents are in danger and afflicted by illness.—(Prose) He purifies the house and himself, eats only clean 'white' food,[24] lights lamps and burns incense, then he invokes the 'Blue Heaven', to send him an explaining dream (No. 4.21). Asking for a dream of revelation is a motif that is used often in the *bensen üliger* as a literary device to introduce rather unexpected or illogical actions as caused by supernatural powers. In the Mongolian epic, however, the dream is used as a warning of coming mishap.

Geser sees in his dream a person (motif K2085)[25] who reveals to him that his father and mother had been abducted by demons (No. 8.1-3).[26] They are both still alive, but they must be fed in an old temple on top of a high cliff in a place some thousand miles away in the west. In the dream the history of this old temple is furthermore revealed: In a world period (*kalpa*) long ago, the temple was used for worshipping the seven planets, which were represented by seven statues. In the course of thousands of years, the statues had lost their splendour and colour while the world and its inhabitants fell into a bad and evil state. People had forgotten the filial piety they owed to their ancestors so that the Earth was ordered by Heaven to disjoint the bones of those who had caused parents to suffer and to punish those who had deceived their spouses. (As early as 1614, similar punishments for such offences are mentioned in various didactic sayings ascribed to Geser.[27])

The Earth-planet, however, after receiving such heavenly commands, went home and got drunk, whereupon he forgot his orders completely. Shortly after Geser's incarnation, seven fire-doves also came to the world and searched for a place to nest. They found the old temple with its dilapidated statues, took possession of the seven statues and obtained the permission to feed on human beings. When one of these fire-doves woke up after a three years' sleep and flew out of the temple to look around, it observed Geser's return to his home after a campaign against the *mangɣus* monster. As the seven doves become aware of the fact that Geser had fought with the big sea-monster for nine days and nine nights, they realize that they had no chance of capturing and eating Geser. Hovering around Geser's place for three days and nights without getting any prey, they succeed finally in abducting Geser's parents and their five servants and bring them to the old temple. Happy to have found food, they now search for a big bronze-cauldron to cook the flesh and bones of their seven prisoners so that the meat will become soft and tender. After three years of forced abstinence they would otherwise not be satiated. Before they leave to look for a cauldron, they secure the door of the temple with a sturdy lock. Geser learns all this from the heavenly appariation in his dream, who orders him not to tarry on the next morning when he rides to the temple on the cliff to free his father and mother and bring them back alive and safe.

(Verse) Sampilnorbu repeats in a poem (62 lines) the lengthy instructions. In this section Sampilnorbu combines a few motifs of alien origin: firebirds which turn into three fireballs and burn down the precincts of a rich family are mentioned in a *bensen üliger*;[28] a similar situation can be traced back to the famous Chinese novel *Hsi yu-chi* (The Journey to the West).[29] The cooking of enemies is mentioned in the Mongolian literary tradition for the first time in the *Secret History of the Mongols* from the middle of the thirteenth century: the magical powers of an enemy are transferred to the people who cook and consume his flesh.[30]

The number seven as applied to the carnivorous birds is also used in the sixth *Geser* story told by Lubsang,[31] in which seven *mangɣus* brothers can transform themselves into seven mountains by magic. These are finally destroyed and scattered by Geser's magic arrows. Sampilnorbu's reference to Geser's fight with a sea-monster gives a clue that this story in Lubsang's *Qor Geser*[32] was known to him. Parallels like these necessitate the compilation of a catalogue of all motifs in the 'new' Mongolian *Geser* and collation with previously complied motifs. The comparison might then eluminate the source of the newer chapters. The chapter in *Qor Geser*[33] describes the fight of Geser with a sea-monster (motif B16.5.1) that demands a girl as human offering every year (motif S262 'Periodic sacrifices to a monster'). Geser subdues the sea-monster and transforms it into a docile mount for his visit to the dragon-

king; there he wins the hand of the dragon-king's valiant daughter *Nurusuɣma,* with whom he returns to earth. No other *Geser* story tells this adventure beneath the sea, an incident which combines two motifs popular with the Mongols: 1) the yearly human offering to a monster[34] and 2) the grateful dragon-king granting his daughter to the helpful hero. The presentation of a golden casket with the soul of the dragon-king's daughter to the hero is told in many Chinese and Mongolian fairytales (motif B11.6.1 'Dragon helps hero out of gratitude'), while Geser's fight with the seamonster is told only by Lubsang (and referred to by Sampilnorbu), but it is not mentioned at all in the thirty-three Tibetan *Geser* tales.[35]

V (Prose) In the morning after the heaven-sent dream, Geser, after saddling his horse (No. 6.2-2), sets out in fulfilment of the dream to search for the old temple (No. 6.1.4-1) and liberate his imprisoned parents. When he has arrived there, he dismounts in front of the locked gate and breaks it to pieces with a single heavy kick of his foot. His father and mother and the five household members rush out, ask him how he found them and tell him that they had been carried off by seven terrible creatures, more cruel than devils.

(Verse) The tense prose of this report is followed in Sampilnorbu's version by a poem (36 lines) which elaborates the motif of the 'milk test' (motif H175.1 'Recognition of son by gushing up of milk in mother's breasts'; cf. T592). The poem reveals again the close affiliation of Sampilnorbu's poetical expression with the didactic poem *The Teachings of Geser* of his old teacher Toɣtoqu, as for instance when he says:

> Buman mangɣus-un darulɣa Geser
> Buman kümün-degen sitügen bolbaču
> Buɣurul eji-degen bayibai tere
> Bübeyilenden bayiju la öšsčei si ye.
> Tümen-ü mangɣus-i daruɣad
> (10) Törü-yin olan-daɣan tulɣaɣuri boluɣad
> Tüidker mangɣus-i sönügedeg bolbaču
> Törögsen eji-degen bayibai si ye.
> Üre-ben üjegsen eji-yin gini
> Örü sedkil ni tasuna uu
> (15) Angɣ-a nilq-a mini irejei le ged
> Alaɣ nidün-eče ben asqaraɣulju bayin-a
> Ama mömü-yin sedkil gedeg
> Aɣar tngri-yin qur-a la si ye
> Eji kümün-ü sedkil gedeg
> (20) Ečige tngri-yin ariɣun qur-a.
> Engkürei üre-ben üjeged tasun-a uu
> Engger-ün tobči-ban tayiluɣad tegel-e
> Esi-ben ire. eji-ben körü-ei ged
> Endei kökü-ben ɣarɣaɣad ögkül-e
> (25) Eji-yin iyen kökü-yi öščei
> Ečige-yin manglai Geser boɣda
> Elberil jirum tuyil-un boɣda
> Eji-yin kökü-yi teberiged tegel-e
> Eke-yin köküged. soruɣad tegel-e

(30) Emüged kööged. soruγad tegel-e
     Önügen čaγan eke-yin uγuraγ
     Aγsiraju ireged dusulayiγad tegel-e
     Ama mönü ni küü-tei ben aγuljil-a
     Ayil-un bükün aγuljiγad tegel-e
(35) Ende-ben bayiγsan doluγula
     Esi-ben ireged jiγuraγad tegel-e.

Geser, obstacle for a hundred thousand monsters,
He became the idol of a hundred thousand people,
     yet
He too had a greyhaired mother,
Who reared him and sang lullabies to him!
He has subdued ten thousand monsters and
(10) Has become the support of many citizens!
He has destroyed the devilish monsters,
Yet he was born of a mother!
Did she hold back her compassionate feelings?
(15) She said 'My little babe has come!'
And shed tears from her hazelbrown eyes.
The mind of a mother is like
Heavenly rain.
What is called the mother's mind is like
(20) Pure rain falling from father Heaven!
Has it stopped after seeing her beloved child?
She unbuttoned now the garment's flap,
Said, 'Come close, suck from your mother's
     breast!'
She took out her breasts, tenderly, so that he
(25) Sucked strength from his mother's breasts.
Holy Geser, his father's best,
Having extreme filial piety,
Has he refused, when seeing his mother's breasts?
He clasped his mother's breast and
(30) Drained it, sucking and gulping down the
Helpful white mother's milk,
Drying it up even to the last drop.
Thus met the mother with her son,
Then he met all others from the household,
(35) These seven who had been there, and
They came home and met the others . . .[36]

The motif of the milk test as a sign of recognition, when the mother's dried up breasts begin to flow with milk as soon as she sees her missing son, is found in a number of Mongolian *bensen üliger*[37] as well as in epics of the Central Asian Turks.[38] By using this motif, Sampilnorbu follows here the very old literary topos of expressing piety and gratitude towards one's parents, as it is found already in Uighur manuscripts and xylographs of the twelfth and thirteenth centuries[39] on the subject of the return of motherly love.[40] This topos seems to supply a sentence in the *Teachings of Geser*, the poem which made Sampilnorbu famous:[41]

     'In your clean, white belly
     You did carry me ten months.'

His repeated remark that even the heaven-sent hero Geser had a 'greyhaired mother' can also be traced to a line from the same *Teachings of Geser*: 'We originate from fathers and mothers!'[42] Its occurrence illustrates the subconscious remoulding of literary devices.

VI (Prose). Geser has then finally found all the missing people.—(Verse) He now presses in a poem (29 lines) for an urgent return. He loads all seven on his winged horse[43] and returns home. The joy about their homecoming and liberation is great. Geser's father takes his throne, lamps are lighted and incense is burned in gratitude.

VII (Prose) There follows a prose passage in accordance with the pattern of the *bensen üliger*.—(Verse) Sampilnorbu announces then (18 lines) the change of the place of action to the old temple, to which the seven monsters return with a cauldron obtained for cooking their prisoners. When the monsters arrive, they immediately realize that Geser had been there. The door is broken and wide open, and the captives are gone. All they have is an empty cauldron.

VIII (Prose) Disconcerted, the seven take counsel on the steps to be taken. They have no more than a cauldron: the food is gone. Finally they reach the decision to kill Geser, since they will otherwise have no chance of remaining on earth.—(Verse) They take up arms and decide to attack Geser. The approach of the seven *mangγus* monsters is narrated with all the literary devices customarily found in the Mongolian epic when the destruction of the *mangγus* monster is described: dense fog bars the sight, cold winds are blowing, announcing their arrival (No. 9.2-4). With raucous voices the seven fire-doves declare that they have come to kill Geser and get back their human food, of which he had deprived them (43 lines).

IX (Prose) Geser's gatekeeper rushes in and announces the arrival of seven terrible-looking creatures which shout out Geser's name. Geser, still wearing his coat-of mail and helmet as at his return, loses no time in stating his intention to fight. He therefore orders the gatekeeper to have the seven monsters wait on a square outside his house till he comes out to fight with them and defeat one after the other. This answer is greeted with scorn and ridicule by the monsters. The description of Geser's coat of mail and the helmet differs from that in the xylograph of the *Geser* epic, which was printed in Peking in 1716 (and in its attached 'new' chapters), where it is called a 'bluish-black coat of mail'.[44] Sampilnorbu's description is more in line with the formulaic poems in the *bensen üliger*, where generally a number of coats of mail are described, worn by the hero one above the other, with the uppermost made of steel. Sampilnorbu's description embroiders on the remarks, found in some Mongolian epics, concerning the techniques of forging steel,[45] when he states that 'a hundred years of beating make six ching (3.5 kg) of iron, ten thousand years of forging make such a coat of mail[46] which is light and hard, cool in summer and warm in winter . . .'— (Verse) The topic of the following poem (18 lines) is the saddling of the horse (No. 4.9-7).

X (Prose) Geser rides proudly into battle (No. 6.1-6).—(Verse) Stopping in front from the enemies, he asks them to discuss the pending issue civilly (12 lines).

XI (Prose) The narrative continues.—(Verse) Geser's words are met with wild accusations of the seven monsters, claiming that they want only to eat his flesh and to drink his blood (30 lines).

XII (Prose) Continuation.—(Verse) One of the seven monsters asks his six brothers to let him fight alone against Geser, a valiant gesture which belongs to the canon of martial behaviour in the *bensen üliger* (15 lines).

XIII (Prose) Geser, on hearing the boast, laughs, turns his horse round and attacks the seven creatures with his lance.—(Verse) Geser and the seven fire-doves fight with one another with spears. In the lengthy poem (108 lines) the various cuts and thrusts are named in accordance with the classic Chinese art of lance-fighting,[47] while the description of the fight follows the pattern set by renowned Mongolian rhapsodes.[48]

XIV (Prose) The seven strange creatures see that they have no chance of killing Geser and remaining on earth.—(Verse) Geser's fight against the seven enemies, who spout fire and smoke, continues for seven days and seven nights (33 lines).

XV (Prose) When finally the seven beg Geser for an intermission of the fight until next day at noon, Geser is happy to agree. The monsters sheath their weapons and take leave to return to their temple, while Geser returns to his home. The seven evil creatures, after cooling their heated bodies in a lake, return to their temple and confer on a new strategy to defeat Geser. When the enemy is too tired or takes to flight, fighting is often suspended until the next day in the *bensen üliger*, not only as a magnanimous chivalric gesture, but as an often used device for repeating once again a battle-scene to the gusto of the audience.—(Verse) After his return, Geser explains his failure to subdue the aggressors to his parents, who try to caution him (20 lines).

XVI (Prose) Geser again eats only clean, white food. In the night he stays between dreaming and waking (No. 8.3-1). At daybreak he has a dream, telling him to use the piercing sun-and-moon-sword, dangling on his hip, his fire-kindling steel (*kete čing*) and the 'horse sweat comb',[49] which is hanging by his side. With these three magic utensils he has nothing to fear! (None of these three utensils is mentioned in the classical Mongolian *Geser* epic.)

In the morning Geser looks for the three things as demanded in his dream; then he waits for another meeting with the seven demons. The seven strange creatures arrive at noon as agreed and wait outside on the square, discussing once more the ruse by which they plan to kill Geser. They rejoice when they see Geser approaching on foot. He sees the weapons held by the seven, unfastens (No. 11.1.3-2) the horse sweat comb on his back and orders it to keep the seven monsters far away (motif D1413 'Magic object holds person fast'). As if petrified, the spellbound monsters are immobilized. Geser then draws his magic sword (motif D1081.1 'Sword of magic origin') and beheads the demons one after the other. Afterwards he takes his fire-steel box, which has eighteen magic powers (motif D1252.1; D1175.2),[50] and strikes fire. The flames rise immediately and burn the seven beheaded demons to ashes. The speedy burning of the evil creatures turns bad to good, 'iron to gold!' Geser returns to his home and reports the defeat of the seven monsters to his wife and to his father and mother. Peace is brought to the world. A big feast is arranged for everybody, for which plenty of camels are slaughtered and cattle killed.

At the end of this **Geser** adventure Sampilnorbu used motifs associated with the tale 'Three magic objects' (AT 566), which is found in another form in Mongolian fairy tales.[51] The sword of Geser is named differently in the classical **Geser** tradition of the Mongols, i.e. 'black sword of a nine fathom point'.[52] The other two utensils appear with other magical powers in many epics and fairy-tales. The steel and flint box has often the function of hiding the magically shrunk figures of the hero, his horse, his weapons or other possessions. The magic power to root someone to the spot, given here to the sweat comb—generally used by Mongolian horsemen to dry the sweat from the flanks of a horse—shows a certain similarity to the magic powers attributed to other kinds of combs, namely to turn any evil into stone or wood.[53]

The cremation of the seven dead monsters is in agreement with the motif of burning the dead *mangγus* to ashes in order to prevent his reanimation, often used in the Mongolian epic (No. 10.6.9-1). For the resuscitation of a dead body a complete skeleton is needed; this is a belief which is found among hunter-groups, i.e. that the 'lord of the wild animals' can only reanimate complete skeletons when replacing killed animals.

Sampilnorbu's *Geser-yin tuγuji* gives an interesting insight into the structure and composition of a recent oral epic and the individual additions by the singer. It propagates the idea of filial piety, showing how even the heaven-sent Geser observes these rules by using the patterns typical of the 'epics of the recovery of lost possessions and relatives': the hero has to fight to regain his parents, who were abducted by a monster. This is the only concession to the classical **Geser** epic of 1716, the Peking xylograph. The same holds true for the other

Mongolian *Geser* epics recently collected from the singers Lubsang, Sulfungɣa, Bökečilaɣu and others with their new structures and mythicised motifs. Yet contrary to these, Sampilnorbu tells his story in the form of the *bensen üliger,* in which the old, constant use of verse has been replaced by the prosimetrum, the alternating sequence of prose narration and poetry.[54] With the transfer of the prose into the hitherto fully versified **Geser** tradition, a new form of narrating the **Geser** story has been introduced, changing the poetic character and poetic structure of these epics. Sampilnorbu, who is named together with Loozar[55] as Bagharin singer of the **Geser** epic, is believed to have a repertoire of eighteen **Geser** chapters, of which so far only the text discussed above is accessible.

CONCLUSION

There are, however, a few more indications of the spread of prosimetrum. In September 1991 I recorded in the Inner-Mongolian district of Silinghool a chapter of the *Jangɣar* epic. The *Jangɣar* epic has been known to the Western public since 1804/1805, when Benjamin Bergmann published a short chapter of the epic, which he had heard from the Volga Kalmucks.[56] The *Jangɣar* epic is the main epic of the West-Mongolian Kalmucks, as well as of the Western Mongols living in the Chinese province of Sinkiang, from where it has also spread to Northern Mongolia. It certainly is one of the best-documented Mongolian epics,[57] belonging to the type of 'power-delegating epics',[58] wherein the retinue (*comitatus*) of the ruler Jangɣar, who are comparable to the Arthurian knights of the Round Table, are delegated to fight against a varying number of aggressors and enemies.[59] All of the known oral versions of *Jangɣar* are in verse, and none of them has found its way to Inner Mongolia.

Rinčin, a professional singer born in 1930 in the Inner-Mongolian Bagharin-district and living now in Siliqota (administrative centre of Siling-hool), whose epic I recorded in 1991, claimed to have learned his two *Jangɣar* chapters from his uncle, a widely travelled lama (monk) called Čoyiraɣ, when he was eleven years old (1941). Since then he had read printed *Jangɣar* versions too. Both sources have certainly influenced his version of the *Abduction of the Enemy-Ruler Kürmün Khan by Lord Jangɣar's Retinue Mingjan.* Čoyiraɣ considered Jangɣar to be the incarnation of *Adai ulaɣan tngri,* the head of the forty-four gods (*tngri*) of the East, and equated the thirteen heroes of Jangɣar with some of the forty-four *tngri* (see Burčina 1990). Repeating the teaching of his uncle, Rinčin brought a flavour of Lamaism into his telling of *Jangɣar.* He performed the epic, however, in a mixture of verse and prose according to the style of the *bensen üliger.* His *Jangɣar,* so far a rare example of this West-Mongolian epic in Inner Mongolia, is further proof of the beginning of a process introducing the prosimetric form into the hitherto versified Mongolian epic.

Notes

1. See Poppe 1937; 1979; Vladimircov 1983-84; Bawden 1980; Nekljudov 1984; Bürinbeki and Buyankesig 1988; Heissig 1988.

2. See Narantuyaa 1988.

3. Thirteen volumes of translations have appeared to date under the title *Mongolische Epen* in the series *Asiatische Forschungen*: vols. 1 and 2 translations of Rintchen's *Folklore Mongol,* second and third vol. (Poppe 1975a; 1975b); vols. 3, 4, and 5 translations of the collections by Rinčinsambuu, Xorloo, and Zagdsürén, respectively (Poppe 1975c; 1975d; 1977a); vols. 6 and 9 translations of two collections by Žamcarono (Poppe 1977b; 1980); vol. 7 a translation of three South Mongolian epics (Veit 1977); vol. 8 a translation of six East Mongolian epics (Heissig 1979); vol. 10 a translation of eight North Mongolian epics (Bawden 1982); vol. 11 a translation of nine songs from the collection of Žanh'r, II. bot' (Poppe 1985); vol. 12 the translation of two epics collected by P. Chorloo [Xorloo] (Koppe 1992); and vol. 13 a translation of five Oirat epics from Xinjiang (Koppe 1993).

4. See Bormanshinov 1981.

5. See Heissig 1983.

6. See Heissig 1987.

7. See *Kökenaɣur Geser-ün tuɣuji* (3) in *GČB* 1986.

8. See Öljei 1991.

9. See *Baɣarin Geser-ün tuɣuji* 1984; *Baɣarin Geser-un tuɣuji* (2) in *GČB* 1985.

10. See *Baɣarin Geser-ün tuɣuji* (3) in *GČB* 1985.

11. Cf. *Ulaɣančab Qor Geser-un tuɣuji* 1986; Yü 1993.

12. Cf. Yü 1993, 77.

13. Cf. Nekljudov and Tumurceren [Tömörceren] 1982; 1985 (German translation).

14. See *Baɣarin Geser-ün domoɣ* (1) in *GČB* 1985.

15. See Buyankesig 1993.

16. Cf. Nima 1988, 207-10.

17. Cf. Nima 1988, 211-71. This poem has not yet been identified.

18. Cf. Mendübayar 1990, 119.

19. Cf. Heissig 1992b.

20. Cf. Damdinsüren 1961.

21. See Bawden 1976.

22. Nima 1988, 211-71.

23. The motif numbers refer to Heissig 1988, a motif-index of Mongolian epic.

24. Only milk products and water, no meat or fat.

25. Motif numbers preceded by a letter refer to Thompson 1955-58, here motif K2085 'Supernatural person seen in dream gives advice'.

26. Mongolian scholars have recently published some material on the nomenclature of devilish powers and ghosts, with interesting details; see Sayinčoγtu 1993.

27. Cf. Heissig 1978; Sárközi 1992.

28. Cf. Heissig 1992a, 60-61.

29. Cf. Heissig 1972, 2: 105.

30. Cf. Uray-Kõhalmi 1987, 90-91.

31. Cf. Yü 1993, 73.

32. Cf. *Ulaγančab Qor Geser-ün tuγuji* 1986, 53-86.

33. 'Geser mang simnus-i dorungγuyilaju emüne dalai-yin luus-un qaγan-u ökin Nurusuγma-yi qatun bolγaju abuγsan ni.'

34. See Heissig 1995; Öljei 1991, 80-81.

35. Cf. Karmay 1993.

36. Tape recording of 4 November 1988.

37. See Heissig 1988, 1: 348; Heissig 1992a, 61-62.

38. Cf. Hatto 1993.

39. Cf. Zieme 1985, 68-86.

40. See Heissig 1994.

41. Nima 1988, 222: 'Ariγun tungγalaγ kebeli doturaban / Arban sara-bar ačiyalaju bayiγad . . .'

42. Nima 1988, 216: 'Ečige eke-eče ben egüsčü bütübe uu . . .'

43. For Central Asiatic Turkic parallels, see Hatto 1993.

44. See Heissig 1983, 442-46.

45. Cf. Hatto 1993.

46. Tape recording 4 November 1988: '. . . ˇJaγun jil dabtamajin / jirγuγan jing bolγaju / tümen jil dabtaju bayinam / temür quyaγ γarγaγsan . . .'

47. Cf. Riftin 1992.

48. Cf. Nima 1988, 373-74: Šuγara 1983, 309; Heissig 1992a, 103-5, 113. Nine of ten denominations reappear in Sampilnorbu's text.

49. Mongolian *sigür*, a piece of wood to brush off the sweat from the horse's flanks.

50. 'Magic steel'; 'Magic fire-steel (flint, strike-a-light)'; cf. also AT 562 (Aarne and Thompson 1961).

51. Cf. Lőrincz 1979, 266; Aarne and Thompson 1961.

52. Heissig 1983, 445: Yisün alda šoru bolod.

53. Heissig 1988, 2: 729; Heissig 1985, 41.

54. In recognition of their function, the Mongols call these prose parts *aγulγa* 'summary of contents', distinguishing them thereby from the *silüg* 'poem'. See Süke, Kürelša and Buyantoγtaqu 1983, 367-72.

55. Cf. Anba 1993, 86.

56. Bergmann 1804-5, 257-59 [1969, 181-214].

57. See Bormanshinov 1981, 957-963; *Jangγar* 1986.

58. Cf. Heissig (forthcoming).

59. Cf. Kičikov 1992.

Bibliography

Anba. 1993. 'Čaγanmüren γool-un kin-u Geser-i sitükü yosun (On the Custom of Offering Sacrifice to Geser in the Chaganmüren Area).' *Mongolian Language and Literature* 5: 82-87.

Aarne, Antti, and Stith Thompson. 1961. *The Types of the Folktale: A Classification and Bibliography.* Folklore Fellows Communications 184. 2nd ed. Helsinki: Suomalainen Tiedeakatemia.

Baγarin Geser-ün tuγuji. Arban tabuduγar bölüg. Kökehota, 1984.

Bawden, Charles R. 1976. 'On the Evils of Strong Drink: A Mongol Tract from the Early Twentieth Century.' In *Tractata Altaica.* Denis Sinor sexagenario optime de rebus altaicis merito dedicata redegerunt Walther Heissig, John R. Krueger, Felix J. Oinas, et Edmond Schütz. Wiesbaden: Harrassowitz. 57-79.

———. 1980. 'Mongol: The Contemporary Tradition.' In *Traditions of Heroic and Epic Poetry.* Vol 1. *The Traditions.* Ed. A. T. Hatto. Vol. 2. *Characteristics and Techniques.* Ed. J. B. Hainsworth. 2 vols. London: Modern Humanities Research Association, 1980-89. 1: 268-99.

———, tr. 1982. *Mongolische Epen. X. Eight North Mongolian Epic Poems.* Asiatische Forschungen 75. Wiesbaden: Harrassowitz.

Bergmann, Benjamin von. 1804-5. *Benjamin Bergmann's nomadische Streifereien unter den Kalmüken in den Jahren 1802 und 1803.* 4 pts. in 2 vols. Riga. [Rpt. Oosterhout: Anthropological Publications, 1969.]

Bormanshinov, Arash. 1981. 'Džangar.' In *Enzyklopädie des Märchens.* Ed. Kurt Ranke et al. Vol. 3. Berlin: de Gruyter. Coll. 957-63.

Burčina, Darima A. 1990. *Geseriada zapadnyx burjat. Ukazatel' proizvendenij i ix variantov.* Otvetstvennyj redaktor Ju. I. Smirnov. Novosibirsk: Nauka.

Bürinbeki and N. Buyankesig. 1988. *Mongγol ündüsüten-ü baγaturliγ tuulis songγumal. I/II.* Kökehota and Ulaγanhota.

Buyankesig, N. 1993. 'Baγarin Geser-ün domoγ. Süme tayilaγa-yin tuqai.' *Mongolian Language and Literature* 6: 84-91.

Damdinsüren, ed. 1961. *Ačilaltu nom-un tuqai.* Studia Mongolica. Tomus III, fasc. 12. Ulan Bator.

GČB 1985: *Geser-ün čuburil bičig.* Kökehota, 1985.

GČB 1986: *Geser-ün čuburil bičig.* Kökehota, 1986.

Hatto, A. T. 1993 'Reflections of a Non-Mongolist on W. Heissig's Erzählstoffe.' *Ural-altaische Jahrbücher,* NF 12: 269-78.

Heissig, Walther. 1972. *Geschichte der mongolischen Literatur.* 2 vols. Wiesbaden: Harrassowitz.

———. 1978. 'Geser Khan als Heilsgottheit.' In *Proceedings of the Csoma de Körös Memorial Symposium, Held at Matrafured, Hungary, 24-30 September, 1976.* Ed. Louis Ligeti. Bibliotheca Orientalis Hungarica 23. Budapest: Akadémiai Kiadó. 125-52.

———, tr. 1979. *Mongolische Epen. VIII. Übersetzung von sechs ostmongolischen Epen nach den Aufzeichnungen von Lhisürün, Ganjurjab, Orgil, Dorongγa und Pajai.* Asiatische Forschungen 60. Wiesbaden: Harrassowitz.

———. 1983. *Geser-Studien. Untersuchungen zu den Erzählstoffen in den 'neuen' Kapiteln des mongolischen Geser-Zyklus.* Abhandlungen der Rheinisch-Westfälischen Akademie der Wissenschaften 69. Opladen: Westdeutscher Verlag. 442-46.

———. 1985. *Tsakhar-Märchen. Nach Aufzeichnungen aus dem Jahre 1938/39.* Asiatische Forschungen 87. Wiesbaden: Harrassowitz.

———. 1987. 'Geser Khan.' In *Enzyklopädie des Märchens.* Ed. Kurt Ranke et al. Vol. 5. Berlin: de Gruyter. Coll. 1151-62.

———. 1988. *Erzählstoffe rezenter mongolischer Heldendichtung.* 2 vols. Asiatische Forschungen 100. Wiesbaden: Harrassowitz.

———. 1992a. *Oralität und Schriftlichkeit mongolischer Spielmanns-Dichtung.* Rheinisch-Westfälische Akademie der Wissenschaften: Geisteswissenschaften, Vorträge G 317. Opladen: Westdeutscher Verlag.

———. 1992b. 'Zur Re-Mythisierung des ostmongolischen Epos.' In *Fragen der mongolischen Heldendichtung. V.* Ed. Walther Heissig. Asiatische Forschungen 120. Wiesbaden: Harrassowitz. 92-112.

———. 1994. 'Der Dank an die Mutter und seine mongolischen Varianten.' In *Memoriae Munusculum. Gedenkband für Annemarie von Gabain.* Ed. Klaus Röhrborn and Wolfgang Veenker. Veröffentlichungen der Societas Uralo-Altaica 39. Wiesbaden: Harrassowitz. 65-71.

———. 1995. 'Vom "Dank des Drachenkönigs" (B 375) zum todbringenden "Kleidertausch des Königs" (K 527) im mongolischen Märchen.' In *Studien zur Stoff- und Motivgeschichte der Volkserzählung. Berichte und Referate des achten bis zehnten Symposiums zur Volkserzählung, Brunnenburg/Südtirol 1991-1993.* Beiträge zur europäischen Ethnologie und Folklore, Reihe B, Tagungsberichte und Materialien 6. Ed. Leander Petzold and Siegfried de Rachewiltz. Frankfurt a. M.: Lang. 237-50.

———. Forthcoming. 'The Present State of the Mongolian Epic and Some Topics of Future Research.' Paper read at the UNESCO-Workshop, Turku, 1993.

Jangγar. 1986. 2 vols. Kökehota: Inner Mongolian Academy of Social Sciences.

Karmay, S. M. 1993. 'The Theoretical Basis of the Tibetan Epic with References to a "Chronological Order" of Various Episodes in the Geser Epic.' *Bulletin of the School of Oriental and African Studies* 56: 234-46.

Kičikov, A. Š. 1992. *Geroičeskij èpos 'Džangar'.* Moscow: Nauka.

Koppe, Klaus, tr. 1992. *Mongolische Epen. XII. Jula aldar Qayan und Uyan mönggün qadayasun.* Aufnahme von Pürėvijn Chorloo. Asiatische Forschungen 118. Wiesbaden: Harrassowitz.

———, tr. 1993. *Mongolische Epen. XIII. 'Oiratische Epen'. Fünf Epen aus Sinkiang.* Asiatische Forschungen 127. Wiesbaden: Harrassowitz.

Lőrincz, László. 1979. *Mongolische Märchentypen.* Asiatische Forschungen 61. Wiesbaden: Harrassowitz.

Mendübayar. 1990. *Tuuli tuγuji üliger qolboγan-u iji aya-yin songγumal.* Peking.

Narantuyaa, R. 1988. 'Mongol tuulijn bürtgel.' *Studia Folclorica* (Ulan Bator) 8: 78-154.

Nekljudov, S. Ju. 1984. *Geroičeskij èpos mongol'skix narodov. Ustnye i literarnye tradicii.* Issledovanija po fol'kloru i mirfologii Vostoka. Moscow: Izd. Nauka.

———, and Ž. Tumurceren, eds. and tr. 1982. *Mongol'skie skazanija o Gesere. Novye zapisi.* AN SSSR, Inst. mirovoj lit. Moscow: Izd. Nauka.

———, eds. and tr. 1985. *Mongolische Erzählungen über Geser. Neue Aufzeichnungen.* Tr. J. Bäcker. Asiatische Forschungen 92. Wiesbaden: Harrassowitz.

Nima. 1988. *Kelen-ü uran darqad.* Peking.

Öljei, M. A. 1991. *Mongγol töbed 'Geser'-ün Qaričaγa.* Peking.

Poppe, N. N. 1937. *Xalxa-mongol'skij geroičeskij èpos.* Moscow and Leningrad: Izd. Nauka.

———, tr. 1975a. *Mongolische Epen. I. Übersetzung der Sammlung B. Rintchen, Folklore Mongol, Livre deuxième.* Asiatische Forschungen 42. Wiesbaden: Harrassowitz.

———, tr. 1975b. *Mongolische Epen. II. Übersetzung der Sammlung B. Rintchen, Folklore Mongol, Livre troisième.* Asiatische Forschungen 43. Wiesbaden: Harrassowitz.

———, tr. 1975c. *Mongolische Epen. III. Übersetzung der Sammlung G. Rinčinsambuu, Mongol ardyn baatarlag tuul's.* Asiatische Forschungen 47. Wiesbaden: Harrassowitz.

———, tr. 1975d. *Mongolische Epen. IV. Übersetzung der Sammlung P. Xorloo, Xalx Ardyn Tuul'.* Asiatische Forschungen 48. Wiesbaden: Harrassowitz.

———, tr. 1977a. *Mongolische Epen. V. Übersetzung der Sammlung U. Zagdsürèn, Žangaryn Tuul's.* Asiatische Forschungen 50. Wiesbaden: Harrassowitz.

———, tr. 1977b. *Mongolische Epen. VI. Übersetzung der Sammlung C. Ž. Žamcarano, Büxü Xara Xübüün Ül'gèrnüüd.* Asiatische Forschungen 53. Wiesbaden: Harrassowitz.

———. 1979. *The Heroic Epic of the Khalkha Mongols.* Tr. J. Krueger, D. Montgomery, and M. Walter. Publ. of the Mongolia Soc., Occasional Paper 11. 2nd ed. Bloomington: The Mongolia Society. [English tr. of Poppe 1937.]

———, tr. 1980. *Mongolische Epen. IX. Übersetzung der Sammlung C. Ž. Žamcarano, Proizvedenija narodnoj slovestnosti mongol'skich plemen.* Asiatische Forschungen 65. Wiesbaden: Harrassowitz.

———, tr. 1985. *Mongolische Epen. XI. Übersetzung von neun Gesängen aus der Sammlung Žanh'r, II. bot'.* Asiatische Forschungen 89. Wiesbaden: Harrassowitz.

Riftin, Boris. L. 1992. 'Die Beschreibung des heldischen Zweikampfes im ostmongolischen Epos.' In *Fragen der mongolischen Heldendichtung. V.* Ed. Walther Heissig. Asiatische Forschungen 120. Wiesbaden: Harrassowitz. 145-93.

Sárközi, Alice. 1992. *Political Prophecies in Mongolia in the 17th—20th Centuries.* Asiatische Forschungen 116. Wiesbaden: Harrassowitz.

Sayinčoγtu. 1993. 'Mongγol-un čidkür-ün soyal.' *Journal of the Inner Mongolia Normal University* 1993.4: 20-36.

Šuγara, Ü., ed. 1983. *Pajai-yin jokiyal-un tegübüri.* Kökehota.

Süke, B., Kürelša and Buyantoγtaqu. 1983. *Qorčin uran jokiyal-un tobčiya.* Peking.

Thompson, Stith. 1955-58. *Motif-Index of Folk-Literature.* 6 vols. Rev. ed. Bloomington: Indiana UP.

Ulaγančab Qor Geser-un tuγuji. Kökehota, 1986.

Uray-Kőohalmi, Käthe. 1987. 'Herd und Kessel in der epischen Dichtung der innerasiatischen und sibirischen Völker.' In *Fragen der mongolischen Heldendichtung. IV.* Ed. Walther Heissig. Asiatische Forschungen 101. Wiesbaden: Harrassowitz. 82-94.

Veit, Veronika, tr. 1977. *Mongolische Epen. VII. Übersetzung von drei südmongolischen Epen.* Asiatische Forschungen 54. Wiesbaden: Harrassowitz.

Vladimircov, B. Ja. 1983-84. 'The Oirat-Mongolian Heroic Epic.' In *Mongolian Studies. VIII.* Tr. J. R. Krueger. Bloomington: The Mongolia Society. 6-58.

Yü, Lüngmei. 1993. 'Geserči kiged tegün-ü Qor Geser-ün tuγuji.' *Mongolian Language and Literature* 2: 73-84.

Zieme, Peter. 1985. *Buddhistische Stabreimdichtungen der Uiguren.* Berlin: Akademie-Verlag.

Li Lianrong (essay date October 2001)

SOURCE: Lianrong, Li. "History and the Tibetan Epic *Gesar*." *Oral Tradition* 16, no. 2 (October 2001): 317-42.

[*In the following essay, Lianrong provides an overview of modern* Gesar *epic scholarship and discusses new critical trends of the last twenty years.*]

Looking back on the achievements of half a century devoted to studying the Tibetan epic *Gling rje Gesar rgyal povi mam tar* (later *Gesar*), one finds a particular school of research whose province is the relationship between the epic and historical truth. This is a school that should not be neglected. I believe a historical study of the epic ought to research written records under the assumption that King Gesar and his deeds could have existed. Was there a person called Gling Gesar? Where is Gling? What is the particular time of origin of the hero's story? Who is the author? What is the relationship between the Tibetan *Gesar* and versions popular among other ethnic groups? Because this school has spent much of its energy on the question of the epic's diachronic origin, this kind of study is called historical research on the origin of the epic.

The approach embodied by the questions above was common for early epic researchers of *Gesar.* There is also evidence of this approach among foreign scholars, who were studying the epic before most Tibetan, Mongolian, and Chinese scholarship on this subject began. To be more precise, before 1959 most of the publications on *Gesar* outside China centered on the historical problems of the epic (Stein 1993:12-14; Khomonov 1986:1-38; Nekljudov 1991:1-85[1]). In China, without exception, this problem has been the focus since the first explorations into the Tibetan *Gesar.* After nearly a half-century of research, scholars have reached basic agreement on the following three points. 1) Either the epic's protagonist Gling Gesar was a real person or he is a synthetic character created by the combination of historical figures. 2) Tibetan versions of the epic serve as the source for branches of *Gesar* found among other ethnic groups. Being branches, they have features of their own. 3) Though many views exist, there is basic agreement about the time of the epic's origin. However, with regard to Gling Gesar legends, research into folklore—rather than history—is the appropriate avenue.

This [essay] provides a review of the scholarly discourse on problems of the Tibetan epic *Gesar*'s time of origin, in hopes of summarizing the achievements and shortcomings of the previous generations, finding a basis for solving problems, and showing how basic agreements have been reached.

EARLY THEORIES ABOUT *GESAR*'S TIME OF
ORIGIN

In the 1930s and 1940s pioneering Chinese Tibetologists (largely Han scholars) gathering in Sichuan began to notice this great epic. Those who gave attention to the epic in varying degrees or promoted its exploration included Li Anzhai, Peng Gonghou, Xie Guoan, Liu Liquian, Zhuang Xueben, Chen Zongxiang, Li Jianming, and in particular Han Rulin and Ren Naiqiang. Others contributed to *Gesar* studies in a number of ways: by collecting handwritten copies and photocopies of *Gesar*; by translating and thus introducing the achievements in collection of and research on *Gesar* at home and abroad; by offering relevant information and materials; and by giving guidance to the scholars who devoted themselves to the cause of *Gesar* studies. All of these often uncredited scholars and researchers influenced the study of *Gesar.*

In fact, these early Tibetologists should be categorized as borderland specialists. They came from different professions; some were merchants, teachers, officials, and even religious believers (such as Li Jianming mentioned above), but most were sociologists, anthropologists, or ethnologists, such as the renowned ethnologist Li Anzhai. Li encouraged Chen Zongxiang, who planned to translate *The Superhuman Life of Gesar of Ling* (David-Neel 1984:1[2]). At the same time, Li provided assistance to this book's author, David-Neel, and her colleague Yongdun Lama while they were investigating *Gesar* in Sichuan, as well as wrote an article in praise of their scholarship (Li 1945, 1992:149; David-Neel 1984:1).

During this period, teachers from the Department of Frontier Languages of Lanzhou University, following in the footsteps of their colleagues from the Tibetan Research Society in Qinghai, actively pioneered China's Tibet Studies (called "Frontier Studies" at that time). Tibetologists should not forget those pioneers, such as Yang Zhifu, Wu Jun and others, who made decisive contributions to the cause of collecting, translating, and researching *Gesar* after Tibet was incorporated into China. Wu Jun in particular delineated important arguments concerning the historical research of the epic *Gesar.*

In the nascent stages of Tibet Studies, *Gesar* was treated as a work of literature; however, due to circumstances this direction has received little attention. When Tibet Studies became Frontier Studies, the aforementioned scholars treated *Gesar* as historical fiction: "This book is a record of Gesar of Ling. The Han people call it a Tibetan version of *The Story of the Three Kingdoms, Gesar Langte* in Tibetan, or *A Record of Gesar* in translation. It can also be translated as *A Poetic History of Gesar,* because it usually relies on a form of poetic narration similar to our *Xujuan Tanci*" (Ren N. 1944:1). From this attitude it may be inferred that in the ethnically mixed northwestern Sichuan province people consider the epic *Gesar* equal to *The Story of the Three Kingdoms.*[3] Thus, those scholars who devoted themselves to borderlands research found that on the one hand *Gesar* was not *The Story of the Three Kingdoms*; on the other hand, driven by interest at that time, they sought to study the epic from the perspectives of folklore and history.

According to Ren Xinjian, when his father Ren Naiqiang returned from fieldwork in Xinlong in 1928, he included his first notes on *Gesar* in his *Xikang Guiyilu (The Peculiar Things in Xikang)* (1931), and had it published under the titles of *A Tibetan Version of the Story of the Three Kingdoms* and *Samples of A Tibetan Version of the Story of the Three Kingdoms* (1934). Later, Ren Naiqiang included these pieces on *Gesar* in his chapter on folklore in *A Pictorial Record of Xikang,* a book he devoted to the historical geography of Xikang Tujing (Ren X. 1991:54-55). Though Ren N. noted that *Gesar* is a "poetic history," a "historical romance," "Like the *Baijuan* in the Han dynasty," "a novel that develops Buddhist ideals," and a work replete with absorbing literary features, his main interest remained historical research of the epic. In his writings, Ren N. included collections of the epic's remnants and sayings about the epic. He also gave a very valuable preliminary textual analysis of the number of its parts. But it must be pointed out that he paid little attention to the epic as verbal art, although it is certain that he read David-Neel's *The Superhuman Life of Gesar of Ling,* which more than once emphasized its nature as an epic. Ren N. used the term "epic," but he considered *Gesar* to be history and did not attend to its artistic value.

He made large conceptual leaps when analyzing the historical authenticity of *Gesar.* He claims that there was such a person in history, but has trouble settling on a historical personage. In his initial paper Ren N. proposes for the first time in the history of *Gesar* studies that Kings Gesar and Gu si luo[4] are one and the same (Ren N. 1944:7). He later describes Gesar as the offspring of Gu si luo's enemy Danxiang (Jiangbian 1986:15). But he eventually explains away this opinion derived from Tibetan sources by saying that "Tibetans did not have a correct sense of epoch and should not be trusted for such a conception" (*idem*). Finally, he returns to his original position and asserts that Gesar was in fact Gu si luo (Jiangbian 1986:19). In order to discover the epic's date of composition, he surmises that "the Tibetan version of *The Story of the Three Kingdoms* seems to be written by the lamas from the Sakya sect in the Yuan dynasty" (Jiangbian 1986:16). The possible span of time for the epic's origin is further narrowed on the basis of his argument that it must have appeared before Bsod nams rgyal mtshan began writing, because in his *Rgyal rabs gsal bavi me long* (1982) the king speaks of the militant King Gesar as he proposes to the Princess Wenching. This text can be traced to the close of the twelfth century. Ren N. conjectures that the loss of any printed copy as evidence for his position may be blamed on the turbulent change from Bon shamanism to Tibetan Buddhism.

Ren N. laid the groundwork for exploration of the epic *Gesar.* His research called attention to the role of *Gesar* in Han culture and his work in epic studies was also groundbreaking. In addition to his introduction to and analysis of literature, history, and folklore noted above, he also objectively and scientifically reviewed a number of the epic volumes, their core content, and the view of the so-called "hesitant Guan Yu" put forward by foreign scholars.[5] Ren N.'s argument that Gesar and Guan Yu had separate origins was not accepted until 1959, when Stein published his summary of the studies in the West over the past one hundred years. On the whole, it may be asserted that the greatest contribution on the part of Ren N. is that he established a precedent for Chinese *Gesar* studies.

Another famous frontier researcher, Han Rulin (1988), also deserves mention. Han was a contemporary of Ren's, and similarly possessed great insight into the Guan Yu problem. His 1941 paper on Guan Yu in Tibet was not lengthy, but the problems he raised were quite valuable. It provided a very good summary of *Gesar* research outside of China, which for the last one hundred years had posited that King Gesar and Guan Yu were the same. Han reveals that this was a mistake by referring to the principle of variation in folklore,[6] and attributes the cause of such a mistake to the features of Tibetan folk culture. According to this theory, the association of the two figures may be linked to the historical changes in the Manchu and Han cultures in the course of their exchanges with Tibetan culture. In addition, Han criticizes the far-fetched claim that *Gesar* was Caesar of Rome. However, his criticism did not reach *Gesar* researchers outside China, who continued to follow in their predecessors' footsteps (see Stein 1993:396). Han's perspective has served as the primary vehicle for epic researchers to criticize the association of Gesar with Caesar. He noted that their conflation is very influential in the West and that this fact would anticipate the epic's reemergence as an object of study.[7]

Han did not concentrate specifically on the time of origin of the epic; however, like the Tibetans he believed that Gesar was a man of the early Tang dynasty. For him, this theory was given credence by "The Legend of the Wedding of Princess Wencheng" in *Ma ni bkav vbum* and *La dwags rgyal rabs.*[8] That Han could put forward such a view is really quite reasonable when one considers that he had no access to reference materials and that the *Gesar* fragments provided by Ren Naiqiang were his only available evidence.

On the whole, Tibetologists in the 1930s and 1940s were inclined to research the historical origin of the epic, an agenda that was inextricable from the core problem of frontier studies at that time: opening up the frontier and consolidating the state. Of course, the roles played by religious and ethnological researchers should not be overlooked. Generally speaking, however, Ren N. opened new horizons for historical epic studies with an eye to the home country and fieldwork. For his part, Han criticized foreign scholars for misguided historical research, summarized the achievements and shortcomings of historical epic studies outside China over the past hundred years, and opened up new prospects for Chinese *Gesar* studies. However, due to limitations at that time and the unsteadiness of the situation, this exploration into the historical origins of the epic failed to find a foothold. It did not reemerge until conditions matured again.

In addition, there were a few Tibetologists who concentrated on the study of *Gesar* as an epic per se. Most were invested in the more traditional forms of religious and historical research and approached *Gesar* using the rubrics of myth and ritual studies. Scholars like Dge vdun chos vphel, who used innovative scholarly approaches and discussed the epic's variation and its transmission, were few in number (cf. 1990 vol. 1:182; vol. 2:96).

EMERGENCE OF NEW APPROACHES

After the founding of New China, early frontier scholars assisted in the great state project of conducting nationwide surveys, research, and identification of minority nationalities with regard to their culture, customs, social history, population, organization, and other characteristics. Hence surveying and data collection were the major tasks for this period.

Under the new art guidelines, the slogan "All in the interest of the laboring masses, all for the purpose of serving the people" became the basic principle motivating academic activities. As a project of vital importance to the new socialist society, folklore studies received more attention in this period. Nationwide collecting of folklore began in full swing. The newly established Chinese Research Society of Folk Literature and Art played a leading role in the collecting. A top-down approach was instituted for China's folklore studies, resulting in the standardization of academic activities.

It was in this atmosphere that a grand-scale collection of the epic *Gesar* was launched. In a matter of a few years, surprisingly great achievements resulted; however, to our sorrow, the work of collection suffered from anti-superstitious and anti-feudalist movements during which a great quantity of *Gesar* cantos was thrown on the flames. As those who assisted the collection work commented, "We were competing with the fire god for treasure" (Xu 1993:183). To add to our dismay, none of those early scholars who conducted *Gesar* research in the 1930s and 1940s assisted with the later collection work. As a result, such work suffered many drawbacks.

After many cantos and records relevant to *Gesar* had been amassed, these new scholars were faced with the problem of interpretation. *Gesar*'s time of origin did not receive much attention at this point, but as an unavoidable issue it was included on the agenda for discussion. It was not that scholars and researchers were too busy to investigate such a problem; rather, they lacked the proper conditions and techniques for such research. Some individual scholars did their best to cope with the question of origins in a truthful way, making every use of their available resources and

knowledge and performing basic preparatory work. Because scholarship is a cumulative process, the current level of understanding could not have been reached without the explorations of the 1950s and 1960s.

In 1956 Lao She published the abstract of his report at the second council meeting of the Association of Chinese Writers under the title "A Report on the Literature of Ethnic Groups in China." This article appeared simultaneously in the *People's Daily* and *Folklore* and registered a strong impact on the scholarly community. As a result, some collectors, such as Xu Guoqiong, made *Gesar* their lifelong study (Xu 1993:1). The importance of Lao's report lies in the fact that it directly inspired a large-scale effort to collect the epic *Gesar* and served as a touchstone from then on. The power of his comments may be attributed partially to his status as vice-chair of the council for China's Research Society of Folk Literature and Art.

In this report Lao demonstrates that the Tibetan epic *Gesar* had formed in the late Yuan and early Ming dynasties, the earliest time of origin that had been proposed since the incoporation of Tibet into China (Lao 1956:3). With respect to the Mongolian version of the epic, he remarks that "the *Story of Gesar,* came into being two centuries prior to the time when Chinggis appeared on the historical stage!" (*ibid*). According to Lao, the materials cited in his paper were provided by 11 colleagues from eight minority nationalities and by two Han colleagues well acquainted with the varieties of brotherly ethnic literature.[9] Among these collectors there were Mongols but no Tibetans—a discrepancy also common outside China. When the Mongolian *Geser* was searched for associations with Chinggis Khan, either the ethnic scholars assisting Lao She believed that Gesar was Chinggis Khan, having been influenced by the perspective of Soviet scholars, or they knew the outcome of the seminar on *Gesar* held in 1953 in Ulan-Ude of the Soviet Union and did not equate Gesar with Chinggis Khan (Khomonov 1986:21-22). What were the grounds for placing the origin of *Gesar* between the late Yuan and early Ming periods? It seems either that Lao was well versed in Ren Naiqiang's perspective, or that he was familiar with *Gesar* and its history in the Tibetan Dege District, Sichuan, or that the fieldwork conducted by David-Neel had influenced him. No matter the source, a time of origin between the late Yuan and early Ming periods did not vary far from that proposed by Chinese scholars in the 1930s and 1940s. It marked a good starting point for the study of *Gesar* in the New China.

When *Gesar* was being researched in the Qinghai province, some pre-liberation scholars were included in the team. They were largely teachers at the Department of Frontier Languages of Lanzhou University, and their most important job was to translate the collected handwritten manuscripts. Due to their special status as data providers, they introduced Tibetan culture, especially folk culture and *Gesar.* The Qinghai Union of Writers and Artists compiled and published the *Reference Materials for Collecting and Researching Tibetan Literature in Qinghai* (1959:1-2)[10] as "inside only" materials. With regard to the time of its origin, Yang Zhifu argues that if *Gesar* has been written by Rdo ring sras chung (commonly known as Rdo ring bandita), its date of composition should be set between the late Kangxi of the Qing dynasty and Qianlong—or between the seventeenth and eighteenth centuries. His evidence derives from the historical records of Rdo ring bandita. Yang Z. adds that *Gesar* might have been written by the Red-sect Lamas in Xikang, but this view and the previous one are based primarily on oral legends. He believes that there are no records of *Gesar* in Tibetan literature (Yang Z. 1959:9).

Wu Jun, similarly attributing the composition of *Gesar* to Rdo ring bandita, sets the date of its origin in the early Qing dynasty, or the seventeenth century. His perspective somewhat differs from Yang, who thinks that Rdo ring bandita was a contemporary of the Seventh Dalai Lama; Wu believes, in accordance with popular legends, that he was a contemporary of the Fifth Dalai Lama. Both Wu and Yang Z. cite cases in which parts of the Tibetan *Gesar* were recorded by various parties; thus we may infer that the entire epic had not been written down in one place and time. Even a single copy of *Gesar* could sustain notable scribal inconsistencies—"it was not written by a single hand nor was it written at one time. Its content was gradually shaped by folk legends and the interests of individual artists and their audiences" (Wu 1959:1).

With reference to the process of compiling and composing, Wu points out that "people continually blended the contents of *Gesar* stories with popular legends and myths, using the rich, demotic language to enliven its drama. By fixing the epic in written form, it became the nine-part, twelve-part, and twenty-four-part versions that are now popular in Xikang, Qinghai, and Tibet" (*idem*). Wu's understanding of *Gesar* reflects not only his grasp of the rules of folklore but also his personal involvement with the epic. He writes that "fifteen years ago, I was in Yushu, Gansu, and Qinghai, where I heard this printed version of the *Record of King Gesar* recited many times" (*idem*). This simple statement influenced later generations of scholars to seek out and experience live performances of *Gesar.*

In their articles Yang Z. and Wu criticize Ren N. and Han for linking *The Barbarous Version of the Story of the Three Kingdoms*[11] with *Gesar,* as well as for believing that either Caesar or Guan Yu could be Gesar. Yang

Z. also argues against the proposition that Gesar could have been Gu si luo, but Wu supports this idea until the 1980s. Though Yang Z. and Wu criticize the perspectives of Ren N. and Han, they participate in the same scholarly tradition: if all views, including those of Lao, stemmed at last from Ren Naiqiang's work, then a tradition of historical research has always underlain the study of *Gesar* in China.[12]

One month after Yang Z. and Wu had contributed to the Union of Writers and Artists of Qinghai, *Folklore* published Shan Chao's "Notes on Tibetan Folk Literature" (1959). In the article Shan states that "among the long stories that are spreading, the most well known is the *Record of King Gesar.* It was collectively created in the eleventh century, and its hero, Gesar, was an ideal figure among the masses" (81). Shan does not supply evidence for his argument, but it probably was influenced by the Tibetan scholars he encountered during his fieldwork.[13] In the 1980s many Tibetan scholars insisted on the validity of this perspective.

In the late 1950s and early 1960s the folklorist Xu Guoqiong was more concerned with *Gesar*'s time of origin than any other scholar. Xu devoted himself to the development of epic studies in the New China, giving his life to the work of collecting and compiling early versions of *Gesar.* He pursued field work among the Tibetan people and actively popularized *Gesar,* ensuring future exploration of the epic. To some extent, his work directly determined the fate of *Gesar.* Xu was determined to brave all difficulties, even death, to save the tradition, and this devotion has influenced and inspired much of the subsequent work on the epic, even to the present day. Stories about his efforts to compile such a great magnitude of cantos and documents not only advanced the preservation of *Gesar* in writing but also served as a powerful model for the development and recovery of folklore throughout China.

Xu played a strong role in early epic preservation, frequently traveling between Beijing and Qinghai, a trip that other scholars seldom if ever made at the time. Scholars serving jail sentences, such as Yang Z. and Wu, obviously had little opportunity to travel. In this way Xu's voice set the tone for the study of *Gesar.* His first article, a comprehensive introduction to *Gesar,* has retained its position in the *Selected Papers on Chinese Folk Literature, 1949-1979,* and has been widely quoted (1959). This paper secured his position in the academic history of *Gesar* studies both then and now. Xu devoted two subsections to the time of origin of the epic, summarizing all the perspectives common during that period. He agreed with the argument that the epic came into being in the eleventh century, and provided his own support (305-10).[14]

By the end of the 1950s[15] *Gesar* researchers at home and abroad subscribed to one of the following four theories about the origin of *Gesar.* First, some European scholars traced the epic's origin to the seventh or eighth century—in his work Han appears to agree with this opinion (1988). This argument was largely based on the Tubo legends ("The Wedding of the Princess Wencheng") and "historical memory" of the Tubo wars. Second, according to Ren N. the thirteenth century was *Gesar*'s time of origin. Lao continued in the same vein by speculating on the time of the author's birth and death. Third, some scholars from the former Soviet Union insisted that the seventeenth or the eighteenth century was the period of genesis; Yang Z. and Wu concurred, also founding their arguments on the author's dates of birth and death. Finally, Xu argued for the eleventh century, a time of origin earlier proposed by David-Neel.[16] Shan agreed with this opinion, and Ts. Damdinsüreng gave the most persuasive argument for the eleventh century in the papers he published around 1957. At that moment Ts. Damdinsüreng was studying in the Soviet Union, where he closely followed the theoretical trends concerning the epic. He was influenced by Soviet theories on the historical origin of epic and its creation by particular people.[17] That Xu agreed with this perspective probably had something to do with the predisposition of the Chinese academic community at that time to Soviet theories—learning from the Soviets was a nationwide trend.

Xu cites Ts. Damdinsüreng's grounds for arguing against the seventh and eighth centuries, making use of the basic perspectives of Tibetan scholars and artists whom he had encountered while collecting *Gesar* cantos. The character of Gesar himself serves as the main point in his discussion of the epic's time of origin, as it had for Ts. Damdinsüreng. Xu, however, has new evidence: a description of the birth of Gesar in *Mdo smad chos vbyung* by the nineteenth-century historian Brag dgon pa dkon mchog bstan pa rab rgyas mentioned that the hero was born on the very first day of the Tibetan traditional calendar in 1027 (1982:234). It was later discovered that this was commonly believed by Tibetan scholars in the Qing dynasty.

In addition, Xu lists three dates close to those in the *Politico-Religious History of Amdo.* It is important to note that these dates were mentioned in the text in accordance with the epic's attempt to present Gesar as a historical figure. The accessibility of copies of the epic, which before the 1950s had not been available for scholarly research, enable Xu to introduce these dates. Based on the text's own assertions he argues that Gesar was a man of the eleventh century: his fame spread after his death, leading his contemporary Nor bu chos vphel to perform his story as an epic. Subsequently, oral performances and written versions of *Gesar* have

influenced each other up to the present moment. In making this argument, Xu draws upon his knowledge of the characteristic variations inherent to folklore. The role of variation and recognition of its importance were gradually surfacing in the works of a later generation of researchers.

It was Huang Jingtao who brought an end to various origin theories in early *Gesar* studies and provided a correct line of thinking. He believed that scholars from different disciplines needed to cooperate in order to analyze the epic from all angles; only in this way, he argues, can we reach reasonable conclusions. Noting the epic's common folklore features, Huang determines that it was a folk creation and recognizes that it is problematic to speak of a "primary draft" or a "present draft" (Huang J. 1962:323-24). He warns against confusion and simplification without sidestepping the issue itself. Huang's line of thinking—in particular, the importance of a multidisciplinary approach and of *Gesar*'s folk characteristics—took root among Chinese researchers, resulting in the strength of present-day *Gesar* studies.

THE EVOLUTION OF THEORY FROM THE 1970s ONWARD

In the late 1970s, after *Gesar* research and collection had been suspended for twelve years due to the Cultural Revolution and its aftermath,[18] scholars bravely stepped forward and reasserted the value of epic studies (Xu 1978:16-18; Wang Yinuan 1979a:6-16). There had been a similar gap of nearly twelve years when *Gesar* studies halted in the 1940s and began again in the late 1950s. During these periods Chinese scholars endured many hardships with respect to the collection and research of this great epic; it is through such vicissitudes that our epic studies have gradually been set on course.

Wang Yinuan had completed the first Chinese translation of *Gesar* in 1981 (see Wang Yinuan and Huajia 1981), reentering the arena of *Gesar* studies with great relish. In a succession of four articles published between 1978 and 1981, he vigorously expresses his understanding and recognition of this epic. Like previous researchers, Wang Yinuan mistakenly applies literary methods to the study of an oral epic. Of course, it was not without great difficulty that he used such methods to determine the time of origin: he attempted to locate a single author in order to ascertain the date of the epic's composition, and eventually comes to share the opinion of other scholars that this author was the fifteenth-century Tibetan figure Nor bu chos vphel (1980:353-55).

Although Wang Yinuan's inference violates the basic principles of transformation and variation in folklore, his research has been valuable in that it provided a later generation of researchers with important clues about how the epic had been compiled, recorded, and composed by scribes and learned men in the past. Searching for an "author" has assisted researchers who wish to learn more about the time of recording and to identify a scribe for a variant of a certain part of the epic. Xu adopts Wang Yinuan's methods in his discussion of the author and compiler of the epic and of the chronological background of its particular parts and chapters (1984:76; 1985:108). However, this search is limited to a particular manuscript from a particular period, and even these results are uncertain.

Shortly after Wang Yinuan published his theories, Wang Yingchuan and Shangguan Jianbi (1981) approached the problem of origin by considering the epic's historical background. Wang weaves Marxist literary theory into her argument, contending that typical environments create typical characters (1986:174-75). This perspective was adopted and elaborated by Tong Jinghua, who points out that the epic has absorbed the rich heritage of ancient Tibetan folklore (1985:192).

In his "On Discussions of the Historical Contents of *Gesar*," Huang Wenhuan surmises that *Gesar* closely reflects history, based on the epic's representation of social reality during the Tubo period, its attitude toward the royal family, and its representation of both Han-Tibetan relations and great and small wars. Characteristics of the Tubo period form the core of the epic; for this reason, "we can say that *Gesar* is basically a long poetic work created by the Tubo people according to the basic historical facts of the Tubo period" (Huang W. 1986:148). In addition, Huang claims that *Gesar* has historical authenticity, and is an "epic about the Tubo," a treasure house for the study of Tibetan society (1985:90-102). His perspective, however, represents a step backward in *Gesar* studies (Stein 1993:8-9). The theory that epics serve as "historical memory" was proposed by European scholars and later criticized by both Mongologists and the European scholars themselves. Nevertheless, in the process of championing his perspective Huang outlines the basic constituents of the epic and pioneers work on its historical features. From this point of view his paper establishes a new arena for historical study.

Following Huang's article, many papers on the historical content of the epic appeared, influenced by his method. For example, Danzhu Angben reached the conclusion that *Gesar* developed from historical fact to story to epic (1985:133). He Feng adopted this approach in his monographic study and achieved similar results (1995:1-20). In addition, scholars made inferences about the epic's time of origin from a related perspective. For example, based on the idea that the social milieu is reflected in the epic, Jianbai Pingcuo argued that the

Record of King Gesar originated during the thirteenth century, when it is believed that the Tibetan people hoped a hero would rescue them from a fragmented society (1982). This theory has been included in *History of Literature of Chinese Minority Nationalities* (Mao 1984:424).

With the discovery of the huge field of Tibetan verbal art, research and criticism began to be more closely scrutinized (cf. Xu 1986:1046). As explorations into all aspects of the epic grew more sophisticated, it became clear that no absolute time of origin could ever be established; on the contrary, epic is cumulative. The search for an Ur-text ceded to a desire to understand its ongoing process of formation. How did *Gesar* develop? Jiangbian Jiacuo was the first Chinese scholar to fully address this question, and his work remains the greatest advance on the issue of *Gesar*'s origins. *The Historical Fate of Gesar* (1989) makes use of popular epic theories and a basic knowledge of folklore, and investigates the epic by periods against the rich background of Tibetan culture. The basic concepts developed by Jiangbian were likewise included in the authoritative two-volume *A History of Tibetan Literature* (Ma 1994:185-200).

One may well ask how, after Chinese scholars had pursued the idea of an Ur-text for more than half a century, Jiangbian was able to set aside this question in favor of asking how *Gesar* formed and changed through the centuries? No doubt he was influenced by V. I. Propp's discussion of the Russian "Song of the Hero": "To raise the question about when (in which year and which century) the 'Song of the Hero' was created is itself probably wrong, since its formation might have lasted for centuries. The question of its origins calls for a special study on the part of researchers of folk literature and art" (1964:131). In addition, Jiangbian's perspective was affected by Huang Jingtao's "Preface" to *Gesar 4* (1962), which highlights *Gesar*'s status as a collective work that undergoes continual recomposition, and by Mao Dun's comments (1981) on the formation of the Homeric epics. Both of these authors regard oral poetry as a dynamic process and return it to the reality of folk culture for discussion.

To put it another way, before considering the problem of origin, the nature of *Gesar* ought to be defined. Is it literature written by an author or a a work belonging to the oral tradition of a people? Though many scholars regarded the epic as a creative work of the folk, they took too narrow a view when investigating the issue of authorship. Centuries after the composition of a literary work its authorship may grow obscure; we know even less of the epic as part of an oral tradition whose roots extend deep into the past. To locate the epic's origin in time by making use of its authorship is an errant methodology. As Propp observed, "for any discipline, methodological correctness is the determining factor among many. Wrong methodology could not lead to a correct conclusion" (1955:353).

Jiangbian first defined **Gesar** as folk art characterized by inheritance and variation. Such a work may embody the span of thousands of years, and any performance heard today cannot be equated to a written record from another century. As Jiangbian has put it, "**Gesar** is really a spectrum that reflects the ancient history of Tibet" (1986:50) and "a running river" (1994:76). Furthermore, folk creations keep changing and no version is the ultimate version—as the Tibetan saying goes, "every group of Tibetans has a version of **Gesar**." In the context of an oral tradition one need not be so concerned about whether or not Gesar was a real historical figure, or try to pin down the date of his existence in order to determine when the epic first was composed. Jiangbian has shown why this train of thought leads nowhere.

Instead he turned his attention to identification of the sociocultural influences on **Gesar,** using his familiarity with ancient Tibetan culture and his detailed knowledge of the history of exchange between the Han and Tibetan peoples. In order to locate the core content of the epic, he analyzed the typical scene "Horse-racing and Claiming the Kingship," studying both oral and written versions. He describes the epic's ancient content and aesthetic appeal, noting that these serve as "an important marker for a clan society" (1985:50) and reaches the following conclusions about **Gesar**'s historical development (37-38):

> The origin, development, and evolution of **Gesar** has undergone several important stages. It took shape in a historical period when Tibetan clan society started to fall apart and the state power of slavery was forming. This period fell between the birth of Christ and fifth to sixth century CE During the reign of the Tubo Dynasty, or the seventh to ninth centuries, **Gesar** gradually took shape. The epic further developed and spread after the collapse of the Tubo Dynasty, or tenth century CE.

Jiangbian pointed out that the foundation for the origin of epic is ethnic folk culture. He conjectured that before epics came into being, the Tibetan people "already had a corpus of stories that described the formation of the heavens and the earth, their ethnic origin, and ethnic heroes; these stories provided a foundation for creating the character Gesar, also known as Sgrung in early history. After further polishing by the oral poets, especially the ballad singers, **Gesar** became a great epic" (1986:51). As to the complicated cultural contents of different eras in the epic, the early part centers on Sgrung, Rdevu, and Bon consecutively. Other elements of the plot were later woven into the epic, serving as "clues" for misguided time-of-origin guesswork (41, 51). In 1994, Jiangbian gave full expression to his

exploration of the epic's origins in Tibetan culture in **Gesar and Tibetan Culture,** which provides strong evidence for his claims about the epic's various sources.

During the mid-1990s certain Tibetan scholars also freed themselves from the issue of the epic's time of origin by approaching the subject from other angles. Their efforts were strongly influenced by Jiangbian's summary in Tibetan of the common features in **Gesar** (1988:59). Blo gros rgya mtsho, Gcod pa don grub, Rta mgrin, and others made bold inferences by analyzing the epic's rhetoric and by comparing it with *Snyan ngag me long*[19] and folk ballads. Blo gros rgya mtsho (1996:33) suggests that based on its rhetorical structure, the epic may have been finished after 1883. Gcod pa don grub and Rta mgrin (1994:52) proposed that the epic took shape between the Song and Yuan Dynasties (tenth to eleventh century), when people were thirsty for a more settled life and looked to Srong btsan sgam po and other great heroes for hope. These scholars believed that **Gesar** synthesizes many folk ideals and develops continually. Though their conclusions are still affected by viewing the epic as a form of history, their methodology has taken a new direction and their study is in-depth. If they can bypass the shortcomings of "epic-historicism," their work will do much to promote research on the formation and development of oral epic and on the emergence of epic manuscripts.

Many Tibetan scholars have regarded the epic as a historical record, but this viewpoint is shifting. In general these scholars have achieved a great deal, especially with multi-perspective discussions that have been emerging since the early 1990s. Work by scholars like Chab vgag rdo rje tshe ring (1995) on the relationship between "mother-epic" and "son-epic" is worth our attention. No doubt the growth of Tibetan scholarship will create many possibilities for **Gesar** exploration.

THE DEATH OF THEORY ON A SPECIFIC TIME OF ORIGIN

Looking back at how **Gesar** has been explored at home and abroad, we can see that the theory on the epic's origin has come a long way. Not many scholars realized the complexity of the epic; in fact, generally they have clung to their own theories and in the process of seeking historical evidence have remained blind to the nature of the epic as folk art. However, we must recognize that their work has also contributed to the deeper level of understanding we have today.

For historical reasons, Chinese epic study in its true sense has not existed for very long, and herein lies a great discrepancy with research outside China. Epic research began only 70 years ago, while the period devoted to in-depth analysis has been even briefer—

approximately 20 years. Achieving progress and surpassing prior research are time-consuming, and it is a fact that some scholars are not fully qualified. We must recognize that research is a gradual process.

In addition, we need to shift our methodology away from treating the epic as a history whose content may be used to determine its time of origin.[20] This kind of methodology first took root in the Russian poetic circle with regard to the Russian poem entitled *The Hero's Song.* Russian scholars tried to locate the time when the epic poem originated in actual history:

> When trying to prove that a heroic ballad belongs to this or that historical period, they used a method of far-fetched association on the basis of personal and place names. Their conclusions are thus untenable. When defining the historical layers or sediments, V. F. Meller and his followers tried to find the oldest text of heroic ballads without taking account of the distinctive characteristics of folk art.

> (Sidorova 1955:69)

This critique remains pertinent for Chinese *Gesar* researchers. From the point of view of folklore studies an epic does not equal historical reality; in many cases, authenticity exists in only a figurative sense—it cannot solve the basic problem concerning origin. Of course, place-names, historical figures, and history in the epic may themselves be real: a people's history is an endless resource for verbal art. But when history enters the domain of traditional art, it does not submit to documentation; historical figures in an epic no longer belong to history, but to art and culture.

Another method belonging to the "epic-as-history" school involves locating the epic's time of origin according to the actual biographies of its heroic figures. Researchers begin with an epic character and look for his or her prototype in real life; conclusions about the epic's origins are drawn by reference to the era of that prototypical figure. With the further discovery of epic texts and the "history" that records Gesar in Tibetan literature, things have grown more complicated. Due to textual confirmation of historical figures in Tibetan and Chinese literature, the view that the epic *Gesar* originates among the Tibetans has become inarguable. For this reason scholars unanimously concentrate attention on the tenth and eleventh centuries, or even later. However, one may still find fault with this approach because the epic itself reveals a long history of development. By narrowing the period of its creation to the tenth and eleventh centuries, the dynamic of literary composition is erroneously attributed to an oral epic. Furthermore, the epic reflects Tibetan society during the sixth to ninth centuries rather than the tenth century. Thus a satisfactory conclusion about the epic's origins cannot be drawn based on the lifespans of historical heroic figures.

Still another method has been to pinpoint the epic's time of origin according to its authorship. Though scholars may have freed themselves from the restrictions of viewing the epic as straightforward history, they still confuse oral poetry with written literature. Generally speaking, oral epic has no particular author; so-called authors are those who record the epic and those who disseminate it. The common bearers of folk art are those who enjoy traditional culture, while the bearers of the epic are professional or semi-professional bards. Therefore the claim that Nor bu chos vphel, who was the historical King Gesar's contemporary, created the epic should be revised to admit that even he was merely someone like Bu thub dgav—a scribe.[21]

Only when *Gesar* is returned to the vast context of Tibetan culture, especially Tibetan folk culture, and considered stage by stage and century by century can our methodology be defensible. And only via a defensible methodology can we come to correct conclusions; this is Jiangbian's main point. As for stage-by-stage research on *Gesar*'s possible origins, there is no single investigation that can serve as a model.[22] To make a breakthrough, we need to study each stage of development. Only after an analysis of many aspects of the epic can a new level of understanding be reached.

Notes

1. These are the seminal works on *Gesar* outside of China. With the exception of the origin and variants of the Mongolian and Tibetan *Gesar,* which is the focus of Stein's work, many non-Chinese authors have given less attention to the authenticity of *Gesar* and its time of origin. However, by the 1980s, as Nekljudov comments, this problem "is no longer worth pursuing . . . ; for most specialists, it is crystal clear [that both the Mongolian *Gesser* and Tibetan *Gesar* originated in Tibet]" (1991:192).

2. Originally written in French.

3. *The Story of the Three Kingdoms* is one of four very famous fictional stories about Chinese history. It first appeared during the Ming Dynasty. Because the name of one of the main heroes, Guan Gong, sounds like "Gesar," some believed these characters to be one and the same.

4. The Tibetan King Gu si luo established his kingdom in the region of Qinghai in the eleventh century.

5. Guan Yu, the hero of *The Story of the Three Kingdoms,* is commonly called Guan Gong and has many temples in China. Some foreign scholars believed that King Gesar was related to Guan Yu.

6. He observed that "storytellers among the folk like to 'worship heroes,' so they will not only build

temples for Gesar and offer him joss sticks, but also confuse him with different gods and mistake him for the Sacred King Guan Yu" (Han 1998:3403).

7. He cited the Peking edition of the Mongolian *Gesar* that was popular in the West as an example and remarked that "European Mongologists believed that this book had something to do with the contacts between the East and West, and thus I. G. Schmidt, W. Schot, and P. Pelliot would have studied it for a hundred years to come" (Han 1998:3404).

8. *La dwags rgyal rabs* also mentions Khrom gesar vdan ma (Anonymous 1986:5). Both *Ma ni bkav vbum* and *La dwags rgyal rabs* are very famous books in Tibetan history. *Ma ni bkav vbum* is a Tibetan historical document concerning the twelfth through the fourteenth century. *La dwags rgyal rabs* is a history from approximately the eighteenth century. "The Legend of the Wedding of Princess Wencheng" has been popular in Tibetan and Chinese areas; the history reflected in this legend began to be recorded in the Tang dynasty's document.

9. It is customary for the Chinese to regard themselves as "elder brother" figures to their minority populations. Thus, ethnic verbal art is referred to as "brotherly ethnic literature."

10. Collected by Yang Zhifu and Wu Jun.

11. *The Barbarous Version of the Story of the Three Kingdoms* (or *Zang San Guo,* the "Tibetan" Three Kingdoms) was created by scholars in order to equate the Chinese *The Story of the Three Kingdoms* with *Gesar.*

12. Although some of Yang Z. and Wu's ideas may not be entirely persuasive, they tried their best to introduce their criticism and scholarship during a period of time when the political climate was not friendly to the study of "feudalist" literature. They maintained an objective attitude and used an epistemological approach in their papers. Their responsible methodology has some value in the academic history of our *Gesar* studies.

13. Citing Shan's perspective, Xu Guoqiong observed (1959): "After liberation, comrade Shan Chao worked in Tibet for a long time collecting and compiling Tibetan folklore." From this we may infer that Tibetan scholars influenced Shan Chao's perspective.

14. The following paragraph paraphrases Xu's summary (1959).

15. Before the work of R. A. Stein became known.

16. "During the tenth or the twelfth century there were probably only two or three songs" (David-Neel 1984:2).

17. Cf. Propp 1956; 1999: Foreword; and Chicherov 1961:68-84.

18. Huang Jingtao (1962) emphasizes the difficulties suffered by *Gesar* studies during this period of history.

19. A famous seventh-century Indian classic known throughout Mongolia and Tibet and also known as "The Mirror of Poetry" (*K'avy' adarsah*), composed by the Indian philosopher Dandin (cf. Zhao K. 1989). Translated into Tibetan in the thirteenth century, it deeply influenced Tibetan literary theory and literature.

20. *Gesar*'s representations of events have long been treated as faithful history by Tibetan scholars. We cannot neglect the force of tradition, and yet we need to adjust ourselves to a new academic atmosphere and actively promote deeper exploration into the epic, combining the typically strong analytical skills of Tibetans with a new methodology.

21. Bu thub dgav of Qinghai, Yushu, was well known as the "non-stop *Gesar* scribe" because he copied copious amounts of *Gesar* cantos. Cf. Yang E. 1995:330-48.

22. See Lang Ying's chronological approach to *Manas* (1991:26) and Rinchindorji's similar approach to *Jangar* (1999:203).

References

Anonymous 1986: *The King-lineages of La dwags State* (*La dwags rgyal rabs*). Lhasa: Tibetan People's Publishing House.

Blo gros rgya mtsho 1996: Blo gros rgya mtsho. "A Brief Account of King Gesar and the epic *King Gesar.*" ("Gesar rgyal po dang Gesar rgyal povi sgrung yig skor rags tsam gleng ba"). In *Selected Papers on King Gesar* (*Gling sgrung dpyad rtsom bdams bsgrigs*). Xining: Qinghai Nationalities Publishing House. pp. 1-39.

Brag dgon pa dkon mchog bstan pa rab rgyas 1982: Brag dgon pa dkon mchog bstan pa rab rgyas. *The History of Buddhism in Mdo smad District* (*Mdo smad chos vbyung*). Lanzhou: Gansu Nationalities Publishing House.

Bsod nams rgyal mtshan 1982: Bsod nams rgyal mtshan. *The King-lineages of Tibet* (*Rgyal rabs gsal bavi me long*). Beijing: Ethnic Publishing House.

Chab vgag rdo rje tshe ring 1995: Chab vgag rdo rje tshe ring. "On the Originating or Mother-Epic of *Gesar,* the Son-epic" ("Gling Gesar rgal povi sgung las ma sgrung gi skor gleng ba"). *Tibetan Studies* (*Bod ljong zhib vjugs*), 4:75-86.

Chicherov 1961: V. I. Chicherov. "Some Issues for the Study of Epics of Soviet Norodnosti." Trans. from Russian to Chinese by Zhou Guangyuan. *Folk Literature*, November:68-81.

Damdinsüreng 1956: Ts. Damdinsüreng. "A Record of King Gesar." (In Chinese). In *Mongolian Literature and Language*, 7:43-52.

David-Neel 1984: Alexandra David-Neel. *A Record of Superhuman Gesar from Gling.* Ed. by Yang Yuanfang. Trans. into Chinese by Chen Zongxiang. Institute of Nationality Studies, Southwestern Institute for Nationalities. (Also publ. as *La Vie surhumanine de Guesar de Ling, le Heros thibetain, racontée par les Bardes de son pays.* Paris: Adyar, 1959.)

Danzhu 1985: Danzhu Angben. "Tribal Wars and *A Record of Gesar.*" In *Gesar Studies.* Vol. 1. (In Chinese). Chinese Folk Literature and Arts Press. pp. 119-33.

Dge vdun chos vphel 1990: Dge vdun chos vphel. *A Collection of Works by Dge vdun chos vphel*, vols. 1-2. (In Tibetan). Ed. by Chab spel tshe brtan phun tshogs. Lhasa: Bod ljong mi dmangs Press.

Gcod pa don grub and Rta mgrin 1994: Gcod pa don grub and Rta mgrin. *A New Perspective on the Epic Gesar (Gling Gesar rgyal povi sgrung la dpyad pa kun gsal vphrul gyi me long).* Xining: Mtsho sngon mi rigs Press.

Han 1990: Han Rulin. "Guan Yu in Tibet (*Guan Yu Zai Xi* Zang)" In *Collected Papers on Gesar Studies (Ge Sa Er Xue Ji Cheng).* 2 vols. Ed. by Zhao Bingli. Lanzhou: Gansu People's Publishing House. pp. 3403-7.

He 1995: He Feng. *Gesar and Tibetan Tribes.* (In Chinese). Xining: Qinghai People's Publishing House.

Huang J. 1962: Huang Jingtao. "Preface" In *Gesar 4.* (In Chinese). Shanghai: Shanghai Literature and Arts Press. Rpt. in *Selected Papers on China's Folk Literature, 1949-1979.* Ed. by Shanghai Research Society of Folk Literature. Shanghai: Shanghai Press of Literature and Arts, 1980.

Huang W. 1985: Huang Wenhuan. "Reexploration of the Historical Contents of *Gesar.*" (In Chinese). *Gesar Studies*, 1:90-102.

Huang W. 1986: ———. "On Discussions of the Historical Contents of *Gesar.*" (In Chinese). In *A Collection of Papers on Gesar Studies*, vol. 1. Ed. by Jiangbian Jiacuo et al. pp. 128-49.

Jianbai 1990: Jianbai Pingcuo. "Several Problems in the Epic *Gesar (Guan Yu Ge Sa Er Wang Zhuan De Ji Ge Wen Ti).*" In *Collected Papers on Gesar Studies (Ge Sa Er Xue Ji Cheng.)* 2 vols. Ed. by Zhao Bingli. Lanzhou: Gansu People's Publishing House. pp. 793-94.

Jiangbian 1985: Jiangbian Jiacuo. "On the Year of Origin of *Gesar.*" *Qinghai Social Sciences*, 6. Rpt. in *Collected Papers on Gesar Studies (Ge Sa Er Xue Ji Cheng.)* 2 vols. Ed. by Zhao Bingli. Lanzhou: Gansu People's Publishing House, 1990. pp. 1058-70.

Jiangbian 1986: ———. *Primary Exploration on Gesar.* (In Chinese). Xining: Qinghai People's Publishing House.

Jiangbian 1988: ———. "A General Survey of the Epic *Gesar (Gesar* rgyal povi sgrung gi bshad pa)." *Sbrang char*, 1:59.

Jiangbian 1989: ———. *The Historical Fate of Gesar.* (In Chinese). Chengdu: Sichuan Nationalities Publishing House.

Jiangbian 1994: ———. *Gesar and Tibetan Culture.* (In Chinese). Hohhot: Inner Mongolia University Press.

Jiangbian et al. 1986: Jiangbian Jiacuo et al, eds. *A Collection of Papers on Gesar Studies.* Vol. 1. Chengdu: Sichuan Nationalities Publishing House.

Khomonov 1986: M. P. Khomonov. *The Buriat Epic Gesar.* Ed. by The Institute of Literature Research of IMASS. Trans. from Russian to Chinese by Has. Hohhot: Inner Mongolian Academy of Social Sciences.

Lang 1991: Lang Ying. *On Gesar.* (In Chinese). Hohhot: Inner Mongolia University Press.

Lao 1956: Lao She. "A Report on the Literature of Ethnic Groups in China." Presented at the 1956 Conference of the Writers' Society of China. Rpt. in *Collected Papers on Gesar Studies (Ge Sa Er Xue Ji Cheng)*, vol. 1. Ed. by Zhao Bingli. Lanzhou: Gansu People's Publishing House, 1990. pp. 3-6.

Li 1945: Li Anzhai. "Introducing Two Specialists on Tibetan Affairs." (In Chinese). *Kangdao Yuekan*, 6:145-48.

Li 1992: ———. *Collected Essays on Tibetology by Li Anzhai.* (In Chinese). Bejing: China Tibetology Press.

Ma, Dge vdun chos vphel, and Tong 1994: Ma Xueliang, Dge vdun chos vphel, and Tong Jinhua, eds. *A History of Tibetan Literature.* (In Chinese and Tibetan). Chengdu: Sichuan Nationalities Publishing House.

Mao D. 1981: Mao Dun. *A Study of Myth.* (In Chinese). Tianjin: Baihua Literature and Arts Press.

Mao X. 1984: Mao Xing, ed. *Literature of Minority Nationalities in China.* Vol. 1. (In Chinese). Changsha: Hunan People's Publishing House.

Mikhajlov 1959: Mikhajlov. "We Must Treasure Our Cultural Heritage: About the Epic *Gesar,* its Contents, and its Characteristics" ("Bi Xu Zhen Xi Wen Hua Yi Chan—Guan Yu Ge Si Er Shi Shi De Nei Rong Te Se"). *Qianghai Ethnic Folk Literature Material (Qianghai Min Zu Min Jian Wen Xue Zi Liao)*, 4:2.

Nekljudov 1991: S. Ju. Nekljudov. *Mongolian People's Heroic Epic* (*Meng Gu Ren Minde Ying Xiong Shi Shi*). Trans. from Russian to Chinese by Xu Changhan and Gao Wenfeng Zhang Jizhi. Hohhot: Inner Mongolia University Press.

Propp 1956: Vladimier Iakovlevich Propp. "Some Methodological Issues in the Study of Epics." (In Russian). In *Russian Epics*. Leningrad: Leningrad University Press. pp. 91-99. 2nd ed. Moskow Labirint Press, 1999. Rpt. in *Folk Literature*, 1956:93-98. Trans. into Chinese by Wang Zhiliang.

Propp 1964: ———. "Basic Stages of Russian Epics." Trans. into Chinese by Cao Zhishou. *References to the Studies of Folk Literature and Arts*, 9:131-41.

Ren N. 1931: Ren Naiqiang. *The Peculiar Things in Xikang* (*Xikang Guiyilu*). Chengdu: Sichuan Daily Publishing House.

Ren N. 1934: ———. *An Outline of Xikang Province* (*Xikang Tujing*). New Asian Society Publishers.

Ren N. 1944: ———. "A Primary Introduction to A Tibetan Version of *The Three Kingdoms*." (In Chinese). *Bianzheng Gonglun*, 4:4-6.

Ren X. 1991: Ren Xinjian. "Introducing the Earliest Chinese Translation of *Gesar*." (In Chinese). In *Reference on the Epic Gesar*, vol. 10. Ed. by the Sichuan Gesar Office. pp. 54-60.

Rinchindorji 1999: Rinchindorji. *On Jangar*. (In Chinese). Hohhot: Inner Mongolia University Press.

Shangguan 1981: Shangguan Jianbi. "The State of Gling and Gling Gesar." (In Chinese). *Literature Studies of Minority Nationalities*, 1 and 2. Rpt. in *Collected Papers on Gesar Studies (Ge Sa Er Xue Ji Cheng)*. 2 vols. Ed. by Zhao Bingli. Lanzhou: Gansu People's Publishing House, 1990. pp. 1582-86.

Shan 1959: Shan Chao. "Notes on Tibetan Folk Literature." (In Chinese). *Folklore*, May:80-82.

Shanghai 1980: Shanghai Research Society of Folk Literature, ed. *Selected Papers on Chinese Folk Literature, 1949-1979*. (In Chinese). Shanghai: Shanghai Press of Literature and Arts.

Sidorova 1955: Sidorova. "Bourgeois Schools in Russian Folk Literature and Arts Circles and Struggles against Them." Trans. into Chinese by Yu Sun. *Folk Literature*, June:57-70.

Stein 1993: R. A. Stein. *A Study of Tibetan Epics and Ballads* (*Xi Zang Shi Shi Yu Shuo Chang Yi Ren de Yan Jiu*). Trans. into Chinese by Geng Sheng. Lhasa: Tibetan People's Publishing House. pp. 12-41.

Tong 1985: Tong Jinhua. "The Relationship between King Gesar and Historical Figures." (In Chinese). *Tribune of Folk Literature*, 1:24-37.

Wang Yinuan 1979a: Wang Yinuan. "A Brief Introduction to *A Record of King Gesar*." (In Chinese). *Newsletter for Folk Literature Fellows*: 6-16.

Wang Yinuan 1979b: ———. "Gesar in *A Record of King Gesar*." (In Chinese). *Journal of Northwestern Institute for Nationalites*, 1. Rpt. in *Folk Literature*, 5:10-18.

Wang Yinuan 1980: ———. "A Brief Introduction to the Tibetan Long Poem, *A Record of King Gesar*." (In Chinese). *Newsletter for Workers on Folk Literature*, 5. Rpt. in *Selected Papers on Chinese Folk Literature, 1949-1979*. Ed. by Shanghai Research Society of Folk Literature. Shanghai: Shanghai Press of Literature and Arts, 1980. pp. 345-56.

Wang Yinuan 1981: ———. "The Tibetan Epic *A Record of King Gesar*." (In Chinese). *Journal of Central University for Nationalities*, 3. Rpt. in *Collected Papers on Gesar Studies (Ge Sa Er Xue Ji Cheng)*. 2 vols. Ed. by Zhao Bingli. Lanzhou: Gansu People's Publishing House, 1990. pp. 788-93.

Wang Yinuan and Huajia 1981: ———and Huajia, trans. *A Guide to Reading Gesar*. (In Chinese). Lanzhou: Gansu People's Publishing House.

Wang Yingchuan 1986: Wang Yingchuan. "Characterization of King Gesar and the Historical Background of the Epic." (In Chinese). *Literature Studies of Minority Nationalities*, 1 and 2. Rpt. in *A Collection of Papers on Gesar Studies*, vol. 1. Ed. by Jiangbian Jiacuo et al. Chengdu: Sichuan Nationalities Publishing House, 1986. pp. 162-79.

Wu 1959: Wu Jun. "Data Linking *Gesar* to the *Story of Gu si luo*." (In Chinese). In *Reference Materials for Collecting and Researching Tibetan Literature in Qinghai*. Vol. 2. Xining: Qinghai Association of Letters and Arts. pp. 1-30.

Xu 1959: Xu Guoqiong. "The Tibetan Epic *A Record of King Gesar*." (In Chinese). *Literature Review*, 6:45-54. Rpt. in *Selected Papers on Chinese Folk Literature, 1949-1979*. Ed. by Shanghai Research Society of Folk Literature. Shanghai: Shanghai Press of Literature and Arts, 1980. pp. 301-18.

Xu 1978: ———. "Strong Condemnation of the 'Gang-of-Four' for the Destruction They Brought to the Cause of Folk Literature." (In Chinese). *Newsletter of Folk Literature Workers*, 2:16-18.

Xu 1984: ———. "About the Author and Collector of the Epic *Gesar*." (In Chinese). *Tibetology*, 4:76-80.

Xu 1985: ———. "About the Origin and Historical Background of the Canto *Story of Ga Gling*." (In Chinese). *Journal of Gesar Studies*, 1:103-18.

Xu 1986: ———. "The Year of Gesar's Birth and the Time of the Epic *Gesar*." (In Chinese). *Journal of the Tibetan Institute of Nationalities*, 3:43-52. Rpt. in *Col-*

lected Papers on Gesar Studies (*Ge Sa Er Xue Ji Cheng*), vol 2. Ed. by Zhao Bingli. Lanzhou: Gansu People's Publishing House, 1990. pp. 1039-46.

Xu 1993: ———. *A Recorded Survey of Gesar.* (In Chinese). Kunming: Yunnan People's Publishing House.

Yang E. 1995: Yang Enhong. *Folk God of Poetry: A Study on the Ballad Singers of Gesar.* (In Chinese). Beijing: China Tibetology Press.

Yang Z. 1959: Yang Zhifu. "Data on Tibetan Literature." In *Reference Materials for Collecting and Researching Tibetan Literature in Qinghai,* vol. 1. Xining: Qinghai Association of Letters and Arts.

Zhao B. 1990: Zhao Bingli, ed. *Collected Papers on Gesar Studies (Ge Sa Er Xue Ji Cheng).* 2 vols. Lanzhou: Gansu People's Publishing House.

Zhao K. 1989: Zhao Kang, ed. and trans. from Tibetan into Chinese. "The Mirror of Poetry (*Shi Jing*)." In *The Corpus of Ancient Aesthetic Philosophy of Ethnic Groups in China (Zhong guo shao shu min zu gu dai mei xue si xiang ziliao chu bian).* Chengdu: Sichuan Nationalities Publishing House. pp. 115-275.

FURTHER READING

Criticism

Enhong, Yang. "On the Study of the Narrative Structure of Tibetan Epic: *A Record of King Gesar.*" *Oral Tradition* 16, no. 2 (October 2001): 294-316.

Considers the narrative structure of the *Gesar* epic and explains how the tradition of fixed formulas helps in the process of memorizing it.

Hamayon, Roberte. "The One in the Middle: Unwelcome Third as a Brother, Irreplaceable Mediator as a Son." In *Fragen der Mongolischen Heldendichtung, Volume III,* pp. 373-409. Wiesbaden, Germany: Otto Harrassowitz, 1985.

Compares variations in three different Buryat versions of the *Gesar* epic.

Jiacuo, Jiangbian. "The Emergence of the Tibetan Epic *Gesar.*" In *Fragen der Mongolischen Heldendichtung,* Volume V, pp. 343-49. Wiesbaden, Germany: Harrassowitz Verlag, 1992.

Examines different theories regarding the time period of the creation of the *Gesar* epic.

Kapstein, Matthew T. "Mulian in the Land of Snows and King Gesar in Hell: A Chinese Tale of Parental Death in Its Tibetan Transformations." In *The Buddhist Dead: Practices, Discourses, Representations,* edited by Bryan J. Cuevas and Jacqueline I. Stone, pp. 345-77. Honolulu: University of Hawai'i Press, 2007.

Discusses the evolution of the *Transformation Text on Mulian Saving His Mother from Hell,* including its transposition into a Tibetan setting.

Nekljudov, S. Ju. "The Mechanisms of Epic Plot and the Mongolian *Geseriad.*" *Oral Tradition* 11, no. 1 (October, 1996): 133-43.

Discusses how the plot of the *Gesar* epic developed through the improvisation process of oral tradition.

Pharsalia

Lucan

Roman epic poem. Also known as *Bellum Civile, Civil War,* and *De Bello Civili.*

The following entry provides a critical overview of Lucan's epic poem *Pharsalia* (c. 61-5). For discussion of Lucan's complete career, see *CMLC,* Volume 33.

INTRODUCTION

Pharsalia is a history of the civil war waged from 49 to 48 B.C. between Julius Caesar and Pompey, written by the Roman poet Lucan. Pompey, a major rival of Caesar's, supported the conservative Optimates in the Senate. The epic work was left unfinished at the time of Lucan's death by suicide in the year 65. Lucan used cynicism, paradox, satire, and hyperbole throughout the *Pharsalia,* breaking with tradition by not championing its main protagonist, Caesar. In the work Lucan is pro-republican and extremely hostile to Caesarism; he included many passages that clearly would displease Nero (Roman Emperor from 54-68 A.D.). Lucan viewed the decisive battle of Pharsalia as ushering in the end of constitutional government. George M. Logan writes that Lucan was "a master, perhaps the supreme master, of the typical Silver Latin poetic style." The *Pharsalia* served as a standard Latin textbook in sixteenth-century England. Called an "eccentric masterpiece" by P. F. Widdows, it is Lucan's sole surviving work.

BIOGRAPHICAL INFORMATION

Marcus Annaeus Lucanus was born in Corduba, present-day Spain, in 39, to Marcus Annaeus Mela, a wealthy Roman knight, and his wife, Acilia. Lucan's grandfather was Seneca the Elder and his uncle was Seneca the Younger. At the age of seven months, Lucan was taken to Rome, where he was later educated in literature, rhetoric, and philosophy. He was taught the latter subject by the noted Stoic philosopher Annaeus Cornutus. In 59, while continuing his education in Athens, Lucan was summoned by Nero to serve as his tutor. It is believed that for some time they were good friends, and in 60 Lucan won a prize for the poem "Laudes Neronis," in praise of Nero. In 62 or 63 Lucan was ap-pointed quaestor, a rare preferment for one not of royal blood. But in 64, for assorted and unclear reasons, Nero banned Lucan from speaking in public, effectively ending his career. Speculation by historians about what caused the break between the two men includes political differences, Nero's jealousy of Lucan's poetic ability and fame, and a likely public pronouncement by Lucan in opposition to Nero. In 65 Lucan became a member of a plot, led by Senator Caius Calpurnius Piso, to assassinate Nero. The plot was discovered and its conspirators were given the option of being put to death or committing suicide; Lucan chose suicide. Tacitus reports that as the blood flowed freely from his open veins, Lucan recited some lines of original poetry concerning a wounded soldier dying a similar kind of death. Nero had Lucan's father killed when he came to claim his son's property, and later disposed of his uncle as well.

TEXTUAL HISTORY

Scholars do not know exactly when Lucan began composing the *Pharsalia,* although some have suggested c. 61. It was not complete by the time of Lucan's death. It is assumed that some of the more openly hostile portions were written after Nero's order that Lucan be banned from giving public readings. Although Lucan read only three volumes of the work in public, nine complete books and part of a tenth are extant, comprising 8060 lines. Critics surmise that Lucan had anticipated twelve volumes for the entire work, although some think that the work could have been extended to sixteen books.

PLOT AND MAJOR CHARACTERS

The *Pharsalia* was based on a now-lost historical work by Livy. Rich with allusions and epigrams, it includes more than one hundred speeches exhibiting a tremendous range of rhetorical devices. Its three major characters are Caesar, Pompey, and Cato. Caesar is introduced as a near-superhuman warrior; Pompey is an old and tired man, but one who nevertheless elicits devotion from the public; Cato is a Stoic whose overriding concern is the welfare of the state. None of them is treated as a hero in the traditional manner of literature. Through these individuals Lucan relates a story based on actual events concerning the war between Caesar and Pompey. One of Lucan's stylistic innovations is his rejection of the gods and divine machinery; supernatural elements are replaced largely with fate and fortune.

MAJOR THEMES

Lucan continually expresses revulsion for the civil war that pits fellow Romans agains each other. As an anti-imperialist, he anticipates the self-destruction of the republic of Rome as he knew it, as Nero becomes more and more tyrannical.

CRITICAL RECEPTION

Although it appears likely that Lucan enjoyed a large and appreciative audience of senators and knights, his work was sometimes compared unfavorably with that of Vergil, albeit Lucan's verse was not meant to be like Vergil's. Shortly after Lucan's death his reputation lapsed and he was little commented upon. Lucan's reputation soared during the Middle Ages, however, and would stay elevated for centuries. Logan writes that, with its contained speeches of "unmatched brilliance," *Pharsalia* was a respected classic in sixteenth-century England. Christopher Marlowe began a translation of it in 1593 and published the first book in 1600 under the title *Lucans first Booke, translated line for line,* before dropping the project. Lucan was also highly regarded by the Romantics in the nineteenth century. Percy Bysshe Shelley considered him a genius superior to Vergil. But with the advent of new political ideas, Lucan's popularity plummeted again. By the end of the 1800s, Caesar was admired and Lucan vilified. In the first half of the twentieth century, Lucan was once again largely ignored, or else criticized for obscurity or failing to develop thematic unity. In modern times, he has attracted renewed attention, but not always praise. Robert Graves, who has translated an edition of Lucan's epic into English, writes that it is difficult to convey Lucan's sense in simple English prose. O. A. W. Dilke takes Graves to task for his modern, conversational prose translation of Lucan, contending that such an approach cannot "hope to reproduce more than a fraction of the spirit of the Latin." Dilke insists that Lucan is best translated into blank verse, with great care taken in the rhythm. P. F. Widdows is also highly critical of Graves's translation, faulting its absence of rhythm and explaining that a fine translation of Lucan must contain "rhythm, energy, and point" and that a good translator must recognize the poet's "energy, odd-

ness, and passion." In her translation, Jane Wilson Joyce explains that she always strives for lines that work well when read aloud, in keeping with the fact that Lucan wrote the *Pharsalia* for public performance. Widdows defends the *Pharsalia* from the relatively common charge that it lacks unity, pointing out that it is, after all, incomplete.

PRINCIPAL WORKS

Pharsalia [also known as *Bellum Civile*] (epic poem) c. 61-5

Principal English Translations

Pharsalia: Dramatic Episodes of the Civil Wars (translated by Robert Graves) 1957
The Battle of Pharsalia: A Verse Translation of Lucan, Book VII (translated by O. A. W. Dilke) 1971
Lucan's Civil War (translated by P. F. Widdows) 1988
Civil War (translated by Susan H. Braund) 1992
Pharsalia (translated by Jane Wilson Joyce) 1993

CRITICISM

Robert Graves (essay date 1957)

SOURCE: Graves, Robert. Introduction to *Pharsalia: Dramatic Episodes of the Civil War,* by Lucan, translated by Robert Graves, pp. 7-24. Baltimore, Md.: Penguin Books, 1957.

[*In the following essay, Graves describes Lucan as a melodramatic rhetorician, the father of yellow journalism, and a writer with hysterical tendencies, also noting some of the challenges posed by translating his writings.*]

Suetonius's *Life of Lucan* begins:

> Marcus Annaeus Lucanus of Cordoba made his first public appearance as a poet at the Neronia, a literary and musical contest held every five years. Later he gave a public reading of his epic poem about the Civil War between Pompey and Caesar; and compared himself, in a prologue, with Virgil as he had been at the same age. Here he was bold enough to ask:
>
>> And tell me now, am I still at
>> The stage when Virgil wrote his *Gnat*?

While still a boy he heard that his father was living deep in the country because he had made an unhappy marriage . . .

Here some sentences are missing. From the *Life* written by Vacca four centuries later, and from references in Statius's *Silvae*, Tacitus, the *Eusebian Chronicle,* and Sidonius Apollinaris, a few more facts can be added to Suetonius's account. Lucan was born on November 3rd, A.D. 39, in the third year of Caligula's reign, and taken from Cordoba to Rome at the age of seven months. His father, Marcus Annaeus Mella, was a Spanish provincial of equestrian rank who had grown immensely rich as Comptroller of the Revenue; but did not seek advancement in literature or politics like his brothers Lucius Annaeus Seneca and Junius Gallio. The 'unhappy marriage' may have followed the divorce of Lucan's mother Acilia. At Rome Lucan received the best education then available, the emphasis being on literature and rhetoric, and was something of an infant prodigy. He studied Stoic philosophy under Cornutius, with the poet Persius as a fellow-pupil. Lucan's uncle Seneca, another professed Stoic and the most famous writer of the day, had been appointed tutor to the young Emperor Nero; he used his position to amass a fortune of some £4,000,000 in gold, by most questionable means; and became Consul in A.D. 56. Lucan was two years older than Nero, by whom he was for awhile greatly admired. His earliest poems, which no longer exist, concerned the recovery of Hector's dead body by Priam; the descent of Orpheus to the Underworld in pursuit of Eurydice; and a letter to his wife Polla Argentaria, whom he loved dearly and who had youth, beauty, wealth, virtue, and intellect to commend her. Other early short poems appear to have been worked into his *Civil War*: Hercules's wrestling match with Antaeus in Book IV, Perseus's killing of Medusa in Book IX, the account of the Nile in Book X. From Rome he went to study Greek literature at Athens.

Nero recalled Lucan from Athens and made him one of his intimates, besides bestowing a quaestorship on him; but this favour did not last long. Nero interrupted a reading of Lucan's poetry by suddenly summoning a meeting of the Senate, and going out himself, with the sole object of ruining the performance. The hostility that Lucan thereafter showed him, in word and deed, is still notorious. Once, after relieving himself explosively in a public convenience, he declaimed a half-line of Nero's:

'. . . and it sounded like underground thunder—'

which made a number of men who had been easing themselves beside him take to their heels and run. He also satirized Nero, and his own influential friends as well, in a most bitter and damaging poem. Finally he became, so to speak, the standard-bearer of Piso's ill-fated conspiracy, ranting publicly about how glorious it was to murder a tyrant, and even offering to present his friends with Nero's head. When the conspiracy came to light, however, he lost his cocksureness and was easily compelled to make a confession; after which he resorted to the most abject pleas for pardon, going so far as to accuse his own innocent mother of being one of the conspirators. Apparently he thought that, since Nero was a matricide, he would appreciate this lack of decent devotion. Nero did indeed allow him to choose the manner of his death. Lucan took advantage of the respite by writing his father a letter which contained amendments to some of his verses; then ate a huge dinner, and told a physician to cut the arteries in his wrists.

I remember that his poems were published by all sorts of editors, reputable and disreputable, and even lectured on by professors of rhetoric.

. . . . .

Lucan's quaestorship, during which he staged some gladiatorial shows, was a great mark of Imperial favour, since he had not yet reached the age at which a man could legally hold public office. Nero also appointed him to the exclusive College of Augurs. According to one account the cause of Lucan's animosity was that Nero, who had reserved the Latin Verse Prize at the Neronia for himself, grew jealous when the audience in the theatre applauded Lucan's *Orpheus and Eurydice* somewhat too enthusiastically, and forbade him to give poetry recitals even in private. Lucan died on April 30th, 65 A.D., at the age of twenty-five; declaiming some lines of his own about how a Macedonian soldier bled to death. He still had two and a half books of the *Civil Wars* to write, and seven to revise. His reckless and inept behaviour during the conspiracy forced his father and both his uncles to commit suicide as well. Polla Argentaria buried him in the garden, and continued to celebrate his birthday for many years; there were no children of the marriage. Nero acknowledged Lucan's talents, briefly but adequately, in a memorial tablet:

MARCO ANNAEO LUCANO CORDUBENSI POETAE, BENEFICIO NERONIS, FAMA SERVATA.

. . . . .

The eloquent Quintilian, Lucan's contemporary and fellow-Spaniard, wrote of the *Civil Wars*: 'This poem is full of fire and energy and famous for its epigrammatic wit; but in my opinion affords a safer model to the rhetorician than to the poet.' Agreed; yet except for Ennius and Lucretius, both of whom had something urgent to say, and Catullus, whose Celtiberian passion marked him off from his stolid or frivolous fellows, very few Latin writers recognized the distinction between poetry and verse-rhetoric; nor did the educational system countenance it.

Rhetoric and poetry were both imported to Rome from Greek cities in Italy. When the Republic, enlarged by hard and ruthless fighting, needed diplomats to consolidate her gains by cleverly playing off one enemy against another, the traditional virtue of blunt and laconic speech could be questioned. In ancient days, a Roman envoy might draw a circle around some enemy king with the ferrule of his staff, saying: 'We offer you peace at the price of a million gold pieces, payable before the moon wanes. Leave this circle without accepting our terms, and you will live to rue it.' Not every king, however, could be overawed so simply; and it began to be realized from certain hard bargains driven by eloquent foreign embassies that Rome had often involved herself in unnecessary fighting by a simple lack of suppleness and tact. A few far-sighted senators resolved to educate their sons as diplomats; very much as they had once resolved to challenge the Carthaginians at sea, though wholly ignorant of ship-building or naval tactics. This inspired decision was taken only after much heart-searching; for in 161 B.C., the Senate ordered the Praetor Marcus Pomponius to prevent rhetoricians—who seem to have been Italian-Greeks—from settling at Rome; and as late as 92 B.C. the Censors Gnaeus Domitius Ahenobarbus and Lucius Licinius Crassus published an edict against rhetorical schools as nurseries of idleness. Yet Suetonius records: 'Little by little, rhetoric came to seem useful and honourable, and many addicted themselves to it as a defence and for glory'—in fact, the diplomatic corps, by following the principle 'Divide and conquer', were worth many legions to the military establishment.

It became fashionable to study at Athens, the centre of Greek culture. There the Roman student discovered that he could hope to graduate as a diplomat only after taking a master's degree in rhetoric; and that rhetoric, the art of persuading an opponent by flattery, threats, or fraud to accept one's own proposition, however unsound, would help him to win magistratial elections and plead public causes with confidence, besides being a valuable adjunct to warfare. Yet before being allowed to rhetorize in the schools, he must take the prescribed course in Homeric study and learn as much as possible of the *Iliad* and *Odyssey* by heart. This was a *sine qua non,* because the Sons of Homer, the original disseminators of polite culture at early Greek courts, had won such scriptural authority whenever disputes arose on history, geography, genealogy, religion, science, or morals, that an apt quotation from 'the poet' (as he was simply called) clinched every argument, unless the opposing orator could contrive to cap it. A civilized attitude to poetry is said to have first been adopted at Rome, which so far had known only ballads and rough military marching songs, as the result of a typically Roman street-accident: Crates the Milesian, sent as ambassador by King Attalus of Pergamus in 167 B.C., broke his leg by falling into an uncovered sewer, and spent his convalescence giving lectures on poetry—meaning, of course, Homer. Thus the quantitative hexameter, though awkward in Latin, an accentual language,

became the main literary metre at Rome, displacing the native Saturnian; and Ennius, the father of Latin poetry, adopted archaisms and invented novelties to make the change possible.

Because the rhetorician's art, securely based on the *Iliad* and *Odyssey,* was to persuade his hearers, regardless of truth, Roman students understood that Homer must have been a consummate diplomat; from which it followed that, since one could not always establish what special pleading had prompted the poet's lines, his art in concealing art should be all the more admired. Literary education branched from Homer into prose-rhetoric and verse-rhetoric. In the prose direction lay history, philosophy, law, literary criticism, scientific theory; in the other, epics, drama, satires, didactic pieces, pastorals, odes, and so forth. The student worked industriously to rid himself of a natural preference for simple, practical language, and to outdo his professors in a passionate slipperiness of expression.

When at last Latin literature could challenge Greek in all departments of prose-rhetoric, and all departments of verse-rhetoric except the Homeric corpus, the Romans began to ask why they should perpetually yield the epic palm to crabbed old Homer. Could they not find and build up a Homer of their own? They could. Inevitably the choice fell on Virgil, who had shown such exquisite craftsmanship that the rhetorical object in his *Aeneid,* namely glorification of the divinely-descended Caesars as destined rulers of the world, was pervasive without being patently offensive. The Court lent Virgil such strong support that he had scarcely set about his task before Sextus Propertius wrote an epigram proclaiming it 'greater than the *Iliad*'; and a loyal Senate supplied much the same hearty glow of enthusiasm as leads patriotic Scots to rank Robert Burns above William Shakespeare. Suetonius in his *Lives of the Roman Poets* dutifully remarks that 'Virgil never lacked for detractors; which is not strange, because neither did Homer.' These detractors listed his pilferings and historical errors, but they envied his talents no less than his financial success; and only the independent-minded admiral, Marcus Vipsanius Agrippa, made a really brutal comment. 'Virgil,' he said, 'is a suppositious child of Maecenas, and has invented a new type of rhetoric which steers a careful course between bombast and baldness of expression, concealing its artificiality by the use of every-day phrases.' Virgil's shyness, his literary perfectionism, his temperance, his idealism, his valetudinarianism, his avoidance of bawdy society, and his notorious passion for beautiful boys—which in those days could be gratified without loss of reputation—combine to make a recognizable picture. How exquisite the interior decorations of his house on the Esquiline (a gift from Augustus) must have been: especially the gilded bedrooms where sleep kissed the eyelids of Alexander and Cebes, his poetical boy-slaves! This Alexander, the 'Alexis' of the *Bucolics,* had been a present from Asinius Pollio, the most enlightened man of his age.

Virgil became a school classic overnight; and though Lucan—born two generations later and brought up on *Arma virumque cano*—seems to have felt jealously resentful, he knew that it would be foolish to challenge Virgil in his own field. I suspect that he also disguised his jealousy by decrying Virgil as an effeminate old today. He decided to stop writing mythological fables in the approved Augustan style and launch a modernist movement which would confine the *Aeneid* to the school-room, where it was obviously due to last as long as the Latin language itself.

A sophisticated reaction against Virgil had begun some twenty years before, when the Emperor Caligula nearly carried out his plan of suppressing Virgil's 'dull and uneducated' works; but an Augustan revival under Claudius gave them a reprieve. Lucan's Neronian modernism was well calculated: he had chosen a historical rather than a legendary theme for his neo-epic, and in Book IX gives a drily realistic account of how Caesar visited Troy, by then a run-down tourist centre. So far from being divinely welcomed by Venus in person (as he would have been in the *Aeneid*), Caesar is taken by a garrulous guide to see the sights, including the grove where the Goddess had first seduced his ancestor Anchises. Nor does Lucan send the heroic Cato to consult his ancestral ghosts in Virgilian style, but lets a horror-comic witch called Erichtho resuscitate a dead Pompeian soldier with grisly spells and then threaten him with eternal punishment unless he prophesies the future. This modernism is equally anti-Virgilian in its deliberate neglect of craftsmanship; the rhythms are monotonous; often words are clumsily iterated before the memory of their first use has faded from the reader's ear; the argument is broken by impudent philosophical, geographical or historical asides. Lucan lacks religious conviction; dwells lovingly on the macabre; hates his times; and allows his readers to assume that he is as self-centred, degenerate, cruel, and cowardly as the next man. His hyperboles are patently ridiculous: the Thracian cranes, for instance, delay their winter migration in order to gorge on Roman corpses at Pharsalus—though Pharsalus was not fought until the Spring, and cranes are non-carnivorous. Yet his occasional polished epigrams make highly serviceable quotations:

> *Victrix causa deis placuit, sed victa Catoni*
> 'The conquering cause pleased the Gods; the conquered pleased Cato.'

> *Nulla fides unquam miseros elegit amicos*
> 'Nobody ever chooses the already unfortunate as objects of his loyal friendship.'

> *Nescit plebes ieiuna timere*
> 'Starve the mob, and it grows restless.'

> *Metiri sua regna decet, vires-que fateri*
> 'It is best to take stock of the resources at your command, and admit their inadequacy.'

Lucan may be called the father of yellow journalism, for his love of sensational detail, his unprincipled reportage, and his disregard of continuity between today's and yesterday's rhetoric. Thus the Roman Senate who disgrace themselves by a panic-stricken rush from Rome, because of wild rumours that Caesar intends to sack the City, become, two books later, the courageous, dignified, truly Roman Senate who reassemble in Epirus, and appoint Pompey dictator. Again, Pompey calmly leaves the field of Pharsalus when the battle is going against him, hoping that this unselfish action will limit Roman bloodshed; but in the next book spurs his jaded horse towards Tempe with a panic-stricken heart; and presently sends his ally Deiotarus to arrange for a merciless Parthian invasion of Italy—yet still remains Rome's most devoted son. Caesar is more consistently maligned as a ferocious and treacherous ogre; feels disappointed to meet so little opposition during his march on Rome; picnics heartily on the battlefield of Pharsalus, delighting in the already stinking mounds of corpses; and sheds crocodile tears when presented with Pompey's head. His remarkable clemency is denounced as a diabolical trick to humiliate and enslave Rome; his treacherous assassins win rapturous applause; Pompey's own breaches of the Constitution are glossed over. Lucan claimed that posterity, reading his epic, would be sure to take Pompey's side; which was to hope that Caesar's own unrhetorical and obviously truthful commentaries on the war would no longer be extant. Yet posterity has recognized that, for Lucan, Caesar's crime lay principally in his name, which Nero had inherited; and Nero's not in absolutism and cruelty, but in having offended Lucan by thwarting his poetic career. The case is given away when Lucan forgets his brief for awhile, and mentions the totally false picture of Caesar the Monster which hatred and fear conjured up at Rome, after the crossing of the Rubicon, among men who should have known better.

Lucan may also be called the father of the costume-film. If lopped of all digressive rhodomontade, the *Civil Wars* is a script which could be put almost straight on the floor. It consists of carefully chosen, cunningly varied, brutally sensational scenes, linked by a tenuous thread of historical probability; and alternated with soft interludes in which deathless courage, supreme self-sacrifice, memorable piety, Stoic virtue, and wifely devotion are expected to win favour from the great sentimental box-office public. He used his own beautiful, high-spirited wife Polla Argentaria—said to have helped in the revision of his manuscripts—as a model for Pompey's Cornelia; and so strong was the Roman taboo on any display of uxoriousness, that Pompey's low spirits when he sends Cornelia away to safety in Lesbos must have seemed an indecently modern touch. Yet if Lucan was sincere in his most commendable plea for closer ties between husband and wife, how sincere can he have been in eulogizing Pompey's supporter Cato? Cato treated his wife Marcia as though she were a brood-mare, allowing himself no sensual pleasure during the act of procreation, and selling her, while pregnant of a fourth child, to a noble friend who wished to have his empty cradles filled with good stock.

Lucan must, I think, have been so single-minded a rhetorician that all his values were melodramatic ones. Unless a situation yielded a surprising paradox—the cruelty of Caesar's clemency, the loyal comradeship that the Oderzo Gauls showed by mutual murder, or the unkindness of the Roman refugee who gave Pompey's body decent burial—it did not interest him. Was the grand paradox, then, that neither his wife, his mother, his father, nor his own moral reputation meant anything at all to Lucan, compared with poetic ambition—which he based on an outstanding command of rhetoric? Was his account of Caesar's attempt to cross the Adriatic in a two-oared dinghy, though waves rose two or three thousand feet high, symbolic of his own insane self-assurance? He seems, however, to have had twinges of doubt. Valerius Probus, in his life of Lucan's friend, the poet Persius, 'who was gentle, virginally modest, handsome, good and pure, and showed an exemplary devotion to his mother, sister and aunt,' records Lucan's immense admiration for him. 'When Persius read his poems aloud, Lucan could hardly wait until he had finished before crying out that this was true poetry; and his own, mere fooling.' Yet all Persius's virtue did not make him much of a poet, at that.

. . . . .

Christopher Marlow first attempted the formidable task of translating Lucan into English. Perhaps it should here be explained that the Fathers of the Christian Church had experienced much the same difficulty in consolidating their empire as had the Fathers of the Republican Senate. How were they to combat the clever arguments of pagan sophists? Faith in timely inspiration by the Holy Ghost was not reckoned enough; and Paul's tactical success when he caused a division between Sadducees and Pharisees in the Sanhedrin offered so hopeful a precedent that they allowed their deacons to study under professors of rhetoric. The Classical curriculum, with certain necessary changes, became the basis of clerkly education throughout Christendom—though Virgil and Cicero ousted Homer and Demosthenes—and Virgil was actually credited with divine inspiration. In Marlow's London, Classical rhetoric still

flourished as vigorously as in Lucan's Rome; and it was claimed that Elizabethan English could take an even higher polish than Latin.

Now, these are the opening lines of the *Civil Wars*:

Bella per Emathois plus quam ciuilia campos
iusque datum sceleri canimus, populumque potentem
in sua uictrici conuersum uiscera dextra
cognatasque acies, et rupto foedere regni
certatum totis concussi uiribus orbis
in commune nefas, infestisque obuia signis
signa, pares aquilas et pila minantia pilis.
   quis furor, o ciues, quae tanta licentia ferri?
gentibus inuisis Latium praebere cruorem
cumque superba foret Babylon spolianda tropaeis
Ausoniis umbraque erraret Crassus inulta
bella geri placuit nullos habitura a triumphos?

Marlow rendered them magnificently:

Wars worse than ciuill on Thessalian playnes,
And outrage strangling law & people strong,
We sing, whose conquering swords their own breasts
   launcht,
Armies a lied, the kingdoms league vprooted,
Th' affrighted worlds force bent on publique spoile,
Trumpets, and drums like deadly threatning other,
Eagles alike displaide, darts answering darts.
Romans, what madnes, what huge lust of warre
Hath made Barbarians drunke with Latin bloud?
Now Babilon, (proud through our spoile) should stoop,
While slaughtred Crassus ghost walks vnreueng'd,
Will ye wadge war, for which you shall not triumph?

However, he never got beyond the first book; this was perhaps a reconnaissance, rather than a serious attempt to turn the whole 48,000 lines into English. Nobody else in those pre-Commonwealth days proved capable of continuing in the same strain, though both Sir F. Gorges and Thomas May tried. By 1718, when Nicholas Rowe made the translation which Dr Johnson subsequently pronounced 'one of the greatest productions of English poetry', the language had lost its exuberance.

Emathian plains with slaughter cover'd o'er,
And rage unknown to civil wars before,
Establish'd violence, and lawless might,
Avow'd and hallow'd by the name of right;
A race renown'd, the world's victorious lords,
Turn'd on themselves with their own hostile swords;
Piles against piles oppos'd in impious fight,
And eagles against eagles bending flight;
Of blood by friends, by kindred, parent, spilt,
One common horrour and [Illegible Text] guilt;
A shatter'd world in wild disorder tost,
Leagues, laws, and empire, in confusion lost;
Of all the woes which civil discords bring,
And Rome o'ercome by Roman arms, I sing.

What blind, detested madness could afford
Such horrid licence to the murdering sword?

Say, Romans, whence so dire a fury rose,
To glut with Latian blood your barbarous foes?
Could you in wars like these provoke your fate?
Wars, where no triumphs on the victor wait!
While Babylon's proud spires yet rise so high,
And rich in Roman spoils invade the sky;
While yet no vengeance is to Crassus paid,
But unatton'd repines the wandering shade . . .

It may be argued that Marlow's poetic fire honours Lucan above his deserts; and that the monotony of Rowe's eighteenth-century rhymed couplets matches Lucan's use of the hexameter more exactly. Rowe's translation went into several editions and can be bought second-hand without trouble. But, though readers capable of facing a verse epic are rare nowadays, and though it may seem easy enough to convey Lucan's sense in simple English prose, anyone who tries will soon find Latin rearing its ugly head and winding its absurd coils about him. In 1890, H. T. Riley provided a literal version, with valuable notes, for *Bohn's Library.* This is how he began:

Wars more than civil upon the Emathian plains, and licence conceded to lawlessness, I sing; and a powerful people turning with victorious right-hand against its own vitals, and kindred armies engaged; and, the compact of rule rent asunder, a contest waged with all the might of the shaken earth for the universal woe, and standards meeting with hostile standards, the eagles alike, and darts threatening darts.

What madness, this, O citizens! what lawlessness so great of the sword, while nations are your hate, for you to shed the Latin blood? And, while proud Babylon was to be spoiled of the Ausonian trophies, and the shade of Crassus was wandering unavenged, has it pleased you that wars, doomed to produce no triumphs, should be waged?

It is a valuable crib to the Latin original; but the more literal the rendering the less comprehensible to readers ignorant of Latin. A closer approximation to English was made by J. D. Duff for *Loeb* (1928):

Of war I sing, war worse than civil, waged over the plains of Emathia, and on legality conferred on crime; I tell how an imperial people turned their victorious right hands against their own vitals; how kindred fought against kindred; how, when the compact of tyranny was shattered, all the forces of the shaken world contended to make mankind guilty; how standards confronted hostile standards, eagles were matched against each other, and pilum threatened pilum.

What madness was this, my countrymen, what fierce orgy of slaughter? While the ghost of Crassus still wandered unavenged, and it was your duty to rob proud Babylon of her trophies over Italy, did you choose to give to hated nations the spectacle of Roman bloodshed, and to wage wars that could win no triumphs?

Yet just how much can the general reader understand of this? Where is Emathia? What is worse than civil war? What Ausonian trophies were laid up in Babylon?

Only Marlow, of all these translations, changed Emathia to 'Thessaly'; aware that Lucan had been using thoroughly off-target geographical terms. Emathia was part of Macedonia and lay not far from Thessaly; so, because *Thessalios* would not scan after *Bella per,* Lucan wrote *Emathios,* with the excuse that Thessaly had at one time formed part of the Macedonian Empire. *Ausoniis,* again, is a nicely scanning word, like *Emathios;* it originally referred to the Oscan city of Ausona. When the Ausonians revolted (Livy: ix. 25), the Romans of the early Republic massacred them to a man. But since the Alexandrian Greeks used *Ausonia* as a handy poetic term for the whole Italian peninsula, and Virgil adopted this convention in the *Aeneid,* Lucan makes it mean 'Rome'. Even Marlow retains 'Babylon', which Lucan uses as a more manageable word than 'Seleuceia', the name of the Parthian capital since Hellenistic times, though Babylon had lost its importance long before the Civil Wars. To say that the Ausonian trophies—meaning the Roman eagles captured from Marcus Licinius Crassus by the Parthian king in 53 B.C.—had been laid up at Babylon, was rather like saying that Pictish trophies had been laid up at Winchester—meaning that Scottish standards captured at Flodden in 1513 were brought to London, which had now succeeded Winchester as capital of England. The war was 'worse than civil' because Caesar and Pompey had been related by marriage; but since the general reader cannot be expected to know this, or the meanings of 'Emathia', 'Ausonia', and 'Babylon', I have decided to bring up into the text what most translators either leave to the reader's historical apprehension, or supply in footnote form.

I give this version:

The theme of my poem is the Civil War which was decided on the plains of Pharsalus in Thessaly; yet 'Civil War' is an understatement, since Pompey and Caesar, the opposing leaders, were not only fellow-citizens but relatives: the whole struggle was indeed no better than one of licensed fratricide. I shall here describe how, after the breakdown of the First Triumvirate, Rome turned the imperial sword against her own breast: how kinsman faced kinsman on the field of battle, each line of legionaries armed with identical javelins and carrying the same familiar eagle-standards as its opponents; and how the civilized world reeled under this contest of iniquity.

What made our forefathers embark on such an orgy of self-destruction? And why were their hated enemies permitted to enjoy the spectacle? Why was proud Parthia not first obliged to disgorge the Eagles taken from Crassus, whose ghost still wandered unavenged over her plains?

Latin poetry, as established by Ennius, had its own special vocabulary, devised to assist versification. A number of common Latin words were excluded by their scansion from the hexameter: for instance, Nero's family name, Domitius Ahenobarbus. 'Domitius' contains too many short syllables in a row, and 'Ahenobarbus' has a short syllable hopelessly imprisoned between two long ones. So if one wished to write the hexameter: 'And Domitius Ahenobarbus also came,' the only way out would be to address him in the vocative, which is a manageable anapaest; and use the historical present for 'came'; and explain 'Ahenobarbus' as meaning 'Brazen Beard':

> Tu-que venis, Domiti, quem signat ahenea
> barba
> 'And thou comest also, Domitius, whom a brazen beard distinguishes.'

Naturally, circumlocution of this sort need not, and should not, be reproduced in English prose—who would translate the French *'Qu'est-ce que c'est que ça?'* as anything but 'What's that?' The morbidities of this Latin poetical convention have been summarized in the well-known Victorian *Gradus ad Parnassum* ('Steps to Parnassus'); but even this distressing handbook withholds a full description of the disease.

One remarkable symptom was the poet's readiness to perpetuate any foolish mistake made by a reputable predecessor; thus, since Ovid in a moment of aberrancy had recorded Procne's transformation into a nightingale and Philomela's into a swallow (not contrariwise), 'Procne' was thereafter legitimized as a synonym for 'nightingale', whenever 'Philomela' would not fit the line. And when Virgil assumed that the decisive Battle of Philippi fought between Augustus and Brutus in 44 B.C., had taken place on the same field as the equally decisive one between Caesar and Pompey in 48 B.C.—having heard the name 'Philippi' mentioned in both connexions—he was followed by Ovid, Manilius, Florus, Petronius, and Lucan. These poets were highly educated, and must have known that the large Thracian Philippi lay 150 miles or so north-east from the small Thessalian Philippi; yet they all continued to descant on this strange poetical coincidence. Horace alone failed to follow suit; he doubtless had clear memories of Philippi, where he had fought on the wrong side and, not very gloriously, cast away his shield.

In another context, Lucan writes:

> Invidus annoso qui fama derogat aevo,
> Qui vates ad vera vocat.

> 'It would be churlish to challenge the authority of legend and expect poets to be truthful.'

and the Romans held that lies are necessary to poetry. Practical anatomic experience told them, for example, that Centaurs could not exist, because they were popularly depicted with two more limbs and one more stomach than any mammal was known to possess. However, since Homer had mentioned them in the *Iliad* and *Odyssey,* and Pindar had described their monstrous origin, Centaurs formed a necessary part of poetry—along with the one-eyed Cyclops, the winged horse Pegasus, and the fire-breathing Chimaera. Since no one troubled to discover the original poetic meaning of these anomalous concepts, disciplined students took the view: 'If our professor of rhetoric tells us to employ absurd mythical figures, it is our duty not only to obey but to convince our verse-audience that we believe in their practical reality.'

Lucan liked to pretend that poetic artifice had not been forced on him merely by metrical requirement and a study of the best models, but that he honoured Apollo by deliberately making verses as dark as some of the Delphic oracles; and therefore strained sense almost, though not quite, to breaking point. Thus:

> Mitis Atax Latias gaudet non ferre carinas
> finis et Hesperiae, promoto limite, Varus;
> quaque sub Herculeo sacratus nomine portus
> urguet rupe caua pelagus: non Corus in illum
> ius habet aut Zephyrus, solus sua litora turbat
> Circius et tuta prohibet statione Monoeci. . .

which appears in the *Bohn* translation as:

> . . . the placid Atax rejoices at no longer bearing the Latian keels; the Varus, too, the limit of Hesperia, her boundaries now extended; where, too, beneath the divine authority of Hercules, the consecrated harbour adjoins the sea with its hollowed rocks; no Corus holds sway over it, nor yet the Zephyr; alone does Circius disturb the shores his own, and withholds the ships from the safe harbour of Monoecus.

and which Marlow versified as follows:

> Mild Atax glad it beares no Roman boats,
> And frontier Varus that the campe is farre,
> Sent aide; so did Alcides port, whose seas
> Eate hollow rocks, and where the north-west wind
> Nor Zephir rules not, but the north alone
> Turmoiles the coast, and enterance forbids . . .

but which, when reduced to simple English, means:

> Caesar's galleys no longer patrolled either the slow-flowing Aude, or the Var which now formed the frontier of Greater Italy. Moreover, his flotilla had been withdrawn from the rocky cove of Monaco, sacred to Hercules who touched there during his Tenth Labour—it offers safe anchorage when the wind blows from the north-west, but no protection against the dreaded Sirocco.

And here is another puzzle:

*. . . excepta quis morte potest? secreta tenebis
litoris Euboici memorando condite busto,
qua maris angustat fauces saxosa Carystos
et, tumidis infesta colit quae numina, Rhamnus,
artatus rapido feruet qua gurgite pontus
Euripusque trahit, cursum mutantibus undis,
Chalcidicas puppes ad iniquam classibus Aulin.*

which has been translated in *Bohn*:

The secret recesses of the Euboean shore thou shalt
possess, buried in a memorable tomb, where rocky
Carystos straitens the outlets of the sea, and where
Rhamnus worships the Deity hostile to the proud;
where the sea boils, enclosed in its rapid tide, and the
Euripus hurries along, with waves that change their
course, the ships of Chalcis to Aulis, hostile to fleets.

The person concerned is Appius Claudius who had been
told by the Pythoness, when he consulted the Delphic
Oracle, that he could escape the Civil War by 'taking
his solitary ease in Euboea, that heaven of refuge.'

The sense is:

'Appius, you are fated to take your solitary ease in Euboea: by being buried in a sequestered but famous tomb
near the quarries of Carystos. It will face across the
narrow sea towards the town of Rhamnos in Attica,
sacred to Nemesis, the goddess who punishes human
ambition. In between lie the so-called Hollows of Euboea, where the sea is disturbed by the rapid,
constantly-shifting current from the Straits of Euripus:
a current which sets the ships of Calchis adrift and
swings them across to Aulis in Boeotia—that fatal shore
where long ago Agamemnon's ships assembled before
sailing to Troy.'

Since this is what these passages mean, surely they
should be so rendered? I see no point in letting them
remain obscure, just because a few Latinists can nod
appreciatively at the concealed references to Hercules's
Tenth Labour, and Agamemnon's expedition to Troy,
and the Goddess Nemesis's temple at Rhamnus, and the
asbestos quarries of Carystus; or can recognize *Portus
Menoecus* as the present Principality of Monaco, and
Atax as the River Aude. Granted, I have denied Lucan
credit for his *Gradus ad Parnassum* dexterity, letting
him read more like Herodotus or Pausanias; but the
lover of rhetoric may always, if he prefers, consult
Rowe's version, which here adds mistranslation to Lucan's obscurity.

Convinced that it would be 'churlish to demand truth
from poets', Lucan reaches the pitch of grotesqueness
in his Ninth Book. Cato's was a bold and exhausting
march along the eastern coast of the Gulf of Sirte, and
took six days; the men carried their own rations and at
night camped by scanty water-holes. Lucan, however,
sends him on a two-months' march for thousands of

miles in a wide semi-circle through the waterless
Sahara; meanwhile the troops battle day and night, apparently without any food but sand, against fantastically
unzoological serpents. Sir John Mandeville pales beside
Lucan:

. . . An unlucky soldier named Sabellus felt the barbed
fangs of a tiny seps fixed in his leg. He pulled it off
and pinned it to the ground with the point of his javelin.
This seps is the most destructive of all snakes, despite
its smallness. The skin next to the bite began to break
and the flesh to melt away until the white thigh-bone
showed; then, as the wound widened farther, the body
swam in corruption and slowly disappeared, starting
with the calves, knees, and thighs. Black matter dripped
from the thighs, the muscles which held the belly in
place snapped and the intestines slid out. Sabellus, in
fact, slowly trickled into the ground, and there was
unexpectedly little of him left, because the seps' venom
reduces the limbs by a chemical process to a puddle of
filth. His anatomy was for awhile revealed with painful
clearness: ligaments, sinews, the structure of the lungs,
the bones of the chest, and all the inner organs. Slowly
the strong shoulders and arms and neck and head liqui-
fied, as it were snow when the warm South Wind blows,
or wax exposed to the Sun. It is not much to record
that the flesh was eaten away—that happens whenever
corpses are cremated—but no pyre reduces bones to
nothing as this venom did . . .

Nasidius, once a Marsian farmer, died in a very different manner: by expansion, not liquefaction. When a
fiery prester struck at him, his face turned red as a
glowing coal and began to swell until the features could
no longer be recognized. Then the virus spread and
puffed him out to the gigantic proportions of ship's
canvas in a storm. The man himself was buried deep
inside this bloated mass, and the breastplate flew off
like the lid of a fiercely steaming cauldron. Soon Nasidius became a great mountain of flesh in which limbs
were indistinguishable from trunk; no vultures or wild
beasts could have ventured to feast on him, and even
his comrades dared not consign him to a pyre. They
fled in horror, and as they glanced back the body was
still swelling in every direction.

In 1927, A. E. Housman, better known as the author of
A Shropshire Lad, stabilized the text of the **Civil Wars.**
Prevented by the self-denying ordinance to which
textual critics subscribe from expressing any poetic
judgement, he merely allows himself a few dry comments, in an appendix, on Lucan's astronomical
ignorance. But the savagery of his attack on former editors suggests that he is using them as whipping-boys
for Lucan; did not Lucan himself use Caesar as a
whipping-boy for Nero? After charging Cortius with
egotism and tediousness; Burman with diffuseness and
triviality; Bentley with senile ill-temper; Weise with
ludicrous ignorance; 'passing over C. F. Weber's
perfectly useless edition'; and saying hard words about
Hosius, Housman writes:

An elaborate edition with apparatus criticus and commentary was produced in 1896 and 1897 by C. M.

Francken. Hardly a page of it can be read without anger and disgust. Francken was a born blunderer, marked cross from the womb and perverse; and he had not the shrewdness or modesty to suspect that others saw clearer than he did nor the prudence and decency to acquaint himself with what he might have learned from those whom he preferred to contradict. For stupidity of plan and slovenliness of execution his apparatus criticus is worse than Breiter's apparatus of Manilius; and I never saw another of which that could be said.

. . . . .

Why has Lucan's reputation flared up so high, every now and then, and always at the expense of Virgil, to whom as a verse technician at least, he could not hold a candle? One may equally ask why the modernist movement in Anglo-American poetry which Ezra Pound, T. S. Eliot, T. E. Hulme, and others started over forty years ago, by way of revolt against the Virgilian tradition of Tennyson, Longfellow, William Morris and others, has enjoyed such success. The truth is that at the close of the First World War much the same moral and aesthetic gap separated neo-Georgian from Victorian London, as had separated Neronian from Augustan Rome. Standards had changed radically and the smooth, languid, pellucid verse—*splendidior vitro*—hitherto demanded by critics could no longer adequately express the consequent malaise. To poets whom loss of faith in their own national institutions, ethics, religion, and even in themselves, sends marching and counter-marching through the Waste Land, Lucan can be as much a 'standard-bearer' as he was for Piso's ill-considered conspiracy. His un-Virgilian rhetoric, and all the modernist traits mentioned above—impatience with craftsmanship, digressive irrelevances, emphasis on the macabre, lack of religious conviction, turgid hyperbole, inconsistency, appeal to violence, and occasional flashes of real brilliance—have been rediscovered by this new disagreeable world. Accounts of the extravagant and tyrannical behaviour to which ordinary Romans were ready to submit under Nero do not now read so fantastically as they did before the rise of totalitarianism in Europe; and many people who to-day pass as Stoics are hardly more able to stand the test of violent moral suasion than was Lucan.

Shelley has been taken to task for preferring Lucan to Virgil, but he too lived in a cranky age and showed extreme emotional instability; the melodramatic sublime of his *Cenci* often spills over into the bathetic ridiculous, like Lucan's account of Cato's heroic struggle with the Libyan serpents. It is only to be expected, similarly, that Pound (the most Lucan-like of modernists) should please the young and disorientated better than Tennyson. Yet surely there are poetic alternatives to the soft-voiced skilful rhetorician, 'wielder of the stateliest measure ever moulded by the lips of man' (Tennyson on Virgil), who prides himself on his *ars est celare ar-*

tem technique, and the brassy-voiced intemperate rhetorician, for whom *ars est in arte praeconari* (art lies in advertising, rather than concealing, artistry)? The Romans, for example, could choose the unrhetorical Catullus who was tender without being soft, and manly without being strident: a true poet. But although the two-thousand-year-old tradition of rhetorical education has at last lapsed at the Universities, its effects are still apparent in popular literary taste. The verse-reading public has always preferred sound to sense; and since the rhetorician disguised as a poet is no longer challenged to justify his tropes logically, he can get away (so to speak) with rape, arson, and murder.

Why then, if I dislike Lucan so much (as Dr E. V. Rieu, the Editor of these *Penguin Classics,* very pertinently asks) have I chosen to spend six months in translating **The Civil Wars**? Because the book is a historical phenomenon that cannot be argued away, and because like other prodigiously vital writers with hysterical tendencies—Rudyard Kipling is a convenient instance—Lucan exerts a strange fascination on even the reluctant reader; and because, as I have tried to show, he anticipated so many of the literary *genres* dominant to-day that it would be unfair not to put him in modern dress for the admiration of the great majority whose tastes differ from mine.

George M. Logan (essay date winter 1971)

SOURCE: Logan, George M. "Daniel's *Civil Wars* and Lucan's *Pharsalia.*" *Studies in English Literature, 1500-1900* 11, no. 1 (winter 1971): 53-68.

[*In the following essay, Logan presents specific passages of Samuel Daniel's* Civil Wars *that are modeled on or inspired by the* Pharsalia.]

Meres's *Palladis Tamia* contains the earliest recorded comparison of Samuel Daniel with Lucan: "As Lucan hath mournefully depainted the ciuil wars of Pompey and Caesar: so hath Daniel the civill wars of Yorke and Lancaster, and Drayton the civill wars of Edward the second and the Barons."[1] Everard Guilpin, in his *Skialetheia* (licensed a few days after Meres's work in September 1598), versified the comparison:

> *Daniel* (as some holds) might mount if he list,
> But others say that he's a Lucanist.[2]

This remark is apparently intended as a slur; probably Guilpin has in mind the commonplace that Lucan, whose epic treats historical subject matter in strictly chronological order, was a prosaic historian rather than a poet. Daniel's friend Camden gave the identification semiofficial status by calling the author of *The Civil*

Wars "our Lucan" in the *Remains*,[3] and Daniel evidently remained "the English Lucan" until Thomas May took the title away from him in the 1630's.[4]

In sixteenth-century England, the *Pharsalia* occupied the position of a major classic. Lucan was a master, perhaps the supreme master, of the typical Silver Latin poetic style. His epigrams are terser than any others, his hyperboles more ingeniously extreme; the speeches that he puts into the mouths of his characters are of unmatched brilliance and clangor. For as long as Western education was anchored in the teaching of Latin rhetoric, the *Pharsalia* was a standard textbook. The famous list of the books that John Dorne sold at Oxford in 1520 mentions, among other works, thirty-seven copies of various works of Cicero and the same number of Terence, twenty-nine copies of Vergil, twenty-three of Ovid, eight of Horace and Pliny, six of Sallust, and fourteen of Lucan.[5] From about the middle of the sixteenth century, the *Pharsalia* constituted a part of the curriculum at the better English grammar schools.[6] Concomitant to Lucan's use in the schools was the wide availability of copies of his epic. The *editio princeps* had appeared in Rome in 1469, only four years after the earliest editions of Cicero and before the printing of any other poet (with the possible exception of Vergil).[7] There were several sixteenth-century editions, the first English edition being published in 1588.[8] Translations of the *Pharsalia,* "none the easiest work of that kind," as Clarendon says, were attempted and abandoned by Barnabe Googe (ca. 1560) and George Turberville (ca. 1570).[9] The line-for-line rendering of Book I attributed to Marlowe was registered in September 1593 and finally published in 1600.

In addition to its usefulness as a compendium of Stoic epigrams and rhetorical flowers, the *Pharsalia* appealed strongly to sixteenth-century Englishmen as a major classical authority on the problems of civil war. Erasmian humanism was everywhere marked by pacifistic tendencies; in the context of contemporary English history, Lucan's depiction of the horrors of internal dissension must have seemed especially pertinent. From the point of view of the creative artist, the *Pharsalia*—a standard commentary on the most famous of all civil wars—had obvious value as a model. In a period when verse, and particularly the epic genre, was still regarded as an appropriate medium for serious historical writing, Lucan's poem could provide precedents for turning military incident into poetry and important assistance to writers engaged in the attempt to impose order and dignity on the squalid panorama of the civil wars of the English fifteenth century.

It is not surprising, then, that Daniel, writing a poetic history of these wars, should have taken the *Pharsalia* as a guide. His imitations of Lucan must have been eas-

ily recognized by contemporary readers, and a significant part of the enjoyment of his poem must have come from its implicit invitation to rethink the wars of York and Lancaster in terms of the war between Caesar and Pompey. To the modern reader, though, who lacks the close verbal familiarity with the *Pharsalia* that educated Elizabethans enjoyed, this aspect of *The Civil Wars* is hardly perceptible. Daniel's modern critics have not attempted precise definition of the English poet's debt to Lucan. Laurence Michel, the only twentieth-century editor of Daniel's epic, is vague and misleading on the subject.[10] Thus a detailed account of the connection between the two poems seems a desideratum.

That Daniel went out of his way to invite comparison between his epic and the *Pharsalia* becomes clear when the openings of the two poems are put side by side. Daniel's first three stanzas are little more than a condensed paraphrase of Lucan's introductory passage:

> I Sing the ciuill Warres,
>   tumultuous Broyles,
> And Bloody factions of a
>   mightie Land:
> Whose people hautie, proud
>   with forraine spoyles,
> Vpon themselues turn-backe
>   their conquering hand;
> Whil'st Kin their Kin,
>   Brother the Brother foyles;
> Like Ensignes all against
>   like Ensignes band;
> Bowes against Bowes,
>   the Crowne against
>   the Crowne;
> Whil'st all pretending right,
>   all right's throwne downe.
>
> What furie, ô what madnes
>   held thee so,
> Deare *England* (too too
>   prodigall of blood)
> To waste so much, and
>   warre without a foe,
> Whilst *Fraunce,* to see thy
>   spoyles, at pleasure stood!
> How much might'st thou haue
>   purchast with lesse woe,
> T'haue done thee honour and
>   thy people good?
> Thine might haue beene
>   what-euer lies betweene
> The *Alps* and vs, the
>   *Pyrenei* and *Rhene.*
>
> Yet now what reason
>   haue we to complaine?
> Since hereby came the
>   calme we did inioy;
> The blisse of thee *Eliza*;
>   happie gaine
> For all our losse: when-as

        no other way
The heauens could finde,
    but to vnite againe
The fatall sev'red Families,
        that they
Might bring foorth thee: that
    in thy peace might growe
That glorie, which few
    Times could euer showe.[11]

                                        (*CW,* I.i-iii)

Bella per Emathios plus
    quan civilia campos,
Iusque datum sceleri canimus,
    populumque potentem
In sua victrici conversum
    viscera dextra,
Cognatasque acies, et rupto
    foedere regni
Certatum totis concussi
    viribus orbis
In commune nefas, infestisque
    obvia signis
Signa, pares aquilas et
    pila minantia pilis.

Quis furor, o cives, quae
    tanta licentia ferri?
Gentibus invisis Latium
    praebere cruorem,
Cumque superba foret
    Babylon spolianda tropaeis
Ausoniis umbraque erraret
    Crassus inulta,
Bella geri placuit nullos
    habitura triumphos?
Heu, quantum terrae potuit
    pelagique parari
Hoc quem civiles hauserunt
    sanguine dextrae,
Unde venit Titan, et
    nox ubi sidera condit.

                        . . . . .

Quod si non aliam venturo
    fata Neroni
Invenere viam magnoque
    aeterna parantur
Regna deis caelumque suo
    servire Tonanti
Non nisi saevorum potuit
    post bella gigantum,
Iam nihil, o superi, querimur;
    scelera ista nefasque
Hac mercede placent; diros
    Pharsalia campos
Inpleat et Poeni saturentur
    sanguine manes;
Ultima funesta concurrant
    proelia Munda;
His, Caesar, Perusina
    fames Mutinaeque labores
Accedant fatis et quas
    premit aspera classes
Leucas et ardenti servilia

bella sub Aetna:
Multum Roma tamen
    debet civilibus armis,
Quod tibi res acta est.[12]

        (***Phars.*** [***Pharsalia***], I.1-15, 33-45)

The imitation is close, but one may point out suggestive differences between the passages. In the first place, Daniel's paraphrase is only about half as long as the original. Daniel has nothing that corresponds to lines 21-32 in the Latin, and he has reduced to a verse and a half Lucan's detailed, six-line survey of the foreign territory that might have been conquered with the blood wasted on civil war (omitted here; ***Phars.,*** I.15-20). One notices, also, that in Daniel's version these foreign conquests would have required "lesse woe," whereas Lucan is not at all concerned about the length of the casualty lists, so long as the cause be suitably imperialistic. Nor can Daniel quite bring himself to the hyperbolic pitch of Lucan's "Multum Roma tamen debet civilibus armis." Lucan's nauseating flattery of the monarch—which continues through line 63—is cut to one stanza in Daniel's version. Lucan goes on to assert that Nero is a wholly sufficient muse for his purposes. Daniel in 1595 invoked Elizabeth. After her death, in a characteristic revision, Daniel's second-favorite abstraction (after "Order") succeeded: "Come sacred *Virtue*: I no *Muse,* but thee, / Inuoke, in this great labour I intend" (I.iv.1-2).[13]

One must read some seven hundred lines farther into Daniel's poem to find another extended passage clearly modeled on Lucan.[14] Upon Bolingbroke's return from exile, his first night's rest is disturbed by a "fearefull vision" of the Genius of England. The apparition reproves the Duke's ambition and blames him for the civil strife that will inevitably result from the further pursuit of his aims. E. M. W. Tillyard has suggested that Daniel here employs "the Morality motive of Respublica,"[15] but in fact the poet is simply adapting the vision of Roma that Caesar encounters when about to cross the Rubicon. Lucan writes:

Ingens visa duci patriae trepidantis imago
Clara per obscuram voltu maestissima noctem,
Turrigero canos effundens vertice crines,
Caesarie lacera nudisque adstare lacertis
Et gemitu permixta loqui: "Quo tenditis ultra?
Quo fertis mea signa, viri? si iure venitis,
Si cives, huc usque licet."

                                        (I.186-192)

Similarly, Bolingbroke seems to see,

        in reuerent forme appeare
A faire and goodly woman all distrest;
Which, with full-weeping eyes and rented haire,[16]
Wringing her hands (as one that griev'd and prayd)

With sighes commixt with words, vnto him said;
   "O! whither dost thou tend, my vnkinde Sonne?

     . . . . .

   "Stay here thy foote, thy yet vnguilty foote,
   That canst not stay when thou art farther in."

         (I.lxxxvii.4-8, lxxxviii.1, lxxxix.1-2)

The rebels offer the same sophism in excuse:

   Roma, fave coeptis; non
      te furialibus armis
   Persequor; en adsum victor
      terraque marique
   Caesar, ubique tuus—liceat
      modo, nunc quoque—miles.
   Ille erit, ille nocens, qui
      me tibi fecerit hostem.

         (I.200-203)

   Deare Countrey, ô I haue not
      hither brought
   These Armes to spoyle, but
      for thy liberties:
   The sinne be on their head,
      that this haue wrought;
   Who wrongd me first, and
      thee do tyrannise.
   I am thy Champion, and I
      seeke my right:
   Prouok't I am to this,
      by others spight.

         (I.xc.3-8)

The account of generalized panic and despair that closes the first book of *The Civil Wars* (stanzas 107-118) is also modeled on the parallel episode of the *Pharsalia* (I.466-695, II.1-66). At three points the imitation is close. Daniel writes that aged citizens "blame their many yeeres that liue so long, / To see the horrour of these miseries" (I.cviii.1-2), recalling three verses of Lucan's second book:

   At miseros angit sua cura parentes,
   Oderuntque gravis vivacia fata senectae
   Servatosque iterum bellis civilibus annos.

         (II.64-66)

Similarly, a passage in which Daniel has English women congregate in the "Temples"—"there to vow and pray / For husbands, brothers, or their sonnes gone out" (I.cix.2-3)—is modeled on the behavior of Lucan's Roman matrons in *Pharsalia*, II.28-33. In a powerful stanza, "graue religious Fathers" pray that foreign enemies may arise:

   Conspire against vs, neighbour nations all,
   That enuie at the height whereto w'are growne:
   Coniure the barbarous North, and let them call
   Strange furie from farre distant shores vnknowne;
   And let them altogether on vs fall,

So to diuert the ruine of our owne:
That we, forgetting what doth so incense,
May turne the hand of malice, to defence.

         (I.cxi)

Lucan has the men setting out for war voice this hope:

   Non pacem petimus, superi: date gentibus iras,
   Nunc urbes excite feras; coniuret in arma
   Mundus, Achaemeniis decurrant Medica Susis
   Agmina, Massageten Scythicus non adliget Hister,
   Fundat ab extremo flavos aquilone Suebos
   Albis et indomitum Rheni caput; omnibus hostes
   Reddite nos populis: civile avertite bellum.

         (II.47-53)

In both epics, the beginning of civil war is heralded by numerous portents (*CW*, I.cxiii-cxv; ***Phars.***, I.522-583). Daniel's list is considerably shorter and less sensational than Lucan's, but it is clear from the particular prodigies included, as well as their order, that Daniel has the Roman poet's collection in mind.

In Book II of *The Civil Wars* there is evidence that Daniel, who had a weakness for star-crossed lovers, was greatly moved by Lucan's portrait of Pompey and Cornelia. Daniel's conception of Richard II and Isabel is modeled to a substantial extent on Lucan's tragic pair. The first hint of this partial identification comes toward the middle of the book. On the first night of his captivity, Richard is deceived by a happy dream. Daniel's verse takes on the rhythmic ebb and flow that is characteristic of his most emotional passages:

   His new misfortune makes deluding sleepe
   Say 'twas not so (False dreames the trueth denie).
   Wherewith he starts; feels waking cares do creepe
   Vpon his soule, and giues his dreame the lie;
   Then sleepes againe: and then againe, as deepe
   Deceites of darknes mocke his miserie.
   So hard believ'd was sorrow in her youth:
   That he thinks truth was dreams, & dreams were truth.

         (II.liii)

Although there are no close parallels, subsequent borrowings make it seem probable that Daniel was inspired by the famous passage at the beginning of Lucan's climactic seventh book:

   At nox felicis Magno pars ultima vitae
   Sollicitos vana decepit imagine somnos.

     . . . . .

     seu fine bonorum
   Anxia venturis ad tempora laeta refugit,
   Sive per ambages solitas contraria visis
   Vaticinata quies magni tulit omina planctus,
   Seu vetito patrias ultra tibi cernere sedes
   Sic Romam Fortuna dedit. Ne rumpite somnos,
   Castrorum vigiles, nullas tuba verberet aures.

         (VII.7-8, 19-25)

The account of the reunion and final parting of Richard and Isabel that follows (II.lxvi-xciii) constitutes one of Daniel's most interesting debts to the *Pharsalia*. The episode, which marks the only appearance of Isabel in Daniel's poem, is completely unhistorical. Isabel was actually not quite eleven years old at the time of Richard's capture. Here Daniel does not simply grind out an obvious paraphrase of a familiar Lucanic passage, as he often had in Book I: his imagination is heated to the point of transforming and fusing material from two different episodes of the *Pharsalia.*

At the beginning of the passage, Isabel stands at a window as Bolingbroke leads Richard into London. Her situation parallels that of Cornelia watching (from a cliff) at Delos as Pompey comes from Pharsalia in defeat. Neither wife has been fully informed of what has befallen her husband (*CW*, II.lxvii.3-4; *Phars.,* VIII.51-53); both husbands come into sight downcast and disheveled (*CW*, II.lxxiv.5-7; *Phars.,* VIII.54-57); both wives swoon. Isabel's swoon was doubtless more or less inevitable, but Daniel probably has the description of Cornelia's unusually severe attack in mind:

Obvia nox miserae caelum
　　lucemque tenebris
Abstulit, atque animam
　　clausit dolor; omnia nervis
Membra relicta labant,
　　riguerunt corda, diuque
Spe mortis decepta iacet.

(VIII.58-61)

Sorrow keepes full
　　possession in her heart,
Lockes it within, stops vp
　　the way of breath,
Shuts senses out of doore
　　from euerie part;
And so long holdes there,
　　as it hazardeth
Oppressed Nature, and is
　　forc't to part,
Or else must be constrain'd
　　to stay with death.

(II.lxxx.1-6)

Reviving, both wives protest their faithfulness (*CW*, II.lxxxi-lxxxvii; *Phars.,* VIII.86-105). From a hint in Lucan—"incipe Magnum / Sola sequi" (VIII.80-81)—Daniel develops two graceful stanzas:

And yet, deare Lord, though thy vngratefull Land
Hath left thee thus; yet I will take thy part:
I doo remaine the same, vnder thy hand;
Thou still dost rule the kingdome of my hart:
If all be lost, that gouernment doth stand;
And that shall neuer from thy rule depart:
And so thou bee, I care not how thou bee:
Let Greatnes goe; so it goe without thee.

(II.lxxxlv; see also lxxxv)

With this passage one might also compare Pompey's ungracious rebuke:

Deformis adhuc vivente marito
Summus et augeri vetitus dolor: ultima debet
Esse fides lugere virum. Tu nulla tulisti
Bello damna meo: vivit post proelia Magnus
Sed fortuna perit. Quod defles, illud amasti.[17]

(VIII.81-85)

For the second part of the episode, which narrates Richard's and Isabel's last night together, Daniel seems to have drawn upon the parallel scene between Pompey and Cornelia. When Pompey means to tell Cornelia that he must send her away from the danger of battle, the words will not come: "Mentem iam verba paratam / Destituunt" (V.731-732). In Daniel's episode both lovers find themselves struck dumb, though it is Isabel who cannot deliver a prepared speech:

Shee that was come with a resolved hart,
And with a mouth full stor'd, with wordes well chose;
Thinking, This comfort wil I first impart
Vnto my Lord, and thus my speach dispose:

· · · · ·

When being come, all this prov'd nought but winde;
Teares, lookes, and sighes, do only tell her minde.

Thus both stood silent and confused so,
Their eyes relating how their hearts did morne:
Both bigge with sorrow, and both great with wo
In labour with what was not to be borne:
This mightie burthen, wherewithall they goe,
Dies vndeliuered, perishes vnborne.

(II.xci.1-4, 7-8, xcii.1-6)

More significant than this sort of parallel, though, is the general resemblance of setting and atmosphere in these two fine scenes. Thus the last stanza quoted is illuminated by the following lines from Lucan's episode, even though there are no close verbal parallels between the passages:

Exiluit stratis amens tormentaque nulla
Vult differre mora. Non maesti pectora Magni
Sustinet amplexu dulci, non colla tenere,
Extremusque perit tam longi fructus amoris,
Praecipitantque suos luctus, neuterque recedens
Sustinuit dixisse "vale"; vitamque per omnem
Nulla fuit tam maesta dies.

(V.791-797)

In the remaining books of *The Civil Wars,* Daniel seems to remember the *Pharsalia* only when there is a battle to be described—a task for which, as Jonson's *mot* suggests, Daniel was not by nature suited.[18] The heroic last stand of Talbot at Châtillon is probably Daniel's greatest success in this kind, and the episode echoes several passages of the **Pharsalia**. Talbot's speech to his soldiers seems to be modeled on the speech of Caesar's lieutenant Vulteius, urging his men to resolve on a noble death:

> Neuer had worthy men, for any fact,
> A more faire glorious Theater, then we;
> Whereon true Magnanimitie might act
> Braue deedes, which better witnessed could be.
> For, lo, from yonder Turrets, yet vnsackt,
> Your valiant fellowes stand, your worth to see,
> T'auouch your valour, if you liue to gaine;
> And if we die, that we di'd not in vaine.
>
> (VI.lxxxii)

Vulteius's forces are trapped on a raft at sea:

> Non tamen in caeca bellorum nube cadendum est,
> Aut cum permixtas acies sua tela tenebris
> Involvent. Conferta iacent cum corpora campo,
> In medium mors omnis abit, perit obruta virtus:
> Nos in conspicua sociis hostique carina
> Constituere dei. Praebebunt aequora testes,
> Praebebunt terrae, summis dabit insula saxis,
> Spectabunt geminae diverso litore partes.
> Nescio quod nostris magnum et memorabile fatis
> Exemplum, Fortuna, paras.
>
> (IV.488-497)

The two speeches have the same effect: Talbot's men, like Vulteius's, now are impatient for battle to begin (*CW*, VI. lxxxv.1-3); **Phars.**, IV.524-525); they are not merely willing, but actually eager to die (*CW*, VI.lxxxix.1-3, 7-8; **Phars.**, IV. 514-517). Both groups fight with deadly efficiency:

> nec quemquam dextra
>   fefellit,
> Cum feriat moriente manu.[19]
>
> (IV.559-560)

> No stroke they giue, but
>   wounds; no wound, but
>   kills:
> Neere to their hate, close
>   to their work they stood,
> Hit where they would, their
>   hand obeyes their wills.
>
> (VI.xc.2-4)

In both cases, this unusual effectiveness is explained by the fact that the soldiers had already ratified an agreement to die:

> Stabat devota iuventus
> Damnata iam luce ferox
>   securaque pugnae
> Promisso sibi fine manu.
>
> (IV.533-535)

> So much, true resolution
> wrought in those

> Who had made couenant
>   with death before. . . .
>
> (VI.xci.1-2)

Talbot's personal leadership of his forces is probably imitated from Caesar's conduct at Pharsalia (*CW*, VI.xciii.7-8, xciv; **Phars.**, VII.557-559, 574-577), and the simile comparing the English commander to an aged oak was certainly suggested by Lucan's famous description of Pompey (*CW*, VI.xcv; **Phars.**, I.135-143).[20]

The last of Daniel's debts to Lucan comes in his account of the battle of Towton (VIII.iii-xxxv). This climactic encounter the poet dignifies by calling it the English Pharsalia—"Shew, how our great Pharsalian Field was fought / At *Towton* in the North" (VIII.iii.1-2)—although he notes sadly that no counterpart of one of the Lucanic actors was present: "But, here no *Cato* with a Senate stood / For Common-wealth" (VIII.vii.1-2). As one might expect, Daniel feels obliged to imitate, not very interestingly, several Lucanic details. The incredible magnitude of the contending armies is stressed and exaggerated. Lucan says of Pharsalia that "Hic patriae perit omne decus" (VII.597); Daniel echoes the line: "*Yorke*, by his attempt hath ouer-throwne / All the best glorie wherein *England* stood" (VIII.xxxv.5-6). There is an apostrophe very much in Lucan's vein:

> What rage, what madness, *England*, do we see?
> That this braue people, in such multitude
> Run to confound themselues, and all to be
> Thus mad for *Lords*, and for meere Seruitude.[21]
>
> (VIII.vi.1-4)

Edward's speech to his men resembles Caesar's *real-politisch* exhortation before Pharsalia:

> Com'n is the day, sayd he, wherein who can
> Obtaine the best, is Best: this day must try
> Who hath the wrong, and whence our ills haue beene:
> And tis our swords must make vs honest men.
>
> (VIII.ix.5-8)

The Latin is quite similar:

> Haec est illa dies, mihi quam Rubiconis ad undas
> Promissam memini, cuius spe movimus arma,
> In quam distulimus vetitos remeare triumphos,
> Haec, fato quae teste probet, quis iustius arma
> Sumpserit; haec acies victum factura nocentem est.
> Si pro me patriam ferro flammisque petistis,
> Nunc pugnate truces gladioque exsolvite culpam:
> Nulla manus, belli mutato iudice, pura est.[22]
>
> (VII.254-263)

The most interesting parallel involves Pompey's withdrawal, when the battle is clearly lost, to an elevated vantage point:

Stetit aggere campi,
Eminus unde omnes sparsas per Thessala rura
Aspiceret clades, quae bello obstante latebant.
Tot telis sua fata peti, tot corpora fusa
Ac se tam multo pereuntem sanguine vidit.
Nec, sicut mos est miseris, trahere omnia secum
Mersa iuvat gentesque suae miscere ruinae:
Ut Latiae post se vivat pars maxima turbae,
Sustinuit dignos etiamnunc credere votis
Caelicolas vovitque, sui solacia casus.
"Parcite," ait "superi, cunctas prosternere gentes.
Stante potest mundo Romaque superstite Magnus
Esse miser.

. . . . .

Civiline parum est bello, si meque meosque
Obruit? exiguae clades sumus orbe remoto?
Omnia quid laceras? quid perdere cuncta laboras?"

(VII.649-661, 663-665)

Again Lucan's tragic Pompey provides the inspiration for one of Daniel's best passages, three stanzas in the repetitive, melancholy style that we encountered before in the episode of Richard and Isabel:

Vnhappy *Henrie,* from a little Hill,
Plac't not far off (whence he might view the fight)
Had all th'intire full prospect of this ill,
With all the scattered slaughter, in his sight:
Saw how the victor rag'd, and spoil'd at wil,
And left not off when all was in his might:
Saw, with how great adoo himselfe was wonne;
And with what store of blood Kings are vndone.

We are not worth so much, nor I, nor he,
As hath beene spent for vs, by you this day,
Deare people, said he: therefore, O, agree,
And leaue off mischiefe, and your malice stay.
Stay, *Edward,* stay. They must a People bee,
When we shall not be Kings.

. . . . .

For me, I could be pleas'd t'haue nought to doe
With Fortune; and content, my selfe were ill,
So *England* might be well; and that t'vndoe
Me, might suffice the sword, without more ill.[23]

(VIII.xxii, xxiii.1-6, xxiv.1-4)

When he began *The Civil Wars,* Daniel probably intended a poem modeled closely on the *Pharsalia.* The opening stanzas of his poem seem to promise a Lucanic epic, and the structure of the first book as a whole, as well as numerous individual episodes and details in that book and the second, are patterned after the *Pharsalia.* Moreover, one finds in several of these imitated passages tacit identifications of Bolingbroke with the ruthless and evil Caesar of the *Pharsalia* and of Richard II with Lucan's tragic Pompey. It is clear from reflective passages in the early books of the poem that Daniel in 1595 conceived of his theme in terms of a simple opposition between legitimacy and usurpation,[24] and since

Lucan's account of the Roman civil war is for the most part cast in similar black-and-white terms, the prestigious *Pharsalia* must have seemed an inevitable and perfect model.

Many of the Lucanic imitations are obvious and rather mechanical paraphrases of well-known passages of the *Pharsalia,* and one would guess that these paraphrases reflect Daniel's desire to gain for his epic some of the dignity and authority of his classical model rather than his genuine personal response to the Latin. Occasionally, though, Lucan's powerful writing kindled Daniel's imagination, with profitable results. One is glad, for example, that Lucan's "coniuret in arma / Mundus," with the list of sonorous, colorful names that follows, inspired two spacious and romantic lines in Daniel's first book:

Coniure the barbarous North, and let them call
Strange furie from farre distant shores vnknowne.

Again, the passages inspired by Lucan's portrayal of Pompey are among the finest in Daniel's poem. Nor can it be doubted that Daniel learned much from Lucan about the nature of civil strife and the downward spiral of moral debilitation that accompanies it. Such a passage as the final thirty-eight stanzas of Daniel's first book, timeless in the validity and importance of its insights into the pathology of disturbed states, could not have been written without attention to the *Pharsalia.*

Lucan's epigrammatic insights into the nature of politics and war stuck in Daniel's mind, and they come up, in English guise, throughout *The Civil Wars.* So also do Lucan's striking descriptions of combat, which were obviously valuable to the very unmartial Daniel. But as the poem moves beyond Richard and Bolingbroke and as Daniel's conception of his material becomes more complex—or more confused—the large-scale Lucanic imitations disappear almost entirely. There are long stretches of the poem in which Lucan is quite absent from Daniel's thoughts.

Daniel was, after all, increasingly a quiet and sober poet, conservative and mature. Lucan, who died at twenty-six, was an extraordinarily noisy and flamboyant writer. Viewed in some lights, it seems remarkable that Daniel should have thought to imitate Lucan at all. The fact that he did, and that some poetry resulted from the confluence, suggests both an unlooked-for dimension in the English poet and forgotten merit in the Roman.

Notes

1. *Elizabethan Critical Essays,* ed. G. Gregory Smith (Oxford, 1904), II, 316. Drayton's debt to Lucan is discussed by Anthony LaBranche, "Drayton's

The Barons Warres and the Rhetoric of Historical Poetry," *JEGP* [*Journal of English and Germanic Poetry*], LXII (1963), 82-95.

2. "Satire VI," *Skialetheia*, Shakespeare Association Facsimiles, No. 2 (Oxford, 1931).

3. *Remains Concerning Britain*, Library of Old Authors (London, 1870), p. 10. The phrase was picked up by Speed in his *History of Great Britain* (1611). The relevant passage is quoted in Samuel Daniel, *The Civil Wars*, ed. Laurence Michel (New Haven, 1958), p. 6. In the *Defence of Ryme* Daniel speaks admiringly of "my Homer-Lucan," but it is not clear what book or person he intends.

4. See Homer Nearing, *English Historical Poetry 1599-1641* (Philadelphia, 1945), p. 86.

5. T. M. Lindsay, "Englishmen and the Classical Renascence," *Cambridge History of English Literature*, III, 19-20.

6. For sample curricula, see Thomas W. Baldwin, *William Shakspere's Small Latine & Lesse Greeke* (Urbana, 1944), I, 338, 352, 357, 382, 387, 413, 457.

7. Sir John Sandys, *A History of Classical Scholarship*, 2nd ed. (Cambridge, 1908), II, 103. Sandys dates the first edition of Vergil "c. 1469."

8. Henrietta R. Palmer, *List of English Editions and Translations of Greek and Latin Classics Printed before 1641* (London, 1911), p. 69.

9. Carey H. Conley, *The First English Translators of the Classics* (New Haven, 1927), p. 20 and note.

10. Michel says only that "the kind of indebtedness Daniel lay in to Lucan is illustrated" by Daniel's first three stanzas (p. 7). It will be seen that the extended close paraphrase that Daniel produces in these stanzas is not at all typical of his use of Lucan.

11. I quote from Michel's edition of the text of 1609. In order to avoid impossible complexities I have based my comparisons on this revision throughout.

12. Citations are to Marcus Annaeus Lucanus, *The Civil War*, ed. J. D. Duff, Loeb Classical Library (London and Cambridge, Mass., 1928). Duff's text is based on A. E. Housman's standard edition (Oxford and Cambridge, Mass., 1926).

13. Revising with his usual economy, Daniel changed only the first half-line of the stanza: *1595* reads "O sacred Goddesse: I no Muse, but thee. . . ."

14. In between, there are a few smaller borrowings. One of Caesar's epigrams—"Arma tenenti / Omnia dat, qui iusta negat" (I.348-349)—is appropri-

ated by Daniel as a comment on the foolishness of Richard II's confiscation of Bolingbroke's inheritance: "to a man so strong, and of such might, / He giues him more, that takes away his right" (I.lxxvi. 7-8). Daniel's impressive passage on the causes of the war is modeled on a similar passage in Lucan's first book (*CW*, I.lxxx-lxxxi; *Phars.*, I.160-161, 173-177, 181-182). The episode in which Richard has Gloucester put to death without a trial may have been expanded from the colorless accounts in the chronicles with Lucan's Pothinus in mind. Cf. *CW*, I.xliii-li with Pothinus's speech recommending the assassination of Pompey (*Phars.*, VIII.482-535). Similarly, Nearing (p. 86) suggests that the debate between Richard's advisers in *CW*, II.xxviii-xlvii may be modeled on the debate in Pompey's camp whether to engage Caesar in battle at Pharsalia (VII.45-123; cf. also VIII.258-455).

15. *Shakespeare's History Plays* (London, 1944), p. 240.

16. In earlier editions of the poem the parallel was even closer. *1595* reads "rent-white" for "rented." In *1609* the Genius is described as "A faire and goodly woman"; the earlier version was "A naked goodly woman," perhaps suggested by Lucan's "nudis . . . lacertis."

17. Cornelia's behavior in *Phars.*, VIII.591-592 may have suggested another element of Daniel's picture of Isabel at the window, namely, her desire to look and fear to see. Daniel develops this pretty vacillation at length (stanzas 68, 72-73, 78).

Daniel's episode has close verbal connections with the corresponding scene of *Richard II* (V.i). The fact that Daniel's scene also contains Lucanic parallels that are absent from Shakespeare's version perhaps reinforces the view that Shakespeare borrowed from Daniel rather than the converse. Since the possibility of assigning a *terminus a quo* for the composition of *Richard II* depends upon the establishment of Shakespeare's indebtedness to Daniel, the matter is not trivial. I hope to deal with it in detail in another paper.

18. "Daniel wrott Civill Warres, and yett hath not one batle in all his book." "Conversations of Ben Jonson and William Drummond of Hawthornden 1619," *Critical Essays of the Seventeenth Century*, ed. J. E. Spingarn (Oxford, 1908), I, 213.

19. Lucan, of course, is speaking of the mass suicide by which Vulteius's troops conclude their resistance: "totum . . . in partibus unis / Bellorum fecere nefas" (IV.548-549).

20. A few stanzas farther on one finds another striking image derived from the *Pharsalia*. Describing the

first battle of St. Albans, Daniel ventures a bold hyperbole: "Which, slaughter, and no battaile, might be thought; / Sith that side vs'd their swords, and this their throat" (VI.cx.7-8). He is remembering Lucan's description of the rout of Pompey's forces: "Perdidit inde modum caedes, ac nulla secuta est / Pugna, sed hinc iugulis, hinc ferro bella geruntur" (VII.532-533).

In view of the Lucanic context, there may be some significance in the description of Talbot as superior to his fortune (VI.lxxviii.5-6). Cf. Lucan on Pompey (VII.682-686). The other epic simile in Daniel's passage may also have been suggested by Lucan. Cf. *CW,* VI.xcii with *Phars.,* II.454-460.

21. Cf., e.g., *Phars.,* I.8 ff., VII.95-96, and VI.262.

22. Cf. also *CW,* III.xlvii.8: "No hand of strife is pure, but that which wins." *CW,* VIII.xi may have been suggested by *Phars.,* V.321-334. In Daniel's battle, fallen arrows are gathered up and returned "like clowdes of steele; which powre / Destruction downe, and did new-night the sky" (VIII.xvi.2-3). The image is borrowed from Lucan's account of Pharsalia: "Ferro subtexitur aether, / Noxque super campos telis conserta pependit" (VII.519-520).

23. This passage cannot fail to remind the reader of *3H6,* II.v. But the scenes differ in many respects, and there is little beyond Shakespeare's "O that my death would stay these ruthful deeds!" (II.v.95) to suggest a close connection between them. On the other hand, Shakespeare, like Daniel, may have had Lucan in mind.

A few other Lucanic echoes are scattered through Daniel's poem. *CW,* II.xxxi.6-7—"it selfe when Greatnesse cannot beare, / With her owne waight, must needes confus'dly fall"—echoes Lucan on the collapse of the Republic (*Phars.,* I. 70-72; cf. also *CW,* VI.xliii-xliv). In Book IV, Hotspur asks: "What? haue we hands, and shall we seruile bee? / Why were swordes made? but, to preserue men free" (IV.xxxviii.7-8). Daniel appropriated the epigram from the *Pharsalia:* "Ignorantque datos, ne quisquam serviat, enses" (IV.579)). Daniel's lament that Hotspur's bravery, expended in an evil cause, can win no glory may have been imitated from Lucan's similar passage on Caesar's centurion Scaeva (*CW,* IV.lv; *Phars.,* VI.257-262). In fact, the notions that valor is a vice in civil war and that victory is only the worst misery in such a war pervade both *The Civil Wars* and the *Pharsalia.*

A few similes (in addition to those already mentioned) are modeled on Lucan. Gloucester stood as an isthmus between Henry VI and the Duke of York, just as Crassus did between Pompey and Caesar (*CW,* V.lxxxlx.3-8; *Phars.,* I.99-106). In Book VI, York's increase of strength is compared to the swelling of the Severn in its course to the sea (stanza 107): Lucan had compared Pompey, in his irresistible force, to the Po at flood stage (VI.272-278). Louis F. Ball, "The Background of the Minor English Renaissance Epics," *ELH* [*English Literary History*], I (1934), 84, says that the similes in *CW,* II.xi, xcix, III.iv, and VII.xcvii are "in part gathered from Lucan." *CW,* III.iv may owe something to *Phars.,* VI. 263-267, 272-278, and *CW,* VII.xcvii probably takes at least the adjective "Libyan" from *Phars.,* I.205-212. I wish Ball had been more specific about the others.

One may add here that Kenneth Muir, in his review of Michel's edition (*Shakespeare Quarterly,* X [1959], 443), has pointed out that Daniel's Latin note to *CW,* V.xxiii is misquoted from *Phars.,* IX.588-589.

24. See Joan Rees, *Samuel Daniel: A Critical and Biographical Study* (Liverpool, 1964), pp. 137 ff.

O. A. W. Dilke (essay date 1971)

SOURCE: Dilke, O. A. W. Introduction to *The Battle of Pharsalia: A Verse Translation of Lucan, Book VII,* translated by O. A. W. Dilke, pp. 225-33. Leeds, U. K.: Leeds Philosophical and Literary Society, 1971.

[*In the following essay, Dilke discusses how Lucan should be rendered in translation, the change he makes in tone from Book IV of* Pharsalia *onward, and the status of his reputation during the Middle Ages.*]

LUCAN AND HIS WORK

In translating ancient poetry, every age consciously or unconsciously reinterprets the original. Thus in the eighteenth century elegance was the keynote, and the rhyming couplet was used to render not only elegiac verse, for which it is fitted, but epic, for which it is not. Today's fashion is to translate ancient epic into modern conversational prose. The picturesque phrases of the *Iliad* are watered down to everyday expressions: Homer's stock question 'What is this word that has escaped the barriers of your teeth?' has become 'This is absurd' or 'What nonsense!'[1] In the case of the *Odyssey* there is much to commend this transformation, since the story is in itself so entertaining that in this form the Greekless reader, although he loses something, is given a version which he can race through and enjoy.

But such a translation of Lucan, which Robert Graves has given us,[2] cannot, though one is grateful to him for introducing the poet to a wider public, hope to reproduce more than a fraction of the spirit of the Latin. Original epic in English has not been switched from verse to prose, it has ceased to be written; as John Wain has observed, some of its work has been taken over by the novel, some by the cinema. Thus there is no advantage in translating epic into prose, and there may well be disadvantages. Lucan was rightly called by Quintilian more a pattern for orators than for poets; nevertheless, he has flashes of poetic inspiration. His work belongs to a well-recognized poetic genre, historical epic, the finest Latin specimen of which, rugged in its archaism, is perhaps Ennius' *Annals,* a poem on the early history of Rome surviving only in fragments.

As to the rhetorical tone which permeates the hexameters of Lucan's **Civil War,** this was the natural result of Roman upbringing.[3] Secondary education in Rome was based largely on oratorical declamation. This consisted of two types of exercise: *suasoriae,* advisory speeches (e.g. 'advise Cicero whether to buy his life from Antony by burning his books') and *controversiae,* speeches on one side or the other of an imaginary legal case, often of a melodramatic nature. The rhetorical tone can sometimes be reproduced in prose (though this has seldom been attained in Robert Graves's version), but it can be rendered even better in epic blank verse, the vehicle of Shakespeare's historical dramas. This does not mean that Lucan, no archaizer, should be translated into Shakespearian English: the effect is gained by the rhythm, not by obsolete wording. Historical epic and historical drama have much in common: in each the writer selects his material from the annals of history to suit his purpose, in each an important part is played by speeches, and each is bound from time to time to descend to the prosaic.

Marcus Annaeus Lucanus was born in Corduba (Córdova), Spain, in A.D. 89 of a literary family. Of his two grandfathers one was the elder Seneca, writer on rhetoric, the other was an orator of Corduba. His uncle the younger Seneca achieved fame as Stoic philosopher, millionaire, writer of tragedies not designed for the public stage, and as tutor to the young Nero and virtual prime minister until his retirement in A.D. 64. Lucan's parents took him to Rome as a baby, and he was educated there. We are told that he wrote poetry while still very young. He had the usual training in Greek and Latin literature and in rhetoric, and learnt to make speeches on both sides. The place of a university education was filled largely by the philosophic schools, and Lucan, whose family was of Stoic persuasion, sat at the feet of Lucius Annaeus Cornutus, a well-known Stoic philosopher.

He was nearly fifteen years old when Nero, two years his senior, became emperor. Nero too was a poet, and five years later collected round him a clique of young poets, of whom Lucan was one. Poetry was stimulated partly by a five-yearly festival instituted by Nero, which included poetic and rhetorical competitions (Lucan was successful in one of the former), and partly by the *recitationes,* readings of new literary works, which had been popular in Rome since Augustus' times. At these sessions the authors read extracts from their own works either to an invited group of to the public. We can well imagine that at first the young poet was keen to show Nero that he was grateful for this patronage of the arts.

We are told that at one of these *recitationes* Nero suddenly summoned a meeting of Senate and walked out, 'just to get a breath of fresh air'.[4] This was probably only one cause of offence in a quarrel which resulted in the emperor's forbidding Lucan to recite poetry or plead in the law-courts. Thwarted by this, in A.D. 65 the poet joined the conspiracy to assassinate Nero organized by Gaius Calpurnius Piso. When it failed he, like Piso, committed suicide by opening his veins. To him, as a Stoic, submission to an emperor who took away his freedom of speech seemed no better than being a slave. Suicide in the tradition of Cato of Utica was held by Stoics to be an honourable way out in the last resort. He was only 25 years old at his death, and had completed only 9½ books of his historical epic, **Bellum Civile** or **De Bello Civili, The Civil War.** The old title, **Pharsalia,** seems to have arisen out of a misunderstanding of 9.985-6 *Pharsalia nostra vivet,* which, addressed to Caesar, means 'the battle of Pharsalia, fought by you and sung of by me, shall live on'.

It must be admitted that the work is not uniformly good. After the death of Virgil, Horace and Ovid no great poets emerged, and it was clearly felt by some that a vacuum had been left which could not be filled. With the development of a more rhetorical and epigrammatic style, which we call Silver Latin, the tragedies of Seneca and the epic of Lucan represent a reaction against the sublimity and perfection of Virgil. In his language Lucan aims at being forceful and epigrammatic rather than smooth and beautiful. Historical accuracy is sacrificed, if he thinks it necessary, to dramatic effect; for example, Cicero is made to be present and deliver a speech on the plain of Pharsalia, whereas we knew he was in Epirus at the time. Moreover Lucan was still, at his death, immature as a poet: he piles up horror and exaggeration; he is childishly irreverent; he introduces lengthy, learned excursuses; he has no conception of impartiality, at least from the fourth book onwards[5]. Almost all that Pompey does is excused, almost all actions of Caesar blamed, cursed or derided.

Against these defects there is much to be said in praise of Lucan. Quintilian rightly calls him 'fiery and galloping'. The listener or reader is swept along from one impassioned episode to another. The selection of episodes is on the whole judicious: humdrum history is skirted over. The rhetoric, even if unnatural to the Anglo-Saxon temperament, is at times superb, with fine epigrammatic touches (*sententiae*), while poetic passages, where they are not overlaid by too much rhetoric, are striking. Martial (14.194) puts this epigram into the mouth of Lucan:

> Some say I write no poetry;
> My publisher does not agree.[6]

Lucan is an angry young man. Throughout the poem he is infuriated at the horror and futility of civil war, which must still have seemed very real, and after a while he is angry at Nero and the whole imperial régime too. For him Pompey and Cato, the Republicans, while they are not exactly heroes of the epic, stand for freedom—freedom of thought, of the pen, of the person, of political action. When the translator was in South Africa for two years, as Professor of Classics at Rhodes University, he was struck by the parallels between that country, which still remembers well the Anglo-Boer War and its effects, and the Rome of Lucan's day.[7] It is this idealism of Lucan's that lifts the poem above a soured complaint or a prosaic work of propaganda. And despite his reaction against Virgil he has frequent echoes of the *Aeneid*.[8]

There is no doubt that the chief source of the *Civil War* was a part of Livy's history which is now lost apart from short summaries. A typical incident which we know came from Livy is that of the augur Cornelius, 7.192 ff. Tacitus tells us that Livy praised Pompey so highly that Augustus called him a Pompeian, and this accords well with Lucan's attitude. There is no sign of his having followed Caesar's *Civil War*. Lucan is often unreliable on historical and geographical points; examples of this are given in the notes. he used freely the prose works and tragedies of his uncle Seneca.

The present writer believes, with Boissier[9] and others, that there is a marked difference of approach from Book IV onwards. The opening of Book I, as has been seen, has an extravagant panegyric on Nero. True, in ll. 669-72 the Neo-Pythagorean Nigidius Figulus prophesies that civil war will last many years, and that when it ends Rome will be controlled by an overlord (*dominus*); only till then will she be free. But this is only an isolated and comparatively mild expression of the Republicanism and love of freedom natural to one brought up as a Stoic. There are, on the other hand, virulent attacks on the Principate from the second half of Book IV onwards. In 4.692 is the first reference to Rome's becoming a *regnum*, kingdom. Ever since the expulsion of the Tarquins, the name of *rex* had been hated in Rome, and Julius Caesar had not dared to call

himself king. In 4.822 Lucan complains that Sulla, Marius, Cinna and all the line of Caesars have secured the right to use the sword against Romans. This type of protest will be seen in several passages of Books VII and VIII. It is only surprising that Domitius, an ancestor of Nero's, is made to die a heroic death; but no doubt the poet wished to preserve the character of this obstinate fighter as he had drawn it in Book II.

Lucan's attitude towards the gods and fate[10] marks a new development. Virgil, following Homer and others, had incorporated into the *Aeneid* individual gods and goddesses fighting or intriguing with one side or the other. There were two reasons why such divine interference, customary as it had become, would not work well in Lucan's epic. One was that he was dealing with events which took place only 110 years before, so that the introduction of divine machinery would have seemed absurd. The other was that Lucan as a Stoic did not believe in anthropomorphic gods. The Stoics acknowledged some underlying force in the universe, which they variously called Zeus (Jupiter), Universal or Eternal Law (7.1), Nature, Providence or Destiny. In the *Civil War* this underlying force may appear as 'the gods', Fortune, fate or the fates. The chief difference in Lucan between Fortune and fate is that the former, who in fact as a goddess had a widespread cult, represents a greater degree of personification.

THE BATTLE

With the aid of Caesar's *Civil War*, Appian and other authorities we are able to reconstruct the forces and tactics of the two sides, though the siting of the battle is disputed.[11] The battle of Pharsalia was fought in summer 48 B.C., some distance from the town of Pharsalus (Farsala).

Both sides had received reinforcements from Macedonia, but Pompey's forces far outnumbered Caesar's. Pompey had about 47,500 legionaries and 2,000 veterans of the reserve, 7,000 cavalry and a countless horde of auxiliary forces, mostly from Asia Minor and Syria. Caesar had about 22,500 legionaries and 1,000 cavalry, but his forces were far more experienced than Pompey's. The two sides took up positions 6 km. apart, and only skirmishes ensued for some days. But the Pompeians kept clamouring for battle, and Pompey reluctantly agreed, trusting in his superior cavalry to rout the enemy quickly. Since Pompey did not at first advance beyond a suitable position in the plain, Caesar decided to move camp repeatedly, and was about to start this new plan when Pompey's army began advancing. The order of battle was somewhat as follows (ancient authorities differ):

CAESAR'S ARMY

Cavalry, light-armed troops	Sulla, Caesar	Domitius	Antony	S
		Calvinus		T
				R
Over 6,000 cavalry, light-armed troops	Pompey	Scipio	Lentulus	E
				A
		some cavalry		M

POMPEY'S ARMY

The battle started when Gaius Crastinus, an ex-centurion, dashed forward from Caesar's right wing. When the legionaries had closed, Pompey ordered his left-wing cavalry, over 6,000 in all, supported by slingers and archers, to charge Caesar's cavalry. These fell back, but Caesar then gave the signal to a 'fourth line', detached from the third line of each of his legions and posted facing the flank, to charge Pompey's cavalry with weapons aimed at their faces. This resulted in the Pompeian cavalry fleeing to the hills in panic. For a fair time Pompey's legionaries stood their ground well. But then Caesar's 'fourth line' went on to attack the left wing of Pompey's army in the rear. When Caesar's third line also attacked, the Pompeians fled to their camp. This too was attacked, and while most of the survivors made for the hills, Pompey galloped off to Larissa.

After a meal at the camp, which they found full of every kind of luxury, Caesar's troops were divided. Four legions pursued the Pompeians for six miles, besieged them on a mountain and cut them off from water. By the following morning they had surrendered. As many as 30 centurions but only 200 other ranks fell on Caesar's side. The Pompeians lost 15,000 men according to Caesar, 6,000 according to Pollio; over 24,000 surrendered, and others escaped.

The battle of Pharsalia must be reckoned among the most decisive in all Roman history. Although the losses of the losers were high, it was not the number of killed that made it decisive. Pharsalia effectively marks the end of senatorial rule and of Pompey's prestige. Up to now, whoever the important politicians had been, the Senate, or a ruling clique of it, had held a varying degree of power. From now on to his assassination Caesar alone was to hold it, and from the battle of Actium (31 B.C.) up to Lucan's time a succession of emperors related to Caesar or closely tied by marriage to the imperial house.

LUCAN UNDER THE EMPIRE AND IN THE MIDDLE AGES

The poet Statius was a friend of Lucan's widow and writes an anniversary poem (*Silvae*, ii. 7) in his honour. Quintilian says the poem is fiery and goes with a swing, but thinks it is more to be imitated by orators than by poets. Martial defends Lucan against those who consider him no poet. In the fourth and fifth centuries and in the Middle Ages and Renaissance the **Civil War** was well-known and imitated. Servius has a number of quotations from Lucan in his commentary on Virgil. Claudian borrows from him both in his court poetry and in the *De Raptu Proserpinae*. St Augustine has occasional reminiscences, while Dracontius and Corippus borrow extensively from him.

In the Middle Ages, manuscripts of Lucan multiplied, and quotations or reminiscences have been observed in over sixty authors.[12] He tended to be regarded as a historian, and the Gonville and Caius College manuscript actually says of him *historiam composuit et non poema*.[13] But in at least one respect there is a distinct shift of emphasis. Caesar, of whom Lucan gives us an increasingly hostile picture, is glorified in the Middle Ages: in Chapter 4 of *Li hystoire de Julius Cesar*, which claims to be based on the ten books of Lucan, we read of the 'gentillece, ki en son cor estoit'. This transformed picture of Caesar caused Alexander Neckam to praise Lucan for showing how much destruction Pompey's *invidia* of his father-in-law had brought upon the world.

Lucan came to be studied in schools, together with Virgil, Horace and Ovid, as a master of Latin style. The lengthy twelfth-century commentary by Arnulfus[14] shows some knowledge of rhetoric combined with abysmal ignorance of Roman history and institutions; for example, Arnulfus did not even know that Roman legions were numbered. We possess fragments of a manuscript of Lucan dating from the fourth or fifth century; our earliest manuscript of the whole poem dates from the ninth century.

Chaucer (*House of Fame*, ll. 1497 ff.) depicts him on an iron pillar, carrying on his shoulders the fame of Caesar and Pompey. Dante calls him *admirabilis* and 'quello grande poeta'. In *Inferno* 4.88 ff. he makes Virgil point out four other outstanding poets of antiquity, Homer, 'poeta sovrano', Horace, described as the satirist, Ovid and Lucan. Among the passages which influenced Dante was that in the ninth book of the **De Bello Civili** in which gruesome descriptions are given of the fate of men bitten by North African snakes.

ENGLISH ADAPTERS AND TRANSLATORS OF LUCAN[15]

It was, appropriately enough, in his native Spain that Lucan was first translated, as far as we can tell. This earliest extant translation, a prose rendering of the whole of the poem, was published probably in Madrid about 1530 by M. Lasso de Oropesa. Its title is **La Historia que escrivìò en Latin el Poeta Lucano**; here we have echoes of the earlier idea that Lucan was a historian.

The original of the poem was well known in England in Elizabethan times, but no translation of it in English was published until 1600, and then of one book only. Thomas Hughes has been called 'Lucan's first translator',[16] but it would be more correct to call him an adapter. It was in the thirtieth year of Queen Elizabeth's reign that the members of Grey's Inn put on at her court in Greenwich 'certaine deuises and shewes'. Among these was a tragedy called *The Misfortunes of Arthur,* by Hughes, which was published in 1587. It was based on the Arthur legends, but drew heavily, particularly in the battle scenes, on Lucan and to a lesser extent on Seneca's tragedies. Some of Hughes's adaptations from Lucan are mentioned by the present writer in *Notes and Queries,* 208 (1963), 93-4, and they have more recently been investigated by G. M. Logan.[17]

In 1595 Samuel Daniel published the first four books of his *Civile Wars between the two Houses of Lancaster and Yorke*; another four followed, and the poem was revised but never completed. Daniel is sometimes called 'the English Lucan', and indeed the first three stanzas of his first book are closely modelled on the opening of Book I of Lucan. The first two imitate Lucan's opening lines:

> (1) I Sing the ciuill Warres, tumultuous Broyles,
> And Bloody factions of a mightie land:
> Whose people hautie, proud with foraine spoyles,
> Vpon themselves turn-back their conquering hand;
> Whil'st kin their kin, Brother the Brother foyles;
> Like Ensignes all against like Ensignes band,
> Bowes against Bowes, the Crowne against the Crowne;
> Whil'st all pretending right, all right's throwne downe.

> (2) What furie, ô what madnes held thee so,
> Deare *England* (too too prodigall of blood)
> To waste so much, and warre without a foe,
> Whil'st *France,* to see thy spoyles, at pleasure stood!
> How much might'st thou have purchast with lesse woe,
> T' haue done thee honour and thy people good?
> Thine might haue beene what-euer lies betweene
> The *Alps* and vs, the *Pyrenei* and *Rhene.*

In the third stanza Daniel acclaims the Queen in an adaptation of the lines (1. 33 f.) in which Lucan acclaims Nero:

> (3) Yet now what reason haue we to complaine?
> Since hereby came the calme we did inioy;

> The blisse of thee *Eliza*; happie gaine
> For all our losse; when-as no other way
> The heauens could finde, but to vnite againe
> The fatall sev'red Families, that they
> Might bring foorth thee; that on thy peace might growe
> That glorie, which few Times could euer showe.

The first English translation of Lucan was made by a famous poet. In 1600 Christopher Marlowe published **Lucans first Booke, translated line for line,** which had been entered on the Stationers' Registers in 1593. The dedication was signed by Thomas Thorpe, publisher of Shakespeare's *Sonnets*. This is a mature work of Marlowe's, in epic blank verse, but suffers from undue condensation in parts, since it attempts the difficult task of keeping to the original number of lines. The opening verses are:

> Wars worse then civill on *Thessalian* playnes,
> And outrage strangling law & people strong,
> We sing, whose conquering swords their own breasts launcht,
> Armies alied, the kingdoms league vprooted,
> Th' affrighted worlds force bent on publique spoile,
> Thrumpets, and drums like deadly threatning other,
> Eagles alike displaide, darts answering darts.

As the present translation will show, it is not always easy to preserve the entire sense while keeping to the metre. But Marlowe, as well as condensing, admits much looseness of expression in places. This can be illustrated from ll.10-11, *cumque superba foret Babylon spolianda tropaeis Ausoniis,* literally 'and when haughty Babylon (i.e. Parthia) should have been despoiled of Italian trophies', which becomes 'Now Babylon, proud through our spoil, should stoop'.

The first English translation of the whole of Lucan was by Sir Arthur Gorges, whose mother was cousin to Sir Walter Raleigh. It was a verse translation, published in 1614. The opening lines are:

> A More than ciuill warre I sing,
> That through th' *Emathian* fields did ring,
> Where reins let loose to headstrong pride,
> A potent people did misguide:
> Whose conquering hand enrag'd rebounds
> On his owne bowels with deep wounds.
> When Hosts confronting neare alies,
> All faith and Empires Lawes defies.
> A world of force in faction meetes,
> And common guilt like torrents fleets.

Of the next translation, also in verse, by Thomas May, the first three books appeared in 1626 and the whole in 1627. His opening lines are:

> Warres more than ciuill on Æmathian plaines
> We sing; rage licensd; where great Rome distaines

In her owne bowels her victorious swords;
Where kindred hoasts encounter, all accords
Of Empire broke: where arm'd to impious warre
The strength of all the shaken world from farre
Is met; knowne Ensignes Ensignes do defie,
Piles against Piles, 'gainst Eagles Eagles fly.

Not content with this translation, May wrote a supplement to Lucan in seven books in both Latin and English, bringing the epic down to the death of Caesar.[18] He was permitted to dedicate this supplement to Charles I, so that an epigram on him ran:

Thou son of Mercury, whose fluent tongue
Made Lucan finish his Pharsalian song,
Thy fame is equal, better is thy fate,
Thou hast got Charles his love, he Nero's hate.

'Son of Mercury' must be a pun on May's name (*Maius* in Latin), since Mercury (Hermes) was son of Main. In 1629 selections from Lucan were translated by Sir John Beaumont.

Nicholas Rowe, poet laureate, civil servant and editor of Shakespeare, published in 1710 a translation, in rhyming couplets, of Book IX, which was included in 'Tonson's *Miscellanies*'. Immediately after his death in 1718 his translation of the whole of Lucan appeared, and the following year it was reprinted with a life of the translator and some literary criticism by J. Welwood. These are Rowe's opening lines:

Emathian Plains with Slaughter cover'd o'er,
And Rage unknown to Civil Wars before,
Establish'd Violence, and lawless Might,
Avow'd and hallow'd by the name of Right;
A Race Renown'd, the world's victorious Lords,
Turn'd on themselves with their own hostile Swords;
Piles against Piles oppos'd in impious Fight,
And Eagles against Eagles bending Flight:
Of Blood by Friends, by Kindred, Parents, spilt,
One common Horror and promiscuous Guilt,
A shatter'd World in wild Disorder tost,
Leagues, Laws, and Empire in Confusion lost;
Of all the woes which Civil Discords bring,
And *Rome* o'ercome by *Roman* Arms, I sing.

As will be seen, he expands his translation into an unduly large number of lines, so that Book I, which in Lucan has 695 lines, has 1170 in Rowe, and the longest book, IX, which in Lucan has 1108 lines, reaches 1857 lines in Rowe. He is also at times inaccurate: thus 1. 10 f., quoted above . . . , becomes:

While *Babylon*'s proud Spires yet rise so high,
And rich in *Roman* Spoils invade the sky.

All these are verse translations of Lucan. All aim, with more or less success, at capturing something of the rhetorical quality of the verse which Quintilian defined as *ardens et concitatus*. The modern love of prose translations has caused our poet to be regarded, in the eyes of the general reader, as a flat and prosaic writer. If this defect must be admitted of parts, it is far from true of the whole.

Notes

1. Homer, *Iliad* and *Odyssey,* translated by E. V. Rieu (Penguin, 1950, 1945).

2. Lucan, *Pharsalia: Dramatic Episodes of the Civil Wars* (Penguin, 1956).

3. M. P. O. Morford, *The Poet Lucan* (Oxford, 1967); M. L. Clarke, *Rhetoric at Rome* (London, 1953), and *Higher Education in the Ancient World* (London, 1971); S. F. Bonner, 'Lucan and the Declamation Schools', *Am J Philol.* [*American Journal of Philology*] 87 (1966), 257-96; W. Rutz, 'Lucan und die Rhetorik', Fondation Hardt, *Entretiens* 15 (Geneva, 1968), 235-65.

4. *Life of Lucan* attributed to Suetonius. Literally 'to cool himself off'; not necessarily 'with the sole object of ruining the performance' (Robert Graves). The prevailing view of the introduction to the epic (I. 1-66), with its instant deification of Nero, is that it is to be taken at its face value, as a typical specimen of Silver Latin flattery of the great; so, for example, P. Grimal, 'L'éloge de Néron au début de la Pharsale est-il ironique?', *Revue des Etudes Latines,* 38 (1960), 296-305.

5. In a chapter by the present translator entitled 'Lucan's Political Views and the Caesars', which will appear in the series *Studies in Latin Literature and its Influence,* ed. D. R. Dudley, it is argued that in the earlier part of his work Lucan does make some attempt at impartiality.

6. *Bibliopola* (*bybliopola*) is 'bookseller'; these acted also as publishers.

7. O. A. W. Dilke, *Lucan, Poet of Freedom* (inaugural lecture, Grahamstown, 1961).

8. Id. 'Virgil and Lucan', *Proc. Virgil Soc.* 8 (1968-9), 1-12: M. von Albrecht, 'Der Dichter Lucan und die epische Tradition', Fondation Hardt, *Entritiens* 15 (1968, publ. 1970), 269-308.

9. G. Boissier, *L' oppositions sous les Cesars* 3rd edn, Paris, 1892), pp. 272 ff. For a contrary view see Jacqueline Brisset, *Les idees politiques de Lucain* (Paris, 1964), pp. 176 ff.; the reference to a comet in l. 529, which she quotes as hostile to Nero, seems purely general.

10. B. F. Dick, 'Fatum and Fortuna in Lucan's *Bellum Civile*', *Class. Philol.,* 62 (1967), 235-42, and 'Lucain et la religion'. Fondation Hardt (n. 3), 161-95.

11. Lucan VII, revised from the edition of J. P. Postgate by O. A. W. Dilke (Cambridge, 1960), pp. 41-50.

12. M. Manitius, *Geschichle der lateinischen Literatur des Mittelalters* (Mullers Handbuch ix.ii.3), index Epic[3], *Mod. Lang. Rev.* 25 (1930), 32-51; Eva M. Sanford, 'Quotations from Lucan in Medieval Latin Authors', *Am. J. Philol.* 55 (1934), 1-19.

13. C. H. Haskins, *Studies in the History of Mediaeval Science* (Cambridge, Mass., 2nd edn, 1927), p. 372.

14. Arnulfi Aurelianensis *Glosule super Lucanum,* ed. Berthe M. Marti (American Academy in Rome, 1958).

15. A chapter by the present translator entitled 'Lucan and English Literature' will appear in 1972 in the series *Studies in Latin Literature and its Influence,* ed. D. R. Dudley.

16. J. C. Maxwell in *Notes & Queries* 192 (1947), 521-2.

17. *Rev. Engl. Stud.* n.s. 20 (1969), 22-32, with reference to earlier work on the subject.

18. The order of composition was (a) 50 lines of Latin, to 'complete' Book X; (b) a seven-book supplement in English; (c) a seven-book supplement in Latin, revised from the English version. See R. T. Bruere, 'The Latin and English Versions of Thomas May's *Supplementum Lucani*', *CPh* xliv (1949), 145-63.

Bibliography

EDITIONS AND MODERN TRANSLATIONS

Lucan, ed. A. E. Housman, Oxford, 1926 and reprinted.

Lucan, tr. J. D. Duff (Loeb translation), London, 1943.

Lucan, ed. C. E. Haskins, with introduction by W. E. Heitland, and notes, London, 1887. (Text out of date.)

Lucan, ed. A. Bourgery and M. Ponchont (Budé), 2 vols, Paris, 1926-9.

Lucan, tr. Robert Graves (Penguin), London, 1956.

Lucan I, ed. P. Lejay, Paris, 1894.

Lucan I, ed. R. J. Getty, Cambridge, 1940 and reprinted.

Lucan I, ed. P. Wuilleumier and H. le Bonniec, Paris, 1962.

Lucan VII, ed. J. P. Postgate, revised by O. A. W. Dilke, Cambridge, 1960 and reprinted.

Lucan VIII, ed. J. P. Postgate, Cambridge, 1917.

EARLY ADAPTATIONS AND TRANSLATIONS

Early English Tragedies, ed. J. W. Cunliffe, Oxford, 1912.

Samuel Daniel, *The Civil Wars,* ed. L. Michel, Yale University Press, 1958.

Christopher Marlowe, *Lucans first Booke translated line for line.* In Marlowe's poems, ed. L. C. Martin, London, 1931.

Sir Arthur Gorges, *Lucan's Pharsalia. Translated into English. Whereunto is annexed the life of the Authour.* 1614.

T[homas] M[ay], *Lucan's Pharsalia,* 1626 (Books I-III), 1627 (complete), 1631, 1635, 1650, 1659.

Nicholas Rowe, *Pharsalia,* 1718; 2 vols 1720, 1722, 1753.

P. F. Widdows (essay date 1988)

SOURCE: Widdows, P. F. Introduction to *Lucan's* Civil War, translated by P. F. Widdows, pp. xi-xxv. Bloomington: Indiana University Press, 1988.

[*In the following excerpt, Widdows weighs Lucan's reputation, analyzes the unity of the* Pharsalia, *and presents a general assessment of the work.*]

LIFE

Our knowledge of the life of Marcus Annæus Lucanus—known variously in the modern vernacular as Lucan, Lucain, and Lucano—is derived principally from two short "lives" prefixed to medieval manuscripts of his poem, one attributed to Suetonius (c. A.D. 70-160), and the other to a grammarian named Vacca, who is thought to have lived in the sixth century, but who derived his material from a much earlier source, Lucan came from a distinguished family of Spanish Romans living in Corduba. His father, M. Annæus Mela, a wealthy knight and businessman, had two brothers, the philosopher Seneca, and Lucius Annæus Junius Gallio, proconsul of the Roman province of Achæa (i.e., Greece) in the days of St. Paul's missionary journeys.[1] His mother, Acilia, came from a talented family, also. Her father was Acilius Lucanus (hence Lucan's name), a well-known lawyer and writer.

Lucan was born in A.D. 39 in Corduba and was taken to Rome in his first year to be brought up and educated. He went through the traditional education of the Roman upper classes, first studying with a grammarian; then with a rhetorician, under whose tutelage he became a star in the art of declamation (see below); and finally with the Stoic philosopher Cornutus. Thus the two chief talents of his family, rhetoric and philosophy, especially Stoic philosophy, were further reinforced by his education. Lucan also acquired in his short life an encyclopedic knowledge (some of it inaccurate, but that was not his fault) of a remarkably wide range of other subjects, including geography, ethnology, astronomy, astrology, mythology, history, and politics.

In about the year A.D. 60 Lucan attracted the attention of Nero (two years younger than Lucan), who appointed him *quæstor* (the first step in a political career at Rome) before the statutory age of twenty-five, and then made him a member of the College of Augurs, a position of great prestige from which he derived his detailed knowledge of the pseudo-science of augury. At the same time he was active on the literary scene, producing, according to Vacca, a poem on Troy, a Saturnalia, a Catachthonion (Descent to the Underworld), an unfinished tragedy on the myth of Medea, fourteen dramatic ballets, some epigrams, a speech in prose against one Octavius Sagitta and another in his defense, a speech (?) on the burning of the city, and letters from Campania—none of which have survived. Of his **Civil War** we have nine complete books and half of the tenth, although he published only three books in his lifetime.

In the same year that he was made *quæstor,* Lucan won the prize in a public contest of poetry at the Neronian Games, for a poem in praise of Nero. There is no knowing what resentment was building up in Nero's jealous and suspicious mind, but relations seem to have continued to be outwardly friendly until 64, the year in which Nero broke up a poetry recital by Lucan and forbade him to publish poetry or practice in the law courts.

In the end Nero's extravagance and eccentricity led, in A.D. 65, to the formation of a conspiracy under a senator named Caius Calpurnius Piso. Many of the leading senators and knights joined it, including Lucan. Their purpose was to assassinate Nero and replace him with Piso. Two days before the planned assassination, the conspiracy was betrayed, and all the participants were either executed or ordered to kill themselves. Lucan, one of the last to be given the order, opened his veins, reciting as he died, according to Tacitus, some lines that he had written about a soldier who had suffered a similar fate.

LUCAN, NERO, AND *THE CIVIL WAR*

The relationship between Lucan, his epic poem, and Nero is a complicated one, and little is certain beyond the facts that Lucan recited and published three books of **The Civil War** while he was a friend and fellow poet of Nero; that he quarrelled with Nero and was forbidden to publish any more; and that he joined the conspiracy of Piso and was among those ordered to commit suicide when it was detected.

It would be neat and convenient to be able to say that the first three books were favorable to Nero and free from strong libertarian sentiments, and that the remaining seven were strongly libertarian and republican and openly offensive to the emperor. Unfortunately, there is no such clear division. For example, one of the strongest expressions of libertarian sentiment is in Book 1, the paradoxical wish expressed by Nigidius Figulus at the end of his prophecy (lines 669/739-672/743). [Here and elsewhere such double notation indicates the numbers of the original Latin lines and those of the translation.] And, contrariwise, in Book 7 Lucan goes out of his way to give Nero's ancestor L. Domitius a heroic death at the battle of Pharsalia (lines 599/656-616/675), when he must have known, as we know from Cæsar's account, that Domitius escaped from the battle and was overtaken and killed by Cæsar's cavalry. The only apparent reason for this distortion is the desire to please Nero.

In any case, the writing and partial publication of **The Civil War** came late in Lucan's short life, probably in the last three or four years of it; and it is disconcerting to realize that he remained on good terms with Nero long after most men of goodwill had become disgusted with the emperor's behavior. Certainly, Nero's reign started well. In his first speech to the senators, in A.D. 54, Nero promised to share power with them and to exercise generosity and clemency; and it seems that in the first five years, with the excellent Burrus as commander of the prætorian guard, Seneca to advise him, and his mother, Agrippina, as a controlling influence on his personal behavior, he did carry out that policy.

It is generally agreed that the turning point in his reign was the murder of Agrippina in A.D. 59, after which Nero became increasingly capricious and uncontrolled. Seneca continued his efforts to influence him for another three years, until he retired from public life in 62; and Lucan seems to have remained in favor until the ban on publication in 64. This suggests that Lucan's quarrel with Nero was artistic rather than political, although by 64 personal differences would have been aggravated by the suspicion, widely held, that Nero himself had started the Great Fire of Rome in that year. It must be remembered that Nero was not only unbelievably vain but also genuinely proud of his artistic ability, especially as a poet, and that he considered Lucan a serious rival. How, in the circumstances of 64 and 65, Lucan can have expected to publish a poem that, whatever the conditions under which it was written, breathes Stoic fervor and hatred of tyranny from almost every page, is a mystery. Perhaps, at least from the year 64 onward, he did not. Perhaps he was writing with a view to a future when everything would be different, when the struggle between Liberty and a Cæsar would be over, and when freedom would once more exist.

REPUTATION

It is unlikely today that the average reader, if asked to name the greatest poets of Rome, would reply with Virgil, Horace, Ovid, and Lucan. Yet from the Middle Ages to the early part of the nineteenth century the inclusion of Lucan in the list would have occasioned no surprise. Even so, right from the beginning there has been something equivocal about his reputation. Martial, his compatriot, coeval, and friend, represents Lucan in an epigram as saying:

> Sunt quidam qui me dicunt non esse poetam:
> Sed qui me vendit bibliopola putat.

> (There are some people around who deny that I am a poet:
> Not so my publisher; he sells me and thinks that I am.)

The basis of criticism by his contemporaries was that Lucan was not like Virgil. Like most artists who react against the influence of a towering figure from the recent past, he went too far, from the strictly classical point of view, in the opposite direction. His reaction against Virgil (with whose work he was well acquainted) took two salient forms: abandonment of a notable feature traditional to epic poetry since Homer, namely, the intervention of the gods in the affairs of mortals; and the retention of certain features, for example, storms at sea and single combat between heroes, but in a wildly exaggerated form, as if to out-Virgil Virgil.

A little later, Quintilian, another Spaniard, prominent in Rome as a teacher and practitioner of rhetoric, continued the note of uncertainty in the thumbnail sketch of Lucan as a poet which is perhaps the best-known description of his special qualities:

> Lucanus ardens et concitatus et sententiis clarissimus, et, ut dicam quod sentio, magis oratoribus quam poetis imitandus.

> (Lucan is full of passion and energy and remarkable for his *sententiæ,* and, to give my honest opinion, more suitable as a model for orators than for poets.)

Nevertheless, Lucan's reputation was firmly established by the time of Tacitus, who, in the mouth of a character in a dialogue, ranked him with Horace and Virgil.[2] His popularity continued through the Middle Ages, as is attested by the number of manuscripts of the **Bellum Civile,**[3] the constant quotation from him by other authors, and his presence in the *florilegia,* or anthologies, compiled for purposes of quotation by speakers and writers. It continued through the Renaissance, whose scholars set to work compiling manuscripts and editing the **Bellum Civile.**

It was, as mentioned above, in the early part of the nineteenth century that Lucan's reputation began to decline, at least in England and Germany—less so in France, where people are more tolerant of rhetoric. In England, the spirit of Victorianism that disparaged Lucan was the same as the spirit that disparaged the poetry of Pope. Poetry to the Victorians had to be "poetic" in their limited sense of the term, with a strong emphasis on melancholy, sentiment, and moral purpose; whereas the qualities that immediately strike the reader in Lucan are energy, passion, indignation, cleverness, and wit. He was indeed a "rhetorical" poet, but not in the sense that is usually understood by the term today. This requires some explanation.

RHETORIC

It is impossible to understand the special flavor of Lucan's manner of writing without some consideration of its source, namely, the practice of declamation, which was the stage to which rhetoric had been reduced. Declamation had already existed in the time of Cicero, and he practiced it, but only as an amusement. To him oratory was the great glory of man. It comprehended knowledge of history, philosophy, literature, and language, all enrolled in the cause of persuasion, and persuasion in defense of justice and truth. By those exalted standards declamation was a sorry thing, no more than an intellectual game.

Declamation was, nevertheless, the main part of rhetorical education in the age of Nero. Its teachers taught it in school and practiced it in performance. "Performance" is the *mot juste.* It took place in public and had its experts and its stars. It took two specific forms, the *Suasoria* and the *Controversia.*

The *Suasoria* is easily described. The student or performer chose a theme and spoke persuasively for or against it. Naturally after a time the supply of themes ran out, and it became a stereotyped exercise on a limited number of well-worn subjects. Juvenal, in a characteristically oblique and memorable way of expressing the fact that he had had a conventional education, phrases it as follows:

> Et nos ergo manum ferulae subduximus, et nos
> Consilium dedimus Sullæ, privatus ut altum
> Dormiret.

> (Well, I too have withdrawn my hand from the cane of the tutor,

I too have given advice to Sulla to lay down the reins
of
Power, and slumber away in peace as a private
person.)

Typical *Suasoriæ,* as recorded by Seneca the Elder and
Quintilian, are:

"Cicero deliberates whether to ask pardon from Antony."

"Alexander, having reached India, deliberates whether
to set sail across the Ocean."

"Agamemnon deliberates whether to sacrifice Iphige-
neia."

"Antony promises to spare Cicero's life if he burns his
writings. Cicero deliberates whether to do so."

Lucan was a star at these student exercises, and clear
signs of his education can be seen in the *Civil War.* For
example:

Curio persuades Cæsar to cross the Rubicon and seize
sole power (Book 1, lines 273-291).

On the morning of Pharsalia Cicero urges the hesitant
Pompey to engage in battle against Cæsar (Book 7,
lines 67-85).

At a council of war in Cilicia, the senator Lentulus
persuades the defeated Pompey to take refuge in Egypt
rather than, as he intended, in Parthia (Book 8, lines
331-453).

In Egypt, the councillor Pothinus persuades King
Ptolemy to murder Pompey (Book 8, lines 484-535).

The other and more difficult type of declamation was
the *Controversia.* It was based on a law, sometimes
real, sometimes imaginary, and a legal case was
constructed in relation to it, in which the students took
opposing sides. To develop nimbleness of wit they
would sometimes take one side, sometimes the other.
One example will suffice to give an idea of what was
involved:

The Brave Man Who Had Lost His Hands (Seneca,
Controversiæ, i, 4)

The law: Whoever catches an adulterer with his wife,
so long as he kills them both, may not be prosecuted.
A son, also, may punish adultery by his mother.

The case: A brave man has lost his hands in a war. He
caught an adulterer with his wife, by whom he had a
grown-up son. He ordered the son to kill the guilty
pair. The son refused: the adulterer escaped. The man
disinherited his son.

In this preposterous situation passionate speeches were
made on both sides, marked by ingenious *colores* and
startling *sententiæ* (see below), the cleverer and more
unexpected the better.

In the framing of such arguments there were two main
techniques: *colores* and *sententiæ. Color* was the technical term for the line of argument, the approach, the
interpretation of the facts, whether for or against,
depending on the side of the speaker. The reader of the
Bellum Civile will find widespread use of this technique,
sometimes with alternate *colores* piled on top of one
another. They are not always in support of or against an
argument, but are possible explanations or interpretations of an event or state of affairs. An example of the
latter is the series of explanations for the source and
behavior of the Nile in Book 10. In Book 1, the
introduction to the controversial passage in praise of
Nero (lines 33-45) is a typical *color.* Having graphically
described the disastrous results to Italy of the civil war,
and having considered other, more useful, ways in
which the blood of Romans could have been shed, Lucan retracts and says that if this suffering was the necessary price to pay for the advent of Nero as ruler, then it
was well worth it.

The word *sententia,* as understood by the declaimers,
had developed well beyond its meaning of "aphorism."
It has been well described as follows: "the *sententia* of
the Silver Age was no longer necessarily aphoristic: it
included the making of a hit, a point, a terse culminating effect, by various devices of thought or language."[4]
Since there is no English word that covers all this, I
shall use the Latin *sententia.* In Lucan it is all-pervasive.
It is found at its most striking, perhaps, at the end of an
argument or a speech, neatly and memorably summing
up. A few examples from Book 1 will give an idea of
Lucan's skill at *sententiæ:*

[Lines 98-99]

Temporis angusti mansit concordia discors,
Paxque fuit non sponte ducum.
(Concord there was of a sort, albeit short-lived and
    discordant,
Peace in spite of the marshals.)

[Lines 126-128]

            Quis iustius induit arma,
Scire nefas; magno se iudice quisque tuetur:
Victrix causa deis placuit, sed victa Catoni.
                    (Impossible to determine
Which had the juster cause, for both had impeccable
    sanction:
Gods on the conquering side, but Cato choosing the
    conquered.)

[Lines 503-504]

            Sic urbe relicta
In bellum fugitur.
(So at Rome: premature abandonment of the city,
Flight into battle.)

[Lines 670-672]

"Cum domino pax ista venit. Duc, Roma, malorum
Continuam seriem clademque in tempora multa
Extrahe, civili tantum iam libera bello."
("When it comes, that peace, it will come combined
   with a tyrant.
Better that Rome should endure an endless chain of
   disaster,
On and on; civil war is the sole condition of freedom.")

An epigram attached to one of the old commentaries well expresses Lucan's peculiar qualities. It is in the form of an epitaph, and the writer puts it in Lucan's mouth:

Corduba me genuit; rapuit Nero; proelia dixi
   Quæ gessere pares, hinc gener, inde socer.
Continuo numquam direxi carmina ductu
   Quæ tractim serpant: plus mihi comma placet.
Fulminis in morem quæ sunt miranda citentur;
   Hæc vere sapiet dictio quæ feriet.

(Corduba bore me; Nero destroyed me; I wrote of the
   battles
   Fought by the riva pair, father and husband of one.
None of my verses flow in an ordered symmetry,
   winding
   Slowly along: I prefer sentences short, to the point.
Startling events should be phrased like a sudden vol-
   ley of thunder;
   Language, to strike the mind, needs to have flavor
   and bite.)

CRITICAL QUESTIONS

There has been much discussion among scholars about the unity, or lack of it, of the **Civil War,** and about the question of who, if anyone, is its hero.

As to its unity, the matter is to some extent bedeviled by uncertainty as to the intended length of the poem and what the contents of the unwritten part would have been. Clearly it is difficult to talk about the unity of an incomplete work. Certain views that were once held can now be dismissed, namely, at one extreme that the poem as we have it is complete, and at the other that it was planned to continue in perhaps twenty-four books to the victory of Augustus over Antony and Cleopatra at the Battle of Actium. The two most probable answers are that the poem would have concluded with the suicide of Cato at Utica, in a total of twelve books; and that it would have continued to a total of perhaps sixteen books and ended with the assassination of Cæsar.

Great ingenuity has been displayed on behalf of both these solutions, but neither can be considered proven. My own opinion inclines toward the first, on the grounds that after the death of Cato, who alone represented for Lucan genuine human virtue and the hope of political freedom, anything else would be an anticlimax; and that Lucan had already poured such passion and indignation into his account of the conflict that it would have been very difficult to avoid duplication and staleness, two defects from which the poem as we have it is notably free. Lucan needed no more space and no more events beyond the death of Cato. All his points would have been made.

Assuming that one of these two conclusions is correct, we may tentatively broach the question of unity. It is generally accepted that Lucan's main source for his historical narrative was Livy. Livy's books on the Civil War are lost, but there survives from antiquity a series of summaries of these lost books, known as the *Perio-chæ*. Comparison of Lucan with the *Periochæ* leaves little doubt that Lucan was indeed following Livy.[5] That being so, he had only a limited choice in his narrative line. Certainly he could select and omit, emphasize and dilute; he could indulge in digressions; he could concentrate and amalgamate similar episodes into one. All these things he could and did do: but he was ultimately constrained by the unfolding events of history. Constrained, though, is not really the word. After all, he chose that period rather than another, and for a purpose; and it served him well. Like all writers of epic since Homer, he stated his theme at the outset: it is civil war and the guilt that it engenders, spreading from Rome to taint the world:

War, civil war and worse, fought out on the plains of
   Thessalia,
Times when injustice reigned and a crime was legally
   sanctioned,
Times when a powerful race, whose prowess had won
   it an empire,
Turned its swords on itself, with opposing armies of
   kinsmen—
This is my theme. I shall tell of the compact of tyranny
   broken,
Huge contention throughout the shattered world, to
   engender
Universal guilt, and of spears and standards and eagles
Facing each other in battle, of Roman arms against
   Roman.

This passage is not as specific as the introductions to the *Iliad* or the *Æneid,* but it nevertheless tells us what Lucan's subject is: guilt and fratricide, and all the evils that stem from them.

I would say, then, that although the poem does not have unity in the conventional Aristotelian sense, it does have a unity of mood and of shape. It is entirely pessimistic. It starts with the bad (Cæsar's crossing of the Rubicon); it continues through the worse (fratricidal fighting in Spain and the senatorial defeat at Pharsalia);

and hypothetically it ends (after a brief glimpse in Book 9 of what virtue can really be like) with the worst, the death of Cato. Of course the narrative is interrupted constantly, but the line is clear, one long decline from relative grace to infamy, from relative freedom to servitude. This is on the assumption that the poem ends with the death of Cato. If it continued to the assassination of Cæsar, then the harmony and consistency would have been upset, and the poem would have ended on a false note of hope with that one short-lived and meaningless flaring up of freedom which was soon to be lost again under Augustus and his successors.

The poem has no single hero. The person nearest to being its hero is Cato, Lucan's ideal, the Stoic saint. But he is not near enough to the center of action throughout the poem to be given that title. Rather, one could say that there are heroes of individual books or episodes: Vulteius, the brave fighter on the wrong side in Book 4; the centurion Scæva, also on Cæsar's side, in Book 6; Cornelia, Pompey's wife, the epitome of womanly virtue and courage, in the early part of Book 8; Pompey himself, that ambivalent character, during the scene of his death in the last part of Book 8; and Cato, leading his men through the dangers of the Libyan desert, in Book 9. The dominating character of the whole poem is Cæsar, and he, so far from being its hero, is its evil genius. On him Lucan lavishes a marvelous extravagance of hatred, mitigated only by touches of grudging admiration for his demoniac energy.

EVALUATION

Like all great poetic achievements, Lucan's *Civil War* is at once a very simple and a very elaborate work. Its claim to be an epic poem, rather than imaginative history or versified rhetoric, rests on the splendor of its language and on the enormous and encyclopedic superstructure of episode and commentary, so elaborate that the story line sometimes gets lost or is reduced to an insignificant minimum.

Much of the professional criticism of Lucan has been devoted to relating him to his predecessors and contemporaries in the epic tradition. This is not without value: it is always interesting to examine the provenance of a work of art. But the thing that strikes readers who come to Lucan for the first time is the way he differs from all other Latin writers, his originality. For example, in Book 6 of the *Æneid*, Virgil describes the descent of Æneas to the Underworld, where he receives a prophecy of the future greatness of Rome; while in Book 6 of the *Civil War* the witch Erictho resuscitates a dead soldier at the request of Sextus Pompeius, and when she asks the soldier to prophesy the outcome of the civil war, he does so in very vague and perfunctory terms. What is striking is not the fact that Lucan gives us in his sixth

book, parallel to Virgil's, a scene that is in some sense concerned with the Underworld. What is striking is the total difference between the two authors. Æneas' descent to the Underworld is the center of the whole poem, uniting what has been and what will be; and the grand vision of Rome's future that is vouchsafed is what more than anything else made the *Æneid* Rome's national epic. In Lucan all is different. The visitor is Sextus Pompeius,

> Pompey's unworthy son, who was later to prowl as an exile
> Over Sicilian waters, and stain as a pirate the triumph
> Won by his father precisely for clearing the sea of the pirates.

His motive is fear for the outcome of the civil war and desire to know that outcome, whatever it may be. Instead of trying the various reputable forms of prophecy, he resorts to the worst and lowest—witchcraft. Lucan's description of Erictho, the witch he consults, is a masterpiece of the macabre. So is the description of the bringing to life of a dead soldier, whom she summons from the Underworld to prophesy. Incidentally, it is typical of Lucan that the provenance of this dead soldier is mysterious. We are in the period before the battle of Pharsalia. Commentators dutifully suggest that there must have been some preliminary skirmishing. Very likely there was, but Lucan is not interested in such background details. He simply needs a soldier for Erictho to raise, that being the only means of answering Sextus Pompeius' far-reaching question. His interest is in the raising of the soldier (he paradoxically dies backwards, as it were), the questioning, the prophecy, and the return to death.

Similarly, all epics had a storm, and Lucan therefore gives us, in Book 5, a storm to outdo all storms. The occasion of it is Cæsar's crossing from Epirus to Italy to rouse the lethargic Marcus Antonius, whom he had been fruitlessly summoning to cross with his reinforcements. Cæsar eludes the guards on his camp (complaining, in a Lucanian aside, that he was able to do so), rouses a poor fisherman, and persuades him, against his will and against the signs of the weather, to sail him across. So great is Lucan's absorption in the tremendous storm that overtakes them, and so small is his concern for the facts of the situation, that the reader has to study the ending of the episode quite carefully to discover that Cæsar never got across the Adriatic at all, but was driven back to his place of departure. The point again is the description of the unprecedented storm and its unsuccessful challenge to Cæsar's invincible self-confidence.

Lucan is capable of quiet and moving effects, such as the fraternization of the soldiers on opposing sides in Spain, in Book 4, or the visit of Cato to the oracle of

Juppiter Hammon, in Book 9. There are many such passages. But the key words in the criticism of Lucan's style are "surpassing," "outdoing," "exaggerating"; and the consequences of them cannot be avoided. The sea battle at Massilia in the third book, the heroic stand of the centurion Scæva in the sixth, and the deaths by snakebite during Cato's march through the Libyan desert in the ninth—these are the usual targets for critical scorn. Of course they are grotesque and sometimes even inadvertently comic, as excessive enthusiasm usually is to the sober viewer, but credit, however grudging, must be given to their vigor and inventiveness. Lucan is never half-hearted. He explores every thought and situation to the limit. He does so relentlessly, in matters great and small. The resulting impression is overwhelming. It is not to everybody's taste, but it is this furious commitment to his task, together with a mastery of language that lives up to every demand made on it, that makes the *Civil War* an eccentric masterpiece.

Translation

The first translation of Lucan into English that is likely to interest the general reader is Nicholas Rowe's, published in 1719.[6] Rowe was a person of some consequence in his time, being among other things poet laureate and the first editor of Shakespeare's plays. He was a member of the Whig literary circle and imbued with their tradition of opposition to royal usurpation and tyranny. Hence, probably, his interest in Lucan, than whom no Latin poet was a more passionate or eloquent upholder of freedom against tyranny (for which reason he later appealed strongly to Shelley). Rowe was also heir to the poetic tradition of Dryden, and at the time when he was writing there was probably no alternative to the form he chose for his translation of Lucan: the heroic couplet. For the translation of rhetorical epic, the heroic couplet has two fatal disadvantages: the inevitable distortion and expansion imposed by the use of rhyme, and the strong tendency to limit the sense and syntax of the sentences to the couplet. Add to this Rowe's natural diffuseness and the tolerance of the age for extreme freedom in translation, and the result is a mannered poem of 12,275 lines for Lucan's 8,060, roughly one extra line for every two of the original. A short passage will give an idea of Rowe's style. Early in Book 1 the narrative begins with Cæsar's arrival at the Rubicon:

[Lines 183-190]

Iam gelidas Cæsar cursu superaverat Alpes
Ingentisque animo motus bellumque futurum
Ceperat. Ut ventum est parvi Rubiconis ad undas,
Ingens visa duci patriæ trepidantis imago
Clara per obscuram voltu mæstissima noctem
Turrigero canos effundens vertice crines
Cæsarie lacera nudisque adstare lacertis

Et gemitu per nixta loqui.

[As Translated by Rowe]

Now Cæsar, marching swift with winged haste,
The summits of the frozen Alps had past.
The vast events and enterprizes fraught,
And future wars revolving in his thought,
Now near the banks of Rubicon he stood;
When lo! as he survey'd the narrow flood,
Amidst the dusky horrors of the night,
A wondrous vision stood confest to sight.
Her awful head Rome's rev'rend image rear'd,
Trembling and sad the matron form appear'd:
A tow'ry crown her hoary temples bound,
And her torn tresses rudely hung around:
Her naked arms uplifting e'er she spoke,
Then groaning, thus the mournful silence broke.

Rowe's Lucan was highly esteemed in its day, and it is, by its own standards, a workmanlike job: but Lucan it is not. It has none of the latter's energy, oddness, and passion, and I do not think that a modern reader could easily make his way through it.

Nevertheless, Rowe's translation held the field for 200 years. The next verse translation came in 1896, a version by Edward Ridley in blank verse. It has never, I think, been reprinted, and there is nothing to say about it except that it is a fairly accurate rendering of the Latin in undistinguished language, relying heavily on Victorian "poetic" diction. Here is Ridley's translation of the above passage:

Cæsar had crossed the Alps, his mighty soul
Great tumults pondering and the coming shock.
Now on the marge of Rubicon, he saw,
In face most sorrowful and ghostly guise,
His trembling country's image; huge it seemed
Through mists of night obscure; and hoary hair
Streamed from the lofty front with turrets crowned:
Torn were her locks and naked were her arms.
Then thus, with broken sighs, the vision spake.

In 1928 there appeared a prose translation by J. D. Duff for the Loeb Classical Library. It was based on A. E. Housman's text (see below), and Duff had the great scholarly advantage of having attended Housman's lectures on Lucan at Cambridge. It serves its purpose well in the Loeb series, which is to guide the reader through the Latin printed on the opposite page. It is written in pedestrian prose which nevertheless makes a serious attempt to catch the subtleties of Lucan's highly condensed expressions, and sometimes it succeeds. But, being in prose, it fails even to suggest the powerful élan of the original.

Robert Graves, in his translation of 1956 for the Penguin Classics, also chose to translate Lucan into prose, but prose of a very different sort from Duff's—

clean, modern, and lively. Here is Graves's version of our specimen passage:

> Cæsar had crossed the icy Alps before he began to consider the disastrous and far-reaching effects of this war; but on his arrival at the Rubicon, a small river which divides the pastures of Gaul from the cornfields of Italy, he was granted a night vision of Rome, his own distressed motherland. She stood bare-armed, her features expressing profound sorrow and her white hairs streaming dishevelled from underneath a mural crown. "Where are you bound, soldiers?" she asked, sighing deeply.

Graves avowedly disliked Lucan and took all kinds of liberties with his text. He does convey something of his spirit and is at least readable; but again, it is not Lucan.

In the matter of translation, it seems that every age requires a different interpretation of the great masters of the past who have something permanent to say. Rowe satisfied the taste of the eighteenth century, Ridley perhaps that of the nineteenth, and Graves in certain limited respects that of the twentieth. But beyond questions of taste and fashion, there are three things that a translation of Lucan should ideally have: rhythm, energy, and point. Rowe's version had rhythm and sometimes point; Ridley's had not enough of any; and Graves's has point and a certain energy, but not rhythm.

One of the first things a verse translator has to decide is what meter to use. For translating Lucan the choices were: firstly, conventional iambic pentameters—dismissed as being too short a line and too tired a form (nobody, I think, writes long poems in straight iambic pentameters any more); secondly, a six-foot iambic line, the line used in speeches and dialogue in all of Greek tragedy and Seneca's plays—dismissed as being artificial (it has never taken root in the English poetic tradition, and for some mysterious psychometrical reason it reads unsatisfactorily); thirdly, a modified form of iambic pentameter, fashionable at the moment and usually described as "a loose iambic line of five beats," with anything from ten to about seventeen syllables—dismissed on the grounds of insufficiency of rhythm and uncertainty of stress; fourthly, "a loose line of six beats," with a style based on speech rhythms. There was much to be said for the last, and it is the meter used in C. Day Lewis's admirable Æneid. However, I felt that a more driving and regular rhythm was needed for Lucan, whose versification is closer to Ovid's than to Virgil's. This left Lucan's own meter, the hexameter. There were two objections to it: it is dactylic rather than iambic, which is the metrical unit into which English speech most naturally falls; and it is unfamiliar to most readers. The latter point is not a serious objection. The reader soon gets used to it, and I have never heard of anyone having any difficulty reading Evangeline (although admittedly Longfellow's hexameters are much smoother and more dactylic than mine). As to the former point, I am of the opinion that a translator needs the discipline of a limiting form, which paradoxically sharpens the language. This, of course, is a matter of degree. At one extreme, rhyme is too limiting a discipline, and at the other, "loose iambic lines" and free verse are not limiting enough. In fact, I found that the hexameter was the most satisfactory meter of all. It is a long line, comparable to the original (my version averages eleven lines to every ten of the Latin), and it has a strong, identifiable rhythm—in particular a swinging and memorable line ending well suited for the expression of pointed language. As for its supposed unsuitability to English, I would point (apart from Evangeline and Miles Standish) to Arthur Hugh Clough's fascinating poetic novella, Amours de Voyage, whose versification is lively, natural, and unmonotonous. As to its success as a medium for translation, I must leave that for readers to judge for themselves.

METER

. . . The line tends to have a break between words (cæsural) in the third foot, though I have been less regular in observing it than Latin writers were. The stress, which in English is the predominant factor, comes on the first syllable of each foot, and thus the first syllable of every line is always stressed, even if it is an unimportant word (in which case the stress should not be exaggerated). . . .

One of the advantages of this meter is that it admits of great variety within its strict framework. Although these four lines have the same controlling beats, they are all different in the distribution of dactyls, spondees, and trochees. In spite of the technicalities, this meter is not difficult, and once the principle is grasped the lines should read quite naturally.

TEXT

The text used here is that established by A. E. Housman in 1926.[7] The text of Lucan is on the whole good, but before Housman's time it had been spoiled by poor choice of readings from the available manuscripts and particularly by misleading punctuation. By the correction of these two faults and by other contributions of his own, Housman produced, with marvelously steady and scholarly judgment, a text that, by comparison with all previous ones, gives the effect of a cleaned picture—livelier color, sharpened detail, and enhanced meaning. I have departed from his text at Book 1, line 282; Book 2, line 292; Book 7, line 43; and Book 9, line 568; all cases of doubtful readings.

Notes

1. He was the Gallio who "cared for none of these things" (Acts 18:17).

2. *Dialogus de Oratoribus* 20, 5.

3. All the medieval manuscripts call this poem either *Bellum Civile* or *De Bello Civili,* and I have followed them in calling it *The Civil War.* It has more commonly been known in modern times, until recently, as *The Pharsalia,* a title that originated in the Renaissance based on a misunderstanding of Book 9, lines 935-986. This title is really a misnomer: its only advantages are that it has become familiar from long usage and avoids confusion with Cæsar's *De Bello Civili.* The tendency nowadays is to be purist and go back to the title of the manuscripts.

4. E. Phillips Barker, *The Poet in the Forcing House,* Occasional Publications of the Classical Association, number 2 (Cambridge: Cambridge University Press, 1917), p. 13.

5. For the whole question, see René Pichon, *Les Sources de Lucain* (Paris: Ernest Leroux, 1912).

6. For a description of the few earlier versions, see O. A. W. Dilke, "Lucan and English Literature," in *Neronians and Flavians,* edited by D. R. Dudley (London and Boston: Routledge and Kegan Paul, 1972).

7. *M. Annæi Lucani Belli Civilis Libri Decem,* edited by A. E. Housman (Oxford: Basil Blackwell, 1926 and later impressions).

Selected Bibliography

Ahl, Frederick M. *Lucan: An Introduction.* Ithaca and London: Cornell University Press, 1976. (The best general introduction to Lucan, discussing all the standard questions and problems, and containing a useful bibliography.)

Dilke, O. A. W. "Lucan and English Literature" and "Lucan's Political Views and the Caesars." Both in *Neronians and Flavians: Silver Latin* I, edited by D. R. Dudley. London and Boston: Routledge and Kegan Paul, 1972.

Due, Otto Steen. "An Essay on Lucan." *Classical Medievalia* 22 (1962):68-132. (Discusses Lucan's reputation through the ages and the questions of the unity and purpose of the *Civil War.*)

Durry, Marcel, ed. *Entretiens sur l'antiquité classique,* XV: *Lucain.* Geneva: Fondation Hardt, 1970. (A wide-ranging and interesting collection of essays, five in French and two in German, on Lucan and history, art, religion, philosophy, rhetoric, and the epic tradition.)

Haskins, C. E., ed. M. *Annaei Lucani Pharsalia.* London: Bell and Sons, 1887. (The only reasonably modern commentary in English on the whole of Lucan. Long and useful introduction by W. E. Heitland.)

Jal, Paul. *La guerre civile à Rome.* Paris: Presses Universitaires de France, 1963. (Covers civil wars from the times of Marius and Sulla to A.D. 69. Both learned and readable, with a wealth of references to Lucan.)

Marti, Berthe M. "The Meaning of the Pharsalia." *American Journal of Philology* 66 (1945):352-376. (A discussion of the structure, characters, and intent of Lucan's poem, particularly from the point of view of his Stoic background.)

Morford, M. P. O. *The Poet Lucan: Studies in Rhetorical Epic.* Oxford: Basil Blackwell, 1967. (More about rhetoric than poetry, but a useful corrective to the standard, rather depreciative, assessments of Lucan in earlier studies of Latin literature.)

Pichon, René, *Les sources de Lucain,* Paris: Ernest Leroux, 1912. (An exhaustive work whose salient contribution is to show that Lucan's main historical source was Livy.)

Riley, H. T., trans. *Lucan's Pharsalia, Literally Translated into English Prose.* Bohn's Classical Library. London and New York: George Bell and Sons, 1853, and reprinted since. ("Literally" is the word. Unreadable as a translation, but containing the most helpful continuous historical commentary on the poem to be found anywhere.)

Rutz, Werner, ed. *Lucan. Wege der Forschung,* no. 235. Darmstadt: Wissenschaftlich Buchgesellschaft, 1970. (A comprehensive and learned collection of essays, all in German, including a justly celebrated essay by Eduard Fraenkel, "Lucan als Mittler der antiken Pathos.")

For those interested in studying Lucan in detail, there are three exhaustive bibliographies:

Helm, Rudolf. "Lucan, 1925-1942." *Lustrum* 1 (1956):163-228. (A chronological commentary on all work on Lucan in the period.)

Rutz, Werner. "Lucan, 1943-1963." *Lustrum* 9 (1964):243-334. (An excellent descriptive list, clearly arranged under categories.)

Rutz, Werner. "Lucan, 1964-1983." *Lustrum* 26 (1984):105-203. (Continuation of the above on the same system.)

For subsequent work on Lucan, see individual annual volumes of *L'Année Philologique.*

Jane Wilson Joyce (essay date 1993)

SOURCE: Joyce, Jane Wilson. Introduction to *Pharsalia,* by Lucan, translated by Jane Wilson Joyce, pp. ix-xxv. Ithaca, N.Y.: Cornell University Press, 1993.

[*In the following essay, Joyce discusses the life of Lucan, his close links with politics, and his literary reputation and influence.*]

POET

Lucan (Marcus Annaeus Lucanus) was born 3 November 39 C. E. at Cordoba, son of the Spanish financier Marcus Annaeus Mela and member of a remarkable family.[1] His grandfather Lucius Annaeus Seneca ("the Elder"), a successful businessman, wrote a history of Rome, now lost, beginning with the civil war that forms the subject of Lucan's **Pharsalia**; blessed with longevity (he lived to be nearly a hundred) and a phenomenal memory, a keen critic of Roman rhetoric, he could quote at length even from speeches heard in boyhood; some of his work on oratory is extant. One of Lucan's two uncles, Lucius Annaeus Gallio (later adopted and renamed Lucius Iunius Novatus Gallio), is the Gallio who, as governor of Achaea in 52 C. E., threw out the Jews' case against St. Paul in Acts 18:12ff. The other, Lucius Annaeus Seneca, was Rome's richest citizer, the most popular living author of his day, and, for a short while, virtual co-ruler of the Roman world.

Within a few months of Lucan's birth, his father moved the family to Rome; he then retired to a house deep in the country. While it is possible that Lucan received his early education at home in the old Roman style, all indications are that he was educated at Rome. Perhaps he lived there with his uncle Gallio while attending a grammar school. Here he would have learned to read and write both Latin and Greek until he was about eleven (51 C. E.); then, for the next five years, he would have studied grammar and literature and other subjects intended to give pupils a good general education and a foundation for advanced study of rhetoric. In 49, a shift in the kaleidoscope of Roman imperial politics and intrigue brought his uncle Seneca home from exile on Corsica, and Seneca may well have taken an interest in his gifted nephew's education.

An exceptional student, Lucan continued his studies under the tutelage of Lucius Annaeus Cornutus (born circa 20 C. E.). Possibly related to Lucan or in some other way connected with his family, this young Stoic teacher of rhetoric and philosophy was author of works in both Greek and Latin, including a critique of Vergil's poetry and a handbook of Stoic allegorical interpretations of Greek mythology. In the classroom with Lucan was another gifted young poet, Persius, whose satires still exist. After two or three years' study under Cornutus, Lucan went abroad sometime in the late 50s C. E. for a final year of schooling at Athens. According to Suetonius' biographical sketch of Lucan, it is at this point that the poet's life intertwines with that of the emperor Nero, who summoned Lucan home to make him a member of the "cadre of friends" (*cohors amicorum*).[2]

It seems highly likely, however, that poet and emperor had become well acquainted much earlier, for, from 49

to 54, Lucan's uncle Seneca served as Nero's tutor. What would have been more natural than that he bring the two youths together in those years? They were almost of an age, Lucan being only about eleven months younger than Nero, and they shared a passionate interest in literature. Indeed, in 60 C. E., Nero established games patterned on Apollo's Pythian Games, with contests for poets as well as for athletes and horsemen; Lucan won top honors in these games with a poem praising Nero (*Laudes Neronis*).

The cordial, even friendly, relations implied by these events continued. In 62 or 63 C. E., Nero appointed Lucan quaestor and augur both. The normal age for a quaestorship (the lowest rung of the Roman political ladder) was twenty-five. Even if we accept the later date, Lucan, who turned twenty-four only in November, was still too young to hold such an office; in fact, early appointment to the quaestorship was an honor usually reserved for members of the imperial family. The augurate, too, was an honor: the College of Augurs was restricted to sixteen members.

The motives of princes, however, are notoriously difficult to read, and it is well to remember that, also in 62, Seneca had begged permission to cede the bulk of his huge fortune to Nero and to be allowed to go into retirement. While refusing the first request for a while, Nero granted the second.[3] Considering the reckless course of action Nero had set himself in the late 50s (the infamous murder of his mother occurred in 59), it is unlikely that Seneca's retirement was an entirely simple matter. Seneca may have been maneuvered into making the request, or he may have felt himself in danger and hoped to avoid trouble. In any case, it is possible that, despite the honors accorded him, Lucan was beginning to feel uneasy about Nero's friendship; it is equally possible that his own friendly feelings were fading. Nor should we overlook the possibility that Nero was using the nephew to get at the uncle.

The dual honors awarded to Lucan carried with them dual responsibilities. As quaestor, he became a member of the Senate and organized a show of gladiatorial games; as augur, he had many ceremonial functions to perform. In the meantime, he kept up his writing—something that can be said of few Roman authors, who tended either to be uninvolved in official duties or to postpone literary activity until their political careers had ended. Though only his unfinished epic remains, we know the titles of many more works by Lucan. Among those on mythological themes were *Iliacon* (*Song of Troy*), *Catachthonion* (*Trip to the Underworld*), *Orpheus, Medea* (an unfinished tragedy), and libretti for fourteen pantomimes (*Salticae Fabulae*). There were ten books of occasional verse (called *Silvae*), a collection of epigrams, another of *Saturnalia,* and a third of

Letters from Campania; we hear of an *Address to Polla* (Lucan's wife) and of a pair of speeches in the declamatory style—one for, one against Octavius Sagitta (involved in 58 C. E. in a sex-and-murder scandal recounted by Tacitus in *Annales* 13.44). In addition to the *Laudes Neronis* (*In Praise of Nero*) already mentioned, a poem titled *About the Burning of the City* (*De Incendio Urbis*) is also listed.

Vacca, Lucan's only ancient biographer other than Suetonius, says that these works were all extant in his day (four or five centuries after Lucan's death). While some titles may refer to juvenilia, the output is nonetheless prodigious; equally, we should note their longevity. And even if some works date as early as 55, or even 52 C. E., still we must be impressed by a writer who produced so much in little more than a decade.

The strands of literature and politics in Lucan's life become more tightly interwoven from this point on. Indeed, it may have been in 62 or 63 that he set to work on the *Pharsalia,* though chronology for events in the last two or three years of his life is hazy. We hear from Vacca that up through the year of his quaestorship, relations between poet and emperor were friendly; then things changed drastically as Lucan incurred Nero's envy and hatred (*equidem hactenus tempora habuit secunda. quae autem sequuntur mutata invidia et odio Neronis. . .*).

Like Vacca, Suetonius suggests that Nero's jealousy of Lucan created the rift between them. He sees the turning point in an act of deliberate humiliation. While Lucan was giving a public reading, Nero suddenly called a meeting of the Senate and departed, his sole intention being to give Lucan "the freeze" (*nulla nisi refrigerandi sui causa*). Suetonius goes on to say that Lucan read a "libelous poem" (*carmen famosum*) in which he gave both the emperor and his most powerful friends a severe tongue-lashing; it is at least possible that Suetonius is referring to Lucan's *De Incendio Urbis,* which, if it was about the Great Fire at Rome, would have to have been written sometime after July 64 C. E. Towards the end of that same year, according to Tacitus, Dio, and Vacca, Nero imposed a ban on all Lucan's public speaking. (Suetonius makes no mention of such a ban.)[4]

Early in 65 C. E., Lucan joined a conspiracy of senators headed by Calpurnius Piso and sworn to assassinate Nero.[5] Vacca says Lucan was led astray by the older senator (*deceptus est*), while Suetonius describes him as the virtual standard-bearer of the group (*paene signifer*). The conspiracy was discovered, and Lucan, along with his uncles Seneca and Gallio, was forced to commit suicide. When his father came forward to claim Lucan's property, he, too, was compelled to kill himself.[6]

Lucan's relationship with Nero traces a meteoric trajectory—a steep climb to the heights swiftly followed by a plunge into oblivion. Throughout his life run twin themes of literature and politics, the two elements gradually drawing together and intermingling until, in the end, Lucan the political conspirator, compelled by Nero to die, sends his father corrections of verses in the *Pharsalia* before ordering the surgeon to open his veins. He died 30 April 65 C.E.[7]

* * *

For most of the twentieth century, Lucan has been a shadowy literary presence, an author little read and largely ignored. Yet, as we have seen, his literary output was vast; his talent was recognized in his own day; and his many works were all still available long after his death. A brief history of Lucan's fluctuating literary reputation is in order here, beginning with his reputation as author in his lifetime.

In the ancient world, the first step in publication was often the public reading. Who listened when Lucan read his *Pharsalia*? The emperor did, for one. In his *Life* of Lucan as we have seen, Suetonius tells us that Nero walked out of one of Lucan's recitations; ergo, he was there. Clearly, if the emperor was present, then the audience must have been large and prestigious. Given Nero's passion for the arts, even those with little genuine interest in poetry would have felt compelled to feign interest, would have wanted to see and be seen at such gatherings. So it seems likely that Lucan could have counted on a large audience of distinguished and well-educated men and women—or at least he could before the break with Nero.

What would such a reading have been like? The Younger Pliny, whose letters are our principal source of information, tells us that an author, having decided to give a reading, would issue invitations.[8] One can imagine that an invitation from the well-connected Lucan must have been much sought after. Readings could last an afternoon or continue over the space of several days. Poetry, especially epic and tragedy, was most commonly the type of work presented. It was also the author's responsibility to hire a hall or theater for his recitation, and he had to supply the seating and platform as well—no problem for the wealthy Lucan, although these expenses must often have been prohibitive for a man of limited means.[9] Once his guests had assembled, the author spoke a few words, then sat to read from his new work. At intervals, the audience cheered or even rose to its feet if especially stirred. (Occasionally an author would ensure the stirring by judicious disbursements of money beforehand.)

Such readings were very much a feature of the social landscape in Lucan's day and had been so since their inception in the 30s B.C.E. Asinius Pollio, friend of Vergil and Horace, and founder of Rome's first public library, started the fashion.[10] Juvenal, writing a generation after Lucan, complains of the large number and low quality of these public readings (*Satires* 1.1 and 3.9).

It seems likely, than, that Lucan, the courtier shown preferential treatment by the emperor, nephew of the emperor's chief counselor, and a wealthy senator and augur in his own right, could have counted on a glittering assembly of senators and knights, their womenfolk and hangers-on, even had his work been mediocre. But, in addition to his political connections, Lucan the author seems to have been popular. Statius, in his poem in honor of Lucan's birthday (*Silvae* 2.7), has the mother of Orpheus, the Muse Calliopê, make an implicit comparison between her mythological son and the infant Lucan; leaning over the baby's cradle, she predicts:

> No stream, no herds of wild creatures will you stir
> with your plectrum, nor yet the Getic ash-trees,
> but the Seven Hills, Mars' river Tiber,
> learned Knights and the Senate clad in purple—
> these you'll charm and lead with your eloquent song
> . . .
>
>   (vv. 43-47)

The implication is clearly that Lucan will be an urban, a specifically Roman, Orpheus.

In addition to full-blown public performances, there were also private readings, to which, after Nero imposed the ban, Lucan may have resorted. Perhaps we should think of his uncle's well-appointed villa (where Seneca, too, may have presented private readings or even productions of his tragedies). And, if the author was Lucan and the text his *Pharsalia,* very private indeed such readings must have been, for, with Nero's ban in effect, both reader and listener were subject to the treason laws. Certainly the overt and violent hostility to Caesarism expressed in *Pharsalia* Seven would not have been safe for public recitation at any time, even in the heyday of Lucan's intimacy with Nero.

* * *

Lucan's influence since his death has been variable. In the decades immediately afterward, as in much of the twentieth century, interest in his work was muted; but in the centuries between—especially in the Middle Ages—it was considerable.

Presumably, Lucan's papers, including the manuscript of the *Pharsalia,* came into the hands of Polla Argentaria after the deaths of her husband, his uncles, and his father in 65 C. E. It might seem more appropriate that the poet's former master of rhetoric, rather than his widow, should have become Lucan's literary executor; after all, Cornutus filled that role for his other famous

pupil, Persius. But Cornutus would seem not to have been a candidate for literary executor, since it is unclear when or if he ever returned from exile after his banishment in the early 60s C. E. At the end of his *Life* of Lucan, Suetonius says that he can recall public lectures on the *Pharsalia,* and he mentions that several copies, some of them better than others, were available at the booksellers' stalls in his day (c. 100 C. E.). The poet Martial, in an unflattering epigram published about the same time, confirms that sales of the *Pharsalia* were brisk.[11]

Though his epic was recognized to be ground-breaking, though he was an author much admired during most of his short life, Lucan found no imitators, no poets in his audience ready to take up his principles. In antiquity, it was not his poetry or his rhetoric that stopped Lucan's contemporaries from following his innovative lead in the creation of epic: it was his politics and his death. Although the influence of Lucan's epic may be discerned in the *Punica* of Silius Italicus (composed c. 88-98 C. E.), in the *Argonautica* of Valerius Flaccus (composed c. 80-92 C. E.), and in Statius' *Thebaid* (also composed in the 80s), none of these imperial epics could be said to have been modelled on the *Pharsalia*; only the *Punica* uses history rather than mythology as its subject, but even so, the Second Punic War was safely in the distant and glorious past. Silius Italicus, despite his historical subject, joins the other two poets in reverting to the traditional epic device of divine machinery. As Frederick M. Ahl has put it, "If Vergil proved to be a poet the Flavian writers could not rival, Lucan was one they dared not rival."[12]

The clearest indication that this was the tenor of the times is the criticism levelled at the *Pharsalia* in Petronius' *Satyricon* (paragraphs 118-124), published (perhaps) shortly after Lucan's death. Although Lucan is never mentioned by name, Petronius clearly means that he is the poet who would profit from a study of the sample *Civil War* sketched out there. Petronius, a literary conservative, is alarmed and a little affronted by Lucan's innovativeness. In particular, Petronius advocates in his sample epic a return to traditional use of the gods to explain motivation and events.

Other notices about Lucan and his work from the next generation were equally unflattering. In his *Dialogue* on the Roman literary tradition, Tacitus—never a friend of Lucan—has one of his less-imposing characters praise Lucan, only to be outdone in the debate by a more traditionalist speaker. Quintilian, the eminent teacher of rhetoric, has left us a famous assessment of the *Pharsalia*: "Lucan is intense and keyed up and best known for his epigrams; also, speaking for myself, he is a model more useful to orators than to poets" (*Lucanus ardens et concitatus et sententiis clarissimus et, ut dicam quod sentio, magis oratoribus quam poetis imitandus*). But after this flurry of interest on the part of Lucan's younger contemporaries, there was a period of silence lasting nearly two and a half centuries.

Then, in late antiquity and the early Middle Ages, Lucan came into his own. Around 350 C. E., a learned commentary was composed on the *Pharsalia*; it survives, with many later additions, in two separate manuscripts—the *Commenta Bernensia* and the *Adnotationes super Lucanum*. Early in the 400s, the poets Claudian and Prudentius were great admirers of Lucan; Vacca probably wrote his *Life* of Lucan in the fifth or sixth century. In the ninth through eleventh centuries, what are now the major manuscripts of the *Pharsalia* were copied and circulated, and from the mid-tenth century to the 1400s, Lucan was listed in the top category of meritorious pagan authors, along with Terence, Vergil, Horace, Ovid, Statius, Juvenal, Persius, and Sallust. A little later, Lucan's epic seems to have been readily available for classroom use.

The most important admirer of the *Pharsalia* in medieval Europe was Dante, who, guided by Vergil ("the Prince of Poets") to the First Circle of Hell, sees a brilliant band of pagan poets: Homer, Horace, Ovid—and Lucan. As Dante-Pilgrim says:

> . . . I saw gathered at the edge of light
> the masters of that highest school whose song
> outsoars all others like an eagle's flight.
>
> (*Inferno,* Canto IV, 94-96)[13]

The Renaissance, too, evinced interest in the *Pharsalia*. Thus, Lucan's epic is the only poem from the classical era included among the *editiones principes,* classical texts printed between 1465 and 1469, the first five years of the printing press. Montaigne often quotes from and makes favorable mention of Lucan's epic. Translations into French, Italian, and Spanish appeared from the fifteenth century to the seventeenth century.[14] Christopher Marlowe's splendid translation of the first book of Lucan's poem was published in 1600.[15]

Again, the eighteenth century, which began in a period of literary classicism and which ended with the reactionary Romantics, was—despite its diverse tastes—friendly to Lucan throughout. Nicholas Rowe's translation of the epic appeared in 1718 and was hailed near the end of the century by Dr. Johnson as "one of the greatest productions of English poetry."[16] In 1815, Shelley wrote to Thomas Jefferson Hogg, twice, indicating his preference for Lucan over Vergil (probably on political rather than poetic grounds).[17] Later, in 1821, Shelley still expressed admiration for Lucan, this time in the "sincerest form of flattery": in a passage from the *Adonais* strikingly reminiscent of Pompey's apotheosis in the

opening lines of *Pharsalia* Nine, Shelley links Lucan with Thomas Chatterton and Sir Philip Sidney; as the souls of poets who died young, they will greet the spirit of John Keats as it enters the fiery non-material world above (*Adonais* 45).

In contrast, the climate of the modern world has not been favorable to Lucan. For much of the twentieth century, the word "rhetorical" has been devalued in popular idiom to the extent that it now means little more than "bad (and probably deceitful)." Classical scholars themselves have too often been among the first to close Lucan out. This exclusion seems surprising, for, whatever one may think of the literary merits of the work, it is a document from antiquity; more than this, it is a rare example of an ancient work in progress as well as an indicator of the political sentiments of a suppressed opposition. Fortunately, in recent years, Lucan has received more of the attention he deserves.

POEM

At one level, Lucan's poem is about the battle of Pharsalus, the decisive conflict of 48 B. C. E. fought on the Emathian fields of Thessaly in northern Greece and pitting forces led by Julius Caesar against those led by his kinsman Pompey Magnus; it recounts events that prefigure Pharsalus, the battle itself, and the aftermath; it also portrays the dominant personalities of the time—Caesar, Pompey, and Cato. This battle, according to the more traditional view, ushers in the last chapter in the long, ugly chronicle of Roman civil war which stretches back nearly a century. Although it was decisive, the battle of Pharsalus was by no means the end of this struggle, for the war raged on until 31 B. C. E., when Octavian (later the emperor Augustus) won out. Equally, although Pharsalus is the first major engagement after Caesar crossed the Rubicon, it was but one battle of many fought by Roman factions in the last century of the Republic. For Lucan, however, more than any previous or subsequent episode in the civil war, Pharsalus was the death scene of the Roman Republic.

At another level, the poem is about Lucan's Rome, how Roman folly and disaster led to the establishment of the Julio-Claudian dynasty; it is about the price paid to purchase Nero.

At its deepest level, the poem is a meditation on liberty in the state and free will in the individual. Lucan wrestles with questions of courage and patriotic ideals, even tyrannicide. Perhaps the most intriguing aspect of the poem is how it seems to reveal the poet's own swings of mood, his ups and downs during the last years of his life, the period of his involvement in the Pisonian conspiracy.

The poem, then, is not so much an account of historical events as it is a study of politics and psychology, of disastrous patterns of behavior and the compulsion to repeat them, the compulsion of Rome to destroy itself. In Lucan's poem, Pharsalus stands for all such acts of political self-destruction; it is the pure "type," the gladiatorial match between Liberty and a Caesar. Pharsalus is to Lucan a doomsday; that day, almost a century before his birth, changed Lucan's world for the worse. As the surrealistic vision of the battlefield at the end of Book Seven clearly shows, Pharsalus was for Lucan the event that brought the forces of death and destruction to power at Rome.

It is because the battle of Pharsalus holds such sway in Lucan's imagination that **Bellum Civile** seems a less satisfactory choice for the title of the poem than **Pharsalia.** Lucan's poem is not only about the civil war between Caesar and the Senate: it is about *bella plus quam civilia* (1.1), "wars worse than civil"; it is about the day Romans brought the Roman Republic to an end, the day the world turned its sword against its own vitals.

* * *

The **Pharsalia** is undoubtedly an epic poem; equally certainly, it is a quirky one. First and foremost (by ancient standards at any rate) among those characteristics of a traditional epic which the **Pharsalia** does maintain is its use of dactylic hexameters, the definitive meter of epic poetry from Homer on. Second, with its ten books averaging 800 lines each, the **Pharsalia** is long. Third, it is a continuous narrative. Fourth, the style is generally elevated.

Lucan's choice of subject matter naturally dictates his choice of characters, accounting, to some extent, for one of the more radical aspects of Lucan's epic—the presence of not one but *three* heroes. Or rather, one anti-hero, one would-be-again hero, and one philosopher-hero whom Lucan seems not to like very much. Caesar, Pompey, and Cato have all had their share of critics to say that *he* is the one true hero of the epic. Rather, Lucan's point seems to be that no one man is the center of his epic; he prefers to concentrate on the self-destruction of Rome at Pharsalus and the brood of evils hatched there.

The fact that the subject matter of the **Pharsalia** is drawn not from myth but from history—and fairly recent history at that—is not without precedent: Naevius (third century B. C. E.) wrote an epic in native Italian verse-form about the First Punic War, which had dominated his youth and early manhood; soon after, Ennius ("the Father of Roman Poetry") wrote an epic in hexameters called the *Annales* in which he traced Roman history from the Fall of Troy down through the war with Hannibal (the Second Punic War). Although

Lucan's use of a severely restricted chronological focus represents a new development in the course of Roman epic, his choice of historical subject matter does not.

But subject matter alone cannot account for the spirit of innovation which suffuses Lucan's **Pharsalia.** There is no getting round the fact that this poem, while it is recognizably an epic, is deeply, radically new and different. We might call it a "slant epic" as "road" and "read" would be called a "slant rhyme."

Perhaps the most noticeable difference between Lucan's epic and a traditional epic is the drastically diminished role played by members of the old Greco-Roman pantheon; no gods as puppeteers here, no Jupiter with the scroll of destiny on his knees, no solicitous Venus or Juno to whisk a beloved son out of danger. In fact, in a sequence of three parallel scenes (in Books Five, Six, and Nine), Lucan makes it abundantly clear that these deities are moribund and that supernatural power has passed into the hands of Thessalian witches and foreigners' gods. When Appius goes to Apollo's Delphic oracle (5.65-236) to learn his future, he finds the place shut down; when Sextus approaches the witch Erictho to learn *his* future (6.570-830), she is only too willing and able to oblige. The third scene, in which Cato refuses to consult Ammon's flourishing African oracle when urged by Labienus to do so (9.511-586), seems des gned to suggest that Romans have driven away the old simple gods or become too corruptly sophisticated for them. A few men, true Stoics of the Roman school like Cato, heirs to the ideals preserved in their exemplary tales, have that philosophy to sustain them. Ordinary Romans, however, represented by Appius, Sextus, and Labienus, lump oracles and witchcraft together as mildly amusing carnival tricks and possible sources of information useful to themselves personally.

The usual reason given for Lucan's shift away from the Olympians is that the events he narrates are too recent to make their inclusion plausible. It does make literary sense to leave out the (dilapidated) divine machinery, to use the exotic African oracle as a means of displaying Cato's Stoic virtues in yet another light. But the negligible role of Jupiter, Juno & Co. also points up a political message.

In the first place, Lucan's avoidance of traditional divine machinery emphasizes one of his major premises in the **Pharsalia,** namely, that Caesar's defeat of the Republican forces proves that, if there are gods, either they are not omnipotent or they do not have Rome's best interests at heart. In the second place (and here Lucan is putting effect before cause), the attitude of ordinary Romans to divinity and the supernatural is, Lucan seems to say, directly attributable to the Julio-Claudian practice of emperor deification. If godhood may be conferred on a mortal man by decree of a fawning Senate, then bona fide gods are devalued, and the fabric of belief weakened or destroyed. Philosophy is the only alternative. In the address to Nero (1.33-66), Lucan suggests that his emperor, when deified, will enter Olympus as a usurper or as an actor choosing a role to play; by contrast, the apotheosis of Pompey (9.1-18) takes the form of a soul soaring through a Platonic universe.

The divine and the supernatural are not entirely absent from the *Pharsalia*. On the contrary, omens and clairvoyants abound, especially in the first six books. In a satiric reenactment of Aeneas' encounter with Venus (*Aeneid* 1.305ff.), Caesar experiences a visitation from Roma (*Pharsalia* 1.183-203). In Africa, that simpler and purer country, Lucan finds a congenial setting for his accounts of Hercules and Antaeus (4.581-660), of Hercules and the Apples of the Hesperides (9.348-367), of Perseus and Medusa (9.619-699).

Above all, the forces of fortune and fate (sometimes appearing in mythological form as the Three Sisters) rule the Lucanian universe. Fate was a force in the *Aeneid*, too, but Vergil's concept was one of harmony between fate and Roman destiny; Lucan's contrasting outlook is summed up in his pithy observation *In se magna ruunt*— "Great things fall in on themselves" (1.81).

As when we first learn that the Parthenon was intended to be not merely virginal white marble, but marble resplendent with paint and ornament, so we may be taken aback to find that, while the *Pharsalia* is an epic, it is not all solemnity and high-mindedness. In fact, some parts of it are downright funny. Take Book Five, for example: what of the scene with the Pythia trying to fob Appius off with a simulated trance (vv. 120-161)? Having given a long, admiring description of the oracle and having lamented its decline, Lucan presents the Roman Senator Appius determined at the outbreak of hostilities to use the oracle to find out his own personal fortunes in the war ahead. First, the reluctant Pythia (who has grown fond of retirement) thinks up a dozen reasons why the shrine is out of order, each more pseudo-scientific than the one before. Then, when forced into the shrine, she hangs back at the door and fakes a prophecy—a ruse the not-too-shrewd Appius notices only after the poet has given him eight lines of hints.

Or take Caesar's scene with the poor fisherman (5.510-559), an episode that reads like a fractured fairy tale. Caesar slips out of his camp at night, disguised as a commoner, and goes in search of a ship to take him from Greece back to Italy (he's tired of waiting for Antony and wants to hurry him up). When Caesar, larger than life, knocks at the door of a fisherman's hut (shades of Odysseus at the door of Eumaios the swineherd!), he makes the roof tiles rattle; nor is Caesar

(in actuality, renowned for his mastery of the plain style) able to stop himself from speaking in a high, not to say high-handed, style. The poor fisherman gives Caesar sixteen hexameters explaining why the voyage is impossible on such a night, then says with comic abruptness, "But, if you must go, we'll go—either we'll get there or we won't" (vv. 557-559).

Later in Book Five, we have another example of Lucan's wry humor—the send-up of Caesar as Hero Toss'd Upon Stormy Seas (vv. 577-596). Having described a ferocious storm at sea, Lucan has Caesar make a similarly blustering speech of self-aggrandizement, whereupon Lucan unleashes a storm of even greater ferocity. And yet, after fifty lines of lashing winds and crashing waves, all that happens is that Caesar is gently deposited on the very shore from which he set out (vv. 672-678).

* * *

We have seen how closely linked politics and literature are in the life of Lucan. There is a similar interweaving of intent in his epic. The *Pharsalia* is the vehicle for Lucan's political as well as his literary ideas.

Lucan excels at the deft mixture of humor and horror, as in his long description of the witch Erictho (6.507-569) or in the retelling of the myth of Medusa (9.624-629). A particularly effective example of this aspect of the *Pharsalia* occurs at 6.564-569, where Lucan gleefully describes the witch engaged in necrophilia. Indeed, Lucan seems spurred to increasingly wild and grotesque flights of fancy as he describes the witch. In a sense, Erictho becomes for him an image of himself as poet, for she is able to mimic all animals and forces of nature. He says of her, *Tot rerum vox una fuit* ("One voice was all of Nature." See 6.685-693). Like Erictho, Lucan has simulated many voices; like her, he is attempting to raise up the dead and make them speak—but not just Caesar and Pompey and their generation: Lucan is trying to reanimate the corpse of the Republic.

As this comparison implies, antiestablishment politics is the most potent force in the *Pharsalia*; not surprisingly, then, the most noticeable type of humor in Lucan's epic is political satire. Lucan's uncle Seneca had a flair for this genre, too: he wrote a farcical account (wickedly entitled the *Apocolocyntosis* or "*Gourdification*") of the arrival in Olympus of the emperor Claudius, recently deceased, recently deified, and depicted by Seneca as a drooling idiot. The best example of political satire in the *Pharsalia* is perhaps the zombie's description of insurrection in the underworld (6.777-802), with Elysian Romans pitted against Tartarean; but the episode in Book Nine (vv. 950-979) where Caesar, accompanied by an overzealous guide, tours the dusty briar patch that once was Troy, runs a close second. Both these passages stand Vergil's *Aeneid* on its head—yet another example of Lucan's habit of seeing politics and literature as two sides of a single coin.

Caesar is not the only major figure to serve as a target for Lucan's barbs; Cato gets his, too. For example, in Book Two (vv. 350-380), Lucan (like a disdainful society editor) gives us a catalogue of all the refinements that Cato's remarriage to Marcia lacked: there was no fancy clothing (the bride wore black), no elaborate ceremony, no guests or toasts or bawdy jokes, and no resumption of conjugal rights, either. The fun Lucan pokes at Pompey is much milder: Pompey's dream at the beginning of Book Seven, for instance, is more sad than funny, and if we smile at moments during Cordus' hasty burial of Pompey at the end of Book Eight, then Pompey's spirit joins us in that smile at the opening of Book Nine.

In fact, Lucan's most startling innovation as epic poet may hinge on his outlook: more than its multiplicity of heroes or its paucity of gods, ultimately what sets the *Pharsalia* apart is mood. This difference shows up most clearly in contrast to the *Aeneid.* Vergil's poem is the work of a gentle but gloomy optimist; Lucan's, of a witty but angry pessimist. While anger is the poem's pervasive, underlying mood, its surface displays many tones. It is tender and elegiac in scenes between Pompey and Cornelia, eerie and evocative in its descriptions of deserted farmlands and ghost towns, lush and exotic at Cleopatra's banquet, and so on. Each scene has its own flavor. The poem may owe its tonal diversity to the poet's nature as much as to his education. Perhaps, too, he is indebted to Ovid, whose *Metamorphoses* is similarly an epic remarkable for its constantly shifting tone and mood.

The pervasive anger of the *Pharsalia,* though often in the cloak of satiric humor, is black and bitter nonetheless. Why must *his* generation pay with its liberty for the cowardice and ineffectiveness of previous generations? This sense of personal grievance and the conviction that the world died at Pharsalus nearly a century before he was born account in large measure for the quirkiness of Lucan's *Pharsalia.*

TRANSLATION

Living in an age of rhetorical elegance and ebullience, Lucan was a member of a family especially noted, even in that age, for its literary skill and sophistication. Lawyer, politician, courtier, conspirator, and poet, Lucan was accustomed to turn the phrase that could turn heads. While we, who read silently and to ourselves, eyes flicking down a printed page, are accustomed to think of poetry as a private experience, Lucan and his contemporaries read aloud; to them, poetry, especially epic poetry, was a public experience; indeed, it was often a public performance and, as such, demanded the language of declamation. In the case of the *Pharsalia,* this purpose is heightened since Lucan meant to persuade his listeners to look at their recent history anew and to reassess life under the Caesars.

We see the workings of all these factors in Lucan's poem. We see what Lucan's audience heard. In translating, I have tried to keep in mind always the paramount importance to Lucan of the spoken word, the heard image. Working in a six-beat line, I have tried to match his content line for line, to maintain the shapes of his sentences, and to preserve his rhetorical figures, including the many apostrophes. I have tried to give some sense of alliteration and other poetic devices, and also to honor his choice of word at key points in the lines (most notably at the beginnings and ends). I have also tried to keep to his sequence of images. Most of all I have tried to produce a translation that follows natural English rhythms, while still conveying some sense of the Latin rhetoric. Ideally, I want mine to be a translation that can be read aloud.

But, because our culture is so oriented toward seeing words rather than hearing them, I have "translated" some rhetorical effects by various typographical means: (1) Some sections of the poem, where Lucan or a character is thinking to himself, or where the poet suddenly steps either into or out of his narrative, appear in italics to indicate the changed tone. (2) I have followed Robert Fitzgerald's lead (*Odyssey,* 1961; *Iliad,* 1974; *Aeneid,* 1981) in making free use of paragraphing and formal divisions within the books to highlight change of speaker or focus and to point up structure. (3) For the catalogues and more lyrical passages, I have broken up the six-beat lines as Richmond Lattimore did in his translation of Hesiod's poems (1968). Let me stress, however, that none of these devices is present in the original Latin text. They are purely typographical elements which I am using to suggest changes in tempo, voice, or emphasis, changes which would have been readily apparent to a listening audience, and which still could affect us if we heard rather than saw the poem.

* * *

I have followed the justly famous text of A. E. Housman (1927) with one exception: I am indebted to Peter Green for the reading *disturbavisti* at 1.86. Line numbers refer to the Latin text, although they do also match the English text fairly closely. Line numbers marked with an asterisk point up lines deleted or rearranged by Housman; any deviation from his text is indicated in the notes.

To make Lucan's poem most readily accessible to a general audience, I have decided on the following practices: (1) For stylistic reasons, I have not used "silent glosses"; Lucan's style is densely allusive, and to bring such a wealth of additional material up into the body of the text would have made it too clotted. (2) I have tried to help with pronunciation of Greek and Latin names that might possibly be unfamiliar to non-classicists by placing a circumflex above the vowel in any sounded syllable that an English reader might not guess should be sounded (for example, "Agavê"—three syllables, not two); in the case of two vowels, both of which are sounded, I have placed an umlaut over the second vowel in the usual way ("Phaëthon," for example); very rarely, I have indicated a stressed syllable with an acute accent. (3) In most cases I have used modern place names if they derive from the ancient, but in some instances I have rather arbitrarily decided to keep the ancient name even if the modern name is a derivative ("Marseilles," for example, seemed to set up too many inappropriate associations to use in place of "Massilia"); but generally speaking, the modern names are used. (4) There is an extensive glossary at the end of the poem to help with the myriad allusions to people and places. (5) I have tried to keep footnotes to a minimum; after the first reference to any one item, no further notes are given unless absolutely necessary. (6) Each individual book has a preface which gives a brief synopsis and addresses a few literary questions; in addition, some glossary entries suggest literary sources and antecedents. (7) All dates throughout are Before the Common Era (B. C. E.) unless otherwise specified. . . .

Notes

1. The Latin sources for Lucan's life are gathered in W. E. Heitland's Introduction to C. E. Haskins' edition of Lucan's epic, xiii-xx. Frederick M. Ahl gives a detailed analysis of the sources in the first chapter and in the Appendix of *Lucan: An Introduction* (Cornell University Press, 1976). Dates for events in Lucan's life (other than birth and death) are conjectural, based on Ahl, pp. 36-47 and 333-353.

2. Most easily found in English translation in J. C. Rolfe's *Suetonius* in the Loeb Classical Library series (Harvard University Press, 1959), vol. 2, pp. 500-503.

3. See Tacitus *Annales* 14.52-56.

4. For ancient testimony to the ban, see Tacitus *Annales* 15.49; Vacca, vv. 24-32 (Heitland); Dio 62.29.4.

5. Member of a family which had long demonstrated strong Republican feelings, Calpurnius Piso had already come into conflict with Gaius (Caligula) in 40 C. E. over the deification of his wife.

6. Tacitus describes the discovery of the Pisonian conspiracy at *Annales* 15.54-57 and the suicides of Lucan (15.70), Seneca (15.60-64), Gallio (15.73), and Mela (16.17).

7. See Suetonius' *Life* of Lucan, pp. 502-503 (Loeb).

8. See his *Letters* 7.17.11-12 and 9.34.2.

9. See Tacitus *Dialogus de Oratoribus* (*Dialogue about Orators*) par. 9.

10. Lucan's grandfather Lucius Annaeus Seneca (c. 55 B. C. E. to C. E. 37) tells us this in the preface (par. 2) to his fourth book of *Controversiae* (*Debates*), a collection of school exercises in oratory, debating imaginary cases before the law court.

11. Martial *Epigrams* 14.104; see also 7.23 and 25.

12. Ahl, *Lucan: An Introduction,* p. 80.

13. Dante Alighieri, *The Inferno,* trans. John Ciardi (New York: Mentor Books/New American Library, 1954), p. 52.

14. Some examples of translations made of the *Pharsalia* in the fifteenth through seventeenth centuries include: P. Le Rouge's French prose paraphrase of 7.62ff. (Paris, 1490, 1500), Michel de Marolles' translation (1623), and Brébeuf's French verse translation (1655); Montechiello's Italian version of 1492, Giulio Morigi's of 1579, and Alberto Campani's of 1640; in Spanish we have Juan de Jauregui's *Farsalia* (trans., 1614; pub. 1684).

15. See *Marlowe's Poems,* L. C. Martin, ed. (New York: Gordian Press, Inc., 1966), pp. 261-295.

16. In his *Life* of Nicholas Rowe (in *Lives of the Poets,* 1779), Samuel Johnson (himself partial to Lucan) goes on to say: "There is, perhaps, [no other translation] that so completely exhibits the genius and spirit of the original. Lucan is distinguished by a kind of dictatorial or philosophick dignity . . . full of ambitious morality and pointed sentences, comprised in vigorous and animated lines." And Johnson goes on to commend Rowe's translation further for its melody and force and its adherence to the original.

17. See Letters 254 and 257 in *The Complete Works of Percy Bysshe Shelley,* vol. 9, edited by Roger Ingpen and Walter E. Peck (New York: Gordian Press, 1965), pp. 116 and 119.

Matthew Leigh (essay date 1997)

SOURCE: Leigh, Matthew. "Pharsalus—Wishing and Watching." In *Lucan: Spectacle and Engagement,* pp. 77-109. Oxford: Clarendon Press, 1997.

[*In the following excerpt, Leigh analyzes three episodes in Book 7 of the* Pharsalia *in which Lucan inserts himself into the action as narrator.*]

If the narrator of the **Pharsalia** is repeatedly subject to intense emotional involvement in the various crises of the Spanish campaign, there is nevertheless a discernible heightening of engagement as the epic reaches its decisive conflict, Pharsalus. One passage from the Pharsalus narrative, 7. 185-213, has . . . been discussed as a programme for Lucan's anguished and involved narrative voice; two others, 7. 1-44 and 7. 647-711, provide the focus for investigation in the following chapter. The purpose of this [essay] is to consider three further points in Book 7 where the narrator invades the world of the action, or the action that of the narrator. These are all analysed with a view to their complexity and reflexivity. Once again, the impassioned manner of the narrator is contrasted with an alternative perspective, that of the indolent spectator Jupiter.

Pharsalia 7. 630-46: 'We Are All Laid Low'

Mors nulla querella
digna sua est, nullosque hominum lugere vacamus.
Non istas habuit pugnae Pharsalia partes
quas aliae clades: *illic* per fata virorum,
per populos *hic* Roma perit; quod militis *illic,*
mors *hic* gentis erat: sanguis ibi fluxit Achaeus,
Ponticus, Assyrius; cunctos haerere cruores
Romanus campisque vetat consistere torrens.
Maius ab hac acie quam quod sua saecula ferrent
volnus habent populi; plus est quam vita salusque
quod perit: in totum mundi prosternimur aevum.
Vincitur his gladiis omnis quae serviet aetas.
Proxim a quid suboles aut quid meruere nepotes
in regnum nasci? Pavide num gessimus arma
teximus aut iugulos? Alieni poena timoris
in nostra cervice sedet. Post proelia natis
si dominum, Fortuna, et bella dedisses.

No death is worthy of its own lament and we have no room to mourn individuals. Pharsalia did not have those features of battle which other massacres have: there Rome died through the destinies of men, here through whole peoples; what there was the death of soldiers, here was the death of a race—there flowed Achaean, Pontic, Assyrian blood; the Roman torrent prevents all that gore from sticking or from settling on the fields. The peoples suffered a greater wound from this battle than their generations could endure; it is more than life and salvation that is lost—we are laid low for all the time of the world to come. Every age which shall be enslaved is conquered by these swords. Why did the next generation, why did the grandsons deserve to be born into a monarchy? Did we bear arms like cowards or cover our throats? The penalty of another's fear sits on our necks. Fortune, if you gave those born after the battle a master, you should also have given them wars.

I begin my discussion of Lucan's Pharsalus narrative with this brief passage because it features, in condensed form, almost all the elements of his literary style and political outlook to be highlighted in this chapter.[1] In its

anger and search for someone to blame, it also raises issues which will form the central preoccupation of the ensuing discussion of the heroism and *devotio* of Pompey.[2]

Lines 7. 597-616 describe the heroic death of Domitius. Yet this is not to be a poem of individual *aristeiai*. This is the message of 7. 617-30, where Lucan's expression of shame at discussing individual deaths goes hand in hand with a grotesque account of the violence done by Roman to Roman, kinsman to kinsman.

Lines 7. 630-46 return to the futility of mourning individuals: Pharsalus is a universal disaster. Moreover, it is this expression of universality, conceived both spatially and temporally, which underpins the striking intensification of involvement visible in this scene.

The universal impact of Pharsalus is expressed spatially at lines 7. 632-40. These lines represent all other battles as more distant (*illic . . . illic*) while presenting Pharsalus as 'here' (*hic . . . hic . . . hac*). Lucan moves beyond the standard adversative relationship of *hic* and *ille,* emphasizing the nearness of 'this' battle. Just as all the kings and races of the world are drawn into the confined space of Pharsalus, so the narrator undergoes a transformation, taking on an engaged presence at the scene of the conflict. At times, his presence is that of a character intervening in the action, at others the *hic* of Pharsalus represents the horribly vivid reality of a battle which the Neronian narrator must recount. This second aspect of Lucan's use of deixis emerges very strongly at 7. 545-59, where the immediacy of *hic* gives body to the place considered in memory.[3]

The temporal universality of the battle emerges most powerfully at 7. 638-41:

Maius ab hac acie quam quod sua saecula ferrent
volnus habent populi; plus est quam vita salusque
quod perit: in totum mundi prosternimur aevum.
Vincitur his gladiis omnis quae serviet aetas.

The peoples suffered a greater wound from this battle than their generations could endure; it is more than life and salvation that is lost—we are laid low for all the time of the world to come. Every age which shall be enslaved is conquered by these swords.

These lines outline the historical significance of Pharsalus. They treat the battle as the great transformatory episode, and exploit the Vergilian conception of epic as aetiology or foundation myth. The depiction of Pharsalus as the evil cause of present woes coheres with a radical engagement with Vergilian prophecy and Augustan intimations of immortality at 7. 385-459.[4]

Yet the battle is not just an αἴτιον. The temporalities are not so much bridged as merged. The narrator engages with the battle as something continuous and present—we are all still being laid low. This merger of times and perspectives is achieved through the introduction of those normal tenses and voices already familiar from the previous chapter.

Variation of tense emerges in the lines just quoted. The imperfect subjunctive 'could endure' (*ferrent*) suggests that 'suffered' (*habent*) is present historic; 'is lost' (*perit*) can be either present or progressive present historic; but 'we are laid low' (*prosternimur*) marks a clear shift. While its tone is of soldiers laid low in battle, the use of the first-person plural and the expansion of the temporal focus (*in totum mundi . . . aevum*) makes it clear that the people being laid low are not just the soldiers, but all Romans to come; both those, one might say, between the battle and the time of Lucan, and those who will live after him. This is peculiarly resonant for a civil war. In conventional narratives of war, it is possible to use notions of 'us' to imply the Romans against the foreign enemy (*milites nostri*).[5] Here, 'we are laid low' has an entirely different implication.[6]

Prosternimur thus allows Lucan both to associate himself with the immediacy of death in battle and to point to Pharsalus as the αἴτιον for Rome's destruction. Line 7. 641 has the same double effect:

> Vincitur his gladiis omnis quae serviet aetas.

> Every age which shall be enslaved is conquered by these swords.

The combination of 'these swords' (*his gladiis*) with 'shall be enslaved' (*serviet*) may be taken as an instance in miniature of the phenomenon which was first noted with reference to 4. 254-9: the illusion of immediate presence undermined by the self-conscious reference to historical information available only to one living after the battle.[7] The future historic again features as a distancing, analytical device. Alternatively, the sense of merged temporalities, of *his gladiis* still drawn and ready for use, allows 'omnis quae serviet aetas' a further sense: that is, of the future faced by the Neronian narrator and his readers, the very future to which he refers at 7. 205-13 and 9. 980-6. In either case, the main point of reference, the focus of pathos, is the Neronian world of the unfree survivors. The interaction of different conceptions of futurity is prominent at 7. 385-459.

With lines 7. 638-41, Lucan achieves a smooth but complex transition to 7. 642-7, where the concluding focus is explicitly that of the subsequent generations, hence the first-person plural perfect tense of 'did we bear?' (*gessimus*) and 'did we cover?' (*teximus*). Lucan wishes 'you should also have given them wars' (*et bella dedisses*) and laments that his time did not have the chance to fight against monarchy. 'He' was beaten at Pharsalus.

On one level, these closing lines are entirely consonant with the engaged, Republican Lucan prominent in Books 4 and 5: they reverse the terms of Vergilian epic, the αἴτια, the sense of foundation and futurity, in order to write a dissenter's anti-*Aeneid*. However, the hatred of Caesarism is now combined with a second and equally violent resentment, that of those who 'let us down':

> Proxima quid suboles aut quid meruere nepotes
> in regnum nasci? Pavide num gessimus arma
> teximus aut iugulos? Alieni poena timoris
> in nostra cervice sedet. Post proelia natis
> si dominum, Fortuna, et bella dedisses.

> Why did the next generation, why did the grandsons deserve to be born into a monarchy? Did we bear arms like cowards or cover our throats? The penalty of another's fear sits on our necks. Fortune, if you gave those born after the battle a master, you should also have given them wars.

These are the words of a generation not just defeated but sure that it has been betrayed. 'The penalty of another's fear' (*Alieni poena timoris*) is a markedly unspecific expression, and one which begs some obvious questions: 'Who let us down? Whose cowardice?' On the surface, the answer to these questions may seem clear. Lucan, after all, gives the reader a positive answer. Rambaud,[8] Lounsbury,[9] and Heyke[10] all point to 7. 525-7 and the collapse of the barbarian cavalry:

> Inmemores pugnae *nulloque pudore timendi*
> praecipites fecere palam civilia bella
> non bene barbaricis umquam commissa catervis.

> Forgetful of battle and unashamed of their fear, by their headlong flight they made it evident that civil wars are never well entrusted to barbarian troops.

To this they add the summary of the collapse at 7. 543-4:

> Semel ortus in omnis
> it timor, et fatis datus est pro Caesare cursus.

> Once it rose, the fear spread to all and the fates allowed things to run in favour of Caesar.

Yet it is a measure of the complexity of the question that Lucan also feels bound to give a second, negative answer, and one which replies to his complaint in its own terms. Pompey, the reader is assured, was not afraid, 7. 669-70:

> Nec derat robur in enses
> ire duci iuguloque pati vel pectore letum.

> Nor did the general lack the courage to enter the fight and meet death with a blow to the throat or the breast.

Blame attributed and blame denied are an intriguing combination. Blame attributed bespeaks the need to blame someone, the sense that the defeat of the

Republic was not just due to the positive superiority of the opposition. Blame denied reveals the suspicion which the denial controverts, gives air to the notion that Pompey's generalship was perhaps cowardly or his conduct reprehensible.[11] It is the purpose of my chapter on Pompey closely to investigate the suspicion that Lucan's ostentatious refusal to blame Pompey is not as simple as it may appear. In this chapter, my analysis of 7. 545-96 examines the actions of the senators, and shows how the address to Brutus may be taken as the sarcastic and frustrated complaint of the die-hard oppositionist revealed in these lines. As in the mutiny and the appeal to Discordia, it is thus possible to measure the true degree of Lucan's disillusion, of his rage against history.

PHARSALIA 7. 385-459: HEADING FOR THE
BATTLEFIELD

This is a complete and complex narrative movement, which should be printed in full:

Ergo utrimque pari procurrunt agmina motu
irarum; metus hos regni, spes excitat illos.
Hae *facient* dextrae, quidquid non expleat aetas
ulla nec humanum genus reparet omnibus annis,
ut vacet a ferro.[12] Gentes Mars iste futuras
obruet et populos aevi venientis in orbem   (390)
erepto natale *feret*. Tunc omne Latinum
fabula nomen *erit*; Gabios Veiosque Coramque
pulvere vix tectae *poterunt* monstrare ruinae
Albanosque lares Laurentinosque penates,
rus vacuum, quod non habitet nisi nocte coacta
invitus questusque Numam iussisse senator.
Non aetas haec carpsit edax monimentaque rerum
putria destituit: crimen civile videmus
tot vacuas urbes. Generis quo turba redacta est
humani! Toto populi qui nascimur orbe   (400)
nec muros inplere viris nec possumus agros:
urbs nos una capit. Vincto fossore coluntur
Hesperiae segetes, stat tectis putris avitis
in nullos ruitura domus, nulloque frequentem
cive suo Romam sed mundi faece repletam
cladis eo dedimus, ne tanto in corpore bellum
iam possit civile geri. Pharsalia tanti
causa mali. Cedant feralia nomina Cannae
et damnata diu Romanis Allia fastis.
Tempora signavit leviorum Roma malorum,   (410)
hunc voluit nescire diem. Pro tristia fata!
Aera pestiferum tractu morbosque fluentis
insanamque famem permissasque ignibus urbes
moeniaque in praeceps laturos plena tremores
hi *possunt*[13] explere viri, quos undique traxit
in miseram Fortuna necem, dum munera longi
explicat eripiens aevi populosque ducesque
constituit campis, per quos tibi, Roma, ruenti
ostendat quam magna cadas. Quae latius orbem
possedit, citius per prospera fata cucurrit?   (420)
Omne tibi bellum gentis dedit, omnibus annis
te geminum Titan procedere vidit in axem;
haud multum terrae spatium restabat Eoae,
ut tibi nox, tibi tota dies, tibi curreret aether,

omniaque errantes stellae Romana viderent.
Sed retro tua fata tulit par omnibus annis
Emathiae funesta dies. Hac luce cruenta
effectum, ut Latios non horreat India fasces,
nec vetitos errare Dahas in moenia ducat
Sarmaticumque premat succinctus consul
aratrum,   (430)
quod semper saevas debet tibi Parthia poenas,
quod fugiens civile nefas redituraque numquam
libertas ultra Tigrim Rhenumque recessit
ac, totiens nobis iugulo quaesita, vagatur
Germanum Scythicumque bonum, nec respicit ultra
Ausoniam, vellem populis incognita nostris.
Volturis ut primum laevo fundata volatu
Romulus infami conplevit moenia luco,
usque ad Thessalicas servisses, Roma,
ruinas.   (440)
De Brutis, Fortuna, queror. Quid tempora legum
egimus aut annos a consule nomen habentis?
Felices Arabes Medique Eoaque tellus,
quam sub perpetuis tenuerunt fata tyrannis.
Ex populis qui regna ferunt sors ultima nostra est,
quos servire pudet. Sunt nobis nulla profecto
numina: cum caeco rapiantur saecula casu,
mentimur regnare Iovem. *Spectabit* ab alto
aethere Thessalicas, teneat cum fulmina, caedes?
Scilicet ipse petet *Pholoen,* petet *ignibus*
Oeten   (450)
inmeritaeque nemus Rhodopes pinusque Mimantis,
Cassius hoc potius *feriet* caput? Astra Thyestae
intulit et subitis damnavit noctibus Argos:
tot similis fratrum gladios patrumque gerenti
Thessaliae *dabit* ille diem? Mortalia nulli
sunt curata deo. Cladis tamen huius habemus
vindictam, quantam terris dare numina fas est:
bella pares superis *facient* civilia divos,
fulminibus manes radiisque *ornabit* et astris
inque deum templis *iurabit* Roma per umbras.

Therefore from both sides the armies ran forwards each with as great an angry impulse; fear of monarchy aroused one side, hope the other. These right hands will do a deed which no age can make right nor can the human race in all the years repair, even if it desists from warfare. This fight will destroy the nations of the future and will take away the peoples of the time still to come to the world, stealing their birth from them. Then all the Latin name will be a tale; the ruins covered in dust will scarce be able to indicate Gabii and Veii and Cora and the houses of Alba and the settlements of Laurentum, an empty stretch of country which nobody inhabits save the senator who is compelled against his will to spend the night there and who complains of Numa's orders. The tooth of time did not eat away at these things and bring down the crumbling monuments of the past: we see in so many empty cities the sin of civil war. To what has the mob of the human race been reduced! We peoples who are born all over the world can neither fill the walls nor the fields with men: one city holds us. The corn of Hesperia is cultivated by a chained ditcher; the house stands crumbling with its ancient roof, doomed to fall but on no occupants; and Rome, populated by no citizens of her own but full of the dregs of the world, we have brought to such a point of destruction that in so great a body it is no longer possible to fight a civil war. Pharsalia is responsible for so great an ill. Let the fatal names give way, Cannae and the Allia long damned on the Roman calendar. Rome marked the date of lesser ills, this day she preferred not to know. O sorry fates! These men can satiate air poisonous to inhale and the spread of plagues and mad hunger and cities set on fire and earthquakes that will bring full cities to the ground—these men whom Fortune has drawn from every side to wretched slaughter, the gifts of long ages which she steals away as she displays them to you, the peoples and the generals whom she has set on the field, by whom she may show you, Rome, in collapse how great you are as you fall. Which city possessed a greater expanse of the globe, which ran faster from one success to another? Every war gave you nations, every year the Sun saw you move further towards the North and South; very little of the Eastern land remained before all of night and day, all the heavens, should run for you and the wandering stars should see nothing that was not Roman. Yet the fatal day of Emathia, a match for all the years, turned back your destiny. By this bloody day it was ensured that India should not tremble at the Latin rods; that the consul should not forbid the Dahae to roam and lead them into city walls or gird himself up and lean on a Sarmatian plough; that still Parthia should owe you savage retribution; that Freedom, fleeing the crimes of civil strife and never to return, has retreated beyond the Tigris and the Rhine and, so often sought by us at the expense of our lives, wanders, the property of the Germans and the Scythians, and never more looks back on Ausonia—if only she had never been known to our peoples! Would that, ever since Romulus filled the city walls he had founded on the auspices of a vulture's flight on the left with the people of the notorious grove, you had been a slave, Rome, right down to the disaster of Thessaly! Fortune, I complain of the Bruti. Why did we enjoy times of legal administration and years which took their names from the consuls? Lucky are the Arabs, the Medes and the Eastern land, which destiny has held under a succession of tyrants. Of the peoples who endure monarchies our lot is the worst, for we are ashamed to be slaves. Truly we have no divine powers: when the generations are carried along by blind chance, we lie to say that Jupiter rules. Will he watch the slaughter of Thessaly from the heights of heaven, though he holds the thunderbolts? Will he, of course, attack Pholoe, will he attack with his fires Oeta and the grove of innocent Rhodope and the pines of Mimas, will Cassius strike this head instead? He brought night to Thyestes and damned Argos to sudden darkness: will he grant day to Thessaly as she bears so many like swords of brothers and of fathers? No god has cared for mortal affairs. Yet we have as great a revenge for this slaughter as it is right for the divine powers to give to mortals: civil wars will make gods equal to those above; Rome will decorate shades with thunderbolts and haloes and stars and in the temples of the gods will swear by ghosts.

This is a classic example of Lucan's technique of narrative delay. Lines 7. 382-4 round off the *paraceleusis* of Pompey, and are then followed by two lines of consequent action:

Ergo utrimque pari procurrunt agmina motu irarum; metus hos regni, spes excitat illos.

Therefore from both sides the armies ran forwards with equal angry emotion; fear of monarchy aroused one side, hope the other.

The reader is then treated to seventy-two lines of magniloquent analysis and exclamation from the narrator, itself rounded off by the surely ironic 7. 460-1:

Ut *rapido cursu* fati suprema *morantem consumpsere locum*. . .

When with rapid dash they crossed the ground that delayed the final ends of fate . . .[14]

Needless to say, Lucan shares none of the haste of his characters.

These brief segments of narrative advance encircle a remarkable instance of the indignant reflection and final intervention of Lucan's narrator. It is my contention that the movement of the passage demands its reading as a unified whole, that the temptation should be resisted to mark off certain sections as coming from the primary narrator, others from an anonymous chorus.[15] The case for a resulting architectonic unity may be made by a series of observations.

It is essential from the outset to emphasize the significance of 7. 386, 'fear of monarchy aroused one side, hope the other' (*metus hos regni, spes excitat illos*). Lucan fills his characters with the very emotions which he expects to generate in his readers at 7. 211. Of course, the distinction applies to the emotions of the Pompeians on the one hand, and of the Caesarians on the other, and thus summarizes the reactions to the speeches of the two generals; but it is also programmatic for the dramatic involvement of the narrator in this segment.[16]

The text printed at 7. 387-9 is not free from suspicion but the possible corruption is not such as to obscure the sweeping movement and complex literary effects at which Lucan aims through 387-407. These lines divide into two answering sections. The first, 387-96, takes its inspiration from the anticipatory emotions of the troops at 386. The primary narrator, by employing a succession of future indicatives, evokes the immediacy of expectation: 'will do . . . will destroy . . . will take away . . . will be . . . will scarce be able' (*facient . . . obruet . . . feret . . . erit . . . poterunt*). Though it soon becomes apparent that the future is not open, that these verbs use a prospective mode of expression to convey a strictly historical proposition, it is essential to the functioning of the passage as a whole that the sense of some potential vivid presence should be injected from the start.

The future historic again serves to underline the extreme significance of the event.[17] That these are future historics and not the vivid futures of a separate character or chorus is made explicit by the answering movement of perfects and presents at 7. 397-407, outlining the state of the world 'in which we live'. Essential here are the expressions in the first person plural: 'we see the sin of civil war . . . we are born . . . we can . . . one city holds us . . . we have brought to such a point of destruction' (*crimen civile videmus . . . nascimur . . . possumus . . . urbs nos una capit . . . cladis eo dedimus*).

The two answering movements at 387-407 combine to produce a two-pronged attack on Augustan poetry: at once assaulting directly its optimistic prophecies and, more subtly, providing an exegesis of the points of anxiety already present within them. It is the second tendency, in particular, that is apparent at lines 391-6, which enter into a complex dialectic with the prophecy of Anchises at *Aeneid* 6. 773-6:

> 'Hi tibi Nomentum et Gabios urbemque Fidenam,
> hi Collatinas imponent montibus arces,
> Pometics Castrumque Inui Bolamque Coramque;
> haec tum nomina erunt, nunc sunt sine nomine terrae.'

> 'These men will put Nomentum and Gabii and the city of Fidenae and the Collatine citadel atop the mountains for you, and Pometii and Castrum Inui and Bola and Cora; these then will be famous names, now they are lands without name.'[18]

Anchises understands the power of naming as one imposes one's civilization, one's buildings, on the countryside. Yet the names evoked have a particular and troubling resonance. Anchises tells of the future glory of cities, but it is not an unconditional future. It is the destiny of Rome as she expands to render other civilizations mere ghost-towns, and it cannot escape the Augustan reader that, by his time, Gabii and Fidenae are mere names because destroyed by Rome.[19]

The speech of Anchises is a complex phenomenon. It is impossible to escape the sense that, in its totality, this is an 'eternal' statement of Roman destiny and identity. At the same time, a detailed reading of the speech reveals an indisputable partiality and selectivity. The downplaying or exclusion of the creative arts at 6. 847-53, which has long been recognized as highly incongruous in the context of Vergil's poetry, is also marked by Ovid as true only for an early period of Roman history.[20] And the celebration of Gabii and Fidenae is a classic instance of the 'optimistic prophecy'[21] in the *Aeneid*: a prophecy delivered by one character to another, often with the effect of consoling the listener, but which reveals its own omissions and obfuscations to the 'Augustan' reader. It is this inconcinnity which Lucan exploits at 7. 391-6:

> Tunc omne Latinum
> fabula nomen erit; Gabios Veiosque Coramque
> pulvere vix tectae poterunt monstrare ruinae
> Albanosque lares Laurentinosque penates,
> rus vacuum, quod non habitat nisi nocte coacta
> invitus questusque Numam iussisse senator.

> Then all the Latin name will be a tale; the ruins covered in dust will scarce be able to indicate Gabii and Veii and Cora and the houses of Alba and the settlements of Laurentum, an empty stretch of country which nobody inhabits save the senator who is compelled against his will to spend the night there and who complains of Numa's orders.

Lucan blames on the civil wars the destruction of cities ruined years earlier and by the expansion of Rome. The function of this anachronism is surely to point up the literary relationship to Vergil and to offer an exegesis of his predecessor's text.[22] Lucan does not so much write an anti-*Aeneid* as draw out the troubling 'further voice' audible in the prophecy of Anchises.[23]

Lucan's prospective, prophetic voice at 387-96 interacts strikingly with its retrospective counterpart at 397-407. If the former offers an exegesis of the problems which Vergil discreetly invites the reader to perceive in Anchises' prophecy, the latter noisily rebuts the illusions of Horace's Augustan verse. *Pharsalia* 7. 397-8 opens:

> Non aetas haec carpsit edax monimentaque rerum
> putria destituit.

> The tooth of time did not eat away at these things and bring down the crumbling monuments of the past.

Lucan thus savages the conceits of Horace at *Carm.* 3. 30. 1-5:

> Exegi monumentum aere perennius
> regalique situ pyramidum altius,
> quod non imber edax, non Aquilo impotens
> possit diruere aut innumerabilis
> annor im series et fuga temporum.

> I have built a monument more lasting than bronze and higher than the regal pomp of the pyramids which neither biting rain nor mighty Aquilo nor the numberless succession of the years and the flight of times can bring down.

Another target is perhaps the boast of Ovid at *Met.* 15. 871-2:

> Iamque opus exegi, quod nec Iovis ira nec ignis
> nec poterit ferrum nec edax abolere vetustas.

> And now I have built a work, which neither the anger of Jupiter nor fire nor steel nor the tooth of time can destroy.[24]

What is significant about both these Augustan claims to immortality is that the survival they claim is conditional on the continuation of the political culture which can make sense of them. Though *Carm.* 3. 30 begins with the claim of longer life for the poet's verse than for mere physical monuments, it closes with the assertion of the vital interrelation of Roman verse and the public buildings of the Roman state, *Carm.* 3. 30. 7-9:

> Usque ego postera
> crescam laude recens, dum Capitolium
> scandet cum tacita Virgine pontifex.

> I shall ever rise, fresh with the praises of posterity, as long as the priest climbs the Capitol with the silent Virgin.[25]

This association of the immortality of Augustan verse with the survival of the political buildings of the Augustan State also underpins the apostrophe of Vergil to Nisus and Euryalus at *Aeneid* 9. 446-9,[26] is parodied in Apollo's words to Daphne the laurel tree at Ovid, *Met.* 1. 557-67, and explored much more seriously at the very close of the poem, especially 15. 877-9:

> Quaque patet domitis Romana potentia terris,
> ore legar populi, perque omnia saecula fama,
> siquid habent veri vatum praesagia, vivam.

> And where Roman power opens out over the conquered lands, I shall be read in the mouths of the people, and through all the generations, if the prophecies of the poets have any truth, I shall live in fame.[27]

The Augustan poets premise their claim of immortality on the survival of Augustan Rome.[28] Lucan, however, protests that Rome has been destroyed, and, what's more, that it was destroyed by the very war, the *crimen civile* which brought their Augustus to power. The poets who praise the new regime are not the celebrants of the great Rome but the lackeys of its destroyer. This is powerfully expressed at 7. 402-3, where 'The corn of Hesperia is cultivated by a chained ditcher' (*Vincto fossore coluntur | Hesperiae segetes*), an allusion to the replacement of the native Italian farmer with the chain-gang labour of the *ergastulum*, also bears the stamp of Ovid's exile poetry, of the latter's final experience of tyranny. For Ovid, in *Tristia* 4. 1. 5-6, apologizing for the inadequacy of his verse, claims that he writes only for *requies* and compares his motivation to that of the chained ditcher:

> Hoc est cur cantet vinctus quoque compede fossor,
> indocili numero cum grave mollit opus.

> This is why even the ditcher bound in fetters sings as he eases his hard labour with an untaught tune.

The same poet, at *Epistulae ex Ponto* 1. 6. 31-2, protests that he has not yet lost hope, and adds that:

> Haec [i.e. spes] facit ut vivat fossor quoque compede
> vinctus
> liberaque a ferro crura futura putet.

> This [hope] makes even the ditcher bound in fetters live and hope that his legs will be free from the irons.[29]

Lines 387-407 introduce the notion of the narrator operating on two different stages at once. The Neronian narrator is able also to speak as if he is a character watching the drama develop. This perspective will now come to prominence. At the same time, the presence and prospection of the narrator at 387-96 is not that of a dramatically involved and naïve character, but a highly self-conscious production constantly entangled intertextually with the Augustan visions of Rome it unmasks or deplores. The intertextual dimension will again become prominent at the close of the speech.

All the emphasis of 397-407 is on what has happened, does happen, no longer can happen. The explanation is simple and brief, 7. 407-8:

> . . . Pharsalia tanti
> causa mali.

> Pharsalia is responsible for so great an ill.[30]

From here, the emotion of the narrator grows. The reference to Cannae and Allia at 7. 408-11 is in the form of what one might call an imperative of literary immortality, and one which derives its force from the response of the Roman calendar: 'only Pharsalus have we refused to recall'. The perspective here is still firmly that of the Neronian poet looking back on and analysing the battle and its consequences, but a slightly different movement seems to emerge in the following lines, 7. 411-19. The initial exclamation 'O sorry fates!' (*Pro tristia fata!*) seems still to maintain the position of retrospection. On the other hand, *fata* can be viewed as coming as well as past, and this interpretation is consonant with the easiest translation of the following sentence: that is, that it is addressed by the 'narrator as character' to Rome, the best part of which are the men who die, as he stands on or by the field of battle. As they fall, so does Rome (*quam magna cadas*). Thus, *possunt* is read 'can glut', *traxit* and *constituit* as 'has drawn' and 'has arrayed'. The apostrophe to 'you, Rome, in collapse' (*tibi, Roma, ruenti*) and the purpose clause 'by whom she may show you' (*per quos . . . ostendat*) would seem to support this interpretation.[31]

The intervention of the narrator is only fleeting. It acts as much as anything to demonstrate the emotional pressure generated by awareness that Pharsalus is the one great and destructive day. The address to Rome at 7. 418-19 is an address to the men of Rome on the battlefield, who, by destroying themselves, destroy the city as well, but it is also an address to the idealizing conception of Rome. This ideal of Rome remains Lucan's addressee throughout the section introduced with the rhetorical question at 419-20:

> Quae latius orbem
> possedit, citius per prospera fata cucurrit?

> Which city possessed a greater expanse of the globe,
> which ran faster from one success to another?

The rise and fall of the city is traced in the second person.[32] It is as if the ideal of Rome is to be separated from the men, the generation which is to be blamed. For the point of this passage is again that Pharsalus destroyed everything, 7. 426-7:

> Sed retro tua fata tulit par omnibus annis
> Emathiae funesta dies.

> Yet the fatal day of Emathia, a match for all the years,
> turned back your destiny.

The true nadir is the world of Nero and of Lucan.

At 7. 427-36, the narrator gives four lines of external, imperial decline (7. 428-31) and five of internal (7. 432-6), and all the product of Pharsalus. Again, we are in the territory of the αἴτιον. The civil wars were the period of transformation which created the Rome in which Lucan lives. The theme of lost liberty now prompts the narrator to a retrospective and paradoxical mode of expression, offering a wish (7. 437-9, esp. *servisses*), a complaint (7. 440, *queror*), a rhetorical question (7. 440-1), and a tortured *sententia* (7. 442-5). Finally, as his emotion and indignation builds, the narrator draws what ought to be his climactic conclusion: that is, that the fact of the civil wars proves that there are no gods, or at least no caring gods. However, lines 7. 445-7, self-consciously literary in their final swipe at Horace,[33] do not so much complete the process of retrospection as act as the pivot to introduce the emergence of the narrator as *dramatis persona*:

> Sunt nobis nulla profecto
> numina: cum caeco rapiantur saecula casu,
> mentimur regnare Iovem.

> Truly we have no divine powers: when the generations
> are carried along by blind chance, we lie to say that
> Jupiter rules.

At this point, it is important to recapitulate. *Pharsalia* 7. 387-459 is a consistent sweeping movement, deploying a variety of perspectives to evoke the significance for Lucan's Rome of the coming battle. While Pharsalus and its consequences are past, historical events for the narrator and his audience, it is a past which remains alive in the world it created. The inclusion of so long a piece of intense analysis at this point in the action is in violation of any traditional conception of epic narration. What is seen, in fact, is a radical transformation of customary epic practice, though one which, by its assault on the imperial aetiology, the bridging of temporalities of the *Aeneid,* can be seen as an explosion of forces inherent in previous *Romana carmina*.

The variation of perspective, the appeal to futurity—all this will now return as the movement, architectonic in its structure, reaches its climax. 7. 387-96 begins with a series of future historics, which act to underline the significance of the battle, also to disconcert the reader by their likeness to those futures which express a contingent situation or which promise immortality in a literary work.[34] Similarly, 7. 411-19 hints at the actual intervention of the narrator as character, this being treated as the paradoxical extension of his retrospective rage. At 7. 447-54, where previously this was only a possible interpretation, now it is evident. The contingent future of the narrator emerges directly from the conclusion to his retrospection:

> *Spectabit* ab alto
> aethere Thessalicas, teneat cum fulmina, caedes?
> Scilicet ipse *petet* Pholoen, *petet* ignibus Oeten
> inmeritaeque nemus Rhodopes pinusque Mimantis,
> Cassius hoc potius *feriet* caput? Astra Thyestae
> intulit et subitis damnavit noctibus Argos:
> tot similis fratrum gladios patrumque gerenti
> Thessaliae *dabit* ille diem?

> Will he watch the slaughter of Thessaly from the heights of heaven, though he holds the thunderbolts? Will he, of course, attack Pholoe, will he attack with his fires Oeta and the grove of innocent Rhodope and the pines of Mimas, will Cassius strike this head instead? He brought night to Thyestes and damned Argos to sudden darkness: will he grant day to Thessaly as she bears so many like swords of brothers and of fathers?

The sentiment expressed accuses Jupiter of watching, of reading the **Pharsalia** with a culpable absence of passion.[35] The contrast between the anguished engagement of the poet and the apathy attributed to the god recalls the terms of Cato's question at 2. 289-92 and Lucan's own comment at 4. 400-1. The wishes implicit in Lucan's question are those which he anticipates in his readers at 7. 211. Moreover, it is surely possible to envisage the manner of the complaint. Just as Lucan's readers will feel as if they are present at the battle, so too here the 'narrator as character' seems to stand on the field of battle, to hold up his hands to heaven, to point to the high mountains all around him, and thus to deliver his despairing complaint: history must be reversed.

Further, all the above observations take on a particular point when one considers two passages of Seneca of obvious intertextual importance for the narrator's complaint. The first of these is *De Otio* 4. 2, where one of the catalogue of philosophical questions listed by Seneca is:

> Qui sit deus; *deses* opus suum *spectet* an tractet.

> Who is god; whether he indolently watches his creation
> or takes it in hand.[36]

The implication of Jupiter's spectatorship in Lucan is the same as that posited here by Seneca, that it stands for his inaction, his want of care.[37] The second passage is more complex. My discussion of spectatorship and spectacle in Lucan stresses his allusion to the experience of the audience in the amphitheatre.[38] Yet consideration is also given to Rosenmeyer's discussion of Seneca, where the world is a stage on which man acts out the good life for the gods to observe.[39] The two conceptions of spectacle are scarcely separate from each other; for the amphitheatre, in Seneca as much as in Cicero, is a constant source of exemplary deeds of various sorts.[40] This blending is apparent in the second passage to be examined, Seneca, *De Providentia* 2. 7-9:

> Miraris tu, si deus ille bonorum amantissimus, qui illos quam optimos esse atque excellentissimos vult, fortunam illis cum qua exerceantur adsignat? Ego vero non miror, si aliquando impetum capiunt spectandi magnos viros conluctantis cum aliqua ca amitate. *Nobis interdum voluptati est, si adulescens constantis animi inruentem feram venabulo excepit, si leonis incursum interritus pertulit, tantoque hoc spectaculum est gratius quanto id honestior fecit.* Non sunt ista quae possint deorum in se vultum convertere, puerilia et humanae oblectamenta levitatis: *ecce spectaculum dignum ad quod respiciat intentus operi suo deus,* ecce par deo dignum, vir fortis cum fortuna mala compositus, utique si et provocavit. *Non video, inquam, quid habeat in terris Iuppiter pulchrius, si&{eo}; convertere animum velit, quam ut spectet Catonem iam partibus non semel fractis stantem nihilo minus inter ruinas publicas rectum.*

> Are you surprised if that god, who is most devoted to good men, who wishes them to be as good and as excellent as possible, assigns them a fortune with which they may be exercised. I indeed am not surprised, if sometimes they get the urge to watch great men wrestling with some calamity. Occasionally it is a source of pleasure for us if a young man of unflinching mind has caught an onrushing beast with his spear, if unshaken he has borne the attack of a lion, and this spectacle is the more pleasing the more virtuous is the man who has provided it. Those things are not the sort which can attract the attention of the gods, the puerile entertainments of human folly: lo! a spectacle worthy of the observation of a god intent on his work, lo! a pair worthy of a god—a hero pitted against ill fortune just as if he had issued the challenge. I tell you, I cannot see what Jupiter can have on earth more fair, if thither he should wish to turn his mind, than to watch Cato, his party already broken more than once, still standing no less straight amidst the disaster of the State.

The argument is complex, in that the exemplarity of the young hunter goes hand in hand with the entertainment of the watching audience. On the other hand, Seneca the philosopher denies the element of simple pleasure for Jupiter in watching the struggles of a Cato and emphasizes that our actions amidst disaster are not futile, for they are there to be observed and judged by the gods.[41] The voice of the narrator in Lucan is very different: it takes Seneca's hypothetical situation, gives it a dramatic reality, and condemns Jupiter the spectator for his disengagement. This has two obvious effects. On the one hand, it accuses Jupiter of an attitude too close to the 'pleasure' (*voluptas*) and 'folly' (*levitas*) of the human audience at the amphitheatre; on the other, it makes Seneca sound uncannily like his second self, the Seneca of the tragedies: the narrator of the *Pharsalia* now sounds far more like the chorus at *Phaedra* 959-88 than he does like Seneca in *De Providentia* 2. 7.

This is one way of looking at this passage. As in the flood episode, however, there are further elements, local and temporal, which undermine the surface naturalism of the intervention. On the local level, for instance, it is somewhat disingenuous to describe the narrator as holding his hands up to the mountains of Thessaly all around. While Mount Oeta is genuinely Thessalian, Pholoe is Arcadian, Rhodope Thracian and Mount Mimas Ionian. Though Keil presumes that there existed a second, Thracian Mount Mimas, it is evident that Lucan's juxtaposition of Rhodope with Mimas is owed rather to his quotation of Ov. *Met.* 2. 222-3:

> Et tanden nivibus Rhodope caritura Mimasque Dindymaque et Mycale natusque ad sacra Cithaeron.

> And Rhodope at last set to lose its snow and Mimas and Dindyma and Mycale and Cithaeron born for holy rites.

While some may take this as evidence of Lucan's geographical incompetence, it is surely more rewarding to follow Kroll and regard this and the subsequent imitation at Sil. *Pun.* 3. 494, *Rhodopeque adiuncta Mimanti,* as the self-conscious acknowledgement of the poetic inheritance.[42] There is an inevitable distancing effect in the recognition that the character we see so directly engaged with the crisis of civil war is also a poet rather knowingly quoting his predecessor, Ovid.

Temporal naturalism lasts little longer. Where the futures of 7. 387-96 were all historics, 'will he watch . . . will he attack . . . will he attack . . . will he strike . . . will he grant' (*spectabit, petet, petet, feriet,* and *dabit*) might all be taken as contingent. This is especially obvious for *spectabit* and *dabit*. The problem emerges with the second question, and particularly with *feriet*. This question plays on the Neronian narrator's knowledge of history subsequent to Pharsalus and of the assassination of Caesar. 'This head' (*hoc . . . caput*) imagines the character pointing to Caesar in person, but the information offered, the reference to Cassius, contradicts the implications of the deictic. In other words, even in those moments where Lucan feigns to seek the reversal of history, he displays great self-consciousness, reverses his own illusion, and puts the weight of the pathos on the Neronian narrator. It is in these terms that the close of this passage achieves its special point.

The passage concludes with a return to the perspective of the opening lines and demonstrates the capacity of the future tense as a formal device, 7. 454-9:

> Mortalia nulli
> sunt curata deo. Cladis tamen huius habemus
> vindictam, quantam terris dare numina fas est:
> bella pares superis facient civilia divos,
> fulminibus manes radiisque ornabit et astris
> inque deum templis iurabit Roma per umbras.

No god has cared for mortal affairs. Yet we have as great a revenge for this slaughter as it is right for the divine powers to give to mortals: civil wars will make gods equal to those above; Rome will decorate shades with thunderbolts and haloes and stars and in the temples of the gods will swear by ghosts.

The theology of the passage has been commented on by many.[43] The Epicurean statement with which it begins can also be read as atheism if we treat *nulli* as indicating simply that there are no gods out there to care.[44] The atheism of the last lines, asserting that the old gods are equal to the new in the sense of being only shades and ghosts, may also indicate another revenge: the crazily antagonistic spirit of the Caesars will bring civil war, the amphitheatre even, to heaven (*pares*).[45] This is just what the spectator Jupiter of 7. 447 deserves.[46] At the same time, however, little has been said about the return to the future historic as a coda to the movement begun at 7. 387-96. Where that section began with a 'will do/make' (*facient*), so does this one, closely followed by 'will decorate' (*ornabit*) and 'will swear' (*iurabit*). The notion of futurity serves as the leitmotiv of the passage, but only a futurity cruelly conditioned and closed. At 7. 447-54, indignant recollection turns into an impotent plea for reversal; the narrator enacts the emotions anticipated at 7. 211; but he also, with *feriet,* includes at the height of his intervention a necessary intellectualizing distance. As his rhetoric sweeps on, and the future form avoids any change in the mode of locution, gradually we become aware of the change in the propositional content of his words. The promise of 7. 205-13 is now completely fulfilled: fate is still fate; it may be coming and not past but is still immutable. The prayers perish on their speaker's lips.

Pharsalia 7. 545-96: Caesar Attacks the Senators

> Ventum erat ad robur Magni mediasque catervas.
> Quod totos errore vago perfuderat agros
> constitit *hic* bellum, fortunaque Caesaris haesit.
> Non *illic* regum auxiliis collecta iuventus
> bella gerit ferrumque manus movere rogatae:
> *ille* locus fratres habuit, locus *ille* parentis.   (550)
> *Hic* furor, *hic* rabies, *hic* sunt tua crimina, *Caesar.*

> *Hanc* fuge, *mens,* partem belli tenebrisque relinque,
> nullaque tantorum discat *me vate* malorum,
> quam multum bellis liceat civilibus, aetas.
> A potius pereant lacrimae pereantque querellae:
> quidquid in *hac* acie gessisti, *Roma,* tacebo.
> *Hic* Caesar, rabies populis stimulusque furorum,
> nequa parte sui pereat scelus, agmina circum
> it vagus atque ignes animis flagrantibus addit.
> Inspicit et gladios, qui toti sanguine manent,   (560)
> qui niteant primo tantum mucrone cruenti,
> quae presso tremat ense manus, quis languida tela,
> quis contenta ferat, quis praestet bella iubenti,
> quem pugnare iuvet, quis voltum cive perempto
> mutet; obit latis proiecta cadavera campis;
> volnera multorum totum fusura cruorem
> opposita premit ipse manu. Quacumque vagatur,
> sanguineum veluti quatiens Bellona flagellum
> Bistonas aut Mavors agitans si verbere saevo
> Palladia stimulet turbatos aegide currus,   (570)
> nox ingens scelerum est; caedes oriuntur et instar
> inmensae vocis gemitus, et pondere lapsi
> pectoris arma sonant confractique ensibus enses.
> Ipse manu subicit gladios ac tela ministrat
> adversosque iubet ferro confundere voltus,
> promovet ipse acies, inpellit terga suorum,
> verbere conversae cessantis excitat hastae,
> in plebem vetat ire manus monstratque senatum:
> scit cruor imperii qui sit, quae viscera rerum,
> unde petat Romam, libertas ultima mundi   (580)
> *quo steterit ferienda loco.* Permixta secundo
> ordine nobilitas venerandaque corpora ferro
> urguentur; *caedunt Lepidos caeduntque Metellos*
> *Corvinosque simul Torquataque nomina,* rerum
> saepe duces summosque hominum te, Magne, remoto.
> Illic plebeia contectus casside voltus
> ignotusque hosti quod ferrum, Brute, tenebas!
> O decus imperii, spes o suprema senatus,
> extremum tanti generis per saecula nomen,
> ne rue per medios nimium temerarius hostis,   (590)
> nec tibi fatales admoveris ante Philippos,
> Thessalia periture tua. Nil proficis istic
> Caesaris intentus iugulo: nondum attigit arcem,
> iuris et humani columen, quo cuncta premuntur,
> egressus meruit fatis tam nobile letum.
> Vivat et, ut Bruti procumbat victima, regnet.

The fight had come to the strong-point of Magnus and to the middle of his troops. The war which had spread in random wandering all over the fields stopped here and Caesar's fortune was checked. Not there did young men wage war who had been collected from the auxiliaries of kings, but hands unbidden plied the steel: that place held brothers, that place fathers. Here is madness, here rage, here is your damnation, Caesar. O mind, flee this part of the war and leave it to the darkness, and let no age learn from my vatic recollection of such great evils how much is possible in civil wars. O rather let our tears be shed, our laments be uttered in vain: whatever you did in this battle, Rome, I shall not report. Here Caesar, rage and goad to madness of the peoples, lest criminality be lost in any part of his force, goes wandering around the ranks and adds fires to burning minds. And he inspects the swords, to see which drip all over with blood, which shine and are bespattered only at the very end of the blade, which hand trembles as it grips the sword, who bears his weapons weakly, who with exertion, who goes into action when ordered, who is delighted to fight, who changes his expression when he has slain a citizen; he goes around the corpses scattered on the broad fields; he himself uses his hand to staunch the wounds which would otherwise shed all the blood of many men. Wherever he wanders, like Bellona brandishing her bloody whip or Mars as he urges on the Bistones, when with savage blows he lashes on his horses that have been thrown into confusion by the aegis of Pallas, there is a huge night of crimes; slaughter rises and a groaning the size of a huge voice, and the breastplates resound with their own weight as a man falls, so too swords broken on swords. He himself with his own hand supplies swords and hands out spears and orders the men to disfigure with the steel the faces of their enemies. He himself pushes forward the line, drives onward the backs of his men, rouses the dawdlers with a blow from the butt of his spear, orders his men not to attack the ordinary soldiers and points the way to the Senate; he knows which is the lifeblood of the empire, which are the guts of the State, from where to attack Rome, in which place what remains of freedom in the world has taken her stand, ready to be struck. Senators commingled with knights and venerable bodies are pressed by the steel; they chop the Lepidi and they chop the Metelli and at the same time the Corvini and the famous Torquati, often leaders of the State and, you apart, Magnus, the loftiest of men. There, masking your face in a plebeian helmet and unnoticed by the enemy, what a sword did you hold, Brutus! O glory of the empire, O final hope of the Senate, the last name of a family so great across the centuries, do not rush too rashly through the midst of the enemy and do not bring on yourself ahead of time the doom of Philippi, you who are destined to die in your own Thessaly. [T]here you achieve nothing by aiming at Caesar's throat: he has not yet reached the citadel, and, by passing the summit of human law to which all things are subject, has not yet by his destiny earned so famous/noble a death. Let him live and, that he may fall a victim to Brutus, let him reign.

This is the worst moment of the war. The point at which Caesar's attack turns away from the foreign cavalry to assault the leaders of Rome is when the war becomes most truly civil. The narrator twice breaks into the narrative, and it is on these interventions that I wish to concentrate. While the first derives all its pathos from the evil of Caesar, the second may be interpreted as expressing equal frustration with the pious inertia of the Pompeians.

Pharsalia 7. 545-57 Refusal to Narrate

Lucan's introduction is very striking, *Pharsalia* 7. 545-57:

Ventum erat ad robur Magni mediasque catervas.
Quod totos errore vago perfuderat agros
constitit *hic* bellum, fortunaque Caesaris haesit.
Non *illic* regum auxiliis collecta iuventus
bella gerit ferrumque manus movere rogatae:

ille locus fratres habuit, locus *ille* parentis.
Hic furor, *hic* rabies, *hic* sunt tua crimina, *Caesar*.
Hanc fuge, *mens*, partem belli tenebrisque relinque,
nullaque tantorum discat *me vate* malorum,
quam multum bellis liceat civilibus, aetas.
A potius pereant lacrimae pereantque querellae:
quidquid in *hac* acie gessisti, *Roma, tacebo*.
Hic Caesar . . .

The fight had come to the strong-point of Magnus and to the middle of his troops. The war which had spread in random wandering all over the fields stopped here and Caesar's fortune was checked. Not there did young men wage war who had been collected from the auxiliaries of kings, but hands unbidden plied the steel: that place held brothers, that place fathers. Here is madness, here rage, here is your damnation, Caesar. O mind, flee this part of the war and leave it to the darkness, and let no age learn from my vatic recollection of such great evils how much is possible in civil wars. O rather let our tears be shed, our laments be uttered in vain: whatever you did in this battle, Rome, I shall not report. Here Caesar . . .

The situation described is just that which brought the soldiers to full consciousness of the horrors of civil war at 4. 169-79 and at 7. 463-9.[47] The peculiar problems posed by this for the narrator are underlined by Lucan's self-description at 7. 553 as a *vates,* that is, the Augustan national priest-prophet-poet. Chapter 1 has already discussed the connection of the term *vates* with patriotic verse (and implicitly its contingent problems for Lucan). The poet's attitude to his inheritance is illustrated not only by this passage but also by the final lines of the proem to the **Pharsalia,** 1. 63-6 and by the reaction to Caesar's visit to Troy at 9. 980-6. In each instance, the usage of the term is founded on the irony of gesturing at a tradition to which Lucan knows that he cannot belong. It is surprising how little Newman makes of this tension;[48] far more is to be gained from the analysis both of Lucan as *vates* and of the various surrogate *vates* appearing in the **Pharsalia** given by Masters and O'Higgins.[49] The latter in particular far outdoes her predecessors in showing how Lucan plays on the mixture of prospection and retrospection in the prophet-poet.[50] It is surely this concept of telling a story from the past in order to set a prescription for the future which fuels Lucan's constant dialectic with the Augustan poets as *vates.* At this of all moments in Lucan's epic, the collapse of their national, patriotic role is most keenly felt.[51]

Lucan's use of apostrophe is intense and complex.[52] He addresses *Caesar, mens,* and *Roma,* all as characters or composers of literature, always with a retrospective stance, never himself intervening as a character in the action. As at 7. 418, the address to *Roma* is effectively an address to the soldiers on the battlefield, refusing to recall what she/they did at Pharsalus. More complicated is the sentence in which Lucan addresses first Caesar and then his own mind. This sentence is dense with *hic*-form deictics. These contrast with the *illic . . . / ille . . . ille* of the previous sentence, and serve to show how the objective, distanced 'there' suddenly becomes an immediately present 'here' for the poet. The first impression given by the combination of *hic* deixis with address to Caesar is that the narrator has intervened as a character on the field of battle, but it is soon revealed that *hanc . . . partem belli* is, so to speak, a 'part of the narrative of war'. The address to Caesar as a character is similar to Vergil's address to Nisus and Euryalus at *Aeneid* 9. 446-9 or to Lausus at 10. 791-3, but while the promise of fame seems a favour happily granted by Vergil to his characters, Caesar forces his way into Lucan's Roman songs, and later, when Lucan promises his villain poetic immortality, the offer can be taken as a menace as well as a boon (*Pharsalia*, 9. 980-6).

Dear Brutus: *Pharsalia* 7. 586-96

The poet's reluctance to narrate is, of course, a feint. Lines 7. 557-85 take us through a long description of the actions of Caesar, conducted as a grotesque parody of the conduct of the archetypal 'good general'. At 7. 578-85, much stress is placed on the cutting-down of the representatives of the great aristocratic families, and this then introduces the address to Brutus at 7. 586-96, which closes the scene. This extended apostrophe places the whole scene in a most interesting light and it is on this section that analysis will be concentrated:

> Illic plebeia contectus casside voltus
> ignotusque hosti quod ferrum, Brute, tenebas!
> O decus imperii, spes o suprema senatus,
> extremum tanti generis per saecula nomen,
> ne rue per medios nimium temerarius hostis,
> nec tibi fatales admoveris ante Philippos,
> Thessalia periture tua. Nil proficis istic
> Caesaris intentus iugulo: nondum attigit arcem,
> iuris et humani columen, quo cuncta premuntur,
> egressus meruit fatis tam nobile letum.
> Vivat et, ut Bruti procumbat victima, regnet.

There, masking your face in a plebeian helmet and unnoticed by the enemy, what a sword did you hold, Brutus! O glory of the empire, O final hope of the Senate, the last name of a family so great across the centuries, do not rush too rashly through the midst of the enemy and do not bring on yourself ahead of time the doom of Philippi, you who are destined to die in your own Thessaly. [T]here you achieve nothing by aiming at Caesar's throat: he has not yet reached the citadel, and, by passing the summit of human law to which all things are subject, has not yet by his destiny earned so famous/noble a death. Let him live and, that he may fall a victim to Brutus, let him reign.

Caesar is depicted at 7. 557-81 as the great immoralist, the one who 'ordered them to mangle the faces of the enemy with their steel' (*adversosque iubet ferro confun-*

dere voltus). He is also a figure of immense activity, always on the move, always driving men forward. As Aeneas becomes like Aegaeon at *Aeneid* 10. 565-70, so here Caesar is like Bellona and Mars (*Pharsalia* 7. 567-71). At 7. 578, Caesar urges his men to turn their destructive energy on the senators. The massacre of the great names of Rome must call forth particular lament, for with them dies freedom, *Pharsalia* 7. 579-85:

> Scit, cruor imperii qui sit, quae viscera rerum,
> unde petat Romam, libertas ultima mundi
> quo steterit ferienda loco. Permixta secundo
> ordine nobilitas venerandaque corpora ferro
> urguentur; caedunt Lepidos caeduntque Metellos
> Corvinosque simul Torquataque nomina, rerum
> saepe duces summosque hominum te, Magne, remoto.

He knows which is the lifeblood of the empire, which are the guts of the State, from where to attack Rome, in which place what remains of freedom on the earth has taken her stand, ready to be struck. Senators commingled with knights and venerable bodies are pressed by the steel; they chop the Lepidi and they chop the Metelli and at the same time the Corvini and the famous Torquati, often leaders of the State and, you apart, Magnus, the loftiest of men.

This scene effectively excludes the senators from the accusation of *timor* at 7. 644. This need not have been the case. It has been noted above that 7. 575 records Caesar's order to his men to 'mangle the faces of the enemy with their steel' (*adversos . . . confundere voltus*). This is Lucan's version of Caesar's famous stratagem to combat the aristocratic *jeunesse dorée* who had followed Pompey, by exploiting their reluctance to receive the scars of which men would be proud.[53] This sounds very like the anti-aristocratic, Marian rhetoric that later will be identified as typical of Caesar in my discussion of the Caesarian centurion.[54] Yet Lucan does not reproduce the slur, insists that the aristocrats did not run.

If this scene excludes the senators from accusations of cowardice, it does not spare them the frustration often shown at the Pompeians' propensity for moral victories. The senators do not run, but they do not fight either. Rather, the frenzied mobility of Caesar is contrasted with the saintly inaction of the Pompeians, a vice which they share with or derive from their general. The contrast between the constant movement of Caesar and the inertia of Pompey is first brought out at *Pharsalia* 1. 135-57 in the comparison of the former to lightning, the latter to an ancient oak tree,[55] and there is surely an allusion to this fatal weakness of the Pompeian side when, at the start of this passage, Lucan announces that 'The fight had come to the strong-point of Magnus' (*Ventum erat ad robur Magni*). Caesar's Commentaries blame Pompey for ordering his men to stand and await the attack of the Caesarians at Pharsal is,[56] and the fatal passivity of the Pompeians has already been evoked at *Pharsalia* 7. 501-3:

> Civilia bella
> una acies patitur, gerit altera; frigidus inde
> stat gladius, calet omne nocens a Caesare ferrum.

> One side suffers civil war, the other wages it; on one side the sword stands cold, on Caesar's side every guilty weapon is hot.[57]

The combination of the arboreal and the culpably passive is well evoked at 7. 580-5 with *steterit*,[58] *ferienda*,[59] and *caedunt*,[60] and the theme is rounded off at 7. 597-8, when:

> Iacet *aggere* magno
> patricium campis non mixta plebe cadaver.

> The patrician corpses lie in a huge mound on the fields, unadulterated with the common soldiers.[61]

Lucan may loathe civil war, but he also yearns for someone, even a Sulla, with the spirit to resist Caesar.[62] It is in this context that the apostrophe to Brutus gains its special bite.

The notion suggested by 7. 545-56 of Lucan wrestling with the composition of the *Pharsalia* and the narration of the battle, thus addressing his characters as literary figures, is enhanced by the address to Brutus. It is true that the 'narrator as character' appears to intervene on the battlefield and urge a course of action on Brutus, but any sense of immediacy is disrupted by a glaring anachronism the impact of which is heightened by Lucan's cruel intertextual allusion.

The narrative of 7. 557-85 does not endeavour to create immediacy. It is conducted throughout in the present historic but only one apostrophe (7. 585, *Magne*) appears and no attempt is made to set up a vivid present or to depict a possible turning-point. When Lucan first addresses Brutus, he assiduously maintains temporal separation by simply asking him what he was doing then:

> Illic plebeia contectus casside voltus
> ignotuscue hosti quod ferrum, Brute, tenebas!

> There, masking your face in a plebeian helmet and unnoticed by the enemy, what a sword did you hold Brutus!

If the sentence is punctuated with an exclamation mark at the end, the effect approximates to the sarcastic 'What a brave man you were!' If it is punctuated with a question mark, there emerges the probing 'What exactly were you doing?'[63] For there is an obvious question as to why Brutus, amidst the nobles and himself 'the last name of a family so great across the centuries'

(*extremum tanti generis per saecula nomen*), should be skulking in a plebeian helmet.[64] Evidently, Brutus here stands as a representative of the inadequacies of the aristocrats at Pharsalus. This is then brought out in the imperative of the 'narrator as character'. After two lines of laudatory epithets, Lucan then urges his 'hero':

> Ne rue per medios nimium temerarius hostis,
> nec tibi fatales admoveris ante Philippos,
> Thessalia periture tua.

> Do not rush too rashly through the midst of the enemy and do not bring on yourself ahead of time the doom of Philippi, you who are destined to die in your own Thessaly.

The first aspect of this sentence which one notes is that it functions in the same way as the reference to Cassius discussed above: in the very sentence in which the narrator appears as a character on the field of battle, the reference to information available only to one living after the battle, that is to Philippi, reverses the illusion. This architectonic linking of temporalities and perspectives should now be familiar. The second aspect is that the imperative from 'narrator as character' to 'character' alludes to the repeated Vergilian formula in which the noble warrior rushes into the middle of the enemy *moriturus* or *periturus*, that is, essentially, 'intending to die'.[65] This action, which takes on a stylized religious function in the *devotio* of the Decii in Livy, is fundamentally a response to the political pressure on the aristocratic general to show personal *virtus* in the line of battle when his troops are in retreat or facing defeat.[66] It is thus peculiarly appropriate that Brutus should be the focus of one of its central appearances in the *Pharsalia.* On the other hand, the formula is here used with a sarcastic edge to it. For, *periture* here means 'destined to die' or 'later to die', not 'intending to die'.[67] Lucan plays cruelly on the question: 'Brutus, what did you do in the war?' This is easy to see when we consider the particular intertextual referent invoked by Lucan. This is the address of Aeneas to Lausus at *Aeneid* 10. 811-12:

> 'Quo moriture ruis maioraque viribus audes?
> Fallit te incautum pietas tua.'

> 'Why do you rush to your death, why do you dare deeds too great for your strength? Your sense of responsibility betrays you in your heedlessness.'

The reading of *Pharsalia* 7. 385-459 offered above showed how Lucan extracted effects from the narrator speaking lines which in Vergil are left to a character, Anchises. Here, the effect is no less radical. Where Aeneas upbraided Lausus for his death-rush (*moriture ruis*)—the future participle indicating perhaps a mixture of intent and inevitable consequences—and called the loyal youth 'heedless' (*incautus*), now Lucan urges Brutus not to rush through the enemy and calls him 'too rash' (*nimium temerarius*). Yet the use of the future participle *periture* and the reference to Philippi emphasize that there was never any question of Brutus acting with foolish bravery at Pharsalus, and the great aristocrat hiding in a plebeian helmet hardly seems a figure of headstrong heroism and loyalty.[68] When the narrator observes that Caesar has not yet earned 'so famous / noble a death' (*tam nobile letum*), one is reminded also of Brutus' failure to die like the aristocrat that he is.[69] *Pharsalia* 7. 596, 'Let him live and, that he may fall a victim to Brutus, let him reign' (*Vivat et, ut Bruti procumbat victima, regnet*), it is true, draws from the episode a form of long-term consolation in the assassination of Caesar which emerges throughout the poem, but this instance is charged with further, more troubling implications.[70]. . .

Notes

1. A similar approach to that taken here is apparent in Quint (1993) 147-51, which analyses this scene in the context of the ongoing opposition of the defeated, of the literary and political refusal of an ending. For Quint, Luc. 7. 630-46 is the most pessimistic moment in the poem.

2. See [Leigh, Matthew. *Lucan: Spectacle and Engagement*. Oxford: Clarendon Press, 1997] Ch. 4.

3. See below . . . .

4. See below . . . .

5. For *milites nostri* in Caesar, see *B. Gall.* 1. 52. 5, 2. 11. 5, 2. 33. 6, etc. For *nostri* as 'the Roman soldiers', see Caes. *B. Gall.* 1. 26. 4 and 5, 1. 52. 3, 1. 53. 3.

6. The effect of *prosternimur* is enhanced by its double sense: 'We prostrate ourselves before a tyrant' (*OLD* 'prosterno' 3) and 'We are defeated/ slain' (*OLD* 'prosterno' 5).

7. See Ch. 2 [Leigh, 1997], pp. 52-3.

8. Rambaud (1955) 271-2.

9. Lounsbury (1976) 214-17.

10. Heyke (1970) 86, esp. n. 2.

11. Or, as Serv. at Verg. *Aen.* 1. 242 would have it when discussing the tradition that Aeneas and Antenor betrayed Troy, Horace's reference to 'ardentem sine fraude Troiam' does not work because 'nemo . . . excusat nisi rem plenam suspicionis'.

12. The text printed at 387-9 is that transmitted and restored by Shackleton-Bailey in his Teubner edition. The Latin is difficult, and the text cannot be free from suspicion, but it is possible to translate adequately if 'ut vacet a ferro' is taken as concessive. Housman's 'Hae facient dextrae quidquid nona explicat aetas | ut vacet a ferro' objects to 388 as pleonastic, and presumes that it is an interpolation designed to explain 387 and 9. However, his 'nona aetas' is suspect, and does not express the absolute desolation wrought by the battle.

13. 'possunt' = PGV, Housman, 'possint' = (M), Shackleton Bailey, 'possent' = ZUC, Haskins and Luck. Housman's 'fingit se proelio adesse' can be applied to any of the conditions created by the variant readings.

14. For *mora,* see Masters (1992) 3-10, 43, 54-5, 60, 95-6, 119-22, 183 and [Leigh, 1997] Ch. 5, pp. 186-7. For *locus* as textual space or rhetorical theme, see *OLD* 'locus' 23 and 24.

15. For the approach here resisted, see Marti (1975).

16. The density of reference to the anticipatory emotions grows ever greater the closer Pharsalus approaches. O'Higgins (1988) and Masters (1992) argue for the metapoetic quality of the Erictho scene at the close of Book 6. It is striking therefore that Sextus Pompeius should travel to visit her at a time when his comrades, 6. 419, '*spemque metumque* ferunt' and when his emotional state can be described as, 6. 423-4, '*stimulante metu* fati praenoscere cursus, | inpatiensque *morae venturisque* omnibus aeger'. For further references to anticipation at the start of Book 7, see 7. 20 for Pompey's rest 'anxia venturis' (contra Housman 'anxia mens curis'), 7. 105 'venturi timor', cf. 106 'metuenda', 7. 133-8, esp. 'maiore metu', 'timeat sibi', 'pro se ferre metus', 'urbi Magnoque timetur', 7. 248 for Caesar advancing 'formidine mersa', 7. 252 'nil opus est votis', 7. 297 'spe trepido', 7. 298-9 'camporum limite parvo | absumus a votis', etc. One of the aims of this chapter is to demonstrate that while this community of emotion between characters, readers, and narrator is in part a literary device to create suspense, it is also something much more than this.

17. This function of the future historic is underlined in [Leigh, 1997] App. 3.

18. For previous treatments of this intertext, see Guillemin (1951) 221-2, Thompson and Bruère (1968), Feeney (1986b) 7-8, and Labate (1991) 179.

19. Already in the Augustan period, Hor. *Epist.* 1. 11. 7-8 describes a 'Gabiis desertior atque | Fidenis vicus', while of Veii, Prop. 4. 10. 29-30 states: 'Nunc intra muros pastoris bucina lenti | cantat, et in vestris ossibus arva metunt'. For Cora, Gagliardi

(1975) gives Livy 2. 16, Serv. at Verg. *Aen.* 7. 672, and ps.-Aur. Vict. *Orig.* 17. See Feeney (1986*b*) for the fate of all the cities cited.

20. For Vergil's own discomfort, see Lyne (1987) 214-16, but most importantly Broch (1983) 268-9. Hine (1987) collects a mass of material on this issue but does not entirely dispel anxiety. For Ovid's attitude, see *Fast.* 3. 79-104, esp. 101-2, and Hinds (1992) 124-7.

21. See O'Hara (1990).

22. Dilke (1960) ad loc. finds it 'somewhat strange' to blame the destruction of Veii on Pharsalus but does not perceive the Vergilian intertext.

23. At the same time, 7. 391-2, 'omne nomen Latinum | fabula erit', recalls first the description at 3. 211-13 of Caesar's claim to descent from Iulus and Troy as a *fabula,* that is as Vergil's literary fiction; second 6. 48-9 (Troy), 6. 355-9, and 8. 406-7 (both Thebes) where the greatness of cities is attested only by a *fabula.*

24. For *edax* and the tooth of time, cf. Ov. *Am.* 1. 15. 41-2, 'Ergo etiam cum me supremus adederit ignis, | vivam, parsque mei multa superstes erit' and *Anth. Lat.* 415. 8 (SB), 'edetque'.

25. The contrast between the immortality of poetry and the mortality of buildings is traced back to Ennius, *Ann.* frr. 12-13 and 404-5 (Skutsch) in Zwierlein (1982). It is still apparent in *Anth. Lat.* 415 and 416 (SB) and is appropriated for philosophy in Sen. *Brev.* 15. 4, 17. 1, 19. 1. By contrast, the association between immortal verse and State building seems typically Augustan.

26. Verg. *Aen.* 9. 446-9: 'Fortunati ambo! Si quid mea carmina possunt, | nulla dies umquam memori vos eximet aevo, | dum domus Aeneae Capitoli immobile saxum | accolet imperiumque pater Romanus tenebit'.

27. Anderson (1963) 26-7 notes that Ov. *Met.* 15. 876-9 first acknowledges dependence on Roman power, then defiantly transcends it. This connects to the song of Pythagoras at the beginning of the book with its uncomfortable implications for *Roma aeterna* in its account of the rise and fall of cities.

28. This is not true, however, of Ov. *Am.* 1. 15. Galinsky (1969) 95-6 contrasts the unconditional immortality claimed by Ovid for his own verse at *Am.* 1. 15. 33-4 with the conditional survival of Vergil at 1. 15. 25-6, 'Tityrus et fruges [segetes (Mckeown)] Aeneiaque arma legentur, | Roma triumphati dum caput orbis erit'. Galinsky treats this as evidence of the dissident mentality of the *Amores.*

29. 'Hesperiae segetes' at Luc. 7. 403 raises two further issues. First, *Hesperia* is used regularly by Lucan as a term for *Italia* in deliberate allusion to Ennius and Vergil and thus as an extension of his anti-*Aeneid.* Second, *segetes* has a Vergilian resonance of its own, used at Prop. 2. 34. 78, as an encapsulation of the *Georgics,* alluding to Verg. *G.* 1. 1, 'Quid faciat laetas segetes . . .'. It is for this reason that McKeown at Ov. *Am.* 1. 15. 26 emends 'fruges' to 'segetes'.

30. Lucan employs a version of the ἀρχὴ κακῶν motif. For this, see Pease (1935) at Verg. *Aen.* 4. 169.

31. See n. 13 for the alternative readings 'possint' and 'possent', neither of which invalidates the suggestion of immediate presence.

32. Luc. 7. 421-31, 'tibi . . . te . . . tibi . . . tibi . . . tibi . . . tua . . . tibi'.

33. Hor. *Carm.* 3. 5. 1-2, 'Caelo tonantem credidimus Iovem | regnare' associates the power of Augustus over the world with that of Jupiter over the heavens. Now, Lucan cites the coming of the emperors as proof of the non-existence or unconcern of Jove. See Zetzel (1980) and Feeney (1991) 281-2. Assaults on Hor. *Carm.* 3. 5 open and close this section of Lucan, for Luc. 7. 390, 'aevi venientis in orbem' must be an echo of 'veniens in aevum' at Hor. *Carm.* 3. 5 16.

34. For these distinctions, see [Leigh, 1997] App. 3.

35. Stat. *Theb.* 1. 79-80 picks up on the terms of Lucan's complaint when Oedipus, lamenting his mistreatment by his sons, exclaims, 'Et videt ista deorum | ignavus genitor?'

36. The Latin text printed is the emendation of Gertz, which I prefer to the version offered by Reynolds in the OCT, '. . . quae sit dei sedes, opus suum spectet an tractet'.

37. *Comm. Bern.* at Luc. 7. 447-8 explains that Lucan 'astruit deos non curare terrena'. It is interesting to note that while Seneca cites this as one of many questions to be considered in *otium,* Cato's refusal to hold his hands together and watch the end of the universe is expressed in the context of a debate with Brutus over whether the correct response to civil war is to engage or to pursue the philosophical *otium* of retreat. Thus, Brutus at Luc. 2. 266-7 urges that 'melius tranquilla sine armis | otia solus ages', while Cato responds at 2. 292-5, 'Gentesne furorem | Hesperium ignotae Romanaque bella sequentur | diductique fretis alio sub sidere reges, | *otia solus agam*?'

38. See [Leigh, 1997] Ch. 7, 'A View to a Kill'.

39. Rosenmeyer (1989). For my response to Rosenmeyer, see esp. the discussions of Cato and Vulteius.

40. For Lucan's contamination of the exemplary with the amphitheatrical, see [Leigh, 1997] Ch. 7, esp. pp. 236-40.

41. Note that at *Prov.* 1. 1 Seneca promises that 'deorum causam agam'. This is hardly Lucan's perspective.

42. For the presumed Thracian Mt. Mimas, see Keil at Pauly, *RE* xv. 2. 1714. Kroll (1924) 153 is far more plausible. Bömer (1969-86) at Ov. *Met.* 2. 222 is also sceptical. *Adiuncta* in Silius points to his awareness of the chain of imitation he is joining—the sense is as much rhetorical as geographical. *Adiunctus* has the geographical sense of 'next to' at Curt. 8. 11. 25 and 10. 10. 2, while *adiungere, adiunctus,* and *adiunctio* have a range of different rhetorical senses, of which Cic. *De Or.* 3. 206 and *Part Or.* 16 would seem to conform to the sense of putting two or more words together.

43. Due (1962) 101-2 and (1970) 213-14 argues that Lucan denies the existence of the gods absolutely and then revels in the absurdity of any idea of mortal revenge. Feeney (1991) 281-2 sees Lucan protesting against divine unconcern. Gagliardi (1985) 2054 and Johnson (1987) 89-90 are surely correct to see Lucan flirting with both positions.

44. *Comm. Bern.* at Luc. 7. 449 notes the movement between the two poles of atheism and Epicureanism, 'Duas opiniones posuit: prima non esse deos, secunda non curare mortales'.

45. Cf. Feeney (1991) 297-8. A similar form of civil war seems to be going on in the Underworld at 6. 797-9, 'Aeternis chalybis nodis et carcere Ditis | constrictae plausere manus, camposque piorum | poscit turba nocens'.

46. One thinks of Plin. *Pan.* 33. 1: 'e spectatore spectaculum factus'.

47. For more on this, see [Leigh, 1997] Ch. 2, pp. 46-8. For the particular problem of facing one's relatives as *adversi*, see my discussion of Lucan's development of the traditional paradigm of the front and the back in [Leigh, 1997] Ch. 6, pp. 206-20.

48. Newman (1967) 99-206 cf. (1986) 204-6 and esp. 219.

49. O'Higgins (1988) cf. Masters (1992), esp. 138-9 and 205-6 and the surrounding discussions of Phemonoe and Erictho. Discussing this passage, in particular, both emphasize Lucan's simultaneous reluctance and urge to narrate. Thus, O'Higgins (1988) 215 compares Lucan at 7. 552-5 to Apollo and Phemonoe in Book 5, and observes that 'A similar abhorrence of the "nefas" of civil war is detectable in Lucan. If Apollo hesitates to create a world so alien to the gods, Lucan—to an extent—shrinks from recreating it. Although the impulse to write is stronger, there is evident a counter-impulse to maintain a decent silence'. O'Higgins then (p. 216) talks of him proceeding 'in spite of his scruples', despite knowing that as *vates* he will win an 'invidious distinction'. Masters (1992) 148 talks of the split in Lucan's poetic persona, the will to silence represented by Phemonoe, the 'grisly relish and Silver Latin exuberance' by her fellow *vates,* Erictho. 'Infandum, regina, iubes renovare dolorem' is, of course, a chat-up line.

50. Moore (1921), esp. 142-51, and Dick (1963) 46-9 offer little more than brief catalogues of instances.

51. O'Higgins (1988) 211 n. 11 notes that 'Newman . . . has shown how "vates" was, in part, a political concept for the Augustan poets. There is a political element in Lucan's understanding of his role also', but then abandons the point in favour of some more general reflections on Lucan's politics. Johnson (1987) 98-9 has something to say on the point, but does not stray into specifics. Gagliardi (1970) ch. 5, 'Aspetti della Nuova Tecnica Epica e Letteraria', 104-39 is perhaps the best discussion of the political aspect of the *vates*.

52. A significant factor is that noted by Gagliardi (1975) ad loc., namely that apostrophe to abstracts such as *mens* is an innovation which Lucan has drawn from tragedy, e.g. Eur. *Heracl.* 433 (with Wilkins (1993) ad loc.) and *Bacch.* 1287. This is thus 'un altro elemento significativo . . . della trasformazione dell'epica tradizionale in Lucano dietro la spinta della nuova vocazione drammatica a cui è portato dalla storia'. The comparison of Lucan's narrative voice to a tragic chorus is an important element in the tradition of likening him to a tragic historian discussed in [Leigh, 1997] Ch. 1.

53. Plut. *Caes.* 45. 1-3, *Pomp.* 71. 4-5; Appian *B. Civ.* 2. 76. 318; Flor. *Epit.* 2. 13. 50; Frontin. *Str.* 4. 7. 32; Polyaenus, 8. 23. 25; Oros., 6. 15. 26.

54. See [Leigh, 1997] Ch. 6, pp. 194-206 and 228-31.

55. See Rosner-Siegel (1983).

56. See Caes. *B. Civ.* 3. 92 and cf. Plut. *Caes.* 44. 4, Plut. *Pomp.* 69. 4-5, and App. *B. Civ.* 2. 79. 33, who states that Caesar also voiced this criticism in his letters.

57. Cf. Luc. 7. 485-7 and 533.

58. At Luc. 1. 135, the simile of Pompey as oak tree begins famously 'Stat magni nominis umbra'. At 7. 502-3, Lucan says of the Pompeians 'frigidus inde | stat gladius'.

59. Used relatively rarely of chopping a tree, but cf. Columella, *Arb.* 10. 3, Claud. *De Rept. Proserp.* 3. 378, and particularly Luc. 3. 430, where the soldiers are fearful for the consequences 'si robora sacra feirent'.

60. Constantly used of chopping. See *TLL* iii. 56 A. For *caedere* in Lucan *re* trees, see 2. 670, 3. 413, 3. 450, 9. 332. Further, at 2. 172 and 6. 584, *caedere* vel. sim. is used of humans now described as *truncus*. Masters (1992) 27 n. 40 notes the argument that Caesar's cutting-down of the sacred grove in Book 3 of the *Pharsalia* is symbolic of his defeat of Pompey, while 29 n. 44 notes of 3. 450 that 'caesi nemoris' 'plays on the name "Caesar"'. One might add that Ovid uses the term *incaeduus* to describe sacred groves at *Fast.* 1. 243 and 2. 435-6 and at *Am.* 3. 1. 1, while *Met.* 2. 418 talks of 'nemus, quod nulla ceciderat aetas', *Met.* 8. 329 of the 'silva' 'quam nulla ceciderat aetas', cf. *Met.* 8. 769, 'repetitaque robora caedit'. The destruction of the sacred grove in Lucan is discussed in Phillips (1968) and in Dyson (1970). Of the two parallels attested, Dyson's contemporary historical parallel has been less well received than Phillips's comparison with Erysichthon in Ov. *Met.* 8. However, the manner in which Caesar dares 'primus' to wield the axe and fell an oak suggests a blasphemous perversion of the famed leadership-skills of Alexander. I would therefore like to suggest a third source in the story of Alexander at Aornus. Curt. 8. 11. 8 reads: 'ipse primus truncam arborem iecit, clamorque exercitus, index alacritatis, secutus est, nullo detrectante munus quod rex occupavit'. In support of this parallel, one might note that Curt. 8. 9. 34 underlines the sacred status of trees among the Indians ('Deos putant quidquid colere coeperunt, arbores maxime, quas violare capital est'). Finally, if it is protested that Curtius is probably subsequent to Lucan and therefore imitating the Caesar of the *Pharsalia*, one might respond that Alexander is also depicted as leading the way at Arr. *Anab.* 4. 29. 7 (esp. καὶ αὐτὸς ἐχώννυεν), allowing us to speculate that the claim is made earlier still in the Alexander tradition. For another instance of this 'topos' in Curt., see 5. 6. 14 for Alexander leading his men across the ice. Very similar is Sil. *Pun.* 1. 242-4 on Hannibal: 'primus sumpsisse laborem, | primus iter carpsisse pedes partemque subire, | si valli festinet opus'. Spaltenstein (1986-90) ad loc. discusses the topos. Examples include Luc. 9.

394-5 and 618; Sil. *Pun.* 3. 516, 4. 216-19, 4. 512-15, 8. 551-5; Livy 10. 41. 4 and 21. 4. 8; Tac. *Hist.* 2. 5. 1; Suet. *Jul.* 57. 2; Dio Cass. 69. 9. 3; and, for the topos reversed, Just. *Epit.* 2. 10. 23.

61. For the importance of the Caesarian *agger* in Lucan, see Masters (1992) 29-34.

62. For the wish that Pompey should act as Sulla, see Luc. 6. 299-313.

63. It is striking that Duff (1928) prints the Latin text with an exclamation mark and the English translation with a question mark.

64. Another similarity between the arboreal senators and Pompey is that they are now merely *nomina*. Apart from Brutus, Caesar also cuts down the 'Torquata . . . nomina'. Pompey, we recall, 1. 135, 'Stat magni nominis umbra'. For Brutus in plebeian armour, cf. Masters (1994) n. 65.

65. This formula is investigated in Ch. 4 [Leigh, 1997] and in Leigh (1993). The anthropological and political assertions which I now make are all based on the evidence collected in these two pieces.

66. See Leigh (1993) 98-103 and [Leigh, 1997] Ch. 4, pp. 128-34.

67. Gagliardi (1975) ad loc. is clearly confused by the ambiguity, first translating 'periture' as 'esponendoti a morte certa', then suggesting that the future participle actually has a 'funzione predicativa'. *Periturus* and *moriturus* mean doomed to die at Luc. 2. 74, 3. 211, 3. 665, 4. 748, 4. 776, 6. 788, 7. 329, 7. 730, 8. 692, 9. 318, 9. 611 but the distinction between fate and intention is blurred in the soliloquy of Domitius at 2. 523-5, 'in medios belli non ire furores | iam dudum *moriture* paras? *Rue* certus et omnes | lucis rumpe moras et Caesaris effuge munus', while the sense of 'intending to die' is clear at 4. 277, for which cf. 4. 271-2, 'ut effuso Caesar decurrere passu | vidit et ad certam *devotos* tendere mortem'.

68. For another example of the 'narrator as character' quoting Vergil while urging a course of action on his characters, see Conte (1974) at Luc. 6. 196-201. The effect of the intertextuality is again to give the 'involved' imperative a sarcastic distance.

69. When we consider the failure of Brutus' aristocratic valour, it is useful to bear in mind the intervening imitation of Vergil in the address of the narrator to the Fabii at Ov. *Fast.* 2. 225-6: 'Quo ruitis, generosa domus? Male creditis hosti! | Simplex nobilitas, perfida tela cave!' The episode of the Fabii seems to have exercised some hold over Lucan's imagination, for the description of the swollen Cremera and the comparison of the

Fabii to Libyan lions at *Fast.* 2. 205-13 is highly reminiscent of Luc. 1. 185 and 213-19 on the swollen Rubicon and of 1. 205-12 for Caesar as a suicidal Libyan lion.

70. It is in these terms that Ahl (1976) 45-6 and Feeney (1991) 282 interpret the apostrophe. For Ahl, it is the first instance of the 'secretive confidence' increasingly often displayed by Lucan in 8-10; Feeney emphasizes 'fatales' and sees Lucan recovering faith in destiny. For other anticipations of Brutus' role in the assassination of Caesar, see Luc. 5. 206-8, 6. 791-2, 10. 338-44. None of these has anything to equate to the ironies of 'periture'.

Bibliography

Ahl, F. (1976), *Lucan. An Introduction* (Ithaca).

Anderson, W. S. (1963), 'Multiple Change in the Metamorphoses', *TAPhA* 94: 1-27.

Broch, H. (1983), *The Death of Vergil,* trans. J. S. Untermeyer (Oxford).

Conte, G. B. (1974), *Saggio di commento a Lucano. Pharsalia 6. 118-260. L'Aristia di Sceva* (Pisa).

Dick, B. F. (1963), 'The Technique of Prophecy in Lucan', *TAPhA* 94: 37-49.

Dilke, O. A. W. (1960), *M. Annaei Lucani De Bello Civili Liber VII,* revision of J. P. Postgate ed. (Cambridge).

Due, O. S. (1962), 'An Essay on Lucan', *C&M* 23: 68-132.

———, (1970), 'Lucain et la philosophie', in *Entretiens de la Fondation Hardt,* 15, *Lucain,* 203-32 (Geneva).

Duff, J. D. (1928), *Lucan with an English Translation* (Cambridge, Mass.).

Dyson, S. (1970), 'Caepio, Tacitus and Lucan's Sacred Grove', *CPh* 65: 36-8.

Feeney, D. C. (1986*b*), 'History and Revelation in Vergil's Underworld', *PCPhS* NS 32: 1-24.

———, (1991), *The Gods in Epic* (Oxford).

Gagliardi, D. (1970), *Lucano: Poeta della libertà* (2nd edn., Naples).

———, (1985), 'La letteratura dell'irrazionale in età neroniana', *ANRW* II.32.3: 2047-65.

———, (1975) (ed.), *M. Annaei Lucani Belli Civilis Liber VII* (Florence).

Galinsky, K. (1969), 'The Triumph Theme in the Roman Elegy', *WS* 82: 75-107.

Guillemin, A. (1951), 'L'inspiration virgilienne dans la Pharsale', *REL* 29: 214-27.

Heyke, W. (1970), *Zur Rolle der Pietas bei Lucan,* Diss. (Heidelberg).

Hine, H. (1987), 'Aeneas and the Arts (Vergil, *Aeneid* 6.847-50)', in M. Whitby, P. Hardie and M. Whitby (eds.), *Homo Viator: Classical Essays for John Bramble* (Bristol), 173-84.

Johnson, W. R. (1987), *Momentary Monsters* (Ithaca, NY).

Kroll, W. (1924), *Studien zum Verständnis der römischen Literatur* (Stuttgart).

Labate, M. (1991), 'Città morte, città future: Un tema della poesia augustea', *Maia,* 43.3: 167-84.

Leigh, M. G. L. (1993), 'Hopelessly Devoted to You: Traces of the Decii in Vergil's Aeneid', *PVS* 21: 89-110.

Lounsbury, R. (1976), 'History and Motive in Book Seven of Lucan's Pharsalia', *Hermes,* 104: 210-39.

Lyne, R. O. A. M. (1987), *Further Voices in Vergil's Aeneid* (Oxford).

Mckeown, J. C. (1989), *Ovid: Amores, Text, Prolegomena and Commentary in Four Volumes,* ii. *A Commentary on Book One* (Leeds).

Marti, B. (1975), 'Lucan's Narrative Techniques', *Parola del passato,* 30: 74-90.

Masters, J. (1992), *Poetry and Civil War in Lucan's Bellum Civile* (Cambridge).

———, (1994), 'Deceiving the Reader: The Political Mission of Lucan Book 7', in J. Elsner and J. Masters (eds.) *Reflections of Nero* (London), 151-77.

Moore, C. H. (1921), 'Prophecy in the Ancient Epic', *HSPh* 32: 99-175.

Newman, J. K. (1967), *Augustus and the New Poetry* (Brussels).

———, (1986), *The Classical Epic Tradition* (Madison, Wis.).

O'Hara, J. J. (1990), *Death and the Optimistic Prophecy in Vergil's Aeneid* (Princeton).

O'Higgins, D. (1988), 'Lucan as Vates', *ClAnt* 7.2: 208-26.

Pease, A. S. (1935), *P. Vergili Maronis Aeneidos Liber Quartus* (Cambridge, Mass.).

Phillips, O. C. (1968), 'Lucan's Grove', *CPh* 63: 296-300.

Quint, D. (1993), *Epic and Empire* (Princeton).

Rambaud, M. (1955), 'L'Apologie de Pompée par Lucain au Livre VII de la Pharsale', *REL* 33: 258-96.

Rosenmeyer, T. (1989), *Senecan Drama and Stoic Cosmology* (Berkeley, Los Angeles, and London).

Rosner-Siegel, J. (1983), 'The Oak and the Lightning: Lucan, Bellum Civile 1. 135-57', *Athenaeum,* NS 61: 165-77.

Thompson, L., and Bruère, R. T. (1968), 'Lucan's Use of Virgilian Reminiscence', *CPh* 63.1: 2-21.

Wilkins, J. (1993) (ed.), *Euripides Heraclidae with Introduction and Commentary* (Oxford).

Zetzel, J. E. G. (1980), 'Two Imitations in Lucan', *CQ* NS 30: 257.

Zwierlein, O. (1982), 'Der Ruhm der Dichtung bei Ennius und seinen Nachfolgern, *Hermes,* 110: 85-102.

Abbreviations

ANRW: *Aufstieg und Niedergang der Römischen Welt*

ClAnt: *Classical Antiquity*

C&M: *Classica et Mediaevalia*

CPh: *Classical Philology*

CQ: *Classical Quarterly*

HSPh: *Harvard Studies in Classical Philology*

OLD: *Oxford Latin Dictionary,* ed. P. G. W. Glare (Oxford, 1968-82)

PCPhS: *Proceedings of the Cambridge Philological Society*

PVS: *Proceedings of the Virgil Society*

REL: *Revue des études latines*

TAPhA: *Transactions and Proceedings of the American Philological Association*

WS: *Wiener Studien*

TEXTS OF LUCAN

The text of Lucan used throughout this study is the magisterial edition of A. E. Housman (Oxford, 1926). Where I disagree with Housman or print an alternative reading, this is noted in the text. Other editions referred to in the notes are:

C. E. Haskins (1887), *M. Annaei Lucani Pharsalia* (London)

G. Luck (1985), *Lukan: Der Bürgerkrieg* (Berlin)

D. R. Shackleton Bailey (1988), *Lucanus De Bello Civili* (Stuttgart)

FURTHER READING

Criticism

Ahl, Frederick M. "Some Minor Characters of the *Pharsalia*." In *Lucan: An Introduction,* pp. 116-49. Ithaca, N.Y.: Cornell University Press, 1976.

> Character sketches of the minor players in the *Pharsalia,* noting Lucan's "genius for capturing the moods and faces of the civil wars."

Additional coverage of Lucan's life and career is contained in the following sources published by Gale: *Classical and Medieval Literature Criticism,* Vol. 33; *Epics for Students,* Vol. 2; and *Literature Resource Center.*

How to Use This Index

The main references

Calvino, Italo
1923-1985 .... CLC **5, 8, 11, 22, 33, 39,**
73; SSC 3, 48

list all author entries in the following Gale Literary Criticism series:

AAL = *Asian American Literature*
BG = *The Beat Generation: A Gale Critical Companion*
BLC = *Black Literature Criticism*
BLCS = *Black Literature Criticism Supplement*
CLC = *Contemporary Literary Criticism*
CLR = *Children's Literature Review*
CMLC = *Classical and Medieval Literature Criticism*
DC = *Drama Criticism*
FL = *Feminism in Literature: A Gale Critical Companion*
GL = *Gothic Literature: A Gale Critical Companion*
HLC = *Hispanic Literature Criticism*
HLCS = *Hispanic Literature Criticism Supplement*
HR = *Harlem Renaissance: A Gale Critical Companion*
LC = *Literature Criticism from 1400 to 1800*
NCLC = *Nineteenth-Century Literature Criticism*
NNAL = *Native North American Literature*
PC = *Poetry Criticism*
SSC = *Short Story Criticism*
TCLC = *Twentieth-Century Literary Criticism*
WLC = *World Literature Criticism, 1500 to the Present*
WLCS = *World Literature Criticism Supplement*

The cross-references

See also CA 85-88, 116; CANR 23, 61;
DAM NOV; DLB 196; EW 13; MTCW 1, 2;
RGSF 2; RGWL 2; SFW 4; SSFS 12

list all author entries in the following Gale biographical and literary sources:

AAYA = *Authors & Artists for Young Adults*
AFAW = *African American Writers*
AFW = *African Writers*
AITN = *Authors in the News*
AMW = *American Writers*
AMWR = *American Writers Retrospective Supplement*
AMWS = *American Writers Supplement*
ANW = *American Nature Writers*
AW = *Ancient Writers*
BEST = *Bestsellers*
BPFB = *Beacham's Encyclopedia of Popular Fiction: Biography and Resources*
BRW = *British Writers*
BRWS = *British Writers Supplement*
BW = *Black Writers*
BYA = *Beacham's Guide to Literature for Young Adults*
CA = *Contemporary Authors*
CAAS = *Contemporary Authors Autobiography Series*
CABS = *Contemporary Authors Bibliographical Series*
CAD = *Contemporary American Dramatists*
CANR = *Contemporary Authors New Revision Series*
CAP = *Contemporary Authors Permanent Series*
CBD = *Contemporary British Dramatists*
CCA = *Contemporary Canadian Authors*
CD = *Contemporary Dramatists*
CDALB = *Concise Dictionary of American Literary Biography*

CDALBS = Concise Dictionary of American Literary Biography Supplement
CDBLB = Concise Dictionary of British Literary Biography
CMW = St. James Guide to Crime & Mystery Writers
CN = Contemporary Novelists
CP = Contemporary Poets
CPW = Contemporary Popular Writers
CSW = Contemporary Southern Writers
CWD = Contemporary Women Dramatists
CWP = Contemporary Women Poets
CWRI = St. James Guide to Children's Writers
CWW = Contemporary World Writers
DA = DISCovering Authors
DA3 = DISCovering Authors 3.0
DAB = DISCovering Authors: British Edition
DAC = DISCovering Authors: Canadian Edition
DAM = DISCovering Authors: Modules
   DRAM: Dramatists Module; **MST:** Most-studied Authors Module;
   MULT: Multicultural Authors Module; **NOV:** Novelists Module;
   POET: Poets Module; **POP:** Popular Fiction and Genre Authors Module
DFS = Drama for Students
DLB = Dictionary of Literary Biography
DLBD = Dictionary of Literary Biography Documentary Series
DLBY = Dictionary of Literary Biography Yearbook
DNFS = Literature of Developing Nations for Students
EFS = Epics for Students
EW = European Writers
EWL = Encyclopedia of World Literature in the 20th Century
EXPN = Exploring Novels
EXPP = Exploring Poetry
EXPS = Exploring Short Stories
FANT = St. James Guide to Fantasy Writers
FW = Feminist Writers
GFL = Guide to French Literature, Beginnings to 1789, 1798 to the Present
GLL = Gay and Lesbian Literature
HGG = St. James Guide to Horror, Ghost & Gothic Writers
HW = Hispanic Writers
IDFW = International Dictionary of Films and Filmmakers: Writers and Production Artists
IDTP = International Dictionary of Theatre: Playwrights
LAIT = Literature and Its Times
LAW = Latin American Writers
JRDA = Junior DISCovering Authors
MAICYA = Major Authors and Illustrators for Children and Young Adults
MAICYAS = Major Authors and Illustrators for Children and Young Adults Supplement
MAWW = Modern American Women Writers
MJW = Modern Japanese Writers
MTCW = Major 20th-Century Writers
NCFS = Nonfiction Classics for Students
NFS = Novels for Students
PAB = Poets: American and British
PFS = Poetry for Students
RGAL = Reference Guide to American Literature
RGEL = Reference Guide to English Literature
RGSF = Reference Guide to Short Fiction
RGWL = Reference Guide to World Literature
RHW = Twentieth-Century Romance and Historical Writers
SAAS = Something about the Author Autobiography Series
SATA = Something about the Author
SFW = St. James Guide to Science Fiction Writers
SSFS = Short Stories for Students
TCWW = Twentieth-Century Western Writers
WLIT = World Literature and Its Times
WP = World Poets
YABC = Yesterday's Authors of Books for Children
YAW = St. James Guide to Young Adult Writers

Literary Criticism Series
Cumulative Author Index

Alexander, Barbara
  See Ehrenreich, Barbara
Alexander, Lloyd 1924-2007 .... **CLC 35**
  See also AAYA 1, 27; BPFB 1; BYA 5, 6, 7, 9, 10, 11; CA 1-4R; 260; CANR 1, 24, 38, 55, 113; CLR 1, 5, 48; CWRI 5; DLB 52; FANT; JRDA; MAICYA 1, 2; MAIC-YAS 1; MTCW 1; SAAS 19; SATA 3, 49, 81, 129, 135; SATA-Obit 182; SUFW; TUS; WYA; YAW
Alexander, Lloyd Chudley
  See Alexander, Lloyd
Alexander, Meena 1951- .... **CLC 121**
  See also CA 115; CANR 38, 70, 146; CP 5, 6, 7; CWP; DLB 323; FW
Alexander, Rae Pace
  See Alexander, Raymond Pace
Alexander, Raymond Pace
  1898-1974 .... **SSC 62**
  See also CA 97-100; SATA 22; SSFS 4
Alexander, Samuel 1859-1938 .... **TCLC 77**
Alexeiev, Konstantin
  See Stanislavsky, Constantin
Alexeyev, Constantin Sergeivich
  See Stanislavsky, Constantin
Alexeyev, Konstantin Sergeyevich
  See Stanislavsky, Constantin
Alexie, Sherman 1966- .... **CLC 96, 154;**
  NNAL; PC 53; SSC 107
  See also AAYA 28; BYA 15; CA 138; CANR 65, 95, 133, 174; CN 7; DA3; DAM MULT; DLB 175, 206, 278; LATS 1:2; MTCW 2; MTFW 2005; NFS 17; SSFS 18
Alexie, Sherman Joseph, Jr.
  See Alexie, Sherman
al-Farabi 870(?)-950 .... **CMLC 58**
  See also DLB 115
Alfau, Felipe 1902-1999 .... **CLC 66**
  See also CA 137
Alfieri, Vittorio 1749-1803 .... **NCLC 101**
  See also EW 4; RGWL 2, 3; WLIT 7
Alfonso X 1221-1284 .... **CMLC 78**
Alfred, Jean Gaston
  See Ponge, Francis
Alger, Horatio, Jr. 1832-1899 .... **NCLC 8, 83**
  See also CLR 87; DLB 42; LAIT 2; RGAL 4; SATA 16; TUS
Al-Ghazali, Muhammad ibn Muhammad
  1058-1111 .... **CMLC 50**
  See also DLB 115
Algren, Nelson 1909-1981 ..... **CLC 4, 10, 33;**
  SSC 33
  See also AMWS 9; BPFB 1; CA 13-16R; 103; CANR 20, 61; CDALB 1941-1968; CN 1, 2; DLB 9; DLBY 1981, 1982, 2000; EWL 3; MAL 5; MTCW 1, 2; MTFW 2005; RGAL 4; RGSF 2
al-Hamadhani 967-1007 .... **CMLC 93**
  See also WLIT 6
al-Hariri, al-Qasim ibn 'Ali Abu
  Muhammad al-Basri
  1054-1122 .... **CMLC 63**
  See also RGWL 3
Ali, Ahmed 1908-1998 .... **CLC 69**
  See also CA 25-28R; CANR 15, 34; CN 1, 2, 3, 4, 5; DLB 323; EWL 3
Ali, Tariq 1943- .... **CLC 173**
  See also CA 25-28R; CANR 10, 99, 161
Alighieri, Dante
  See Dante
al-Kindi, Abu Yusuf Ya'qub ibn Ishaq c.
  801-c. 873 .... **CMLC 80**
Allan, John B.
  See Westlake, Donald E.
Allan, Sidney
  See Hartmann, Sadakichi

Allan, Sydney
  See Hartmann, Sadakichi
Allard, Janet **CLC 59**
Allen, Betsy
  See Harrison, Elizabeth (Allen) Cavanna
Allen, Edward 1948- .... **CLC 59**
Allen, Fred 1894-1956 .... **TCLC 87**
Allen, Paula Gunn 1939-2008 . **CLC 84, 202;**
  NNAL
  See also AMWS 4; CA 112; 143; 272; CANR 63, 130; CWP; DA3; DAM MULT; DLB 175; FW; MTCW 2; MTFW 2005; RGAL 4; TCWW 2
Allen, Roland
  See Ayckbourn, Alan
Allen, Sarah A.
  See Hopkins, Pauline Elizabeth
Allen, Sidney H.
  See Hartmann, Sadakichi
Allen, Woody 1935- .... **CLC 16, 52, 195**
  See also AAYA 10, 51; AMWS 15; CA 33-36R; CANR 27, 38, 63, 128, 172; DAM POP; DLB 44; MTCW 1; SSFS 21
Allende, Isabel 1942- ... **CLC 39, 57, 97, 170,**
  264; HLC 1; SSC 65; WLCS
  See also AAYA 18, 70; CA 125; 130; CANR 51, 74, 129, 165; CDWLB 3; CWW 2; DA3; DAM MULT, NOV; DLB 145; DNFS 1; EWL 3; FL 1:5; FW; HW 1, 2; INT CA-130; LAIT 5; LAWS 1; LMFS 2; MTCW 1, 2; MTFW 2005; NCFS 1; NFS 6, 18, 29; RGSF 2; RGWL 3; SATA 163; SSFS 11, 16; WLIT 1
Alleyn, Ellen
  See Rossetti, Christina
Alleyne, Carla D. **CLC 65**
Allingham, Margery (Louise)
  1904-1966 .... **CLC 19**
  See also CA 5-8R; 25-28R; CANR 4, 58; CMW 4; DLB 77; MSW; MTCW 1, 2
Allingham, William 1824-1889 ...... **NCLC 25**
  See also DLB 35; RGEL 2
Allison, Dorothy E. 1949- .... **CLC 78, 153**
  See also AAYA 53; CA 140; CANR 66, 107; CN 7; CSW; DA3; FW; MTCW 2; MTFW 2005; NFS 11; RGAL 4
Alloula, Malek **CLC 65**
Allston, Washington 1779-1843 .... **NCLC 2**
  See also DLB 1, 235
Almedingen, E. M.
  See Almedingen, Martha Edith von
Almedingen, Martha Edith von
  1898-1971 .... **CLC 12**
  See also CA 1-4R; CANR 1; SATA 3
Almodovar, Pedro 1949(?)- .... **CLC 114, 229;**
  HLCS 1
  See also CA 133; CANR 72, 151; HW 2
Almqvist, Carl Jonas Love
  1793-1866 .... **NCLC 42**
al-Mutanabbi, Ahmad ibn al-Husayn Abu
  al-Tayyib al-Jufi al-Kindi
  915-965 .... **CMLC 66**
  See also RGWL 3; WLIT 6
Alonso, Damaso 1898-1990 .... **CLC 14**
  See also CA 110; 131; 130; CANR 72; DLB 108; EWL 3; HW 1, 2
Alov
  See Gogol, Nikolai (Vasilyevich)
al'Sadaawi, Nawal
  See El Saadawi, Nawal
al-Shaykh, Hanan 1945- .... **CLC 218**
  See also CA 135; CANR 111; CWW 2; DLB 346; EWL 3; WLIT 6
Al Siddik
  See Rolfe, Frederick (William Serafino Austin Lewis Mary)
Alta 1942- .... **CLC 19**
  See also CA 57-60

Alter, Robert B. 1935- .... **CLC 34**
  See also CA 49-52; CANR 1, 47, 100, 160
Alter, Robert Bernard
  See Alter, Robert B.
Alther, Lisa 1944- .... **CLC 7, 41**
  See also BPFB 1; CA 65-68; CAAS 30; CANR 12, 30, 51, 180; CN 4, 5, 6, 7; CSW; GLL 2; MTCW 1
Althusser, L.
  See Althusser, Louis
Althusser, Louis 1918-1990 .... **CLC 106**
  See also CA 131; 132; CANR 102; DLB 242
Altman, Robert 1925-2006 .... **CLC 16, 116,**
  242
  See also CA 73-76; 254; CANR 43
Alurista
  See Urista (Heredia), Alberto (Baltazar)
Alvarez, A. 1929- .... **CLC 5, 13**
  See also CA 1-4R; CANR 3, 33, 63, 101, 134; CN 3, 4, 5, 6; CP 1, 2, 3, 4, 5, 6, 7; DLB 14, 40; MTFW 2005
Alvarez, Alejandro Rodriguez
  1903-1965 . **CLC 49; DC 32; TCLC 199**
  See also CA 131; 93-96; EWL 3; HW 1
Alvarez, Julia 1950- .. **CLC 93, 274; HLCS 1**
  See also AAYA 25; AMWS 7; CA 147; CANR 69, 101, 133, 166; DA3; DLB 282; LATS 1:2; LLW; MTCW 2; MTFW 2005; NFS 5, 9; SATA 129; SSFS 27; WLIT 1
Alvaro, Corrado 1896-1956 .... **TCLC 60**
  See also CA 163; DLB 264; EWL 3
Amado, Jorge 1912-2001 ... **CLC 13, 40, 106,**
  232; HLC 1
  See also CA 77-80; 201; CANR 35, 74, 135; CWW 2; DAM MULT, NOV; DLB 113, 307; EWL 3; HW 2; LAW; LAWS 1; MTCW 1, 2; MTFW 2005; RGWL 2, 3; TWA; WLIT 1
Ambler, Eric 1909-1998 .... **CLC 4, 6, 9**
  See also BRWS 4; CA 9-12R; 171; CANR 7, 38, 74; CMW 4; CN 1, 2, 3, 4, 5, 6; DLB 77; MSW; MTCW 1, 2; TEA
Ambrose c. 339-c. 397 .... **CMLC 103**
Ambrose, Stephen E. 1936-2002 .... **CLC 145**
  See also AAYA 44; CA 1-4R; 209; CANR 3, 43, 57, 83, 105; MTFW 2005; NCFS 2; SATA 40, 138
Amichai, Yehuda 1924-2000 .. **CLC 9, 22, 57,**
  116; PC 38
  See also CA 85-88; 189; CANR 46, 60, 99, 132; CWW 2; EWL 3; MTCW 1, 2; MTFW 2005; PFS 24; RGHL; WLIT 6
Amichai, Yehudah
  See Amichai, Yehuda
Amiel, Henri Frederic 1821-1881 .... **NCLC 4**
  See also DLB 217
Amis, Kingsley 1922-1995 . **CLC 1, 2, 3, 5, 8,**
  13, 40, 44, 129
  See also AAYA 77; AITN 2; BPFB 1; BRWS 2; CA 9-12R; 150; CANR 8, 28, 54; CDBLB 1945-1960; CN 1, 2, 3, 4, 5, 6; CP 1, 2, 3, 4; DA; DA3; DAB; DAC; DAM MST, NOV; DLB 15, 27, 100, 139, 326; DLBY 1996; EWL 3; HGG; INT CANR-8; MTCW 1, 2; MTFW 2005; RGEL 2; RGSF 2; SFW 4
Amis, Martin 1949- ... **CLC 4, 9, 38, 62, 101,**
  213; SSC 112
  See also BEST 90:3; BRWS 4; CA 65-68; CANR 8, 27, 54, 73, 95, 132, 166; CN 5, 6, 7; DA3; DLB 14, 194; EWL 3; INT CANR-27; MTCW 2; MTFW 2005
Amis, Martin Louis
  See Amis, Martin
Ammianus Marcellinus c. 330-c.
  395 .... **CMLC 60**
  See also AW 2; DLB 211

Boot, William
　　See Stoppard, Tom
Booth, Irwin
　　See Hoch, Edward D.
Booth, Martin 1944-2004 .... **CLC 13**
　　See also CA 93-96, 188; 223; CAAE 188;
　　CAAS 2; CANR 92; CP 1, 2, 3, 4
Booth, Philip 1925-2007 .... **CLC 23**
　　See also CA 5-8R; 262; CANR 5, 88; CP 1,
　　2, 3, 4, 5, 6, 7; DLBY 1982
Booth, Philip Edmund
　　See Booth, Philip
Booth, Wayne C. 1921-2005 .... **CLC 24**
　　See also CA 1-4R; 244; CAAS 5; CANR 3,
　　43, 117; DLB 67
Booth, Wayne Clayson
　　See Booth, Wayne C.
Borchert, Wolfgang 1921-1947 .... **TCLC 5**
　　See also CA 104; 188; DLB 69, 124; EWL
　　3
Borel, Petrus 1809-1859 .... **NCLC 41**
　　See also DLB 119; GFL 1789 to the Present
Borges, Jorge Luis 1899-1986 ... **CLC 1, 2, 3,**
　　4, 6, 8, 9, 10, 13, 19, 44, 48, 83; HLC 1;
　　PC 22, 32; SSC 4, 41, 100; TCLC 109;
　　WLC 1
　　See also AAYA 26; BPFB 1; CA 21-24R;
　　CANR 19, 33, 75, 105, 133; CDWLB 3;
　　DA; DA3; DAB; DAC; DAM MST,
　　MULT; DLB 113, 283; DLBY 1986;
　　DNFS 1, 2; EWL 3; HW 1, 2; LAW;
　　LMFS 2; MSW; MTCW 1, 2; MTFW
　　2005; PFS 27; RGHL; RGSF 2; RGWL
　　2, 3; SFW 4; SSFS 17; TWA; WLIT 1
Borne, Ludwig 1786-1837 .... **NCLC 193**
　　See also DLB 90
Borowski, Tadeusz 1922-1951 .... **SSC 48;**
　　TCLC 9
　　See also CA 106; 154; CDWLB 4; DLB
　　215; EWL 3; RGHL; RGSF 2; RGWL 3;
　　SSFS 13
Borrow, George (Henry)
　　1803-1881 .... **NCLC 9**
　　See also BRWS 12; DLB 21, 55, 166
Bosch (Gavino), Juan 1909-2001 ..... **HLCS 1**
　　See also CA 151; 204; DAM MST, MULT;
　　DLB 145; HW 1, 2
Bosman, Herman Charles
　　1905-1951 .... **TCLC 49**
　　See also CA 160; DLB 225; RGSF 2
Bosschere, Jean de 1878(?)-1953 ... **TCLC 19**
　　See also CA 115; 186
Boswell, James 1740-1795 ... **LC 4, 50; WLC**
　　1
　　See also BRW 3; CDBLB 1660-1789; DA;
　　DAB; DAC; DAM MST; DLB 104, 142;
　　TEA; WLIT 3
Boto, Eza
　　See Biyidi, Alexandre
Bottomley, Gordon 1874-1948 ..... **TCLC 107**
　　See also CA 120; 192; DLB 10
Bottoms, David 1949- .... **CLC 53**
　　See also CA 105; CANR 22; CSW; DLB
　　120; DLBY 1983
Boucicault, Dion 1820-1890 .... **NCLC 41**
　　See also DLB 344
Boucolon, Maryse
　　See Conde, Maryse
Bourcicault, Dion
　　See Boucicault, Dion
Bourdieu, Pierre 1930-2002 .... **CLC 198**
　　See also CA 130; 204
Bourget, Paul (Charles Joseph)
　　1852-1935 .... **TCLC 12**
　　See also CA 107; 196; DLB 123; GFL 1789
　　to the Present

Bourjaily, Vance (Nye) 1922- .... **CLC 8, 62**
　　See also CA 1-4R; CAAS 1; CANR 2, 72;
　　CN 1, 2, 3, 4, 5, 6, 7; DLB 2, 143; MAL
　　5
Bourne, Randolph S(illiman)
　　1886-1918 .... **TCLC 16**
　　See also AMW; CA 117; 155; DLB 63;
　　MAL 5
Boursiquot, Dionysius
　　See Boucicault, Dion
Bova, Ben 1932- .... **CLC 45**
　　See also AAYA 16; CA 5-8R; CAAS 18;
　　CANR 11, 56, 94, 111, 157; CLR 3, 96;
　　DLBY 1981; INT CANR-11; MAICYA 1,
　　2; MTCW 1; SATA 6, 68, 133; SFW 4
Bova, Benjamin William
　　See Bova, Ben
Bowen, Elizabeth (Dorothea Cole)
　　1899-1973 . **CLC 1, 3, 6, 11, 15, 22, 118;**
　　SSC 3, 28, 66; TCLC 148
　　See also BRWS 2; CA 17-18; 41-44R;
　　CANR 35, 105; CAP 2; CDBLB 1945-
　　1960; CN 1; DA3; DAM NOV; DLB 15,
　　162; EWL 3; EXPS; FW; HGG; MTCW
　　1, 2; MTFW 2005; NFS 13; RGSF 2;
　　SSFS 5, 22; SUFW 1; TEA; WLIT 4
Bowering, George 1935- .... **CLC 15, 47**
　　See also CA 21-24R; CAAS 16; CANR 10;
　　CN 7; CP 1, 2, 3, 4, 5, 6, 7; DLB 53
Bowering, Marilyn R(uthe) 1949- .... **CLC 32**
　　See also CA 101; CANR 49; CP 4, 5, 6, 7;
　　CWP; DLB 334
Bowers, Edgar 1924-2000 .... **CLC 9**
　　See also CA 5-8R; 188; CANR 24; CP 1, 2,
　　3, 4, 5, 6, 7; CSW; DLB 5
Bowers, Mrs. J. Milton 1842-1914
　　See Bierce, Ambrose (Gwinett)
Bowie, David
　　See Jones, David Robert
Bowles, Jane (Sydney) 1917-1973 ..... **CLC 3,**
　　68
　　See also CA 19-20; 41-44R; CAP 2; CN 1;
　　EWL 3; MAL 5
Bowles, Jane Auer
　　See Bowles, Jane (Sydney)
Bowles, Paul 1910-1999 ..... **CLC 1, 2, 19, 53;**
　　SSC 3, 98; TCLC 209
　　See also AMWS 4; CA 1-4R; 186; CAAS
　　1; CANR 1, 19, 50, 75; CN 1, 2, 3, 4, 5,
　　6; DLB 5, 6, 218; EWL 3; MAL 5;
　　MTCW 1, 2; MTFW 2005; RGAL 4;
　　SSFS 17
Bowles, William Lisle 1762-1850 . **NCLC 103**
　　See also DLB 93
Box, Edgar
　　See Vidal, Gore
Boyd, James 1888-1944 .... **TCLC 115**
　　See also CA 186; DLB 9; DLBD 16; RGAL
　　4; RHW
Boyd, Nancy
　　See Millay, Edna St. Vincent
Boyd, Thomas (Alexander)
　　1898-1935 .... **TCLC 111**
　　See also CA 111; 183; DLB 9; DLBD 16,
　　316
Boyd, William 1952- .... **CLC 28, 53, 70**
　　See also CA 114; 120; CANR 51, 71, 131,
　　174; CN 4, 5, 6, 7; DLB 231
Boyesen, Hjalmar Hjorth
　　1848-1895 .... **NCLC 135**
　　See also DLB 12, 71; DLBD 13; RGAL 4
Boyle, Kay 1902-1992 .... **CLC 1, 5, 19, 58,**
　　121; SSC 5, 102
　　See also CA 13-16R; 140; CAAS 1; CANR
　　29, 61, 110; CN 1, 2, 3, 4; CP 1, 2, 3,
　　4, 5; DLB 4, 9, 48, 86; DLBY 1993; EWL
　　3; MAL 5; MTCW 1, 2; MTFW 2005;
　　RGAL 4; RGSF 2; SSFS 10, 13, 14

Boyle, Mark
　　See Kienzle, William X.
Boyle, Patrick 1905-1982 .... **CLC 19**
　　See also CA 127
Boyle, T. C.
　　See Boyle, T. Coraghessan
Boyle, T. Coraghessan 1948- ..... **CLC 36, 55,**
　　90; SSC 16
　　See also AAYA 47; AMWS 8; BEST 90:4;
　　BPFB 1; CA 120; CANR 44, 76, 89, 132;
　　CN 6, 7; CPW; DA3; DAM POP; DLB
　　218, 278; DLBY 1986; EWL 3; MAL 5;
　　MTCW 2; MTFW 2005; SSFS 13, 19
Boz
　　See Dickens, Charles (John Huffam)
Brackenridge, Hugh Henry
　　1748-1816 .... **NCLC 7**
　　See also DLB 11, 37; RGAL 4
Bradbury, Edward P.
　　See Moorcock, Michael
Bradbury, Malcolm (Stanley)
　　1932-2000 .... **CLC 32, 61**
　　See also CA 1-4R; CANR 1, 33, 91, 98,
　　137; CN 1, 2, 3, 4, 5, 6; CP 1; DA3;
　　DAM NOV; DLB 14, 207; EWL 3;
　　MTCW 1, 2; MTFW 2005
Bradbury, Ray 1920- ... **CLC 1, 3, 10, 15, 42,**
　　98, 235; SSC 29, 53; WLC 1
　　See also AAYA 15; AITN 1, 2; AMWS 4;
　　BPFB 1; BYA 4, 5, 11; CA 1-4R; CANR
　　2, 30, 75, 125, 186; CDALB 1968-1988;
　　CN 1, 2, 3, 4, 5, 6, 7; CPW; DA; DA3;
　　DAB; DAC; DAM MST, NOV, POP;
　　DLB 2, 8; EXPN; EXPS; HGG; LAIT 3,
　　5; LATS 1:2; LMFS 2; MAL 5; MTCW
　　1, 2; MTFW 2005; NFS 1, 22, 29; RGAL
　　4; RGSF 2; SATA 11, 64, 123; SCFW 1,
　　2; SFW 4; SSFS 1, 20; SUFW 1, 2; TUS;
　　YAW
Bradbury, Ray Douglas
　　See Bradbury, Ray
Braddon, Mary Elizabeth
　　1837-1915 .... **TCLC 111**
　　See also BRWS 8; CA 108; 179; CMW 4;
　　DLB 18, 70, 156; HGG
Bradfield, Scott 1955- .... **SSC 65**
　　See also CA 147; CANR 90; HGG; SUFW
　　2
Bradfield, Scott Michael
　　See Bradfield, Scott
Bradford, Gamaliel 1863-1932 .... **TCLC 36**
　　See also CA 160; DLB 17
Bradford, William 1590-1657 .... **LC 64**
　　See also DLB 24, 30; RGAL 4
Bradley, David, Jr. 1950- ...... **BLC 1:1; CLC**
　　23, 118
　　See also BW 1, 3; CA 104; CANR 26, 81;
　　CN 4, 5, 6, 7; DAM MULT; DLB 33
Bradley, David Henry, Jr.
　　See Bradley, David, Jr.
Bradley, John Ed 1958- .... **CLC 55**
　　See also CA 139; CANR 99; CN 6, 7; CSW
Bradley, John Edmund, Jr.
　　See Bradley, John Ed
Bradley, Marion Zimmer
　　1930-1999 .... **CLC 30**
　　See also AAYA 40; BPFB 1; CA 57-60; 185;
　　CAAS 10; CANR 7, 31, 51, 75, 107;
　　CPW; DA3; DAM POP; DLB 8; FANT;
　　FW; GLL 1; MTCW 1, 2; MTFW 2005;
　　SATA 90, 139; SATA-Obit 116; SFW 4;
　　SUFW 2; YAW
Bradshaw, John 1933- .... **CLC 70**
　　See also CA 138; CANR 61
Bradstreet, Anne 1612(?)-1672 .... **LC 4, 30,**
　　130; PC 10
　　See also AMWS 1; CDALB 1640-1865;
　　DA; DA3; DAC; DAM MST, POET; DLB
　　24; EXPP; FW; PFS 6; RGAL 4; TUS;
　　WP

Brontes
See Bronte, Anne; Bronte, (Patrick) Branwell; Bronte, Charlotte; Bronte, Emily (Jane)

Brooke, Frances 1724-1789 .... **LC 6, 48**
See also DLB 39, 99

Brooke, Henry 1703(?)-1783 .... **LC 1**
See also DLB 39

Brooke, Rupert (Chawner)
1887-1915 .. **PC 24; TCLC 2, 7; WLC 1**
See also BRWS 3; CA 104; 132; CANR 61; CDBLB 1914-1945; DA; DAB; DAC; DAM MST, POET; DLB 19, 216; EXPP; GLL 2; MTCW 1, 2; MTFW 2005; PFS 7; TEA

Brooke-Haven, P.
See Wodehouse, P(elham) G(renville)

Brooke-Rose, Christine 1923(?)- ..... **CLC 40, 184**
See also BRWS 4; CA 13-16R; CANR 58, 118, 183; CN 1, 2, 3, 4, 5, 6, 7; DLB 14, 231; EWL 3; SFW 4

Brookner, Anita 1928- . **CLC 32, 34, 51, 136, 237**
See also BRWS 4; CA 114; 120; CANR 37, 56, 87, 130; CN 4, 5, 6, 7; CPW; DA3; DAB; DAM POP; DLB 194, 326; DLBY 1987; EWL 3; MTCW 1, 2; MTFW 2005; NFS 23; TEA

Brooks, Cleanth 1906-1994 . **CLC 24, 86, 110**
See also AMWS 14; CA 17-20R; 145; CANR 33, 35; CSW; DLB 63; DLBY 1994; EWL 3; INT CANR-35; MAL 5; MTCW 1, 2; MTFW 2005

Brooks, George
See Baum, L(yman) Frank

Brooks, Gwendolyn 1917-2000 .... **BLC 1:1, 2:1; CLC 1, 2, 4, 5, 15, 49, 125; PC 7; WLC 1**
See also AAYA 20; AFAW 1, 2; AITN 1; AMWS 3; BW 2, 3; CA 1-4R; 190; CANR 1, 27, 52, 75, 132; CDALB 1941-1968; CLR 27; CP 1, 2, 3, 4, 5, 6, 7; CWP; DA; DA3; DAC; DAM MST, MULT, POET; DLB 5, 76, 165; EWL 3; EXPP; FL 1:5; MAL 5; MBL; MTCW 1, 2; MTFW 2005; PFS 1, 2, 4, 6; RGAL 4; SATA 6; SATA-Obit 123; TUS; WP

Brooks, Mel 1926-
See Kaminsky, Melvin
See also CA 65-68; CANR 16; DFS 21

Brooks, Peter 1938- .... **CLC 34**
See also CA 45-48; CANR 1, 107, 182

Brooks, Peter Preston
See Brooks, Peter

Brooks, Van Wyck 1886-1963 .... **CLC 29**
See also AMW; CA 1-4R; CANR 6; DLB 45, 63, 103; MAL 5; TUS

Brophy, Brigid (Antonia)
1929-1995 .... **CLC 6, 11, 29, 105**
See also CA 5-8R; 149; CAAS 4; CANR 25, 53; CBD; CN 1, 2, 3, 4, 5, 6; CWD; DA3; DLB 14, 271; EWL 3; MTCW 1, 2

Brosman, Catharine Savage 1934- ..... **CLC 9**
See also CA 61-64; CANR 21, 46, 149

Brossard, Nicole 1943- .... **CLC 115, 169; PC 80**
See also CA 122; CAAS 16; CANR 140; CCA 1; CWP; CWW 2; DLB 53; EWL 3; FW; GLL 2; RGWL 3

Brother Antoninus
See Everson, William (Oliver)

Brothers Grimm
See Grimm, Jacob Ludwig Karl; Grimm, Wilhelm Karl

The Brothers Quay
See Quay, Stephen; Quay, Timothy

Broughton, T(homas) Alan 1936- ..... **CLC 19**
See also CA 45-48; CANR 2, 23, 48, 111

Broumas, Olga 1949- .... **CLC 10, 73**
See also CA 85-88; CANR 20, 69, 110; CP 5, 6, 7; CWP; GLL 2

Broun, Heywood 1888-1939 .... **TCLC 104**
See also DLB 29, 171

Brown, Alan 1950- .... **CLC 99**
See also CA 156

Brown, Charles Brockden
1771-1810 .... **NCLC 22, 74, 122**
See also AMWS 1; CDALB 1640-1865; DLB 37, 59, 73; FW; GL 2; HGG; LMFS 1; RGAL 4; TUS

Brown, Christy 1932-1981 .... **CLC 63**
See also BYA 13; CA 105; 104; CANR 72; DLB 14

Brown, Claude 1937-2002 ..... **BLC 1:1; CLC 30**
See also AAYA 7; BW 1, 3; CA 73-76; 205; CANR 81; DAM MULT

Brown, Dan 1964- .... **CLC 209**
See also AAYA 55; CA 217; MTFW 2005

Brown, Dee 1908-2002 .... **CLC 18, 47**
See also AAYA 30; CA 13-16R; 212; CAAS 6; CANR 11, 45, 60, 150; CPW; CSW; DA3; DAM POP; DLBY 1980; LAIT 2; MTCW 1, 2; MTFW 2005; NCFS 5; SATA 5, 110; SATA-Obit 141; TCWW 1, 2

Brown, Dee Alexander
See Brown, Dee

Brown, George
See Wertmueller, Lina

Brown, George Douglas
1869-1902 .... **TCLC 28**
See also CA 162; RGEL 2

Brown, George Mackay 1921-1996 ... **CLC 5, 48, 100**
See also BRWS 6; CA 21-24R; 151; CAAS 6; CANR 12, 37, 67; CN 1, 2, 3, 4, 5, 6; CP 1, 2, 3, 4, 5, 6; DLB 14, 27, 139, 271; MTCW 1; RGSF 2; SATA 35

Brown, James Willie
See Komunyakaa, Yusef

Brown, James Willie, Jr.
See Komunyakaa, Yusef

Brown, Larry 1951-2004 .... **CLC 73**
See also CA 130; 134; 233; CANR 117, 145; CSW; DLB 234; INT CA-134

Brown, Moses
See Barrett, William (Christopher)

Brown, Rita Mae 1944- .... **CLC 18, 43, 79, 259**
See also BPFB 1; CA 45-48; CANR 2, 11, 35, 62, 95, 138, 183; CN 5, 6, 7; CPW; CSW; DA3; DAM NOV, POP; FW; INT CANR-11; MAL 5; MTCW 1, 2; MTFW 2005; NFS 9; RGAL 4; TUS

Brown, Roderick (Langmere) Haig-
See Haig-Brown, Roderick (Langmere)

Brown, Rosellen 1939- .... **CLC 32, 170**
See also CA 77-80; CAAS 10; CANR 14, 44, 98; CN 6, 7

Brown, Sterling Allen 1901-1989 ...... **BLC 1; CLC 1, 23, 59; HR 1:2; PC 55**
See also AFAW 1, 2; BW 1, 3; CA 85-88; 127; CANR 26; CP 3, 4; DA3; DAM MULT, POET; DLB 48, 51, 63; MAL 5; MTCW 1, 2; MTFW 2005; RGAL 4; WP

Brown, Will
See Ainsworth, William Harrison

Brown, William Hill 1765-1793 .... **LC 93**
See also DLB 37

Brown, William Larry
See Brown, Larry

Brown, William Wells 1815-1884 ... **BLC 1:1; DC 1; NCLC 2, 89**
See also DAM MULT; DLB 3, 50, 183, 248; RGAL 4

Browne, Clyde Jackson
See Browne, Jackson

Browne, Jackson 1948(?)- .... **CLC 21**
See also CA 120

Browne, Sir Thomas 1605-1682 .... **LC 111**
See also BRW 2; DLB 151

Browning, Robert 1812-1889 . **NCLC 19, 79; PC 2, 61, 97; WLCS**
See also BRW 4; BRWC 2; BRWR 2; CDBLB 1832-1890; CLR 97; DA; DA3; DAB; DAC; DAM MST, POET; DLB 32, 163; EXPP; LATS 1:1; PAB; PFS 1, 15; RGEL 2; TEA; WLIT 4; WP; YABC 1

Browning, Tod 1882-1962 .... **CLC 16**
See also CA 141; 117

Brownmiller, Susan 1935- .... **CLC 159**
See also CA 103; CANR 35, 75, 137; DAM NOV; FW; MTCW 1, 2; MTFW 2005

Brownson, Orestes Augustus
1803-1876 .... **NCLC 50**
See also DLB 1, 59, 73, 243

Bruccoli, Matthew J. 1931-2008 .... **CLC 34**
See also CA 9-12R; 274; CANR 7, 87; DLB 103

Bruccoli, Matthew Joseph
See Bruccoli, Matthew J.

Bruce, Lenny
See Schneider, Leonard Alfred

Bruchac, Joseph 1942- .... **NNAL**
See also AAYA 19; CA 33-36R, 256; CAAE 256; CANR 13, 47, 75, 94, 137, 161; CLR 46; CWRI 5; DAM MULT; DLB 342; JRDA; MAICYA 2; MAICYAS 1; MTCW 2; MTFW 2005; SATA 42, 89, 131, 176; SATA-Essay 176

Bruin, John
See Brutus, Dennis

Brulard, Henri
See Stendhal

Brulls, Christian
See Simenon, Georges (Jacques Christian)

Brunetto Latini c. 1220-1294 .... **CMLC 73**

Brunner, John (Kilian Houston)
1934-1995 .... **CLC 8, 10**
See also CA 1-4R; 149; CAAS 8; CANR 2, 37; CPW; DAM POP; DLB 261; MTCW 1, 2; SCFW 1, 2; SFW 4

Bruno, Giordano 1548-1600 .... **LC 27, 167**
See also RGWL 2, 3

Brutus, Dennis 1924- ..... **BLC 1:1; CLC 43; PC 24**
See also AFW; BW 2, 3; CA 49-52; CAAS 14; CANR 2, 27, 42, 81; CDWLB 3; CP 1, 2, 3, 4, 5, 6, 7; DAM MULT, POET; DLB 117, 225; EWL 3

Bryan, C(ourtlandt) D(ixon) B(arnes)
1936- .... **CLC 29**
See also CA 73-76; CANR 13, 68; DLB 185; INT CANR-13

Bryan, Michael
See Moore, Brian

Bryan, William Jennings
1860-1925 .... **TCLC 99**
See also DLB 303

Bryant, William Cullen 1794-1878 . **NCLC 6, 46; PC 20**
See also AMWS 1; CDALB 1640-1865; DA; DAB; DAC; DAM MST, POET; DLB 3, 43, 59, 189, 250; EXPP; PAB; PFS 30; RGAL 4; TUS

Bryusov, Valery Yakovlevich
1873-1924 .... **TCLC 10**
See also CA 107; 155; EWL 3; SFW 4

Buchan, John 1875-1940 .... **TCLC 41**
See also CA 108; 145; CMW 4; DAB; DAM POP; DLB 34, 70, 156; HGG; MSW; MTCW 2; RGEL 2; RHW; YABC 2

Butler, Samuel 1835-1902 .... **TCLC 1, 33; WLC 1**
See also BRWS 2; CA 143; CDBLB 1890-1914; DA; DA3; DAB; DAC; DAM MST, NOV; DLB 18, 57, 174; RGEL 2; SFW 4; TEA

Butler, Walter C.
See Faust, Frederick (Schiller)

Butor, Michel (Marie Francois)
1926- .... **CLC 1, 3, 8, 11, 15, 161**
See also CA 9-12R; CANR 33, 66; CWW 2; DLB 83; EW 13; EWL 3; GFL 1789 to the Present; MTCW 1, 2; MTFW 2005

Butts, Mary 1890(?)-1937 ... **SSC 124; TCLC 77**
See also CA 148; DLB 240

Buxton, Ralph
See Silverstein, Alvin; Silverstein, Virginia B(arbara Opshelor)

Buzo, Alex
See Buzo, Alexander (John)

Buzo, Alexander (John) 1944- .... **CLC 61**
See also CA 97-100; CANR 17, 39, 69; CD 5, 6; DLB 289

Buzzati, Dino 1906-1972 .... **CLC 36**
See also CA 160; 33-36R; DLB 177; RGWL 2, 3; SFW 4

Byars, Betsy 1928- .... **CLC 35**
See also AAYA 19; BYA 3; CA 33-36R, 183; CAAE 183; CANR 18, 36, 57, 102, 148; CLR 1, 16, 72; DLB 52; INT CANR-18; JRDA; MAICYA 1, 2; MAICYAS 1; MTCW 1; SAAS 1; SATA 4, 46, 80, 163; SATA-Essay 108; WYA; YAW

Byars, Betsy Cromer
See Byars, Betsy

Byatt, Antonia Susan Drabble
See Byatt, A.S.

Byatt, A.S. 1936- .... **CLC 19, 65, 136, 223; SSC 91**
See also BPFB 1; BRWC 2; BRWS 4; CA 13-16R; CANR 13, 33, 50, 75, 96, 133; CN 1, 2, 3, 4, 5, 6; DA3; DAM NOV, POP; DLB 14, 194, 319, 326; EWL 3; MTCW 1, 2; MTFW 2005; RGSF 2; RHW; SSFS 26; TEA

Byrd, William II 1674-1744 .... **LC 112**
See also DLB 24, 140; RGAL 4

Byrne, David 1952- .... **CLC 26**
See also CA 127

Byrne, John Keyes 1926-2009 .... **CLC 19**
See also CA 102; CANR 78, 140; CBD; CD 5, 6; DFS 13, 24; DLB 13; INT CA-102

Byron, George Gordon (Noel)
1788-1824 ..... **DC 24; NCLC 2, 12, 109, 149; PC 16, 95; WLC 1**
See also AAYA 64; BRW 4; BRWC 2; CD-BLB 1789-1832; DA; DA3; DAB; DAC; DAM MST, POET; DLB 96, 110; EXPP; LMFS 1; PAB; PFS 1, 14, 29; RGEL 2; TEA; WLIT 3; WP

Byron, Robert 1905-1941 .... **TCLC 67**
See also CA 160; DLB 195

C. 3. 3.
See Wilde, Oscar

Caballero, Fernan 1796-1877 .... **NCLC 10**

Cabell, Branch
See Cabell, James Branch

Cabell, James Branch 1879-1958 .... **TCLC 6**
See also CA 105; 152; DLB 9, 78; FANT; MAL 5; MTCW 2; RGAL 4; SUFW 1

Cabeza de Vaca, Alvar Nunez
1490-1557(?) .... **LC 61**

Cable, George Washington
1844-1925 .... **SSC 4; TCLC 4**
See also CA 104; 155; DLB 12, 74; DLBD 13; RGAL 4; TUS

Cabral de Melo Neto, Joao
1920-1999 .... **CLC 76**
See also CA 151; CWW 2; DAM MULT; DLB 307; EWL 3; LAW; LAWS 1

Cabrera Infante, G. 1929-2005 ... **CLC 5, 25, 45, 120; HLC 1; SSC 39**
See also CA 85-88; 236; CANR 29, 65, 110; CDWLB 3; CWW 2; DA3; DAM MULT; DLB 113; EWL 3; HW 1, 2; LAW; LAWS 1; MTCW 1, 2; MTFW 2005; RGSF 2; WLIT 1

Cabrera Infante, Guillermo
See Cabrera Infante, G.

Cade, Toni
See Bambara, Toni Cade

Cadmus and Harmonia
See Buchan, John

Caedmon fl. 658-680 .... **CMLC 7**
See also DLB 146

Caeiro, Alberto
See Pessoa, Fernando

Caesar, Julius
See Julius Caesar

Cage, John (Milton), (Jr.)
1912-1992 .... **CLC 41; PC 58**
See also CA 13-16R; 169; CANR 9, 78; DLB 193; INT CANR-9; TCLE 1:1

Cahan, Abraham 1860-1951 .... **TCLC 71**
See also CA 108; 154; DLB 9, 25, 28; MAL 5; RGAL 4

Cain, Christopher
See Fleming, Thomas

Cain, G.
See Cabrera Infante, G.

Cain, Guillermo
See Cabrera Infante, G.

Cain, James M(allahan) 1892-1977 .. **CLC 3, 11, 28**
See also AITN 1; BPFB 1; CA 17-20R; 73-76; CANR 8, 34, 61; CMW 4; CN 1, 2; DLB 226; EWL 3; MAL 5; MSW; MTCW 1; RGAL 4

Caine, Hall 1853-1931 .... **TCLC 97**
See also RHW

Caine, Mark
See Raphael, Frederic (Michael)

Calasso, Roberto 1941- .... **CLC 81**
See also CA 143; CANR 89

Calderon de la Barca, Pedro
1600-1681 . **DC 3; HLCS 1; LC 23, 136**
See also DFS 23; EW 2; RGWL 2, 3; TWA

Caldwell, Erskine 1903-1987 ... **CLC 1, 8, 14, 50, 60; SSC 19; TCLC 117**
See also AITN 1; AMW; BPFB 1; CA 1-4R; 121; CAAS 1; CANR 2, 33; CN 1, 2, 3, 4; DA3; DAM NOV; DLB 9, 86; EWL 3; MAL 5; MTCW 1, 2; MTFW 2005; RGAL 4; RGSF 2; TUS

Caldwell, (Janet Miriam) Taylor (Holland)
1900-1985 .... **CLC 2, 28, 39**
See also BPFB 1; CA 5-8R; 116; CANR 5; DA3; DAM NOV, POP; DLBD 17; MTCW 2; RHW

Calhoun, John Caldwell
1782-1850 .... **NCLC 15**
See also DLB 3, 248

Calisher, Hortense 1911-2009 .... **CLC 2, 4, 8, 38, 134; SSC 15**
See also CA 1-4R; CANR 1, 22, 117; CN 1, 2, 3, 4, 5, 6, 7; DA3; DAM NOV; DLB 2, 218; INT CANR-22; MAL 5; MTCW 1, 2; MTFW 2005; RGAL 4; RGSF 2

Callaghan, Morley Edward
1903-1990 ..... **CLC 3, 14, 41, 65; TCLC 145**
See also CA 9-12R; 132; CANR 33, 73; CN 1, 2, 3, 4; DAC; DAM MST; DLB 68; EWL 3; MTCW 1, 2; MTFW 2005; RGEL 2; RGSF 2; SSFS 19

Callimachus c. 305B.C.-c.
240B.C. .... **CMLC 18**
See also AW 1; DLB 176; RGWL 2, 3

Calvin, Jean
See Calvin, John

Calvin, John 1509-1564 .... **LC 37**
See also DLB 327; GFL Beginnings to 1789

Calvino, Italo 1923-1985 .... **CLC 5, 8, 11, 22, 33, 39, 73; SSC 3, 48; TCLC 183**
See also AAYA 58; CA 85-88; 116; CANR 23, 61, 132; DAM NOV; DLB 196; EW 13; EWL 3; MTCW 1, 2; MTFW 2005; RGHL; RGSF 2; RGWL 2, 3; SFW 4; SSFS 12; WLIT 7

Camara Laye
See Laye, Camara

Cambridge, A Gentleman of the University of
See Crowley, Edward Alexander

Camden, William 1551-1623 .... **LC 77**
See also DLB 172

Cameron, Carey 1952- .... **CLC 59**
See also CA 135

Cameron, Peter 1959- .... **CLC 44**
See also AMWS 12; CA 125; CANR 50, 117, 188; DLB 234; GLL 2

Camoens, Luis Vaz de 1524(?)-1580
See Camoes, Luis de

Camoes, Luis de 1524(?)-1580 . **HLCS 1; LC 62; PC 31**
See also DLB 287; EW 2; RGWL 2, 3

Camp, Madeleine L'Engle
See L'Engle, Madeleine

Campana, Dino 1885-1932 .... **TCLC 20**
See also CA 117; 246; DLB 114; EWL 3

Campanella, Tommaso 1568-1639 .... **LC 32**
See also RGWL 2, 3

Campbell, Bebe Moore 1950-2006 . **BLC 2:1; CLC 246**
See also AAYA 26; BW 2, 3; CA 139; 254; CANR 81, 134; DLB 227; MTCW 2; MTFW 2005

Campbell, John Ramsey
See Campbell, Ramsey

Campbell, John W(ood, Jr.)
1910-1971 .... **CLC 32**
See also CA 21-22; 29-32R; CANR 34; CAP 2; DLB 8; MTCW 1; SCFW 1, 2; SFW 4

Campbell, Joseph 1904-1987 .... **CLC 69; TCLC 140**
See also AAYA 3, 66; BEST 89:2; CA 1-4R; 124; CANR 3, 28, 61, 107; DA3; MTCW 1, 2

Campbell, Maria 1940- .... **CLC 85; NNAL**
See also CA 102; CANR 54; CCA 1; DAC

Campbell, Ramsey 1946- ... **CLC 42; SSC 19**
See also AAYA 51; CA 57-60; 228; CAAE 228; CANR 7, 102, 171; DLB 261; HGG; INT CANR-7; SUFW 1, 2

Campbell, (Ignatius) Roy (Dunnachie)
1901-1957 .... **TCLC 5**
See also AFW; CA 104; 155; DLB 20, 225; EWL 3; MTCW 2; RGEL 2

Campbell, Thomas 1777-1844 .... **NCLC 19**
See also DLB 93, 144; RGEL 2

Campbell, Wilfred
See Campbell, William

Campbell, William 1858(?)-1918 ..... **TCLC 9**
See also CA 106; DLB 92

Campbell, William Edward March
1893-1954 .... **TCLC 96**
See also CA 108; 216; DLB 9, 86, 316; MAL 5

Campion, Jane 1954- .... **CLC 95, 229**
See also AAYA 33; CA 138; CANR 87

Campion, Thomas 1567-1620 . **LC 78; PC 87**
See also CDBLB Before 1660; DAM POET; DLB 58, 172; RGEL 2

Child, Mrs.
See Child, Lydia Maria
Child, Philip 1898-1978 .... **CLC 19, 68**
See also CA 13-14; CAP 1; CP 1; DLB 68;
RHW; SATA 47
Childers, (Robert) Erskine
1870-1922 .... **TCLC 65**
See also CA 113; 153; DLB 70
Childress, Alice 1920-1994 .... **BLC 1:1; CLC**
12, 15, 86, 96; DC 4; TCLC 116
See also AAYA 8; BW 2, 3; BYA 2; CA 45-
48; 146; CAD; CANR 3, 27, 50, 74; CLR
14; CWD; DA3; DAM DRAM, MULT,
NOV; DFS 2, 8, 14, 26; DLB 7, 38, 249;
JRDA; LAIT 5; MAICYA 1, 2; MAIC-
YAS 1; MAL 5; MTCW 1, 2; MTFW
2005; RGAL 4; SATA 7, 48, 81; TUS;
WYA; YAW
Chin, Frank (Chew, Jr.) 1940- .... **AAL; CLC**
135; DC 7
See also CA 33-36R; CAD; CANR 71; CD
5, 6; DAM MULT; DLB 206, 312; LAIT
5; RGAL 4
Chin, Marilyn (Mei Ling) 1955- .... **PC 40**
See also CA 129; CANR 70, 113; CWP;
DLB 312; PFS 28
Chislett, (Margaret) Anne 1943- ...... **CLC 34**
See also CA 151
Chitty, Thomas Willes 1926- .... **CLC 6, 11**
See also CA 5-8R; CN 1, 2, 3, 4, 5, 6; EWL
3
Chivers, Thomas Holley
1809-1858 .... **NCLC 49**
See also DLB 3, 248; RGAL 4
Chlamyda, Jehudil
See Peshkov, Alexei Maximovich
Ch'o, Chou
See Shu-Jen, Chou
Choi, Susan 1969- .... **CLC 119**
See also CA 223; CANR 188
Chomette, Rene Lucien 1898-1981 .. **CLC 20**
See also CA 103
Chomsky, Avram Noam
See Chomsky, Noam
Chomsky, Noam 1928- .... **CLC 132**
See also CA 17-20R; CANR 28, 62, 110,
132, 179; DA3; DLB 246; MTCW 1, 2;
MTFW 2005
Chona, Maria 1845(?)-1936 .... **NNAL**
See also CA 144
Chopin, Kate
See Chopin, Katherine
Chopin, Katherine 1851-1904 .... **SSC 8, 68,**
110; TCLC 127; WLCS
See also AAYA 33; AMWR 2; BYA 11, 15;
CA 104; 122; CDALB 1865-1917; DA3;
DAB; DAC; DAM MST, NOV; DLB 12,
78; EXPN; EXPS; FL 1:3; FW; LAIT 3;
MAL 5; MBL; NFS 3; RGAL 4; RGSF 2;
SSFS 2, 13, 17, 26; TUS
Chretien de Troyes c. 12th cent. - . **CMLC 10**
See also DLB 208; EW 1; RGWL 2, 3;
TWA
Christie
See Ichikawa, Kon
Christie, Agatha (Mary Clarissa)
1890-1976 .. **CLC 1, 6, 8, 12, 39, 48, 110**
See also AAYA 9; AITN 1, 2; BPFB 1;
BRWS 2; CA 17-20R; 61-64; CANR 10,
37, 108; CBD; CDBLB 1914-1945; CMW
4; CN 1, 2; CPW; CWD; DA3; DAB;
DAC; DAM NOV; DFS 2; DLB 13, 77,
245; MSW; MTCW 1, 2; MTFW 2005;
NFS 8; RGEL 2; RHW; SATA 36; TEA;
YAW
Christie, Ann Philippa
See Pearce, Philippa
Christie, Philippa
See Pearce, Philippa

Christine de Pisan
See Christine de Pizan
Christine de Pizan 1365(?)-1431(?) ...... **LC 9,**
130; PC 68
See also DLB 208; FL 1:1; FW; RGWL 2,
3
Chuang-Tzu c. 369B.C.-c.
286B.C. .... **CMLC 57**
Chubb, Elmer
See Masters, Edgar Lee
Chulkov, Mikhail Dmitrievich
1743-1792 .... **LC 2**
See also DLB 150
Churchill, Caryl 1938- .... **CLC 31, 55, 157;**
DC 5
See also BRWS 4; CA 102; CANR 22, 46,
108; CBD; CD 5, 6; CWD; DFS 25; DLB
13, 310; EWL 3; FW; MTCW 1; RGEL 2
Churchill, Charles 1731-1764 .... **LC 3**
See also DLB 109; RGEL 2
Churchill, Chick
See Churchill, Caryl
Churchill, Sir Winston (Leonard Spencer)
1874-1965 .... **TCLC 113**
See also BRW 6; CA 97-100; CDBLB
1890-1914; DA3; DLB 100, 329; DLBD
16; LAIT 4; MTCW 1, 2
Chute, Carolyn 1947- .... **CLC 39**
See also CA 123; CANR 135; CN 7
Ciardi, John (Anthony) 1916-1986 . **CLC 10,**
40, 44, 129; PC 69
See also CA 5-8R; 118; CAAS 2; CANR 5,
33; CLR 19; CP 1, 2, 3, 4; CWRI 5; DAM
POET; DLB 5; DLBY 1986; INT
CANR-5; MAICYA 1, 2; MAL 5; MTCW
1, 2; MTFW 2005; RGAL 4; SAAS 26;
SATA 1, 65; SATA-Obit 46
Cibber, Colley 1671-1757 .... **LC 66**
See also DLB 84; RGEL 2
Cicero, Marcus Tullius
106B.C.-43B.C. .... **CMLC 3, 81**
See also AW 1; CDWLB 1; DLB 211;
RGWL 2, 3; WLIT 8
Cimino, Michael 1943- .... **CLC 16**
See also CA 105
Cioran, E(mil) M. 1911-1995 .... **CLC 64**
See also CA 25-28R; 149; CANR 91; DLB
220; EWL 3
Circus, Anthony
See Hoch, Edward D.
Cisneros, Sandra 1954- .... **CLC 69, 118, 193;**
HLC 1; PC 52; SSC 32, 72
See also AAYA 9, 53; AMWS 7; CA 131;
CANR 64, 118; CLR 123; CN 7; CWP;
DA3; DAM MULT; DLB 122, 152; EWL
3; EXPN; FL 1:5; FW; HW 1, 2; LAIT 5;
LATS 1:2; LLW; MAICYA 2; MAL 5;
MTCW 2; MTFW 2005; NFS 2; PFS 19;
RGAL 4; RGSF 2; SSFS 3, 13, 27; WLIT
1; YAW
Cixous, Helene 1937- .... **CLC 92, 253**
See also CA 126; CANR 55, 123; CWW 2;
DLB 83, 242; EWL 3; FL 1:5; FW; GLL
2; MTCW 1, 2; MTFW 2005; TWA
Clair, Rene
See Chomette, Rene Lucien
Clampitt, Amy 1920-1994 .... **CLC 32; PC 19**
See also AMWS 9; CA 110; 146; CANR
29, 79; CP 4, 5; DLB 105; MAL 5; PFS
27
Clancy, Thomas L., Jr. 1947- .... **CLC 45, 112**
See also AAYA 9, 51; BEST 89:1, 90:1;
BPFB 1; BYA 10, 11; CA 125; 131;
CANR 62, 105, 132; CMW 4; CPW;
DA3; DAM NOV, POP; DLB 227; INT
CA-131; MTCW 1, 2; MTFW 2005
Clancy, Tom
See Clancy, Thomas L., Jr.

Clare, John 1793-1864 .. **NCLC 9, 86; PC 23**
See also BRWS 11; DAB; DAM POET;
DLB 55, 96; RGEL 2
Clarin
See Alas (y Urena), Leopoldo (Enrique
Garcia)
Clark, Al C.
See Goines, Donald
Clark, Brian (Robert)
See Clark, (Robert) Brian
Clark, (Robert) Brian 1932- .... **CLC 29**
See also CA 41-44R; CANR 67; CBD; CD
5, 6
Clark, Curt
See Westlake, Donald E.
Clark, Eleanor 1913-1996 .... **CLC 5, 19**
See also CA 9-12R; 151; CANR 41; CN 1,
2, 3, 4, 5, 6; DLB 6
Clark, J. P.
See Clark Bekederemo, J.P.
Clark, John Pepper
See Clark Bekederemo, J.P.
See also AFW; CD 5; CP 1, 2, 3, 4, 5, 6, 7;
RGEL 2
Clark, Kenneth (Mackenzie)
1903-1983 .... **TCLC 147**
See also CA 93-96; 109; CANR 36; MTCW
1, 2; MTFW 2005
Clark, M. R.
See Clark, Mavis Thorpe
Clark, Mavis Thorpe 1909-1999 ...... **CLC 12**
See also CA 57-60; CANR 8, 37, 107; CLR
30; CWRI 5; MAICYA 1, 2; SAAS 5;
SATA 8, 74
Clark, Walter Van Tilburg
1909-1971 .... **CLC 28**
See also CA 9-12R; 33-36R; CANR 63,
113; CN 1; DLB 9, 206; LAIT 2; MAL 5;
RGAL 4; SATA 8; TCWW 1, 2
Clark Bekederemo, J.P. 1935- .... **BLC 1:1;**
CLC 38; DC 5
See Clark, John Pepper
See also AAYA 79; BW 1; CA 65-68;
CANR 16, 72; CD 6; CDWLB 3; DAM
DRAM, MULT; DFS 13; DLB 117; EWL
3; MTCW 2; MTFW 2005
Clarke, Arthur
See Clarke, Arthur C.
Clarke, Arthur C. 1917-2008 .. **CLC 1, 4, 13,**
18, 35, 136; SSC 3
See also AAYA 4, 33; BPFB 1; BYA 13;
CA 1-4R; 270; CANR 2, 28, 55, 74, 130;
CLR 119; CN 1, 2, 3, 4, 5, 6, 7; CPW;
DA3; DAM POP; DLB 261; JRDA; LAIT
5; MAICYA 1, 2; MTCW 1, 2; MTFW
2005; SATA 13, 70, 115; SATA-Obit 191;
SCFW 1, 2; SFW 4; SSFS 4, 18; TCLE
1:1; YAW
Clarke, Arthur Charles
See Clarke, Arthur C.
Clarke, Austin 1896-1974 .... **CLC 6, 9**
See also CA 29-32; 49-52; CAP 2; CP 1, 2;
DAM POET; DLB 10, 20; EWL 3; RGEL
2
Clarke, Austin C. 1934- .... **BLC 1:1; CLC 8,**
53; SSC 45, 116
See also BW 1; CA 25-28R; CAAS 16;
CANR 14, 32, 68, 140; CN 1, 2, 3, 4, 5,
6, 7; DAC; DAM MULT; DLB 53, 125;
DNFS 2; MTCW 2; MTFW 2005; RGSF
2
Clarke, Gillian 1937- .... **CLC 61**
See also CA 106; CP 3, 4, 5, 6, 7; CWP;
DLB 40
Clarke, Marcus (Andrew Hislop)
1846-1881 .... **NCLC 19; SSC 94**
See also DLB 230; RGEL 2; RGSF 2
Clarke, Shirley 1925-1997 .... **CLC 16**
See also CA 189

Colum, Padraic 1881-1972 .... **CLC 28**
 See also BYA 4; CA 73-76; 33-36R; CANR
 35; CLR 36; CP 1; CWRI 5; DLB 19;
 MAICYA 1, 2; MTCW 1; RGEL 2; SATA
 15; WCH

Colvin, James
 See Moorcock, Michael

Colwin, Laurie (E.) 1944-1992 .... **CLC 5, 13,
 23, 84**
 See also CA 89-92; 139; CANR 20, 46;
 DLB 218; DLBY 1980; MTCW 1

Comfort, Alex(ander) 1920-2000 .... **CLC 7**
 See also CA 1-4R; 190; CANR 1, 45; CN
 1, 2, 3, 4; CP 1, 2, 3, 4, 5, 6, 7; DAM
 POP; MTCW 2

Comfort, Montgomery
 See Campbell, Ramsey

Compton-Burnett, I(vy)
 1892(?)-1969 .... **CLC 1, 3, 10, 15, 34;
 TCLC 180**
 See also BRW 7; CA 1-4R; 25-28R; CANR
 4; DAM NOV; DLB 36; EWL 3; MTCW
 1, 2; RGEL 2

Comstock, Anthony 1844-1915 ...... **TCLC 13**
 See also CA 110; 169

Comte, Auguste 1798-1857 .... **NCLC 54**

Conan Doyle, Arthur
 See Doyle, Sir Arthur Conan

Conde (Abellan), Carmen
 1901-1996 .... **HLCS 1**
 See also CA 177; CWW 2; DLB 108; EWL
 3; HW 2

Conde, Maryse 1937- .... **BLC 2:1; BLCS;
 CLC 52, 92, 247**
 See also BW 2, 3; CA 110, 190; CAAE 190;
 CANR 30, 53, 76, 171; CWW 2; DAM
 MULT; EWL 3; MTCW 2; MTFW 2005

Condillac, Etienne Bonnot de
 1714-1780 .... **LC 26**
 See also DLB 313

Condon, Richard 1915-1996 ...... **CLC 4, 6, 8,
 10, 45, 100**
 See also BEST 90:3; BPFB 1; CA 1-4R;
 151; CAAS 1; CANR 2, 23, 164; CMW
 4; CN 1, 2, 3, 4, 5, 6; DAM NOV; INT
 CANR-23; MAL 5; MTCW 1, 2

Condon, Richard Thomas
 See Condon, Richard

Condorcet
 See Condorcet, marquis de Marie-Jean-
 Antoine-Nicolas Caritat

**Condorcet, marquis de
 Marie-Jean-Antoine-Nicolas Caritat**
 1743-1794 .... **LC 104**
 See also DLB 313; GFL Beginnings to 1789

Confucius 551B.C.-479B.C. .... **CMLC 19, 65;
 WLCS**
 See also DA; DA3; DAB; DAC; DAM
 MST

Congreve, William 1670-1729 ... **DC 2; LC 5,
 21; WLC 2**
 See also BRW 2; CDBLB 1660-1789; DA;
 DAB; DAC; DAM DRAM, MST, POET;
 DFS 15; DLB 39, 84; RGEL 2; WLIT 3

Conley, Robert J. 1940- .... **NNAL**
 See also CA 41-44R; CANR 15, 34, 45, 96,
 186; DAM MULT; TCWW 2

Connell, Evan S., Jr. 1924- .... **CLC 4, 6, 45**
 See also AAYA 7; AMWS 14; CA 1-4R;
 CAAS 2; CANR 2, 39, 76, 97, 140; CN
 1, 2, 3, 4, 5, 6; DAM NOV; DLB 2, 335;
 DLBY 1981; MAL 5; MTCW 1, 2;
 MTFW 2005

Connelly, Marc(us Cook) 1890-1980 . **CLC 7**
 See also CA 85-88; 102; CAD; CANR 30;
 DFS 12; DLB 7; DLBY 1980; MAL 5;
 RGAL 4; SATA-Obit 25

Connolly, Paul
 See Wicker, Tom

Connor, Ralph
 See Gordon, Charles William

Conrad, Joseph 1857-1924 ..... **SSC 9, 67, 69,
 71; TCLC 1, 6, 13, 25, 43, 57; WLC 2**
 See also AAYA 26; BPFB 1; BRW 6;
 BRWC 1; BRWR 2; BYA 2; CA 104; 131;
 CANR 60; CDBLB 1890-1914; DA; DA3;
 DAB; DAC; DAM MST, NOV; DLB 10,
 34, 98, 156; EWL 3; EXPN; EXPS; LAIT
 2; LATS 1:1; LMFS 1; MTCW 1, 2;
 MTFW 2005; NFS 2, 16; RGEL 2; RGSF
 2; SATA 27; SSFS 1, 12; TEA; WLIT 4

Conrad, Robert Arnold
 See Hart, Moss

Conroy, Pat 1945- .... **CLC 30, 74**
 See also AAYA 8, 52; AITN 1; BPFB 1;
 CA 85-88; CANR 24, 53, 129; CN 7;
 CPW; CSW; DA3; DAM NOV, POP;
 DLB 6; LAIT 5; MAL 5; MTCW 1, 2;
 MTFW 2005

Constant (de Rebecque), (Henri) Benjamin
 1767-1830 .... **NCLC 6, 182**
 See also DLB 119; EW 4; GFL 1789 to the
 Present

Conway, Jill K. 1934- .... **CLC 152**
 See also CA 130; CANR 94

Conway, Jill Kathryn Ker
 See Conway, Jill K.

Conybeare, Charles Augustus
 See Eliot, T(homas) S(tearns)

Cook, Michael 1933-1994 .... **CLC 58**
 See also CA 93-96; CANR 68; DLB 53

Cook, Robin 1940- .... **CLC 14**
 See also AAYA 32; BEST 90:2; BPFB 1;
 CA 108; 111; CANR 41, 90, 109, 181;
 CPW; DA3; DAM POP; HGG; INT CA-
 111

Cook, Roy
 See Silverberg, Robert

Cooke, Elizabeth 1948- .... **CLC 55**
 See also CA 129

Cooke, John Esten 1830-1886 .... **NCLC 5**
 See also DLB 3, 248; RGAL 4

Cooke, John Estes
 See Baum, L(yman) Frank

Cooke, M. E.
 See Creasey, John

Cooke, Margaret
 See Creasey, John

Cooke, Rose Terry 1827-1892 ...... **NCLC 110**
 See also DLB 12, 74

Cook-Lynn, Elizabeth 1930- .... **CLC 93;
 NNAL**
 See also CA 133; DAM MULT; DLB 175

Cooney, Ray **CLC 62**
 See also CBD

Cooper, Anthony Ashley 1671-1713 .. **LC 107**
 See also DLB 101, 336

Cooper, Dennis 1953- .... **CLC 203**
 See also CA 133; CANR 72, 86; GLL 1;
 HGG

Cooper, Douglas 1960- .... **CLC 86**

Cooper, Henry St. John
 See Creasey, John

Cooper, J. California (?)- .... **CLC 56**
 See also AAYA 12; BW 1; CA 125; CANR
 55; DAM MULT; DLB 212

Cooper, James Fenimore
 1789-1851 .... **NCLC 1, 27, 54, 203**
 See also AAYA 22; AMW; BPFB 1;
 CDALB 1640-1865; CLR 105; DA3;
 DLB 3, 183, 250, 254; LAIT 1; NFS 25;
 RGAL 4; SATA 19; TUS; WCH

Cooper, Susan Fenimore
 1813-1894 .... **NCLC 129**
 See also ANW; DLB 239, 254

Coover, Robert 1932- .. **CLC 3, 7, 15, 32, 46,
 87, 161; SSC 15, 101**
 See also AMWS 5; BPFB 1; CA 45-48;
 CANR 3, 37, 58, 115; CN 1, 2, 3, 4, 5, 6,
 7; DAM NOV; DLB 2, 227; DLBY 1981;
 EWL 3; MAL 5; MTCW 1, 2; MTFW
 2005; RGAL 4; RGSF 2

Copeland, Stewart (Armstrong)
 1952- .... **CLC 26**

Copernicus, Nicolaus 1473-1543 .... **LC 45**

Coppard, A(lfred) E(dgar)
 1878-1957 .... **SSC 21; TCLC 5**
 See also BRWS 8; CA 114; 167; DLB 162;
 EWL 3; HGG; RGEL 2; RGSF 2; SUFW
 1; YABC 1

Coppee, Francois 1842-1908 .... **TCLC 25**
 See also CA 170; DLB 217

Coppola, Francis Ford 1939- ... **CLC 16, 126**
 See also AAYA 39; CA 77-80; CANR 40,
 78; DLB 44

Copway, George 1818-1869 .... **NNAL**
 See also DAM MULT; DLB 175, 183

Corbiere, Tristan 1845-1875 .... **NCLC 43**
 See also DLB 217; GFL 1789 to the Present

Corcoran, Barbara (Asenath)
 1911- .... **CLC 17**
 See also AAYA 14; CA 21-24R, 191; CAAE
 191; CAAS 2; CANR 11, 28, 48; CLR
 50; DLB 52; JRDA; MAICYA 2; MAIC-
 YAS 1; RHW; SAAS 20; SATA 3, 77;
 SATA-Essay 125

Cordelier, Maurice
 See Giraudoux, Jean(-Hippolyte)

Cordier, Gilbert
 See Scherer, Jean-Marie Maurice

Corelli, Marie
 See Mackay, Mary

Corinna c. 225B.C.-c. 305B.C. ...... **CMLC 72**

Corman, Cid 1924-2004 .... **CLC 9**
 See also CA 85-88; 225; CAAS 2; CANR
 44; CP 1, 2, 3, 4, 5, 6, 7; DAM POET;
 DLB 5, 193

Corman, Sidney
 See Corman, Cid

Cormier, Robert 1925-2000 .... **CLC 12, 30**
 See also AAYA 3, 19; BYA 1, 2, 6, 8, 9;
 CA 1-4R; CANR 5, 23, 76, 93; CDALB
 1968-1988; CLR 12, 55; DA; DAB; DAC;
 DAM MST, NOV; DLB 52; EXPN; INT
 CANR-23; JRDA; LAIT 5; MAICYA 1,
 2; MTCW 1, 2; MTFW 2005; NFS 2, 18;
 SATA 10, 45, 83; SATA-Obit 122; WYA;
 YAW

Corn, Alfred (DeWitt III) 1943- .... **CLC 33**
 See also CA 179; CAAE 179; CAAS 25;
 CANR 44; CP 3, 4, 5, 6, 7; CSW; DLB
 120, 282; DLBY 1980

Corneille, Pierre 1606-1684 .. **DC 21; LC 28,
 135**
 See also DAB; DAM MST; DFS 21; DLB
 268; EW 3; GFL Beginnings to 1789;
 RGWL 2, 3; TWA

Cornwell, David
 See le Carre, John

Cornwell, David John Moore
 See le Carre, John

Cornwell, Patricia 1956- .... **CLC 155**
 See also AAYA 16, 56; BPFB 1; CA 134;
 CANR 53, 131; CMW 4; CPW; CSW;
 DAM POP; DLB 306; MSW; MTCW 2;
 MTFW 2005

Cornwell, Patricia Daniels
 See Cornwell, Patricia

Cornwell, Smith
 See Smith, David (Jeddie)

Corso, Gregory 1930-2001 .... **CLC 1, 11; PC 33**
See also AMWS 12; BG 1:2; CA 5-8R; 193; CANR 41, 76, 132; CP 1, 2, 3, 4, 5, 6, 7; DA3; DLB 5, 16, 237; LMFS 2; MAL 5; MTCW 1, 2; MTFW 2005; WP

Cortazar, Julio 1914-1984 ... **CLC 2, 3, 5, 10, 13, 15, 33, 34, 92; HLC 1; SSC 7, 76**
See also BPFB 1; CA 21-24R; CANR 12, 32, 81; CDWLB 3; DA3; DAM MULT, NOV; DLB 113; EWL 3; EXPS; HW 1, 2; LAW; MTCW 1, 2; MTFW 2005; RGSF 2; RGWL 2, 3; SSFS 3, 20; TWA; WLIT 1

Cortes, Hernan 1485-1547 .... **LC 31**

Cortez, Jayne 1936- .... **BLC 2:1**
See also BW 2, 3; CA 73-76; CANR 13, 31, 68, 126; CWP; DLB 41; EWL 3

Corvinus, Jakob
See Raabe, Wilhelm (Karl)

Corwin, Cecil
See Kornbluth, C(yril) M.

Cosic, Dobrica 1921- .... **CLC 14**
See also CA 122; 138; CDWLB 4; CWW 2; DLB 181; EWL 3

Costain, Thomas B(ertram) 1885-1965 .... **CLC 30**
See also BYA 3; CA 5-8R; 25-28R; DLB 9; RHW

Costantini, Humberto 1924(?)-1987 . **CLC 49**
See also CA 131; 122; EWL 3; HW 1

Costello, Elvis 1954- .... **CLC 21**
See also CA 204

Costenoble, Philostene
See Ghelderode, Michel de

Cotes, Cecil V.
See Duncan, Sara Jeannette

Cotter, Joseph Seamon Sr. 1861-1949 .... **BLC 1:1; TCLC 28**
See also BW 1; CA 124; DAM MULT; DLB 50

Couch, Arthur Thomas Quiller
See Quiller-Couch, Sir Arthur (Thomas)

Coulton, James
See Hansen, Joseph

Couperus, Louis (Marie Anne) 1863-1923 .... **TCLC 15**
See also CA 115; EWL 3; RGWL 2, 3

Coupland, Douglas 1961- .... **CLC 85, 133**
See also AAYA 34; CA 142; CANR 57, 90, 130, 172; CCA 1; CN 7; CPW; DAC; DAM POP; DLB 334

Coupland, Douglas Campbell
See Coupland, Douglas

Court, Wesli
See Turco, Lewis

Courtenay, Bryce 1933- .... **CLC 59**
See also CA 138; CPW

Courtney, Robert
See Ellison, Harlan

Cousteau, Jacques-Yves 1910-1997 .. **CLC 30**
See also CA 65-68; 159; CANR 15, 67; MTCW 1; SATA 38, 98

Coventry, Francis 1725-1754 .... **LC 46**
See also DLB 39

Coverdale, Miles c. 1487-1569 .... **LC 77**
See also DLB 167

Cowan, Peter (Walkinshaw) 1914-2002 .... **SSC 28**
See also CA 21-24R; CANR 9, 25, 50, 83; CN 1, 2, 3, 4, 5, 6, 7; DLB 260; RGSF 2

Coward, Noel (Peirce) 1899-1973 . **CLC 1, 9, 29, 51**
See also AITN 1; BRWS 2; CA 17-18; 41-44R; CANR 35, 132; CAP 2; CBD; CD-BLB 1914-1945; DA3; DAM DRAM; DFS 3, 6; DLB 10, 245; EWL 3; IDFW 3, 4; MTCW 1, 2; MTFW 2005; RGEL 2; TEA

Cowley, Abraham 1618-1667 .. **LC 43; PC 90**
See also BRW 2; DLB 131, 151; PAB; RGEL 2

Cowley, Malcolm 1898-1989 .... **CLC 39**
See also AMWS 2; CA 5-8R; 128; CANR 3, 55; CP 1, 2, 3, 4; DLB 4, 48; DLBY 1981, 1989; EWL 3; MAL 5; MTCW 1, 2; MTFW 2005

Cowper, William 1731-1800 ..... **NCLC 8, 94; PC 40**
See also BRW 3; DA3; DAM POET; DLB 104, 109; RGEL 2

Cox, William Trevor
See Trevor, William

Coyne, P. J.
See Masters, Hilary

Coyne, P.J.
See Masters, Hilary

Cozzens, James Gould 1903-1978 . **CLC 1, 4, 11, 92**
See also AMW; BPFB 1; CA 9-12R; 81-84; CANR 19; CDALB 1941-1968; CN 1, 2; DLB 9, 294; DLBD 2; DLBY 1984, 1997; EWL 3; MAL 5; MTCW 1, 2; MTFW 2005; RGAL 4

Crabbe, George 1754-1832 ... **NCLC 26, 121; PC 97**
See also BRW 3; DLB 93; RGEL 2

Crace, Jim 1946- .... **CLC 157; SSC 61**
See also BRWS 14; CA 128; 135; CANR 55, 70, 123, 180; CN 5, 6, 7; DLB 231; INT CA-135

Craddock, Charles Egbert
See Murfree, Mary Noailles

Craig, A. A.
See Anderson, Poul

Craik, Mrs.
See Craik, Dinah Maria (Mulock)

Craik, Dinah Maria (Mulock) 1826-1887 .... **NCLC 38**
See also DLB 35, 163; MAICYA 1, 2; RGEL 2; SATA 34

Cram, Ralph Adams 1863-1942 ..... **TCLC 45**
See also CA 160

Cranch, Christopher Pearse 1813-1892 .... **NCLC 115**
See also DLB 1, 42, 243

Crane, (Harold) Hart 1899-1932 .... **PC 3; TCLC 2, 5, 80; WLC 2**
See also AMW; AMWR 2; CA 104; 127; CDALB 1917-1929; DA; DA3; DAB; DAC; DAM MST, POET; DLB 4, 48; EWL 3; MAL 5; MTCW 1, 2; MTFW 2005; RGAL 4; TUS

Crane, R(onald) S(almon) 1886-1967 .... **CLC 27**
See also CA 85-88; DLB 63

Crane, Stephen (Townley) 1871-1900 .... **PC 80; SSC 7, 56, 70; TCLC 11, 17, 32, 216; WLC 2**
See also AAYA 21; AMW; AMWC 1; BPFB 1; BYA 3; CA 109; 140; CANR 84; CDALB 1865-1917; CLR 132; DA; DA3; DAB; DAC; DAM MST, NOV, POET; DLB 12, 54, 78; EXPN; EXPS; LAIT 2; LMFS 2; MAL 5; NFS 4, 20; PFS 9; RGAL 4; RGSF 2; SSFS 4; TUS; WYA; YABC 2

Cranmer, Thomas 1489-1556 .... **LC 95**
See also DLB 132, 213

Cranshaw, Stanley
See Fisher, Dorothy (Frances) Canfield

Crase, Douglas 1944- .... **CLC 58**
See also CA 106

Crashaw, Richard 1612(?)-1649 .. **LC 24; PC 84**
See also BRW 2; DLB 126; PAB; RGEL 2

Cratinus c. 519B.C.-c. 422B.C. ..... **CMLC 54**
See also LMFS 1

Craven, Margaret 1901-1980 .... **CLC 17**
See also BYA 2; CA 103; CCA 1; DAC; LAIT 5

Crawford, F(rancis) Marion 1854-1909 .... **TCLC 10**
See also CA 107; 168; DLB 71; HGG; RGAL 4; SUFW 1

Crawford, Isabella Valancy 1850-1887 .... **NCLC 12, 127**
See also DLB 92; RGEL 2

Crayon, Geoffrey
See Irving, Washington

Creasey, John 1908-1973 .... **CLC 11**
See also CA 5-8R; 41-44R; CANR 8, 59; CMW 4; DLB 77; MTCW 1

Crebillon, Claude Prosper Jolyot de (fils) 1707-1777 .... **LC 1, 28**
See also DLB 313; GFL Beginnings to 1789

Credo
See Creasey, John

Credo, Alvaro J. de
See Prado (Calvo), Pedro

Creeley, Robert 1926-2005 .... **CLC 1, 2, 4, 8, 11, 15, 36, 78, 266; PC 73**
See also AMWS 4; CA 1-4R; 237; CAAS 10; CANR 23, 43, 89, 137; CP 1, 2, 3, 4, 5, 6, 7; DA3; DAM POET; DLB 5, 16, 169; DLBD 17; EWL 3; MAL 5; MTCW 1, 2; MTFW 2005; PFS 21; RGAL 4; WP

Creeley, Robert White
See Creeley, Robert

Crenne, Helisenne de 1510-1560 .... **LC 113**
See also DLB 327

Crevecoeur, Hector St. John de
See Crevecoeur, Michel Guillaume Jean de

Crevecoeur, Michel Guillaume Jean de 1735-1813 .... **NCLC 105**
See also AMWS 1; ANW; DLB 37

Crevel, Rene 1900-1935 .... **TCLC 112**
See also GLL 2

Crews, Harry 1935- .... **CLC 6, 23, 49**
See also AITN 1; AMWS 11; BPFB 1; CA 25-28R; CANR 20, 57; CN 3, 4, 5, 6, 7; CSW; DA3; DLB 6, 143, 185; MTCW 1, 2; MTFW 2005; RGAL 4

Crichton, John Michael
See Crichton, Michael

Crichton, Michael 1942-2008 .. **CLC 2, 6, 54, 90, 242**
See also AAYA 10, 49; AITN 2; BPFB 1; CA 25-28R; 279; CANR 13, 40, 54, 76, 127, 179; CMW 4; CN 2, 3, 6, 7; CPW; DA3; DAM NOV, POP; DLB 292; DLBY 1981; INT CANR-13; JRDA; MTCW 1, 2; MTFW 2005; SATA 9, 88; SATA-Obit 199; SFW 4; YAW

Crispin, Edmund
See Montgomery, (Robert) Bruce

Cristina of Sweden 1626-1689 .... **LC 124**

Cristofer, Michael 1945(?)- .... **CLC 28**
See also CA 110; 152; CAD; CANR 150; CD 5, 6; DAM DRAM; DFS 15; DLB 7

Cristofer, Michael Ivan
See Cristofer, Michael

Criton
See Alain

Croce, Benedetto 1866-1952 .... **TCLC 37**
See also CA 120; 155; EW 8; EWL 3; WLIT 7

Crockett, David 1786-1836 .... **NCLC 8**
See also DLB 3, 11, 183, 248

Crockett, Davy
See Crockett, David

Crofts, Freeman Wills 1879-1957 .. **TCLC 55**
See also CA 115; 195; CMW 4; DLB 77; MSW

Croker, John Wilson 1780-1857 .... **NCLC 10**
See also DLB 110

Crommelynck, Fernand 1885-1970 .. **CLC 75**
See also CA 189; 89-92; EWL 3

Cromwell, Oliver 1599-1658 .... **LC 43**

Cronenberg, David 1943- .... **CLC 143**
See also CA 138; CCA 1

Cronin, A(rchibald) J(oseph)
1896-1981 .... **CLC 32**
See also BPFB 1; CA 1-4R; 102; CANR 5;
CN 2; DLB 191; SATA 47; SATA-Obit 25

Cross, Amanda
See Heilbrun, Carolyn G(old)

Crothers, Rachel 1878-1958 .... **TCLC 19**
See also CA 113; 194; CAD; CWD; DLB
7, 266; RGAL 4

Croves, Hal
See Traven, B.

Crow Dog, Mary (?)- .... **CLC 93; NNAL**
See also CA 154

Crowfield, Christopher
See Stowe, Harriet (Elizabeth) Beecher

Crowley, Aleister
See Crowley, Edward Alexander

Crowley, Edward Alexander
1875-1947 .... **TCLC 7**
See also CA 104; GLL 1; HGG

Crowley, John 1942- .... **CLC 57**
See also AAYA 57; BPFB 1; CA 61-64;
CANR 43, 98, 138, 177; DLBY 1982;
FANT; MTFW 2005; SATA 65, 140; SFW
4; SUFW 2

Crowne, John 1641-1712 .... **LC 104**
See also DLB 80; RGEL 2

Crud
See Crumb, R.

Crumarums
See Crumb, R.

Crumb, R. 1943- .... **CLC 17**
See also CA 106; CANR 107, 150

Crumb, Robert
See Crumb, R.

Crumbum
See Crumb, R.

Crumski
See Crumb, R.

Crum the Bum
See Crumb, R.

Crunk
See Crumb, R.

Crustt
See Crumb, R.

Crutchfield, Les
See Trumbo, Dalton

Cruz, Victor Hernandez 1949- ... **HLC 1; PC
37**
See also BW 2; CA 65-68, 271; CAAE 271;
CAAS 17; CANR 14, 32, 74, 132; CP 1,
2, 3, 4, 5, 6, 7; DAM MULT, POET; DLB
41; DNFS 1; EXPP; HW 1, 2; LLW;
MTCW 2; MTFW 2005; PFS 16; WP

Cryer, Gretchen (Kiger) 1935- .... **CLC 21**
See also CA 114; 123

Csath, Geza
See Brenner, Jozef

Cudlip, David R(ockwell) 1933- .... **CLC 34**
See also CA 177

Cullen, Countee 1903-1946 ..... **BLC 1:1; HR
1:2; PC 20; TCLC 4, 37, 220; WLCS**
See also AAYA 78; AFAW 2; AMWS 4; BW
1; CA 108; 124; CDALB 1917-1929; DA;
DA3; DAC; DAM MST, MULT, POET;
DLB 4, 48, 51; EWL 3; EXPP; LMFS 2;
MAL 5; MTCW 1, 2; MTFW 2005; PFS
3; RGAL 4; SATA 18; WP

Culleton, Beatrice 1949- .... **NNAL**
See also CA 120; CANR 83; DAC

Culver, Timothy J.
See Westlake, Donald E.

Culver, Timothy J.
See Westlake, Donald E.

Cum, R.
See Crumb, R.

Cumberland, Richard
1732-1811 .... **NCLC 167**
See also DLB 89; RGEL 2

Cummings, Bruce F(rederick)
1889-1919 .... **TCLC 24**
See also CA 123

Cummings, E(dward) E(stlin)
1894-1962 .. **CLC 1, 3, 8, 12, 15, 68; PC
5; TCLC 137; WLC 2**
See also AAYA 41; AMW; CA 73-76;
CANR 31; CDALB 1929-1941; DA;
DA3; DAB; DAC; DAM MST, POET;
DLB 4, 48; EWL 3; EXPP; MAL 5;
MTCW 1, 2; MTFW 2005; PAB; PFS 1,
3, 12, 13, 19, 30; RGAL 4; TUS; WP

Cummins, Maria Susanna
1827-1866 .... **NCLC 139**
See also DLB 42; YABC 1

Cunha, Euclides (Rodrigues Pimenta) da
1866-1909 .... **TCLC 24**
See also CA 123; 219; DLB 307; LAW;
WLIT 1

Cunningham, E. V.
See Fast, Howard

Cunningham, J. Morgan
See Westlake, Donald E.

Cunningham, J(ames) V(incent)
1911-1985 .... **CLC 3, 31; PC 92**
See also CA 1-4R; 115; CANR 1, 72; CP 1,
2, 3, 4; DLB 5

Cunningham, Julia (Woolfolk)
1916- .... **CLC 12**
See also CA 9-12R; CANR 4, 19, 36; CWRI
5; JRDA; MAICYA 1, 2; SAAS 2; SATA
1, 26, 132

Cunningham, Michael 1952- .... **CLC 34, 243**
See also AMWS 15; CA 136; CANR 96,
160; CN 7; DLB 292; GLL 2; MTFW
2005; NFS 23

Cunninghame Graham, R. B.
See Cunninghame Graham, Robert
(Gallnigad) Bontine

Cunninghame Graham, Robert (Gallnigad)
Bontine 1852-1936 .... **TCLC 19**
See also CA 119; 184; DLB 98, 135, 174;
RGEL 2; RGSF 2

Curnow, (Thomas) Allen (Monro)
1911-2001 .... **PC 48**
See also CA 69-72; 202; CANR 48, 99; CP
1, 2, 3, 4, 5, 6, 7; EWL 3; RGEL 2

Currie, Ellen 19(?)- .... **CLC 44**

Curtin, Philip
See Lowndes, Marie Adelaide (Belloc)

Curtin, Phillip
See Lowndes, Marie Adelaide (Belloc)

Curtis, Price
See Ellison, Harlan

Cusanus, Nicolaus 1401-1464
See Nicholas of Cusa

Cutrate, Joe
See Spiegelman, Art

Cynewulf c. 770- .... **CMLC 23**
See also DLB 146; RGEL 2

Cyrano de Bergerac, Savinien de
1619-1655 .... **LC 65**
See also DLB 268; GFL Beginnings to
1789; RGWL 2, 3

Cyril of Alexandria c. 375-c. 430 . **CMLC 59**

Czaczkes, Shmuel Yosef Halevi
See Agnon, S.Y.

Dabrowska, Maria (Szumska)
1889-1965 .... **CLC 15**
See also CA 106; CDWLB 4; DLB 215;
EWL 3

Dabydeen, David 1955- .... **CLC 34**
See also BW 1; CA 125; CANR 56, 92; CN
6, 7; CP 5, 6, 7; DLB 347

Dacey, Philip 1939- .... **CLC 51**
See also CA 37-40R, 231; CAAE 231;
CAAS 17; CANR 14, 32, 64; CP 4, 5, 6,
7; DLB 105

Dacre, Charlotte c. 1772-1825(?) . **NCLC 151**

Dafydd ap Gwilym c. 1320-c. 1380 ..... **PC 56**

Dagerman, Stig (Halvard)
1923-1954 .... **TCLC 17**
See also CA 117; 155; DLB 259; EWL 3

D'Aguiar, Fred 1960- ..... **BLC 2:1; CLC 145**
See also CA 148; CANR 83, 101; CN 7;
CP 5, 6, 7; DLB 157; EWL 3

Dahl, Roald 1916-1990 ...... **CLC 1, 6, 18, 79;
TCLC 173**
See also AAYA 15; BPFB 1; BRWS 4; BYA
5; CA 1-4R; 133; CANR 6, 32, 37, 62;
CLR 1, 7, 41, 111; CN 1, 2, 3, 4; CPW;
DA3; DAB; DAC; DAM MST, NOV,
POP; DLB 139, 255; HGG; JRDA; MAI-
CYA 1, 2; MTCW 1, 2; MTFW 2005;
RGSF 2; SATA 1, 26, 73; SATA-Obit 65;
SSFS 4; TEA; YAW

Dahlberg, Edward 1900-1977 . **CLC 1, 7, 14;
TCLC 208**
See also CA 9-12R; 69-72; CANR 31, 62;
CN 1, 2; DLB 48; MAL 5; MTCW 1;
RGAL 4

Daitch, Susan 1954- .... **CLC 103**
See also CA 161

Dale, Colin
See Lawrence, T(homas) E(dward)

Dale, George E.
See Asimov, Isaac

d'Alembert, Jean Le Rond
1717-1783 .... **LC 126**

Dalton, Roque 1935-1975(?) ..... **HLCS 1; PC
36**
See also CA 176; DLB 283; HW 2

Daly, Elizabeth 1878-1967 .... **CLC 52**
See also CA 23-24; 25-28R; CANR 60;
CAP 2; CMW 4

Daly, Mary 1928- .... **CLC 173**
See also CA 25-28R; CANR 30, 62, 166;
FW; GLL 1; MTCW 1

Daly, Maureen 1921-2006 .... **CLC 17**
See also AAYA 5, 58; BYA 6; CA 253;
CANR 37, 83, 108; CLR 96; JRDA; MAI-
CYA 1, 2; SAAS 1; SATA 2, 129; SATA-
Obit 176; WYA; YAW

Damas, Leon-Gontran 1912-1978 ... **CLC 84;
TCLC 204**
See also BW 1; CA 125; 73-76; EWL 3

Dana, Richard Henry Sr.
1787-1879 .... **NCLC 53**

Dangarembga, Tsitsi 1959- .... **BLC 2:1**
See also BW 3; CA 163; NFS 28; WLIT 2

Daniel, Samuel 1562(?)-1619 .... **LC 24**
See also DLB 62; RGEL 2

Daniels, Brett
See Adler, Renata

Dannay, Frederic 1905-1982 .... **CLC 3, 11**
See also BPFB 3; CA 1-4R; 107; CANR 1,
39; CMW 4; DAM POP; DLB 137; MSW;
MTCW 1; RGAL 4

D'Annunzio, Gabriele 1863-1938 ... **TCLC 6,
40, 215**
See also CA 104; 155; EW 8; EWL 3;
RGWL 2, 3; TWA; WLIT 7

Danois, N. le
See Gourmont, Remy(-Marie-Charles) de

Dante 1265-1321 .... **CMLC 3, 18, 39, 70; PC
21; WLCS**
See also DA; DA3; DAB; DAC; DAM
MST, POET; EFS 1; EW 1; LAIT 1;
RGWL 2, 3; TWA; WLIT 7; WP

Deighton, Leonard Cyril 1929- ..... **CLC 4, 7, 22, 46**
See also AAYA 57, 6; BEST 89:2; BPFB 1; CA 9-12R; CANR 19, 33, 68; CDBLB 1960- Present; CMW 4; CN 1, 2, 3, 4, 5, 6, 7; CPW; DA3; DAM NOV, POP; DLB 87; MTCW 1, 2; MTFW 2005

Dekker, Thomas 1572(?)-1632 ..... **DC 12; LC 22, 159**
See also CDBLB Before 1660; DAM DRAM; DLB 62, 172; LMFS 1; RGEL 2

de Laclos, Pierre Ambroise Franois
See Laclos, Pierre-Ambroise Francois

Delacroix, (Ferdinand-Victor-)Eugene 1798-1863 .... **NCLC 133**
See also EW 5

Delafield, E. M.
See Dashwood, Edmee Elizabeth Monica de la Pasture

de la Mare, Walter (John) 1873-1956 ..... **PC 77; SSC 14; TCLC 4, 53; WLC 2**
See also CA 163; CDBLB 1914-1945; CLR 23; CWRI 5; DA3; DAB; DAC; DAM MST, POET; DLB 19, 153, 162, 255, 284; EWL 3; EXPP; HGG; MAICYA 1, 2; MTCW 2; MTFW 2005; RGEL 2; RGSF 2; SATA 16; SUFW 1; TEA; WCH

de Lamartine, Alphonse (Marie Louis Prat)
See Lamartine, Alphonse (Marie Louis Prat) de

Delaney, Franey
See O'Hara, John (Henry)

Delaney, Shelagh 1939- .... **CLC 29**
See also CA 17-20R; CANR 30, 67; CBD; CD 5, 6; CDBLB 1960 to Present; CWD; DAM DRAM; DFS 7; DLB 13; MTCW 1

Delany, Martin Robison 1812-1885 .... **NCLC 93**
See also DLB 50; RGAL 4

Delany, Mary (Granville Pendarves) 1700-1788 .... **LC 12**

Delany, Samuel R., Jr. 1942- .... **BLC 1:1; CLC 8, 14, 38, 141**
See also AAYA 24; AFAW 2; BPFB 1; BW 2, 3; CA 81-84; CANR 27, 43, 116, 172; CN 2, 3, 4, 5, 6, 7; DAM MULT; DLB 8, 33; FANT; MAL 5; MTCW 1, 2; RGAL 4; SATA 92; SCFW 1, 2; SFW 4; SUFW 2

Delany, Samuel Ray
See Delany, Samuel R., Jr.

de la Parra, (Ana) Teresa (Sonojo) 1890(?)-1936 .... **HLCS 2; TCLC 185**
See also CA 178; HW 2; LAW

Delaporte, Theophile
See Green, Julien (Hartridge)

De La Ramee, Marie Louise 1839-1908 .... **TCLC 43**
See also CA 204; DLB 18, 156; RGEL 2; SATA 20

de la Roche, Mazo 1879-1961 .... **CLC 14**
See also CA 85-88; CANR 30; DLB 68; RGEL 2; RHW; SATA 64

De La Salle, Innocent
See Hartmann, Sadakichi

de Laureamont, Comte
See Lautreamont

Delbanco, Nicholas 1942- ..... **CLC 6, 13, 167**
See also CA 17-20R, 189; CAAE 189; CAAS 2; CANR 29, 55, 116, 150; CN 7; DLB 6, 234

Delbanco, Nicholas Franklin
See Delbanco, Nicholas

del Castillo, Michel 1933- .... **CLC 38**
See also CA 109; CANR 77

Deledda, Grazia (Cosima) 1875(?)-1936 .... **TCLC 23**
See also CA 123; 205; DLB 264, 329; EWL 3; RGWL 2, 3; WLIT 7

Deleuze, Gilles 1925-1995 .... **TCLC 116**
See also DLB 296

Delgado, Abelardo (Lalo) B(arrientos) 1930-2004 .... **HLC 1**
See also CA 131; 230; CAAS 15; CANR 90; DAM MST, MULT; DLB 82; HW 1, 2

Delibes, Miguel
See Delibes Setien, Miguel

Delibes Setien, Miguel 1920- .... **CLC 8, 18**
See also CA 45-48; CANR 1, 32; CWW 2; DLB 322; EWL 3; HW 1; MTCW 1

DeLillo, Don 1936- ..... **CLC 8, 10, 13, 27, 39, 54, 76, 143, 210, 213**
See also AMWC 2; AMWS 6; BEST 89:1; BPFB 1; CA 81-84; CANR 21, 76, 92, 133, 173; CN 3, 4, 5, 6, 7; CPW; DA3; DAM NOV, POP; DLB 6, 173; EWL 3; MAL 5; MTCW 1, 2; MTFW 2005; NFS 28; RGAL 4; TUS

de Lisser, H. G.
See De Lisser, H(erbert) G(eorge)

De Lisser, H(erbert) G(eorge) 1878-1944 .... **TCLC 12**
See also BW 2; CA 109; 152; DLB 117

Deloire, Pierre
See Peguy, Charles (Pierre)

Deloney, Thomas 1543(?)-1600 .... **LC 41; PC 79**
See also DLB 167; RGEL 2

Deloria, Ella (Cara) 1889-1971(?) ..... **NNAL**
See also CA 152; DAM MULT; DLB 175

Deloria, Vine, Jr. 1933-2005 .... **CLC 21, 122; NNAL**
See also CA 53-56; 245; CANR 5, 20, 48, 98; DAM MULT; DLB 175; MTCW 1; SATA 21; SATA-Obit 171

Deloria, Vine Victor, Jr.
See Deloria, Vine, Jr.

del Valle-Inclan, Ramon (Maria)
See Valle-Inclan, Ramon (Maria) del

Del Vecchio, John M(ichael) 1947- .. **CLC 29**
See also CA 110; DLBD 9

de Man, Paul (Adolph Michel) 1919-1983 .... **CLC 55**
See also CA 128; 111; CANR 61; DLB 67; MTCW 1, 2

de Mandiargues, Andre Pieyre
See Pieyre de Mandiargues, Andre

DeMarinis, Rick 1934- .... **CLC 54**
See also CA 57-60, 184; CAAE 184; CAAS 24; CANR 9, 25, 50, 160; DLB 218; TCWW 2

de Maupassant, (Henri Rene Albert) Guy
See Maupassant, (Henri Rene Albert) Guy de

Dembry, R. Emmet
See Murfree, Mary Noailles

Demby, William 1922- ...... **BLC 1:1; CLC 53**
See also BW 1, 3; CA 81-84; CANR 81; DAM MULT; DLB 33

de Menton, Francisco
See Chin, Frank (Chew, Jr.)

Demetrius of Phalerum c. 307B.C.- .... **CMLC 34**

Demijohn, Thom
See Disch, Thomas M.

De Mille, James 1833-1880 .... **NCLC 123**
See also DLB 99, 251

Democritus c. 460B.C.-c. 370B.C. . **CMLC 47**

de Montaigne, Michel (Eyquem)
See Montaigne, Michel (Eyquem) de

de Montherlant, Henry (Milon)
See Montherlant, Henry (Milon) de

Demosthenes 384B.C.-322B.C. ...... **CMLC 13**
See also AW 1; DLB 176; RGWL 2, 3; WLIT 8

de Musset, (Louis Charles) Alfred
See Musset, Alfred de

de Natale, Francine
See Malzberg, Barry N(athaniel)

de Navarre, Marguerite 1492-1549 .... **LC 61, 167; SSC 85**
See also DLB 327; GFL Beginnings to 1789; RGWL 2, 3

Denby, Edwin (Orr) 1903-1983 .... **CLC 48**
See also CA 138; 110; CP 1

de Nerval, Gerard
See Nerval, Gerard de

Denham, John 1615-1669 .... **LC 73**
See also DLB 58, 126; RGEL 2

Denis, Julio
See Cortazar, Julio

Denmark, Harrison
See Zelazny, Roger

Dennis, John 1658-1734 .... **LC 11, 154**
See also DLB 101; RGEL 2

Dennis, Nigel (Forbes) 1912-1989 ...... **CLC 8**
See also CA 25-28R; 129; CN 1, 2, 3, 4; DLB 13, 15, 233; EWL 3; MTCW 1

Dent, Lester 1904-1959 .... **TCLC 72**
See also CA 112; 161; CMW 4; DLB 306; SFW 4

Dentinger, Stephen
See Hoch, Edward D.

De Palma, Brian 1940- .... **CLC 20, 247**
See also CA 109

De Palma, Brian Russell
See De Palma, Brian

de Pizan, Christine
See Christine de Pizan

De Quincey, Thomas 1785-1859 ..... **NCLC 4, 87, 198**
See also BRW 4; CDBLB 1789-1832; DLB 110, 144; RGEL 2

De Ray, Jill
See Moore, Alan

Deren, Eleanora 1908(?)-1961 .. **CLC 16, 102**
See also CA 192; 111

Deren, Maya
See Deren, Eleanora

Derleth, August (William) 1909-1971 .... **CLC 31**
See also BPFB 1; BYA 9, 10; CA 1-4R; 29-32R; CANR 4; CMW 4; CN 1; DLB 9; DLBD 17; HGG; SATA 5; SUFW 1

Der Nister 1884-1950 .... **TCLC 56**
See also DLB 333; EWL 3

de Routisie, Albert
See Aragon, Louis

Derrida, Jacques 1930-2004 ...... **CLC 24, 87, 225**
See also CA 124; 127; 232; CANR 76, 98, 133; DLB 242; EWL 3; LMFS 2; MTCW 2; TWA

Derry Down Derry
See Lear, Edward

Dersonnes, Jacques
See Simenon, Georges (Jacques Christian)

Der Stricker c. 1190-c. 1250 .... **CMLC 75**
See also DLB 138

Desai, Anita 1937- . **CLC 19, 37, 97, 175, 271**
See also BRWS 5; CA 81-84; CANR 33, 53, 95, 133; CN 1, 2, 3, 4, 5, 6, 7; CWRI 5; DA3; DAB; DAM NOV; DLB 271, 323; DNFS 2; EWL 3; FW; MTCW 1, 2; MTFW 2005; SATA 63, 126

Desai, Kiran 1971- .... **CLC 119**
See also BYA 16; CA 171; CANR 127; NFS 28

de Saint-Luc, Jean
See Glassco, John

EWL 3; LAIT 3; MAL 5; MTCW 1, 2; MTFW 2005; NFS 6; RGAL 4; RGHL; RHW; SSFS 27; TCLE 1:1; TCWW 1, 2; TUS

Dodgson, Charles Lutwidge
See Carroll, Lewis

Dodsley, Robert 1703-1764 .... LC 97
See also DLB 95; RGEL 2

Dodson, Owen (Vincent)
1914-1983 .... BLC 1:1; CLC 79
See also BW 1; CA 65-68; 110; CANR 24; DAM MULT; DLB 76

Doeblin, Alfred 1878-1957 .... TCLC 13
See also CA 110; 141; CDWLB 2; DLB 66; EWL 3; RGWL 2, 3

Doerr, Harriet 1910-2002 .... CLC 34
See also CA 117; 122; 213; CANR 47; INT CA-122; LATS 1:2

Domecq, H(onorio) Bustos
See Bioy Casares, Adolfo; Borges, Jorge Luis

Domini, Rey
See Lorde, Audre

Dominic, R. B.
See Hennissart, Martha

Dominique
See Proust, (Valentin-Louis-George-Eugene) Marcel

Don, A
See Stephen, Sir Leslie

Donaldson, Stephen R. 1947- ... CLC 46, 138
See also AAYA 36; BPFB 1; CA 89-92; CANR 13, 55, 99; CPW; DAM POP; FANT; INT CANR-13; SATA 121; SFW 4; SUFW 1, 2

Donleavy, J(ames) P(atrick) 1926- .... CLC 1, 4, 6, 10, 45
See also AITN 2; BPFB 1; CA 9-12R; CANR 24, 49, 62, 80, 124; CBD; CD 5, 6; CN 1, 2, 3, 4, 5, 6, 7; DLB 6, 173; INT CANR-24; MAL 5; MTCW 1, 2; MTFW 2005; RGAL 4

Donnadieu, Marguerite
See Duras, Marguerite

Donne, John 1572-1631 ... LC 10, 24, 91; PC 1, 43; WLC 2
See also AAYA 67; BRW 1; BRWC 1; BRWR 2; CDBLB Before 1660; DA; DAB; DAC; DAM MST, POET; DLB 121, 151; EXPP; PAB; PFS 2, 11; RGEL 3; TEA; WLIT 3; WP

Donnell, David 1939(?)- .... CLC 34
See also CA 197

Donoghue, Denis 1928- .... CLC 209
See also CA 17-20R; CANR 16, 102

Donoghue, Emma 1969- .... CLC 239
See also CA 155; CANR 103, 152; DLB 267; GLL 2; SATA 101

Donoghue, P.S.
See Hunt, E. Howard

Donoso (Yanez), Jose 1924-1996 ... CLC 4, 8, 11, 32, 99; HLC 1; SSC 34; TCLC 133
See also CA 81-84; 155; CANR 32, 73; CDWLB 3; CWW 2; DAM MULT; DLB 113; EWL 3; HW 1, 2; LAW; LAWS 1; MTCW 1, 2; MTFW 2005; RGSF 2; WLIT 1

Donovan, John 1928-1992 .... CLC 35
See also AAYA 20; CA 97-100; 137; CLR 3; MAICYA 1, 2; SATA 72; SATA-Brief 29; YAW

Don Roberto
See Cunninghame Graham, Robert (Gallnigad) Bontine

Doolittle, Hilda 1886-1961 . CLC 3, 8, 14, 31, 34, 73; PC 5; WLC 3
See also AAYA 66; AMWS 1; CA 97-100; CANR 35, 131; DA; DAC; DAM MST, POET; DLB 4, 45; EWL 3; FL 1:5; FW; GLL 1; LMFS 2; MAL 5; MBL; MTCW 1, 2; MTFW 2005; PFS 6, 28; RGAL 4

Doppo
See Kunikida Doppo

Doppo, Kunikida
See Kunikida Doppo

Dorfman, Ariel 1942- .... CLC 48, 77, 189; HLC 1
See also CA 124; 130; CANR 67, 70, 135; CWW 2; DAM MULT; DFS 4; EWL 3; HW 1, 2; INT CA-130; WLIT 1

Dorn, Edward (Merton)
1929-1999 .... CLC 10, 18
See also CA 93-96; 187; CANR 42, 79; CP 1, 2, 3, 4, 5, 6, 7; DLB 5; INT CA-93-96; WP

Dor-Ner, Zvi CLC 70

Dorris, Michael 1945-1997 .... CLC 109; NNAL
See also AAYA 20; BEST 90:1; BYA 12; CA 102; 157; CANR 19, 46, 75; CLR 58; DA3; DAM MULT, NOV; DLB 175; LAIT 5; MTCW 2; MTFW 2005; NFS 3; RGAL 4; SATA 75; SATA-Obit 94; TCWW 2; YAW

Dorris, Michael A.
See Dorris, Michael

Dorsan, Luc
See Simenon, Georges (Jacques Christian)

Dorsange, Jean
See Simenon, Georges (Jacques Christian)

Dorset
See Sackville, Thomas

Dos Passos, John (Roderigo)
1896-1970 ... CLC 1, 4, 8, 11, 15, 25, 34, 82; WLC 2
See also AMW; BPFB 1; CA 1-4R; 29-32R; CANR 3; CDALB 1929-1941; DA; DA3; DAB; DAC; DAM MST, NOV; DLB 4, 9, 274, 316; DLBD 1, 15; DLBY 1996; EWL 3; MAL 5; MTCW 1, 2; MTFW 2005; NFS 14; RGAL 4; TUS

Dossage, Jean
See Simenon, Georges (Jacques Christian)

Dostoevsky, Fedor Mikhailovich
1821-1881 .. NCLC 2, 7, 21, 33, 43, 119, 167, 202; SSC 2, 33, 44; WLC 2
See also AAYA 40; DA; DA3; DAB; DAC; DAM MST, NOV; DLB 238; EW 7; EXPN; LATS 1:1; LMFS 1, 2; NFS 28; RGSF 2; RGWL 2, 3; SSFS 8; TWA

Dostoevsky, Fyodor
See Dostoevsky, Fedor Mikhailovich

Doty, Mark 1953(?)- .... CLC 176; PC 53
See also AMWS 11; CA 161, 183; CAAE 183; CANR 110, 173; CP 7; PFS 28

Doty, Mark A.
See Doty, Mark

Doty, Mark Alan
See Doty, Mark

Doty, M.R.
See Doty, Mark

Doughty, Charles M(ontagu)
1843-1926 .... TCLC 27
See also CA 115; 178; DLB 19, 57, 174

Douglas, Ellen 1921- .... CLC 73
See also CA 115; CANR 41, 83; CN 5, 6, 7; CSW; DLB 292

Douglas, Gavin 1475(?)-1522 .... LC 20
See also DLB 132; RGEL 2

Douglas, George
See Brown, George Douglas

Douglas, Keith (Castellain)
1920-1944 .... TCLC 40
See also BRW 7; CA 160; DLB 27; EWL 3; PAB; RGEL 2

Douglas, Leonard
See Bradbury, Ray

Douglas, Michael
See Crichton, Michael

Douglas, Michael
See Crichton, Michael

Douglas, (George) Norman
1868-1952 .... TCLC 68
See also BRW 6; CA 119; 157; DLB 34, 195; RGEL 2

Douglas, William
See Brown, George Douglas

Douglass, Frederick 1817(?)-1895 .. BLC 1:1; NCLC 7, 55, 141; WLC 2
See also AAYA 48; AFAW 1, 2; AMWC 1; AMWS 3; CDALB 1640-1865; DA; DA3; DAC; DAM MST, MULT; DLB 1, 43, 50, 79, 243; FW; LAIT 2; NCFS 2; RGAL 4; SATA 29

Dourado, (Waldomiro Freitas) Autran
1926- .... CLC 23, 60
See also CA 25-28R; 179; CANR 34, 81; DLB 145, 307; HW 2

Dourado, Waldomiro Freitas Autran
See Dourado, (Waldomiro Freitas) Autran

Dove, Rita 1952- . BLC 2:1; BLCS; CLC 50, 81; PC 6
See also AAYA 46; AMWS 4; BW 2; CA 109; CAAS 19; CANR 27, 42, 68, 76, 97, 132; CDALBS; CP 5, 6, 7; CSW; CWP; DA3; DAM MULT, POET; DLB 120; EWL 3; EXPP; MAL 5; MTCW 2; MTFW 2005; PFS 1, 15; RGAL 4

Dove, Rita Frances
See Dove, Rita

Doveglion
See Villa, Jose Garcia

Dowell, Coleman 1925-1985 .... CLC 60
See also CA 25-28R; 117; CANR 10; DLB 130; GLL 2

Downing, Major Jack
See Smith, Seba

Dowson, Ernest (Christopher)
1867-1900 .... TCLC 4
See also CA 105; 150; DLB 19, 135; RGEL 2

Doyle, A. Conan
See Doyle, Sir Arthur Conan

Doyle, Sir Arthur Conan
1859-1930 ..... SSC 12, 83, 95; TCLC 7; WLC 2
See also AAYA 14; BPFB 1; BRWS 2; BYA 4, 5, 11; CA 104; 122; CANR 131; CDBLB 1890-1914; CLR 106; CMW 4; DA; DA3; DAB; DAC; DAM MST, NOV; DLB 18, 70, 156, 178; EXPS; HGG; LAIT 2; MSW; MTCW 1, 2; MTFW 2005; NFS 28; RGEL 2; RGSF 2; RHW; SATA 24; SCFW 1, 2; SFW 4; SSFS 2; TEA; WCH; WLIT 4; WYA; YAW

Doyle, Conan
See Doyle, Sir Arthur Conan

Doyle, John
See Graves, Robert

Doyle, Roddy 1958- .... CLC 81, 178
See also AAYA 14; BRWS 5; CA 143; CANR 73, 128, 168; CN 6, 7; DA3; DLB 194, 326; MTCW 2; MTFW 2005

Doyle, Sir A. Conan
See Doyle, Sir Arthur Conan

Dr. A
See Asimov, Isaac; Silverstein, Alvin; Silverstein, Virginia B(arbara Opshelor)

Drabble, Margaret 1939- ...... CLC 2, 3, 5, 8, 10, 22, 53, 129
See also BRWS 4; CA 13-16R; CANR 18, 35, 63, 112, 131, 174; CDBLB 1960 to Present; CN 1, 2, 3, 4, 5, 6, 7; CPW; DA3; DAB; DAC; DAM MST, NOV, POP; DLB 14, 155, 231; EWL 3; FW; MTCW 1, 2; MTFW 2005; RGEL 2; SATA 48; TEA

Drakulic, Slavenka 1949- .... CLC 173
See also CA 144; CANR 92

Duong, Thu Huong 1947- .... **CLC 273**
See also CA 152; CANR 106, 166; DLB
348; NFS 23

Duong Thu Huong
See Duong, Thu Huong

du Perry, Jean
See Simenon, Georges (Jacques Christian)

Durang, Christopher 1949- .... **CLC 27, 38**
See also CA 105; CAD; CANR 50, 76, 130;
CD 5, 6; MTCW 2; MTFW 2005

Durang, Christopher Ferdinand
See Durang, Christopher

Duras, Claire de 1777-1832 .... **NCLC 154**

Duras, Marguerite 1914-1996 . **CLC 3, 6, 11,
20, 34, 40, 68, 100; SSC 40**
See also BPFB 1; CA 25-28R; 151; CANR
50; CWW 2; DFS 21; DLB 83, 321; EWL
3; FL 1:5; GFL 1789 to the Present; IDFW
4; MTCW 1, 2; RGWL 2, 3; TWA

Durban, (Rosa) Pam 1947- .... **CLC 39**
See also CA 123; CANR 98; CSW

Durcan, Paul 1944- .... **CLC 43, 70**
See also CA 134; CANR 123; CP 1, 5, 6, 7;
DAM POET; EWL 3

d'Urfe, Honore
See Urfe, Honore d'

Durfey, Thomas 1653-1723 .... **LC 94**
See also DLB 80; RGEL 2

Durkheim, Emile 1858-1917 .... **TCLC 55**
See also CA 249

Durrell, Lawrence (George)
1912-1990 ..... **CLC 1, 4, 6, 8, 13, 27, 41**
See also BPFB 1; BRWS 1; CA 9-12R; 132;
CANR 40, 77; CDBLB 1945-1960; CN 1,
2, 3, 4; CP 1, 2, 3, 4, 5; DAM NOV; DLB
15, 27, 204; DLBY 1990; EWL 3; MTCW
1, 2; RGEL 2; SFW 4; TEA

Durrenmatt, Friedrich
See Duerrenmatt, Friedrich

Dutt, Michael Madhusudan
1824-1873 .... **NCLC 118**

Dutt, Toru 1856-1877 .... **NCLC 29**
See also DLB 240

Dwight, Timothy 1752-1817 .... **NCLC 13**
See also DLB 37; RGAL 4

Dworkin, Andrea 1946-2005 ..... **CLC 43, 123**
See also CA 77-80; 238; CAAS 21; CANR
16, 39, 76, 96; FL 1:5; FW; GLL 1; INT
CANR-16; MTCW 1, 2; MTFW 2005

Dwyer, Deanna
See Koontz, Dean R.

Dwyer, K.R.
See Koontz, Dean R.

Dybek, Stuart 1942- .... **CLC 114; SSC 55**
See also CA 97-100; CANR 39; DLB 130;
SSFS 23

Dye, Richard
See De Voto, Bernard (Augustine)

Dyer, Geoff 1958- .... **CLC 149**
See also CA 125; CANR 88

Dyer, George 1755-1841 .... **NCLC 129**
See also DLB 93

Dylan, Bob 1941- .... **CLC 3, 4, 6, 12, 77; PC
37**
See also AMWS 18; CA 41-44R; CANR
108; CP 1, 2, 3, 4, 5, 6, 7; DLB 16

Dyson, John 1943- .... **CLC 70**
See also CA 144

Dzyubin, Eduard Georgievich
1895-1934 .... **TCLC 60**
See also CA 170; EWL 3

E. V. L.
See Lucas, E(dward) V(errall)

Eagleton, Terence (Francis) 1943- .. **CLC 63,
132**
See also CA 57-60; CANR 7, 23, 68, 115;
DLB 242; LMFS 2; MTCW 1, 2; MTFW
2005

Eagleton, Terry
See Eagleton, Terence (Francis)

Early, Jack
See Scoppettone, Sandra

East, Michael
See West, Morris L(anglo)

Eastaway, Edward
See Thomas, (Philip) Edward

Eastlake, William (Derry)
1917-1997 .... **CLC 8**
See also CA 5-8R; 158; CAAS 1; CANR 5,
63; CN 1, 2, 3, 4, 5, 6; DLB 6, 206; INT
CANR-5; MAL 5; TCWW 1, 2

Eastman, Charles A(lexander)
1858-1939 .... **NNAL; TCLC 55**
See also CA 179; CANR 91; DAM MULT;
DLB 175; YABC 1

Eaton, Edith Maude 1865-1914 .... **AAL**
See also CA 154; DLB 221, 312; FW

Eaton, (Lillie) Winnifred 1875-1954 .... **AAL**
See also CA 217; DLB 221, 312; RGAL 4

Eberhart, Richard 1904-2005 ...... **CLC 3, 11,
19, 56; PC 76**
See also AMW; CA 1-4R; 240; CANR 2,
125; CDALB 1941-1968; CP 1, 2, 3, 4, 5,
6, 7; DAM POET; DLB 48; MAL 5;
MTCW 1; RGAL 4

Eberhart, Richard Ghormley
See Eberhart, Richard

Eberstadt, Fernanda 1960- .... **CLC 39**
See also CA 136; CANR 69, 128

Ebner, Margaret c. 1291-1351 ...... **CMLC 98**

**Echegaray (y Eizaguirre), Jose (Maria
Waldo)** 1832-1916 .... **HLCS 1; TCLC 4**
See also CA 104; CANR 32; DLB 329;
EWL 3; HW 1; MTCW 1

Echeverria, (Jose) Esteban (Antonino)
1805-1851 .... **NCLC 18**
See also LAW

Echo
See Proust, (Valentin-Louis-George-Eugene)
Marcel

Eckert, Allan W. 1931- .... **CLC 17**
See also AAYA 18; BYA 2; CA 13-16R;
CANR 14, 45; INT CANR-14; MAICYA
2; MAICYAS 1; SAAS 21; SATA 29, 91;
SATA-Brief 27

Eckhart, Meister 1260(?)-1327(?) .. **CMLC 9,
80**
See also DLB 115; LMFS 1

Eckmar, F. R.
See de Hartog, Jan

Eco, Umberto 1932- .... **CLC 28, 60, 142, 248**
See also BEST 90:1; BPFB 1; CA 77-80;
CANR 12, 33, 55, 110, 131; CPW; CWW
2; DA3; DAM NOV, POP; DLB 196, 242;
EWL 3; MSW; MTCW 1, 2; MTFW
2005; NFS 22; RGWL 3; WLIT 7

Eddison, E(ric) R(ucker)
1882-1945 .... **TCLC 15**
See also CA 109; 156; DLB 255; FANT;
SFW 4; SUFW 1

Eddy, Mary (Ann Morse) Baker
1821-1910 .... **TCLC 71**
See also CA 113; 174

Edel, (Joseph) Leon 1907-1997 .. **CLC 29, 34**
See also CA 1-4R; 161; CANR 1, 22, 112;
DLB 103; INT CANR-22

Eden, Emily 1797-1869 .... **NCLC 10**

Edgar, David 1948- .... **CLC 42**
See also CA 57-60; CANR 12, 61, 112;
CBD; CD 5, 6; DAM DRAM; DFS 15;
DLB 13, 233; MTCW 1

Edgerton, Clyde (Carlyle) 1944- ...... **CLC 39**
See also AAYA 17; CA 118; 134; CANR
64, 125; CN 7; CSW; DLB 278; INT CA-
134; TCLE 1:1; YAW

Edgeworth, Maria 1768-1849 ... **NCLC 1, 51,
158; SSC 86**
See also BRWS 3; DLB 116, 159, 163; FL
1:3; FW; RGEL 2; SATA 21; TEA; WLIT
3

Edmonds, Paul
See Kuttner, Henry

Edmonds, Walter D(umaux)
1903-1998 .... **CLC 35**
See also BYA 2; CA 5-8R; CANR 2; CWRI
5; DLB 9; LAIT 1; MAICYA 1, 2; MAL
5; RHW; SAAS 4; SATA 1, 27; SATA-
Obit 99

Edmondson, Wallace
See Ellison, Harlan

Edson, Margaret 1961- ...... **CLC 199; DC 24**
See also AMWS 18; CA 190; DFS 13; DLB
266

Edson, Russell 1935- .... **CLC 13**
See also CA 33-36R; CANR 115; CP 2, 3,
4, 5, 6, 7; DLB 244; WP

Edwards, Bronwen Elizabeth
See Rose, Wendy

Edwards, Eli
See McKay, Festus Claudius

Edwards, G(erald) B(asil)
1899-1976 .... **CLC 25**
See also CA 201; 110

Edwards, Gus 1939- .... **CLC 43**
See also CA 108; INT CA-108

Edwards, Jonathan 1703-1758 .... **LC 7, 54**
See also AMW; DA; DAC; DAM MST;
DLB 24, 270; RGAL 4; TUS

Edwards, Sarah Pierpont 1710-1758 .. **LC 87**
See also DLB 200

Efron, Marina Ivanovna Tsvetaeva
See Tsvetaeva (Efron), Marina (Ivanovna)

Egeria fl. 4th cent. - .... **CMLC 70**

Eggers, Dave 1970- .... **CLC 241**
See also AAYA 56; CA 198; CANR 138;
MTFW 2005

Egoyan, Atom 1960- .... **CLC 151**
See also AAYA 63; CA 157; CANR 151

Ehle, John (Marsden, Jr.) 1925- ...... **CLC 27**
See also CA 9-12R; CSW

Ehrenbourg, Ilya (Grigoryevich)
See Ehrenburg, Ilya (Grigoryevich)

Ehrenburg, Ilya (Grigoryevich)
1891-1967 .... **CLC 18, 34, 62**
See Erenburg, Ilya (Grigoryevich)
See also CA 102; 25-28R; EWL 3

Ehrenburg, Ilyo (Grigoryevich)
See Ehrenburg, Ilya (Grigoryevich)

Ehrenreich, Barbara 1941- ..... **CLC 110, 267**
See also BEST 90:4; CA 73-76; CANR 16,
37, 62, 117, 167; DLB 246; FW; MTCW
1, 2; MTFW 2005

Ehrlich, Gretel 1946- .... **CLC 249**
See also ANW; CA 140; CANR 74, 146;
DLB 212, 275; TCWW 2

Eich, Gunter
See Eich, Gunter

Eich, Gunter 1907-1972 .... **CLC 15**
See also CA 111; 93-96; DLB 69, 124;
EWL 3; RGWL 2, 3

Eichendorff, Joseph 1788-1857 .... **NCLC 8**
See also DLB 90; RGWL 2, 3

Eigner, Larry
See Eigner, Laurence (Joel)

Eigner, Laurence (Joel) 1927-1996 ..... **CLC 9**
See also CA 9-12R; 151; CAAS 23; CANR
6, 84; CP 1, 2, 3, 4, 5, 6, 7; DLB 5; WP

Eilhart von Oberge c. 1140-c.
1195 .... **CMLC 67**
See also DLB 148

Einhard c. 770-840 .... **CMLC 50**
See also DLB 148

Engelhardt, Frederick
See Hubbard, L. Ron

Engels, Friedrich 1820-1895 .. **NCLC 85, 114**
See also DLB 129; LATS 1:1

Enquist, Per Olov 1934- .... **CLC 257**
See also CA 109; 193; CANR 155; CWW
2; DLB 257; EWL 3

Enright, D(ennis) J(oseph)
1920-2002 .... **CLC 4, 8, 31; PC 93**
See also CA 1-4R; 211; CANR 1, 42, 83;
CN 1, 2; CP 1, 2, 3, 4, 5, 6, 7; DLB 27;
EWL 3; SATA 25; SATA-Obit 140

Ensler, Eve 1953- .... **CLC 212**
See also CA 172; CANR 126, 163; DFS 23

Enzensberger, Hans Magnus
1929- .... **CLC 43; PC 28**
See also CA 116; 119; CANR 103; CWW
2; EWL 3

Ephron, Nora 1941- .... **CLC 17, 31**
See also AAYA 35; AITN 2; CA 65-68;
CANR 12, 39, 83, 161; DFS 22

Epicurus 341B.C.-270B.C. .... **CMLC 21**
See also DLB 176

Epinay, Louise d' 1726-1783 .... **LC 138**
See also DLB 313

Epsilon
See Betjeman, John

Epstein, Daniel Mark 1948- .... **CLC 7**
See also CA 49-52; CANR 2, 53, 90

Epstein, Jacob 1956- .... **CLC 19**
See also CA 114

Epstein, Jean 1897-1953 .... **TCLC 92**

Epstein, Joseph 1937- .... **CLC 39, 204**
See also AMWS 14; CA 112; 119; CANR
50, 65, 117, 164

Epstein, Leslie 1938- .... **CLC 27**
See also AMWS 12; CA 73-76, 215; CAAE
215; CAAS 12; CANR 23, 69, 162; DLB
299; RGHL

Equiano, Olaudah 1745(?)-1797 ..... **BLC 1:2;
LC 16, 143**
See also AFAW 1, 2; CDWLB 3; DAM
MULT; DLB 37, 50; WLIT 2

Erasmus, Desiderius 1469(?)-1536 ..... **LC 16,
93**
See also DLB 136; EW 2; LMFS 1; RGWL
2, 3; TWA

Erdman, Paul E. 1932-2007 .... **CLC 25**
See also AITN 1; CA 61-64; 259; CANR
13, 43, 84

Erdman, Paul Emil
See Erdman, Paul E.

Erdrich, Karen Louise
See Erdrich, Louise

Erdrich, Louise 1954- .... **CLC 39, 54, 120,
176; NNAL; PC 52; SSC 121**
See also AAYA 10, 47; AMWS 4; BEST
89:1; BPFB 1; CA 114; CANR 41, 62,
118, 138; CDALBS; CN 5, 6, 7; CP 6, 7;
CPW; CWP; DA3; DAM MULT, NOV,
POP; DLB 152, 175, 206; EWL 3; EXPP;
FL 1:5; LAIT 5; LATS 1:2; MAL 5;
MTCW 1, 2; MTFW 2005; NFS 5; PFS
14; RGAL 4; SATA 94, 141; SSFS 14,
22; TCWW 2

Erenburg, Ilya (Grigoryevich)
See Ehrenburg, Ilya (Grigoryevich)
See also DLB 272

Erickson, Stephen Michael
See Erickson, Steve

Erickson, Steve 1950- .... **CLC 64**
See also CA 129; CANR 60, 68, 136;
MTFW 2005; SFW 4; SUFW 2

Erickson, Walter
See Fast, Howard

Ericson, Walter
See Fast, Howard

Eriksson, Buntel
See Bergman, Ingmar

Eriugena, John Scottus c.
810-877 .... **CMLC 65**
See also DLB 115

Ernaux, Annie 1940- .... **CLC 88, 184**
See also CA 147; CANR 93; MTFW 2005;
NCFS 3, 5

Erskine, John 1879-1951 .... **TCLC 84**
See also CA 112; 159; DLB 9, 102; FANT

Erwin, Will
See Eisner, Will

Eschenbach, Wolfram von
See von Eschenbach, Wolfram

Eseki, Bruno
See Mphahlele, Es'kia

Esekie, Bruno
See Mphahlele, Es'kia

Esenin, S.A.
See Esenin, Sergei

Esenin, Sergei 1895-1925 .... **TCLC 4**
See also CA 104; EWL 3; RGWL 2, 3

Esenin, Sergei Aleksandrovich
See Esenin, Sergei

Eshleman, Clayton 1935- .... **CLC 7**
See also CA 33-36R, 212; CAAE 212;
CAAS 6; CANR 93; CP 1, 2, 3, 4, 5, 6,
7; DLB 5

Espada, Martin 1957- .... **PC 74**
See also CA 159; CANR 80; CP 7; EXPP;
LLW; MAL 5; PFS 13, 16

Espriella, Don Manuel Alvarez
See Southey, Robert

Espriu, Salvador 1913-1985 .... **CLC 9**
See also CA 154; 115; DLB 134; EWL 3

Espronceda, Jose de 1808-1842 ..... **NCLC 39**

Esquivel, Laura 1950(?)- ... **CLC 141; HLCS
1**
See also AAYA 29; CA 143; CANR 68, 113,
161; DA3; DNFS 2; LAIT 3; LMFS 2;
MTCW 2; MTFW 2005; NFS 5; WLIT 1

Esse, James
See Stephens, James

Esterbrook, Tom
See Hubbard, L. Ron

Esterhazy, Peter 1950- .... **CLC 251**
See also CA 140; CANR 137; CDWLB 4;
CWW 2; DLB 232; EWL 3; RGWL 3

Estleman, Loren D. 1952- .... **CLC 48**
See also AAYA 27; CA 85-88; CANR 27,
74, 139, 177; CMW 4; CPW; DA3; DAM
NOV, POP; DLB 226; INT CANR-27;
MTCW 1, 2; MTFW 2005; TCWW 1, 2

Etherege, Sir George 1636-1692 . **DC 23; LC
78**
See also BRW 2; DAM DRAM; DLB 80;
PAB; RGEL 2

Euclid 306B.C.-283B.C. .... **CMLC 25**

Eugenides, Jeffrey 1960- .... **CLC 81, 212**
See also AAYA 51; CA 144; CANR 120;
MTFW 2005; NFS 24

Euripides c. 484B.C.-406B.C. .... **CMLC 23,
51; DC 4; WLCS**
See also AW 1; CDWLB 1; DA; DA3;
DAB; DAC; DAM DRAM, MST; DFS 1,
4, 6, 25; DLB 176; LAIT 1; LMFS 1;
RGWL 2, 3; WLIT 8

Eusebius c. 263-c. 339 .... **CMLC 103**

Evan, Evin
See Faust, Frederick (Schiller)

Evans, Caradoc 1878-1945 ... **SSC 43; TCLC
85**
See also DLB 162

Evans, Evan
See Faust, Frederick (Schiller)

Evans, Marian
See Eliot, George

Evans, Mary Ann
See Eliot, George

Evarts, Esther
See Benson, Sally

Evelyn, John 1620-1706 .... **LC 144**
See also BRW 2; RGEL 2

Everett, Percival 1956- .... **CLC 57**
See Everett, Percival L.
See also AMWS 18; BW 2; CA 129; CANR
94, 134, 179; CN 7; MTFW 2005

Everett, Percival L.
See Everett, Percival
See also CSW

Everson, R(onald) G(ilmour)
1903-1992 .... **CLC 27**
See also CA 17-20R; CP 1, 2, 3, 4; DLB 88

Everson, William (Oliver)
1912-1994 .... **CLC 1, 5, 14**
See also BG 1:2; CA 9-12R; 145; CANR
20; CP 1; DLB 5, 16, 212; MTCW 1

Evtushenko, Evgenii Aleksandrovich
See Yevtushenko, Yevgeny (Alexandrovich)

Ewart, Gavin (Buchanan)
1916-1995 .... **CLC 13, 46**
See also BRWS 7; CA 89-92; 150; CANR
17, 46; CP 1, 2, 3, 4, 5, 6; DLB 40;
MTCW 1

Ewers, Hanns Heinz 1871-1943 ..... **TCLC 12**
See also CA 109; 149

Ewing, Frederick R.
See Sturgeon, Theodore (Hamilton)

Exley, Frederick (Earl) 1929-1992 .... **CLC 6,
11**
See also AITN 2; BPFB 1; CA 81-84; 138;
CANR 117; DLB 143; DLBY 1981

Eynhardt, Guillermo
See Quiroga, Horacio (Sylvestre)

Ezekiel, Nissim (Moses) 1924-2004 .. **CLC 61**
See also CA 61-64; 223; CP 1, 2, 3, 4, 5, 6,
7; DLB 323; EWL 3

Ezekiel, Tish O'Dowd 1943- .... **CLC 34**
See also CA 129

Fadeev, Aleksandr Aleksandrovich
See Bulgya, Alexander Alexandrovich

Fadeev, Alexandr Alexandrovich
See Bulgya, Alexander Alexandrovich

Fadeyev, A.
See Bulgya, Alexander Alexandrovich

Fadeyev, Alexander
See Bulgya, Alexander Alexandrovich

Fagen, Donald 1948- .... **CLC 26**

Fainzil'berg, Il'ia Arnol'dovich
See Fainzilberg, Ilya Arnoldovich

Fainzilberg, Ilya Arnoldovich
1897-1937 .... **TCLC 21**
See also CA 120; 165; DLB 272; EWL 3

Fair, Ronald L. 1932- .... **CLC 18**
See also BW 1; CA 69-72; CANR 25; DLB
33

Fairbairn, Roger
See Carr, John Dickson

Fairbairns, Zoe (Ann) 1948- .... **CLC 32**
See also CA 103; CANR 21, 85; CN 4, 5,
6, 7

Fairfield, Flora
See Alcott, Louisa May

Falco, Gian
See Papini, Giovanni

Falconer, James
See Kirkup, James

Falconer, Kenneth
See Kornbluth, C(yril) M.

Falkland, Samuel
See Heijermans, Herman

Fallaci, Oriana 1930-2006 .... **CLC 11, 110**
See also CA 77-80; 253; CANR 15, 58, 134;
FW; MTCW 1

Faludi, Susan 1959- .... **CLC 140**
See also CA 138; CANR 126; FW; MTCW
2; MTFW 2005; NCFS 3

Faludy, George 1913- .... **CLC 42**
  See also CA 21-24R
Faludy, Gyoergy
  See Faludy, George
Fanon, Frantz 1925-1961 ...... **BLC 1:2; CLC 74; TCLC 188**
  See also BW 1; CA 116; 89-92; DAM MULT; DLB 296; LMFS 2; WLIT 2
Fanshawe, Ann 1625-1680 .... **LC 11**
Fante, John (Thomas) 1911-1983 .... **CLC 60; SSC 65**
  See also AMWS 11; CA 69-72; 109; CANR 23, 104; DLB 130; DLBY 1983
Farah, Nuruddin 1945- .. **BLC 1:2, 2:2; CLC 53, 137**
  See also AFW; BW 2, 3; CA 106; CANR 81, 148; CDWLB 3; CN 4, 5, 6, 7; DAM MULT; DLB 125; EWL 3; WLIT 2
Fardusi
  See Ferdowsi, Abu'l Qasem
Fargue, Leon-Paul 1876(?)-1947 .... **TCLC 11**
  See also CA 109; CANR 107; DLB 258; EWL 3
Farigoule, Louis
  See Romains, Jules
Farina, Richard 1936(?)-1966 .... **CLC 9**
  See also CA 81-84; 25-28R
Farley, Walter (Lorimer) 1915-1989 .... **CLC 17**
  See also AAYA 58; BYA 14; CA 17-20R; CANR 8, 29, 84; DLB 22; JRDA; MAICYA 1, 2; SATA 2, 43, 132; YAW
Farmer, Philip Jose 1918-2009 ..... **CLC 1, 19**
  See also AAYA 28; BPFB 1; CA 1-4R; CANR 4, 35, 111; DLB 8; MTCW 1; SATA 93; SCFW 1, 2; SFW 4
Farquhar, George 1677-1707 .... **LC 21**
  See also BRW 2; DAM DRAM; DLB 84; RGEL 2
Farrell, J(ames) G(ordon) 1935-1979 .... **CLC 6**
  See also CA 73-76; 89-92; CANR 36; CN 1, 2; DLB 14, 271, 326; MTCW 1; RGEL 2; RHW; WLIT 4
Farrell, James T(homas) 1904-1979 . **CLC 1, 4, 8, 11, 66; SSC 28**
  See also AMW; BPFB 1; CA 5-8R; 89-92; CANR 9, 61; CN 1, 2; DLB 4, 9, 86; DLBD 2; EWL 3; MAL 5; MTCW 1, 2; MTFW 2005; RGAL 4
Farrell, M. J.
  See Keane, Mary Nesta (Skrine)
Farrell, Warren (Thomas) 1943- ...... **CLC 70**
  See also CA 146; CANR 120
Farren, Richard J.
  See Betjeman, John
Farren, Richard M.
  See Betjeman, John
Fassbinder, Rainer Werner 1946-1982 .... **CLC 20**
  See also CA 93-96; 106; CANR 31
Fast, Howard 1914-2003 .... **CLC 23, 131**
  See also AAYA 16; BPFB 1; CA 1-4R, 181; 214; CAAE 181; CAAS 18; CANR 1, 33, 54, 75, 98, 140; CMW 4; CN 1, 2, 3, 4, 5, 6, 7; CPW; DAM NOV; DLB 9; INT CANR-33; LATS 1:1; MAL 5; MTCW 2; MTFW 2005; RHW; SATA 7; SATA-Essay 107; TCWW 1, 2; YAW
Faulcon, Robert
  See Holdstock, Robert
Faulkner, William (Cuthbert) 1897-1962 .... **CLC 1, 3, 6, 8, 9, 11, 14, 18, 28, 52, 68; SSC 1, 35, 42, 92, 97; TCLC 141; WLC 2**
  See also AAYA 7; AMW; AMWR 1; BPFB 1; BYA 5, 15; CA 81-84; CANR 33; CDALB 1929-1941; DA; DA3; DAB; DAC; DAM MST, NOV; DLB 9, 11, 44,

102, 316, 330; DLBD 2; DLBY 1986, 1997; EWL 3; EXPN; EXPS; GL 2; LAIT 2; LATS 1:1; LMFS 2; MAL 5; MTCW 1, 2; MTFW 2005; NFS 4, 8, 13, 24; RGAL 4; RGSF 2; SSFS 2, 5, 6, 12, 27; TUS
Fauset, Jessie Redmon 1882(?)-1961 ...... **BLC 1:2; CLC 19, 54; HR 1:2**
  See also AFAW 2; BW 1; CA 109; CANR 83; DAM MULT; DLB 51; FW; LMFS 2; MAL 5; MBL
Faust, Frederick (Schiller) 1892-1944 .... **TCLC 49**
  See also BPFB 1; CA 108; 152; CANR 143; DAM POP; DLB 256; TCWW 1, 2; TUS
Faust, Irvin 1924- .... **CLC 8**
  See also CA 33-36R; CANR 28, 67; CN 1, 2, 3, 4, 5, 6, 7; DLB 2, 28, 218, 278; DLBY 1980
Fawkes, Guy
  See Benchley, Robert (Charles)
Fearing, Kenneth (Flexner) 1902-1961 .... **CLC 51**
  See also CA 93-96; CANR 59; CMW 4; DLB 9; MAL 5; RGAL 4
Fecamps, Elise
  See Creasey, John
Federman, Raymond 1928- .... **CLC 6, 47**
  See also CA 17-20R, 208; CAAE 208; CAAS 8; CANR 10, 43, 83, 108; CN 3, 4, 5, 6; DLBY 1980
Federspiel, J.F. 1931-2007 .... **CLC 42**
  See also CA 146; 257
Federspiel, Juerg F.
  See Federspiel, J.F.
Federspiel, Jurg F.
  See Federspiel, J.F.
Feiffer, Jules 1929- .... **CLC 2, 8, 64**
  See also AAYA 3, 62; CA 17-20R; CAD; CANR 30, 59, 129, 161; CD 5, 6; DAM DRAM; DLB 7, 44; INT CANR-30; MTCW 1; SATA 8, 61, 111, 157
Feiffer, Jules Ralph
  See Feiffer, Jules
Feige, Hermann Albert Otto Maximilian
  See Traven, B.
Fei-Kan, Li
  See Jin, Ba
Feinberg, David B. 1956-1994 .... **CLC 59**
  See also CA 135; 147
Feinstein, Elaine 1930- .... **CLC 36**
  See also CA 69-72; CAAS 1; CANR 31, 68, 121, 162; CN 3, 4, 5, 6, 7; CP 2, 3, 4, 5, 6, 7; CWP; DLB 14, 40; MTCW 1
Feke, Gilbert David 1965 **CLC 65**
Feldman, Irving (Mordecai) 1928- ..... **CLC 7**
  See also CA 1-4R; CANR 1; CP 1, 2, 3, 4, 5, 6, 7; DLB 169; TCLE 1:1
Felix-Tchicaya, Gerald
  See Tchicaya, Gerald Felix
Fellini, Federico 1920-1993 .... **CLC 16, 85**
  See also CA 65-68; 143; CANR 33
Felltham, Owen 1602(?)-1668 .... **LC 92**
  See also DLB 126, 151
Felsen, Henry Gregor 1916-1995 ..... **CLC 17**
  See also CA 1-4R; 180; CANR 1; SAAS 2; SATA 1
Felski, Rita **CLC 65**
Fenelon, Francois de Pons de Salignac de la Mothe- 1651-1715 .... **LC 134**
  See also DLB 268; EW 3; GFL Beginnings to 1789
Fenno, Jack
  See Calisher, Hortense

Fenollosa, Ernest (Francisco) 1853-1908 .... **TCLC 91**
Fenton, James 1949- .... **CLC 32, 209**
  See also CA 102; CANR 108, 160; CP 2, 3, 4, 5, 6, 7; DLB 40; PFS 11
Fenton, James Martin
  See Fenton, James
Ferber, Edna 1887-1968 .... **CLC 18, 93**
  See also AITN 1; CA 5-8R; 25-28R; CANR 68, 105; DLB 9, 28, 86, 266; MAL 5; MTCW 1, 2; MTFW 2005; RGAL 4; RHW; SATA 7; TCWW 1, 2
Ferdousi
  See Ferdowsi, Abu'l Qasem
Ferdovsi
  See Ferdowsi, Abu'l Qasem
Ferdowsi
  See Ferdowsi, Abu'l Qasem
Ferdowsi, Abolghasem Mansour
  See Ferdowsi, Abu'l Qasem
Ferdowsi, Abolqasem
  See Ferdowsi, Abu'l Qasem
Ferdowsi, Abol-Qasem
  See Ferdowsi, Abu'l Qasem
Ferdowsi, Abu'l Qasem 940-1020(?) .... **CMLC 43**
  See also CA 276; RGWL 2, 3; WLIT 6
Ferdowsi, A.M.
  See Ferdowsi, Abu'l Qasem
Ferdowsi, Hakim Abolghasem
  See Ferdowsi, Abu'l Qasem
Ferguson, Helen
  See Kavan, Anna
Ferguson, Niall 1964- .... **CLC 134, 250**
  See also CA 190; CANR 154
Ferguson, Niall Campbell
  See Ferguson, Niall
Ferguson, Samuel 1810-1886 .... **NCLC 33**
  See also DLB 32; RGEL 2
Fergusson, Robert 1750-1774 .... **LC 29**
  See also DLB 109; RGEL 2
Ferling, Lawrence
  See Ferlinghetti, Lawrence
Ferlinghetti, Lawrence 1919(?)- .... **CLC 2, 6, 10, 27, 111; PC 1**
  See also AAYA 74; BG 1:2; CA 5-8R; CAD; CANR 3, 41, 73, 125, 172; CDALB 1941-1968; CP 1, 2, 3, 4, 5, 6, 7; DA3; DAM POET; DLB 5, 16; MAL 5; MTCW 1, 2; MTFW 2005; PFS 28; RGAL 4; WP
Ferlinghetti, Lawrence Monsanto
  See Ferlinghetti, Lawrence
Fern, Fanny
  See Parton, Sara Payson Willis
Fernandez, Vicente Garcia Huidobro
  See Huidobro Fernandez, Vicente Garcia
Fernandez-Armesto, Felipe **CLC 70**
  See also CA 142; CANR 93, 153, 189
Fernandez-Armesto, Felipe Fermin Ricardo 1950-
  See Fernandez-Armesto, Felipe
Fernandez de Lizardi, Jose Joaquin
  See Lizardi, Jose Joaquin Fernandez de
Ferre, Rosario 1938- ...... **CLC 139; HLCS 1; SSC 36, 106**
  See also CA 131; CANR 55, 81, 134; CWW 2; DLB 145; EWL 3; HW 1, 2; LAWS 1; MTCW 2; MTFW 2005; WLIT 1
Ferrer, Gabriel (Francisco Victor) Miro
  See Miro (Ferrer), Gabriel (Francisco Victor)
Ferrier, Susan (Edmonstone) 1782-1854 .... **NCLC 8**
  See also DLB 116; RGEL 2
Ferrigno, Robert 1947- .... **CLC 65**
  See also CA 140; CANR 125, 161

Ferron, Jacques 1921-1985 .... **CLC 94**
  See also CA 117; 129; CCA 1; DAC; DLB
  60; EWL 3

Feuchtwanger, Lion 1884-1958 .... **TCLC 3**
  See also CA 104; 187; DLB 66; EWL 3;
  RGHL

Feuerbach, Ludwig 1804-1872 ..... **NCLC 139**
  See also DLB 133

Feuillet, Octave 1821-1890 .... **NCLC 45**
  See also DLB 192

Feydeau, Georges (Leon Jules Marie)
  1862-1921 .... **TCLC 22**
  See also CA 113; 152; CANR 84; DAM
  DRAM; DLB 192; EWL 3; GFL 1789 to
  the Present; RGWL 2, 3

Fichte, Johann Gottlieb
  1762-1814 .... **NCLC 62**
  See also DLB 90

Ficino, Marsilio 1433-1499 .... **LC 12, 152**
  See also LMFS 1

Fiedeler, Hans
  See Doeblin, Alfred

Fiedler, Leslie A(aron) 1917-2003 ..... **CLC 4,
  13, 24**
  See also AMWS 13; CA 9-12R; 212; CANR
  7, 63; CN 1, 2, 3, 4, 5, 6; DLB 28, 67;
  EWL 3; MAL 5; MTCW 1, 2; RGAL 4;
  TUS

Field, Andrew 1938- .... **CLC 44**
  See also CA 97-100; CANR 25

Field, Eugene 1850-1895 .... **NCLC 3**
  See also DLB 23, 42, 140; DLBD 13; MAI-
  CYA 1, 2; RGAL 4; SATA 16

Field, Gans T.
  See Wellman, Manly Wade

Field, Michael 1915-1971 .... **TCLC 43**
  See also CA 29-32R

Fielding, Helen 1958- .... **CLC 146, 217**
  See also AAYA 65; CA 172; CANR 127;
  DLB 231; MTFW 2005

Fielding, Henry 1707-1754 .... **LC 1, 46, 85,
  151, 154; WLC 2**
  See also BRW 3; BRWR 1; CDBLB 1660-
  1789; DA; DA3; DAB; DAC; DAM
  DRAM, MST, NOV; DLB 39, 84, 101;
  NFS 18; RGEL 2; TEA; WLIT 3

Fielding, Sarah 1710-1768 .... **LC 1, 44**
  See also DLB 39; RGEL 2; TEA

Fields, W. C. 1880-1946 .... **TCLC 80**
  See also DLB 44

Fierstein, Harvey (Forbes) 1954- ..... **CLC 33**
  See also CA 123; 129; CAD; CD 5, 6;
  CPW; DA3; DAM DRAM, POP; DFS 6;
  DLB 266; GLL 1; MAL 5

Figes, Eva 1932- .... **CLC 31**
  See also CA 53-56; CANR 4, 44, 83; CN 2,
  3, 4, 5, 6, 7; DLB 14, 271; FW; RGHL

Filippo, Eduardo de
  See de Filippo, Eduardo

Finch, Anne 1661-1720 ..... **LC 3, 137; PC 21**
  See also BRWS 9; DLB 95; PFS 30

Finch, Robert (Duer Claydon)
  1900-1995 .... **CLC 18**
  See also CA 57-60; CANR 9, 24, 49; CP 1,
  2, 3, 4, 5, 6; DLB 88

Findley, Timothy (Irving Frederick)
  1930-2002 .... **CLC 27, 102**
  See also CA 25-28R; 206; CANR 12, 42,
  69, 109; CCA 1; CN 4, 5, 6, 7; DAC;
  DAM MST; DLB 53; FANT; RHW

Fink, William
  See Mencken, H(enry) L(ouis)

Firbank, Louis 1942- .... **CLC 21**
  See also CA 117

Firbank, (Arthur Annesley) Ronald
  1886-1926 .... **TCLC 1**
  See also BRWS 2; CA 104; 177; DLB 36;
  EWL 3; RGEL 2

Firdaosi
  See Ferdowsi, Abu'l Qasem

Firdausi
  See Ferdowsi, Abu'l Qasem

Firdavsi, Abulqosimi
  See Ferdowsi, Abu'l Qasem

Firdavsii, Abulqosim
  See Ferdowsi, Abu'l Qasem

Firdawsi, Abu al-Qasim
  See Ferdowsi, Abu'l Qasem

Firdosi
  See Ferdowsi, Abu'l Qasem

Firdousi
  See Ferdowsi, Abu'l Qasem

Firdousi, Abu'l-Qasim
  See Ferdowsi, Abu'l Qasem

Firdovsi, A.
  See Ferdowsi, Abu'l Qasem

Firdovsi, Abulgasim
  See Ferdowsi, Abu'l Qasem

Firdusi
  See Ferdowsi, Abu'l Qasem

Fish, Stanley
  See Fish, Stanley Eugene

Fish, Stanley E.
  See Fish, Stanley Eugene

Fish, Stanley Eugene 1938- .... **CLC 142**
  See also CA 112; 132; CANR 90; DLB 67

Fisher, Dorothy (Frances) Canfield
  1879-1958 .... **TCLC 87**
  See also CA 114; 136; CANR 80; CLR 71;
  CWRI 5; DLB 9, 102, 284; MAICYA 1,
  2; MAL 5; YABC 1

Fisher, M(ary) F(rances) K(ennedy)
  1908-1992 .... **CLC 76, 87**
  See also AMWS 17; CA 77-80; 138; CANR
  44; MTCW 2

Fisher, Roy 1930- .... **CLC 25**
  See also CA 81-84; CAAS 10; CANR 16;
  CP 1, 2, 3, 4, 5, 6, 7; DLB 40

Fisher, Rudolph 1897-1934 ...... **BLC 1:2; HR
  1:2; SSC 25; TCLC 11**
  See also BW 1, 3; CA 107; 124; CANR 80;
  DAM MULT; DLB 51, 102

Fisher, Vardis (Alvero) 1895-1968 .... **CLC 7;
  TCLC 140**
  See also CA 5-8R; 25-28R; CANR 68; DLB
  9, 206; MAL 5; RGAL 4; TCWW 1, 2

Fiske, Tarleton
  See Bloch, Robert (Albert)

Fitch, Clarke
  See Sinclair, Upton

Fitch, John IV
  See Cormier, Robert

Fitzgerald, Captain Hugh
  See Baum, L(yman) Frank

FitzGerald, Edward 1809-1883 ...... **NCLC 9,
  153; PC 79**
  See also BRW 4; DLB 32; RGEL 2

Fitzgerald, F(rancis) Scott (Key)
  1896-1940 ... **SSC 6, 31, 75; TCLC 1, 6,
  14, 28, 55, 157; WLC 2**
  See also AAYA 24; AITN 1; AMW; AMWC
  2; AMWR 1; BPFB 1; CA 110; 123;
  CDALB 1917-1929; DA; DA3; DAB;
  DAC; DAM MST, NOV; DLB 4, 9, 86,
  219, 273; DLBD 1, 15, 16; DLBY 1981,
  1996; EWL 3; EXPN; EXPS; LAIT 3;
  MAL 5; MTCW 1, 2; MTFW 2005; NFS
  2, 19, 20; RGAL 4; RGSF 2; SSFS 4, 15,
  21, 25; TUS

Fitzgerald, Penelope 1916-2000 . **CLC 19, 51,
  61, 143**
  See also BRWS 5; CA 85-88; 190; CAAS
  10; CANR 56, 86, 131; CN 3, 4, 5, 6, 7;
  DLB 14, 194, 326; EWL 3; MTCW 2;
  MTFW 2005

Fitzgerald, Robert (Stuart)
  1910-1985 .... **CLC 39**
  See also CA 1-4R; 114; CANR 1; CP 1, 2,
  3, 4; DLBY 1980; MAL 5

FitzGerald, Robert D(avid)
  1902-1987 .... **CLC 19**
  See also CA 17-20R; CP 1, 2, 3, 4; DLB
  260; RGEL 2

Fitzgerald, Zelda (Sayre)
  1900-1948 .... **TCLC 52**
  See also AMWS 9; CA 117; 126; DLBY
  1984

Flanagan, Thomas (James Bonner)
  1923-2002 .... **CLC 25, 52**
  See also CA 108; 206; CANR 55; CN 3, 4,
  5, 6, 7; DLBY 1980; INT CA-108; MTCW
  1; RHW; TCLE 1:1

Flaubert, Gustave 1821-1880 .... **NCLC 2, 10,
  19, 62, 66, 135, 179, 185; SSC 11, 60;
  WLC 2**
  See also DA; DA3; DAB; DAC; DAM
  MST, NOV; DLB 119, 301; EW 7; EXPS;
  GFL 1789 to the Present; LAIT 2; LMFS
  1; NFS 14; RGSF 2; RGWL 2, 3; SSFS
  6; TWA

Flavius Josephus
  See Josephus, Flavius

Flecker, Herman Elroy
  See Flecker, (Herman) James Elroy

Flecker, (Herman) James Elroy
  1884-1915 .... **TCLC 43**
  See also CA 109; 150; DLB 10, 19; RGEL
  2

Fleming, Ian 1908-1964 ... **CLC 3, 30; TCLC
  193**
  See also AAYA 26; BPFB 1; BRWS 14; CA
  5-8R; CANR 59; CDBLB 1945-1960;
  CMW 4; CPW; DA3; DAM POP; DLB
  87, 201; MSW; MTCW 1, 2; MTFW
  2005; RGEL 2; SATA 9; TEA; YAW

Fleming, Ian Lancaster
  See Fleming, Ian

Fleming, Thomas 1927- .... **CLC 37**
  See also CA 5-8R; CANR 10, 102, 155;
  INT CANR-10; SATA 8

Fleming, Thomas James
  See Fleming, Thomas

Fletcher, John 1579-1625 . **DC 6; LC 33, 151**
  See also BRW 2; CDBLB Before 1660;
  DLB 58; RGEL 2; TEA

Fletcher, John Gould 1886-1950 .... **TCLC 35**
  See also CA 107; 167; DLB 4, 45; LMFS
  2; MAL 5; RGAL 4

Fleur, Paul
  See Pohl, Frederik

Flieg, Helmut
  See Heym, Stefan

Flooglebuckle, Al
  See Spiegelman, Art

Flying Officer X
  See Bates, H(erbert) E(rnest)

Fo, Dario 1926- .... **CLC 32, 109, 227; DC 10**
  See also CA 116; 128; CANR 68, 114, 134,
  164; CWW 2; DA3; DAM DRAM; DFS
  23; DLB 330; DLBY 1997; EWL 3;
  MTCW 1, 2; MTFW 2005; WLIT 7

Foden, Giles 1967- .... **CLC 231**
  See also CA 240; DLB 267; NFS 15

Fogarty, Jonathan Titulescu Esq.
  See Farrell, James T(homas)

Follett, Ken 1949- .... **CLC 18**
  See also AAYA 6, 50; BEST 89:4; BPFB 1;
  CA 81-84; CANR 13, 33, 54, 102, 156;
  CMW 4; CPW; DA3; DAM NOV, POP;
  DLB 87; DLBY 1981; INT CANR-33;
  MTCW 1

Follett, Kenneth Martin
  See Follett, Ken

Author Index

Garro, Elena 1920(?)-1998 .. **HLCS 1; TCLC 153**
See also CA 131; 169; CWW 2; DLB 145; EWL 3; HW 1; LAWS 1; WLIT 1

Garth, Will
See Hamilton, Edmond; Kuttner, Henry

Garvey, Marcus (Moziah, Jr.)
1887-1940 ..... **BLC 1:2; HR 1:2; TCLC 41**
See also BW 1; CA 120; 124; CANR 79; DAM MULT; DLB 345

Gary, Romain
See Kacew, Romain

Gascar, Pierre
See Fournier, Pierre

Gascoigne, George 1539-1577 .... **LC 108**
See also DLB 136; RGEL 2

Gascoyne, David (Emery)
1916-2001 .... **CLC 45**
See also CA 65-68; 200; CANR 10, 28, 54; CP 1, 2, 3, 4, 5, 6, 7; DLB 20; MTCW 1; RGEL 2

Gaskell, Elizabeth Cleghorn
1810-1865 .... **NCLC 5, 70, 97, 137; SSC 25, 97**
See also BRW 5; CDBLB 1832-1890; DAB; DAM MST; DLB 21, 144, 159; RGEL 2; RGSF 2; TEA

Gass, William H. 1924- . **CLC 1, 2, 8, 11, 15, 39, 132; SSC 12**
See also AMWS 6; CA 17-20R; CANR 30, 71, 100; CN 1, 2, 3, 4, 5, 6, 7; DLB 2, 227; EWL 3; MAL 5; MTCW 1, 2; MTFW 2005; RGAL 4

Gassendi, Pierre 1592-1655 .... **LC 54**
See also GFL Beginnings to 1789

Gasset, Jose Ortega y
See Ortega y Gasset, Jose

Gates, Henry Louis, Jr. 1950- ... **BLCS; CLC 65**
See also BW 2, 3; CA 109; CANR 25, 53, 75, 125; CSW; DA3; DAM MULT; DLB 67; EWL 3; MAL 5; MTCW 2; MTFW 2005; RGAL 4

Gatos, Stephanie
See Katz, Steve

Gautier, Theophile 1811-1872 .. **NCLC 1, 59; PC 18; SSC 20**
See also DAM POET; DLB 119; EW 6; GFL 1789 to the Present; RGWL 2, 3; SUFW; TWA

Gautreaux, Tim 1947- .... **CLC 270**
See also CA 187; CSW; DLB 292

Gay, John 1685-1732 .... **LC 49**
See also BRW 3; DAM DRAM; DLB 84, 95; RGEL 2; WLIT 3

Gay, Oliver
See Gogarty, Oliver St. John

Gay, Peter 1923- .... **CLC 158**
See also CA 13-16R; CANR 18, 41, 77, 147; INT CANR-18; RGHL

Gay, Peter Jack
See Gay, Peter

Gaye, Marvin (Pentz, Jr.)
1939-1984 .... **CLC 26**
See also CA 195; 112

Gebler, Carlo 1954- .... **CLC 39**
See also CA 119; 133; CANR 96, 186; DLB 271

Gebler, Carlo Ernest
See Gebler, Carlo

Gee, Maggie 1948- .... **CLC 57**
See also CA 130; CANR 125; CN 4, 5, 6, 7; DLB 207; MTFW 2005

Gee, Maurice 1931- .... **CLC 29**
See also AAYA 42; CA 97-100; CANR 67, 123; CLR 56; CN 2, 3, 4, 5, 6, 7; CWRI 5; EWL 3; MAICYA 2; RGSF 2; SATA 46, 101

Gee, Maurice Gough
See Gee, Maurice

Geiogamah, Hanay 1945- .... **NNAL**
See also CA 153; DAM MULT; DLB 175

Gelbart, Larry
See Gelbart, Larry (Simon)

Gelbart, Larry (Simon) 1928- .... **CLC 21, 61**
See also CA 73-76; CAD; CANR 45, 94; CD 5, 6

Gelber, Jack 1932-2003 ...... **CLC 1, 6, 14, 79**
See also CA 1-4R; 216; CAD; CANR 2; DLB 7, 228; MAL 5

Gellhorn, Martha (Ellis)
1908-1998 .... **CLC 14, 60**
See also CA 77-80; 164; CANR 44; CN 1, 2, 3, 4, 5, 6 7; DLBY 1982, 1998

Genet, Jean 1910-1986 .. **CLC 1, 2, 5, 10, 14, 44, 46; DC 25; TCLC 128**
See also CA 13-16R; CANR 18; DA3; DAM DRAM; DFS 10; DLB 72, 321; DLBY 1986; EW 13; EWL 3; GFL 1789 to the Present; GLL 1; LMFS 2; MTCW 1, 2; MTFW 2005; RGWL 2, 3; TWA

Genlis, Stephanie-Felicite Ducrest
1746-1830 .... **NCLC 166**
See also DLB 313

Gent, Peter 1942- .... **CLC 29**
See also AITN 1; CA 89-92; DLBY 1982

Gentile, Giovanni 1875-1944 .... **TCLC 96**
See also CA 119

Geoffrey of Monmouth c.
1100-1155 .... **CMLC 44**
See also DLB 146; TEA

George, Jean
See George, Jean Craighead

George, Jean Craighead 1919- .... **CLC 35**
See also AAYA 8, 69; BYA 2, 4; CA 5-8R; CANR 25; CLR 1, 80, 136; DLB 52; JRDA; MAICYA 1, 2; SATA 2, 68, 124, 170; WYA; YAW

George, Stefan (Anton) 1868-1933 . **TCLC 2, 14**
See also CA 104; 193; EW 8; EWL 3

Georges, Georges Martin
See Simenon, Georges (Jacques Christian)

Gerald of Wales c. 1146-c. 1223 ... **CMLC 60**

Gerhardi, William Alexander
See Gerhardie, William Alexander

Gerhardie, William Alexander
1895-1977 .... **CLC 5**
See also CA 25-28R; 73-76; CANR 18; CN 1, 2; DLB 36; RGEL 2

Gerome
See Thibault, Jacques Anatole Francois

Gerson, Jean 1363-1429 .... **LC 77**
See also DLB 208

Gersonides 1288-1344 .... **CMLC 49**
See also DLB 115

Gerstler, Amy 1956- .... **CLC 70**
See also CA 146; CANR 99

Gertler, T. CLC 34
See also CA 116; 121

Gertrude of Helfta c. 1256-c.
1301 .... **CMLC 105**

Gertsen, Aleksandr Ivanovich
See Herzen, Aleksandr Ivanovich

Ghalib
See Ghalib, Asadullah Khan

Ghalib, Asadullah Khan
1797-1869 .... **NCLC 39, 78**
See also DAM POET; RGWL 2, 3

Ghelderode, Michel de 1898-1962 ..... **CLC 6, 11; DC 15; TCLC 187**
See also CA 85-88; CANR 40, 77; DAM DRAM; DLB 321; EW 11; EWL 3; TWA

Ghiselin, Brewster 1903-2001 .... **CLC 23**
See also CA 13-16R; CAAS 10; CANR 13; CP 1, 2, 3, 4, 5, 6, 7

Ghose, Aurabinda 1872-1950 .... **TCLC 63**
See also CA 163; EWL 3

Ghose, Aurobindo
See Ghose, Aurabinda

Ghose, Zulfikar 1935- .... **CLC 42, 200**
See also CA 65-68; CANR 67; CN 1, 2, 3, 4, 5, 6, 7; CP 1, 2, 3, 4, 5, 6, 7; DLB 323; EWL 3

Ghosh, Amitav 1956- .... **CLC 44, 153**
See also CA 147; CANR 80, 158; CN 6, 7; DLB 323; WWE 1

Giacosa, Giuseppe 1847-1906 .... **TCLC 7**
See also CA 104

Gibb, Lee
See Waterhouse, Keith (Spencer)

Gibbon, Edward 1737-1794 .... **LC 97**
See also BRW 3; DLB 104, 336; RGEL 2

Gibbon, Lewis Grassic
See Mitchell, James Leslie

Gibbons, Kaye 1960- .... **CLC 50, 88, 145**
See also AAYA 34; AMWS 10; CA 151; CANR 75, 127; CN 7; CSW; DA3; DAM POP; DLB 292; MTCW 2; MTFW 2005; NFS 3; RGAL 4; SATA 117

Gibran, Kahlil 1883-1931 ..... **PC 9; TCLC 1, 9, 205**
See also CA 104; 150; DA3; DAM POET, POP; DLB 346; EWL 3; MTCW 2; WLIT 6

Gibran, Khalil
See Gibran, Kahlil

Gibson, Mel 1956- .... **CLC 215**

Gibson, William 1914-2008 .... **CLC 23**
See also CA 9-12R; 279; CAD; CANR 9, 42, 75, 125; CD 5, 6; DA; DAB; DAC; DAM DRAM, MST; DFS 2; DLB 7; LAIT 2; MAL 5; MTCW 2; MTFW 2005; SATA 66; SATA-Obit 199; YAW

Gibson, William 1948- .... **CLC 39, 63, 186, 192; SSC 52**
See also AAYA 12, 59; AMWS 16; BPFB 2; CA 126; 133; CANR 52, 90, 106, 172; CN 6, 7; CPW; DA3; DAM POP; DLB 251; MTCW 2; MTFW 2005; SCFW 2; SFW 4; SSFS 26

Gibson, William Ford
See Gibson, William

Gide, Andre (Paul Guillaume)
1869-1951 ...... **SSC 13; TCLC 5, 12, 36, 177; WLC 3**
See also CA 104; 124; DA; DA3; DAB; DAC; DAM MST, NOV; DLB 65, 321, 330; EW 8; EWL 3; GFL 1789 to the Present; MTCW 1, 2; MTFW 2005; NFS 21; RGSF 2; RGWL 2, 3; TWA

Gifford, Barry 1946- .... **CLC 34**
See also CA 65-68; CANR 9, 30, 40, 90, 180

Gifford, Barry Colby
See Gifford, Barry

Gilbert, Frank
See De Voto, Bernard (Augustine)

Gilbert, W(illiam) S(chwenck)
1836-1911 .... **TCLC 3**
See also CA 104; 173; DAM DRAM, POET; DLB 344; RGEL 2; SATA 36

Gilbert of Poitiers c. 1085-1154 .... **CMLC 85**

Gilbreth, Frank B(unker), Jr.
1911-2001 .... **CLC 17**
See also CA 9-12R; SATA 2

Gilchrist, Ellen (Louise) 1935- .. **CLC 34, 48, 143, 264; SSC 14, 63**
See also BPFB 2; CA 113; 116; CANR 41, 61, 104; CN 4, 5, 6, 7; CSW; DAM POP; DLB 130; EWL 3; EXPS; MTCW 1, 2; MTFW 2005; RGAL 4; RGSF 2; SSFS 9

Gildas fl. 6th cent. - .... **CMLC 99**
Giles, Molly 1942- .... **CLC 39**
See also CA 126; CANR 98
Gill, Eric
See Gill, (Arthur) Eric (Rowton Peter Joseph)
Gill, (Arthur) Eric (Rowton Peter Joseph)
1882-1940 .... **TCLC 85**
See also CA 120; DLB 98
Gill, Patrick
See Creasey, John
Gillette, Douglas CLC 70
Gilliam, Terry 1940- .... **CLC 21, 141**
See also AAYA 19, 59; CA 108; 113; CANR 35; INT CA-113
Gilliam, Terry Vance
See Gilliam, Terry
Gillian, Jerry
See Gilliam, Terry
Gilliatt, Penelope (Ann Douglass)
1932-1993 .... **CLC 2, 10, 13, 53**
See also AITN 2; CA 13-16R; 141; CANR 49; CN 1, 2, 3, 4, 5; DLB 14
Gilligan, Carol 1936- .... **CLC 208**
See also CA 142; CANR 121, 187; FW
Gilman, Charlotte (Anna) Perkins (Stetson)
1860-1935 ...... **SSC 13, 62; TCLC 9, 37, 117, 201**
See also AAYA 75; AMWS 11; BYA 11; CA 106; 150; DLB 221; EXPS; FL 1:5; FW; HGG; LAIT 2; MBL; MTCW 2; MTFW 2005; RGAL 4; RGSF 2; SFW 4; SSFS 1, 18
Gilmore, Mary (Jean Cameron)
1865-1962 .... **PC 87**
See also CA 114; DLB 260; RGEL 2; SATA 49
Gilmour, David 1946- .... **CLC 35**
Gilpin, William 1724-1804 .... **NCLC 30**
Gilray, J. D.
See Mencken, H(enry) L(ouis)
Gilroy, Frank D(aniel) 1925- .... **CLC 2**
See also CA 81-84; CAD; CANR 32, 64, 86; CD 5, 6; DFS 17; DLB 7
Gilstrap, John 1957(?)- .... **CLC 99**
See also AAYA 67; CA 160; CANR 101
Ginsberg, Allen 1926-1997 .... **CLC 1, 2, 3, 4, 6, 13, 36, 69, 109; PC 4, 47; TCLC 120; WLC 3**
See also AAYA 33; AITN 1; AMWC 1; AMWS 2; BG 1:2; CA 1-4R; 157; CANR 2, 41, 63, 95; CDALB 1941-1968; CP 1, 2, 3, 4, 5, 6; DA; DA3; DAB; DAC; DAM MST, POET; DLB 5, 16, 169, 237; EWL 3; GLL 1; LMFS 2; MAL 5; MTCW 1, 2; MTFW 2005; PAB; PFS 29; RGAL 4; TUS; WP
Ginzburg, Eugenia
See Ginzburg, Evgeniia
Ginzburg, Evgeniia 1904-1977 .... **CLC 59**
See also DLB 302
Ginzburg, Natalia 1916-1991 .... **CLC 5, 11, 54, 70; SSC 65; TCLC 156**
See also CA 85-88; 135; CANR 33; DFS 14; DLB 177; EW 13; EWL 3; MTCW 1, 2; MTFW 2005; RGHL; RGWL 2, 3
Gioia, (Michael) Dana 1950- .... **CLC 251**
See also AMWS 15; CA 130; CANR 70, 88; CP 6, 7; DLB 120, 282; PFS 24
Giono, Jean 1895-1970 .... **CLC 4, 11; TCLC 124**
See also CA 45-48; 29-32R; CANR 2, 35; DLB 72, 321; EWL 3; GFL 1789 to the Present; MTCW 1; RGWL 2, 3
Giovanni, Nikki 1943- ... **BLC 1:2; CLC 2, 4, 19, 64, 117; PC 19; WLCS**
See also AAYA 22; AITN 1; BW 2, 3; CA 29-32R; CAAS 6; CANR 18, 41, 60, 91, 130, 175; CDALBS; CLR 6, 73; CP 2, 3,

4, 5, 6, 7; CSW; CWP; CWRI 5; DA; DA3; DAB; DAC; DAM MST, MULT, POET; DLB 5, 41; EWL 3; EXPP; INT CANR-18; MAICYA 1, 2; MAL 5; MTCW 1, 2; MTFW 2005; PFS 17, 28; RGAL 4; SATA 24, 107; TUS; YAW
Giovanni, Yolanda Cornelia
See Giovanni, Nikki
Giovanni, Yolande Cornelia
See Giovanni, Nikki
Giovanni, Yolande Cornelia, Jr.
See Giovanni, Nikki
Giovene, Andrea 1904-1998 .... **CLC 7**
See also CA 85-88
Gippius, Zinaida (Nikolaevna)
1869-1945 .... **TCLC 9**
See also CA 106; 212; DLB 295; EWL 3
Giraudoux, Jean(-Hippolyte)
1882-1944 .... **TCLC 2, 7**
See also CA 104; 196; DAM DRAM; DLB 65, 321; EW 9; EWL 3; GFL 1789 to the Present; RGWL 2, 3; TWA
Gironella, Jose Maria (Pous)
1917-2003 .... **CLC 11**
See also CA 101; 212; EWL 3; RGWL 2, 3
Gissing, George (Robert)
1857-1903 .... **SSC 37, 113; TCLC 3, 24, 47**
See also BRW 5; CA 105; 167; DLB 18, 135, 184; RGEL 2; TEA
Gitlin, Todd 1943- .... **CLC 201**
See also CA 29-32R; CANR 25, 50, 88, 179
Giurlani, Aldo
See Palazzeschi, Aldo
Gladkov, Fedor Vasil'evich
See Gladkov, Fyodor (Vasilyevich)
Gladkov, Fyodor (Vasilyevich)
1883-1958 .... **TCLC 27**
See also CA 170; DLB 272; EWL 3
Glancy, Diane 1941- .... **CLC 210; NNAL**
See also CA 136, 225; CAAE 225; CAAS 24; CANR 87, 162; DLB 175
Glanville, Brian (Lester) 1931- .... **CLC 6**
See also CA 5-8R; CAAS 9; CANR 3, 70; CN 1, 2, 3, 4, 5, 6, 7; DLB 15, 139; SATA 42
Glasgow, Ellen (Anderson Gholson)
1873-1945 .... **SSC 34; TCLC 2, 7**
See also AMW; CA 104; 164; DLB 9, 12; MAL 5; MBL; MTCW 2; MTFW 2005; RGAL 4; RHW; SSFS 9; TUS
Glaspell, Susan 1882(?)-1948 ..... **DC 10; SSC 41; TCLC 55, 175**
See also AMWS 3; CA 110; 154; DFS 8, 18, 24; DLB 7, 9, 78, 228; MBL; RGAL 4; SSFS 3; TCWW 2; TUS; YABC 2
Glassco, John 1909-1981 .... **CLC 9**
See also CA 13-16R; 102; CANR 15; CN 1, 2; CP 1, 2, 3; DLB 68
Glasscock, Amnesia
See Steinbeck, John (Ernst)
Glasser, Ronald J. 1940(?)- .... **CLC 37**
See also CA 209
Glassman, Joyce
See Johnson, Joyce
Gleick, James (W.) 1954- .... **CLC 147**
See also CA 131; 137; CANR 97; INT CA-137
Glendinning, Victoria 1937- .... **CLC 50**
See also CA 120; 127; CANR 59, 89, 166; DLB 155
Glissant, Edouard (Mathieu)
1928- .... **CLC 10, 68**
See also CA 153; CANR 111; CWW 2; DAM MULT; EWL 3; RGWL 3
Gloag, Julian 1930- .... **CLC 40**
See also AITN 1; CA 65-68; CANR 10, 70; CN 1, 2, 3, 4, 5, 6

Glowacki, Aleksander
See Prus, Boleslaw
Gluck, Louise 1943- .... **CLC 7, 22, 44, 81, 160; PC 16**
See also AMWS 5; CA 33-36R; CANR 40, 69, 108, 133, 182; CP 1, 2, 3, 4, 5, 6, 7; CWP; DA3; DAM POET; DLB 5; MAL 5; MTCW 2; MTFW 2005; PFS 5, 15; RGAL 4; TCLE 1:1
Gluck, Louise Elisabeth
See Gluck, Louise
Glyn, Elinor 1864-1943 .... **TCLC 72**
See also DLB 153; RHW
Gobineau, Joseph-Arthur
1816-1882 .... **NCLC 17**
See also DLB 123; GFL 1789 to the Present
Godard, Jean-Luc 1930- .... **CLC 20**
See also CA 93-96
Godden, (Margaret) Rumer
1907-1998 .... **CLC 53**
See also AAYA 6; BPFB 2; BYA 2, 5; CA 5-8R; 172; CANR 4, 27, 36, 55, 80; CLR 20; CN 1, 2, 3, 4, 5, 6; CWRI 5; DLB 161; MAICYA 1, 2; RHW; SAAS 12; SATA 3, 36; SATA-Obit 109; TEA
Godoy Alcayaga, Lucila 1899-1957 .. **HLC 2; PC 32; TCLC 2**
See also BW 2; CA 104; 131; CANR 81; DAM MULT; DLB 283, 331; DNFS; EWL 3; HW 1, 2; LAW; MTCW 1, 2; MTFW 2005; RGWL 2, 3; WP
Godwin, Gail 1937- .... **CLC 5, 8, 22, 31, 69, 125**
See also BPFB 2; CA 29-32R; CANR 15, 43, 69, 132; CN 3, 4, 5, 6, 7; CPW; CSW; DA3; DAM POP; DLB 6, 234; INT CANR-15; MAL 5; MTCW 1, 2; MTFW 2005
Godwin, Gail Kathleen
See Godwin, Gail
Godwin, William 1756-1836 .. **NCLC 14, 130**
See also CDBLB 1789-1832; CMW 4; DLB 39, 104, 142, 158, 163, 262, 336; GL 2; HGG; RGEL 2
Goebbels, Josef
See Goebbels, (Paul) Joseph
Goebbels, (Paul) Joseph
1897-1945 .... **TCLC 68**
See also CA 115; 148
Goebbels, Joseph Paul
See Goebbels, (Paul) Joseph
Goethe, Johann Wolfgang von
1749-1832 . **DC 20; NCLC 4, 22, 34, 90, 154; PC 5; SSC 38; WLC 3**
See also CDWLB 2; DA; DA3; DAB; DAC; DAM DRAM, MST, POET; DLB 94; EW 5; GL 2; LATS 1; LMFS 1:1; RGWL 2, 3; TWA
Gogarty, Oliver St. John
1878-1957 .... **TCLC 15**
See also CA 109; 150; DLB 15, 19; RGEL 2
Gogol, Nikolai (Vasilyevich)
1809-1852 .... **DC 1; NCLC 5, 15, 31, 162; SSC 4, 29, 52; WLC 3**
See also DA; DAB; DAC; DAM DRAM, MST; DFS 12; DLB 198; EW 6; EXPS; RGSF 2; RGWL 2, 3; SSFS 7; TWA
Goines, Donald 1937(?)-1974 .... **BLC 1:2; CLC 80**
See also AITN 1; BW 1, 3; CA 124; 114; CANR 82; CMW 4; DA3; DAM MULT, POP; DLB 33
Gold, Herbert 1924- ... **CLC 4, 7, 14, 42, 152**
See also CA 9-12R; CANR 17, 45, 125; CN 1, 2, 3, 4, 5, 6, 7; DLB 2; DLBY 1981; MAL 5
Goldbarth, Albert 1948- .... **CLC 5, 38**
See also AMWS 12; CA 53-56; CANR 6, 40; CP 3, 4, 5, 6, 7; DLB 120

Goldberg, Anatol 1910-1982 .... **CLC 34**
See also CA 131; 117
Goldemberg, Isaac 1945- .... **CLC 52**
See also CA 69-72; CAAS 12; CANR 11,
32; EWL 3; HW 1; WLIT 1
Golding, Arthur 1536-1606 .... **LC 101**
See also DLB 136
Golding, William 1911-1993 . **CLC 1, 2, 3, 8,
10, 17, 27, 58, 81; WLC 3**
See also AAYA 5, 44; BPFB 2; BRWR 1;
BRWS 1; BYA 2; CA 5-8R; 141; CANR
13, 33, 54; CD 5; CDBLB 1945-1960;
CLR 94, 130; CN 1, 2, 3, 4; DA; DA3;
DAB; DAC; DAM MST, NOV; DLB 15,
100, 255, 326, 330; EWL 3; EXPN; HGG;
LAIT 4; MTCW 1, 2; MTFW 2005; NFS
2; RGEL 2; RHW; SFW 4; TEA; WLIT
4; YAW
Golding, William Gerald
See Golding, William
Goldman, Emma 1869-1940 .... **TCLC 13**
See also CA 110; 150; DLB 221; FW;
RGAL 4; TUS
Goldman, Francisco 1954- .... **CLC 76**
See also CA 162; CANR 185
Goldman, William 1931- .... **CLC 1, 48**
See also BPFB 2; CA 9-12R; CANR 29,
69, 106; CN 1, 2, 3, 4, 5, 6, 7; DLB 44;
FANT; IDFW 3, 4
Goldman, William W.
See Goldman, William
Goldmann, Lucien 1913-1970 .... **CLC 24**
See also CA 25-28; CAP 2
Goldoni, Carlo 1707-1793 .... **LC 4, 152**
See also DAM DRAM; EW 4; RGWL 2, 3;
WLIT 7
Goldsberry, Steven 1949- .... **CLC 34**
See also CA 131
Goldsmith, Oliver 1730(?)-1774 .... **DC 8; LC
2, 48, 122; PC 77; WLC 3**
See also BRW 3; CDBLB 1660-1789; DA;
DAB; DAC; DAM DRAM, MST, NOV,
POET; DFS 1; DLB 39, 89, 104, 109, 142,
336; IDTP; RGEL 2; SATA 26; TEA;
WLIT 3
Goldsmith, Peter
See Priestley, J(ohn) B(oynton)
Goldstein, Rebecca 1950- .... **CLC 239**
See also CA 144; CANR 99, 165; TCLE
1:1
Goldstein, Rebecca Newberger
See Goldstein, Rebecca
Gombrowicz, Witold 1904-1969 .... **CLC 4, 7,
11, 49**
See also CA 19-20; 25-28R; CANR 105;
CAP 2; CDWLB 4; DAM DRAM; DLB
215; EW 12; EWL 3; RGWL 2, 3; TWA
Gomez de Avellaneda, Gertrudis
1814-1873 .... **NCLC 111**
See also LAW
Gomez de la Serna, Ramon
1888-1963 .... **CLC 9**
See also CA 153; 116; CANR 79; EWL 3;
HW 1, 2
Goncharov, Ivan Alexandrovich
1812-1891 .... **NCLC 1, 63**
See also DLB 238; EW 6; RGWL 2, 3
Goncourt, Edmond (Louis Antoine Huot) de
1822-1896 .... **NCLC 7**
See also DLB 123; EW 7; GFL 1789 to the
Present; RGWL 2, 3
Goncourt, Jules (Alfred Huot) de
1830-1870 .... **NCLC 7**
See also DLB 123; EW 7; GFL 1789 to the
Present; RGWL 2, 3
Gongora (y Argote), Luis de
1561-1627 .... **LC 72**
See also RGWL 2, 3

Gontier, Fernande 19(?)- .... **CLC 50**
Gonzalez Martinez, Enrique
See Gonzalez Martinez, Enrique
Gonzalez Martinez, Enrique
1871-1952 .... **TCLC 72**
See also CA 166; CANR 81; DLB 290;
EWL 3; HW 1, 2
Goodison, Lorna 1947- .... **BLC 2:2; PC 36**
See also CA 142; CANR 88, 189; CP 5, 6,
7; CWP; DLB 157; EWL 3; PFS 25
Goodman, Allegra 1967- .... **CLC 241**
See also CA 204; CANR 162; DLB 244
Goodman, Paul 1911-1972 ..... **CLC 1, 2, 4, 7**
See also CA 19-20; 37-40R; CAD; CANR
34; CAP 2; CN 1; DLB 130, 246; MAL
5; MTCW 1; RGAL 4
Goodweather, Hartley
See King, Thomas
GoodWeather, Hartley
See King, Thomas
Googe, Barnabe 1540-1594 .... **LC 94**
See also DLB 132; RGEL 2
Gordimer, Nadine 1923- ...... **CLC 3, 5, 7, 10,
18, 33, 51, 70, 123, 160, 161, 263; SSC
17, 80; WLCS**
See also AAYA 39; AFW; BRWS 2; CA
5-8R; CANR 3, 28, 56, 88, 131; CN 1, 2,
3, 4, 5, 6, 7; DA; DA3; DAB; DAC; DAM
MST, NOV; DLB 225, 326, 330; EWL 3;
EXPS; INT CANR-28; LATS 1:2; MTCW
1, 2; MTFW 2005; NFS 4; RGEL 2;
RGSF 2; SSFS 2, 14, 19; TWA; WLIT 2;
YAW
Gordon, Adam Lindsay
1833-1870 .... **NCLC 21**
See also DLB 230
Gordon, Caroline 1895-1981 . **CLC 6, 13, 29,
83; SSC 15**
See also AMW; CA 11-12; 103; CANR 36;
CAP 1; CN 1, 2; DLB 4, 9, 102; DLBD
17; DLBY 1981; EWL 3; MAL 5; MTCW
1, 2; MTFW 2005; RGAL 4; RGSF 2
Gordon, Charles William
1860-1937 .... **TCLC 31**
See also CA 109; DLB 92; TCWW 1, 2
Gordon, Mary 1949- .. **CLC 13, 22, 128, 216;
SSC 59**
See also AMWS 4; BPFB 2; CA 102;
CANR 44, 92, 154, 179; CN 4, 5, 6, 7;
DLB 6; DLBY 1981; FW; INT CA-102;
MAL 5; MTCW 1
Gordon, Mary Catherine
See Gordon, Mary
Gordon, N. J.
See Bosman, Herman Charles
Gordon, Sol 1923- .... **CLC 26**
See also CA 53-56; CANR 4; SATA 11
Gordone, Charles 1925-1995 .... **BLC 2:2;
CLC 1, 4; DC 8**
See also BW 1, 3; CA 93-96; 180; 150;
CAAE 180; CAD; CANR 55; DAM
DRAM; DLB 7; INT CA-93-96; MTCW
1
Gore, Catherine 1800-1861 .... **NCLC 65**
See also DLB 116, 344; RGEL 2
Gorenko, Anna Andreevna
See Akhmatova, Anna
Gor'kii, Maksim
See Peshkov, Alexei Maximovich
Gorky, Maxim
See Peshkov, Alexei Maximovich
Goryan, Sirak
See Saroyan, William
Gosse, Edmund (William)
1849-1928 .... **TCLC 28**
See also CA 117; DLB 57, 144, 184; RGEL
2

Gotlieb, Phyllis (Fay Bloom) 1926- .. **CLC 18**
See also CA 13-16R; CANR 7, 135; CN 7;
CP 1, 2, 3, 4; DLB 88, 251; SFW 4
Gottesman, S. D.
See Kornbluth, C(yril) M.; Pohl, Frederik
Gottfried von Strassburg fl. c.
1170-1215 .... **CMLC 10, 96**
See also CDWLB 2; DLB 138; EW 1;
RGWL 2, 3
Gotthelf, Jeremias 1797-1854 .... **NCLC 117**
See also DLB 133; RGWL 2, 3
Gottschalk, Laura Riding
See Jackson, Laura (Riding)
Gould, Lois 1932(?)-2002 .... **CLC 4, 10**
See also CA 77-80; 208; CANR 29; MTCW
1
Gould, Stephen Jay 1941-2002 .... **CLC 163**
See also AAYA 26; BEST 90:2; CA 77-80;
205; CANR 10, 27, 56, 75, 125; CPW;
INT CANR-27; MTCW 1, 2; MTFW 2005
Gourmont, Remy(-Marie-Charles) de
1858-1915 .... **TCLC 17**
See also CA 109; 150; GFL 1789 to the
Present; MTCW 2
Gournay, Marie le Jars de
See de Gournay, Marie le Jars
Govier, Katherine 1948- .... **CLC 51**
See also CA 101; CANR 18, 40, 128; CCA
1
Gower, John c. 1330-1408 .... **LC 76; PC 59**
See also BRW 1; DLB 146; RGEL 2
Goyen, (Charles) William
1915-1983 .... **CLC 5, 8, 14, 40**
See also AITN 2; CA 5-8R; 110; CANR 6,
71; CN 1, 2, 3; DLB 2, 218; DLBY 1983;
EWL 3; INT CANR-6; MAL 5
Goytisolo, Juan 1931- .... **CLC 5, 10, 23, 133;
HLC 1**
See also CA 85-88; CANR 32, 61, 131, 182;
CWW 2; DAM MULT; DLB 322; EWL
3; GLL 2; HW 1, 2; MTCW 1, 2; MTFW
2005
Gozzano, Guido 1883-1916 .... **PC 10**
See also CA 154; DLB 114; EWL 3
Gozzi, (Conte) Carlo 1720-1806 .... **NCLC 23**
Grabbe, Christian Dietrich
1801-1836 .... **NCLC 2**
See also DLB 133; RGWL 2, 3
Grace, Patricia Frances 1937- .... **CLC 56**
See also CA 176; CANR 118; CN 4, 5, 6,
7; EWL 3; RGSF 2
Gracian, Baltasar 1601-1658 .... **LC 15, 160**
Gracian y Morales, Baltasar
See Gracian, Baltasar
Gracq, Julien 1910-2007 ..... **CLC 11, 48, 259**
See also CA 122; 126; 267; CANR 141;
CWW 2; DLB 83; GFL 1789 to the
present
Grade, Chaim 1910-1982 .... **CLC 10**
See also CA 93-96; 107; DLB 333; EWL 3;
RGHL
Grade, Khayim
See Grade, Chaim
Graduate of Oxford, A
See Ruskin, John
Grafton, Garth
See Duncan, Sara Jeannette
Grafton, Sue 1940- .... **CLC 163**
See also AAYA 11, 49; BEST 90:3; CA 108;
CANR 31, 55, 111, 134; CMW 4; CPW;
CSW; DA3; DAM POP; DLB 226; FW;
MSW; MTFW 2005
Graham, John
See Phillips, David Graham
Graham, Jorie 1950- .... **CLC 48, 118; PC 59**
See also AAYA 67; CA 111; CANR 63, 118;
CP 4, 5, 6, 7; CWP; DLB 120; EWL 3;
MTFW 2005; PFS 10, 17; TCLE 1:1

Graham, R(obert) B(ontine) Cunninghame
See Cunninghame Graham, Robert (Gallnigad) Bontine
Graham, Robert
See Haldeman, Joe
Graham, Tom
See Lewis, (Harry) Sinclair
Graham, W(illiam) S(ydney)
1918-1986 .... **CLC 29**
See also BRWS 7; CA 73-76; 118; CP 1, 2, 3, 4; DLB 20; RGEL 2
Graham, Winston (Mawdsley)
1910-2003 .... **CLC 23**
See also CA 49-52; 218; CANR 2, 22, 45, 66; CMW 4; CN 1, 2, 3, 4, 5, 6, 7; DLB 77; RHW
Grahame, Kenneth 1859-1932 ...... **TCLC 64, 136**
See also BYA 5; CA 108; 136; CANR 80; CLR 5, 135; CWRI 5; DA3; DAB; DLB 34, 141, 178; FANT; MAICYA 1, 2; MTCW 2; NFS 20; RGEL 2; SATA 100; TEA; WCH; YABC 1
Granger, Darius John
See Marlowe, Stephen
Granin, Daniil 1918- .... **CLC 59**
See also DLB 302
Granovsky, Timofei Nikolaevich
1813-1855 .... **NCLC 75**
See also DLB 198
Grant, Skeeter
See Spiegelman, Art
Granville-Barker, Harley
1877-1946 .... **TCLC 2**
See also CA 104; 204; DAM DRAM; DLB 10; RGEL 2
Granzotto, Gianni
See Granzotto, Giovanni Battista
Granzotto, Giovanni Battista
1914-1985 .... **CLC 70**
See also CA 166
Grasemann, Ruth Barbara
See Rendell, Ruth
Grass, Guenter
See Grass, Gunter
Grass, Gunter 1927- .. **CLC 1, 2, 4, 6, 11, 15, 22, 32, 49, 88, 207; WLC 3**
See also BPFB 2; CA 13-16R; CANR 20, 75, 93, 133, 174; CDWLB 2; CWW 2; DA; DA3; DAB; DAC; DAM MST, NOV; DLB 330; EW 13; EWL 3; MTCW 1, 2; MTFW 2005; RGHL; RGWL 2, 3; TWA
Grass, Gunter Wilhelm
See Grass, Gunter
Gratton, Thomas
See Hulme, T(homas) E(rnest)
Grau, Shirley Ann 1929- .... **CLC 4, 9, 146; SSC 15**
See also CA 89-92; CANR 22, 69; CN 1, 2, 3, 4, 5, 6, 7; CSW; DLB 2, 218; INT CA-89-92; CANR-22; MTCW 1
Gravel, Fern
See Hall, James Norman
Graver, Elizabeth 1964- .... **CLC 70**
See also CA 135; CANR 71, 129
Graves, Richard Perceval
1895-1985 .... **CLC 44**
See also CA 65-68; CANR 9, 26, 51
Graves, Robert 1895-1985 ... **CLC 1, 2, 6, 11, 39, 44, 45; PC 6**
See also BPFB 2; BRW 7; BYA 4; CA 5-8R; 117; CANR 5, 36; CDBLB 1914-1945; CN 1, 2, 3; CP 1, 2, 3, 4; DA3; DAB; DAC; DAM MST, POET; DLB 20, 100, 191; DLBD 18; DLBY 1985; EWL 3; LATS 1:1; MTCW 1, 2; MTFW 2005; NCFS 2; NFS 21; RGEL 2; RHW; SATA 45; TEA

Graves, Valerie
See Bradley, Marion Zimmer
Gray, Alasdair 1934- .... **CLC 41**
See also BRWS 9; CA 126; CANR 47, 69, 106, 140; CN 4, 5, 6, 7; DLB 194, 261, 319; HGG; INT CA-126; MTCW 1, 2; MTFW 2005; RGSF 2; SUFW 2
Gray, Amlin 1946- .... **CLC 29**
See also CA 138
Gray, Francine du Plessix 1930- ..... **CLC 22, 153**
See also BEST 90:3; CA 61-64; CAAS 2; CANR 11, 33, 75, 81; DAM NOV; INT CANR-11; MTCW 1, 2; MTFW 2005
Gray, John (Henry) 1866-1934 ...... **TCLC 19**
See also CA 119; 162; RGEL 2
Gray, John Lee
See Jakes, John
Gray, Simon 1936-2008 .... **CLC 9, 14, 36**
See also AITN 1; CA 21-24R; 275; CAAS 3; CANR 32, 69; CBD; CD 5, 6; CN 1, 2, 3; DLB 13; EWL 3; MTCW 1; RGEL 2
Gray, Simon James Holliday
See Gray, Simon
Gray, Spalding 1941-2004 .... **CLC 49, 112; DC 7**
See also AAYA 62; CA 128; 225; CAD; CANR 74, 138; CD 5, 6; CPW; DAM POP; MTCW 2; MTFW 2005
Gray, Thomas 1716-1771 ..... **LC 4, 40; PC 2, 80; WLC 3**
See also BRW 3; CDBLB 1660-1789; DA; DA3; DAB; DAC; DAM MST; DLB 109; EXPP; PAB; PFS 9; RGEL 2; TEA; WP
Grayson, David
See Baker, Ray Stannard
Grayson, Richard (A.) 1951- .... **CLC 38**
See also CA 85-88; 210; CAAE 210; CANR 14, 31, 57; DLB 234
Greeley, Andrew M. 1928- .... **CLC 28**
See also BPFB 2; CA 5-8R; CAAS 7; CANR 7, 43, 69, 104, 136, 184; CMW 4; CPW; DA3; DAM POP; MTCW 1, 2; MTFW 2005
Green, Anna Katharine
1846-1935 .... **TCLC 63**
See also CA 112; 159; CMW 4; DLB 202, 221; MSW
Green, Brian
See Card, Orson Scott
Green, Hannah
See Greenberg, Joanne (Goldenberg)
Green, Hannah 1927(?)-1996 .... **CLC 3**
See also CA 73-76; CANR 59, 93; NFS 10
Green, Henry
See Yorke, Henry Vincent
Green, Julian
See Green, Julien (Hartridge)
Green, Julien (Hartridge)
1900-1998 .... **CLC 3, 11, 77**
See also CA 21-24R; 169; CANR 33, 87; CWW 2; DLB 4, 72; EWL 3; GFL 1789 to the Present; MTCW 2; MTFW 2005
Green, Paul (Eliot) 1894-1981 .... **CLC 25**
See also AITN 1; CA 5-8R; 103; CAD; CANR 3; DAM DRAM; DLB 7, 9, 249; DLBY 1981; MAL 5; RGAL 4
Greenaway, Peter 1942- .... **CLC 159**
See also CA 127
Greenberg, Ivan 1908-1973 .... **CLC 24**
See also CA 85-88; DLB 137; MAL 5
Greenberg, Joanne (Goldenberg)
1932- .... **CLC 7, 30**
See also AAYA 12, 67; CA 5-8R; CANR 14, 32, 69; CN 6, 7; DLB 335; NFS 23; SATA 25; YAW
Greenberg, Richard 1959(?)- .... **CLC 57**
See also CA 138; CAD; CD 5, 6; DFS 24

Greenblatt, Stephen J(ay) 1943- ...... **CLC 70**
See also CA 49-52; CANR 115
Greene, Bette 1934- .... **CLC 30**
See also AAYA 7, 69; BYA 3; CA 53-56; CANR 4, 146; CLR 2, 140; CWRI 5; JRDA; LAIT 4; MAICYA 1, 2; NFS 10; SAAS 16; SATA 8, 102, 161; WYA; YAW
Greene, Gael CLC 8
See also CA 13-16R; CANR 10, 166
Greene, Graham 1904-1991 .. **CLC 1, 3, 6, 9, 14, 18, 27, 37, 70, 72, 125; SSC 29, 121; WLC 3**
See also AAYA 61; AITN 2; BPFB 2; BRWR 2; BRWS 1; BYA 3; CA 13-16R; 133; CANR 35, 61, 131; CBD; CDBLB 1945-1960; CMW 4; CN 1, 2, 3, 4; DA; DA3; DAB; DAC; DAM MST, NOV; DLB 13, 15, 77, 100, 162, 201, 204; DLBY 1991; EWL 3; MSW; MTCW 1, 2; MTFW 2005; NFS 16; RGEL 2; SATA 20; SSFS 14; TEA; WLIT 4
Greene, Robert 1558-1592 .... **LC 41**
See also BRWS 8; DLB 62, 167; IDTP; RGEL 2; TEA
Greer, Germaine 1939- .... **CLC 131**
See also AITN 1; CA 81-84; CANR 33, 70, 115, 133; FW; MTCW 1, 2; MTFW 2005
Greer, Richard
See Silverberg, Robert
Gregor, Arthur 1923- .... **CLC 9**
See also CA 25-28R; CAAS 10; CANR 11; CP 1, 2, 3, 4, 5, 6, 7; SATA 36
Gregor, Lee
See Pohl, Frederik
Gregory, Lady Isabella Augusta (Persse)
1852-1932 .... **TCLC 1, 176**
See also BRW 6; CA 104; 184; DLB 10; IDTP; RGEL 2
Gregory, J. Dennis
See Williams, John A(lfred)
Gregory of Nazianzus, St.
329-389 .... **CMLC 82**
Gregory of Rimini 1300(?)-1358 . **CMLC 109**
See also DLB 115
Grekova, I.
See Ventsel, Elena Sergeevna
Grekova, Irina
See Ventsel, Elena Sergeevna
Grendon, Stephen
See Derleth, August (William)
Grenville, Kate 1950- .... **CLC 61**
See also CA 118; CANR 53, 93, 156; CN 7; DLB 325
Grenville, Pelham
See Wodehouse, P(elham) G(renville)
Greve, Felix Paul (Berthold Friedrich)
1879-1948 .... **TCLC 4**
See also CA 104; 141, 175; CANR 79; DAC; DAM MST; DLB 92; RGEL 2; TCWW 1, 2
Greville, Fulke 1554-1628 .... **LC 79**
See also BRWS 11; DLB 62, 172; RGEL 2
Grey, Lady Jane 1537-1554 .... **LC 93**
See also DLB 132
Grey, Zane 1872-1939 .... **TCLC 6**
See also BPFB 2; CA 104; 132; DA3; DAM POP; DLB 9, 212; MTCW 1, 2; MTFW 2005; RGAL 4; TCWW 1, 2; TUS
Griboedov, Aleksandr Sergeevich
1795(?)-1829 .... **NCLC 129**
See also DLB 205; RGWL 2, 3
Grieg, (Johan) Nordahl (Brun)
1902-1943 .... **TCLC 10**
See also CA 107; 189; EWL 3
Grieve, C(hristopher) M(urray)
1892-1978 ... **CLC 2, 4, 11, 19, 63; PC 9**
See also BRWS 12; CA 5-8R; 85-88; CANR 33, 107; CDBLB 1945-1960; CP 1, 2; DAM POET; DLB 20; EWL 3; MTCW 1; RGEL 2

Gustafson, Ralph (Barker)
1909-1995 .... **CLC 36**
See also CA 21-24R; CANR 8, 45, 84; CP
1, 2, 3, 4, 5, 6; DLB 88; RGEL 2

Gut, Gom
See Simenon, Georges (Jacques Christian)

Guterson, David 1956- .... **CLC 91**
See also CA 132; CANR 73, 126; CN 7;
DLB 292; MTCW 2; MTFW 2005; NFS
13

Guthrie, A(lfred) B(ertram), Jr.
1901-1991 .... **CLC 23**
See also CA 57-60; 134; CANR 24; CN 1,
2, 3; DLB 6, 212; MAL 5; SATA 62;
SATA-Obit 67; TCWW 1, 2

Guthrie, Isobel
See Grieve, C(hristopher) M(urray)

Gutierrez Najera, Manuel
1859-1895 .... **HLCS 2; NCLC 133**
See also DLB 290; LAW

Guy, Rosa (Cuthbert) 1925- .... **CLC 26**
See also AAYA 4, 37; BW 2; CA 17-20R;
CANR 14, 34, 83; CLR 13, 137; DLB 33;
DNFS 1; JRDA; MAICYA 1, 2; SATA 14,
62, 122; YAW

Gwendolyn
See Bennett, (Enoch) Arnold

H. D.
See Doolittle, Hilda

H. de V.
See Buchan, John

Haavikko, Paavo Juhani 1931- .. **CLC 18, 34**
See also CA 106; CWW 2; EWL 3

Habbema, Koos
See Heijermans, Herman

Habermas, Juergen 1929- .... **CLC 104**
See also CA 109; CANR 85, 162; DLB 242

Habermas, Jurgen
See Habermas, Juergen

Hacker, Marilyn 1942- ...... **CLC 5, 9, 23, 72,**
91; PC 47
See also CA 77-80; CANR 68, 129; CP 3,
4, 5, 6, 7; CWP; DAM POET; DLB 120,
282; FW; GLL 2; MAL 5; PFS 19

Hadewijch of Antwerp fl. 1250- ... **CMLC 61**
See also RGWL 3

Hadrian 76-138 .... **CMLC 52**

Haeckel, Ernst Heinrich (Philipp August)
1834-1919 .... **TCLC 83**
See also CA 157

Hafiz c. 1326-1389(?) .... **CMLC 34**
See also RGWL 2, 3; WLIT 6

Hagedorn, Jessica T(arahata)
1949- .... **CLC 185**
See also CA 139; CANR 69; CWP; DLB
312; RGAL 4

Haggard, H(enry) Rider
1856-1925 .... **TCLC 11**
See also BRWS 3; BYA 4, 5; CA 108; 148;
CANR 112; DLB 70, 156, 174, 178;
FANT; LMFS 1; MTCW 2; RGEL 2;
RHW; SATA 16; SCFW 1, 2; SFW 4;
SUFW 1; WLIT 4

Hagiosy, L.
See Larbaud, Valery (Nicolas)

Hagiwara, Sakutaro 1886-1942 .... **PC 18;**
TCLC 60
See also CA 154; EWL 3; RGWL 3

Hagiwara Sakutaro
See Hagiwara, Sakutaro

Haig, Fenil
See Ford, Ford Madox

Haig-Brown, Roderick (Langmere)
1908-1976 .... **CLC 21**
See also CA 5-8R; 69-72; CANR 4, 38, 83;
CLR 31; CWRI 5; DLB 88; MAICYA 1,
2; SATA 12; TCWW 2

Haight, Rip
See Carpenter, John (Howard)

Haij, Vera
See Jansson, Tove (Marika)

Hailey, Arthur 1920-2004 .... **CLC 5**
See also AITN 2; BEST 90:3; BPFB 2; CA
1-4R; 233; CANR 2, 36, 75; CCA 1; CN
1, 2, 3, 4, 5, 6, 7; CPW; DAM NOV, POP;
DLB 88; DLBY 1982; MTCW 1, 2;
MTFW 2005

Hailey, Elizabeth Forsythe 1938- ..... **CLC 40**
See also CA 93-96, 188; CAAE 188; CAAS
1; CANR 15, 48; INT CANR-15

Haines, John (Meade) 1924- .... **CLC 58**
See also AMWS 12; CA 17-20R; CANR
13, 34; CP 1, 2, 3, 4, 5; CSW; DLB 5,
212; TCLE 1:1

Ha Jin
See Jin, Xuefei

Hakluyt, Richard 1552-1616 .... **LC 31**
See also DLB 136; RGEL 2

Haldeman, Joe 1943- .... **CLC 61**
See also AAYA 38; CA 53-56, 179; CAAE
179; CAAS 25; CANR 6, 70, 72, 130,
171; DLB 8; INT CANR-6; SCFW 2;
SFW 4

Haldeman, Joe William
See Haldeman, Joe

Hale, Janet Campbell 1947- .... **NNAL**
See also CA 49-52; CANR 45, 75; DAM
MULT; DLB 175; MTCW 2; MTFW 2005

Hale, Sarah Josepha (Buell)
1788-1879 .... **NCLC 75**
See also DLB 1, 42, 73, 243

Halevy, Elie 1870-1937 .... **TCLC 104**

Haley, Alex(ander Murray Palmer)
1921-1992 ...... **BLC 1:2; CLC 8, 12, 76;**
TCLC 147
See also AAYA 26; BPFB 2; BW 2, 3; CA
77-80; 136; CANR 61; CDALBS; CPW;
CSW; DA; DA3; DAB; DAC; DAM MST,
MULT, POP; DLB 38; LAIT 5; MTCW
1, 2; NFS 9

Haliburton, Thomas Chandler
1796-1865 .... **NCLC 15, 149**
See also DLB 11, 99; RGEL 2; RGSF 2

Hall, Donald 1928- ... **CLC 1, 13, 37, 59, 151,**
240; PC 70
See also AAYA 63; CA 5-8R; CAAS 7;
CANR 2, 44, 64, 106, 133; CP 1, 2, 3, 4,
5, 6, 7; DAM POET; DLB 5, 342; MAL
5; MTCW 2; MTFW 2005; RGAL 4;
SATA 23, 97

Hall, Donald Andrew, Jr.
See Hall, Donald

Hall, Frederic Sauser
See Sauser-Hall, Frederic

Hall, James
See Kuttner, Henry

Hall, James Norman 1887-1951 ..... **TCLC 23**
See also CA 123; 173; LAIT 1; RHW 1;
SATA 21

Hall, Joseph 1574-1656 .... **LC 91**
See also DLB 121, 151; RGEL 2

Hall, Marguerite Radclyffe
See Hall, Radclyffe

Hall, Radclyffe 1880-1943 ...... **TCLC 12, 215**
See also BRWS 6; CA 110; 150; CANR 83;
DLB 191; MTCW 2; MTFW 2005; RGEL
2; RHW

Hall, Rodney 1935- .... **CLC 51**
See also CA 109; CANR 69; CN 6, 7; CP
1, 2, 3, 4, 5, 6, 7; DLB 289

Hallam, Arthur Henry
1811-1833 .... **NCLC 110**
See also DLB 32

Halldor Laxness
See Gudjonsson, Halldor Kiljan

Halleck, Fitz-Greene 1790-1867 .... **NCLC 47**
See also DLB 3, 250; RGAL 4

Halliday, Michael
See Creasey, John

Halpern, Daniel 1945- .... **CLC 14**
See also CA 33-36R; CANR 93, 174; CP 3,
4, 5, 6, 7

Hamburger, Michael 1924-2007 ... **CLC 5, 14**
See also CA 5-8R, 196; 261; CAAE 196;
CAAS 4; CANR 2, 47; CP 1, 2, 3, 4, 5, 6,
7; DLB 27

Hamburger, Michael Peter Leopold
See Hamburger, Michael

Hamill, Pete 1935- .... **CLC 10, 261**
See also CA 25-28R; CANR 18, 71, 127,
180

Hamill, William Peter
See Hamill, Pete

Hamilton, Alexander 1712-1756 .... **LC 150**
See also DLB 31

Hamilton, Alexander
1755(?)-1804 .... **NCLC 49**
See also DLB 37

Hamilton, Clive
See Lewis, C.S.

Hamilton, Edmond 1904-1977 .... **CLC 1**
See also CA 1-4R; CANR 3, 84; DLB 8;
SATA 118; SFW 4

Hamilton, Elizabeth 1758-1816 ... **NCLC 153**
See also DLB 116, 158

Hamilton, Eugene (Jacob) Lee
See Lee-Hamilton, Eugene (Jacob)

Hamilton, Franklin
See Silverberg, Robert

Hamilton, Gail
See Corcoran, Barbara (Asenath)

Hamilton, (Robert) Ian 1938-2001 . **CLC 191**
See also CA 106; 203; CANR 41, 67; CP 1,
2, 3, 4, 5, 6, 7; DLB 40, 155

Hamilton, Jane 1957- .... **CLC 179**
See also CA 147; CANR 85, 128; CN 7;
MTFW 2005

Hamilton, Mollie
See Kaye, M.M.

Hamilton, (Anthony Walter) Patrick
1904-1962 .... **CLC 51**
See also CA 176; 113; DLB 10, 191

Hamilton, Virginia 1936-2002 .... **CLC 26**
See also AAYA 2, 21; BW 2, 3; BYA 1, 2,
8; CA 25-28R; 206; CANR 20, 37, 73,
126; CLR 1, 11, 40, 127; DAM MULT;
DLB 33, 52; DLBY 2001; INT CANR-
20; JRDA; LAIT 5; MAICYA 1, 2; MAI-
CYAS 1; MTCW 1, 2; MTFW 2005;
SATA 4, 56, 79, 123; SATA-Obit 132;
WYA; YAW

Hammett, (Samuel) Dashiell
1894-1961 .... **CLC 3, 5, 10, 19, 47; SSC**
17; TCLC 187
See also AAYA 59; AITN 1; AMWS 4;
BPFB 2; CA 81-84; CANR 42; CDALB
1929-1941; CMW 4; DA3; DLB 226, 280;
DLBD 6; DLBY 1996; EWL 3; LAIT 3;
MAL 5; MSW; MTCW 1, 2; MTFW
2005; NFS 21; RGAL 4; RGSF 2; TUS

Hammon, Jupiter 1720(?)-1800(?) . **BLC 1:2;**
NCLC 5; PC 16
See also DAM MULT, POET; DLB 31, 50

Hammond, Keith
See Kuttner, Henry

Hamner, Earl (Henry), Jr. 1923- ...... **CLC 12**
See also AITN 2; CA 73-76; DLB 6

Hampton, Christopher 1946- .... **CLC 4**
See also CA 25-28R; CD 5, 6; DLB 13;
MTCW 1

Hampton, Christopher James
See Hampton, Christopher

Hamsun, Knut
See Pedersen, Knut

Hamsund, Knut Pedersen
See Pedersen, Knut

Author Index

Handke, Peter 1942- .... **CLC 5, 8, 10, 15, 38, 134; DC 17**
See also CA 77-80; CANR 33, 75, 104, 133, 180; CWW 2; DAM DRAM, NOV; DLB 85, 124; EWL 3; MTCW 1, 2; MTFW 2005; TWA

Handler, Chelsea 1976(?)- .... **CLC 269**
See also CA 243

Handy, W(illiam) C(hristopher) 1873-1958 .... **TCLC 97**
See also BW 3; CA 121; 167

Hanley, James 1901-1985 ..... **CLC 3, 5, 8, 13**
See also CA 73-76; 117; CANR 36; CBD; CN 1, 2, 3; DLB 191; EWL 3; MTCW 1; RGEL 2

Hannah, Barry 1942- .. **CLC 23, 38, 90, 270; SSC 94**
See also BPFB 2; CA 108; 110; CANR 43, 68, 113; CN 4, 5, 6, 7; CSW; DLB 6, 234; INT CA-110; MTCW 1; RGSF 2

Hannon, Ezra
See Hunter, Evan

Hanrahan, Barbara 1939-1991 .... **TCLC 219**
See also CA 121; 127; CN 4, 5; DLB 289

Hansberry, Lorraine (Vivian) 1930-1965 ... **BLC 1:2, 2:2; CLC 17, 62; DC 2; TCLC 192**
See also AAYA 25; AFAW 1, 2; AMWS 4; BW 1, 3; CA 109; 25-28R; CABS 3; CAD; CANR 58; CDALB 1941-1968; CWD; DA; DA3; DAB; DAC; DAM DRAM, MST, MULT; DFS 2; DLB 7, 38; EWL 3; FL 1:6; FW; LAIT 4; MAL 5; MTCW 1, 2; MTFW 2005; RGAL 4; TUS

Hansen, Joseph 1923-2004 .... **CLC 38**
See also BPFB 2; CA 29-32R; 233; CAAS 17; CANR 16, 44, 66, 125; CMW 4; DLB 226; GLL 1; INT CANR-16

Hansen, Karen V. 1955- .... **CLC 65**
See also CA 149; CANR 102

Hansen, Martin A(lfred) 1909-1955 .... **TCLC 32**
See also CA 167; DLB 214; EWL 3

Hanson, Kenneth O(stlin) 1922- .... **CLC 13**
See also CA 53-56; CANR 7; CP 1, 2, 3, 4, 5

Hardwick, Elizabeth 1916-2007 .... **CLC 13**
See also AMWS 3; CA 5-8R; 267; CANR 3, 32, 70, 100, 139; CN 4, 5, 6; CSW; DA3; DAM NOV; DLB 6; MBL; MTCW 1, 2; MTFW 2005; TCLE 1:1

Hardwick, Elizabeth Bruce
See Hardwick, Elizabeth

Hardwick, Elizabeth Bruce
See Hardwick, Elizabeth

Hardy, Thomas 1840-1928 . **PC 8, 92; SSC 2, 60, 113; TCLC 4, 10, 18, 32, 48, 53, 72, 143, 153; WLC 3**
See also AAYA 69; BRW 6; BRWC 1, 2; BRWR 1; CA 104; 123; CDBLB 1890-1914; DA; DA3; DAB; DAC; DAM MST, NOV, POET; DLB 18, 19, 135, 284; EWL 3; EXPN; EXPP; LAIT 2; MTCW 1, 2; MTFW 2005; NFS 3, 11, 15, 19; PFS 3, 4, 18; RGEL 2; RGSF 2; TEA; WLIT 4

Hare, David 1947- . **CLC 29, 58, 136; DC 26**
See also BRWS 4; CA 97-100; CANR 39, 91; CBD; CD 5, 6; DFS 4, 7, 16; DLB 13, 310; MTCW 1; TEA

Harewood, John
See Van Druten, John (William)

Harford, Henry
See Hudson, W(illiam) H(enry)

Hargrave, Leonie
See Disch, Thomas M.

Hariri, Al- al-Qasim ibn 'Ali Abu Muhammad al-Basri
See al-Hariri, al-Qasim ibn 'Ali Abu Muhammad al-Basri

Harjo, Joy 1951- ..... **CLC 83; NNAL; PC 27**
See also AMWS 12; CA 114; CANR 35, 67, 91, 129; CP 6, 7; CWP; DAM MULT; DLB 120, 175, 342; EWL 3; MTCW 2; MTFW 2005; PFS 15; RGAL 4

Harlan, Louis R(udolph) 1922- .... **CLC 34**
See also CA 21-24R; CANR 25, 55, 80

Harling, Robert 1951(?)- .... **CLC 53**
See also CA 147

Harmon, William (Ruth) 1938- .... **CLC 38**
See also CA 33-36R; CANR 14, 32, 35; SATA 65

Harper, F. E. W.
See Harper, Frances Ellen Watkins

Harper, Frances E. W.
See Harper, Frances Ellen Watkins

Harper, Frances E. Watkins
See Harper, Frances Ellen Watkins

Harper, Frances Ellen
See Harper, Frances Ellen Watkins

Harper, Frances Ellen Watkins 1825-1911 . **BLC 1:2; PC 21; TCLC 14, 217**
See also AFAW 1, 2; BW 1, 3; CA 111; 125; CANR 79; DAM MULT, POET; DLB 50, 221; MBL; RGAL 4

Harper, Michael S(teven) 1938- ..... **BLC 2:2; CLC 7, 22**
See also AFAW 2; BW 1; CA 33-36R; 224; CAAE 224; CANR 24, 108; CP 2, 3, 4, 5, 6, 7; DLB 41; RGAL 4; TCLE 1:1

Harper, Mrs. F. E. W.
See Harper, Frances Ellen Watkins

Harpur, Charles 1813-1868 .... **NCLC 114**
See also DLB 230; RGEL 2

Harris, Christie
See Harris, Christie (Lucy) Irwin

Harris, Christie (Lucy) Irwin 1907-2002 .... **CLC 12**
See also CA 5-8R; CANR 6, 83; CLR 47; DLB 88; JRDA; MAICYA 1, 2; SAAS 10; SATA 6, 74; SATA-Essay 116

Harris, Frank 1856-1931 .... **TCLC 24**
See also CA 109; 150; CANR 80; DLB 156, 197; RGEL 2

Harris, George Washington 1814-1869 .... **NCLC 23, 165**
See also DLB 3, 11, 248; RGAL 4

Harris, Joel Chandler 1848-1908 ..... **SSC 19, 103; TCLC 2**
See also CA 104; 137; CANR 80; CLR 49, 128; DLB 11, 23, 42, 78, 91; LAIT 2; MAICYA 1, 2; RGSF 2; SATA 100; WCH; YABC 1

Harris, John (Wyndham Parkes Lucas) Beynon 1903-1969 .... **CLC 19**
See also BRWS 13; CA 102; 89-92; CANR 84; DLB 255; SATA 118; SCFW 1, 2; SFW 4

Harris, MacDonald
See Heiney, Donald (William)

Harris, Mark 1922-2007 .... **CLC 19**
See also CA 5-8R; 260; CAAS 3; CANR 2, 55, 83; CN 1, 2, 3, 4, 5, 6, 7; DLB 2; DLBY 1980

Harris, Norman **CLC 65**

Harris, (Theodore) Wilson 1921- ... **BLC 2:2; CLC 25, 159**
See also BRWS 5; BW 2, 3; CA 65-68; CAAS 16; CANR 11, 27, 69, 114; CDWLB 3; CN 1, 2, 3, 4, 5, 6, 7; CP 1, 2, 3, 4, 5, 6, 7; DLB 117; EWL 3; MTCW 1; RGEL 2

Harrison, Barbara Grizzuti 1934-2002 .... **CLC 144**
See also CA 77-80; 205; CANR 15, 48; INT CANR-15

Harrison, Elizabeth (Allen) Cavanna 1909-2001 .... **CLC 12**
See also CA 9-12R; 200; CANR 6, 27, 85, 104, 121; JRDA; MAICYA 1; SAAS 4; SATA 1, 30; YAW

Harrison, Harry 1925- .... **CLC 42**
See also CA 1-4R; CANR 5, 21, 84; DLB 8; SATA 4; SCFW 4; SFW 4

Harrison, Harry Max
See Harrison, Harry

Harrison, James
See Harrison, Jim

Harrison, James Thomas
See Harrison, Jim

Harrison, Jim 1937- .... **CLC 6, 14, 33, 66, 143; SSC 19**
See also AMWS 8; CA 13-16R; CANR 8, 51, 79, 142; CN 5, 6; CP 1, 2, 3, 4, 5, 6; DLBY 1982; INT CANR-8; RGAL 4; TCWW 2; TUS

Harrison, Kathryn 1961- .... **CLC 70, 151**
See also CA 144; CANR 68, 122

Harrison, Tony 1937- .... **CLC 43, 129**
See also BRWS 5; CA 65-68; CANR 44, 98; CBD; CD 5, 6; CP 2, 3, 4, 5, 6, 7; DLB 40, 245; MTCW 1; RGEL 2

Harriss, Will(ard Irvin) 1922- .... **CLC 34**
See also CA 111

Hart, Ellis
See Ellison, Harlan

Hart, Josephine 1942(?)- .... **CLC 70**
See also CA 138; CANR 70, 149; CPW; DAM POP

Hart, Moss 1904-1961 .... **CLC 66**
See also CA 109; 89-92; CANR 84; DAM DRAM; DFS 1; DLB 7, 266; RGAL 4

Harte, (Francis) Bret(t) 1836(?)-1902 ... **SSC 8, 59; TCLC 1, 25; WLC 3**
See also AMWS 2; CA 104; 140; CANR 80; CDALB 1865-1917; DA; DA3; DAC; DAM MST; DLB 12, 64, 74, 79, 186; EXPS; LAIT 2; RGAL 4; RGSF 2; SATA 26; SSFS 3; TUS

Hartley, L(eslie) P(oles) 1895-1972 ... **CLC 2, 22**
See also BRWS 7; CA 45-48; 37-40R; CANR 33; CN 1; DLB 15, 139; EWL 3; HGG; MTCW 1, 2; MTFW 2005; RGEL 2; RGSF 2; SUFW 1

Hartman, Geoffrey H. 1929- .... **CLC 27**
See also CA 117; 125; CANR 79; DLB 67

Hartmann, Sadakichi 1869-1944 ...... **TCLC 73**
See also CA 157; DLB 54

Hartmann von Aue c. 1170-c. 1210 .... **CMLC 15**
See also CDWLB 2; DLB 138; RGWL 2, 3

Hartog, Jan de
See de Hartog, Jan

Haruf, Kent 1943- .... **CLC 34**
See also AAYA 44; CA 149; CANR 91, 131

Harvey, Caroline
See Trollope, Joanna

Harvey, Gabriel 1550(?)-1631 .... **LC 88**
See also DLB 167, 213, 281

Harvey, Jack
See Rankin, Ian

Harwood, Ronald 1934- .... **CLC 32**
See also CA 1-4R; CANR 4, 55, 150; CBD; CD 5, 6; DAM DRAM, MST; DLB 13

Hasegawa Tatsunosuke
See Futabatei, Shimei

Hasek, Jaroslav (Matej Frantisek) 1883-1923 .... **SSC 69; TCLC 4**
See also CA 104; 129; CDWLB 4; DLB 215; EW 9; EWL 3; MTCW 1, 2; RGSF 2; RGWL 2, 3

NOV, POP; DLB 2, 28, 227; DLBY 1980, 2002; EWL 3; EXPN; INT CANR-8; LAIT 4; MAL 5; MTCW 1, 2; MTFW 2005; NFS 1; RGAL 4; TUS; YAW

Hellman, Lillian 1905-1984 .. **CLC 2, 4, 8, 14, 18, 34, 44, 52; DC 1; TCLC 119**
See also AAYA 47; AITN 1, 2; AMWS 1; CA 13-16R; 112; CAD; CANR 33; CWD; DA3; DAM DRAM; DFS 1, 3, 14; DLB 7, 228; DLBY 1984; EWL 3; FL 1:6; FW; LAIT 3; MAL 5; MBL; MTCW 1, 2; MTFW 2005; RGAL 4; TUS

Helprin, Mark 1947- .... **CLC 7, 10, 22, 32**
See also CA 81-84; CANR 47, 64, 124; CDALBS; CN 7; CPW; DA3; DAM NOV, POP; DLB 335; DLBY 1985; FANT; MAL 5; MTCW 1, 2; MTFW 2005; SSFS 25; SUFW 2

Helvetius, Claude-Adrien 1715-1771 .. **LC 26**
See also DLB 313

Helyar, Jane Penelope Josephine
1933- .... **CLC 17**
See also CA 21-24R; CANR 10, 26; CWRI 5; SAAS 2; SATA 5; SATA-Essay 138

Hemans, Felicia 1793-1835 ...... **NCLC 29, 71**
See also DLB 96; RGEL 2

Hemingway, Ernest (Miller)
1899-1961 .... **CLC 1, 3, 6, 8, 10, 13, 19, 30, 34, 39, 41, 44, 50, 61, 80; SSC 1, 25, 36, 40, 63, 117; TCLC 115, 203; WLC 3**
See also AAYA 19; AMW; AMWC 1; AMWR 1; BPFB 2; BYA 2, 3, 13, 15; CA 77-80; CANR 34; CDALB 1917-1929; DA; DA3; DAB; DAC; DAM MST, NOV; DLB 4, 9, 102, 210, 308, 316, 330; DLBD 1, 15, 16; DLBY 1981, 1987, 1996, 1998; EWL 3; EXPN; EXPS; LAIT 3, 4; LATS 1:1; MAL 5; MTCW 1, 2; MTFW 2005; NFS 1, 5, 6, 14; RGAL 4; RGSF 2; SSFS 17; TUS; WYA

Hempel, Amy 1951- .... **CLC 39**
See also CA 118; 137; CANR 70, 166; DA3; DLB 218; EXPS; MTCW 2; MTFW 2005; SSFS 2

Henderson, F. C.
See Mencken, H(enry) L(ouis)

Henderson, Mary
See Mavor, Osborne Henry

Henderson, Sylvia
See Ashton-Warner, Sylvia (Constance)

Henderson, Zenna (Chlarson)
1917-1983 .... **SSC 29**
See also CA 1-4R; 133; CANR 1, 84; DLB 8; SATA 5; SFW 4

Henkin, Joshua 1964- .... **CLC 119**
See also CA 161; CANR 186

Henley, Beth **CLC 23, 255; DC 6, 14**
See Henley, Elizabeth Becker
See also CABS 3; CAD; CD 5, 6; CSW; CWD; DFS 2, 21, 26; DLBY 1986; FW

Henley, Elizabeth Becker 1952- ...... **CLC 23, 255; DC 6, 14**
See Henley, Beth
See also AAYA 70; CA 107; CABS 3; CAD; CANR 32, 73, 140; CD 5, 6; CSW; DA3; DAM DRAM, MST; DFS 2, 21; DLBY 1986; FW; MTCW 1, 2; MTFW 2005

Henley, William Ernest 1849-1903 .. **TCLC 8**
See also CA 105; 234; DLB 19; RGEL 2

Hennissart, Martha 1929- .... **CLC 2**
See also BPFB 2; CA 85-88; CANR 64; CMW 4; DLB 306

Henry VIII 1491-1547 .... **LC 10**
See also DLB 132

Henry, O. 1862-1910 . **SSC 5, 49, 117; TCLC 1, 19; WLC 3**
See also AAYA 41; AMWS 2; CA 104; 131; CDALB 1865-1917; DA; DA3; DAB; DAC; DAM MST; DLB 12, 78, 79; EXPS;

MAL 5; MTCW 1, 2; MTFW 2005; RGAL 4; RGSF 2; SSFS 2, 18, 27; TCWW 1, 2; TUS; YABC 2

Henry, Oliver
See Henry, O.

Henry, Patrick 1736-1799 .... **LC 25**
See also LAIT 1

Henryson, Robert 1430(?)-1506(?) ..... **LC 20, 110; PC 65**
See also BRWS 7; DLB 146; RGEL 2

Henschke, Alfred
See Klabund

Henson, Lance 1944- .... **NNAL**
See also CA 146; DLB 175

Hentoff, Nat(han Irving) 1925- .... **CLC 26**
See also AAYA 4, 42; BYA 6; CA 1-4R; CAAS 6; CANR 5, 25, 77, 114; CLR 1, 52; DLB 345; INT CANR-25; JRDA; MAICYA 1, 2; SATA 42, 69, 133; SATA-Brief 27; WYA; YAW

Heppenstall, (John) Rayner
1911-1981 .... **CLC 10**
See also CA 1-4R; 103; CANR 29; CN 1, 2; CP 1, 2, 3; EWL 3

Heraclitus c. 540B.C.-c. 450B.C. ... **CMLC 22**
See also DLB 176

Herbert, Frank 1920-1986 ... **CLC 12, 23, 35, 44, 85**
See also AAYA 21; BPFB 2; BYA 4, 14; CA 53-56; 118; CANR 5, 43; CDALBS; CPW; DAM POP; DLB 8; INT CANR-5; LAIT 5; MTCW 1, 2; MTFW 2005; NFS 17; SATA 9, 37; SATA-Obit 47; SCFW 1, 2; SFW 4; YAW

Herbert, George 1593-1633 . **LC 24, 121; PC 4**
See also BRW 2; BRWR 2; CDBLB Before 1660; DAB; DAM POET; DLB 126; EXPP; PFS 25; RGEL 2; TEA; WP

Herbert, Zbigniew 1924-1998 ..... **CLC 9, 43; PC 50; TCLC 168**
See also CA 89-92; 169; CANR 36, 74, 177; CDWLB 4; CWW 2; DAM POET; DLB 232; EWL 3; MTCW 1; PFS 22

Herbst, Josephine (Frey)
1897-1969 .... **CLC 34**
See also CA 5-8R; 25-28R; DLB 9

Herder, Johann Gottfried von
1744-1803 .... **NCLC 8, 186**
See also DLB 97; EW 4; TWA

Heredia, Jose Maria 1803-1839 ...... **HLCS 2; NCLC 209**
See also LAW

Hergesheimer, Joseph 1880-1954 ... **TCLC 11**
See also CA 109; 194; DLB 102, 9; RGAL 4

Herlihy, James Leo 1927-1993 .... **CLC 6**
See also CA 1-4R; 143; CAD; CANR 2; CN 1, 2, 3, 4, 5

Herman, William
See Bierce, Ambrose (Gwinett)

Hermogenes fl. c. 175- .... **CMLC 6**

Hernandez, Jose 1834-1886 .... **NCLC 17**
See also LAW; RGWL 2, 3; WLIT 1

Herodotus c. 484B.C.-c. 420B.C. .. **CMLC 17**
See also AW 1; CDWLB 1; DLB 176; RGWL 2, 3; TWA; WLIT 8

Herr, Michael 1940(?)- .... **CLC 231**
See also CA 89-92; CANR 68, 142; DLB 185; MTCW 1

Herrick, Robert 1591-1674 .. **LC 13, 145; PC 9**
See also BRW 2; BRWC 2; DA; DAB; DAC; DAM MST, POP; DLB 126; EXPP; PFS 13, 29; RGAL 4; RGEL 2; TEA; WP

Herring, Guilles
See Somerville, Edith Oenone

Herriot, James 1916-1995
See Wight, James Alfred

Herris, Violet
See Hunt, Violet

Herrmann, Dorothy 1941- .... **CLC 44**
See also CA 107

Herrmann, Taffy
See Herrmann, Dorothy

Hersey, John 1914-1993 .. **CLC 1, 2, 7, 9, 40, 81, 97**
See also AAYA 29; BPFB 2; CA 17-20R; 140; CANR 33; CDALBS; CN 1, 2, 3, 4, 5; CPW; DAM POP; DLB 6, 185, 278, 299; MAL 5; MTCW 1, 2; MTFW 2005; RGHL; SATA 25; SATA-Obit 76; TUS

Hervent, Maurice
See Grindel, Eugene

Herzen, Aleksandr Ivanovich
1812-1870 .... **NCLC 10, 61**
See also DLB 277

Herzen, Alexander
See Herzen, Aleksandr Ivanovich

Herzl, Theodor 1860-1904 .... **TCLC 36**
See also CA 168

Herzog, Werner 1942- .... **CLC 16, 236**
See also CA 89-92

Hesiod fl. 8th cent. B.C.- .... **CMLC 5, 102**
See also AW 1; DLB 176; RGWL 2, 3; WLIT 8

Hesse, Hermann 1877-1962 ... **CLC 1, 2, 3, 6, 11, 17, 25, 69; SSC 9, 49; TCLC 148, 196; WLC 3**
See also AAYA 43; BPFB 2; CA 17-18; CAP 2; CDWLB 2; DA; DA3; DAB; DAC; DAM MST, NOV; DLB 66, 330; EW 9; EWL 3; EXPN; LAIT 1; MTCW 1, 2; MTFW 2005; NFS 6, 15, 24; RGWL 2, 3; SATA 50; TWA

Hewes, Cady
See De Voto, Bernard (Augustine)

Heyen, William 1940- .... **CLC 13, 18**
See also CA 33-36R; 220; CAAE 220; CAAS 9; CANR 98, 188; CP 3, 4, 5, 6, 7; DLB 5; RGHL

Heyerdahl, Thor 1914-2002 .... **CLC 26**
See also CA 5-8R; 207; CANR 5, 22, 66, 73; LAIT 4; MTCW 1, 2; MTFW 2005; SATA 2, 52

Heym, Georg (Theodor Franz Arthur)
1887-1912 .... **TCLC 9**
See also CA 106; 181

Heym, Stefan 1913-2001 .... **CLC 41**
See also CA 9-12R; 203; CANR 4; CWW 2; DLB 69; EWL 3

Heyse, Paul (Johann Ludwig von)
1830-1914 .... **TCLC 8**
See also CA 104; 209; DLB 129, 330

Heyward, (Edwin) DuBose
1885-1940 .... **HR 1:2; TCLC 59**
See also CA 108; 157; DLB 7, 9, 45, 249; MAL 5; SATA 21

Heywood, John 1497(?)-1580(?) .... **LC 65**
See also DLB 136; RGEL 2

Heywood, Thomas 1573(?)-1641 . **DC 29; LC 111**
See also DAM DRAM; DLB 62; LMFS 1; RGEL 2; TEA

Hiaasen, Carl 1953- .... **CLC 238**
See also CA 105; CANR 22, 45, 65, 113, 133, 168; CMW 4; CPW; CSW; DA3; DLB 292; MTCW 2; MTFW 2005

Hibbert, Eleanor Alice Burford
1906-1993 .... **CLC 7**
See also BEST 90:4; BPFB 2; CA 17-20R; 140; CANR 9, 28, 59; CMW 4; CPW; DAM POP; MTCW 2; MTFW 2005; RHW; SATA 2; SATA-Obit 74

Hichens, Robert (Smythe)
1864-1950 .... **TCLC 64**
See also CA 162; DLB 153; HGG; RHW; SUFW

Hogarth, Charles
　See Creasey, John
Hogarth, Emmett
　See Polonsky, Abraham (Lincoln)
Hogarth, William 1697-1764 .... **LC 112**
　See also AAYA 56
Hogg, James 1770-1835 .... **NCLC 4, 109**
　See also BRWS 10; DLB 93, 116, 159; GL
　2; HGG; RGEL 2; SUFW 1
Holbach, Paul-Henri Thiry
　1723-1789 .... **LC 14**
　See also DLB 313
Holberg, Ludvig 1684-1754 .... **LC 6**
　See also DLB 300; RGWL 2, 3
Holbrook, John
　See Vance, Jack
Holcroft, Thomas 1745-1809 .... **NCLC 85**
　See also DLB 39, 89, 158; RGEL 2
Holden, Ursula 1921- .... **CLC 18**
　See also CA 101; CAAS 8; CANR 22
Holderlin, (Johann Christian) Friedrich
　1770-1843 .... **NCLC 16, 187; PC 4**
　See also CDWLB 2; DLB 90; EW 5; RGWL
　2, 3
Holdstock, Robert 1948- .... **CLC 39**
　See also CA 131; CANR 81; DLB 261;
　FANT; HGG; SFW 4; SUFW 2
Holdstock, Robert P.
　See Holdstock, Robert
Holinshed, Raphael fl. 1580- .... **LC 69**
　See also DLB 167; RGEL 2
Holland, Isabelle (Christian)
　1920-2002 .... **CLC 21**
　See also AAYA 11, 64; CA 21-24R; 205;
　CAAE 181; CANR 10, 25, 47; CLR 57;
　CWRI 5; JRDA; LAIT 4; MAICYA 1, 2;
　SATA 8, 70; SATA-Essay 103; SATA-Obit
　132; WYA
Holland, Marcus
　See Caldwell, (Janet Miriam) Taylor
　(Holland)
Hollander, John 1929- .... **CLC 2, 5, 8, 14**
　See also CA 1-4R; CANR 1, 52, 136; CP 1,
　2, 3, 4, 5, 6, 7; DLB 5; MAL 5; SATA 13
Hollander, Paul
　See Silverberg, Robert
Holleran, Andrew
　See Garber, Eric
Holley, Marietta 1836(?)-1926 .... **TCLC 99**
　See also CA 118; DLB 11; FL 1:3
Hollinghurst, Alan 1954- .... **CLC 55, 91**
　See also BRWS 10; CA 114; CN 5, 6, 7;
　DLB 207, 326; GLL 1
Hollis, Jim
　See Summers, Hollis (Spurgeon, Jr.)
Holly, Buddy 1936-1959 .... **TCLC 65**
　See also CA 213
Holmes, Gordon
　See Shiel, M(atthew) P(hipps)
Holmes, John
　See Souster, (Holmes) Raymond
Holmes, John Clellon 1926-1988 ...... **CLC 56**
　See also BG 1:2; CA 9-12R; 125; CANR 4;
　CN 1, 2, 3, 4; DLB 16, 237
Holmes, Oliver Wendell, Jr.
　1841-1935 .... **TCLC 77**
　See also CA 114; 186
Holmes, Oliver Wendell
　1809-1894 .... **NCLC 14, 81; PC 71**
　See also AMWS 1; CDALB 1640-1865;
　DLB 1, 189, 235; EXPP; PFS 24; RGAL
　4; SATA 34
Holmes, Raymond
　See Souster, (Holmes) Raymond
Holt, Samuel
　See Westlake, Donald E.
Holt, Victoria
　See Hibbert, Eleanor Alice Burford

Holub, Miroslav 1923-1998 .... **CLC 4**
　See also CA 21-24R; 169; CANR 10; CD-
　WLB 4; CWW 2; DLB 232; EWL 3;
　RGWL 3
Holz, Detlev
　See Benjamin, Walter
Homer c. 8th cent. B.C.- .... **CMLC 1, 16, 61;**
　PC 23; WLCS
　See also AW 1; CDWLB 1; DA; DA3;
　DAB; DAC; DAM MST, POET; DLB
　176; EFS 1; LAIT 1; LMFS 1; RGWL 2,
　3; TWA; WLIT 8; WP
Hong, Maxine Ting Ting
　See Kingston, Maxine Hong
Hongo, Garrett Kaoru 1951- .... **PC 23**
　See also CA 133; CAAS 22; CP 5, 6, 7;
　DLB 120, 312; EWL 3; EXPP; PFS 25;
　RGAL 4
Honig, Edwin 1919- .... **CLC 33**
　See also CA 5-8R; CAAS 8; CANR 4, 45,
　144; CP 1, 2, 3, 4, 5, 6, 7; DLB 5
Hood, Hugh (John Blagdon) 1928- . **CLC 15,**
　28, 273; SSC 42
　See also CA 49-52; CAAS 17; CANR 1,
　33, 87; CN 1, 2, 3, 4, 5, 6, 7; DLB 53;
　RGSF 2
Hood, Thomas 1799-1845 . **NCLC 16; PC 93**
　See also BRW 4; DLB 96; RGEL 2
Hooker, (Peter) Jeremy 1941- .... **CLC 43**
　See also CA 77-80; CANR 22; CP 2, 3, 4,
　5, 6, 7; DLB 40
Hooker, Richard 1554-1600 .... **LC 95**
　See also BRW 1; DLB 132; RGEL 2
Hooker, Thomas 1586-1647 .... **LC 137**
　See also DLB 24
hooks, bell 1952(?)- .... **BLCS; CLC 94**
　See also BW 2; CA 143; CANR 87, 126;
　DLB 246; MTCW 2; MTFW 2005; SATA
　115, 170
Hooper, Johnson Jones
　1815-1862 .... **NCLC 177**
　See also DLB 3, 11, 248; RGAL 4
Hope, A(lec) D(erwent) 1907-2000 .... **CLC 3,**
　51; PC 56
　See also BRWS 7; CA 21-24R; 188; CANR
　33, 74; CP 1, 2, 3, 4, 5; DLB 289; EWL
　3; MTCW 1, 2; MTFW 2005; PFS 8;
　RGEL 2
Hope, Anthony 1863-1933 .... **TCLC 83**
　See also CA 157; DLB 153, 156; RGEL 2;
　RHW
Hope, Brian
　See Creasey, John
Hope, Christopher 1944- .... **CLC 52**
　See also AFW; CA 106; CANR 47, 101,
　177; CN 4, 5, 6, 7; DLB 225; SATA 62
Hope, Christopher David Tully
　See Hope, Christopher
Hopkins, Gerard Manley
　1844-1889 .... **NCLC 17, 189; PC 15;**
　WLC 3
　See also BRW 5; BRWR 2; CDBLB 1890-
　1914; DA; DA3; DAB; DAC; DAM MST,
　POET; DLB 35, 57; EXPP; PAB; PFS 26;
　RGEL 2; TEA; WP
Hopkins, John (Richard) 1931-1998 .. **CLC 4**
　See also CA 85-88; 169; CBD; CD 5, 6
Hopkins, Pauline Elizabeth
　1859-1930 .... **BLC 1:2; TCLC 28**
　See also AFAW 2; BW 2, 3; CA 141; CANR
　82; DAM MULT; DLB 50
Hopkinson, Francis 1737-1791 .... **LC 25**
　See also DLB 31; RGAL 4
Hopley, George
　See Hopley-Woolrich, Cornell George
Hopley-Woolrich, Cornell George
　1903-1968 .... **CLC 77**
　See also CA 13-14; CANR 58, 156; CAP 1;
　CMW 4; DLB 226; MSW; MTCW 2

Horace 65B.C.-8B.C. .... **CMLC 39; PC 46**
　See also AW 2; CDWLB 1; DLB 211;
　RGWL 2, 3; WLIT 8
Horatio
　See Proust, (Valentin-Louis-George-Eugene)
　Marcel
Horgan, Paul (George Vincent
　O'Shaughnessy) 1903-1995 .. **CLC 9, 53**
　See also BPFB 2; CA 13-16R; 147; CANR
　9, 35; CN 1, 2, 3, 4, 5; DAM NOV; DLB
　102, 212; DLBY 1985; INT CANR-9;
　MTCW 1, 2; MTFW 2005; SATA 13;
　SATA-Obit 84; TCWW 1, 2
Horkheimer, Max 1895-1973 .... **TCLC 132**
　See also CA 216; 41-44R; DLB 296
Horn, Peter
　See Kuttner, Henry
Hornby, Nick 1957(?)- .... **CLC 243**
　See also AAYA 74; CA 151; CANR 104,
　151; CN 7; DLB 207
Horne, Frank (Smith) 1899-1974 ...... **HR 1:2**
　See also BW 1; CA 125; 53-56; DLB 51;
　WP
Horne, Richard Henry Hengist
　1802(?)-1884 .... **NCLC 127**
　See also DLB 32; SATA 29
Hornem, Horace Esq.
　See Byron, George Gordon (Noel)
Horne Tooke, John 1736-1812 ..... **NCLC 195**
Horney, Karen (Clementine Theodore
　Danielsen) 1885-1952 .... **TCLC 71**
　See also CA 114; 165; DLB 246; FW
Hornung, E(rnest) W(illiam)
　1866-1921 .... **TCLC 59**
　See also CA 108; 160; CMW 4; DLB 70
Horovitz, Israel 1939- .... **CLC 56**
　See also CA 33-36R; CAD; CANR 46, 59;
　CD 5, 6; DAM DRAM; DLB 7, 341;
　MAL 5
Horton, George Moses
　1797(?)-1883(?) .... **NCLC 87**
　See also DLB 50
Horvath, odon von 1901-1938
　See von Horvath, Odon
　See also EWL 3
Horvath, Oedoen von -1938
　See von Horvath, Odon
Horwitz, Julius 1920-1986 .... **CLC 14**
　See also CA 9-12R; 119; CANR 12
Horwitz, Ronald
　See Harwood, Ronald
Hospital, Janette Turner 1942- .... **CLC 42,**
　145
　See also CA 108; CANR 48, 166; CN 5, 6,
　7; DLB 325; DLBY 2002; RGSF 2
Hosseini, Khaled 1965- .... **CLC 254**
　See also CA 225; SATA 156
Hostos, E. M. de
　See Hostos (y Bonilla), Eugenio Maria de
Hostos, Eugenio M. de
　See Hostos (y Bonilla), Eugenio Maria de
Hostos, Eugenio Maria
　See Hostos (y Bonilla), Eugenio Maria de
Hostos (y Bonilla), Eugenio Maria de
　1839-1903 .... **TCLC 24**
　See also CA 123; 131; HW 1
Houdini
　See Lovecraft, H. P.
Houellebecq, Michel 1958- .... **CLC 179**
　See also CA 185; CANR 140; MTFW 2005
Hougan, Carolyn 1943-2007 .... **CLC 34**
　See also CA 139; 257
Household, Geoffrey (Edward West)
　1900-1988 .... **CLC 11**
　See also CA 77-80; 126; CANR 58; CMW
　4; CN 1, 2, 3, 4; DLB 87; SATA 14;
　SATA-Obit 59

Housman, A(lfred) E(dward)
1859-1936 .... **PC 2, 43; TCLC 1, 10; WLCS**
See also AAYA 66; BRW 6; CA 104; 125; DA; DA3; DAB; DAC; DAM MST, POET; DLB 19, 284; EWL 3; EXPP; MTCW 1, 2; MTFW 2005; PAB; PFS 4, 7; RGEL 2; TEA; WP

Housman, Laurence 1865-1959 .... **TCLC 7**
See also CA 106; 155; DLB 10; FANT; RGEL 2; SATA 25

Houston, Jeanne Wakatsuki 1934- .... **AAL**
See also AAYA 49; CA 103, 232; CAAE 232; CAAS 16; CANR 29, 123, 167; LAIT 4; SATA 78, 168; SATA-Essay 168

Hove, Chenjerai 1956- .... **BLC 2:2**
See also CP 7

Howard, Elizabeth Jane 1923- ..... **CLC 7, 29**
See also BRWS 11; CA 5-8R; CANR 8, 62, 146; CN 1, 2, 3, 4, 5, 6, 7

Howard, Maureen 1930- .... **CLC 5, 14, 46, 151**
See also CA 53-56; CANR 31, 75, 140; CN 4, 5, 6, 7; DLBY 1983; INT CANR-31; MTCW 1, 2; MTFW 2005

Howard, Richard 1929- .... **CLC 7, 10, 47**
See also AITN 1; CA 85-88; CANR 25, 80, 154; CP 1, 2, 3, 4, 5, 6, 7; DLB 5; INT CANR-25; MAL 5

Howard, Robert E 1906-1936 .... **TCLC 8**
See also BPFB 2; BYA 5; CA 105; 157; CANR 155; FANT; SUFW 1; TCWW 1, 2

Howard, Robert Ervin
See Howard, Robert E

Howard, Warren F.
See Pohl, Frederik

Howe, Fanny 1940- .... **CLC 47**
See also CA 117, 187; CAAE 187; CAAS 27; CANR 70, 116, 184; CP 6, 7; CWP; SATA-Brief 52

Howe, Fanny Quincy
See Howe, Fanny

Howe, Irving 1920-1993 .... **CLC 85**
See also AMWS 6; CA 9-12R; 141; CANR 21, 50; DLB 67; EWL 3; MAL 5; MTCW 1, 2; MTFW 2005

Howe, Julia Ward 1819-1910 . **PC 81; TCLC 21**
See also CA 117; 191; DLB 1, 189, 235; FW

Howe, Susan 1937- .... **CLC 72, 152; PC 54**
See also AMWS 4; CA 160; CP 5, 6, 7; CWP; DLB 120; FW; RGAL 4

Howe, Tina 1937- .... **CLC 48**
See also CA 109; CAD; CANR 125; CD 5, 6; CWD; DLB 341

Howell, James 1594(?)-1666 .... **LC 13**
See also DLB 151

Howells, W. D.
See Howells, William Dean

Howells, William D.
See Howells, William Dean

Howells, William Dean 1837-1920 ... **SSC 36; TCLC 7, 17, 41**
See also AMW; CA 104; 134; CDALB 1865-1917; DLB 12, 64, 74, 79, 189; LMFS 1; MAL 5; MTCW 2; RGAL 4; TUS

Howes, Barbara 1914-1996 .... **CLC 15**
See also CA 9-12R; 151; CAAS 3; CANR 53; CP 1, 2, 3, 4, 5, 6; SATA 5; TCLE 1:1

Hrabal, Bohumil 1914-1997 ...... **CLC 13, 67; TCLC 155**
See also CA 106; 156; CAAS 12; CANR 57; CWW 2; DLB 232; EWL 3; RGSF 2

Hrabanus Maurus 776(?)-856 .... **CMLC 78**
See also DLB 148

Hrotsvit of Gandersheim c. 935-c. 1000 .... **CMLC 29**
See also DLB 148

Hsi, Chu 1130-1200 .... **CMLC 42**

Hsun, Lu
See Shu-Jen, Chou

Hubbard, L. Ron 1911-1986 .... **CLC 43**
See also AAYA 64; CA 77-80; 118; CANR 52; CPW; DA3; DAM POP; FANT; MTCW 2; MTFW 2005; SFW 4

Hubbard, Lafayette Ronald
See Hubbard, L. Ron

Huch, Ricarda (Octavia)
1864-1947 .... **TCLC 13**
See also CA 111; 189; DLB 66; EWL 3

Huddle, David 1942- .... **CLC 49**
See also CA 57-60, 261; CAAS 20; CANR 89; DLB 130

Hudson, Jeffery
See Crichton, Michael

Hudson, Jeffrey
See Crichton, Michael

Hudson, W(illiam) H(enry)
1841-1922 .... **TCLC 29**
See also CA 115; 190; DLB 98, 153, 174; RGEL 2; SATA 35

Hueffer, Ford Madox
See Ford, Ford Madox

Hughart, Barry 1934- .... **CLC 39**
See also CA 137; FANT; SFW 4; SUFW 2

Hughes, Colin
See Creasey, John

Hughes, David (John) 1930-2005 ..... **CLC 48**
See also CA 116; 129; 238; CN 4, 5, 6, 7; DLB 14

Hughes, Edward James
See Hughes, Ted

Hughes, (James Mercer) Langston
1902-1967 .. **BLC 1:2; CLC 1, 5, 10, 15, 35, 44, 108; DC 3; HR 1:2; PC 1, 53; SSC 6, 90; WLC 3**
See also AAYA 12; AFAW 1, 2; AMWR 1; AMWS 1; BW 1, 3; CA 1-4R; 25-28R; CANR 1, 34, 82; CDALB 1929-1941; CLR 17; DA; DA3; DAB; DAC; DAM DRAM, MST, MULT, POET; DFS 6, 18; DLB 4, 7, 48, 51, 86, 228, 315; EWL 3; EXPP; EXPS; JRDA; LAIT 3; LMFS 2; MAICYA 1, 2; MAL 5; MTCW 1, 2; MTFW 2005; NFS 21; PAB; PFS 1, 3, 6, 10, 15, 30; RGAL 4; RGSF 2; SATA 4, 33; SSFS 4, 7; TUS; WCH; WP; YAW

Hughes, Richard (Arthur Warren)
1900-1976 .... **CLC 1, 11; TCLC 204**
See also CA 5-8R; 65-68; CANR 4; CN 1, 2; DAM NOV; DLB 15, 161; EWL 3; MTCW 1; RGEL 2; SATA 8; SATA-Obit 25

Hughes, Ted 1930-1998 . **CLC 2, 4, 9, 14, 37, 119; PC 7, 89**
See also BRWC 2; BRWR 2; BRWS 1; CA 1-4R; 171; CANR 1, 33, 66, 108; CLR 3, 131; CP 1, 2, 3, 4, 5, 6; DA3; DAB; DAC; DAM MST, POET; DLB 40, 161; EWL 3; EXPP; MAICYA 1, 2; MTCW 1, 2; MTFW 2005; PAB; PFS 4, 19; RGEL 2; SATA 49; SATA-Brief 27; SATA-Obit 107; TEA; YAW

Hughes, Thomas 1822-1896 .... **NCLC 207**
See also BYA 3; DLB 18, 163; LAIT 2; RGEL 2; SATA 31

Hugo, Richard
See Huch, Ricarda (Octavia)

Hugo, Richard F(ranklin)
1923-1982 .... **CLC 6, 18, 32; PC 68**
See also AMWS 6; CA 49-52; 108; CANR 3; CP 1, 2, 3; DAM POET; DLB 5, 206; EWL 3; MAL 5; PFS 17; RGAL 4

Hugo, Victor (Marie) 1802-1885 .... **NCLC 3, 10, 21, 161, 189; PC 17; WLC 3**
See also AAYA 28; DA; DA3; DAB; DAC; DAM DRAM, MST, NOV, POET; DLB 119, 192, 217; EFS 2; EW 6; EXPN; GFL 1789 to the Present; LAIT 1, 2; NFS 5, 20; RGWL 2, 3; SATA 47; TWA

Huidobro, Vicente
See Huidobro Fernandez, Vicente Garcia

Huidobro Fernandez, Vicente Garcia
1893-1948 .... **TCLC 31**
See also CA 131; DLB 283; EWL 3; HW 1; LAW

Hulme, Keri 1947- .... **CLC 39, 130**
See also CA 125; CANR 69; CN 4, 5, 6, 7; CP 6, 7; CWP; DLB 326; EWL 3; FW; INT CA-125; NFS 24

Hulme, T(homas) E(rnest)
1883-1917 .... **TCLC 21**
See also BRWS 6; CA 117; 203; DLB 19

Humboldt, Alexander von
1769-1859 .... **NCLC 170**
See also DLB 90

Humboldt, Wilhelm von
1767-1835 .... **NCLC 134**
See also DLB 90

Hume, David 1711-1776 .. **LC 7, 56, 156, 157**
See also BRWS 3; DLB 104, 252, 336; LMFS 1; TEA

Humphrey, William 1924-1997 .... **CLC 45**
See also AMWS 9; CA 77-80; 160; CANR 68; CN 1, 2, 3, 4, 5, 6; CSW; DLB 6, 212, 234, 278; TCWW 1, 2

Humphreys, Emyr Owen 1919- .... **CLC 47**
See also CA 5-8R; CANR 3, 24; CN 1, 2, 3, 4, 5, 6, 7; DLB 15

Humphreys, Josephine 1945- ..... **CLC 34, 57**
See also CA 121; 127; CANR 97; CSW; DLB 292; INT CA-127

Huneker, James Gibbons
1860-1921 .... **TCLC 65**
See also CA 193; DLB 71; RGAL 4

Hungerford, Hesba Fay
See Brinsmead, H(esba) F(ay)

Hungerford, Pixie
See Brinsmead, H(esba) F(ay)

Hunt, E. Howard 1918-2007 .... **CLC 3**
See also AITN 1; CA 45-48; 256; CANR 2, 47, 103, 160; CMW 4

Hunt, Everette Howard, Jr.
See Hunt, E. Howard

Hunt, Francesca
See Holland, Isabelle (Christian)

Hunt, Howard
See Hunt, E. Howard

Hunt, Kyle
See Creasey, John

Hunt, (James Henry) Leigh
1784-1859 .... **NCLC 1, 70; PC 73**
See also DAM POET; DLB 96, 110, 144; RGEL 2; TEA

Hunt, Marsha 1946- .... **CLC 70**
See also BW 2, 3; CA 143; CANR 79

Hunt, Violet 1866(?)-1942 .... **TCLC 53**
See also CA 184; DLB 162, 197

Hunter, E. Waldo
See Sturgeon, Theodore (Hamilton)

Hunter, Evan 1926-2005 .... **CLC 11, 31**
See also AAYA 39; BPFB 2; CA 5-8R; 241; CANR 5, 38, 62, 97, 149; CMW 4; CN 1, 2, 3, 4, 5, 6, 7; CPW; DAM POP; DLB 306; DLBY 1982; INT CANR-5; MSW; MTCW 1; SATA 25; SATA-Obit 167; SFW 4

Hunter, Kristin
See Lattany, Kristin (Elaine Eggleston) Hunter

Hunter, Mary
See Austin, Mary (Hunter)

Jones, Everett LeRoi
    See Baraka, Amiri
Jones, Gayl 1949- .. **BLC 1:2; CLC 6, 9, 131, 270**
    See also AFAW 1, 2; BW 2, 3; CA 77-80; CANR 27, 66, 122; CN 4, 5, 6, 7; CSW; DA3; DAM MULT; DLB 33, 278; MAL 5; MTCW 1, 2; MTFW 2005; RGAL 4
Jones, James 1921-1977 ...... **CLC 1, 3, 10, 39**
    See also AITN 1, 2; AMWS 11; BPFB 2; CA 1-4R; 69-72; CANR 6; CN 1, 2; DLB 2, 143; DLBD 17; DLBY 1998; EWL 3; MAL 5; MTCW 1; RGAL 4
Jones, John J.
    See Lovecraft, H. P.
Jones, LeRoi
    See Baraka, Amiri
Jones, Louis B. 1953- .... **CLC 65**
    See also CA 141; CANR 73
Jones, Madison 1925- .... **CLC 4**
    See also CA 13-16R; CAAS 11; CANR 7, 54, 83, 158; CN 1, 2, 3, 4, 5, 6, 7; CSW; DLB 152
Jones, Madison Percy, Jr.
    See Jones, Madison
Jones, Mervyn 1922- .... **CLC 10, 52**
    See also CA 45-48; CAAS 5; CANR 1, 91; CN 1, 2, 3, 4, 5, 6, 7; MTCW 1
Jones, Mick 1956(?)- .... **CLC 30**
Jones, Nettie (Pearl) 1941- .... **CLC 34**
    See also BW 2; CA 137; CAAS 20; CANR 88
Jones, Peter 1802-1856 .... **NNAL**
Jones, Preston 1936-1979 .... **CLC 10**
    See also CA 73-76; 89-92; DLB 7
Jones, Robert F(rancis) 1934-2003 .... **CLC 7**
    See also CA 49-52; CANR 2, 61, 118
Jones, Rod 1953- .... **CLC 50**
    See also CA 128
Jones, Terence Graham Parry
    1942- .... **CLC 21**
    See also CA 112; 116; CANR 35, 93, 173; INT CA-116; SATA 67, 127; SATA-Brief 51
Jones, Terry
    See Jones, Terence Graham Parry
Jones, Thom (Douglas) 1945(?)- ..... **CLC 81; SSC 56**
    See also CA 157; CANR 88; DLB 244; SSFS 23
Jong, Erica 1942- .... **CLC 4, 6, 8, 18, 83**
    See also AITN 1; AMWS 5; BEST 90:2; BPFB 2; CA 73-76; CANR 26, 52, 75, 132, 166; CN 3, 4, 5, 6, 7; CP 2, 3, 4, 5, 6, 7; CPW; DA3; DAM NOV, POP; DLB 2, 5, 28, 152; FW; INT CANR-26; MAL 5; MTCW 1, 2; MTFW 2005
Jonson, Ben(jamin) 1572(?)-1637 . **DC 4; LC 6, 33, 110, 158; PC 17; WLC 3**
    See also BRW 1; BRWC 1; BRWR 1; CD-BLB Before 1660; DA; DAB; DAC; DAM DRAM, MST, POET; DFS 4, 10; DLB 62, 121; LMFS 1; PFS 23; RGEL 2; TEA; WLIT 3
Jordan, June 1936-2002 .. **BLCS; CLC 5, 11, 23, 114, 230; PC 38**
    See also AAYA 2, 66; AFAW 1, 2; BW 2, 3; CA 33-36R; 206; CANR 25, 70, 114, 154; CLR 10; CP 3, 4, 5, 6, 7; CWP; DAM MULT, POET; DLB 38; GLL 2; LAIT 5; MAICYA 1, 2; MTCW 1; SATA 4, 136; YAW
Jordan, June Meyer
    See Jordan, June
Jordan, Neil 1950- .... **CLC 110**
    See also CA 124; 130; CANR 54, 154; CN 4, 5, 6, 7; GLL 2; INT CA-130
Jordan, Neil Patrick
    See Jordan, Neil

Jordan, Pat(rick M.) 1941- .... **CLC 37**
    See also CA 33-36R; CANR 121
Jorgensen, Ivar
    See Ellison, Harlan
Jorgenson, Ivar
    See Silverberg, Robert
Joseph, George Ghevarughese CLC 70
Josephson, Mary
    See O'Doherty, Brian
Josephus, Flavius c. 37-100 ..... **CMLC 13, 93**
    See also AW 2; DLB 176; WLIT 8
Josh
    See Twain, Mark
Josiah Allen's Wife
    See Holley, Marietta
Josipovici, Gabriel 1940- ...... **CLC 6, 43, 153**
    See also CA 37-40R; 224; CAAE 224; CAAS 8; CANR 47, 84; CN 3, 4, 5, 6, 7; DLB 14, 319
Josipovici, Gabriel David
    See Josipovici, Gabriel
Joubert, Joseph 1754-1824 .... **NCLC 9**
Jouve, Pierre Jean 1887-1976 .... **CLC 47**
    See also CA 252; 65-68; DLB 258; EWL 3
Jovine, Francesco 1902-1950 .... **TCLC 79**
    See also DLB 264; EWL 3
Joyaux, Julia
    See Kristeva, Julia
Joyce, James (Augustine Aloysius)
    1882-1941 .... **DC 16; PC 22; SSC 3, 26, 44, 64, 118, 122; TCLC 3, 8, 16, 35, 52, 159; WLC 3**
    See also AAYA 42; BRW 7; BRWC 1; BRWR 1; BYA 11, 13; CA 104; 126; CD-BLB 1914-1945; DA; DA3; DAB; DAC; DAM MST, NOV, POET; DLB 10, 19, 36, 162, 247; EWL 3; EXPN; EXPS; LAIT 3; LMFS 1, 2; MTCW 1, 2; MTFW 2005; NFS 7, 26; RGSF 2; SSFS 1, 19; TEA; WLIT 4
Jozsef, Attila 1905-1937 .... **TCLC 22**
    See also CA 116; 230; CDWLB 4; DLB 215; EWL 3
Juana Ines de la Cruz, Sor
    1651(?)-1695 ... **HLCS 1; LC 5, 136; PC 24**
    See also DLB 305; FW; LAW; RGWL 2, 3; WLIT 1
Juana Inez de La Cruz, Sor
    See Juana Ines de la Cruz, Sor
Juan Manuel, Don 1282-1348 .... **CMLC 88**
Judd, Cyril
    See Kornbluth, C(yril) M.; Pohl, Frederik
Juenger, Ernst 1895-1998 .... **CLC 125**
    See also CA 101; 167; CANR 21, 47, 106; CDWLB 2; DLB 56; EWL 3; RGWL 2, 3
Julian of Norwich 1342(?)-1416(?) . **LC 6, 52**
    See also BRWS 12; DLB 146; LMFS 1
Julius Caesar 100B.C.-44B.C. .... **CMLC 47**
    See also AW 1; CDWLB 1; DLB 211; RGWL 2, 3; WLIT 8
Jung, Patricia B.
    See Hope, Christopher
Junger, Ernst
    See Juenger, Ernst
Junger, Sebastian 1962- .... **CLC 109**
    See also AAYA 28; CA 165; CANR 130, 171; MTFW 2005
Juniper, Alex
    See Hospital, Janette Turner
Junius
    See Luxemburg, Rosa
Junzaburo, Nishiwaki
    See Nishiwaki, Junzaburo
Just, Ward 1935- .... **CLC 4, 27**
    See also CA 25-28R; CANR 32, 87; CN 6, 7; DLB 335; INT CANR-32

Just, Ward Swift
    See Just, Ward
Justice, Donald 1925-2004 ... **CLC 6, 19, 102; PC 64**
    See also AMWS 7; CA 5-8R; 230; CANR 26, 54, 74, 121, 122, 169; CP 1, 2, 3, 4, 5, 6, 7; CSW; DAM POET; DLBY 1983; EWL 3; INT CANR-26; MAL 5; MTCW 2; PFS 14; TCLE 1:1
Justice, Donald Rodney
    See Justice, Donald
Juvenal c. 60-c. 130 .... **CMLC 8**
    See also AW 2; CDWLB 1; DLB 211; RGWL 2, 3; WLIT 8
Juvenis
    See Bourne, Randolph S(illiman)
K., Alice
    See Knapp, Caroline
Kabakov, Sasha CLC 59
Kabir 1398(?)-1448(?) .... **LC 109; PC 56**
    See also RGWL 2, 3
Kacew, Romain 1914-1980 .... **CLC 25**
    See also CA 108; 102; DLB 83, 299; RGHL
Kacew, Roman
    See Kacew, Romain
Kadare, Ismail 1936- .... **CLC 52, 190**
    See also CA 161; CANR 165; EWL 3; RGWL 3
Kadohata, Cynthia 1956(?)- ..... **CLC 59, 122**
    See also AAYA 71; CA 140; CANR 124; CLR 121; SATA 155, 180
Kafka, Franz 1883-1924 ... **SSC 5, 29, 35, 60; TCLC 2, 6, 13, 29, 47, 53, 112, 179; WLC 3**
    See also AAYA 31; BPFB 2; CA 105; 126; CDWLB 2; DA; DA3; DAB; DAC; DAM MST, NOV; DLB 81; EW 9; EWL 3; EXPS; LATS 1:1; LMFS 2; MTCW 1, 2; MTFW 2005; NFS 7; RGSF 2; RGWL 2, 3; SFW 4; SSFS 3, 7, 12; TWA
Kafu
    See Nagai, Kafu
Kahanovitch, Pinchas
    See Der Nister
Kahanovitsch, Pinkhes
    See Der Nister
Kahanovitsh, Pinkhes
    See Der Nister
Kahn, Roger 1927- .... **CLC 30**
    See also CA 25-28R; CANR 44, 69, 152; DLB 171; SATA 37
Kain, Saul
    See Sassoon, Siegfried (Lorraine)
Kaiser, Georg 1878-1945 .... **TCLC 9, 220**
    See also CA 106; 190; CDWLB 2; DLB 124; EWL 3; LMFS 2; RGWL 2, 3
Kaledin, Sergei CLC 59
Kaletski, Alexander 1946- .... **CLC 39**
    See also CA 118; 143
Kalidasa fl. c. 400-455 .... **CMLC 9; PC 22**
    See also RGWL 2, 3
Kallman, Chester (Simon)
    1921-1975 .... **CLC 2**
    See also CA 45-48; 53-56; CANR 3; CP 1, 2
Kaminsky, Melvin CLC 12, 217
    See Brooks, Mel
    See also AAYA 13, 48; DLB 26
Kaminsky, Stuart M. 1934- .... **CLC 59**
    See also CA 73-76; CANR 29, 53, 89, 161; CMW 4
Kaminsky, Stuart Melvin
    See Kaminsky, Stuart M.
Kamo no Chomei 1153(?)-1216 .... **CMLC 66**
    See also DLB 203
Kamo no Nagaakira
    See Kamo no Chomei

Kandinsky, Wassily 1866-1944 .... **TCLC 92**
See also AAYA 64; CA 118; 155

Kane, Francis
See Robbins, Harold

Kane, Paul
See Simon, Paul

Kane, Sarah 1971-1999 .... **DC 31**
See also BRWS 8; CA 190; CD 5, 6; DLB 310

Kanin, Garson 1912-1999 .... **CLC 22**
See also AITN 1; CA 5-8R; 177; CAD; CANR 7, 78; DLB 7; IDFW 3, 4

Kaniuk, Yoram 1930- .... **CLC 19**
See also CA 134; DLB 299; RGHL

Kant, Immanuel 1724-1804 ..... **NCLC 27, 67**
See also DLB 94

Kantor, MacKinlay 1904-1977 .... **CLC 7**
See also CA 61-64; 73-76; CANR 60, 63; CN 1, 2; DLB 9, 102; MAL 5; MTCW 2; RHW; TCWW 1, 2

Kanze Motokiyo
See Zeami

Kaplan, David Michael 1946- .... **CLC 50**
See also CA 187

Kaplan, James 1951- .... **CLC 59**
See also CA 135; CANR 121

Karadzic, Vuk Stefanovic
1787-1864 .... **NCLC 115**
See also CDWLB 4; DLB 147

Karageorge, Michael
See Anderson, Poul

Karamzin, Nikolai Mikhailovich
1766-1826 .... **NCLC 3, 173**
See also DLB 150; RGSF 2

Karapanou, Margarita 1946- .... **CLC 13**
See also CA 101

Karinthy, Frigyes 1887-1938 .... **TCLC 47**
See also CA 170; DLB 215; EWL 3

Karl, Frederick R(obert)
1927-2004 .... **CLC 34**
See also CA 5-8R; 226; CANR 3, 44, 143

Karr, Mary 1955- .... **CLC 188**
See also AMWS 11; CA 151; CANR 100; MTFW 2005; NCFS 5

Kastel, Warren
See Silverberg, Robert

Kataev, Evgeny Petrovich
1903-1942 .... **TCLC 21**
See also CA 120; DLB 272

Kataphusin
See Ruskin, John

Katz, Steve 1935- .... **CLC 47**
See also CA 25-28R; CAAS 14, 64; CANR 12; CN 4, 5, 6, 7; DLBY 1983

Kauffman, Janet 1945- .... **CLC 42**
See also CA 117; CANR 43, 84; DLB 218; DLBY 1986

Kaufman, Bob (Garnell)
1925-1986 .... **CLC 49; PC 74**
See also BG 1:3; BW 1; CA 41-44R; 118; CANR 22; CP 1; DLB 16, 41

Kaufman, George S. 1889-1961 ...... **CLC 38; DC 17**
See also CA 108; 93-96; DAM DRAM; DFS 1, 10; DLB 7; INT CA-108; MTCW 2; MTFW 2005; RGAL 4; TUS

Kaufman, Moises 1964- .... **DC 26**
See also CA 211; DFS 22; MTFW 2005

Kaufman, Sue
See Barondess, Sue K(aufman)

Kavafis, Konstantinos Petrou
1863-1933 .... **PC 36; TCLC 2, 7**
See also CA 104; 148; DA3; DAM POET; EW 8; EWL 3; MTCW 2; PFS 19; RGWL 2, 3; WP

Kavan, Anna 1901-1968 .... **CLC 5, 13, 82**
See also BRWS 7; CA 5-8R; CANR 6, 57; DLB 255; MTCW 1; RGEL 2; SFW 4

Kavanagh, Dan
See Barnes, Julian

Kavanagh, Julie 1952- .... **CLC 119**
See also CA 163; CANR 186

Kavanagh, Patrick (Joseph)
1904-1967 .... **CLC 22; PC 33**
See also BRWS 7; CA 123; 25-28R; DLB 15, 20; EWL 3; MTCW 1; RGEL 2

Kawabata, Yasunari 1899-1972 ..... **CLC 2, 5, 9, 18, 107; SSC 17**
See also CA 93-96; 33-36R; CANR 88; DAM MULT; DLB 180, 330; EWL 3; MJW; MTCW 2; MTFW 2005; RGSF 2; RGWL 2, 3

Kawabata Yasunari
See Kawabata, Yasunari

Kaye, Mary Margaret
See Kaye, M.M.

Kaye, M.M. 1908-2004 .... **CLC 28**
See also CA 89-92; 223; CANR 24, 60, 102, 142; MTCW 1, 2; MTFW 2005; RHW; SATA 62; SATA-Obit 152

Kaye, Mollie
See Kaye, M.M.

Kaye-Smith, Sheila 1887-1956 .... **TCLC 20**
See also CA 118; 203; DLB 36

Kaymor, Patrice Maguilene
See Senghor, Leopold Sedar

Kazakov, Iurii Pavlovich
See Kazakov, Yuri Pavlovich

Kazakov, Yuri Pavlovich 1927-1982 . **SSC 43**
See also CA 5-8R; CANR 36; DLB 302; EWL 3; MTCW 1; RGSF 2

Kazakov, Yury
See Kazakov, Yuri Pavlovich

Kazan, Elia 1909-2003 .... **CLC 6, 16, 63**
See also CA 21-24R; 220; CANR 32, 78

Kazantzakis, Nikos 1883(?)-1957 .... **TCLC 2, 5, 33, 181**
See also BPFB 2; CA 105; 132; DA3; EW 9; EWL 3; MTCW 1, 2; MTFW 2005; RGWL 2, 3

Kazin, Alfred 1915-1998 ..... **CLC 34, 38, 119**
See also AMWS 8; CA 1-4R; CAAS 7; CANR 1, 45, 79; DLB 67; EWL 3

Keane, Mary Nesta (Skrine)
1904-1996 .... **CLC 31**
See also CA 108; 114; 151; CN 5, 6; INT CA-114; RHW; TCLE 1:1

Keane, Molly
See Keane, Mary Nesta (Skrine)

Keates, Jonathan 1946(?)- .... **CLC 34**
See also CA 163; CANR 126

Keaton, Buster 1895-1966 .... **CLC 20**
See also AAYA 79; CA 194

Keats, John 1795-1821 ...... **NCLC 8, 73, 121; PC 1, 96; WLC 3**
See also AAYA 58; BRW 4; BRWR 1; CD-BLB 1789-1832; DA; DA3; DAB; DAC; DAM MST, POET; DLB 96, 110; EXPP; LMFS 1; PAB; PFS 1, 2, 3, 9, 17; RGEL 2; TEA; WLIT 3; WP

Keble, John 1792-1866 .... **NCLC 87**
See also DLB 32, 55; RGEL 2

Keene, Donald 1922- .... **CLC 34**
See also CA 1-4R; CANR 5, 119

Keillor, Garrison 1942- ..... **CLC 40, 115, 222**
See also AAYA 2, 62; AMWS 16; BEST 89:3; BPFB 2; CA 111; 117; CANR 36, 59, 124, 180; CPW; DA3; DAM POP; DLBY 1987; EWL 3; MTCW 1, 2; MTFW 2005; SATA 58; TUS

Keith, Carlos
See Lewton, Val

Keith, Michael
See Hubbard, L. Ron

Kell, Joseph
See Burgess, Anthony

Keller, Gottfried 1819-1890 .... **NCLC 2; SSC 26, 107**
See also CDWLB 2; DLB 129; EW; RGSF 2; RGWL 2, 3

Keller, Nora Okja 1965- .... **CLC 109**
See also CA 187

Kellerman, Jonathan 1949- .... **CLC 44**
See also AAYA 35; BEST 90:1; CA 106; CANR 29, 51, 150, 183; CMW 4; CPW; DA3; DAM POP; INT CANR-29

Kelley, William Melvin 1937- .... **BLC 2:2; CLC 22**
See also BW 1; CA 77-80; CANR 27, 83; CN 1, 2, 3, 4, 5, 6, 7; DLB 33; EWL 3

Kellock, Archibald P.
See Mavor, Osborne Henry

Kellogg, Marjorie 1922-2005 .... **CLC 2**
See also CA 81-84; 246

Kellow, Kathleen
See Hibbert, Eleanor Alice Burford

Kelly, Lauren
See Oates, Joyce Carol

Kelly, M(ilton) T(errence) 1947- ...... **CLC 55**
See also CA 97-100; CAAS 22; CANR 19, 43, 84; CN 6

Kelly, Robert 1935- .... **SSC 50**
See also CA 17-20R; CAAS 19; CANR 47; CP 1, 2, 3, 4, 5, 6, 7; DLB 5, 130, 165

Kelman, James 1946- .... **CLC 58, 86**
See also BRWS 5; CA 148; CANR 85, 130; CN 5, 6, 7; DLB 194, 319, 326; RGSF 2; WLIT 4

Kemal, Yasar
See Kemal, Yashar

Kemal, Yashar 1923(?)- .... **CLC 14, 29**
See also CA 89-92; CANR 44; CWW 2; EWL 3; WLIT 6

Kemble, Fanny 1809-1893 .... **NCLC 18**
See also DLB 32

Kemelman, Harry 1908-1996 .... **CLC 2**
See also AITN 1; BPFB 2; CA 9-12R; 155; CANR 6, 71; CMW 4; DLB 28

Kempe, Margery 1373(?)-1440(?) ... **LC 6, 56**
See also BRWS 12; DLB 146; FL 1:1; RGEL 2

Kempis, Thomas a 1380-1471 .... **LC 11**

Kenan, Randall (G.) 1963- .... **BLC 2:2**
See also BW 2, 3; CA 142; CANR 86; CN 7; CSW; DLB 292; GLL 1

Kendall, Henry 1839-1882 .... **NCLC 12**
See also DLB 230

Keneally, Thomas 1935- .... **CLC 5, 8, 10, 14, 19, 27, 43, 117**
See also BRWS 4; CA 85-88; CANR 10, 50, 74, 130, 165; CN 1, 2, 3, 4, 5, 6, 7; CPW; DA3; DAM NOV; DLB 289, 299, 326; EWL 3; MTCW 1, 2; MTFW 2005; NFS 17; RGEL 2; RGHL; RHW

Keneally, Thomas Michael
See Keneally, Thomas

Kennedy, A. L. 1965- .... **CLC 188**
See also CA 168; 213; CAAE 213; CANR 108; CD 5, 6; CN 6, 7; DLB 271; RGSF 2

Kennedy, Adrienne (Lita) 1931- .... **BLC 1:2; CLC 66; DC 5**
See also AFAW 2; BW 2, 3; CA 103; CAAS 20; CABS 3; CAD; CANR 26, 53, 82; CD 5, 6; DAM MULT; DFS 9; DLB 38, 341; FW; MAL 5

Kennedy, Alison Louise
See Kennedy, A. L.

Kennedy, John Pendleton
1795-1870 .... **NCLC 2**
See also DLB 3, 248, 254; RGAL 4

CANR-34; MAL 5; MTCW 1, 2; MTFW 2005; PAB; PFS 9, 26; RGAL 4; TCLE 1:1; WP

Kinsella, Thomas 1928- .... **CLC 4, 19, 138, 274; PC 69**
See also BRWS 5; CA 17-20R; CANR 15, 122; CP 1, 2, 3, 4, 5, 6, 7; DLB 27; EWL 3; MTCW 1, 2; MTFW 2005; RGEL 2; TEA

Kinsella, W.P. 1935- .... **CLC 27, 43, 166**
See also AAYA 7, 60; BPFB 2; CA 97-100, 222; CAAE 222; CAAS 7; CANR 21, 35, 66, 75, 129; CN 4, 5, 6, 7; CPW; DAC; DAM NOV, POP; FANT; INT CANR-21; LAIT 5; MTCW 1, 2; MTFW 2005; NFS 15; RGSF 2

Kinsey, Alfred C(harles)
1894-1956 .... **TCLC 91**
See also CA 115; 170; MTCW 2

Kipling, (Joseph) Rudyard 1865-1936 . **PC 3, 91; SSC 5, 54, 110; TCLC 8, 17, 167; WLC 3**
See also AAYA 32; BRW 6; BRWC 1, 2; BYA 4; CA 105; 120; CANR 33; CDBLB 1890-1914; CLR 39, 65; CWRI 5; DA; DA3; DAB; DAC; DAM MST, POET; DLB 19, 34, 141, 156, 330; EWL 3; EXPS; FANT; LAIT 3; LMFS 1; MAICYA 1, 2; MTCW 1, 2; MTFW 2005; NFS 21; PFS 22; RGEL 2; RGSF 2; SATA 100; SFW 4; SSFS 8, 21, 22; SUFW 1; TEA; WCH; WLIT 4; YABC 2

Kircher, Athanasius 1602-1680 .... **LC 121**
See also DLB 164

Kirk, Russell (Amos) 1918-1994 .. **TCLC 119**
See also AITN 1; CA 1-4R; 145; CAAS 9; CANR 1, 20, 60; HGG; INT CANR-20; MTCW 1, 2

Kirkham, Dinah
See Card, Orson Scott

Kirkland, Caroline M. 1801-1864 . **NCLC 85**
See also DLB 3, 73, 74, 250, 254; DLBD 13

Kirkup, James 1918- .... **CLC 1**
See also CA 1-4R; CAAS 4; CANR 2; CP 1, 2, 3, 4, 5, 6, 7; DLB 27; SATA 12

Kirkwood, James 1930(?)-1989 .... **CLC 9**
See also AITN 2; CA 1-4R; 128; CANR 6, 40; GLL 2

Kirsch, Sarah 1935- .... **CLC 176**
See also CA 178; CWW 2; DLB 75; EWL 3

Kirshner, Sidney
See Kingsley, Sidney

Kis, Danilo 1935-1989 .... **CLC 57**
See also CA 109; 118; 129; CANR 61; CD-WLB 4; DLB 181; EWL 3; MTCW 1; RGSF 2; RGWL 2, 3

Kissinger, Henry A(lfred) 1923- ..... **CLC 137**
See also CA 1-4R; CANR 2, 33, 66, 109; MTCW 1

Kittel, Frederick August
See Wilson, August

Kivi, Aleksis 1834-1872 .... **NCLC 30**

Kizer, Carolyn 1925- ..... **CLC 15, 39, 80; PC 66**
See also CA 65-68; CAAS 5; CANR 24, 70, 134; CP 1, 2, 3, 4, 5, 6, 7; CWP; DAM POET; DLB 5, 169; EWL 3; MAL 5; MTCW 2; MTFW 2005; PFS 18; TCLE 1:1

Klabund 1890-1928 .... **TCLC 44**
See also CA 162; DLB 66

Klappert, Peter 1942- .... **CLC 57**
See also CA 33-36R; CSW; DLB 5

Klausner, Amos
See Oz, Amos

Klein, A(braham) M(oses)
1909-1972 .... **CLC 19**
See also CA 101; 37-40R; CP 1; DAB; DAC; DAM MST; DLB 68; EWL 3; RGEL 2; RGHL

Klein, Joe
See Klein, Joseph

Klein, Joseph 1946- .... **CLC 154**
See also CA 85-88; CANR 55, 164

Klein, Norma 1938-1989 .... **CLC 30**
See also AAYA 2, 35; BPFB 2; BYA 6, 7, 8; CA 41-44R; 128; CANR 15, 37; CLR 2, 19; INT CANR-15; JRDA; MAICYA 1, 2; SAAS 1; SATA 7, 57; WYA; YAW

Klein, T.E.D. 1947- .... **CLC 34**
See also CA 119; CANR 44, 75, 167; HGG

Klein, Theodore Eibon Donald
See Klein, T.E.D.

Kleist, Heinrich von 1777-1811 .... **DC 29; NCLC 2, 37; SSC 22**
See also CDWLB 2; DAM DRAM; DLB 90; EW 5; RGSF 2; RGWL 2, 3

Klima, Ivan 1931- .... **CLC 56, 172**
See also CA 25-28R; CANR 17, 50, 91; CDWLB 4; CWW 2; DAM NOV; DLB 232; EWL 3; RGWL 3

Klimentev, Andrei Platonovich
See Klimentov, Andrei Platonovich

Klimentov, Andrei Platonovich
1899-1951 .... **SSC 42; TCLC 14**
See also CA 108; 232; DLB 272; EWL 3

Klinger, Friedrich Maximilian von
1752-1831 .... **NCLC 1**
See also DLB 94

Klingsor the Magician
See Hartmann, Sadakichi

Klopstock, Friedrich Gottlieb
1724-1803 .... **NCLC 11**
See also DLB 97; EW 4; RGWL 2, 3

Kluge, Alexander 1932- .... **SSC 61**
See also CA 81-84; CANR 163; DLB 75

Knapp, Caroline 1959-2002 .... **CLC 99**
See also CA 154; 207

Knebel, Fletcher 1911-1993 .... **CLC 14**
See also AITN 1; CA 1-4R; 140; CAAS 3; CANR 1, 36; CN 1, 2, 3, 4, 5; SATA 36; SATA-Obit 75

Knickerbocker, Diedrich
See Irving, Washington

Knight, Etheridge 1931-1991 .... **BLC 1:2; CLC 40; PC 14**
See also BW 1, 3; CA 21-24R; 133; CANR 23, 82; CP 1, 2, 3, 4, 5; DAM POET; DLB 41; MTCW 2; MTFW 2005; RGAL 4; TCLE 1:1

Knight, Sarah Kemble 1666-1727 .... **LC 7**
See also DLB 24, 200

Knister, Raymond 1899-1932 .... **TCLC 56**
See also CA 186; DLB 68; RGEL 2

Knowles, John 1926-2001 ... **CLC 1, 4, 10, 26**
See also AAYA 10, 72; AMWS 12; BPFB 2; BYA 3; CA 17-20R; 203; CANR 40, 74, 76, 132; CDALB 1968-1988; CLR 98; CN 1, 2, 3, 4, 5, 6, 7; DA; DAC; DAM MST, NOV; DLB 6; EXPN; MTCW 1, 2; MTFW 2005; NFS 2; RGAL 4; SATA 8, 89; SATA-Obit 134; YAW

Knox, Calvin M.
See Silverberg, Robert

Knox, John c. 1505-1572 .... **LC 37**
See also DLB 132

Knye, Cassandra
See Disch, Thomas M.

Koch, C(hristopher) J(ohn) 1932- .... **CLC 42**
See also CA 127; CANR 84; CN 3, 4, 5, 6, 7; DLB 289

Koch, Christopher
See Koch, C(hristopher) J(ohn)

Koch, Kenneth 1925-2002 .... **CLC 5, 8, 44; PC 80**
See also AMWS 15; CA 1-4R; 207; CAD; CANR 6, 36, 57, 97, 131; CD 5, 6; CP 1, 2, 3, 4, 5, 6, 7; DAM POET; DLB 5; INT CANR-36; MAL 5; MTCW 2; MTFW 2005; PFS 20; SATA 65; WP

Kochanowski, Jan 1530-1584 .... **LC 10**
See also RGWL 2, 3

Kock, Charles Paul de 1794-1871 . **NCLC 16**

Koda Rohan
See Koda Shigeyuki

Koda Rohan
See Koda Shigeyuki

Koda Shigeyuki 1867-1947 .... **TCLC 22**
See also CA 121; 183; DLB 180

Koestler, Arthur 1905-1983 ... **CLC 1, 3, 6, 8, 15, 33**
See also BRWS 1; CA 1-4R; 109; CANR 1, 33; CDBLB 1945-1960; CN 1, 2, 3; DLBY 1983; EWL 3; MTCW 1, 2; MTFW 2005; NFS 19; RGEL 2

Kogawa, Joy Nozomi 1935- ..... **CLC 78, 129, 262, 268**
See also AAYA 47; CA 101; CANR 19, 62, 126; CN 6, 7; CP 1; CWP; DAC; DAM MST, MULT; DLB 334; FW; MTCW 2; MTFW 2005; NFS 3; SATA 99

Kohout, Pavel 1928- .... **CLC 13**
See also CA 45-48; CANR 3

Koizumi, Yakumo
See Hearn, (Patricio) Lafcadio (Tessima Carlos)

Kolmar, Gertrud 1894-1943 .... **TCLC 40**
See also CA 167; EWL 3; RGHL

Komunyakaa, Yusef 1947- . **BLC 2:2; BLCS; CLC 86, 94, 207; PC 51**
See also AFAW 2; AMWS 13; CA 147; CANR 83, 164; CP 6, 7; CSW; DLB 120; EWL 3; PFS 5, 20, 30; RGAL 4

Konigsberg, Alan Stewart
See Allen, Woody

Konrad, George
See Konrad, Gyorgy

Konrad, George
See Konrad, Gyorgy

Konrad, Gyorgy 1933- .... **CLC 4, 10, 73**
See also CA 85-88; CANR 97, 171; CD-WLB 4; CWW 2; DLB 232; EWL 3

Konwicki, Tadeusz 1926- .... **CLC 8, 28, 54, 117**
See also CA 101; CAAS 9; CANR 39, 59; CWW 2; DLB 232; EWL 3; IDFW 3; MTCW 1

Koontz, Dean
See Koontz, Dean R.

Koontz, Dean R. 1945- .... **CLC 78, 206**
See also AAYA 9, 31; BEST 89:3, 90:2; CA 108; CANR 19, 36, 52, 95, 138, 176; CMW 4; CPW; DA3; DAM NOV, POP; DLB 292; HGG; MTCW 1; MTFW 2005; SATA 92, 165; SFW 4; SUFW 2; YAW

Koontz, Dean Ray
See Koontz, Dean R.

Kopernik, Mikolaj
See Copernicus, Nicolaus

Kopit, Arthur (Lee) 1937- ...... **CLC 1, 18, 33**
See also AITN 1; CA 81-84; CABS 3; CAD; CD 5, 6; DAM DRAM; DFS 7, 14, 24; DLB 7; MAL 5; MTCW 1; RGAL 4

Kopitar, Jernej (Bartholomaus)
1780-1844 .... **NCLC 117**

Kops, Bernard 1926- .... **CLC 4**
See also CA 5-8R; CANR 84, 159; CBD; CN 1, 2, 3, 4, 5, 6, 7; CP 1, 2, 3, 4, 5, 6, 7; DLB 13; RGHL

Kornbluth, C(yril) M. 1923-1958 .... **TCLC 8**
See also CA 105; 160; DLB 8; SCFW 1, 2; SFW 4

La Fontaine, Jean de 1621-1695 .... **LC 50**
　　See also DLB 268; EW 3; GFL Beginnings
　　to 1789; MAICYA 1, 2; RGWL 2, 3;
　　SATA 18
LaForet, Carmen 1921-2004 .... **CLC 219**
　　See also CA 246; CWW 2; DLB 322; EWL
　　3
LaForet Diaz, Carmen
　　See LaForet, Carmen
Laforgue, Jules 1860-1887 . **NCLC 5, 53; PC**
　　14; SSC 20
　　See also DLB 217; EW 7; GFL 1789 to the
　　Present; RGWL 2, 3
Lagerkvist, Paer (Fabian)
　　1891-1974 .. **CLC 7, 10, 13, 54; SSC 12;**
　　TCLC 144
　　See also CA 85-88; 49-52; DA3; DAM
　　DRAM, NOV; DLB 259, 331; EW 10;
　　EWL 3; MTCW 1, 2; MTFW 2005; RGSF
　　2; RGWL 2, 3; TWA
Lagerkvist, Par
　　See Lagerkvist, Paer (Fabian)
Lagerloef, Selma (Ottiliana Lovisa)
　　See Lagerlof, Selma (Ottiliana Lovisa)
Lagerlof, Selma (Ottiliana Lovisa)
　　1858-1940 .... **TCLC 4, 36**
　　See also CA 108; 188; CLR 7; DLB 259,
　　331; MTCW 2; RGWL 2, 3; SATA 15;
　　SSFS 18
La Guma, Alex 1925-1985 .. **BLCS; CLC 19;**
　　TCLC 140
　　See also AFW; BW 1, 3; CA 49-52; 118;
　　CANR 25, 81; CDWLB 3; CN 1, 2, 3;
　　CP 1; DAM NOV; DLB 117, 225; EWL
　　3; MTCW 1, 2; MTFW 2005; WLIT 2;
　　WWE 1
Lahiri, Jhumpa 1967- .... **SSC 96**
　　See also AAYA 56; CA 193; CANR 134,
　　184; DLB 323; MTFW 2005; SSFS 19,
　　27
Laidlaw, A. K.
　　See Grieve, C(hristopher) M(urray)
Lainez, Manuel Mujica
　　See Mujica Lainez, Manuel
Laing, R(onald) D(avid) 1927-1989 . **CLC 95**
　　See also CA 107; 129; CANR 34; MTCW 1
Laishley, Alex
　　See Booth, Martin
Lamartine, Alphonse (Marie Louis Prat) de
　　1790-1869 .... **NCLC 11, 190; PC 16**
　　See also DAM POET; DLB 217; GFL 1789
　　to the Present; RGWL 2, 3
Lamb, Charles 1775-1834 ..... **NCLC 10, 113;**
　　SSC 112; WLC 3
　　See also BRW 4; CDBLB 1789-1832; DA;
　　DAB; DAC; DAM MST; DLB 93, 107,
　　163; RGEL 2; SATA 17; TEA
Lamb, Lady Caroline 1785-1828 ... **NCLC 38**
　　See also DLB 116
Lamb, Mary Ann 1764-1847 ...... **NCLC 125;**
　　SSC 112
　　See also DLB 163; SATA 17
Lame Deer 1903(?)-1976 .... **NNAL**
　　See also CA 69-72
Lamming, George (William)
　　1927- . **BLC 1:2, 2:2; CLC 2, 4, 66, 144**
　　See also BW 2, 3; CA 85-88; CANR 26,
　　76; CDWLB 3; CN 1, 2, 3, 4, 5, 6, 7; CP
　　1; DAM MULT; DLB 125; EWL 3;
　　MTCW 1, 2; MTFW 2005; NFS 15;
　　RGEL 2
L'Amour, Louis 1908-1988 .... **CLC 25, 55**
　　See also AAYA 16; AITN 2; BEST 89:2;
　　BPFB 2; CA 1-4R; 125; CANR 3, 25, 40;
　　CPW; DA3; DAM NOV, POP; DLB 206;
　　DLBY 1980; MTCW 1, 2; MTFW 2005;
　　RGAL 4; TCWW 1, 2
Lampedusa, Giuseppe (Tomasi) di
　　See Tomasi di Lampedusa, Giuseppe

Lampman, Archibald 1861-1899 .. **NCLC 25,**
　　194
　　See also DLB 92; RGEL 2; TWA
Lancaster, Bruce 1896-1963 .... **CLC 36**
　　See also CA 9-10; CANR 70; CAP 1; SATA
　　9
Lanchester, John 1962- .... **CLC 99**
　　See also CA 194; DLB 267
Landau, Mark Alexandrovich
　　See Aldanov, Mark (Alexandrovich)
Landau-Aldanov, Mark Alexandrovich
　　See Aldanov, Mark (Alexandrovich)
Landis, Jerry
　　See Simon, Paul
Landis, John 1950- .... **CLC 26**
　　See also CA 112; 122; CANR 128
Landolfi, Tommaso 1908-1979 .... **CLC 11, 49**
　　See also CA 127; 117; DLB 177; EWL 3
Landon, Letitia Elizabeth
　　1802-1838 .... **NCLC 15**
　　See also DLB 96
Landor, Walter Savage
　　1775-1864 .... **NCLC 14**
　　See also BRW 4; DLB 93, 107; RGEL 2
Landwirth, Heinz
　　See Lind, Jakov
Lane, Patrick 1939- .... **CLC 25**
　　See also CA 97-100; CANR 54; CP 3, 4, 5,
　　6, 7; DAM POET; DLB 53; INT CA-97-
　　100
Lane, Rose Wilder 1887-1968 ...... **TCLC 177**
　　See also CA 102; CANR 63; SATA 29;
　　SATA-Brief 28; TCWW 2
Lang, Andrew 1844-1912 .... **TCLC 16**
　　See also CA 114; 137; CANR 85; CLR 101;
　　DLB 98, 141, 184; FANT; MAICYA 1, 2;
　　RGEL 2; SATA 16; WCH
Lang, Fritz 1890-1976 .... **CLC 20, 103**
　　See also AAYA 65; CA 77-80; 69-72;
　　CANR 30
Lange, John
　　See Crichton, Michael
Langer, Elinor 1939- .... **CLC 34**
　　See also CA 121
Langland, William 1332(?)-1400(?) .... **LC 19,**
　　120
　　See also BRW 1; DA; DAB; DAC; DAM
　　MST, POET; DLB 146; RGEL 2; TEA;
　　WLIT 3
Langstaff, Launcelot
　　See Irving, Washington
Lanier, Sidney 1842-1881 . **NCLC 6, 118; PC**
　　50
　　See also AMWS 1; DAM POET; DLB 64;
　　DLBD 13; EXPP; MAICYA 1; PFS 14;
　　RGAL 4; SATA 18
Lanyer, Aemilia 1569-1645 .... **LC 10, 30, 83;**
　　PC 60
　　See also DLB 121
Lao-Tzu
　　See Lao Tzu
Lao Tzu c. 6th cent. B.C.-3rd cent.
　　B.C. .... **CMLC 7**
Lapine, James (Elliot) 1949- .... **CLC 39**
　　See also CA 123; 130; CANR 54, 128; DFS
　　25; DLB 341; INT CA-130
Larbaud, Valery (Nicolas)
　　1881-1957 .... **TCLC 9**
　　See also CA 106; 152; EWL 3; GFL 1789
　　to the Present
Larcom, Lucy 1824-1893 .... **NCLC 179**
　　See also AMWS 13; DLB 221, 243
Lardner, Ring
　　See Lardner, Ring(gold) W(ilmer)
Lardner, Ring W., Jr.
　　See Lardner, Ring(gold) W(ilmer)

Lardner, Ring(gold) W(ilmer)
　　1885-1933 ..... **SSC 32, 118; TCLC 2, 14**
　　See also AMW; BPFB 2; CA 104; 131;
　　CDALB 1917-1929; DLB 11, 25, 86, 171;
　　DLBD 16; MAL 5; MTCW 1, 2; MTFW
　　2005; RGAL 4; RGSF 2; TUS
Laredo, Betty
　　See Codrescu, Andrei
Larkin, Maia
　　See Wojciechowska, Maia (Teresa)
Larkin, Philip (Arthur) 1922-1985 ... **CLC 3,**
　　5, 8, 9, 13, 18, 33, 39, 64; PC 21
　　See also BRWS 1; CA 5-8R; 117; CANR
　　24, 62; CDBLB 1960 to Present; CP 1, 2,
　　3, 4; DA3; DAB; DAM MST, POET;
　　DLB 27; EWL 3; MTCW 1, 2; MTFW
　　2005; PFS 3, 4, 12; RGEL 2
La Roche, Sophie von
　　1730-1807 .... **NCLC 121**
　　See also DLB 94
La Rochefoucauld, Francois
　　1613-1680 .... **LC 108**
　　See also DLB 268; EW 3; GFL Beginnings
　　to 1789; RGWL 2, 3
Larra (y Sanchez de Castro), Mariano Jose
　　de 1809-1837 .... **NCLC 17, 130**
Larsen, Eric 1941- .... **CLC 55**
　　See also CA 132
Larsen, Nella 1893(?)-1963 ... **BLC 1:2; CLC**
　　37; HR 1:3; TCLC 200
　　See also AFAW 1, 2; AMWS 18; BW 1;
　　CA 125; CANR 83; DAM MULT; DLB
　　51; FW; LATS 1:1; LMFS 2
Larson, Charles R(aymond) 1938- ... **CLC 31**
　　See also CA 53-56; CANR 4, 121
Larson, Jonathan 1960-1996 .... **CLC 99**
　　See also AAYA 28; CA 156; DFS 23;
　　MTFW 2005
La Sale, Antoine de c. 1386-1460(?) . **LC 104**
　　See also DLB 208
Las Casas, Bartolome de
　　1474-1566 .... **HLCS; LC 31**
　　See also DLB 318; LAW; WLIT 1
Lasch, Christopher 1932-1994 .... **CLC 102**
　　See also CA 73-76; 144; CANR 25, 118;
　　DLB 246; MTCW 1, 2; MTFW 2005
Lasker-Schueler, Else 1869-1945 ... **TCLC 57**
　　See also CA 183; DLB 66, 124; EWL 3
Lasker-Schuler, Else
　　See Lasker-Schueler, Else
Laski, Harold J(oseph) 1893-1950 . **TCLC 79**
　　See also CA 188
Latham, Jean Lee 1902-1995 .... **CLC 12**
　　See also AITN 1; BYA 1; CA 5-8R; CANR
　　7, 84; CLR 50; MAICYA 1, 2; SATA 2,
　　68; YAW
Latham, Mavis
　　See Clark, Mavis Thorpe
Lathen, Emma
　　See Hennissart, Martha
Lathrop, Francis
　　See Leiber, Fritz (Reuter, Jr.)
Lathen, Emma
　　See Lattany, Kristin (Elaine Eggleston)
　　Hunter
Lattany, Kristin (Elaine Eggleston) Hunter
　　1931- .... **CLC 35**
　　See also AITN 1; BW 1; BYA 3; CA 13-
　　16R; CANR 13, 108; CLR 3; CN 1, 2, 3,
　　4, 5, 6; DLB 33; INT CANR-13; MAI-
　　CYA 1, 2; SAAS 10; SATA 12, 132; YAW
Lattimore, Richmond (Alexander)
　　1906-1984 .... **CLC 3**
　　See also CA 1-4R; 112; CANR 1; CP 1, 2,
　　3; MAL 5
Laughlin, James 1914-1997 .... **CLC 49**
　　See also CA 21-24R; 162; CAAS 22; CANR
　　9, 47; CP 1, 2, 3, 4, 5, 6; DLB 48; DLBY
　　1996, 1997

Laurence, Jean Margaret Wemyss
See Laurence, Margaret
Laurence, Margaret 1926-1987 ..... **CLC 3, 6, 13, 50, 62; SSC 7**
See also BYA 13; CA 5-8R; 121; CANR 33; CN 1, 2, 3, 4; DAC; DAM MST; DLB 53; EWL 3; FW; MTCW 1, 2; MTFW 2005; NFS 11; RGEL 2; RGSF 2; SATA-Obit 50; TCWW 2
Laurent, Antoine 1952- .... **CLC 50**
Lauscher, Hermann
See Hesse, Hermann
Lautreamont 1846-1870 .... **NCLC 12, 194; SSC 14**
See also DLB 217; GFL 1789 to the Present; RGWL 2, 3
Lautreamont, Isidore Lucien Ducasse
See Lautreamont
Lavater, Johann Kaspar 1741-1801 .... **NCLC 142**
See also DLB 97
Laverty, Donald
See Blish, James (Benjamin)
Lavin, Mary 1912-1996 . **CLC 4, 18, 99; SSC 4, 67**
See also CA 9-12R; 151; CANR 33; CN 1, 2, 3, 4, 5, 6; DLB 15, 319; FW; MTCW 1; RGEL 2; RGSF 2; SSFS 23
Lavond, Paul Dennis
See Kornbluth, C(yril) M.; Pohl, Frederik
Lawes, Henry 1596-1662 .... **LC 113**
See also DLB 126
Lawler, Ray
See Lawler, Raymond Evenor
Lawler, Raymond Evenor 1922- .... **CLC 58**
See also CA 103; CD 5, 6; DLB 289; RGEL 2
Lawrence, D(avid) H(erbert Richards)
1885-1930 .... **PC 54; SSC 4, 19, 73; TCLC 2, 9, 16, 33, 48, 61, 93; WLC 3**
See also BPFB 2; BRW 7; BRWR 2; CA 104; 121; CANR 131; CDBLB 1914-1945; DA; DA3; DAB; DAC; DAM MST, NOV, POET; DLB 10, 19, 36, 98, 162, 195; EWL 3; EXPP; EXPS; GLL 1; LAIT 2, 3; MTCW 1, 2; MTFW 2005; NFS 18, 26; PFS 6; RGEL 2; RGSF 2; SSFS 2, 6; TEA; WLIT 4; WP
Lawrence, T(homas) E(dward)
1888-1935 .... **TCLC 18, 204**
See also BRWS 2; CA 115; 167; DLB 195
Lawrence of Arabia
See Lawrence, T(homas) E(dward)
Lawson, Henry (Archibald Hertzberg)
1867-1922 .... **SSC 18; TCLC 27**
See also CA 120; 181; DLB 230; RGEL 2; RGSF 2
Lawton, Dennis
See Faust, Frederick (Schiller)
Laxness, Halldor (Kiljan)
See Gudjonsson, Halldor Kiljan
Layamon fl. c. 1200- .... **CMLC 10, 105**
See also DLB 146; RGEL 2
Laye, Camara 1928-1980 .. **BLC 1:2; CLC 4, 38**
See also AFW; BW 1; CA 85-88; 97-100; CANR 25; DAM MULT; EWL 3; MTCW 1, 2; WLIT 2
Layton, Irving 1912-2006 ..... **CLC 2, 15, 164**
See also CA 1-4R; 247; CANR 2, 33, 43, 66, 129; CP 1, 2, 3, 4, 5, 6, 7; DAC; DAM MST, POET; DLB 88; EWL 3; MTCW 1, 2; PFS 12; RGEL 2
Layton, Irving Peter
See Layton, Irving
Lazarus, Emma 1849-1887 ...... **NCLC 8, 109**
Lazarus, Felix
See Cable, George Washington

Lazarus, Henry
See Slavitt, David R.
Lea, Joan
See Neufeld, John (Arthur)
Leacock, Stephen (Butler)
1869-1944 .... **SSC 39; TCLC 2**
See also CA 104; 141; CANR 80; DAC; DAM MST; DLB 92; EWL 3; MTCW 2; MTFW 2005; RGEL 2; RGSF 2
Lead, Jane Ward 1623-1704 .... **LC 72**
See also DLB 131
Leapor, Mary 1722-1746 .... **LC 80; PC 85**
See also DLB 109
Lear, Edward 1812-1888 ..... **NCLC 3; PC 65**
See also AAYA 48; BRW 5; CLR 1, 75; DLB 32, 163, 166; MAICYA 1, 2; RGEL 2; SATA 18, 100; WCH; WP
Lear, Norman (Milton) 1922- .... **CLC 12**
See also CA 73-76
Least Heat-Moon, William
See Trogdon, William (Lewis)
Leautaud, Paul 1872-1956 .... **TCLC 83**
See also CA 203; DLB 65; GFL 1789 to the Present
Leavis, F(rank) R(aymond)
1895-1978 .... **CLC 24**
See also BRW 7; CA 21-24R; 77-80; CANR 44; DLB 242; EWL 3; MTCW 1, 2; RGEL 2
Leavitt, David 1961- .... **CLC 34**
See also CA 116; 122; CANR 50, 62, 101, 134, 177; CPW; DA3; DAM POP; DLB 130; GLL 1; INT CA-122; MAL 5; MTCW 2; MTFW 2005
Leblanc, Maurice (Marie Emile)
1864-1941 .... **TCLC 49**
See also CA 110; CMW 4
Lebowitz, Fran(ces Ann) 1951(?)- ... **CLC 11, 36**
See also CA 81-84; CANR 14, 60, 70; INT CANR-14; MTCW 1
Lebrecht, Peter
See Tieck, (Johann) Ludwig
le Cagat, Benat
See Whitaker, Rod
le Carre, John
See le Carre, John
le Carre, John 1931- .... **CLC 9, 15**
See also AAYA 42; BEST 89:4; BPFB 2; BRWS 2; CA 5-8R; CANR 13, 33, 59, 107, 132, 172; CDBLB 1960 to Present; CMW 4; CN 1, 2, 3, 4, 5, 6, 7; CPW; DA3; DAM POP; DLB 87; EWL 3; MSW; MTCW 1, 2; MTFW 2005; RGEL 2; TEA
Le Clezio, J. M.G. 1940- . **CLC 31, 155; SSC 122**
See also CA 116; 128; CANR 147; CWW 2; DLB 83; EWL 3; GFL 1789 to the Present; RGSF 2
Le Clezio, Jean Marie Gustave
See Le Clezio, J. M.G.
Leconte de Lisle, Charles-Marie-Rene
1818-1894 .... **NCLC 29**
See also DLB 217; EW 6; GFL 1789 to the Present
Le Coq, Monsieur
See Simenon, Georges (Jacques Christian)
Leduc, Violette 1907-1972 .... **CLC 22**
See also CA 13-14; 33-36R; CANR 69; CAP 1; EWL 3; GFL 1789 to the Present; GLL 1
Ledwidge, Francis 1887(?)-1917 .... **TCLC 23**
See also CA 123; 203; DLB 20
Lee, Andrea 1953- .... **BLC 1:2; CLC 36**
See also BW 1, 3; CA 125; CANR 82; DAM MULT
Lee, Andrew
See Auchincloss, Louis

Lee, Chang-rae 1965- .... **CLC 91, 268, 274**
See also CA 148; CANR 89; CN 7; DLB 312; LATS 1:2
Lee, Don L.
See Madhubuti, Haki R.
Lee, George W(ashington)
1894-1976 .... **BLC 1:2; CLC 52**
See also BW 1; CA 125; CANR 83; DAM MULT; DLB 51
Lee, Harper 1926- ... **CLC 12, 60, 194; WLC 4**
See also AAYA 13; AMWS 8; BPFB 2; BYA 3; CA 13-16R; CANR 51, 128; CDALB 1941-1968; CSW; DA; DA3; DAB; DAC; DAM MST, NOV; DLB 6; EXPN; LAIT 3; MAL 5; MTCW 1, 2; MTFW 2005; NFS 2; SATA 11; WYA; YAW
Lee, Helen Elaine 1959(?)- .... **CLC 86**
See also CA 148
Lee, John CLC 70
Lee, Julian
See Latham, Jean Lee
Lee, Larry
See Lee, Lawrence
Lee, Laurie 1914-1997 .... **CLC 90**
See also CA 77-80; 158; CANR 33, 73; CP 1, 2, 3, 4, 5, 6; CPW; DAB; DAM POP; DLB 27; MTCW 1; RGEL 2
Lee, Lawrence 1941-1990 .... **CLC 34**
See also CA 131; CANR 43
Lee, Li-Young 1957- .... **CLC 164; PC 24**
See also AMWS 15; CA 153; CANR 118; CP 6, 7; DLB 165, 312; LMFS 2; PFS 11, 15, 17
Lee, Manfred B. 1905-1971 .... **CLC 11**
See also CA 1-4R; 29-32R; CANR 2, 150; CMW 4; DLB 137
Lee, Manfred Bennington
See Lee, Manfred B.
Lee, Nathaniel 1645(?)-1692 .... **LC 103**
See also DLB 80; RGEL 2
Lee, Nelle Harper
See Lee, Harper
Lee, Shelton Jackson
See Lee, Spike
Lee, Sophia 1750-1824 .... **NCLC 191**
See also DLB 39
Lee, Spike 1957(?)- .... **BLCS; CLC 105**
See also AAYA 4, 29; BW 2, 3; CA 125; CANR 42, 164; DAM MULT
Lee, Stan 1922- .... **CLC 17**
See also AAYA 5, 49; CA 108; 111; CANR 129; INT CA-111; MTFW 2005
Lee, Tanith 1947- .... **CLC 46**
See also AAYA 15; CA 37-40R; CANR 53, 102, 145, 170; DLB 261; FANT; SATA 8, 88, 134, 185; SFW 4; SUFW 1, 2; YAW
Lee, Vernon
See Paget, Violet
Lee, William
See Burroughs, William S.
Lee, Willy
See Burroughs, William S.
Lee-Hamilton, Eugene (Jacob)
1845-1907 .... **TCLC 22**
See also CA 117; 234
Leet, Judith 1935- .... **CLC 11**
See also CA 187
Le Fanu, Joseph Sheridan
1814-1873 .... **NCLC 9, 58; SSC 14, 84**
See also CMW 4; DA3; DAM POP; DLB 21, 70, 159, 178; GL 3; HGG; RGEL 2; RGSF 2; SUFW 1
Leffland, Ella 1931- .... **CLC 19**
See also CA 29-32R; CANR 35, 78, 82; DLBY 1984; INT CANR-35; SATA 65; SSFS 24

Lively, Penelope 1933- .... **CLC 32, 50**
See also BPFB 2; CA 41-44R; CANR 29, 67, 79, 131, 172; CLR 7; CN 5, 6, 7; CWRI 5; DAM NOV; DLB 14, 161, 207, 326; FANT; JRDA; MAICYA 1, 2; MTCW 1, 2; MTFW 2005; SATA 7, 60, 101, 164; TEA
Lively, Penelope Margaret
See Lively, Penelope
Livesay, Dorothy (Kathleen)
1909-1996 .... **CLC 4, 15, 79**
See also AITN 2; CA 25-28R; CAAS 8; CANR 36, 67; CP 1, 2, 3, 4, 5; DAC; DAM MST, POET; DLB 68; FW; MTCW 1; RGEL 2; TWA
Livius Andronicus c. 284B.C.-c.
204B.C. .... **CMLC 102**
Livy c. 59B.C.-c. 12 .... **CMLC 11**
See also AW 2; CDWLB 1; DLB 211; RGWL 2, 3; WLIT 8
Li Yaotang
See Jin, Ba
Lizardi, Jose Joaquin Fernandez de
1776-1827 .... **NCLC 30**
See also LAW
Llewellyn, Richard
See Llewellyn Lloyd, Richard Dafydd Vivian
Llewellyn Lloyd, Richard Dafydd Vivian
1906-1983 .... **CLC 7, 80**
See also CA 53-56; 111; CANR 7, 71; DLB 15; SATA 11; SATA-Obit 37
Llosa, Jorge Mario Pedro Vargas
See Vargas Llosa, Mario
Llosa, Mario Vargas
See Vargas Llosa, Mario
Lloyd, Manda
See Mander, (Mary) Jane
Lloyd Webber, Andrew 1948- .... **CLC 21**
See also AAYA 1, 38; CA 116; 149; DAM DRAM; DFS 7; SATA 56
Llull, Ramon c. 1235-c. 1316 .... **CMLC 12**
Lobb, Ebenezer
See Upward, Allen
Locke, Alain (Le Roy)
1886-1954 .... **BLCS; HR 1:3; TCLC 43**
See also AMWS 14; BW 1, 3; CA 106; 124; CANR 79; DLB 51; LMFS 2; MAL 5; RGAL 4
Locke, John 1632-1704 .... **LC 7, 35, 135**
See also DLB 31, 101, 213, 252; RGEL 2; WLIT 3
Locke-Elliott, Sumner
See Elliott, Sumner Locke
Lockhart, John Gibson 1794-1854 .. **NCLC 6**
See also DLB 110, 116, 144
Lockridge, Ross (Franklin), Jr.
1914-1948 .... **TCLC 111**
See also CA 108; 145; CANR 79; DLB 143; DLBY 1980; MAL 5; RGAL 4; RHW
Lockwood, Robert
See Johnson, Robert
Lodge, David 1935- .... **CLC 36, 141**
See also BEST 90:1; BRWS 4; CA 17-20R; CANR 19, 53, 92, 139; CN 1, 2, 3, 4, 5, 6, 7; CPW; DAM POP; DLB 14, 194; EWL 3; INT CANR-19; MTCW 1, 2; MTFW 2005
Lodge, Thomas 1558-1625 .... **LC 41**
See also DLB 172; RGEL 2
Loewinsohn, Ron(ald William)
1937- .... **CLC 52**
See also CA 25-28R; CANR 71; CP 1, 2, 3, 4
Logan, Jake
See Smith, Martin Cruz
Logan, John (Burton) 1923-1987 .... **CLC 5**
See also CA 77-80; 124; CANR 45; CP 1, 2, 3, 4; DLB 5

Lo-Johansson, (Karl) Ivar
1901-1990 .... **TCLC 216**
See also CA 102; 131; CANR 20, 79, 137; DLB 259; EWL 3; RGWL 2, 3
Lo Kuan-chung 1330(?)-1400(?) .... **LC 12**
Lomax, Pearl
See Cleage, Pearl
Lomax, Pearl Cleage
See Cleage, Pearl
Lombard, Nap
See Johnson, Pamela Hansford
Lombard, Peter 1100(?)-1160(?) ... **CMLC 72**
Lombino, Salvatore
See Hunter, Evan
London, Jack 1876-1916
See London, John Griffith
London, John Griffith 1876-1916 .... **SSC 4, 49; TCLC 9, 15, 39; WLC 4**
See also AAYA 13, 75; AITN 2; AMW; BPFB 2; BYA 4, 13; CA 110; 119; CANR 73; CDALB 1865-1917; CLR 108; DA; DA3; DAB; DAC; DAM MST, NOV; DLB 8, 12, 78, 212; EWL 3; EXPS; JRDA; LAIT 3; MAICYA 1, 2; MAL 5; MTCW 1, 2; MTFW 2005; NFS 8, 19; RGAL 4; RGSF 2; SATA 18; SFW 4; SSFS 7; TCWW 1, 2; TUS; WYA; YAW
Long, Emmett
See Leonard, Elmore
Longbaugh, Harry
See Goldman, William
Longfellow, Henry Wadsworth
1807-1882 .... **NCLC 2, 45, 101, 103; PC 30; WLCS**
See also AMW; AMWR 2; CDALB 1640-1865; CLR 99; DA; DA3; DAB; DAC; DAM MST, POET; DLB 1, 59, 235; EXPP; PAB; PFS 2, 7, 17; RGAL 4; SATA 19; TUS; WP
Longinus c. 1st cent. - .... **CMLC 27**
See also AW 2; DLB 176
Longley, Michael 1939- .... **CLC 29**
See also BRWS 8; CA 102; CP 1, 2, 3, 4, 5, 6, 7; DLB 40
Longstreet, Augustus Baldwin
1790-1870 .... **NCLC 159**
See also DLB 3, 11, 74, 248; RGAL 4
Longus fl. c. 2nd cent. - .... **CMLC 7**
Longway, A. Hugh
See Lang, Andrew
Lonnbohm, Armas Eino Leopold
See Lonnbohm, Armas Eino Leopold
Lonnbohm, Armas Eino Leopold
1878-1926 .... **TCLC 24**
See also CA 123; EWL 3
Lonnrot, Elias 1802-1884 .... **NCLC 53**
See also EFS 1
Lonsdale, Roger CLC 65
Lopate, Phillip 1943- .... **CLC 29**
See also CA 97-100; CANR 88, 157; DLBY 1980; INT CA-97-100
Lopez, Barry (Holstun) 1945- .... **CLC 70**
See also AAYA 9, 63; ANW; CA 65-68; CANR 7, 23, 47, 68, 92; DLB 256, 275, 335; INT CANR-7, CANR-23; MTCW 1; RGAL 4; SATA 67
Lopez de Mendoza, Inigo
See Santillana, Inigo Lopez de Mendoza, Marques de
Lopez Portillo (y Pacheco), Jose
1920-2004 .... **CLC 46**
See also CA 129; 224; HW 1
Lopez y Fuentes, Gregorio
1897(?)-1966 .... **CLC 32**
See also CA 131; EWL 3; HW 1
Lorca, Federico Garcia
See Garcia Lorca, Federico
Lord, Audre
See Lorde, Audre

Lord, Bette Bao 1938- .... **AAL; CLC 23**
See also BEST 90:3; BPFB 2; CA 107; CANR 41, 79; INT CA-107; SATA 58
Lord Auch
See Bataille, Georges
Lord Brooke
See Greville, Fulke
Lord Byron
See Byron, George Gordon (Noel)
Lord Dunsany
See Dunsany, Edward John Moreton Drax Plunkett
Lorde, Audre 1934-1992 .... **BLC 1:2, 2:2; CLC 18, 71; PC 12; TCLC 173**
See also AFAW 1, 2; BW 1, 3; CA 25-28R; 142; CANR 16, 26, 46, 82; CP 2, 3, 4, 5; DA3; DAM MULT, POET; DLB 41; EWL 3; FW; GLL 1; MAL 5; MTCW 1, 2; MTFW 2005; PFS 16; RGAL 4
Lorde, Audre Geraldine
See Lorde, Audre
Lord Houghton
See Milnes, Richard Monckton
Lord Jeffrey
See Jeffrey, Francis
Loreaux, Nichol CLC 65
Lorenzini, Carlo 1826-1890 .... **NCLC 54**
See also CLR 5, 120; MAICYA 1, 2; SATA 29, 100; WCH; WLIT 7
Lorenzo, Heberto Padilla
See Padilla (Lorenzo), Heberto
Loris
See Hofmannsthal, Hugo von
Loti, Pierre
See Viaud, (Louis Marie) Julien
Lottie
See Grimke, Charlotte L(ottie) Forten
Lou, Henri
See Andreas-Salome, Lou
Louie, David Wong 1954- .... **CLC 70**
See also CA 139; CANR 120
Louis, Adrian C. NNAL
See also CA 223
Louis, Father M.
See Merton, Thomas (James)
Louise, Heidi
See Erdrich, Louise
Lovecraft, H. P. 1890-1937 .... **SSC 3, 52; TCLC 4, 22**
See also AAYA 14; BPFB 2; CA 104; 133; CANR 106; DA3; DAM POP; HGG; MTCW 1, 2; MTFW 2005; RGAL 4; SCFW 1, 2; SFW 4; SUFW
Lovecraft, Howard Phillips
See Lovecraft, H. P.
Lovelace, Earl 1935- .... **CLC 51**
See also BW 2; CA 77-80; CANR 41, 72, 114; CD 5, 6; CDWLB 3; CN 1, 2, 3, 4, 5, 6, 7; DLB 125; EWL 3; MTCW 1
Lovelace, Richard 1618-1658 ..... **LC 24, 158; PC 69**
See also BRW 2; DLB 131; EXPP; PAB; RGEL 2
Low, Penelope Margaret
See Lively, Penelope
Lowe, Pardee 1904- .... **AAL**
Lowell, Amy 1874-1925 ... **PC 13; TCLC 1, 8**
See also AAYA 57; AMW; CA 104; 151; DAM POET; DLB 54, 140; EWL 3; EXPP; LMFS 2; MAL 5; MBL; MTCW 2; MTFW 2005; PFS 30; RGAL 4; TUS
Lowell, James Russell 1819-1891 ... **NCLC 2, 90**
See also AMWS 1; CDALB 1640-1865; DLB 1, 11, 64, 79, 189, 235; RGAL 4

Machiavelli, Niccolo 1469-1527 ... **DC 16; LC 8, 36, 140; WLCS**
See also AAYA 58; DA; DAB; DAC; DAM MST; EW 2; LAIT 1; LMFS 1; NFS 9; RGWL 2, 3; TWA; WLIT 7

MacInnes, Colin 1914-1976 .... **CLC 4, 23**
See also CA 69-72; 65-68; CANR 21; CN 1, 2; DLB 14; MTCW 1, 2; RGEL 2; RHW

MacInnes, Helen (Clark)
1907-1985 .... **CLC 27, 39**
See also BPFB 2; CA 1-4R; 117; CANR 1, 28, 58; CMW 4; CN 1, 2; CPW; DAM POP; DLB 87; MSW; MTCW 1, 2; MTFW 2005; SATA 22; SATA-Obit 44

Mackay, Mary 1855-1924 .... **TCLC 51**
See also CA 118; 177; DLB 34, 156; FANT; RGEL 2; RHW; SUFW 1

Mackay, Shena 1944- .... **CLC 195**
See also CA 104; CANR 88, 139; DLB 231, 319; MTFW 2005

Mackenzie, Compton (Edward Montague)
1883-1972 .... **CLC 18; TCLC 116**
See also CA 21-22; 37-40R; CAP 2; CN 1; DLB 34, 100; RGEL 2

Mackenzie, Henry 1745-1831 .... **NCLC 41**
See also DLB 39; RGEL 2

Mackey, Nathaniel 1947- .... **BLC 2:3; PC 49**
See also CA 153; CANR 114; CP 6, 7; DLB 169

Mackey, Nathaniel Ernest
See Mackey, Nathaniel

MacKinnon, Catharine A. 1946- .... **CLC 181**
See also CA 128; 132; CANR 73, 140, 189; FW; MTCW 2; MTFW 2005

Mackintosh, Elizabeth
1896(?)-1952 .... **TCLC 14**
See also CA 110; CMW 4; DLB 10, 77; MSW

Macklin, Charles 1699-1797 .... **LC 132**
See also DLB 89; RGEL 2

MacLaren, James
See Grieve, C(hristopher) M(urray)

MacLaverty, Bernard 1942- .... **CLC 31, 243**
See also CA 116; 118; CANR 43, 88, 168; CN 5, 6, 7; DLB 267; INT CA-118; RGSF 2

MacLean, Alistair (Stuart)
1922(?)-1987 .... **CLC 3, 13, 50, 63**
See also CA 57-60; 121; CANR 28, 61; CMW 4; CP 2, 3, 4, 5, 6, 7; CPW; DAM POP; DLB 276; MTCW 1; SATA 23; SATA-Obit 50; TCWW 2

Maclean, Norman (Fitzroy)
1902-1990 .... **CLC 78; SSC 13**
See also AMWS 14; CA 102; 132; CANR 49; CPW; DAM POP; DLB 206; TCWW 2

MacLeish, Archibald 1892-1982 ... **CLC 3, 8, 14, 68; PC 47**
See also AMW; CA 9-12R; 106; CAD; CANR 33, 63; CDALBS; CP 1, 2; DAM POET; DFS 15; DLB 4, 7, 45; DLBY 1982; EWL 3; EXPP; MAL 5; MTCW 1, 2; MTFW 2005; PAB; PFS 5; RGAL 4; TUS

MacLennan, (John) Hugh
1907-1990 .... **CLC 2, 14, 92**
See also CA 5-8R; 142; CANR 33; CN 1, 2, 3, 4; DAC; DAM MST; DLB 68; EWL 3; MTCW 1, 2; MTFW 2005; RGEL 2; TWA

MacLeod, Alistair 1936- .. **CLC 56, 165; SSC 90**
See also CA 123; CCA 1; DAC; DAM MST; DLB 60; MTCW 2; MTFW 2005; RGSF 2; TCLE 1:2

Macleod, Fiona
See Sharp, William

MacNeice, (Frederick) Louis
1907-1963 .... **CLC 1, 4, 10, 53; PC 61**
See also BRW 7; CA 85-88; CANR 61; DAB; DAM POET; DLB 10, 20; EWL 3; MTCW 1, 2; MTFW 2005; RGEL 2

MacNeill, Dand
See Fraser, George MacDonald

Macpherson, James 1736-1796 .... **CMLC 28; LC 29; PC 97**
See also BRWS 8; DLB 109, 336; RGEL 2

Macpherson, (Jean) Jay 1931- .... **CLC 14**
See also CA 5-8R; CANR 90; CP 1, 2, 3, 4, 6, 7; CWP; DLB 53

Macrobius fl. 430- .... **CMLC 48**

MacShane, Frank 1927-1999 .... **CLC 39**
See also CA 9-12R; 186; CANR 3, 33; DLB 111

Macumber, Mari
See Sandoz, Mari(e Susette)

Madach, Imre 1823-1864 .... **NCLC 19**

Madden, (Jerry) David 1933- .... **CLC 5, 15**
See also CA 1-4R; CAAS 3; CANR 4, 45; CN 3, 4, 5, 6, 7; CSW; DLB 6; MTCW 1

Maddern, Al(an)
See Ellison, Harlan

Madhubuti, Haki R. 1942- .... **BLC 1:2; CLC 2; PC 5**
See also BW 2, 3; CA 73-76; CANR 24, 51, 73, 139; CP 2, 3, 4, 5, 6, 7; CSW; DAM MULT, POET; DLB 5, 41; DLBD 8; EWL 3; MAL 5; MTCW 2; MTFW 2005; RGAL 4

Madison, James 1751-1836 .... **NCLC 126**
See also DLB 37

Maepenn, Hugh
See Kuttner, Henry

Maepenn, K. H.
See Kuttner, Henry

Maeterlinck, Maurice 1862-1949 .... **DC 32; TCLC 3**
See also CA 104; 136; CANR 80; DAM DRAM; DLB 192, 331; EW 8; EWL 3; GFL 1789 to the Present; LMFS 2; RGWL 2, 3; SATA 66; TWA

Maginn, William 1794-1842 .... **NCLC 8**
See also DLB 110, 159

Mahapatra, Jayanta 1928- .... **CLC 33**
See also CA 73-76; CAAS 9; CANR 15, 33, 66, 87; CP 4, 5, 6, 7; DAM MULT; DLB 323

Mahfouz, Nagib
See Mahfouz, Naguib

Mahfouz, Naguib 1911(?)-2006 . **CLC 52, 55, 153; SSC 66**
See also AAYA 49; AFW; BEST 89:2; CA 128; 253; CANR 55, 101; DA3; DAM NOV; DLB 346; DLBY 1988; MTCW 1, 2; MTFW 2005; RGSF 2; RGWL 2, 3; SSFS 9; WLIT 2

Mahfouz, Naguib Abdel Aziz Al-Sabilgi
See Mahfouz, Naguib

Mahfouz, Najib
See Mahfouz, Naguib

Mahfuz, Najib
See Mahfouz, Naguib

Mahon, Derek 1941- .... **CLC 27; PC 60**
See also BRWS 6; CA 113; 128; CANR 88; CP 1, 2, 3, 4, 5, 6, 7; DLB 40; EWL 3

Maiakovskii, Vladimir
See Mayakovski, Vladimir (Vladimirovich)

Mailer, Norman 1923-2007 ... **CLC 1, 2, 3, 4, 5, 8, 11, 14, 28, 39, 74, 111, 234**
See also AAYA 31; AITN 2; AMW; AMWC 2; AMWR 2; BPFB 2; CA 9-12R; 266; CABS 1; CANR 28, 74, 77, 130; CDALB 1968-1988; CN 1, 2, 3, 4, 5, 6, 7; CPW; DA; DA3; DAB; DAC; DAM MST, NOV, POP; DLB 2, 16, 28, 185, 278; DLBD 3; DLBY 1980, 1983; EWL 3; MAL 5; MTCW 1, 2; MTFW 2005; NFS 10; RGAL 4; TUS

Mailer, Norman Kingsley
See Mailer, Norman

Maillet, Antonine 1929- .... **CLC 54, 118**
See also CA 115; 120; CANR 46, 74, 77, 134; CCA 1; CWW 2; DAC; DLB 60; INT CA-120; MTCW 2; MTFW 2005

Maimonides, Moses 1135-1204 ..... **CMLC 76**
See also DLB 115

Mais, Roger 1905-1955 .... **TCLC 8**
See also BW 1, 3; CA 105; 124; CANR 82; CDWLB 3; DLB 125; EWL 3; MTCW 1; RGEL 2

Maistre, Joseph 1753-1821 .... **NCLC 37**
See also GFL 1789 to the Present

Maitland, Frederic William
1850-1906 .... **TCLC 65**

Maitland, Sara (Louise) 1950- .... **CLC 49**
See also BRWS 11; CA 69-72; CANR 13, 59; DLB 271; FW

Major, Clarence 1936- ...... **BLC 1:2; CLC 3, 19, 48**
See also AFAW 2; BW 2, 3; CA 21-24R; CAAS 6; CANR 13, 25, 53, 82; CN 3, 4, 5, 6, 7; CP 2, 3, 4, 5, 6, 7; CSW; DAM MULT; DLB 33; EWL 3; MAL 5; MSW

Major, Kevin (Gerald) 1949- .... **CLC 26**
See also AAYA 16; CA 97-100; CANR 21, 38, 112; CLR 11; DAC; DLB 60; INT CANR-21; JRDA; MAICYA 1, 2; MAIC-YAS 1; SATA 32, 82, 134; WYA; YAW

Maki, James
See Ozu, Yasujiro

Makin, Bathsua 1600-1675(?) .... **LC 137**

Makine, Andrei 1957-
See Makine, Andrei

Makine, Andrei 1957- .... **CLC 198**
See also CA 176; CANR 103, 162; MTFW 2005

Malabaila, Damiano
See Levi, Primo

Malamud, Bernard 1914-1986 .. **CLC 1, 2, 3, 5, 8, 9, 11, 18, 27, 44, 78, 85; SSC 15; TCLC 129, 184; WLC 4**
See also AAYA 16; AMWS 1; BPFB 2; BYA 15; CA 5-8R; 118; CABS 1; CANR 28, 62, 114; CDALB 1941-1968; CN 1, 2, 3, 4; CPW; DA; DA3; DAB; DAC; DAM MST, NOV, POP; DLB 2, 28, 152; DLBY 1980, 1986; EWL 3; EXPS; LAIT 4; LATS 1:1; MAL 5; MTCW 1, 2; MTFW 2005; NFS 27; RGAL 4; RGHL; RGSF 2; SSFS 8, 13, 16; TUS

Malan, Herman
See Bosman, Herman Charles; Bosman, Herman Charles

Malaparte, Curzio 1898-1957 .... **TCLC 52**
See also DLB 264

Malcolm, Dan
See Silverberg, Robert

Malcolm, Janet 1934- .... **CLC 201**
See also CA 123; CANR 89; NCFS 1

Malcolm X
See Little, Malcolm

Malebranche, Nicolas 1638-1715 .... **LC 133**
See also GFL Beginnings to 1789

Malherbe, Francois de 1555-1628 .... **LC 5**
See also DLB 327; GFL Beginnings to 1789

Mallarme, Stephane 1842-1898 ...... **NCLC 4, 41, 210; PC 4**
See also DAM POET; DLB 217; EW 7; GFL 1789 to the Present; LMFS 2; RGWL 2, 3; TWA

Mallet-Joris, Francoise 1930- .... **CLC 11**
See also CA 65-68; CANR 17; CWW 2; DLB 83; EWL 3; GFL 1789 to the Present

Malley, Ern
See McAuley, James Phillip
Mallon, Thomas 1951- .... **CLC 172**
See also CA 110; CANR 29, 57, 92
Mallowan, Agatha Christie
See Christie, Agatha (Mary Clarissa)
Maloff, Saul 1922- .... **CLC 5**
See also CA 33-36R
Malone, Louis
See MacNeice, (Frederick) Louis
Malone, Michael (Christopher)
1942- .... **CLC 43**
See also CA 77-80; CANR 14, 32, 57, 114
Malory, Sir Thomas 1410(?)-1471(?) . **LC 11,**
88; WLCS
See also BRW 1; BRWR 2; CDBLB Before
1660; DA; DAB; DAC; DAM MST; DLB
146; EFS 2; RGEL 2; SATA 59; SATA-
Brief 33; TEA; WLIT 3
Malouf, David 1934- .... **CLC 28, 86, 245**
See also BRWS 12; CA 124; CANR 50, 76,
180; CN 3, 4, 5, 6, 7; CP 1, 3, 4, 5, 6, 7;
DLB 289; EWL 3; MTCW 2; MTFW
2005; SSFS 24
Malouf, George Joseph David
See Malouf, David
Malraux, (Georges-)Andre
1901-1976 .... **CLC 1, 4, 9, 13, 15, 57;**
TCLC 209
See also BPFB 2; CA 21-22; 69-72; CANR
34, 58; CAP 2; DA3; DAM NOV; DLB
72; EW 12; EWL 3; GFL 1789 to the
Present; MTCW 1, 2; MTFW 2005;
RGWL 2, 3; TWA
Malthus, Thomas Robert
1766-1834 .... **NCLC 145**
See also DLB 107, 158; RGEL 2
Malzberg, Barry N(athaniel) 1939- ... **CLC 7**
See also CA 61-64; CAAS 4; CANR 16;
CMW 4; DLB 8; SFW 4
Mamet, David 1947- .. **CLC 9, 15, 34, 46, 91,**
166; DC 4, 24
See also AAYA 3, 60; AMWS 14; CA 81-
84; CABS 3; CAD; CANR 15, 41, 67, 72,
129, 172; CD 5, 6; DA3; DAM DRAM;
DFS 2, 3, 6, 12, 15; DLB 7; EWL 3;
IDFW 4; MAL 5; MTCW 1, 2; MTFW
2005; RGAL 4
Mamet, David Alan
See Mamet, David
Mamoulian, Rouben (Zachary)
1897-1987 .... **CLC 16**
See also CA 25-28R; 124; CANR 85
Mandelshtam, Osip
See Mandelstam, Osip (Emilievich)
See also DLB 295
Mandelstam, Osip (Emilievich)
1891(?)-1943(?) .... **PC 14; TCLC 2, 6**
See Mandelshtam, Osip
See also CA 104; 150; EW 10; EWL 3;
MTCW 2; RGWL 2, 3; TWA
Mander, (Mary) Jane 1877-1949 ... **TCLC 31**
See also CA 162; RGEL 2
Mandeville, Bernard 1670-1733 .... **LC 82**
See also DLB 101
Mandeville, Sir John fl. 1350- ...... **CMLC 19**
See also DLB 146
Mandiargues, Andre Pieyre de
See Pieyre de Mandiargues, Andre
Mandrake, Ethel Belle
See Thurman, Wallace (Henry)
Mangan, James Clarence
1803-1849 .... **NCLC 27**
See also BRWS 13; RGEL 2
Maniere, J.-E.
See Giraudoux, Jean(-Hippolyte)
Mankiewicz, Herman (Jacob)
1897-1953 .... **TCLC 85**
See also CA 120; 169; DLB 26; IDFW 3, 4

Manley, (Mary) Delariviere
1672(?)-1724 .... **LC 1, 42**
See also DLB 39, 80; RGEL 2
Mann, Abel
See Creasey, John
Mann, Emily 1952- .... **DC 7**
See also CA 130; CAD; CANR 55; CD 5,
6; CWD; DLB 266
Mann, (Luiz) Heinrich 1871-1950 ... **TCLC 9**
See also CA 106; 164, 181; DLB 66, 118;
EW 8; EWL 3; RGWL 2, 3
Mann, (Paul) Thomas 1875-1955 . **SSC 5, 80,**
82; TCLC 2, 8, 14, 21, 35, 44, 60, 168;
WLC 4
See also BPFB 2; CA 104; 128; CANR 133;
CDWLB 2; DA; DA3; DAB; DAC; DAM
MST, NOV; DLB 66, 331; EW 9; EWL 3;
GLL 1; LATS 1:1; LMFS 1; MTCW 1, 2;
MTFW 2005; NFS 17; RGSF 2; RGWL
2, 3; SSFS 4, 9; TWA
Mannheim, Karl 1893-1947 .... **TCLC 65**
See also CA 204
Manning, David
See Faust, Frederick (Schiller)
Manning, Frederic 1882-1935 .... **TCLC 25**
See also CA 124; 216; DLB 260
Manning, Olivia 1915-1980 .... **CLC 5, 19**
See also CA 5-8R; 101; CANR 29; CN 1,
2; EWL 3; FW; MTCW 1; RGEL 2
Mannyng, Robert c. 1264-c.
1340 .... **CMLC 83**
See also DLB 146
Mano, D. Keith 1942- .... **CLC 2, 10**
See also CA 25-28R; CAAS 6; CANR 26,
57; DLB 6
Mansfield, Katherine
See Beauchamp, Kathleen Mansfield
Manso, Peter 1940- .... **CLC 39**
See also CA 29-32R; CANR 44, 156
Mantecon, Juan Jimenez
See Jimenez (Mantecon), Juan Ramon
Mantel, Hilary 1952- .... **CLC 144**
See also CA 125; CANR 54, 101, 161; CN
5, 6, 7; DLB 271; RHW
Mantel, Hilary Mary
See Mantel, Hilary
Manton, Peter
See Creasey, John
Man Without a Spleen, A
See Chekhov, Anton (Pavlovich)
Manzano, Juan Franciso
1797(?)-1854 .... **NCLC 155**
Manzoni, Alessandro 1785-1873 ... **NCLC 29,**
98
See also EW 5; RGWL 2, 3; TWA; WLIT 7
Map, Walter 1140-1209 .... **CMLC 32**
Mapu, Abraham (ben Jekutiel)
1808-1867 .... **NCLC 18**
Mara, Sally
See Queneau, Raymond
Maracle, Lee 1950- .... **NNAL**
See also CA 149
Marat, Jean Paul 1743-1793 .... **LC 10**
Marcel, Gabriel Honore 1889-1973 . **CLC 15**
See also CA 102; 45-48; EWL 3; MTCW 1,
2
March, William
See Campbell, William Edward March
Marchbanks, Samuel
See Davies, Robertson
Marchi, Giacomo
See Bassani, Giorgio
Marcus Aurelius
See Aurelius, Marcus
Marcuse, Herbert 1898-1979 .... **TCLC 207**
See also CA 188; 89-92; DLB 242
Marguerite
See de Navarre, Marguerite

Marguerite d'Angouleme
See de Navarre, Marguerite
Marguerite de Navarre
See de Navarre, Marguerite
Margulies, Donald 1954- .... **CLC 76**
See also AAYA 57; CA 200; CD 6; DFS 13;
DLB 228
Marias, Javier 1951- .... **CLC 239**
See also CA 167; CANR 109, 139; DLB
322; HW 2; MTFW 2005
Marie de France c. 12th cent. - ...... **CMLC 8,**
111; PC 22
See also DLB 208; FW; RGWL 2, 3
Marie de l'Incarnation 1599-1672 ...... **LC 10**
Marier, Captain Victor
See Griffith, D.W.
Mariner, Scott
See Pohl, Frederik
Marinetti, Filippo Tommaso
1876-1944 .... **TCLC 10**
See also CA 107; DLB 114, 264; EW 9;
EWL 3; WLIT 7
Marivaux, Pierre Carlet de Chamblain de
1688-1763 .... **DC 7; LC 4, 123**
See also DLB 314; GFL Beginnings to
1789; RGWL 2, 3; TWA
Markandaya, Kamala
See Taylor, Kamala
Markfield, Wallace (Arthur)
1926-2002 .... **CLC 8**
See also CA 69-72; 208; CAAS 3; CN 1, 2,
3, 4, 5, 6, 7; DLB 2, 28; DLBY 2002
Markham, Edwin 1852-1940 .... **TCLC 47**
See also CA 160; DLB 54, 186; MAL 5;
RGAL 4
Markham, Robert
See Amis, Kingsley
Marks, J.
See Highwater, Jamake (Mamake)
Marks-Highwater, J.
See Highwater, Jamake (Mamake)
Markson, David M. 1927- .... **CLC 67**
See also AMWS 17; CA 49-52; CANR 1,
91, 158; CN 5, 6
Markson, David Merrill
See Markson, David M.
Marlatt, Daphne (Buckle) 1942- .... **CLC 168**
See also CA 25-28R; CANR 17, 39; CN 6,
7; CP 4, 5, 6, 7; CWP; DLB 60; FW
Marley, Bob
See Marley, Robert Nesta
Marley, Robert Nesta 1945-1981 ...... **CLC 17**
See also CA 107; 103
Marlowe, Christopher 1564-1593 . **DC 1; LC**
22, 47, 117; PC 57; WLC 4
See also BRW 1; BRWR 1; CDBLB Before
1660; DA; DA3; DAB; DAC; DAM
DRAM, MST; DFS 1, 5, 13, 21; DLB 62;
EXPP; LMFS 1; PFS 22; RGEL 2; TEA;
WLIT 3
Marlowe, Stephen 1928-2008 .... **CLC 70**
See also CA 13-16R; 269; CANR 6, 55;
CMW 4; SFW 4
Marmion, Shakerley 1603-1639 .... **LC 89**
See also DLB 58; RGEL 2
Marmontel, Jean-Francois 1723-1799 .. **LC 2**
See also DLB 314
Maron, Monika 1941- .... **CLC 165**
See also CA 201
Marot, Clement c. 1496-1544 .... **LC 133**
See also DLB 327; GFL Beginnings to 1789
Marquand, John P(hillips)
1893-1960 .... **CLC 2, 10**
See also AMW; BPFB 2; CA 85-88; CANR
73; CMW 4; DLB 9, 102; EWL 3; MAL
5; MTCW 2; RGAL 4

Marques, Rene 1919-1979 .. **CLC 96; HLC 2**
See also CA 97-100; 85-88; CANR 78; DAM MULT; DLB 305; EWL 3; HW 1, 2; LAW; RGSF 2

Marquez, Gabriel Garcia
See Garcia Marquez, Gabriel

Marquis, Don(ald Robert Perry)
1878-1937 .... **TCLC 7**
See also CA 104; 166; DLB 11, 25; MAL 5; RGAL 4

Marquis de Sade
See Sade, Donatien Alphonse Francois

Marric, J. J.
See Creasey, John

Marryat, Frederick 1792-1848 .... **NCLC 3**
See also DLB 21, 163; RGEL 2; WCH

Marsden, James
See Creasey, John

Marsh, Edward 1872-1953 .... **TCLC 99**

Marsh, (Edith) Ngaio 1895-1982 .. **CLC 7, 53**
See also CA 9-12R; CANR 6, 58; CMW 4; CN 1, 2, 3; CPW; DAM POP; DLB 77; MSW; MTCW 1, 2; RGEL 2; TEA

Marshall, Alan
See Westlake, Donald E.

Marshall, Allen
See Westlake, Donald E.

Marshall, Garry 1934- .... **CLC 17**
See also AAYA 3; CA 111; SATA 60

Marshall, Paule 1929- .... **BLC 1:3, 2:3; CLC 27, 72, 253; SSC 3**
See also AFAW 1, 2; AMWS 11; BPFB 2; BW 2, 3; CA 77-80; CANR 25, 73, 129; CN 1, 2, 3, 4, 5, 6, 7; DA3; DAM MULT; DLB 33, 157, 227; EWL 3; LATS 1:2; MAL 5; MTCW 1, 2; MTFW 2005; RGAL 4; SSFS 15

Marshallik
See Zangwill, Israel

Marsilius of Inghen c.
1340-1396 .... **CMLC 106**

Marsten, Richard
See Hunter, Evan

Marston, John 1576-1634 .... **LC 33**
See also BRW 2; DAM DRAM; DLB 58, 172; RGEL 2

Martel, Yann 1963- .... **CLC 192**
See also AAYA 67; CA 146; CANR 114; DLB 326, 334; MTFW 2005; NFS 27

Martens, Adolphe-Adhemar
See Ghelderode, Michel de

Martha, Henry
See Harris, Mark

Marti, Jose
See Marti (y Perez), Jose (Julian)

Marti (y Perez), Jose (Julian)
1853-1895 ..... **HLC 2; NCLC 63; PC 76**
See also DAM MULT; DLB 290; HW 2; LAW; RGWL 2, 3; WLIT 1

Martial c. 40-c. 104 .... **CMLC 35; PC 10**
See also AW 2; CDWLB 1; DLB 211; RGWL 2, 3

Martin, Ken
See Hubbard, L. Ron

Martin, Richard
See Creasey, John

Martin, Steve 1945- .... **CLC 30, 217**
See also AAYA 53; CA 97-100; CANR 30, 100, 140; DFS 19; MTCW 1; MTFW 2005

Martin, Valerie 1948- .... **CLC 89**
See also BEST 90:2; CA 85-88; CANR 49, 89, 165

Martin, Violet Florence 1862-1915 .. **SSC 56; TCLC 51**

Martin, Webber
See Silverberg, Robert

Martindale, Patrick Victor
See White, Patrick (Victor Martindale)

Martin du Gard, Roger
1881-1958 .... **TCLC 24**
See also CA 118; CANR 94; DLB 65, 331; EWL 3; GFL 1789 to the Present; RGWL 2, 3

Martineau, Harriet 1802-1876 ...... **NCLC 26, 137**
See also DLB 21, 55, 159, 163, 166, 190; FW; RGEL 2; YABC 2

Martines, Julia
See O'Faolain, Julia

Martinez, Enrique Gonzalez
See Gonzalez Martinez, Enrique

Martinez, Jacinto Benavente y
See Benavente (y Martinez), Jacinto

Martinez de la Rosa, Francisco de Paula
1787-1862 .... **NCLC 102**
See also TWA

Martinez Ruiz, Jose 1873-1967 .... **CLC 11**
See also CA 93-96; DLB 322; EW 3; EWL 3; HW 1

Martinez Sierra, Gregorio
See Martinez Sierra, Maria

Martinez Sierra, Gregorio
1881-1947 .... **TCLC 6**
See also CA 115; EWL 3

Martinez Sierra, Maria 1874-1974 .. **TCLC 6**
See also CA 250; 115; EWL 3

Martinsen, Martin
See Follett, Ken

Martinson, Harry (Edmund)
1904-1978 .... **CLC 14**
See also CA 77-80; CANR 34, 130; DLB 259, 331; EWL 3

Martyn, Edward 1859-1923 .... **TCLC 131**
See also CA 179; DLB 10; RGEL 2

Marut, Ret
See Traven, B.

Marut, Robert
See Traven, B.

Marvell, Andrew 1621-1678 .... **LC 4, 43; PC 10, 86; WLC 4**
See also BRW 2; BRWR 2; CDBLB 1660-1789; DA; DAB; DAC; DAM MST, POET; DLB 131; EXPP; PFS 5; RGEL 2; TEA; WP

Marx, Karl (Heinrich)
1818-1883 .... **NCLC 17, 114**
See also DLB 129; LATS 1:1; TWA

Masaoka, Shiki -1902
See Masaoka, Tsunenori

Masaoka, Tsunenori 1867-1902 ..... **TCLC 18**
See also CA 117; 191; EWL 3; RGWL 3; TWA

Masaoka Shiki
See Masaoka, Tsunenori

Masefield, John (Edward)
1878-1967 .... **CLC 11, 47; PC 78**
See also CA 19-20; 25-28R; CANR 33; CAP 2; CDBLB 1890-1914; DAM POET; DLB 10, 19, 153, 160; EWL 3; EXPP; FANT; MTCW 1, 2; PFS 5; RGEL 2; SATA 19

Maso, Carole 1955(?)- .... **CLC 44**
See also CA 170; CANR 148; CN 7; GLL 2; RGAL 4

Mason, Bobbie Ann 1940- ... **CLC 28, 43, 82, 154; SSC 4, 101**
See also AAYA 5, 42; AMWS 8; BPFB 2; CA 53-56; CANR 11, 31, 58, 83, 125, 169; CDALBS; CN 5, 6, 7; CSW; DA3; DLB 173; DLBY 1987; EWL 3; EXPS; INT CANR-31; MAL 5; MTCW 1, 2; MTFW 2005; NFS 4; RGAL 4; RGSF 2; SSFS 3, 8, 20; TCLE 1:2; YAW

Mason, Ernst
See Pohl, Frederik

Mason, Hunni B.
See Sternheim, (William Adolf) Carl

Mason, Lee W.
See Malzberg, Barry N(athaniel)

Mason, Nick 1945- .... **CLC 35**

Mason, Tally
See Derleth, August (William)

Mass, Anna CLC 59

Mass, William
See Gibson, William

Massinger, Philip 1583-1640 .... **LC 70**
See also BRWS 11; DLB 58; RGEL 2

Master Lao
See Lao Tzu

Masters, Edgar Lee 1868-1950 ...... **PC 1, 36; TCLC 2, 25; WLCS**
See also AMWS 1; CA 104; 133; CDALB 1865-1917; DA; DAC; DAM MST, POET; DLB 54; EWL 3; EXPP; MAL 5; MTCW 1, 2; MTFW 2005; RGAL 4; TUS; WP

Masters, Hilary 1928- .... **CLC 48**
See also CA 25-28R, 217; CAAE 217; CANR 13, 47, 97, 171; CN 6, 7; DLB 244

Masters, Hilary Thomas
See Masters, Hilary

Mastrosimone, William 1947- .... **CLC 36**
See also CA 186; CAD; CD 5, 6

Mathe, Albert
See Camus, Albert

Mather, Cotton 1663-1728 .... **LC 38**
See also AMWS 2; CDALB 1640-1865; DLB 24, 30, 140; RGAL 4; TUS

Mather, Increase 1639-1723 .... **LC 38, 161**
See also DLB 24

Mathers, Marshall
See Eminem

Mathers, Marshall Bruce
See Eminem

Matheson, Richard 1926- .... **CLC 37, 267**
See also AAYA 31; CA 97-100; CANR 88, 99; DLB 8, 44; HGG; INT CA-97-100; SCFW 1, 2; SFW 4; SUFW 2

Matheson, Richard Burton
See Matheson, Richard

Mathews, Harry 1930- .... **CLC 6, 52**
See also CA 21-24R; CAAS 6; CANR 18, 40, 98, 160; CN 5, 6, 7

Mathews, John Joseph 1894-1979 .. **CLC 84; NNAL**
See also CA 19-20; 142; CANR 45; CAP 2; DAM MULT; DLB 175; TCWW 1, 2

Mathias, Roland 1915-2007 .... **CLC 45**
See also CA 97-100; 263; CANR 19, 41; CP 1, 2, 3, 4, 5, 6, 7; DLB 27

Mathias, Roland Glyn
See Mathias, Roland

Matsuo Basho 1644(?)-1694 ...... **LC 62; PC 3**
See also DAM POET; PFS 2, 7, 18; RGWL 2, 3; WP

Mattheson, Rodney
See Creasey, John

Matthew of Vendome c. 1130-c.
1200 .... **CMLC 99**
See also DLB 208

Matthews, (James) Brander
1852-1929 .... **TCLC 95**
See also CA 181; DLB 71, 78; DLBD 13

Matthews, Greg 1949- .... **CLC 45**
See also CA 135

Matthews, William (Procter III)
1942-1997 .... **CLC 40**
See also AMWS 9; CA 29-32R; 162; CAAS 18; CANR 12, 57; CP 2, 3, 4, 5, 6; DLB 5

Matthias, John (Edward) 1941- .... **CLC 9**
See also CA 33-36R; CANR 56; CP 4, 5, 6,
7

Matthiessen, F(rancis) O(tto)
1902-1950 .... **TCLC 100**
See also CA 185; DLB 63; MAL 5

Matthiessen, Peter 1927- ... **CLC 5, 7, 11, 32,
64, 245**
See also AAYA 6, 40; AMWS 5; ANW;
BEST 90:4; BPFB 2; CA 9-12R; CANR
21, 50, 73, 100, 138; CN 1, 2, 3, 4, 5, 6,
7; DA3; DAM NOV; DLB 6, 173, 275;
MAL 5; MTCW 1, 2; MTFW 2005; SATA
27

Maturin, Charles Robert
1780(?)-1824 .... **NCLC 6, 169**
See also BRWS 8; DLB 178; GL 3; HGG;
LMFS 1; RGEL 2; SUFW

Matute (Ausejo), Ana Maria 1925- .. **CLC 11**
See also CA 89-92; CANR 129; CWW 2;
DLB 322; EWL 3; MTCW 1; RGSF 2

Maugham, W. S.
See Maugham, W(illiam) Somerset

Maugham, W(illiam) Somerset
1874-1965 .. **CLC 1, 11, 15, 67, 93; SSC
8, 94; TCLC 208; WLC 4**
See also AAYA 55; BPFB 2; BRW 6; CA
5-8R; 25-28R; CANR 40, 127; CDBLB
1914-1945; CMW 4; DA; DA3; DAB;
DAC; DAM DRAM, MST, NOV; DFS
22; DLB 10, 36, 77, 100, 162, 195; EWL
3; LAIT 3; MTCW 1, 2; MTFW 2005;
NFS 23; RGEL 2; RGSF 2; SATA 54;
SSFS 17

Maugham, William Somerset
See Maugham, W(illiam) Somerset

Maupassant, (Henri Rene Albert) Guy de
1850-1893 . **NCLC 1, 42, 83; SSC 1, 64;
WLC 4**
See also BYA 14; DA; DA3; DAB; DAC;
DAM MST; DLB 123; EW 7; EXPS; GFL
1789 to the Present; LAIT 2; LMFS 1;
RGSF 2; RGWL 2, 3; SSFS 4, 21; SUFW;
TWA

Maupin, Armistead 1944- .... **CLC 95**
See also CA 125; 130; CANR 58, 101, 183;
CPW; DA3; DAM POP; DLB 278; GLL
1; INT CA-130; MTCW 2; MTFW 2005

Maupin, Armistead Jones, Jr.
See Maupin, Armistead

Maurhut, Richard
See Traven, B.

Mauriac, Claude 1914-1996 .... **CLC 9**
See also CA 89-92; 152; CWW 2; DLB 83;
EWL 3; GFL 1789 to the Present

Mauriac, Francois (Charles)
1885-1970 .... **CLC 4, 9, 56; SSC 24**
See also CA 25-28; CAP 2; DLB 65, 331;
EW 10; EWL 3; GFL 1789 to the Present;
MTCW 1, 2; MTFW 2005; RGWL 2, 3;
TWA

Mavor, Osborne Henry 1888-1951 .. **TCLC 3**
See also CA 104; DLB 10; EWL 3

Maxwell, Glyn 1962- .... **CLC 238**
See also CA 154; CANR 88, 183; CP 6, 7;
PFS 23

Maxwell, William (Keepers, Jr.)
1908-2000 .... **CLC 19**
See also AMWS 8; CA 93-96; 189; CANR
54, 95; CN 1, 2, 3, 4, 5, 6, 7; DLB 218,
278; DLBY 1980; INT CA-93-96; MAL
5; SATA-Obit 128

May, Elaine 1932- .... **CLC 16**
See also CA 124; 142; CAD; CWD; DLB
44

Mayakovski, Vladimir (Vladimirovich)
1893-1930 .... **TCLC 4, 18**
See also CA 104; 158; EW 11; EWL 3;
IDTP; MTCW 2; MTFW 2005; RGWL 2,
3; SFW 4; TWA; WP

Mayakovsky, Vladimir
See Mayakovski, Vladimir (Vladimirovich)

Mayhew, Henry 1812-1887 .... **NCLC 31**
See also DLB 18, 55, 190

Mayle, Peter 1939(?)- .... **CLC 89**
See also CA 139; CANR 64, 109, 168

Maynard, Joyce 1953- .... **CLC 23**
See also CA 111; 129; CANR 64, 169

Mayne, William (James Carter)
1928- .... **CLC 12**
See also AAYA 20; CA 9-12R; CANR 37,
80, 100; CLR 25, 123; FANT; JRDA;
MAICYA 1, 2; MAICYAS 1; SAAS 11;
SATA 6, 68, 122; SUFW 2; YAW

Mayo, Jim
See L'Amour, Louis

Maysles, Albert 1926- .... **CLC 16**
See also CA 29-32R

Maysles, David 1932-1987 .... **CLC 16**
See also CA 191

Mazer, Norma Fox 1931- .... **CLC 26**
See also AAYA 5, 36; BYA 1, 8; CA 69-72;
CANR 12, 32, 66, 129, 189; CLR 23;
JRDA; MAICYA 1, 2; SAAS 1; SATA 24,
67, 105, 168, 198; WYA; YAW

Mazzini, Guiseppe 1805-1872 .... **NCLC 34**

McAlmon, Robert (Menzies)
1895-1956 .... **TCLC 97**
See also CA 107; 168; DLB 4, 45; DLBD
15; GLL 1

McAuley, James Phillip 1917-1976 .. **CLC 45**
See also CA 97-100; CP 1, 2; DLB 260;
RGEL 2

McBain, Ed
See Hunter, Evan

McBrien, William (Augustine)
1930- .... **CLC 44**
See also CA 107; CANR 90

McCabe, Patrick 1955- .... **CLC 133**
See also BRWS 9; CA 130; CANR 50, 90,
168; CN 6, 7; DLB 194

McCaffrey, Anne 1926- .... **CLC 17**
See also AAYA 6, 34; AITN 2; BEST 89:2;
BPFB 2; BYA 5; CA 25-28R, 227; CAAE
227; CANR 15, 35, 55, 96, 169; CLR 49,
130; CPW; DA3; DAM NOV, POP; DLB
8; JRDA; MAICYA 1, 2; MTCW 1, 2;
MTFW 2005; SAAS 11; SATA 8, 70, 116,
152; SATA-Essay 152; SFW 4; SUFW 2;
WYA; YAW

McCaffrey, Anne Inez
See McCaffrey, Anne

McCall, Nathan 1955(?)- .... **CLC 86**
See also AAYA 59; BW 3; CA 146; CANR
88, 186

McCann, Arthur
See Campbell, John W(ood, Jr.)

McCann, Edson
See Pohl, Frederik

McCarthy, Charles
See McCarthy, Cormac

McCarthy, Charles, Jr.
See McCarthy, Cormac

McCarthy, Cormac 1933- .... **CLC 4, 57, 101,
204**
See also AAYA 41; AMWS 8; BPFB 2; CA
13-16R; CANR 10, 42, 69, 101, 161, 171;
CN 6, 7; CPW; CSW; DA3; DAM POP;
DLB 6, 143, 256; EWL 3; LATS 1:2;
MAL 5; MTCW 2; MTFW 2005; TCLE
1:2; TCWW 2

McCarthy, Mary (Therese)
1912-1989 .. **CLC 1, 3, 5, 14, 24, 39, 59;
SSC 24**
See also AMW; BPFB 2; CA 5-8R; 129;
CANR 16, 50, 64; CN 1, 2, 3, 4; DA3;
DLB 2; DLBY 1981; EWL 3; FW; INT
CANR-16; MAL 5; MBL; MTCW 1, 2;
MTFW 2005; RGAL 4; TUS

McCartney, James Paul
See McCartney, Paul

McCartney, Paul 1942- .... **CLC 12, 35**
See also CA 146; CANR 111

McCauley, Stephen (D.) 1955- .... **CLC 50**
See also CA 141

McClaren, Peter **CLC 70**

McClure, Michael (Thomas) 1932- ... **CLC 6,
10**
See also BG 1:3; CA 21-24R; CAD; CANR
17, 46, 77, 131; CD 5, 6; CP 1, 2, 3, 4, 5,
6, 7; DLB 16; WP

McCorkle, Jill (Collins) 1958- .... **CLC 51**
See also CA 121; CANR 113; CSW; DLB
234; DLBY 1987; SSFS 24

McCourt, Frank 1930- .... **CLC 109**
See also AAYA 61; AMWS 12; CA 157;
CANR 97, 138; MTFW 2005; NCFS 1

McCourt, James 1941- .... **CLC 5**
See also CA 57-60; CANR 98, 152, 186

McCourt, Malachy 1931- .... **CLC 119**
See also SATA 126

McCoy, Edmund
See Gardner, John

McCoy, Horace (Stanley)
1897-1955 .... **TCLC 28**
See also AMWS 13; CA 108; 155; CMW 4;
DLB 9

McCrae, John 1872-1918 .... **TCLC 12**
See also CA 109; DLB 92; PFS 5

McCreigh, James
See Pohl, Frederik

McCullers, (Lula) Carson (Smith)
1917-1967 .... **CLC 1, 4, 10, 12, 48, 100;
SSC 9, 24, 99; TCLC 155; WLC 4**
See also AAYA 21; AMW; AMWC 2; BPFB
2; CA 5-8R; 25-28R; CABS 1, 3; CANR
18, 132; CDALB 1941-1968; DA; DA3;
DAB; DAC; DAM MST, NOV; DFS 5,
18; DLB 2, 7, 173, 228; EWL 3; EXPS;
FW; GLL 1; LAIT 3, 4; MAL 5; MBL;
MTCW 1, 2; MTFW 2005; NFS 6, 13;
RGAL 4; RGSF 2; SATA 27; SSFS 5;
TUS; YAW

McCulloch, John Tyler
See Burroughs, Edgar Rice

McCullough, Colleen 1937- ...... **CLC 27, 107**
See also AAYA 36; BPFB 2; CA 81-84;
CANR 17, 46, 67, 98, 139; CPW; DA3;
DAM NOV, POP; MTCW 1, 2; MTFW
2005; RHW

McCunn, Ruthanne Lum 1946- .... **AAL**
See also CA 119; CANR 43, 96; DLB 312;
LAIT 2; SATA 63

McDermott, Alice 1953- .... **CLC 90**
See also AMWS 18; CA 109; CANR 40,
90, 126, 181; CN 7; DLB 292; MTFW
2005; NFS 23

McElroy, Joseph 1930- .... **CLC 5, 47**
See also CA 17-20R; CANR 149; CN 3, 4,
5, 6, 7

McElroy, Joseph Prince
See McElroy, Joseph

McEwan, Ian 1948- ... **CLC 13, 66, 169, 269;
SSC 106**
See also BEST 90:4; BRWS 4; CA 61-64;
CANR 14, 41, 69, 87, 132, 179; CN 3, 4,
5, 6, 7; DAM NOV; DLB 14, 194, 319,
326; HGG; MTCW 1, 2; MTFW 2005;
RGSF 2; SUFW 2; TEA

McEwan, Ian Russell
See McEwan, Ian

McFadden, David 1940- .... **CLC 48**
See also CA 104; CP 1, 2, 3, 4, 5, 6, 7; DLB
60; INT CA-104

McFarland, Dennis 1950- .... **CLC 65**
See also CA 165; CANR 110, 179

Miller, Sue 1943- .... **CLC 44**
See also AMWS 12; BEST 90:3; CA 139;
CANR 59, 91, 128; DA3; DAM POP;
DLB 143

Miller, Walter M(ichael, Jr.)
1923-1996 .... **CLC 4, 30**
See also BPFB 2; CA 85-88; CANR 108;
DLB 8; SCFW 1, 2; SFW 4

Millett, Kate 1934- .... **CLC 67**
See also AITN 1; CA 73-76; CANR 32, 53,
76, 110; DA3; DLB 246; FW; GLL 1;
MTCW 1, 2; MTFW 2005

Millhauser, Steven 1943- ... **CLC 21, 54, 109;
SSC 57**
See also AAYA 76; CA 110; 111; CANR
63, 114, 133, 189; CN 6, 7; DA3; DLB 2;
FANT; INT CA-111; MAL 5; MTCW 2;
MTFW 2005

Millhauser, Steven Lewis
See Millhauser, Steven

Millin, Sarah Gertrude 1889-1968 ... **CLC 49**
See also CA 102; 93-96; DLB 225; EWL 3

Milne, A. A. 1882-1956 .... **TCLC 6, 88**
See also BRWS 5; CA 104; 133; CLR 1,
26, 108; CMW 4; CWRI 5; DA3; DAB;
DAC; DAM MST; DLB 10, 77, 100, 160;
FANT; MAICYA 1, 2; MTCW 1, 2;
MTFW 2005; RGEL 2; SATA 100; WCH;
YABC 1

Milne, Alan Alexander
See Milne, A. A.

Milner, Ron(ald) 1938-2004 .. **BLC 1:3; CLC
56**
See also AITN 1; BW 1; CA 73-76; 230;
CAD; CANR 24, 81; CD 5, 6; DAM
MULT; DLB 38; MAL 5; MTCW 1

Milnes, Richard Monckton
1809-1885 .... **NCLC 61**
See also DLB 32, 184

Milosz, Czeslaw 1911-2004 .... **CLC 5, 11, 22,
31, 56, 82, 253; PC 8; WLCS**
See also AAYA 62; CA 81-84; 230; CANR
23, 51, 91, 126; CDWLB 4; CWW 2;
DA3; DAM MST, POET; DLB 215, 331;
EW 13; EWL 3; MTCW 1, 2; MTFW
2005; PFS 16, 29; RGHL; RGWL 2, 3

Milton, John 1608-1674 ..... **LC 9, 43, 92; PC
19, 29; WLC 4**
See also AAYA 65; BRW 2; BRWR 2; CD-
BLB 1660-1789; DA; DA3; DAB; DAC;
DAM MST, POET; DLB 131, 151, 281;
EFS 1; EXPP; LAIT 1; PAB; PFS 3, 17;
RGEL 2; TEA; WLIT 3; WP

Min, Anchee 1957- .... **CLC 86**
See also CA 146; CANR 94, 137; MTFW
2005

Minehaha, Cornelius
See Wedekind, Frank

Miner, Valerie 1947- .... **CLC 40**
See also CA 97-100; CANR 59, 177; FW;
GLL 2

Minimo, Duca
See D'Annunzio, Gabriele

Minot, Susan (Anderson) 1956- ...... **CLC 44,
159**
See also AMWS 6; CA 134; CANR 118;
CN 6, 7

Minus, Ed 1938- .... **CLC 39**
See also CA 185

Mirabai 1498(?)-1550(?) .... **LC 143; PC 48**
See also PFS 24

Miranda, Javier
See Bioy Casares, Adolfo

Mirbeau, Octave 1848-1917 .... **TCLC 55**
See also CA 216; DLB 123, 192; GFL 1789
to the Present

Mirikitani, Janice 1942- .... **AAL**
See also CA 211; DLB 312; RGAL 4

Mirk, John (?)-c. 1414 .... **LC 105**
See also DLB 146

Miro (Ferrer), Gabriel (Francisco Victor)
1879-1930 .... **TCLC 5**
See also CA 104; 185; DLB 322; EWL 3

Misharin, Alexandr CLC 59

Mishima, Yukio
See Hiraoka, Kimitake

Mishima Yukio
See Hiraoka, Kimitake

Miss C. L. F.
See Grimke, Charlotte L(ottie) Forten

Mister X
See Hoch, Edward D.

Mistral, Frederic 1830-1914 .... **TCLC 51**
See also CA 122; 213; DLB 331; GFL 1789
to the Present

Mistral, Gabriela
See Godoy Alcayaga, Lucila

Mistry, Rohinton 1952- ... **CLC 71, 196, 274;
SSC 73**
See also BRWS 10; CA 141; CANR 86,
114; CCA 1; CN 6, 7; DAC; DLB 334;
SSFS 6

Mitchell, Clyde
See Ellison, Harlan; Silverberg, Robert

Mitchell, Emerson Blackhorse Barney
1945- .... **NNAL**
See also CA 45-48

Mitchell, James Leslie 1901-1935 .... **TCLC 4**
See also BRWS 14; CA 104; 188; DLB 15;
RGEL 2

Mitchell, Joni 1943- .... **CLC 12**
See also CA 112; CCA 1

Mitchell, Joseph (Quincy)
1908-1996 .... **CLC 98**
See also CA 77-80; 152; CANR 69; CN 1,
2, 3, 4, 5, 6; CSW; DLB 185; DLBY 1996

Mitchell, Margaret (Munnerlyn)
1900-1949 .... **TCLC 11, 170**
See also AAYA 23; BPFB 2; BYA 1; CA
109; 125; CANR 55, 94; CDALBS; DA3;
DAM NOV, POP; DLB 9; LAIT 2; MAL
5; MTCW 1, 2; MTFW 2005; NFS 9;
RGAL 4; RHW; TUS; WYAS 1; YAW

Mitchell, Peggy
See Mitchell, Margaret (Munnerlyn)

Mitchell, S(ilas) Weir 1829-1914 .... **TCLC 36**
See also CA 165; DLB 202; RGAL 4

Mitchell, W(illiam) O(rmond)
1914-1998 .... **CLC 25**
See also CA 77-80; 165; CANR 15, 43; CN
1, 2, 3, 4, 5, 6; DAC; DAM MST; DLB
88; TCLE 1:2

Mitchell, William (Lendrum)
1879-1936 .... **TCLC 81**
See also CA 213

Mitford, Mary Russell 1787-1855 ... **NCLC 4**
See also DLB 110, 116; RGEL 2

Mitford, Nancy 1904-1973 .... **CLC 44**
See also BRWS 10; CA 9-12R; CN 1; DLB
191; RGEL 2

Miyamoto, (Chujo) Yuriko
1899-1951 .... **TCLC 37**
See also CA 170, 174; DLB 180

Miyamoto Yuriko
See Miyamoto, (Chujo) Yuriko

Miyazawa, Kenji 1896-1933 .... **TCLC 76**
See also CA 157; EWL 3; RGWL 3

Miyazawa Kenji
See Miyazawa, Kenji

Mizoguchi, Kenji 1898-1956 .... **TCLC 72**
See also CA 167

Mo, Timothy (Peter) 1950- .... **CLC 46, 134**
See also CA 117; CANR 128; CN 5, 6, 7;
DLB 194; MTCW 1; WLIT 4; WWE 1

Modarressi, Taghi (M.) 1931-1997 ... **CLC 44**
See also CA 121; 134; INT CA-134

Modiano, Patrick (Jean) 1945- .... **CLC 18,
218**
See also CA 85-88; CANR 17, 40, 115;
CWW 2; DLB 83, 299; EWL 3; RGHL

Mofolo, Thomas (Mokopu)
1875(?)-1948 .... **BLC 1:3; TCLC 22**
See also AFW; CA 121; 153; CANR 83;
DAM MULT; DLB 225; EWL 3; MTCW
2; MTFW 2005; WLIT 2

Mohr, Nicholasa 1938- .... **CLC 12; HLC 2**
See also AAYA 8, 46; CA 49-52; CANR 1,
32, 64; CLR 22; DAM MULT; DLB 145;
HW 1, 2; JRDA; LAIT 5; LLW; MAICYA
2; MAICYAS 1; RGAL 4; SAAS 8; SATA
8, 97; SATA-Essay 113; WYA; YAW

Moi, Toril 1953- .... **CLC 172**
See also CA 154; CANR 102; FW

Mojtabai, A(nn) G(race) 1938- ..... **CLC 5, 9,
15, 29**
See also CA 85-88; CANR 88

Moliere 1622-1673 ..... **DC 13; LC 10, 28, 64,
125, 127; WLC 4**
See also DA; DA3; DAB; DAC; DAM
DRAM, MST; DFS 13, 18, 20; DLB 268;
EW 3; GFL Beginnings to 1789; LATS
1:1; RGWL 2, 3; TWA

Molin, Charles
See Mayne, William (James Carter)

Molnar, Ferenc 1878-1952 .... **TCLC 20**
See also CA 109; 153; CANR 83; CDWLB
4; DAM DRAM; DLB 215; EWL 3;
RGWL 2, 3

Momaday, N. Scott 1934- ...... **CLC 2, 19, 85,
95, 160; NNAL; PC 25; WLCS**
See also AAYA 11, 64; AMWS 4; ANW;
BPFB 2; BYA 12; CA 25-28R; CANR 14,
34, 68, 134; CDALBS; CN 2, 3, 4, 5, 6,
7; CPW; DA; DA3; DAB; DAC; DAM
MST, MULT, NOV, POP; DLB 143, 175,
256; EWL 3; EXPP; INT CANR-14;
LAIT 4; LATS 1:2; MAL 5; MTCW 1, 2;
MTFW 2005; NFS 10; PFS 2, 11; RGAL
4; SATA 48; SATA-Brief 30; TCWW 1,
2; WP; YAW

Monette, Paul 1945-1995 .... **CLC 82**
See also AMWS 10; CA 139; 147; CN 6;
GLL 1

Monroe, Harriet 1860-1936 .... **TCLC 12**
See also CA 109; 204; DLB 54, 91

Monroe, Lyle
See Heinlein, Robert A.

Montagu, Elizabeth 1720-1800 .... **NCLC 7,
117**
See also FW

Montagu, Mary (Pierrepont) Wortley
1689-1762 .... **LC 9, 57; PC 16**
See also DLB 95, 101; FL 1:1; RGEL 2

Montagu, W. H.
See Coleridge, Samuel Taylor

Montague, John (Patrick) 1929- ..... **CLC 13,
46**
See also CA 9-12R; CANR 9, 69, 121; CP
1, 2, 3, 4, 5, 6, 7; DLB 40; EWL 3;
MTCW 1; PFS 12; RGEL 2; TCLE 1:2

Montaigne, Michel (Eyquem) de
1533-1592 .... **LC 8, 105; WLC 4**
See also DA; DAB; DAC; DAM MST;
DLB 327; EW 2; GFL Beginnings to
1789; LMFS 1; RGWL 2, 3; TWA

Montale, Eugenio 1896-1981 ... **CLC 7, 9, 18;
PC 13**
See also CA 17-20R; 104; CANR 30; DLB
114, 331; EW 11; EWL 3; MTCW 1; PFS
22; RGWL 2, 3; TWA; WLIT 7

Montesquieu, Charles-Louis de Secondat
1689-1755 .... **LC 7, 69**
See also DLB 314; EW 3; GFL Beginnings
to 1789; TWA

Montessori, Maria 1870-1952 ...... **TCLC 103**
See also CA 115; 147

2; MAL 5; MBL; MTCW 1, 2; MTFW 2005; NFS 1, 6, 8, 14; RGAL 4; RHW; SATA 57, 144; SSFS 5; TCLE 1:2; TUS; YAW

Morrison, Van 1945- .... **CLC 21**
See also CA 116; 168

Morrissy, Mary 1957- .... **CLC 99**
See also CA 205; DLB 267

Mortimer, John 1923-2009 .... **CLC 28, 43**
See also CA 13-16R; CANR 21, 69, 109, 172; CBD; CD 5, 6; CDBLB 1960 to Present; CMW 4; CN 5, 6, 7; CPW; DA3; DAM DRAM, POP; DLB 13, 245, 271; INT CANR-21; MSW; MTCW 1, 2; MTFW 2005; RGEL 2

Mortimer, John Clifford
See Mortimer, John

Mortimer, Penelope (Ruth)
1918-1999 .... **CLC 5**
See also CA 57-60; 187; CANR 45, 88; CN 1, 2, 3, 4, 5, 6

Mortimer, Sir John
See Mortimer, John

Morton, Anthony
See Creasey, John

Morton, Thomas 1579(?)-1647(?) .... **LC 72**
See also DLB 24; RGEL 2

Mosca, Gaetano 1858-1941 .... **TCLC 75**

Moses, Daniel David 1952- .... **NNAL**
See also CA 186; CANR 160; DLB 334

Mosher, Howard Frank 1943- .... **CLC 62**
See also CA 139; CANR 65, 115, 181

Mosley, Nicholas 1923- .... **CLC 43, 70**
See also CA 69-72; CANR 41, 60, 108, 158; CN 1, 2, 3, 4, 5, 6, 7; DLB 14, 207

Mosley, Walter 1952- .... **BLCS; CLC 97, 184**
See also AAYA 57; AMWS 13; BPFB 2; BW 2; CA 142; CANR 57, 92, 136, 172; CMW 4; CN 7; CPW; DA3; DAM MULT, POP; DLB 306; MSW; MTCW 2; MTFW 2005

Moss, Howard 1922-1987 . **CLC 7, 14, 45, 50**
See also CA 1-4R; 123; CANR 1, 44; CP 1, 2, 3, 4; DAM POET; DLB 5

Mossgiel, Rab
See Burns, Robert

Motion, Andrew 1952- .... **CLC 47**
See also BRWS 7; CA 146; CANR 90, 142; CP 4, 5, 6, 7; DLB 40; MTFW 2005

Motion, Andrew Peter
See Motion, Andrew

Motley, Willard (Francis)
1909-1965 .... **CLC 18**
See also AMWS 17; BW 1; CA 117; 106; CANR 88; DLB 76, 143

Motoori, Norinaga 1730-1801 .... **NCLC 45**

Mott, Michael (Charles Alston)
1930- .... **CLC 15, 34**
See also CA 5-8R; CAAS 7; CANR 7, 29

Mountain Wolf Woman 1884-1960 . **CLC 92;
NNAL**
See also CA 144; CANR 90

Moure, Erin 1955- .... **CLC 88**
See also CA 113; CP 5, 6, 7; CWP; DLB 60

Mourning Dove 1885(?)-1936 .... **NNAL**
See also CA 144; CANR 90; DAM MULT; DLB 175, 221

Mowat, Farley 1921- .... **CLC 26**
See also AAYA 1, 50; BYA 2; CA 1-4R; CANR 4, 24, 42, 68, 108; CLR 20; CPW; DAC; DAM MST; DLB 68; INT CANR-24; JRDA; MAICYA 1, 2; MTCW 1, 2; MTFW 2005; SATA 3, 55; YAW

Mowat, Farley McGill
See Mowat, Farley

Mowatt, Anna Cora 1819-1870 ..... **NCLC 74**
See also RGAL 4

Mo Yan
See Moye, Guan

Moye, Guan 1956(?)- .... **CLC 257**
See also CA 201; EWL 3; RGWL 3

Mo Yen
See Moye, Guan

Moyers, Bill 1934- .... **CLC 74**
See also AITN 2; CA 61-64; CANR 31, 52, 148

Mphahlele, Es'kia 1919-2008 .... **BLC 1:3;
CLC 25, 133**
See also AFW; BW 2, 3; CA 81-84; 278; CANR 26, 76; CDWLB 3; CN 4, 5, 6; DA3; DAM MULT; DLB 125, 225; EWL 3; MTCW 2; MTFW 2005; RGSF 2; SATA 119; SATA-Obit 198; SSFS 11

Mphahlele, Ezekiel
See Mphahlele, Es'kia

Mphahlele, Zeke
See Mphahlele, Es'kia

Mqhayi, S(amuel) E(dward) K(rune Loliwe)
1875-1945 .... **BLC 1:3; TCLC 25**
See also CA 153; CANR 87; DAM MULT

Mrozek, Slawomir 1930- .... **CLC 3, 13**
See also CA 13-16R; CAAS 10; CANR 29; CDWLB 4; CWW 2; DLB 232; EWL 3; MTCW 1

Mrs. Belloc-Lowndes
See Lowndes, Marie Adelaide (Belloc)

Mrs. Fairstar
See Horne, Richard Henry Hengist

M'Taggart, John M'Taggart Ellis
See McTaggart, John McTaggart Ellis

Mtwa, Percy (?)- .... **CLC 47**
See also CD 6

Mueller, Lisel 1924- .... **CLC 13, 51; PC 33**
See also CA 93-96; CP 6, 7; DLB 105; PFS 9, 13

Muggeridge, Malcolm (Thomas)
1903-1990 .... **TCLC 120**
See also AITN 1; CA 101; CANR 33, 63; MTCW 1, 2

Muhammad 570-632 .... **WLCS**
See also DA; DAB; DAC; DAM MST; DLB 311

Muir, Edwin 1887-1959 . **PC 49; TCLC 2, 87**
See also BRWS 6; CA 104; 193; DLB 20, 100, 191; EWL 3; RGEL 2

Muir, John 1838-1914 .... **TCLC 28**
See also AMWS 9; ANW; CA 165; DLB 186, 275

Mujica Lainez, Manuel 1910-1984 ... **CLC 31**
See also CA 81-84; 112; CANR 32; EWL 3; HW 1

Mukherjee, Bharati 1940- ..... **AAL; CLC 53, 115, 235; SSC 38**
See also AAYA 46; BEST 89:2; CA 107, 232; CAAE 232; CANR 45, 72, 128; CN 5, 6, 7; DAM NOV; DLB 60, 218, 323; DNFS 1, 2; EWL 3; FW; MAL 5; MTCW 1, 2; MTFW 2005; RGAL 4; RGSF 2; SSFS 7, 24; TUS; WWE 1

Muldoon, Paul 1951- .... **CLC 32, 72, 166**
See also BRWS 4; CA 113; 129; CANR 52, 91, 176; CP 2, 3, 4, 5, 6, 7; DAM POET; DLB 40; INT CA-129; PFS 7, 22; TCLE 1:2

Mulisch, Harry (Kurt Victor)
1927- .... **CLC 42, 270**
See also CA 9-12R; CANR 6, 26, 56, 110; CWW 2; DLB 299; EWL 3

Mull, Martin 1943- .... **CLC 17**
See also CA 105

Muller, Wilhelm .... **NCLC 73**

Mulock, Dinah Maria
See Craik, Dinah Maria (Mulock)

Multatuli 1820-1881 .... **NCLC 165**
See also RGWL 2, 3

Munday, Anthony 1560-1633 .... **LC 87**
See also DLB 62, 172; RGEL 2

Munford, Robert 1737(?)-1783 .... **LC 5**
See also DLB 31

Mungo, Raymond 1946- .... **CLC 72**
See also CA 49-52; CANR 2

Munro, Alice 1931- .... **CLC 6, 10, 19, 50, 95, 222; SSC 3, 95; WLCS**
See also AITN 2; BPFB 2; CA 33-36R; CANR 33, 53, 75, 114, 177; CCA 1; CN 1, 2, 3, 4, 5, 6, 7; DA3; DAC; DAM MST, NOV; DLB 53; EWL 3; MTCW 1, 2; MTFW 2005; NFS 27; RGEL 2; RGSF 2; SATA 29; SSFS 5, 13, 19; TCLE 1:2; WWE 1

Munro, H(ector) H(ugh) 1870-1916 . **SSC 12, 115; TCLC 3; WLC 5**
See also AAYA 56; BRWS 6; BYA 11; CA 104; 130; CANR 104; CDBLB 1890-1914; DA; DA3; DAB; DAC; DAM MST, NOV; DLB 34, 162; EXPS; LAIT 2; MTCW 1, 2; MTFW 2005; RGEL 2; SSFS 1, 15; SUFW

Munro, Hector H.
See Munro, H(ector) H(ugh)

Murakami, Haruki 1949- .... **CLC 150, 274**
See also CA 165; CANR 102, 146; CWW 2; DLB 182; EWL 3; MJW; RGWL 3; SFW 4; SSFS 23

Murakami Haruki
See Murakami, Haruki

Murasaki, Lady
See Murasaki Shikibu

Murasaki Shikibu 978(?)-1026(?) .. **CMLC 1, 79**
See also EFS 2; LATS 1:1; RGWL 2, 3

Murdoch, Iris 1919-1999 .. **CLC 1, 2, 3, 4, 6, 8, 11, 15, 22, 31, 51; TCLC 171**
See also BRWS 1; CA 13-16R; 179; CANR 8, 43, 68, 103, 142; CBD; CDBLB 1960 to Present; CN 1, 2, 3, 4, 5, 6; CWD; DA3; DAB; DAC; DAM MST, NOV; DLB 14, 194, 233, 326; EWL 3; INT CANR-8; MTCW 1, 2; MTFW 2005; NFS 18; RGEL 2; TCLE 1:2; TEA; WLIT 4

Murfree, Mary Noailles 1850-1922 .. **SSC 22; TCLC 135**
See also CA 122; 176; DLB 12, 74; RGAL 4

Murglie
See Murnau, F.W.

Murnau, Friedrich Wilhelm
See Murnau, F.W.

Murnau, F.W. 1888-1931 .... **TCLC 53**
See also CA 112

Murphy, Richard 1927- .... **CLC 41**
See also BRWS 5; CA 29-32R; CP 1, 2, 3, 4, 5, 6, 7; DLB 40; EWL 3

Murphy, Sylvia 1937- .... **CLC 34**
See also CA 121

Murphy, Thomas (Bernard) 1935- ... **CLC 51**
See also CA 101; DLB 310

Murphy, Tom
See Murphy, Thomas (Bernard)

Murray, Albert 1916- .... **BLC 2:3; CLC 73**
See also BW 2; CA 49-52; CANR 26, 52, 78, 160; CN 7; CSW; DLB 38; MTFW 2005

Murray, Albert L.
See Murray, Albert

Murray, James Augustus Henry
1837-1915 .... **TCLC 117**

Murray, Judith Sargent
1751-1820 .... **NCLC 63**
See also DLB 37, 200

Newman, Charles 1938-2006 .... **CLC 2, 8**
See also CA 21-24R; 249; CANR 84; CN
3, 4, 5, 6

Newman, Charles Hamilton
See Newman, Charles

Newman, Edwin (Harold) 1919- ...... **CLC 14**
See also AITN 1; CA 69-72; CANR 5

Newman, John Henry 1801-1890 . **NCLC 38, 99**
See also BRWS 7; DLB 18, 32, 55; RGEL
2

Newton, (Sir) Isaac 1642-1727 ...... **LC 35, 53**
See also DLB 252

Newton, Suzanne 1936- .... **CLC 35**
See also BYA 7; CA 41-44R; CANR 14;
JRDA; SATA 5, 77

New York Dept. of Ed. CLC 70

Nexo, Martin Andersen
1869-1954 .... **TCLC 43**
See also CA 202; DLB 214; EWL 3

Nezval, Vitezslav 1900-1958 .... **TCLC 44**
See also CA 123; CDWLB 4; DLB 215;
EWL 3

Ng, Fae Myenne 1956- .... **CLC 81**
See also BYA 11; CA 146

Ngcobo, Lauretta 1931- .... **BLC 2:3**
See also CA 165

Ngema, Mbongeni 1955- .... **CLC 57**
See also BW 2; CA 143; CANR 84; CD 5,
6

Ngugi, James T.
See Ngugi wa Thiong'o

Ngugi, James Thiong'o
See Ngugi wa Thiong'o

Ngugi wa Thiong'o 1938- .... **BLC 1:3, 2:3;
CLC 3, 7, 13, 36, 182**
See also AFW; BRWS 8; BW 2; CA 81-84;
CANR 27, 58, 164; CD 3, 4, 5, 6, 7; CD-
WLB 3; CN 1, 2; DAM MULT, NOV;
DLB 125; DNFS 2; EWL 3; MTCW 1, 2;
MTFW 2005; RGEL 2; WWE 1

Niatum, Duane 1938- .... **NNAL**
See also CA 41-44R; CANR 21, 45, 83;
DLB 175

Nichol, B(arrie) P(hillip) 1944-1988 . **CLC 18**
See also CA 53-56; CP 1, 2, 3, 4; DLB 53;
SATA 66

Nicholas of Autrecourt c.
1298-1369 .... **CMLC 108**

Nicholas of Cusa 1401-1464 .... **LC 80**
See also DLB 115

Nichols, John 1940- .... **CLC 38**
See also AMWS 13; CA 9-12R, 190; CAAE
190; CAAS 2; CANR 6, 70, 121, 185;
DLBY 1982; LATS 1:2; MTFW 2005;
TCWW 1, 2

Nichols, Leigh
See Koontz, Dean R.

Nichols, Peter (Richard) 1927- .... **CLC 5, 36, 65**
See also CA 104; CANR 33, 86; CBD; CD
5, 6; DLB 13, 245; MTCW 1

Nicholson, Linda CLC 65

Ni Chuilleanain, Eilean 1942- .... **PC 34**
See also CA 126; CANR 53, 83; CP 5, 6, 7;
CWP; DLB 40

Nicolas, F. R. E.
See Freeling, Nicolas

Niedecker, Lorine 1903-1970 ..... **CLC 10, 42;
PC 42**
See also CA 25-28; CAP 2; DAM POET;
DLB 48

Nietzsche, Friedrich (Wilhelm)
1844-1900 .... **TCLC 10, 18, 55**
See also CA 107; 121; CDWLB 2; DLB
129; EW 7; RGWL 2, 3; TWA

Nievo, Ippolito 1831-1861 .... **NCLC 22**

Nightingale, Anne Redmon 1943- .... **CLC 22**
See also CA 103; DLBY 1986

Nightingale, Florence 1820-1910 ... **TCLC 85**
See also CA 188; DLB 166

Nijo Yoshimoto 1320-1388 .... **CMLC 49**
See also DLB 203

Nik. T. O.
See Annensky, Innokenty (Fyodorovich)

Nin, Anais 1903-1977 ..... **CLC 1, 4, 8, 11, 14,
60, 127; SSC 10**
See also AITN 2; AMWS 10; BPFB 2; CA
13-16R; 69-72; CANR 22, 53; CN 1, 2;
DAM NOV, POP; DLB 2, 4, 152; EWL
3; GLL 2; MAL 5; MBL; MTCW 1, 2;
MTFW 2005; RGAL 4; RGSF 2

Nisbet, Robert A(lexander)
1913-1996 .... **TCLC 117**
See also CA 25-28R; 153; CANR 17; INT
CANR-17

Nishida, Kitaro 1870-1945 .... **TCLC 83**

Nishiwaki, Junzaburo 1894-1982 .... **PC 15**
See also CA 194; 107; EWL 3; MJW;
RGWL 3

Nissenson, Hugh 1933- .... **CLC 4, 9**
See also CA 17-20R; CANR 27, 108, 151;
CN 5, 6; DLB 28, 335

Nister, Der
See Der Nister

Niven, Larry 1938- .... **CLC 8**
See also AAYA 27; BPFB 2; BYA 10; CA
21-24R, 207; CAAE 207; CAAS 12;
CANR 14, 44, 66, 113, 155; CPW; DAM
POP; DLB 8; MTCW 1, 2; SATA 95, 171;
SCFW 1, 2; SFW 4

Niven, Laurence VanCott
See Niven, Larry

Nixon, Agnes Eckhardt 1927- .... **CLC 21**
See also CA 110

Nizan, Paul 1905-1940 .... **TCLC 40**
See also CA 161; DLB 72; EWL 3; GFL
1789 to the Present

Nkosi, Lewis 1936- .... **BLC 1:3; CLC 45**
See also BW 1, 3; CA 65-68; CANR 27,
81; CBD; CD 5, 6; DAM MULT; DLB
157, 225; WWE 1

Nodier, (Jean) Charles (Emmanuel)
1780-1844 .... **NCLC 19**
See also DLB 119; GFL 1789 to the Present

Noguchi, Yone 1875-1947 .... **TCLC 80**

Nolan, Brian
See O Nuallain, Brian

Nolan, Christopher 1965-2009 .... **CLC 58**
See also CA 111; CANR 88

Noon, Jeff 1957- .... **CLC 91**
See also CA 148; CANR 83; DLB 267;
SFW 4

Norden, Charles
See Durrell, Lawrence (George)

Nordhoff, Charles Bernard
1887-1947 .... **TCLC 23**
See also CA 108; 211; DLB 9; LAIT 1;
RHW 1; SATA 23

Norfolk, Lawrence 1963- .... **CLC 76**
See also CA 144; CANR 85; CN 6, 7; DLB
267

Norman, Marsha (Williams) 1947- . **CLC 28,
186; DC 8**
See also CA 105; CABS 3; CAD; CANR
41, 131; CD 5, 6; CSW; CWD; DAM
DRAM; DFS 2; DLB 266; DLBY 1984;
FW; MAL 5

Normyx
See Douglas, (George) Norman

Norris, (Benjamin) Frank(lin, Jr.)
1870-1902 . **SSC 28; TCLC 24, 155, 211**
See also AAYA 57; AMW; AMWC 2; BPFB
2; CA 110; 160; CDALB 1865-1917; DLB
12, 71, 186; LMFS 2; MAL 5; NFS 12;
RGAL 4; TCWW 1, 2; TUS

Norris, Kathleen 1947- .... **CLC 248**
See also CA 160; CANR 113

Norris, Leslie 1921-2006 .... **CLC 14**
See also CA 11-12; 251; CANR 14, 117;
CAP 1; CP 1, 2, 3, 4, 5, 6, 7; DLB 27,
256

North, Andrew
See Norton, Andre

North, Anthony
See Koontz, Dean R.

North, Captain George
See Stevenson, Robert Louis (Balfour)

North, Captain George
See Stevenson, Robert Louis (Balfour)

North, Milou
See Erdrich, Louise

Northrup, B. A.
See Hubbard, L. Ron

North Staffs
See Hulme, T(homas) E(rnest)

Northup, Solomon 1808-1863 ...... **NCLC 105**

Norton, Alice Mary
See Norton, Andre

Norton, Andre 1912-2005 .... **CLC 12**
See also AAYA 14; BPFB 2; BYA 4, 10,
12; CA 1-4R; 237; CANR 2, 31, 68, 108,
149; CLR 50; DLB 8, 52; JRDA; MAI-
CYA 1, 2; MTCW 1; SATA 1, 43, 91;
SUFW 1, 2; YAW

Norton, Caroline 1808-1877 .. **NCLC 47, 205**
See also DLB 21, 159, 199

Norway, Nevil Shute 1899-1960 .... **CLC 30**
See also BPFB 3; CA 102; 93-96; CANR
85; DLB 255; MTCW 2; NFS 9; RHW 4;
SFW 4

Norwid, Cyprian Kamil
1821-1883 .... **NCLC 17**
See also RGWL 3

Nosille, Nabrah
See Ellison, Harlan

Nossack, Hans Erich 1901-1977 .... **CLC 6**
See also CA 93-96; 85-88; CANR 156;
DLB 69; EWL 3

Nostradamus 1503-1566 .... **LC 27**

Nosu, Chuji
See Ozu, Yasujiro

Notenburg, Eleanora (Genrikhovna) von
See Guro, Elena (Genrikhovna)

Nova, Craig 1945- .... **CLC 7, 31**
See also CA 45-48; CANR 2, 53, 127

Novak, Joseph
See Kosinski, Jerzy

Novalis 1772-1801 .... **NCLC 13, 178**
See also CDWLB 2; DLB 90; EW 5; RGWL
2, 3

Novick, Peter 1934- .... **CLC 164**
See also CA 188

Novis, Emile
See Weil, Simone (Adolphine)

Nowlan, Alden (Albert) 1933-1983 ... **CLC 15**
See also CA 9-12R; CANR 5; CP 1, 2, 3;
DAC; DAM MST; DLB 53; PFS 12

Noyes, Alfred 1880-1958 ...... **PC 27; TCLC 7**
See also CA 104; 188; DLB 20; EXPP;
FANT; PFS 4; RGEL 2

Nugent, Richard Bruce
1906(?)-1987 .... **HR 1:3**
See also BW 1; CA 125; DLB 51; GLL 2

Nunez, Elizabeth 1944- .... **BLC 2:3**
See also CA 223

Nunn, Kem CLC 34
See also CA 159

Nussbaum, Martha Craven 1947- .. **CLC 203**
See also CA 134; CANR 102, 176

Nwapa, Flora (Nwanzuruaha)
1931-1993 .... **BLCS; CLC 133**
See also BW 2; CA 143; CANR 83; CD-
WLB 3; CWRI 5; DLB 125; EWL 3;
WLIT 2

Olson, Toby 1937- .... **CLC 28**
See also CA 65-68; CAAS 11; CANR 9,
31, 84, 175; CP 3, 4, 5, 6, 7

Olyesha, Yuri
See Olesha, Yuri (Karlovich)

Olympiodorus of Thebes c. 375-c.
430 .... **CMLC 59**

Omar Khayyam
See Khayyam, Omar

Ondaatje, Michael 1943- ..... **CLC 14, 29, 51,
76, 180, 258; PC 28**
See also AAYA 66; CA 77-80; CANR 42,
74, 109, 133, 172; CN 5, 6, 7; CP 1, 2, 3,
4, 5, 6, 7; DA3; DAB; DAC; DAM MST;
DLB 60, 323, 326; EWL 3; LATS 1:2;
LMFS 2; MTCW 2; MTFW 2005; NFS
23; PFS 8, 19; TCLE 1:2; TWA; WWE 1

Ondaatje, Philip Michael
See Ondaatje, Michael

Oneal, Elizabeth 1934- .... **CLC 30**
See also AAYA 5, 41; BYA 13; CA 106;
CANR 28, 84; CLR 13; JRDA; MAICYA
1, 2; SATA 30, 82; WYA; YAW

Oneal, Zibby
See Oneal, Elizabeth

O'Neill, Eugene (Gladstone)
1888-1953 ... **DC 20; TCLC 1, 6, 27, 49;
WLC 4**
See also AAYA 54; AITN 1; AMW; AMWC
1; CA 110; 132; CAD; CANR 131;
CDALB 1929-1941; DA; DA3; DAB;
DAC; DAM DRAM, MST; DFS 2, 4, 5,
6, 9, 11, 12, 16, 20, 26; DLB 7, 331; EWL
3; LAIT 3; LMFS 2; MAL 5; MTCW 1,
2; MTFW 2005; RGAL 4; TUS

Onetti, Juan Carlos 1909-1994 ... **CLC 7, 10;
HLCS 2; SSC 23; TCLC 131**
See also CA 85-88; 145; CANR 32, 63; CD-
WLB 3; CWW 2; DAM MULT, NOV;
DLB 113; EWL 3; HW 1, 2; LAW;
MTCW 1, 2; MTFW 2005; RGSF 2

O'Nolan, Brian
See O Nuallain, Brian

O Nuallain, Brian 1911-1966 .... **CLC 1, 4, 5,
7, 10, 47**
See also BRWS 2; CA 21-22; 25-28R; CAP
2; DLB 231; EWL 3; FANT; RGEL 2;
TEA

Ophuls, Max
See Ophuls, Max

Ophuls, Max 1902-1957 .... **TCLC 79**
See also CA 113

Opie, Amelia 1769-1853 .... **NCLC 65**
See also DLB 116, 159; RGEL 2

Oppen, George 1908-1984 ..... **CLC 7, 13, 34;
PC 35; TCLC 107**
See also CA 13-16R; 113; CANR 8, 82; CP
1, 2, 3; DLB 5, 165

Oppenheim, E(dward) Phillips
1866-1946 .... **TCLC 45**
See also CA 111; 202; CMW 4; DLB 70

Oppenheimer, Max
See Ophuls, Max

Opuls, Max
See Ophuls, Max

Orage, A(lfred) R(ichard)
1873-1934 .... **TCLC 157**
See also CA 122

Origen c. 185-c. 254 .... **CMLC 19**

Orlovitz, Gil 1918-1973 .... **CLC 22**
See also CA 77-80; 45-48; CN 1; CP 1, 2;
DLB 2, 5

Orosius c. 385-c. 420 .... **CMLC 100**

O'Rourke, Patrick Jake
See O'Rourke, P.J.

O'Rourke, P.J. 1947- .... **CLC 209**
See also CA 77-80; CANR 13, 41, 67, 111,
155; CPW; DAM POP; DLB 185

Orris
See Ingelow, Jean

Ortega y Gasset, Jose 1883-1955 ...... **HLC 2;
TCLC 9**
See also CA 106; 130; DAM MULT; EW 9;
EWL 3; HW 1, 2; MTCW 1, 2; MTFW
2005

Ortese, Anna Maria 1914-1998 .... **CLC 89**
See also DLB 177; EWL 3

Ortiz, Simon
See Ortiz, Simon J.

Ortiz, Simon J. 1941- . **CLC 45, 208; NNAL;
PC 17**
See also AMWS 4; CA 134; CANR 69, 118,
164; CP 3, 4, 5, 6, 7; DAM MULT, POET;
DLB 120, 175, 256, 342; EXPP; MAL 5;
PFS 4, 16; RGAL 4; SSFS 22; TCWW 2

Ortiz, Simon Joseph
See Ortiz, Simon J.

Orton, Joe
See Orton, John Kingsley

Orton, John Kingsley 1933-1967 .... **CLC 4,
13, 43; DC 3; TCLC 157**
See also BRWS 5; CA 85-88; CANR 35,
66; CBD; CDBLB 1960 to Present; DAM
DRAM; DFS 3, 6; DLB 13, 310; GLL 1;
MTCW 1, 2; MTFW 2005; RGEL 2;
TEA; WLIT 4

Orwell, George
See Blair, Eric (Arthur)

Osborne, David
See Silverberg, Robert

Osborne, Dorothy 1627-1695 .... **LC 141**

Osborne, George
See Silverberg, Robert

Osborne, John 1929-1994 .... **CLC 1, 2, 5, 11,
45; TCLC 153; WLC 4**
See also BRWS 1; CA 13-16R; 147; CANR
21, 56; CBD; CDBLB 1945-1960; DA;
DAB; DAC; DAM DRAM, MST; DFS 4,
19, 24; DLB 13; EWL 3; MTCW 1, 2;
MTFW 2005; RGEL 2

Osborne, Lawrence 1958- .... **CLC 50**
See also CA 189; CANR 152

Osbourne, Lloyd 1868-1947 .... **TCLC 93**

Osceola
See Blixen, Karen (Christentze Dinesen)

Osgood, Frances Sargent
1811-1850 .... **NCLC 141**
See also DLB 250

Oshima, Nagisa 1932- .... **CLC 20**
See also CA 116; 121; CANR 78

Oskison, John Milton
1874-1947 .... **NNAL; TCLC 35**
See also CA 144; CANR 84; DAM MULT;
DLB 175

Ossoli, Sarah Margaret (Fuller)
1810-1850 .... **NCLC 5, 50, 211**
See also AMWS 2; CDALB 1640-1865;
DLB 1, 59, 73, 183, 223, 239; FW; LMFS
1; SATA 25

Ostriker, Alicia 1937- .... **CLC 132**
See also CA 25-28R; CAAS 24; CANR 10,
30, 62, 99, 167; CWP; DLB 120; EXPP;
PFS 19, 26

Ostriker, Alicia Suskin
See Ostriker, Alicia

Ostrovsky, Aleksandr Nikolaevich
See Ostrovsky, Alexander

Ostrovsky, Alexander 1823-1886 .. **NCLC 30,
57**
See also DLB 277

Osundare, Niyi 1947- .... **BLC 2:3**
See also AFW; BW 3; CA 176; CDWLB 3;
CP 7; DLB 157

Otero, Blas de 1916-1979 .... **CLC 11**
See also CA 89-92; DLB 134; EWL 3

O'Trigger, Sir Lucius
See Horne, Richard Henry Hengist

Otto, Rudolf 1869-1937 .... **TCLC 85**

Otto, Whitney 1955- .... **CLC 70**
See also CA 140; CANR 120

Otway, Thomas 1652-1685 ... **DC 24; LC 106**
See also DAM DRAM; DLB 80; RGEL 2

Ouida
See De La Ramee, Marie Louise

Ouologuem, Yambo 1940- .... **CLC 146**
See also CA 111; 176

Ousmane, Sembene 1923-2007 .... **BLC 1:3,
2:3; CLC 66**
See also AFW; BW 1, 3; CA 117; 125; 261;
CANR 81; CWW 2; EWL 3; MTCW 1;
WLIT 2

Ovid 43B.C.-17 .... **CMLC 7, 108; PC 2**
See also AW 2; CDWLB 1; DA3; DAM
POET; DLB 211; PFS 22; RGWL 2, 3;
WLIT 8; WP

Owen, Hugh
See Faust, Frederick (Schiller)

Owen, Wilfred (Edward Salter)
1893-1918 ... **PC 19; TCLC 5, 27; WLC
4**
See also BRW 6; CA 104; 141; CDBLB
1914-1945; DA; DAB; DAC; DAM MST,
POET; DLB 20; EWL 3; EXPP; MTCW
2; MTFW 2005; PFS 10; RGEL 2; WLIT
4

Owens, Louis (Dean) 1948-2002 .... **NNAL**
See also CA 137, 179; 207; CAAE 179;
CAAS 24; CANR 71

Owens, Rochelle 1936- .... **CLC 8**
See also CA 17-20R; CAAS 2; CAD;
CANR 39; CD 5, 6; CP 1, 2, 3, 4, 5, 6, 7;
CWD; CWP

Oz, Amos 1939- ...... **CLC 5, 8, 11, 27, 33, 54;
SSC 66**
See also CA 53-56; CANR 27, 47, 65, 113,
138, 175; CWW 2; DAM NOV; EWL 3;
MTCW 1, 2; MTFW 2005; RGHL; RGSF
2; RGWL 3; WLIT 6

Ozick, Cynthia 1928- . **CLC 3, 7, 28, 62, 155,
262; SSC 15, 60, 123**
See also AMWS 5; BEST 90:1; CA 17-20R;
CANR 23, 58, 116, 160, 187; CN 3, 4, 5,
6, 7; CPW; DA3; DAM NOV, POP; DLB
28, 152, 299; DLBY 1982; EWL 3; EXPS;
INT CANR-23; MAL 5; MTCW 1, 2;
MTFW 2005; RGAL 4; RGHL; RGSF 2;
SSFS 3, 12, 22

Ozu, Yasujiro 1903-1963 .... **CLC 16**
See also CA 112

Pabst, G. W. 1885-1967 .... **TCLC 127**

Pacheco, C.
See Pessoa, Fernando

Pacheco, Jose Emilio 1939- .... **HLC 2**
See also CA 111; 131; CANR 65; CWW 2;
DAM MULT; DLB 290; EWL 3; HW 1,
2; RGSF 2

Pa Chin
See Jin, Ba

Pack, Robert 1929- .... **CLC 13**
See also CA 1-4R; CANR 3, 44, 82; CP 1,
2, 3, 4, 5, 6, 7; DLB 5; SATA 118

Packer, Vin
See Meaker, Marijane

Padgett, Lewis
See Kuttner, Henry

Padilla (Lorenzo), Heberto
1932-2000 .... **CLC 38**
See also AITN 1; CA 123; 131; 189; CWW
2; EWL 3; HW 1

Paerdurabo, Frater
See Crowley, Edward Alexander

Page, James Patrick 1944- .... **CLC 12**
See also CA 204

Page, Jimmy 1944-
See Page, James Patrick

Perez Galdos, Benito 1843-1920 ..... **HLCS 2; TCLC 27**
See also CA 125; 153; EW 7; EWL 3; HW 1; RGWL 2, 3

Peri Rossi, Cristina 1941- .. **CLC 156; HLCS 2**
See also CA 131; CANR 59, 81; CWW 2; DLB 145, 290; EWL 3; HW 1, 2

Perlata
See Peret, Benjamin

Perloff, Marjorie G(abrielle)
1931- .... **CLC 137**
See also CA 57-60; CANR 7, 22, 49, 104

Perrault, Charles 1628-1703 .... **LC 2, 56**
See also BYA 4; CLR 79, 134; DLB 268; GFL Beginnings to 1789; MAICYA 1, 2; RGWL 2, 3; SATA 25; WCH

Perrotta, Tom 1961- .... **CLC 266**
See also CA 162; CANR 99, 155

Perry, Anne 1938- .... **CLC 126**
See also CA 101; CANR 22, 50, 84, 150, 177; CMW 4; CN 6, 7; CPW; DLB 276

Perry, Brighton
See Sherwood, Robert E(mmet)

Perse, St.-John
See Leger, (Marie-Rene Auguste) Alexis Saint-Leger

Perse, Saint-John
See Leger, (Marie-Rene Auguste) Alexis Saint-Leger

Persius 34-62 .... **CMLC 74**
See also AW 2; DLB 211; RGWL 2, 3

Perutz, Leo(pold) 1882-1957 .... **TCLC 60**
See also CA 147; DLB 81

Peseenz, Tulio F.
See Lopez y Fuentes, Gregorio

Pesetsky, Bette 1932- .... **CLC 28**
See also CA 133; DLB 130

Peshkov, Alexei Maximovich
1868-1936 .... **SSC 28; TCLC 8; WLC 3**
See also CA 105; 141; CANR 83; DA; DAB; DAC; DAM DRAM, MST, NOV; DFS 9; DLB 295; EW 8; EWL 3; MTCW 2; MTFW 2005; RGSF 2; RGWL 2, 3; TWA

Pessoa, Fernando 1888-1935 .... **HLC 2; PC 20; TCLC 27**
See also CA 125; 183; CANR 182; DAM MULT; DLB 287; EW 10; EWL 3; RGWL 2, 3; WP

Pessoa, Fernando Antonio Nogueira
See Pessoa, Fernando

Peterkin, Julia Mood 1880-1961 ...... **CLC 31**
See also CA 102; DLB 9

Peters, Joan K(aren) 1945- .... **CLC 39**
See also CA 158; CANR 109

Peters, Robert L(ouis) 1924- .... **CLC 7**
See also CA 13-16R; CAAS 8; CP 1, 5, 6, 7; DLB 105

Peters, S. H.
See Henry, O.

Petofi, Sandor 1823-1849 .... **NCLC 21**
See also RGWL 2, 3

Petrakis, Harry Mark 1923- .... **CLC 3**
See also CA 9-12R; CANR 4, 30, 85, 155; CN 1, 2, 3, 4, 5, 6, 7

Petrarch 1304-1374 .... **CMLC 20; PC 8**
See also DA3; DAM POET; EW 2; LMFS 1; RGWL 2, 3; WLIT 7

Petronius c. 20-66 .... **CMLC 34**
See also AW 2; CDWLB 1; DLB 211; RGWL 2, 3; WLIT 8

Petrov, Eugene
See Kataev, Evgeny Petrovich

Petrov, Evgenii
See Kataev, Evgeny Petrovich

Petrov, Evgeny
See Kataev, Evgeny Petrovich

Petrovsky, Boris
See Beauchamp, Kathleen Mansfield

Petry, Ann (Lane) 1908-1997 .. **CLC 1, 7, 18; TCLC 112**
See also AFAW 1, 2; BPFB 3; BW 1, 3; BYA 2; CA 5-8R; 157; CAAS 6; CANR 4, 46; CLR 12; CN 1, 2, 3, 4, 5, 6; DLB 76; EWL 3; JRDA; LAIT 1; MAICYA 1, 2; MAICYAS 1; MTCW 1; RGAL 4; SATA 5; SATA-Obit 94; TUS

Petursson, Halligrimur 1614-1674 .... **LC 8**

Peychinovich
See Vazov, Ivan (Minchov)

Phaedrus c. 15B.C.-c. 50 .... **CMLC 25**
See also DLB 211

Phelge, Nanker
See Richards, Keith

Phelps (Ward), Elizabeth Stuart
See Phelps, Elizabeth Stuart

Phelps, Elizabeth Stuart
1844-1911 .... **TCLC 113**
See also CA 242; DLB 74; FW

Pheradausi
See Ferdowsi, Abu'l Qasem

Philippe de Remi c. 1247-1296 ... **CMLC 102**

Philips, Katherine 1632-1664 ..... **LC 30, 145; PC 40**
See also DLB 131; RGEL 2

Philipson, Ilene J. 1950- .... **CLC 65**
See also CA 219

Philipson, Morris H. 1926- .... **CLC 53**
See also CA 1-4R; CANR 4

Phillips, Caryl 1958- ..... **BLCS; CLC 96, 224**
See also BRWS 5; BW 2; CA 141; CANR 63, 104, 140; CBD; CD 5, 6; CN 5, 6, 7; DA3; DAM MULT; DLB 157; EWL 3; MTCW 2; MTFW 2005; WLIT 4; WWE 1

Phillips, David Graham
1867-1911 .... **TCLC 44**
See also CA 108; 176; DLB 9, 12, 303; RGAL 4

Phillips, Jack
See Sandburg, Carl (August)

Phillips, Jayne Anne 1952- .... **CLC 15, 33, 139; SSC 16**
See also AAYA 57; BPFB 3; CA 101; CANR 24, 50, 96; CN 4, 5, 6, 7; CSW; DLBY 1980; INT CANR-24; MTCW 1, 2; MTFW 2005; RGAL 4; RGSF 2; SSFS 4

Phillips, Richard
See Dick, Philip K.

Phillips, Robert (Schaeffer) 1938- .... **CLC 28**
See also CA 17-20R; CAAS 13; CANR 8; DLB 105

Phillips, Ward
See Lovecraft, H. P.

Philo c. 20B.C.-c. 50 .... **CMLC 100**
See also DLB 176

Philostratus, Flavius c. 179-c. 244 .... **CMLC 62**

Phiradausi
See Ferdowsi, Abu'l Qasem

Piccolo, Lucio 1901-1969 .... **CLC 13**
See also CA 97-100; DLB 114; EWL 3

Pickthall, Marjorie L(owry) C(hristie)
1883-1922 .... **TCLC 21**
See also CA 107; DLB 92

Pico della Mirandola, Giovanni
1463-1494 .... **LC 15**
See also LMFS 1

Piercy, Marge 1936- .... **CLC 3, 6, 14, 18, 27, 62, 128; PC 29**
See also BPFB 3; CA 21-24R, 187; CAAE 187; CAAS 1; CANR 13, 43, 66, 111; CN 3, 4, 5, 6, 7; CP 1, 2, 3, 4, 5, 6, 7; CWP; DLB 120, 227; EXPP; FW; MAL 5; MTCW 1, 2; MTFW 2005; PFS 9, 22; SFW 4

Piers, Robert
See Anthony, Piers

Pieyre de Mandiargues, Andre
1909-1991 .... **CLC 41**
See also CA 103; 136; CANR 22, 82; DLB 83; EWL 3; GFL 1789 to the Present

Pil'niak, Boris
See Vogau, Boris Andreyevich

Pil'niak, Boris Andreevich
See Vogau, Boris Andreyevich

Pilnyak, Boris 1894-1938
See Vogau, Boris Andreyevich

Pinchback, Eugene
See Toomer, Jean

Pincherle, Alberto 1907-1990 .. **CLC 2, 7, 11, 27, 46; SSC 26**
See also CA 25-28R; 132; CANR 33, 63, 142; DAM NOV; DLB 127; EW 12; EWL 3; MTCW 2; MTFW 2005; RGSF 2; RGWL 2, 3; WLIT 7

Pinckney, Darryl 1953- .... **CLC 76**
See also BW 2, 3; CA 143; CANR 79

Pindar 518(?)B.C.-438(?)B.C. .... **CMLC 12; PC 19**
See also AW 1; CDWLB 1; DLB 176; RGWL 2

Pineda, Cecile 1942- .... **CLC 39**
See also CA 118; DLB 209

Pinero, Arthur Wing 1855-1934 .... **TCLC 32**
See also CA 110; 153; DAM DRAM; DLB 10, 344; RGEL 2

Pinero, Miguel (Antonio Gomez)
1946-1988 .... **CLC 4, 55**
See also CA 61-64; 125; CAD; CANR 29, 90; DLB 266; HW 1; LLW

Pinget, Robert 1919-1997 ..... **CLC 7, 13, 37**
See also CA 85-88; 160; CWW 2; DLB 83; EWL 3; GFL 1789 to the Present

Pink Floyd
See Barrett, (Roger) Syd; Gilmour, David; Mason, Nick; Waters, Roger; Wright, Rick

Pinkney, Edward 1802-1828 .... **NCLC 31**
See also DLB 248

Pinkwater, D. Manus
See Pinkwater, Daniel

Pinkwater, Daniel Manus
See Pinkwater, Daniel

Pinkwater, Daniel M.
See Pinkwater, Daniel

Pinkwater, Daniel 1941- .... **CLC 35**
See also AAYA 1, 46; BYA 9; CA 29-32R; CANR 12, 38, 89, 143; CLR 4; CSW; FANT; JRDA; MAICYA 1, 2; SAAS 3; SATA 8, 46, 76, 114, 158; SFW 4; YAW

Pinkwater, Manus
See Pinkwater, Daniel

Pinsky, Robert 1940- .... **CLC 9, 19, 38, 94, 121, 216; PC 27**
See also AMWS 6; CA 29-32R; CAAS 4; CANR 58, 97, 138, 177; CP 3, 4, 5, 6, 7; DA3; DAM POET; DLBY 1982, 1998; MAL 5; MTCW 2; MTFW 2005; PFS 18; RGAL 4; TCLE 1:2

Pinta, Harold
See Pinter, Harold

Pinter, Harold 1930-2008 ...... **CLC 1, 3, 6, 9, 11, 15, 27, 58, 73, 199; DC 15; WLC 4**
See also BRWR 1; BRWS 1; CA 5-8R; 280; CANR 33, 65, 112, 145; CBD; CD 5, 6; CDBLB 1960 to Present; CP 1; DA; DA3; DAB; DAC; DAM DRAM, MST; DFS 3, 5, 7, 14, 25; DLB 13, 310, 331; EWL 3; IDFW 3, 4; LMFS 2; MTCW 1, 2; MTFW 2005; RGEL 2; RGHL; TEA

Piozzi, Hester Lynch (Thrale)
1741-1821 .... **NCLC 57**
See also DLB 104, 142

Pirandello, Luigi 1867-1936 .. DC 5; SSC 22;
TCLC 4, 29, 172; WLC 4
See also CA 104; 153; CANR 103; DA;
DA3; DAB; DAC; DAM DRAM; MST;
DFS 4, 9; DLB 264, 331; EW 8; EWL 3;
MTCW 2; MTFW 2005; RGSF 2; RGWL
2, 3; WLIT 7

Pirdousi
See Ferdowsi, Abu'l Qasem

Pirdousi, Abu-l-Qasim
See Ferdowsi, Abu'l Qasem

Pirsig, Robert M(aynard) 1928- ... CLC 4, 6,
73
See also CA 53-56; CANR 42, 74; CPW 1;
DA3; DAM POP; MTCW 1, 2; MTFW
2005; SATA 39

Pisan, Christine de
See Christine de Pizan

Pisarev, Dmitrii Ivanovich
See Pisarev, Dmitry Ivanovich

Pisarev, Dmitry Ivanovich
1840-1868 .... NCLC 25
See also DLB 277

Pix, Mary (Griffith) 1666-1709 ..... LC 8, 149
See also DLB 80

Pixerecourt, (Rene Charles) Guilbert de
1773-1844 .... NCLC 39
See also DLB 192; GFL 1789 to the Present

Plaatje, Sol(omon) T(shekisho)
1878-1932 .... BLCS; TCLC 73
See also BW 2, 3; CA 141; CANR 79; DLB
125, 225

Plaidy, Jean
See Hibbert, Eleanor Alice Burford

Planche, James Robinson
1796-1880 .... NCLC 42
See also RGEL 2

Plant, Robert 1948- .... CLC 12

Plante, David 1940- .... CLC 7, 23, 38
See also CA 37-40R; CANR 12, 36, 58, 82,
152; CN 2, 3, 4, 5, 6, 7; DAM NOV;
DLBY 1983; INT CANR-12; MTCW 1

Plante, David Robert
See Plante, David

Plath, Sylvia 1932-1963 ..... CLC 1, 2, 3, 5, 9,
11, 14, 17, 50, 51, 62, 111; PC 1, 37;
WLC 4
See also AAYA 13; AMWR 2; AMWS 1;
BPFB 3; CA 19-20; CANR 34, 101; CAP
2; CDALB 1941-1968; DA; DA3; DAB;
DAC; DAM MST, POET; DLB 5, 6, 152;
EWL 3; EXPN; EXPP; FL 1:6; FW; LAIT
4; MAL 5; MBL; MTCW 1, 2; MTFW
2005; NFS 1; PAB; PFS 1, 15, 28; RGAL
4; SATA 96; TUS; WP; YAW

Plato c. 428B.C.-347B.C. .... CMLC 8, 75, 98;
WLCS
See also AW 1; CDWLB 1; DA; DA3;
DAB; DAC; DAM MST; DLB 176; LAIT
1; LATS 1:1; RGWL 2, 3; WLIT 8

Platonov, Andrei
See Klimentov, Andrei Platonovich

Platonov, Andrei Platonovich
See Klimentov, Andrei Platonovich

Platonov, Andrey Platonovich
See Klimentov, Andrei Platonovich

Platt, Kin 1911- .... CLC 26
See also AAYA 11; CA 17-20R; CANR 11;
JRDA; SAAS 17; SATA 21, 86; WYA

Plautus c. 254B.C.-c. 184B.C. .... CMLC 24,
92; DC 6
See also AW 1; CDWLB 1; DLB 211;
RGWL 2, 3; WLIT 8

Plick et Plock
See Simenon, Georges (Jacques Christian)

Plieksans, Janis
See Rainis, Janis

Plimpton, George 1927-2003 .... CLC 36
See also AITN 1; AMWS 16; CA 21-24R;
224; CANR 32, 70, 103, 133; DLB 185,
241; MTCW 1, 2; MTFW 2005; SATA
10; SATA-Obit 150

Pliny the Elder c. 23-79 .... CMLC 23
See also DLB 211

Pliny the Younger c. 61-c. 112 ...... CMLC 62
See also AW 2; DLB 211

Plomer, William Charles Franklin
1903-1973 .... CLC 4, 8
See also AFW; BRWS 11; CA 21-22; CANR
34; CAP 2; CN 1; CP 1, 2; DLB 20, 162,
191, 225; EWL 3; MTCW 1; RGEL 2;
RGSF 2; SATA 24

Plotinus 204-270 .... CMLC 46
See also CDWLB 1; DLB 176

Plowman, Piers
See Kavanagh, Patrick (Joseph)

Plum, J.
See Wodehouse, P(elham) G(renville)

Plumly, Stanley 1939- .... CLC 33
See also CA 108; 110; CANR 97, 185; CP
3, 4, 5, 6, 7; DLB 5, 193; INT CA-110

Plumly, Stanley Ross
See Plumly, Stanley

Plumpe, Friedrich Wilhelm
See Murnau, F.W.

Plutarch c. 46-c. 120 .... CMLC 60
See also AW 2; CDWLB 1; DLB 176;
RGWL 2; TWA; WLIT 8

Po Chu-i 772-846 .... CMLC 24

Podhoretz, Norman 1930- .... CLC 189
See also AMWS 8; CA 9-12R; CANR 7,
78, 135, 179

Poe, Edgar Allan 1809-1849 ..... NCLC 1, 16,
55, 78, 94, 97, 117, 211; PC 1, 54; SSC
1, 22, 34, 35, 54, 88, 111; WLC 4
See also AAYA 14; AMW; AMWC 1;
AMWR 2; BPFB 3; BYA 5, 11; CDALB
1640-1865; CMW 4; DA; DA3; DAB;
DAC; DAM MST, POET; DLB 3, 59, 73,
74, 248, 254; EXPP; EXPS; GL 3; HGG;
LAIT 2; LATS 1:1; LMFS 1; MSW; PAB;
PFS 1, 3, 9; RGAL 4; RGSF 2; SATA 23;
SCFW 1, 2; SFW 4; SSFS 2, 4, 7, 8, 16,
26; SUFW; TUS; WP; WYA

Poet of Titchfield Street, The
See Pound, Ezra (Weston Loomis)

Poggio Bracciolini, Gian Francesco
1380-1459 .... LC 125

Pohl, Frederik 1919- .... CLC 18; SSC 25
See also AAYA 24; CA 61-64, 188; CAAE
188; CAAS 1; CANR 11, 37, 81, 140; CN
1, 2, 3, 4, 5, 6; DLB 8; INT CANR-11;
MTCW 1, 2; MTFW 2005; SATA 24;
SCFW 1, 2; SFW 4

Poirier, Louis
See Gracq, Julien

Poitier, Sidney 1927- .... CLC 26
See also AAYA 60; BW 1; CA 117; CANR
94

Pokagon, Simon 1830-1899 .... NNAL
See also DAM MULT

Polanski, Roman 1933- .... CLC 16, 178
See also CA 77-80

Poliakoff, Stephen 1952- .... CLC 38
See also CA 106; CANR 116; CBD; CD 5,
6; DLB 13

Police, The
See Copeland, Stewart (Armstrong); Sting;
Summers, Andy

Polidori, John William
1795-1821 .... NCLC 51; SSC 97
See also DLB 116; HGG

Poliziano, Angelo 1454-1494 .... LC 120
See also WLIT 7

Pollitt, Katha 1949- .... CLC 28, 122
See also CA 120; 122; CANR 66, 108, 164;
MTCW 1, 2; MTFW 2005

Pollock, (Mary) Sharon 1936- .... CLC 50
See also CA 141; CANR 132; CD 5; CWD;
DAC; DAM DRAM, MST; DFS 3; DLB
60; FW

Pollock, Sharon 1936- .... DC 20
See also CD 6

Polo, Marco 1254-1324 .... CMLC 15
See also WLIT 7

Polonsky, Abraham (Lincoln)
1910-1999 .... CLC 92
See also CA 104; 187; DLB 26; INT CA-
104

Polybius c. 200B.C.-c. 118B.C. ...... CMLC 17
See also AW 1; DLB 176; RGWL 2, 3

Pomerance, Bernard 1940- .... CLC 13
See also CA 101; CAD; CANR 49, 134;
CD 5, 6; DAM DRAM; DFS 9; LAIT 2

Ponge, Francis 1899-1988 .... CLC 6, 18
See also CA 85-88; 126; CANR 40, 86;
DAM POET; DLBY 2002; EWL 3; GFL
1789 to the Present; RGWL 2, 3

Poniatowska, Elena 1932- . CLC 140; HLC 2
See also CA 101; CANR 32, 66, 107, 156;
CDWLB 3; CWW 2; DAM MULT; DLB
113; EWL 3; HW 1, 2; LAWS 1; WLIT 1

Pontoppidan, Henrik 1857-1943 .... TCLC 29
See also CA 170; DLB 300, 331

Ponty, Maurice Merleau
See Merleau-Ponty, Maurice

Poole, (Jane Penelope) Josephine
See Helyar, Jane Penelope Josephine

Poole, Josephine
See Helyar, Jane Penelope Josephine

Popa, Vasko 1922-1991 . CLC 19; TCLC 167
See also CA 112; 148; CDWLB 4; DLB
181; EWL 3; RGWL 2, 3

Pope, Alexander 1688-1744 ...... LC 3, 58, 60,
64, 164; PC 26; WLC 5
See also BRW 3; BRWC 1; BRWR 1; CD-
BLB 1660-1789; DA; DA3; DAB; DAC;
DAM MST, POET; DLB 95, 101, 213;
EXPP; PAB; PFS 12; RGEL 2; WLIT 3;
WP

Popov, Evgenii Anatol'evich
See Popov, Yevgeny

Popov, Yevgeny CLC 59
See also DLB 285

Poquelin, Jean-Baptiste
See Moliere

Porete, Marguerite (?)-1310 .... CMLC 73
See also DLB 208

Porphyry c. 233-c. 305 .... CMLC 71

Porter, Connie (Rose) 1959(?)- .... CLC 70
See also AAYA 65; BW 2, 3; CA 142;
CANR 90, 109; SATA 81, 129

Porter, Gene(va Grace) Stratton
See Stratton-Porter, Gene(va Grace)

Porter, Katherine Anne 1890-1980 ... CLC 1,
3, 7, 10, 13, 15, 27, 101; SSC 4, 31, 43,
108
See also AAYA 42; AITN 2; AMW; BPFB
3; CA 1-4R; 101; CANR 1, 65; CDALBS;
CN 1, 2; DA; DA3; DAB; DAC; DAM
MST, NOV; DLB 4, 9, 102; DLBD 12;
DLBY 1980; EWL 3; EXPS; LAIT 3;
MAL 5; MBL; MTCW 1, 2; MTFW 2005;
NFS 14; RGAL 4; RGSF 2; SATA 39;
SATA-Obit 23; SSFS 1, 8, 11, 16, 23;
TCWW 2; TUS

Porter, Peter (Neville Frederick)
1929- .... CLC 5, 13, 33
See also CA 85-88; CP 1, 2, 3, 4, 5, 6, 7;
DLB 40, 289; WWE 1

Porter, William Sydney
See Henry, O.

Prudhomme, Rene Francois Armand
1839-1907
See Sully Prudhomme, Rene-Francois-Armand
Prus, Boleslaw 1845-1912 .... **TCLC 48**
See also RGWL 2, 3
Prynne, William 1600-1669 .... **LC 148**
Prynne, Xavier
See Hardwick, Elizabeth
Pryor, Aaron Richard
See Pryor, Richard
Pryor, Richard 1940-2005 .... **CLC 26**
See also CA 122; 152; 246
Pryor, Richard Franklin Lenox Thomas
See Pryor, Richard
Przybyszewski, Stanislaw
1868-1927 .... **TCLC 36**
See also CA 160; DLB 66; EWL 3
Pseudo-Dionysius the Areopagite fl. c. 5th
cent. - .... **CMLC 89**
See also DLB 115
Pteleon
See Grieve, C(hristopher) M(urray)
Puckett, Lute
See Masters, Edgar Lee
Puig, Manuel 1932-1990 .... **CLC 3, 5, 10, 28,**
65, 133; HLC 2
See also BPFB 3; CA 45-48; CANR 2, 32,
63; CDWLB 3; DA3; DAM MULT; DLB
113; DNFS 1; EWL 3; GLL 1; HW 1, 2;
LAW; MTCW 1, 2; MTFW 2005; RGWL
2, 3; TWA; WLIT 1
Pulitzer, Joseph 1847-1911 .... **TCLC 76**
See also CA 114; DLB 23
Pullman, Philip 1946- .... **CLC 245**
See also AAYA 15, 41; BRWS 13; BYA 8,
13; CA 127; CANR 50, 77, 105, 134;
CLR 20, 62, 84; JRDA; MAICYA 1, 2;
MAICYAS 1; MTFW 2005; SAAS 17;
SATA 65, 103, 150, 198; SUFW 2; WYAS
1; YAW
Purchas, Samuel 1577(?)-1626 .... **LC 70**
See also DLB 151
Purdy, A(lfred) W(ellington)
1918-2000 .... **CLC 3, 6, 14, 50**
See also CA 81-84; 189; CAAS 17; CANR
42, 66; CP 1, 2, 3, 4, 5, 6, 7; DAC; DAM
MST, POET; DLB 88; PFS 5; RGEL 2
Purdy, James 1923-2009 .... **CLC 2, 4, 10, 28,**
52
See also AMWS 7; CA 33-36R; CAAS 1;
CANR 19, 51, 132; CN 1, 2, 3, 4, 5, 6, 7;
DLB 2, 218; EWL 3; INT CANR-19;
MAL 5; MTCW 1; RGAL 4
Purdy, James Amos
See Purdy, James
Pure, Simon
See Swinnerton, Frank Arthur
Pushkin, Aleksandr Sergeevich
See Pushkin, Alexander (Sergeyevich)
Pushkin, Alexander (Sergeyevich)
1799-1837 .... **NCLC 3, 27, 83; PC 10;**
SSC 27, 55, 99; WLC 5
See also DA; DA3; DAB; DAC; DAM
DRAM, MST, POET; DLB 205; EW 5;
EXPS; PFS 28; RGSF 2; RGWL 2, 3;
SATA 61; SSFS 9; TWA
P'u Sung-ling 1640-1715 .... **LC 49; SSC 31**
Putnam, Arthur Lee
See Alger, Horatio, Jr.
Puttenham, George 1529(?)-1590 ...... **LC 116**
See also DLB 281
Puzo, Mario 1920-1999 .... **CLC 1, 2, 6, 36,**
107
See also BPFB 3; CA 65-68; 185; CANR 4,
42, 65, 99, 131; CN 1, 2, 3, 4, 5, 6; CPW;
DA3; DAM NOV, POP; DLB 6; MTCW
1, 2; MTFW 2005; NFS 16; RGAL 4

Pygge, Edward
See Barnes, Julian
Pyle, Ernest Taylor 1900-1945 .... **TCLC 75**
See also CA 115; 160; DLB 29; MTCW 2
Pyle, Ernie
See Pyle, Ernest Taylor
Pyle, Howard 1853-1911 .... **TCLC 81**
See also AAYA 57; BYA 2, 4; CA 109; 137;
CLR 22, 117; DLB 42, 188; DLBD 13;
LAIT 1; MAICYA 1, 2; SATA 16, 100;
WCH; YAW
Pym, Barbara (Mary Crampton)
1913-1980 .... **CLC 13, 19, 37, 111**
See also BPFB 3; BRWS 2; CA 13-14; 97-
100; CANR 13, 34; CAP 1; DLB 14, 207;
DLBY 1987; EWL 3; MTCW 1, 2; MTFW
2005; RGEL 2; TEA
Pynchon, Thomas 1937- .. **CLC 2, 3, 6, 9, 11,**
18, 33, 62, 72, 123, 192, 213; SSC 14,
84; WLC 5
See also AMWS 2; BEST 90:2; BPFB 3;
CA 17-20R; CANR 22, 46, 73, 142; CN
1, 2, 3, 4, 5, 6, 7; CPW 1; DA; DA3;
DAB; DAC; DAM MST, NOV, POP;
DLB 2, 173; EWL 3; MAL 5; MTCW 1,
2; MTFW 2005; NFS 23; RGAL 4; SFW
4; TCLE 1:2; TUS
Pythagoras c. 582B.C.-c. 507B.C. . **CMLC 22**
See also DLB 176
Q
See Quiller-Couch, Sir Arthur (Thomas)
Qian, Chongzhu
See Ch'ien, Chung-shu
Qian, Sima 145B.C.-c. 89B.C. .... **CMLC 72**
Qian Zhongshu
See Ch'ien, Chung-shu
Qroll
See Dagerman, Stig (Halvard)
Quarles, Francis 1592-1644 .... **LC 117**
See also DLB 126; RGEL 2
Quarrington, Paul 1953- .... **CLC 65**
See also CA 129; CANR 62, 95
Quarrington, Paul Lewis
See Quarrington, Paul
Quasimodo, Salvatore 1901-1968 .... **CLC 10;**
PC 47
See also CA 13-16; 25-28R; CAP 1; DLB
114, 332; EW 12; EWL 3; MTCW 1;
RGWL 2, 3
Quatermass, Martin
See Carpenter, John (Howard)
Quay, Stephen 1947- .... **CLC 95**
See also CA 189
Quay, Timothy 1947- .... **CLC 95**
See also CA 189
Queen, Ellery
See Dannay, Frederic; Hoch, Edward D.;
Lee, Manfred B.; Marlowe, Stephen;
Sturgeon, Theodore (Hamilton); Vance,
Jack
Queneau, Raymond 1903-1976 ..... **CLC 2, 5,**
10, 42
See also CA 77-80; 69-72; CANR 32; DLB
72, 258; EW 12; EWL 3; GFL 1789 to
the Present; MTCW 1, 2; RGWL 2, 3
Quevedo, Francisco de 1580-1645 ...... **LC 23,**
160
Quiller-Couch, Sir Arthur (Thomas)
1863-1944 .... **TCLC 53**
See also CA 118; 166; DLB 135, 153, 190;
HGG; RGEL 2; SUFW 1
Quin, Ann 1936-1973 .... **CLC 6**
See also CA 9-12R; 45-48; CANR 148; CN
1; DLB 14, 231
Quin, Ann Marie
See Quin, Ann
Quincey, Thomas de
See De Quincey, Thomas

Quindlen, Anna 1953- .... **CLC 191**
See also AAYA 35; AMWS 17; CA 138;
CANR 73, 126; DA3; DLB 292; MTCW
2; MTFW 2005
Quinn, Martin
See Smith, Martin Cruz
Quinn, Peter 1947- .... **CLC 91**
See also CA 197; CANR 147
Quinn, Peter A.
See Quinn, Peter
Quinn, Simon
See Smith, Martin Cruz
Quintana, Leroy V. 1944- ...... **HLC 2; PC 36**
See also CA 131; CANR 65, 139; DAM
MULT; DLB 82; HW 1, 2
Quintilian c. 40-c. 100 .... **CMLC 77**
See also AW 2; DLB 211; RGWL 2, 3
Quiroga, Horacio (Sylvestre)
1878-1937 ... **HLC 2; SSC 89; TCLC 20**
See also CA 117; 131; DAM MULT; EWL
3; HW 1; LAW; MTCW 1; RGSF 2;
WLIT 1
Quoirez, Francoise 1935-2004 ... **CLC 3, 6, 9,**
17, 36
See also CA 49-52; 231; CANR 6, 39, 73;
CWW 2; DLB 83; EWL 3; GFL 1789 to
the Present; MTCW 1, 2; MTFW 2005;
TWA
Raabe, Wilhelm (Karl) 1831-1910 . **TCLC 45**
See also CA 167; DLB 129
Rabe, David (William) 1940- .. **CLC 4, 8, 33,**
200; DC 16
See also CA 85-88; CABS 3; CAD; CANR
59, 129; CD 5, 6; DAM DRAM; DFS 3,
8, 13; DLB 7, 228; EWL 3; MAL 5
Rabelais, Francois 1494-1553 .... **LC 5, 60;**
WLC 5
See also DA; DAB; DAC; DAM MST;
DLB 327; EW 2; GFL Beginnings to
1789; LMFS 1; RGWL 2, 3; TWA
Rabi'a al-'Adawiyya c. 717-c.
801 .... **CMLC 83**
See also DLB 311
Rabinovitch, Sholem 1859-1916 .... **SSC 33;**
TCLC 1, 35
See also CA 104; DLB 333; TWA
Rabinovitsh, Sholem Yankev
See Rabinovitch, Sholem
Rabinowitz, Sholem Yakov
See Rabinovitch, Sholem
Rabinowitz, Solomon
See Rabinovitch, Sholem
Rabinyan, Dorit 1972- .... **CLC 119**
See also CA 170; CANR 147
Rachilde
See Vallette, Marguerite Eymery; Vallette,
Marguerite Eymery
Racine, Jean 1639-1699 .. **DC 32; LC 28, 113**
See also DA3; DAB; DAM MST; DLB 268;
EW 3; GFL Beginnings to 1789; LMFS
1; RGWL 2, 3; TWA
Radcliffe, Ann (Ward) 1764-1823 ... **NCLC 6,**
55, 106
See also DLB 39, 178; GL 3; HGG; LMFS
1; RGEL 2; SUFW; WLIT 3
Radclyffe-Hall, Marguerite
See Hall, Radclyffe
Radiguet, Raymond 1903-1923 ...... **TCLC 29**
See also CA 162; DLB 65; EWL 3; GFL
1789 to the Present; RGWL 2, 3
Radishchev, Aleksandr Nikolaevich
1749-1802 .... **NCLC 190**
See also DLB 150
Radishchev, Alexander
See Radishchev, Aleksandr Nikolaevich
Radnoti, Miklos 1909-1944 .... **TCLC 16**
See also CA 118; 212; CDWLB 4; DLB
215; EWL 3; RGHL; RGWL 2, 3

Romains, Jules 1885-1972 .... **CLC 7**
See also CA 85-88; CANR 34; DLB 65, 321; EWL 3; GFL 1789 to the Present; MTCW 1

Romero, Jose Ruben 1890-1952 .... **TCLC 14**
See also CA 114; 131; EWL 3; HW 1; LAW

Ronsard, Pierre de 1524-1585 . **LC 6, 54; PC 11**
See also DLB 327; EW 2; GFL Beginnings to 1789; RGWL 2, 3; TWA

Rooke, Leon 1934- .... **CLC 25, 34**
See also CA 25-28R; CANR 23, 53; CCA 1; CPW; DAM POP

Roosevelt, Franklin Delano 1882-1945 .... **TCLC 93**
See also CA 116; 173; LAIT 3

Roosevelt, Theodore 1858-1919 ..... **TCLC 69**
See also CA 115; 170; DLB 47, 186, 275

Roper, Margaret c. 1505-1544 .... **LC 147**

Roper, William 1498-1578 .... **LC 10**

Roquelaure, A. N.
See Rice, Anne

Rosa, Joao Guimaraes 1908-1967
See Guimaraes Rosa, Joao

Rose, Wendy 1948- . **CLC 85; NNAL; PC 13**
See also CA 53-56; CANR 5, 51; CWP; DAM MULT; DLB 175; PFS 13; RGAL 4; SATA 12

Rosen, R.D. 1949- .... **CLC 39**
See also CA 77-80; CANR 62, 120, 175; CMW 4; INT CANR-30

Rosen, Richard
See Rosen, R.D.

Rosen, Richard Dean
See Rosen, R.D.

Rosenberg, Isaac 1890-1918 .... **TCLC 12**
See also BRW 6; CA 107; 188; DLB 20, 216; EWL 3; PAB; RGEL 2

Rosenblatt, Joe
See Rosenblatt, Joseph

Rosenblatt, Joseph 1933- .... **CLC 15**
See also CA 89-92; CP 3, 4, 5, 6, 7; INT CA-89-92

Rosenfeld, Samuel
See Tzara, Tristan

Rosenstock, Sami
See Tzara, Tristan

Rosenstock, Samuel
See Tzara, Tristan

Rosenthal, M(acha) L(ouis) 1917-1996 .... **CLC 28**
See also CA 1-4R; 152; CAAS 6; CANR 4, 51; CP 1, 2, 3, 4, 5, 6; DLB 5; SATA 59

Ross, Barnaby
See Dannay, Frederic; Lee, Manfred B.

Ross, Bernard L.
See Follett, Ken

Ross, J. H.
See Lawrence, T(homas) E(dward)

Ross, John Hume
See Lawrence, T(homas) E(dward)

Ross, Martin 1862-1915
See Martin, Violet Florence
See also DLB 135; GLL 2; RGEL 2; RGSF 2

Ross, (James) Sinclair 1908-1996 ... **CLC 13; SSC 24**
See also CA 73-76; CANR 81; CN 1, 2, 3, 4, 5, 6; DAC; DAM MST; DLB 88; RGEL 2; RGSF 2; TCWW 1, 2

Rossetti, Christina 1830-1894 ... **NCLC 2, 50, 66, 186; PC 7; WLC 5**
See also AAYA 51; BRW 5; BYA 4; CLR 115; DA; DA3; DAB; DAC; DAM MST, POET; DLB 35, 163, 240; EXPP; FL 1:3; LATS 1:1; MAICYA 1, 2; PFS 10, 14, 27; RGEL 2; SATA 20; TEA; WCH

Rossetti, Christina Georgina
See Rossetti, Christina

Rossetti, Dante Gabriel 1828-1882 . **NCLC 4, 77; PC 44; WLC 5**
See also AAYA 51; BRW 5; CDBLB 1832-1890; DA; DAB; DAC; DAM MST, POET; DLB 35; EXPP; RGEL 2; TEA

Rossi, Cristina Peri
See Peri Rossi, Cristina

Rossi, Jean-Baptiste 1931-2003 .... **CLC 90**
See also CA 201; 215; CMW 4; NFS 18

Rossner, Judith 1935-2005 .... **CLC 6, 9, 29**
See also AITN 2; BEST 90:3; BPFB 3; CA 17-20R; 242; CANR 18, 51, 73; CN 4, 5, 6, 7; DLB 6; INT CANR-18; MAL 5; MTCW 1, 2; MTFW 2005

Rossner, Judith Perelman
See Rossner, Judith

Rostand, Edmond (Eugene Alexis) 1868-1918 .... **DC 10; TCLC 6, 37**
See also CA 104; 126; DA; DA3; DAB; DAC; DAM DRAM, MST; DFS 1; DLB 192; LAIT 1; MTCW 1; RGWL 2, 3; TWA

Roth, Henry 1906-1995 ..... **CLC 2, 6, 11, 104**
See also AMWS 9; CA 11-12; 149; CANR 38, 63; CAP 1; CN 1, 2, 3, 4, 5, 6; DA3; DLB 28; EWL 3; MAL 5; MTCW 1, 2; MTFW 2005; RGAL 4

Roth, (Moses) Joseph 1894-1939 ... **TCLC 33**
See also CA 160; DLB 85; EWL 3; RGWL 2, 3

Roth, Philip 1933- ... **CLC 1, 2, 3, 4, 6, 9, 15, 22, 31, 47, 66, 86, 119, 201; SSC 26, 102; WLC 5**
See also AAYA 67; AMWR 2; AMWS 3; BEST 90:3; BPFB 3; CA 1-4R; CANR 1, 22, 36, 55, 89, 132, 170; CDALB 1968-1988; CN 3, 4, 5, 6, 7; CPW 1; DA; DA3; DAB; DAC; DAM MST, NOV, POP; DLB 2, 28, 173; DLBY 1982; EWL 3; MAL 5; MTCW 1, 2; MTFW 2005; NFS 25; RGAL 4; RGHL; RGSF 2; SSFS 12, 18; TUS

Roth, Philip Milton
See Roth, Philip

Rothenberg, Jerome 1931- .... **CLC 6, 57**
See also CA 45-48; CANR 1, 106; CP 1, 2, 3, 4, 5, 6, 7; DLB 5, 193

Rotter, Pat **CLC 65**

Roumain, Jacques (Jean Baptiste) 1907-1944 .... **BLC 1:3; TCLC 19**
See also BW 1; CA 117; 125; DAM MULT; EWL 3

Rourke, Constance Mayfield 1885-1941 .... **TCLC 12**
See also CA 107; 200; MAL 5; YABC 1

Rousseau, Jean-Baptiste 1671-1741 ...... **LC 9**

Rousseau, Jean-Jacques 1712-1778 .... **LC 14, 36, 122; WLC 5**
See also DA; DA3; DAB; DAC; DAM MST; DLB 314; EW 4; GFL Beginnings to 1789; LMFS 1; RGWL 2, 3; TWA

Roussel, Raymond 1877-1933 .... **TCLC 20**
See also CA 117; 201; EWL 3; GFL 1789 to the Present

Rovit, Earl (Herbert) 1927- .... **CLC 7**
See also CA 5-8R; CANR 12

Rowe, Elizabeth Singer 1674-1737 ..... **LC 44**
See also DLB 39, 95

Rowe, Nicholas 1674-1718 .... **LC 8**
See also DLB 84; RGEL 2

Rowlandson, Mary 1637(?)-1678 .... **LC 66**
See also DLB 24, 200; RGAL 4

Rowley, Ames Dorrance
See Lovecraft, H. P.

Rowley, William 1585(?)-1626 ... **LC 100, 123**
See also DFS 22; DLB 58; RGEL 2

Rowling, J.K. 1965- .... **CLC 137, 217**
See also AAYA 34; BYA 11, 13, 14; CA 173; CANR 128, 157; CLR 66, 80, 112; MAICYA 2; MTFW 2005; SATA 109, 174; SUFW 2

Rowling, Joanne Kathleen
See Rowling, J.K.

Rowson, Susanna Haswell 1762(?)-1824 .... **NCLC 5, 69, 182**
See also AMWS 15; DLB 37, 200; RGAL 4

Roy, Arundhati 1960(?)- .... **CLC 109, 210**
See also CA 163; CANR 90, 126; CN 7; DLB 323, 326; DLBY 1997; EWL 3; LATS 1:2; MTFW 2005; NFS 22; WWE 1

Roy, Gabrielle 1909-1983 .... **CLC 10, 14**
See also CA 53-56; 110; CANR 5, 61; CCA 1; DAB; DAC; DAM MST; DLB 68; EWL 3; MTCW 1; RGWL 2, 3; SATA 104; TCLE 1:2

Royko, Mike 1932-1997 .... **CLC 109**
See also CA 89-92; 157; CANR 26, 111; CPW

Rozanov, Vasilii Vasil'evich
See Rozanov, Vassili

Rozanov, Vasily Vasilyevich
See Rozanov, Vassili

Rozanov, Vassili 1856-1919 .... **TCLC 104**
See also DLB 295; EWL 3

Rozewicz, Tadeusz 1921- ...... **CLC 9, 23, 139**
See also CA 108; CANR 36; CWW 2; DA3; DAM POET; DLB 232; EWL 3; MTCW 1, 2; MTFW 2005; RGHL; RGWL 3

Ruark, Gibbons 1941- .... **CLC 3**
See also CA 33-36R; CAAS 23; CANR 14, 31, 57; DLB 120

Rubens, Bernice (Ruth) 1923-2004 . **CLC 19, 31**
See also CA 25-28R; 232; CANR 33, 65, 128; CN 1, 2, 3, 4, 5, 6, 7; DLB 14, 207, 326; MTCW 1

Rubin, Harold
See Robbins, Harold

Rudkin, (James) David 1936- .... **CLC 14**
See also CA 89-92; CBD; CD 5, 6; DLB 13

Rudnik, Raphael 1933- .... **CLC 7**
See also CA 29-32R

Ruffian, M.
See Hasek, Jaroslav (Matej Frantisek)

Rufinus c. 345-410 .... **CMLC 111**

Ruiz, Jose Martinez
See Martinez Ruiz, Jose

Ruiz, Juan c. 1283-c. 1350 .... **CMLC 66**

Rukeyser, Muriel 1913-1980 . **CLC 6, 10, 15, 27; PC 12**
See also AMWS 6; CA 5-8R; 93-96; CANR 26, 60; CP 1, 2, 3; DA3; DAM POET; DLB 48; EWL 3; FW; GLL 2; MAL 5; MTCW 1, 2; PFS 10, 29; RGAL 4; SATA-Obit 22

Rule, Jane 1931-2007 .... **CLC 27, 265**
See also CA 25-28R; 266; CAAS 18; CANR 12, 87; CN 4, 5, 6, 7; DLB 60; FW

Rule, Jane Vance
See Rule, Jane

Rulfo, Juan 1918-1986 .. **CLC 8, 80; HLC 2; SSC 25**
See also CA 85-88; 118; CANR 26; CD-WLB 3; DAM MULT; DLB 113; EWL 3; HW 1, 2; LAW; MTCW 1, 2; RGSF 2; RGWL 2, 3; WLIT 1

Rumi, Jalal al-Din 1207-1273 ...... **CMLC 20; PC 45**
See also AAYA 64; RGWL 2, 3; WLIT 6; WP

EWL 3; EXPN; LAIT 4; MAICYA 1, 2;
MAL 5; MTCW 1, 2; MTFW 2005; NFS
1; RGAL 4; RGSF 2; SATA 67; SSFS 17;
TUS; WYA; YAW

Salisbury, John
See Caute, (John) David

Sallust c. 86B.C.-35B.C. .... **CMLC 68**
See also AW 2; CDWLB 1; DLB 211;
RGWL 2, 3

Salter, James 1925- .... **CLC 7, 52, 59; SSC 58**
See also AMWS 9; CA 73-76; CANR 107,
160; DLB 130; SSFS 25

Saltus, Edgar (Everton) 1855-1921 . **TCLC 8**
See also CA 105; DLB 202; RGAL 4

Saltykov, Mikhail Evgrafovich
1826-1889 .... **NCLC 16**
See also DLB 238:

Saltykov-Shchedrin, N.
See Saltykov, Mikhail Evgrafovich

Samarakis, Andonis
See Samarakis, Antonis

Samarakis, Antonis 1919-2003 .... **CLC 5**
See also CA 25-28R; 224; CAAS 16; CANR
36; EWL 3

Samigli, E.
See Schmitz, Aron Hector

Sanchez, Florencio 1875-1910 .... **TCLC 37**
See also CA 153; DLB 305; EWL 3; HW 1;
LAW

Sanchez, Luis Rafael 1936- .... **CLC 23**
See also CA 128; DLB 305; EWL 3; HW 1;
WLIT 1

Sanchez, Sonia 1934- . **BLC 1:3, 2:3; CLC 5,
116, 215; PC 9**
See also BW 2, 3; CA 33-36R; CANR 24,
49, 74, 115; CLR 18; CP 2, 3, 4, 5, 6, 7;
CSW; CWP; DA3; DAM MULT; DLB 41;
DLBD 8; EWL 3; MAICYA 1, 2; MAL 5;
MTCW 1, 2; MTFW 2005; PFS 26; SATA
22, 136; WP

Sancho, Ignatius 1729-1780 .... **LC 84**

Sand, George 1804-1876 .... **DC 29; NCLC 2,
42, 57, 174; WLC 5**
See also DA; DA3; DAB; DAC; DAM
MST, NOV; DLB 119, 192; EW 6; FL 1:3;
FW; GFL 1789 to the Present; RGWL 2,
3; TWA

Sandburg, Carl (August) 1878-1967 . **CLC 1,
4, 10, 15, 35; PC 2, 41; WLC 5**
See also AAYA 24; AMW; BYA 1, 3; CA
5-8R; 25-28R; CANR 35; CDALB 1865-
1917; CLR 67; DA; DA3; DAB; DAC;
DAM MST, POET; DLB 17, 54, 284;
EWL 3; EXPP; LAIT 2; MAICYA 1, 2;
MAL 5; MTCW 1, 2; MTFW 2005; PAB;
PFS 3, 6, 12; RGAL 4; SATA 8; TUS;
WCH; WP; WYA

Sandburg, Charles
See Sandburg, Carl (August)

Sandburg, Charles A.
See Sandburg, Carl (August)

Sanders, (James) Ed(ward) 1939- .... **CLC 53**
See also BG 1:3; CA 13-16R; CAAS 21;
CANR 13, 44, 78; CP 1, 2, 3, 4, 5, 6, 7;
DAM POET; DLB 16, 244

Sanders, Edward
See Sanders, (James) Ed(ward)

Sanders, Lawrence 1920-1998 .... **CLC 41**
See also BEST 89:4; BPFB 3; CA 81-84;
165; CANR 33, 62; CMW 4; CPW; DA3;
DAM POP; MTCW 1

Sanders, Noah
See Blount, Roy, Jr.

Sanders, Winston P.
See Anderson, Poul

Sandoz, Mari(e Susette) 1900-1966 .. **CLC 28**
See also CA 1-4R; 25-28R; CANR 17, 64;
DLB 9, 212; LAIT 2; MTCW 1, 2; SATA
5; TCWW 1, 2

Sandys, George 1578-1644 .... **LC 80**
See also DLB 24, 121

Saner, Reg(inald Anthony) 1931- .... **CLC 9**
See also CA 65-68; CP 3, 4, 5, 6, 7

Sankara 788-820 .... **CMLC 32**

Sannazaro, Jacopo 1456(?)-1530 .... **LC 8**
See also RGWL 2, 3; WLIT 7

Sansom, William 1912-1976 . **CLC 2, 6; SSC
21**
See also CA 5-8R; 65-68; CANR 42; CN 1,
2; DAM NOV; DLB 139; EWL 3; MTCW
1; RGEL 2; RGSF 2

Santayana, George 1863-1952 .... **TCLC 40**
See also AMW; CA 115; 194; DLB 54, 71,
246, 270; DLBD 13; EWL 3; MAL 5;
RGAL 4; TUS

Santiago, Danny
See James, Daniel (Lewis)

**Santillana, Inigo Lopez de Mendoza,
Marques de** 1398-1458 .... **LC 111**
See also DLB 286

Santmyer, Helen Hooven
1895-1986 .... **CLC 33; TCLC 133**
See also CA 1-4R; 118; CANR 15, 33;
DLBY 1984; MTCW 1; RHW

Santoka, Taneda 1882-1940 .... **TCLC 72**

Santos, Bienvenido N(uqui)
1911-1996 .... **AAL; CLC 22; TCLC 156**
See also CA 101; 151; CANR 19, 46; CP 1;
DAM MULT; DLB 312, 348; EWL;
RGAL 4; SSFS 19

Santos, Miguel
See Mihura, Miguel

Sapir, Edward 1884-1939 .... **TCLC 108**
See also CA 211; DLB 92

Sapper
See McNeile, Herman Cyril

Sapphire 1950- .... **CLC 99**
See also CA 262

Sapphire, Brenda
See Sapphire

Sappho fl. 6th cent. B.C.- ... **CMLC 3, 67; PC
5**
See also CDWLB 1; DA3; DAM POET;
DLB 176; FL 1:1; PFS 20; RGWL 2, 3;
WLIT 8; WP

Saramago, Jose 1922- ..... **CLC 119; HLCS 1**
See also CA 153; CANR 96, 164; CWW 2;
DLB 287, 332; EWL 3; LATS 1:2; NFS
27; SSFS 23

Sarduy, Severo 1937-1993 .... **CLC 6, 97;
HLCS 2; TCLC 167**
See also CA 89-92; 142; CANR 58, 81;
CWW 2; DLB 113; EWL 3; HW 1, 2;
LAW

Sargeson, Frank 1903-1982 ..... **CLC 31; SSC
99**
See also CA 25-28R; 106; CANR 38, 79;
CN 1, 2, 3; EWL 3; GLL 2; RGEL 2;
RGSF 2; SSFS 20

Sarmiento, Domingo Faustino
1811-1888 .... **HLCS 2; NCLC 123**
See also LAW; WLIT 1

Sarmiento, Felix Ruben Garcia
See Dario, Ruben

Saro-Wiwa, Ken(ule Beeson)
1941-1995 .... **CLC 114; TCLC 200**
See also BW 2; CA 142; 150; CANR 60;
DLB 157

Saroyan, William 1908-1981 ... **CLC 1, 8, 10,
29, 34, 56; DC 28; SSC 21; TCLC 137;
WLC 5**
See also AAYA 66; CA 5-8R; 103; CAD;
CANR 30; CDALBS; CN 1, 2; DA; DA3;
DAB; DAC; DAM DRAM, MST, NOV;
DFS 17; DLB 7, 9, 86; DLBY 1981; EWL
3; LAIT 4; MAL 5; MTCW 1, 2; MTFW
2005; RGAL 4; RGSF 2; SATA 23; SATA-
Obit 24; SSFS 14; TUS

Sarraute, Nathalie 1900-1999 .... **CLC 1, 2, 4,
8, 10, 31, 80; TCLC 145**
See also BPFB 3; CA 9-12R; 187; CANR
23, 66, 134; CWW 2; DLB 83, 321; EW
12; EWL 3; GFL 1789 to the Present;
MTCW 1, 2; MTFW 2005; RGWL 2, 3

Sarton, May 1912-1995 ... **CLC 4, 14, 49, 91;
PC 39; TCLC 120**
See also AMWS 8; CA 1-4R; 149; CANR
1, 34, 55, 116; CN 1, 2, 3, 4, 5, 6; CP 1,
2, 3, 4, 5, 6; DAM POET; DLB 48; DLBY
1981; EWL 3; FW; INT CANR-34; MAL
5; MTCW 1, 2; MTFW 2005; RGAL 4;
SATA 36; SATA-Obit 86; TUS

Sartre, Jean-Paul 1905-1980 . **CLC 1, 4, 7, 9,
13, 18, 24, 44, 50, 52; DC 3; SSC 32;
WLC 5**
See also AAYA 62; CA 9-12R; 97-100;
CANR 21; DA; DA3; DAB; DAC; DAM
DRAM, MST, NOV; DFS 5, 26; DLB 72,
296, 321, 332; EW 12; EWL 3; GFL 1789
to the Present; LMFS 2; MTCW 1, 2;
MTFW 2005; NFS 21; RGHL; RGSF 2;
RGWL 2, 3; SSFS 9; TWA

Sassoon, Siegfried (Lorraine)
1886-1967 .... **CLC 36, 130; PC 12**
See also BRW 6; CA 104; 25-28R; CANR
36; DAB; DAM MST, NOV, POET; DLB
20, 191; DLBD 18; EWL 3; MTCW 1, 2;
MTFW 2005; PAB; PFS 28; RGEL 2;
TEA

Satterfield, Charles
See Pohl, Frederik

Satyremont
See Peret, Benjamin

Saul, John III
See Saul, John

Saul, John 1942- .... **CLC 46**
See also AAYA 10, 62; BEST 90:4; CA 81-
84; CANR 16, 40, 81, 176; CPW; DAM
NOV, POP; HGG; SATA 98

Saul, John W.
See Saul, John

Saul, John W. III
See Saul, John

Saul, John Woodruff III
See Saul, John

Saunders, Caleb
See Heinlein, Robert A.

Saura (Atares), Carlos 1932-1998 .... **CLC 20**
See also CA 114; 131; CANR 79; HW 1

Sauser, Frederic Louis
See Sauser-Hall, Frederic

Sauser-Hall, Frederic 1887-1961 ..... **CLC 18,
106**
See also CA 102; 93-96; CANR 36, 62;
DLB 258; EWL 3; GFL 1789 to the
Present; MTCW 1; WP

Saussure, Ferdinand de
1857-1913 .... **TCLC 49**
See also DLB 242

Savage, Catharine
See Brosman, Catharine Savage

Savage, Richard 1697(?)-1743 .... **LC 96**
See also DLB 95; RGEL 2

Savage, Thomas 1915-2003 .... **CLC 40**
See also CA 126; 132; 218; CAAS 15; CN
6, 7; INT CA-132; SATA-Obit 147;
TCWW 2

Savan, Glenn 1953-2003 .... **CLC 50**
See also CA 225

Savonarola, Girolamo 1452-1498 ...... **LC 152**
See also LMFS 1

Sax, Robert
See Johnson, Robert

Saxo Grammaticus c. 1150-c.
1222 .... **CMLC 58**

Saxton, Robert
See Johnson, Robert

Scribe, (Augustin) Eugene 1791-1861 . **DC 5; NCLC 16**
See also DAM DRAM; DLB 192; GFL 1789 to the Present; RGWL 2, 3

Scrum, R.
See Crumb, R.

Scudery, Georges de 1601-1667 .... **LC 75**
See also GFL Beginnings to 1789

Scudery, Madeleine de 1607-1701 .. **LC 2, 58**
See also DLB 268; GFL Beginnings to 1789

Scum
See Crumb, R.

Scumbag, Little Bobby
See Crumb, R.

Seabrook, John
See Hubbard, L. Ron

Seacole, Mary Jane Grant
1805-1881 .... **NCLC 147**
See also DLB 166

Sealy, I(rwin) Allan 1951- .... **CLC 55**
See also CA 136; CN 6, 7

Search, Alexander
See Pessoa, Fernando

Seare, Nicholas
See Whitaker, Rod

Sebald, W(infried) G(eorg)
1944-2001 .... **CLC 194**
See also BRWS 8; CA 159; 202; CANR 98; MTFW 2005; RGHL

Sebastian, Lee
See Silverberg, Robert

Sebastian Owl
See Thompson, Hunter S.

Sebestyen, Igen
See Sebestyen, Ouida

Sebestyen, Ouida 1924- .... **CLC 30**
See also AAYA 8; BYA 7; CA 107; CANR 40, 114; CLR 17; JRDA; MAICYA 1, 2; SAAS 10; SATA 39, 140; WYA; YAW

Sebold, Alice 1963- .... **CLC 193**
See also AAYA 56; CA 203; CANR 181; MTFW 2005

Second Duke of Buckingham
See Villiers, George

Secundus, H. Scriblerus
See Fielding, Henry

Sedges, John
See Buck, Pearl S(ydenstricker)

Sedgwick, Catharine Maria
1789-1867 .... **NCLC 19, 98**
See also DLB 1, 74, 183, 239, 243, 254; FL 1:3; RGAL 4

Sedulius Scottus 9th cent. -c. 874 .. **CMLC 86**

Seebohm, Victoria
See Glendinning, Victoria

Seelye, John (Douglas) 1931- .... **CLC 7**
See also CA 97-100; CANR 70; INT CA-97-100; TCWW 1, 2

Seferiades, Giorgos Stylianou
1900-1971 .... **CLC 5, 11; TCLC 213**
See also CA 5-8R; 33-36R; CANR 5, 36; DLB 332; EW 12; EWL 3; MTCW 1; RGWL 2, 3

Seferis, George
See Seferiades, Giorgos Stylianou

Segal, Erich (Wolf) 1937- .... **CLC 3, 10**
See also BEST 89:1; BPFB 3; CA 25-28R; CANR 20, 36, 65, 113; CPW; DAM POP; DLBY 1986; INT CANR-20; MTCW 1

Seger, Bob 1945- .... **CLC 35**

Seghers
See Radvanyi, Netty

Seghers, Anna
See Radvanyi, Netty

Seidel, Frederick 1936- .... **CLC 18**
See also CA 13-16R; CANR 8, 99, 180; CP 1, 2, 3, 4, 5, 6, 7; DLBY 1984

Seidel, Frederick Lewis
See Seidel, Frederick

Seifert, Jaroslav 1901-1986 . **CLC 34, 44, 93; PC 47**
See also CA 127; CDWLB 4; DLB 215, 332; EWL 3; MTCW 1, 2

Sei Shonagon c. 966-1017(?) ..... **CMLC 6, 89**

Sejour, Victor 1817-1874 .... **DC 10**
See also DLB 50

Sejour Marcou et Ferrand, Juan Victor
See Sejour, Victor

Selby, Hubert, Jr. 1928-2004 ..... **CLC 1, 2, 4, 8; SSC 20**
See also CA 13-16R; 226; CANR 33, 85; CN 1, 2, 3, 4, 5, 6, 7; DLB 2, 227; MAL 5

Selzer, Richard 1928- .... **CLC 74**
See also CA 65-68; CANR 14, 106

Sembene, Ousmane
See Ousmane, Sembene

Senancour, Etienne Pivert de
1770-1846 .... **NCLC 16**
See also DLB 119; GFL 1789 to the Present

Sender, Ramon (Jose) 1902-1982 ...... **CLC 8; HLC 2; TCLC 136**
See also CA 5-8R; 105; CANR 8; DAM MULT; DLB 322; EWL 3; HW 1; MTCW 1; RGWL 2, 3

Seneca, Lucius Annaeus c. 1B.C.-c. 65 .... **CMLC 6, 107; DC 5**
See also AW 2; CDWLB 1; DAM DRAM; DLB 211; RGWL 2, 3; TWA; WLIT 8

Senghor, Leopold Sedar
1906-2001 .. **BLC 1:3; CLC 54, 130; PC 25**
See also AFW; BW 2; CA 116; 125; 203; CANR 47, 74, 134; CWW 2; DAM MULT, POET; DNFS 2; EWL 3; GFL 1789 to the Present; MTCW 1, 2; MTFW 2005; TWA

Senior, Olive (Marjorie) 1941- .... **SSC 78**
See also BW 3; CA 154; CANR 86, 126; CN 6; CP 6, 7; CWP; DLB 157; EWL 3; RGSF 2

Senna, Danzy 1970- .... **CLC 119**
See also CA 169; CANR 130, 184

Sepheriades, Georgios
See Seferiades, Giorgos Stylianou

Serling, (Edward) Rod(man)
1924-1975 .... **CLC 30**
See also AAYA 14; AITN 1; CA 162; 57-60; DLB 26; SFW 4

Serna, Ramon Gomez de la
See Gomez de la Serna, Ramon

Serpieres
See Guillevic, (Eugene)

Service, Robert
See Service, Robert W(illiam)

Service, Robert W(illiam)
1874(?)-1958 ... **PC 70; TCLC 15; WLC 5**
See also BYA 4; CA 115; 140; CANR 84; DA; DAB; DAC; DAM MST, POET; DLB 92; PFS 10; RGEL 2; SATA 20

Seth, Vikram 1952- .... **CLC 43, 90**
See also BRWS 10; CA 121; 127; CANR 50, 74, 131; CN 6, 7; CP 5, 6, 7; DA3; DAM MULT; DLB 120, 271, 282, 323; EWL 3; INT CA-127; MTCW 2; MTFW 2005; WWE 1

Setien, Miguel Delibes
See Delibes Setien, Miguel

Seton, Cynthia Propper 1926-1982 .. **CLC 27**
See also CA 5-8R; 108; CANR 7

Seton, Ernest (Evan) Thompson
1860-1946 .... **TCLC 31**
See also ANW; BYA 3; CA 109; 204; CLR 59; DLB 92; DLBD 13; JRDA; SATA 18

Seton-Thompson, Ernest
See Seton, Ernest (Evan) Thompson

Settle, Mary Lee 1918-2005 .... **CLC 19, 61, 273**
See also BPFB 3; CA 89-92; 243; CAAS 1; CANR 44, 87, 126, 182; CN 6, 7; CSW; DLB 6; INT CA-89-92

Seuphor, Michel
See Arp, Jean

Sevigne, Marie (de Rabutin-Chantal)
1626-1696 .... **LC 11, 144**
See also DLB 268; GFL Beginnings to 1789; TWA

Sevigne, Marie de Rabutin Chantal
See Sevigne, Marie (de Rabutin-Chantal)

Sewall, Samuel 1652-1730 .... **LC 38**
See also DLB 24; RGAL 4

Sexton, Anne (Harvey) 1928-1974 ..... **CLC 2, 4, 6, 8, 10, 15, 53, 123; PC 2, 79; WLC 5**
See also AMWS 2; CA 1-4R; 53-56; CABS 2; CANR 3, 36; CDALB 1941-1968; CP 1, 2; DA; DA3; DAB; DAC; DAM MST, POET; DLB 5, 169; EWL 3; EXPP; FL 1:6; FW; MAL 5; MBL; MTCW 1, 2; MTFW 2005; PAB; PFS 4, 14, 30; RGAL 4; RGHL; SATA 10; TUS

Shaara, Jeff 1952- .... **CLC 119**
See also AAYA 70; CA 163; CANR 109, 172; CN 7; MTFW 2005

Shaara, Michael 1929-1988 .... **CLC 15**
See also AAYA 71; AITN 1; BPFB 3; CA 102; 125; CANR 52, 85; DAM POP; DLBY 1983; MTFW 2005; NFS 26

Shackleton, C.C.
See Aldiss, Brian W.

Shacochis, Bob
See Shacochis, Robert G.

Shacochis, Robert G. 1951- .... **CLC 39**
See also CA 119; 124; CANR 100; INT CA-124

Shadwell, Thomas 1641(?)-1692 .... **LC 114**
See also DLB 80; IDTP; RGEL 2

Shaffer, Anthony 1926-2001 .... **CLC 19**
See also CA 110; 116; 200; CBD; CD 5, 6; DAM DRAM; DFS 13; DLB 13

Shaffer, Anthony Joshua
See Shaffer, Anthony

Shaffer, Peter 1926- ... **CLC 5, 14, 18, 37, 60; DC 7**
See also BRWS 1; CA 25-28R; CANR 25, 47, 74, 118; CBD; CD 5, 6; CDBLB 1960 to Present; DA3; DAB; DAM DRAM, MST; DFS 5, 13; DLB 13, 233; EWL 3; MTCW 1, 2; MTFW 2005; RGEL 2; TEA

Shakespeare, William 1564-1616 . **PC 84, 89, 98; WLC 5**
See also AAYA 35; BRW 1; CDBLB Before 1660; DA; DA3; DAB; DAC; DAM DRAM, MST, POET; DFS 20, 21; DLB 62, 172, 263; EXPP; LAIT 1; LATS 1:1; LMFS 1; PAB; PFS 1, 2, 3, 4, 5, 8, 9; RGEL 2; TEA; WLIT 3; WP; WS; WYA

Shakey, Bernard
See Young, Neil

Shalamov, Varlam (Tikhonovich)
1907-1982 .... **CLC 18**
See also CA 129; 105; DLB 302; RGSF 2

Shamloo, Ahmad
See Shamlu, Ahmad

Shamlou, Ahmad
See Shamlu, Ahmad

Shamlu, Ahmad 1925-2000 .... **CLC 10**
See also CA 216; CWW 2

Shammas, Anton 1951- .... **CLC 55**
See also CA 199; DLB 346

Shandling, Arline
See Berriault, Gina

Sidney, Mary 1561-1621 .... **LC 19, 39**
See also DLB 167

Sidney, Sir Philip 1554-1586 .... **LC 19, 39, 131; PC 32**
See also BRW 1; BRWR 2; CDBLB Before 1660; DA; DA3; DAB; DAC; DAM MST, POET; DLB 167; EXPP; PAB; PFS 30; RGEL 2; TEA; WP

Sidney Herbert, Mary
See Sidney, Mary

Siegel, Jerome 1914-1996 .... **CLC 21**
See also AAYA 50; CA 116; 169; 151

Siegel, Jerry
See Siegel, Jerome

Sienkiewicz, Henryk (Adam Alexander Pius) 1846-1916 .... **TCLC 3**
See also CA 104; 134; CANR 84; DLB 332; EWL 3; RGSF 2; RGWL 2, 3

Sierra, Gregorio Martinez
See Martinez Sierra, Gregorio

Sierra, Maria de la O'LeJarraga Martinez
See Martinez Sierra, Maria

Sigal, Clancy 1926- .... **CLC 7**
See also CA 1-4R; CANR 85, 184; CN 1, 2, 3, 4, 5, 6, 7

Siger of Brabant 1240(?)-1284(?) . **CMLC 69**
See also DLB 115

Sigourney, Lydia H.
See Sigourney, Lydia Howard (Huntley)
See also DLB 73, 183

Sigourney, Lydia Howard (Huntley) 1791-1865 .... **NCLC 21, 87**
See also Sigourney, Lydia H.
See also DLB 1, 42, 239, 243

Sigourney, Lydia Huntley
See Sigourney, Lydia Howard (Huntley)

Siguenza y Gongora, Carlos de 1645-1700 .... **HLCS 2; LC 8**
See also LAW

Sigurjonsson, Johann
See Sigurjonsson, Johann

Sigurjonsson, Johann 1880-1919 ... **TCLC 27**
See also CA 170; DLB 293; EWL 3

Sikelianos, Angelos 1884-1951 .... **PC 29; TCLC 39**
See also EWL 3; RGWL 2, 3

Silkin, Jon 1930-1997 .... **CLC 2, 6, 43**
See also CA 5-8R; CAAS 5; CANR 89; CP 1, 2, 3, 4, 5, 6; DLB 27

Silko, Leslie 1948- ...... **CLC 23, 74, 114, 211; NNAL; SSC 37, 66; WLCS**
See also AAYA 14; AMWS 4; ANW; BYA 12; CA 115; 122; CANR 45, 65, 118; CN 4, 5, 6, 7; CP 4, 5, 6, 7; CPW 1; CWP; DA; DA3; DAC; DAM MST, MULT, POP; DLB 143, 175, 256, 275; EWL 3; EXPP; EXPS; LAIT 4; MAL 5; MTCW 2; MTFW 2005; NFS 4; PFS 9, 16; RGAL 4; RGSF 2; SSFS 4, 8, 10, 11; TCWW 1, 2

Sillanpaa, Frans Eemil 1888-1964 ... **CLC 19**
See also CA 129; 93-96; DLB 332; EWL 3; MTCW 1

Sillitoe, Alan 1928- .. **CLC 1, 3, 6, 10, 19, 57, 148**
See also AITN 1; BRWS 5; CA 9-12R, 191; CAAE 191; CAAS 2; CANR 8, 26, 55, 139; CDBLB 1960 to Present; CN 1, 2, 3, 4, 5, 6; CP 1, 2, 3, 4, 5; DLB 14, 139; EWL 3; MTCW 1, 2; MTFW 2005; RGEL 2; RGSF 2; SATA 61

Silone, Ignazio 1900-1978 .... **CLC 4**
See also CA 25-28; 81-84; CANR 34; CAP 2; DLB 264; EW 12; EWL 3; MTCW 1; RGSF 2; RGWL 2, 3

Silone, Ignazione
See Silone, Ignazio

Siluriensis, Leolinus
See Jones, Arthur Llewellyn

Silver, Joan Micklin 1935- .... **CLC 20**
See also CA 114; 121; INT CA-121

Silver, Nicholas
See Faust, Frederick (Schiller)

Silverberg, Robert 1935- .... **CLC 7, 140**
See also AAYA 24; BPFB 3; BYA 7, 9; CA 1-4R, 186; CAAE 186; CAAS 3; CANR 1, 20, 36, 85, 140, 175; CLR 59; CN 6, 7; CPW; DAM POP; DLB 8; INT CANR-20; MAICYA 1, 2; MTCW 1, 2; MTFW 2005; SATA 13, 91; SATA-Essay 104; SCFW 1, 2; SFW 4; SUFW 2

Silverstein, Alvin 1933- .... **CLC 17**
See also CA 49-52; CANR 2; CLR 25; JRDA; MAICYA 1, 2; SATA 8, 69, 124

Silverstein, Shel 1932-1999 .... **PC 49**
See also AAYA 40; BW 3; CA 107; 179; CANR 47, 74, 81; CLR 5, 96; CWRI 5; JRDA; MAICYA 1, 2; MTCW 2; MTFW 2005; SATA 33, 92; SATA-Brief 27; SATA-Obit 116

Silverstein, Virginia B(arbara Opshelor) 1937- .... **CLC 17**
See also CA 49-52; CANR 2; CLR 25; JRDA; MAICYA 1, 2; SATA 8, 69, 124

Sim, Georges
See Simenon, Georges (Jacques Christian)

Simak, Clifford D(onald) 1904-1988 . **CLC 1, 55**
See also CA 1-4R; 125; CANR 1, 35; DLB 8; MTCW 1; SATA-Obit 56; SCFW 1, 2; SFW 4

Simenon, Georges (Jacques Christian) 1903-1989 .... **CLC 1, 2, 3, 8, 18, 47**
See also BPFB 3; CA 85-88; 129; CANR 35; CMW 4; DA3; DAM POP; DLB 72; DLBY 1989; EW 12; EWL 3; GFL 1789 to the Present; MSW; MTCW 1, 2; MTFW 2005; RGWL 2, 3

Simic, Charles 1938- .... **CLC 6, 9, 22, 49, 68, 130, 256; PC 69**
See also AAYA 78; AMWS 8; CA 29-32R; CAAS 4; CANR 12, 33, 52, 61, 96, 140; CP 2, 3, 4, 5, 6, 7; DA3; DAM POET; DLB 105; MAL 5; MTCW 2; MTFW 2005; PFS 7; RGAL 4; WP

Simmel, Georg 1858-1918 .... **TCLC 64**
See also CA 157; DLB 296

Simmons, Charles (Paul) 1924- .... **CLC 57**
See also CA 89-92; INT CA-89-92

Simmons, Dan 1948- .... **CLC 44**
See also AAYA 16, 54; CA 138; CANR 53, 81, 126, 174; CPW; DAM POP; HGG; SUFW 2

Simmons, James (Stewart Alexander) 1933- .... **CLC 43**
See also CA 105; CAAS 21; CP 1, 2, 3, 4, 5, 6, 7; DLB 40

Simmons, Richard
See Simmons, Dan

Simms, William Gilmore 1806-1870 .... **NCLC 3**
See also DLB 3, 30, 59, 73, 248, 254; RGAL 4

Simon, Carly 1945- .... **CLC 26**
See also CA 105

Simon, Claude 1913-2005 ... **CLC 4, 9, 15, 39**
See also CA 89-92; 241; CANR 33, 117; CWW 2; DAM NOV; DLB 83, 332; EW 13; EWL 3; GFL 1789 to the Present; MTCW 1

Simon, Claude Eugene Henri
See Simon, Claude

Simon, Claude Henri Eugene
See Simon, Claude

Simon, Marvin Neil
See Simon, Neil

Simon, Myles
See Follett, Ken

Simon, Neil 1927- .... **CLC 6, 11, 31, 39, 70, 233; DC 14**
See also AAYA 32; AITN 1; AMWS 4; CA 21-24R; CAD; CANR 26, 54, 87, 126; CD 5, 6; DA3; DAM DRAM; DFS 2, 6, 12, 18,, 24; DLB 7, 266; LAIT 4; MAL 5; MTCW 1, 2; MTFW 2005; RGAL 4; TUS

Simon, Paul 1941(?)- .... **CLC 17**
See also CA 116; 153; CANR 152

Simon, Paul Frederick
See Simon, Paul

Simonon, Paul 1956(?)- .... **CLC 30**

Simonson, Rick CLC 70

Simpson, Harriette
See Arnow, Harriette (Louisa) Simpson

Simpson, Louis 1923- ... **CLC 4, 7, 9, 32, 149**
See also AMWS 9; CA 1-4R; CAAS 4; CANR 1, 61, 140; CP 1, 2, 3, 4, 5, 6, 7; DAM POET; DLB 5; MAL 5; MTCW 1, 2; MTFW 2005; PFS 7, 11, 14; RGAL 4

Simpson, Mona 1957- .... **CLC 44, 146**
See also CA 122; 135; CANR 68, 103; CN 6, 7; EWL 3

Simpson, Mona Elizabeth
See Simpson, Mona

Simpson, N(orman) F(rederick) 1919- .... **CLC 29**
See also CA 13-16R; CBD; DLB 13; RGEL 2

Sinclair, Andrew (Annandale) 1935- . **CLC 2, 14**
See also CA 9-12R; CAAS 5; CANR 14, 38, 91; CN 1, 2, 3, 4, 5, 6, 7; DLB 14; FANT; MTCW 1

Sinclair, Emil
See Hesse, Hermann

Sinclair, Iain 1943- .... **CLC 76**
See also BRWS 14; CA 132; CANR 81, 157; CP 5, 6, 7; HGG

Sinclair, Iain MacGregor
See Sinclair, Iain

Sinclair, Irene
See Griffith, D.W.

Sinclair, Julian
See Sinclair, May

Sinclair, Mary Amelia St. Clair (?)-
See Sinclair, May

Sinclair, May 1865-1946 .... **TCLC 3, 11**
See also CA 104; 166; DLB 36, 135; EWL 3; HGG; RGEL 2; RHW; SUFW

Sinclair, Roy
See Griffith, D.W.

Sinclair, Upton 1878-1968 ...... **CLC 1, 11, 15, 63; TCLC 160; WLC 5**
See also AAYA 63; AMWS 5; BPFB 3; BYA 2; CA 5-8R; 25-28R; CANR 7; CDALB 1929-1941; DA; DA3; DAB; DAC; DAM MST, NOV; DLB 9; EWL 3; INT CANR-7; LAIT 3; MAL 5; MTCW 1, 2; MTFW 2005; NFS 6; RGAL 4; SATA 9; TUS; YAW

Sinclair, Upton Beall
See Sinclair, Upton

Singe, (Edmund) J(ohn) M(illington) 1871-1909 .... **WLC**

Singer, Isaac
See Singer, Isaac Bashevis

Singer, Isaac Bashevis 1904-1991 .. **CLC 1, 3, 6, 9, 11, 15, 23, 38, 69, 111; SSC 3, 53, 80; WLC 5**
See also AAYA 32; AITN 1, 2; AMW; AMWR 2; BPFB 3; BYA 1, 4; CA 1-4R; 134; CANR 1, 39, 106; CDALB 1941-1968; CLR 1; CN 1, 2, 3, 4; CWRI 5; DA; DA3; DAB; DAC; DAM MST, NOV; DLB 6, 28, 52, 278, 332, 333; DLBY 1991; EWL 3; EXPS; HGG; JRDA; LAIT

Snyder, Zilpha Keatley 1927- .... **CLC 17**
See also AAYA 15; BYA 1; CA 9-12R, 252;
CAAE 252; CANR 38; CLR 31, 121;
JRDA; MAICYA 1, 2; SAAS 2; SATA 1,
28, 75, 110, 163; SATA-Essay 112, 163;
YAW

Soares, Bernardo
See Pessoa, Fernando

Sobh, A.
See Shamlu, Ahmad

Sobh, Alef
See Shamlu, Ahmad

Sobol, Joshua 1939- .... **CLC 60**
See also CA 200; CWW 2; RGHL

Sobol, Yehoshua 1939-
See Sobol, Joshua

Socrates 470B.C.-399B.C. .... **CMLC 27**

Soderberg, Hjalmar 1869-1941 ...... **TCLC 39**
See also DLB 259; EWL 3; RGSF 2

Soderbergh, Steven 1963- .... **CLC 154**
See also AAYA 43; CA 243

Soderbergh, Steven Andrew
See Soderbergh, Steven

Sodergran, Edith (Irene) 1892-1923
See Soedergran, Edith (Irene)

Soedergran, Edith (Irene)
1892-1923 .... **TCLC 31**
See also CA 202; DLB 259; EW 11; EWL
3; RGWL 2, 3

Softly, Edgar
See Lovecraft, H. P.

Softly, Edward
See Lovecraft, H. P.

Sokolov, Alexander V(sevolodovich)
1943- .... **CLC 59**
See also CA 73-76; CWW 2; DLB 285;
EWL 3; RGWL 2, 3

Sokolov, Raymond 1941- .... **CLC 7**
See also CA 85-88

Sokolov, Sasha
See Sokolov, Alexander V(sevolodovich)

Solo, Jay
See Ellison, Harlan

Sologub, Fedor
See Teternikov, Fyodor Kuzmich

Sologub, Feodor
See Teternikov, Fyodor Kuzmich

Sologub, Fyodor
See Teternikov, Fyodor Kuzmich

Solomons, Ikey Esquir
See Thackeray, William Makepeace

Solomos, Dionysios 1798-1857 .... **NCLC 15**

Solwoska, Mara
See French, Marilyn

Solzhenitsyn, Aleksandr 1918-2008 ... **CLC 1,
2, 4, 7, 9, 10, 18, 26, 34, 78, 134, 235;
SSC 32, 105; WLC 5**
See also AAYA 49; AITN 1; BPFB 3; CA
69-72; CANR 40, 65, 116; CWW 2; DA;
DA3; DAB; DAC; DAM MST, NOV;
DLB 302, 332; EW 13; EWL 3; EXPS;
LAIT 4; MTCW 1, 2; MTFW 2005; NFS
6; RGSF 2; RGWL 2, 3; SSFS 9; TWA

Solzhenitsyn, Aleksandr I.
See Solzhenitsyn, Aleksandr

Solzhenitsyn, Aleksandr Isayevich
See Solzhenitsyn, Aleksandr

Somers, Jane
See Lessing, Doris

Somerville, Edith Oenone
1858-1949 .... **SSC 56; TCLC 51**
See also CA 196; DLB 135; RGEL 2; RGSF
2

Somerville & Ross
See Martin, Violet Florence; Somerville,
Edith Oenone

Sommer, Scott 1951- .... **CLC 25**
See also CA 106

Sommers, Christina Hoff 1950- ...... **CLC 197**
See also CA 153; CANR 95

Sondheim, Stephen 1930- .. **CLC 30, 39, 147;
DC 22**
See also AAYA 11, 66; CA 103; CANR 47,
67, 125; DAM DRAM; DFS 25; LAIT 4

Sondheim, Stephen Joshua
See Sondheim, Stephen

Sone, Monica 1919- .... **AAL**
See also DLB 312

Song, Cathy 1955- .... **AAL; PC 21**
See also CA 154; CANR 118; CWP; DLB
169, 312; EXPP; FW; PFS 5

Sontag, Susan 1933-2004 ... **CLC 1, 2, 10, 13,
31, 105, 195**
See also AMWS 3; CA 17-20R; 234; CANR
25, 51, 74, 97, 184; CN 1, 2, 3, 4, 5, 6, 7;
CPW; DA3; DAM POP; DLB 2, 67; EWL
3; MAL 5; MBL; MTCW 1, 2; MTFW
2005; RGAL 4; RHW; SSFS 10

Sophocles 496(?)B.C.-406(?)B.C. .... **CMLC 2,
47, 51, 86; DC 1; WLCS**
See also AW 1; CDWLB 1; DA; DA3;
DAB; DAC; DAM DRAM, MST; DFS 1,
4, 8, 24; DLB 176; LAIT 1; LATS 1:1;
LMFS 1; RGWL 2, 3; TWA; WLIT 8

Sordello 1189-1269 .... **CMLC 15**

Sorel, Georges 1847-1922 .... **TCLC 91**
See also CA 118; 188

Sorel, Julia
See Drexler, Rosalyn

Sorokin, Vladimir **CLC 59**
See also CA 258; DLB 285

Sorokin, Vladimir Georgievich
See Sorokin, Vladimir

Sorrentino, Gilbert 1929-2006 .... **CLC 3, 7,
14, 22, 40, 247**
See also CA 77-80; 250; CANR 14, 33, 115,
157; CN 3, 4, 5, 6, 7; CP 1, 2, 3, 4, 5, 6,
7; DLB 5, 173; DLBY 1980; INT
CANR-14

Soseki
See Natsume, Soseki

Soto, Gary 1952- ... **CLC 32, 80; HLC 2; PC
28**
See also AAYA 10, 37; BYA 11; CA 119;
125; CANR 50, 74, 107, 157; CLR 38;
CP 4, 5, 6, 7; DAM MULT; DFS 26; DLB
82; EWL 3; EXPP; HW 1, 2; INT CA-
125; JRDA; LLW; MAICYA 2; MAIC-
YAS 1; MAL 5; MTCW 2; MTFW 2005;
PFS 7, 30; RGAL 4; SATA 80, 120, 174;
WYA; YAW

Soupault, Philippe 1897-1990 .... **CLC 68**
See also CA 116; 147; 131; EWL 3; GFL
1789 to the Present; LMFS 2

Souster, (Holmes) Raymond 1921- .... **CLC 5,
14**
See also CA 13-16R; CAAS 14; CANR 13,
29, 53; CP 1, 2, 3, 4, 5, 6, 7; DA3; DAC;
DAM POET; DLB 88; RGEL 2; SATA 63

Southern, Terry 1924(?)-1995 .... **CLC 7**
See also AMWS 11; BPFB 3; CA 1-4R;
150; CANR 1, 55, 107; CN 1, 2, 3, 4, 5,
6; DLB 2; IDFW 3, 4

Southerne, Thomas 1660-1746 .... **LC 99**
See also DLB 80; RGEL 2

Southey, Robert 1774-1843 .... **NCLC 8, 97**
See also BRW 4; DLB 93, 107, 142; RGEL
2; SATA 54

Southwell, Robert 1561(?)-1595 .... **LC 108**
See also DLB 167; RGEL 2; TEA

Southworth, Emma Dorothy Eliza Nevitte
1819-1899 .... **NCLC 26**
See also DLB 239

Souza, Ernest
See Scott, Evelyn

Soyinka, Wole 1934- .. **BLC 1:3, 2:3; CLC 3,
5, 14, 36, 44, 179; DC 2; WLC 5**
See also AFW; BW 2, 3; CA 13-16R;
CANR 27, 39, 82, 136; CD 5, 6; CDWLB
3; CN 6, 7; CP 1, 2, 3, 4, 5, 6 ,7; DA;
DA3; DAB; DAC; DAM DRAM, MST,
MULT; DFS 10, 26; DLB 125, 332; EWL
3; MTCW 1, 2; MTFW 2005; PFS 27;
RGEL 2; TWA; WLIT 2; WWE 1

Spackman, W(illiam) M(ode)
1905-1990 .... **CLC 46**
See also CA 81-84; 132

Spacks, Barry (Bernard) 1931- .... **CLC 14**
See also CA 154; CANR 33, 109; CP 3, 4,
5, 6, 7; DLB 105

Spanidou, Irini 1946- .... **CLC 44**
See also CA 185; CANR 179

Spark, Muriel 1918-2006 .... **CLC 2, 3, 5, 8,
13, 18, 40, 94, 242; PC 72; SSC 10, 115**
See also BRWS 1; CA 5-8R; 251; CANR
12, 36, 76, 89, 131; CDBLB 1945-1960;
CN 1, 2, 3, 4, 5, 6, 7; CP 1, 2, 3, 4, 5, 6,
7; DA3; DAB; DAC; DAM MST, NOV;
DLB 15, 139; EWL 3; FW; INT CANR-
12; LAIT 4; MTCW 1, 2; MTFW 2005;
NFS 22; RGEL 2; TEA; WLIT 4; YAW

Spark, Muriel Sarah
See Spark, Muriel

Spaulding, Douglas
See Bradbury, Ray

Spaulding, Leonard
See Bradbury, Ray

Speght, Rachel 1597-c. 1630 .... **LC 97**
See also DLB 126

Spence, J. A. D.
See Eliot, T(homas) S(tearns)

Spencer, Anne 1882-1975 .... **HR 1:3; PC 77**
See also BW 2; CA 161; DLB 51, 54

Spencer, Elizabeth 1921- .... **CLC 22; SSC 57**
See also CA 13-16R; CANR 32, 65, 87; CN
1, 2, 3, 4, 5, 6, 7; CSW; DLB 6, 218;
EWL 3; MTCW 1; RGAL 4; SATA 14

Spencer, Leonard G.
See Silverberg, Robert

Spencer, Scott 1945- .... **CLC 30**
See also CA 113; CANR 51, 148; DLBY
1986

Spender, Stephen 1909-1995 ..... **CLC 1, 2, 5,
10, 41, 91; PC 71**
See also BRWS 2; CA 9-12R; 149; CANR
31, 54; CDBLB 1945-1960; CP 1, 2, 3, 4,
5, 6; DA3; DAM POET; DLB 20; EWL
3; MTCW 1, 2; MTFW 2005; PAB; PFS
23; RGEL 2; TEA

Spengler, Oswald (Arnold Gottfried)
1880-1936 .... **TCLC 25**
See also CA 118; 189

Spenser, Edmund 1552(?)-1599 ...... **LC 5, 39,
117; PC 8, 42; WLC 5**
See also AAYA 60; BRW 1; CDBLB Before
1660; DA; DA3; DAB; DAC; DAM MST,
POET; DLB 167; EFS 2; EXPP; PAB;
RGEL 2; TEA; WLIT 3; WP

Spicer, Jack 1925-1965 .... **CLC 8, 18, 72**
See also BG 1:3; CA 85-88; DAM POET;
DLB 5, 16, 193; GLL 1; WP

Spiegelman, Art 1948- .... **CLC 76, 178**
See also AAYA 10, 46; CA 125; CANR 41,
55, 74, 124; DLB 299; MTCW 2; MTFW
2005; RGHL; SATA 109, 158; YAW

Spielberg, Peter 1929- .... **CLC 6**
See also CA 5-8R; CANR 4, 48; DLBY
1981

Spielberg, Steven 1947- .... **CLC 20, 188**
See also AAYA 8, 24; CA 77-80; CANR
32; SATA 32

Spillane, Frank Morrison
See Spillane, Mickey

Szymborska, Wislawa 1923- ... **CLC 99, 190; PC 44**
See also AAYA 76; CA 154; CANR 91, 133, 181; CDWLB 4; CWP; CWW 2; DA3; DLB 232, 332; DLBY 1996; EWL 3; MTCW 2; MTFW 2005; PFS 15, 27; RGHL; RGWL 3

T. O., Nik
See Annensky, Innokenty (Fyodorovich)

Tabori, George 1914-2007 .... **CLC 19**
See also CA 49-52; 262; CANR 4, 69; CBD; CD 5, 6; DLB 245; RGHL

Tacitus c. 55-c. 117 .... **CMLC 56**
See also AW 2; CDWLB 1; DLB 211; RGWL 2, 3; WLIT 8

Tadjo, Veronique 1955- .... **BLC 2:3**
See also EWL 3

Tagore, Rabindranath 1861-1941 .... **PC 8; SSC 48; TCLC 3, 53**
See also CA 104; 120; DA3; DAM DRAM, POET; DFS 26; DLB 323, 332; EWL 3; MTCW 1, 2; MTFW 2005; PFS 18; RGEL 2; RGSF 2; RGWL 2, 3; TWA

Taine, Hippolyte Adolphe
1828-1893 .... **NCLC 15**
See also EW 7; GFL 1789 to the Present

Talayesva, Don C. 1890-(?) .... **NNAL**

Talese, Gay 1932- .... **CLC 37, 232**
See also AITN 1; AMWS 17; CA 1-4R; CANR 9, 58, 137, 177; DLB 185; INT CANR-9; MTCW 1, 2; MTFW 2005

Tallent, Elizabeth 1954- .... **CLC 45**
See also CA 117; CANR 72; DLB 130

Tallmountain, Mary 1918-1997 .... **NNAL**
See also CA 146; 161; DLB 193

Tally, Ted 1952- .... **CLC 42**
See also CA 120; 124; CAD; CANR 125; CD 5, 6; INT CA-124

Talvik, Heiti 1904-1947 .... **TCLC 87**
See also EWL 3

Tamayo y Baus, Manuel
1829-1898 .... **NCLC 1**

Tammsaare, A(nton) H(ansen)
1878-1940 .... **TCLC 27**
See also CA 164; CDWLB 4; DLB 220; EWL 3

Tam'si, Tchicaya U
See Tchicaya, Gerald Felix

Tan, Amy 1952- ..... **AAL; CLC 59, 120, 151, 257**
See also AAYA 9, 48; AMWS 10; BEST 89:3; BPFB 3; CA 136; CANR 54, 105, 132; CDALBS; CN 6, 7; CPW 1; DA3; DAM MULT, NOV, POP; DLB 173, 312; EXPN; FL 1:6; FW; LAIT 3, 5; MAL 5; MTCW 2; MTFW 2005; NFS 1, 13, 16; RGAL 4; SATA 75; SSFS 9; YAW

Tandem, Carl Felix
See Spitteler, Carl

Tandem, Felix
See Spitteler, Carl

Tania B.
See Blixen, Karen (Christentze Dinesen)

Tanizaki, Jun'ichiro 1886-1965 ... **CLC 8, 14, 28; SSC 21**
See also CA 93-96; 25-28R; DLB 180; EWL 3; MJW; MTCW 2; MTFW 2005; RGSF 2; RGWL 2

Tanizaki Jun'ichiro
See Tanizaki, Jun'ichiro

Tannen, Deborah 1945- .... **CLC 206**
See also CA 118; CANR 95

Tannen, Deborah Frances
See Tannen, Deborah

Tanner, William
See Amis, Kingsley

Tante, Dilly
See Kunitz, Stanley

Tao Lao
See Storni, Alfonsina

Tapahonso, Luci 1953- .... **NNAL; PC 65**
See also CA 145; CANR 72, 127; DLB 175

Tarantino, Quentin (Jerome)
1963- .... **CLC 125, 230**
See also AAYA 58; CA 171; CANR 125

Tarassoff, Lev
See Troyat, Henri

Tarbell, Ida M(inerva) 1857-1944 . **TCLC 40**
See also CA 122; 181; DLB 47

Tarchetti, Ugo 1839(?)-1869 .... **SSC 119**

Tardieu d'Esclavelles,
Louise-Florence-Petronille
See Epinay, Louise d'

Tarkington, (Newton) Booth
1869-1946 .... **TCLC 9**
See also BPFB 3; BYA 3; CA 110; 143; CWRI 5; DLB 9, 102; MAL 5; MTCW 2; RGAL 4; SATA 17

Tarkovskii, Andrei Arsen'evich
See Tarkovsky, Andrei (Arsenyevich)

Tarkovsky, Andrei (Arsenyevich)
1932-1986 .... **CLC 75**
See also CA 127

Tartt, Donna 1964(?)- .... **CLC 76**
See also AAYA 56; CA 142; CANR 135; MTFW 2005

Tasso, Torquato 1544-1595 .... **LC 5, 94**
See also EFS 2; EW 2; RGWL 2, 3; WLIT 7

Tate, (John Orley) Allen 1899-1979 .. **CLC 2, 4, 6, 9, 11, 14, 24; PC 50**
See also AMW; CA 5-8R; 85-88; CANR 32, 108; CN 1, 2; CP 1, 2; DLB 4, 45, 63; DLBD 17; EWL 3; MAL 5; MTCW 1, 2; MTFW 2005; RGAL 4; RHW

Tate, Ellalice
See Hibbert, Eleanor Alice Burford

Tate, James (Vincent) 1943- ..... **CLC 2, 6, 25**
See also CA 21-24R; CANR 29, 57, 114; CP 1, 2, 3, 4, 5, 6, 7; DLB 5, 169; EWL 3; PFS 10, 15; RGAL 4; WP

Tate, Nahum 1652(?)-1715 .... **LC 109**
See also DLB 80; RGEL 2

Tauler, Johannes c. 1300-1361 ...... **CMLC 37**
See also DLB 179; LMFS 1

Tavel, Ronald 1936-2009 .... **CLC 6**
See also CA 21-24R; CAD; CANR 33; CD 5, 6

Taviani, Paolo 1931- .... **CLC 70**
See also CA 153

Taylor, Bayard 1825-1878 .... **NCLC 89**
See also DLB 3, 189, 250, 254; RGAL 4

Taylor, C(ecil) P(hilip) 1929-1981 .... **CLC 27**
See also CA 25-28R; 105; CANR 47; CBD

Taylor, Edward 1642(?)-1729 ..... **LC 11, 163; PC 63**
See also AMW; DA; DAB; DAC; DAM MST, POET; DLB 24; EXPP; RGAL 4; TUS

Taylor, Eleanor Ross 1920- .... **CLC 5**
See also CA 81-84; CANR 70

Taylor, Elizabeth 1912-1975 .... **CLC 2, 4, 29; SSC 100**
See also CA 13-16R; CANR 9, 70; CN 1, 2; DLB 139; MTCW 1; RGEL 2; SATA 13

Taylor, Frederick Winslow
1856-1915 .... **TCLC 76**
See also CA 188

Taylor, Henry 1942- .... **CLC 44**
See also CA 33-36R; CAAS 7; CANR 31, 178; CP 6, 7; DLB 5; PFS 10

Taylor, Henry Splawn
See Taylor, Henry

Taylor, Kamala 1924-2004 .... **CLC 8, 38**
See also BYA 13; CA 77-80; 227; CN 1, 2, 3, 4, 5, 6, 7; DLB 323; EWL 3; MTFW 2005; NFS 13

Taylor, Mildred D. 1943- .... **CLC 21**
See also AAYA 10, 47; BW 1; BYA 3, 8; CA 85-88; CANR 25, 115, 136; CLR 9, 59, 90; CSW; DLB 52; JRDA; LAIT 3; MAICYA 1, 2; MTFW 2005; SAAS 5; SATA 135; WYA; YAW

Taylor, Peter (Hillsman) 1917-1994 .. **CLC 1, 4, 18, 37, 44, 50, 71; SSC 10, 84**
See also AMWS 5; BPFB 3; CA 13-16R; 147; CANR 9, 50; CN 1, 2, 3, 4, 5; CSW; DLB 218, 278; DLBY 1981, 1994; EWL 3; EXPS; INT CANR-9; MAL 5; MTCW 1, 2; MTFW 2005; RGSF 2; SSFS 9; TUS

Taylor, Robert Lewis 1912-1998 .... **CLC 14**
See also CA 1-4R; 170; CANR 3, 64; CN 1, 2; SATA 10; TCWW 1, 2

Tchekhov, Anton
See Chekhov, Anton (Pavlovich)

Tchicaya, Gerald Felix 1931-1988 .. **CLC 101**
See also CA 129; 125; CANR 81; EWL 3

Tchicaya U Tam'si
See Tchicaya, Gerald Felix

Teasdale, Sara 1884-1933 .... **PC 31; TCLC 4**
See also CA 104; 163; DLB 45; GLL 1; PFS 14; RGAL 4; SATA 32; TUS

Tecumseh 1768-1813 .... **NNAL**
See also DAM MULT

Tegner, Esaias 1782-1846 .... **NCLC 2**

Teilhard de Chardin, (Marie Joseph) Pierre
1881-1955 .... **TCLC 9**
See also CA 105; 210; GFL 1789 to the Present

Temple, Ann
See Mortimer, Penelope (Ruth)

Tennant, Emma 1937- .... **CLC 13, 52**
See also BRWS 9; CA 65-68; CAAS 9; CANR 10, 38, 59, 88, 177; CN 3, 4, 5, 6, 7; DLB 14; EWL 3; SFW 4

Tenneshaw, S.M.
See Silverberg, Robert

Tenney, Tabitha Gilman
1762-1837 .... **NCLC 122**
See also DLB 37, 200

Tennyson, Alfred 1809-1892 ... **NCLC 30, 65, 115, 202; PC 6; WLC 6**
See also AAYA 50; BRW 4; CDBLB 1832-1890; DA; DA3; DAB; DAC; DAM MST, POET; DLB 32; EXPP; PAB; PFS 1, 2, 4, 11, 15, 19; RGEL 2; TEA; WLIT 4; WP

Teran, Lisa St. Aubin de
See St. Aubin de Teran, Lisa

Terence c. 184B.C.-c. 159B.C. ...... **CMLC 14; DC 7**
See also AW 1; CDWLB 1; DLB 211; RGWL 2, 3; TWA; WLIT 8

Teresa de Jesus, St. 1515-1582 .... **LC 18, 149**

Teresa of Avila, St.
See Teresa de Jesus, St.

Terkel, Louis
See Terkel, Studs

Terkel, Studs 1912-2008 .... **CLC 38**
See also AAYA 32; AITN 1; CA 57-60; 278; CANR 18, 45, 67, 132; DA3; MTCW 1, 2; MTFW 2005; TUS

Terkel, Studs Louis
See Terkel, Studs

Terry, C. V.
See Slaughter, Frank G(ill)

Terry, Megan 1932- .... **CLC 19; DC 13**
See also CA 77-80; CABS 3; CAD; CANR 43; CD 5, 6; CWD; DFS 18; DLB 7, 249; GLL 2

Tertullian c. 155-c. 245 .... **CMLC 29**

Tertz, Abram
See Sinyavsky, Andrei (Donatevich)

Underwood, Miles
See Glassco, John

Undset, Sigrid 1882-1949 .... **TCLC 3, 197; WLC 6**
See also AAYA 77; CA 104; 129; DA; DA3; DAB; DAC; DAM MST, NOV; DLB 293, 332; EW 9; EWL 3; FW; MTCW 1, 2; MTFW 2005; RGWL 2, 3

Ungaretti, Giuseppe 1888-1970 ... **CLC 7, 11, 15; PC 57; TCLC 200**
See also CA 19-20; 25-28R; CAP 2; DLB 114; EW 10; EWL 3; PFS 20; RGWL 2, 3; WLIT 7

Unger, Douglas 1952- .... **CLC 34**
See also CA 130; CANR 94, 155

Unsworth, Barry 1930- .... **CLC 76, 127**
See also BRWS 7; CA 25-28R; CANR 30, 54, 125, 171; CN 6, 7; DLB 194, 326

Unsworth, Barry Forster
See Unsworth, Barry

Updike, John 1932-2009 .... **CLC 1, 2, 3, 5, 7, 9, 13, 15, 23, 34, 43, 70, 139, 214; PC 90; SSC 13, 27, 103; WLC 6**
See also AAYA 36; AMW; AMWC 1; AMWR 1; BPFB 3; BYA 12; CA 1-4R; CABS 1; CANR 4, 33, 51, 94, 133; CDALB 1968-1988; CN 1, 3, 4, 5, 6, 7; CP 1, 2, 3, 4, 5, 6, 7; CPW 1; DA; DA3; DAB; DAC; DAM MST, NOV, POET, POP; DLB 2, 5, 143, 218, 227; DLBD 3; DLBY 1980, 1982, 1997; EWL 3; EXPP; HGG; MAL 5; MTCW 1, 2; MTFW 2005; NFS 12, 24; RGAL 4; RGSF 2; SSFS 3, 19; TUS

Updike, John Hoyer
See Updike, John

Upshaw, Margaret Mitchell
See Mitchell, Margaret (Munnerlyn)

Upton, Mark
See Sanders, Lawrence

Upward, Allen 1863-1926 .... **TCLC 85**
See also CA 117; 187; DLB 36

Urdang, Constance (Henriette)
1922-1996 .... **CLC 47**
See also CA 21-24R; CANR 9, 24; CP 1, 2, 3, 4, 5, 6; CWP

Urfe, Honore d' 1567(?)-1625 .... **LC 132**
See also DLB 268; GFL Beginnings to 1789; RGWL 2, 3

Uriel, Henry
See Faust, Frederick (Schiller)

Uris, Leon 1924-2003 .... **CLC 7, 32**
See also AITN 1, 2; BEST 89:2; BPFB 3; CA 1-4R; 217; CANR 1, 40, 65, 123; CN 1, 2, 3, 4, 5, 6; CPW 1; DA3; DAM NOV, POP; MTCW 1, 2; MTFW 2005; RGHL; SATA 49; SATA-Obit 146

Urista (Heredia), Alberto (Baltazar)
1947- .... **HLCS 1; PC 34**
See also CA 45-48R; CANR 2, 32; DLB 82; HW 1; LLW

Urmuz
See Codrescu, Andrei

Urquhart, Guy
See McAlmon, Robert (Menzies)

Urquhart, Jane 1949- .... **CLC 90, 242**
See also CA 113; CANR 32, 68, 116, 157; CCA 1; DAC; DLB 334

Usigli, Rodolfo 1905-1979 .... **HLCS 1**
See also CA 131; DLB 305; EWL 3; HW 1; LAW

Usk, Thomas (?)-1388 .... **CMLC 76**
See also DLB 146

Ustinov, Peter (Alexander)
1921-2004 .... **CLC 1**
See also AITN 1; CA 13-16R; 225; CANR 25, 51; CBD; CD 5, 6; DLB 13; MTCW 2

U Tam'si, Gerald Felix Tchicaya
See Tchicaya, Gerald Felix

U Tam'si, Tchicaya
See Tchicaya, Gerald Felix

Vachss, Andrew 1942- .... **CLC 106**
See also CA 118, 214; CAAE 214; CANR 44, 95, 153; CMW 4

Vachss, Andrew H.
See Vachss, Andrew

Vachss, Andrew Henry
See Vachss, Andrew

Vaculik, Ludvik 1926- .... **CLC 7**
See also CA 53-56; CANR 72; CWW 2; DLB 232; EWL 3

Vaihinger, Hans 1852-1933 .... **TCLC 71**
See also CA 116; 166

Valdez, Luis (Miguel) 1940- ..... **CLC 84; DC 10; HLC 2**
See also CA 101; CAD; CANR 32, 81; CD 5, 6; DAM MULT; DFS 5; DLB 122; EWL 3; HW 1; LAIT 4; LLW

Valenzuela, Luisa 1938- .... **CLC 31, 104; HLCS 2; SSC 14, 82**
See also CA 101; CANR 32, 65, 123; CD-WLB 3; CWW 2; DAM MULT; DLB 113; EWL 3; FW; HW 1, 2; LAW; RGSF 2; RGWL 3

Valera y Alcala-Galiano, Juan
1824-1905 .... **TCLC 10**
See also CA 106

Valerius Maximus CMLC 64
See also DLB 211

Valery, (Ambroise) Paul (Toussaint Jules)
1871-1945 .... **PC 9; TCLC 4, 15**
See also CA 104; 122; DA3; DAM POET; DLB 258; EW 8; EWL 3; GFL 1789 to the Present; MTCW 1, 2; MTFW 2005; RGWL 2, 3; TWA

Valle-Inclan, Ramon (Maria) del
1866-1936 .... **HLC 2; TCLC 5**
See also CA 106; 153; CANR 80; DAM MULT; DLB 134, 322; EW 8; EWL 3; HW 2; RGSF 2; RGWL 2, 3

Vallejo, Antonio Buero
See Buero Vallejo, Antonio

Vallejo, Cesar (Abraham)
1892-1938 .... **HLC 2; TCLC 3, 56**
See also CA 105; 153; DAM MULT; DLB 290; EWL 3; HW 1; LAW; PFS 26; RGWL 2, 3

Valles, Jules 1832-1885 .... **NCLC 71**
See also DLB 123; GFL 1789 to the Present

Vallette, Marguerite Eymery
1860-1953 .... **TCLC 67**
See also CA 182; DLB 123, 192; EWL 3

Valle Y Pena, Ramon del
See Valle-Inclan, Ramon (Maria) del

Van Ash, Cay 1918-1994 .... **CLC 34**
See also CA 220

Vanbrugh, Sir John 1664-1726 .... **LC 21**
See also BRW 2; DAM DRAM; DLB 80; IDTP; RGEL 2

Van Campen, Karl
See Campbell, John W(ood, Jr.)

Vance, Gerald
See Silverberg, Robert

Vance, Jack 1916- .... **CLC 35**
See also CA 29-32R; CANR 17, 65, 154; CMW 4; DLB 8; FANT; MTCW 1; SCFW 1, 2; SFW 4; SUFW 1, 2

Vance, John Holbrook
See Vance, Jack

Van Den Bogarde, Derek Jules Gaspard Ulric Niven 1921-1999 .... **CLC 14**
See also CA 77-80; 179; DLB 14

Vandenburgh, Jane CLC 59
See also CA 168

Vanderhaeghe, Guy 1951- .... **CLC 41**
See also BPFB 3; CA 113; CANR 72, 145; CN 7; DLB 334

van der Post, Laurens (Jan)
1906-1996 .... **CLC 5**
See also AFW; CA 5-8R; 155; CANR 35; CN 1, 2, 3, 4, 5, 6; DLB 204; RGEL 2

van de Wetering, Janwillem
1931-2008 .... **CLC 47**
See also CA 49-52; 274; CANR 4, 62, 90; CMW 4

Van Dine, S. S.
See Wright, Willard Huntington

Van Doren, Carl (Clinton)
1885-1950 .... **TCLC 18**
See also CA 111; 168

Van Doren, Mark 1894-1972 .... **CLC 6, 10**
See also CA 1-4R; 37-40R; CANR 3; CN 1; CP 1; DLB 45, 284, 335; MAL 5; MTCW 1, 2; RGAL 4

Van Druten, John (William)
1901-1957 .... **TCLC 2**
See also CA 104; 161; DLB 10; MAL 5; RGAL 4

Van Duyn, Mona 1921-2004 .... **CLC 3, 7, 63, 116**
See also CA 9-12R; 234; CANR 7, 38, 60, 116; CP 1, 2, 3, 4, 5, 6, 7; CWP; DAM POET; DLB 5; MAL 5; MTFW 2005; PFS 20

Van Dyne, Edith
See Baum, L(yman) Frank

van Herk, Aritha 1954- .... **CLC 249**
See also CA 101; CANR 94; DLB 334

van Itallie, Jean-Claude 1936- .... **CLC 3**
See also CA 45-48; CAAS 2; CAD; CANR 1, 48; CD 5, 6; DLB 7

Van Loot, Cornelius Obenchain
See Roberts, Kenneth (Lewis)

van Ostaijen, Paul 1896-1928 .... **TCLC 33**
See also CA 163

Van Peebles, Melvin 1932- .... **CLC 2, 20**
See also BW 2, 3; CA 85-88; CANR 27, 67, 82; DAM MULT

van Schendel, Arthur(-Francois-Emile)
1874-1946 .... **TCLC 56**
See also EWL 3

Van See, John
See Vance, Jack

Vansittart, Peter 1920-2008 .... **CLC 42**
See also CA 1-4R; 278; CANR 3, 49, 90; CN 4, 5, 6, 7; RHW

Van Vechten, Carl 1880-1964 ... **CLC 33; HR 1:3**
See also AMWS 2; CA 183; 89-92; DLB 4, 9, 51; RGAL 4

van Vogt, A(lfred) E(lton) 1912-2000 . **CLC 1**
See also BPFB 3; BYA 13, 14; CA 21-24R; 190; CANR 28; DLB 8, 251; SATA 14; SATA-Obit 124; SCFW 1, 2; SFW 4

Vara, Madeleine
See Jackson, Laura (Riding)

Varda, Agnes 1928- .... **CLC 16**
See also CA 116; 122

Vargas Llosa, Jorge Mario Pedro
See Vargas Llosa, Mario

Vargas Llosa, Mario 1936- .. **CLC 3, 6, 9, 10, 15, 31, 42, 85, 181; HLC 2**
See also BPFB 3; CA 73-76; CANR 18, 32, 42, 67, 116, 140, 173; CDWLB 3; CWW 2; DA; DA3; DAB; DAC; DAM MST, MULT, NOV; DLB 145; DNFS 2; EWL 3; HW 1, 2; LAIT 5; LATS 1:2; LAW; LAWS 1; MTCW 1, 2; MTFW 2005; RGWL 2, 3; SSFS 14; TWA; WLIT 1

Varnhagen von Ense, Rahel
1771-1833 .... **NCLC 130**
See also DLB 90

von Daniken, Erich
See von Daeniken, Erich
von Eschenbach, Wolfram c. 1170-c.
1220 .... **CMLC 5**
See also CDWLB 2; DLB 138; EW 1;
RGWL 2, 3
von Hartmann, Eduard
1842-1906 .... **TCLC 96**
von Hayek, Friedrich August
See Hayek, F(riedrich) A(ugust von)
von Heidenstam, (Carl Gustaf) Verner
See Heidenstam, (Carl Gustaf) Verner von
von Heyse, Paul (Johann Ludwig)
See Heyse, Paul (Johann Ludwig von)
von Hofmannsthal, Hugo
See Hofmannsthal, Hugo von
von Horvath, Odon
See von Horvath, Odon
von Horvath, Odon
See von Horvath, Odon
von Horvath, Odon 1901-1938 .... **TCLC 45**
See also CA 118; 184, 194; DLB 85, 124;
RGWL 2, 3
von Horvath, Oedoen
See von Horvath, Odon
von Kleist, Heinrich
See Kleist, Heinrich von
Vonnegut, Kurt, Jr.
See Vonnegut, Kurt
Vonnegut, Kurt 1922-2007 .... **CLC 1, 2, 3, 4,**
5, 8, 12, 22, 40, 60, 111, 212, 254; SSC
8; WLC 6
See also AAYA 6, 44; AITN 1; AMWS 2;
BEST 90:4; BPFB 3; BYA 3, 14; CA
1-4R; 259; CANR 1, 25, 49, 75, 92;
CDALB 1968-1988; CN 1, 2, 3, 4, 5, 6,
7; CPW 1; DA; DA3; DAB; DAC; DAM
MST, NOV, POP; DLB 2, 8, 152; DLBD
3; DLBY 1980; EWL 3; EXPN; EXPS;
LAIT 4; LMFS 2; MAL 5; MTCW 1, 2;
MTFW 2005; NFS 3, 28; RGAL 4;
SCFW; SFW 4; SSFS 5; TUS; YAW
Von Rachen, Kurt
See Hubbard, L. Ron
von Sternberg, Josef
See Sternberg, Josef von
Vorster, Gordon 1924- .... **CLC 34**
See also CA 133
Vosce, Trudie
See Ozick, Cynthia
Voznesensky, Andrei (Andreievich)
1933- .... **CLC 1, 15, 57**
See also CA 89-92; CANR 37; CWW 2;
DAM POET; EWL 3; MTCW 1
Voznesensky, Andrey
See Voznesensky, Andrei (Andreievich)
Wace, Robert c. 1100-c. 1175 .... **CMLC 55**
See also DLB 146
Waddington, Miriam 1917-2004 .... **CLC 28**
See also CA 21-24R; 225; CANR 12, 30;
CCA 1; CP 1, 2, 3, 4, 5, 6, 7; DLB 68
Wade, Alan
See Vance, Jack
Wagman, Fredrica 1937- .... **CLC 7**
See also CA 97-100; CANR 166; INT CA-
97-100
Wagner, Linda W.
See Wagner-Martin, Linda (C.)
Wagner, Linda Welshimer
See Wagner-Martin, Linda (C.)
Wagner, Richard 1813-1883 ..... **NCLC 9, 119**
See also DLB 129; EW 6
Wagner-Martin, Linda (C.) 1936- .... **CLC 50**
See also CA 159; CANR 135

Wagoner, David (Russell) 1926- .... **CLC 3, 5,**
15; PC 33
See also AMWS 9; CA 1-4R; CAAS 3;
CANR 2, 71; CN 1, 2, 3, 4, 5, 6, 7; CP 1,
2, 3, 4, 5, 6, 7; DLB 5, 256; SATA 14;
TCWW 1, 2
Wah, Fred(erick James) 1939- .... **CLC 44**
See also CA 107; 141; CP 1, 6, 7; DLB 60
Wahloo, Per 1926-1975 .... **CLC 7**
See also BPFB 3; CA 61-64; CANR 73;
CMW 4; MSW
Wahloo, Peter
See Wahloo, Per
Wain, John (Barrington) 1925-1994 . **CLC 2,**
11, 15, 46
See also CA 5-8R; 145; CAAS 4; CANR
23, 54; CDBLB 1960 to Present; CN 1, 2,
3, 4, 5; CP 1, 2, 3, 4, 5; DLB 15, 27, 139,
155; EWL 3; MTCW 1, 2; MTFW 2005
Wajda, Andrzej 1926- .... **CLC 16, 219**
See also CA 102
Wakefield, Dan 1932- .... **CLC 7**
See also CA 21-24R, 211; CAAE 211;
CAAS 7; CN 4, 5, 6, 7
Wakefield, Herbert Russell
1888-1965 .... **TCLC 120**
See also CA 5-8R; CANR 77; HGG; SUFW
Wakoski, Diane 1937- ...... **CLC 2, 4, 7, 9, 11,**
40; PC 15
See also CA 13-16R, 216; CAAE 216;
CAAS 1; CANR 9, 60, 106; CP 1, 2, 3, 4,
5, 6, 7; CWP; DAM POET; DLB 5; INT
CANR-9; MAL 5; MTCW 2; MTFW
2005
Wakoski-Sherbell, Diane
See Wakoski, Diane
Walcott, Derek 1930- . **BLC 1:3, 2:3; CLC 2,**
4, 9, 14, 25, 42, 67, 76, 160; DC 7; PC
46
See also BW 2; CA 89-92; CANR 26, 47,
75, 80, 130; CBD; CD 5, 6; CDWLB 3;
CP 1, 2, 3, 4, 5, 6, 7; DA3; DAB; DAC;
DAM MST, MULT, POET; DLB 117,
332; DLBY 1981; DNFS 1; EFS 1; EWL
3; LMFS 2; MTCW 1, 2; MTFW 2005;
PFS 6; RGEL 2; TWA; WWE 1
Waldman, Anne (Lesley) 1945- .... **CLC 7**
See also BG 1:3; CA 37-40R; CAAS 17;
CANR 34, 69, 116; CP 1, 2, 3, 4, 5, 6, 7;
CWP; DLB 16
Waldo, E. Hunter
See Sturgeon, Theodore (Hamilton)
Waldo, Edward Hamilton
See Sturgeon, Theodore (Hamilton)
Walker, Alice 1944- .... **BLC 1:3, 2:3; CLC 5,**
6, 9, 19, 27, 46, 58, 103, 167; PC 30;
SSC 5; WLCS
See also AAYA 3, 33; AFAW 1, 2; AMWS
3; BEST 89:4; BPFB 3; BW 2, 3; CA 37-
40R; CANR 9, 27, 49, 66, 82, 131;
CDALB 1968-1988; CN 4, 5, 6, 7; CPW;
CSW; DA; DA3; DAB; DAC; DAM MST,
MULT, NOV, POET, POP; DLB 6, 33,
143; EWL 3; EXPN; EXPS; FL 1:6; FW;
INT CANR-27; LAIT 3; MAL 5; MBL;
MTCW 1, 2; MTFW 2005; NFS 5; PFS
30; RGAL 4; RGSF 2; SATA 31; SSFS 2,
11; TUS; YAW
Walker, Alice Malsenior
See Walker, Alice
Walker, David Harry 1911-1992 ...... **CLC 14**
See also CA 1-4R; 137; CANR 1; CN 1, 2;
CWRI 5; SATA 8; SATA-Obit 71
Walker, Edward Joseph 1934-2004 .. **CLC 13**
See also CA 21-24R; 226; CANR 12, 28,
53; CP 1, 2, 3, 4, 5, 6, 7; DLB 40
Walker, George F(rederick) 1947- .. **CLC 44,**
61
See also CA 103; CANR 21, 43, 59; CD 5,
6; DAB; DAC; DAM MST; DLB 60

Walker, Joseph A. 1935-2003 .... **CLC 19**
See also BW 1, 3; CA 89-92; CAD; CANR
26, 143; CD 5, 6; DAM DRAM, MST;
DFS 12; DLB 38
Walker, Margaret 1915-1998 .... **BLC 1:3;**
CLC 1, 6; PC 20; TCLC 129
See also AFAW 1, 2; BW 2, 3; CA 73-76;
172; CANR 26, 54, 76, 136; CN 1, 2, 3,
4, 5, 6; CP 1, 2, 3, 4, 5, 6; CSW; DAM
MULT; DLB 76, 152; EXPP; FW; MAL
5; MTCW 1, 2; MTFW 2005; RGAL 4;
RHW
Walker, Ted
See Walker, Edward Joseph
Wallace, David Foster 1962-2008 .... **CLC 50,**
114, 271; SSC 68
See also AAYA 50; AMWS 10; CA 132;
277; CANR 59, 133; CN 7; DA3; MTCW
2; MTFW 2005
Wallace, Dexter
See Masters, Edgar Lee
Wallace, (Richard Horatio) Edgar
1875-1932 .... **TCLC 57**
See also CA 115; 218; CMW 4; DLB 70;
MSW; RGEL 2
Wallace, Irving 1916-1990 .... **CLC 7, 13**
See also AITN 1; BPFB 3; CA 1-4R; 132;
CAAS 1; CANR 1, 27; CPW; DAM NOV,
POP; INT CANR-27; MTCW 1, 2
Wallant, Edward Lewis 1926-1962 ... **CLC 5,**
10
See also CA 1-4R; CANR 22; DLB 2, 28,
143, 299; EWL 3; MAL 5; MTCW 1, 2;
RGAL 4; RGHL
Wallas, Graham 1858-1932 .... **TCLC 91**
Waller, Edmund 1606-1687 .... **LC 86; PC 72**
See also BRW 2; DAM POET; DLB 126;
PAB; RGEL 2
Walley, Byron
See Card, Orson Scott
Walpole, Horace 1717-1797 ..... **LC 2, 49, 152**
See also BRW 3; DLB 39, 104, 213; GL 3;
HGG; LMFS 1; RGEL 2; SUFW 1; TEA
Walpole, Hugh (Seymour)
1884-1941 .... **TCLC 5**
See also CA 104; 165; DLB 34; HGG;
MTCW 2; RGEL 2; RHW
Walrond, Eric (Derwent) 1898-1966 . **HR 1:3**
See also BW 1; CA 125; DLB 51
Walser, Martin 1927- .... **CLC 27, 183**
See also CA 57-60; CANR 8, 46, 145;
CWW 2; DLB 75, 124; EWL 3
Walser, Robert 1878-1956 ..... **SSC 20; TCLC**
18
See also CA 118; 165; CANR 100; DLB
66; EWL 3
Walsh, Gillian Paton
See Paton Walsh, Jill
Walsh, Jill Paton
See Paton Walsh, Jill
Walter, Villiam Christian
See Andersen, Hans Christian
Walter of Chatillon c. 1135-c.
1202 .... **CMLC 111**
Walters, Anna L(ee) 1946- .... **NNAL**
See also CA 73-76
Walther von der Vogelweide c.
1170-1228 .... **CMLC 56**
Walton, Izaak 1593-1683 .... **LC 72**
See also BRW 2; CDBLB Before 1660;
DLB 151, 213; RGEL 2
Walzer, Michael (Laban) 1935- ...... **CLC 238**
See also CA 37-40R; CANR 15, 48, 127
Wambaugh, Joseph, Jr. 1937- ...... **CLC 3, 18**
See also AITN 1; BEST 89:3; BPFB 3; CA
33-36R; CANR 42, 65, 115, 167; CMW
4; CPW 1; DA3; DAM NOV, POP; DLB
6; DLBY 1983; MSW; MTCW 1, 2

Weldon, Fay 1931- . **CLC 6, 9, 11, 19, 36, 59, 122**
See also BRWS 4; CA 21-24R; CANR 16, 46, 63, 97, 137; CDBLB 1960 to Present; CN 3, 4, 5, 6, 7; CPW; DAM POP; DLB 14, 194, 319; EWL 3; FW; HGG; INT CANR-16; MTCW 1, 2; MTFW 2005; RGEL 2; RGSF 2

Wellek, Rene 1903-1995 .... **CLC 28**
See also CA 5-8R; 150; CAAS 7; CANR 8; DLB 63; EWL 3; INT CANR-8

Weller, Michael 1942- .... **CLC 10, 53**
See also CA 85-88; CAD; CD 5, 6

Weller, Paul 1958- .... **CLC 26**

Wellershoff, Dieter 1925- .... **CLC 46**
See also CA 89-92; CANR 16, 37

Welles, (George) Orson 1915-1985 .. **CLC 20, 80**
See also AAYA 40; CA 93-96; 117

Wellman, John McDowell 1945- ...... **CLC 65**
See also CA 166; CAD; CD 5, 6; RGAL 4

Wellman, Mac
See Wellman, John McDowell; Wellman, John McDowell

Wellman, Manly Wade 1903-1986 ... **CLC 49**
See also CA 1-4R; 118; CANR 6, 16, 44; FANT; SATA 6; SATA-Obit 47; SFW 4; SUFW

Wells, Carolyn 1869(?)-1942 .... **TCLC 35**
See also CA 113; 185; CMW 4; DLB 11

Wells, H(erbert) G(eorge) 1866-1946 . **SSC 6, 70; TCLC 6, 12, 19, 133; WLC 6**
See also AAYA 18; BPFB 3; BRW 6; CA 110; 121; CDBLB 1914-1945; CLR 64, 133; DA; DA3; DAB; DAC; DAM MST, NOV; DLB 34, 70, 156, 178; EWL 3; EXPS; HGG; LAIT 3; LMFS 2; MTCW 1, 2; MTFW 2005; NFS 17, 20; RGEL 2; RGSF 2; SATA 20; SCFW 1, 2; SFW 4; SSFS 3; SUFW; TEA; WCH; WLIT 4; YAW

Wells, Rosemary 1943- .... **CLC 12**
See also AAYA 13; BYA 7, 8; CA 85-88; CANR 48, 120, 179; CLR 16, 69; CWRI 5; MAICYA 1, 2; SAAS 1; SATA 18, 69, 114, 156; YAW

Wells-Barnett, Ida B(ell) 1862-1931 .... **TCLC 125**
See also CA 182; DLB 23, 221

Welsh, Irvine 1958- .... **CLC 144**
See also CA 173; CANR 146; CN 7; DLB 271

Welty, Eudora 1909-2001 .... **CLC 1, 2, 5, 14, 22, 33, 105, 220; SSC 1, 27, 51, 111; WLC 6**
See also AAYA 48; AMW; AMWR 1; BPFB 3; CA 9-12R; 199; CABS 1; CANR 32, 65, 128; CDALB 1941-1968; CN 1, 2, 3, 4, 5, 6, 7; CSW; DA; DA3; DAB; DAC; DAM MST, NOV; DFS 26; DLB 2, 102, 143; DLBD 12; DLBY 1987, 2001; EWL 3; EXPS; HGG; LAIT 3; MAL 5; MBL; MTCW 1, 2; MTFW 2005; NFS 13, 15; RGAL 4; RGSF 2; RHW; SSFS 2, 10, 26; TUS

Welty, Eudora Alice
See Welty, Eudora

Wen I-to 1899-1946 .... **TCLC 28**
See also EWL 3

Wentworth, Robert
See Hamilton, Edmond

Werewere Liking 1950- .... **BLC 2:2**
See also EWL 3

Werfel, Franz (Viktor) 1890-1945 ... **TCLC 8**
See also CA 104; 161; DLB 81, 124; EWL 3; RGWL 2, 3

Wergeland, Henrik Arnold 1808-1845 .... **NCLC 5**

Werner, Friedrich Ludwig Zacharias 1768-1823 .... **NCLC 189**
See also DLB 94

Werner, Zacharias
See Werner, Friedrich Ludwig Zacharias

Wersba, Barbara 1932- .... **CLC 30**
See also AAYA 2, 30; BYA 6, 12, 13; CA 29-32R, 182; CAAE 182; CANR 16, 38; CLR 3, 78; DLB 52; JRDA; MAICYA 1, 2; SAAS 2; SATA 1, 58; SATA-Essay 103; WYA; YAW

Wertmueller, Lina 1928- .... **CLC 16**
See also CA 97-100; CANR 39, 78

Wescott, Glenway 1901-1987 .. **CLC 13; SSC 35**
See also CA 13-16R; 121; CANR 23, 70; CN 1, 2, 3, 4; DLB 4, 9, 102; MAL 5; RGAL 4

Wesker, Arnold 1932- .... **CLC 3, 5, 42**
See also CA 1-4R; CAAS 7; CANR 1, 33; CBD; CD 5, 6; CDBLB 1960 to Present; DAB; DAM DRAM; DLB 13, 310, 319; EWL 3; MTCW 1; RGEL 2; TEA

Wesley, Charles 1707-1788 .... **LC 128**
See also DLB 95; RGEL 2

Wesley, John 1703-1791 .... **LC 88**
See also DLB 104

Wesley, Richard (Errol) 1945- .... **CLC 7**
See also BW 1; CA 57-60; CAD; CANR 27; CD 5, 6; DLB 38

Wessel, Johan Herman 1742-1785 .... **LC 7**
See also DLB 300

West, Anthony (Panther) 1914-1987 .... **CLC 50**
See also CA 45-48; 124; CANR 3, 19; CN 1, 2, 3, 4; DLB 15

West, C. P.
See Wodehouse, P(elham) G(renville)

West, Cornel 1953- .... **BLCS; CLC 134**
See also CA 144; CANR 91, 159; DLB 246

West, Cornel Ronald
See West, Cornel

West, Delno C(loyde), Jr. 1936- .... **CLC 70**
See also CA 57-60

West, Dorothy 1907-1998 ...... **HR 1:3; TCLC 108**
See also AMWS 18; BW 2; CA 143; 169; DLB 76

West, Edwin
See Westlake, Donald E.

West, (Mary) Jessamyn 1902-1984 ... **CLC 7, 17**
See also CA 9-12R; 112; CANR 27; CN 1, 2, 3; DLB 6; DLBY 1984; MTCW 1, 2; RGAL 4; RHW; SATA-Obit 37; TCWW 2; TUS; YAW

West, Morris L(anglo) 1916-1999 ..... **CLC 6, 33**
See also BPFB 3; CA 5-8R; 187; CANR 24, 49, 64; CN 1, 2, 3, 4, 5, 6; CPW; DLB 289; MTCW 1, 2; MTFW 2005

West, Nathanael 1903-1940 ...... **SSC 16, 116; TCLC 1, 14, 44**
See also AAYA 77; AMW; AMWR 2; BPFB 3; CA 104; 125; CDALB 1929-1941; DA3; DLB 4, 9, 28; EWL 3; MAL 5; MTCW 1, 2; MTFW 2005; NFS 16; RGAL 4; TUS

West, Owen
See Koontz, Dean R.

West, Paul 1930- .... **CLC 7, 14, 96, 226**
See also CA 13-16R; CAAS 7; CANR 22, 53, 76, 89, 136; CN 1, 2, 3, 4, 5, 6, 7; DLB 14; INT CANR-22; MTCW 2; MTFW 2005

West, Rebecca 1892-1983 ... **CLC 7, 9, 31, 50**
See also BPFB 3; BRWS 3; CA 5-8R; 109; CANR 19; CN 1, 2, 3; DLB 36; DLBY 1983; EWL 3; FW; MTCW 1, 2; MTFW 2005; NCFS 4; RGEL 2; TEA

Westall, Robert (Atkinson) 1929-1993 .... **CLC 17**
See also AAYA 12; BYA 2, 6, 7, 8, 9, 15; CA 69-72; 141; CANR 18, 68; CLR 13; FANT; JRDA; MAICYA 1, 2; MAICYAS 1; SAAS 2; SATA 23, 69; SATA-Obit 75; WYA; YAW

Westermarck, Edward 1862-1939 . **TCLC 87**

Westlake, Donald E. 1933-2008 ... **CLC 7, 33**
See also BPFB 3; CA 17-20R; 280; CAAS 13; CANR 16, 44, 65, 94, 137; CMW 4; CPW; DAM POP; INT CANR-16; MSW; MTCW 2; MTFW 2005

Westlake, Donald E. Edmund
See Westlake, Donald E.

Westlake, Donald Edwin
See Westlake, Donald E.

Westlake, Donald Edwin Edmund
See Westlake, Donald E.

Westmacott, Mary
See Christie, Agatha (Mary Clarissa)

Weston, Allen
See Norton, Andre

Wetcheek, J. L.
See Feuchtwanger, Lion

Wetering, Janwillem van de
See van de Wetering, Janwillem

Wetherald, Agnes Ethelwyn 1857-1940 .... **TCLC 81**
See also CA 202; DLB 99

Wetherell, Elizabeth
See Warner, Susan (Bogert)

Whale, James 1889-1957 .... **TCLC 63**
See also AAYA 75

Whalen, Philip (Glenn) 1923-2002 .... **CLC 6, 29**
See also BG 1:3; CA 9-12R; 209; CANR 5, 39; CP 1, 2, 3, 4, 5, 6, 7; DLB 16; WP

Wharton, Edith (Newbold Jones) 1862-1937 . **SSC 6, 84, 120; TCLC 3, 9, 27, 53, 129, 149; WLC 6**
See also AAYA 25; AMW; AMWC 2; AMWR 1; BPFB 3; CA 104; 132; CDALB 1865-1917; CLR 136; DA; DA3; DAB; DAC; DAM MST, NOV; DLB 4, 9, 12, 78, 189; DLBD 13; EWL 3; EXPS; FL 1:6; GL 3; HGG; LAIT 2, 3; LATS 1:1; MAL 5; MBL; MTCW 1, 2; MTFW 2005; NFS 5, 11, 15, 20; RGAL 4; RGSF 2; RHW; SSFS 6, 7; SUFW; TUS

Wharton, James
See Mencken, H(enry) L(ouis)

Wharton, William 1925-2008 ..... **CLC 18, 37**
See also CA 93-96; 278; CN 4, 5, 6, 7; DLBY 1980; INT CA-93-96

Wheatley (Peters), Phillis 1753(?)-1784 .... **BLC 1:3; LC 3, 50; PC 3; WLC 6**
See also AFAW 1, 2; CDALB 1640-1865; DA; DA3; DAC; DAM MST, MULT, POET; DLB 31, 50; EXPP; FL 1:1; PFS 13, 29; RGAL 4

Wheelock, John Hall 1886-1978 .... **CLC 14**
See also CA 13-16R; 77-80; CANR 14; CP 1, 2; DLB 45; MAL 5

Whim-Wham
See Curnow, (Thomas) Allen (Monro)

Whisp, Kennilworthy
See Rowling, J.K.

Whitaker, Rod 1931-2005 .... **CLC 29**
See also CA 29-32R; 246; CANR 45, 153; CMW 4

Whitaker, Rodney
See Whitaker, Rod

Wright, Willard Huntington
1888-1939 .... **TCLC 23**
See also CA 115; 189; CMW 4; DLB 306;
DLBD 16; MSW

Wright, William 1930- .... **CLC 44**
See also CA 53-56; CANR 7, 23, 154

Wroth, Lady Mary 1587-1653(?) .... **LC 30, 139; PC 38**
See also DLB 121

Wu Ch'eng-en 1500(?)-1582(?) .... **LC 7**

Wu Ching-tzu 1701-1754 .... **LC 2**

Wulfstan c. 10th cent. -1023 .... **CMLC 59**

Wurlitzer, Rudolph 1938(?)- .... **CLC 2, 4, 15**
See also CA 85-88; CN 4, 5, 6, 7; DLB 173

Wyatt, Sir Thomas c. 1503-1542 . **LC 70; PC 27**
See also BRW 1; DLB 132; EXPP; PFS 25;
RGEL 2; TEA

Wycherley, William 1640-1716 .... **LC 8, 21, 102, 136**
See also BRW 2; CDBLB 1660-1789; DAM
DRAM; DLB 80; RGEL 2

Wyclif, John c. 1330-1384 .... **CMLC 70**
See also DLB 146

Wylie, Elinor (Morton Hoyt)
1885-1928 .... **PC 23; TCLC 8**
See also AMWS 1; CA 105; 162; DLB 9,
45; EXPP; MAL 5; RGAL 4

Wylie, Philip (Gordon) 1902-1971 ... **CLC 43**
See also CA 21-22; 33-36R; CAP 2; CN 1;
DLB 9; SFW 4

Wyndham, John
See Harris, John (Wyndham Parkes Lucas)
Beynon

Wyss, Johann David Von
1743-1818 .... **NCLC 10**
See also CLR 92; JRDA; MAICYA 1, 2;
SATA 29; SATA-Brief 27

Xenophon c. 430B.C.-c. 354B.C. ... **CMLC 17**
See also AW 1; DLB 176; RGWL 2, 3;
WLIT 8

Xingjian, Gao 1940- .... **CLC 167**
See also CA 193; DFS 21; DLB 330;
MTFW 2005; RGWL 3

Yakamochi 718-785 .... **CMLC 45; PC 48**

Yakumo Koizumi
See Hearn, (Patricio) Lafcadio (Tessima
Carlos)

Yamada, Mitsuye (May) 1923- .... **PC 44**
See also CA 77-80

Yamamoto, Hisaye 1921- .... **AAL; SSC 34**
See also CA 214; DAM MULT; DLB 312;
LAIT 4; SSFS 14

Yamauchi, Wakako 1924- .... **AAL**
See also CA 214; DLB 312

Yan, Mo
See Moye, Guan

Yanez, Jose Donoso
See Donoso (Yanez), Jose

Yanovsky, Basile S.
See Yanovsky, V(assily) S(emenovich)

Yanovsky, V(assily) S(emenovich)
1906-1989 .... **CLC 2, 18**
See also CA 97-100; 129

Yates, Richard 1926-1992 .... **CLC 7, 8, 23**
See also AMWS 11; CA 5-8R; 139; CANR
10, 43; CN 1, 2, 3, 4, 5; DLB 2, 234;
DLBY 1981, 1992; INT CANR-10; SSFS
24

Yau, John 1950- .... **PC 61**
See also CA 154; CANR 89; CP 4, 5, 6, 7;
DLB 234, 312; PFS 26

Yearsley, Ann 1753-1806 .... **NCLC 174**
See also DLB 109

Yeats, W. B.
See Yeats, William Butler

Yeats, William Butler 1865-1939 . **DC 33; PC 20, 51; TCLC 1, 11, 18, 31, 93, 116; WLC 6**
See also AAYA 48; BRW 6; BRWR 1; CA
104; 127; CANR 45; CDBLB 1890-1914;
DA; DA3; DAB; DAC; DAM DRAM,
MST, POET; DLB 10, 19, 98, 156, 332;
EWL 3; EXPP; MTCW 1, 2; MTFW
2005; NCFS 3; PAB; PFS 1, 2, 5, 7, 13,
15; RGEL 2; TEA; WLIT 4; WP

Yehoshua, A.B. 1936- .... **CLC 13, 31, 243**
See also CA 33-36R; CANR 43, 90, 145;
CWW 2; EWL 3; RGHL; RGSF 2; RGWL
3; WLIT 6

Yehoshua, Abraham B.
See Yehoshua, A.B.

Yellow Bird
See Ridge, John Rollin

Yep, Laurence 1948- .... **CLC 35**
See also AAYA 5, 31; BYA 7; CA 49-52;
CANR 1, 46, 92, 161; CLR 3, 17, 54, 132;
DLB 52, 312; FANT; JRDA; MAICYA 1,
2; MAICYAS 1; SATA 7, 69, 123, 176;
WYA; YAW

Yep, Laurence Michael
See Yep, Laurence

Yerby, Frank G(arvin) 1916-1991 . **BLC 1:3; CLC 1, 7, 22**
See also BPFB 3; BW 1, 3; CA 9-12R; 136;
CANR 16, 52; CN 1, 2, 3, 4, 5; DAM
MULT; DLB 76; INT CANR-16; MTCW
1; RGAL 4; RHW

Yesenin, Sergei Aleksandrovich
See Esenin, Sergei

Yevtushenko, Yevgeny (Alexandrovich)
1933- ...... **CLC 1, 3, 13, 26, 51, 126; PC 40**
See also CA 81-84; CANR 33, 54; CWW
2; DAM POET; EWL 3; MTCW 1; PFS
29; RGHL; RGWL 2, 3

Yezierska, Anzia 1885(?)-1970 .... **CLC 46; TCLC 205**
See also CA 126; 89-92; DLB 28, 221; FW;
MTCW 1; NFS 29; RGAL 4; SSFS 15

Yglesias, Helen 1915-2008 .... **CLC 7, 22**
See also CA 37-40R; 272; CAAS 20; CANR
15, 65, 95; CN 4, 5, 6, 7; INT CANR-15;
MTCW 1

Y.O.
See Russell, George William

Yokomitsu, Riichi 1898-1947 .... **TCLC 47**
See also CA 170; EWL 3

Yolen, Jane 1939- .... **CLC 256**
See also AAYA 4, 22; BPFB 3; BYA 9, 10,
11, 14, 16; CA 13-16R; CANR 11, 29, 56,
91, 126, 185; CLR 4, 44; CWRI 5; DLB
52; FANT; INT CANR-29; JRDA; MAI-
CYA 1, 2; MTFW 2005; SAAS 1; SATA
4, 40, 75, 112, 158, 194; SATA-Essay 111;
SFW 4; SUFW 2; WYA; YAW

Yonge, Charlotte (Mary)
1823-1901 .... **TCLC 48**
See also CA 109; 163; DLB 18, 163; RGEL
2; SATA 17; WCH

York, Jeremy
See Creasey, John

York, Simon
See Heinlein, Robert A.

Yorke, Henry Vincent 1905-1974 ...... **CLC 2, 13, 97**
See also BRWS 2; CA 85-88, 175; 49-52;
DLB 15; EWL 3; RGEL 2

Yosano, Akiko 1878-1942 ... **PC 11; TCLC 59**
See also CA 161; EWL 3; RGWL 3

Yoshimoto, Banana
See Yoshimoto, Mahoko

Yoshimoto, Mahoko 1964- .... **CLC 84**
See also AAYA 50; CA 144; CANR 98, 160;
NFS 7; SSFS 16

Young, Al(bert James) 1939- .... **BLC 1:3; CLC 19**
See also BW 2, 3; CA 29-32R; CANR 26,
65, 109; CN 2, 3, 4, 5, 6, 7; CP 1, 2, 3, 4,
5, 6, 7; DAM MULT; DLB 33

Young, Andrew (John) 1885-1971 ...... **CLC 5**
See also CA 5-8R; CANR 7, 29; CP 1;
RGEL 2

Young, Collier
See Bloch, Robert (Albert)

Young, Edward 1683-1765 .... **LC 3, 40**
See also DLB 95; RGEL 2

Young, Marguerite (Vivian)
1909-1995 .... **CLC 82**
See also CA 13-16; 150; CAP 1; CN 1, 2,
3, 4, 5, 6

Young, Neil 1945- .... **CLC 17**
See also CA 110; CCA 1

Young Bear, Ray A. 1950- ... **CLC 94; NNAL**
See also CA 146; DAM MULT; DLB 175;
MAL 5

Yourcenar, Marguerite 1903-1987 ... **CLC 19, 38, 50, 87; TCLC 193**
See also BPFB 3; CA 69-72; CANR 23, 60,
93; DAM NOV; DLB 72; DLBY 1988;
EW 12; EWL 3; GFL 1789 to the Present;
GLL 1; MTCW 1, 2; MTFW 2005;
RGWL 2, 3

Yuan, Chu 340(?)B.C.-278(?)B.C. . **CMLC 36**

Yu Dafu 1896-1945 .... **SSC 122**
See also DLB 328; RGSF 2

Yurick, Sol 1925- .... **CLC 6**
See also CA 13-16R; CANR 25; CN 1, 2,
3, 4, 5, 6, 7; MAL 5

Zabolotsky, Nikolai Alekseevich
1903-1958 .... **TCLC 52**
See also CA 116; 164; EWL 3

Zabolotsky, Nikolay Alekseevich
See Zabolotsky, Nikolai Alekseevich

Zagajewski, Adam 1945- .... **PC 27**
See also CA 186; DLB 232; EWL 3; PFS
25

Zakaria, Fareed 1964- .... **CLC 269**
See also CA 171; CANR 151, 188

Zalygin, Sergei -2000 .... **CLC 59**

Zalygin, Sergei (Pavlovich)
1913-2000 .... **CLC 59**
See also DLB 302

Zamiatin, Evgenii
See Zamyatin, Evgeny Ivanovich

Zamiatin, Evgenii Ivanovich
See Zamyatin, Evgeny Ivanovich

Zamiatin, Yevgenii
See Zamyatin, Evgeny Ivanovich

Zamora, Bernice (B. Ortiz) 1938- .. **CLC 89; HLC 2**
See also CA 151; CANR 80; DAM MULT;
DLB 82; HW 1, 2

Zamyatin, Evgeny Ivanovich
1884-1937 .... **SSC 89; TCLC 8, 37**
See also CA 105; 166; DLB 272; EW 10;
EWL 3; RGSF 2; RGWL 2, 3; SFW 4

Zamyatin, Yevgeny Ivanovich
See Zamyatin, Evgeny Ivanovich

Zangwill, Israel 1864-1926 ... **SSC 44; TCLC 16**
See also CA 109; 167; CMW 4; DLB 10,
135, 197; RGEL 2

Zanzotto, Andrea 1921- .... **PC 65**
See also CA 208; CWW 2; DLB 128; EWL
3

Zappa, Francis Vincent, Jr. 1940-1993
See Zappa, Frank
See also CA 108; 143; CANR 57

Zappa, Frank CLC 17
See Zappa, Francis Vincent, Jr.

Zaturenska, Marya 1902-1982 ..... **CLC 6, 11**
See also CA 13-16R; 105; CANR 22; CP 1,
2, 3

Literary Criticism Series
Cumulative Topic Index

This index lists all topic entries in Gale's *Children's Literature Review* (CLR), *Classical and Medieval Literature Criticism* (CMLC), *Contemporary Literary Criticism* (CLC), *Drama Criticism* (DC), *Literature Criticism from 1400 to 1800* (LC), *Nineteenth-Century Literature Criticism* (NCLC), *Short Story Criticism* (SSC), and *Twentieth-Century Literary Criticism* (TCLC). The index also lists topic entries in the Gale Critical Companion Collection, which includes the following publications: *The Beat Generation* (BG), *Feminism in Literature* (FL), *Gothic Literature* (GL), and *Harlem Renaissance* (HR).

Topic Index

CMLC Cumulative Nationality Index

Nationality Index

CMLC Cumulative Title Index

Title Index

Title Index

Title Index

Title Index

Title Index

Title Index

Title Index

Title Index

Title Index

ISBN-13: 978-1-4144-3926-6
ISBN-10: 1-4144-3926-1

90000

9 781414 439266